TORT LAW

Fifth Edition

TORT LAW

Fifth Edition

Linda L. Edwards, J.D., Ph.D.

J. Stanley Edwards, J.D.

Patricia Kirtley Wells, J.D.

DELMAR
CENGAGE Learning™

Australia • Brazil • Japan • Korea • Mexico • Singapore • Spain • United Kingdom • United States

Tort Law, Fifth Edition
Linda L. Edwards, J.D., Ph.D.
J. Stanley Edwards, J.D.
Patricia Kirtley Wells, J.D.

Vice President, Editorial: Dave Garza

Director of Learning Solutions: Sandy Clark

Senior Acquisitions Editor: Shelley Esposito

Managing Editor: Larry Main

Senior Product Manager: Melissa Riveglia

Editorial Assistant: Diane Chrysler

Vice President, Marketing: Jennifer Baker

Marketing Director: Deborah Yarnell

Marketing Manager: Erin Brennan

Marketing Coordinator: Erin DeAngelo

Senior Production Director: Wendy Troeger

Production Manager: Mark Bernard

Senior Content Project Manager:
Betty L. Dickson

Senior Art Director: Joy Kocsis

Senior Technology Project Manager: Joe Pliss

For product information and technology assistance, contact us at
Cengage Learning Customer & Sales Support, 1-800-354-9706
For permission to use material from this text or product,
submit all requests online at **www.cengage.com/permissions**
Further permissions questions can be e-mailed to
permissionrequest@cengage.com

Library of Congress Control Number: 2011921832

ISBN-13: 978-1-1113-1215-2

ISBN-10: 1-1113-1215-X

Delmar
5 Maxwell Drive
Clifton Park, NY 12065-2919
USA

Cengage Learning is a leading provider of customized learning solutions with office locations around the globe, including Singapore, the United Kingdom, Australia, Mexico, Brazil, and Japan. Locate your local office at:

international.cengage.com/region

Cengage Learning products are represented in Canada by Nelson Education, Ltd.

To learn more about Delmar, visit **www.cengage.com/delmar**
Purchase any of our products at your local college store or at our preferred online store **www.cengagebrain.com**

Cover Photo Credits: Man in protective clothing ©Hugh Burden/Getty Images; Gavel ©Tetra Images/Getty Images; Motorcycle accident ©Martin Shields/Alamy; Wheelchair ©Southern Stock/Getty Images; Coffee spill ©Jeffrey Coolidge/Getty Images; Background light ©Comstock/Legalities

Printed in the United States of America
4 5 6 7 15 14 13

DEDICATION

This edition is dedicated to Stan's mother, Esther Dean. With 86 years on this earth, and still counting, Esther provided the environment and nourishment that allowed Stan and his siblings, Jim Edwards, Bonnie Nelson and Susan Myers to find there place in this hectic world. Together with her late husband, William H. Dean, Esther was, and she still is, the inspiration for the entire family. A special thanks is also due Stan's wife, Lenore Edwards, for her support and gentle prodding that allowed this 5th edition to become a reality.

CONTENTS IN BRIEF

CONTENTS

PREFACE

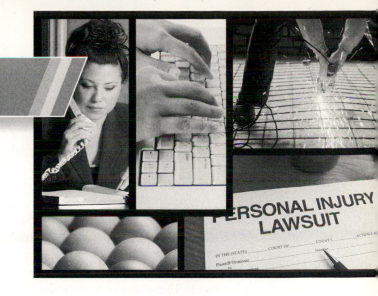

"If it's not broken, don't fix it." This has been our guiding adage throughout the fifth revision of this text. The feedback we have received throughout the years for the first four editions has been so positive, we were reluctant to make major changes for the sake of change alone.

We have updated cases, added new materials due to changes in the law, and revised all of our Internet references to reflect its "current" condition." We hope we have maintained the balance of readability and academic integrity created in the previous editions. The core of the text has remained unchanged except for updates where necessary and additional information where helpful.

The text retains the hypotheticals introducing each chapter and the "Putting It into Practice" exercises that encourage students to immediately put into application concepts to which they have been exposed. The "Practice Pointers" continue to introduce practical procedural skills, such as drafting pleadings, preparing medical authorization requests, documenting damages, writing FOIA letters, and assembling trial exhibits. The "Tort Teasers" at the end of each chapter continue to provide stimulating fact patterns in the form of actual cases, which can be used in class to discuss the tort principles presented in that chapter.

We have retained the features added in the fourth edition. They were:

- **Review Questions and Practice Exams**—The review questions are broad questions that require students to assimilate the concepts in each chapter. The practice exams consist of true-false, multiple-choice, fill-in-the-blank, and matching questions that test knowledge of specific principles and vocabulary. The questions are similar to those provided in the "Test Bank" (in the Instructor's Manual); consequently, students can be assured that if they do well on these practice exams (whose answers are provided in Appendix A), they should do well on the exams given in class. We have also emphasized the need for students to take advantage of this resource and make sure they have sufficiently mastered the materials before moving on to the next chapter.

- **Net News**—Links to a wide variety of websites are liberally sprinkled throughout the text. Some of these links acquaint students with the more commonly used sites; some provide sample documents and explain concepts or principles; some provide links to federal or state agencies; others offer stimulating articles on issues pertinent to tort law.

INTERNET WARNING: Please remember that web addresses change frequently, websites can undergo construction, and web pages can simply disappear. For these reasons, the links that are valid at the time of publication may not be valid by the time they are visited by students. This edition does not use "deep" links to any of the Internet resources. The main web page is given along with instructions for how to reach the desired material. This change was meant to avoid potential copyright issues as well as assure that, to the extent possible, the Internet materials would be accessible to the student regardless of minor changes in the construction of the website referred to.

- **Local Links**—These prompt students and faculty to consider the rules and practices unique to their jurisdiction. While the text is necessarily generic, these inquiries allow faculty to explain the procedures and terms used in their jurisdiction.

- **Internet Inquiries**—Searching the Internet is the best way to build confidence and become familiar with what is available. These exercises provide some structure to that search. Some of these exercises are a fairly structured means of familiarizing students with particular websites whereas other exercises are more exploratory in nature, encouraging students to discover and report what they find.
- **Practical Ponderables**—These exercises include questions that require students to assimilate information they have learned throughout the chapter (sometimes incorporating concepts discussed in previous chapters). The questions are more provocative than those in the Practice Exams and necessitate integration of materials. They could easily serve as the basis for class discussion and homework assignments.

SUPPLEMENTAL TEACHING MATERIALS

This fifth edition is accompanied by a support package that will assist students in learning and aid instructors in teaching:

Paralegal CourseMate

Tort Law, Fifth Edition, has a CourseMate available. This CourseMate includes:

- an interactive eBook, with highlighting, note-taking, and search capabilities
- interactive teaching and learning tools, including:
  - Quizzing
  - Case studies
  - Chapter objectives
  - Flashcards
  - Web links
  - Crossword puzzles
  - PowerPoint® presentations
  - And more!
  - Engagement Tracker, a first-of-its-kind tool that monitors student engagement in the course

To learn more about this resource and access free demo CourseMate resources, go to www.cengagebrain.com, and search by this book's ISBN (9781111312152). To access CourseMate materials that you have purchased, go to login.cengagebrain.com, enter your access code, and create an account or log into your existing account.

Instructor's Manual

The **Instructor's Manual** has been extensively revised to create a larger test bank that also now provides answers to over 200 essay and short-answer questions. Answers to the more than 300 Review Questions in the text are also now included. Suggested responses to the Tort Teasers, Internet Inquiries, and Practical Ponderables are available. Edited cases are provided in the Tort Teasers section so that faculty have an opportunity to read the cited cases when desired. Suggested exercises and discussion questions are included for each chapter, assisting faculty in organizing their in-class presentations.

INSTRUCTOR RESOURCES

Instructor Resources

Spend less time planning and more time teaching. With Delmar Cengage Learning's Instructor Resources to Accompany Tort Law, preparing for class and evaluating students have never been easier!

This invaluable instructor CD-ROM allows you "anywhere, anytime" access to all of your resources.

- The **Instructor's Manual** contains various resources for each chapter of the book.
- The **Computerized Testbank** in ExamView makes generating tests and quizzes a snap. With many questions and different styles to choose from, you can create customized assessments for your students with the click of a button. Add your own unique questions and print rationales for easy class preparation.
- Customizable **PowerPoint® Presentations** focus on key points for each chapter. (PowerPoint® is a registered trademark of the Microsoft Corporation.)

To access additional course materials (including CourseMate), please go to login.cengage.com, then use your SSO (single sign on) login to access the materials.

All of these instructor materials are also posted on our website (http://www.paralegal.delmar.cengage .com/) in the Online Resources section.

WebTUTOR™

WebTutor™

The WebTutor™ supplement allows you, as the instructor, to take learning beyond the classroom. This online courseware is designed to complement the text and benefit students and instructors alike by helping to better manage your time, prepare for exams, organize your notes, and more. WebTutor™ allows you to extend your reach beyond the classroom.

WebPage

Come visit our website at http://www.paralegal.delmar.cengage.com/, where you will find valuable information such as hot links and sample materials to download, as well as other Delmar Cengage Learning products.

Please note the Internet resources are of a time-sensitive nature and URL addresses may often change or be deleted.

Supplements At-a-Glance

SUPPLEMENT:	WHAT IT IS:	WHAT'S IN IT:
Paralegal CourseMate CourseMate	Online interactive teaching and learning tools and an interactive eBook. Go to *login.cengage.com* to access.	Interactive teaching and learning tools, including: • Quizzing • Case studies • Chapter Objectives • Flashcards • Weblinks • Crossword puzzles • PowerPoints® presentations • Interactive eBook • Engagement Tracker
Online Instructor's Manual	Resources for the instructor, posted online at *www.paralegal.delmar.cengage.com* in the Online Resources section and via Cengage Single Sign On	• Instructor's Manual with answers to text questions and test bank and answer key • PowerPoint® presentations
Instructor Resources CD-ROM INSTRUCTOR RESOURCES	Resources for the instructor, available on CD-ROM	• Instructor's Manual with answers to text questions and test bank and answer key • Computerized Testbank in Exam View, with many questions and styles to choose from to create customized assessments for your students • PowerPoint® presentations
WebTutor™ WebTUTOR™	WebTUTOR™ supplemental courseware is the best way to use the Internet to turn everyone in your class into a front-row student. It complements Cengage Learning paralegal textbooks by providing interactive reinforcement that helps students grasp complex concepts. WebTUTOR™ allows you to know quickly what concepts your students are or aren't grasping.	• Automatic and immediate feedback from quizzes and exams • Online exercises that reinforce what students have learned • Flashcards • Greater interaction and involvement through online discussion forums

ACKNOWLEDGMENTS

As with any long-term project, many people are involved in bringing a new edition to completion. We would like to thank Melissa Riveglia, Senior Product Manager; Diane Chrysler, Editorial Assistant; Betty L. Dickson, Senior Content Project Manager; Shelley Esposito, Senior Acquisitions Editor; and Erin Brennan, Marketing Manager, for their dedicated and conscientious assistance. We also want to thank the reviewers who devoted their time and expertise to help make this text better meet the needs of students and faculty. We honor their obvious commitment to the educational process.

Kathleen Fisher
Kennesaw State University Paralegal Studies
Kennesaw, GA

Constance Herinkova
South College
Knoxville, TN

Linda Hibbs
Community College of Philadelphia
Philadelphia, PA

Deborah Winfrey Keene
Lansing Community College
Lansing, MI

LIST OF CASES

ABOUT THE AUTHORS

Dr. Linda L. Edwards (1951–2004) authored or co-authored seven textbooks in the legal assistant field. They were: *Tort Law for Legal Assistants, 3rd edition; Practical Case Analysis; Civil Procedure & Litigation: A Practical Approach; Introduction to Paralegal Studies: A Practical Approach; Guide to Factual Investigations; Introduction to Paralegal Studies & the Law: A Practical Approach, and Law Office Skills.*

Dr. Edwards was an attorney/author in Cave Creek, Arizona. She had been an instructor in the Justice and Legal Studies Department at Phoenix College for 24 years until her retirement in 2001. She served as both program director of the Legal Assisting Program and department chairperson. During her tenure as program director she was involved in obtaining approval for the Legal Assisting program by the American Bar Association. She created dozens of new classes in both legal assisting and criminal justice and was known for her innovations in the field of education.

An individual of many interests, Linda had a B.S. in Chemistry, a M.S. in Criminal Justice and a Ph.D. in Holistic Healing; she was also a certified homeopath, Bowen therapist, and Edu-K practitioner.

J. Stanley Edwards has been an Arizona attorney since 1975. He has been a general practitioner for all but two of those years. Stan co-authored five textbooks with his late wife, Dr. Linda L. Edwards. They are: *Tort Law for Legal Assistants, 3rd edition; Civil Procedure & Litigation: A Practical Approach; Introduction to*
Paralegal Studies: A Practical Approach; Guide to Factual Investigations; and Introduction to Paralegal Studies & the Law: A Practical Approach.

Stan has tried over twenty cases to juries. He previously served as a judge *pro tem* in both the civil and family law divisions of the Maricopa County Superior Court. Stan is a certified arbitrator in the District Court of Arizona. He has twice been named Volunteer Lawyer of the Month by the Volunteer Lawyers Program. He is licensed to practice in Arizona, Colorado (currently on inactive status), the District Court of Arizona, the Ninth Circuit Court of Appeals, and the United States Patent and Trademark Office.

Patricia Kirtley Wells was a litigation associate at Snell & Wilmer before becoming a trial attorney for the E.E.O.C. Trisha has been in private practice since 1999. She has served as a judge *pro tem* for the Maricopa County Justice Courts and for the City of Phoenix Municipal Court. As an adjunct instructor at Phoenix College since 1999, Trisha has taught the tort law class from prior editions of *Tort Law for Legal Assistants.*

Trisha was a law student extern to Stanley Feldman when he served as a Justice of the Arizona Supreme Court. She is licensed to practice in Arizona, the District Court of Arizona, and the Ninth Circuit Court of Appeals.

PART I

Introduction

CHAPTER 1

Overview of Tort Law

CHAPTER OBJECTIVES

After completing the chapter, you should be able to

- Define a tort and distinguish between a tort and a crime, as well as between a tort and a contract.
- Trace the evolution of tort law.
- Recognize the philosophical principles and arguments underpinning tort law.

You come home one evening to find that one of your children has been bitten by your next-door neighbor's pit bull, who was safely secured behind the fence when your child, contrary to your instruction, entered the yard to retrieve a wayward ball. Your neighbor took every precaution of isolating the dog, short of locking the fence. Should the neighbor be held liable?

Someone in your family contracts a deadly disease, the cause of which can be traced to chemical contaminants found in toxic wastes dumped by the city in which you live. The city dumped the waste several decades before the area became residential and, at the time, was totally ignorant of the long-term effects. Should the city be held liable?

A medical student watches as a five-year-old girl falls into the lake at the local park and screams "Help, I can't swim." He walks away as she goes under for the third time. Although he worked as a lifeguard for several years, he has not worked as a lifeguard since entering medical school. Should he be held liable?

An eight-year-old boy trespasses and falls into a hole on your property. Should you be held liable?

Your daughter finally succeeds in becoming a famous actress. Without her permission, a magazine publishes nude photographs of her. Should she be able to sue for invasion of privacy?

Your son is wrongfully detained because a storekeeper suspects him of shoplifting. Should he be able to sue the store for the emotional distress he endures?

Should the attorney for whom you work be held liable for your negligent acts?

Should you be held liable for the intentional torts of your children?

Your home has been burglarized on several occasions and, in a desperate attempt to protect your property, you set up a mechanical protective device. Should you be held liable if a would-be burglar is seriously injured by the device?

These questions, illustrating the broad scope of human experiences that fall under tort law, will be examined in this text. Tort law is an intriguing area of the law that covers virtually every aspect of human endeavor. It not only governs the conduct of many in our society, but also reflects our attitudes and values toward living itself. Within the parameters of tort law can be discovered many of the philosophical underpinnings of our society.

BACKGROUND

It has been said that tort liability is like a tax that makes products and services more costly to all and ultimately unaffordable to some. This "tax," it is argued, has put some medical doctors out of business, prohibited the sale of certain drugs and products, and severely hampered businesses and governmental bodies in their delivery of services.

Advocates of expanded tort liability see tort law as the knight in shining armor, duly anointed to protect the interests of the consumer. In their perception, manufacturers and those who deliver services are better able than consumers to predict and prevent injuries from the use of their products and services. The burden of injury, they reason, should be borne by those who create risks rather than by those who fall prey to them. The philosophical and political debates on the issue of risk allocation have gained new significance in one of the most recent developments in tort law—product liability.

Others argue that we have become too paternalistic in our efforts to protect individuals and that we should allow people to bear the consequences of their decisions. After all, they point out, the process of living comes with no guarantees and the assurance of safety is too high a price to pay for freedom.

In addition to this philosophical concern, there is reluctance to burden a defendant, particularly an industry, with all losses, for fear of financial ruin. As a result, new technological developments may be inhibited or become financially prohibitive.

This problem of distribution of losses continues to haunt those who seek an equitable balance between the needs of plaintiffs and defendants. Judges must decide the proper solution to this controversy. Suffice it to say that whichever philosophical trail they choose to follow predetermines their resolution of many cases.

WHAT IS A TORT?

But what is this thing we call a **tort**? Although the term has evaded concrete definition, it has been described as a civil wrong for which the victim receives a remedy in the form of damages (Exhibit 1–1). Included under this heading are intentional torts (assault, battery, and false imprisonment are some examples), negligence (acts committed without intent but in violation of a reasonable person standard), and strict liability (acts committed with no intent at all).

EXHIBIT 1—1 Definition of a Tort

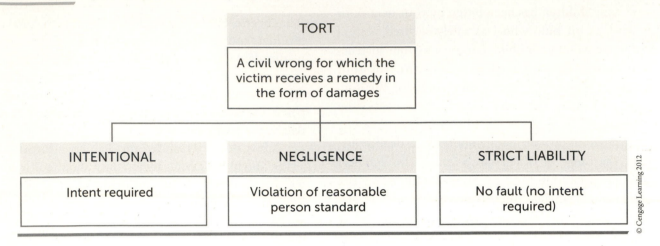

© Cengage Learning 2012

REASONABLENESS OF CONDUCT

The common thread interweaving most torts is the notion that socially unreasonable conduct should be penalized and those who are its victims should be compensated. Of course, determining what is unreasonable is a formidable task, because reasonableness, like beauty, is in the eye of the beholder. The overall goal in defining reasonableness is to balance the plaintiff's need for protection against the defendant's claim of freedom to pursue his own ends. But how does one determine reasonableness of conduct? Should one take into consideration, for example, the parties' religious beliefs, their physical disabilities, their values, emotional idiosyncrasies, or their mental state?

To get a feeling for where you stand on this issue of reasonableness, consider the following. You are sitting as a juror on a case in which the plaintiff, a devoutly religious Catholic woman, was severely injured by the negligent driving of the defendant. The plaintiff was pregnant at the time of her injury and was told that because of the serious pelvic injury she had sustained she would be in grave danger if she carried her baby to term. Because of her intense aversion to abortion, she chose to deliver the baby and died in the process.

Do you think the defendant should be required to compensate the plaintiff's family for her death? How would you determine the reasonableness of the plaintiff's conduct? Would you require her to conform to the conduct of the "average" person, or would you compare her conduct to that of a reasonable person holding her beliefs? These are just some examples of the types of questions with which jurors and courts must grapple in their struggle to assign fault and apportion damages equitably under tort law doctrines.

Sometimes the reasonableness of the defendant's conduct is not at issue because of the far-reaching social consequences of his or her actions. In the area of product liability, for example, even those manufacturers and sellers who act reasonably are held liable to plaintiffs injured by their products. This is done in the name of protecting society. By holding manufacturers and sellers responsible for all such losses, the argument is made, consumers will be better protected and sellers and manufacturers will be more conscientious in the delivery of their services and products. Similarly, one who innocently defames another will be held liable despite his benign intent. The victim's reputation is irreparably tarnished no matter how reasonable the defamer's conduct, goes the rationale, and so compensation is required.

PUBLIC POLICY

Tort law often goes beyond compensating individuals and considers, more broadly, the interests and goals of society at large and the community in which we live. These interests are often referred to by the courts as **public policy** concerns. Most people are familiar with the term *corporate* or *company policy*, which dictates the values and principles of a corporation. Similarly, the local, state, and national communities have "public policies" that dictate the norms of the community or the public based on its beliefs and values regarding justice, fairness, and equality. Judges may consider public policy to determine the impact

NET NEWS

For an overview of tort law and what it encompasses, go to **http://www.law.cornell.edu**. Scroll down to "Popular Topics" and select "Accidents and Injuries."

their rulings or legal principles will have on society as a whole.

All laws, including tort law, are based in some part on the public policy of the society and/or the community. To find the public policy underlying a law, one must look at the rationale or reason for the law. For example, a community may have an ordinance that prohibits the opening of an adult book store within 300 feet of an elementary school. The public policy underlying such an ordinance is the community policy or value that young children should not be exposed to adult book stores and their patrons.

Understanding public policy is essential to understanding tort law.

Why, you might ask, must the interest of society be considered when dealing with a dispute between two individuals? Because our common law system is based on case precedent, every decision rendered by a court has the potential of establishing a rule that must be followed by other courts. Society, therefore, has an interest in ensuring that disputes between litigants are resolved through a process of resolution that is fair and just for all concerned. The very principles set forth today will be those that govern the cases of tomorrow.

MORALITY OF CONDUCT

Is the morality of a defendant's conduct relevant in tort law? Although personal morality may be subject to variation, tort law borrows heavily from a sense of public morality. It can be said that, at least in certain cases, we all have a sense of what is universally regarded as right and wrong. Tort law generally reflects that sense.

There are circumstances, however, in which a defendant can be held liable even though he or she has violated no moral code. One who, for example, trespasses on the land of another in the reasonable belief that it is his own land is still liable for trespass. With the increasing popularity of no-fault torts, such as strict liability, we appear to be moving away from a need to cast moral judgment on a defendant's conduct. In contrast, tort law does not deal with all blatantly immoral acts. Although it may be morally

reprehensible, for example, to allow a stranger to die when you could save her, in most circumstances you will have committed no tort.

SLIPPERY-SLOPE ARGUMENTS

Case precedent, the effect of a ruling on a future case, is a major part of the development of tort law. Courts are often hesitant to crack open a legal door in a particular case for fear of creating a "flood of litigation," an occurrence they are ever on the alert to avoid. For that reason, some types of flagrant misdeeds are not vindicated by tort law. Relatively trivial concerns must also go by the wayside in an effort to minimize the flood of litigation. Many of our most grievous hurts are inflicted in the context of interpersonal relationships and yet most of these must go without redress. Lovers are jilted, children are verbally belittled by parents, friends are "used," and so on. The law cannot become enmeshed in these psychically damaging events if the legal system is to avoid the administrative nightmare created by an onslaught of cases. Clearly, not all human wrong can be remedied.

Perhaps you have heard of the **slippery-slope argument**, which means, essentially, that use of an argument in one case will allow application of that same argument in innumerable other cases. The metaphor is used to show that once you take the first step, it is too easy to fall down the slippery slope to the bottom of the hill, presumably into a morass of undesirable outcomes. The slippery-slope argument is, in essence, an administrative concern. A court fears that if it finds negligence on behalf of the sympathetic plaintiff before it, hundreds of thousands of similarly situated individuals or those whose situations are analogous to the case will also seek similar redress. The precedential effect of arguments regarding physician-assisted suicide, racial composition of juries, and the use of marijuana for medical purposes are among the many slippery-slope issues considered by the courts.

Keep in mind that, although courts are to focus on the long-term in making their decisions, they sometimes are understandably sympathetic to the plight of the individuals before them. In such cases they often render decisions that meet the short-term goals of justice but that prove untenable over the long run. Justice, you will soon discover, is an illusory goal that often eludes capture by even the most conscientious judge.

CREATION OF CASE LAW

Tort law is largely a product of **case law**, which involves case-by-case decision making by the state courts. This decision-making process is affected, to some degree, by statutes, which the courts are mandated to follow unless statutory gaps exist that leave a court with unanswered questions. Some statutes, such as the wrongful death and survival acts, directly address issues that arise in the context of tort law. Others, such as certain criminal statutes, serve as guidelines to the courts in establishing policy. A statute, for example, that makes it a misdemeanor to drive while under the influence of alcohol sets forth the standard of care expected of drivers. A driver having a blood alcohol level in excess of the statutory limit would be considered to have breached the duty of care he owed to those around him.

Another guideline that courts use in formulating their holdings is the *Restatement of the Law of Torts*. The *Restatement* was compiled by eminent legal scholars and practitioners in an attempt to provide lawyers and judges with **black-letter principles** (legal principles generally accepted by the legal community, also referred to as black-letter law) of tort law. Adopted in many jurisdictions, the *Restatement* is frequently cited in court opinions.

Although criticized for creating the impression of uniformity in the law where there is none, the *Restatement* is nevertheless a frequently used guide through the maze of tort law decisions. For this reason, the *Restatement* is often cited throughout this text. Keep in mind, however, that your state may not have adopted the *Restatement* position. Consult the case law in your state when dealing with a specific case.

RELATIONSHIP BETWEEN TORT LAW AND OTHER AREAS OF THE LAW

Torts versus Crimes

How does a tort differ from a crime? Although the two share several similarities, they differ in terms of the interests affected, the remedy granted, standard of proof, and procedural mechanisms used (see Exhibit 1–2). A crime is considered an offense against society, whereas a tort is an offense against another individual or group of individuals. The purpose of prosecuting someone who has committed a crime is to vindicate the interests of society by punishing the offender. The purpose of suing in tort, in contrast, is to compensate the victim.

Although the primary purpose of criminal law is punishment and the primary purpose of tort law is compensation, there is some overlap between the two. Compensation given to the victim of a crime (known as **restitution**) is frequently used by the courts as part of an offender's sentence. By the same token, punitive damages, which are intended to punish the **tortfeasor** (one who has committed a tort), are used in certain circumstances in tort law.

EXHIBIT 1–2 Torts versus Crimes

	TORTS	CRIMES
PURPOSE	Compensation	Punishment
STANDARD OF PROOF	Preponderance of Evidence	Beyond a Reasonable Doubt
INTERESTS VIOLATED	Individual's Interest	Society's Interest
PROCEDURAL RULES	Civil Rules	Criminal Rules

© Cengage Learning 2012

NET NEWS

To learn more about the American Law Institute, which publishes the *Restatements*, and to gain a better understanding of what the *Restatements* are and how they are compiled, go to the library archives at Penn Law http://www.law.upenn.edu/ and locate the archives of the American Law Institute under "Collections."

Despite this overlap, the primary functions of criminal law and tort law remain distinct.

Moreover, the rules of civil procedure are used in tort cases, whereas the rules of criminal procedure are used in criminal cases. Also, the plaintiff's burden of proof in a tort case requires proof by a **preponderance of the evidence**; the state's burden of proof in a criminal case is proof **beyond a reasonable doubt**. The rules of evidence applicable in criminal cases vary from those applicable in civil cases.

Many acts may be both a crime against the state and a tort against the individual. If a drunk driver, for example, is involved in a vehicular accident, she may be charged with a criminal offense as well as sued by the injured parties for negligence. For this reason (among others) those charged with criminal offenses often plead **nolo contendere** (no contest). If they were to plead guilty, their admission of guilt could be used against them in a subsequent civil trial, whereas a plea of nolo contendere could not. This is true, however, only if the issue tried in the criminal case is also relevant to some aspect of the tort action. Because of the lower standard of proof in a civil case, the plaintiff in a tort case will have an easier time establishing liability than the state will have proving guilt in a criminal case. In the trial of the twentieth century, the defendant O.J. Simpson was acquitted of criminal charges and found liable for the same conduct under tort principles in a civil case.

Torts versus Contracts

Tort law differs from contract law in terms of the voluntariness of entering into an agreement. When two or more parties create a contract, they each agree to give up something in return for receiving some benefit. In a contract action, the parties have voluntarily and knowingly assumed duties or obligations to others. In tort law, by contrast, duties are imposed by the law without the express consent or awareness of those involved (Exhibit 1–3). If a guest is injured on a landowner's premises, the landowner is liable, not because he expressly contracted to prevent injury to the guest, but because the law imposes certain obligations on him by virtue of being a landowner.

The remedy in a contract case is to compensate the prevailing party with the benefit of the bargain. In other words, the remedy is to provide them with what was expected under the contract. In a tort case the

EXHIBIT 1–3 Torts versus Contracts

	TORTS	CONTRACTS
DUTIES ASSIGNED	Imposed by Law	By Parties' Consent
OBLIGATIONS MADE TO	Society in General	Specific Individuals

© Cengage Learning 2012

remedy is much broader and the victim of a tort may be awarded monetary damages for pain and suffering, economic damages, and punitive damages.

Just as with criminal law, however, there is an overlap between tort law and contract law. Certain tort duties may coincide with those duties set forth in a contract, for example, so that if a party fails to live up to its obligations, an action may lie in either tort or contract. Additionally, some quasi-contractual obligations (such as the obligation to act in good faith) are imposed by law without the consent of the parties, just as in tort law.

One other distinction between contract and tort law is that in contract law, obligations are made to specific individuals by virtue of an agreement of the parties; whereas in tort law, duties are imposed by law and owed to society. In tort law, one is bound to act as a reasonable person toward all other persons, but in contract law one is bound in contract only to certain chosen individuals. This distinction is not completely valid, however, in that tort law principles impose special duties in some cases because of the relationship one has with another. An employer, for example, owes duties of care to her employees that she does not owe to other persons.

You will find as you pursue your study of torts that this area of law overlaps with most other areas of law. Therefore, you will frequently find yourself referring to knowledge that you have gained from the study of property law, constitutional law, criminal law, contract law, corporate law, and so on.

BRIEF HISTORY OF TORT LAW

If this is the point in most textbooks where you skip ahead, try to persevere. You might be surprised at how interesting the evolution of tort law really is (Exhibit 1–4).

EXHIBIT 1–4 Evolution of Tort Law

Blood feud (no fault)

Action in trespass (no fault)
(Vi et armis)
(Direct use of force)

Trespass on the case (wrongful intent or negligence)
(No force or indirect injury)

Negligence (fault required)

Strict liability (no fault)

© Cengage Learning 2012

In barbaric societies the only "law" that seemed to control group behavior had its roots in the blood feud. The protocol of the blood feud required that the clan go to war against any outsider who inflicted harm on a clan member, thereby dishonoring the clan as a whole. Atonement for the humiliation suffered by the victim's kin seemed the primary goal.

Despite the obvious deterrence this system of justice provided, its inherent violence and its toll on those who were obligated to protect family and clan members prompted reform. Ultimately a negotiation process was developed in which the victim summoned the perpetrator to the "moot"—a forum in which the victim pleaded his case to the community and asked for a redress of his grievance. Community members offered advice about how best to resolve the dispute. When a solution acceptable to both victim and perpetrator was found, the parties dispersed and the blood feud was averted.

When the law first assumed a more civilized veneer, the remedies created served as substitutes for the feuding process, and thus emerged the concept of monetary compensation. Early in Anglo-Saxon history, individuals were assigned a monetary value based principally on their rank. Money instead of blood was offered as a salve for injured clan pride. Compensation was directed toward the clan rather than the individual, and awards were distributed proportionately among the injured person's relatives. There was no distinction between crimes and torts. Furthermore, there seemed to be no concern regarding issues of fault or blameworthiness. Even the most remote causal connection was sufficient to justify the imposition of punishment.

Interestingly enough, during this same time period vengeance was exacted on whatever was determined to be the immediate cause of death, even if it was an animal or inanimate object. The offending object, be it a horse or a sword, might be turned over to the victim or the victim's family to be used as they saw fit, or delivered to the king.

Action in Trespass

Over time the moot process of dispute resolution led to the establishment of certain fundamental rules. Communities discovered, through trial and error, those decisions that led to the greatest peace and harmony. Following the Norman Conquest, the dispute resolution process fell to the royal justices of the king's courts. They soon discovered that following the already established local rules provided optimal efficiency in resolving conflict. As a result, the local rules eventually evolved into what is now known as the common law.

The **action in trespass**, which emerged sometime in the middle of the thirteenth century, was one of the products of the common law evolution. This action, which was basically of a criminal nature, dealt with serious and forcible breaches of peace. One of its requirements was the showing of force and arms, referred to as *vi et armis*.

The plaintiff had to allege that the defendant had used force directly on the plaintiff's person or property, thus the term *vi et armis* appeared in every writ of trespass as a matter of course. No further showing of blameworthiness or fault on the part of the defendant was necessary. As time went on, however, even mild, innocuous physical contact was sufficient for the plaintiff to prevail in a trespass action, and the pleading of *vi et armis* became a mere technical device.

To see an example of a trespass in action, read the whimsically written case of *Tricoli v. Centalanza*. Do not be concerned if you do not fully understand the legal arguments, because we have not yet discussed the legal concepts at issue. In essence, the appellate court concluded that the trial court was justified in requiring only one of the defendants to pay all of the plaintiff's damages and in assessing damages even though the plaintiff's damages were arguably inconsequential.

CASE / *Tricoli v. Centalanza et al.*
126 A. 214 (1924)
Supreme Court of New Jersey.
Oct. 8, 1924

"Run away, Maestro Juan, I am going to kill you." Such was the ferocious threat that disturbed the atmosphere, not of prehistoric Mexico, where upon desolate plains the savage coyote still bays at the moon, nor yet of classic Verona, where dramatic memories of the houses of Montague and Capulet still linger to entrance the romantic wayfarer, but from the undiluted atmosphere of Bloomfield Avenue, where it winds its attractive course through the prim rococo shades of modern Montclair, which upon the day succeeding Christmas in 1923 sat like Roma immortalis upon its seven hills, and from its throne of beauty contemplated with serene satisfaction the peace and tranquility of the modern world.

The Maestro, however, with true chivalric disdain, refused to retreat, but determined at all hazards, like Horatius, to hold the bridge, or rather the stoop, upon which he stood. Like a true Roman, inoculated with the maximum percentage of American patriotism, he turned defiantly to the oncoming house of Centalanza, and proclaimed in the bellicose language of the day, "You too son of a gun."

In the days of the Montague and Capulet, aristocratic rapiers and swords defended the honor of their respective houses; but in this day of popular progress the Maestro and the Centalanza sought only the plebeian defense of fists and a shovel. As a result of a triangular contest, the physician testified that the Maestro was battered "from head to buttocks"—a distribution of punishment, it may be observed, which, while it may not be entirely aesthetic in its selection of a locum tenens, was to say the least equitably administered and distributed. Indeed, so much was the Maestro battered that his daily toil lost him for 12 days, and the trial court estimated that this loss, together with his pain and suffering, and the aggravation of the trespass, entitled him to receive from the house of Centalanza $240.

The latter, however, has appealed, and alleges that the Maestro proved no substantial cause of action against them. But the learned trial court, upon this contested state of facts, concluded, and we think properly, that there was an issue of fact thus presented, since the suit was for assault and battery in the nature of trespass *vi et armis*. But the defendants Centalanza insist that two distinct encounters took place, one by both defendants, and the other by one only, and they ask: How can such a physical contretemps be admeasured, so as to impose upon each member of the house of Centalanza his fair share of compensation for his physical contribution to the melee? The inquiry possesses its latent difficulties, but, since it is an admitted rule of law that the court will not distribute the damages between tortfeasors, upon any theory of equitable admeasurement, the house of Centalanza obviously must bear the entire loss, without seeking a partition thereof. . . .

Indeed, it would prove to be a rare feat of judicial acumen were the court to attempt to give due credit to Donato Centalanza for the prowess he displayed in his fistic endeavors, and to assess to Raffale Centalanza his mead of financial contribution for the dexterity with which he wielded his handy implement of excavation. It is doubtful, even in these days of the mystic prize ring, whether such a metaphysical test may be included among the accredited mental accomplishments of a quasi militant judiciary, which, while it occasionally indulges in a caustic punch, still strenuously endeavors to maintain the proverbial respectability and regal poise of its ancestral prototype. In such a situation we are not inclined to impose this extraordinary and novel field of jurisdiction upon our inferior courts. The occurrence of trespass *vi et armis* confers upon the trial court the right to assess exemplary damages as smart money, and this the trial court properly did under the circumstances of the case. . . .

It is contended, however, that the actual damage sustained by the Maestro was inconsequential, and that the rule, "*De minimis non curat lex,*" applies. It must be obvious, however, that damage which to the attending physician seemed to penetrate the Maestro "from head to buttocks" may seem trivial to us as noncombatants, but to the Maestro it manifestly seemed otherwise, and doubtless punctured his corpus, as well as his sensibilities. Indeed, he well might declare in the language of the gallant Mercutio of Verona, concerning the extent of his wound: "It is not as wide as a church door, or as deep as a well, but' twill serve."

The judgment will be affirmed.

Trespass on the Case

The action in trespass was highly restrictive in that it precluded recovery by those who could show no use or only indirect use of force by the defendant. A companion form of action known as **trespass on the case** arose to allow recovery in the absence of force or in cases where an injury was inflicted indirectly. A plaintiff who was injured when the defendant wielded a plank of wood against him could pursue an action in trespass to redress his injuries, whereas a plaintiff who tripped over that same piece of wood left carelessly in her path by the defendant had to resort to an action on the case.

Although damage to the plaintiff was implied in an action in trespass, the plaintiff in a trespass on the case was required to show injury and damage. Trespass-on-the-case actions demanded proof of the defendant's wrongful intent or negligence, whereas an action in trespass required no showing of fault. Trespass on the case was frequently used as a means of recovering for breach of a legal duty grounded on custom. Those who served the public, such as innkeepers, were frequently the defendants in such cases.

Negligence

The development of public transportation seems to have had a profound influence on the evolution of tort law. As the courts were faced with more traffic-related cases, they came to the realization that decisions mechanically rendered in favor of victims under the trespass theory (which merely required the showing of direct force) would have a prohibitive effect on the use of highways. Under this approach, few could afford to risk traveling on the highways and losing their fortunes as a result of accident. Thus, the idea of negligence emerged as a compromise. Travelers were granted some measure of protection from liability as long as they drove in such a manner that they reduced the risk of accidents.

The rise of negligence as a cause of action coincided with the disintegration of actions in trespass and trespass on the case, although negligence ultimately assumed many of the characteristics of a trespass-on-the-case action. The distinction between trespass and trespass on the case has basically disappeared except in a few states where some trace of the distinction has been retained through common law pleadings. One vestige of the distinction that continues to hang on, however, is the necessity of proving damages. Torts that trace their ancestry back to trespass require no proof of actual damages; those that trace back to trespass on the case do require such proof. Although reminders of these dinosaurs of tort law emerge occasionally, they have for the most part been replaced by the modern torts that are the subject of this text.

COMING FULL CIRCLE

This brief overview of the development of tort law demonstrates the cyclical evolution of our attitude toward the notion of fault. Strict liability (no fault) reigned supreme during early Anglo-Saxon law and was evident in the action in trespass. Only in actions on the case did the notion of duty and neglect arise. Now, at the beginning of the twenty-first century, strict liability has once again assumed importance in our legal system. More and more modern courts are assigning liability even where there is no showing of fault.

How did this notion of no fault assume such importance in tort law? To understand, we must look back to the scientific revolution that followed the Civil War. Influenced by the technological wonders of the Industrial Revolution, intellectuals embraced the supremacy of scientific thought. Legal scholars, led by Oliver Wendell Holmes (an influential Supreme Court Justice), also adopted the scientific paradigm as they sought to create common principles that specified when individuals were entitled to compensation for the wrongs they had suffered. In so doing, these "scientific" scholars created a general duty of care that resulted in a fault theory of tort law.

At the beginning of the twentieth century, problems of poverty and social disadvantage began to be seen as societal rather than individual problems. Increasingly the government was called upon to intervene and redress the wrongs visited upon individuals. The tort "scientists," who had been content to systematically catalog the rules of tort law, gave way to the legal "realists," who saw themselves more as revolutionaries than as mere observers. No longer content with rules that created fair results between parties, these scholars strove for rules that equitably distributed losses. In other words, tort law came to be viewed more as a means of creating a just society than as simply a peaceful resolution of interpersonal disputes. The fault theory of tort law was abandoned in favor of a system that provided social justice. William Prosser, one of the most noted tort scholars and author of one of the most influential treatises on tort law, advocated that the purpose of tort law was to provide justice rather than to simply punish and deter inappropriate conduct. He forcefully and successfully lobbied for the adoption of strict liability in reference to defective products on the premise that liability should be borne by those best able to bear it (the manufacturer).

For what reason have we taken this brief excursion through the historical roots of tort law? Learning tort law is not just about memorizing case law and legal principles. A true understanding of tort law requires a knowledge of the purposes it serves and its relationship to societal goals and needs.

Much ado is being made today about the reform of tort law, but these reforms have essentially arisen as members of society wrestle with certain basic issues. Should society bear the cost of losses suffered by individuals, or should that responsibility be shifted to the individual? What role should fault play in tort law? Is the purpose of tort law merely to resolve disputes, or is it to see that justice is done?

Looking into the mirror of the past often helps us better understand where we are going in the future. Knowing the historical derivation of tort law will give you some insights about the tort reforms advocated today. Knowing how those who have come before us have answered the questions raised above helps us as today's legislators, voters, jurors, and judges struggle to answer these same questions. In Chapter 16 we examine tort reform issues. Those issues cannot be adequately addressed without considering the philosophical implications they raise. Our brief interaction with tort law of the past shows that these philosophical questions are neither new nor easily resolved.

CLASSIFICATION OF TORTS

Today torts are divided into three categories, depending on the nature of the defendant's conduct: intentional torts, negligence, and strict liability. By far the most common is negligence. The bulk of personal injury practice centers around automobile accident cases, "slip and fall" cases, and other types of cases in which someone failed to use reasonable care. Strict liability is found to a lesser degree, usually in the context of product liability. Intentional torts usually involve conduct that also constitutes a crime such as a battery or an assault. Tort law differs from criminal law in terms of the purposes, burden of proof, and procedural rules.

The organization of this text reflects the relative importance of each of these tort classifications. Although considerable coverage is devoted to negligence and related topics, relatively little consideration is given to intentional torts. Although intentional torts are conceptually easier to comprehend than negligence, negligence is addressed in depth because paralegals must have a solid foundation in negligence when they begin practicing, even if their understanding of intention is a bit superficial.

We divide our discussion into three separate areas, but you should be aware that many torts may be based on any one of the three types of conduct. Misrepresentation, for example, can be committed intentionally, negligently, or with no fault (strict liability), as can defamation. Malpractice is a tort based on negligence. Bad faith is primarily an intentional tort. But many other causes of action are hybrids that defy precise classification. Rather than trying to pigeonhole all torts into neat categories, recognize that some distinctions are blurred.

SUMMARY

A tort can be defined as a civil wrong for which the victim receives compensation in the form of damages. The feeling that socially unreasonable conduct should be penalized underlies tort law, and much of the case law is focused on determining what constitutes unreasonable conduct. In some cases, however, reasonableness is not an issue because the goal is to protect society no matter how reasonable the conduct.

Public policy concerns prevail throughout tort law. These concerns center primarily around the ideals of justice, fairness, and equality held by the public or the community and becomes community policies that provide the purpose or rationale underlying the principles of tort law. One of the philosophical dilemmas that permeates tort law is how much weight should be placed on the needs of society when resolving disputes between individuals. In balancing these needs, courts frequently resort to slippery-slope arguments to justify their refusal to grant relief to sympathetic plaintiffs.

Tort law is largely a product of common law, although statutes are, in some instances, relied on. The courts frequently look to the *Restatement of the Law of Torts* in formulating the law.

Although similar in some ways to crimes, torts differ in terms of purpose, burden of proof, and procedural rules. Many acts are considered both a crime and a tort. Torts differ from contracts in that the duties assigned according to tort law are those imposed by law, whereas those assigned in the context of contracts are by virtue of the party's consent. Furthermore, in contract law obligations are assumed toward specific individuals, whereas tort law assumes that obligations are owed to society as a whole.

The origin of tort law can be traced back to the blood feud, which evolved into the "moot" process of dispute resolution and ultimately developed into the common law. When the concept of monetary compensation emerged, it was directed toward the clan rather than the individual. The action in trespass, which evolved in the thirteenth century, required proof that the defendant used force directly on the plaintiff or his property. The plaintiff did not, however, have to prove fault on the part of the defendant. In contrast, trespass on the case allowed recovery even when the defendant did not use force or inflicted injury indirectly. Proof of damages and the defendant's wrongful intent or negligence were, however, required in a trespass-on-the-case action. The concept of negligence developed along with the evolution of public transportation. At the same time, actions in trespass and trespass on the case fell into disfavor and ultimately disappeared. Strict liability has now assumed an important role in tort law and is evidence of its cyclical evolution in that the law began with no fault (action in trespass) and has now culminated in no fault. Tort law bears the imprint of the "scientific" scholars and legal realists who sought its reform.

KEY TERMS

action in trespass (*vi et armis*)
Early cause of action involving serious, forcible breaches of peace that evolved to encompass even minor physical contact; no showing of fault was required

beyond a reasonable doubt
Standard of proof requiring a showing of almost absolute certainty for each element

black-letter law
Legal principles generally accepted by the legal community

case law
Case-by-case decision making by the court

nolo contendere
Pleas of "no contest"; not an admission of guilt

preponderance of the evidence
Standard of proof requiring a showing that each element is more probable than not

public policy
Policy of the public or a community which dictates the norms of the community based on its beliefs and values regarding justice, fairness, and equality

restitution
Compensation for a crime given to the victim

slippery-slope argument
Argument that once you take a first step in allowing something in one instance, you are in danger of sliding the "slippery slope" into a bottomless pit of circumstances requiring comparable treatment

tort
Civil wrong for which victim receives compensation in the form of damages

tortfeasor
One who has committed a tort

trespass on the case
Early cause of action involving injuries inflicted indirectly and requiring some showing of fault

REVIEW QUESTIONS

1. What are some of the purposes of tort law?

2. What is a tort?

3. How does the concept of reasonableness relate to tort law?

4. What place do public policy arguments and morality play in tort law?

5. What is a slippery-slope argument, and how does it affect court decisions?

6. How do each of the following relate to tort law?
   a. case law
   b. statutes
   c. *Restatement-Torts*

7. What are the primary differences between tort law and criminal law?

8. What are the primary differences between tort law and contract law?

9. Describe the evolution of tort law. Identify blood feuds, moots, actions in trespass, and trespass on the case in the process.

PRACTICE EXAM

Students should complete the practice exam after studying each chapter. The answers are in Appendix A. If you score lower than 80%, you should reread the materials.

True-False

1. Some perceive tort liability as a tax because it puts some people out of business, makes some products unaffordable, and hampers some governmental bodies in their delivery of services.

2. Those who believe in the expansion of tort liability believe that tort law should protect the interests of consumers.

3. Those who argue against the expansion of tort law believe that individuals should bear the consequences of their decisions, and that if we burden industry too much, new technological developments will be inhibited or prohibited.

4. A tort is an intentional act for which a victim receives damages.

5. The basic premise of tort law is that socially unreasonable conduct should be penalized.

6. Reasonableness balances the plaintiff's need for protection against the defendant's freedom to pursue his own ends.

7. Reasonableness does not depend on the perceptions of the individual determining reasonableness.

8. In some instances, a defendant can be held liable even if his conduct is reasonable.

9. Public policy arguments do not consider societal interests because the dispute at issue is between individuals.

10. Any blatantly immoral conduct is considered a tort.

11. Tort law is driven exclusively by case law.

12. The *Restatement of the Law of Torts* attempts to provide lawyers with black-letter principles.

13. Compensation is the only purpose of tort law.

14. In tort law the primary goal is to punish the tortfeasor and to deter others from the same conduct.

15. An admission of guilt cannot be used against a defendant in a subsequent civil trial but a plea of *nolo contendere* can.

16. It is harder to prove that a defendant is guilty of a crime than to prove that she is liable for a tort.

17. Tort duties sometimes correspond with contractual duties.

18. Trespass-on-the-case actions required proof of the defendant's negligence or wrongful intent.

19. Negligence arose as a cause of action because of a concern that few could afford to travel under the trespass theory of tort law.

20. Torts that trace their heritage back to trespass on the case require no proof of actual damages.

21. Strict liability was evident in actions in trespass.

22. At the beginning of the twentieth century, tort law came to be viewed as a means of creating a just society and not just a means of resolving disputes.

23. Intent must be proved when suing based on either an intentional tort or negligence.

24. Negligence is the most common tort, whereas intentional torts are rarely encountered in practice.

Fill-in-the-Blank

1. _____ _____ arguments concern issues of fairness, equality, and justice.

2. A_____ _____ argument is used by a court when it is concerned that a decision for a sympathetic plaintiff may lead to innumerable individuals in similar situations seeking redress.

3. A _____ is an offense against society, whereas a(n) _____ is an offense against an individual.

4. In tort law the burden of proof is

_____ _____

_____.

5. The _____ _____
required a clan to go to war against any outsider
who inflicted harm on a clan member. It was
eventually replaced by a(n) _____,
in which a victim would plead his case to the
community and ask for redress of his grievance.

6. A tort that involves the pleading of *vi et armis*
is a(n) _____ _____
_____. A more restrictive tort that
allows recovery in the absence of a showing of force is a(n) _____
_____ _____.

Multiple-Choice

1. Those who argue for the expansion of tort law
believe that
   a. the burden of risk should be borne by those
better able to afford it, such as manufacturers
and providers of services.
   b. the law is too paternalistic.
   c. individuals should bear the burden of the risk
of getting injured.
   d. all of the above.

2. The *Restatement of the Law of Torts*
   a. has been adopted by all states.
   b. is frequently cited by the courts.
   c. is prepared by the courts.
   d. all of the above.

3. Tort law differs from criminal law in terms of
   a. purpose.
   b. burden of proof.
   c. procedural rules.
   d. all of the above.

4. Contracts differ from torts in that
   a. the duties that exist in contract law are
imposed by law.
   b. the duties that exist in tort law are imposed
by law.
   c. in contract law duties are made to the public in
general.
   d. none of the above.

5. In early Anglo-Saxon times,
   a. blood was offered to heal injured clan pride.
   b. there was great emphasis placed on issues of
fault and blameworthiness.
   c. even remote causal connections were considered sufficient to justify punishment.
   d. all of the above.

6. Following the Norman Conquest,
   a. the dispute-resolution process fell to the royal
justices of the king's court.
   b. it was discovered that following local rules led
to maximum efficiency in resolving conflict.
   c. the common law was developed.
   d. all of the above.

7. An action in trespass
   a. required a showing of force and arms.
   b. required a showing of fault.
   c. dealt with nonforcible breaches of peace.
   d. all of the above.

8. In a trespass on the case
   a. the plaintiff had to plead *vi et armis*.
   b. the plaintiff did not have to prove injury or
damage.
   c. recovery was allowed in the absence of force or
where injury was inflicted indirectly.
   d. none of the above.

TORT TEASERS

As indicated in this chapter, the issue of risk allocation is a troublesome matter that the courts and legal scholars have grappled with over the years. To help clarify the questions relating to risk allocation, consider the following hypotheti-cal situation. After unsuccessfully administering Ritalin and several other drugs, as well as using counseling and behavior modification techniques, a psychologist resorts to giving lithium to Lisa, a hyperactive five-year-old who is violent toward others and self-destructive. Lisa's behavior becomes manageable once the dosage is adjusted; she is kept on the lithium for five years. As an adult, she is diagnosed as

having severe, life-threatening liver damage that requires a liver transplant. The doctor traces the liver condition back to Lisa's ongoing lithium usage. Long-term studies indicate that lithium can cause liver damage, especially in children who have had protracted exposure to the drug. These stud-ies were not available when Lisa was given the medication.

Write out all the reasons supporting your belief that the psychologist should or should not be held liable for Lisa's damages. Be sure to include in your discussion public policy arguments you think are relevant.

INTERNET INQUIRIES

The Cornell Law School Legal Information Institute is a major legal resource gateway. At this site you will find links to United States Court of Appeals recent decisions, state court decisions and statutes, and a host of relevant resources. Be sure to bookmark this site; you will use it often.

To become familiar with what this site has to offer, do the following exercises:

a. Go to http://www.law.cornell.edu/ and scroll down and select "Accident & Injuries"

b. Find the link to "Listing by Jurisdictions" by selecting "State Law Resources." Go to your state and make a list of the resources that are available online.

c. Select "Supreme Court," then select the search option. Enter "Tort Law." On the search page that comes up, find *Bates v. Dow Argo Sciences LLC*. In the cases that come up following *Bates*, look for a case involving El Al Israel Airlines. Read the synopsis at the beginning, and write down the holding of the case.

PRACTICAL PONDERABLES

Much ado has been made in the media about the elderly woman who collected a substantial judgment from McDonald's as a result of the injuries she sustained from hot coffee she spilled on her lap. To get more details about this case, go to http://www.lectlaw.com, type "McDonald's" into the search window and choose "Actual Facts About the McDonald's Coffee Case." (Note that this article was written by the American Trial Lawyers Association [ATLA], whose primary members are plaintiffs' attorneys.)

After reading this article, write a short paper on your assessment of the appropriateness of the judgment. In your paper, consider some of the arguments raised in this chapter about the purpose of tort law.

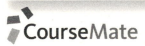

Access an interactive eBook, chapter-specific learning tools, including flashcards, quizzes, and more in your Paralegal CourseMate, accessed through www. CengageBrain.com.

CHAPTER 2

Overview of a Tort Case

© Cengage Learning 2012

CHAPTER OBJECTIVES

In this chapter you will be given a procedural overview of a tort case and will learn the terminology associated with

- The initiation of a complaint and a response to that complaint.
- The conduct of the discovery process.
- The preparation for trial.
- The conduct of a trial.
- The implementation of post-trial procedures.

After leaving work on Friday afternoon, Hanna drove to Happy Valley Bank to cash her paycheck. Leaving the bank, as she prepared to enter Sunshine Avenue, the street on which the bank was located, she came to a complete stop and looked into the mirror provided by the bank to see if there was any oncoming traffic. The bank had found it necessary to install this mirror because customers experienced so much difficulty in seeing any oncoming cars. The curved shape of the street obstructed their view. (See Exhibit 2–1). As fate would have it, rain from earlier that afternoon had caused the mirror to fog over. Consequently, Hanna did not see the car being driven by Fred and pulled out directly in front of it. Fred, being unable to stop in time, rammed into Hanna's car, causing it to spin around and collide with the car being driven by Sunny, which was proceeding in the opposite direction. Fred and Sunny sustained only minor injuries in the accident, but Hanna received a broken leg and a concussion. As a result, Hanna was out of work for a month.

Hanna relates these events to an attorney and then tells the attorney that she wants to sue the bank, which Hanna believes was the ultimate cause of her accident. Hanna is aware that Fred and Sunny may sue her for the property damage and physical injuries they incurred. Let us walk through the likely chain of events that will occur as Hanna enters the legal world (see Exhibit 2–2).

INITIATING A COMPLAINT

First, the attorney must ascertain whether the legal elements of a negligence claim have been met. Did the bank have a duty to maintain the mirror in a safe condition and, if so, did the bank breach that duty by allowing the mirror to fog over? The attorney must also determine whether the mirror was, in fact, the cause of the accident and whether Hanna sustained monetary and other damages as a result of the accident.

To address these questions the attorney will need to find out several things. Who owns the mirror? Who is responsible for maintenance of the mirror?

EXHIBIT 2–1 Bank Parking Lot

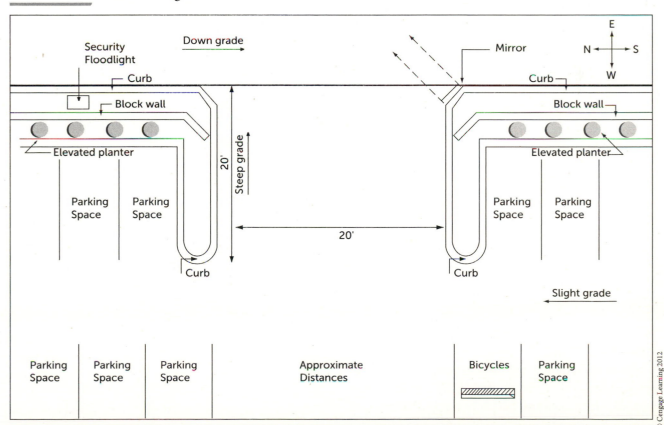

© Cengage Learning 2012

EXHIBIT 2–2 Overview of a Case

INITIATING A COMPLAINT	• Interview • Investigation • Filing of complaint
DEFENDANT RESPONSE	• Answer • File counterclaim or cross-claim • File motions • Default
DISCOVERY	• Interrogatories • Depositions • Disclosure statements • Requests for admissions • Requests for production of documents • Requests for medical or psychological exam • Motions to compel and for protective order • Motions for summary judgment
PRETRIAL PROCEDURES	• Pretrial conference • Motions in limine
TRIAL	• Voir dire (challenges for cause and peremptory challenges) • Opening statements • Direct and cross-examination • Motion for directed verdict • Closing arguments • General or special verdict
POST-TRIAL PROCEDURES	• Motion for new trial • JNOV • Appeal and cross-appeal

© Cengage Learning 2012

EXHIBIT 2–3 Elements of a Complaint

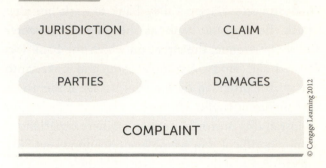

© Cengage Learning 2012

Who owns the bank? Does the bank have any agreements with the city regarding maintenance of the mirror? Is the design of the street itself defective? Was Hanna negligent in her use of the mirror? Were there any witnesses to the accident? Does the extent of Hanna's money damages warrant a lawsuit?

After conducting her investigation, if the attorney concludes that Hanna does have a viable claim, she will send a **demand letter** to Happy Valley Bank. In this letter, she will explain why she believes the bank is liable, she will detail the extent of her client's damages, and she will put forth a demand for settlement of the case. If she cannot negotiate a settlement, she will initiate the case or lawsuit by filing a **complaint** (FRCP 8[a]).[1]

Answers to these questions can be ascertained during interviews with the client and witnesses. A discussion of interviewing practices is available in Appendix B, Interviewing.

A complaint has four basic elements (see Exhibit 2–3). First, a complaint must state that the court has **jurisdiction**, i.e., the authority to hear the case. The attorney must show, for example, that she has met any residence or amount-in-controversy requirements of the court. The plaintiff has the right to choose the court within which to file her complaint so long as she meets the jurisdictional requirements of that court.

Second, the complaint must list the parties to the action. In this case Hanna would be the plaintiff and Happy Valley Bank the defendant.

Third, the complaint must provide a brief summary of each of the elements of the case along with the basic facts that will be used to prove each element. Hanna's attorney must allege that Happy Valley Bank had a duty to maintain the mirror in a safe condition, that it breached that duty, that as a result of the breach Hanna was injured, and that she sustained monetary damages. The degree of factual detail required in this part of the complaint is dictated by the procedural rules of the particular state in which the complaint is being filed (check the Rules of Civil Procedure in your state).

Finally, the complaint must specify the relief being sought by the plaintiff. In Hanna's case, she will be

---

1. The *Federal Rules of Civil Procedure* are cited throughout this text as FRCP.

asking for compensation for her hospital and medical bills and her lost salary, as well as additional monies for the pain and suffering she endured. In some states, a verification must be submitted along with the complaint. The **verification** is an affidavit indicating that the plaintiff has read the complaint and that, to the best of her knowledge, it is true. The *Rules of Civil Procedure* in Hanna's state will determine how defendant Happy Valley Bank should be served with the complaint, where the complaint should be filed, and who may serve it.

DEFENDANT'S RESPONSE

Once Happy Valley Bank has been served, it has several options. If the bank does not file a response or answer to the complaint, Hanna can get a **default judgment** in which the court would resolve the case in Hanna's favor because of Happy Valley Bank's lack of opposition (FRCP 55). The court might set aside the default judgment if Happy Valley Bank can show it had a good reason for failing to respond to the complaint.

Defendant Happy Valley Bank could choose to file an **answer** (FRCP 8[b]). In so doing it would admit those allegations in Hanna's complaint it thought to be true, deny those with which it disagreed, and respond lack of sufficient knowledge for those allegations requiring further investigation. At the same time, the defendant could raise any affirmative defenses it might have, such as contributory negligence. An **affirmative defense** is any defense that the party asserting it must affirmatively prove or, in other words, for which it bears the burden of proof (FRCP 8[d]). So if Happy Valley Bank asserted that Hanna's negligence was the cause of her damages (thus using contributory negligence as an affirmative defense), it would have the burden of proving that negligence.

The defendant may at this time also raise any counterclaims or cross-claims. A **counterclaim** is a claim raised by the defendant against the plaintiff;

a **cross-claim** is a claim raised against a co-party. For example, if Fred sued Hanna and Happy Valley Bank to recover for his injuries and property damage, Hanna could raise a counterclaim against Fred alleging contributory negligence and a cross-claim against Happy Valley Bank alleging negligence.

At the same time Happy Valley Bank answers Hanna's complaint, it could file a motion (FRCP 12). Motions can be filed alleging, among other things, a lack of jurisdiction over the person or subject matter, improper venue, insufficiency of process, or failure to state a claim upon which relief can be granted. The most important of these is the last—failure to state a claim upon which relief can be granted, referred to in some states as a motion for dismissal or a **demurrer**. By filing such a motion, the defendant, in essence, is asserting that the plaintiff has failed to state a legally necessary element of the cause of action. If, for example, Happy Valley Bank did not own the mirror and had no legally recognizable duty to maintain it, the element of duty would be unfulfilled. If that were the case, Happy Valley Bank could file a motion alleging that Hanna had failed to state a claim upon which relief could be granted. By granting the motion, the court would dismiss the case.

DISCOVERY

If the case is not dismissed in these early stages of the process, it will move into the **discovery** phase (FRCP 26). The theory underlying discovery is that the more each side finds out about the other side's case, the more likely it is that the parties will be able to settle the case and that the final outcome will be an equitable one. Discovery can be compared to a game of poker. In this game each party tries to gain as much information as possible about the opposing side's position while revealing as little information as possible about its own position. Admittedly the stakes in litigation are often higher than those in poker, but the strategies employed are remarkably similar. It is fair to say that most cases today are won or lost in

NET NEWS

To read and search the *Federal Rules of Civil Procedure* online, go to **http://www.law.cornell.edu**. Select "Federal Rules", then select "Federal Rules of Civil Procedure". To access the procedural rules of your state, either go to **http://www.llrx.com/** and select "Court Rules, Forms and Dockets", then select your state, or find the web page for your highest state court, which you can do by going to the Directory of Nation's Courts at **http://www.ncsc.org**.

the discovery process. Because legal assistants play a major role in this process, you must become adept at creating and manipulating the tools of discovery.

There are five basic types of discovery: (1) interrogatories, (2) depositions, (3) requests for admission, (4) requests for production of documents, and (5) requests for medical and psychological examinations.

Interrogatories are written questions submitted to the opposing party, which that party must answer in writing and under oath (FRCP 33). Interrogatories are a relatively inexpensive way of soliciting basic objective information. Hanna's counsel, for example, will want to use interrogatories to find out the names, addresses, and duties of the employees of Happy Valley Bank who maintain the mirror, as well as information regarding Happy Valley Bank's relationship to the owner of the property on which the bank is located. Interrogatories are limited in usefulness because they are usually answered by or with the assistance of opposing counsel, whose aim is typically to provide as little information as possible.

A **deposition**, however, is an oral examination of a witness (or a party to the lawsuit) under oath (FRCP 27–32). Because depositions are considerably more time-consuming and more expensive than interrogatories, attorneys carefully select those whom they want to depose. At a deposition, deposing counsel will be able to observe the demeanor and presentation of the witness and assess how a jury might respond to the deponent. The attorney will also be able to pursue lines of questioning more thoroughly than by using interrogatories because he or she can ask follow-up questions and observe the witnesses' body language as they respond to the questions. A court reporter, present during the deposition, prepares a transcript of everything that is said. The transcript can then be introduced at trial. For that reason an attorney may opt to depose a witness whose testimony she wants to use at trial if she believes that witness will not appear for the trial. Counsel can also use the witness's statements made during the deposition to impeach (discredit) his testimony at trial. The deposition may also be videotaped and portions of the videotape may

be shown to the judge and/or jury who can assess the witnesses' demeanor at the deposition.

Happy Valley Bank's counsel would most likely want to depose Hanna to elicit detailed information from her about what she did before the accident, as well as to assess her probable demeanor before a jury. This kind of information would be pertinent to counsel not only in mapping a trial strategy but also in considering the advisability of settlement.

Requests for admissions are simply requests by one party asking that the other party admit certain facts (FRCP 36). If Hanna's attorney, for example, ascertained that the bank did in fact own, install, and maintain the mirror, she would want the bank to admit those facts. Once a party admits a fact, that matter is conclusively established and cannot be argued at trial. Under the *Federal Rules* and the rules in many states, if a party fails to respond to requests for admissions, those matters are deemed admitted.

Documents vital to a case that are in the possession of the opposing party can be obtained via a **request for production of documents** (FRCP 34). Hanna's attorney will want to review any maintenance records pertaining to the maintenance of the mirror and defense counsel will want to examine Hanna's hospital and medical records. Both can do so by propounding or serving a request for production of documents. Because Hanna has put her medical condition at issue in this case, Happy Valley Bank's counsel will also want to select a physician to examine Hanna in order to get a second opinion about the seriousness of her injuries. This can be done through a **request for medical examination** (FRCP 35).

If Hanna lived in a state that required mandatory disclosure, she would have to serve a disclosure statement early on in the case to the opposing parties. A **disclosure statement** must contain certain categories of information about that party's case. To understand how disclosure statements have evolved, you must know something about the reformation of the discovery process.

The last decade has seen the emergence of a reform movement advocating "disclosure-centered"

NET NEWS

To review a portion of a deposition taken of Dr. Jeffrey Wigand (the former vice president and head of research for the tobacco company, Brown & Williamson, whose testimony was the focus of the movie *The Insider*), go to **http://www.jeffreywigand.com/**. Dr. Wigand's testimony was crucial in subsequent litigation against the tobacco companies.

discovery, in which parties are required to disclose information voluntarily without waiting for a request. Under the traditional "request-centered" system, an attorney who wanted information had to ask for it and describe it in clear enough terms that an opponent could not get away with hiding crucial evidence by claiming that the request was ambiguous. That process was inherently inefficient since the requesting party had no knowledge of what information was there to be discovered and he had to ask to see everything. In some ways, traditional discovery was like the game Battleship, in which each player tries to guess where the other player's ships are.

The basis of mandatory disclosure is full and open disclosure. Instead of putting the requesting party to the frustrating task of firing off requests in the dark, mandatory disclosure requires parties to disclose—without being asked—every bit of information in their possession that is relevant to any issue being litigated. This approach eliminates a great deal of the gamesmanship of traditional discovery and much of the paperwork as well. The traditional discovery tools are still needed to flesh out the information voluntarily provided, but their use is now greatly curtailed.

Disclosure statements are the foundation of mandatory disclosure. Under the federal rules, the body of the disclosure statement must address four areas of subject matter. These include the disclosure of

- the name, address, and telephone number of each individual likely to have discoverable information that the disclosing party may use to support its claims or defenses.

- all documents in a party's possession, custody, or control and that the disclosing party may use to support its claims or defenses.

- the computation of damages and the documents and other evidentiary materials upon which such computations are based.

- any insurance policy covering the defendant for the liabilities claimed in the suit.

- the identity of expert witnesses who will be used at trial.

During the pretrial discovery process both parties can make discovery-related motions as well as motions for summary judgment. Discovery-related motions include motions to compel and motions for protective orders. A **motion to compel** is appropriate when the opposing party refuses to produce discoverable material (FRCP 37). A **motion for a protective order**, in contrast, prevents discovery of information that is privileged and therefore not discoverable (FRCP 26[c]).

During the discovery process a party may evaluate the dispute and determine that the other side has failed to prove one or more elements of its case. Consequently, there is no material fact at issue for the jury to decide; instead, the court could render a decision as a matter of law without a trial. In this event the party will file a **motion for summary judgment**, requesting that the court enter a judgment on its behalf, thus dispensing with the need for a trial (FRCP 56). A party can also request a partial summary judgment, which, in effect, eliminates particular issues. If Hanna's attorney filed a motion for a partial summary judgment and the court determined, as a matter of law, that Happy Valley Bank had a duty to maintain the mirror in a safe condition and that it breached that duty, then the only remaining issue to resolve would be the extent of Hanna's injuries and whether Happy Valley Bank was the proximate and actual cause of Hanna's injuries.

To rebut a motion for summary judgment the opponent must show that a genuine factual dispute exists and that a trial will be necessary to resolve that dispute. The mere allegation that a factual dispute exists is, however, insufficient. Using answers from

NET NEWS

To see sample motions in limine, go to **http://www.quojure.com/**. Select "Samples" and enter "motions in limine" as your search term.

interrogatories, deposition answers, and affidavits, the opposing party must show that it can controvert material facts alleged by the other side.

PRETRIAL PROCEDURES

If the parties cannot resolve the dispute during the discovery process, and summary judgment is not granted the case will proceed toward trial. Most courts require a **pretrial conference** to clarify the issues and defenses for trial, to establish the witnesses and exhibits that will be used at trial, and to promote settlement (FRCP 16). How vehemently the judge pushes for settlement depends on his or her philosophical bent. Statistics tell us, however, that most cases settle at or before the pretrial conference.

Before trial the parties will once again have an opportunity to move for dismissal as well as to make motions in limine. The purpose of a **motion in limine** is to resolve whether the evidence should or should not be introduced to the jury because it is unduly prejudicial, irrelevant, or will confuse the jury or waste its time. For example, if Hanna's attorney wanted to introduce testimony that Happy Valley Bank had instituted a new procedure for maintenance of the mirror subsequent to Hanna's accident, Happy Valley Bank's attorney would want to make a motion in limine to prevent that testimony. The generally prevailing argument, by the way, is that a motion such as this should be granted, as admission of this type of evidence would inhibit defendants from taking measures to remove or correct dangerous conditions.

TRIAL

If Hanna's case goes to trial, she will have the opportunity to decide between a bench trial (trial before a judge) and a jury trial (FRCP 39). In a jury trial all factual issues are resolved by the jury while all legal issues are resolved by the judge. In a **bench trial** the judge decides both factual and legal issues. Whether to opt for a jury trial or a bench trial is a strategic decision, although case law does limit the right to a jury in certain types of cases.

Jury selection is conducted through a process known as **voir dire**, which consists of a series of questions asked of potential jurors by the trial judge or the attorneys, depending on local practice (FRCP 47). A party who wants to excuse a particular juror and can show that the juror has already formed a judgment as to how the case should be decided or for some reason is unable to decide the case impartially, may use a **challenge for cause** (FRCP 47[c]). The party who wants to dismiss a particular juror but cannot allege bias may remove the juror using a **peremptory challenge** (FRCP 47[e]). No reason need be given for a peremptory challenge.

Although an attorney has an unlimited number of challenges for cause, he has a limited number of peremptory challenges (the specific number depends on local practice). Hanna's attorney might want to use his peremptory challenges to eliminate jurors engaged in a particular occupation if research has shown that members of that profession are generally reluctant to compensate plaintiffs generously. He will also want to excuse persons that instinct or observation tell him will be unsympathetic to his client's plight.

When the trial begins, Hanna's counsel will be given an opportunity to make **opening statements**. He will probably give an overview of the basic elements of her case, introduce the parties and witnesses that will be involved in the trial, and in general set the tone and theme of her case. Opening statements are not considered part of the evidence, but they are extremely important, especially in light of research showing that the majority of jurors decide the outcome of the case during opening statements and do not change their minds after hearing the testimony. Because Hanna has the burden of proving each element of her case by a preponderance of the evidence, she will be given the opportunity not

NET NEWS

To read the opening statements in famous trials such as the McMartin Preschool and Timothy McVeigh criminal trials, go to **http://www.law.umkc.edu** and enter "opening statements" as your search term.

NET NEWS

To read the *Federal Rules of Evidence*, go to **http://www.azd.uscourts.gov** and select the tab for "Rules/ General Orders". Then select "Federal Rules of Evidence."

only to begin the trial with opening statements but also to end the trial by making the final statement in closing arguments. In order to prove her case by a preponderance of the evidence, Hanna's evidence must be more convincing than Happy Valley Bank's evidence.

The evidence in any civil case consists of witness testimony and exhibits. On **direct examination** questions are posed by the counsel calling the witness; **cross-examination** is conducted by opposing counsel. The function of cross-examination is to impeach (discredit) testimony given by the witness during direct examination. This process continues through redirect and recross-examination and so on until counsel exhaust all their questions.

During the course of the trial, counsel may object to questions being asked or evidence being presented. The trial court will rule on the admissibility of evidence using the rules of evidence appropriate for that court. Each state has adopted rules of evidence for its state courts and the Federal Rules of Evidence are used in federal courts. If the court **sustains** (grants) an objection to a question, that question cannot be asked but if the court **overrules** (denies) an objection, that question can be asked.

After Hanna's counsel finishes presenting Hanna's case to the jury, counsel for Happy Valley Bank will probably move for a **directed verdict**, arguing that Hanna failed to meet the burden of proof on all the elements of her case (FRCP 50). Such motions, though frequently made, are commonly denied, but if a motion for a directed verdict is granted, the case is in essence dismissed. Hanna's counsel will make a similar motion if Happy Valley Bank presents evidence regarding an affirmative defense. At the close of Happy Valley Bank's case, Hanna will be given an opportunity to present rebuttal evidence, which is used to refute evidence presented by the defendant.

Because Hanna has the burden of proof, her counsel will be given the opportunity to present her **closing argument** to the jury first. In this argument Hanna's attorney will summarize the facts of the case, showing how the evidence established each of the legal elements. Using the theme established in her opening statements, she will use her most persuasive rhetoric to convince the jury that Hanna should prevail and that generous damages should be awarded. Counsel for Happy Valley Bank will do likewise in his closing arguments, and then Hanna's attorney will close with a rebuttal argument.

Finally, in a process known as **charging the jury**, the judge will instruct the jury on the rules of law to be applied (FRCP 50). In some states standard jury instructions are used. In others, attorneys draft proposed instructions for the judge's consideration and, in a conference conducted outside the earshot of the jury, argue which instructions should be adopted. Much attention is given to the adoption of jury instructions, and counsel is given an opportunity to object to any instructions the judge gives or fails to give. Jury instructions are important because objections to these instructions are typically the fundamental components of an appeal.

The jury will then be asked to render either a general or special verdict (FRCP 49). In Hanna's case a **general verdict** would require the jury to decide if Happy Valley Bank was liable for Hanna's injuries and to determine what damages should be awarded. If a **special verdict** were requested, the jury would be required to answer special interrogatories, and the judge would have to determine the prevailing party after reviewing the jury's answers. In a case tried before a judge alone, the attorneys may be required to submit trial briefs in which they present the applicable law and show how it would apply to the facts of the particular case.

NET NEWS

To see jury instructions used in specific Federal courts, go to **http://www.uscourts.gov/** and select the court in which you are interested. To read an interesting article about how jury instructions and the whole jury system might be improved, go to **http://www.uchastings.edu/** and enter "improving the jury system" as your search term.

NET NEWS

For an overview of the court system, read the article entitled "The Court System and How it Works" by going to **http://www.lectlaw.com** and enter the name of the article.

POST-TRIAL

If the jury decides against Hanna, she can make a **motion for a new trial**, arguing that errors were committed during the trial (FRCP 59). Or she can move for a **judgment notwithstanding the verdict (JNOV)**, arguing that the verdict reached was contrary to the evidence and law (FRCP 50[b]). Such motions are generally contingent on counsel making appropriate objections during the trial; if counsel fails to do so, these procedural remedies will be denied. Hanna could also **appeal** (see *Federal Rules of Appellate Procedure*) the decision to a higher court, and if Happy Valley Bank were unhappy with part of the outcome at the trial level, it can file a **cross-appeal**. Once a final judgment is entered, however, and all appeals were completed, the issues litigated are **res judicata**, in that they cannot be re-litigated at a later time. The philosophy underlying this rule is that litigation must ultimately come to an end and cannot be allowed to go on forever.

EMPHASIS ON DISCOVERY THROUGHOUT THIS TEXT

Although this overview of a civil case is certainly not exhaustive, lacking many of the subroutes parties can pursue in litigation, it does give you a framework within which to analyze tort problems. Examples will be provided throughout the text of typical discovery tools, and you will be encouraged to consider the information presented in each chapter in the context of how it could be applied in discovery. Keep the importance of discovery foremost in your mind as you work through this book. Remember that a key contribution paralegals can make to the litigation team lies in their ability to create, manipulate, and organize discovery tools.

SUMMARY

To initiate a tort claim, the plaintiff must file a complaint. This complaint must state the basis for the court's jurisdiction, the parties to the action, the elements of the case, and the relief being sought. The defendant may then file an answer admitting or denying allegations in the plaintiff's complaint and raising any affirmative defenses. The defendant may also bring a counterclaim against the plaintiff or a cross-claim against a co-party. Additionally, he or she may file a motion alleging, for example, that the plaintiff failed to state a claim upon which relief can be granted.

In the discovery phase both parties try to find out as much as possible about the other side's case while revealing as little as possible about their own. Interrogatories, depositions, requests for admission, requests for production of documents, and requests for medical and psychological examinations are the most frequently used tools of discovery. A party may also file a motion for summary judgment if no material fact is arguably at issue.

A case that cannot be resolved during the discovery process and is not dismissed on summary judgment moves on to trial. Before trial, most courts require the parties to attend a pretrial conference and to resolve evidentiary questions by making motions in limine. At the trial the parties are allowed to select jurors through a process of voir dire, dismissing jurors on the basis of either a challenge for cause or peremptory challenge. At trial the plaintiff has the burden of proving each element of his or her case by a preponderance of the evidence. Both counsels are given the opportunity to introduce their cases by making opening statements, to elicit testimony through direct examination, and to impeach witnesses through cross-examination. Motions for directed verdict are generally made after opposing counsel has presented his or her case. After both counsel have given closing arguments, the judge charges the jury. The jury is then asked to render either a general or special verdict, the latter of which requires the answering of special interrogatories.

Subsequent to trial, a party can move for a new trial or a judgment notwithstanding the verdict. Appeals and cross-appeals can also be filed, but once a final judgment is entered and all appeals are completed, the issues litigated are considered res judicata.

KEY TERMS

affirmative defense
Any defense that a party asserts for which it bears the burden of proof

answer
A pleading in which the defendant responds to the plaintiff's complaint

appeal
Formal request by a party asking a higher court to review the decision of a lower court

bench trial
Trial before a judge

challenge for cause
Request to remove a potential juror because of his alleged inability to decide the case impartially

charging the jury
Process in which the judge instructs the jurors in rules of law they are to apply

closing argument
Final statement made by an attorney that summarizes the evidence

complaint
An initial pleading filed on behalf of the plaintiff, the purpose of which is to provide the defendant with the material elements of the plaintiff's demand

counterclaim
A claim presented by a defendant in opposition to the plaintiff's claim

cross-appeal
Appeal filed after an appeal is filed by the opposing party

cross-claim
A claim brought by a defendant against a co-defendant in the same action

cross-examination
Examination of a witness called by the opposing party

default judgment
Judgment entered due to lack of opposition on behalf of the opposing party

demand letter
A letter detailing a client's damages and setting forth the reasons for his or her demand

demurrer
Motion for dismissal based on a defect in the form or content of a complaint

deposition
Oral examination of a witness under oath

direct examination
Examination by the attorney that called the witness

directed verdict
Dismissal of a case because of the opposing party's failure to meet the requisite burden of proof

disclosure statement
A document each party is required to prepare and serve on opposing parties shortly after a lawsuit commences. This document must contain certain categories of information about that party's case

discovery
Process through which parties try to find out as much as possible about the other side's case

general verdict
Verdict in which a jury decides issues of liability and damages

interrogatories
Written questions submitted to the opposing party that that party must answer in writing and under oath

judgment notwithstanding the verdict (JNOV)
A decision that the verdict reached was contrary to the evidence and the law

jurisdiction
Power to hear a particular kind of case

motion for a new trial
Motion requesting a new trial based on an alleged error committed by the trial judge

motion for a protective order
Motion that protects a party from having to disclose privileged information

motion for summary judgment
Motion requesting that the court enter a judgment on the party's behalf because there is no material fact at issue

motion in limine
Motion to prevent evidence from being presented to the jury

motion to compel
Motion to force the opposing party to comply with a request for discovery

opening statements
Statements made by counsel to the jury at the beginning of trial

overrule
To deny an objection

peremptory challenge
Request to remove a potential juror for no articulated reason

pretrial conference
Conference involving the judge and parties at which issues and procedures for the trial are clarified and efforts are made at settlement

requests for admissions
Request by one party asking the other party to admit certain facts

request for medical examination
Request that the opposing party be examined by a physician chosen by the party making the request

request for production of documents
Request for document in possession of the opposing party

res judicata
Legal principle stating that issues litigated cannot be relitigated at a later time

special verdict
Verdict in which the jury is required to answer special interrogatories, which the judge must review to determine who the prevailing party is

sustain
To grant an objection

verification
Affidavit indicating that the plaintiff has read the complaint and to the best of her knowledge believes it to be true

voir dire
Process of jury selection involving the use of challenges for cause and peremptory challenges

REVIEW QUESTIONS

1. What will an attorney generally do before initiating a complaint?

2. What are the four elements of a complaint?

3. What possible options does a defendant have in responding to a plaintiff's complaint?

4. What are the five basic discovery tools, and how are they used?

5. What is a disclosure statement, and how does it relate to the concept of mandatory disclosure?

6. Identify each of the following:
   a. motion to compel
   b. motion for a protective order
   c. motion for summary judgment
   d. motion in limine

7. What is the difference between a jury trial and a bench trial?

8. Describe the voir dire process, and distinguish between challenges for cause and peremptory challenges.

9. What is the purpose of each of the following?
   a. opening statements
   b. closing arguments
   c. direct examination
   d. cross-examination
   e. moving for a directed verdict
   f. charging the jury

10. What is the difference between a general and a special verdict?

11. What options do parties have after trial?

PRACTICE EXAM

Students should complete the practice exam after studying each chapter. The answers are in Appendix A. If you score lower than 80%, you should reread the materials.

True-False

1. Before an attorney can file a complaint, she must determine whether the legal elements of a claim have been met.

2. A plaintiff can select any court in which to file a complaint.

3. The amount of detail required in a complaint is dictated by the statutes in the state in which the complaint is filed.

4. A complaint must specify the relief being sought by the plaintiff.

5. In all states a verification must be submitted along with a complaint.

6. Interrogatories are very useful because they are answered by a party without any assistance from counsel.

7. Once a party admits a fact in a request for admission, that matter is conclusively established and cannot be argued at trial.

8. Under the *Federal Rules of Civil Procedure*, if a party fails to respond to requests for admission, those matters are deemed admitted.

9. A party cannot file a motion for a partial summary judgment.

10. To rebut a motion for summary judgment a party need merely allege that a factual dispute does in fact exist.

11. Most cases settle at or before the pretrial conference.

12. Most jurors decide the outcome of a case during opening statements.

13. The plaintiff opens a case by making the first opening statement and ends a case by making the final closing argument.

14. Motions for directed verdict are rarely made but frequently granted.

15. A party that fails to make the appropriate objections during trial will be denied any procedural remedies requested in a post-trial motion.

Matching

GROUP 1

_____ 1. Place where defendant can raise an affirmative defense

_____ 2. Claim raised by defendant against co-party

_____ 3. Claim raised by plaintiff against defendant

_____ 4. Failure to state claim upon which relief can be granted

a. counterclaim
b. cross-claim
c. demurrer
d. answer

GROUP 2

_____ 1. Used to establish facts

_____ 2. Used to assess plaintiff's medical condition

_____ 3. Used to obtain documents

_____ 4. Used to thoroughly question a party

_____ 5. Used to get basic information

_____ 6. Mandatory disclosure

a. interrogatories
b. deposition
c. requests for admission
d. request for production of documents
e. request for medical examination
f. disclosure statement

GROUP 3

_____ 1. Resolves evidentiary questions

_____ 2. No material fact at issue

_____ 3. Prevents discovery of privileged information

_____ 4. Used when party refuses to provide information

_____ 5. Used when judge erred during trial

a. motion to compel
b. motion for protective order
c. motion in limine
d. motion for summary judgment
e. motion for new trial

GROUP 4

_____ 1. Used to impeach witnesses

_____ 2. Conducted by attorney calling a witness

_____ 3. Sets the theme of a case

_____ 4. Directions regarding rules of law

_____ 5. Failure to meet burden of proof

a. opening statements
b. jury instructions
c. directed verdicts
d. cross-examination
e. direct examination

Fill-in-the-Blanks

1. If an attorney determines that a viable claim exists, he may send a _____ letter to the defendant setting forth why the defendant is liable and demanding a certain amount of money to settle the case.

2. A(n) _____ is an affidavit indicating that the plaintiff has read the complaint and that to the best of her knowledge it is true.

3. If a defendant does not respond to a plaintiff's complaint, the plaintiff can seek a _____ _____ in his favor.

4. A(n) _____ _____ is any defense that the party asserting it bears the burden of proving.

5. At the same time it files an answer, a defendant can file a(n) _____ alleging lack of jurisdiction over the person or subject matter.

6. _____ are written questions submitted to a party which that party must answer in writing.

7. An oral examination of a witness before trial is known as a(n) _____.

8. A party can obtain copies of documents in the possession of the opposing party by filing a(n) _____ _____ _____ _____.

9. If a plaintiff has put her medical condition at issue in a case, the defendant can get a second opinion about the seriousness of her injuries through a(n) _____ _____ _____.

10. In states with mandatory disclosure, each party must file a(n) _____ _____ early on in the case.

11. If during discovery a party learns that there is no material issue of fact and that a court could render a decision without hearing evidence, that party should file a(n) _____ _____ _____.

12. To prevent the jury from hearing irrelevant and prejudicial evidence, a party should file a(n) _____ _____ _____ before trial.

13. At a jury trial all _____ issues are decided by the jury and all _____ are decided by the judge. At a(n) _____ trial the judge decides both factual and legal issues.

14. During the process of _____ _____ the judge or the attorneys can ask potential jurors questions.

15. A party that can show that a potential juror is unable to decide the case impartially should use a(n) _____ _____ _____, whereas a party that cannot allege bias but that wants to get rid of a potential juror should use a _____.

16. If a judge _____ an objection, the question can be asked.

17. In some states standard jury instructions are used to _____ the jury.

18. A jury that is asked to render a(n) _____ verdict must decide liability and award damages; a jury that is asked to render a(n) _____ verdict must answer interrogatories, which a judge must review to determine the prevailing party.

19. A losing party can file a motion for a(n) _____ _____ _____ on the basis that the verdict reached was contrary to the evidence.

20. A party that is unhappy with a trial court's decision can _____ that decision to a higher court; the opposing party can then file a(n) _____.

21. An issue that is considered _____ _____ cannot be re-litigated at a later time.

Multiple-Choice

1 A complaint contains
   a. a statement of jurisdiction.
   b. a listing of the parties.
   c. a brief summary of each element of the case.
   d. all of the above.

2. In an answer, a defendant
   a. admits allegations in the complaint believed to be true.
   b. denies allegations in the complaint believed to be false.
   c. indicates lack of sufficient knowledge for those allegations requiring further investigation.
   d. all of the above.

3. Discovery
   a. can be compared to a game of poker.
   b. is a stage of litigation in which legal assistants have little involvement.

    c. has little impact on the final outcome of cases.
    d. all of the above.

4. Depositions
    a. are less expensive than interrogatories.
    b. do not provide as much insight into a party's thinking as do interrogatories.
    c. allow an attorney to assess how a witness will come across to a jury.
    d. all of the above.

5. An attorney
    a. may choose to depose a witness that he believes will not be available for trial.
    b. cannot use a deposition transcript to impeach a witness at trial.
    c. cannot introduce a deposition transcript at trial.
    d. all of the above.

6. Under the federal rules, a disclosure statement must contain
    a. the name, address, and telephone number of each person likely to have discoverable information.
    b. any documents in the possession, custody, or control of a party that are relevant to the disputed facts alleged in the complaint.
    c. information regarding the computation of damages.
    d. all of the above.

7. Disclosure-centered discovery
    a. is less efficient than request-centered discovery.
    b. requires parties to disclose information voluntarily.
    c. is like the game of Battleship in that parties have to guess what information the opposing party has.
    d. all of the above.

8. Mandatory disclosure
    a. eliminates the need for traditional discovery devices.
    b. does little to reduce the gamesmanship of discovery.
    c. is based on full and open disclosure.
    d. all of the above.

9. Discovery-related motions include
    a. motions for summary judgment.
    b. motions to compel.
    c. motions alleging improper venue.
    d. all of the above.

10. Pretrial conferences are used to
    a. establish witnesses and evidence that will be used at trial.
    b. promote settlement.
    c. clarify issues and defenses.
    d. all of the above.

11. Opening statements
    a. allow an attorney to introduce the parties.
    b. are not particularly important.
    c. are considered part of the evidence.
    d. all of the above.

12. During closing arguments an attorney
    a. summarizes the facts of the case.
    b. shows how the evidence established each of the legal elements in the case.
    c. tries to convince the jury that her client should prevail.
    d. all of the above.

13. Jury instructions
    a. are of little importance because jurors are known to pay little attention to them.
    b. cannot be objected to by attorneys.
    c. may be drafted by counsel and argued before the judge.
    d. all of the above.

TORT TEASERS

Make a flowchart of the events and activities leading up to trial, those events that occur at trial, and those events that occur after trial. Which of these events do you think you will be most involved in as a legal assistant?

INTERNET INQUIRIES

This assignment is designed to begin familiarizing you with the provisions of the *Federal Rules of Civil Procedure.* For each of the following questions, find the applicable rule number in the *Federal Rules* that provides an answer.

1. Within what time period must a summons be served after a complaint is filed?

2. What basic elements must be included in any complaint?

3. What are the possible bases for an affirmative defense?

4. What are the possible grounds for a motion to dismiss?

5. Who can serve a subpoena, and where can it be served?

6. How long must a person be given to respond to a subpoena?

7. When must a response to a motion be filed? When must a reply be served?

8. What determines the time limits of oral arguments? Must a judge allow them?

9. What must a party that is filing a motion to compel do before the court will consider the motion?

10. For what reasons can a judge issue a protective order?

11. When must a response to a motion for summary judgment be filed? When must a reply be filed?

12. Who can file a motion to set certificate of readiness?

13. When must discovery be completed?

14. What must a party show if it wants to postpone a trial?

15. What must be included in a settlement conference memorandum, when must it be completed, and to whom must it be given?

16. Who conducts voir dire in the federal courts?

17. To how many peremptory challenges is a party entitled?

18. At what point must a party submit requests for jury instructions?

19. When can a party apply for a default judgment?

20. How are awards for attorneys' fees determined?

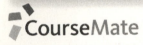 Access an interactive eBook, chapter-specific learning tools, including flashcards, quizzes, and more in your Paralegal CourseMate, accessed through www.CengageBrain.com.

CHAPTER 3

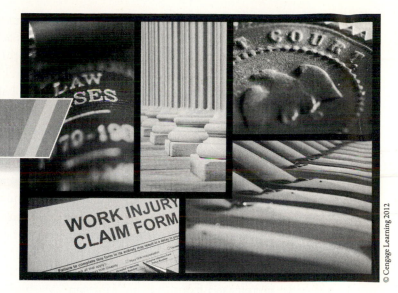

Intentional Torts

CHAPTER OBJECTIVES

After completing the chapter, you should be able to

- Identify the elements of assault, battery, false imprisonment, and infliction of mental distress.
- Identify the elements of trespass to land, trespass to chattels, and conversion.
- Recognize circumstances in which it is appropriate to raise the defenses of consent or necessity.
- Recognize when force can be used to defend self, others, or property, to regain possession of chattels, or to reenter land.

Suppose you come home one evening to discover that your teenage son "borrowed" your car and went on the following spree: First, he dropped by his girlfriend's house to pick her up, but once there met with considerable resistance from her parents. Not to be intimidated by her father, who stood menacingly in front of the car as he started the engine, your son yelled out the window that he would run over her father if he did not get out of the way. The father, who doggedly stood his ground until the last possible moment, barely escaped injury when he finally jumped aside.

Unbeknownst to either your son or his girlfriend, her younger brother had crawled into the back of the car during the fracas with the father. Now, the little boy screamed to be released from the car. Your son, who harbored some latent hostility toward the little brother, took great delight in holding him captive for several miles before letting him out of the car to walk home.

Next, your son and his girlfriend headed to a remote place in the country to enjoy a little privacy. Deeply involved in professing their love for each other, neither noticed the approach of a man brandishing a gun. The man punctuated each demand to get off his land by firing a shot in the air. Thoroughly frightened, the two lovers beat a hasty retreat but, with one last act of bravado, your son took aim at a sign on the man's property and obliterated it with the car. Later, your son, as an afterthought, casually mentioned to you that before leaving the property he took the opportunity to fire a few shots in the man's direction with a gun that he had "borrowed" from the top shelf in your closet.

Ultimately, he arrived safely at home with a car that was only slightly scratched from its close encounter with a sign. In the course of his escapade, what intentional torts did your son commit, and what defenses might he raise to justify his conduct? To answer these questions let us first consider the nature of an intentional tort.

WHAT IS AN INTENTIONAL TORT?

The state of the tortfeasor's mind separates an intentional tort from a negligent one. Although negligent torts can be committed unintentionally, **intentional torts**, as the name implies, require that the tortfeasor intend or have a desire to bring about a particular consequence. The tortfeasor need not desire or plan to harm a person, but he must be aware that certain consequences are substantially certain to result from his acts. If, for example, the defendant intends to do nothing more than play a practical joke on the plaintiff and has absolutely no desire to injure her, he may still be liable if he harms the plaintiff. The intent to bring about a particular result is what is important. The fact that he wishes no harm to the plaintiff has no bearing on his intent.

If a defendant knows with substantial certainty that a result will occur, he will be liable for the consequences. An individual who throws a firecracker into the middle of a dense crowd, for example, may not actually want to hit anyone but if she knows with substantial certainty that someone will get hit, she has acted intentionally. If the consequences are merely highly likely but not substantially certain, the defendant will be considered negligent but will not be deemed to have acted intentionally. Note that intent can be distinguished from motive. Intent is the desire to bring about a consequence; motive is connected to the reason for desiring such a consequence.

You will recall that intentional torts can also be crimes. An assault is both a tort and a crime, as are trespass and false imprisonment. A police officer who deliberately and unlawfully detains an individual can be sued for the damages sustained by the detainee (false imprisonment) and can be punished criminally as well (although the crime is often referred to as unlawful imprisonment). Be cautious, however, in drawing too many analogies between tort law and criminal law. The purposes and historical derivations of criminal and tort law are different, so the terms and concepts used in the criminal arena do not necessarily correspond to those used in tort law. For example, in the criminal arena, defendants can be adjudged guilty or not guilty, while in tort law they are liable or not liable.

Transferred-Intent Doctrine

If a tortfeasor intends to punch A, but A ducks and the tortfeasor inadvertently strikes B, the intent to strike A will be transferred from A to B. Under the **transferred-intent doctrine**, the defendant's intent toward one person is transferred to the person who is actually injured as a result of the defendant's conduct. Therefore, in such cases the tortfeasor is deemed to have committed an intentional tort. This same rule is applicable if the tortfeasor intends to commit one kind of tort and in fact commits another. If the tortfeasor uses his dog to terrorize A (an assault), and the

EXHIBIT 3-1 *Intentional Torts against Persons*

BATTERY	ASSAULT
Intentional infliction of harmful or offensive contact.	Intentional causing of apprehension of harmful or offensive contact.

FALSE IMPRISONMENT	INFLICTION OF MENTAL DISTRESS
Intentional confinement of another.	Intentional infliction of severe emotional or mental distress as a result of extreme and outrageous conduct (can also be committed recklessly).

© Cengage Learning 2012

dog escapes and bites B (a battery), the tortfeasor will be liable for the battery even though he intended an assault.

Categorization of Intentional Torts

Intentional torts are generally divided into two categories: those against persons and those against property. The torts against persons that are discussed in this chapter are battery, assault, false imprisonment, and infliction of mental distress (see Exhibit 3-1). The torts against property that are discussed are trespass to land, trespass to chattels, and conversion.

INTENTIONAL TORTS AGAINST PERSONS

Battery

If two people become engaged in a heated argument and one pushes the other to the ground, the person who does the shoving commits a battery. **Battery** is defined as the intentional infliction of a harmful or offensive contact upon a person. If the tortfeasor intends only to frighten the victim and accidentally makes "harmful or offensive contact," she has still committed a battery. As indicated earlier, whether the tortfeasor intends to actually injure the plaintiff is irrelevant. To satisfy the elements of battery the tortfeasor must only intend to make contact and the contact must actually be made.

What Is Considered Contact?

The function of the law concerning battery is to protect individuals from undesired and unpermitted contacts or invasion of their body. This tort extends to contact with any part of a person's body or anything attached to or identified with the body. Contact with a purse, with an object in the plaintiff's hand, or with the car in which the plaintiff is riding all constitute contact for the purposes of battery. In one case, the defendant argued that he was not liable because he grabbed the victim's purse and did not have any contact with her body. The court rejected the defendant's argument, reasoning that the intentional snatching of an object from a person's hand is as offensive an invasion as having actual contact with the body (*Wal-Mart Stores, Inc. v. Odem*, 929 S.W.2d 513 [Tex. App 1996]).

The defendant need not actually touch the plaintiff with his body. A person who orders his dog to attack or who throws water on someone has committed a battery (*Restatement [Second] of Torts* § 18, cmt. c).

Neither must the plaintiff suffer pain or bodily damage to recover for battery. The contact need only be "offensive." In determining whether a contact is offensive, the question is whether a person with a reasonable sense of dignity would be offended. If a woman gently taps her boyfriend on the shoulder to get his attention, she has not committed a battery. Touching by a friend is not offensive to an ordinary person and therefore is not actionable.

Awareness of Contact

The plaintiff is not required to have any awareness of the contact at the time it occurs. If the plaintiff gives consent for a biopsy to be done and the doctor decides while the patient is under anesthetic to go ahead and perform surgery, the doctor has committed battery. Even though she obtained consent for the biopsy, she lacks the plaintiff's consent to perform the surgery. The fact that the plaintiff is unaware of the doctor's actions at the time of the surgery is irrelevant.

Extent of Liability

The defendant who commits battery is liable for any consequences regardless of how unforeseen they may be. Suppose the defendant grabs the plaintiff around the waist and playfully squeezes her in a manner that would normally cause no bodily harm. Because the plaintiff is suffering from osteoporosis, however, she sustains extensive damage to her ribs, resulting in long suffering. The defendant is liable for the full extent of the plaintiff's bodily harm even though he could not have reasonably anticipated that harm.

Assault

Assault is defined as the intentional causing of an apprehension of harmful or offensive contact. Apprehension does not mean fear but does require the plaintiff to be aware of the impending contact. A woman who shakes her broom at someone to frighten or chase him away has committed assault if the object of her threats believes she is trying to strike him. A defendant can commit assault by either intending to commit a battery or merely intending to frighten the plaintiff, with no intent of actual contact. A defendant, for example, who attempts to strike the plaintiff but misses commits an assault, but so does the defendant who makes a fist at the plaintiff with no intent of actually hitting him.

The doctrine of transferred intent is as applicable to assault as it is to battery. Therefore, if a defendant throws a stone at A and B fears being hit, the defendant will be liable to B for assault even though he never intended to hit or frighten B.

Plaintiff's Attitude

Unlike battery, a plaintiff alleging assault must be aware of the threatened contact. So if A intends to frighten B by discharging a pistol behind him, but B, who is stone deaf, does not hear the pistol, A will not be liable to B for assault (*Restatement [Second] of Torts* § 22, illus. 1).

An individual will not be able to recover for assault if his apprehension is that someone else will be touched and not himself. If a husband, for example, disarms a robber just before he shoots the husband's wife, the husband cannot recover for assault, because the attack was directed at his wife and not himself (*Restatement [Second] of Torts* § 26).

A plaintiff need not be fearful that he will be harmed. A plaintiff confident in his ability to protect himself can still be the victim of assault. His awareness that he could be harmed if he failed to take defensive action is sufficient.

Defendant's Ability to Carry Out Threat

A defendant must appear to the plaintiff to have the present ability to carry out the threatened contact. In one case the defendant repeatedly threatened to kill the plaintiff if she sued him. After the plaintiff filed suit, the defendant came to her home, beat on the door, tried to pry it open, and repeated his threats to kill her. The defendant argued that no assault had been committed because he had made no overt action toward the plaintiff. The court concluded that the evidence supported a finding that the defendant had the apparent ability to carry out the threatened act (*Holcombe v. Whitaker*, 318 So. 2d 289 [Ala. 1975]). If a plaintiff believes the defendant has the ability to carry out his threatened contact, then even though the defendant actually does not, the elements of assault are met.

What Constitutes a Threat?

Any threats of harm must be imminent to constitute an assault. Threats of future harm are not sufficient, although they may satisfy the criteria for the tort of intentional infliction of mental distress. If A threatens to shoot B, for example, but must go to her car to get her revolver, A has not committed assault (*Restatement [Second] of Torts* § 29, illus. 4).

The courts are in some disagreement as to whether words alone constitute an assault. Some courts require that words be accompanied by some overt act that tends to enhance the threatening character of the words; other courts, in accordance with the *Restatement [Second]*, require no accompanying overt act. If a member of a juvenile gang, holding a knife in his hand, approaches a member of another gang and, without movement, says, "You die," many courts would conclude that an assault had been committed.

Note that the tort of assault is complete as soon as the plaintiff apprehends the contact. If, after the plaintiff's apprehension, the defendant suddenly abandons his plan, he will still be liable for assault.

PUTTING IT INTO PRACTICE 3:1

When Mike Tyson steps out of his limousine, he is confronted by a fan who jumps in front of him, assumes a boxing stance, and jabs at him. Tyson laughs at the fan. Has the fan committed a tort?

False Imprisonment

The tort of **false imprisonment** is committed when a person intentionally confines another. Originally, confinement was restricted to actual incarceration, but today confinement includes restraint in an open street or in a moving vehicle. The restraint must be more than a mere obstruction of the plaintiff's right to go wherever she pleases. Blocking the plaintiff's path in one direction only does not constitute confinement as long as alternative routes are available. The doctrine of transferred intent is applicable to this tort. If the defendant, in his intent to confine one person, inadvertently confines another as well, she will be liable to both for false imprisonment.

What Constitutes Confinement?

The plaintiff is not required to subject herself or her property to any risk of harm in an effort to extricate herself from her confinement. Suppose a defendant closes off every exit except one. If the plaintiff can escape only by exposing herself to the possibility of substantial bodily harm, the defendant has confined her. Similarly, if the defendant blocks all doors except one and steals the plaintiff's clothing, leaving the plaintiff naked, and the plaintiff can leave only by walking through a room filled with persons of both sexes, the defendant has confined the plaintiff (*Restatement [Second] of Torts* § 36, illus. 3 and 5).

Confinement can be achieved by something less than physical force. If a defendant threatens by his body language alone to harm the plaintiff if the plaintiff tries to escape, he has still confined the plaintiff. Threats need not be aimed directly at the plaintiff, either. If the defendant threatens to harm another if the plaintiff leaves the confinement area, the defendant has committed false imprisonment. Any threats, however, must be of imminent harm. Threats of future harm are not sufficient. Finally, the plaintiff must be aware of her confinement at the time it occurs. If a person does not discover until after her release that she was confined, she cannot claim she was falsely imprisoned.

False Imprisonment in Law Enforcement

False imprisonment most often occurs in the context of law enforcement. A valid defense to the allegation of false imprisonment is the police officer's assertion of the legal right to make an arrest. An officer can claim such a defense even if the arrest or detention later turns out to be unlawful. He is required only to act reasonably and in good faith in carrying out the arrest. An officer who serves the plaintiff with an invalid arrest warrant but who reasonably believes the warrant to be valid has not committed false imprisonment.

LOCAL LINKS

Consult the statutes and common law in your state to ascertain the rights of merchants in your jurisdiction.

Shoplifting

In most states today a merchant who reasonably believes that a customer has stolen property has a right to detain the suspected individual for a short period of time for the purpose of investigation. The right to detain is very restricted, however, and will be lost if the detention is unreasonably long, if the plaintiff is bullied or insulted, if the plaintiff is publicly accused of shoplifting, or if the detention is used to coerce payment or the signing of a confession. In most states the right to detain is limited to detention on the defendant's premises and is lost when the plaintiff leaves the premises. The pivotal question is whether the merchant had reasonable grounds for the detention.

Infliction of Mental Distress

A relative newcomer to tort law is the claim of infliction of mental distress. This tort can be committed either intentionally or recklessly. If committed intentionally, the tortfeasor must want to bring about a particular consequence or must know with substantial certainty that a specific result is likely to occur. If the tort is committed recklessly, the defendant must act in deliberate disregard of the emotional distress that he knows he is very likely to cause the plaintiff. Such recklessness rises above negligence.

What Is "Extreme and Outrageous" Conduct?

It is not enough for this tort that the defendant act unreasonably; the conduct must be "extreme and outrageous." *Outrageous conduct* is any conduct considered intolerable in any civilized society and is characterized as exceeding all possible bounds of decency. For example, if the defendant tells the plaintiff that her husband has been critically injured in an accident, when in fact

PUTTING IT INTO PRACTICE 3:2

A man and his wife go to a "Private After-Hours Sale" at a department store. The man, who is recovering from a recent kidney transplant, is still partially paralyzed, has bloodshot eyes and visible needle marks, and walks with a faltering gait. He is given a shopping bag by one of the store's employees and believes that he is to use this bag for shopping. He goes to the men's department and selects ties, shirts, and cuff links, which he puts in his bag. When he leaves the men's department and moves toward the escalator, he is apprehended by a store security guard who has been observing his actions. The man is searched and then interrogated for a considerable length of time before he is released. Has this man been falsely imprisoned?

no such accident has occurred, the defendant is liable for any emotional distress the plaintiff suffers (*Restatement [Second] of Torts* § 46, illus. 1).

Mere insults and petty manipulation of others are not sufficient for this tort. However, a defendant who uses his position abusively may be liable for any emotional distress this causes. A high school principal, for example, who browbeats a student, threatening her with public disgrace and even prison unless she confesses to immoral conduct with certain men, will probably be liable for any emotional distress suffered by the student (*Restatement [Second] of Torts* § 46, illus. 6).

The peculiar characteristics of the plaintiff may be taken into consideration in evaluating the defendant's conduct. A defendant who takes advantage of a plaintiff of below-average intelligence may be liable for any distress she causes the plaintiff even though that same conduct would not be deemed outrageous if the plaintiff were an adult of average intelligence.

Considerable differences exist among the courts as to what does and does not constitute "extreme and outrageous" conduct. To illustrate, consider two cases from different jurisdictions. In the first case (*Kentucky Fried Chicken National Management Co. v. Weathersby*, 607 A.2d 8 [Md. 1992]), the employee's supervisor accused her of stealing money from the store safe, ordered her to take a polygraph test, and, in front of customers and other employees, took away her store keys and suspended her for ten days "pending an investigation." Because of personality traits of the employee, of which the employer was unaware, the employer's actions resulted in the employee's hospitalization for depression and severe suicidal and homicidal tendencies. The court held that because the employer had no knowledge of the employee's peculiar sensitivities, no cause of action may have existed. Barring that

knowledge, however, the court concluded that the employer's conduct, however illaudable it may have been, did not rise to the level of intentional infliction of emotional distress. The court also opined that a "certain amount of arbitrary nastiness" in the workplace is a "fact of life we must accept" and that "[t]he workplace is not always a tranquil world where civility reigns."

In the second case (*Doe v. Mills*, 536 N.W.2d 824 [Mich. 1995]), members of a religious order protested outside an abortion clinic, holding up large signs displaying the real names of the plaintiffs and begging them not to "kill their babies." The trial court granted the defendants' motion for summary judgment, but the appellate court reversed on the ground that reasonable persons could conclude that the defendants' conduct was sufficiently outrageous and extreme as to warrant liability. The court observed that the defendants' actions were "more than mere insults, indignities, threats, annoyances, or petty oppressions." Do you believe the outcomes in these two cases are consistent, or do you think each court has a different sense of what constitutes "extreme and outrageous" conduct?

Transferred-Intent Doctrine

The doctrine of transferred intent is generally not applicable in cases of intentional infliction of mental distress. To apply this doctrine would be to open the courthouse doors to all those who suffered emotional distress as a result of viewing tortious acts being intentionally committed against others. An exception to this general prohibition occurs when the defendant directs his conduct against a member of the plaintiff's immediate family and is aware that the plaintiff is present at the time. For example, if a man severely beats a child's father and is aware at the time of the beating that the child is watching, he will be liable for the emotional distress suffered by that child.

NET NEWS

To read about intentional infliction of emotional distress claims in the workplace and to see some summaries of actual cases, go to **http://www.uslaw.com/** and enter "intentional infliction of emotional stress" as your search term.

The transferred-intent doctrine also is not applicable if the defendant fails to commit the tort he intended to commit and succeeds only in causing the plaintiff emotional distress. A defendant who is weary of the incessant barking of his neighbor's dog, and who shoots at the dog with the intent to kill it but misses, will not be liable for the emotional distress suffered by the dog's owner. His intent to commit conversion, in other words, is not transferred to the emotional distress he actually causes (*Restatement [Second] of Torts* § 47, illus. 2).

Type of Harm Suffered

A plaintiff must prove that she actually suffered severe emotional distress and must, at the very least, have sought medical attention. Some courts require that the plaintiff suffer some kind of physical harm, although most modern courts have no such requirement. A plaintiff who suffers harm only because of a peculiar vulnerability or sensitivity will not be allowed to recover if the defendant is not aware of these vulnerabilities or sensitivities.

LOCAL LINKS

Do the courts in your jurisdiction require physical harm to recover for infliction of emotional distress?

Higher Standard for Those in Public Service

Common carriers and public utilities are held to a higher standard of conduct than the rest of the populace and can be held liable, for example, for highly insulting language. Although an insult to an ordinary person would almost never be considered actionable, an insult to a customer by an employee of a utility or carrier would be considered cause for an infliction of mental distress claim. This rule apparently stems from a concern that those who provide such services not be rude to their customers.

NET NEWS

The tort of negligent infliction of emotional distress has not been accepted in all jurisdictions. In the controversial case of *Boyles v. Kerr*, 855 S.W.2d 593 [Tex. 1993] a young man and his friends arranged to secretly videotape him and his girlfriend having intercourse and then showed the tape to others. Locate this case in Findlaw. Despite the fact that Boyles (the girlfriend) was publicly humiliated, was adversely affected in her schoolwork, had problems with subsequent relationships with men, and ultimately sought counseling, the Texas supreme court refused to recognize negligent infliction of emotional distress as an independent cause of action, although it did remand the matter back to the trial court to allow Boyles to pursue a claim of intentional infliction of emotional distress.

PUTTING IT INTO PRACTICE 3:3

The manager of a Radio Shack outlet is told on two occasions about unsatisfactory practices in his store. His supervisor and two security people come to his store to investigate. He is questioned at thirty-minute intervals throughout the day, during which he claims he is cursed at, threatened, and denied his medication. Later that afternoon, he is asked to submit to a polygraph test, which he agrees to, but he is not allowed to take his medication, Valium, because it may interfere with the test. He is brought to the testing place but hyperventilates and must be taken home. He returns to work the next day but cannot remain on the job, and eventually is hospitalized by a psychiatrist. Does he have a viable claim for intentional infliction of emotional distress?

INTENTIONAL TORTS AGAINST PROPERTY

Trespass to Land

A person who enters or wrongfully remains on another's land has committed the tort of **trespass to land** (see Exhibit 3–2). By the same token, trespass occurs if an individual fails to remove an object from another's land if she is under a duty to remove it. Historically, trespass was a strict liability tort, allowing liability even if the defendant's contact with the land was unintentional. Today almost all courts have rejected strict liability except when the defendant is engaging in an abnormally dangerous activity, such as blasting.

Defendant's Intent

The defendant's only intent must be to make physical contact with the plaintiff's land. He need not intend any harm to the plaintiff's property nor even be aware that any harm might occur. A defendant is still liable for trespass even if his contact with the plaintiff's land is the result of a reasonable mistake. An intentional trespass is committed, for example, if a defendant walks on another's land thinking it to be his own or believing he is entitled to enter the land.

Type of Contact Required

The defendant need not enter or make contact with the land herself; an indirect invasion is sufficient. If a child fires his BB gun at the plaintiff's barn, for example, he is liable for trespass even if he never sets foot on the plaintiff's property. Furthermore, a defendant who does not intend to enter the plaintiff's land but who knows that such an entry is reasonably certain to happen is liable for trespass. If a person builds up an embankment next to her adjoining neighbor's land, and during an ordinary rain the dirt washes from her land to the other's land, she is liable for trespass. Even a defendant who allows gases or particles to enter the plaintiff's property will, according to most modern courts, be liable for trespass. Similarly, most courts today hold that a trespass is committed when the defendant sets off a blast that causes concussions or vibrations on the plaintiff's property.

Because landowners, under the common law, are considered to own the airspace above their property and the surface below their property, those who violate such space can be sued for trespass. Someone who fires a gun over the plaintiff's property may be liable for trespass even though no bullet lands on the property. In this day of general aviation, however, landowners cannot be allowed to sue for any invasion of their airspace. The airspace above certain minimum flight altitudes, as established by federal statutes and administrative regulations, is considered public domain. Therefore, damages cannot be awarded for any flights occurring above these altitudes. A landowner who can show that he has suffered actual harm resulting from the flight of aircraft over his property at permissible altitudes may, however, be able to sue on the basis of a nuisance theory. This theory of recovery is discussed in more detail in Chapter 11.

Revocation of Permission to Enter

Trespass is also committed if a defendant who has permission to enter the plaintiff's land refuses to leave when the permission is revoked. Similarly, if the defendant refuses or neglects to remove something when she is supposed to, she may be liable for trespass. For example, a person who is given permission to park his car on the plaintiff's land for a month, and who at the end of the month removes the car but forgets to remove the gas can that he put beside the car, has committed a trespass.

EXHIBIT 3–2 *Intentional Torts against Property*

TRESPASS TO LAND	TRESPASS TO CHATTELS	CONVERSION
Intentionally entering or wrongfully remaining on another's land	Intentional interference with another's use or possession of chattel (personal property)	Intentional interference with another's use or possession of chattel to the extent fairness requires that the defendant pay the full value of the chattel

© Cengage Learning 2012

PUTTING IT INTO PRACTICE 3:4

A veterinarian receives the permission of the Copelands to allow a student interested in a career in veterinary medicine to accompany him as he cares for their cat in their home. The student does not tell the veterinarian or the Copelands that, in addition to being a student, she is an employee of a local television station. She videotapes the veterinarian's session with the cat and parts of that videotape are aired when an investigative report on the veterinarian is broadcast. Do the Copelands have grounds for a trespass claim against the television station?

Extent of Liability

A defendant is liable for almost all consequences of the trespass, no matter how unpredictable those consequences might be. Even if a defendant has no reason to believe that the plaintiff or others will be injured as a result of his trespass, he will be liable. In some courts he will be liable as well for any emotional distress suffered as a result of the trespass, even if the plaintiff suffers no physical harm.

Trespass to Chattels

Trespass to chattels is committed by the intentional interference with the plaintiff's use or possession of **chattel** (personal property). Chattel is property that is visible, tangible, and movable. A defendant who damages the plaintiff's china or who deliberately hides the plaintiff's bicycle so as to deprive him of its use has committed trespass to chattels. The length of the deprivation is irrelevant. Recovery will be allowed even if the loss of possession is only temporary. The owner of the chattel need not be in possession of the chattel at the time the trespass occurs. Both the owner and possessor of a chattel are entitled to sue.

The only intent required for this tort is the intent to interfere in some way with the plaintiff's chattel. The defendant need not intend to cause harm to the property. Neither is the defendant's mistaken belief that the property is his own a defense. Defendant must intend to and actually make physical contact with the property.

Unlike the plaintiff who sues for trespass, however, the plaintiff who sues for trespass to chattels must prove actual harm. A child who climbs on the back of a dog and pulls on its ears has not committed trespass to chattels as long as the dog is not harmed in any way (*Restatement [Second] of Torts* § 218 illus. 2).

Conversion

If the defendant's interference with the plaintiff's property is so substantial that justice demands that she pay the plaintiff the full value of the property, the defendant has committed the tort of **conversion**. As with trespass to land and trespass to chattels, no intent to harm the plaintiff's property or possessory rights is required. An innocent mistake by the defendant is sufficient. The plaintiff must show only that the defendant intended to interfere with her possessory rights. As with trespass to chattels, the plaintiff in a conversion action need not be the owner but can be the person in possession of the property at the time of the conversion.

In recent years some courts have applied the trespass-to-chattels theory to electronic communications. A Virginia court, for example, concluded that sending unauthorized spam to a computer network constituted trespass to chattels (*America Online v. IMS*, 24 F.Supp.2d 548 [1998]). A marketing company that sent 60 million unauthorized electronic mail (e-mail) advertisements ("spam") to an Internet company's subscribers was liable for trespass to chattels. The court found that the marketer's conduct injured the plaintiff's goodwill and diminished the value of the computer network.

NET NEWS

For an analysis of some courts' application of the trespass to chattels theory to electronic communications, go to the Electronic Frontier Foundation site at **http://www.eff.org/**.

For examples of cases dealing with electronic trespass to chattels, go to **http://www.tomwbell.com/** and enter "electronic trespass" as your search term.

Distinction between Conversion and Trespass to Chattels

From the defendant's standpoint the distinction between trespass to chattels and conversion is an important one. A defendant who is in possession of the chattel at the time suit is brought has the right to return the goods in the case of trespass to chattels. Returning the goods is an effort to mitigate the plaintiff's damages. In the case of conversion, however, title is deemed to have transferred from the plaintiff to the defendant because of the defendant's interference. As a result, the defendant is required to pay the full value of the property. In a sense, conversion may be looked on as a "forced sale" because the defendant pays for the full value of the property rather than for just the damage done.

Indicia of Conversion

Six factors are taken into consideration in determining whether a defendant's interference with the plaintiff's property rises to the level of conversion (*Restatement [Second] of Torts* § 222A):

- the extent and duration of the defendant's exercise of control over the property
- the extent and duration of the resulting interference with the plaintiff's right to control
- the defendant's intent to assert a right inconsistent with the plaintiff's right of control
- the defendant's good faith
- the harm done to the chattel
- the inconvenience and expense caused to the plaintiff

To illustrate how these factors are weighed, consider a defendant who, upon leaving a restaurant, mistakenly picks up the plaintiff's hat believing it to be his own. When he reaches the sidewalk he discovers his mistake and promptly reenters the restaurant and returns the hat. Because no harm was done, the defendant acted in good faith, and his interference with the plaintiff's right of control was limited, no conversion would be committed (*Restatement [Second] of Torts* § 222A, illus. 1).

Suppose that the defendant keeps that hat for three months before discovering his mistake and returning the hat. Such a lengthy confiscation of the hat would be considered a conversion because of the defendant's substantial interference with the plaintiff's use of his property. The defendant's acting in good faith would not make it any less a conversion (*Restatement [Second] of Torts* § 222A, illus. 2).

When the defendant gets to the sidewalk, if a sudden gust of wind blows the hat into an open manhole, he will be liable for conversion because the plaintiff's property interest is completely destroyed. Again, the defendant's good faith would not change the outcome (*Restatement [Second] of Torts* § 222A, illus. 3).

Suppose the defendant knowingly takes the plaintiff's hat but returns it to the restaurant because he sees a police officer coming toward him. He has committed a conversion because of his bad faith even though the duration of his control over the hat is relatively short (*Restatement [Second] of Torts* § 222A, illus. 4). Although the distinction between trespass to chattels and conversion is a blurred one, these guidelines will assist you in making reasonable distinctions.

Removal and Transfer of Goods

Conversion can be committed by ways other than taking possession of the plaintiff's property. A defendant may also be liable for conversion by the removal of goods. The removal must create a relatively serious interference with the plaintiff's right to possession and control of his or her property. Suppose, for example, the defendant takes possession of a house of which the plaintiff and defendant are co-owners. If the defendant removes the plaintiff's furniture when they become engaged in a dispute about ownership, he will be liable for conversion if he refuses to make the furniture available when the plaintiff demands it back. However, if the defendant complies with the plaintiff's request, the defendant's interference will constitute trespass to chattels but not conversion. In the latter case the defendant's interference is not so severe as to constitute conversion but is considered intermeddling with the plaintiff's goods, which is the essence of trespass to chattels.

Conversion also occurs when the defendant transfers chattel to someone who is not entitled to it. A parking lot attendant, for example, who gives a car to the wrong person, commits conversion if he creates an interference with the car owner's rights that is sufficiently severe. By the same token, a parking lot attendant who intentionally refuses to return the plaintiff's car to him is liable for conversion if the refusal is done in bad faith and the resultant interference with the plaintiff's right to possession is substantial.

Conversion of Intangibles

In recent years a number of courts have allowed conversion suits for intangibles, such as stock certificates, promissory notes, insurance policies, and savings bank books. Generally, however, these intangible rights must be linked to some kind of document to support a conversion action. A defendant who falsely claims ownership over Internet domain names, for example, is not liable for conversion although he may be liable for some other tort, such as interference with contractual relations (discussed in Chapter 10).

DEFENSES

Mistake

Mistake in and of itself is not a defense to an intentional tort. A defendant who intentionally enters the land of another, acting in the honest and reasonable belief that the land is her own, is still liable for the tort of trespass. Mistake is, however, an element of consideration in some of the other defenses discussed in this chapter. A defendant who reasonably but mistakenly believes that he must defend himself or another can still claim self-defense even though his acts are premised on an erroneous belief. The effect of mistake is considered throughout the remaining sections of this chapter.

Consent

In general, a defendant is not liable for an intentional tort if the plaintiff consents to the defendant's intentional interference (see Exhibit 3–3). In most cases the plaintiff does not explicitly consent, but the consent may be implied from the plaintiff's conduct or from any customs surrounding such conduct. Because defendants are not expected to be mind readers, the issue of whether a plaintiff has consented is determined by objective manifestations and not by the plaintiff's subjective mental state. Simply put, the question is whether a reasonable person in the defendant's shoes would have believed that the plaintiff has consented to an invasion of his interest. Suppose a man announces to his date while they are standing at her front door that he is going to kiss her good night. If she says or does nothing to indicate her displeasure, it can be inferred from her conduct that she has given consent.

Consent or lack of consent can also be inferred from custom. One court, for example, rejected the plaintiff's assertion that he was a licensee when he entered the receiving dock area of the store. The court concluded that the evidence did not prove habitual or customary use of the receiving dock by the store's customers (*Miracle v. Wal-Mart Stores East*, 659 F.Supp. 821 CE.D. [Ky 2009]).

PUTTING IT INTO PRACTICE 3:5

When Matthew moves into a home he has recently rented, he discovers that the former tenant (John) has still not removed his furniture. Matthew wants to bring in his own furniture, so he makes arrangements to have John's furniture stored in a warehouse in John's name. He calls John immediately to let him know of these arrangements but is unable to get in touch with John for a week. Has Matthew committed a conversion?

What if Matthew moved the furniture to a warehouse that was so distant that John was greatly inconvenienced and forced to go to great expense to recover his furniture? Or suppose that instead of moving the furniture, Matthew changed the locks. When John, after being notified of the change, comes to the house to retrieve his furniture, Matthew is not home. Has Matthew committed a conversion if John is able to return the next day and pick up his furniture?

Suppose Matthew loans John his truck to drive to the warehouse to pick up the furniture, but John makes a ten-mile detour to pick up his girlfriend. Has John committed a conversion? Would your answer change if, on the way to his girlfriend's house, John is involved in an accident that causes significant damage to Matthew's truck?

EXHIBIT 3–3 Defenses to Intentional Torts

CONSENT	If a plaintiff who has the capacity to consent to interference with his person or property voluntarily does so, either explicitly or implicitly, the defendant will not be liable for such interference.
SELF-DEFENSE	A defendant is entitled (privileged) to use reasonable force to protect himself or another against imminent harm if he reasonably believes it is necessary to do so (most courts require that any person being aided must be privileged to act in self-defense).
DEFENSE OF PROPERTY	A defendant is entitled to use reasonable (not deadly) force to protect his property against imminent harm if he reasonably believes it is necessary to do so and he verbally demands that the intruder stop first (if circumstances permit).
REGAINING POSSESSION OF CHATTELS	A property owner is entitled to use reasonable force to regain possession of chattel if the chattel was wrongfully taken and the owner is in fresh pursuit.
REENTRY ON LAND	In some states a land owner may use reasonable force to reenter his land, although the majority of courts deny that right to landlords attempting to evict tenants.
PUBLIC NECESSITY	A defendant may harm the property interest of another when necessary to prevent a disaster to the community or a substantial number of people. No reimbursement of the plaintiff is required.
PRIVATE NECESSITY	A defendant may harm the property interest of another if necessary to protect his own interests or those of a few private citizens because no less damaging way to prevent the harm exists. Reimbursement of the plaintiff is required if there is substantial harm to the plaintiff's property.

© Cengage Learning 2012

Capacity to Consent

Consent is not a defense if the plaintiff is incapable of or incompetent to give consent. Someone who is unconscious or obviously intoxicated, for example, is incapable of giving consent. Consent will be implied, however, if emergency action is immediately necessary to save an incapacitated person's life, if no indication exists that he would have refused to give consent, and if a reasonable person would have consented under like circumstances. A patient's consent is implied, for example, when a doctor performs emergency surgery that is immediately necessary to save the patient.

Generally, if a plaintiff consents only because she is mistaken about some material fact, her consent will still be considered effective. If, however, the defendant either knows of or induces the plaintiff's mistake, the plaintiff's consent will be deemed ineffective. If the defendant, for example, induces the plaintiff to engage in sexual intercourse with him by staging what he knows to be a fake wedding ceremony, he will be liable for battery because her consent will be considered ineffective.

The question of mistaken consent most often arises in the context of medical cases in which the plaintiff alleges that the doctor did not adequately inform her about the risks involved in the proposed treatment. Generally, the courts consider consent to be ineffective if the doctor fails to disclose the consequences of a procedure that she knows will definitely follow from the treatment. If, however, the doctor simply fails to mention a minor risk that may or may not be a consequence of the treatment, most courts will consider the plaintiff's consent to be effective.

The courts are split in reference to the effectiveness of a plaintiff's consent to a criminal act. The majority of courts find such consent ineffective. A minority of courts and the *Restatement (Second)* consider the consent effective unless the crime is intended to protect a class of persons against their own poor judgment and the plaintiff is a member of that protected class. A defendant who commits statutory rape, for example, is liable regardless of the plaintiff's consent. Because the plaintiff is a member of the class the statute is intended to protect, she cannot give her consent.

Voluntariness of Consent

If a plaintiff consents only because she is under duress and that duress creates an immediate and serious threat to herself or another, her consent will be deemed involuntary. Threats of future harm and threats involving economic duress are generally not sufficient to render a plaintiff's consent involuntary. A plaintiff who agrees to have sex with the defendant because of his threat to blackmail her in the future cannot claim duress because the threat pertains to future action.

Scope of Consent

A defendant must not exceed the scope of the plaintiff's consent. A defendant who invades a plaintiff's interest in a way that substantially deviates from that consented to will be liable for his act. Suppose a plaintiff consents to gallbladder surgery but the surgeon decides to remove her appendix as well. Because the plaintiff's consent did not extend to her appendix, the doctor will be liable for battery. However, if the condition of the patient's appendix justified an emergency removal, the patient will be deemed to have implicitly consented to that operation. The issue of consent in the area of medical practice is largely academic today because most hospitals require patients to fill out extremely general consent forms, which, unless unduly vague, protect hospitals from liability.

Self-Defense

In the area of self-defense two questions are generally raised: Was the defendant privileged to use force to defend herself, and was the degree of force that she used reasonable? (The answers to these two questions will differ somewhat in the civil arena as compared with the criminal arena.) A person may defend himself against any threatened harmful or offensive bodily contact as well as any threatened confinement. Whether the threat posed is intentional or negligent does not matter. The defendant need not even actually be harmed to invoke this defense.

Defendant's Belief

The defendant must reasonably believe that a threat exists, even if she is wrong. This result is probably based on the idea that "self-preservation is the first law of nature." Suppose a police officer apprehends a suspect known to her to be armed and dangerous. If the suspect reaches into his pocket for what the officer mistakenly believes to be a gun and the officer shoots him, the officer will be deemed to have acted in self-defense so long as her mistaken belief is a reasonable one. If the officer was exceptionally timid or paranoid, unreasonably believed that the suspect was about to shoot her, and no objective facts supported her perception, she could not claim self-defense.

What Constitutes Reasonable Force?

A defendant may use only that force that is reasonably necessary to protect herself against a threatened harm. She cannot use force to defend herself against words alone unless those words are accompanied by some type of hostile act. Nor can she use force to protect herself against future harm. Any threat of harm must appear to the defendant to be imminent. Furthermore,

PUTTING IT INTO PRACTICE 3:6

A patient who has had his larynx removed because of cancer allows the surgeon who removed the larynx to take photographs of him to record the progression of his tumor. The patient gives no written consent but implies through his actions that he is willing to comply with the surgeon's request. On the surgeon's last visit, he once again proceeds to take the patient's photograph, but the patient raises his fist and tries to move his head out of range of the camera. Does the patient's consent to the previous photographs entitle the surgeon to take the last photograph despite the patient's apparent resistance?

she must reasonably believe that she has no reasonable alternative to the use of force to protect herself from the impending danger.

For obvious reasons, a defendant may not claim self-defense if he uses force against someone who is helpless. If A takes a swing at B and in the process slips and falls flat on his back, rendering him incapacitated, B cannot take that opportunity to avenge himself. Nor can self-defense be used to justify any retaliation for a previously committed tort. If a small child throws a snowball at the defendant, hitting her in the eye, the defendant is not justified in using force to punish the child (*Restatement [Second] of Torts* § 63, illus. 4). In summary, the use of force is not considered reasonable if it is used against someone who is helpless in response to a threat of future harm, in retaliation for a previously committed tort, or in response to words unaccompanied by a hostile act.

How much force a defendant may use depends on the degree of force necessary to prevent the impending harm. Suppose A threatens B with clenched fists. B cannot claim self-defense if she responds using a knife, because her response exceeds the amount of force necessary to protect herself. Furthermore, a defendant may not use **deadly force** (defined as that force likely to cause death or serious bodily injury) unless she is in danger of death or serious bodily harm herself (*Restatement [Second] of Torts* §§ 65–66). Consequently, someone threatened with rape or some other type of serious bodily harm may defend herself using deadly force, whereas someone threatened with trespass to chattels may not. This rule is based on an objective standard in that the conduct of the defendant is compared to that of a reasonable person under similar circumstances.

Defense of Home

A common question that arises in the area of self-defense pertains to the use of force when someone invades another's home. The oft-quoted advice that if someone shoots a person who is outside his house, he must drag the body inside in order to claim self-defense, is erroneous. All one need show is that he reasonably believed he was in imminent danger of death or serious bodily harm and that no lesser degree of force was sufficient to prevent the harm.

The courts are split, however, on whether a defendant has a duty to retreat. Some courts, giving homage to individual honor and dignity, allow a defendant to use deadly force even if he can safely retreat. Other courts, attaching more importance to the sanctity of human life, require a defendant to retreat if he can do so safely. Even the latter courts, however, do not require someone who is attacked in his own home to retreat. This result is apparently based on the precept that "one's home is one's castle."

LOCAL LINKS

§ Do your courts require a defendant to retreat before using deadly force?

Prevention of Felonies

According to the *Restatement*, deadly force may also be used to prevent certain types of felonies, such as robbery, kidnapping, and rape. The defendant must believe that the felony cannot otherwise be prevented and the type of harm threatened must involve death or serious bodily injury (*Restatement [Second] of Torts* § 143). Notice that the defendant in this case is entitled to use force even though she is not personally endangered.

Defense of Others

Reasonable force may be used to protect others, including complete strangers. To claim the privilege of defense of another, the defendant must reasonably believe that the circumstances would support a claim of self-defense and that his intervention is immediately necessary for the protection of the other person.

Problems arise when the defendant intervenes on behalf of another, mistakenly believing assistance is necessary. Suppose A sees B being tackled and injured by C and he intervenes on B's behalf. If it turns out that C is an undercover police officer attempting to arrest B, should A be able to claim the privilege of defense of another as long as he reasonably believed that B was in imminent danger? Most courts reason that the intervener (A) "steps into the shoes of the person he has sought to champion (B)." If it turns out that the person being rescued is not privileged to act in self-defense, the intervener is precluded from claiming such a privilege. A minority of courts, including the *Restatement [Second]*, however, allow the intervener to claim the privilege as long as he reasonably believes the person he is aiding would have been privileged to use self-defense.

LOCAL LINKS

What must a defendant prove in your state if he mistakenly intervenes on another's behalf?

Defense of Property

The same rationale used in defense of persons applies to defense of property. A property owner may use only that degree of force that is reasonably necessary to protect the property (some states, such as Texas, allow deadly force to be used to protect property). Furthermore, the owner must verbally insist that an intruder stop before she is justified in using force. An exception to this general rule is allowed if the defendant reasonably perceives that the request to stop will be useless or that the harm will occur immediately (*Restatement [Second] of Torts* § 77[c]). Beyond this an owner may not use deadly force to protect property unless she believes such force is immediately necessary to prevent death or serious bodily harm to herself or another or to prevent certain types of felonies.

LOCAL LINKS

Can you use deadly force in your state to defend property?

Mechanical Devices

Property owners frustrated by frequent burglaries that the local police appear impotent to prevent sometimes turn to mechanical devices for protection. These devices can range from strings of barbed wire to spring guns, which are mechanically rigged guns designed to go off automatically when someone enters the premises. As a general rule, a property owner is entitled to use such a device only if she could use a similar degree of force if she herself were present when the intruder entered. Because such devices are usually considered deadly force, they may be used only to prevent death or serious bodily harm or the commission of certain felonies. A homeowner will be liable, therefore, if a trespasser is seriously injured by an electric fence erected by the homeowner. Because the owner would not be justified in using deadly force against the trespasser if she confronted the trespasser in person, she would not be justified in using a mechanical device that constituted deadly force.

The classic case of *Katko v. Briney*, 183 N.W.2d 657 (Iowa 1971), which you can read on the next page, aptly illustrates the principle regarding the use of mechanical devices. In *Katko* the defendants owned an unoccupied, boarded-up farmhouse that had been broken into many times. To prevent further burglaries the defendants constructed a spring gun that was designed to discharge if a person entered the bedroom. The plaintiff, who broke into the house in an effort to steal bottles and jars that he believed to be antique, was severely injured when the gun went off. The court held that a property owner may not use deadly force against a trespasser unless that trespasser is endangering human life or committing some violent felony.

PUTTING IT INTO PRACTICE /3:7

George is walking his date, Sandy, to the theater when a man suddenly lunges before them, wielding a knife that he slashes menacingly at them. George grabs the gun that he carries in his belt holster and points it at the man. Can he lawfully shoot the man?

Suppose the attacker is mentally ill and likes to scare people but is actually quite harmless. If the "knife" is actually a plastic toy knife and incapable of causing harm, is George still justified in using deadly force to protect himself and Sandy?

CASE

Katko v. Briney
183 N.W. 2d 657 (Iowa 1971)

MOORE, Chief Justice

The primary issue presented here is whether an owner may protect personal property in an unoccupied boarded-up farm house against trespassers and thieves by a spring gun capable of inflicting death or serious injury.

We are not here concerned with a man's right to protect his home and members of his family. Defendants' home was several miles from the scene of the incident to which we refer infra.

Plaintiff's action is for damages resulting from serious injury caused by a shot from a 20-gauge spring shotgun set by defendants in a bedroom of an old farm house which had been uninhabited for several years. Plaintiff and his companion, Marvin McDonough, had broken and entered the house to find and steal old bottles and dated fruit jars which they considered antiques.

At defendants' request plaintiff's action was tried to a jury consisting of residents of the community where defendants' property was located. The jury returned a verdict for plaintiff and against defendants for $20,000 actual and $10,000 punitive damages.

After careful consideration of defendants' motions for judgment notwithstanding the verdict and for new trial, the experienced and capable trial judge overruled them and entered judgment on the verdict. Thus we have this appeal by defendants.

I. In this action our review of the record as made by the parties in the lower court is for the correction of errors at law. We do not review actions at law de novo. Rule 334, *Rules of Civil Procedure.* Findings of fact by the jury are binding upon this court if supported by substantial evidence. Rule 344 (f), par. 1, R.C.P.

II. Most of the facts are not disputed. In 1957 defendant Bertha L. Briney inherited her parents' farm land in Mahaska and Monroe Counties. Included was an 80-acre tract in southwest Mahaska County where her grandparents and parents had lived. No one occupied the house thereafter. Her husband, Edward, attempted to care for the land. He kept no farm machinery thereon. The outbuildings became dilapidated.

For about 10 years, 1957 to 1967, there occurred a series of trespassing and housebreaking events with loss of some household items, the breaking of windows and 'messing up of the property in general'. The latest occurred June 8, 1967, prior to the event on July 16, 1967 herein involved.

Defendants through the years boarded up the windows and doors in an attempt to stop the intrusions. They had posted 'no trespass' signs on the land several years before 1967. The nearest one was 35 feet from the house. On June 11, 1967 defendants set "a shotgun trap" in the north bedroom. After Mr. Briney cleaned and oiled his 20-gauge shotgun, the power of which he was well aware, defendants took it to the old house where they secured it to an iron bed with the barrel pointed at the bedroom door. It was rigged with wire from the doorknob to the gun's trigger so it would fire when the door was opened. Briney first pointed the gun so an intruder would be hit in the stomach but at Mrs. Briney's suggestion it was lowered to hit the legs. He admitted he did so "because I was mad and tired of being tormented," but he "did not intend to injure anyone." He gave no explanation of why he used a loaded shell and set it to hit a person already in the house. Tin was nailed over the bedroom window. The spring gun could not be seen from the outside. No warning of its presence was posted.

Plaintiff lived with his wife and worked regularly as a gasoline station attendant in Eddyville, seven miles from the old house. He had observed it for several years while hunting in the area and considered it as being abandoned. He knew it had long been uninhabited. In 1967 the area around the house was covered with high weeds. Prior to July 16, 1967, plaintiff and McDonough had been to the premises and found several old bottles and fruit jars which they took and added to their collection of antiques. On the latter date about 9:30 p.m. they made a second trip to the Briney property. They entered the old house by removing a board from a porch window which was without glass. While McDonough was looking around the kitchen area plaintiff went to another part of the house. As he started to open the north bedroom door the shotgun went off striking him in the right leg above the ankle bone. Much of his leg, including part of the tibia, was blown away. Only by McDonough's assistance was plaintiff able to get out of the house, and after crawling some distance was put in his vehicle and rushed to a doctor and then to a hospital. He remained in the hospital 40 days.

Plaintiff's doctor testified he seriously considered amputation but eventually the healing process was successful. Some weeks after his release from the hospital plaintiff returned to work on crutches. He was required to keep the injured leg in a cast for approximately a year and wear a special brace for another year. He continued to suffer pain during this period.

There was undisputed medical testimony plaintiff had a permanent deformity, a loss of tissue, and a shortening of the leg.

The record discloses plaintiff to trial time had incurred $710 medical expense, $2056.85 for hospital service, $61.80 for orthopedic service and $750 as loss

(continues)

of earnings. In addition thereto the trial court submitted to the jury the question of damages for pain and suffering and for future disability.

III. Plaintiff testified he knew he had no right to break and enter the house with intent to steal bottles and fruit jars therefrom. He further testified he had entered a plea of guilty to larceny in the nighttime of property of less than $20 value from a private building. He stated he had been fined $50 and costs and paroled during good behavior from a 60-day jail sentence. Other than minor traffic charges this was plaintiff's first brush with the law. On this civil case appeal it is not our prerogative to review the disposition made of the criminal charge against him.

IV. The main thrust of defendants' defense in the trial court and on this appeal is that 'the law permits use of a spring gun in a dwelling or warehouse for the purpose of preventing the unlawful entry of a burglar or thief'. They repeated this contention in their exceptions to the trial court's instructions 2, 5 and 6. They took no exception to the trial court's statement of the issues or to other instructions.

In the statement of issues the trial court stated plaintiff and his companion committed a felony when they broke and entered defendants' house. In instruction 2 the court referred to the early case history of the use of spring guns and stated under the law their use was prohibited except to prevent the commission of felonies of violence and where human life is in danger. The instruction included a statement that breaking and entering is not a felony of violence.

Instruction 5 stated: "You are hereby instructed that one may use reasonable force in the protection of his property, but such right is subject to the qualification that one may not use such means of force as will take human life or inflict great bodily injury. Such is the rule even though the injured party is a trespasser and is in violation of the law himself."

Instruction 6 stated: "An owner of premises is prohibited from willfully or intentionally injuring a trespasser by means of force that either takes life or inflicts great bodily injury; and therefore a person owning a premise is prohibited from setting out 'spring guns' and like dangerous devices which will likely take life or inflict great bodily injury, for the purpose of harming trespassers. The fact that the trespasser may be acting in violation of the law does not change the rule. The only time when such conduct of setting a 'spring gun' or a like dangerous device is justified would be when the trespasser was committing a felony of violence or a felony punishable by death, or where the trespasser was endangering human life by his act."

Instruction 7, to which defendants made no objection or exception, stated: "To entitle the plaintiff to recover for compensatory damages, the burden of proof is upon him to establish by a preponderance of the evidence each and all of the following propositions:

1. That defendants erected a shotgun trap in a vacant house on land owned by defendant, Bertha L. Briney, on or about June 11, 1967, which fact was known only by them, to protect household goods from trespassers and thieves.
2. That the force used by defendants was in excess of that force reasonably necessary and which persons are entitled to use in the protection of their property.
3. That plaintiff was injured and damaged and the amount thereof.
4. That plaintiff's injuries and damages resulted directly from the discharge of the shotgun trap which was set and used by defendants."

The overwhelming weight of authority, both textbook and case law, supports the trial court's statement of the applicable principles of law.

Prosser on Torts, Third Edition, pages 116–118, states:

"... the law has always placed a higher value upon human safety than upon mere rights in property, it is the accepted rule that there is no privilege to use any force calculated to cause death or serious bodily injury to repel the threat to land or chattels, unless there is also such a threat to the defendant's personal safety as to justify a self-defense.... spring guns and other mankilling devices are not justifiable against a mere trespasser, or even a petty thief. They are privileged only against those upon whom the landowner, if he were present in person, would be free to inflict injury of the same kind."

Restatement of Torts, section 85, page 180, states: "The value of human life and limb, not only to the individual concerned but also to society, so outweighs the interest of a possessor of land in excluding from it those whom he is not willing to admit thereto that a possessor of land has, as is stated in § 79, no privilege to use force intended or likely to cause death or serious harm against another whom the possessor sees about to enter his premises or meddle with his chattel, unless the intrusion threatens death or serious bodily harm to the occupiers or users of the premises. * * * A possessor of land cannot do indirectly and by a mechanical device that which, were he present, he could not do immediately and in person: Therefore, he cannot gain a privilege to install, for the purpose of protecting his land from intrusions harmless to the lives and limbs of the occupiers or users of it, a mechanical device whose only purpose is to inflict death or serious harm upon such as may intrude, by giving notice of his intention to inflict, by mechanical

(continues)

means and indirectly, harm which he could not, even after request, inflict directly were he present."

In Volume 2, Harper and James, *The Law of Tort*, section 27.3, pages 1440, 1441, this is found: "The possessor of land may not arrange his premises intentionally so as to cause death or serious bodily harm to a trespasser. The possessor may of course take some steps to repel a trespass. If he is present he may use force to do so, by only that amount which is reasonably necessary to effect the repulse. Moreover if the trespass threatens harm to property only—even a theft of property—the possessor would not be privileged to use deadly force, he may not arrange his premises so that such force will be inflicted by mechanical means. If he does, he will be liable even to a thief who is injured by such device. . . ."

In *Hooker v. Miller*, 37 Iowa 613, we held defendant vineyard owner liable for damages resulting from a spring gun shot although plaintiff was a trespasser and there to steal grapes. At pages 614, 615, this statement is made: "This court has held that a mere trespass against property other than a dwelling is not a sufficient justification to authorize the use of a deadly weapon by the owner in its defense; and that if death results in such a case it will be murder, though the killing be actually necessary to prevent the trespass. *The State v. Vance*, 17 Iowa 138." At page 617 this court said: "(T)respassers and other inconsiderable violators of the law are not to be visited by barbarous punishments or prevented by inhuman inflictions of bodily injuries."

The facts in *Allison v. Fiscus*, 156 Ohio 120, 110 N.E.2d 237, 44 A.L.R.2d 369, decided in 1951, are very similar to the case at bar. There, plaintiff's right to damages was recognized for injuries received when he feloniously broke a door latch and started to enter defendant's warehouse with intent to steal. As he entered, a trap of two sticks of dynamite buried under the doorway by defendant owner was set off and plaintiff seriously injured. The court held the question whether a particular trap was justified as a use of reasonable and necessary force against a trespasser engaged in the commission of a felony should have been submitted to the jury. The Ohio Supreme court recognized plaintiff's right to recover punitive or exemplary damages in addition to compensatory damages.

In *Starkey v. Dameron*, 96 Colo. 459, 45 P.2d 172, plaintiff was allowed to recover compensatory and punitive damages for injuries received from a spring gun which defendant filling station operator had concealed in an automatic gasoline pump as protection against thieves.

In *Wilder v. Gardner*, 39 Ga.App. 608, 147 S.E. 911, judgment for plaintiff for injuries received from a spring gun which defendant had set, the court said: "A person in control of premises may be responsible even to a trespasser for injuries caused by pitfalls, mantraps, or other like contrivances so dangerous in character as to imply a disregard of consequences or a willingness to inflict injury."

In *Phelps v. Hamlett*, Tex.Civ.App., 207 S.W. 425, defendant rigged a bomb inside his outdoor theater so that if anyone came through the door the bomb would explode. The court reversed plaintiff's recovery because of an incorrect instruction but at page 426 said: "While the law authorizes an owner to protect his property by such reasonable means as he may find to be necessary, yet considerations of humanity preclude him from setting out, even on his own property, traps and devices dangerous to the life and limb of those whose appearance and presence may be reasonably anticipated, even though they may be trespassers."

In *United Zinc & Chemical Co. v. Britt*, 258 U.S. 268, 275, 42 S.Ct. 299, 66 L.Ed. 615, 617, the court states: "The liability for spring guns and mantraps arises from the fact that the defendant has . . . expected the trespasser and prepared an injury that is no more justified than if he had held the gun and fired it."

In addition to civil liability, many jurisdictions hold a land owner criminally liable for serious injuries or homicide caused by spring guns or other set devices. See *State v. Childers*, 133 Ohio 508, 14 N.E.2d 767 (melon thief shot by spring gun); *Pierce v. Commonwealth*, 135 Va. 635, 115 S.E. 686 (policeman killed by spring gun when he opened unlocked front door of defendant's shoe repair shop); *State v. Marfaudille*, 48 Wash. 117, 92 P. 939 (murder conviction for death from spring gun set in a trunk); *State v. Beckham*, 306 Mo. 566, 267 S.W. 817 (boy killed by spring gun attached to window of defendant's chili stand); *State v. Green*, 118 S.C. 279, 110 S.E. 145, 19 A.L.R. 1431 (intruder shot by spring gun when he broke and entered vacant house. Manslaughter conviction of owner—affirmed); *State v. Barr*, 11 Wash. 481, 39 P. 1080 (murder conviction affirmed for death of an intruder into a boarded-up cabin in which owner had set a spring gun).

In Wisconsin, Oregon, and England the use of spring guns and similar devices is specifically made unlawful by statute.

The legal principles stated by the trial court in instructions 2, 5 and 6 are well established and supported by the authorities cited and quoted supra. There is no merit in defendants' objections and exceptions thereto. Defendants' various motions based on the same reasons stated in exceptions to instructions were properly overruled.

* * *

Study and careful consideration of defendants' contentions on appeal reveal no reversible error.

Affirmed.

Media reports of this case reflected that the entry was into the Brineys' home rather than into an abandoned farmhouse. As a result, public outcry regarding the decision resulted in the introduction of "Briney Bills" in several state legislatures. These bills legalized the use of any means necessary to protect one's person, family, or property from intrusion.

If an owner intends to use some nonlethal mechanical device, such as barbed wire, he must post some type of warning that will put others on notice that the device is present. Even a warning will not suffice, however, in the case of a mechanical device that constitutes the use of deadly force. No warning of the spring gun, for example, would have relieved the defendants in *Katko* of liability.

(You may find it interesting to know that the Brineys were forced to sell 80 acres of their 120-acre farm in order to satisfy the judgment in this case. Because no bids above the minimum price of $10,000 were made, three neighbors purchased the land for a dollar more, expecting to hold it for the Brineys until they won their appeal. After the Brineys lost their appeal, the neighbors leased the land back to them for enough money to pay their taxes and the interest on the money they had borrowed. Years later the neighbors decided to sell the property; one of them bought it for $16,000 and sold it to his son for $16,500. Briney and Katko then joined together and jointly sued the neighbors. Just before the case came to trial it was settled for a large enough sum that the Brineys were able to pay the remainder of their judgment to Katko.)

LOCAL LINKS

Have any "Briney" bills (or something analogous) been passed in your state?

Regaining Possession of Chattels

Under limited circumstances, a property owner may use force to regain possession of chattels taken from her by someone else. Because the owner becomes an aggressor by her use of force, she is not given the same latitude by the courts as one who is taking a less aggressive stance in defending her possession of chattels.

Reasonable Force

To claim this defense, the owner must first show that he used reasonable force in securing the chattels. Deadly force is never allowable unless justified under the doctrine of self-defense.

Property Wrongfully Taken

Second, the property must have been wrongfully taken. If the owner willingly gives up possession and is later entitled to repossession of the property, she cannot use force to regain it. A seller who attempts to repossess a stereo unit sold to a consumer who has missed several payments cannot break into the consumer's house to regain possession. If, however, the consumer uses fraud to gain possession and the seller promptly discovers the fraud, she may use reasonable force to recover possession (*Restatement [Second] of Torts* §§ 101[1][a] and 106). No greater force than that required can be used, and deadly force is impermissible unless necessary for the defendant to protect herself against ensuing violence.

Fresh Pursuit

Third, the property owner must be in "fresh pursuit." Therefore, if the owner delays for a substantial period of time before attempting to get her property back, he may no longer use reasonable force to secure

---

PUTTING IT INTO PRACTICE 3:8

1. Summarize the facts that are critical to an understanding of the *Katko* case.

2. According to Prosser, why is there no privilege to use force intended to cause death or serious physical injury in order to protect property? Under what conditions may such force be used?

3. Explain this: A possessor of land cannot do indirectly what he could not if he were present.

4. Summarize the theme of the civil cases cited by the *Katko* court.

5. Can a landowner be held criminally liable for serious injuries or homicide caused by a spring gun?

possession. Instead he must turn to the courts for redress. Although the courts have never clearly defined the meaning of *fresh pursuit*, it appears that prompt and persistent efforts must be made to reclaim the property. Owners are privileged to use force to recapture property only because of the concern for the delay created by the cumbersome, time-consuming legal process. If, however, they fail to make timely efforts to regain possession, they will be relegated to the legal process for a remedy.

Mistake

Any mistakes on the part of the owner will cause her to lose the privilege. If, for example, she mistakenly (albeit reasonably) believes that someone is in possession of her goods, she will not be justified in using force to retake the goods. Similarly, if she reasonably but mistakenly believes that force is necessary to reclaim the goods, she will lose the privilege. The owner is expected to bear the consequences of any mistakes.

Detention of Shoplifters

The issue of recapture of goods most frequently occurs in the context of merchants detaining suspected shoplifters. As discussed earlier in this chapter, many courts have granted merchants the privilege of temporarily detaining any person they reasonably suspect of shoplifting. As you will recall, the detention must be relatively short in duration and the merchant or its agent must not attempt to coerce a payment or a confession from the suspect, nor may the merchant or its agent purport to arrest the suspect (*Gortarez By & Through Gortarez v. Smithy's Super Valv, Inc.*, 140 Ariz. 97, 680 P.2d 807 [1984]).

Reentry on Land

The issue of reentry on land typically occurs in the case of a landlord who attempts to forcibly evict a tenant who overstays his lease (referred to as a *holdover tenant*). The majority of American courts do not permit the use of force by landlords. Landlords, it is felt, should be restricted to the legal process to resolve these disputes because the law typically provides procedures allowing for expeditious resolutions. In short, landlords are discouraged from taking the law into their own hands. A landlord may, however, enter the land if he does so without force. Furthermore, if a provision in the lease allows for reentry through the use of force, some courts will uphold a forcible entry as long as only reasonable force is used.

LOCAL LINKS

Do the courts in your state permit landlords to use force to evict holdover tenants?

Necessity

In the privileges discussed thus far, the defendant has prevailed in her cause of action because of some wrongdoing on the plaintiff's part. In some circumstances, however, the defendant is privileged not because the plaintiff has done anything wrong but because of unusual circumstances that justify the defendant's actions. The privilege of **necessity** justifies the defendant's harming of the plaintiff's property in emergencies. For example, a person who trespasses on another's land in an attempt to avoid a criminal attack can claim the privilege of necessity.

PUTTING IT INTO PRACTICE 3:9

Read over the facts in the "Putting It into Practice" question 3:2 for false imprisonment and consider the following additional facts:

- The man being interrogated asked to call his employer and/or his wife and his request was denied.
- One of the store detectives walked around the room repeatedly slapping his gun during the investigation.
- After more than an hour of questioning, the detectives asked the man to sign a civil release form, threatening him with jail if he refused to sign. After he reluctantly signed the form, he was told not to mention this incident to anyone.

Did the detectives exceed their authority in their detention of the suspected shoplifter?

Distinction between Public and Private Necessity

Cases involving necessity fall into two categories: public necessity and private necessity. The conduct of a defendant protecting only his own interests or those of a few private citizens falls into the realm of **private necessity**. By contrast, if the class of persons being protected is the public as a whole or a substantial number of persons, the privilege is referred to as **public necessity**. The only reason for distinguishing between these two kinds of necessities is that the defendant does not have to pay for damages caused in cases of public necessity but is required to do so in cases involving private necessity.

LOCAL LINKS

Do you have state statutes requiring compensation for victims in public necessity cases?

Public Necessity

The privilege of public necessity arises when interference with the land or chattels of another is required to avert a disaster to the community. In one case, for example, the defendant sprayed fire retardant chemicals on the plaintiff's land while fighting a forest fire that threatened the entire county. When the plaintiff sued for the damage incurred by his trees, the court permitted the defendant to raise the privilege of necessity (*Stocking v. Johnson Flying Service*, 387 P.2d 312 [Mont. 1963]). The defendant who successfully claims the privilege of public necessity will not be required to reimburse the plaintiff for the damages he suffers. Although the common law does not require

the community as a whole to compensate the victim, several states have enacted statutes that provide for such compensation.

A utility company may be required to relocate its lines at its own expense if the relocation is demanded by public necessity (*Perrysburg v. Toledo Edison Co.*, 870 N.E.2d 198 [Ohio. App 2007]).

Private Necessity

A person may claim the privilege for private necessity when she damages the property of another to prevent injury to herself or her property. The privilege also extends to the protection of a third person or the property of that person. Furthermore, the privilege requires that no less damaging way of preventing the harm exist. In contrast to cases of public necessity, private necessity applies even when the danger is not severe. A driver, for example, can claim the privilege of private necessity if he is forced to trespass on private land because the public roadway on which he is traveling is obstructed and the only conceivable path of avoidance is through the adjoining land of a private owner.

Damages

In determining whether a privilege exists, the harm to the plaintiff's property must be weighed against the severity and likelihood of the danger the defendant is seeking to avoid (*Restatement [Second] of Torts* § 263, cmt. d). If the defendant causes no substantial harm to the plaintiff's property, the privilege of private necessity is a complete defense. If, however, the defendant causes actual damage to the plaintiff's property, the privilege will be limited and

PUTTING IT INTO PRACTICE 3:10

A fireman arrives at the scene of a raging blaze and removes Maryann's lawfully parked car from the highway to gain access to a fire hydrant. Is the fireman privileged to move the car? Is he liable to Maryann for any unavoidable damages to her vehicle?

Maryann's next-door neighbor, Liz, is bleeding profusely after being hit by flying debris from chemical-containing cans that exploded in the fire. Liz asks Maryann to use her scarf as a tourniquet until the ambulance arrives. Maryann refuses because the scarf is an heirloom and says she will look for something else to use as a tourniquet. Afraid that she will bleed to death before Maryann finds something acceptable, Liz grabs Maryann's scarf. Is Liz privileged to do so? Will she be liable to Maryann for the bloodstains on the scarf?

the defendant will be required to pay for the damages caused. Suppose a man is lost in the forest and comes upon someone's cabin. If he enters the cabin and takes food because he is starving, he will not be liable for the trespass. He will, however, be required to compensate the owner of the cabin for the food he takes.

One of the benefits of invoking the privilege of private necessity is that the person whose property has been harmed has no right to use reasonable force to prevent the exercise of the privilege. Furthermore, one who resorts to such retaliatory force will be liable for any damages she causes (*Restatement [Second] of Torts* § 263, cmt. b).

SUMMARY

An intentional tort requires that the tortfeasor intend or have a desire to bring about a particular consequence. The fact that the defendant wishes no harm to the plaintiff has no bearing on whether he acted intentionally. If he knows with substantial certainty that a result will occur, he will be liable for an intentional tort. Under the transferred-intent doctrine, a tortfeasor's intent with respect to one person may be transferred to the person who is actually injured.

The intentional infliction of a harmful or offensive contact upon a person's body or anything attached to or identified with the body is referred to as *battery*. The plaintiff need not suffer actual pain or bodily injury nor even be aware of the contact at the time it occurs.

If a tortfeasor intentionally causes an apprehension of a harmful or offensive contact, he commits assault. Assault requires an intent either to commit a battery or to frighten the plaintiff. The victim of assault, unlike the victim of battery, must be aware of the threatened contact. The plaintiff need not actually fear that he will be harmed but he must believe that the defendant has the present ability to carry out the threatened contact.

The tortfeasor who intentionally confines another commits the tort of false imprisonment. The plaintiff must be aware of her confinement at the time it occurs but is not required to subject herself to any risk of harm in order to extricate herself from her confinement. As with assault and battery, the doctrine of transferred intent is applicable, and threats of harm must be imminent.

The tort of infliction of mental distress can be committed either intentionally or recklessly, but in either case the defendant's conduct must be "extreme and outrageous." The peculiar characteristics of the plaintiff may be taken into consideration in evaluating the defendant's conduct. Generally, the doctrine of transferred intent is not applicable, although some exceptions exist. A plaintiff must prove she actually suffered severe emotional distress and in some courts must prove she experienced some kind of actual physical harm.

A person who enters or wrongfully remains on another's land commits the tort of trespass. The defendant's only intent must be to make physical contact with the plaintiff's land. He need not intend any harm to the plaintiff's property nor be aware that any harm might occur. An indirect invasion of the land is sufficient, as is an invasion of the airspace above or the surface below the plaintiff's property. A defendant who refuses to leave the plaintiff's land when permission has been terminated also commits trespass.

Intentional interference with the plaintiff's use or possession of chattels constitutes trespass to chattels. As with trespass, the only intent required is the intent to interfere. The defendant need not intend to cause harm to the property. As with trespass, the mistaken belief that the property is his own is not a defense. In contrast with trespass, the plaintiff is required to prove actual harm.

If the defendant's interference with the plaintiff's property is so substantial that the defendant must compensate the plaintiff for the full value of the property, the defendant has committed the tort of conversion. The defendant need not desire to harm the plaintiff's property. With trespass to chattels, the defendant has a right to return the goods to mitigate the plaintiff's damages, but the defendant in a conversion action is required to pay the full value of the property.

One of the defenses that can be raised in response to an intentional tort is consent. If a plaintiff implicitly or explicitly consents to the defendant's intentional interference, the defendant is not liable for his conduct. Consent is determined by objective manifestations of the plaintiff but can be inferred from custom. The plaintiff must be capable of giving consent and must do so voluntarily. If a defendant exceeds the scope of the plaintiff's consent, he will be liable for his conduct.

A defendant may use reasonable force to protect herself against threatened harmful or offensive bodily contact or threatened confinement. She cannot raise the defense in response to threats of future harm or when she is threatened with words alone, unless those words are accompanied by some kind of hostile act. Deadly force may be used only in response to a threat of death or serious bodily injury. A defendant who uses force to protect against the invasion of her home must show that she faced a threat of death or serious bodily harm and that no lesser degree of force was sufficient. The courts are split on whether a defendant has a duty to retreat before resorting to force.

If the circumstances would support a claim of self-defense and the defendant's intervention is immediately necessary for the protection of a third person, a defendant may use reasonable force to protect another. If the person being rescued would not be privileged to act in self-defense, the defendant, according to most courts, will be precluded from claiming the privilege. A minority of courts, however, allow the privilege as long as the defendant reasonably believes that the person he is aiding would have been privileged to use self-defense.

A property owner may use only that degree of force that is reasonably necessary to protect his property. He must first verbally insist that an intruder stop unless it reasonably appears that the request to stop will be useless or that the harm will occur immediately. Mechanical devices used to protect property are generally considered deadly force and may be used only to prevent death, serious bodily harm, or the commission of certain felonies.

In some circumstances a property owner may use force to regain possession of chattels. Reasonable force is required, and deadly force is never allowed unless justified under the doctrine of self-defense. Furthermore, the property must have been wrongfully taken and the property owner must be in fresh pursuit. If the property owner is mistaken in any way, she will lose the privilege even if her mistake is a reasonable one.

The use of force to gain reentry on land is usually not allowed by the courts. Landlords, who most frequently argue that force is necessary to evict a tenant, are generally restricted to the legal process to resolve their disputes.

A defendant who is justified in harming the plaintiff's property because of an emergency may claim the privilege of either public necessity or private necessity. Interference required to avert a disaster to the community is classified as a public necessity; interference necessary to prevent injury to a few private citizens is classified as a private necessity. In a case of public necessity the defendant is not required to reimburse the plaintiff for the damages he suffers.

KEY TERMS

assault
Intentional causing of an apprehension of harmful or offensive contact

battery
Intentional infliction of a harmful or offensive contact upon a person

chattels
Personal property

conversion
Substantial interference with another's property to the extent that justice demands payment for the full value of the property

deadly force
Force likely to cause death or serious bodily injury

false imprisonment
Intentional confinement of another

intentional tort
Tort in which the tortfeasor intends to bring about a particular consequence or knows with substantial certainty that a result will occur

necessity
Privilege that justifies the defendant's harming of the plaintiff's property in an effort to prevent great harm to the defendant or others

private necessity
Privilege that justifies the defendant's harming of the plaintiff's property in order to protect his own interests or those of a few private citizens

public necessity
Privilege that justifies the defendant's harming of the plaintiff's property in an effort to prevent great harm to the public as a whole or to a substantial number of persons

transferred-intent doctrine
Intent with respect to one person (or tort) is transferred to another person (or tort)

trespass to chattels
Intentional interference with another's use or possession of chattels

trespass to land
Intentionally entering or wrongfully remaining on another's land

REVIEW QUESTIONS

1. What must a tortfeasor intend in order to be held liable for an intentional tort?

2. What is the transferred-intent doctrine?

3. What is a battery?

4. How does a battery differ from an assault?

5. How does the tort of false imprisonment arise in law enforcement and in shoplifting cases?

6. Why is it so difficult to hold a defendant liable for the infliction of emotional distress?

7. What are some of the ways a tortfeasor can commit trespass?

8. What is the difference between trespass to chattels and conversion, and what does a court consider when distinguishing between these two torts?

9. What must be shown to prove that a plaintiff consented?

10. Under what conditions is a defendant entitled to use self-defense?

11. When is a defendant justified in using force to defend her property?

12. Under what conditions might a defendant *not* be justified in defending a third person?

13. Why are homeowners not allowed to use spring guns to defend their homes?

14. Under what conditions can a property owner use force to regain possession of chattels?

15. Can a landlord use force to evict a holdover tenant?

16. What are the differences between public and private necessity?

PRACTICE EXAM

Students should complete the practice exam after studying each chapter. The answers are in Appendix A. If you score lower than 80%, you should reread the materials.

True-False

1. To be liable for an intentional tort, a tortfeasor must intend to harm the plaintiff.

2. Tort law and criminal law share the same purpose and historical derivations.

3. The concepts and terms used in tort law do not always correspond to those used in criminal law.

4. The intent to commit one tort cannot be transferred to the tort that is actually committed.

5. Battery includes harmful or offensive contact even if the defendant intended only to frighten but not to harm the plaintiff.

6. Battery must involve contact with the plaintiff's body, not with something attached to the body.

7. To commit battery the defendant must actually touch the plaintiff with his body.

8. To commit battery the defendant must cause the plaintiff pain or bodily harm.

9. In determining whether a contact is offensive, the question is whether any person of reasonable dignity would be offended.

10. The defendant is liable for the full extent of the plaintiff's harm even if he could not have reasonably anticipated that harm.

11. An assault is not committed unless the plaintiff fears the impending contact.

12. An assault is committed when a defendant intends to frighten but not to contact the plaintiff.

13. A plaintiff who believes he can protect himself and who is not fearful that he will be harmed can still be the victim of an assault.

14. A plaintiff can recover for assault even if she knows that someone other than herself will be touched.

15. The defendant need not have the ability to carry out a threatened contact, but the plaintiff must believe the defendant has that ability.

16. An assault occurs even if threats of future harm are made.

17. An assault is complete as soon as the plaintiff apprehends contact.

18. Some courts allow words alone to constitute an assault.

19. Merely obstructing a plaintiff from taking the route she prefers is grounds for false imprisonment.

20. Confinement for purposes of false imprisonment can be achieved by threats even if those threats consist of the defendant's body language or are directed at someone other than the plaintiff.

21. A plaintiff is not required to subject herself or her property to harm in order to extricate herself from confinement.

22. To defend herself against a claim of false imprisonment, an officer must show that the arrest he made was lawful.

23. To defend herself against charges of false imprisonment by a customer detained for shoplifting, the merchant must show that there were reasonable grounds for the detention and that the detention was not unreasonably long.

24. The right to detain someone suspected of shoplifting will be lost if the defendant is coerced into signing a confession or making payment or is publicly accused of shoplifting.

25. To hold a defendant liable for the tort of intentional infliction of emotional distress, a plaintiff must prove that the defendant wanted to bring about a particular consequence or knew with substantial certainty that a specific result would occur.

26. Insults and petty manipulations are often the basis for the tort of infliction of emotional distress.

27. A plaintiff's peculiar characteristics may be taken into consideration in evaluating the defendant's conduct for purposes of the tort of intentional infliction of emotional distress.

28. The courts are not at all uniform in their assessment of extreme and outrageous conduct.

29. The doctrine of transferred intent generally applies to the infliction of emotional distress.

30. If a defendant fails to commit the tort she intends to commit but ends up causing the plaintiff emotional distress, she cannot be held liable for the harmful effects of the emotional distress.

31. A defendant is liable for the emotional distress suffered by a plaintiff only if he suffered some type of physical harm.

32. Common carriers and public utilities are held to a higher standard of care than the rest of the public for purposes of the tort of intentional infliction of emotional distress.

33. Trespass is a strict-liability tort.

34. Trespass does not occur if a defendant's contact with the land is a result of a reasonable mistake.

35. A defendant is liable for allowing gases or particles to enter the plaintiff's land or for setting off a blast that causes vibrations on the plaintiff's land.

36. Landowners cannot necessarily sue for an invasion of their airspace.

37. If a defendant fails to remove something from the plaintiff's property after permission to be on the property has ended, she is liable for trespass.

38. A defendant is liable for all consequences of a trespass as long as those consequences are predictable.

39. Recovery for trespass to chattels is allowed for the owner but not the possessor of property.

40. A viable defense to trespass to chattels is that the defendant mistakenly believed the property was his.

41. A defendant is not liable for trespass to chattels if there was no harm caused to the property.

42. With conversion the plaintiff can recover even if the defendant made an innocent mistake.

43. With both trespass to chattels and conversion, the defendant has a right to return the property to the plaintiff to mitigate his damages.

44. A defendant does *not* commit conversion if she mistakenly picks up the plaintiff's purse and does not realize her mistake until two months later, at which time she returns it.

45. In deciding whether a conversion has been committed, the only thing the courts consider is the extent and duration of the defendant's control of the property.

46. Mistake is a defense to any intentional tort.

47. A plaintiff's consent may be implied by his conduct.

48. A patient's consent to treatment will be considered ineffective if the doctor fails to adequately inform her about the risks involved or the consequences that will definitely follow the treatment.

49. To claim self-defense the defendant must show a threat of imminent or future harm.

50. When determining whether a defendant used a reasonable amount of force to protect herself, a subjective standard is used.

51. A defendant can use deadly force to protect himself in his home if he reasonably believes he is in imminent danger of death or serious bodily harm.

52. A defendant must retreat before using deadly force to protect herself when her home is invaded.

53. According to the *Restatement*, deadly force can be used to prevent any felony.

54. A defendant can use force to defend another even if he is mistaken about that person's need for intervention as long as he reasonably believes that the person he is helping would have been privileged to claim self-defense.

55. Homeowners must post warnings for nonlethal devices, but posting a warning for a deadly device will not absolve them of liability if someone is injured.

56. Property owners lose their privilege of using force to regain possession of property if they make a mistake.

57. Most courts do not allow a landlord to forcibly evict a tenant unless there is a provision in the lease allowing forcible entry and reasonable force is used.

58. If a defendant claims the privilege of necessity, she must pay for any damages she causes.

59. If a defendant has a right to claim the privilege of necessity, the plaintiff has no right to use reasonable force to prevent the defendant from exercising his privilege.

Matching

_____ 1. Desire to attain a certain result

_____ 2. Reason for wanting a certain result

_____ 3. Inflicting offensive contact

_____ 4. Creating fear of harmful contact

_____ 5. Confinement

_____ 6. Conduct exceeding all bounds of decency

a. assault

b. battery

c. false imprisonment

d. motive

e. intent

f. infliction of emotional distress

Fill-in-the-Blanks

1. Under the _____ _____ doctrine the intent with respect to one person is transferred to another person.

2. An assault occurs when a defendant intends to but fails to commit a(n) _____.

3. To prove infliction of emotional distress, a plaintiff must show that the defendant's conduct was _____ and _____.

4. _____ occurs when someone enters or remains unlawfully on another's land.

5. If a defendant's interference with the plaintiff's property is so substantial that he must pay the plaintiff the full value of her property, the tort of trespass to chattels becomes _____.

6. The privilege of _____ _____ allows a defendant to protect her own interests in an emergency situation. The privilege of _____ _____ allows a defendant to protect the interests of the public in an emergency.

7. In determining whether a privilege exists, the harm to plaintiff's property is weighed against the _____ and _____ of danger the defendant is seeking to avoid.

Multiple-Choice

1. A plaintiff must be aware of the contact at the time it occurs for the defendant to be liable for
   a. battery.
   b. assault.
   c. both assault and battery.
   d. neither assault nor battery.

2. The doctrine of transferred intent is applicable to
   a. battery.
   b. assault.
   c. false imprisonment.
   d. all of the above.

3. For a defendant to be held liable for false imprisonment
   a. a plaintiff must be actually incarcerated.
   b. physical force must be used.
   c. a plaintiff must be aware of her confinement.
   d. all of the above.

4. To be liable for trespass a defendant must
   a. intend to harm the plaintiff's property or be aware that harm might occur.
   b. make contact with the land himself.
   c. know that an entry on the plaintiff's land is reasonably certain to happen.
   d. all of the above.

5. Conversion can be committed by
    a. removing goods.
    b. transferring goods to someone who is not entitled to them.
    c. taking possession of intangibles.
    d. all of the above.

6. Consent cannot
    a. be inferred from custom.
    b. be implied in emergency situations.
    c. be given by someone who is incompetent or incapable of giving consent.
    d. all of the above.

7. Consent
    a. is not valid if the defendant exceeds the scope of that consent.
    b. can, in most states, be given to criminal acts.
    c. is not voluntary if it is given as a result of a threat of future harm or economic duress.
    d. all of the above.

8. A defendant cannot use force to defend herself unless
    a. she is actually harmed.
    b. she believes she has no reasonable alternative to the use of force to protect herself against impending harm.
    c. an actual threat exists against her.
    d. all of the above.

9. A homeowner
    a. can use deadly force to defend property.
    b. can use a mechanical device to prevent burglaries only if the owner would be justified in using the same degree of force if she were present when the intruder entered.
    c. is not liable for injuries suffered by a trespasser who is hurt by the homeowner's electric fence.
    d. all of the above.

10. To regain possession of his property, a property owner
    a. may use reasonable force.
    b. may use force if the property was wrongfully taken.
    c. must be in fresh pursuit.
    d. all of the above.

11. The privilege of private necessity
    a. may be claimed only when the danger is severe.
    b. is a complete defense if the defendant causes no substantial harm to the plaintiff's property.
    c. can be invoked on behalf of oneself but not a third person.
    d. all of the above.

PRACTICE POINTERS

Drafting of routine pleadings is a common assignment for litigation paralegals. In offices that handle a large volume of cases in a particular area of specialization, such as personal injury, insurance defense, or debt collection, complaint drafting generally involves making straightforward modifications to form complaints, and paralegals are handed a file and expected to produce a finished complaint, ready to sign and file with the court. In cases of greater complexity or those that present difficult substantive issues, complaint drafting requires a detailed analysis of the issues based on appropriate legal research. Here, research-qualified paralegals may be asked to prepare a draft for review and editing, but the responsible attorney will participate more actively in the pleading process.

Before a paralegal can begin to draft a complaint, she needs to have some basic knowledge of the facts of the case. These facts are obtained by interviewing the client, and by obtaining pertinent facts and documents, such as police reports, from other sources. Certain facts are necessary in every case. Here are some of them:

1. The names of the parties being sued
2. The state and county of residence of the parties being sued. In the case of corporations and other entities, the state in which the entity is incorporated or created must be known as well as the county and state in which the entity has its principal place of business.
3. The main facts that led to the injury that the client is suing for
4. The place where the injury to the client occurred and the date on which it occurred

(continues)

Notice the key elements of the following complaint. The *caption* at the beginning of the complaint contains the names of the court, plaintiffs, and defendants. The caption also indicates that the type of pleading involved is a "complaint." Under the "General Allegations" the jurisdictional element of the complaint is satisfied by showing where the cause of action occurred and where the defendants are doing business. The "General Allegations" also contain a brief summary of the facts supporting the cause of action. Each "count" identifies a cause of action (intentional infliction of emotional distress and conversion) and the relief being sought (general, special, and punitive damages).

J. Stanley Edwards 004190
Edwards & Smith L.L.P
P. O. Box 41033-371
Phoenix, Arizona 85000
(602) 466-9800
Attorney for Plaintiff

IN THE SUPERIOR COURT OF THE STATE OF ARIZONA
IN AND FOR THE COUNTY OF MARICOPA

LINDA MENDOZA, a single woman

      Plaintiff,

      v.

EMMANUEL RUDY LOPEZ and JANE DOE LOPEZ husband and wife; BEVERLY ALLEN POE and JOHN DOE ALLEN POE husband and wife; JOHN DOES I-X; JANE DOES I-X; BLACK CORPORATIONS I-X; and WHITE PARTNERSHIPS I-X.

      Defendants.

No. CV-07-00123

COMPLAINT

Plaintiff Mendoza alleges:

1. Plaintiff Mendoza currently resides in Maricopa County, Arizona and at all times mentioned herein was a resident of Maricopa County, Arizona.
2. Defendants caused events to occur in Maricopa County, Arizona, out of which this claim for relief arises.
3. Defendants are and were at all times mentioned herein residents of Maricopa County, Arizona.
4. All Defendants identified as husband and wife were at all times mentioned herein married to each other and were acting in furtherance of their marital community. At the present time the true name of any spouse identified as Jane Doe or John Doe is unknown to Plaintiff Mendoza, who therefore sue this Defendants by such fictitious name and will seek to amend this complaint when the true name of such spouse is ascertained.
5. All Defendants identified as Arizona Corporations were at all times mentioned herein created, organized, and existing under the laws of the State of Arizona.
6. All Defendants identified as foreign corporations were at all times mentioned herein qualified and authorized to do and were doing business in the State of Arizona.
7. Defendants John Does I-X, Jane Does I-X, Black Corporations I-X, and White Partnerships I-X are those persons and entities whose relationships to the named Defendants or whose acts or omissions give rise to legal responsibility for the damages incurred by Plaintiff Mendoza, but whose true identities are at the present time unknown to Plaintiff Mendoza. These persons and entities hereby are notified of Plaintiff Mendoza's intention to join them as Defendants if and when additional investigation or discovery reveals the appropriateness of such joinder.

(continues)

Count I
Negligence

8. On or about August 7, 1998, in the vicinity of the intersection of Priest Drive and Greenway Drive, in Tempe, Arizona, Linda Mendoza was injured as a result of the negligent and reckless driving of Emmanuel Rudy Lopez and Beverly Allen Poe.

9. Emmanuel Rudy Lopez had over twelve glasses of beer at the local tavern immediately prior to the accident.

10. Beverly Allen Poe was negligent when she reached down to pick up and dial a number on her cell phone, causing her to collide with the Mendoza Lopez accident.

11. Defendant Poe jumped from her car and pulled Mendoza out of her car and began to hit and kick Mendoza repeatedly.

12. As a direct and proximate result of these injuries, Plaintiff Mendoza has incurred and expended medical and related expenses and will, in the future, be required to incur and expend medical and related expenses for the care and treatment of her injuries.

Count II
Assault

13. Plaintiff hereby adopts and incorporates all preceding paragraphs of this Complaint as if set forth herein again in full.

14. The actions of Defendant Poe constituted assault in that the actions were performed with the knowledge and intent to cause Plaintiff harm or offensive contact, or apprehension thereof, and Plaintiff did suffer reasonable apprehension of such imminent contact.

15. Defendant Poe has severely injured and damaged Plaintiff and caused her great and permanent psychological and emotional damage.

16. As a direct and proximate result of the injuries caused by Defendant Poe, Plaintiff has incurred, and will incur in the future, medical bills, miscellaneous expenses and losses, lost earnings, employment and/or loss of earning capacity and other damages in an amount to be proven at the time of trial in this matter.

17. As a further direct and proximate result of the physical and emotional injuries caused by Poe, Plaintiff has incurred, and will incur in the future, pain, suffering, emotional distress, anxiety, loss of reputation, humiliation and inconvenience, and other general damages in the amount to be proven at the time of trial in this matter.

18. The actions of Defendant Poe as described herein, were not only intentional and/or reckless, but were malicious, wanton and willful, and preformed with an evil hand guided by an evil mind, so as to warrant the imposition of punitive damages in the amount to be proven at the time of trial of this matter.

Count III
Battery

19. Plaintiff hereby adopts and incorporates all proceeding of this Complaint as if set forth herein again in full.

20. The actions of Defendant Poe against Plaintiff as described above constitute battery in that offensive contact, or apprehension thereof.

21. The actions as described on the part of Poe constitute violations of Arizona law, statutes and regulations, specifically A.R.S. § 11–9999 *et seq.*

22. As a direct and proximate result of the battery on Plaintiff, Plaintiff has or will sustain the damages referred to in count one.

Count IV
Intentional Infliction of Emotional Distress

23. Plaintiff hereby adopts and incorporates the preceding paragraphs of this Complaint as if set forth herein again in full.

24. The conduct on the part of Defendant Poe as imposed on Plaintiff caused the intentional infliction of emotional distress in that said conduct was extreme, outrageous, was done with either the intent, or the reckless disregard of the near certainty that such conduct would result in severe emotional distress.

25. As a direct and proximate result of the infliction of emotional distress on Plaintiff, she has been severely injured and is entitled to damages.

WHEREFORE, Plaintiff Mendoza respectfully request judgment against Defendants:
A. For medical and related expenses in an amount to be ascertained at the time of arbitration/trial;
B. For loss of earnings in an amount to be ascertained at the time of arbitration/trial;
C. For just and reasonable compensation for pain and suffering in an amount to be ascertained at the time of arbitration/trial;

(continues)

D. For loss of the use of her vehicle in an amount to be ascertained at the time of arbitration/trial;

E. For property damage expenses in an amount to be ascertained at the time of arbitration/trial;

F. For costs incurred by Plaintiff; and

G. For such other and further relief as the Court deems appropriate.
RESPECTFULLY SUBMITTED this 30th of September 2007.

Edwards & Smith L.L.P

By _____

J. Stanley Edwards
Attorney for Plaintiff

TORT TEASERS

1. What intentional torts were committed in the hypothetical scenario given at the beginning of this chapter? What defenses could have been raised by each of the actors who committed a tort?

2. The defendant was charged with violating a city ordinance banning sleeping in designated public areas. Defendant argued that his homelessness stemmed from economic conditions over which he had no control and that on the night in question he had been turned away from every available shelter in town. Was his conduct privileged? *In re Eichorn,* 81 Cal. Rptr.2d 535 (1998).

3. Plaintiff, who suffers from premature ejaculation, goes in for surgery to remove plaque from his penis. When he awakes from surgery, he is told that a prosthesis has been implanted in his penis to "save him from a second operation." Plaintiff now feels "more like a machine than a man," and that the emotional quality of his lovemaking with his wife has suffered. Should the doctor be held liable, or were his actions privileged? *Montgomery v. Bazaz-Sehgal,* 742 A.2d 1125 (Pa. 1999).

4. Defendant sees Plaintiff break into a vending machine. He yells at Plaintiff to stop, drop his weapon, and wait for the police but Plaintiff and his companions continue to run. The thieves are carrying a money box, a tire tool, and a lug wrench. When they are seventy to seventy-five yards away Defendant fires three shots, one of which strikes Plaintiff in the back. Should Defendant be held liable? *Bray v. Isbell,* 458 So. 2d 594 (La. Ct. App. 1984), *cert. denied,* 462 So. 2d 210 (La. 1985).

5. Plaintiff is injured by Defendant's vicious dog when he trespasses on Defendant's land. Defendant has posted a sign warning outsiders of the presence of the dog. Should Defendant be held liable? *Hood v. Waldrum,* 434 S.W.2d 94 (Tenn. Ct. App. 1968).

6. Defendant hotel's security guard informs Plaintiffs, an interracial couple, that the police will be called to place them under arrest if they do not stay in their hotel room. Plaintiffs remain in their hotel room for several hours fearful that they would be arrested. Will the Plaintiffs prevail on a false imprisonment claim? *Dawes v. Motel 6 Operating L.P.,* 2006WL 276928 (E.D.Wash. 2006).

7. What should the defendants in each of the following cases be found liable for?

   a. Auctioneer sells stolen goods. *Judkins v. Sadler-MacNeil,* 376 P.2d 837 (Wash. 1962).

   b. Defendant race steward posted security guards to prevent Plaintiff race horse owner from retrieving his horse from race grounds and required that the horse be raced against the owner's wishes. *Jamgotchian v. Slender,* 170 Cal. App. 4th 1384 (2009).

   c. Plaintiff owns a tract of land on a hill. Defendant discovers the entrance to a cave on the land adjoining his own. The cave extends a considerable distance under Plaintiff's land. Defendant develops the cave, advertises it, and conducts tours through it. *Edwards v. Sims,* 24 S.W.2d 619 (Ky. 1929).

   d. Defendant touches a woman in an indecent manner, *Skousen v. Nidy,* 367 P.2d 248 (Ariz. 1961).

   e. Defendant threatens Plaintiff with an unloaded gun. *Allen v. Hannaford,* 244 P. 700 (Wash. 1926).

f. Plaintiff, a supervisor at an insurance company, terminates an employee because he threatens another employee with a handgun. Immediately after his termination, the employee begins stalking Plaintiff, making "hang-up telephone calls, sending unsolicited merchandise to her home, and making death threats." She asks for help from Defendant's company but is denied assistance and told to call the police. The man is ultimately arrested for stalking and criminal harassment. Plaintiff feels Defendant's company failed to take steps to make her work environment safe. *Snead v.*

Metropolitan Property and Casualty Insurance Co., 909 F. Supp. 775 (Ore. 1996).

g. Defendant, a police officer, observes Plaintiff's dog running loose in violation of the city's "dog leash" ordinance. When Defendant demands that Plaintiff produce her driver's license or go to jail, she refuses to do so, although she does volunteer her name and address. Defendant arrests her, charging her with a violation of the dog leash ordinance. *Enright v. Groves,* 567 P.2d 851 (Colo. Ct. App. 1977).

INTERNET INQUIRIES

This exercise will require you to go to the web page for your highest court. You can use one of two ways to get to there. One way is to go to a frequently used legal portal called FindLaw at http://www.findlaw.com. At that site, enter "state laws [your state]" as your search term and look for a link to your highest court.

Once you find the web page for your highest state, look for links to recent court decisions. (If your state's highest court does not have links to its decisions, go to the Arizona Supreme Court web page.)

1. How far back can you get court decisions for your state's highest court online?

2. Are summaries or full-text opinions available, or both?

3. Can you search for cases? If yes, look for cases on battery. How many cases come up?

4. Must you read each case, or are you provided with an abstract of the case that allows you to scan the cases more quickly?

PRACTICAL PONDERABLES

You have been asked to do an intake interview of a potential client, Murray McDonald. This is what you find out:

Murray was attending a bachelor party for his friend Steve at Steve's house. Sometime during the party Murray made a derogatory comment about the local professional football team—a comment to which many of the men present apparently took great umbrage. About a half hour after he had made the comment, Murray found himself surrounded by at least six men. While he was trying to figure out what was happening, one of them grabbed his glasses. Murray is extremely nearsighted and is virtually blind without his glasses. The men started tossing Murray's glasses around like a football, making snide comments about Murray's "nerdiness" in the process. Eventually someone dropped the glasses and in the process of trying to recover them, they were smashed. Murray, who said he became increasingly nervous as this "game" went on, tried to extricate himself from the circle the men had created, but they would not let him pass. They were standing near the pool when the incident began, and one of the men decided it would be fun to push Murray in the pool. Murray, who was terrified of

going underwater, frantically struggled to get away but was eventually thrown into the deep end of the pool. Not being able to swim, Murray panicked when he felt himself hit the bottom of the pool. The men allowed him to sink under the water several times before anyone attempted to help him. Murray estimates he spent at least twenty terrifying minutes in the pool, during which time he was certain he was going to drown before he was dragged out on the pool deck. He lay there exhausted for about an hour until his friend Willard, who had been cowering in the bushes, got the courage to gather him up and take him to an emergency room, where they treated him for mental trauma and physical exhaustion.

Murray was unable to go to work for several days after this incident, and he is currently undergoing intensive psychotherapy. This experience triggered some longstanding fears and phobias, which his psychiatrist indicates may take several months or even years to treat. Murray continues to have nightmares in which he relives this experience, he has lost considerable weight because of being unable to eat much, and he experiences panic attacks on a daily basis, making it difficult for him to function at work or socially.

One of his coworkers, John, who had also attended the party heard about Murray's plight and stopped by to visit him after work one day, ostensibly to apologize for the men's behavior. Murray told John to leave his house and hinted that he would call his lawyer. John suddenly became verbally abusive and shouted that Murray had "better not do something stupid like file a lawsuit." He warned Murray that he knew where Murray lived and that if Murray caused any trouble for him or any of the other men, he would come back and finish what they started at the party.

1. What potential torts do you think were committed against Murray?
2. What information would you have to gather before a complaint could be filed?

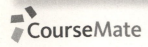 Access an interactive eBook, chapter-specific learning tools, including flashcards, quizzes, and more in your Paralegal CourseMate, accessed through www.CengageBrain.com.

PART II

Reasons to Sue

© Cengage Learning 2012

CHAPTER 4

© Cengage Learning 2012

Negligence: Duty

CHAPTER OBJECTIVES

After completing the chapter, you should be able to

- Describe the standard of care expected of a possessor of land toward those who enter his or her land.
- Describe the standard of care that arises out of certain special relationships (e.g., employer–employee) and special situations (e.g., rendering emergency care).
- Describe the standard of care expected of landlords, tenants, and sellers of land.
- Recognize the concepts of vicarious liability and the family-purpose doctrine.

OVERVIEW OF DUTY

Negligence is conduct that creates an unreasonable risk of harm to another. In any negligence claim, the concept of duty raises the question of whether the defendant is under any obligation to act for the benefit of the plaintiff. A **duty** is a legal obligation to act reasonably and arises out of our relationship to others.

In general terms, the defendant's duty is to act reasonably. In other words, the defendant must exercise the degree of care that any reasonable person would exercise under similar circumstances. You will notice when you read cases that most courts spend relatively little time addressing the question of duty but instead jump directly into an analysis of breach of duty. Nevertheless, duty is a threshold question in every negligence case because a defendant is not liable, no matter how reckless his conduct, unless he owes a duty to the plaintiff. Therefore, we will explore the concept of duty in some depth in this chapter.

The question of duty is essentially a question of whether a defendant is under an obligation to protect the plaintiff. Some courts use the relational approach to answer this question. Under this approach the nature of the relationship between the parties determines whether the defendant has a duty to protect the plaintiff. Parents, for example, owe a duty of care to children, airline companies owe a duty of care to their passengers, and hotels owe a duty of care to their guests. The nature of the duty varies depending on the nature of the relationship. Landowners owe a different duty of care to trespassers than they do to those whom they invite on their premises. Some courts analyze the existence of duty in the context of foreseeability. Under this analysis, a defendant owes a duty only to those persons the defendant could reasonably foresee would be endangered. This was the approach advocated by Justice Cardozo in *Palsgraf v. Long Island*

Railroad (discussed in more detail in Chapter 6). Under this analysis, the tortfeasor may owe a duty of care to those with whom he has no direct contact, such as third parties whom he could reasonably anticipate being injured by his conduct. A tavern owner, for example, could owe a duty of care to those injured by intoxicated patrons whom the tavern owner recognizes as being so intoxicated as to constitute a danger to those about him.

Because the foreseeability approach seems to add to the confusion surrounding the duty question, and because foreseeability is also used to analyze breach of duty and proximate cause, we will rely on the relational approach in this text. Although this approach is based on the concept of relationship between plaintiff and defendant, that relationship need not be a personal or ongoing one. A reckless driver who runs over a pedestrian in a crosswalk owes a duty of care to that pedestrian even though the two have never seen one another before their unfortunate interaction.

Generally, a legal obligation exists only when a direct relationship between the defendant and the plaintiff exists. A duty to the plaintiff may also arise, however, if a relationship exists between the defendant and a third party whose negligence causes injury to the plaintiff. For example, a defendant who loans her automobile to someone who is intoxicated and who injures others could, under certain conditions, be found liable for the injuries caused by the intoxicated individual.

In this chapter we examine the duty of care owed by possessors of land and the duty of care arising out of certain special relationships, such as landlord-tenant, seller-buyer, and lessor-lessee. Be aware, however, that a legal duty arises out of many relationships, such as doctor-patient, parent-child, and employer-employee. We also touch lightly on the issue of vicarious liability (although that subject is discussed in greater detail in Chapter 14) and consider how that doctrine affects employers and car owners.

NET NEWS

General guidance to homeowners regarding the prevention of negligence suits is found in an interesting article by the American Bar Association entitled "Floor Wax and Dog Attack—Homeowner's Guide to Avoiding Liability." The sections on attractive nuisance, social host liability, and artificial hazards are particularly topical for this chapter. You can access this article at **http://www.abanet.org/** and enter "floor wax and dog attack" as your search term.

POSSESSORS OF LAND

Throughout this chapter we refer to "possessors" rather than owners of land. The possessor, not the landowner, was the focus of protection under the common law. The purpose of limiting the liability of possessors was to encourage full utilization of the land, unhampered by burdensome legal obligations to others. For that reason it was the tenant, not the landlord, who generally benefited from the common law rules.

Under the common law the duty of care owed by a possessor was determined by the class into which the plaintiff fell (see Exhibit 4–1). The three classes of plaintiffs were trespassers, licensees, and invitees. A trespasser was one who had no right to be on the defendant's land, a licensee was one who came on the land as a social guest and hence with the owner's consent, and an invitee was one who came on the land with a business purpose. The owner owed the highest duty of care to the invitee and the lowest duty of care to the trespasser. Note that although most courts continue to apply these classifications, the differences between the classes have blurred over time. Some courts have abandoned these distinctions altogether.

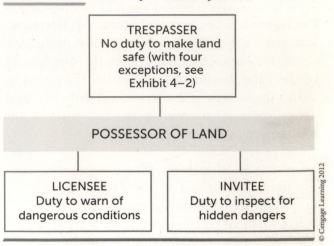

EXHIBIT 4–1 *Duties of Possessor of Land*

© Cengage Learning 2012

TRESPASSERS

Early common law established the principle that possessors of land could not deliberately set traps or spring guns with the intent of injuring a trespasser. From this principle evolved the rule that possessors of land must refrain from willfully or intentionally injuring trespassers. Nevertheless, a trespasser otherwise assumes the risks inherent in entering the land and is responsible for his own safety. In general, a possessor owes no duty of care to a trespasser to make the land safe or to protect the trespasser in any way. If the possessor is pursuing dangerous activities on the property, she need not warn the trespasser of such dangers nor avoid carrying on such activities (*Restatement [Second] of Torts* § 333). There are four exceptions, however, to this general rule (see Exhibit 4–2). Some duty of

LOCAL LINKS

Do the courts in your state classify plaintiffs as trespassers, licensees, and invitees?

EXHIBIT 4–2 *Exceptions to No Duty Rule for Trespassers*

ATTRACTIVE NUISANCE	RESCUERS	KNOWN TRESPASSER	LIMITED TRESPASS
• Knows children are likely to trespass • Knows condition poses unreasonable risk of injury to children • Child is unaware of danger posed by condition • Benefit in maintaining condition is slight compared to risk posed • Possessor fails to use reasonable care to protect children	• Possessor negligently causes harm to person or property • Harm must be imminent, real, and require immediate action	• Possessor is aware of trespasser • Possessor is aware of dangerous condition	• Trespasser uses only limited portion of land

© Cengage Learning 2012

care is owed when the plaintiffs are (1) trespassing children, (2) individuals known to be trespassers, (3) rescuing someone in danger as a result of the defendant possessor's negligence, or (4) trespassing on a very limited portion of the possessor's land. We will discuss each of these exceptions in more depth in the following sections.

Attractive Nuisance

The notion that children who are trespassers should be entitled to greater protection than adults evolved from the **attractive nuisance** doctrine. Under this doctrine a possessor is liable if he maintains a dangerous condition on the land that induces children to enter the premises because it is an enticing item on which to play. A construction site might be considered an attractive nuisance. It is usually replete with lumber, ladders, and other items that make wonderful props for fertile imaginations.

Under the *Restatement*, a possessor can be found liable to a trespassing child if the following conditions are met (*Restatement [Second] of Torts* § 339):

- The possessor has reason to know that the condition is on a place on the land where children are likely to trespass.

- The possessor must have reason to know of the condition and to know that it poses an unreasonable risk of serious injury or death to trespassing children.

- Because of their youth, the children must not have discovered the condition or realized the danger posed by coming into the area made dangerous by the condition.

- The benefit to the possessor in maintaining the condition in its dangerous form must be slight in comparison to the risk posed to the children.

- The possessor must fail to use reasonable care to eliminate the danger or to protect the children.

Suppose a two-year-old child, left unattended for approximately ten minutes, wanders into a neighbor's backyard, falls into the pool, and drowns. Assume the backyard is inadequately fenced and that the owner is aware that on previous occasions children have climbed over the fence into the backyard. Does the swimming pool meet the criteria of an attractive nuisance as set forth in the *Restatement*? Yes. The owner knows that children are likely to trespass, as he is aware they have trespassed in the past. A swimming pool certainly poses an unreasonable risk of serious injury or death to very young children, as they are not usually fully cognizant of the danger posed. The owner has failed to use reasonable care by failing to provide adequate fencing. Any benefit the owner gains from not expending the money to install safe fencing is slight when weighed against the risk of injury posed to trespassing children.

The age, experience, and intelligence of the child may determine whether the attractive-nuisance doctrine applies. The question is whether the child is able to appreciate the risk of the condition involved. Even a relatively young child may be expected to understand the risk of drowning or the risk of falling from a great height. If the defendant can show that the injured child, because of her experience or intelligence, was aware of and appreciated the danger, even if other children of her age might not have been so appreciative, the child will be barred from recovery.

If the condition causing the injury is a "natural" rather than an "artificial" condition, the courts are less likely to allow the child to recover. The reasoning seems to be that it is prohibitively expensive to protect children from a natural condition such as a lake; also, a natural condition is one for which children are more likely to be familiar with the risk involved. The distinction, however, between a natural and an artificial condition is a stilted one and should not be relied on as the sole basis for denying liability.

The bottom line for possessors is that they must take reasonable measures to prevent harm to children. This does not mean that they need to make their premises childproof. Nor does it mean they are required to inspect for dangerous conditions of which they would otherwise have been unaware. Posting a warning may in many instances be sufficient.

Rescue Doctrine

Under the **rescue doctrine**, anyone who negligently causes harm to a person or property may be liable to one who is injured in an effort to rescue the imperiled person or property. The rationale is that the rescuer would not have been injured were it not for the negligence of the tortfeasor. This doctrine prevents a plaintiff from being found contributorily negligent for voluntarily placing herself in a dangerous situation in order to save another. Often dubbed the "danger invites rescue" doctrine, it stems from an opinion written by Judge Cardozo: "Danger invites rescue. . . . The wrong that imperils life is a wrong to the imperiled victim; it is wrong also to his rescuer" (*Wagner v. International Railway Co.*, 133 N.E. 437 [N.Y. 1921]).

PUTTING IT INTO PRACTICE 4:1

1. Is an objective or subjective standard used in assessing whether the attractive-nuisance doctrine applies to a particular child?

2. Suppose a manufacturing company uses a pulley to hoist raw material up to a fifth story of its factory. The company is aware that children like to visit its open yard and its employees actively try to drive the children away. One day an employee forgets to shut off the engine that operates the pulley. A group of children who walk by and see the ball and hook on the pulley going up and down dare one another to grab hold of the pulley and be carried up to the fifth floor. Jed, an eight-year-old, accepts the dare and is being carried up by the pulley when he becomes frightened and lets go of the pulley, falling to the ground and sustaining serious injuries. Does the company owe Jed a duty under the attractive-nuisance doctrine?

3. The owner of a small artificial pond is aware that children in the day-care center next to him often wander away from the center and go near the pond. The owner could prevent this by closing and locking his gate. Marie, a three-year-old child, falls into the pond while attempting to catch some goldfish and almost drowns. Does the pond owner owe Marie a duty of care? Would your answer change if Marie were ten years old?

4. A railroad company has a turntable that it knows creates a risk of unreasonable harm to children, and the company is aware that children often trespass in the area to play on the turntable. The company could easily prevent harm to children by installing a locking device on the turntable that would make it difficult for children to set it in motion. Micki, who is nine, is injured when his foot gets caught in the turntable. Is the railroad company liable to Micki? Would your answer change if installing such a locking device would have prevented its effective operation? What if Micki's father were a railroad engineer and had repeatedly warned Micki about the dangers of playing on the turntable?

Suppose, for example, a motorist were to negligently run into a bicyclist, knocking him to the ground. If another driver who stopped to render aid were run over in the process of helping the bicyclist, the motorist causing the accident would be liable for the injuries of the Good Samaritan. The rationale behind this liability is that the negligent motorist created a chain of events that foreseeably resulted in injury to the rescuer of the tortfeasor's victim. *Restatement (Second) of Torts* § 294, illus. 1, provides a slightly different example involving a person sitting on the curb watching children play ball on the sidewalk. A motorist driving down the street sees the children but fails to slow down or take any preventive measures. One of the children darts in front of the vehicle while in pursuit of the ball, and the observer on the sidewalk lunges forward to pull the child to safety, meanwhile slipping and falling under the car. The motorist is liable for the broken leg sustained by the rescuer even though

the motorist was not driving in a negligent manner in relationship to the rescuer. The driver's negligence in failing to anticipate the actions of the child created a situation that foreseeably justified the intervention of the rescuer.

The rescue doctrine is warranted only when the threatened danger is both imminent and real and requires immediate action if the victim is to be saved. If the defendant's conduct is neither negligent nor intentionally tortious, the doctrine is inapplicable.

Known Trespassers

Another exception to the general rule regarding trespassers involves those trespassers of whom the possessor is aware. Once a possessor knows that a particular person is trespassing on his property, he owes a duty of reasonable care to that person. This duty clearly applies when the danger to the trespasser arises out of something the possessor has done, such as excavate his land. The nature of the duty is less clear, however, when the condition is a natural one. (According to the *Restatement [Second] of Torts* § 337, cmt. b, the duty to exercise reasonable care should still apply when the condition is natural.)

The justification given for the imposition of this duty is that the possessor's continuing tolerance of the trespass constitutes implied permission to use the land. Thus, the trespasser is elevated to the status of a licensee. As a practical matter, however, defendants often do not attempt to thwart trespassing because to do so would be expensive and probably unproductive. Imagine the futility of a railroad company spending time and money trying to deter trespassers from using its tracks. Nevertheless, possessors have been shifted from a position of complete exemption from liability to a more moderate position of limited liability when dealing with known trespassers.

When a possessor knows or has reason to know that trespassers are in dangerous proximity to a hazard and has reason to believe that the trespassers will either not discover the hazard or not realize its hazardous nature, the possessor has a duty to use reasonable care to warn the trespassers of the hazard. In one case, for example, in which the plaintiff ran into an unmarked barbed wire fence while riding on the defendant's land, a court found that the evidence justified a finding that the fence was "dangerously invisible" and could not reasonably be discovered by trespassers (*Webster v. Culbertson*, 761 P.2d 1063 [Ariz. 1988]).

Limited Trespass

Possessors of land also owe a limited duty of care to frequent trespassers who use only a very limited area of their land. Suppose a farmer knows of a well-worn path across the edge of his property created by children taking a shortcut to school. In such a case he would be expected to anticipate the traversal of these children and would be required to use reasonable care in his activities for their protection.

LICENSEES

A **licensee** is one step up from a trespasser. She has the possessor's consent to be on the property but does not have a business purpose for being there. Most licensees are social guests. The duty a possessor owes to a licensee is to warn her of any dangerous conditions if the possessor is aware of that condition and should reasonably anticipate that the licensee may not discover it. Suppose your dinner guest trips on a toy left unattended by one of your children. If you failed to warn your guest of the presence of the toy, and if the lighting conditions were such that he could not reasonably be expected to see it, you could be held liable for his injuries.

The most frequently litigated issue in reference to licensees pertains to the obviousness of a hazardous condition and the warning that is required to prevent harm. A warning that is adequate for an adult, for example, may be inadequate for a child, as a peril that is obvious to an adult may not be so to a child. A posted notice warning of danger is not sufficient when the possessor knows that a licensee is unable to read (e.g., a child, a blind person, or someone from a foreign country) and the possessor may thus be required to use reasonable care to warn in some other way.

The possessor is, however, under no duty to inspect for unknown dangers when dealing with a licensee. As with trespassers, the courts are more likely to find a higher duty of care if the possessor is carrying out activities on the land than if the danger arises out of some natural condition on the land.

Social guests in an automobile are due the same standard of care as are licensees on land. Unless there is a statute to the contrary, most courts have held that the guest is owed no duty of inspection. Therefore, if the owner of a vehicle fails to inspect the car's brakes, which ultimately fail and cause injuries to the guest, the owner will not be liable for the failure to inspect.

NET NEWS

To learn the number of highway rail crossing accidents for any year between 1975 and 2010, you can generate a report based on data compiled by the Federal Administration Office of Safety Analysis. You can generate a report at **http://safetydata.fra.dot.gov**.

INVITEES

Invitees are those persons invited by the possessor onto her land to conduct business. An invitee can be either a public invitee or a business invitee. A **public invitee** is one who is invited and enters the land for the purpose for which the land is held open to the public. If a business owner maintains a free telephone for public use, anyone who enters the premises for purposes of using the telephone is a public invitee. If the land is held open to the public, the visitor need not pay admission to be considered a public invitee. Someone who attends a free public lecture is just as much an invitee as someone who pays admission to an exhibit. A **business invitee** is one who enters the land for a purpose connected with the business dealings of the possessor. A grocery shopper is an invitee, as is a worker who enters to make repairs.

Even if the plaintiff is not engaged in business at the time of his injury, he is considered an invitee so long as he has a general business relationship with the possessor. In *Campbell v. Weathers*, 111 P.2d 72 (Kan. 1941), the plaintiff had been a longstanding customer of the defendant, who operated a lunch counter and cigar stand in an office building. After standing next to the cigar stand for several minutes, the plaintiff used the toilet in the back of the building. On the way he fell into an open trap door in the dark hallway. The defendant argued that the plaintiff was not an invitee because he had made no purchases on the day of his injury and because the toilet was intended for the defendant's employees and not the general public. The court classified the plaintiff as an invitee and pointed out that anyone who goes into a store with the intent of doing business at the present or in the future is an invitee. The court noted that many people shop for hours without making any purchases. Could they be denied invitee status in light of the fact that owners implicitly invite them for their potential business purpose? The *Campbell* court thought not.

A social guest does not rise to the status of an invitee even by performing an incidental service for her host, such as repairing a broken faucet. The host must gain some type of economic benefit before the guest can be considered an invitee. By the same token, a salesperson making an unsolicited call to a private home is not an invitee unless he is invited in (*Restatement [Second] of Torts* § 332, cmt. b). By contrast, a salesperson who calls on a business where she reasonably believes that door-to-door salespeople are typically received is considered an invitee.

The majority of "slip and fall" cases involve invitees. In such cases the question is whether the store owner should be held liable for a customer's slip and fall caused by an unreasonably dangerous condition, such as the proverbial banana peel. The plaintiff must establish that the proprietor either caused the condition (by placing the banana peel on the floor) or that the proprietor was aware of the condition (caused by a third party, such as another customer) and failed to take reasonable measures to remove the hazard.

Losing Invitee Status

An invitee may become a licensee or trespasser if he goes to parts of the premises that extend beyond his invitation. So long as the visitor reasonably believes that the premises are open to the public, however, he will be treated as an invitee even if, unknown to him, the possessor intends that the area be off limits to the general public. However, even if a visitor receives explicit authorization from the possessor to go onto a private portion of the premises, he will lose his invitee status if he enters purely for his own benefit. In one such case a customer who came to a store with the intent of shopping was given permission, in her search for a particular saleswoman, to enter an alteration room reserved for employees. When she entered the room she fell down a stairway. The court held that she was a licensee because she entered the room for her own benefit and without invitation by the owner (although she had its permission to enter). As a licensee she was required to take the premises as she found them (*Lerman Bros. v. Lewis*, 126 S.W.2d 461 [Ky. 1939]).

Compare this case with *Campbell v. Weathers*, in which the plaintiff retained his invitee status because he entered an area that reasonably appeared to him to be open to the public. Reasonable belief of the plaintiff appears to be the operative fact on which the courts focus in these cases.

An invitee also loses her status if she stays on the premises for longer than is reasonably necessary to conduct her business. Once her purpose becomes social rather than business she becomes a licensee.

Nature of Duty to Invitee

A possessor owes a higher duty of care to an invitee than he does to either a licensee or a trespasser. Most importantly, he has a duty to inspect his premises for hidden dangers when dealing with invitees. Although he has no duty to ferret out all hidden dangers, he must use reasonable care in making his inspection (*Restatement [Second] of Torts* § 343). He may even be liable for a dangerous condition resulting from faulty construction or design even if the condition existed before he came into possession of the property.

The definition of *reasonable care* varies depending on the use of the premises. The possessor of a shopping mall, who may readily anticipate the passage of thousands of customers, is held to a higher duty of inspection than the owner of a private home who invites an insurance salesperson in for the purpose of discussing coverage. In some cases the use of a warning of a dangerous condition will meet the requirements of reasonable care, but in other situations affirmative action will be required. If a store owner knows, for example, that customers will be distracted by goods on display and probably will not notice a sign warning them of danger, then a warning will not be sufficient (*Restatement [Second] of Torts* § 343A, illus. 2).

Even if an invitee is aware of and appreciates the danger involved, the possessor may be obligated to take reasonable steps to reduce the danger. In *Wilk v. Georges*, 514 P.2d 877 (Or. 1973), the plaintiff and her husband were shopping for Christmas trees in a nursery operated by the defendant. On the day of the plaintiff's visit it had been raining and the walkways, put together using planks, were slippery and dangerous. The defendant had posted a sign that read:

> Please watch where you are going. This is a nursery where plants grow. There is four seasons: summer and winter, cold and hot, rain, icy spots. Flower petals always falling on the floor, leaves always on the floor.
>
> We are dealing with nature and we are hoping for the best. We are not responsible for anyone get hurt on the premises.
>
> Thank you.

The court found that the defendant should have anticipated an unreasonable risk of harm to the plaintiff despite the posted signs. The defendant, according to the court, had an obligation to take reasonable steps to prevent the harm that occurred to the plaintiff.

In some cases reasonable care may require the possessor to exercise control over third persons. A tavern owner, for example, may be obligated to prevent his patrons from becoming so intoxicated that they cause injury to others. This situation is discussed more in the section dealing with the duty to protect others, later in this chapter.

COMMON LAW DISTINCTIONS TODAY

It is interesting to note that several states have rejected the rigid distinctions between invitee, licensee, and trespasser and have instead adopted a reasonable-person standard of liability. Some states have abolished the invitee/licensee distinction but continue to apply the old rules of liability regarding trespassers. The majority, however, still adhere to the common law classifications.

OUTSIDE THE POSSESSOR'S PROPERTY

The reasons underlying the limitations on landowner liability are less persuasive when the dangerous condition affects those outside the possessor's property. Possessors are generally found liable for conditions that pose an unreasonable risk of harm to persons outside the premises (*Restatement [Second] of Torts* §§ 364–365). This is particularly true where the hazardous condition is artificially created by the possessor. Artificial conditions include man-made structures; additions to the land, such as trees; and alterations to the land, such as excavations. If a possessor of land, for example, alters the condition of the premises so that the normal course of surface water is altered and it flows out onto a highway, she may be held liable for injuries caused by her negligence. Courts are less likely to impose liability, however, if the offending object is something like a telephone pole or mailbox, which are necessities and are also above-ground objects.

In contrast, if the hazardous condition is a natural one, the possessor is under no duty to remove it or protect others from it even if it poses an unreasonable danger of harm to people outside the property (*Restatement [Second] of Torts* § 363[1]). This general rule becomes more complicated when dealing with trees. In urban and suburban areas the courts have obligated possessors to prevent trees from exposing people outside the premises to an unreasonable risk of harm. They have also required the removal of rotten trees and have imposed an affirmative duty to inspect to discover potential defects in trees. In rural areas no duty to remove rotten trees or to inspect for defects has been imposed. Some modern courts have rejected the rural/urban distinction in the case of fallen trees and have held possessors to a reasonable-care standard instead.

PUTTING IT INTO PRACTICE 4:2

1. How would you classify the following?

   a. a salesman soliciting magazines from door-to-door

   b. children playing on a vacant lot where the landowner is aware that the children use the lot to play ball and does nothing to chase them away

   c. children playing on a vacant lot where the landowner has installed playground equipment and has posted a sign welcoming children to play there

   d. a truck driver who delivers goods that have been ordered by the homeowner

   e. a customer who goes behind the counter in a department store without receiving permission to do so

   f. a Jehovah's Witness in your home to teach Bible study

2. A nineteen-month-old child falls into a pool and is seriously injured while her parents are houseguests of the homeowner. The parents have been warned about the pool. Is the homeowner liable for the child's injuries? What duty of care is owed the child?

3. A department store has a weighing scale that protrudes into the aisle. Although the scale is obvious to anyone who is looking, it is surrounded by displays of goods. A customer who is intent on looking at the displays fails to see the scale and trips over it, falling to the ground and injuring her arm. What duty does the department store owe to a customer? Could the store be subject to liability?

LANDLORD/TENANT LIABILITY

Under the common law the reason for limiting a possessor's liability was to promote the possessor's right to use the land to its fullest potential with minimal interference from others. Therefore, protection was given to the actual possessor of the land and not the abstract legal owner. As a result of this principle a tenant who is in possession of the property is entitled to the protection of the common law rules. In addition, members of the tenant's household, as well as those in his employ or working the land for him as independent contractors, are also entitled to the protection of the common law rules. A landlord, accordingly, was relieved of liability under the traditional common law once she surrendered possession of her property to the tenant. (See Exhibit 4–3.)

Tenant's Duties

A tenant is held to the same duty of inspection in reference to invitees as is a landowner. Consequently, a tenant is liable for the injuries to an invitee resulting from a defect that could have been discovered using reasonable care even if the tenant did not in fact discover it. This liability does not extend, however, to common areas such as elevators, stairways, and corridors if the building is an office building or a dwelling with multiple tenants.

EXHIBIT 4–3 *Duties of Tenant versus Landlord*

TENANT'S DUTIES	LANDLORD'S DUTIES
• Same duties as possessor of land • Duty does not extend to common areas	• Liable for dangers he knows or should know about and tenant has no reason to know about • Duty to inspect for dangers when landlord knows property is to be held open to public • Must use reasonable care if he contracts with tenant to keep premises in good repair • If landlord begins to make repairs he must perform reasonably • In some cases has duty to take security precautions to protect tenants from criminal activity

Landlord's Duties

The general rule of non-liability of landlords has been significantly altered today by modern social policy concerns. A landlord is liable, for example, to the tenant and to the tenant's invitees and licensees for those dangers that the landlord knows or should know about and that the tenant has no reason to know about (*Restatement [Second] of Torts* § 358). Most courts do not interpret this as requiring the landlord to inspect the premises. The thrust of this rule is to protect the tenant from hidden dangers of which the landlord is aware or should reasonably anticipate. The landlord has a higher duty if he has reason to believe that the tenant is planning on holding the premises open to the public. In such cases the landlord has an affirmative duty to inspect the premises to find and repair any damages.

What happens if the landlord contracts with the tenant to keep the premises in good repair? Certainly the tenant can sue for breach of contract if the landlord fails to make timely repairs. The question is, however, whether the tenant can sue in tort as well. The majority of courts allow a tort claim to anyone injured as a result of the landlord's breach of his covenant to repair. In such a case the plaintiff must show that the landlord failed to use reasonable care in performing her contractual duties. The landlord, of course, must be given a reasonable time to correct a condition once she has been notified of it.

Even if a landlord has no contractual duty to perform repairs, once he begins performance he must do so reasonably. If he initiates repairs and then fails to complete them, he, in effect, makes the situation worse because tenants are implicitly led to believe that the dangerous condition no longer exists. In such a case anyone on the premises with the tenant's consent who is injured by the landlord's negligence will be allowed to recover against the landlord. However, if the tenant is aware that the repairs were incomplete or were done in a negligent manner, the tenant and not the landlord will be held liable. If the landlord hires an independent contractor to carry out the repairs he will usually be held liable for the contractor's negligence. The reasoning is that a landlord cannot delegate his responsibility to a third party.

Does a landlord have a general duty to protect tenants from a criminal attack? The court in *Walls v. Oxford Management Co., Inc.* 633 A2d 103 (N.H. 1993) examined that question and identified the circumstances under which a landlord owes such a duty to its tenants.

NET NEWS

By going to the Cornell Law site at **http://www.law.cornell.edu/**, you can search and find links to the Uniform Residential Landlord and Tenant Act, state property-law statutes, and federal and state court decisions.

CASE / *Walls v. Oxford Management Co., Inc.*
633 A2d 103 (N.H. 1993)

The United States District Court for the District of New Hampshire (*Loughlin*, J.) has certified to this court the following questions: (1) Does New Hampshire law impose a duty on landlords to provide security to protect tenants from the criminal attacks of third persons? (2) Does this State's law of implied warranty of habitability oblige landlords to provide security to protect tenants from the criminal attacks of third persons?

On December 13, 1988, the plaintiff, Deanna Walls, was sexually assaulted in her vehicle, which was parked on the premises of the Bay Ridge Apartment Complex in Nashua. The plaintiff lived with her mother, who leased an apartment at Bay Ridge. Gerard Buckley was arrested and subsequently convicted of sexually assaulting the plaintiff. Bay Ridge is owned by defendant Nashua-Oxford Bay Associates Limited Partnership (Nashua-Oxford), and managed by defendant Oxford Management Company, Inc. (Oxford). It consists of 412 apartments located in fourteen buildings. During the two years prior to the assault, the Bay Ridge complex had been the site of a number of crimes directed against property, including eleven automobile thefts,

(continues)

three attempted automobile thefts, and thirty-one incidents involving criminal mischief/theft. No sexual assaults or similar attacks against persons had been reported.

The plaintiff brought this action in federal court, charging that the defendants "had a duty to hire and contract with a competent management company, had a duty to provide reasonable security measures for the protection of residents of Bay Ridge, a duty to warn residents of its lack of security, as well as a duty to warn residents of the numerous criminal activities which had taken place on the premises of Bay Ridge and in the vicinity of Bay Ridge." . . .

1. Landlord's Duty to Secure Tenants Against Criminal Attack

The issues raised by the first question place the court at the confluence of two seemingly contradictory principles of law. On one hand lies the accepted maxim that all persons, including landlords, have a duty to exercise reasonable care not to subject others to an unreasonable risk of harm. *See Sargent v. Ross,* 113 N.H. 388, 391, 308 A.2d 528, 534 (1973). On the other hand, a competing rule holds that private persons have no general duty to protect others from the criminal acts of third persons. *See Restatement (Second) of Torts* § 314 (1965); W. Page Keeton *et al., Prosser and Keeton on the Law of Torts,* § 33, at 201 (5th ed. 1984). . . .

At one time, landlords enjoyed considerable immunity from "simple rules of reasonable conduct which govern other persons in their daily activities." *Sargent,* 113 N.H. at 391, 308 A.2d at 530. A landlord owed no general duty to his tenants, and could be found liable for injuries caused by a defective or dangerous condition on leased property only if the injuries were "attributable to (1) a hidden danger in the premises of which the landlord but not the tenant [was] aware, (2) premises leased for public use, (3) premises retained under the landlord's control, such as common stairways, or (4) premises negligently repaired by the landlord." *Id.* at 392, 308 A.2d at 531. In *Sargent,* however, this court abolished landlord immunity, and held that a landlord has a duty to act as a reasonable person under all the circumstances. *Id.* at 397, 308 A.2d at 534. We acknowledged that "[c]onsiderations of human safety within an urban community dictate that the landowner's relative immunity, which is primarily supported by values of the agrarian past, be modified in favor of negligence principles of landowner liability." *Id.* at 396, 308 A.2d at 533 (quotation omitted).

. . . We agree that as a general principle, landlords have no duty to protect tenants from criminal attack.

Without question, there is much to be gained from efforts at curtailing criminal activity. Yet, we will not place on landlords the burden of insuring their tenants against harm from criminal attacks.

Our inquiry is not concluded, however, as we must further consider whether exceptions to the general rule against holding individuals liable for the criminal attacks of others apply to the landlord-tenant relationship. A review of the law in this area suggests four such exceptions. The first arises when a special relationship, such as that of innkeeper-guest, or common carrier-passenger, exists between the parties. *See Restatement (Second) of Torts, supra* § 314A. Courts have repeatedly held, however, that a landlord-tenant relationship is not a special relationship engendering a duty on the part of the landlord to protect tenants from criminal attack. *See, e.g., Rowe,* 125 Ill.2d at 216, 126 Ill.Dec. at 525, 531 N.E.2d at 1364; *Braitman v. Overlook Terrace Corp.,* 68 N.J. 368, 377, 346 A.2d 76, 79 (1975); *Faheen By Hebron v. City Parking Corp.,* 734 S.W.2d 270, 272 (Mo.App.1987). *But see Kline v. 1500 Massachusetts Avenue,* 439 F.2d at 485 (finding landlord-tenant relationship analogous to that of innkeeper-guest).

A second exception arises where "an especial temptation and opportunity for criminal misconduct *brought about by the defendant,* will call upon him to take precautions against it." Keeton, *supra* § 33, at 201 (emphasis added). This exception follows from the rule that a party who realizes or should realize that his conduct has created a condition which involves an unreasonable risk of harm to another has a duty to exercise reasonable care to prevent the risk from taking effect. *Restatement (Second) of Torts, supra* § 321; *see also Restatement (Second) of Torts, supra* § 448 (criminal act of third person is superseding cause of harm to another unless defendant could have foreseen that his negligent conduct increased risk of crime). Accordingly, in the majority of cases in which a landlord has been held liable for a criminal attack upon a tenant, a known physical defect on the premises foreseeably enhanced the risk of that attack. *See, e.g., Braitman,* 68 N.J. at 371, 381, 346 A.2d at 77 (defective deadbolt on apartment door); *Aaron,* 758 S.W.2d at 446 (broken window latch); *Duncavage v. Allen,* 147 Ill.App.3d 88, 100 Ill. Dec. 455, 459, 497 N.E.2d 433, 437 (1986) (inoperable lighting; ladder left unattended near unlocked window).

A third exception is the existence of overriding foreseeability. Some courts have held landlords to a duty to protect tenants from criminal attacks that were clearly foreseeable, even if not causally related to physical

(continues)

defects on the premises. *See, e.g., Trentacost v. Brussel*, 82 N.J. 214, 218, 412 A.2d 436, 438 (1980) (criminal activity apparent in plaintiff's neighborhood); *Holley v. Mt. Zion Terrace Apartments, Inc.*, 382 So.2d 98, 100 (Fla.App.1980) (apartment complex plagued by high incidence of serious crime); *Kline v. 1500 Massachusetts Avenue*, 439 F.2d at 483 (crimes perpetrated against tenants in common area of apartment complex); *Johnston v. Harris*, 387 Mich. 569, 573-74, 198 N.W.2d 409, 410-11 (1972); *Faheen*, 734 S.W.2d at 273.

The fourth exception derives from the general tort principle that one who voluntarily assumes a duty thereafter has a duty to act with reasonable care. *See Restatement (Second) of Torts, supra* §§ 323, 324. Thus, landlords who gratuitously or contractually provide security have been found liable for removing the security in the face of a foreseeable criminal threat. *See Holley*, 382 So.2d at 100; *Kline v. 1500 Massachusetts Avenue*, 439 F.2d at 482-83; *Rowe*, 125 Ill.2d at 217, 126 Ill.Dec. at 525, 531 N.E.2d at 1365.

We hold that while landlords have no general duty to protect tenants from criminal attack, such a duty may arise when a landlord has created, or is responsible for, a known defective condition on a premises that foreseeably enhanced the risk of criminal attack. Moreover, a landlord who undertakes, either gratuitously or by contract, to provide security will thereafter have a duty to act with reasonable care. Where, however, a landlord has made no affirmative attempt to provide security, and is not responsible for a physical defect that enhances the risk of crime, we will not find such a duty. We reject liability based solely on the landlord-tenant relationship or on a doctrine of overriding foreseeability.

A finding that an approved exception applies is not dispositive of the landlord's liability for a tenant's injury. Where a landlord's duty is premised on a defective condition that has foreseeably enhanced the risk of criminal attack, the question whether the defect was a proximate or legal cause of the tenant's injury remains one of fact. Moreover, where a landlord has voluntarily assumed a duty to provide some degree of security, this duty is limited by the extent of the undertaking. *Rowe*, 125 Ill.2d at 218-19, 126 Ill.Dec. at 526, 531 N.E.2d at 1365. For example, a landlord who provides lighting for the exterior of an apartment building might be held liable for failing to insure that the lighting functioned properly, but not for failing to provide additional security measures such as patrol services or protective fencing. The answer to the first certified question is no, subject to the pleading or proof, as appropriate, of facts supporting the approved exceptions.

2. Implied Warranty of Habitability

The second certified question concerns whether a landlord's implied warranty of habitability to provide a reasonably safe premises requires the landlord to secure tenants against criminal attack.

An agreement for the rental of an apartment unit contains an "implied warranty . . . that the apartment is habitable and fit for living," and that "there are no latent defects in facilities vital to the use of the premises for residential purposes." *Kline v. Burns*, 111 N.H. 87, 92, 276 A.2d 248, 251-52 (1971); *see also Javins v. First Nat'l Realty Corp.*, 428 F.2d 1071, 1074 (D.C.Cir.1970). The implied warranty is measured in part by standards set forth in housing codes. *See Kline v. Burns*, 111 N.H. at 91, 276 A.2d at 251. A defect constituting a breach of this warranty "must be of a nature and kind which will render the premises unsafe, or unsanitary and thus unfit for living therein." *Id.* at 93, 276 A.2d at 252.

Until now, this court had not considered whether a landlord's failure to provide security against criminal attack renders a dwelling "unsafe" or "unfit for living," and thus in breach of the implied warranty of habitability. We therefore look for guidance in decisions from other jurisdictions. In *Williams v. William J. Davis, Inc.*, 275 A.2d 231, 231-32 (D.C.1971), the District of Columbia Court of Appeals answered this question in the negative, holding that housing regulations referring to "clean, safe and sanitary conditions," and a "healthy and safe" premises, did not oblige a landlord to furnish protection against criminal attacks. According to the court, the terms "safe" and "safety" referred to structural defects, fire hazards, and unsanitary conditions, not to safety from criminal acts of third parties. *Id.* at 232; *see also Deem v. Charles E. Smith Management, Inc.*, 799 F.2d 944, 946 (4th Cir.1986); *Cooke v. Allstate Management Corp.*, 741 F.Supp. 1205, 1208 (D.S.C.1990). *But see Duncavage*, 147 Ill.App.3d 88, 100 Ill.Dec. 455, 497 N.E.2d at 440; *Trentacost*, 82 N.J. at 228, 412 A.2d at 443.

We hold that the warranty of habitability implied in residential lease agreements protects tenants against structural defects, but does not require landlords to take affirmative measures to provide security against criminal attack. This holding in no way limits a tenant's recovery when a landlord has violated an express agreement to provide security measures, or has invited such an attack through a violation of an express housing code requirement. Our answer to the second certified question is no.

Remanded.

PUTTING IT INTO PRACTICE 4:3

1. Summarize the key facts, i.e., those facts the court relied on in rendering its decision, in *Walls*.

2. What are the issues in this case?

3. Does a private person have a duty to protect another person from criminal attacks?

4. Under what circumstance does a landlord have a duty to protect his tenants from criminal attacks?

5. What reasoning does the court use to arrive at its conclusion regarding the duty landlords owe tenants in reference to preventing criminal attacks?

6. What standard of care does the court apply to landlords in reference to protecting tenants?

7. Suppose that the plaintiff was assaulted when she left her job at an agency of the federal government and that she argues that the assault occurred because the entrance to the building was left unguarded and because the lights were lowered for energy conservation purposes. Further suppose that the agency was in a high-crime area but that no crimes against persons except those involving employees had occurred in the building in the several months preceding the assault on the plaintiff. Do you think a court would find that the agency had a duty to protect the plaintiff from criminal assault if the agency could show that it complied with the community standard of care? In other words, do you think the factual differences between this case and *Kline* would justify a finding of no duty of care?

SELLERS OF LAND

In general, a seller of land is released from tort liability once the buyer takes possession of the property. If, however, the seller fails to disclose a dangerous condition of which she is or should be aware and which she should realize that the buyer will not discover, she will be liable to anyone injured as a result of that condition (*Restatement [Second] of Torts* § 353). Her liability ceases when the buyer has a "reasonable opportunity" to find and correct the defect, even if the buyer does not in fact discover it (*Restatement [Second] of Torts* § 353[2]). If the seller hides the defect or intentionally misleads the buyer into not looking for it, the seller's liability will continue until the buyer actually discovers the condition and has a reasonable time to correct it.

If the seller of a house is also its builder, some courts hold the seller liable for any injuries caused by defects in the house. The courts in such cases analogize to product liability cases, in which both negligence and strict liability theories are utilized. See Chapter 12 for a discussion of liability in this area.

DUTY TO PROTECT OR AID OTHERS

Common Law No-Duty Rule

Under the common law a defendant has no legal obligation to aid a plaintiff in distress unless a special relationship exists between the plaintiff and the defendant. This rule applies even though the defendant could assist the plaintiff without causing any harm to himself. The extent to which this doctrine can be taken is illustrated dramatically in *Yania v. Bigan*, 155 A.2d 343 (Pa. 1959). In this case the defendant enticed his friend to jump into a strip-mine trench with walls eighteen feet high, containing eight to ten feet of water. The defendant refused to rescue his friend when it became obvious that he was drowning. The court found that the defendant was not liable for his friend's death even though he could have easily saved him. For obvious reasons this doctrine has been subject to scathing criticism by legal commentators and seems to be unique to Anglo-American law.

Special Relationships

More imposing than the duty to rescue others is the duty to protect plaintiffs from the negligent, intentional, or criminal acts of third parties—and the law

EXHIBIT 4–4 *Duty of Care*

SPECIAL RELATIONSHIPS THAT MAY CREATE DUTY OF CARE

Parent	Child
Husband	Wife
Teacher	Pupil
Jailor	Prisoner
Common Carrier	Passenger
Employer	Employee
University	Student
Possessor of Land	Licensee/Invitee
Innkeeper	Guest
Rescuer	Victim

DEFENDANT'S RELATIONSHIP WITH THIRD PARTY CREATING DUTY OF CARE TO PLAINTIFF

Attorney	Client
Doctor	Patient
Guardian	Mentally Ill Person
Tavern Owner	Intoxicated Patron
Car Owner	Intoxicated Driver

© Cengage Learning 2012

is loathe to impose this duty. Generally speaking, such a duty arises only in the context of special relationships, such as between parent and child, jailor and prisoner, carrier and passenger, or employer and employee (see Exhibit 4–4). Common carriers such as airline, railroad, and bus companies have a duty to protect their passengers. A bus company may be liable, for example, if a brawl breaks out on a bus, resulting in injury to several passengers, and the bus driver does nothing to intervene. An employer also has a duty to protect employees from those dangers from which they are not able to protect themselves. Such duty is limited to situations within the scope and course of the employees' responsibilities.

In some situations a special relationship may exist even between a university and a student. A court is likely to impose a duty of care on a university, for example, when the harm involved is that of a physical nature, such as a criminal attack. A court is most unlikely, however, to hold a university responsible for the private affairs of its students, particularly when the harm that occurs is of a moral nature.

Defendant's Relationship with Third Parties

In some cases the duty to protect owed by the defendant to the plaintiff arises out of a special relationship the defendant has with a third party. For instance, the guardian of a mentally ill patient who is potentially dangerous may be held liable for injuries inflicted by his dangerous charge.

The obligation to control a third party becomes particularly problematic when the relationship between the defendant and the third party is that of attorney–client or doctor–patient. In the controversial case of *Tarasoff v. Regents of University of California*, 529 P.2d 553 (Cal. 1974), a patient told his psychotherapist that he intended to kill the plaintiff (whom he did, in fact, kill). The court held that the defendant's psychotherapist had a duty to warn the plaintiff of the patient's intentions if a reasonable person in those circumstances would have done so. Admittedly, the doctor-patient privilege was inapplicable in this case because disclosure was necessary to prevent threatened danger. Nevertheless, the *Tarasoff* holding blurs the line between professionals' obligation to protect others and their need to promote open communication between themselves and their clients.

An area in which the defendant's relationship with a negligent third party is becoming increasingly significant involves situations in which the third party is intoxicated. A defendant who loans her vehicle to an intoxicated person, for example, may be liable for injuries caused by that person. Similarly, under the so-called "dram shop" laws, a tavern owner who sells liquor to an obviously intoxicated patron may be liable for injuries inflicted as a result of the patron's negligence. An increasing number of states are extending such liability to social hosts, especially those who violate statutes prohibiting the sale of liquor to minors. As the public becomes more conscious of the potential dangers associated with the immoderate consumption of alcohol (and other drugs), the courts appear to be more inclined to elevate the standard of care to which providers of alcohol are held.

LOCAL LINKS

What are the laws regarding social hosts in your state?

The Court in *Pehle v. Farm Bureau Life Ins.* held that the insurance company requiring a blood test as part of the insurance application process owed a duty to inform its potential policy holders of the results of the blood test. The court found that the relationship of trust and confidence given the insurer by the applicants results in a limited duty.

CASE

Pehle v. Farm Bureau Life Ins. Co., Inc.
397 F.3d 897 C.A.10 (Wyo.), 2005.

LUCERO, Circuit Judge.

Unbeknownst to Wyoming residents Gary and Renna Pehle, husband and wife, they were infected with the Human Immunodeficiency Virus ("HIV") at the time they applied for life insurance from Farm Bureau Life Insurance Company ("Farm Bureau") in 1999. At the time of the application, Farm Bureau collected the initial premium and arranged for blood tests from the Pehles in furtherance of the application. Blood samples were forwarded for analysis to an independent laboratory, LabOne, which in turn reported the HIV status to the insurance company. On receipt of the information, Farm Bureau sent a notice of rejection to the Pehles and advised them that it would disclose the reason for their rejection to their physician if they so wished. No action was taken by the Pehles.

Two years later, Renna Pehle was diagnosed with AIDS and on inquiry she and her husband learned that Farm Bureau records showed the HIV infection at the time of the life insurance rejection. The Pehles sued, alleging that the defendants were negligent in failing to tell them they were HIV-positive. In considering the Pehles' negligence action, the District Court found no duty on the part of Farm Bureau, LabOne, or J. Alexander Lowden, LabOne's Medical Director, and granted summary judgement to all. We agree with the decision as to LabOne and J. Alexander Lowden, but disagree as to Farm Bureau.

I.

We begin our study of the tragedy that shapes this case at the point the Pehles applied for life insurance and Farm Bureau transmitted their blood specimens to LabOne. LabOne is a Kansas corporation and the largest single-site diagnostic testing laboratory in the United States. It provides lab services to insurance companies and employers throughout the country. When LabOne reported the Pehles' HIV status to Farm Bureau, it also did so to the Kansas Department of Health, as required by Kansas law. In its letter denying coverage, Farm Bureau advised each Plaintiff that the applications were denied based on blood results, and offered to send the results to the Pehles' physician upon written authorization, stating: "With your approval, we would be willing to send the results of the blood profile to your physician so that you can discuss the findings with them. Please write the name and address of the physician you want the blood report sent to at the bottom of this letter and return it to me in the enclosed envelope." The Pehles made no inquiry until Mrs. Pehle developed AIDS symptoms in June of 2001, at which point they contacted Farm Bureau and asked it to release the blood test results to their physicians. Farm Bureau duly complied with the request. The underlying action was then filed.

In its analysis of Farm Bureau's motion for Summary Judgment, the district court concluded that the Pehles' case raised no genuine question of material fact because Wyoming law would neither recognize a duty running from a life insurance company to its applicants, nor one running to those applicants from the laboratory hired by the insurance company to test the applicants' blood.

II.
* * *

III.
* * *

(continues)

The Pehles argue that a life insurance company owes a duty under Wyoming common law to notify applicants that they are infected with a sexually transmitted disease when the infection is discovered in the application process. This argument goes farther than the law warrants. Farm Bureau asks us to uphold the lower court's conclusion that there can be no duty owed by an insurance company to mere applicants for its services. This, also, is unwarranted by Wyoming precedent. Balancing all the interests involved as Wyoming law requires, we are compelled to conclude that if an insurance company, through independent investigation by it or a third party for purposes of determining policy eligibility, discovers that an applicant is infected with HIV, the company has a duty to disclose to the applicant information sufficient to cause a reasonable applicant to inquire further.

IV.

Duty under Contract

We are urged by the Pehles to hold that the Notice and Consent agreement they signed creates a duty on the part of Farm Bureau and LabOne to inform them of their HIV status. We decline to do so. The Notice and Consent agreement before us, in and of itself, does not impose a duty upon Farm Bureau to disclose applicants' STD statuses upon discovering them. Similarly, LabOne is not subject to a duty created or suggested by the Notice and Consent agreement.

LabOne is not a party to the Notice and Consent, a form contract that authorizes "the testing of [applicant's] blood" (significantly not specifying who would do the testing), and provides that HIV testing "may be performed," and that if there are "abnormal test results which, in the Insurer's opinion, are significant," "the Insurer may contact" the applicant. Although there were conflicting assertions in the briefs as to who drew applicants' blood, at oral argument it appeared that all parties agreed that it was Farm Bureau and not LabOne that contracted with the nurse who collected the Pehles' samples. A Farm Bureau agent presented the form contract and the nurse sent by Farm Bureau was by the Pehles' side when they signed it. Although LabOne's logo appears at the top of the form and in the Copyright notice, the contract itself does not specify that LabOne would conduct the test. In the clause providing for the invalidity of any modifications or amendments made by the insured, the agreement provides that changes will not be binding "upon *the insurance company* or any of its agents or contractors." (Emphasis added.) As the Wyoming courts have held, "[i]t is axiomatic that an individual not a party to a contract may not be held liable for a breach of that contract." *Worman v. Farmers Coop. Ass'n,* 4 F.Supp.2d 1052, 1054 (D.Wyo.1998) (adjudicating contract dispute under Wyoming law).

Unlike LabOne, Farm Bureau is a party to the Notice and Consent agreement. However, as noted, the agreement does not require the company to inform applicants of their STD status. The Pehles argue that the use of the word "may" in "may contact you" was intended to mean that applicants gave Farm Bureau permission to contact them, rather than expressing the mere possibility that they would be contacted. They also argue that they reasonably read the provision as establishing that the company's standard practice is to inform applicants of abnormalities, having thus requested applicants' permission to do so. A contextual reading of the clause, however, belies the Pehles' position. All other instances of permission employ the word "authorize." Also, in the same paragraph, "may" appears again, and is clearly expressing possibility, not permission: "The Insurer may ask you for the name of a physician or other health care provider." Even if the clause intended "may" to be permissive, permission is by definition not compulsion, and cannot be held to have created a duty on the part of Farm Bureau to inform the Pehles of their HIV status.

Duty under the Common Law

Because there is only the most attenuated relationship between the Pehles and LabOne, we cannot hold LabOne subject to a duty under a traditional common-law negligence theory. In contrast, the Pehles and Farm Bureau had a good deal of contact. Wyoming courts, however, have not decided whether an insurer has a common-law duty to disclose to insurance applicants the results of medical examinations which detect that an applicant is suffering from a life-threatening or debilitating disease. Because Wyoming has not directly addressed this issue, this court must make an Erie-guess as to how the Wyoming Supreme Court would rule. *See United Parcel Service v. Weben Industries,* 794 F.2d 1005, 1008 (5th Cir.1986) ("when making an Erie-guess in the absence of explicit guidance from the state courts, we must attempt to predict state law, not to create or modify it."). We are "free to consider all resources available, including decisions of Wyoming Courts . . . [and] the general . . . trend of authority." *Stuart v. Colorado Interstate Gas Co.,* 271 F.3d 1221, 1228 (10th Cir.2001).

A duty arises when "a relation exists between the parties [such] that the community will impose a legal obligation upon one for the benefit of the other. . . ." *Duncan* 991 P.2d at 742. All parties acknowledge that the list of "relations" under the common law giving rise to a duty is not carved in stone. *Duncan* (which involved a laboratory that stored urine at the wrong temperature, leading to a false-positive alcohol reading) provides the framework for examining such relationships to determine if a duty arises. . . .

(continues)

Because defendants' actions in this case, like those in *Duncan,* could be characterized as either misfeasance or non-feasance, the distinction is not a useful one for our purposes. Putting HIV-positive applicants on notice of their infection could be considered a normal part of testing for HIV, just like keeping urine samples at the proper temperature is a normal part of alcohol-testing in *Duncan.* The wrong allegedly done to the Pehles could be characterized either as an omission in notification (non-feasance) or a negligently performed investigation into their HIV status (misfeasance).

Second, it is not clear whether Wyoming accepts the binary act/omission distinction in tort. Acknowledging that no reported Wyoming case has recognized as much, defendants nonetheless recite the Restatement rule that in the absence of a duty created through a special relationship or through contract, there is no duty to rescue. Section 314 of the Restatement (Second) of Torts lays out the four special relationships giving rise to a duty to protect another from harm as: "(1) carrier/passenger, (2) innkeeper/guest, (3) business invitor/invitee, and (4) voluntary custodian/protected." Farm Bureau's assertion that Wyoming has adopted the Restatement principles, ignores the Wyoming Supreme Court's holding that its precedent "does not . . . adopt or endorse Restatement (Second) of Torts § 314A." *Drew v. LeJay's Sportmen's Cafe,* 806 P.2d 301, 304 (Wyo.1991).

Simply because Wyoming has not adopted Restatement § 314 does not imply a general obligation on the part of Wyoming citizens zealously to guide toddlers away from scissors. It simply means that the approach to duty analysis taken by Wyoming courts is more nuanced. The *Duncan* Court framed the question before it in general terms, as "whether a duty should be imposed based on a particular relationship," *Duncan,* 991 P.2d at 744; it does not say that the analysis is inapplicable to non-feasance cases. Indeed, *Tarasoff,* the case on which *Duncan* in large part models its analysis, was a non-feasance, not a misfeasance, case that rejects the traditional distinction:

[The no-duty rule] derives from the common law's distinction between misfeasance and nonfeasance, and its reluctance to impose liability for the latter. Morally questionable, the rule owes its survival to the difficulties of setting any standards of unselfish service to fellow men, and of making any workable rule to cover possible situations where fifty people might fail to rescue. Because of these practical difficulties, the courts have increased the number of instances in which affirmative duties are imposed not by direct rejection of the common law rule, but by expanding the list of special relationships which will justify departure from that rule.

Tarasoff, 131 Cal.Rptr. 14, 551 P.2d at 343. *Duncan* frames itself as having inquired, in the same manner as *Tarasoff,* whether there is the sort of "particular relationship" that justifies departure from the traditional no-duty rule. *Duncan* 991 P.2d at 744.

Under Wyoming law, then, the inquiry is about the relationship between the parties, and a confidential relationship is one "of trust and confidence" that is "implied in law due to the factual situation surrounding the involved transaction." *Johnson v. Reiger,* 93 P.3d 992, 999 (Wyo.2004). "Such a relationship exists when one party has gained the confidence of the other and purports to act or advise with the other's interests in mind." *Id.*

By encouraging the Pehles to purchase life insurance through them, Farm Bureau purported to act with the Pehles' best interests in mind. In submitting to a procedure for extraction and consenting to an examination of their blood, the Pehles demonstrated that Farm Bureau had gained their confidence. We do not think that insurance companies must exist to treat or diagnose HIV in order for a duty to arise that necessitates that applicants be properly put on notice to inquire further.

This obligates us to return to a balancing analysis. We must inquire who is in "the best position to guard against . . . injury." *Duncan,* 991 P.2d at 745. The Pehles claim that because defendants were in exclusive possession of the information regarding their HIV status, the defendants are in the best position to guard against injury. Although this claim may be true, it is unclear whether, having notified the Pehles as to the reasons for their denial of coverage, Farm Bureau had done what it could do to fulfill the responsibilities of its relationship with the Pehles without putting an unreasonable burden on itself, turning a $2.80 HIV test into a much more expensive and risky proposition. We hold therefore that if an insurance company, through independent investigation by it or a third party for purposes of determining policy eligibility, discovers that an applicant is infected with HIV, the company has a duty to disclose to the applicant information sufficient to cause a reasonable applicant to inquire further. There is a genuine issue of material fact as to whether that duty has been met by Farm Bureau, and that is a question for a factfinder.

Farm Bureau argues, however, that the common law cannot recognize a duty in the Pehles' scenario because such a duty has been preempted by the Wyoming legislature. Unless prevented by constitutional limitation, the common law may, of course, be changed by legislation. *Zancanelli v. Central Coal & Coke,* 25 Wyo. 511, 173 P. 981, 984 (1918). Wyoming's reporting statute provides that "a physician or other health care provider, . . . the administrator of . . . any . . . health care facility . . . and the administrator or operator of a laboratory performing

(continues)

a positive laboratory test for sexually transmitted disease shall report the diagnosis . . . to . . . the department of health." *Wyo. Stat.* § 35-4-132. Farm Bureau says the reporting statute deals with the duties of notification relative to STD's, preempting the field, and clearly does not include insurance companies. But in adopting the foregoing statute, the Wyoming legislature indicates no intent to depart from the common-law rule concerning duties to disclose, and certainly does not purport to cover all aspects of either an infection-notification or an insurance company/applicant duty. It is well established that if an act does not address an area comprehensively, it does not eliminate the relevant common-law concept.

In conclusion, the trust and confidence that the Pehles put in Farm Bureau was sufficient to create a relationship giving rise to a limited duty, informed by the potential burdens and harm to all parties and the public. Wyoming law compels the conclusion that if an insurance company, through independent investigation by it or a third party for purposes of determining policy eligibility, discovers that an applicant is infected with HIV, the company has a duty to disclose to the applicant information sufficient to cause a reasonable applicant to inquire further.

Negligence Per Se

Even though LabOne is not under a contractual duty to the Pehles, it may have a statutory obligation to report their condition indirectly by compliance with applicable Wyoming statutes, and thus we next consider the statutory issue. The Pehles allege that Wyoming statutory law imposes negligence per se on LabOne. This argument is grounded in the common-law doctrine of negligence arising out of a statutory violation. Wyoming Statutes sections 35-4-130 through 35-4-134 require the reporting of communicable diseases. Laboratories are explicitly included in Wyoming's reporting statute, Wyo. Stat. § 35-4-132, but it is unclear whether out-of-state laboratories are covered. We need not reach the question of whether LabOne is obligated to comply with the Wyoming reporting statutes, however, because we conclude that the statutes would not confer negligence per se on LabOne, even if they did apply.

In Wyoming, a violation of a statute constitutes evidence of negligence only if the plaintiff is in the class of persons the statute was intended to protect and the injury is of the type the statute was intended to prevent. *Distad v. Cubin*, 633 P.2d 167, 175 (Wyo.1981). Accordingly, we analyze whether Wyoming's reporting statutes were intended to protect the Pehles from the injury they sustained.

The Pehles cannot sue under a negligence per se theory merely as members of the public. In negligence per se cases, we must ask whether the policy behind the legislative enactment will be appropriately served by using the policy to impose and measure civil damage liability. This is the same inquiry we must make when determining if an implied right of action under a given statute exists. In that context, the Supreme Court has held that there is such a right when "disregard of [a] . . . statute . . . results in damage to one of the class for whose *especial benefit* the statute was enacted." *Gebser v. Lago Vista Indep. Sch. Dist.,* 524 U.S. 274, 295, 118 S.Ct. 1989, 141 L.Ed.2d 277 (1998) (emphasis added). We thus examine the Wyoming reporting statutes to see if the duty they create runs to individuals, or rather to the public at large. *See, e.g., Short v. Ultramar Diamond Shamrock,* 46 F.Supp.2d 1199, 1200 (D.Kan.1999).

Section 133 of the reporting statute provides that health officers upon receipt of a report or notice of an AIDS case "may provide for the examination of the infected individual" and "require the infected individual to seek adequate treatment or . . . submit to treatment at public expense." The Pehles point to this language to argue that victims of diseases themselves are a separate class intended for protection under the statutes. Yet the statute's own statement of its intent refutes this argument; it states unequivocally that its purpose is to benefit the public in preventing the spread of sexually transmitted disease. Wyo. Stat. § 35-4-131(b), Wyo. Stat. § 35-4-132(a).

Some courts have further pointed out that those from whom the law seeks to protect cannot be the class for whose especial benefit the statute was intended. *See, e.g., Bertelmann v. Taas Assoc.,* 69 Haw. 95, 735 P.2d 930, 934 (1987).

Finally, we note that no Wyoming court has ever recognized that a private right of action derives from the Wyoming reporting statutes, nor has one ever used such statutes to define the standard of care in a negligence per se action. To the contrary, Wyoming courts have counseled against such recognition in the absence of legislative guidance. *See Tidwell v. HOM, Inc.,* 896 P.2d 1322, 1326 (Wyo.1995). With that in mind, we must be wary in our *Cubin* analysis not to go beyond the bounds of the state law we are obliged to apply. When "[n]o private cause of action . . . can be discerned," the courts are left on "thin ice" in basing civil damages on a statutory violation. *Id.* Because Wyoming's reporting statutes were primarily intended to protect the general public, and not HIV victims, we cannot conclude that LabOne committed negligence per se by not informing the Pehles of their HIV status.

However, plaintiffs do not assert on appeal, and we do not address, whether there is a right of action against

(continues)

Farm Bureau arising from violation of Wyoming's reporting statutes.

V.

In conclusion, Wyoming common law imposed a limited duty on Farm Bureau. The district court therefore erred in concluding that Farm Bureau owed no duty to the Pehles. We therefore REVERSE the decision of the lower court as relates to Farm Bureau Life. Because the Pehles have neither a sufficient relationship to establish a traditional common-law duty with LabOne, nor membership in the class of protectees that would permit them to sue under a theory of negligence per se, we AFFIRM the lower court's grant of Summary Judgment favoring LabOne and its supervisor J. Alexander Lowden.

Emergency Assistance

Duty also arises out of the special relationship that is created when a defendant begins to render assistance to a person in need. Once assistance is begun it must be administered using reasonable care. Every reasonable means possible must be utilized to keep the plaintiff safe. Part of the rationale underlying this rule is that once a party has begun helping another, others will be less likely to provide aid themselves. Also, if the defendant discontinues aid or gives it in an unreasonable manner, the plaintiff is essentially in a worse position than had the defendant done nothing at all.

One hospital, for example, was found liable for the injuries sustained by a child who was turned away and whose condition was worsened as a result (*Wilmington General Hospital v. Manlove*, 174 A.2d 135 [Del. 1961]). The court reasoned that by maintaining an emergency ward the hospital had in effect induced the plaintiff to forgo other forms of medical assistance. Thus, the hospital was liable for the injuries it created by the delay it had indirectly caused.

Pursuant to the **Good Samaritan statutes** in many jurisdictions, anyone providing emergency medical assistance is not liable for damages arising from that assistance as long as care is provided in good faith and does not constitute gross negligence. The intent of such statutes is to encourage people to render emergency assistance.

The majority of jurisdictions have adopted the **professional rescuer doctrine** (also known as the police or firefighter's rule), which limits the liability of landowners whose property conditions resulted in an injury to firefighters or police officers responding to an emergency. The public policy rationale underlying the rule is that professional rescuers are public servants trained at public expense who receive workers' compensation and/or disability benefits if they are injured. The doctrine of assumption of risk is another reason justifying the doctrine. It is felt that a private citizen has no duty to conduct himself in such a manner not to require the services of a professional rescuer such as a firefighter or police officer. Thus, a tortfeasor has no legal duty to protect the professional rescuer from the very danger that they are employed to confront (*Fordham v. Oldroyd*, 131 P.3d 280 (Utah 2006).

Voluntary-Undertaking Doctrine

A defendant may be found liable even though it has no legal duty to protect the plaintiff. In *Trevino v. Union Pacific R. Co.*, 916 F.2d 1230 (7th Cir. 1990), the defendant railroad company constructed a fence across one side of a railroad track that had not been used for almost a decade. Plaintiff was injured when the car in which he was a passenger collided with several railcars blocking the road. The appellate court remanded the case finding that the plaintiff could potentially establish that the railroad had a duty to maintain a safe crossing and to warn that the crossing was in use. The railroad might have voluntarily assumed such duty when it erected the fence, warning traffic that the road was no longer in use.

Some courts have applied this so-called voluntary-undertaking doctrine even when the plaintiff did not rely on the defendant's undertaking of services. In one Illinois case, for example, the court found an insurance company liable for negligently carrying out a gratuitously undertaken safety inspection and concluded that liability was not restricted to those who relied upon the inspection, but extended to "such persons as defendant could reasonably have foreseen would be endangered as the result of negligent performance" (*Nelson v. Union Wire Rope Corp.*, 199 N.E.2d 769, 779 [Ill. 1964]).

Some modern courts have allowed a plaintiff who relied on a defendant's promise to recover even if the defendant made no overt act of assisting the plaintiff. In one case the sheriff's department was found liable for failing to live up to its promise to warn the plaintiff's wife when a dangerous prisoner, whom she had assisted in having arrested, was released. Shortly after his release he killed her. By inducing the plaintiff's wife to rely on its promise to warn her, the defendant was held liable even though it had done nothing overtly to assist her (*Morgan v. County of Yuba*, 41 Cal. Rptr. 508 [1964]).

Defendants may be liable to third parties as well when they undertake a service they have no legal duty to perform and perform the service negligently. Once again, it is the third party's reliance on the reasonable performance of that service that imposes liability on the defendant. Suppose a business hires a company, for example, to inspect its elevators, and the company negligently reports that the elevators are in good condition when they are not. If someone is injured when one of the elevators falls, the company owes a duty of care to the injured person.

Public Entities

The same theory of duty that applies to private individuals also applies to public entities. In other words, the analysis of duty for a public body is essentially the same as it is for private persons. A state may be liable to an invitee just as if it were a private landowner. Cities, of course, have unique duties, such as providing police and fire protection and keeping the streets safe for purposes of transportation. The defense of limited sovereign immunity (a tort defense that absolves the defendant of liability because of the defendant's status as a governmental entity, discussed in greater detail in Chapter 8) of a governmental body can create some interesting twists, however.

In one fascinating New York case, *Riss v. New York*, 22 N.Y.2d 579 (1968), the court used the doctrine of sovereign immunity to exempt the City of New York from liability even though the plaintiff had begged the New York City Police Department to protect her from the man who hired someone to assault her. The dissent's eloquent rebuttal to the majority's rather curt finding of non-liability is excerpted here. Interestingly, the point of contention between the majority and dissent is largely factual, and the dissent carefully presents facts as well as reasoning to support its conclusion that the city should be liable for providing negligent police protection. You might be interested to know that Burton Pugach, an attorney who hired the man who maimed Linda Riss, served a fourteen-year sentence. After his release he proposed to Ms. Riss and they were ultimately married.

CASE | **Linda Riss, Appellant, v. City of New York, Respondent**
22 N.Y.2d 579 (N.Y. 1968)

KEATING, Judge (dissenting).

Certainly, the record in this case, sound legal analysis, relevant policy considerations and even precedent cannot account for or sustain the result which the majority have here reached. For the result is premised upon a legal rule which long ago should have been abandoned, having lost any justification it might once have had. Despite almost universal condemnation by legal scholars, the rule survives, finding its continuing strength, not in its power to persuade, but in its ability to arouse unwarranted judicial fears of the consequences of overturning it.

Linda Riss, an attractive young woman, was for more than six months terrorized by a rejected suitor well known to the courts of this State, one Burton Pugach. This miscreant, masquerading as a respectable attorney, repeatedly threatened to have Linda killed or maimed if she did not yield to him: "If I can't have you, no one else will have you, and when I get through with you, no one else will want you". In fear for her life, she went to

(continues)

those charged by law with the duty of preserving and safeguarding the lives of the citizens and residents of this State. Linda's repeated and almost pathetic pleas for aid were received with little more than indifference. Whatever help she was given was not commensurate with the identifiable danger. On June 14, 1959 Linda became engaged to another man. At a party held to celebrate the event, she received a phone call warning her that it was her "last chance". Completely distraught, she called the police, begging for help, but was refused. The next day Pugach carried out his dire threats in the very manner he had foretold by having a hired thug throw lye in Linda's face. Linda was blinded in one eye, lost a good portion of her vision in the other, and her face was permanently scarred. After the assault the authorities concluded that there was some basis for Linda's fears, and for the next three and one-half years, she was given around-the-clock protection.

No one questions the proposition that the first duty of government is to assure its citizens the opportunity to live in personal security. And no one who reads the record of Linda's ordeal can reach a conclusion other than that the City of New York, acting through its agents, completely and negligently failed to fulfill this obligation to Linda.

Linda has turned to the courts of this State for redress, asking that the city be held liable in damages for its negligent failure to protect her from harm. With compelling logic, she can point out that, if a stranger, who had absolutely no obligation to aid her, had offered her assistance, and thereafter Burton Pugach was able to injure her as a result of the negligence of the volunteer, the courts would certainly require him to pay damages. (Restatement, 2d, Torts, § 323.) Why then should the city, whose duties are imposed by law and include the prevention of crime . . . and, consequently, extend far beyond that of the Good Samaritan, not be responsible? If a private detective acts carelessly, no one would deny that a jury could find such conduct unacceptable. Why then is the city not required to live up to at least the same minimal standards of professional competence which would be demanded of a private detective?

Linda's reasoning seems so eminently sensible that surely it must come as a shock to her and to every citizen to hear the city argue and to learn that this court decides that the city has no duty to provide police protection to any given individual. What makes the city's position particularly difficult to understand is that, in conformity to the dictates of the law, Linda did not carry any weapon for self-defense. . . . Thus, by a rather bitter irony she was required to rely for protection on the City of New York which now denies all responsibility to her.

It is not a distortion to summarize the essence of the city's case here in the following language: "Because we owe a duty to everybody, we owe it to nobody." Were it not for the fact that this position has been hallowed by much ancient and revered precedent, we would surely dismiss it as preposterous. To say that there is no duty is, of course, to start with the conclusion. The question is whether or not there should be liability for the negligent failure to provide adequate police protection.

The foremost justification repeatedly urged for the existing rule is the claim that the State and the municipalities will be exposed to limitless liability. The city invokes the specter of a "crushing burden" . . . if we should depart from the existing rule and enunciate even the limited proposition that the State and its municipalities can be held liable for the negligent acts of their police employees in executing whatever police services they do in fact provide. . . .

The fear of financial disaster is a myth. The same argument was made a generation ago in opposition to proposals that the State waive its defense of "sovereign immunity". The prophecy proved false then, and it would now. The supposed astronomical financial burden does not and would not exist. No municipality has gone bankrupt because it has had to respond in damages when a policeman causes injury through carelessly driving a police car or in the thousands of other situations where, by judicial fiat or legislative enactment, the State and its subdivisions have been held liable for the tortious conduct of their employees. Thus, in the past four or five years, New York City has been presented with an average of some 10,000 claims each year. The figure would sound ominous except for the fact the city has been paying out less than $8,000,000 on tort claims each year and this amount includes all those sidewalk defect and snow and ice cases about which the courts fret so often. . . . Court delay has reduced the figure paid somewhat, but not substantially. Certainly this is a slight burden in a budget of more than six billion dollars (less than two tenths of 1 percent) and of no importance as compared to the injustice of permitting unredressed wrongs to continue to go unrepaired. That Linda Riss should be asked to bear the loss, which should properly fall on the city if we assume, as we must, in the present posture of the case, that her injuries resulted from the city's failure to provide sufficient police to protect Linda is contrary to the most elementary notions of justice.

The statement in the majority opinion that there are no predictable limits to the potential liability for failure to provide adequate police protection as compared to other areas of municipal liability is, of course, untenable. When immunity in other areas of governmental activity was removed, the same lack of predictable limits existed. Yet, disaster did not ensue.

(continues)

Another variation of the "crushing burden" argument is the contention that, every time a crime is committed, the city will be sued and the claim will be made that it resulted from inadequate police protection. Here, again, is an attempt to arouse the "anxiety of the courts about new theories of liability which may have a far-reaching effect". . . . And here too the underlying assumption of the argument is fallacious because it assumes that a strict liability standard is to be imposed and that the courts would prove completely unable to apply general principles of tort liability in a reasonable fashion in the context of actions arising from the negligent acts of police and fire personnel. The argument is also made as if there were no such legal principles as fault, proximate cause or foreseeability, all of which operate to keep liability within reasonable bounds. No one is contending that the police must be at the scene of every potential crime or must provide a personal bodyguard to every person who walks into a police station and claims to have been threatened. They need only act as a reasonable man would under the circumstances. At first there would be a duty to inquire. If the inquiry indicates nothing to substantiate the alleged threat, the matter may be put aside and other matters attended to. If, however, the claims prove to have some basis, appropriate steps would be necessary.

The instant case provides an excellent illustration of the limits which the courts can draw. No one would claim that, under the facts here, the police were negligent when they did not give Linda protection after her first calls or visits to the police station in February of 1959. The preliminary investigation was sufficient. If Linda had been attacked at this point, clearly there would be no liability here. When, however, as time went on and it was established that Linda was a reputable person, that other verifiable attempts to injure her or intimidate her had taken place, that other witnesses were available to support her claim that her life was being threatened, something more was required—either by way of further investigation or protection—than the statement that was made by one detective to Linda that she would have to be hurt before the police could do anything for her.

In dismissing the complaint, the trial court noted that there are many crimes being committed daily and the police force is inadequate to deal with its "tremendous responsibilities". The point is not addressed to the facts of this case. Even if it were, however, a distinction must be made. It may be quite reasonable to say that the City of New York is not required to hire sufficient police to protect every piece of property threatened during mass riots. The possibility of riots may even be foreseeable, but the occurrence is sufficiently uncommon that the city should not be required to bear the cost of having a redundancy of men for normal operations. But it is going beyond the bounds of required judicial moderation if the city is permitted to escape liability in a situation such as the one at bar. If the police force of the City of New York is so understaffed that it is unable to cope with the everyday problem posed by the relatively few cases where single, known individuals threaten the lives of other persons, then indeed we have reached the danger line and the lives of all of us are in peril. If the police department is in such a deplorable state that the city, because of insufficient manpower, is truly unable to protect persons in Linda Riss' position, then liability not only should, but must be imposed. It will act as an effective inducement for public officials to provide at least a minimally adequate number of police. If local officials are not willing to meet even such a low standard, I see no reason for the courts to abet such irresponsibility.

It is also contended that liability for inadequate police protection will make the courts the arbiters of decisions taken by the Police Commissioner in allocating his manpower and his resources. We are not dealing here with a situation where the injury or loss occurred as a result of a conscious choice of policy made by those exercising high administrative responsibility after a complete and thorough deliberation of various alternatives. There was no major policy decision taken by the Police Commissioner to disregard Linda Riss' appeal for help because there was absolutely no manpower available to deal with Pugach. This "garden variety" negligence case arose in the course of "day-by-day operations of government". . . . Linda Riss' tragedy resulted not from high policy or inadequate manpower, but plain negligence on the part of persons with whom Linda dealt. . . .

More significant, however, is the fundamental flaw in the reasoning behind the argument alleging judicial interference. It is a complete oversimplification of the problem of municipal tort liability. What it ignores is the fact that indirectly courts are reviewing administrative practices in almost every tort case against the State or a municipality, including even decisions of the Police Commissioner. Every time a municipal hospital is held liable for malpractice resulting from inadequate record-keeping, the courts are in effect making a determination that the municipality should have hired or assigned more clerical help or more competent help to medical records or should have done something to improve its record-keeping procedures so that the particular injury would not have occurred. Every time a municipality is held liable for a defective sidewalk, it is as if the courts are saying that more money and resources should have been allocated to sidewalk repair, instead of to other public services.

(continues)

The situation is nowise different in the case of police protection. Whatever effects there may be on police administration will be one of degree, not kind. . . .

The truth of the matter, however, is that the courts are not making policy decisions for public officials. In all these municipal negligence cases, the courts are doing two things. First, they apply the principles of vicarious liability to the operations of government. Courts would not insulate the city from liability for the ordinary negligence of members of the highway department. There is no basis for treating the members of the police department differently.

Second, and most important, to the extent that the injury results from the failure to allocate sufficient funds and resources to meet a minimum standard of public administration, public officials are presented with two alternatives: either improve public administration or accept the cost of compensating injured persons. Thus, if we were to hold the city liable here for the negligence of the police, courts would no more be interfering with the operations of the police department than they "meddle" in the affairs of the highway department when they hold the municipality liable for personal injuries resulting from defective sidewalks, or a private employer for the negligence of his employees. In other words, all the courts do in these municipal negligence cases is require officials to weigh the consequences of their decisions. If Linda Riss' injury resulted from the failure of the city to pay sufficient salaries to attract qualified and sufficient personnel, the full cost of that choice should become acknowledged in the same way as it has in other areas of municipal tort liability. Perhaps officials will find it less costly to choose the alternative of paying damages than changing their existing practices. That may be well and good, but the price for the refusal to provide for an adequate police force should not be borne by Linda Riss and all the other innocent victims of such decisions.

What has existed until now is that the City of New York and other municipalities have been able to engage in a sort of false bookkeeping in which the real costs of inadequate or incompetent police protection have been hidden by charging the expenditures to the individuals who have sustained often catastrophic losses rather than to the community where it belongs, because the latter had the power to prevent the losses.

Although in modern times the compensatory nature of tort law has generally been the one most emphasized, one of its most important functions has been and is its normative aspect. It sets forth standards of conduct which ought to be followed. The penalty for failing to do so is to pay pecuniary damages. At one time the government was completely immunized from this salutary control. This is much less so now, and the imposition of

liability has had healthy side effects. In many areas, it has resulted in the adoption of better and more considered procedures just as workmen's compensation resulted in improved industrial safety practices. To visit liability upon the city here will no doubt have similar constructive effects. No "presumed cure" for the problem of crime is being "foisted" upon the city as the majority opinion charges. The methods of dealing with the problem of crime are left completely to the city's discretion. All that the courts can do is make sure that the costs of the city's and its employees' mistakes are placed where they properly belong. Thus, every reason used to sustain the rule that there is no duty to offer police protection to any individual turns out on close analysis to be of little substance.

* * *

The Appellate Division did not adopt the "no duty" theory, but said there was no negligence here because the danger was not imminent. Despite the fact that the majority of the Appellate Division "agree[d] that certain rulings, and particularly the manner in which they were made, did not add to the appearance of a fair trial", and which, in fact, resulted in a wholly inadequate hearing, the majority found that the "facts brought out on this trial do not show the presence of such imminent danger that extraordinary police activity was so indicated that the failure to take it can be deemed unreasonable conduct." This finding does not stand examination and to its credit the city does not argue that this record would not support a finding of negligence. The danger to Linda was indeed imminent, and this fact could easily have been confirmed had there been competent police work.

Moreover, since this is an appeal from a dismissal of the complaint, we must give the plaintiff the benefit of every favorable inference. The Appellate Division's conclusion could only have been reached by ignoring the thrust of the plaintiff's claim and the evidence in the record. A few examples of the actions of the police should suffice to show the true state of the record. Linda Riss received a telephone call from a person who warned Linda that Pugach was arranging to have her beaten up. A detective learned the identity of the caller. He offered to arrest the caller, but plaintiff rejected that suggestion for the obvious reason that the informant was trying to help Linda. When Linda requested that Pugach be arrested, the detective said he could not do that because she had not yet been hurt. The statement was not so. It was and is a crime to conspire to injure someone. True there was no basis to arrest Pugach then, but that was only because the necessary leg work had not been done. No one went to speak to the informant, who might have furnished additional leads. Linda claimed to be receiving

(continues)

telephone calls almost every day. These calls could have been monitored for a few days to obtain evidence against Pugach. Any number of reasonable alternatives presented themselves. A case against Pugach could have been developed which would have at least put him away for a while or altered the situation entirely. But, if necessary, some police protection should have been afforded.

Perhaps, on a fuller record after a true trial on the merits, the city's position will not appear so damaging as it does now. But with actual notice of danger and ample opportunity to confirm and take reasonable remedial steps, a jury could find that the persons involved acted unreasonably and negligently. Linda Riss is entitled to have a jury determine the issue of the city's liability. This right should not be terminated by the adoption of a question-begging conclusion that there is no duty owed to her. The order of the Appellate Division should be reversed and a new trial granted.

PUTTING IT INTO PRACTICE 4:4

1. According to the dissent in *Riss*, what is the essence of the majority's argument?
2. What is the "crushing burden" argument?
3. How does the dissent counter the "crushing burden" argument?
4. How does the dissent respond to the argument that allowing liability for inadequate police protection will make the courts the arbiters of decisions made by the police commissioner in allocating manpower and resources?
5. Of what kind of false bookkeeping does the dissent accuse the City of New York?
6. What is the "normative" aspect of tort law to which the dissent refers?

PUTTING IT INTO PRACTICE 4:5

Ms. Figueroa is abducted at gunpoint in the parking lot of the Child Care Center, where she has just dropped her child off. She is sexually assaulted and slashed with a knife. The parking lot is owned by North Park College, which both informally and formally (via a letter written to the parents of children attending the Child Care Center) allows parents to use the parking lot. North Park employs off-duty police officers to patrol its campus, including the parking lot. Before this incident only minor crimes had occurred anywhere on campus.

Ms. Figueroa sues North Park for negligent failure to provide adequate security in the parking lot. Should Ms. Figueroa be treated as an invitee or a licensee? Is there any other legal theory she might rely on to establish a duty of protection?

UNBORN CHILDREN

An area that has been subject to considerable controversy of late is whether a duty of care is owed to an unborn child. Suppose a defendant assaults a pregnant woman, recklessly injuring the fetus and causing defects that manifest physically when the child is born. Under the common law the child could not recover for its injuries. Modern courts have reversed this no-duty rule and have allowed recovery in most instances where a causal link between the defendant's act and where the fetus's injury can be proven. This causal link can be highly speculative with a recently conceived embryo, and the *Restatement* suggests that courts require "convincing evidence" of causation in these circumstances (*Restatement [Second] of Torts* § 869, cmt. d).

Some cases have implied in dicta that only fetuses that were viable (capable of surviving outside the uterus) at the time of injury could recover, but all courts directly confronted with the issue have allowed recovery even when the fetus was only a few weeks old at the time of injury. Such reasoning has permitted recovery in cases such as those involving fetuses suffering serious defects in the initial stages of development as a result of their mothers' ingestion of drugs, such as Thalidomide (a medication designed to prevent morning sickness that was later discovered to cause devastating birth defects).

Considerable controversy continues around the question of whether a wrongful death action can be brought if a fetus is stillborn as a result of its injuries. The *Restatement* suggests that recovery should not be allowed "unless the applicable wrongful death statute so provides" (*Restatement [Second] of Torts* § 869[2]). The issue in these wrongful death cases is whether the statutes, which usually refer to "persons," were intended to apply to fetuses. The courts are divided on this issue, although more courts allow recovery than deny it.

CASE

Sarah Elizabeth LEIGHTON, etc., et al., appellants, v. CITY OF NEW YORK, et al., respondents.
Feb. 20, 2007.

GOLDSTEIN, J.

At issue here is whether the law allows a cause of action for damages allegedly sustained by the infant plaintiff as a result of an accident which occurred when she was in utero and not viable outside the womb. We hold that the law allows such a cause of action, since the accident occurred after the infant plaintiff's conception and the infant plaintiff was thereafter born alive.

On January 20, 1999, the infant plaintiff's mother, the plaintiff Esther Portalatin-Leighton, a school teacher who was four months pregnant at the time, allegedly fell as a result of a defective toilet seat. Five minutes after her fall, she felt cramping in her lower abdomen and was taken to Methodist Hospital where she was treated and released. Thereafter, on April 4, 1999, the infant plaintiff was born three months prematurely.

The plaintiffs filed a notice of claim on April 7, 1999. However, the instant action to recover damages, inter alia, for personal injuries, was not commenced until July 23, 2004.

By notice of motion dated April 11, 2005, the defendants moved to dismiss the complaint on the grounds that the mother's causes of action were time barred and the infant plaintiff failed to state a cause of action.

The court dismissed the mother's causes of action as time barred by the one-year and 90 day statute of limitations set forth in General Municipal Law § 50-i. That determination is not challenged on appeal and therefore, is not before this court.

With respect to the infant plaintiff, the defendants claimed she had no cause of action on the ground that "at the time of the alleged breach of duty [she] was a non-viable fetus," and therefore, the defendants did not owe her a duty of care. The plaintiffs in opposition asserted that the defendants were attempting "to add in a new requirement to negligence actions."

The Supreme Court, in the order appealed from, agreed with the defendants that "[i]n order for the infant plaintiff to have a cognizable cause of action it must be a viable fetus at the time of the injury and must be later born alive." Since the infant plaintiff was only a 14-week fetus at the time of the accident who would not have been viable outside the womb had she been born at that juncture, the Supreme Court found that she had no cause of action. We reverse the order insofar as appealed from.

In *Drobner v. Peters,* 232 N.Y. 220, 224, 133 N.E. 567, the Court of Appeals dismissed an action brought by an infant plaintiff to recover damages allegedly sustained as a result of an accident which occurred 11 days before his birth on the ground that the defendant owed no duty to an unborn child apart from the duty to avoid injuring his mother. That determination was overruled by the Court of Appeals in *Woods v. Lancet,* 303 N.Y. 349, 102 N.E.2d 691.

The issue in *Woods v. Lancet, supra* at 356-357, 102 N.E.2d 691 was whether an infant plaintiff could recover damages for injuries allegedly sustained in his mother's womb during the ninth month of pregnancy. The Court of Appeals reversed an order dismissing the infant plaintiff's complaint and overruled its decision in *Drobner v. Peters, supra.* In so doing, the Court of Appeals noted

(continues)

that *Drobner v. Peters, supra* was based upon three principles: (1) lack of precedent in favor of sustaining a cause of action brought by an infant plaintiff for injuries sustained in utero, (2) difficulties in proving causation, and (3) the "purely theoretical" objection "that a foetus in utero has no existence of its own separate from that of its mother, that is, that it is not a being in esse" (*Woods v. Lancet, supra* at 356, 102 N.E.2d 691 [internal quotation marks omitted]).

In answer to these concerns, the Court of Appeals found (1) negligence is a question of common law which may be revised by the courts, (2) difficulties in proving causation should not destroy a legal right, and (3) the case could be decided without dealing with the larger question of whether a fetus has an existence of its own separate from its mother. Apparently to avoid the larger question of whether the fetus was "a being in esse" (*id.*), the court limited the applicability of its ruling "to prepartum injuries to . . . viable children . . . capable of being delivered and of remaining alive, separate from its mother" (*id.* at 357, 102 N.E.2d 691).

Thereafter, the Appellate Division, Third Department, in *Kelly v. Gregory*, 282 App.Div. 542, 125 N.Y.S.2d 696, held that an infant plaintiff could recover damages for injuries allegedly sustained in an accident during the third month of the mother's pregnancy, so long as he could prove causation. In that case, the court noted that "no case imposed as a necessity . . . that actual miscarriage must coincide with the injury" (*id.* at 544, 125 N.Y.S.2d 696). The court further noted that lives in being for inheritance purposes included unborn children and "no distinction between viability or nonviability was attempted to be drawn in determining the point of vestiture of a legal right" (*id.* at 545, 125 N.Y.S.2d 696).

The principles enunciated in *Kelly v. Gregory, supra* were adopted by other jurisdictions (*see e.g., Hornbuckle v. Plantation Pipe Line Co.,* 212 Ga. 504, 93 S.E.2d 727; *Daley v. Meier,* 33 Ill.App.2d 218, 178 N.E.2d 691; *Bennett v. Hymers,* 101 N.H. 483, 147 A.2d 108; *Smith v. Brennan,* 31 N.J. 353, 157 A.2d 497; *Sinkler v. Kneale,* 401 Pa. 267, 164 A.2d 93) and by the Restatement of Torts (*see* Restatement [Second] of Torts, § 869), which states that "[o]ne who tortiously causes harm to an unborn child is subject to liability to the child for the harm if the child is born alive." This principle is "not limited to unborn children who are 'viable' at the time of original injury, that is, capable of independent life . . . [i]f the tortious conduct and the legal causation of the harm can be satisfactorily established" (*id.* § 869, Comment 1[d]).

Based upon the question of viability posed in *Woods v. Lancet, supra,* questions arose in this state as to whether damages were recoverable for the wrongful death of a stillborn fetus that was "viable" and could have survived outside the womb at the time of the injury, had the injury not occurred (*see Matter of Logan,* 3 N.Y.2d 800, 166 N.Y.S.2d 3, 144 N.E.2d 644; *Endresz v. Friedberg,* 24 N.Y.2d 478, 301 N.Y.S.2d 65, 248 N.E.2d 901). In *Endresz v. Friedberg, supra* at 483, 301 N.Y.S.2d 65, 248 N.E.2d 901, the Court of Appeals determined that a wrongful death action cannot be maintained for the death of an unborn child: the child has to be born alive. In reaching that conclusion, the Court of Appeals stated that its decision in *Woods v. Lancet, supra* "simply brought the common law of this State into accord with the demand of natural justice which requires recognition of the legal right of every human being to begin life unimpaired by physical or mental defects resulting from the negligence of another" (*Endresz v. Friedberg, supra* at 483, 301 N.Y.S.2d 65, 248 N.E.2d 901). Thus, the crucial factor is whether the fetus injured in utero is thereafter born alive.

The defendants, in asserting that a child born alive cannot recover for injuries sustained in utero unless the child is capable of viability outside the womb at the time of injury, cite cases relating to the constitutionality of limits on abortion (*see Planned Parenthood v. Casey,* 505 U.S. 833, 860, 112 S.Ct. 2791, 120 L.Ed.2d 674; *Roe v. Wade,* 410 U.S. 113, 160, 93 S.Ct. 705, 35 L.Ed.2d 147). In 1973, the Supreme Court of the United States in *Roe v. Wade, supra* noted that "the traditional rule of tort law denied recovery for prenatal injuries even though the child was born alive" (*id.* at 161, 93 S.Ct. 705, citing Prosser, Torts § 55, at 336-338 [4th ed.]). However, the Supreme Court acknowledged that the traditional rule "has been changed in almost every jurisdiction" (*id.*). As noted in Prosser, Torts (§ 55, at 336), by 1971 the traditional rule had been discarded in "the most spectacular abrupt reversal of a well settled rule in the whole history of the law of torts" in favor of a rule which permitted a child, if born alive, to maintain an action to recover damages for personal injuries sustained in utero.

This court, when faced with a controversy over the constitutionality of legalization of abortion in this state, was able to reconcile legal abortion with the principle established in *Kelly v. Gregory, supra* that "the nonviable unborn child" injured in utero thereafter born alive may sue to recover damages (*Byrn v. New York City Health & Hosps. Corp.,* 38 A.D.2d 316, 329, 329 N.Y.S.2d 722, *affd.* 31 N.Y.2d 194, 335 N.Y.S.2d 390, 286 N.E.2d 887), by holding that "legal personality is not synonymous with separate and vital existence within the womb [and] depending on the circumstances involved, public policy and other factors, legal personality will be accorded or withheld as these extrinsic considerations

(continues)

demand." The Court of Appeals, in affirming our determination, noted that while "unborn children have never been recognized as persons in the law in the whole sense," nevertheless "[f]etuses, if they are born alive, have been entitled in modern times to recover in tort for injuries sustained though the host mother" (*Byrn v. New York City Health & Hosps. Corp.,* 31 N.Y.2d at 200, 335 N.Y.S.2d 390, 286 N.E.2d 887, citing *Kelly v. Gregory, supra*).

Abortion cases are generally distinguishable from the instant case, since fetuses which are aborted are not born alive (*see generally Group Health Assn. v. Blumenthal,* 295 Md. 104, 453 A.2d 1198). However, if the abortion fails and causes injury to the fetus who is later born alive, the child may have a cause of action sounding in medical malpractice to recover damages for the injuries sustained (*see Sheppard-Mobley v. King,* 4 N.Y.3d 627, 797 N.Y.S.2d 403, 830 N.E.2d 301).

In *Albala v. City of New York,* 54 N.Y.2d 269, 271, 445 N.Y.S.2d 108, 429 N.E.2d 786, relied upon by the Supreme Court, the Court of Appeals held that "no cause of action for preconception tort is cognizable" under the common law of this State. Accordingly, the incident allegedly giving rise to liability must occur after conception when there is, in fact, a fetus (*see Enright v. Lilly & Co.,* 77 N.Y.2d 377, 568 N.Y.S.2d 550, 570 N.E.2d 198, *cert. denied* 502 U.S. 868, 112 S.Ct. 197, 116 L.Ed.2d 157; *Hymowitz v. Lilly & Co.,* 73 N.Y.2d 487, 541 N.Y.S.2d 941, 539 N.E.2d 1069, *cert. denied* 493 U.S. 944, 110 S.Ct. 350, 107 L.Ed.2d 338).

In support of its contention that it owed no duty to the infant in utero, the defendant cites *Widera v. Ettco Wire & Cable Corp.,* 204 A.D.2d 306, 611 N.Y.S.2d 569. In that case, the infant plaintiff alleged that his father was exposed to toxic chemicals at his worksite, and the infant was exposed to those chemicals when his mother washed the father's contaminated clothes while he was in utero. This court, in affirming the dismissal of the infant's cause of action sounding in common-law negligence, held that extending the common-law duty to provide a safe place to work to the infant plaintiff would "expand traditional tort concepts beyond manageable bounds and create an almost infinite universe of potential plaintiffs" (*id.* at 307, 611 N.Y.S.2d 569). This case merely stated well-settled law that the duty to provide a safe place to work does not extend to members of the worker's family or household or other third parties who were not physically present on the premises (*see Matter of New York City Asbestos Litig.,* 5 N.Y.3d 486, 806 N.Y.S.2d 146, 840 N.E.2d 115). This principle has no application to the issues in the instant case (*see Mann v. Andersen Prods.,* 246 A.D.2d 68, 676 N.Y.S.2d 658).

Since the infant plaintiff was born alive and alleges that her injuries resulted from an accident which occurred while she was in utero, she has stated a cause of action. Accordingly, the order is reversed insofar as appealed from, on the law, and that branch of the defendants' motion which was pursuant to CPLR 3211(a)(7) to dismiss the infant plaintiff's cause of action is denied.

ORDERED that the order is reversed insofar as appealed from, on the law, with costs, and that branch of the defendants' motion pursuant to CPLR 3211(a)(7) which was to dismiss the infant plaintiff's cause of action is denied.

VICARIOUS LIABILITY

Under the principle of **vicarious liability** a defendant may be liable for the tortious acts of another even though he is not at fault. An employer is vicariously liable for the tortious acts of her employees under the doctrine of **respondeat superior**, which means, literally, "Let the superior respond." Vicarious liability also arises under the **family-purpose doctrine**, which holds the owner of a car vicariously liable for the torts committed by those members of his household whom he allows to drive his car. Because these doctrines impose a duty of care on people who are not directly at fault, we discuss them in this chapter even though they are discussed in greater depth in other chapters.

Under the doctrine of respondeat superior, the employer is liable for any torts committed by an employee during the scope and furtherance of his employment. An employer can escape liability if she can prove that the employee was acting on his own behalf and not the employer's when he committed the tortious act. Suppose an employee is instructed to use a vehicle to run an errand for his employer but, in the course of running the errand, he deviates substantially from his route to see his girlfriend. If the employee negligently causes a vehicular accident upon leaving his girlfriend's house, his employer will be absolved of liability because the employee was acting outside the scope of his employment.

The rationale underpinning this doctrine is that employers, rather than employees, should bear the expense of any accidents resulting from doing business. Such expense, it is reasoned, should be considered part of the price of doing business. The bottom line is that an employer owes a duty of care to any plaintiff injured by an employee acting in the scope and furtherance of his duties as an employee.

Now let us consider vicarious liability in the doctrine of respondeat superior. If a father loans his car to his daughter and she negligently injures someone, the father will be vicariously liable for his daughter's negligence. Some states have extended this liability by statute and have provided that the owner of an automobile is vicariously liable for the negligence of anyone who uses his car with his permission.

APPLICATION

In the case involving Teddy, Mr. Goodright, and Gertrude set forth in the Practice Problem at the end of the chapter and referred to in future chapter, several questions come to mind in reference to duty. Did the Baxters, for example, owe any duty of care to Teddy, who was a trespasser on their land? To answer that question Teddy's attorney will have to determine if Teddy was a known trespasser. Also she will want to consider whether Gertrude is an attractive nuisance. In answering this question she will have to ask whether the Baxters had reason to know that children were likely to trespass in their backyard and whether Gertrude posed an unreasonable risk of injury to trespassing children. Most importantly, she will have to argue that the Baxters failed to use reasonable care in protecting children from Gertrude by failing to keep the gate locked. She will also have to be able to prove that Teddy was not aware of the danger posed by Gertrude and that children of his age, intelligence, and experience would not have perceived the danger.

Another question to be addressed is whether the Baxters owed any duty of care to Mr. Goodright. At first it may appear that Mr. Goodright was a trespasser; however, because he entered the land with the express purpose of rescuing another, he would not be considered a trespasser. Consequently, Teddy's attorney would have to research the standard of care accorded rescuers under the case law in her state.

Mr. Baxter did, in fact, have a duty to assist Mr. Goodright once he saw him being attacked by Gertrude. Remember that although generally there is no duty to render assistance to one in need, an exception exists when the danger has been created by the defendant's own conduct or by an instrument under his control. In this case, because Gertrude was legally under Mr. Baxter's control, Mr. Baxter had a duty to aid Mr. Goodright.

SUMMARY

The first question that arises in any negligence case is one of duty. Generally, a defendant is expected to exercise the same degree of care that any reasonable person would use under similar circumstances. The nature of the relationship between the defendant and the plaintiff is important in determining the duty owed.

The duty owed by possessors of land to those on their land depends on the latter's status as either a trespasser, licensee, or invitee. No duty of care is owed to a trespasser to make the land safe or to protect the trespasser in any way. There are four exceptions, however, to this general rule. Some duty of care is owed to trespassing children, to rescuers, to known trespassers, and to those trespassers using only a very limited portion of the possessor's land. A possessor has the duty to warn a licensee of any dangerous conditions of which the possessor is aware and should reasonably anticipate that the licensee will not discover. Invitees are owed the highest duty of care. A possessor has a duty to inspect her premises for hidden dangers when dealing with invitees. Possessors may be liable for those conditions that pose an unreasonable risk of harm to persons outside their premises, especially if the hazardous condition was artificially created by the possessor. The analysis of duty for public entities is essentially the same as the analysis for private individuals except when the doctrine of sovereign immunity is applicable.

In the special relationship of the landlord and tenant, the tenant is the one entitled to the protection of the common law rules. Although the landlord generally escaped liability under the common law once he transferred possession to the tenant, today he is liable for failure to keep premises in good repair and is liable for those dangers that he knows or should know about and about which the tenant has no reason to know.

Like landlords, sellers of land are released from tort liability once they turn the property over to the buyers. However, if a seller fails to disclose a dangerous condition of which he is or should be aware and which he should realize that the buyer will not discover, he will be liable for any injuries resulting from that dangerous condition.

In Anglo/American law people generally have no obligation to assist others in danger. However, when a special relationship exists between plaintiff and defendant, liability may be found for failure to act. A duty of care may also arise out of a special relationship between the defendant and a third party. Those who render aid to others in need or voluntarily undertake to render services to another establish a temporary special relationship. Once they initiate assistance or perform services, they have an obligation to use every reasonable means possible to keep the plaintiff safe.

Under the common law, children could not recover for injuries sustained by them while in utero. Modern courts are more inclined to allow recovery.

The respondeat superior doctrine and the family-purpose doctrine are examples of vicarious liability, in which the defendant is liable for the tortious acts of another even though the defendant was not at fault. The doctrine of respondeat superior pertains primarily to employers, whereas the family-purpose doctrine applies to car owners who allow members of their household to drive.

KEY TERMS

attractive nuisance
Dangerous condition on the defendant's property that is likely to induce children to trespass

business invitee
One who enters the land for a purpose connected with the business dealings of the possessor

duty
Legal obligation to act reasonably and that arises out of our relationship to others

family-purpose doctrine
Doctrine that makes the owner of a car liable for the tortious acts of family members committed while driving

Good Samaritan statutes
Law providing that anyone who provides medical assistance is not liable for damages arising from that assistance as long as care is provided in good faith and does not constitute gross negligence

invitees
Persons invited by possessor of land onto her property for the purpose of conducting business

licensee
Person who has possessor's consent to be present on land

negligence
Conduct that creates an unreasonable risk of harm to another

professional rescuers doctrine
Limits or bars the liability of tortfeasors to professional rescuers such as police officers and firefighters who sustained injuries as a result of ordinary negligence

public invitee
One who enters the land for the purpose for which the land is held open to the public

rescue doctrine
Doctrine under which anyone who negligently causes harm to a person or property may be liable to one who is injured in an effort to rescue the imperiled person or property

respondeat superior doctrine
Doctrine that makes an employer liable for the tortious acts of employees committed in the scope and furtherance of their employment

vicarious liability
Liability for the tortious acts of others

REVIEW QUESTIONS

1. What duty of care is owed a trespasser?
   a. What are the four exceptions to this general rule?
2. What conditions must be met to have an attractive nuisance?
   a. What characteristics of a child are taken into consideration when deciding whether the attractive-nuisance doctrine applies?
3. What is the rescue doctrine?

4. What duty is owed a known trespasser?
   a. What duty is owed to someone who trespasses on a limited area of a possessor's land?
5. Who is considered a licensee, and what duty of care is owed a licensee?
6. Who is considered an invitee, and what duty of care is owed an invitee?
   a. How can one lose one's invitee status?

7. What duty of care does a possessor owe to those outside her property?

   a. What distinction is made between artificial and natural conditions?

8. What are the duties of a tenant?

9. What are the duties of a landlord?

10. To what extent is a seller of land liable to a plaintiff injured by a defect the seller does not disclose to the buyer?

    a. What if the seller intentionally conceals the defect?

11. Is there a common law duty to rescue someone in distress?

    a. Under what conditions does such a duty exist? Give an example.

12. What duty of care does a person have once he has begun to render emergency aid?

13. What is the voluntary-undertaking doctrine?

14. How does the duty of a public entity compare to that of a private individual?

15. Can a fetus recover for injuries sustained in utero as a result of a defendant's actions?

16. What is the doctrine of respondeat superior?

17. What is the family-purpose doctrine?

PRACTICE EXAM

Students should complete the practice exam after studying each chapter. The answers are in Appendix A. If you score lower than 80%, you should reread the materials.

True-False

1. Under the common law the limitations on the liability of possessors was to encourage full utilization of the land.

2. A possessor must warn trespassers of dangerous activities in which the possessor is engaging on his land.

3. For the attractive-nuisance doctrine to apply, the possessor need not be aware that children are likely to trespass on his land or have reason to know that the condition poses an unreasonable risk of serious injury or death to trespassing children.

4. The applicability of the attractive-nuisance doctrine depends on the age, experience, and intelligence of a child.

5. A posted notice of warning is sufficient for any licensee.

6. A plaintiff is considered an invitee even if she is not engaged in business at the time she is injured.

7. A plaintiff will lose her invitee status if she goes to part of the premises that extend beyond her invitation unless she reasonably believes the premises are open to the public.

8. An invitee does not lose her invitee status just because her reason for being on the premises becomes social rather than for business.

9. What constitutes reasonable care for a possessor depends on the use of the premises.

10. Not all states use the common law distinctions of trespasser, licensee, and invitee.

11. Possessors are generally liable for artificial conditions that pose an unreasonable risk of harm to people outside the premises.

12. All possessors have an obligation to remove trees that expose people outside the possessor's premises to an unreasonable risk of harm.

13. Under the common law, protection was given to the actual possessor of the land and not an abstract legal owner, and landlords were absolved of liability once they surrendered possession of their property to their tenant.

14. A tenant is liable for injuries to an invitee resulting from a defect that could have been discovered using reasonable care even if the tenant did not actually discover it.

15. A tenant is potentially liable for injuries occurring in common areas, such as elevators and stairways.

16. Landlords have a duty to protect a tenant's invitees and licensees from dangers of which the landlord is aware but that the tenant has no reason to know about.

17. A landlord must be given reasonable time to make repairs after being notified of the condition needing repair.

18. If a plaintiff is injured because of the landlord's failure to complete the repairs he started, the plaintiff can sue both the landlord and the tenant.

19. A landlord who hires an independent contractor to do repairs cannot be held liable for the contractor's negligence.

20. In some cases courts have found that landlords do have an obligation to protect tenants from criminal attack.

21. A seller's liability ceases when the buyer takes possession of the land even if the seller fails to disclose a dangerous condition that she should realize the buyer will not discover.

22. If a seller hides a defect, his liability will continue until the buyer actually discovers the defect and has a reasonable time to correct it.

23. Under the common law a defendant has no legal duty to aid a plaintiff in distress unless the defendant can assist the plaintiff without causing harm to himself.

24. Common carriers have a legal duty to protect passengers from criminal attacks.

25. A defendant may be found liable for the actions of an obviously intoxicated individual if she loans her vehicle to this individual.

26. Tavern owners, but not social hosts, can be held liable for the negligent acts of those to whom they served liquor.

27. Even though a defendant begins to render emergency assistance, he is not legally obligated to continue.

28. The Good Samaritan statutes do not protect people who provide aid in good faith if they end up injuring the plaintiff.

29. A defendant cannot be found liable if it has no legal duty to protect the plaintiff.

30. Some courts have applied the voluntary-undertaking doctrine even when the plaintiff did not rely on the defendant's services.

31. The analysis of duty is very different for a public entity than it is for private individuals.

32. Modern courts do not allow recovery for fetuses who have defects because of injuries sustained while in utero, nor are wrongful-death actions allowed for fetuses who are stillborn as a result of injuries sustained by the defendant's actions.

Matching

GROUP 1

_____ 1. Duty to inspect for hidden dangers

_____ 2. Duty to warn of dangerous conditions

_____ 3. Must refrain from intentionally harming

_____ 4. Greater duty owed to children than adults

_____ 5. Elevated to licensee

a. attractive nuisance

b. invitee

c. licensee

d. trespasser

e. known trespasser

GROUP 2

_____ 1. Member of the public invited to enter possessor's land for purposes for which land is held open to the public

_____ 2. Social guest in automobile

_____ 3. Workers who enter store to make repairs

_____ 4. Social guest who performs incidental service for her host

_____ 5. Child drawn to possessor's land who enters without possessor's permission

_____ 6. Adult who enters possessor's land with possessor's awareness but without his permission

a. trespasser

b. licensee

c. invitee

Answers for Matching: Group 2 are either a, b, or c; therefore, some answers will be used more than once.

Fill-in-the-Blanks

1. Under the common law a social guest is classified as a _____, whereas someone with a business purpose is classified as an _____.

2. The _____ _____ doctrine deals with those conditions that attract child trespassers.

3. Under the _____ _____ doctrine, a defendant can be liable to a plaintiff for beginning a service that he subsequently abandons to the plaintiff's detriment.

4. Under the _____ _____ doctrine the owner of a vehicle is liable for those members of the household she allows to drive her vehicle.

5. Employers are _____ liable for any torts committed by an employee during the scope and furtherance of his employment.

Multiple-Choice

1. The question of duty
   a. is a threshold question.
   b. arises only if there is a direct relationship between the plaintiff and the defendant.
   c. bears no relationship to whether the defendant could reasonably foresee that the plaintiff would be endangered.
   d. all of the above.

2. With an attractive nuisance
   a. courts rarely distinguish between natural and artificial conditions when determining whether an injured child can recover.

   b. possessors must childproof their land to avoid liability.
   c. the benefit of maintaining a condition in its dangerous form must be slight compared with the risk posed to the children for the doctrine to apply.
   d. all of the above.

3. The rescue doctrine
   a. does not protect a plaintiff who voluntarily places herself in a dangerous situation to save another.
   b. is based on the premise that the rescuer would not have been injured if not for the negligence of the tortfeasor.
   c. is applicable even if there is no immediate need to save the victim.
   d. all of the above.

4. To frequent trespassers who use only a limited area of their land, possessors owe
   a. no duty of care.
   b. a limited duty of care.
   c. the same care they owe an invitee.
   d. none of the above.

5. A possessor
   a. has a duty to ferret out all hidden dangers for an invitee.
   b. will not be liable for injuries resulting to an invitee as a result of a faulty design or construction that existed before he possessed the property.
   c. may be obligated to take steps to reduce the danger even if an invitee is aware of and appreciates the dangers involved.
   d. all of the above.

6. A landlord
   a. must perform repairs reasonably even if he has no contractual obligation to make the repairs.
   b. cannot be sued in tort by a plaintiff injured as a result of the landlord's breach of her covenant to make repairs.
   c. does not have a duty to inspect his tenant's premises and find and repair damages even if he knows the tenant is holding the land open to the public.
   d. all of the above.

7. The *Tarasoff* holding
   a. blurs the line for professionals between protecting others and preserving the confidentiality of communications between themselves and their clients.
   b. holds professionals responsible for warning plaintiffs that a client intends them harm if a reasonable person in that situation would have believed a warning to be necessary.
   c. has created a lot of controversy.
   d. all of the above.

PRACTICE POINTERS

Jury instructions may be the deciding factor in a case—not because of the influence they have on jurors (most jurors have made up their minds long before they are read the jury instructions), but because of the impact they may have on appeal. Jury instructions that incorrectly state the law may provide grounds for reversal. Therefore, judges are well aware of the significance of jury instructions at the appellate level and place the burden on the attorneys for both sides to draft proposed instructions. These proposals are usually submitted before trial, giving the judge (and opposing counsel) ample time to review them and do any necessary research. After hearing the evidence presented at trial and listening to the arguments of both attorneys regarding jury instructions, the judge prepares instructions that most clearly and accurately present the law as it pertains to the case at hand.

Jury instructions are the definitive statement of the elements of the plaintiff's case. Plaintiff's counsel must make sure that the evidence presented covers each required element (as set forth in the jury instructions), whereas defense counsel must evaluate the weakest elements in the plaintiff's case and focus an attack on those elements. Therefore, from a trial preparation standpoint, jury instructions assist attorneys in focusing on the essential elements of a case and seeing its weakest points.

Attorneys often use legal assistants in the researching and drafting of jury instructions. Jury instructions for the most common causes of action (e.g., motor vehicle accidents and slip-and-fall cases) can be found in books of recommended jury instructions compiled by the court, state bar associations, or some other authoritative source.

An example of a jury instruction that might be used in the case involving Teddy and the Baxters is shown here.

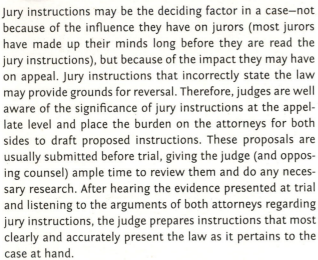

Negligence of a Child
Duty of Adult to Anticipate Behavior of Children

A child is not held to the same standard of care as an adult.

A child who does not use the degree of care that is ordinarily exercised by children of the same age, intelligence, knowledge, and experience under the existing circumstances is negligent.

An adult must anticipate the ordinary behavior of children, and that children might not exercise the same degree of care for their own safety as adults.

NET NEWS
To read sample jury instructions on such topics as res ipsa loquitur, the rescue doctrine, the Good Samaritan rule, and related concepts, go to **http://www.lawca.com,** enter "California Civil Jury Instructions" as your search term and review the result.

PRACTICE PROBLEM

One beautiful summer afternoon Jonathan and Teddy, both age six, were engaged in a particularly rollicking game of football in the backyard of Teddy's house. In an effort to emulate the quarterback hero of his fantasies, Jonathan took aim at Teddy and catapulted the ball into the air. Unfortunately, his aim was off and the ball landed in the backyard of Teddy's neighbors, Mr. and Mrs. Baxter. The Baxter backyard was surrounded by a six-foot wooden fence. Undeterred by this obstacle between him and his ball, Teddy attempted unsuccessfully to scale the fence. Jonathan, who was two months older than Teddy and, therefore, proportionately wiser, suggested that they try the gate to the yard.

Teddy knew that the Baxters always kept the gate locked, and he also remembered that he had been warned repeatedly by both the Baxters and his parents that he should never enter the Baxter yard without supervision. Jonathan urged him to try the gate anyway, but Teddy was hesitant. He was circumspect about entering the yard not only because of his parents' and the Baxters' admonitions, but also because of the presence of Gertrude, the Baxters' German shepherd. Gertrude and Teddy had a somewhat strained relationship because Teddy, in some of his less enlightened moments, had taken a certain perverse pleasure in provoking Gertrude into a barking frenzy by teasing her through the gate. He was reluctant to test her capacity for forgiveness, but, egged on by Jonathan, he tried the gate latch and found, much to his surprise, that it was unlocked. Hesitantly, he opened the gate and peered inside. With Gertrude nowhere in sight he bolted across the yard to retrieve the ball.

Gertrude, her hearing somewhat impaired by advanced age, was deeply immersed in canine daydreams and was oblivious to Teddy's activities. Because of this Teddy might have escaped undetected had he not stubbed his toe on a sprinkler and let out a loud yell. The slumbering Gertrude, awakened by Teddy's cries, sprang to her feet. Somewhat disoriented but drawing on her instincts as a guard dog, Gertrude leaped off the porch in the direction of the unknown intruder. When she was within lunging distance of the now-panicked Teddy, vague memories of loathing filtered into Gertrude's consciousness as she began to recall the many indignities she had endured as a result of Teddy's tormenting.

Goaded by these memories, as well as her instinctual drive to protect her domain, Gertrude took aim for the hapless Teddy. When Teddy felt Gertrude grab hold of one of his pant legs he screamed in terror and tried desperately to kick Gertrude away. Incensed by the kicking, she received from Teddy, Gertrude plunged her teeth deeper, piercing Teddy's flesh. Teddy's continual thrashing about only made Gertrude more determined to maintain her viselike grip on Teddy's leg.

Meanwhile, Jonathan, a spectator to this whole drama, valiantly attempted to rescue his friend by pelting Gertrude with rocks he found in the Baxters' driveway. Unfortunately, the sting of the rocks further enraged Gertrude and, not realizing their source, she reinforced her grip on Teddy's leg.

Drawn by Jonathan's pleas for help and Teddy's screams of terror, a passerby, Mr. Goodright, came running into the Baxters' backyard. Immediately sizing up the situation, Mr. Goodright began kicking at Gertrude with all his might to induce her to release Teddy. Gertrude, stunned by his blows, let loose of Teddy to attack the object that was causing her pain. Seizing this opportunity to escape, Teddy dragged himself toward the gate and Jonathan pulled him to the safety of the driveway.

The courageous Mr. Goodright now pitted his wits against 120 pounds of wrath. Gertrude, enraged by the kicks she had received, lashed out wildly and caught Mr. Goodright's right hand. Pummeling Gertrude's head with his free arm, Mr. Goodright struggled desperately to free his hand from Gertrude's jaws.

The duo might have continued this struggle until one of them collapsed from exhaustion, but, as fate would have it, Mr. Baxter arrived home early from work. As he drove in and caught sight of the fracas taking place in his backyard, he vaulted out of his car, yelling at Gertrude as he ran. When her master's commands finally penetrated her consciousness, Gertrude released her prey.

But the damage had already been wrought. Both Teddy and Mr. Goodright were bleeding profusely from their wounds, and Teddy, his attention no longer diverted by the combat between Mr. Goodright and Gertrude, was beginning to become painfully aware of the full extent of his injuries. Both Mr. Goodright and Teddy sustained serious injuries from their battles with Gertrude.

Teddy would bear emotional as well as physical scars as a result of his encounter with Gertrude. In the future he would experience a phobic disorder connected to dogs, to the extent that the approach of any dog in his direction would trigger an anxiety attack. Mr. Goodright, a longtime animal lover and therefore more sympathetic to Gertrude's acts, would experience no emotional reactions from his trauma but would have to suffer the long-term consequences of his heroic efforts. He would endure several operations to repair the damage to his hand and would never gain full control of his hand again. As a result, his career as a much heralded concert pianist would come to an untimely end, and he would be relegated forever to the humble life of a piano teacher.

One of the first questions that the attorneys representing Teddy and Mr. Goodright in our hypothetical case will have to consider is the question of duty. Did the Baxters owe a duty of care to one who trespassed on their land? Did they owe a different duty of care to a child than to an adult? Did they owe a higher duty of care to a rescuer than they did to an ordinary trespasser?

TORT TEASERS

1. Do the courts in your state classify those who come onto land as invitees, licensees, and trespassers? If not, how are cases involving premises liability analyzed? Is this area of the law controlled by the common law, or statute, or both? What are the applicable statutes?

In each of the following cases, discuss whether a duty of care is owed by the defendant to the plaintiff.

2. Plaintiff, a sixteen-year-old boy, is visiting the home of a friend when he notices a cat at the top of a utility pole in a neighboring yard. He climbs the pole, in part to rescue the cat and in part to see if he can climb the pole. When he arrives at the top of the pole he receives an electric shock and falls, sustaining injuries. *Brown v. Arizona Public Service Co.*, 790 P.2d 290 (Ariz. Ct. App. 1990).

3. Plaintiff, who lives across the street from a baseball park, is struck on the shoulder by a baseball hit from the park. The injury requires corrective surgery. Plaintiff sues Defendant, the owner of the baseball park, for his injuries. *Halliburton v. Town of Halls*, 295 S.W. 3d 636 (Tenn. App. 2008).

4. Plaintiff, who was shopping in Defendant's store, is bitten by Defendant's cat. Defendant promises to lock up the cat for fourteen days so that he can be tested for rabies. Defendant fails to live up to his promise and the cat disappears for a month, requiring Plaintiff to undergo a series of painful rabies shots. After Plaintiff completes the treatment the cat returns in perfect health. *Marsalis v. La Salle*, 90 So. 2d 120 (La. 1957).

5. Plaintiffs allege that homeowner defendant negligently allowed her son who was mentally-ill to keep guns and ammunition on her property, which he used to kill Plaintiffs' relative who was performing yard work. The victim and Defendant were next door neighbors. Defendant testified that she did not know her son kept guns and ammunition on her property and she could not have foreseen that he would shoot anyone as he did not have a history of such violence. *Volpe v. Gallagher*, 821 A.2d 699 (R.I. 2003).

6. Plaintiff golfer was struck in the eyes by a golf ball by a fellow golfer's misdirected ball. *Anand v. Kapoor*, 61 Ad. 3d 787, (N.Y. App. Div Dep't. 2009).

INTERNET INQUIRIES

American Law Sources Online (ALSO) http://www.lawsource.com/ is one of those phenomenal sources of links into federal and state legal resources. From this site you can access United States Supreme Court, Court of

Appeals, bankruptcy panel, and district court decisions as well as a multitude of uniform laws, the United States Code, the United States Constitution, and court rules and practices. At the state level you can find similar resources.

PRACTICAL PONDERABLES

Your firm's client, Arnold, attended a graduation party hosted by an acquaintance of his, Steven. Steven's parents, at Steven's request, agreed to stay out of sight of his guests and they were not seen all evening. They stayed in a guest cottage on the property, watching television and drinking martinis. They were oblivious to the fact that Arnold was severely beaten by one of the guests, Patrick, who has a vicious temper when he has been drinking. Patrick had harbored a grudge against Arnold for comments Arnold made several months previously, but Patrick never had the courage to act on his resentment until this time. Arnold, who was not expecting to be assaulted and who has no self-defense skills, was badly injured.

Some of the guests at the party were minors; Arnold himself is seventeen (below legal drinking age in his state). Assume that a state statute makes it illegal to provide liquor to minors.

1. What argument would you make on behalf of Arnold that Steven's parents had a legal obligation to protect him from being attacked by Patrick?

2. What argument would you anticipate Steven's parents making in response?

3. What are the laws, both statutory and case law, in your state regarding social host liability? In light of those laws, whom do you think would prevail in this scenario and why?

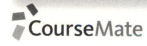 CourseMate   Access an interactive eBook, chapter-specific learning tools, including flashcards, quizzes, and more in your Paralegal CourseMate, accessed through www.CengageBrain.com.

CHAPTER 5

Negligence: Breach of Duty

© Cengage Learning 2012

CHAPTER OBJECTIVES

After completing the chapter, you should be able to

- Identify the criteria used to assess the reasonableness of a person's conduct.
- Distinguish between objective and subjective standards.
- Use the Learned Hand formula.
- Apply the concepts of negligence per se and res ipsa loquitur.

As we first discussed in Chapter 4, if it can be established that the Baxters owed a duty of care to Teddy and to Mr. Goodright, the next question is whether they breached that duty. Because the duty required in most instances is to use reasonable care, that duty is breached by engaging in unreasonable conduct. Did the Baxters exercise the precautions expected of a reasonable person in their maintenance of Gertrude? Was she adequately confined for a dog of her size and temperament? Did the Baxters create an unreasonable risk of harm for Teddy and other children by failing to lock the latch on their gate?

WHAT IS REASONABLE CONDUCT?

Breach of Duty occurs when the defendant fails to conform to the required standard of care. Determining whether a breach of duty has occurred requires (1) a determination of the relevant standard of care and (2) an evaluation of the defendant's conduct in light of that standard. In other words, if the plaintiff is able to prove that she was owed a duty of care by the defendant, that duty gives rise to a general standard of conduct—to use reasonable care. Using reasonable care requires the defendant to recognize the risks created by his actions (or omissions) and to act reasonably in light of those risks. The general standard must then be applied to the specific circumstances of the case to determine the specific standard of care governing the defendant's conduct. The jury is asked to establish this specific standard of care, usually guided by only very general jury instructions defining negligence.

The question of reasonable care boils down to what a reasonable person would have done under similar circumstances. As Prosser and Keeton explain:

> The standard of conduct which the community demands must be an external and objective one, rather than the individual judgment, good or bad, of the particular actor; and it must be, so far as possible, the same for all persons, since the law can have no favorites. At the same time, it must make proper allowance for the risk apparent to the actor, for his capacity to meet it, and for the circumstances under which he must act.
>
> The courts have dealt with this very difficult problem by creating a fictitious person, who never has existed on land or sea: the "reasonable man of ordinary prudence." Sometimes he is described as a reasonable person, or a person of ordinary prudence, or a person of reasonable prudence, or some other blend of reason and caution. (*The Law of Torts* § 32, 173 [5th ed. 1984])

A defendant's conduct must be evaluated at the time of the plaintiff's injury. "Monday-morning quarterbacking" is not allowed. What is important is how reasonable people would perceive the defendant's acts at the time they occurred. The plaintiff, consequently, is not permitted to use the self-serving argument that he was injured as a direct result of the defendant's conduct and that, therefore, the defendant must have been unreasonable.

The characteristics of the proverbial "reasonable person" will be discussed shortly. But first we must consider how our reasonable person decides what to do in a predicament. We can assume that any reasonable person will avoid creating an unreasonable risk of harm for others. The tough question is how he calculates such risks and avoids actions that create unreasonable risks.

LEARNED HAND FORMULA

Judge Learned Hand, an influential jurist well known for his pragmatic approach to determining breach of duty, advocated a type of cost/benefit analysis (see Exhibit 5–1). The judge asked the court to consider the probability that harm would occur as a result of the defendant's conduct (P), the gravity of the potential harm (L), and the burden of precautions that would have to be borne by the defendant to avoid the possible risk (B). He reduced these considerations into a formula and concluded that a defendant breached his duty if

$$P \times L > B$$

EXHIBIT 5–1   Learned Hand Formula

Burden of precautions

Gravity of harm/ Likelihood of harm

Defendant is liable

© Cengage Learning 2012

In other words, according to this equation the defendant would be liable if the probability of harm occurring (P) multiplied by the gravity of such harm (L) exceeded the defendant's burden of taking precautions to avoid the harm (B).

In considering B, the burden of precautions, the courts look not only at the cost involved in taking precautions but also at the social utility of the defendant's conduct. What is the social value of the defendant's conduct? If society would be better served by allowing all defendants in the defendant's position to act as she did, the courts are less likely to require the defendant to alter that course of conduct.

Application of Learned Hand Formula

Let us apply this equation to a hypothetical problem. Suppose an automobile manufacturer discovers a defect in the design of its automobile that under certain circumstances has the potential of creating harm to the occupants of the vehicle. Will the manufacturer be acting unreasonably if it fails to alter this defective design?

In answering that question, one would have to calculate the statistical likelihood of accidents resulting in injury to a vehicle's occupants occurring. Next, one would have to consider the gravity of the types of injuries that would most likely occur, as well as the burden to the manufacturer of altering the design. Suppose it can be anticipated that 100 of those vehicles having this defect will be involved in serious accidents within one year, and that those accidents will result in injuries costing an average of $1 million in medical expenses. If altering the design would cost the manufacturer $1 million, the manufacturer would be obligated to make the alteration because 100 × $1 million > $1 million.

Notice that under the Learned Hand formula, the more serious the potential injury that could be incurred, the less probable its occurrence must be before the defendant is obligated to guard against it. Suppose, for example, the risk of injury is less than 20 percent and yet the type of injury likely to occur is death or serious physical injury. The court would be more likely to find the defendant negligent for failure to redesign the vehicle under those circumstances than if there was a 40 percent chance of an accident but the anticipated injuries were relatively minor.

In assigning a value to B, the courts would not only calculate the cost of altering the design but would also consider the social consequences of requiring similarly situated defendants to alter their comparably defective designs. If consumers could no longer afford a redesigned vehicle, the new design would have little social utility. Suppose the court in our hypothetical case concludes that the cost of redesigning the vehicle would be prohibitive and that the likelihood and gravity of injuries resulting from the defect would be relatively slight. The court would then conclude that the defendant manufacturer had not breached its duty of care to its consumers. Note, however, that the plaintiffs in such cases could still opt for strict liability and warranty causes of action (both discussed in Chapter 12).

To see the Learned Hand formula applied in an actual case, read *Eimann v. Soldier of Fortune Magazine*, 880 F.2d 830 (5th Cir. 1989), excerpted here. In deciding whether the son and mother of a murder victim should be able to bring a wrongful-death action against the magazine that published an ad through which the victim's husband hired an assassin to kill her, the Texas Court applied the Learned Hand risk-utility analysis.

CASE / *Eimann v. Soldier of Fortune Magazine, Inc.*
880 F.2d 830 (5th Cir. 1989)

W. EUGENE DAVIS, Circuit Judge:

Soldier of Fortune Magazine, Inc. appeals a $9.4 million jury verdict against it in a wrongful death action brought by the son and mother of a murder victim. The jury found that Soldier of Fortune acted with negligence and gross negligence in publishing a personal services classified advertisement through which the

victim's husband hired an assassin to kill her. We reverse the judgment entered on the jury's verdict.

I. FACTS
John Wayne Hearn shot and killed Sandra Black at the behest of her husband, Robert, who offered to pay Hearn $10,000 for doing so. Robert Black contacted

(continues)

Hearn through a classified advertisement that Hearn ran in Soldier of Fortune Magazine, Inc. (SOF), a publication that focuses on mercenary activities and military affairs.

The ad, which ran in the September, October and November 1984 issues of SOF, read:

> EX-MARINES—67–69 'Nam Vets, Ex-DI, weapons specialist—jungle warfare, pilot, M.E., high risk assignments, U.S. or overseas. (404) 991–2684.

Hearn testified that "Ex-DI" meant ex-drill instructor; "M.E." meant multi-engine planes; and "high risk assignments" referred to work as a bodyguard or security specialist. Hearn testified that he and another former Marine placed the ad to recruit Vietnam veterans for work as bodyguards and security men for executives. Hearn's partner testified that they also hoped to train troops in South America. This partner never participated in any ad-related jobs and quit the venture shortly after the ad first ran.

Hearn and his partner testified that they did not place the ad with intent to solicit criminal employment. However, Hearn stated that about 90 percent of the callers who responded to the ad sought his participation in illegal activities including beatings, kidnappings, jailbreaks, bombings and murders. It also generated at least one lawful inquiry from an oil conglomerate in Lebanon seeking ten bodyguards; Hearn received a commission for placing seven men with the company.

Between 1982 and January 1984, Black had asked at least four friends or coworkers from Bryan, Texas to kill Sandra Black or help him kill her. All four refused. Black called Hearn in October 1984 after seeing his ad in SOF.

Hearn testified that his initial conversations with Black focused on Black's inquiries about getting bodyguard work through Hearn. In later calls they discussed the sale of Black's gun collection to Hearn. Hearn testified that he traveled from his home in Atlanta to Black's home in Bryan on January 9, 1985 to look at Black's gun collection. Hearn stated that Black discussed his plans for murdering his wife during the meeting and "hinted" that he wanted Hearn to participate, but did not ask Hearn directly to kill his wife. Hearn did not act on the hint and returned to Atlanta.

Black called Hearn repeatedly after Hearn returned to Atlanta. During one call Black spoke with Hearn's girlfriend, Debbie Bannister. Hearn and Bannister met after she called him in response to his SOF ad.

Black proposed directly that Hearn kill his wife during the call to Bannister. She passed the proposal on to Hearn, who called Black and said he would consider doing it. The two talked by phone several times in the following weeks. After an aborted murder attempt about

three weeks later—during which Hearn was to help Black himself kill his wife—Hearn killed Sandra Black on February 21, 1985. By that time Hearn also had killed the ex-husband of Bannister's sister on January 6, 1985 and Bannister's husband on February 2, 1985.

Neither Hearn, who was sentenced to concurrent life sentences for the murders, nor his partner had criminal records when they placed their ad in SOF. Neither had received a dishonorable discharge from the Marines. Further, Hearn included his real name and correct address in submitting the ad to SOF; the ad itself listed Hearn's correct home telephone number.

Sandra Black's son, Gary Wayne Black, and her mother, Marjorie Eimann, sued SOF and its parent, Omega Group, Ltd., for wrongful death under Texas law on the theory that SOF negligently published Hearn's classified ad.

Eimann introduced into evidence about three dozen personal service classified ads selected from the 2,000 or so classified ads that SOF had printed from its inception in 1975 until September 1984. Some ads offered services as a "Mercenary for Hire," "bounty hunter," or "mechanic"; others promised to perform "dirty work," "high risk contracts" or to "do anything, anywhere at the right price."

Eimann presented evidence that seven and perhaps as many as nine classified ads had been tied to crimes or criminal plots. Eimann introduced stories from sources including the Associated Press, United Press International, The Rocky Mountain News, The Denver Post, Time and Newsweek that reported on links between SOF classified ads and at least five of these crimes.

Eimann also presented evidence that law enforcement officials had contacted SOF staffers during investigations of two crimes linked to SOF personal service classifieds. In one case, SOF had provided correspondence from its files—along with two affidavits signed by SOF's managing editor—that were used in the 1982 criminal trial of a Houston man who was convicted of soliciting the murder of his wife; during his effort the man had tried to hire a poisons expert by placing a classified ad in the October 1981 issue of SOF. Eimann also presented testimony from a New Jersey detective, who stated that in April 1984, SOF's advertising manager had helped him to identify a man who placed a classified ad in SOF.

In addition, Eimann presented expert testimony from Dr. Park Dietz, a forensic psychiatrist who had studied SOF, its ads and readership. Dietz testified that an average SOF subscriber—a male who owns camouflage clothing and more than one gun—would understand some phrases in SOF's classified ads as solicitations for illegal activity given the "context" of those ads.

(continues)

The context included other classified ads in SOF, display ads for semiautomatic rifles and books with titles such as "How to Kill," and SOF articles including "Harassing the Bear, New Afghan Tactics Stall Soviet Victory," "Pipestone Canyon, Summertime in 'Nam and the Dyin' was Easy," and "Night Raiders on Russia's Border." Dietz also described his visit to a SOF convention in summer 1987, where he photographed exhibits of weapons and tactical gear.

Based on his studies, Dietz concluded that the Hearn ad "or any other personal service ad in Soldier of Fortune in 1984 foreseeably is related to the commission of domestic crimes." He suggested that classified ads such as Hearn's would not carry such connotations if they appeared in Esquire or Vanity Fair.

Dietz conceded, however, that he had abandoned an effort to distinguish lawful SOF classified ads from criminal ones on the basis of specific code words such as "gun for hire," "mechanic," and "hunter" because some ads were too ambiguous to assign an illegal meaning to them with any certainty. He also noted that crimes had been linked to SOF classified ads that "seemed relatively innocuous." For example, one ad tied to a kidnapping and extortion plot read:

> Recovery and collection. International agents guarantee results on any type of recover[y].
> Reply to Delta Enterprises, P.O. Box 5241, Rockford, Illinois 61125.

As Dietz stated, "The code system doesn't work."

SOF relied primarily on the testimony of its president, Robert K. Brown, who stated he did not know or suspect in 1984 that some of the SOF classified ads had been linked to criminal plots. Other SOF staffers and readers echoed these denials. SOF's advertising manager, Joan Steele, testified that she understood the phrase "high risk assignments" in Hearn's ad to mean "gun for hire," but in the sense of a professional bodyguard or security consultant rather than a contract killer.

The district court's first special interrogatory asked the jury whether Hearn's ad "related to" illegal activity. The court's second interrogatory asked, "Did [SOF]…know or should it have known from the face or the context of the Hearn advertisement that the advertisement could reasonably be interpreted as an offer to engage in illegal activity?"

The court's instructions charged SOF with knowledge that Hearn's ad reasonably could be interpreted as such an offer when (1) the relation to illegal activity appears on the ad's face; or (2) "the advertisement, embroidered by its context, would lead a reasonable publisher of ordinary prudence under the same or similar circumstances to conclude that the advertisement could reasonably be interpreted" as an offer to commit crimes. The court went on to define "context" as the

magazine's (1) "nature"; (2) other advertisements; (3) articles; (4) readership; and (5) knowledge, if any, that other advertisements in the magazine could reasonably be interpreted as an offer to engage in illegal activity.

The jury answered "yes" to the first two interrogatories, and found that SOF's negligence was a proximate cause of Sandra Black's death in response to Interrogatory Three. The court then asked the jury whether SOF's negligence constituted "gross negligence," defined as "conscious indifference." The jury answered "yes" to this interrogatory as well. The jury awarded Eimann $1.9 million in compensatory damages and $7.5 million in punitive damages; the district court entered judgment on the verdict. SOF appeals.

II. ANALYSIS
A. Overview

Eimann presented this case as a straightforward negligence action revolving around one primary issue: whether SOF knew or should have known from the face or context of Hearn's ad that it represented an offer to perform illegal acts. Based on evidence that SOF knew of links between other classified ads and other criminal plots, she contends that SOF owed a duty to recognize ads such as Hearn's that reasonably might be interpreted as criminal solicitations and refrain from publishing them.

SOF argues first that no liability can attach under these facts because the criminal activities of Hearn and Robert Black, rather than Hearn's ad, were the proximate cause of Sandra Black's murder. SOF also argues that imposition of tort liability here contravenes first amendment protection for commercial speech because (1) the judgment below impermissibly imposed a duty on publishers to investigate its advertisers and their ads; and (2) the district court's all-encompassing definition of "context," combined with Dietz's testimony, allowed the jury to penalize SOF for the mercenary and military focus of the magazine's articles and other ads.

We need not address SOF's first amendment attacks on the judgment to resolve this appeal. Assuming without deciding that a Texas court would apply general negligence principles to this case, we conclude that no liability can attach under these principles as a matter of law. SOF owed no duty to refrain from publishing a facially innocuous classified advertisement when the ad's context—at most—made its message ambiguous.

Under Texas law, negligence liability requires the existence of a duty, breach of that duty, and an injury proximately resulting from that breach. The existence of a duty presents a threshold question of law for the court; the jury determines breach and proximate cause only after the court concludes that a duty exists. Our resolution of this case hinges on the initial duty question.

(continues)

B. Duty

In essence, a duty represents a legally enforceable obligation to conform to a particular standard of conduct. Whether the defendant in a negligence action owes a duty involves consideration of two related issues: (1) whether the defendant owes an obligation to this particular plaintiff to act as a reasonable person would in the circumstances; and (2) the standard of conduct required to satisfy that obligation.

Texas courts have applied risk-utility balancing tests in resolving both aspects of the duty question. Thus, in deciding whether an actor owes a duty of reasonable care to the public at large, the Supreme Court of Texas has weighed the risk, foreseeability and likelihood of injury from certain conduct against the conduct's social utility and the burden of guarding against injury.

Similarly, Texas courts have applied risk-utility analysis in determining the second duty issue—whether a defendant who owes an established duty of reasonable care to specified parties must take precautions against particular dangers. Courts have described this aspect of duty as the defendant's obligation to protect those parties against unreasonable risks. A risk becomes unreasonable when its magnitude outweighs the social utility of the act or omission that creates it.

Our analysis here assumes that SOF owes a duty of reasonable care to the public; we focus on the second prong of the duty issue: whether SOF's decision to print Hearn's ad violated the standard of conduct.

In answering this question we look to Judge Learned Hand's concise expression of these balancing principles in *United States v. Carroll Towing*, 159 F.2d 169, 173 (2d Cir.1947). As he described it in algebraic terms, liability turns on whether the burden of adequate precautions, B, is less than the probability of harm, P, multiplied by the gravity of the resulting injury, L. In other words, an actor falls below the standard of conduct and liability attaches when B is less than PL. Conversely, the actor satisfies the obligation to protect against unreasonable risks when the burden of adequate precautions—examined in light of the challenged action's value—outweighs the probability and gravity of the threatened harm.

We now turn to these individual factors.

1. The Probability and Gravity of the Threatened Harm

In assessing the threatened harm we note that "nearly all human acts . . . carry some recognizable but remote possibility of harm to another." The SOF classified ads presented more than a remote risk. Of the 2,000 or so personal service classified ads that SOF printed between 1975 and 1984, Eimann's evidence established that as many as nine had served as links in criminal plots. Of these nine, the evidence revealed that SOF staffers had participated in at least two police investigations of crimes in which classified ads played a role; other crimes tied to the ads received varying amounts of media coverage.

As noted above, the gravity of the threatened harm may require precautions against even unlikely events. For example, the standard of care may require those who own oil storage tanks to take precautions against fires caused by an unpredictable lightning strike. The prospect of ad-inspired crime represents a threat of serious harm. Eimann presented evidence that SOF classified ads played a role in other crimes ranging from extortion to jail-breaks. Sandra Black's murder illustrates one aspect of the crime linked to SOF classified advertisements.

2. The Burden of Preventing the Harm

SOF contends that the standard of conduct applied by the district court impermissibly required the magazine to guard against criminal solicitation by investigating its advertisers and their ads. It relies on a series of cases holding that newspaper publishers owe no duty in tort to investigate their advertisers for the accuracy of ads placed for publication.

However, in our view the standard of conduct against which the jury measured SOF's actions was more exacting than a duty to investigate; it requires publishers to recognize ads that "reasonably could be interpreted as an offer to engage in illegal activity" based on their words or "context" and refrain from printing them. Based on evidence that SOF knew other ads had been tied to crimes, Eimann's counsel contended at oral argument that SOF should have refrained from publishing Hearn's ad and all other personal service classified ads—suggestive ones and bland ones alike. This represents an especially heavy burden given (1) the ambiguous nature of Hearn's ad; and (2) the pervasiveness of advertising in our society.

At most, the residence reveals that Hearn submitted a facially innocuous ad. Standing alone, the phrase "high risk assignments" plausibly encompassed Hearn's professed goal of recruiting candidates for bodyguard jobs. Hearn performed precisely that function for at least one client who contacted him through the ad.

Eimann's effort to portray Hearn's ad as a readily identifiable criminal solicitation falls with Dr. Dietz's repudiation of his effort to identify specific code words signalling criminal intent. At one point in his testimony, Dr. Dietz analyzed a classified ad from the February 1980 issue of SOF. In terms that parallel Hearn's ad, this 1980 ad recruited SOF readers for "exciting high risk

(continues)

undercover stateside work." A court later convicted the individual who submitted it of mailing a threatening communication after he sent a letter instructing someone who had responded to the ad to "terminate" a person in Oklahoma City. Dr. Dietz stated:

> In 1984, in my opinion, someone familiar with the classified ads that have been run for years in Soldier of Fortune would be able to recognize from that ad that this is possibly someone who would be willing to be involved in criminal activity; but they might be wrong when they thought that. We knew that sometimes there were honest advertisers, and we know that some of the readers who responded to ads were honest too....

Dr. Dietz's description applies with equal force to Hearn's ad. Its bare terms reveal no identifiable offer to commit crimes, just as a locksmith's ad in the telephone directory reveals nothing about that particular advertiser's willingness to commit burglaries or steal cars.

This ambiguity persists even if we assume that SOF knew other ads had been tied to criminal plots. No evidence linked the other ads and crimes to Hearn. And as Eimann conceded, even if SOF had investigated Hearn and his partner in 1984, it would have discovered no criminal records and no false information that might have aroused suspicion.

Further, Eimann's heavy reliance on "context" cannot compensate for the fundamental ambiguity of Hearn's ad even if we assume that the district court properly defined that context. The presence in SOF of other ads and articles with violent themes provides no realistic method for gauging the likelihood that a particular ad will foster illegal activity. Do ads touting high-performance cars become solicitations for illegal activity when buyers drive them beyond the speed limit? Only when the ads run in Car and Driver magazine? Or, only when the ads run in magazines that also contain ads for radar detectors?

While we do not reach SOF's first amendment arguments, the Supreme Court's recognition of limited first amendment protection for commercial speech nonetheless highlights the important role of such communication for purposes of risk-benefit analysis. As the Court has noted, "[T]he particular consumer's interest in the free flow of commercial information...may be as keen, if not keener by far, than his interest in the day's most urgent political debate"....

Eimann seeks to discount the importance of SOF's classified ads by stressing that (1) SOF's publisher promoted the ads because they added to the "flavor and mystique" of the magazine; and (2) the jury found that Hearn's ad "relate[d] to" illegal activity. She notes that the Supreme Court has excluded advertising of illegal activity from the scope of first amendment protection. However, in the constitutional arena we have noted that the possibility of illegal results does not necessarily strip an ad of its commercial speech protection.

* * *

Similarly, a standard of conduct that imposes tort liability whenever the advertised product "could reasonably be interpreted as an offer to engage in illegal activity"—or might "relate to" criminal conduct—imposes an especially heavy burden.

3. Balancing the Burdens and Risks

We conclude that the standard of conduct imposed by the district court does not strike the proper balance between the risks of harm from ambiguous advertisement and the burden of preventing harm from this source under these facts. The appreciable risk that ads such as Hearn's will cause harm, combined with the gravity of that harm, does not outweigh the onerous burden Eimann asks us to endorse.

Hearn's ad presents a risk of serious harm. But everyday activities, such as driving on high-speed, closed access roadways, also carry definite risks that we as a society choose to accept in return for the activity's usefulness and convenience. To take a more extreme example, courts have almost uniformly rejected efforts to hold handgun manufacturers liable under negligence or strict liability theories to gunshot victims injured during crimes, despite the real possibility that such products can be used for criminal purposes. Given the pervasiveness of advertising in our society and the important role it plays, we decline to impose on publishers the obligation to reject all ambiguous advertisements for products or services that might pose a threat of harm.

III. CONCLUSION

The standard of conduct imposed by the district court against SOF is too high; it allows a jury to visit liability on a publisher for untoward consequences that flow from his decision to publish any suspicious, ambiguous ad that might cause serious harm. The burden on a publisher to avoid liability from suits of this type is too great: he must reject all such advertisements.

The range of foreseeable misuses of advertised products and services is as limitless as the forms and functions of the products themselves. Without a more specific indication of illegal intent than Hearn's ad or its context provided, we conclude that SOF did not violate the required standard of conduct by publishing an ad that later played a role in criminal activity.

The judgment of the district court is REVERSED and RENDERED.

PUTTING IT INTO PRACTICE 5:1

1. Of the 2,000 ads printed in *Soldier of Fortune* magazine (SOF) between 1975 and 1984, how many served as links in criminal plots? What kinds of crimes did these include?

2. Did the Hearn ad indicate a clearly identifiable offer to commit crimes?

3. What did Dietz testify in regard to the "context" of some of the ads in SOF? Could he distinguish lawful from unlawful classified ads in the magazine?

4. What did the court hold?

5. How have the Texas courts used the risk-utility test in relationship to the question of duty? When does a risk become unreasonable under the risk-utility test?

6. Did SOF owe a duty of reasonable care to the public?

7. Did the SOF ads create more than a remote risk of harm? What evidence did the court use to support its answer to this question?

8. Against what standard of conduct did the court feel the jury measured SOF's actions? Why did the court feel that standard imposed too heavy a burden?

9. For what reason did the court conclude that the district court did not strike the proper balance between the risks of harm from ambiguous ads and the burden of preventing harm arising from these ads?

RESTATEMENT POSITION

The *Restatement (Second) of Torts* § 291 basically incorporates the Learned Hand formula and states that an act is negligent if "the risk is of such magnitude as to outweigh what the law regards as the utility of the act or of the particular manner in which it is done." The following factors are considered in determining the utility of the defendant's conduct:

1. "the social value which the law attaches to the interest which is to be advanced or protected by the conduct"

2. "the extent of the chance that this interest will be advanced or protected by the particular course of conduct"

3. "the extent of the chance that such interest can be adequately advanced or protected by another less dangerous course of conduct" (*Restatement [Second] of Torts* § 292)"

The factors to be considered in determining the magnitude of the risk are

1. "the social value which the law attaches to the interests which are imperiled"

2. "the extent of the chance that the actor's conduct will cause an invasion of any interest of the other or of one of the class of which the other is a member"

3. "the extent of the harm likely to be caused to the interests imperiled"

4. "the number of persons whose interest are likely to be invaded if the risk takes effect in harm" (*Restatement [Second] of Torts* § 293)

PUTTING IT INTO PRACTICE 5:2

David, who is fifteen years old, goes camping with his friends at a state park. On their third day, one of his friends tells the group about a cove located about sixty yards from their campsite. David and the others take a boat to the cove about 7:00 P.M. At least fifteen people are swimming and wading in the cove; one of David's friends dives into the cove and swims away unharmed. David then dives in and hits his head on a ledge or sandbar below the surface and is permanently paralyzed.

David had never seen the cove before he dove into it and did not check the depth of the water before diving into it because he saw his friend dive in without harm and because others had evidently used the diving spot before; there was a "well-worn" path leading up to it. He is an accomplished swimmer and testifies in his deposition that he would not have dived in without checking the depth of the water if he had seen any signs prohibiting diving or warnings of any kind posted in the area or at the park entrance.

If David is classified as an invitee, did the state take reasonable precautions to protect him from harm? Did the state have an obligation to discover the danger posed by the shallow waters of the cove? Would a reasonable landowner have posted signs prohibiting diving if it could not remove the danger? Use the criteria set forth in the *Restatement (Second) of Torts* in §§ 291–293 to help you answer these questions.

REASONABLE-PERSON STANDARD— OBJECTIVE VERSUS SUBJECTIVE

In assessing whether the defendant imposed an unreasonable risk of harm to others, her conduct is compared to that of a reasonable person (see Exhibit 5–2). In essence, the question put before a jury in a negligence case is whether a reasonable person of ordinary prudence standing in the defendant's shoes would have done the same thing the defendant did. Phrasing the question this way requires the use of an **objective standard** in that the defendant's conduct is compared to that of a hypothetical reasonable person. By contrast, if a **subjective standard** were used, the question would be whether the defendant believed that she was behaving in a reasonable manner. Under a subjective standard the reasonableness of one's acts vary depending on one's perception.

EXHIBIT 5–2 *Factors Taken into Consideration in Determining Reasonableness*

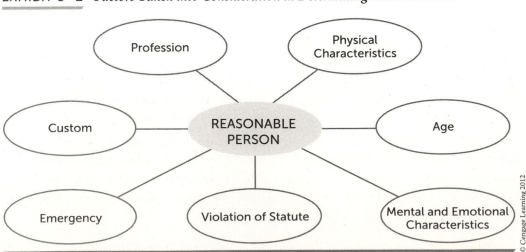

© Cengage Learning 2012

Let us illustrate the difference in outcome of these two standards by using a hypothetical problem. Suppose a driver pulled out in front of oncoming traffic, causing an accident. The driver had poor depth perception and was unable to accurately estimate the distance between himself and other vehicles. If an objective standard were used, one would ask whether a reasonable driver of ordinary prudence would have pulled out in front of the traffic. If the driver did not conform to that reasonable standard, his conduct would be considered negligent. In contrast, under a subjective standard, one would ask whether the driver himself perceived any risks. If he did not, he would be deemed to have used reasonable care and, hence, would not be negligent.

From this example you can probably deduce why the objective and not the subjective standard is used in most instances in tort law. To reduce the uncertainty in our legal system and to maximize safety to members of society, the peculiar frailties and idiosyncrasies of defendants generally are not taken into consideration in assessing the reasonableness of their conduct. With few exceptions, then, in tort law we use an objective standard.

WHAT THE REASONABLE PERSON IS EXPECTED TO KNOW

If the reasonable-person standard serves as the barometer for all negligence cases, just what can we expect from the reasonable person? Reasonable persons are expected to know the "qualities and habits of human beings and animals and the qualities, characteristics, and capacities of things and forces in so far as they are matters of common knowledge at the time and in the community" as well as "common law, legislative enactments, and general customs in so far as they are likely to affect the conduct of the other or third persons" (*Restatement [Second] of Torts* § 290).

PUTTING IT INTO PRACTICE 5:3

1. Grant drives his car at high speeds on an icy road. Having lived in the tropics all his life, he is totally oblivious to the dangerousness of what he is doing and is shocked when he loses control of his car and careens into a parked vehicle. Has he behaved negligently?

2. Margaret detects an odor of gas in her basement and lights a match to look for the leak. She is unaware of the danger of explosion until she wakes up in the emergency room. Do her visitors at the time of the explosion have grounds to recover damages for the injuries they sustain?

3. A city ordinance requires trolley cars to stop at the near side of every boulevard crossing. Susan is following behind a trolley car and intends to pass between the trolley and the curb. As the trolley approaches the boulevard crossing, Susan speeds up to pass. As a visitor to the city, she is unaware of the ordinance and sees no evidence that the trolley is preparing to stop. When she is suddenly aware of the trolley stopping and a passenger stepping out of the car, she is going too fast to stop and runs over the trolley passenger. Is she negligent?

4. Frank invites Carole to ride his daughter's eleven-year-old show horse, "Blue." Carole tells Frank she is a novice rider, so Frank gives her some basic riding instructions before she mounts Blue, but does not explain how to mount, sit, use the reins, turn, stop, or dismount. Allison observes Carole as she rides Blue around the ring; Frank is riding another horse in the same ring. After about twenty-five minutes Carole brings Blue over to Allison to dismount and as she does she drags her right foot over Blue's rump and jabs her foot into his left side. Blue suddenly bolts, runs through an open gate, and knocks off Carole (who has since regained her seat) as he runs beneath a metal overhang. Carole sues. Frank argues that he used reasonable care in assisting Carole to ride and that it was unforeseeable that Blue, a previously gentle, predictable horse, would suddenly bolt. Do you agree?

Reasonable persons are assumed to possess knowledge of scientific and natural laws that is common to laypersons in the community. They are, for example, presumed to be aware of the poisonous qualities of certain animals, insects, drugs, and chemicals; to appreciate the explosive nature of certain compounds and dangerous potential of high-voltage power lines, and to anticipate basic weather phenomena (frigid weather in the Northeast in the winter and extremely hot temperatures in the deserts of the Southwest in the summer). Even if he has never been on a farm, the reasonable person is presumed to understand that stallions and bulls are potentially dangerous, that horses are likely to be frightened by certain objects and actions, and that even the most gentle of bitches may bite an intruding hand while she is nursing her pups. He should also be aware of the peculiarities and behavioral traits of particular groups of people. He should anticipate, for example, that children may behave recklessly and should take precautions when driving to prevent injury to them. He should be aware that foreign visitors and immigrants are likely not to speak English and should therefore realize that warnings written in English will not be adequate. Furthermore, the reasonable person is expected to conform to statutory law and judicial decisions and cannot claim ignorance of the law even if the standard of conduct required by the law contradicts the custom of the community. In short, ignorance of the law is no excuse under the reasonable-person standard.

DEFENDANTS WITH SPECIAL CHARACTERISTICS

Special allowances are not made for defendants who are emotionally unstable or of substandard intelligence. The *Restatement (Second) of Torts* maintains this position even for persons whose intelligence is so low that they are not aware that their conduct creates any danger. The majority rule is, however, at odds with the *Restatement* and does not impose liability where there is an extreme mental deficiency. An intoxicated person is held to the standard of a reasonable sober person (*Restatement [Second] of Torts* § 283C, cmt. d). For policy reasons a person who voluntarily consumes alcohol or becomes intoxicated, and thereby deliberately risks creating harm to others, cannot be absolved of liability simply because he lacks the physical and mental faculties of a sober person.

Even insane people are generally held to a reasonable-person standard, although some courts are beginning to deviate from that standard when the insane person is unable to understand or avoid the danger. Three policy considerations are used to justify this apparently harsh rule. First, the allowance of an insanity defense would lead to fraudulent claims of insanity in an effort to avoid liability. Second, when injury results from an interaction between two innocent persons, the one causing the injury should bear the consequences. Third, the potential of liability provides an incentive to the wards of the mentally incompetent to supervise their charges closely and to prevent them from harming others.

In considering the attributes of the reasonable person, the physical characteristics of the defendant are taken into consideration. A blind person, for example, is held to the standard of a reasonable blind person. Such a person may be expected to use a cane, a Seeing Eye dog, or some other form of assistance to make her way through town. If such a person fails to use any form of assistance and sues the city for injuries resulting from falling into a depression in the sidewalk, she may be precluded from recovering because of her own negligence.

This rule applies to known physical conditions. A defendant who suffers a heart attack while driving and has an accident will not be found negligent because he lost control of his car. If, however, he had had several previous heart attacks, he might be found to be negligent merely because he was driving a car (*Restatement [Second] of Torts* § 283C, cmt. c).

CHILDREN

Children are not held to the standard of care expected of an adult but instead are held to the standard of a "reasonable person of like age, intelligence, and experience under like circumstances" (*Restatement [Second] of Torts* § 283A). This is somewhat of a subjective standard because the intelligence and experience of the child, both of which are relative, are taken into consideration. Therefore, a ten-year-old child of above-average intelligence is held to a higher standard of conduct than a ten-year-old child of below-average intelligence.

Children are held to an adult standard when they engage in potentially dangerous activities that are

PUTTING IT INTO PRACTICE 5:4

1. A driver suddenly becomes convinced that God is taking control of her steering wheel, and as she nears a truck she accelerates "in order to become airborne because she knew she could fly because Batman does it." Will she be held liable for the injuries sustained by the truck driver?

2. A seventeen-year-old negligently shoots his minor companion while they are out deer hunting. To what standard of care should he be held?

3. A driver with a history of epilepsy, for which he has been successfully treated (seizure-free) for more than ten years, suffers an epileptic seizure and is involved in an accident. To what standard of care should he be held?

normally reserved for adults. A child who drives a car is held to the standard of care expected of a reasonable adult driver. The courts are split as far as the standard of care to be applied when children engage in dangerous activities that are not necessarily pursued only by adults. For example, should a child who goes hunting be held to the standard of care of a child or an adult? Some courts reason that because we can reasonably anticipate that children will engage in this activity, they should be held to a standard of care of other children. Others emphasize the inherent dangerousness of the activity and hold children to an adult standard.

LOCAL LINKS

How do the courts in your state deal with children who negligently engage in activities not necessarily reserved for adults, such as hunting?

EMERGENCIES

In addition to considering the age and unique characteristics of the defendant, the courts also look at the circumstances in which the defendant was operating. In an emergency, for example, people are not expected to act with the same rational and calm consideration that one would expect in a less stressful situation. But even in an emergency a defendant is expected to act reasonably, and if he does not, he can be found liable for his actions. For example, in the process of rendering emergency medical assistance, a person who takes no reasonable precautions in moving the victim from one position to another may be found negligent for any injuries she causes. A case that is illustrative (in content, not form) of the analysis employed by the courts in emergency situations is *Cordas v. Peerless Transportation Co.*, 27 N.Y.S.2d 198 (1941). The court's whimsical presentation of the facts makes this a particularly entertaining opinion to read.

CASE *Cordas v. Peerless Transportation Co.*
27 N.Y.S.2d 198 (N.Y. City Ct. 1941)

CARLIN, Justice.

This case presents the ordinary man—that problem child of the law—in a most bizarre setting. As a lowly chauffeur in defendant's employ he became in a trice the protagonist in a breath-bating drama with a denouement almost tragic. It appears that a man, whose identity it would be indelicate to divulge was feloniously relieved of his portable goods by two nondescript highwaymen—in an alley near 26th Street and Third Avenue, Manhattan; they induced him to relinquish his possessions by a strong argument ad hominem couched in the convincing cant of the criminal and pressed at the point of a most persuasive pistol. Laden with their loot, but not thereby impeded, they took an abrupt departure and he, shuffling off the coil of that discretion which enmeshed him in the alley, quickly gave chase through

(continues)

26th Street toward 2d Avenue, whither they were resorting "with expedition swift as thought" for most obvious reasons. Somewhere on that thoroughfare of escape they indulged the stratagem of separation ostensibly to disconcert their pursuer and allay the ardor of his pursuit. He then centered on for capture the man with the pistol whom he saw board defendant's taxicab, which quickly veered south toward 25th Street on 2d Avenue where he saw the chauffeur jump out while the cab, still in motion, continued toward 24th Street; after the chauffeur relieved himself of the cumbersome burden of his fare the latter also is said to have similarly departed from the cab before it reached 24th Street. The chauffeur's story is substantially the same except that he states that his uninvited guest boarded the cab at 25th Street while it was at a standstill waiting for a less colorful fare; that his "passenger" immediately advised him "to stand not upon the order of his going but to go at once" and added finality to his command by an appropriate gesture with a pistol addressed to his sacroiliac. The chauffeur in reluctant acquiescence proceeded about fifteen feet, when his hair, like unto the quills of the fretful porcupine, was made to stand on end by the hue and cry of the man despoiled accompanied by a clamorous concourse of the law-abiding which paced him as he ran; the concatenation of "stop thief," to which the patter of persistent feet did maddingly beat time, rang in his ears as the pursuing posse all the while gained on the receding cab with its quarry therein contained. The hold-up man sensing his insecurity suggested to the chauffeur that in the event there was the slightest lapse in obedience to his curt command that he, the chauffeur, would suffer the loss of his brains, a prospect as horrible to an humble chauffeur as it undoubtedly would be to one of the intelligentsia. The chauffeur apprehensive of certain dissolution from either Scylla, the pursuers, or Charybdis, the pursued, quickly threw his car out of first speed in which he was proceeding, pulled on the emergency, jammed on his brakes and, although he thinks the motor was still running, swung open the door to his left and jumped out of his car. He confesses that the only act that smacked of intelligence was that by which he jammed the brakes in order to throw off balance the hold-up man who was half-standing and half-sitting with his pistol menacingly poised. Thus abandoning his car and passenger the chauffeur sped toward 26th Street and then turned to look; he saw the cab proceeding south toward 24th Street where it mounted the sidewalk. The plaintiff-mother and her two infant children were there injured by the cab which, at the time, appeared to be also minus its passenger who, it appears, was apprehended in the cellar of a local hospital where he was pointed out to a police officer by a remnant of the posse, hereinbefore mentioned. He did not appear at the trial. The three aforesaid plaintiffs and the husband-father sue the defendant for damages predicating their respective causes of action upon the contention that the chauffeur was negligent in abandoning the cab under the aforesaid circumstances. Fortunately the injuries sustained were comparatively slight. . . . In *Steinbrenner v. M. W. Forney Co.* [cite omitted], it is said, "The test of actionable negligence is what reasonably prudent men would have done under the same circumstances"; *Connell v. New York Central & Hudson River Railroad Co.* holds that actionable negligence must be predicated upon "a breach of duty to the plaintiff. Negligence is 'not absolute or intrinsic,' but 'is always relevant to some circumstances of time, place or person.'" In slight paraphrase of the world's first bard it may be truly observed that the expedition of the chauffeur's violent love of his own security outran the pauser, reason, when he was suddenly confronted with unusual emergency which "took his reason prisoner." The learned attorney for the plaintiffs concedes that the chauffeur acted in an emergency but claims a right to recovery upon the following proposition taken verbatim from his brief: "It is respectfully submitted that the value of the interests of the public at large to be immune from being injured by a dangerous instrumentality such as a car unattended while in motion is very superior to the right of a driver of a motor vehicle to abandon same while it is in motion even when acting under the belief that his life is in danger and by abandoning same he will save his life." To hold thus under the facts adduced herein would be tantamount to a repeal by implication of the primal law of nature written in indelible characters upon the fleshy tablets of sentient creation by the Almighty Law-giver, "the supernal Judge who sits on high." There are those who stem the turbulent current for bubble fame, or who bridge the yawning chasm with a leap for the leap's sake or who "outstare the sternest eyes that look, outbrave the heart most daring on the earth, pluck the young sucking cubs from the she-bear, yea, mock the lion when he roars for prey" to win a fair lady and these are the admiration of the generality of men; but they are made of sterner stuff than the ordinary man upon whom the law places no duty of emulation. The law would indeed be fond if it imposed upon the ordinary man the obligation to so demean himself when suddenly confronted with a danger, not of his creation, disregarding the likelihood that such a contingency may darken the intellect and palsy the will of the common legion of the earth, the fraternity of ordinary men,—whose acts or omissions under certain conditions or circumstances make the yardstick by which the law measures culpability or innocence, negligence or

(continues)

care. If a person is placed in a sudden peril from which death might ensue, the law does not impel another to the rescue of the person endangered nor does it condemn him for his unmoral failure to rescue when he can; this is in recognition of the immutable law written in frail flesh. Returning to our chauffeur. If the philosophic Horatio and the martial companions of his watch were "distilled almost to jelly with the act of fear" when they beheld "in the dead vast and middle of the night" the disembodied spirit of Hamlet's father stalk majestically by "with a countenance more in sorrow than in anger" was not the chauffeur, though unacquainted with the example of these eminent men-at-arms, more amply justified in his fearsome reactions when he was more palpably confronted by a thing of flesh and blood bearing in its hand an engine of destruction which depended for its lethal purpose upon the quiver of a hair? When Macbeth was cross-examined by Macduff as to any reason he could advance for his sudden despatch of Duncan's grooms, he said in plausible answer "Who can be wise, amazed, temperate and furious, loyal and neutral, in a moment? No man." Macbeth did not by a "tricksy word" thereby stand justified as he criminally created the emergency from which he sought escape by indulgence in added felonies to divert suspicion to the innocent. However, his words may be wrested to the advantage of the defendant's chauffeur whose acts cannot be legally construed as the proximate cause of plaintiff's injuries, however regrettable, unless nature's first law is arbitrarily disregarded. * * * "The law presumes that *an act or omission done or neglected under the influence of pressing danger was done or neglected involuntarily*. It is there

said that this rule seems to be founded upon the maxim that self-preservation is the first law of nature, and that, where it is a question whether one of two men shall suffer, each is justified in doing the best he can for himself." *Laidlaw v. Sage.* (Italics ours.) *Kolanka v. Erie Railroad Co.* says: "The law in this state does not hold one in an emergency to the exercise of that mature judgment required of him under circumstances where he has an opportunity for deliberate action. He is not required to exercise unerring judgment, which would be expected of him, were he not confronted with an emergency requiring prompt action." The circumstances provide the foil by which the act is brought into relief to determine whether it is or is not negligent. If under normal circumstances an act is done which might be considered negligent it does not follow as a corollary that a similar act is negligent if performed by a person acting under an emergency, not of his own making, in which he suddenly is faced with a patent danger with a moment left to adopt a means of extrication. The chauffeur—the ordinary man in this case—acted in a split second in a most harrowing experience. To call him negligent would be to brand him coward; the court does not do so in spite of what those swaggering heroes, "whose valor plucks dead lions by the beard," may bluster to the contrary. The court is loathe to see the plaintiffs go without recovery even though their damages were slight, but cannot hold the defendant liable upon the facts adduced at the trial. Motions, upon which decision was reserved, to dismiss the complaint are granted with exceptions to plaintiffs. Judgment for defendant against plaintiffs dismissing their complaint upon the merits.

In some situations the reasonable person will be expected to anticipate the actions of others. A driver making her way down a residential street where children are playing will be expected to anticipate that children may run into the street. She will be expected to exercise special care to guard against their carelessness. A reasonable person is not, however, expected to anticipate the crimes or intentional torts of another unless her relationship with that person is such that she should reasonably anticipate such behavior.

CUSTOM

Custom may also be considered in determining reasonable care. Courts will look at the standard practices of a trade or community in assessing the reasonableness

of the defendant's conduct. Adherence to custom is persuasive evidence of the reasonableness of conduct but is not necessarily conclusive. It is possible, although not likely, that a court might conclude that an entire industry is negligent if it fails to adopt certain safety precautions.

PROFESSIONS

A defendant who possesses a higher degree of knowledge or skill as a result of training or experience will be held to a higher standard of care. Lawyers, doctors, accountants, and police officers, among others, are held to the standard of care commonly exercised by members in good standing of their profession (*Restatement [Second] of Torts* § 299A). A medical doctor who administers first aid to someone injured

NET NEWS

To read about the standard of care in medical malpractice cases, including a discussion of res ipsa loquitur and negligence per se, go to **http://www.lectlaw.com/** and enter "establishing medical standard of care" as your search term.

on the street is held to a higher standard of care than someone lacking that training. Professionals who have specialized in a particular area are held to a specialist's standard of care, which exceeds that of the minimal standard of care expected of other members of the profession.

The standard of care applied to professionals is an objective one. Therefore, the question in malpractice cases is whether the professional met the standard of care expected of members of the profession. Relative inexperience is not taken into consideration. Novices in the profession are held to the same standard of competence as more experienced members of the profession. We discuss malpractice in greater depth in Chapter 9.

NEGLIGENCE PER SE

In some cases reasonable conduct is established by statute. A statute mandating that freeway drivers are limited to speeds under 65 mph establishes a safety standard. A defendant who violates this statute and who injures someone as a result of this violation will be considered *negligent per se* ("negligent in itself") in most courts. This doctrine, as applied by the majority of the courts, requires that (1) the violated statute be applicable to the facts of the case, and (2) a causal link between the act constituting a violation of the statute and the plaintiff's injury be established (see Exhibit 5–3). In a few courts, however, a statutory violation is considered merely evidence of negligence and may be outweighed by other evidence of due care.

EXHIBIT 5–3 *Questions Relating to Negligence Per Se Cases*

NEGLIGENCE PER SE

- Is violated statute applicable to facts of case?
- Is plaintiff a member of a class protected by statute?
- Is act causing injury a violation of the statute?
- Is harm that occurred intended to be prevented by statute?

To prove negligence per se the plaintiff must first show that he is a member of the class of persons whom the statute was intended to protect. The plaintiff must also show that the statute was designed to protect against the kind of harm that was sustained.

LOCAL LINKS

How do the courts in your state treat evidence of a statutory violation?

The following case illustrates these two requirements: Plaintiffs were driving along a country dirt road when they approached an intersection. At the intersection they looked for cars, and when they saw none they entered the intersection; there they were hit by an oncoming car. The plaintiffs claimed that their view was obstructed by weeds growing in a ditch along the roadway. Pointing to a statute criminalizing the "shipping, selling, or permitting [of] growing of noxious weeds," they sued the county for negligence per se.

They argued that the county had violated the statute by permitting weeds to grow in the ditch. The court, however, held that the defendants were not negligent per se because the plaintiffs did not belong to the class of persons whom the statute was designed to protect. The statute, the court reasoned, was designed to protect farmers and ranchers from an infestation of weeds and was not designed to protect travelers on the highway (*Hidalgo v. Cochise County*, 13 Ariz. App. 27 [1970]). Note also that the harm the statute was intended to protect against was the spread of weeds, not accidents on the highways. The determination as to whether the type of harm that occurred was that anticipated by statute has been particularly problematic in cases involving keys left in cars. In such cases someone usually uses the keys to steal the car and ultimately becomes involved in an accident. The question then becomes whether the driver who left the keys in the car should be liable for the injuries caused by the person who stole the car. Plaintiffs in states having statutes that prohibit the leaving of keys in a car have argued negligence per se in these cases. If the purpose of the statute

"REASONABLE PERSON" DEFINED

It is impossible to travel anywhere or to travel for long in that confusing forest of learned judgments which constitutes the Common Law of England without encountering the Reasonable Man...The Reasonable Man is always thinking of others; prudence is his guide, and "Safety First," if I may borrow a contemporary catchword, is his rule of life. All solid virtues are his, save only that peculiar quality by which the affection of other men is won...While any given example of his behavior must command our admiration, which taken in the mass his acts create a very different set of impressions. He is one who invariably looks where he is going, and is careful to examine the immediate foreground before he executes a leap or a bound; who neither stargazes nor is lost in meditation when approaching trap doors or the margin of a dock; who records in every case upon the counterfoils of checks such ample details as are desirable, scrupulously substitutes the word "Order" for the word "Bearer," crosses the instrument "a/c Payee only" and registers the package in which it is dispatched; who never mounts a moving omnibus and does not alight from any car while the train is in motion; who investigates exhaustively the bona fides of every mendicant before distributing alms, and will inform himself of the history and habits of a dog before administering a caress; who believes no gossip, nor repeats it, without firm basis for believing it to be true; who never drives his ball till those in front of him have definitely vacated the putting-green which is his own objective; who never from one year's end to another makes an excessive demand upon his wife, his neighbors, his servants, his ox, or his ass...Devoid, in short, of any human weakness, with not one single saving vice, sans prejudice, procrastination, ill-nature, avarice, and absence of mind, as careful for his own safety as he is for that of others, this excellent but odious character stands like a monument in our courts of Justice, vainly appealing to his fellow-citizens to order their lives after his own example. (*Newman v. Maricopa County*, 808 P.2d 1253 [Ariz. Ct. App. 1991], quoting from A.P. Herbert, *Uncommon Law* [1955].)

is to prevent reckless driving by thieves, plaintiffs making this argument should prevail, but if there is some other purpose for the statute, the elements of negligence per se are not satisfied. Even if negligence per se cannot be proved, plaintiffs can cite statutory violations as evidence of negligence.

In some cases the statute in question is a criminal one. Some penal statutes specifically provide that their violation will result in civil liability, but ambiguity exists when no reference to civil liability is made. Under the majority rule and out of deference to the legislature, the courts will apply the criminal statutory standard to civil cases as a matter of law.

Defenses to Negligence Per Se

In rare instances courts have found an absolute duty to comply with a statute and have refused to accept even reasonable excuses for failure to comply. A defendant violating a statute prohibiting the sale of firearms to minors would likely be found negligent despite his good-faith argument that he believed the minor to be an adult.

For the most part, however, statutes are not deemed to impose an absolute duty of compliance. In some jurisdictions the violation of a statute is construed as setting forth a presumption of negligence, which the defendant can rebut by introducing evidence of reasonable care. Other courts treat a statutory violation as negligence per se but accept excuses for noncompliance. Under the *Restatement (Second) of Torts* "excuse" approach, violation of a statute is excused for the following reasons:

1. "the violation is reasonable because of the actor's incapacity"
2. "he neither knows nor should know of the occasion for compliance"
3. "he is unable after reasonable diligence or care to comply"
4. "he is confronted by an emergency not due to his own misconduct"
5. "compliance would involve a greater risk of harm to the actor or to others" (*Restatement [Second] of Torts* § 288A[2])

Even if negligence per se is established, the defendant can still assert the defenses of contributory negligence and assumption of risk so long as the statute does not impose an absolute duty on the defendant.

One might conclude from the foregoing discussion that compliance with a statute establishes that a defendant was not negligent. But that is not true. The trier of fact is always free to conclude that a reasonable person would have taken precautions beyond those mandated by statute. A reasonable person, for example, would be expected to drive below the speed limit on icy roads.

PUTTING IT INTO PRACTICE 5:5

1. A statute requires railroads to fence their tracks. The ABA railroad fails to fence its track; as a result two of a rancher's cows wander onto the track. One is killed by a train and the other is poisoned by weeds growing next to the track. The purpose of the statute is to prevent animals that stray onto the track from being hit. Is the railroad negligent per se?

2. A man holds himself out as being able to diagnose and treat disease, but he is in fact not licensed to practice medicine as required by the New York Public Health Law. He gives a woman chiropractic treatment, after which she suffers paralysis, allegedly resulting from the treatment. Is the man negligent per se?

3. Marjorie, an employee, and her friend Helena, who is visiting Marjorie at her workplace, are both injured when an elevator falls because of the lack of a safety device. A statute requires all factory elevators to have a particular safety device for the express purpose of protecting employees from injury. Can Marjorie and Helena rely on this statute to establish the standard of care?

4. Harold is shot six times when police officers burst into his house in an effort to serve a search warrant. The officers claim that they acted in self-defense when Harold picked up a rifle, but Harold claims he picked up the rifle because the officers startled him from his sleep when they burst into his house unannounced and without identifying themselves.

    At trial the police argue that Harold is negligent per se if the jury finds he violated the criminal statutes regarding assault (whose definition is similar to that of civil assault). Their reasoning is that the plaintiff's negligent conduct in assaulting the police caused the police to shoot him and that, therefore, he was injured as a result of his own negligent conduct. Do you think the assault statute was intended to protect the police or Harold? In other words, who was intended to be protected from the harm of assaultive behavior, Harold or the police?

CASE

Sanders v. Acclaim Entertainment, Inc.
188 F.Supp.2d 1264 (D. Colo. 2002)

BABCOCK, Chief Judge.

I. FACTS

Plaintiffs allege that Columbine High School (Columbine) students Dylan Klebold and/or Eric Harris, both approximately 17 years of age, were co-conspirators in a plot and scheme to assault, terrorize and kill Columbine teachers and students. On April 20, 1999 at approximately 11:20 a.m., Klebold and Harris approached the school armed with multiple guns and other "weapons of destruction" including explosive devices. See Amended C/O, § 3-4.

After shooting at people outside the school, the pair entered the school building and continued their deadly assault inside Columbine. Twelve students and teacher William Sanders were killed. Dozens of others were injured. Id. at § 4.

In the aftermath of the massacre the police allegedly learned that Harris and Klebold were avid, fanatical and excessive consumers of violent...video games...[and] consumers of movies containing obscenity, obscenity for minors, pornography, sexual violence, and/or violence. Amended C/O §§ 6-7. One movie the pair viewed was

(continues)

"The Basketball Diaries" in which "a student massacres his classmates with a shotgun." Amended C/O § 7.

According to Plaintiffs, "but for the actions of the Video Game Defendants and the Movie Defendants, in conjunction with the acts of the other defendants herein, the multiple killings at Columbine High School would not have occurred." Id. at §§ 17, 32. Based on the foregoing, Plaintiffs filed this action on April 19, 2001.

II. CLAIMS AND DEFENDANTS
Plaintiffs bring the following claims against Defendants:

1. Claim One for negligence and strict liability against Defendants Time Warner, Palm Pictures, Island Pictures, New Line Cinema and Polygram;

2. Claim Two for negligence and strict liability against Defendants Acclaim Entertainment, Inc., Activision, Inc., Apogee Software, Inc., Atari Corporation, Capcom Entertainment, Inc., EIDOS Interactive; ID Software, Inc., Infogrames, Inc., f/k/a GT Interactive Software Corporation, Interplay Entertainment Corp., Midway Home Entertainment, Nintendo of America, Sega of America, Inc., and Sony Computer Entertainment America Inc.; Square Soft, *1269 Inc. d/b/a Square USA, Inc. and Virgin Entertainment Group, Inc.,

3. Claim Three for negligence and strict liability against Defendants Meow Media, Inc. d/b/a www.persiankitty.com and Network Authentication Systems, Inc. d/b/a www.adultkey.com and www.porntech.com; and

4. RICO activity by Defendants Meow Media, Inc. d/b/a www.persiankitty.com and Network Authentication Systems, Inc. d/b/a www.adultkey.com and www.porntech.com.

III. CLAIMS AND ALLEGATIONS
A. Claim One for Negligence and Strict Liability
Plaintiffs sue Defendants Time Warner, Palm Pictures, Island Pictures, New Line Cinema, and Polygram as the makers and distributors of "The Basketball Diaries." Defendants Time Warner and Palm Pictures (Movie Defendants) filed Rule 12(b)(6) motions which I resolve in this Memorandum Opinion and Order.

According to Plaintiffs, in "The Basketball Diaries, the protagonist inexplicably guns down his teacher and some of his classmates in cold blood, among other acts of gratuitous violence." Amended C/O § 11. Purportedly, this had the effect of "harmfully influencing impressionable minors such as Harris and Klebold and of thereby causing the shootings." Id. at § 12.

B. Claim Two for Negligence and Strict Liability
Plaintiffs sue Defendants Acclaim Entertainment, Inc. (Mortal Kombat and Mortal Kombat II), Activision,

Inc. (Wolfenstein, Mech Warrior, Mech Warrior 2, and Nightmare Creatures), Apogee Software, Inc. (Wolfenstein and Doom), Atari Corporation (Doom), Capcom Entertainment, Inc. (Resident Evil), EIDOS Interactive (Final Fantasy), ID Software, Inc. (Quake and Doom), Infogrames, Inc. f/k/a GT Interactive Software Corp. (Doom), Interplay Entertainment Corp., (Redneck Rampage), Midway Home Entertainment (Quake and Doom), Nintendo of America (Nightmare Creatures), Sega of America, Inc. (Quake), Sony Computer Entertainment America (Final Fantasy), Square Soft, Inc. d/b/a Square USA, Inc. (Final Fantasy) and Virgin Entertainment Group, Inc. (Resident Evil) for manufacturing and/or supplying the designated violent video games allegedly frequently played by Harris and Klebold. See Am C/O §§ 20-21.

Video Game Defendants Acclaim Entertainment, Inc., Activision, Inc., Capcom Entertainment, Inc., EIDOS Interactive, ID Software, Inc., Infogrames, Inc. f/k/a GT Interactive Software Corp., Interplay Entertainment Corp., Midway Home Entertainment, Nintendo of America, Sony Computer Entertainment America, Inc., filed Rule 12(b)(6) motions addressed in this Memorandum Opinion and Order. Plaintiffs allege that the Video Game Defendants manufactured and/or supplied to Harris and Klebold these video games which made violence pleasurable and attractive and disconnected the violence from the natural consequences thereof, thereby causing Harris and Klebold to act out the violence…[and] trained [them] how to point and shoot a gun effectively without teaching either of them any of the constraints, responsibilities, or consequences necessary to inhibit such an extremely dangerous killing capacity. Amended C/O §§ 25-25.

C. Claim Three for Negligence and Strict Liability and Claim Four for RICO Activity
Plaintiffs bring Claims Three and Four against Defendants Meow Media, Inc. *1270 d/b/a www.persiankitty.com and Network Authentication Systems, Inc. d/b/a www.adultkey.com and www.porntech.com. (Internet Defendants). No Rule 12(b)(6) motions have been filed by the Internet Defendants. Consequently, I do not address Claims Three or Four in this Memorandum Opinion and Order.

D. Allegations Common to the Movie and Video Game Defendants
The negligence and strict products liability Claims One and Two against the Movie and Video Game Defendants contain the following common allegations:

1. Defendants knew that copycat violence would result from the use of their products and materials. See Amended C/O §§ 16(a), 29(b);

(continues)

2. Defendants knew that their products and materials created an unreasonable risk of harm because minors would be influenced by the effect of their products and materials and then would cause harm. See Amended C/O §§ 16(k), 29(h);

3. Defendants knew or should have known that their products and materials were in an unreasonably defective condition and likely to be dangerous for the use for which they were supplied. See Amended C/O §§ 16(v), 29(v); and

4. Defendants failed to exercise reasonable care to inform consumers of the dangerous condition of their products and materials or of the facts which made their products and materials likely to be dangerous. See Amended C/O §§ 16(i), 29(k).

5. Scientific research shows that children who witness acts of violence often tend to act more violently themselves and to sometimes recreate those violent acts. See Amended C/O § 13 (Movie Defendants); and

6. Massive volumes of scientific research show that children who witness acts of violence and/or who are interactively involved with creating violence or violent images often act more violently themselves and sometimes recreate the violence to which they have been exposed. See Amended C/O § 24 (Video Game Defendants).

IV. FED.R.CIV.P. 12(b)(6)

Under Rule 12(b)(6), a district court may dismiss a complaint for failure to state a claim upon which relief can be granted if it appears beyond doubt that the plaintiff can prove no set of facts in support of his claim which would entitle him to relief. *Conley v. Gibson*, 355 U.S. 41, 45-46, 78 S.Ct. 99, 2 L.Ed.2d 80 (1957). If the plaintiff has pleaded facts that would support a legally cognizable claim for relief, a motion to dismiss should be denied. Id. I accept as true all well-pleaded facts, as distinguished from conclusory allegations, and view those facts in the light most favorable to the nonmoving party. *Maher v. Durango Metals*, 144 F.3d 1302, 1304 (10th Cir.1998). All reasonable inferences must be construed in the plaintiff's favor. See *Dill v. City of Edmond*, 155 F.3d 1193, 1201 (10th Cir.1998). Id.

Fed.R.Civ.P. 12(b) provides that if matters outside the complaint are presented to and not excluded by the court, it should treat the motion to dismiss as a summary judgment motion. Fed.R.Civ.P. 12(b); *Carter v. Stanton*, 405 U.S. 669, 671, 92 S.Ct. 1232, 31 L.Ed.2d 569 (1972); *Foremaster v. St. George*, 882 F.2d 1485, 1491 (10th Cir.1989). Failure to convert a motion to dismiss so postured to a motion for summary judgment

under Fed.R.Civ.P. 56 is reversible error. *Miller v. Glanz*, 948 F.2d 1562, 1565 (10th Cir.1991).

Several Video Game Defendants and Movie Defendant Palm Pictures attached*1271 exhibits to briefs in support of their Rule 12(b)(6) motions. These exhibits include the complaint filed in *James v. Meow Media, Inc.*, 90 F.Supp.2d 798 (W.D.Ky.2000), a copy of a hearing transcript, copies of several opinions, and portions of the *Restatement of (Third) Torts* relied on in their briefs by Defendants. I have not read or relied on the *James v. Meow Media* complaint or on the hearing transcript. Defendants' exhibits containing copies of case law and Restatement (Third) of Torts merely supplement and inform my legal research. Also, Plaintiffs attached a letter to its response briefs to Defendants ID Software's and Midway Home Entertainment's Fed.R.Civ.P. 12(b)(6) opening briefs. I have not read or relied on the content of the attached letter. Thus, I need not treat the motions to dismiss as summary judgment motions. See Fed.R.Civ.P. 12(b); *Carter v. Stanton*, 405 U.S. at 671, 92 S.Ct. 1232; Foremaster, 882 F.2d at 1491. The Rule 12(b)(6) motions, briefs in support and briefs in opposition were filed before Plaintiffs filed their Amended Complaint as a matter of right. After careful review I conclude that further briefing is unnecessary. The motions and briefs before me can be fully applied to and resolved in light of the Amended Complaint.

V. CLAIMS ANALYSIS
A. Negligence

Plaintiffs allege negligence in Claim One against the Movie Defendants and in Claim Two against the Video Game Defendants. Under Colorado law, to recover for the negligent conduct of another, a plaintiff must establish: 1) the existence of a legal duty owed to the plaintiff by the defendant; 2) breach of that duty; 3) injury to the plaintiff; and 4) actual and proximate causation. *Leake v. Cain*, 720 P.2d 152, 155 (Colo.1986).

1. Duty

"The court determines, as a matter of law, the existence and scope of [any] duty...." *Metropolitan Gas Repair Serv., Inc. v. Kulik*, 621 P.2d 313, 317 (Colo.1980). See *Perreira v. Colorado*, 768 P.2d 1198, 1208 (Colo.1989). If the law imposes no duty of care under the circumstances, a negligence claim cannot be sustained even though injury may have occurred. *University of Denver v. Whitlock*, 744 P.2d 54 (Colo.1987).

In resolving the threshold legal question whether the Video Game and Movie Defendants have a cognizable duty to the Plaintiffs, I consider: 1) foreseeability of the injury or harm that occurred; 2) the social utility of

(continues)

Defendants' conduct; 3) the magnitude of the burden of guarding against the injury or harm; and 4) the consequences of placing the burden on the Defendants. See *Bailey v. Huggins Diagnostic & Rehabilitation Center*, 952 P.2d 768 (Colo.App.1997), cert. denied, (Colo.1998); *Smith v. City & County of Denver*, 726 P.2d 1125, 1127 (Colo.1986). No single factor is controlling. Whitlock, 744 P.2d at 57.

The question whether a duty should be imposed in a particular case is "essentially one of fairness under contemporary standards-whether reasonable persons would recognize a duty and agree that it exists." *Taco Bell, Inc. v. Lannon*, 744 P.2d 43, 46 (Colo.1987). Generally, a person does not have a duty to prevent a third person from harming another absent special circumstances warranting imposition of such a duty. See *Davenport v. Community Corrections*, 962 P.2d 963, 967 (Colo.1998), cert. denied, 526 U.S. 1068, 119 S.Ct. 1462, 143 L.Ed.2d 547 (1999).

a. Foreseeability
The Colorado Supreme Court teaches that foreseeability is "based on common sense *1272 perceptions of the risks created by various conditions and circumstances and includes whatever is likely enough in the setting of modern life that a reasonably thoughtful person would take account of it in guiding practical conduct." *Perreira*, 768 P.2d at 1209.

Generally, under Colorado law a person has no responsibility to foresee intentional violent acts by others. See *Walcott v. Total Petroleum, Inc.*, 964 P.2d 609, 612 (Colo.App.1998), cert. denied, (Colo.1999) (Gas station owner could not reasonably foresee that a purchaser would intentionally throw gasoline on a victim and set the victim on fire); see also *Solano v. Goff*, 985 P.2d 53, 54-55 (Colo.App.), cert. denied, (Colo.1999) (a murder committed by an escaped inmate who had not committed any prior violent crimes was not foreseeable by the sheriff).

In the circumstances alleged here, the Video Game and Movie Defendants likewise had no reason to suppose that Harris and Klebold would decide to murder or injure their fellow classmates and teachers. Plaintiffs do not allege that these Defendants had any knowledge of Harris' and Klebold's identities, let alone their violent proclivities. Nor, for that matter, did the Video Game and Movie Defendants have any reason to believe that a shooting spree was a likely or probable consequence of exposure to their movie or video games. At most, based on Plaintiffs' allegations that children who witness acts of violence and/or who interactively involved with creating violence or violent images often act more violently themselves and sometimes recreate the violence, see Amended C/O § 24, these Defendants might have

speculated that their motion picture or video games had the potential to stimulate an idiosyncratic reaction in the mind of some disturbed individuals. A speculative possibility, however, is not enough to create a legal duty. See *Davenport*, 962 P.2d at 968 ("While it is foreseeable that reintroducing convicted criminals into the community will result in some aberrant behavior, the dangers associated with community corrections in general are insufficient to establish the requisite foreseeability needed to impose a duty of care [on community corrections facility]").

Although other courts have addressed this question, the Colorado courts have not had the occasion to consider foreseeability in the similar circumstances alleged here. Applying analogous foreseeability principles, two federal courts have rejected imposition of any such duty on video game makers and movie producers or their distributors. In *Watters v. TSR, Inc.*, 904 F.2d 378 (6th Cir.1990), the Sixth Circuit held that a game manufacturer did not have any duty under Kentucky tort law to anticipate and prevent the suicide of a disturbed player because such idiosyncratic reactions are not legally foreseeable. The Court held that to impose liability in such circumstances "would be to stretch the concept of foreseeability...to lengths that would deprive them of all normal meaning." Id. at 381. More recently, in *James v. Meow Media, Inc.*, 90 F.Supp.2d 798, the Court dismissed Plaintiffs' complaint asserting virtually identical claims filed by Plaintiffs in this case. *James v. Meow Media, Inc.* involved a student shooting at a Kentucky high school during which three students were killed and several others seriously injured. The Court accepted as true, as do I, the identical allegations in this case that: 1) the shooter[s] viewed "The Basketball Diaries" film; 2) were "avid consumer[s]" of video games; and 3) were influenced by the film and video games. Stating that "[n]othing Defendants did or failed to do could have been reasonably foreseen as a cause of injury," the Court held that reasonable people could not conclude*1273 that the shooter's exposure to video games and the movie made the shooter's actions foreseeable to the video game makers and the movie producers and distributers. See id. at 804, 806.

Courts around the country have rejected similar claims brought against media or entertainment defendants. In *Zamora v. Columbia Broadcasting System*, 480 F.Supp. 199 (S.D.Fla.1979), the Court held that it was not foreseeable to three television networks that a teenager would shoot and kill his neighbor after viewing comparable violence on television over a ten year period. Plaintiff alleged also that watching television had desensitized the teenager to violence and caused

(continues)

him to develop a sociopathic personality. In granting the defendants' motion to dismiss, the Zamora Court noted that the three major networks are charged with anticipating: 1) the minor's alleged voracious intake of television violence; 2) his parents' apparent acquiescence in his television viewing, presumably without recognition of any problem; and 3) that Zamora would respond with a violent criminal act. See id. at 202. Based in part on the lack of foreseeability, the Court declined to "create such a wide expansion in the law of torts." Id. at 203. See also *Brandt v. Weather Channel, Inc.*, 42 F.Supp.2d 1344, 1345-46 (S.D.Fla.1999), aff'd, 204 F.3d 1123 (11th Cir.1999) (rejecting "novel and unprecedented expansion of...tort law [ ] to impose on a television broadcaster of weather forecasts" a duty to viewer of forecast who drowned when unpredicted adverse weather conditions caused him to be thrown from a fishing boat); *Davidson v. Time Warner. Inc.*, 1997 WL 405907 *13 (S.D.Tex.1997) (rejecting claim that "rap" song caused listener to commit murder because murder "was an irrational and illegal act," the defendants had no duty "to foresee and plan against such conduct"); *McCollum v. CBS, Inc.* 202 Cal.App.3d 989, 996, 1005, 249 Cal.Rptr. 187 (1988) (dismissing claim against defendants who created and disseminated a song called "Suicide Solution" and who allegedly knew or should have known the song might influence susceptible individuals because decedent's suicide was unforeseeable); *Way v. Boy Scouts of America*, 856 S.W.2d 230, 236, 239 (Tex.App.Dallas 1993) (holding decedent's fatal experimentation with gun was not reasonably foreseeable consequence of publishing a shooting sports supplement); *Sakon v. Pepsico, Inc.*, 553 So.2d 163, 166 (Fla.1989) (concluding, at pleadings stage, that young viewer's injury, which allegedly was inspired by defendant's television advertisement depicting dangerous activity, was not foreseeable consequence of advertisement, even though advertisement targeted audience of young viewers).

I find persuasive the reasoning set out in these cases. Consequently, I conclude under similar Colorado tort law, there is no basis for determining that violence would be considered the likely consequence of exposure to video games or movies. This factor weighs heavily against imposing a duty on the Movie and Video Game Defendants.

b. Social Utility of Defendants' Conduct
Creating and distributing works of imagination, whether in the form of video games, movies, television, books, visual art, or song, is an integral component of a society dedicated to the principle of free expression. See U.S. CONST., amend. 1; COLO. CONST., art. 11, § 10 ("[n]o law shall be passed impairing the freedom of speech [and] that every person shall be free to speak,

write or publish whatever he will on any subject"); see also U.S. CONST. art. I, § 8 (giving Congress the power to "promote the Progress of Science and useful Arts, by securing for limited Times to Authors and Inventors the exclusive*1274 Right to their respective Writings and Discoveries."). Accordingly, the creation of such works significantly contributes to social utility. See. e.g., *Joseph Burstyn, Inc. v. Wilson*, 343 U.S. 495, 72 S.Ct. 777, 96 L.Ed. 1098 (1952) (recognizing that movies are a significant medium for the communication of ideas because "[t]hey may affect public attitudes and behavior in a variety of ways, ranging from direct espousal of a political or social doctrine to the subtle shaping of thought which characterizes all artistic expression," and that movies are an important "organ of public opinion."). Id. at 501, 72 S.Ct. 777.

Plaintiffs' characterization of the Video Game and Movie Defendants' creative works as "violent" does not alter the social utility analysis. In the context of ordering entry of a preliminary injunction against a city ordinance that limited minors' access to violent video games, the Seventh Circuit observed, "[v]iolence has always been and remains a central interest of humankind and a recurrent, even obsessive theme of culture both high and low." *American Amusement Mach. Ass'n v. Kendrick*, 244 F.3d 572, 577 (7th Cir.2001), cert. denied, 534 U.S. 994, 122 S.Ct. 462, 151 L.Ed.2d 379 (2001). Indeed, "[c]lassic literature and art, and not merely today's popular culture, are saturated with graphic scenes of violence, whether narrated or pictorial." Id. at 575. Moreover, the Kendrick Court acknowledged that video games that include pictorial representations of violence are "stories" and contain "age-old themes of literature." Id. at 577-78. The Court flatly rejected the notion that society is better served by insulating the vulnerable from exposure to such images:

To shield children...from exposure to violent descriptions and images would not only be quixotic, but deforming; it would leave them unequipped to cope with the world as we know it. Id. at 577.

Setting aside any personal distaste, as I must, it is manifest that there is social utility in expressive and imaginative forms of entertainment even if they contain violence. See *Kendrick*, 244 F.3d at 577. Hence, the social utility factor weighs heavily against imposing a duty against the Video Game and Movie Defendants.

c. and d. Magnitude of the Burden of Guarding against Injury or Harm and Consequences of Placing the Burden on the Defendant

In *Bailey*, 952 P.2d at 772-73, the Colorado Court of Appeals analyzed the question of tort law duty where imposition of such a duty would seriously encroach

(continues)

upon First Amendment values. There, the author of a book appeared on a television program to discuss his controversial views about a particular dental procedure. The plaintiff followed his advice and was injured. In the resulting lawsuit, the Court held that as a general rule, "an author or interviewee on a public television program owes [no] legal duty of due care to those members of the public who may read the book or view the program." Id. at 772. Furthermore, the Court expressed serious doubts about the foreseeability of the harm. See id. at 772-73. The Court then explained that even if the harms were foreseeable, the First Amendment values at stake counseled against imposing a tort duty based on the contents of an author's ideas. See id. at 773.

Colorado courts have repeatedly rejected efforts to impose overly burdensome and impractical obligations on defendants, including the obligation to identify potential dangers. This is especially so where those obligations would interfere with the social utility of a defendant's conduct or *1275 other important societal values. See e.g., *Davenport*, 962 P.2d at 969 (rejecting duty on community corrections program to screen out offenders posing a threat to the public and to restrict offenders' community access where such measures would make the program the "insurer of its residents" and would subvert the effectiveness of the program). See also *Observatory Corp. v. Daly*, 780 P.2d 462, 469 (Colo.1989) (rejecting imposition of a duty on tavern owners to all persons on its premises because "[t]o impose such a duty would be tantamount to requiring a tavern employee to divine future violence on the part of a tavern patron notwithstanding the absence of any objective evidence indicating that the patron constituted an unreasonable risk to the safety of others," thereby making the tavern owner a "virtual insurer of the safety of all persons").

Given the First Amendment values at stake, the magnitude of the burden that Plaintiffs seek to impose on the Video Game and Movie Defendants is daunting. Furthermore, the practical consequences of such liability are unworkable. Plaintiffs would essentially obligate these Defendants, indeed all speakers, to anticipate and prevent the idiosyncratic, violent reactions of unidentified, vulnerable individuals to their creative works. As the Sixth Circuit recognized in *Watters*:

The defendant cannot be faulted, obviously, for putting its game on the market without attempting to ascertain the mental condition of each and every prospective player. The only practicable way of insuring that the game could never reach a "mentally fragile" individual would be to refrain from selling it at all.

Id. at 381; *McCollum*, 202 Cal.App.3d 989, 249 Cal. Rptr. 187. ("[I]t is simply not acceptable to a free and democratic society to impose a duty upon performing artists to limit and restrict their creativity in order to avoid the dissemination of ideas in artistic speech which may adversely affect emotionally troubled individuals.") Id. at 1005-06, 249 Cal.Rptr. 187; *Zamora*, 480 F.Supp. at 202 (recognizing the "impositions pregnant" in charging television networks with the duty of anticipating minors' criminal response to television programs). Because Plaintiffs' legal theory would effectively compel Defendants not to market their works and, thus, refrain from expressing the ideas contained in those works, the burden imposed would be immense and the consequences dire for a free and open society.

In this case, Plaintiffs do not allege that the Video Game and Movie Defendants illegally produced or distributed the movie and video games Harris and Klebold allegedly viewed or played. Finding that these Defendants owed Plaintiffs a duty of care would burden these Defendants' First Amendment rights to freedom of expression. These considerations compel the conclusion that makers of works of imagination including video games and movies may not be held liable in tort based merely on the content or ideas expressed in their creative works. Placing a duty of care on Defendants in the circumstances alleged would chill their rights of free expression. Therefore, these factors also weigh heavily against imposing a duty on Defendants.

All four factors weigh heavily against imposing a duty of care on Defendants. Consequently, I hold that the Video Game and Movie Defendants owed no duty to Plaintiffs as a matter of law. Thus, the Video Game and Movie Defendants are entitled to Rule 12(b)(6) dismissal of Plaintiffs' negligence claims.

2. Causation

Even assuming a duty, the Video Game and Movie Defendants argue that they *1276 were not the legal cause of Plaintiffs' injuries. I agree.

To prevail on their negligence claim, Plaintiffs must show that Defendants' tortious conduct proximately caused Mr. Sanders' death. See *Leake*, 720 P.2d at 155. "[Proximate cause] is the cause without which the claimed injury would not have been sustained." *City of Aurora v. Loveless*, 639 P.2d 1061, 1063 (Colo.1981). In Colorado, causation is generally a question of fact for a jury. But a court may decide the issue as a matter of law where the alleged chain of causation is too attenuated to impose liability. See *Largo Corp. v. Crespin*, 727 P.2d 1098, 1103 (Colo.1986); *Smith v. State Compensation Ins. Fund*, 749 P.2d 462, 464 (Colo.App. 1987). Here, proximate cause requires that Defendants' conduct produced Mr. Sanders' death "in the natural

(continues)

and probable sequence of things." See *Loveless,* 639 P.2d at 1063; *Schneider v. Midtown Motor Co.,* 854 P.2d 1322 (Colo.App.1992).

Where the circumstances make it likely that a defendant's negligence will result in injuries to others and where this negligence is a substantial factor in causing the injuries sustained, proximate causation is satisfied. The intervening or superseding act of a third party, in this case Harris and Klebold, including a third-party's intentionally tortious or criminal conduct does not absolve a defendant from responsibility if the third-party's conduct is reasonably and generally foreseeable. See *Ekberg v. Greene,* 196 Colo. 494, 496-97, 588 P.2d 375, 376-77(1978).

It is undisputed that Harris and Klebold murdered or injured the Columbine victims including Mr. Sanders. The issue is whether Harris' and Klebold's intentional criminal acts constitute a superseding cause of the harm inflicted by them, thus relieving the Movie and Video Game Defendants' of liability.

A superseding cause exists when: 1) an extraordinary and unforeseeable act intervenes between a defendant's original tortious act and the injury or harm sustained by plaintiffs and inflicted by a third party; and 2) the original tortious act is itself capable of bringing about the injury. Just as foreseeability is central to finding that a duty is owed, it is also "the touchstone of proximate cause" and of the superseding cause doctrine. *Walcott,* 964 P.2d 609; see also *Smith,* 749 P.2d at 462-63; *Ekberg,* 588 P.2d at 376. Moreover, a superseding cause relieves the original actor of liability when "the harm is intentionally caused by a third person and is not within the scope of the risk created by the actor's conduct." *Webb v. Dessert Seed Co.,* 718 P.2d 1057, 1062-63 (Colo.1986) (quoting *Restatement (Second) of Torts* § 442B).

I hold in this case that Harris' and Klebold's intentional violent acts were the superseding cause of Mr. Sanders' death. Moreover, as I have determined, their acts were not foreseeable. Their criminal acts, therefore, were not within the scope of any risk purportedly created by Defendants. In this case as in *James v. Meow Media, Inc.,* 90 F.Supp.2d at 806-08, the school shooting was not a normal response to dissemination of movies and videos.

I conclude as a matter of law that no reasonable jury could find that the Video Game and Movie Defendants' conduct resulted in Mr. Sanders' death in "the natural and probable sequence of events." See *Loveless,* 639 P.2d at 1063. Therefore, Defendants were not a proximate cause of Mr. Sanders' injuries. Defendants are entitled to Rule 12(b)(6) dismissal as to the negligence claims in Claims One and Two.

B. Strict Liability

Plaintiffs also assert strict liability in Claims One and Two. Plaintiffs allege that *1277 the Movie and Video Game Defendants produced and distributed their "products" in "a defective . . . and unreasonably dangerous condition." See Amended C/O §§ 16(v), 29(v); *Restatement (Second) of Torts* § 402A.

Plaintiffs allege that these Defendants manufactured and/or supplied to Harris and Klebold video games:

[that] trained Harris and Klebold how to point and shoot a gun effectively without teaching either of them any of the constraints, responsibilities or consequences necessary to inhibit such an extremely dangerous killing capacity.

Amended C/O §§ 25-26.

There is no allegation that anyone was injured while Harris and Klebold actually played the video games or watched "The Basketball Diaries." The actual use of the movie and video games, then, did not result in any injury. Rather, Plaintiffs contend that Mr. Sanders' death was caused by the way Harris and Klebold interpreted and reacted to the messages contained in the movie and the video games. So, any alleged defect stems from the intangible thoughts, ideas and messages contained within the movie and video games but not their tangible physical characteristics.

To recover on a theory of strict products liability under Colorado law, Plaintiffs must establish that the: 1) products are in a defective condition unreasonably dangerous to the user or consumer; 2) products were expected to and did reach Harris and Klebold without substantial change in the condition in which they were sold; 3) alleged defects caused Mr. Sanders' death; 4) Video Game and Movie Defendants sold the product and are engaged in the business of selling products; and 5) Plaintiffs sustained damages as a result of the Video Game and Movie Defendants' acts. See *Barton v. Adams Rental,* 938 P.2d 532, 536-37 (Colo.1997). This strict liability theory requires the existence of a "product" within the meaning of the law. *St. Luke's Hospital, v. Schmaltz,* 188 Colo. 353, 358, 534 P.2d 781, 783–84 (1975). The threshold question is whether Mr. Sanders' death was caused by a "product." See *Hidalgo v. Fagen, Inc.,* 206 F.3d 1013, 1018 (10th Cir.2000) citing *Schmaltz,* 534 P.2d at 784.

1. Definition of Product

Colorado's products liability statute does not define the term "product." See § 13-21-401, C.R.S. Section 402A of the *Restatement (Second) of Torts,* adopted by the Colorado courts, see e.g., *Camacho v. Honda Motor Co.,* 741 P.2d 1240, 1244 (Colo.1987), also does not define "product." As a result, whether something is a "product" is a question of law for the

(continues)

Court to answer. *Smith v. Home Light & Power Co.*, 695 P.2d 788, 789-90 (Colo.App.1984). Therefore, as an initial matter I must determine whether thoughts, images, ideas, and messages contained in movies and video games constitute "products" for purposes of strict products liability.

Colorado courts have not yet considered whether thoughts, images, ideas, and messages are "products" pursuant to the strict liability doctrine. Significantly, however, in considering whether to recognize a new tort recovery theory, the Colorado courts give great weight to the theory's impact on free expression. See *Bailey*, 952 P.2d 768. (dentist did not owe duty of care to patients with respect to statements made on television program and in book in light of free speech implications).

To aid my anticipation as to how Colorado courts would resolve this question, I look to other jurisdictions which have addressed whether the content of video games and movies is a "product" for purposes of determining strict liability. In *Watters*, the Court reviewed existing precedents *1278 and concluded, "[a]s far as we have been able to ascertain,…the doctrine of strict liability has never been extended to words or pictures. Other courts have looked in vain for decisions so expanding the scope of the strict liability doctrine." Id. at 381. For this reason, the Watters Court rejected plaintiff's contention that the video game defendant was strictly liable for causing her son, who had repeatedly played defendant's fantasy adventure game, to commit suicide. Id. Based in part on Watters' reasoning, the *James v. Meow Media, Inc.* Court also rejected as a matter of law the plaintiffs' claims, identical to the claims asserted in this case, that The Basketball Diaries and the video games were "products" for purposes of the strict liability doctrine. See *James v. Meow Media, Inc.*, 90 F.Supp.2d at 811.

Plaintiffs argue that "intangibles" such as images, thoughts, ideas, and messages are products and "subject to strict liability [when] the 'intangibles' are sold to and consumed by the public." Plaintiffs rely on *Comshare, Inc. v. United States*, 27 F.3d 1142 (6th Cir.1994) and *Advent Systems Ltd. v. Unisys Corp.*, 925 F.2d 670 (3d Cir.1991). These cases are distinguishable.

In Comshare, a computer software company sued the government to obtain an income tax refund because the company had spent millions of dollars purchasing computer program source codes but had not been given a tangible property investment tax credit. See id. The Sixth Circuit held that Comshare was entitled to the tangible property tax credit because "the intangible information on Comshare's master source code tapes and discs could not exist in usable form without the tangible

medium." Id. at 1149. In Advent Systems, a commercial transactions case, the Third Circuit held that once a computer program is downloaded onto a diskette, it becomes a "good" under the Uniform Commercial Code. See id. at 675.

Contrary to Plaintiffs' analysis, these holdings are inapposite because they do not discuss strict liability theories and are unrelated to products liability law. While computer source codes and programs may be construed as "tangible property" for tax purposes and as "goods" for commercial purposes, these classifications do not establish that intangible thoughts, ideas, and messages contained in computer video games or movies should be treated as products for purposes of strict liability.

Plaintiffs fail to appreciate the critical distinction between intangible properties and tangible properties for which strict liability can be imposed. The Ninth Circuit explained this distinction in *Winter v. G.P. Putnam's Sons*, 938 F.2d 1033 (9th Cir.1991):

A book containing Shakespeare's sonnets consists of two parts, the material and the print therein, and the ideas and expression thereof. The first may be a product, but the second is not. The latter, were Shakespeare alive, would be governed by copyright laws; the laws of libel to the extent consistent with the First Amendment; and the laws of misrepresentation, negligent misrepresentation, negligence, and mistake. These doctrines applicable to the second part are aimed at the delicate issues that arise with respect to intangibles such as ideas and expression. Products liability law is geared to the tangible world.

Id. at 1034.

The reasoning of Watters and Meow Media is buttressed by the *Restatement (Third) of Torts*. Although Colorado courts have yet to adopt sections of *Restatement (Third) of Torts*, I predict that the Colorado Supreme Court, as it has often done in the past, will selectively adopt relevant sections in the *Restatement *1279 (Third) of Torts*. There, the word "product" is defined and a distinction is made between tangible and intangible properties. See *Restatement (Third) of Torts* 19(a); comment d. to § 19(a). Moreover, the commentary for § 19(a) of the *Restatement (Third) of Torts* notes that courts "have, appropriately refused to impose strict product liability" in cases where the plaintiff's grievances were "with the information, not with the tangible medium." Id. at comment d.

Based on the persuasive reasoning set out in Watters, James, Winter, and the *Restatement (Third) of Torts*, I hold that intangible thoughts, ideas, and expressive content are not "products" as contemplated by the strict liability doctrine.

(continues)

2. Causation

Assuming arguendo that the strict liability doctrine could be extended to include the thoughts, ideas, images and messages contained in video games and movies, Plaintiffs nevertheless would be required to allege adequately causation in order to state a claim based on strict liability. As I have stated, causation is trumped by an intervening act that constitutes a superseding cause. I determined as a matter of law that Harris' and Klebold's actions constituted a superseding cause which broke any chain of causation. See § V(A)(1)(a). Therefore, in the alternative, Plaintiffs' strict liability claims fail for lack of causation.

C. First Amendment Considerations

1. Protection of Video Games

Relying on the following cases, Plaintiffs contend that video games are not protected by the First Amendment. See *America's Best Family Showplace Corp. v. New York*, 536 F.Supp. 170 (E.D.N.Y.1982); *Rothner v. Chicago*, 929 F.2d 297 (7th Cir.1991) (affirming district court ruling that video games lack a vital informative element and therefore are not protected by the First Amendment). These cases are not persuasive because they have been superseded or are directly contrary to established precedent. Rothner was superseded by the Seventh Circuit's recent decision in Kendrick, 244 F.3d at 577-78 (recognizing that video games contain stories, imagery, "age-old themes of literature,"and "messages, even an 'ideology,' just as books and movies do"). The America's Best Court expressed the premise that video games are not protected by the First Amendment because they contain "pure entertainment with no informational element." This premise is directly contrary to the Supreme Court's teaching that the distinction between information and entertainment is so minuscule, that both forms of expression are entitled to First Amendment protection. See *Time, Inc. v. Hill*, 385 U.S. 374, 388, 87 S.Ct. 534, 17 L.Ed.2d 456 (1967). Plaintiffs have failed to show that video games deserve anything less than full First Amendment protection.

2. Brandenburg Test

Whether expressive content is protected under the First Amendment is subject to the test set forth in *Brandenburg v. Ohio*, 395 U.S. 444, 89 S.Ct. 1827, 23 L.Ed.2d 430 (1969). Under Brandenburg, even speech that expressly advocates criminal activity cannot be the basis for liability, unless the speech is "directed to inciting or producing imminent lawless action and is likely to incite or produce such action." Id. at 447, 89 S.Ct. 1827.

The Brandenburg test is exacting. Other courts uniformly reject claims similar to those of Plaintiffs' here.

I reject Plaintiffs' invitation to dilute the Brandenburg test in this case.

Plaintiffs contend that Brandenburg protects only "marginalized political speakers." See Resp., p. 16. I disagree. Brandenburg*1280 did not limit its test to political speech or political speech of marginalized speakers. Nor have lower courts accepted such a limitation. See e.g. *Herceg v. Hustler Magazine, Inc.*, 814 F.2d 1017 (5th Cir.1987), cert. denied, 485 U.S. 959, 108 S.Ct. 1219, 99 L.Ed.2d 420 (1988) in which the Fifth Circuit stated:

[T]he Supreme Court generally has not attempted to differentiate between different categories of protected speech for the purposes of deciding how much constitutional protection is required. Such an endeavor would not only be hopelessly complicated but would raise substantial concern that the worthiness of speech might be judged by majoritarian notions of political and social propriety and morality. If the shield of the First Amendment can be eliminated by proving after publication that an article discussing a dangerous idea negligently helped bring about a real injury simply because the idea can be identified as "bad," all free speech becomes threatened. An article discussing the nature and danger of "crack" usage-or of hang-gliding-might lead to liability just as easily. As is made clear in the Supreme Court's decision in Hess, the "tendency to lead to violence" is not enough.

Id. at 1024.

Alternatively, Plaintiffs argue that Brandenburg's imminence requirement is met by the advocacy of illegal action "at some future time. . . ." See Resp., p. 17. This argument is contrary to binding precedent. "The First Amendment does not permit someone to be punished for advocating illegal conduct at some indefinite future time." *National Gay Task Force v. Board of Education*, 729 F.2d 1270, 1274 (10th Cir.1984) citing *Hess v. Indiana*, 414 U.S. 105, 94 S.Ct. 326, 38 L.Ed.2d 303 (1973), aff'd, 470 U.S. 903, 105 S.Ct. 1858, 84 L.Ed.2d 776 (1985). Hess holds that speech cannot be deemed unprotected when, as is the case here, defendants' speech, is "not directed to any person or group of persons." See *Hess*, 414 U.S. at 108, 94 S.Ct. 326.

Plaintiffs rely also on *Rice v. Paladin Enterprises, Inc.*, 128 F.3d 233 (4th Cir.1997), cert. denied, 523 U.S. 1074, 118 S.Ct. 1515, 140 L.Ed.2d 668 (1998) in which the Fourth Circuit held that the publisher of a book entitled "Hit Man: A Technical Manual for Independent Contractors" might be held liable in a wrongful death action. However, the defendant stipulated that [it] not

(continues)

only knew that its instructions might be used by murderers, but that it actually intended to provide assistance to murderers and would-be murderers which would be used by them 'upon receipt,' and that it in fact assisted [the murderer] in particular in the commission of the murders [at issue].

Id. at 242. Largely based on this stipulation, the Rice Court reached the narrow holding that civil liability for aiding and abetting criminal conduct is constitutionally permissible where a publisher "has the specific purpose of assisting and encouraging commission of such conduct and the alleged assistance and encouragement takes a form other than abstract advocacy." Id. at 243.

Plaintiffs' Complaint is devoid of any allegation that the Movie and Video Game Defendants had any intent, let alone a specific intent, to assist and encourage anyone to engage in acts of criminal violence. Moreover, Rice distinguished the "copycat" theory presented here, where "someone imitates or 'copies' conduct... described or depicted in their broadcasts, publications, or movies." Id. at 265. The Rice Court stated that "it will presumably never be the case that the broadcaster or publisher actually intends" to assist or encourage a crime. Consequently "an inference*1281 of impermissible intent on the part of the producer...would be unwarranted as a matter of law." Id. at 265-66. Rice's limited holding is inapplicable in this case.

Plaintiffs do not discuss compliance with Brandenburg's second requirement that the speech at issue must be "likely" to produce imminent lawless action. See Brandenburg, 395 U.S. at 447-48, 89 S.Ct. 1827. As explained in section V(A)(1)(a), Plaintiffs cannot, as a matter of law, demonstrate that the video games and movie were "likely" to cause any harm, let alone imminent lawless action.

3. Restriction of the First Amendment Rights of Children

Next, Plaintiffs contend that even if video games invoke First Amendment protections, the right to free speech of children may be restricted in a reasonable manner. I disagree.

It is well-established that Brandenburg remains the applicable standard even where the individual allegedly incited to commit unlawful acts is a minor. See e.g. Miller v. California, 413 U.S. 15, 33, 93 S.Ct. 2607, 37 L.Ed.2d 419 (1973) ("likely" impact of speech must judged by its effect on "average person[s], rather than a particularly susceptible or sensitive person").

Assuming the State of Colorado has a compelling interest in broadly extending its tort law to protect

the physical and psychological well-being of minors, the restriction must be "narrowly tailored" to serve that compelling interest in order to withstand First Amendment scrutiny. See Reno v. ACLU, 521 U.S. 844, 879, 117 S.Ct. 2329, 138 L.Ed.2d 874 (1997). The United States Supreme Court has been particularly wary of governmental restrictions, such as those seemingly advocated by Plaintiffs here, that rest "on a common law concept of the most general and undefined nature." See Bridges v. California, 314 U.S. 252, 260, 62 S.Ct. 190, 86 L.Ed. 192 (1941) quoting Cantwell v. Connecticut 310 U.S. 296, 308, 60 S.Ct. 900, 84 L.Ed. 1213 (1940).

Plaintiffs' theory fails the narrow tailoring test because it is not limited to the protection of minors. It would apply even when an adult allegedly commits violence in response to video games or movies. Thus, adults' access to movies and video games would be restricted as well. The theory is, as a matter of law, overbroad. See Reno, 521 U.S. at 875, 878-89, 117 S.Ct. 2329.

Furthermore, because the Movie and Video Game Defendants cannot possibly control who gains access to their games and movies, they could avoid liability under Plaintiffs' theory only by ceasing production and distribution of their creative works. See Watters, 904 F.2d at 381. Such a sweeping theory of liability and the chilling of free expression cannot be considered narrowly tailored.

VI. CONCLUSION
A. Negligence Claims

Plaintiffs' negligence claims fail because as a matter of law the Video Game and Movie Defendants owed no duty to Plaintiffs or Mr. Sanders. In the alternative, Plaintiffs' negligence claims cannot stand because Harris' and Klebold's actions on April 20, 1999 were a superseding cause of Mr. Sanders' death.

B. Strict Liability Claims

Plaintiffs' strict liability claims against the Video Game and Movie Defendants fail as a matter of law because the intangible thoughts, ideas, images, and messages contained in "The Basketball Diaries" and video games allegedly played by Harris and Klebold are not products as required by the strict liability doctrine. Furthermore,*1282 I have determined that Harris' and Klebold's actions on April 20, 1999 constituted a superseding cause relieving Defendants of liability.

C. First Amendment

Plaintiffs' negligence and strict liability claims fail the Brandenburg test.

Accordingly, IT IS ORDERED that: . . .

NET NEWS

Administrative regulations can be used as well as statutes to establish the standard of care. If you need to find a federal regulation, you can start by going to the web page for the federal agency in which you are interested. Listings of website addresses for federal agencies can also be found at **http://www.fedworld .gov**, and **http://www.usgovsearch.com**.

Following are website addresses for some of the more commonly used agencies:

Department of Justice:	http://www.usdoj.gov
Environmental Protection Agency:	http://www.epa.gov
Federal Bureau of Investigation:	http://www.fbi.gov
Federal Election Commission:	http://www.fec.gov
Federal Trade Commission:	http://www.ftc.gov
Food and Drug Administration:	http://www.fda.gov
Internal Revenue Service:	http://www.irs.gov
Occupational Safety and Health Administration:	http://www.osha.gov
Securities and Exchange Commission:	http://www.sec.gov
Social Security Administration:	http://www.ssa.gov

Regulations for the federal agencies are compiled in the *Code of Federal Regulations* (CFR), which can be located in the search section of **http://www.usasearch.gov**. The *Federal Register* is published daily and informs readers of the status of proposed new and amended regulations and can also be found by searching in **http://www.usasearch.gov**.

AUTOMOBILE-GUEST STATUTES

Whereas some statutes have been used to establish a minimal standard of care, other statutes, specifically the **automobile-guest statutes**, have been used to limit the duty of care. such statutes hold a driver of a vehicle liable to a guest in his car only under circumstances of extreme misconduct. Typically such statutes require that the driver's misconduct be willful and wanton, grossly negligent, or reckless before she will be held liable.

The rationale underlying these statutes was two-fold. First, at the time these statutes were enacted, automobile liability insurance was not widely available, so drivers who were successfully sued by their guests had to bear the cost themselves. Many legislatures thought that such "ingratitude" should be discouraged. Second, when insurance was available, collusion between driver and guest (who were most likely friends or relatives) was feared. In other words, some thought that the owner (defendant) of the vehicle might concede negligence to assist the guest (plaintiff) in recovering damages.

In an effort to evade these statutes, plaintiffs have spent considerable effort litigating the question of who is a "guest," as well as what specific acts by the driver constitute the conduct defined by statute. Beginning in the 1970s a number of automobile-guest statutes were either repealed or found unconstitutional. Today only a few states still have such statutes in effect.

LOCAL LINKS

Does your state have an automobile-guest statute?

RES IPSA LOQUITUR

Suppose the plaintiff in a medical malpractice case is injured while on the operating table. If several doctors and nurses were present during the operation and could have contributed to the plaintiff's injuries, the plaintiff, because she was unconscious, will have difficulty proving who did and who did not act negligently. A court-developed doctrine that makes the plaintiff's task easier is the doctrine of res ipsa loquitur, which means, literally, "the thing speaks for itself." This doctrine allows the plaintiff to create an implication that the defendant was negligent without providing direct evidence of that negligence (see Exhibit 5–4).

EXHIBIT 5–4 *Elements of Res Ipsa Loquitur*

- Event that resulted in plaintiff's injuries does not usually happen except as a result of negligence.

- Instrument that caused plaintiff's injury was under the defendant's exclusive control.

- Plaintiff did not cause his own injuries.

- Defendant is in better position to explain events causing plaintiff's injuries than is plaintiff.*

*Not all courts require proof of this element.

© Cengage Learning 2012

Before a plaintiff can rely on the doctrine of res ipsa loquitur, he or she must prove the following:

- The instrument that caused the plaintiff's injury was under the exclusive control of the defendant or, stated another way, the negligence was probably due to the defendant.

- The injury suffered by the plaintiff was of a type that does not ordinarily occur except as a result of someone's negligence.

- The plaintiff did not voluntarily contribute to his or her own injuries.

- Some courts also require that the plaintiff show that the defendant is better able to explain the events that transpired than the plaintiff.

Let us examine each of these factors in some detail.

Defendant in Control or Cause of Injuries

Older cases required the plaintiff to show that the instrumentality that caused the harm was under the exclusive control of the defendant. Modern courts have required instead that the plaintiff show that the negligence was due to the defendant and not to someone else. To do this the plaintiff must often produce evidence demonstrating that it is more probable that the defendant caused the plaintiff's injuries than that someone else did. If it is just as likely that someone other than the defendant caused the injury, res ipsa loquitur will not apply.

A classic "falling chair" case is often used to illustrate the importance of the defendant having exclusive control. In this case the plaintiff was hurt when she was struck by a falling armchair that hit her when she was walking near the St. Francis Hotel during a particularly exuberant celebration of V-J day on August 14, 1945.

The court concluded that res ipsa loquitur was inapplicable because the hotel did not have exclusive control over its furniture and that the "mishap would quite as likely be due to the fault of a guest or other person" as to hotel employees (*Larson v. St. Francis Hotel*, 188 P.2d 513 [Cal. 1948]). In contrast, in a later case, the same court allowed the doctrine to apply when the plaintiff slipped and fell on garbage lying on the sidewalk at the rear of the defendant's restaurant. The court reasoned that the employees were in a position to have caused the accident and the probability of anyone else causing it was very remote (*Noble v. Cavalier Restaurant*, 235 P.2d 396 [Cal. 1951]).

Proving responsibility becomes particularly problematic in cases involving multiple defendants. In such cases the plaintiff may be able to demonstrate that the injury was caused by the negligence of at least one of the defendants but may not be able to show which defendant. In one famous case (*Ybarra v. Spangard*, 154 P.2d 687 [Cal. 1944]), for example, a man had an appendectomy and after the surgery suffered pains in his right shoulder, having sustained injuries while being operated on that he could not explain. He sued the surgeon, attending physician, anesthesiologist, and owner of the hospital, claiming that at least one of them (or a nurse they were supervising) must have been negligent. The court held that res ipsa loquitur applied because it was unreasonable to require someone who was unconscious to identify the negligent defendant. In this case each of the defendants had interrelated responsibilities and therefore a concomitant duty to prevent harm to the plaintiff. The courts seem less willing, however, to apply res ipsa loquitur if the defendants are strangers to one another and act independently of one another.

Injury Is Consequence of Negligence

The plaintiff must demonstrate that the accident would have been unlikely to occur in the absence of negligence. He is not required to show that only negligence is the cause of such events but must prove that such events are generally a consequence of negligence. In some cases that awareness will lie within the experience of the jury and will not have to be proved explicitly by the plaintiff.

In a case in which an airplane disappeared over the Pacific Ocean, leaving no debris that was ever found, the plaintiff (suing on behalf of one of the deceased passengers) was unable to produce evidence of actual negligence. Even though the defendant airline produced evidence that the plane was properly maintained, that the weather was normal, and that the personnel were adequately trained, the court allowed the fact finder the right to infer that negligence was more probably than not the cause of the accident. The plaintiff was not required to disprove every possible cause of the accident in order for the inference of negligence to be allowed (*Cox v. Northwest Airlines, Inc.*, 379 F.2d 893 [7th Cir. 1967]).

Lack of Contributory Negligence

The plaintiff must also provide evidence showing that she acted properly. If the plaintiff was contributorily negligent, the doctrine is probably not applicable. Suppose, for example, that a boiler on a locomotive explodes, killing the engineer whose job includes keeping the right amount of water in the boiler. If testimony is offered that the engineer properly tended the boiler and did nothing to cause the explosion, the doctrine of res ipsa loquitur may apply; in the absence of such testimony, the doctrine may not apply (*Restatement [Second] of Torts* § 328D, illust. 11). In contrast, if the engineer was negligent in running the train at an unsafe speed but that negligence had nothing to do with the explosion, the doctrine could still apply. In the latter case, the plaintiff's contributory negligence would do nothing to reduce the likelihood that the defendant was also negligent.

Evidence More Available to Defendant

Some courts also require the plaintiff to show that evidence of negligence was more available to the defendant(s) than to the plaintiff. Most courts, however, apply the doctrine of res ipsa loquitur even when evidence is no more available to the defendant than to the plaintiff. This element seems to be more of a rationale for applying the doctrine than an evidentiary requirement.

This rationale was used in *Ybarra v. Spangard*, involving the doctors who testified that they knew no reason why the plaintiff's shoulder became painful after his appendectomy. Application of the doctrine in cases such as this requires the defendants either to explain what happened or to risk being found liable.

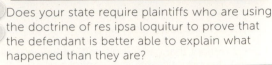

LOCAL LINKS

Does your state require plaintiffs who are using the doctrine of res ipsa loquitur to prove that the defendant is better able to explain what happened than they are?

Procedural Consequences

In a res ipsa loquitur case the jury is allowed to infer negligence. In some courts, meeting the requirements of the doctrine creates a presumption of negligence, which the defendant must rebut to avoid a directed verdict. In a few courts, once res ipsa loquitur applies, the defendant must prove by a preponderance of the evidence that she did not act negligently.

LOCAL LINKS

In your state what is the consequence of a plaintiff proving the elements of res ipsa loquitur?

APPLICATION

Breach of duty is the key question in the case against the Baxters. Teddy and Mr. Goodright will have to prove that the Baxters acted unreasonably by failing to lock the gate to their backyard. If statutes or ordinances within their jurisdiction mandate that dogs be confined in an area that is inaccessible to children, the Baxters could be found negligent per se. At the very least, statutes and ordinances could be used to establish the reasonable standard of care expected of dog owners. Compliance with these statutory requirements would not necessarily absolve the Baxters, however, because their conduct could still be deemed unreasonable. Even if found negligent per se, they could assert that the defendants were contributorily negligent or assumed the risk.

The plaintiffs could integrate the Learned Hand formula into any arguments before the court by showing that the probability of harm occurring if Gertrude was not locked in the yard and the gravity of injuries that would occur if she attacked someone greatly outweighed the minimal inconvenience of ensuring that the gate was locked. They would have to assign numerical figures to these factors to make this formula

NET NEWS

Jury instructions for res ipsa loquitur can be found at **http://www.justia.com** by entering "jury instructions res ipsa loquitur" as your search term. Select Justia : California Civil Jury Instructions (CACI) 417.

meaningful. This formula is somewhat esoteric and is designed to provide a guideline to the courts in assessing the defendants' conduct, so the attorneys would present the formula in arguments to the court and not to the jury.

The Baxters would argue that Teddy fell short of the conduct expected of a child of his age, intelligence, and experience. They would especially want to emphasize that Teddy was aware of Gertrude's propensity to defend her domain and that, having been forewarned to stay out of the Baxters' yard, he was aware of the danger inherent in entering that yard without the Baxters being present. If the Baxters tried to argue that Mr. Goodright behaved negligently by interjecting himself in the altercation between Teddy and Gertrude, they would probably fail. As long as Mr. Goodright acted reasonably considering the frightening circumstances in which he became involved, he would not be found negligent. Reasonableness does not preclude acts of heroism.

SUMMARY

Breach of duty raises the question of whether the defendant engaged in unreasonable conduct. We presume that a reasonable person will avoid creating an unreasonable risk of harm for others. Under the Learned Hand formula, a defendant has breached his duty if the probability of the harm his act presents multiplied by the gravity of such harm exceeds the defendant's burden of taking precautions to avoid the harm. An objective standard is used in assessing the defendant's conduct.

Generally, special allowances are not made for defendants who are emotionally unstable, of substandard intelligence, or insane. The physical characteristics of a defendant are, however, taken into consideration. Children are held to the standard of care of a child of similar age, intelligence, and experience. The fact that a defendant acted in an emergency situation is taken into consideration in determining the reasonableness of the conduct. The custom of a particular industry or community is looked at in reviewing the reasonableness of a defendant's conduct. Professionals are held to the standard of care commonly exercised by members in good standing of their profession, whereas specialists are held to a specialist's standard of care.

If a defendant violates a statute that is applicable to the facts of the case and if someone is injured as a result of that violation, the defendant will be considered negligent per se. The plaintiff must show that she is a member of the class of persons whom the statute is intended to protect and that the statute was designed to protect against the type of harm sustained. Criminal as well as civil statutes may be used to prove negligence per se. Generally, however, statutes do not impose an absolute duty of compliance, and their violation may be excused for a number of reasons.

In contrast to the doctrine of negligence per se, automobile-guest statutes absolve defendants of liability unless their conduct is willful and wanton, grossly negligent, or reckless. Few states still have such statutes in operation.

In some cases the plaintiff is unable to prove negligence because he lacks any direct evidence. The doctrine of res ipsa loquitur allows the plaintiff to create an inference of negligence. Under this doctrine the plaintiff must prove that (1) the negligence was due to the defendant and not to someone else; (2) the experience suffered by the plaintiff was of a sort that does not ordinarily occur except as a result of negligence; (3) the plaintiff did not voluntarily contribute to his own injuries; and, in some courts, (4) the defendant is better able to explain the event that occurred than is the plaintiff.

KEY TERMS

automobile-guest statutes
Laws holding a driver of a vehicle liable to a guest in his car only under circumstances of extreme misconduct

breach of duty
Failure to conform to the required standard of care

objective standard
Comparison of a defendant's conduct to that of a reasonable person

subjective standard
Use of the defendant's own subjective perceptions to determine whether the defendant behaved reasonably

REVIEW QUESTIONS

1. What is the essence of the question regarding reasonable care, and why is the determination of reasonableness sometimes problematic?

2. What is the Learned Hand formula, and how does it help in assessing reasonableness?

3. Explain how the Learned Hand formula could be used to assess whether defendants who fail to provide a childproof lock on the gate that leads to their swimming pool should be liable for the drowning death of their neighbor's two-year-old child.

4. Why is an objective standard used to evaluate the reasonableness of a defendant's conduct?

5. What is a reasonable person expected to know?

6. Which of the following characteristics of a defendant are taken into consideration when assessing reasonableness?
   a. mental state
   b. intelligence
   c. emotional state
   d. intoxication
   e. physical challenges, such as blindness

7. To what standard of care are children held?

8. To what standard of care are people held in emergency situations?

9. How does custom affect the evaluation of reasonableness?

10. To what standard of care are professionals held?

11. What is negligence per se and how does it assist a plaintiff in proving negligence?

12. What must a plaintiff show to prove negligence per se?

13. What are automobile-guest statutes and why were they introduced?

14. What is the status of automobile-guest statutes today?

15. What is the doctrine of res ipsa loquitur and how does it help plaintiffs?

16. What must a plaintiff prove before being able to rely on the doctrine of res ipsa loquitur?

17. What are the possible consequences to the defendant if the plaintiff proves all of the elements of res ipsa loquitur?

PRACTICE EXAM

Students should complete the practice exam after studying each chapter. The answers are in Appendix A. If you score lower than 80%, you should reread the materials.

True-False

1. To assess whether a defendant breached his duty of care, it must be determined whether the defendant acted reasonably.

2. In evaluating a defendant's conduct, a jury is allowed the benefit of information the defendant did not have at the time she acted.

3. Under the Learned Hand formula a cost/benefit analysis is rejected.

4. In determining whether a defendant acted reasonably, the jury must consider the situation from the defendant's perspective.

5. In most instances in tort law an objective standard is used to assess the reasonableness of a defendant's conduct, because doing so reduces the uncertainties in the legal system and maximizes safety to members of the community.

6. A reasonable person is expected to know matters of common knowledge and scientific and natural laws of common knowledge to laypersons.

7. Ignorance of the law is no excuse even if the law contradicts the custom of the community.

8. Courts generally do not hold insane people to a reasonable-person standard because they should not be held responsible for their actions.

9. The physical characteristics of a defendant are never taken into consideration when determining the reasonable-person standard.

10. Children who engage in activities not necessarily reserved for adults are always held to the standard of care of a reasonable adult.

11. Defendants acting under emergency conditions must act reasonably, but they are not held to the standard of care demanded of one in non-emergency conditions.

12. A reasonable person is never expected to anticipate the criminal acts or intentional torts of others.

13. Adherence to custom is conclusive evidence of reasonableness of conduct.

14. The courts can find an entire industry negligent even if no one in the industry has adopted adequate safety measures.

15. Professionals who are novices are not held to the same standard of care as other more experienced members of the profession.

16. Specialists are held to a higher standard of care than other members of the profession.

17. Most courts consider a defendant's violation of a statute as evidence of mere negligence rather than negligence per se, and mere negligence can be negated by evidence of due care.

18. In states that prohibit leaving keys in a parked car, a defendant is not necessarily negligent per se if he leaves his keys in his car and the thief who steals the car is involved in an accident causing injury to the plaintiff.

19. Violation of a statute always imposes an absolute duty of compliance.

20. Under the majority rule, when a criminal statute is violated, courts do not apply the criminal statutory standard to civil cases.

21. Compliance with a statute does not necessarily establish that a defendant was not negligent.

22. The purpose of automobile-guest statutes was to discourage guests from suing their host drivers and prevent collusion between drivers and their guests.

23. Res ipsa loquitur is a court-created doctrine that allows plaintiffs to create an inference of negligence without having to provide direct evidence of negligence.

24. To prove res ipsa loquitur, the plaintiff must show that the negligence was due to the defendant and not someone else, and that the injury the plaintiff suffered was of the type that does not ordinarily occur except as a result of negligence.

25. A plaintiff can be contributorily negligent and still rely on the doctrine of res ipsa loquitur.

26. The courts are less willing to apply the doctrine of res ipsa loquitur in cases in which the defendants are strangers and act independently.

27. Most courts require plaintiffs to prove that the evidence is more available to the defendant than to the plaintiff before they will allow the doctrine of res ipsa loquitur to be applied.

28. If the plaintiff is able to prove the elements of res ipsa loquitur, all courts allow juries to infer negligence but do not allow a presumption of negligence to be created that the defendant would have to rebut.

Fill-in-the-Blanks

1. Under the Learned Hand formula, the _____ and _____ of harm created by the defendant's conduct are considered.

2. When determining the standard of care for a child, the _____, _____ and _____ of the child are taken into consideration.

3. Professionals are held to a _____ standard of care than those outside the profession.

4. _____ _____ statutes hold drivers of vehicles liable for injuries resulting to guests in their car only under circumstances of extreme misconduct.

5. _____ _____ _____ means "the thing speaks for itself."

Multiple-Choice

1. In considering the burden-of-precaution factor in the Learned Hand formula, courts
   a. consider the cost to the defendant in taking precautions.
   b. consider the social utility of the defendant's conduct.
   c. consider both a and b.
   d. do not consider either a or b.

2. Under the Learned Hand formula a defendant is liable
   a. if the burden of precaution outweighs the gravity of harm multiplied by the likelihood of harm.
   b. if the likelihood of harm times the gravity of harm outweighs the burden of precaution.
   c. if the burden of precaution equals the gravity of harm multiplied by the likelihood of harm.
   d. none of the above.

3. Those who are generally held to the standard of care of a reasonable person include
   a. intoxicated people.
   b. people who are emotionally unstable.
   c. people who are of substandard intelligence.
   d. all of the above.

4. When a defendant violates a statute, he is negligent per se if
   a. the statute applies to the facts of the case.
   b. there is a causal link between the defendant's act and the plaintiff's injury.
   c. both a and b.
   d. neither a nor b.

5. To prove negligence per se, the plaintiff must show that the defendant violated a statute and that the
   a. statute was designed to protect against the kind of harm sustained by the plaintiff.
   b. the plaintiff was a member of the class the statute was intended to protect.
   c. both a and b.
   d. neither a nor b.

6. A plaintiff cannot resort to the doctrine of res ipsa loquitur if
   a. it is just as likely that someone other than the defendant caused the plaintiff's injury.
   b. there are multiple defendants.
   c. she cannot show that negligence is the only possible cause of her injuries.
   d. all of the above.

PRACTICE POINTERS

In cases of negligence per se, the task of locating the appropriate statutory standard may fall to the paralegal. Therefore, you should be aware of the most common sources of statutory law. When laws are first enacted they are published separately as "slip laws"; at the end of a legislative session the slip laws for that session are bound in volumes referred to as "session laws." The official source of session laws is a government publication, *United States Statutes at Large*, which orders the session laws by public law numbers (e.g., Pub. L. No. 97-334). Session laws are difficult to access because they are arranged chronologically rather than by subject. Therefore, federal statutes are easier to locate using arrangements of laws by subject matter, referred to as "codes." Unless you are looking for a recently enacted law, you will begin statutory research at the federal level using one of three federal codes: *United States Code* (the official version published by the government), *United States Code Annotated* (published by West Publishing); or *United States Code Service* (published by Lawyers Cooperative Publishing). The official version contains only the text of the federal code, but the two unofficial versions also contain annotations (information about decisions that have applied or discussed certain sections of the code), historical notes, and references to other sources that interpret and analyze the code.

Codes are updated using supplementary volumes or pamphlets or by pocket parts (annual supplements found in the back inside cover of the hardbound volume). Codes can be accessed using the index, which lists statutes alphabetically according to subject matter, or the titles listed in the front of each volume. The *United States Code* is divided into fifty titles and then further subdivided into chapters and subchapters.

All states have subject compilations of state statutes; these compilations may be referred to as "Statutes," "Codes," "Revisions," "Compilations," or by other terms. All state codes are organized based on subject matter, but the numbering schemes vary from state to state. Many jurisdictions have both official and unofficial codes; some have annotated codes and others are unannotated. Consult your law librarian to familiarize yourself with the organizational structure, frequency of updates, and research features of the codes published in your state.

NET NEWS

To read the *United States Code* or any state statutory code, go to **http://www.gpo.gov** and select "FDsys." Then select "United States Code" from the Featured Collections.

TORT TEASERS

1. How would you go about determining whether the Baxters had breached their duty to Teddy and Mr. Goodright? Suppose in your research you found a statute in your state that read as follows: "Owners of dogs known to have dangerous propensities must adequately restrain such dogs so as to prevent injury to others." The *Restatement (Second) of Torts* § 509 provides that

   > A possessor of a domestic animal that he knows or has reason to know has dangerous propensities abnormal to its class, is subject to liability for harm done by the animal to another, although he has used the utmost care to prevent it from doing the harm.

   What arguments would you make on behalf of the Baxters? On behalf of Teddy and Mr. Goodright?

2. If you were to interview Teddy and his parents, what questions would you ask them to help establish that the Baxters had violated their duty of care?

3. Suppose the Baxters alleged that Teddy and Mr. Goodright were both contributorily negligent. If you were representing the Baxters, what arguments would you raise to show that Teddy's conduct was unreasonable? What arguments would you make to show that Mr. Goodright's actions were unreasonable?

4. Plaintiff and Defendant are both driving down the road when Defendant attempts to pass Plaintiff's vehicle. In doing so his left rear tire blows out, causing him to swerve into Plaintiff's vehicle. Testimony is presented showing that the tire was very worn but Defendant claims that he was unaware of the dangerous condition of the tire. Was Defendant's failure to examine his tire unreasonable conduct? *Delair v. McAdoo*, 188 A.181 (Pa. 1936).

5. Defending attorney represents a wife in a divorce proceeding. Under California community-property law she is entitled to a claim to her husband's retirement benefits. Defendant fails to make this claim for his client because he erroneously believes that the wife is not entitled to the benefits. The law, in fact, is relatively clear on this issue and provides that retirement rights are community property. Defendant does not research the issue. Was Defendant negligent? How would you assess the reasonableness of his actions? *Smith v. Lewis*, 530 P.2d 589 (Cal. 1975).

6. A statute requires banks to perform background checks and fingerprint applications of job candidates before employing them. Plaintiff was shot by the bank's security guard who was attempting to rob the bank. The bank failed to fingerprint and perform a background check on the guard. What information do you need to determine if the bank was negligent *per se*? *Mahan v. Am-Gard, Inc.*, 841 A.2d 1052 (PA.Supper 2003).

7. Plaintiff drinks from a bottle of Coca-Cola he purchased from the drugstore and spits up a fly. Defendant introduces evidence that the bottling plant was operated under sanitary conditions and that Coca-Cola bottles can be opened and their caps replaced without any obvious indication of tampering. Is the doctrine of res ipsa loquitur applicable? *Crystal Coca-Cola Bottling Co. v. Cathey*, 317 P.2d 1094 (Ariz. 1957).

INTERNET INQUIRIES

1. Paralegals are frequently asked to conduct statutory research. You can do this online by going to http://www.law.cornell.edu and select "State law resources." Follow the link to your state code, and find a statute(s) relating to the selling of liquor to underage minors.

   a. Give the number(s) of the statute(s) you find.

   b. Summarize the provisions of each statute.

2. Paralegals are generally expected to serve as liaisons with court personnel. Most state trial courts have websites that provide basic information to the public and helpful links to legal professionals. To become familiar with legal resources in your jurisdiction go to http://www.findlaw.com and select the appropriate link.

PRACTICAL PONDERABLES

Your firm has a client, Marvin, who was injured when he ran into a disabled truck on the highway. The accident occurred shortly after sundown. Marvin said he did not see the truck until shortly before he ran into it. The driver of the truck concedes that he had not put any reflectors around the truck to warn oncoming motorists.

Your supervising attorney asks you to find a statute in your state that pertains to this situation. You can either go to the library and get a hard copy of your state's statute, or you can find them online by going to http://www.findlaw.com.

1. What statute(s) do you find that are applicable, and what do they provide?
2. What will you have to prove if you want to use these statutes in proving Marvin's case?
3. How will these statutes make the proof of negligence easier?

 Access an interactive eBook, chapter-specific learning tools, including flashcards, quizzes, and more in your Paralegal CourseMate, accessed through www.CengageBrain.com.

CHAPTER 6

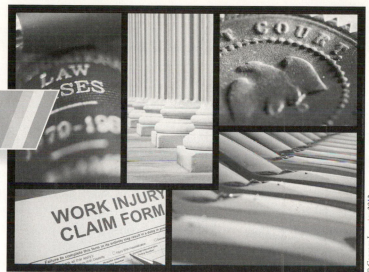

© Cengage Learning 2012

Negligence: Causation

CHAPTER OBJECTIVES

After completing the chapter, you should be able to

- Distinguish between actual cause and proximate cause.
- Prove the element of actual cause.
- Distinguish between the Cardozo and Andrews approaches to proximate cause.
- Identify the exceptions to the Cardozo rule of foreseeability.
- Distinguish between an intervening and a superseding cause.

If Teddy and Mr. Goodright are able to hurdle the "duty" and "breach of duty" obstacles, they must then set their sights on the element of causation. Causation entails two separate considerations: actual cause (sometimes referred to as causation in fact) and proximate cause (or legal cause). **Actual cause** means, quite literally, that the defendant's actions were the direct, factual cause of the plaintiff's injuries. **Proximate cause**, in contrast, means that the defendant's conduct was so closely connected to the plaintiff's injuries that the defendant should be held liable. If the plaintiff is injured by a bizarre and extraordinary chain of events that is only remotely connected to the defendant's negligence, proximate cause is lacking.

ACTUAL CAUSE

But-For Test

The question of whether the defendant was the actual cause of the plaintiff's injuries is usually a factual one (see Exhibit 6–1). The "but-for" or "sine qua non" test is usually used to determine actual cause. Under this test, if the plaintiff's injuries would not have occurred *but for* the defendant's negligence, the defendant will be deemed the actual cause of the plaintiff's injuries (*Restatement [Second] of Torts* § 432).

Let us apply this test to an actual situation. The mate of the defendant's steam trawler falls overboard and disappears immediately. The defendant's lifeboat is equipped with only one oar, which is lashed to the deck instead of being suspended from the davits. As a result, the lashings have to be cut before the boat can be launched. Is the defendant's negligence the actual cause of the plaintiff's death (*Ford v. Trident Fisheries Co.*, 232 Mass. 400,

122 N.E. 389 [1919]). Because the plaintiff disappeared immediately after falling overboard and no evidence shows that the defendant's negligence in any way contributed to the plaintiff's death, the defendant would not be considered the actual cause of the plaintiff's death.

In a more modern context, actual cause arises in cases involving tavern owners who negligently serve liquor to patrons who are obviously intoxicated. If those patrons drive and injure someone, the question is whether the tavern owner's serving of liquor was the actual cause of the harm done to the injured person. In a case that is excerpted later in this chapter (*Ontiveros v. Borak*, 667 P.2d 200 [Ariz. 1983]), the court allowed a jury to find actual causation when a tavern owner served at least thirty beers to a patron who was involved in an accident after he left the bar. The court reasoned that a "defendant may be held liable if his conduct contributed to the result and if that result would not have occurred 'but for' defendant's conduct." The court noted, however, that some factual scenarios would not support a finding of actual causation. If, for example, the patron had consumed thirty beers at the defendant's bar and then had gone across the street for "one for the road," the court opined that "it would be difficult to argue that the accident would not have happened 'but for' the last drink."

Substantial-Factor Test

Notice that the but-for test makes for an extremely broad net into which many a defendant can be snared. But as sweeping as the but-for test is, it does not encompass situations involving concurrent causes of harm to the plaintiff. *Concurrent causes* are those events that combine (concur) to cause the plaintiff's harm, although either one of them alone

---

EXHIBIT 6–1 Actual Cause

BUT-FOR TEST	SUBSTANTIAL FACTOR TEST	BURDEN OF PROOF
But for defendant's negligence plaintiff would not have been injured.	Two or more concurrent or successive events combine to cause the plaintiff's injury and each of them is a substantial factor in producing the injury.	Plaintiff bears burden of proof Except: 1. Alternate liability (*Summers v. Tice*) 2. Market share liability (*Sindell v. Abbott Labs*) 3. Concerted action

could cause the harm without any contribution from the other. Under the substantial-factor test, an alternative to the but-for test, the question is whether the defendant was a substantial factor in producing the plaintiff's injury. If the concurrent causes produce a single, indivisible harm in which the damage from one event cannot be separated from that caused by the other, the courts have generally found both events to be a substantial factor in producing the plaintiff's injuries.

To illustrate the application of this test, suppose the plaintiff is riding down a narrow road in his horse-drawn wagon when two motorcycles roar around him, one on each side. The frightened horse bolts, and the plaintiff is injured. Although either motorcycle by itself would have been sufficient to frighten the horse, the harm created by both of the motorcycles produces a single, indivisible harm. Consequently, both motorcyclists are the actual cause of the plaintiff's injuries (*Corey v. Havener*, 65 N.E. 69 [Mass. 1902]).

Modern courts have struggled with the concept of causation in "toxic tort" cases and have often adopted the less stringent substantial-factor test in concurrent-cause cases. In one case the plaintiffs, who lived downwind from a nuclear test site, alleged that their exposure to radioactive fallout had caused them to develop various forms of cancer. The court adopted a substantial-factor test. In rejecting the but-for test, the court reasoned that the "use of any kind of 'but for' analysis—whether plaintiff's injury would not have occurred but for the conduct of the defendant— to determine factual causation is problematical at best; where likely 'causes' co-exist [such as fallout exposure, background radiation, medical x-rays, etc.], it is wholly inadequate to the task." In considering whether the radiation was a substantial factor in causing the cancers suffered by the plaintiffs, the court looked at whether the plaintiffs' injuries were consistent with the harm caused by exposure to radiation, the length of time the plaintiffs had lived near the test site, the probability that they were exposed to radiation in excess of natural background radiation, the estimated dose of radiation they had received, and whether the statistical incidence of cancer in the plaintiffs was greater than the expected incidence of cancer (*Allen v. United States*, 588 F. Supp. 247 [D. Utah 1984]).

The problem in cases of this sort is proving that the toxin at issue, and not some other factor, was the cause of the plaintiff's injury. To illustrate, in another radiation case the plaintiffs were unable to prove causation because the defense produced evidence that one plaintiff's smoking of 1.5 packs of cigarettes per day for forty-five years was just as much a cause of his lung cancer as the radiation to which he had been exposed, and that another plaintiff's high-cholesterol/low-fiber diet was just as likely a cause of his colon cancer as his exposure to radiation (*Prescott v. United States*, 858 F. Supp. 1461 [D. Nev. 1994]).

To prove causation, plaintiffs in toxic tort cases must often rely on expert testimony, epidemiological studies (studies that demonstrate a statistical association between a disease and a toxic substance), and experimental studies conducted on humans and animals that measure and observe the effects of exposure to chemicals. The evidence presented by plaintiffs must not only prove that the toxin in question is capable of producing the type of injury suffered by the plaintiffs, but also that each individual plaintiff's injury was caused by that particular toxin. The evidentiary rules governing the admissibility of such evidence go beyond the scope of this text, but suffice it to say that plaintiffs must surmount a number of evidentiary obstacles before they can introduce evidence to prove their allegations of causation.

Causation Problems in Mass Tort Cases

Mass torts involving generic products that are inherently toxic present complex causation issues. The plaintiff is not able to identify the specific product, brand, retailer, or manufacturer because of the generic nature of the product. The *risk-contribution theory* has been used to relax the plaintiff's burden of proof to establish causation in a mass tort case where a young boy ingested lead paint resulting in brain damage. The plaintiff was not able to identify the manufacturer of the paint he ingested. In applying the risk-contribution theory to the case the court found that many of the individual defendants knew of the harm caused by white lead carbonate pigments and continued production and promotion of the product. The court held that each industry defendant contributed to the creation of a risk of harm to the public generally and the plaintiff specifically (*Thomas v. Mallett* 701 N.W.2d 523 [Wis. 2005]).

Proof of Actual Cause

The plaintiff bears the burden of proving actual causation by a preponderance of the evidence. In other words, she must prove that it is probable that the injury would not have occurred but for the defendant's acts. Suppose, however, the defendant argues that the plaintiff would have been injured even if the defendant had not been negligent. The plaintiff must then show that the defendant's negligence greatly enhanced the chances of harm occurring in order to sustain the burden of proof.

If two defendants are negligent but only one could have caused the plaintiff's injury, the burden of proof will be thrust back on the defendants to show who actually caused the harm (*Resatement [Second] of Torts* § 433B[3]). Under the theory of *alternate liability*, as developed in *Summers v. Tice*, 199 P.2d 1 (Cal. 1948), each negligent tortfeasor must prove that his actions did not cause the plaintiff's injuries. If one fails to make such proof, both defendants will be found liable. In *Summers v. Tice* the plaintiff and the two defendants went hunting together. The defendants simultaneously shot at a quail and the plaintiff was struck by one of the shots. Because it could not be determined from which gun the bullet was fired, the court held that each of the defendants had the burden to show that it was the other's shot that wounded the plaintiff.

This theory has been expanded to encompass three or more defendants in the area of product liability. The so-called *market-share liability* theory was developed in *Sindell v. Abbott Laboratories*, 607 P.2d 924 (Cal. 1980) to allow recovery to the plaintiff who can show that the defendants were negligent but cannot prove which of the defendants caused the injury. In *Sindell* at least 200 manufacturers used an identical formula to produce diethylstilbestrol (DES). The plaintiff, whose mother took the drug during pregnancy, alleged that her cancer was a direct result of her mother's consumption of DES. The plaintiff sued five drug companies, which she maintained manufactured 90 percent of the DES ever marketed, but was unable to show which of the manufacturers produced the drug that her mother actually took.

The court concluded that it was impossible for the plaintiff to provide such proof, in part because the ill effects caused by the drug did not become apparent for many years after consumption. The court reasoned that when it came down to a conflict between an innocent plaintiff and negligent defendants, the latter should bear the cost of any injuries. The court also opined that the defendants were better able to bear the cost of injury, as they could discover and guard against any defects and could also warn consumers of potential harmful effects. Any defendant unable to prove that it did not produce the particular dosages consumed by the plaintiff's mother would be liable for the portion of the judgment that represented the defendant's share of the overall DES market at the time of the mother's consumption.

Notice that market share liability differs from res ipsa loquitur in that the latter is used when a plaintiff has no way of proving the nature of the defendant's conduct. If the plaintiff can meet the proof requirements of res ipsa loquitur the defendant's negligence will be inferred. With market-share liability the plaintiff can show that all of the defendants were negligent (or produced a dangerous product) but is unable to pin the injuries on one specific defendant.

Other courts, when confronted with multiple defendants, have imposed liability using a *concerted-action theory* set forth in the *Restatement [Second] of Torts* § 876. Under this theory, plaintiffs must show that a tacit agreement existed among the defendants to perform a tortious act. To do this the plaintiff must show the existence of a common plan or that the defendants assisted or encouraged each other in accomplishing a tortious result. Regardless of which theory the court relies on, clearly a defendant may be considered the actual cause of the plaintiff's injury even if another defendant's negligence also contributed to that harm.

Proof of actual cause can be particularly problematic in medical malpractice cases in which a doctor's failure to diagnose may have contributed to a patient's death. One such case (*Wollen v. DePaul Health Center*, 828 S.W.2d 681 [Mo. 1992]), in which the doctors failed to diagnose gastric cancer, is excerpted here. Note the court's rejection of both the but-for and substantial-factor tests because of the impossibility of the plaintiff being able to prove causation under either of these tests. The court develops an alternate theory of recovery—the "lost chance of recovery" theory. This theory allows medical malpractice plaintiffs to recover if they can prove a loss of the chance to recover, even if they cannot prove that the doctor's negligence resulted in a loss of life.

CASE

Wollen v. DePaul Health Center
828 S.W.2d 681 (Mo. 1992)

BENTON, Judge.

Linda F. Wollen appeals the dismissal, for failure to state a cause of action, of her petition for damages filed under the wrongful death statute, [Mo. Rev. Stat.] § 537.080 [1986]. The decision below is vacated; and this case is remanded for further proceedings in accordance with this opinion.

I.

Assuming for the purposes of appellate review that the allegations in appellant's pleadings are true, the facts of this case are: On January 26, 1988, David L. Wollen went to respondent Richard F. Jotte, Sr. M.D., for medical treatment. Dr. Jotte referred Mr. Wollen to the other respondents, DePaul Health Center, Ernst Radiology Clinic, Inc., and Edwin Ernst, III, M.D., for tests. If respondents had performed appropriate tests, or had correctly interpreted the tests that they had conducted, respondents would have diagnosed that Mr. Wollen was suffering from gastric cancer on January 28, 1988. If Mr. Wollen had been correctly diagnosed, and given appropriate treatment, he would have "had a thirty percent (30%) chance of survival and cure."

Mr. Wollen died from gastric cancer on July 2, 1989. On January 17, 1990, Linda F. Wollen, Mr. Wollen's widow, filed a wrongful death action against respondents. Each respondent filed a motion to dismiss the action on the ground that the petition failed to plead a causal connection between respondents' negligence and the death of Mr. Wollen. The circuit court sustained respondents' motions, and appellant refused leave to file an amended petition on May 7, 1990. After appeal to the Court of Appeals, Eastern District, and on application by appellant, this Court ordered this case transferred here on September 10, 1991.

II.

This case turns on the issues of proof and causation. At this initial stage of the case, courts are required to assume that the evidence introduced at the trial will prove the facts as pled by the plaintiff. The question remains, however, whether the ultimate legal fact of causation can be inferred from those facts.

As in the case with most petitions, in addition to pleading the alleged facts, the petition before this Court pleads, as facts, elements of the cause of action—negligence, causation, and damages. Such "facts"/elements are, in reality, merely legal conclusions. In the simple negligence case, the inference from the real pleadings of fact to these legal conclusions is simple and straightforward. A statement that the plaintiff slipped on a patch of ice creates an inference that the ice caused the plaintiff to slip. The inference in this case is not that easy.

In the failure-to-diagnose case, the fact pleaded to show causation often has to be a statistic. This problem can be avoided if the plaintiff can plead that there is a reasonable medical or scientific certainty that defendant's negligence caused the harm.

The cases on reasonable medical certainty, however, reflect the lack of clarity that can occur when the legal profession tries to impose its terms on other professions. In this Court's understanding of the medical issues involved, there are three possibilities: two of which involve "reasonable medical certainty," and a third that does not.

The first possibility is the circumstance that could be phrased as "but for" causation. In this circumstance, the patient has a disease for which, at the stage the patient seeks diagnosis, there is a cure that works in the overwhelming majority of cases. Death from this type of disease caught at this stage is rare unless either the patient or the doctor is negligent at some stage of the treatment process.

The second possibility is exactly the opposite. In this circumstance, there is no known cure for the disease. Medical science can only, at best, extend the patient's life a short time. In the overwhelming majority of cases, the disease is fatal except for a small number of spontaneous remissions or cures.

The third possibility is the one that appears in this case. Doctors have a treatment that works in a large number of cases and fails in a large number of cases. Because there is a real chance that the patient will survive and a real chance that the patient will die from the disease—even if it is diagnosed—it is impossible for a medical expert to state with "reasonable medical certainty" the effect of the failure to diagnose on a specific patient, other than the fact that the failure to diagnose eliminated whatever chance the patient would have had.

III.

Appellant proposes analyzing this case under the theory that respondents' negligence was a "substantial factor" that contributed to Mr. Wollen's death. Prior cases do not support appellant's interpretation of the substantial factor theory.

In this case, appellant can only allege that, even when all of the tortfeasors are taken together, the negligence of the respondents might have contributed to the death of Mr. Wollen. In these circumstances, the petition fails to allege facts that indicate that respondents'

(continues)

negligence was a substantial factor in causing the death of Mr. Wollen.

IV.

In argument before this Court, all parties have discussed whether this Court should recognize an alternative theory of recovery based on the *Restatement (Second) of Torts*, section 323(a). As Missouri is a fact-pleading state, this Court will consider whether the facts as pled entitle appellant to relief under a "lost chance of recovery" theory.

In the past this Court has recognized that section 323 creates a duty of care. In creating this duty, this section of the *Restatement* defines a type of negligent behavior but does not alter the rules of causation. For the reasons discussed in Parts III and V, the petition fails to allege facts that show that respondents' alleged negligence caused Mr. Wollen's death. The petition does, however, allege facts that would support an action for lost chance of recovery.

* * *

The arguments against recognizing such a cause of action, however, are not totally without merit. Traditionally, causation has been treated as a "yes-or-no" or "all-or-nothing" question. There has been a trend towards apportioning fault among various parties in law suits but such apportionment occurs only after the jury has decided that the evidence shows causation. This traditional view of causation does aid the goal—which should be shared by the entire legal profession—of avoiding unnecessary barriers to ordinary people understanding their rights and responsibilities under the law.

On the other hand, there are compelling reasons for granting compensation in this type of cause of action. The traditional yes-no view of the world in causation theory does not match the "maybe" view of the world found in probability, statistics, and everyday life. To both the statistician and the patient seeking care from a doctor, there is no meaningful difference between a 50.001% and a 49.999% chance of recovery.

Medical science has given patients real chances to recover, sometimes only a small chance, but still a chance, in circumstances that used to be hopeless. When patients go to doctors with serious illnesses, they expect to have those chances that medical science has provided. To the individual patient, if the doctor's negligence destroys the chance of recovery, it is irrelevant what that chance originally was. The courts of this state implicitly recognized this fact as far back as 1923.

A patient with cancer, like Mr. Wollen, would pay to have a choice between three unmarked doors—behind two of which were death, with life the third option. A physician who deprived a patient of this opportunity, even though only a one-third chance, would have caused her real harm.

In light of this reality, the patient does suffer a harm when the doctor fails to diagnose or adequately treat a serious injury or disease. The harm suffered is not, however, the loss of life or limb. The harm is the loss of the chance of recovery. While, in the end, damages can only be expressed by multiplying the value of a lost life or limb by the chance of recovery lost, the proper place for such an inquiry is in the damages stage rather than in the liability/causation determination. Therefore, rather than adopting a theory of proportional causation, this Court chooses to recognize a cause of action for lost chance of recovery in medical malpractice cases.

PUTTING IT INTO PRACTICE 6:1

1. What was the question the appellate court was trying to answer?

2. In what types of cases did the court believe but-for causation existed?

3. Why did the court feel the substantial-factor test was ineffective in this case?

4. Did the plaintiff's petition alleged facts support an allegation that the defendants' negligence caused the plaintiff's husband's death? What did it support?

5. How does the "lost chance of recovery" theory assist medical malpractice plaintiffs?

PROXIMATE CAUSE

If the plaintiff is successful in showing that the defendant's negligence was the actual cause of the injury, she must then show that the defendant proximately caused the injury. Some writers feel that the term *legal cause* is more descriptive because it reflects a judicial concern that limits should be put on a defendant's liability. This judicial constraint arises from a sense that a defendant should not be liable for a highly improbable or extraordinary consequence stemming from his negligence—to do so would be unfair. In reading cases you will discover that some courts blur the concepts of actual causation and proximate cause. For example, if a court finds that a defendant's conduct was not the actual cause of the plaintiff's harm, it may label this a failure of proximate cause. Throughout this text, however, we treat these two concepts separately.

Foreseeability

The question of proximate cause basically boils down to a question of foreseeability. Was the plaintiff's injury a reasonably foreseeable consequence of the defendant's conduct? The difficulty that the courts grapple with is where to draw the line in holding defendants liable.

Suppose a defendant and plaintiff are playing around and the defendant accidentally but negligently cuts the plaintiff with a knife, causing relatively mild injuries. In which of the following circumstances do you think the defendant should be held liable for the plaintiff's death?

1. The plaintiff panics at the sight of blood, blindly runs in front of a car, and is killed.
2. The plaintiff contracts gangrene and dies as a result of negligence on the part of the doctor who treats him.
3. The ambulance transporting the plaintiff to a hospital is involved in an accident in which the plaintiff dies.
4. The plaintiff refuses medical care, contracts an infection that can be traced to the injuries he received from the defendant, and dies as a result of that infection.

We will deal with these situations later on in this chapter. But be aware that only limited consensus exists in the area of proximate cause. The courts have struggled, and continue to struggle, with their determination of what is fair to a defendant.

Palsgraf

The most famous case dealing with the issue of foreseeability is *Palsgraf v. Long Island Rail Co.*, 162 N.E. 99 (N.Y. 1928). In *Palsgraf* one of the defendant railroad's employees, attempting to assist a man

---

PUTTING IT INTO PRACTICE 6:2

1. A buyer purchases a condominium based on a false statement by the bank's broker that the association dues are $100 per month when they are in fact $500 per month. One month after the purchase the plumbing breaks down and the buyer has to pay $25,000 to replace the pipes. The buyer says she relied on the statement about the dues in purchasing the condominium and would not have bought it had it not been for the broker's misrepresentation. Does the buyer have a claim against the bank for the broken pipes?
2. Ford Dealers Advertising Association sponsors a $1 million drag race. Although its logo is used in promotional materials, Ford takes no part in preparing the materials nor in making any of the representations that are made in the materials. The winner of the race sues Ford when the promoters of the race refuse to give him his prize money. Does he have a valid claim against Ford?
3. Veterans of the Vietnam War sue the government for damages they claim to have suffered as a result of exposure to Agent Orange. What problems in relationship to actual causation do you anticipate they will have? What types of evidence will they have to present?

running to board the defendant's train, accidentally dislodged a package from the passenger's arm. Unbeknownst to anyone, the package contained fireworks, which exploded when they fell. As a result of the shock of the explosion some scales at the other end of the platform fell and hit the plaintiff.

Arguably, the defendant's employee was negligent in pushing the passenger in the effort to assist him. The real question, however, was whether the defendant's negligence toward the passenger should give rise to liability to the plaintiff, who was injured by a series of fluke events.

CASE // Palsgraf v. Long Island Rail Co.
162 N.E. 99 (N.Y. 1928)

CARDOZO, C.J.

Plaintiff was standing on a platform of defendant's railroad after buying a ticket to go to Rockaway Beach. A train stopped at the station, bound for another place. Two men ran forward to catch it. One of the men reached the platform of the car without mishap, though the train was already moving. The other man, carrying a package, jumped aboard the car, but seemed unsteady as if about to fall. A guard on the car, who had held the door open, reached forward to help him in, and another guard on the platform pushed him from behind. In this act, the package was dislodged, and fell upon the rails. It was a package of small size, about fifteen inches long, and was covered by a newspaper. In fact it contained fireworks, but there was nothing in its appearance to give notice of its contents. The fireworks when they fell exploded. The shock of the explosion threw down some scales at the other end of the platform many feet away. The scales struck the plaintiff, causing injuries for which she sues.

The conduct of the defendant's guard, if a wrong in its relation to the holder of the package, was not a wrong in its relation to the plaintiff, standing far away. Relatively to her it was not negligence at all. Nothing in the situation gave notice that the falling package had in it the potency of peril to persons thus removed. Negligence is not actionable unless it involves the invasion of a legally protected interest, the violation of a right. "Proof of negligence in the air, so to speak, will not do."... "Negligence is the absence of care, according to the circumstances."... The plaintiff, as she stood upon the platform of the station, might claim to be protected against intentional invasion of her bodily security. Such invasion is not charged. She might claim to be protected against unintentional invasion by conduct involving in the thought of reasonable men an unreasonable hazard that such invasion would ensue. These, from the point of view of the law, were the bounds of her immunity, with perhaps some rare exceptions, survivals for the most part of ancient forms of liability, where conduct is held to be at the peril of the actor....If no hazard was apparent to the eye of ordinary vigilance, an act innocent and harmless, at least to outward seeming, with reference

to her, did not take to itself the quality of a tort because it happened to be a wrong, though apparently not one involving the risk of bodily insecurity, with reference to some one else. "In every instance, before negligence can be predicated of a given act, back of the act must be sought and found a duty to the individual complaining, the observance of which would have averted or avoided the injury."... "The ideas of negligence and duty are strictly correlative."... The plaintiff sues in her own right for a wrong personal to her, and not as the vicarious beneficiary of a breach of duty to another.

* * *

A different conclusion will involve us, and swiftly too, in a maze of contradictions. A guard stumbles over a package which has been left upon the platform. It seems to be a bundle of newspapers. It turns out to be a can of dynamite. To the eye of ordinary vigilance, the bundle is abandoned waste, which may be kicked or trod on with impunity. Is a passenger at the other end of the platform protected by the law against the unsuspected hazard concealed beneath the waste? If not, is the result to be any different, so far as the distant passenger is concerned, when the guard stumbles over a valise which a truckman or a porter has left upon the walk? The passenger far away, if the victim of a wrong at all, has a cause of action, not derivative, but original and primary. His claim to be protected against invasion of his bodily security is neither greater nor less because the act resulting in the invasion is a wrong to another far removed. In this case, the rights that are said to have been violated, the interests said to have been invaded, are not even of the same order. The man was not injured in his person nor even put in danger. The purpose of the act, as well as its effect, was to make his person safe. If there was a wrong to him at all, which may very well be doubted, it was a wrong to a property interest only, the safety of his package. Out of this wrong to property, which threatened injury to nothing else, there has passed, we are told, to the plaintiff by derivation or succession a right of action for the invasion of an interest of another order, the right

(continues)

to bodily security. The diversity of interests emphasizes the futility of the effort to build the plaintiff's right upon the basis of a wrong to some one else. The gain is one of emphasis, for a like result would follow if the interests were the same. Even then, the orbit of the danger as disclosed to the eye of reasonable vigilance would be the orbit of the duty. One who jostles one's neighbor in a crowd does not invade the rights of others standing at the outer fringe when the unintended contact casts a bomb upon the ground. The wrong-doer as to them is the man who carries the bomb, not the one who explodes it without suspicion of the danger. Life will have to be made over, and human nature transformed, before prevision so extravagant can be accepted as the norm of conduct, the customary standard to which behavior must conform.

* * *

The argument for the plaintiff is built upon the shifting meanings of such words as "wrong" and "wrongful," and shares their instability. What the plaintiff must show is "a wrong" to herself; i.e., a violation of her own right, and not merely a wrong to someone else, nor conduct "wrongful" because unsocial, but not "a wrong" to any one. We are told that one who drives at reckless speed through a crowded city street is guilty of a negligent act and therefore of a wrongful one, irrespective of the consequences. Negligent the act is, and wrongful in the sense that it is unsocial, but wrongful and unsocial in relation to other travelers, only because the eye of vigilance perceives the risk of damage. If the same act were to be committed on a speedway or a race course, it would lose its wrongful quality. The risk seasonably to be perceived defines the duty to be obeyed, and risk imports relation; it is risk to another or to others within the range of apprehension.... This does not mean, of course, that one who launches a destructive force is always relieved of liability, if the force, though known to be destructive, pursues an unexpected path. "It was not necessary that the defendant should have had notice of the particular method in which an accident would occur, if the possibility of an accident was clear to the ordinarily prudent eye."... Some acts, such as shooting are so imminently dangerous to any one who may come within reach of the missile however unexpectedly, as to impose a duty of prevision not far from that of an insurer. Even to-day, and much oftener in earlier stages of the law, one acts sometimes at one's peril.... Under this head, it may be, fall certain cases of what is known as transferred intent, an act willfully dangerous to A resulting by misadventure in injury to B.... These cases aside, wrong is defined in terms of the natural or probable, at least

when unintentional.... The range of reasonable apprehension is at times a question for the court, and at times, if varying inferences are possible, a question for the jury. Here, by concession, there was nothing in the situation to suggest to the most cautious mind that the parcel wrapped in newspaper would spread wreckage through the station. If the guard had thrown it down knowingly and willfully, he would not have threatened the plaintiff's safety, so far as appearances could warn him. His conduct would not have involved, even then, an unreasonable probability of invasion of her bodily security. Liability can be no greater where the act is inadvertent.

Negligence, like risk, is thus a term of relation. Negligence in the abstract, apart from things related, is surely not a tort, if indeed it is understandable at all.... Negligence is not a tort unless it results in the commission of a wrong, and the commission of a wrong imports the violation of a right, in this case, we are told, the right to be protected against interference with one's bodily security. But bodily security is protected, not against all forms of interference or aggression, but only against some. One who seeks redress at law does not make out a cause of action by showing without more that there has been damage to his person. If the harm was not willful, he must show that the act as to him had possibilities of danger so many and apparent as to entitle him to be protected against the doing of it though the harm was unintended. Affront to personality is still the keynote of the wrong....

The law of causation, remote or proximate, is thus foreign to the case before us. The question of liability is always anterior to the question of the measure of the consequences that go with liability. If there is no tort to be redressed, there is no occasion to consider what damage might be recovered if there were a finding of a tort. We may assume, without deciding, that negligence, not at large or in the abstract, but in relation to the plaintiff, would entail liability for any and all consequences, however novel or extraordinary.... There is room for argument that a distinction is to be drawn according to the diversity of interests invaded by the act, as where conduct negligent in that it threatens an insignificant invasion of an interest in property results in an unforeseeable invasion of an interest of another order, as, e.g., one of bodily security. Perhaps other distinctions may be necessary. We do not go into the question now. The consequences to be followed must first be rooted in a wrong.

* * *

The Judgment of the Appellate Division and that of the Trial Term should be reversed, and the complaint dismissed, with costs in all courts.

(continues)

ANDREWS, J. (dissenting). Assisting a passenger to board a train, the defendant's servant negligently knocked a package from his arms. It fell between the platform and the cars. Of its contents the servant knew and could know nothing. A violent explosion followed. The concussion broke some scales standing a considerable distance away. In falling, they injured the plaintiff, an intending passenger.

Upon these facts, may she recover the damages she has suffered in an action brought against the master? The result we shall reach depends upon our theory as to the nature of negligence. Is it a relative concept—the breach of some duty owing to a particular person or to particular persons? Or, where there is an act which unreasonably threatens the safety of others, is the doer liable for all its proximate consequences, even where they result in injury to one who would generally be thought to be outside the radius of danger? This is not a mere dispute as to words. We might not believe that to the average mind the dropping of the bundle would seem to involve the probability of harm to the plaintiff standing many feet away whatever might be the case as to the owner or to one so near as to be likely to be struck by its fall. If, however, we adopt the second hypothesis, we have to inquire only as to the relation between cause and effect. We deal in terms of proximate cause, not of negligence.

Negligence may be defined roughly as an act or omission which unreasonably does or may affect the rights of others, or which unreasonably fails to protect one's self from the dangers resulting from such acts. Here I confine myself to the first branch of the definition. Nor do I comment on the word "unreasonable." For present purposes it sufficiently describes that average of conduct that society requires of its members.

There must be both the act or the omission, and the right. It is the act itself, not the intent of the actor, that is important.... In criminal law both the intent and the result are to be considered. Intent again is material in tort actions, where punitive damages are sought, dependent on actual malice—not on merely reckless conduct. But here neither insanity nor infancy lessens responsibility....

As has been said, except in cases of contributory negligence, there must be rights which are or may be affected. Often though injury has occurred, no rights of him who suffers have been touched. A licensee or trespasser upon my land has no claim to affirmative care on my part that the land be made safe.... Where a railroad is required to fence its tracks against cattle, no man's rights are injured should he wander upon the road because such fence is absent.... An unborn child may not demand immunity from personal harm....

But we are told that "there is no negligence unless there is in the particular case a legal duty to take care, and this duty must be one which is owed to the plaintiff himself and not merely to others.".... This I think too narrow a conception. Where there is the unreasonable act, and some right that may be affected there is negligence whether damage does or does not result. That is immaterial. Should we drive down Broadway at a reckless speed, we are negligent whether we strike an approaching car or miss it by an inch. The act itself is wrongful. It is a wrong not only to those who happen to be within the radius of danger, but to all who might have been there—a wrong to the public at large. Such is the language of the street. Such is the language of the courts when speaking of contributory negligence. Such again and again their language in speaking of the duty of some defendant and discussing proximate cause in cases where such a discussion is wholly irrelevant on any other theory.

Due care is a duty imposed on each one of us to protect society from unnecessary danger, not to protect A, B, or C alone.

It may well be that there is no such thing as negligence in the abstract. "Proof of negligence in the air, so to speak, will not do." In an empty world negligence would not exist. It does involve a relationship between man and his fellows, but not merely a relationship between man and those whom he might reasonably expect his act would injure; rather, a relationship between him and those whom he does in fact injure. If his act has a tendency to harm some one, it harms him a mile away as surely as it does those on the scene. We now permit children to recover for the negligent killing of the father. It was never prevented on the theory that no duty was owing to them. A husband may be compensated for the loss of his wife's services. To say the wrongdoer was negligent as to the husband as well as to the wife is merely an attempt to fit facts to theory. An insurance company paying a fire loss recovers its payment of the negligent incendiary. We speak of subrogation—of suing in the right of the insured. Behind the cloud of words in the fact they hide, that the act, wrongful as to the insured, has also injured the company. Even if it be true that the fault of father, wife, or insured will prevent recovery, it is because we consider the original negligence, not the proximate cause of the injury....

In the well-known *Polemis* Case,... Scrutton, L. J., said that the dropping of a plank was negligent, for it might injure "workman or cargo or ship." Because of either possibility, the owner of the vessel was to be made good for his loss. The act being wrongful, the doer was liable for its proximate results. Criticized and explained

(continues)

as this statement may have been, I think it states the law as it should be and as it is. . . .

The proposition is this: Everyone owes to the world at large the duty of refraining from those acts that may unreasonably threaten the safety of others. Such an act occurs. Not only is he wronged to whom harm might reasonably be expected to result, but he also who is in fact injured, even if he be outside what would generally be thought the danger zone. There needs be duty due the one complaining, but this is not a duty to a particular individual because as to him harm might be expected. Harm to some one being the natural result of the act, not only that one alone, but all those in fact injured may complain. We have never, I think, held otherwise. . . .

If this be so, we do not have a plaintiff suing by "derivation or succession." Her action is original and primary. Her claim is for a breach of duty to herself— not that she is subrogated to any right of action of the owner of the parcel or of a passenger standing at the scene of the explosion.

The right to recover damages rests on additional considerations. The plaintiff's rights must be injured, and this injury must be caused by the negligence. We build a dam, but are negligent as to its foundations. Breaking, it injures property down stream. We are not liable if all this happened because of some reason other than the insecure foundation. But, when injuries do result from our unlawful act, we are liable for the consequences. It does not matter that they are unusual, unexpected, unforeseen, and unforeseeable. But there is one limitation. The damages must be so connected with the negligence that the latter may be said to be the proximate cause of the former.

These two words have never been given an inclusive definition. What is a cause in a legal sense, still more what is a proximate cause, depend in each case upon many considerations, as does the existence of negligence itself. Any philosophical doctrine of causation does not help us. A boy throws a stone into a pond. The ripples spread. The water level rises. The history of that pond is altered to all eternity. It will be altered by other causes also. Yet it will be forever the resultant of all causes combined. Each one will have an influence. How great only omniscience can say. You may speak of a chain, or, if you please, a net. An analogy is of little aid. Each cause brings about future events. Without each the future would not be the same. Each is proximate in the sense it is essential. But that is not what we mean by the word. Nor on the other hand do we mean sole cause. There is no such thing.

Should analogy be thought helpful, however, I prefer that of a stream. The spring, starting on its journey, is joined by tributary after tributary. The river, reaching the ocean, comes from a hundred sources. No man may say whence any drop of water is derived. Yet for a time distinction may be possible. Into the clear creek, brown swamp water flows from the left. Later, from the right comes water stained by its clay bed. The three may remain for a space, sharply divided. But at least inevitable no trace of separation remains. They are so commingled that all distinction is lost.

As we have said, we cannot trace the effect of an act to the end, if end there is. Again however, we may trace it part of the way. A murder at Serajevo may be the necessary antecedent to an assassination in London twenty years hence. An overturned lantern may burn all Chicago. We may follow the fire from the shed to the last building. We rightly say the fire started by the lantern caused its destruction.

A cause, but not the proximate cause. What we do mean by the word "proximate" is that, because of convenience, of public policy, of a rough sense of justice, the law arbitrarily declines to trace a series of events beyond a certain point. This is not logic. It is practical politics. Take our rule as to fires. Sparks from my burning haystack set on fire my house and my neighbor's. I may recover from a negligent railroad. He may not. Yet the wrongful act as directly harmed the one as the other. We may regret that the line was drawn just where it was, but drawn somewhere it had to be. We said the act of the railroad was not the proximate cause of our neighbor's fire. Cause it surely was. The words we used were simply indicative of our notions of public policy. Other courts think differently. But somewhere they reach the point where they cannot say the stream comes from any one source.

Take an illustration given in an unpublished manuscript by a distinguished and helpful writer on the law of torts. A chauffeur negligently collides with another car which is filled with dynamite, although he could not know it. An explosion follows. A, walking on the sidewalk nearby, is killed. B, sitting in a window of a building opposite, is cut by flying glass. C, likewise sitting in a window a block away, is similarly injured. And a further illustration: A nursemaid, ten blocks away, startled by the noise, involuntarily drops a baby from her arms to the walk. We are told that C may not recover while A may. As to B it is a question for court or jury. We will all agree that the baby might not. Because, we are again told, the chauffeur had no reason to believe his conduct involved any risk of injuring either C or the baby. As to them he was not negligent.

But the chauffeur, being negligent in risking the collision, his belief that the scope of the harm he might do would be limited is immaterial. His act unreasonably jeopardized the safety of anyone who might be affected

(continues)

by it. C's injury and that of the baby were directly traceable to the collision. Without that, the injury would not have happened. C had the right to sit in his office, secure from such dangers. The baby was entitled to use the sidewalk with reasonable safety.

The true theory is, it seems to me, that the injury to C, if in truth he is to be denied recovery, and the injury to the baby, is that their several injuries were not the proximate reason of the negligence. And here not what the chauffeur had reason to believe would be the result of his conduct, but what the prudent would foresee, may have a bearing—may have some bearing, for the problem of proximate cause is not to be solved by any one consideration. It is all a question of expediency. There are no fixed rules to govern our judgment. There are simply matters of which we may take account. We have in a somewhat different connection spoken of "the stream of events." We have asked whether that stream was deflected—whether it was forced into new and unexpected channels. . . . This is rather rhetoric than law. There is in truth little to guide us other than common sense.

There are some hints that may help us. The proximate cause, involved as it may be with many other causes, must be, at the least, something without which the event would not happen. The court must ask itself whether there was a natural and continuous sequence between cause and effect. Was the one a substantial factor in producing the other? Was there a direct connection between them, without too many intervening causes? Is the effect of cause on result not too attenuated? Is the cause likely, in the usual judgment of mankind, to produce the result? Or by the exercise of prudent foresight, could the result be foreseen? Is the result too remote from the cause, and here we consider remoteness in time and space. . . . Clearly we must so consider, for the greater the distance either in time or space, the more surely do other causes intervene to affect the result. When a lantern is overturned, the firing of a shed is a fairly direct consequence. Many things contribute to the spread of the conflagration—the force of the wind, the direction and width of streets, the character of intervening structures, other factors. We draw an uncertain and wavering line, but draw it we must as best we can.

Once again, it is all a question of fair judgment, always keeping in mind the fact that we endeavor to make a rule in each case that will be practical and in keeping with the general understanding of mankind.

Here another question must be answered. In the case supposed, it is said, and said correctly, that the chauffeur is liable for the direct effect of the explosion, although he had no reason to suppose it would follow a collision. "The fact that the injury occurred in a different manner than that which might have been expected does not prevent the chauffeur's negligence from being in law the cause of the injury." But the natural results of a negligent act—the results which a prudent man would or should foresee—do have a bearing upon the decision as to proximate cause. We have said so repeatedly. What should be foreseen? No human foresight would suggest that a collision itself might injure one a block away. On the contrary, given an explosion, such a possibility might be reasonably expected. I think the direct connection, the foresight of which the courts speak, assumes prevision of the explosion, for the immediate results of which, at least, the chauffeur is responsible.

It may be said this is unjust. Why? In fairness he should make good every injury flowing from his negligence. Not because of tenderness toward him we say he need not answer for all that follows his wrong. We look back to the catastrophe, the fire kindled by the spark, or the explosion. We trace the consequences, not indefinitely, but to a certain point. And to aid us in fixing that point we ask what might ordinarily be expected to follow the fire or the explosion.

This last suggestion is the factor which must determine the case before us. The act upon which defendant's liability rests is knocking an apparently harmless package onto the platform. The act was negligent. For its proximate consequences the defendant is liable. If its contents were broken, to the owner; if it fell upon and crushed a passenger's foot, then to him; if it exploded and injured one in the immediate vicinity, to him also as to A in the illustration. Mrs. Palsgraf was standing some distance away. How far cannot be told from the record—apparently 25 or 30 feet, perhaps less. Except for the explosion, she would not have been injured. We are told by the appellant in his brief, "It cannot be denied that the explosion was the direct cause of the plaintiff's injuries." So it was a substantial factor in producing the result—there was here a natural and continuous sequence—direct connection. The only intervening cause was that, instead of blowing her to the ground, the concussion smashed the weighing machine which in turn fell upon her. There was no remoteness in time, little in space. And surely, given such an explosion as here, it needed no great foresight to predict that the natural result would be to injure one on the platform at no greater distance from its scene than was the plaintiff. Just how, no one might be able to predict. Whether by flying fragments, by broken glass, by wreckage of machines or structures, no one could say. But injury in some form was most probable.

Under these circumstances I cannot say as a matter of law that the plaintiff's injuries were not the proximate result of the negligence. That is all we have before us.

(continues)

CASE
(CONTINUED)

The court refused to so charge. No request was made to submit the matter to the jury as a question of fact, even would that have been proper upon the record before us.

The judgment appealed from should be affirmed, with costs.

POUND, LEHMAN, and KELLOGG, JJ., concur with CARDOZO, C. J.

ANDREWS, J., dissents in opinion in which CRANE and O'BRIEN, JJ., concur.

Judgment reversed, etc.

The court, in an oft-quoted decision authored by Judge Cardozo, held that the defendant was not liable (see Exhibit 6–2). The court reasoned that the defendant's conduct did not create an unreasonable risk of harm to the plaintiff and that the injury she sustained was not a foreseeable one. "Proof of negligence in the air," the court said, "will not do." The wrong in relationship to the passenger holding the package did not extend to the plaintiff. According to the Cardozo rule, which is generally followed today, "[a] wrong is defined in terms of the natural and probable, at least when unintentional."

Judge Andrews, in his famous dissent, argued that the defendant had a duty to "protect society from unnecessary danger, not to protect A, B, or C alone." According to Andrews, "every one owes to the world at large the duty of refraining from those acts that may unreasonably threaten the safety of others. . . . Not only is he wronged to whom harm might reasonably be expected to result, but he also who is in fact injured, even if he be outside what would generally be thought the danger zone." (Cardozo's formulation of foreseeability is often referred to as the "zone of danger" test.) Judge Andrews did realize that liability must be cut off at some point. Although he fell short of defining the cutoff point, he suggested that if the result were "too remote from the cause" in terms of time and space or if there were too many "intervening causes," the defendant's negligence should not be considered the proximate cause of the plaintiff's injuries.

LOCAL LINKS

Do the courts in your jurisdiction follow the Cardozo or Andrews rule in reference to proximate cause?

EXHIBIT 6–2 *Proximate Cause*

MAJORITY RULE	MINORITY RULE
CARDOZO • Defendant is liable for all reasonably foreseeable consequences of his negligence. He owes a duty of care to the reasonably foreseeable plaintiff.	ANDREWS • Defendant owes a duty to world at large and not just to those in "danger zone." • Similar to "direct causation": defendant is liable for all consequences flowing directly from his actions no matter how unforeseeable.

EXCEPTIONS TO CARDOZO RULE
• "Eggshell skull" rule—defendant must take plaintiff as he finds him. • Defendant is liable for harm occurring in an unforeseen manner if harm is of the same general type that made defendant's conduct negligent. • Defendant is liable if plaintiff is member of class to which there is general foreseeability of harm even if plaintiff was not particularly foreseeable. • Defendant is liable even if there is an unforeseeable intervening cause leading to same type of harm threatened by defendant's negligence.

PUTTING IT INTO PRACTICE 6:3

1. In *Palsgraf*, was the defendant's conduct negligent in relationship to the passenger carrying the package? Did the negligence to this passenger transfer to Mrs. Palsgraf?

2. Before negligence can be found, what must be found "back of the act," according to Justice Cardozo?

3. According to the majority, what must a plaintiff show in reference to being "wronged"? How does the majority define a "wrong"?

4. When does negligence become a tort, according to the majority?

5. Does negligence at large or in the abstract "entail liability for any and all consequences, however novel or extraordinary"?

6. How does the dissent define "due care"?

7. How does the dissent view the duty to the world at large? Is this duty restricted to those within the "danger zone"?

8. How does the dissent define "proximate cause"? Is this definition a matter of logic or practical politics? Is proximate cause a matter of expediency, or is it bound by fixed rules?

9. According to the dissent, why might C and the baby in the hypothetical case involving the chauffeur not be expected to recover? What argument does the dissent give to support C's recovery?

10. Can a clear line be drawn between proximate cause and causes that are too remote in time and space? What does the question of proximate cause ultimately boil down to, according to the dissent?

11. Was Mrs. Palsgraf's injury a natural and probable consequence of the explosion, according to the dissent?

Direct Causation

Andrews's position parallels that of a view commonly known as *direct causation*. Under this view a defendant is liable for all consequences of his negligent acts, no matter how unforeseeable those consequences may be, so long as they flow directly from his actions. A famous case that illustrates the direct causation view is *In re Polemis*, 3 K.B. 560 (Eng. 1921). In *Polemis*, while the defendants were unloading a ship, which they had chartered from the plaintiffs, they negligently dropped a plank into the hold. Somehow the plank struck a spark, which ignited petroleum the ship was carrying, and the resulting fire destroyed the ship. Although plainly no one could reasonably have foreseen that dropping a plank would strike a spark and destroy the entire ship, the defendants were held liable because the fire was the direct result of their negligent act.

Although the direct-causation rule is commonly criticized because a logical extension of the rule would result in limitless liability, proponents of the view argue that a loss should be borne by the guilty rather than by the innocent. The courts that follow the direct-causation rule will not take into account the extent of the harm, the foreseeability of the result, the manner in which the injury occurred, or the timing of the cause and effect.

Duty versus Proximate Cause

You will probably notice in the course of reading opinions that courts frequently blur the issues of duty and proximate cause together. In fact, the *Palsgraf* opinion itself was centered around a discussion of duty. The question, as posed by Cardozo, was whether the defendant had a duty of care to the plaintiff. Whether phrased in terms of duty or proximate cause, the question is essentially the same. A defendant is liable only if her conduct poses a foreseeable risk to the plaintiff. Similarly, a defendant owes a duty of care only if there is a foreseeable risk to the plaintiff. Keep in

PUTTING IT INTO PRACTICE 6:4

Read the facts for "Putting It into Practice 5:2" (the boy who was paralyzed when he dove into the water without first checking its depth). Is the state's failure to post warning signs the cause of David's injuries? How would you analyze the question of actual cause? How would that analysis differ from an analysis of proximate cause?

mind, however, that proximate cause is basically a policy question. It allows the courts to cut off liability in cases in which it would be inherently unfair to hold a defendant liable.

EXCEPTIONS TO THE CARDOZO RULE

Although the Cardozo position has generally been followed by American courts, there are a few notable exceptions. Under these exceptions recovery is allowed even though the consequences are arguably unforeseeable.

"Eggshell Skull" Rule

The first exception requires that a defendant "take his plaintiff as he finds him." In *Watson v. Rinderknecht*, 84 N.W. 798 (Minn. 1901), the case that set forth this exception, the plaintiff, a sixty-year-old man who was receiving a pension resulting from injuries he had sustained during a war, was assaulted by a much younger and more vigorous defendant. The court held the defendant liable for the full extent of the plaintiff's injuries even though the average person in that same confrontation would have suffered much lesser injuries. Under the so-called "eggshell skull" rule, if the plaintiff suffers any foreseeable injury, the defendant is also liable for any additional unforeseen physical consequences. In other words, if a defendant inflicts a relatively minor impact on a plaintiff who dies because he has a skull of eggshell thinness, the defendant will be liable for his death. Suppose a defendant assaults a plaintiff who, unknown to him, has cancer or AIDS. If the plaintiff dies from these injuries because of his weakened condition, the defendant will be liable for his death even though such injuries would have been minor to any healthy individual.

Same General Type of Harm but Unusual Manner

In the second exception to the *Palsgraf* general rule, a defendant is liable if the harm suffered by the plaintiff is of the general type that made the defendant's conduct negligent even if the harm occurs in an unusual manner. Suppose a defendant hands a loaded pistol to a small child, who carries it over to the plaintiff. In the process of handing the pistol to the plaintiff, if the child drops it and the gun goes off and wounds the plaintiff, the defendant is liable. The rationale is that the risk of accidental discharge is the same kind of general risk that made the defendant's conduct negligent initially. The fact that the discharge occurs by an unforeseeable means (dropping the gun) is irrelevant.

If, however, the child drops the gun on someone's foot, causing injuries, the defendant is not liable. The risk of injuring someone by dropping a gun on his foot is not one of the risks that makes the defendant's conduct negligent (*Restatement [Second] of Torts* § 281, illus. 3).

Plaintiff Member of Foreseeable Class

The same rationale is applicable when injury occurs to a plaintiff who is not a particularly foreseeable plaintiff. As long as the plaintiff is a member of a class to which there is a general foreseeability of harm, the defendant is liable. To illustrate, suppose a defendant's car carelessly collides with a car containing dynamite and the plaintiff, a pedestrian on a sidewalk near the collision point, is injured by the ensuing explosion. Even though there is no way she could have known the car contained dynamite, the defendant is liable because a reasonable driver should realize that careless driving can injure pedestrians. Therefore, the plaintiff is a member of a class (pedestrians) to whom harm is a foreseeable consequence of reckless driving. The fact that the harm occurs in a different manner than might

PUTTING IT INTO PRACTICE 6:5

1. As a result of a shipping company negligently mooring its ship, ice and debris cause the ship to run adrift and it collides with a properly moored ship. Both ships smash into a drawbridge, which is not raised in time because the employees who operate it are not on duty. The bridge topples and a dam is created by the collapsed bridge, the two ships, and ice. The resulting flood creates tremendous damage to the adjoining land. If the river-bank landowners bring suit against the shipping company and the City of Buffalo, which operates the drawbridge, will they be able to prove proximate cause in light of the bizarre turn of events?

2. Helen is a worker in a government munitions plant where she handles nitroglycerine. After working at the plant for a few months, Helen begins experiencing chest pains (on the weekends only), severe enough on one occasion to require hospitalization. Ultimately, she is diagnosed as having suffered a heart attack or coronary insufficiency (inadequate blood flow to the heart). After her return to work she experiences weekend chest pains with increasing frequency until she leaves her job four years later.

   Helen is convinced that her handling of nitroglycerine is causing her heart problems. Only one of the many doctors she consults agrees with her. Helen continues to experience health problems after she leaves the plant (continuing but less severe chest pains, dizziness, fatigue, high blood pressure, and coughing spells that lead to vomiting). At trial the district court judge finds the government to be negligent and the cause of her heart disease. She is awarded $53,000 in damages. The judge refuses, however, to make an award for what doctors determine to be hypochondriasis (a neurotic behavior that results in obsessive concern over the state of one's health). If the government's negligence is the actual cause of Helen's hypochondriasis, should the government be considered the proximate cause of her continuing poor health?

---

be anticipated does not absolve the defendant of liability (*Restatement [Second] of Torts* § 281, illus. 2).

INTERVENING CAUSES

An **intervening cause** is anything that occurs after the defendant's negligent act and that contributes to the plaintiff's injury (*Restatement [Second] of Torts* § 441[1]). If the intervening cause rises to such a level of importance that it precludes the defendant's negligence from being the proximate cause of the plaintiff's injury, it becomes a superseding cause (*Restatement [Second] of Torts* § 440). A **superseding cause** supersedes, or cancels out, the defendant's liability. If the defendant should have foreseen the possibility that an intervening cause or one like it might occur, she remains liable (see Exhibit 6–3).

Examples of intervening forces can be seen in the hypothetical situations listed earlier in the section on foreseeability. In the scenario in which the wounded plaintiff died as a result of the doctor's malpractice,

the doctor would be considered an intervening cause. Similarly, the person who caused the accident in which the plaintiff's ambulance was involved would also be an intervening cause. The question in these cases is whether the negligence of others was sufficiently foreseeable that the defendant was negligent in not anticipating and guarding against such negligence. If the negligence of third persons is not surprising, then any acts of the defendant that precipitate the third person's conduct will be considered a proximate cause of the plaintiff's injuries.

Is it surprising that an ambulance might be involved in an accident as a result of someone's negligence? Probably not, and if not, the defendant will remain the proximate cause of the plaintiff's injuries. Is it surprising that someone admitted to a hospital might be further injured as a result of the negligence of his caretaker? Most courts have found medical malpractice to be sufficiently foreseeable, as long as it is not gross malpractice, and therefore not a superseding cause. Similarly, if the defendant causes the

EXHIBIT 6–3 **Liability**

DEFENDANT IS LIABLE	DEFENDANT IS NOT LIABLE
INTERVENING ACTS	Superseding acts
ACCIDENTS	"Acts of God"
MEDICAL MALPRACTICE OF DOCTOR OCCURRING AFTER DEFENDANT'S NEGLIGENCE	Gross medical malpractice of doctor occurring after defendant's negligence
ESCAPE ATTEMPTS	Bizarre escape response to defendant's negligence
RESCUE	Grossly careless acts of rescuer
FORESEEABLE NEGLIGENCE OF OTHERS	Unforeseeable negligence of others
FORESEEABLE CRIMINAL OR INTENTIONALLY TORTIOUS CONDUCT	Unforeseeable criminal or intentionally tortious conduct

plaintiff to be in a weakened state, making him susceptible to disease or accidents, he will be held liable for any subsequent disease or accidents the plaintiff suffers. In the scenario in which the plaintiff is killed in an attempt to flee from the defendant, the plaintiff's attempted escape will not be a superseding cause as long as the plaintiff's response was not totally extraordinary or bizarre. If someone attempts to rescue the plaintiff and causes part or all of the plaintiff's injuries, the defendant will be liable to the plaintiff and to the rescuer as well for any injuries sustained by either. However, if the rescuer is grossly negligent, his conduct will be considered a superseding cause.

The rationale that the foreseeable negligence of others will not be considered a superseding cause has been used to hold tavern owners liable for the negligence of their intoxicated patrons. Although courts are less likely to impose such liability on social hosts, some courts have done so when the guest served was known to the host to be one who would be driving.

A third person's criminal conduct or intentional tortious act may also, in some cases, be sufficiently foreseeable that such conduct will not be considered a superseding cause. As a practical matter, however, proving that the risk of such criminal or tortious conduct was actually foreseeable is often difficult.

To illustrate foreseeable criminal conduct, consider the case in which an alarm company installed a burglar alarm in a pawnshop but, for the convenience of its maintenance people, left the key to the control box (which regulated the sensitivity of the alarm system) on top of the box. A burglar used the key to lower the sensitivity of the alarm so that he could carry out his illegal mission without detection. The court found the alarm company's negligence to be the proximate cause of the pawnshop's loss, refusing to classify the burglary as a superseding cause, in that the burglary was no doubt foreseeable considering that the whole purpose of the alarm system was to prevent such burglaries (*Central Alarm v. Ganem*, 567 P.2d 1203 [Ariz. 1977]).

Superseding Causes

An "act of God," such as being struck by lightning, is considered a superseding cause, as it is an act of nature that is extraordinary and not foreseeable. If our plaintiff in the hypothetical case given earlier was killed by a bolt of lightning while in the process of running from the defendant, the lightning would be considered a superseding cause that would relieve the defendant of liability.

Another example of a superseding cause is a common carrier's negligent delay in the transporting of goods, resulting in the destruction of the goods by a natural catastrophe, such as a flood or fire. Even though the delay might clearly be the cause of the damage—the goods would not have been destroyed had there been no delay—most courts would consider the act of nature a superseding cause. To avoid this holding a plaintiff must show that an increase in the risk of such a catastrophe as a result of the delay was foreseeable.

A contemporary problem that aptly illustrates the issue of superseding causes is the liability of tavern owners for serving obviously intoxicated patrons who inflict injuries on others when they drink and drive. The question is whether the drinking by the patron supersedes the negligence of the tavern owner. As you read the excerpt from *Ontiveros v. Borak*, note the public policy concerns that drive the court to overrule the common law in Arizona. Some of these same public policy concerns have prompted this court, as well as courts in some other states, to apply the same reasoning to cases involving social hosts.

CASE — *Ontiveros v. Borak*
667 P.2nd 200 (Ariz. 1983)

FELDMAN, Justice.

Plaintiff brought this tort action for damages against the defendant, Peter Borak, Sr., d/b/a/ Max's Terminal Buffet (Borak), and others. The action against Borak, the owner of a tavern, was based on the claim that Borak's negligence in serving liquor to an intoxicated patron, Reuben Flores, had been a cause of a subsequent motor vehicle accident in which Flores had inflicted serious injuries on plaintiff. Flores was joined as a defendant.

* * *

This case presents the issue of a tavern owner's common law liability for negligence in serving his or her patrons. Believing the question is of considerable importance and that the public interest requires a speedy and final decision, we granted the petition for transfer in order to meet and finally resolve the issue so squarely presented by the facts of this case. While the evidence is conflicting, the case was decided on motion for a summary judgment and we are therefore required to review the facts in the light most favorable to the party against whom summary judgment was taken. Acknowledging this principle, defendant properly conceded in oral argument that for the purpose of deciding the question of law presented on this appeal the facts are as follows:

On May 22, 1975, Flores left work and, as was his custom, went to Borak's bar before going home. According to Flores' statement and deposition, he there had "quite a few" beers, which were served by the owner's son, and then went across the street to another bar for a short time. He returned to Borak's bar and remained there until closing time was announced at approximately 8:00 P.M. During the afternoon and early evening Flores consumed approximately 30 beers. Unfortunately, he was able to leave the bar and get in his car, which was parked in the bar's parking lot, and headed for home. A few blocks from the bar, he hit a fire hydrant, then swerved, saw cars from the other direction, swerved again, and then "all of a sudden a man was there and I hit him. I told the police officer there was no need to take a breath test because I was drunk." Nevertheless, the police did administer a breathalyzer test; the result was a reading of .33, more than triple the point at which the law now forbids driving.

Plaintiff survived the accident, but received a fractured skull, subdural hematomas, and liver damage. These injuries allegedly resulted in partial paralysis and mental retardation. Plaintiff has been unable to work since the accident.

COMMON LAW

* * *

At common law, . . . a tavern owner is not liable for injuries sustained off-premises by third persons as the result of the acts of an intoxicated patron, even though the tavern owner's negligence in serving the patron was a contributing cause of the accident. The seminal cases in Arizona on tavern owner ("dram shop") liability are *Pratt v. Daly*, 55 Ariz. 535, 104 P.2d 147, and *Collier v. Stamatis*, 63 Ariz. 285, 162 P.2d 125, decided in 1940 and 1945, respectively. Plaintiff argues correctly that neither case explicitly held that a tavern owner could not be held liable under the common law in a fact situation similar to the one presented by the case at bench. We agree; however, implicit, if not explicit, in both *Pratt* and *Collier* is the acceptance of the common law rule. Thus, it was recognized both within and without Arizona that *Pratt v. Daly* had approved and adopted the common law rule of nonliability. . . . We conclude, therefore, that the rule of nonliability for tavern owners has been the common law in Arizona.

However, the common law, which is judge-made and judge-applied, can and will be changed when changed conditions and circumstances establish that it is unjust or has become bad public policy. In reevaluating previous decisions in light of present facts and circumstances, we do not depart from the proper role of the judiciary. . . .

We turn, therefore, to reexamine the present common law rule, its basis and its applicability under the present conditions. In doing so, we are mindful of our words in *Noland v. Wootan*: We take judicial notice of the terrible toll taken, both in personal injuries and property damage, by drivers who mix alcohol and gasoline. . . .

(continues)

CAUSATION

All counsel agreed at oral argument that the common law rule was not a rule of immunity. Indeed, it is impossible to imagine why, of all occupations, those who furnish liquor should be singled out for a judicially conferred blessing of immunity to respond in damages for their wrongful acts. The common law rule was one of nonliability, founded, as indicated in both *Pratt* and *Collier*, upon concepts of causation. In *Pratt*, this court indicated that the drinking of the liquor, and not the selling of it, is the act which causes the injury. We again acknowledge the obvious fact, mentioned in *Pratt*, that one cannot become intoxicated if one does not drink. However, the obverse is equally true: one cannot become intoxicated by drinking liquor unless someone furnishes it. Our common sense tells us that both the furnishing and the drinking are part of the chain of cause and effect that produces accidents such as the one in this case.

Arizona law holds that cause-in-fact exists if the defendant's act helped cause the final result and if that result would not have happened without the defendant's act. Defendant's act need not have been a "large" or "abundant" cause of the final result; there is liability if the result would not have occurred but for defendant's conduct, even if that conduct contributed "only a little" to plaintiff's injuries. Arizona also recognizes that more than one person may be liable for causing an injury and that a particular defendant may not avoid liability for his causative act by claiming that the conduct of some other person was also a contributing cause....

Therefore, as far as causation-in-fact is concerned, the general rule is that a defendant may be held liable if his conduct contributed to the result and if that result would not have occurred "but for" defendant's conduct. There are some dram shop cases where it would be possible to say as a matter of law that the defendant's acts did not contribute to the result,[1] and there are other cases, such as this, where cause-in-fact remains a question for the jury. Certainly no court can say as a matter of law that there can never be a causal relation between serving liquor to an underaged, incompetent or already intoxicated patron and the subsequent accident in which that patron becomes involved when he or she leaves the premises. In so far as *Pratt v. Daly* or *Collier v. Stamatis* stand for such a principle, they are wrong.

Another part of the causation question is the concept of superseding cause.

> [This] is sometimes said to be a question of whether the [defendant's] conduct has been so significant and important a cause that the defendant should be legally responsible. But both significance and importance turn upon conclusions in terms of legal policy, so that this becomes essentially a question of whether the policy of the law will extend the responsibility for the conduct to the consequences which have in fact occurred.

The basic issue of intervening and superseding causes is whether a defendant "is to be held liable for an injury to which he has in fact made a substantial contribution, when it is brought about by a later cause of independent origin, for which he is not responsible."

The common law rule of tavern owner nonliability was mainly based upon the concept that the chain of legal causation between the selling of the alcohol and the injury was broken or "superseded by the voluntary act of the purchaser in imbibing the drink." We acknowledge, of course, that the customer who drinks to excess or the underage patron who drinks at all is at fault. To say that the immediate actor is at fault, however, is not to say that there is no liability to be imposed upon the remote actor. The policy of the law on questions of intervening and superseding cause has evolved to the rule that the original actor is relieved from liability for the final result when, and only when, an intervening act of another was unforeseeable by a reasonable person in the position of the original actor and when, looking backward, after the event, the intervening act appears extraordinary. However, where the negligent conduct of the first actor increases the foreseeable risk of a particular harm occurring through the conduct of a second actor, the "fact that the harm is brought about through the intervention of another force does not relieve the [first] actor of liability."

The test, then, for whether the actions of a patron, such as Flores, constitute a superseding cause which relieves the tavern owner from liability is whether Flores' conduct was unforeseeable to one in Borak's position and whether the court can say with the benefit of hindsight that the occurrence of the harm through the conduct of the intervening actor was both unforeseeable and extraordinary. Even if there were no authority on the issue, we could find it neither unforeseeable nor unexpected that a patron who was served 30 beers over the space of five or six hours became quite drunk. The only thing extraordinary about the whole situation is that this patron, with a blood-alcohol level of .33, was able to walk to his car. It was certainly neither unforeseeable nor unexpected that once Flores began driving he would become involved in an accident likely to cause death

---

1. Suppose, for instance, that Flores had consumed 30 beers at Borak's and "one more for the road" at the bar across the street. Without specific evidence it would be difficult to argue that the accident would not have happened "but for" the last drink.

(continues)

or serious injury. This elemental point has not escaped other courts.

> When alcoholic beverages are sold by a tavern keeper to a minor or to an intoxicated person, the unreasonable risk of harm...to members of the traveling public may readily be recognized and foreseen; this is particularly evident in current times when traveling by car to and from the tavern is so commonplace and accidents resulting from drinking are so frequent.

In fact, courts have recognized that the injury-producing conduct of the patron who has been served more alcohol while intoxicated is one of the very hazards which make the tavern owner's act negligent. The trend of modern authority is well summarized by the following words of the Supreme Court of Hawaii:

> We hold that the consequences of serving liquor to an intoxicated motorist, in light of the universal use of automobiles and the increasing frequency of accidents involving drunk drivers, are foreseeable to a tavern owner....The consumption, resulting inebriation and injurious conduct are therefore foreseeable intervening acts which will not relieve the tavern of liability.

Common sense, common experience and authority all combine to produce the irrefutable conclusion that furnishing alcohol, consumption of alcohol and subsequent driving of a vehicle which is then involved in an accident are all foreseeable, ordinary links in the chain of causation leading from the sale to the injury. Under the facts of this case, a jury could find that Borak's furnishing of additional liquor to Flores after he became intoxicated was a cause of the injuries sustained by plaintiff.

Borak argues, however, that as a matter of policy we should continue to hold that there is no "proximate cause" in dram shop cases. He contends that it will be difficult to sort out cause and effect in many cases since a patron who has already become intoxicated may be involved in an accident even without the "help" of the defendant who furnishes more alcohol. This contention is answered in the dissent in *Meade v. Freeman*, 93 Idaho 389, 462 P.2d 54 (1969). In criticizing the common law rule, Judge Prather stated:

> It is quite ordinary to observe that persons who commence drinking intoxicants pass through various stages from complete sobriety to incapacitating intoxication and unconsciousness....When the person has imbibed sufficient liquor that the effects thereof are becoming obvious to the ordinary person, the imbiber is still able to control himself and his actions sufficiently to avoid injury to others. If the imbiber continues to drink intoxicants, however, his condition will worsen until he reaches the point that he can not control his thought or muscular processes. After the first signs of apparent and obvious intoxication have begun to show on a person who is drinking, it is within the knowledge and experience of nearly all people that such person should not indulge in any further use of intoxicants until his body has rid itself of that which he has already imbibed. When so viewed, I perceive no difference in regarding the sale of further intoxicants to one already drunk as a proximate cause of ensuing injuries [as] in those cases wherein the sale of firearms to minors or incompetents, the sale of dangerous drugs to those known to be addicted, or the manufacture and release upon the market of dangerously defective commodities are held to form a basis for liability. The underlying principle of all of these cases is that the seller is sending out into the public a thing of danger which a reasonably prudent person under like circumstances would apprehend would be likely to cause injury to someone else. When most people walked and few had horses or carriages, ... it may have been that the common rule of law of nonliability arising from the sale of liquor to an intoxicated person was satisfactory. But the situation then and the problem in today's society of the imbiber going upon the public highways and operating a machine that requires quick response of mind and muscle and capable of producing mass death and destruction are vastly different.

Judge Prather's words are even truer today, fourteen years after they were written. The statistics cited in the concurring opinion in *State ex rel. Ekstrom v. Justice Court*, —Ariz.—, 663 P.2d 992 (1983), indicate a frightful toll—25,000 deaths and 650,000 injuries each year in motor vehicle accidents in which alcohol is a contributing cause. We believe, therefore, that the words of Division II of our Court of Appeals are correct:

> It seems clear that the common law rule is an anachronism, unsuitable to our present society, and that its reasoning is repugnant to modern tort theories.

We agree with the Pennsylvania Supreme Court that "[t]o serve an intoxicated person more liquor is to light the fuse." Therefore, *Pratt v. Daly, supra*, and *Collier v. Stamatis, supra*, are overruled insofar as they stand for the proposition that the negligence of a tavern owner in continuing to serve liquor to a patron who is or has become intoxicated can never be the legal cause of a subsequent accident.

PUTTING IT INTO PRACTICE 6:6

1. What was the common law rule in Arizona regarding the liability of tavern owners?

2. What did the court take judicial notice of?

3. On what basis did the court in *Pratt v. Daly* reach the conclusion that tavern owners were not liable?

4. Using the but-for test, did the court believe that a causal relation can exist between the serving of liquor to a patron and that patron's subsequent involvement in an accident?

5. Under the common law of non-liability, what was considered the superseding cause that broke the chain of causation between the selling of the liquor and the subsequent accident?

6. On what basis did the court conclude that Flores's conduct was not a superseding cause?

7. Why did the defendant believe that proximate cause should not exist in "dramshop" cases?

8. How did the court respond to the defendant's argument?

9. What was the consequence to *Pratt v. Daly* and *Collier v. Stamatis* as a result of this opinion?

Unforeseeable Intervention

Thus far we have looked at cases in which the intervening cause was foreseeable. If the intervention was not foreseeable but, in fact, led to the same type of harm as that threatened by the defendant's negligence, the courts typically find the intervention not to be a superseding cause (*Restatement [Second] of Torts* § 442B). The reasoning is that the defendant exposed the plaintiff to an unreasonable risk of harm of the same type as that which occurred. Allowing the defendant to escape liability simply because the harm was produced by an unforeseeable intervention would be unfair.

Let us consider the case of *Derdiarian v. Felix Contracting Corp.*, 414 N.E.2d 666 (N.Y. 1981) as an illustration of this principle. In this case the plaintiff, an employee of a subcontractor, was sealing a gas main at a work site in the street when he was struck by a driver who had just suffered an epileptic seizure and lost control of his vehicle. When struck, the plaintiff was catapulted into the air and landed in 400°F liquid enamel, causing him to be ignited into a fireball, which he miraculously survived. The plaintiff alleged that the defendant contracting company had failed to take adequate measures to ensure the safety of workers on the excavation site. The defendant argued that the plaintiff was injured as a result of the driver's negligence and that there was no causal link between the defendant's breach of duty and the plaintiff's injuries. The court refused to find the driver's negligence a superseding cause, noting that an intervening act does not serve as a superseding cause "where the risk of the intervening act occurring is the very same risk which renders the actor negligent."

JURY QUESTION

The issue of proximate cause is a jury question as long as there is a possibility that reasonable persons could differ on this issue. The judge must first formulate the appropriate legal rule in the form of a jury instruction. But once that standard has been formulated, the final decision is a factual one left to the jury.

APPLICATION

In the case of Gertrude's attack on Teddy and Mr. Goodright, Gertrude was unquestionably the actual cause of Teddy's and Mr. Goodright's injuries. Of course, the Baxters might argue that Mr. Goodright's injuries were due to Teddy's negligence in entering their backyard. Under the but-for test, however, the rebuttal would be that but for the Baxters' negligence in leaving their gate unlocked Teddy would

PUTTING IT INTO PRACTICE 6:7

1. Marilyn negligently runs over Lucinda, breaking her leg. While Lucinda is learning to walk on crutches, she slips, falls, and breaks her arm. Is Lucinda's fall a superseding cause of her broken arm? Would your answer change if you knew that at the time Lucinda was trying to walk across an extremely narrow walkway and that she was doing this on a dare from her friends?

2. Charles is in a phone booth making a call; he looks up and sees a vehicle coming toward him. He attempts to flee the booth but cannot because of the faulty design, maintenance, and repair of the booth by Pacific Telephone and Western Electric. At trial Charles also alleges that the telephone booth was too close to the stream of "habitually speeding, dangerous traffic." Will Pacific Telephone and Western Electric be successful in arguing that the intoxicated driver in the vehicle that hit Charles was the superseding cause of his injuries?

3. The Exxon tanker, the *Houston*, was delivering oil into a pipeline through two floating hoses when a storm arose, causing the line linking the tanker to the single point mooring system (SPM) to break. During this "breakout," when the hoses were disengaged from the SPM and threatening to damage the ship's propeller, another vessel arrived and helped the crew of the *Houston* to regain control of the hoses. The captain was able to safely navigate the ship back out to sea so that it was no longer in danger of being stranded. While the crew was working to disconnect the hoses, the captain negligently failed to have someone plot the ship's position. Without knowing this position the captain could not effectively use a navigational chart to check for hazards. Failure to fix the ship's position constituted gross and extraordinary negligence. When the captain did order someone to plot the ship's position, he noticed too late that the ship was heading for a reef, and moments later the ship ran aground.

   Exxon sues the owner and operator of the mooring facility for the losses incurred by the loss of its ship. Do you think Exxon is likely to be successful in its suit?

---

not have been able to enter the yard. Even under the substantial-factor test the Baxters' failure to lock their gate would be a significant factor in the cause of Mr. Goodright's injuries. Assuming that Teddy would not have been able to enter the Baxters' backyard except for the presence of the unlocked gate, both he and the Baxters would be considered causes of Mr. Goodright's injuries. As such they would both be liable for his injuries.

The Baxters would also be considered the proximate cause of Teddy's and Mr. Goodright's injuries. It is reasonably foreseeable that if a person fails to lock a gate to a yard housing a watchdog, someone, especially a child, will enter the yard and be attacked.

The Baxters might argue that Mr. Goodright's volunteering to rescue Teddy, which was of his own volition and not a duty imposed upon him, was a superseding cause that should absolve them of liability. Remember, however, that rescue is not considered an intervening cause unless it is performed in a grossly negligent manner. Based on the famous Cardozo rationale that "danger invites rescue," a rescue is foreseeable when the defendant's negligence has created a danger that could result in injury to somebody. An argument on the part of the Baxters that Teddy's negligence was a superseding cause would also fail. Such negligence was reasonably foreseeable if children were able to gain access to the Baxters' backyard via the unlocked gate.

SUMMARY

The issue of causation consists of two separate considerations—actual cause (causation of fact) and proximate cause (legal cause). If the plaintiff can prove that the defendant's actions were the actual and factual cause of her injuries, she has proven actual cause. If the plaintiff can further prove that her injuries were a reasonably foreseeable result of the defendant's conduct, she can show proximate cause.

The but-for and substantial-factor tests are used in proving actual cause. The plaintiff bears the burden of proving actual cause and must do so by a preponderance of the evidence. If the plaintiff cannot prove which defendant actually caused his injuries, he can shift the burden back on the defendants to show who actually caused the harm using the theory of alternate liability or market-share liability. If the tortfeasors are unable to prove that they did not cause the plaintiff's injuries, they will all be found liable. If a plaintiff can prove the existence of a common plan or that the defendants assisted or encouraged each other in accomplishing a tortious result, he has proved actual causation using the concerted action theory.

The purpose of proximate, or legal, cause is to restrict a defendant's liability by absolving her of liability when the plaintiff's injury occurred as a result of a series of highly improbable or extraordinary events stemming from the defendant's negligence. The question of proximate cause is a policy question; the question of actual cause is a factual one. The issue of foreseeability was addressed most notably in *Palsgraf*, in which Judge Cardozo denied recovery to the plaintiff because of a lack of foreseeability. Justice Andrews, in contrast, argued that one owes a duty to the "world at large" and not just to those in the "danger zone." Andrews's position parallels the view of courts that espouse the theory of direct causation.

The Cardozo position is generally followed by most American courts. There are, however, a few notable exceptions. First, under the "eggshell skull" rule, if a plaintiff suffers any foreseeable injury, the defendant is liable for any additional unforeseeable physical consequences. Second, a defendant is liable if the harm suffered by the plaintiff is of the general type that made the defendant's conduct negligent, even if the harm occurs in an unanticipated manner. Third, a defendant is liable as long as the plaintiff is a member of a class to which there is a reasonable foreseeability of harm, even if the plaintiff herself is not a particularly foreseeable plaintiff.

A defendant is expected to foresee the possibility of an intervening cause. Even if the intervening cause is not foreseeable but the kind of harm suffered by the plaintiff is, the defendant will remain liable. If an intervening cause rises to such a level that it becomes a superseding cause, the defendant is absolved of liability. The foreseeable negligence of others is not considered a superseding cause. Neither is a person's criminal or intentionally tortious conduct considered a superseding cause if it is sufficiently foreseeable.

KEY TERMS

actual cause
  Cause in fact of the plaintiff's injuries
custodian of the records
  The person in an organization who knows about its filing system and records
intervening cause
  Act that contributes to the plaintiff's injuries but does not relieve the defendant of liability

proximate cause
  Legal cause of the plaintiff's injuries; emphasis is on the concept of foreseeability
superseding cause
  Act that contributes to the plaintiff's injuries to the extent that the defendant is relieved of liability

REVIEW QUESTIONS

1. What is the difference between actual cause and proximate cause?

2. Describe how each of the following is used to prove actual cause.
   a. but-for test
   b. substantial-factor test
   c. alternate-liability theory
   d. market-share-liability theory
   e. concerted-action theory

3. In what circumstances have courts opted to use the substantial-factor test rather than the but-for test?

4. How do the alternative-liability and market-share-liability theories assist plaintiffs in proving their case?

5. What is the "lost chance of recovery" theory, and how does it help plaintiffs?

6. What does the issue of proximate cause boil down to, and why do courts struggle with this concept?

7. What are the facts in *Palsgraf*?
   a. What was the issue before the court?
   b. What did the majority rule, and why?
   c. Why did the dissent disagree?
   d. Do most courts follow the majority or the dissent?

8. What is the direct-causation rule?
   a. How was it developed in *Polemis*?
   b. Why is this rule criticized?

9. What is the relationship between duty and proximate cause?

10. Give examples of three exceptions to the Cardozo rule of foreseeability.

11. Explain the difference between intervening and superseding causes.
    a. Give an example of an intervening cause.
    b. Give an example of a superseding cause.

12. Under what circumstances will the courts find an unforeseeable intervening cause not to be a superseding cause?

13. Is proximate cause a jury question or a question for the judge?

PRACTICE EXAM

Students should complete the practice exam after studying each chapter. The answers are in Appendix A. If you score lower than 80%, you should reread the materials.

True-False

1. Actual causation relates to the closeness of the connection between the defendant's conduct and the plaintiff's injuries.

2. The but-for test does not encompass situations involving concurrent causes.

3. Under the substantial-factor test, if concurrent causes produce a single, indivisible harm, both factors can be deemed the actual cause of the plaintiff's injuries.

4. The plaintiff must prove with clear and convincing evidence that the defendant was the cause of her injuries.

5. If two defendants are negligent but only one could have caused the plaintiff's injury, the burden is on the plaintiff to prove which defendant caused her injury.

6. Under the market-share-liability theory, a plaintiff can recover even if she cannot prove which defendant from among multiple defendants actually caused her injury.

7. With the market-share-liability theory, the plaintiff can prevail even if he cannot prove the nature of the defendant's conduct.

8. Under the lost-chance-of-recovery theory, a plaintiff can recover even if he cannot prove that the defendant's negligence resulted in a loss of life.

9. Proximate cause reflects a judicial concern that defendants should not be liable for highly improbable consequences stemming from their negligence.

10. Direct causation holds defendants liable for the consequences arising from their actions that are unforeseeable.

11. A defendant is liable for the harm suffered by the plaintiff even if the harm occurs in an unusual manner, as long as the harm is of the same general type that made the defendant's conduct negligent.

12. A third person's criminal or intentionally tortious conduct is never considered a superseding cause.

13. If the acts of a third party are not surprising, they will be considered intervening causes, and the acts of the defendant that precipitate the third party's conduct will be considered the proximate cause of the plaintiff's injuries.

14. If an intervening cause is unforeseeable, a defendant is never liable.

Matching

GROUP 1

_____ 1. Legal cause

_____ 2. Factual cause

_____ 3. Concurrent causes

_____ 4. Broadest test for causation

_____ 5. *Sindell v. Abbott Labs*

_____ 6. Tacit agreement

a. substantial-factor test

b. but-for test

c. concerted-action theory

d. actual cause

e. proximate cause

f. market-share theory

GROUP 2

_____ 1. Negligence in the air will not do

_____ 2. Duty to the world at large

_____ 3. Opinion followed by most courts

_____ 4. Majority opinion for *Palsgraf*

_____ 5. Duty to protect those in danger zone

_____ 6. Duty to protect society from unnecessary danger

a. Andrews

b. Cardozo

c. concerted-action theory

Answers for Matching: Group 2 are either a or b; therefore, answers will be used more than once.

GROUP 3

_____ 1. Cause that precludes defendant liability

_____ 2. Cause that contributes to plaintiff's injury

_____ 3. Virtually limitless liability

_____ 4. Liability for unforeseen consequences suffered by plaintiff

a. eggshell-skull rule

b. direct cause

c. superseding cause

d. intervening cause

Fill-in-the-Blanks

1. Under the _____ _____ test the defendant will be considered the actual cause of the plaintiff's injuries if those injuries would not have occurred but for the defendant's negligence.

2. With the _____ _____ _____ theory the plaintiff can prevail if she can prove the defendants were negligent even though she cannot show which defendant caused her injury.

3. Under the _____ _____ theory the plaintiff must show that the defendants encouraged or assisted each other in performing a tortious act.

4. Proximate cause boils down to a question of _____ .

5. Courts sometimes blur the concept of proximate cause and _____ .

6. Courts that follow the _____ causation rules do not take into account the foreseeability of the result and the extent of the harm.

7. Under the _____ _____ rule a defendant must take his plaintiff as he finds him.

8. Ordinary medical malpractice is an example of a(n) _____ cause whereas a fire or flood is an example of a(n) _____ cause.

Multiple-Choice

1. In toxic tort cases
    a. the problem faced by plaintiffs in toxic tort cases is proving that the toxin in question is capable of producing the type of injury suffered by the plaintiffs.
    b. plaintiffs must rely on expert testimony but not epidemiological studies.
    c. plaintiffs do not have to prove that the toxin in question and not some other toxin caused their injury.
    d. all of the above.

2. In *Sindell v. Abbott Laboratories,* the court
   a. felt that the defendants were in a better position to bear the cost of the plaintiff's injuries than was the plaintiff.
   b. reasoned that when there was a conflict between an innocent plaintiff and negligent defendants, the plaintiff should prevail.
   c. concluded that any defendant manufacturer that could not prove that it had not produced the dosages of DES consumed by the plaintiff's mother would be liable for the portion of the judgment that represented its share of the DES market at the time of the mother's consumption.
   d. all of the above.

3. In *Palsgraf*
   a. the question was whether the defendant was negligent in pushing a passenger to help that passenger board a train.
   b. Justice Cardozo concluded that the harm that occurred to the plaintiff was reasonably foreseeable.
   c. Andrews felt liability should be cut off if there were too many intervening causes or if the result was too remote from the cause in terms of time or space.
   d. all of the above

4. A superseding cause
   a. does not relieve the defendant of liability.
   b. is not an issue when it comes to the liability of tavern owners.
   c. is exemplified by gross negligence by a rescuer.
   d. all of the above.

5. Proximate cause
   a. is a policy question.
   b. is a question only the judge can answer.
   c. is an easy questions for courts to answer.
   d. all of the above.

PRACTICE POINTERS

Plaintiffs are not entitled to compensation for *preexisting conditions*, i.e., physical or emotional conditions that existed prior to the damage inflicted by the defendant. Suppose, for example, the plaintiff was a horse trainer who had suffered a number of riding accidents prior to her vehicular accident involving the defendant. If the plaintiff was suffering from the pain of lower back injury due to these riding accidents, she could not recover damages for her lower back injuries from the defendant if the vehicular accident had not contributed in any way to her preexisting condition. If, however, the vehicular accident had aggravated her preexisting back condition or had caused additional injuries, she could still recover. Remember that under the "eggshell skull" rule she could recover for the full extent of her injuries even if she was more susceptible to injury than a normally healthy individual, and even if the healthy individual might not have suffered similar injuries.

Paralegals are often assigned the task of determining the nature and extent of preexisting conditions. To do so they must meticulously review the medical records of the plaintiff. If their firm represents the plaintiff, they must interview the plaintiff to gain a clear comprehension of the plaintiff's preexisting complaints and to distinguish them from the currently existing injuries. They will also need to examine employment records and any previous insurance or workers' compensation claims. All these records must be compiled in preparation for a review by the medical expert(s). Such careful preparation prevents surprise at subsequent depositions or at trial. Preexisting conditions are a hotly contested issue at all stages of a case and therefore must be carefully documented by both sides in personal injury cases.

Medical records are confidential. Therefore, the client must sign a written authorization before the doctor's office or hospital will release them. Most firms have standard release forms. The form should be reviewed, however, before using it to make sure it provides everything that you need. If clients are asked to sign several authorization forms in advance, they will not need to return to the office every time an authorization is needed. Some institutions will not accept copies, so a duplicate original should be sent. Other institutions require authorizations to be notarized; time can be saved by having them all notarized at once.

Before requesting medical records, the health care facility should be contacted to see what procedures it requires. Are any fees charged, and if so, must they be paid before the records will be released? Many doctors charge nominal fees for their notes and several hundred dollars for their narrative reports; others charge substantial fees for both. Inquiries should be made about the name of the **custodian of the records** (the person in an organization who knows about its filing system and records) from whom the records should be requested.

Following is an example at a medical authorization release.

AUTHORIZATION FOR USE AND DISCLOSURE OF PRIVATE HEALTH INFORMATION AND MEDICAL RECORDS

Patient Identification	Provider Identification	Identification of Records Recipient
Elizabeth Scotty	**Custodian of Records Kino Hospital**	**The Ceasar Law Office**
3155 Montgomery Way Tucson, AZ 89563	2455 E. Ajo Way Tucson, AZ 89563	3800 North Central Avenue, Suite 615, Phoenix, AZ 85012
SSN: 611-77-5025		
DOB: 09-30-83		602-267-1945

I, **Elizabeth Scotty**, hereby authorize the above-identified health care provider to disclose and release to The Ceasar **Law Office**, its representatives, employees, consultants, experts, co-counsel or others designated by the firm, the following from my medical chart to include **all dates of treatment** between **March 31, 2005** and **the present:**

All Records, Reports, Bills and Correspondence, including, but not limited to:

X Assessments
X Consultations
X Discharge Summaries
X Diagnostic Tests
X Diagnostic Imaging Reports/Films
X ER Reports
X Physicians' Notes and Orders
X Nursing Assessments/Notes

X Pathology Reports
X Laboratory Reports and Results
X X-ray Films
X MRI Films
X Bills (or equivalents)
X Therapy Evaluations and Notes
X Plans of Care
X Operative Reports

In addition, I authorize release of any and all records that may contain references to, or specific information about, the following:

X Diagnosis and/or treatment for alcoholism and/or drug abuse
X Diagnosis and/or treatment of mental health issues
X HIV antibody test results and/or AIDS diagnosis and treatment
X Genetic test results and/or related treatment.

This Authorization will expire within one-hundred twenty (120) days from the date of my signature below, or on _____.

This Authorization shall be considered renewed upon my request or upon the request of my attorney, Silly Ceasar and may be revoked by me at any time. It is my intention that this Authorization revoke and replace all other Authorizations signed by me or on my behalf by any and all parties.

I hereby authorize use of photostatic copies of this Authorization in place of the original by The Ceasar **Law Office.**

SIGNATURE

I have had the opportunity to consider and review the contents of this Authorization and confirm that the contents are consistent with my direction to the health care provider. I understand that by signing this Authorization, I do hereby confirm that the health care provider may release and disclose my private health care information to: Ceasar Law Office, 3800 North Central Avenue, Suite 615, Phoenix, AZ 85012. I understand that by release of my medical records from the care of the above-identified provider, that they may be seen by others not intended or identified.

_____
Patient Signature

_____
DATE

(continues)

Custodian of Records
Kino Hospital
2455 E. Ajo Way
Tucson, AZ 89563

Re: Your Patient/JLO Client: Elizabeth Scotty
Dear Sir or Madam:

The Ceasar Law Office represents Elizabeth Scotty. Enclosed, please find an Authorization For Release of Medical Records signed by Ms. Scotty **authorizing you to provide us with any and all medical records, billing records/statements related to services/treatment she received from you** during the time period of March 31, 2005 to the present.

Please provide us with copies of the requested medical records and itemized billing statements as soon as possible. If advanced payment for copying the requested records is required, please contact me and we will forward the payment.

Thank you for your anticipated cooperation. If you have any questions, please do not hesitate to call me.

Respectfully,

**Liliani G. Mendoza
Paralegal**

TORT TEASERS

1. Plaintiff boilermaker welder is injured as a result of exposure to manganese fumes over the course of his career of twenty-seven years as a welder. Defendant manufacturers began placing a product label on welding-rod containers warning that welding may produce fumes and gases hazardous to one's health and cautioned users to avoid breathing the fumes and gas and to use proper ventilation. Plaintiff failed to read the warnings on the welding-rod containers. Is Defendant's failure to warn an actual cause of Plaintiff's injury? *Boyd v. Lincoln Elec. Co.,* 902 N.E 2d 1023 (Ohio App.8 Dist. 2008).

2. Just before Defendant's industrial "dinky" engine collides with a train on a crossing, the engineer of the "dinky" reverses the engine, shuts off the steam, and jumps. The collision causes the throttle to jar loose, and the "dinky" engine backs up, gathers momentum, and travels around a loop to a second crossing where it collides with a train. Plaintiff, who is a passenger on the train, is injured in the second collision. Even though the second collision occurred in an unforeseeable manner, should Defendant be held liable? *Bunting v. Hogsett,* 21 A.31 (Pa. 1890).

3. Suppose Defendant drives a truck at excessive speed. Which of the following consequences do you think are foreseeable?

   a. The truck narrowly misses a pregnant woman, who is frightened into a miscarriage. *Mitnick v. Whelan Bros.,* 163 A. 414 (Conn. 1932).

   b. Defendant injures a man who suffers a second accident six months later while he is walking on crutches as a result of the first accident. *Squires v. Reynolds,* 5 A.2d 877 (Conn. 1939).

   c. A truck knocks a taxi cab up against a stone wall, the wall is weakened, and as a result a stone falls off the top of the wall as the taxi is being disengaged from the wall. A pedestrian is injured when the stone falls on her. *In re Guardian Casualty Co.,* 2 N.Y.S.2d 232 (N.Y. Sup. Ct. 1938).

4. A waitress employed at Defendant's restaurant spills hot coffee on Plaintiff's lap, resulting in first-degree burns. When Plaintiff jumps up she strikes her knee on an adjoining stool, requiring her leg to be put in a cast. Because of her obesity and neurotic anxiety, Plaintiff is disabled for eight months.

If the normal recovery time is one to two weeks, should Defendant be held liable for the full extent of damages? *Thompson v. Lupone*, 62 A.2d 861 (Conn. 1948).

5. Defendant railroad company carries a young girl past her station and puts her off the train near a "hobo jungle," the favorite haunt of many unsavory criminal characters. On the way back to town she is raped by two unidentified persons. Is the defendant the proximate cause of the plaintiff's injuries? *Hines v. Garrett*, 108 S.E. 690 (Va. 1921).

6. A rock radio station with an extensive teenage audience sponsors a contest that rewards the first contestant to locate a particular disc jockey. Two minors, driving in separate automobiles in pursuit of the illustrious disc jockey, reach speeds of up to 80 mph. One of the minors negligently forces another car off the highway, killing the driver. A wrongful death action is filed against the radio station. Should the rock station be held liable, or is the negligence of the minor a superseding cause? *Weirum v. RKO General Inc.*, 539 P.2d 36 (Cal. 1975).

INTERNET INQUIRIES

Parties to litigation often find it helpful to learn about the litigation history of their opponents. Are they, for example, frequent participants in the litigation process, either as plaintiffs or defendants? Do they have a number of judgments recorded against them? Are they currently involved in litigation pertaining to an issue similar to which the parties are now litigating or planning to litigate? Information about existing or previous court cases is relatively easy to find and many times worth the time and effort invested.

Local courts at the county and city levels typically house files of active and inactive cases. They may be stored online, on microfilm, or in paper files. Older cases are often stored in remote places within the court clerk's office or even in another building so it can sometimes take days to retrieve an older case. Cases are typically filed under the plaintiffs' names, defendants' names, and case number. Note that if more than one plaintiff or defendant is involved, the case may be filed under the first plaintiff's name, which means you may not find the case using the name of the plaintiff or defendant for whom you are looking. Courts have indexes organized according to the names of the parties. These indexes give the names of all the parties, the disposition of the case, and the assigned case number. Giving the court clerk this number will allow you to get a copy of the entire file. The beauty of getting the actual court file is that it contains all the documents prepared by the litigants, motions that were made, discovery materials, and many other potentially useful pieces of information about the parties and the witnesses.

Federal district court records can be accessed in one of three ways: (1) going to the district court and asking for an individual's records; (2) subscribing to a database called "PACER" (Public Access to Electronic Records) that allows you to look up specific records; (3) paying a national information retrieval company to pull up the desired records. Additionally, certified copies of decrees, orders and petitions relating to district court proceedings can be obtained through the clerk's office. In every case you will need either the individual's or business entity's name or the case number.

Go to the Internet and, using the name of a local state court in your jurisdiction as search terms, find out if this court has a web page.

1. How far back can you get court decisions for your state's highest court online?

   a. Can you access this court online? If yes, describe the steps you must take to pull up court records. If no, find a court in your state that does have a web page, and use it to answer the following questions. (Go to the National Center for State Courts site at http://www.ncsc.org and select "information & resources" and "browse by states" to find links to courts in your state.)

   b. How far back do these records go online?

   c. Can you access both active and inactive cases online?

   d. Call the court clerk for your local court and find out what procedure you must follow to get court records?

      (1) What information must you have?

      (2) Are these records on microfilm or paper files?

      (3) How much does it cost to make copies of documents in these files?

      (4) What kinds of information are contained in the court files in this court? Are, for example, discovery materials available?

PRACTICAL PONDERABLES

Your firm has agreed to represent Michael, the victim of a school shooting. The evidence your investigator has been able to gather at this point indicates that the suspected assailants had been avid fans of an incredibly violent movie, *Teenage Stalkers*, and that they shot Michael as part of their attempt to replicate what happened in that movie. Your supervising attorneys want to sue the company that produced this movie, but they are concerned about being able to prove causation.

1. What will they have to show to prove the link between the movie company and Michael's shooting?
2. Why do you think causation may be a problem?
3. What evidence will need to be presented if they are going to meet their burden of proof?

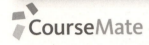 Access an interactive eBook, chapter-specific learning tools, including flashcards, quizzes, and more in your Paralegal CourseMate, accessed through www.CengageBrain.com.

CHAPTER 7

© Cengage Learning 2012

Negligence: Damages

CHAPTER OBJECTIVES

After completing the chapter, you should be able to

- Categorize damages.
- Recognize the various components of damages.
- Appreciate the practical problems inherent in calculating damages.
- Recognize the limitations on what a plaintiff can recover.
- Appreciate the controversy surrounding punitive damages.
- Distinguish between wrongful-death and survival actions.

Liability without damages is like a car with no wheels. If the defendant is clearly liable but the plaintiff suffers minimal injuries, recovery will also be minimal. Clearly, if the attorney's fees exceed the anticipated recovery, the client cannot afford to have an attorney take the case. Therefore, the attorneys representing Teddy and Mr. Goodright will want to determine early if the anticipated damages warrant the expenditure of time and resources necessary to litigate the case. (For organizational purposes, damages are discussed throughout this chapter in the context of negligence only, even though damages can certainly be awarded in cases involving intentional torts and strict liability as well.)

CATEGORIES OF DAMAGES

Damages are generally divided into three categories: compensatory damages, punitive damages, and nominal damages (see Exhibit 7–1). **Compensatory damages** are designed to compensate the victim for her losses and restore her to the position she was in before she sustained her injuries. **Punitive damages** are intended to punish the defendant for reckless or egregious misconduct and deter others from engaging in the same or similar wrongful conduct. **Nominal damages** are awarded when no actual damages are proved but a tort is shown to have been committed. Because actual damages must be proved in negligence cases, nominal damages are not available in negligence suits.

Compensatory damages are further divided into two categories: general damages and special damages. **General damages** are of the type that generally result from the kind of conduct engaged in by the defendant; **special damages** are specific or unique to the plaintiff. A good example of general damages is compensation for pain and suffering. Anyone injured in a motor vehicle accident, for example, will be expected to endure a certain amount of pain and suffering as a result of the injuries. Examples of special damages are medical expenses, lost wages, and future impairment of earnings. In most cases, special damages must be specifically pleaded in a complaint, whereas general damages need not be.

Punitive damages are not intended to make the plaintiff whole but instead are used to punish defendants who have acted with ill will or in conscious disregard for the welfare of others. An additional purpose of punitive damages is to deter future misconduct by the defendant and similarly situated defendants. Punitive damages are not awarded against all defendants, they are awarded against defendants who act in a particularly egregious manner.

Nominal damages are awarded in intentional and strict liability cases in which liability is established but where no actual harm occurred. A jury could find the defendant liable for assaulting the plaintiff yet conclude that the plaintiff, although wronged, suffered no actual harm and thus could award nominal damages of only $10. Nominal damages cannot be awarded in a negligence case, because negligence requires proof of an actual injury. Nominal damages allow a plaintiff to be vindicated but do nothing in the way of compensating either the plaintiff or the attorneys involved. If nominal damages are anticipated, an hourly or set fee will usually be the basis for an attorney's reimbursement rather than a contingency-fee arrangement.

Exhibit 7–2 lists some questions plaintiffs and defendants may have about damages. The remainder of the chapter is structured around these questions.

ILLUSTRATION OF DAMAGES

Let us consider the facts of a real case to illustrate the various components of damages. In *Anderson v. Sears, Roebuck & Co.*, 377 F. Supp. 136 (E.D. La. 1974), the plaintiff was a young child who was severely burned

EXHIBIT 7–1 Categories of Damages

COMPENSATORY	PUNITIVE	NOMINAL
• To compensate and restore 1. Special damages are damages that are specific to plaintiff. 2. General damages are damages that are generally anticipated.	• Designed to punish	• No actual damages

© Cengage Learning 2012

EXHIBIT 7–2 *Questions About Damages*

QUESTIONS PLAINTIFFS ASK ABOUT DAMAGES

- Can they prove pain and suffering?
- Can they prove impaired present and future earning capacity?
- Are they entitled to recover for shortened life expectancy?
- Can they recover for expenses for which they have already been reimbursed?
- Can they recover attorney's fees?
- Are they entitled to punitive damages?
- What can they recover for property damage?
- Can spouses, parents, or children of victims recover for loss of consortium?
- Can spouses, parents, or children recover if the victim dies?

QUESTIONS DEFENDANTS ASK ABOUT DAMAGES

- Should plaintiffs be compensated for pain and suffering?
- Can an award be discounted to present value?
- Can an award be paid using a structured settlement?
- Did the plaintiff mitigate her damages?
- Did the plaintiff suffer actual physical harm?

© Cengage Learning 2012

in a house fire that was started by a heater negligently manufactured by the defendant. The child was burned over 40 percent of her body, with third-degree burns covering 80 percent of her scalp. She was hospitalized for twenty-eight days, during which time she developed infections and related problems and underwent repeated skin grafts. Furthermore, she had to undergo extensive subsequent operations and treatment.

The plaintiff's compensatory damages were divided into five categories: past and future medical expenses, past physical and mental pain, future physical and mental pain, permanent disability and disfigurement, and impaired earning capacity. Future medical expenses included the anticipated cost for plastic surgeons, psychiatrists, sociologists, and private tutors. The $250,000 allocated for these damages was also intended to cover the cost of future operations.

Pain and Suffering

The jury awarded the plaintiff $600,000 for past physical and mental pain. The pain included the pain she endured during her initial and subsequent hospitalizations as well as the mental and emotional trauma she underwent, manifesting in bedwetting, having nightmares, withdrawing, and developing speech impediments. She was further awarded $750,000 for future

physical and mental pain. The pain anticipated here was that of an estimated twenty-seven future operations, along with the pain and crippling caused by the extensive scarring she had sustained. These damages were also intended to compensate her for the likely deprivation of social life that she would surely suffer.

The jury awarded $1 million for permanent disability and disfigurement. Examples of the types of permanent losses she was expected to suffer included permanent loss of use of her legs, permanent injury to the left elbow and left arm, permanent destruction of 40 percent of her skin, permanent impairment of speech, and permanent impairment of a normal social, recreational, and educational life. The obvious problem in awarding damages in this area is that no accurate monetary value can be affixed. How does one assign a monetary value to a person's suffering? Could $1 million, $2 million, or any amount of money compensate the plaintiff in this case for the excruciating pain she suffered and the social rejection she would experience in the future?

"Day-in-the-life" videos are often used by plaintiffs' attorneys to graphically represent the plaintiff's suffering. These films document the everyday activities of the plaintiff and are designed to display in concrete and poignant terms the plaintiff's everyday activities prior to the incident and the full extent of how the plaintiff's injuries have limited and complicated her life. Although criticized by defense attorneys as unfairly appealing to jurors' sympathies and prejudicing them against the defendant, they are generally admissible and often used by plaintiffs to buttress damage claims.

Some attorneys have attempted to concretize this process by assigning a numerical value to the amount of suffering experienced on a daily, hourly, or even minute-by-minute basis. That number is then multiplied by the total number of days, hours, or minutes the pain is expected to last. This so-called "per diem" technique has been disallowed by some courts because it can lead to deceptively high figures. The majority of courts have, however, allowed the use of this argument and leave it up to defendants to dissuade juries as to its reasonableness.

Melvin Belli, who first advocated the per diem argument, gave the following closing argument to illustrate how one might use this approach. The case involved a man with an irreparably injured back and a thirty-year life expectancy.

> You are asked to evaluate in dollars and cents what pain and suffering is. This honorable court will instruct you that a man of this age has a life expectancy of thirty years. Let's put it to you bluntly, what's pain and suffering worth? You've got to answer this question. You've got to award for this as well as the special damages and loss of wages. Let's take Pat, my client, down to the waterfront. He sees Mike, an old friend. He goes up to him and says, "Mike, I've got a job for you. It's a perfect job. You're not going to have to work any more for the rest of your life. . . . You don't have to work even one second. All you have to do is to trade me your good back for my bad one and I'll give you $5.00 a day for the rest of your life. Do you know what $5.00 a day for the rest of your life is? Why, that's $60,000.00! Of course, I realize that you're not going to be able to do any walking, or any swimming, or driving an automobile, or be able to sit in a movie picture show; you're going to have excruciating pain and suffering with this job, 31,000,000 seconds a year, and once you take it on, you'll never be able to relieve yourself of this, but you get $60,000.00!" Do you think Mike would take on that job for $60,000.00? (The Use of Demonstrative Evidence in Achieving "The More Adequate Award" [Asae and Pinney, 1952, pp. 33–34])

Criticism of Pain and Suffering Awards

The problem of subjectivity in reference to the awarding of damages for pain and suffering has been the subject of much debate. Quantification of such damages is often difficult. Nevertheless, some argue that if the law is able to redress a businessperson who sustains commercial damage, it can do no less for those who have suffered "a more poignant infliction" (*Gray v. Washington Power Co.*, 71 P. 206 [Wash. 1930]). Even though no gauge is available for measuring such damages, which are to some degree sentimental, sentiment, it has been observed, is an element in all damages. Furthermore, the reasoning goes, the lack of precision in assessing damages should not preclude their approximate measurement, and they should be submitted to the best judgment of the jury.

The concept of compensating plaintiffs for their pain has been criticized, however. Some maintain that such damages should be allowed only when there is a physiological basis for the pain. Cornelius Peck, at the University of Washington Law School, argues that pain is a social and psychological as well as a physiological phenomenon (Peck, *Compensation for Pain: A Reappraisal in Light of New Medical Evidence*, 72 Mich. L. Rev. 1355 [1974]). One study he uses to illustrate his point involves a comparison between soldiers wounded in battle and civilians who had undergone surgery. Although the battle wounds probably provided a greater physiological basis for pain than did the incisions required by surgery, only a little more than 25 percent of the soldiers required relief for pain, whereas 87 percent of the civilians requested treatment for pain (Beecher, *Relationship of Significance of Wound to Pain Experienced*, 161 J.A.M.A. 1609 [1956]). This study seems to indicate that the cause of the injury creating the pain has some bearing on the individual's perception of that pain.

NET NEWS

Suggestions to attorneys regarding the presentation of evidence relating to pain and suffering can be found at **http://www.medleague.com** by entering the "Services" link and selecting "Presentations."

Therefore, pain sustained as a result of some noble endeavor may be more easily borne than pain stemming from some capricious or inexplicable cause.

The usual argument given to justify compensation for pain is that compensation brings consolation to one who has suffered. Peck argues, however, that this consolation may actually provide reinforcement for pain behavior and may serve to increase the pain of those who are to be consoled.

Equitable compensation of victims remains an illusory albeit noble goal of tort law. The struggle continues in the allocation of damages to balance the needs of plaintiffs, defendants, and the rest of society.

Impaired Earning Capacity

The last item addressed in *Anderson* is that of impaired earning capacity. The court concluded that the plaintiff's injuries would prevent her from earning a living for the rest of her life and that, therefore, the jury's award of $330,000 for impaired earning capacity was appropriate.

Two types of recovery fall under the category of impaired earnings: recovery for past earnings and recovery for prospective future losses. In dealing with past earnings, recovery is relatively simple to calculate if the plaintiff was employed at fixed wages. If he was unemployed or if the wages cannot be computed exactly, the plaintiff will have to use circumstantial evidence to show impairment of earning capacity.

Future loss of earning capacity is more difficult to compute. Jurors must first determine how long a plaintiff might be expected to live. Mortality tables published by insurance actuaries are used in this process. Jurors are also allowed to take into consideration the plaintiff's personal habits, prior health, and individual characteristics in determining the plaintiff's projected life span. Some creative attorneys use economists as experts to testify to a diminution of the plaintiff's earning capacity. Loss of future earnings is, of course, applicable only when the plaintiff can show that the injuries are permanent.

SHORTENED LIFE EXPECTANCY

Although damages for loss of prospective earnings have been allowed, damages for the shortening of the plaintiff's life expectancy traditionally have been

PUTTING IT INTO PRACTICE 7:1

A twenty-nine-year-old veteran is rendered paraplegic as a result of a negligently performed lung operation. Before his operation he had been pronounced completely cured of tuberculosis, for which he had previously been classified as 100 percent disabled. As a result of his injuries the man suffers frequent leg spasms, burning and swelling in his legs and feet, involuntary bowel movements, and occasional urinary accidents due to blockage in his catheter. His future medical treatment will include intensive rehabilitation, possible reconstructive procedures, and ongoing evaluations by neurologists, psychiatrists, urologists, and plastic surgeons. He runs the risk of kidney and bladder infections. He has become depressed, has lost his ability to procreate, his sleep is interrupted every night as he changes his position to prevent bed sores, and he has no hope of recovering the use of his legs. He has endured numerous operations stemming from his paraplegia and will probably have to have several more.

Prior to his lung operation he lived a normal social life, participated in athletics, had received a bachelor's degree in aeronautical engineering after receiving an honorable discharge from the army, and was working as an associate engineer with a salary of $110 per week. With rehabilitation he could secure work in a related engineering field, and with intensive medical care he had a projected life expectancy of forty years. Had he not been injured he probably could have worked for thirty years. His medical expenses have been paid for by the government, and he is receiving monthly VA disability payments.

What kinds of damages is he entitled to? How would you go about proving his damages?

denied. Under the common law, damages for loss of life were precluded unless provided for by statute. The courts have reasoned that the same rule must be applicable to damages for a shortened life. Furthermore, there has been a desire to avoid an issue so fraught with incalculable variables as well as a fear that such compensation would result in a duplication of damages. A few courts have, however, considered shortening of life expectancy as a distinct compensable harm.

In one case, for example, a ten-month-old boy developed a severe case of meningitis after being negligently examined and treated at a military hospital. He subsequently became profoundly retarded and suffered severe physical disabilities. The court concluded that damages for shortened life expectancy were appropriate and awarded $900,000 for the child's reduced life expectancy as a separate element of damages (*McNeill v. United States*, 519 F. Supp. 283 [D.S.C. 1981]).

COLLATERAL-SOURCE RULE

A plaintiff is often reimbursed for her out-of-pocket expenses, including lost wages and payments for medical care, by her insurance company. Nevertheless, under the **collateral-source rule** she is entitled to recover these damages again from the defendant. Therefore under the rule, a plaintiff can recover for lost wages even if he has been reimbursed through sick pay provided by his employer or by disability benefits through workers' compensation. Social Security disability benefits, welfare payments, vacation pay, sick pay, and Medicare payments also do not count against a plaintiff's recovery under this rule. Even if a plaintiff receives free services from friends or family members, she may recover the reasonable value of those services.

The rule precludes the admission of evidence to the jury regarding payment of benefits to the injured party from a source other than the tortfeasor. In many cases the benefits are one for which the plaintiff has directly or indirectly paid. If a plaintiff has paid premiums on an insurance policy, or earned vacation or sick pay denying him double recovery would deprive him of the benefits of his investment and/or time. Furthermore, allowing the defendant to benefit from the plaintiff's investment would be unfair. The rationale for this rule dates back to 1854 and is intended to promote justice and prevent the tortfeasor from benefiting or mitigating damages in the amount of payments or compensation that the injured party received from a collateral source. The public policy underlying this rule is that the tortfeasor is responsible

to compensate the victim for the total harm caused by the tortfeasor's conduct. Additionally, plaintiff's recovery were offset by collateral benefits, the deterrent effect of tort law would be diminished. Under this rule, the plaintiff is assured full compensation for all medical, physical, and emotional injuries.

Today, however, legal sentiment no longer favors double recovery for the same injury. At least thirty-eight states have passed statutes forbidding or limiting duplication in awards from multiple sources (Schap and Freely, *Much More on the Collateral Source Rule*, Working Papers 0605. College of the Holy Cross, Dept. of Economic [June 2006]). The reasoning is that plaintiffs should be allowed to recover only an amount that provides compensation for actual injuries. The ability to admit evidence of supplemental benefits at trial ensures that liability is divided among all tortfeasors in accordance with their respective degrees of culpability.

In many cases the company making the plaintiff's payment has a right of reimbursement out of any judgment the plaintiff receives, known as the right of **subrogation**. A medical insurance plan typically requires that the plaintiff reimburse the company out of any judgment he receives, thereby preventing double recovery. Most courts have held that evidence of collateral benefits is inadmissible. (To read about the changes to the collateral-source rule proposed by tort reform advocates, see Chapter 16.)

EXPENSES OF LITIGATION

Although in England the winning party is entitled to recover her expenses of litigation, including attorney's fees, such is not the case in the United States. Most personal injury cases are handled on a contingency-fee basis, in which the attorney agrees to provide services for a fee based on a percentage of the client's recovery. If there is no recovery, the attorney receives nothing. Typically, the percentage of the fee depends on whether the case is settled or litigated. A common contingency-fee arrangement provides for payment of 33 1/3 percent of the settlement and 40 percent of a final judgment. Some have suggested that, as a practical matter, punitive damages and awards for pain and suffering in effect allow a plaintiff to pay attorney's fees and still retain compensation for her own losses.

The contingency-fee arrangement has been the subject of frequent criticism. Some maintain that it creates a conflict of interest between the attorney and the client in reference to settlement offers. In some cases attorneys receive much more than would be considered a reasonable fee for the efforts they expended. However, such a fee arrangement allows those persons who would ordinarily be financially incapable of pursuing their claims to do so. Also, remember that attorneys do not win every case; therefore, cases in which they receive nothing may balance those for which they are overcompensated.

DAMAGES FOR PHYSICAL HARM TO PROPERTY

Damages for physical harm to property are tied to the value of the property. If the property is completely destroyed, damages are measured according to the value of the property at the time and place the tort occurred. If the property is damaged but not destroyed, the damages are measured by the difference in value before and after the tort, although the amount cannot exceed the replacement cost. If the plaintiff is merely deprived of use of the property, damages consist of the value of the use of which the plaintiff was deprived.

When we refer to value of property we are alluding to its **fair market value**, which is the amount that the property could have been sold for on the open market. The assumption is that fair market value involves a voluntary sale by a leisurely seller to a willing buyer. Note that market value is usually determined on the basis of the market at the place and time that the wrong occurred. Furthermore, market value constitutes the highest price one seeking to sell the property could have realized and not the lowest price at which it could have been sold.

Market value does not always provide adequate compensation, particularly in cases in which the property has personal value to the plaintiff and no one else. Jane and Les, an elderly couple, lost their twelve-year-old dachshund, Cutie, when she was hit by a car. The negligent driver paid $300 for Cutie, whom Jane and Les purchased as a puppy for $300 when they lost both of their kids due to a tragic accident. The value of Cutie was $300. In such cases the court considers the original cost of the property, the use made of the property, and its condition at the time of the tort. The mental distress that the plaintiff suffers as a result of being deprived of the property is, however, not usually compensable. Several courts have held that the "actual value to owner" standard applies when the pet has no fair market value.

DAMAGES IN PRODUCT LIABILITY CASES

Damages in the context of product liability cases require special consideration and are treated separately in Chapter 12.

PUNITIVE DAMAGES

Punitive damages, which are sometimes referred to as **exemplary damages**, are designed to punish the tortfeasor for egregious misconduct and to deter similarly situated wrongdoers. In negligence cases they can be awarded only when the defendant's conduct is egregious or almost criminal. Some jurisdictions require that the jury find defendant's conduct was "reckless," "willful or wanton," or "with an evil mind." Punitive damages are also permitted when the defendant commits an intentional tort, such as assault or intentional infliction of emotional harm. Punitive damages are considered a windfall to the plaintiff, and a jury can use its discretion to refrain from awarding them. These damages are often appealed and successfully reduced or **remitted** by the judge. The judge also has the ability to increase a jury award called **additur**.

Punitive damages have been criticized as constituting undue compensation to the plaintiff because they are not related to the plaintiff's injury. Some maintain that punitive damages are in essence criminal fines that should be paid to the state and not to the plaintiff. The counterargument is that such damages act as a deterrent to those with evil motivations. They also compensate plaintiffs for the expenses of litigation, such as attorney's fees, which they would normally have to bear themselves.

Punitive damages are more and more commonly being awarded in product liability cases. A defendant who knows of a defect and makes the product anyway is liable for punitive damages. As explained by the *Grimshaw* court (in the Ford Pinto case discussed later):

> Punitive damages thus remain as the most effective remedy for consumer protection against defectively designed mass produced articles. They provide a motive for private individuals to enforce rules of law and enable them to recoup the expenses of doing so, which can be considerable and not otherwise recoverable.

A problem in this area that has concerned some commentators and judges is that a defendant could be

NET NEWS
To read decisions of the United States Supreme Court regarding punitive damage award in a tobacco case, go to http://www.tobacco.neu.edu and enter "Memo Supporting Punitive Damages" as your search term.

bankrupted by significant punitive damages for some plaintiffs before other plaintiffs recovered even compensatory damages. Hundreds of potential victims might exist to whom the defendant might be liable for millions of dollars in punitive damages. As a result the defendant could become bankrupt and future plaintiffs could be precluded from recovering even compensatory damages.

One question that arises in the area of punitive damages is whether employers, who are generally liable for the torts of their employees, should be made to pay punitive damages. The courts are split in this area, but many follow the *Restatement (Second) of Torts* § 909, which requires the payment of punitive damages only in cases where the employer had personal culpability or where the employee was working in a managerial capacity.

Punitive damages have been the target of extensive criticism, and tort reform advocates have focused their energies on remedying what they perceive as the excessiveness of many such awards. (For a more detailed consideration of the tort reform movement in reference to punitive damages, see the discussion in Chapter 16.) A comprehensive list of the pitfalls of punitive damages is outlined below:

The permissibility of punitive damages in negligence cases:

1. inflames the cupidity of plaintiffs.

2. adds a grossly intangible element to a negligence case grievously interfering with rational settlement negotiations.

3. leads to lengthy and rancorous discovery process and disputes.

4. places before the jury inflammatory evidence affecting their dispassionate judgment as to negligence (often, this is its principal purpose) and compensatory damages.

5. moreover, . . . if the plaintiff can inject the issue of punitive damages in a case, he can show the wealth of the defendant. This results in the trial of a negligence case becoming a field day with the issue of the defendant's wealth.

6. places upon the defendants the risk of vast, unforeseeable damages for which usually no insurance protection is available (thus thwarting the policy of the law of spreading the risk and the cost thereof).

7. places a social policy decision in the hands of a jury without giving them access to the huge and broad array of facts necessary to reach an intelligent and useful decision.

8. outrageously gives a windfall to a few plaintiffs who are fortunate enough to be injured by a millionaire (or a billionaire corporation).

9. imposes punishment for conduct (rather than reimbursement for loss), a decision usually, and better, left to the criminal law and the decision for the legislative, judicial or administrative representatives of the people, not a small group of hap-hazardly selected citizens.

10. jury punitive damage awards of an unpredictable nature and appalling inconsistency continue to proliferate. Neither the Legislature nor the appellate courts have been able to formulate coherent, reasonable guidelines and limitations for the remedy. Perhaps the quest is utopian and unrealizable. In practice, it lacks any semblance of consistency between defendants, or even the same defendant, in cases tried by different juries.

Because the Legislature has not prescribed guidelines for punitive damages, they may be awarded by juries at whim. Those who favor abolishing the doctrine of punitive damages argue that the lack of clear standards governing the amount of punitive awards frees the jury to act irrationally, out of passion and prejudice.

11. the extreme unpredictability of punitive damages and the occasional crushing amount set by a vindictive jury approaches a due process

violation because, in a practical sense, the defendant lacks notice [that] his conduct may result in loss of his entire assets.

12. to the extent that the defendant has been, or will be, punished for his conduct by the criminal process, the imposition of punitive damages constitutes double punishment.

13. if the punitive damage issue is injected into accident cases, the jury must be informed as to whether the compensatory award will come out of the defendant's pocket or be paid by an insurance carrier, for otherwise damages cannot be sensibly assessed. This has the evil of injecting the issue of insurance coverage in the case in violation of statutory policy.

14. punitive damages awarded as a result of a fortuitous or accidental result rather than an intended result will have no deterrent effect, for the negligent actor just assumes they will not occur.

15. because insurance carriers do not have to pay for injuries resulting from conduct that merits punitive damages, plaintiffs will only ask for punitive damages in negligence cases where defendant is uninsured or the defendant is wealthy. This will reduce the deterrent effect of permitting punitive damages in negligence cases.

16. the "punishment" of punitive damages is assessed without the constitutional safe-guards of criminal punishment. The punishment is imposed by only a preponderance of the evidence. Although the remedy is quasi-criminal, the defendant does not have the protections of a criminal defendant, such as freedom from self-incrimination, prohibition of excessive fines, etc.

17. the doctrine developed in the common law to provide full compensation to the plaintiff. But now that the scope of damages has increased markedly in negligence cases to include compensation for various intangible injuries (including negligent infliction of emotional distress without proof of physical injury), the extra remedy is no longer necessary. . . .

18. because compensatory damages include recovery for such intangibles as shock, loss of comfort and society, loss of enjoyment of life, etc., they probably often contain an element of retribution.

19. a closely related argument is that civil juries are inexperienced and ill-equipped to mete out punishment that would be in the best interests of society.

The most frequently stated benefits of permitting punitive damage awards are:

1. to provide a plaintiff who has suffered only nominal damages with an incentive to litigate.
2. to punish the defendant for the transgression.
3. to deter the defendant and others from committing similar acts in the future.

It is obvious that the first rationale does not apply to negligence cases, and the second and third should not apply to ordinary negligence cases, but only those with an element of outrageous conduct.

Moreover, the second rationale (punishment) infringes on the sphere of the criminal law and the third (deterrence) is wholly unsupported by any objective or scientific proof that it is effective (*Woolstrum v. Mailloux*, 141 Cal. App. 3d Supp. 1 [1983] [citations omitted]).

Ford Pinto Case

In the infamous Ford Pinto case, defendant Ford Motor Company argued that it should not be liable for punitive damages because no evidence of corporate ratification of the alleged misconduct was presented (*Grimshaw v. Ford Motor Co.*, 119 Cal. App. 3d 757, 174 Cal. Rptr. 348 [1981]). The facts are summarized by the court:

The Accident:

In November 1971, the Grays purchased a new 1972 Pinto hatchback manufactured by Ford in October 1971. The Grays had trouble with the car from the outset. During the first few months of ownership, they had to return the car to the dealer for repairs a number of times. Their car problems included excessive gas and oil consumption, down shifting of the automatic transmission, lack of power, and occasional stalling. It was later learned that the stalling and excessive fuel consumption were caused by a heavy carburetor float.

On May 28, 1972, Mrs. Gray, accompanied by 13-year-old Richard Grimshaw, set out in the Pinto from Anaheim for Barstow to meet Mr. Gray. The Pinto was then six months old and had been driven approximately 3,000 miles. Mrs. Gray stopped in San Bernardino for gasoline, got back onto the freeway (Interstate 15) and proceeded toward her destination at 60–65 miles per hour. As she approached the Route 30 off-ramp where traffic was congested, she moved from the outer fast lane to the middle lane of the freeway. Shortly after this lane change, the Pinto suddenly stalled and coasted to a halt in the middle lane. It was later established that the carburetor float had become so saturated with gasoline that it suddenly sank, opening the float chamber and causing the engine to flood and stall. A car traveling immediately behind the Pinto was able to swerve and pass it but the driver of a 1962 Ford Galaxie was unable to avoid colliding with the Pinto. The Galaxie had been traveling from 50 to 55 miles per hour, but before the impact had been braked to a speed of from 28 to 37 miles per hour.

At the moment of impact, the Pinto caught fire and its interior was engulfed in flames. According to plaintiffs' expert, the impact of the Galaxie had driven the Pinto's gas tank forward and caused it to be punctured by the flange or one of the bolts on the differential housing so that fuel sprayed from the punctured tank and entered the passenger compartment through gaps resulting from the separation of the rear wheel well sections from the floor pan. By the time the Pinto came to rest after the collision, both occupants had sustained serious burns. When they emerged from the vehicle, their clothing was almost completely burned off. Mrs. Gray died a few days later of congestive heart failure as a result of the burns. Grimshaw managed to survive but only through heroic medical measures. He has undergone numerous and extensive surgeries and skin grafts and must undergo additional surgeries over the next 10 years. He lost portions of several fingers on his left hand and portions of his left ear, while his face required many skin grafts from various portions of his body. Because Ford does not contest the amount of compensatory damages awarded to Grimshaw and the Grays, no purpose would be served by further description of the injuries suffered by Grimshaw or the damages sustained by the Grays.

Design of the Pinto Fuel System:

In 1968, Ford began designing a new subcompact automobile which ultimately became the Pinto. Mr. Iacocca, then a Ford Vice President, conceived the project and was its moving force. Ford's objective was to build a car at or below 2,000 pounds to sell for no more than $2,000.

Ordinarily, marketing surveys and preliminary engineering studies precede the styling of a new automobile line. Pinto, however, was a rush project, so that styling preceded engineering and dictated engineering design to a greater degree than usual. Among the engineering decisions dictated by styling was the placement of the fuel tank. It was then the preferred practice in Europe and Japan to locate the gas tank over the rear axle in subcompacts because a small vehicle has less "crush space" between the rear axle and the bumper than larger cars. The Pinto's styling, however, required the tank to be placed behind the rear axle leaving only 9 or 10 inches of "crush space," far less than in any other American automobile or Ford overseas subcompact. In addition, the Pinto was designed so that its bumper was little more than a chrome strip, less substantial than the bumper of any other American car produced then or later. The Pinto's rear structure also lacked reinforcing members known as "hat sections" (2 longitudinal side members) and horizontal cross-members running between them such as were found in cars of larger unitized construction and in all automobiles produced by Ford's overseas operations. The absence of the reinforcing members rendered the Pinto less crush resistant than other vehicles. Finally, the differential housing selected for the Pinto had an exposed flange and a line of exposed bolt heads. These protrusions were sufficient to puncture a gas tank driven forward against the differential upon rear impact.

Crash Tests:

During the development of the Pinto, prototypes were built and tested. Some were "mechanical prototypes" which duplicated mechanical features of the design but not its appearance while others, referred to as "engineering prototypes," were true duplicates of the design car. These prototypes as well as two production Pintos were crash tested by Ford to determine, among other things, the integrity of the fuel system in rear-end accidents. Ford also conducted the tests to see if the Pinto as designed would meet a proposed federal regulation requiring all automobiles manufactured in 1972 to be able to withstand a 20-mile-per-hour fixed barrier impact without significant fuel spillage and all automobiles manufactured after January 1, 1973, to withstand a 30-mile-per-hour fixed barrier impact without significant fuel spillage.

The crash tests revealed that the Pinto's fuel system as designed could not meet the 20-mile-per-hour proposed standard. Mechanical prototypes struck from the rear with a moving barrier at 21-miles-per-hour caused the fuel tank to be driven forward and to be punctured, causing fuel leakage in excess of the standard prescribed by the proposed regulation. A production Pinto crash tested at 21-miles-per-hour into a fixed barrier caused the fuel neck to be torn from the gas tank and the tank to be punctured by a bolt head on the differential housing. In at least one test, spilled fuel entered the driver's compartment through gaps resulting from the separation of the seams joining the rear wheel wells to the floor pan. The seam separation was occasioned by the lack of reinforcement in the rear structure and insufficient welds of the wheel wells to the floor pan.

Tests conducted by Ford on other vehicles, including modified or reinforced mechanical Pinto prototypes, proved safe at speeds at which the Pinto failed. Where rubber bladders had been installed in the tank, crash tests into fixed barriers at 21-miles-per-hour withstood leakage from punctures in the gas tank. Vehicles with fuel tanks installed above rather than behind the rear axle passed the fuel system integrity test at 31-miles-per-hour fixed barrier. A Pinto with two longitudinal hat sections added to firm up the rear structure passed a 20-mile-per-hour rear impact fixed barrier test with no fuel leakage.

The Cost to Remedy Design Deficiencies:

When a prototype failed the fuel system integrity test, the standard of care for engineers in the industry was to redesign and retest it. The vulnerability of the production Pinto's fuel tank at speeds of 20 and 30-miles-per-hour fixed barrier tests could have been remedied by inexpensive "fixes," but Ford produced and sold the Pinto to the public without doing anything to remedy the defects. Design changes that would have enhanced the integrity of the fuel tank system at relatively little cost per car included the following: Longitudinal side members and cross members at $2.40 and $1.80, respectively; a single shock absorbent "flak suit" to protect the tank at $4; a tank within a tank and placement of the tank over the axle at $5.08 to $5.79; a nylon bladder within the tank at $5.25 to $8; placement of the tank over the axle surrounded with a protective barrier at a cost of $9.95 per car; substitution of a rear axle with a smooth differential housing at a cost of $2.10; imposition of a protective shield between the differential housing and the tank at $2.35; improvement and reinforcement of the bumper at $2.60; addition of eight inches of crush space at a cost of $6.40. Equipping the car with a reinforced rear structure, smooth axle, improved bumper and additional crush space at a total cost of $15.30 would have made the fuel tank safe in a 34 to 38-mile-per-hour rear end collision by a vehicle the size of the Ford Galaxie.

If, in addition to the foregoing, a bladder or tank within a tank were used or if the tank were protected with a shield, it would have been safe in a 40 to 45-mile-per-hour rear impact. If the tank had been located over the rear axle, it would have been safe in a rear impact at 50 miles per hour or more.

Management's Decision to Go Forward with Knowledge of Defects:

The idea for the Pinto, as has been noted, was conceived by Mr. Iacocca, then Executive Vice President of Ford. The feasibility study was conducted under the supervision of Mr. Robert Alexander, Vice President of Car Engineering. Ford's Product Planning Committee, whose members included Mr. Iacocca, Mr. Robert Alexander, and Mr. Harold MacDonald, Ford's Group Vice President of Car Engineering, approved the Pinto's concept and made the decision to go forward with the project. During the course of the project, regular product review meetings were held which were chaired by Mr. MacDonald and attended by Mr. Alexander. As the project approached actual production, the engineers responsible for the components of the project "signed off" to their immediate supervisors who in turn "signed off" to their superiors and so on up the chain of command until the entire project was approved for public release by Vice Presidents Alexander and MacDonald and ultimately by Mr. Iacocca. The Pinto crash tests results had been forwarded up the chain of command to the ultimate decision-makers and were known to the Ford officials who decided to go forward with production.

Harley Copp, a former Ford engineer and executive in charge of the crash testing program, testified that the highest level of Ford's management made the decision to go forward with the production of the Pinto, knowing that the gas tank was vulnerable to puncture and rupture at low rear impact speeds creating a significant risk of death or injury from fire and knowing that "fixes" were feasible at nominal cost. He testified that management's decision was based on the cost savings which would inure from omitting or delaying the "fixes."

Mr. Copp's testimony concerning management's awareness of the crash tests results and the vulnerability of the Pinto fuel system was corroborated by other evidence. At an April 1971 product review meeting chaired by Mr. MacDonald, those present received and discussed a report (Exhibit 125) prepared by Ford engineers pertaining to the financial impact of a proposed federal standard on fuel system integrity and the cost savings which would accrue from deferring even minimal "fixes" [footnote omitted]. The report refers to crash tests of the integrity of the fuel system of Ford vehicles and design changes needed to meet anticipated federal standards. Also in evidence was a September 23, 1970, report (Exhibit 124) by Ford's "Chassis Design Office" concerning a program "to establish a corporate (Ford) position and reply to the government" on the proposed federal fuel system integrity standard which included zero fuel spillage at 20-miles-per-hour fixed barrier crash by January 1, 1972, and 30-miles-per-hour by January 1, 1973. The report states in part: "The 20 and 30 mph rear fixed barrier crashes will probably require repackaging the fuel tanks in a protected area such as above the rear axle. This is based on moving barrier crash tests of a Chevelle and a Ford at 30 mph and other Ford products at 20 mph. Currently there are no plans for forward models to repackage the fuel tanks. Tests must be conducted to prove that repackaged tanks will live without significantly strengthening rear structure for added protection." The report also notes that the Pinto was the "(s)mallest car line with most difficulty in achieving compliance." It is reasonable to infer that the report was prepared for and known to Ford officials in policy-making positions.

The fact that two of the crash tests were run at the request of the Ford Chassis and Vehicle Engineering Department for the specific purpose of demonstrating the advisability of moving the fuel tank over the axle as a possible "fix" further corroborated Mr. Copp's testimony that management knew the results of the crash tests. Mr. Kennedy, who succeeded Mr. Copp as the engineer in charge of Ford's crash testing program, admitted that the test results had been forwarded up the chain of command to his superiors.

Finally, Mr. Copp testified to conversations in late 1968 or early 1969 with the chief assistant research engineer in charge of cost-weight evaluation of the Pinto, and to a later conversation with the chief chassis engineer who was then in charge of crash testing the early prototype. In these conversations, both men expressed concern about the integrity of the Pinto's fuel system and complained about management's unwillingness to deviate from the design if the change would cost money.

The appellate court concluded that substantial evidence was presented from which the jury could reasonably have inferred that Ford's management went ahead with the production of the Pinto with full knowledge of the design defect. The defect rendered the fuel tank extremely vulnerable on rear impact at low speeds and endangered the safety and lives of its occupants. The court categorized Ford's executive decision-making process as corporate malice and the jury awarded $125 million in punitive damages, which was later reduced by the trial judge to $3.5 million.

One of the issues raised in this case was the propriety of the punitive-damage award. Ford contended that the $3.5 million award exceeded, many times over, the highest award ever upheld in California as well as the maximum civil penalties that could be enforced under federal and state statutes against a manufacturer.

As can be seen, the court was unpersuaded by this argument:

> In determining whether an award of punitive damages is excessive, comparison of the amount awarded with other awards in other cases is not a valid consideration. . . . Nor does "[t]he fact that an award may set a precedent by its size" in and of itself render it suspect; whether the award was excessive must be assessed by examining the circumstances of the particular case. . . . In deciding whether an award is excessive as a matter of law or was so grossly disproportionate as to raise the presumption that it was the product of passion or prejudice, the following factors should be weighed: The degree of reprehensibility of defendant's conduct, the wealth of the defendant, the amount of compensatory damages, and an amount which would serve as a deterrent effect on like conduct by defendant and others who may be so inclined. . . . Applying the foregoing criteria to the instant case, the punitive damage award as reduced by the trial court was well within reason.[1]

---

1. A quantitative formula whereby the amount of punitive damages can be determined in a given case with mathematical certainty is manifestly impossible as well as undesirable. . . . The authors advocate abandonment of the rule that a reasonable relationship must exist between punitive damages and actual damages. They suggest that courts balance society's interest against defendant's interest by focusing on the following factors: Severity of threatened harm; degree of reprehensibility of defendant's conduct, profitability of the conduct, wealth of defendant, amount of compensatory damages (whether it was high in relation to injury), cost of litigation, potential criminal sanctions and other civil actions against defendant based on same conduct. . . . In the present case, the amount of the award as reduced by the judge was reasonable under the suggested factors, including the factor of any other potential liability—civil or criminal.

In assessing the propriety of a punitive damage award, as in assessing the propriety of any other judicial ruling based upon factual determinations, the evidence must be viewed in the light most favorable to the judgment. . . . Viewing the record thusly in the instant case, the conduct of Ford's management was reprehensible in the extreme. It exhibited a conscious and callous disregard of public safety in order to maximize corporate profits. Ford's self-evaluation of its conduct is based on a review of the evidence most favorable to it instead of on the basis of the evidence most favorable to the judgment. Unlike malicious conduct directed toward a single specific individual, Ford's tortious conduct endangered the lives of thousands of Pinto purchasers. Weighed against the factor of reprehensibility, the punitive damage award as reduced by the trial judge was not excessive.

Nor was the reduced award excessive taking into account defendant's wealth and the size of the compensatory award. Ford's net worth was 7.7 billion dollars and its income after taxes for 1976 was over 983 million dollars. The punitive award was approximately .005% of Ford's net worth and approximately .03% of its 1976 net income. The ratio of the punitive damages to compensatory damages was approximately 1.4 to one. Significantly, Ford does not quarrel with the amount of the compensatory award to Grimshaw.

Nor was the size of the award excessive in light of its deterrent purpose. An award which is so small that it can be simply written off as a part of the cost of doing business would have no deterrent effect. An award which affects the company's pricing of its product and thereby affects its competitive advantage would serve as a deterrent. The award in question was far from excessive as a deterrent against future wrongful conduct by Ford and others.

Ford complains that the punitive award is far greater than the maximum penalty that may be imposed under California or federal law prohibiting the sale of defective automobiles or other products. For example, Ford notes that California statutes provide a maximum fine of only $50 for the first offense and $100 for a second offense for a dealer who sells an automobile that fails to conform to federal safety laws or is not equipped with required lights or brakes . . .; that a manufacturer who sells brake fluid in this state failing to meet statutory standards is subject to a maximum of only $50 . . .; and that the maximum penalty that may be imposed under federal law for violation of automobile safety standards if $1,000 per vehicle up to a maximum of $800,000 for any related series of offenses. . . . It is precisely because monetary penalties under government regulations prescribing business standards or the criminal law are so inadequate and ineffective as deterrents against a manufacturer and distributor of mass produced defective products that punitive damages must be of sufficient amount to discourage such practices. Instead of showing that the punitive damage award was excessive, the comparison between the award and the maximum penalties under state and federal statutes and regulations governing automotive safety demonstrates the propriety of the amount of punitive damages awarded.

The United States Supreme Court found the award in *Campbell* "excessive" in relationship to the state's legitimate interest. The Court concluded that

CASE

State Farm Mut. Auto. Ins. Co. v. Campbell
123 S. Ct. 1513 (2003)

Justice KENNEDY delivered the opinion of the Court.

We address once again the measure of punishment, by means of punitive damages, a State may impose upon a defendant in a civil case. The question is whether, in the circumstances we shall recount, an award of $145 million in punitive damages, where full compensatory damages are $1 million, is excessive and in violation of the Due Process Clause of the Fourteenth Amendment to the Constitution of the United States.

* * *

In 1981, Curtis Campbell (Campbell) was driving with his wife, Inez Preece Campbell, in Cache County, Utah. He decided to pass six vans traveling ahead of them on a two-lane highway. Todd Ospital was driving a small car approaching from the opposite direction. To avoid a head-on collision with Campbell, who by then was driving on the wrong side of the highway and toward oncoming traffic, Ospital swerved onto the

(continues)

shoulder, lost control of his automobile, and collided with a vehicle driven by Robert G. Slusher. Ospital was killed, and Slusher was rendered permanently disabled. The Campbells escaped unscathed.

In the ensuing wrongful death and tort action, Campbell insisted he was not at fault. Early investigations did support differing conclusions as to who caused the accident, but "a consensus was reached early on by the investigators and witnesses that Mr. Campbell's unsafe pass had indeed caused the crash." 65 P.3d 1134, 1141 (Utah 2001). Campbell's insurance company, petitioner State Farm Mutual Automobile Insurance Company (State Farm), nonetheless decided to contest liability and declined offers by Slusher and Ospital's estate (Ospital) to settle the claims for the policy limit of $50,000 ($25,000 per claimant). State Farm also ignored the advice of one of its own investigators and took the case to trial, assuring the Campbells that "their assets were safe, that they had no liability for the accident, that [State Farm] would represent their interests, and that they did not need to procure separate counsel." *Id.*, at 1142. To the contrary, a jury determined that Campbell was 100 percent at fault, and a judgment was returned for $185,849, far more than the amount offered in settlement.

At first State Farm refused to cover the $135,849 in excess liability. Its counsel made this clear to the Campbells: "'You may want to put for sale signs on your property to get things moving.'" Nor was State Farm willing to post a supersedeas bond to allow Campbell to appeal the judgment against him. Campbell obtained his own counsel to appeal the verdict. During the pendency of the appeal, in late 1984, Slusher, Ospital, and the Campbells reached an agreement whereby Slusher and Ospital agreed not to seek satisfaction of their claims against the Campbells. In exchange the Campbells agreed to pursue a bad faith action against State Farm and to be represented by Slusher's and Ospital's attorneys. The Campbells also agreed that Slusher and Ospital would have a right to play a part in all major decisions concerning the bad-faith action. No settlement could be concluded without Slusher's and Ospital's approval, and Slusher and Ospital would receive 90 percent of any verdict against State Farm.

In 1989, the Utah Supreme Court denied Campbell's appeal in the wrongful-death and tort actions. *Slusher v. Ospital*, 777 P.2d 437 (Utah 1989). State Farm then paid the entire judgment, including the amounts in excess of the policy limits. The Campbells nonetheless filed a complaint against State Farm alleging bad faith, fraud, and intentional infliction of emotional distress. The trial court initially granted State Farm's motion for summary judgment because State Farm had paid the

excess verdict, but that ruling was reversed on appeal. 840 P.2d 130 (Utah App.1992). On remand State Farm moved *in limine* to exclude evidence of alleged conduct that occurred in unrelated cases outside of Utah, but the trial court denied the motion. At State Farm's request the trial court bifurcated the trial into two phases conducted before different juries. In the first phase the jury determined that State Farm's decision not to settle was unreasonable because there was a substantial likelihood of an excess verdict.

Before the second phase of the action against State Farm we decided *BMW of North America, Inc. v. Gore*, 517 U.S. 559, 116 S.Ct. 1589, 134 L.Ed.2d 809 (1996), and refused to sustain a $2 million punitive damages award which accompanied a verdict of only $4,000 in compensatory damages. Based on that decision, State Farm again moved for the exclusion of evidence of dissimilar out-of-state conduct. App. to Pet. for Cert. 168a–172a. The trial court denied State Farm's motion. *Id.*, at 189a.

The second phase addressed State Farm's liability for fraud and intentional infliction of emotional distress, as well as compensatory and punitive damages. The Utah Supreme Court aptly characterized this phase of the trial:

> "State Farm argued during phase II that its decision to take the case to trial was an 'honest mistake' that did not warrant punitive damages. In contrast, the Campbells introduced evidence that State Farm's decision to take the case to trial was a result of a national scheme to meet corporate fiscal goals by capping payouts on claims company wide. This scheme was referred to as State Farm's 'Performance, Planning and Review,' or PP & R, policy. To prove the existence of this scheme, the trial court allowed the Campbells to introduce extensive expert testimony regarding fraudulent practices by State Farm in its nationwide operations. Although State Farm moved prior to phase II of the trial for the exclusion of such evidence and continued to object to it at trial, the trial court ruled that such evidence was admissible to determine whether State Farm's conduct in the Campbell case was indeed intentional and sufficiently egregious to warrant punitive damages." 65 P.3d, at 1143.

Evidence pertaining to the PP & R policy concerned State Farm's business practices for over 20 years in numerous States. Most of these practices bore no relation to third-party automobile insurance claims, the type of claim underlying the Campbells' complaint against the company. The jury awarded the Campbells $2.6 million in compensatory damages and $145 million in punitive damages, which the trial court reduced to

(continues)

$1 million and $25 million respectively. Both parties appealed.

The Utah Supreme Court sought to apply the three guideposts we identified in *Gore, supra,* at 574–575, 116 S.Ct. 1589, and it reinstated the $145 million punitive damages award. Relying in large part on the extensive evidence concerning the PP & R policy, the court concluded State Farm's conduct was reprehensible. The court also relied upon State Farm's "massive wealth" and on testimony indicating that "State Farm's actions, because of their clandestine nature, will be punished at most in one out of every 50,000 cases as a matter of statistical probability," 65 P.3d, at 1153, and concluded that the ratio between punitive and compensatory damages was not unwarranted. Finally, the court noted that the punitive damages award was not excessive when compared to various civil and criminal penalties State Farm could have faced, including $10,000 for each act of fraud, the suspension of its license to conduct business in Utah, the disgorgement of profits, and imprisonment. *Id.,* at 1154–1155. We granted certiorari. 535 U.S. 1111, 122 S.Ct. 2326, 153 L.Ed.2d 158 (2002).

II.

We recognized in *Cooper Industries, Inc. v. Leatherman Tool Group, Inc.,* 532 U.S. 424, 121 S.Ct. 1678, 149 L.Ed.2d 674 (2001), that in our judicial system compensatory and punitive damages, although usually awarded at the same time by the same decisionmaker, serve different purposes. *Id.,* at 432, 121 S.Ct. 1678. Compensatory damages "are intended to redress the concrete loss that the plaintiff has suffered by reason of the defendant's wrongful conduct." *Ibid.* (citing Restatement (Second) of Torts § 903, pp. 453–454 (1979)). By contrast, punitive damages serve a broader function; they are aimed at deterrence and retribution. *Cooper Industries, supra,* at 432, 121 S.Ct. 1678; see also *Gore, supra,* at 568, 116 S.Ct. 1589 ("Punitive damages may properly be imposed to further a State's legitimate interests in punishing unlawful conduct and deterring its repetition"); *Pacific Mut. Life Ins. Co. v. Haslip,* 499 U.S. 1, 19, 111 S.Ct. 1032, 113 L.Ed.2d 1 (1991) ("[P]unitive damages are imposed for purposes of retribution and deterrence").

While States possess discretion over the imposition of punitive damages, it is well established that there are procedural and substantive constitutional limitations on these awards. *Cooper Industries, supra; Gore, supra,* at 559, 116 S.Ct. 1589; *Honda Motor Co. v. Oberg,* 512 U.S. 415, 114 S.Ct. 2331, 129 L.Ed.2d 336 (1994); *TXO Production Corp. v. Alliance Resources Corp.,* 509 U.S. 443, 113 S.Ct. 2711, 125 L.Ed.2d 366 (1993); *Haslip, supra* The Due Process Clause of the Fourteenth Amendment

prohibits the imposition of grossly excessive or arbitrary punishments on a tortfeasor. *Cooper Industries, supra,* at 433, 121 S.Ct. 1678; *Gore,* 517 U.S., at 562, 116 S.Ct. 1589; see also *id.,* at 587, 116 S.Ct. 1589 (BREYER, J., concurring) ("This constitutional concern, itself harkening back to the Magna Carta, arises out of the basic unfairness of depriving citizens of life, liberty, or property, through the application, not of law and legal processes, but of arbitrary coercion"). The reason is that "[e]lementary notions of fairness enshrined in our constitutional jurisprudence dictate that a person receive fair notice not only of the conduct that will subject him to punishment, but also of the severity of the penalty that a State may impose." *Id.,* at 574, 116 S.Ct. 1589; *Cooper Industries, supra,* at 433, 121 S.Ct. 1678 ("Despite the broad discretion that States possess with respect to the imposition of criminal penalties and punitive damages, the Due Process Clause of the Fourteenth Amendment to the Federal Constitution imposes substantive limits on that discretion"). To the extent an award is grossly excessive, it furthers no legitimate purpose and constitutes an arbitrary deprivation of property. *Haslip, supra,* at 42, 111 S.Ct. 1032 (O'CONNOR, J., dissenting) ("Punitive damages are a powerful weapon. Imposed wisely and with restraint, they have the potential to advance legitimate state interests. Imposed indiscriminately, however, they have a devastating potential for harm. Regrettably, common-law procedures for awarding punitive damages fall into the latter category").

Although these awards serve the same purposes as criminal penalties, defendants subjected to punitive damages in civil cases have not been accorded the protections applicable in a criminal proceeding. This increases our concerns over the imprecise manner in which punitive damages systems are administered. We have admonished that "[p]unitive damages pose an acute danger of arbitrary deprivation of property. Jury instructions typically leave the jury with wide discretion in choosing amounts, and the presentation of evidence of a defendant's net worth creates the potential that juries will use their verdicts to express biases against big businesses, particularly those without strong local presences." *Honda Motor, supra,* at 432, 114 S.Ct. 2331; see also *Haslip, supra,* at 59, 111 S.Ct. 1032 (O'CONNOR, J., dissenting) ("[T]he Due Process Clause does not permit a State to classify arbitrariness as a virtue. Indeed, the point of due process-of the law in general-is to allow citizens to order their behavior. A State can have no legitimate interest in deliberately making the law so arbitrary that citizens will be unable to avoid punishment based solely upon bias or whim"). Our concerns are heightened when the decision-maker is presented, as we shall discuss, with

(continues)

evidence that has little bearing as to the amount of punitive damages that should be awarded. Vague instructions, or those that merely inform the jury to avoid "passion or prejudice," App. to Pet. for Cert. 108a-109a, do little to aid the decisionmaker in its task of assigning appropriate weight to evidence that is relevant and evidence that is tangential or only inflammatory.

In light of these concerns, in *Gore, supra,* we instructed courts reviewing punitive damages to consider three guideposts: (1) the degree of reprehensibility of the defendant's misconduct; (2) the disparity between the actual or potential harm suffered by the plaintiff and the punitive damages award; and (3) the difference between the punitive damages awarded by the jury and the civil penalties authorized or imposed in comparable cases. *Id.,* at 575, 116 S.Ct. 1589. We reiterated the importance of these three guideposts in *Cooper Industries* and mandated appellate courts to conduct *de novo* review of a trial court's application of them to the jury's award. 532 U.S. 424, 121 S.Ct. 1678. Exacting appellate review ensures that an award of punitive damages is based upon an " 'application of law, rather than a decisionmaker's caprice.' " *Id.,* at 436, 121 S.Ct. 1678 (quoting *Gore, supra,* at 587, 116 S.Ct. 1589 (BREYER, J., concurring)).

III.

Under the principles outlined in *BMW of North America, Inc. v. Gore,* this case is neither close nor difficult. It was error to reinstate the jury's $145 million punitive damages award. We address each guidepost of *Gore* in some detail.

"[T]he most important indicium of the reasonableness of a punitive damages award is the degree of reprehensibility of the defendant's conduct." *Gore,* 517 U.S., at 575, 116 S.Ct. 1589. We have instructed courts to determine the reprehensibility of a defendant by considering whether: the harm caused was physical as opposed to economic; the tortious conduct evinced an indifference to or a reckless disregard of the health or safety of others; the target of the conduct had financial vulnerability; the conduct involved repeated actions or was an isolated incident; and the harm was the result of intentional malice, trickery, or deceit, or mere accident. *Id.,* at 576–577, 116 S.Ct. 1589. The existence of any one of these factors weighing in favor of a plaintiff may not be sufficient to sustain a punitive damages award; and the absence of all of them renders any award suspect. It should be presumed a plaintiff has been made whole for his injuries by compensatory damages, so punitive damages should only be awarded if the defendant's culpability, after having paid compensatory damages, is so reprehensible as to warrant the imposition of

further sanctions to achieve punishment or deterrence. *Id.,* at 575, 116 S.Ct. 1589.

Applying these factors in the instant case, we must acknowledge that State Farm's handling of the claims against the Campbells merits no praise. The trial court found that State Farm's employees altered the company's records to make Campbell appear less culpable. State Farm disregarded the overwhelming likelihood of liability and the near-certain probability that, by taking the case to trial, a judgment in excess of the policy limits would be awarded. State Farm amplified the harm by at first assuring the Campbells their assets would be safe from any verdict and by later telling them, postjudgment, to put a for-sale sign on their house. While we do not suggest there was error in awarding punitive damages based upon State Farm's conduct toward the Campbells, a more modest punishment for this reprehensible conduct could have satisfied the State's legitimate objectives, and the Utah courts should have gone no further.

This case, instead, was used as a platform to expose, and punish, the perceived deficiencies of State Farm's operations throughout the country. The Utah Supreme Court's opinion makes explicit that State Farm was being condemned for its nationwide policies rather than for the conduct directed toward the Campbells. 65 P.3d, at 1143 ("[T]he Campbells introduced evidence that State Farm's decision to take the case to trial was a result of a national scheme to meet corporate fiscal goals by capping payouts on claims company wide"). This was, as well, an explicit rationale of the trial court's decision in approving the award, though reduced from $145 million to $25 million. App. to Pet. for Cert. 120a ("[T]he Campbells demonstrated, through the testimony of State Farm employees who had worked outside of Utah, and through expert testimony, that this pattern of claims adjustment under the PP & R program was not a local anomaly, but was a consistent, nationwide feature of State Farm's business operations, orchestrated from the highest levels of corporate management").

The Campbells contend that State Farm has only itself to blame for the reliance upon dissimilar and out-of-state conduct evidence. The record does not support this contention. From their opening statements onward the Campbells framed this case as a chance to rebuke State Farm for its nationwide activities. App. 208 ("You're going to hear evidence that even the insurance commission in Utah and around the country are unwilling or inept at protecting people against abuses"); *id.,* at 242 ("[T]his is a very important case. . . . [I]t transcends the Campbell file. It involves a nationwide practice. And you, here, are

(continues)

going to be evaluating and assessing, and hopefully requiring State Farm to stand accountable for what it's doing across the country, which is the purpose of punitive damages"). This was a position maintained throughout the litigation. In opposing State Farm's motion to exclude such evidence under *Gore* the Campbells' counsel convinced the trial court that there was no limitation on the scope of evidence that could be considered under our precedents. App. to Pet. for Cert. 172a ("As I read the case *[Gore],* I was struck with the fact that a clear message in the case . . . seems to be that courts in punitive damages cases should receive more evidence, not less. And that the court seems to be inviting an even broader area of evidence than the current rulings of the court would indicate"); *id.,* at 189a (trial court ruling).

A State cannot punish a defendant for conduct that may have been lawful where it occurred. *Gore, supra,* at 572, 116 S.Ct. 1589; *Bigelow v. Virginia,* 421 U.S. 809, 824, 95 S.Ct. 2222, 44 L.Ed.2d 600 (1975) ("A State does not acquire power or supervision over the internal affairs of another State merely because the welfare and health of its own citizens may be affected when they travel to that State"); *New York Life Ins. Co. v. Head,* 234 U.S. 149, 161, 34 S.Ct. 879, 58 L.Ed. 1259 (1914) ("[I]t would be impossible to permit the statutes of Missouri to operate beyond the jurisdiction of that State . . . without throwing down the constitutional barriers by which all the States are restricted within the orbits of their lawful authority and upon the preservation of which the Government under the Constitution depends. This is so obviously the necessary result of the Constitution that it has rarely been called in question and hence authorities directly dealing with it do not abound"); *Huntington v. Attrill,* 146 U.S. 657, 669, 13 S.Ct. 224, 36 L.Ed. 1123 (1892) ("Laws have no force of themselves beyond the jurisdiction of the State which enacts them, and can have extra-territorial effect only by the comity of other States"). Nor, as a general rule, does a State have a legitimate concern in imposing punitive damages to punish a defendant for unlawful acts committed outside of the State's jurisdiction. Any proper adjudication of conduct that occurred outside Utah to other persons would require their inclusion, and, to those parties, the Utah courts, in the usual case, would need to apply the laws of their relevant jurisdiction. *Phillips Petroleum Co. v. Shutts,* 472 U.S. 797, 821–822, 105 S.Ct. 2965, 86 L.Ed.2d 628 (1985).

Here, the Campbells do not dispute that much of the out-of-state conduct was lawful where it occurred. They argue, however, that such evidence was not the primary basis for the punitive damages award and was relevant to the extent it demonstrated, in a general sense, State Farm's motive against its insured. Brief for Respondents 46–47 ("[E]ven if the practices described by State Farm were not malum in se or malum prohibitum, they became relevant to punitive damages to the extent they were used as tools to implement State Farm's wrongful PP & R policy"). This argument misses the mark. Lawful out-of-state conduct may be probative when it demonstrates the deliberateness and culpability of the defendant's action in the State where it is tortious, but that conduct must have a nexus to the specific harm suffered by the plaintiff. A jury must be instructed, furthermore, that it may not use evidence of out-of-state conduct to punish a defendant for action that was lawful in the jurisdiction where it occurred. *Gore,* 517 U.S., at 572–573, 116 S.Ct. 1589 (noting that a State "does not have the power . . . to punish [a defendant] for conduct that was lawful where it occurred and that had no impact on [the State] or its residents"). A basic principle of federalism is that each State may make its own reasoned judgment about what conduct is permitted or proscribed within its borders, and each State alone can determine what measure of punishment, if any, to impose on a defendant who acts within its jurisdiction. *Id.,* at 569, 116 S.Ct. 1589 ("[T]he States need not, and in fact do not, provide such protection in a uniform manner").

For a more fundamental reason, however, the Utah courts erred in relying upon this and other evidence: The courts awarded punitive damages to punish and deter conduct that bore no relation to the Campbells' harm. A defendant's dissimilar acts, independent from the acts upon which liability was premised, may not serve as the basis for punitive damages. A defendant should be punished for the conduct that harmed the plaintiff, not for being an unsavory individual or business. Due process does not permit courts, in the calculation of punitive damages, to adjudicate the merits of other parties' hypothetical claims against a defendant under the guise of the reprehensibility analysis, but we have no doubt the Utah Supreme Court did that here. 65 P.3d, at 1149 ("Even if the harm to the Campbells can be appropriately characterized as minimal, the trial court's assessment of the situation is on target: 'The harm is minor to the individual but massive in the aggregate'"). Punishment on these bases creates the possibility of multiple punitive damages awards for the same conduct; for in the usual case nonparties are not bound by the judgment some other plaintiff obtains. *Gore, supra,* at 593, 116 S.Ct. 1589 (BREYER, J., concurring) ("Larger damages might also 'double count' by including in the punitive damages award some of the compensatory, or punitive, damages that subsequent plaintiffs would also recover").

(continues)

The same reasons lead us to conclude the Utah Supreme Court's decision cannot be justified on the grounds that State Farm was a recidivist. Although "[o]ur holdings that a recidivist may be punished more severely than a first offender recognize that repeated misconduct is more reprehensible than an individual instance of malfeasance," *Gore, supra,* at 577, 116 S.Ct. 1589, in the context of civil actions courts must ensure the conduct in question replicates the prior transgressions. *TXO,* 509 U.S., at 462, n. 28, 113 S.Ct. 2711 (noting that courts should look to " 'the existence and frequency of similar past conduct' " (quoting *Haslip,* 499 U.S., at 21–22, 111 S.Ct. 1032)).

The Campbells have identified scant evidence of repeated misconduct of the sort that injured them. Nor does our review of the Utah courts' decisions convince us that State Farm was only punished for its actions toward the Campbells. Although evidence of other acts need not be identical to have relevance in the calculation of punitive damages, the Utah court erred here because evidence pertaining to claims that had nothing to do with a third-party lawsuit was introduced at length. Other evidence concerning reprehensibility was even more tangential. For example, the Utah Supreme Court criticized State Farm's investigation into the personal life of one of its employees and, in a broader approach, the manner in which State Farm's policies corrupted its employees. 65 P.3d, at 1148, 1150 The Campbells attempt to justify the courts' reliance upon this unrelated testimony on the theory that each dollar of profit made by underpaying a third-party claimant is the same as a dollar made by underpaying a first-party one. Brief for Respondents 45; see also 65 P.3d at 1150 ("State Farm's continuing illicit practice created market disadvantages for other honest insurance companies because these practices increased profits. As plaintiffs' expert witnesses established, such wrongfully obtained competitive advantages have the potential to pressure other companies to adopt similar fraudulent tactics, or to force them out of business. Thus, such actions cause distortions throughout the insurance market and ultimately hurt all consumers"). For the reasons already stated, this argument is unconvincing. The reprehensibility guidepost does not permit courts to expand the scope of the case so that a defendant may be punished for any malfeasance, which in this case extended for a 20-year period. In this case, because the Campbells have shown no conduct by State Farm similar to that which harmed them, the conduct that harmed them is the only conduct relevant to the reprehensibility analysis.

Turning to the second *Gore* guidepost, we have been reluctant to identify concrete constitutional limits on the ratio between harm, or potential harm, to the plaintiff and the punitive damages award. 517 U.S., at 582, 116 S.Ct. 1589 ("[W]e have consistently rejected the notion that the constitutional line is marked by a simple mathematical formula, even one that compares actual *and potential* damages to the punitive award"); *TXO, supra,* at 458, 113 S.Ct. 2711. We decline again to impose a bright-line ratio which a punitive damages award cannot exceed. Our jurisprudence and the principles it has now established demonstrate, however, that, in practice, few awards exceeding a single-digit ratio between punitive and compensatory damages, to a significant degree, will satisfy due process. In *Haslip,* in upholding a punitive damages award, we concluded that an award of more than four times the amount of compensatory damages might be close to the line of constitutional impropriety. 499 U.S., at 23–24, 111 S.Ct. 1032. We cited that 4-to-1 ratio again in *Gore.* 517 U.S., at 581, 116 S.Ct. 1589. The Court further referenced a long legislative history, dating back over 700 years and going forward to today, providing for sanctions of double, treble, or quadruple damages to deter and punish. *Id.,* at 581, and n. 33, 116 S.Ct. 1589. While these ratios are not binding, they are instructive. They demonstrate what should be obvious: Single-digit multipliers are more likely to comport with due process, while still achieving the State's goals of deterrence and retribution, than awards with ratios in range of 500 to 1, *id.,* at 582, 116 S.Ct. 1589, or, in this case, of 145 to 1.

Nonetheless, because there are no rigid benchmarks that a punitive damages award may not surpass, ratios greater than those we have previously upheld may comport with due process where "a particularly egregious act has resulted in only a small amount of economic damages." *Ibid.;* see also *ibid.*(positing that a higher ratio *might* be necessary where "the injury is hard to detect or the monetary value of noneconomic harm might have been difficult to determine"). The converse is also true, however. When compensatory damages are substantial, then a lesser ratio, perhaps only equal to compensatory damages, can reach the outermost limit of the due process guarantee. The precise award in any case, of course, must be based upon the facts and circumstances of the defendant's conduct and the harm to the plaintiff.

In sum, courts must ensure that the measure of punishment is both reasonable and proportionate to the amount of harm to the plaintiff and to the general damages recovered. In the context of this case, we have no doubt that there is a presumption against an award that has a 145-to-1 ratio. The compensatory award in this case was substantial; the Campbells were awarded $1 million for a year and a half of emotional distress. This was complete compensation. The harm arose from a transaction in the economic realm, not from

(continues)

some physical assault or trauma; there were no physical injuries; and State Farm paid the excess verdict before the complaint was filed, so the Campbells suffered only minor economic injuries for the 18-month period in which State Farm refused to resolve the claim against them. The compensatory damages for the injury suffered here, moreover, likely were based on a component which was duplicated in the punitive award. Much of the distress was caused by the outrage and humiliation the Campbells suffered at the actions of their insurer; and it is a major role of punitive damages to condemn such conduct. Compensatory damages, however, already contain this punitive element. See Restatement (Second) of Torts § 908, Comment c, p. 466 (1977) ("In many cases in which compensatory damages include an amount for emotional distress, such as humiliation or indignation aroused by the defendant's act, there is no clear line of demarcation between punishment and compensation and a verdict for a specified amount frequently includes elements of both").

The Utah Supreme Court sought to justify the massive award by pointing to State Farm's purported failure to report a prior $100 million punitive damages award in Texas to its corporate headquarters; the fact that State Farm's policies have affected numerous Utah consumers; the fact that State Farm will only be punished in one out of every 50,000 cases as a matter of statistical probability; and State Farm's enormous wealth. 65 P.3d, at 1153. Since the Supreme Court of Utah discussed the Texas award when applying the ratio guidepost, we discuss it here. The Texas award, however, should have been analyzed in the context of the reprehensibility guidepost only. The failure of the company to report the Texas award is out-of-state conduct that, if the conduct were similar, might have had some bearing on the degree of reprehensibility, subject to the limitations we have described. Here, it was dissimilar, and of such marginal relevance that it should have been accorded little or no weight. The award was rendered in a first-party lawsuit; no judgment was entered in the case; and it was later settled for a fraction of the verdict. With respect to the Utah Supreme Court's second justification, the Campbells' inability to direct us to testimony demonstrating harm to the people of Utah (other than those directly involved in this case) indicates that the adverse effect on the State's general population was in fact minor.

The remaining premises for the Utah Supreme Court's decision bear no relation to the award's reasonableness or proportionality to the harm. They are, rather, arguments that seek to defend a departure from well-established constraints on punitive damages. While States enjoy considerable discretion in deducing when punitive damages are warranted, each award must comport with the principles set forth in *Gore.* Here the argument that State Farm will be punished in only the rare case, coupled with reference to its assets (which, of course, are what other insured parties in Utah and other States must rely upon for payment of claims) had little to do with the actual harm sustained by the Campbells. The wealth of a defendant cannot justify an otherwise unconstitutional punitive damages award. *Gore,* 517 U.S., at 585, 116 S.Ct. 1589 ("The fact that BMW is a large corporation rather than an impecunious individual does not diminish its entitlement to fair notice of the demands that the several States impose on the conduct of its business"); see also *id.,* at 591, 116 S.Ct. 1589 (BREYER, J., concurring) ("[Wealth] provides an open-ended basis for inflating awards when the defendant is wealthy. . . . That does not make its use unlawful or inappropriate; it simply means that this factor cannot make up for the failure of other factors, such as 'reprehensibility,' to constrain significantly an award that purports to punish a defendant's conduct"). The principles set forth in *Gore* must be implemented with care, to ensure both reasonableness and proportionality.

The third guidepost in *Gore* is the disparity between the punitive damages award and the "civil penalties authorized or imposed in comparable cases." *Id.,* at 575, 116 S.Ct. 1589. We note that, in the past, we have also looked to criminal penalties that could be imposed. *Id.,* at 583, 116 S.Ct. 1589; *Haslip,* 499 U.S., at 23, 111 S.Ct. 1032. The existence of a criminal penalty does have bearing on the seriousness with which a State views the wrongful action. When used to determine the dollar amount of the award, however, the criminal penalty has less utility. Great care must be taken to avoid use of the civil process to assess criminal penalties that can be imposed only after the heightened protections of a criminal trial have been observed, including, of course, its higher standards of proof. Punitive damages are not a substitute for the criminal process, and the remote possibility of a criminal sanction does not automatically sustain a punitive damages award.

Here, we need not dwell long on this guidepost. The most relevant civil sanction under Utah state law for the wrong done to the Campbells appears to be a $10,000 fine for an act of fraud, 65 P.3d, at 1154, an amount dwarfed by the $145 million punitive damages award. The Supreme Court of Utah speculated about the loss of State Farm's business license, the disgorgement of profits, and possible imprisonment, but here again its references were to the broad fraudulent scheme drawn from evidence of out-of-state and dissimilar conduct. This analysis was insufficient to justify the award.

(continues)

IV.

An application of the *Gore* guideposts to the facts of this case, especially in light of the substantial compensatory damages awarded (a portion of which contained a punitive element), likely would justify a punitive damages award at or near the amount of compensatory damages. The punitive award of $145 million, therefore, was neither reasonable nor proportionate to the wrong committed, and it was

an irrational and arbitrary deprivation of the property of the defendant. The proper calculation of punitive damages under the principles we have discussed should be resolved, in the first instance, by the Utah courts.

The judgment of the Utah Supreme Court is reversed, and the case is remanded for further proceedings not inconsistent with this opinion.

It is so ordered.

PUTTING IT INTO PRACTICE 7:2

1. For what reason did the plaintiff argue that punitive damages were justified?
2. What evidence did the plaintiff produce to support his claim for punitive damages?
3. On what basis did State Farm argue that the punitive-damage award was unjustified?
4. Why did the Supreme Court conclude that the punitive-damage award was not justified?

State Farm's conduct was not egregious enough to warrant a $145 million award: its actions were not sufficiently reprehensible; the ratio between the plaintiff's compensatory damages and his punitive damages was outside the bounds of reasonableness; and the award exceeded the sanctions for comparable misconduct in Utah and elsewhere.

RECOVERY FOR LOSS OF CONSORTIUM

Under the common law, a husband and wife were considered one. Therefore, if the wife were injured the husband could recover for **loss of consortium**, which encompasses recovery for lost services, such as companionship, sex, earnings outside the home, and so on. But because the wife had no right to services from her husband, she could recover nothing if he were injured. Evolution of the common law and equal-protection attacks on statutes have resulted in both husbands and wives being entitled to recover for loss of services.

A loss of consortium claim is a **derivative claim** in that it is derived from the spouse's underlying claim. If a husband, for example, is injured in a motor vehicle accident and successfully sues the negligent

driver, the wife can then sue for loss of her husband's consortium.

Because both spouses can recover, this leads to the possibility of double recovery. If the spouses were to sue in two separate actions, the wife might recover for medical expenses in one action, and the husband might later recover for the same expenses by arguing that he was the one who in fact paid the expenses. To preclude double recovery, many states require that such actions be brought together.

In most jurisdictions parents can recover for medical expenses incurred as a result of injury to a child. They are also entitled to recovery for the lost services and earnings of a minor child. In cases in which the child has died, more and more courts are allowing recovery for loss of the child's companionship.

Typically, children have not been allowed to recover for loss of companionship of a parent who has been injured. More recently, however, a few courts have allowed such recovery when the child is a minor and is dependent on the parent for its nurturing and development. Courts have been reluctant to get involved in this area because of the difficulty in quantifying the damages. Furthermore, the potential for duplicative claims exists when the injured parent has several minor children.

PUTTING IT INTO PRACTICE 7:3

1. A cow escapes from the defendant's enclosed pasture through an opening in the fence and strikes the plaintiffs' car, causing damage to the car and injury to the plaintiffs. Some of defendants' cows had escaped over the prior ten years, but none had done so through this part of the fence. How the fence broke cannot be shown by either party. Ranchers are required by law to fence their land and to exercise ordinary care to keep their cattle inside. The defendants are found negligent despite their claims of diligence in repairing the fence. Are punitive damages justified in this case?

2. A workman, employed by a contractor hired by Standard Oil to repair a road on its refinery property, is injured by the explosive leaking of a sulfuric acid from the shallowly buried underground Standard Oil pipeline. The facts are summarized by the appellate court according to the plaintiff's testimony and then according to the defendant's testimony.

The plaintiff's testimony showed

    a. fifty leaks had been reported in the pipeline throughout its life.

    b. the line was twenty years old and its life expectancy at the time of the accident could have been measured in months.

    c. the defendant knew the roadwork would be in the vicinity of the line.

    d. a Standard Oil inspector had recommended replacement of the line.

    e. that the company, because of the daily use of the pipe and the loss of profit if the line shut down, decided to "run it to failure."

    f. that the defendant did not post a warning at the work site or place a guard there.

    g. the sulfuric acid at the refinery had caused twenty to twenty-five injuries.

The defendant, on the other hand, showed

    a. that the previous leaks had occurred over a twenty-year period and over a line four miles long.

    b. that all leaks had been promptly repaired on the day of occurrence.

    c. that all of the leaks except one or possibly two had occurred at valves or at defective welds, rather than because of pipe erosion, as in the present case.

    d. that the line had a remaining life of four or five years and substantial loss would result from its being shut down for more than repair time.

    e. that no leak had ever occurred near the section of the pipe where the plaintiff was injured.

    f. that in a faraway area where the company had decided to "run to failure" rather than replace (after several ruptures), the company had placed a heavy redwood covering around the pipe.

    g. that the defendant company had inspected the whole line with special equipment a few years before the accident and found no need of repair.

    h. that in the area where the inspection showed a need for replacement, the company had been quite willing to shut down the line for several days.

    i. that of the thirty-two sulfuric acid injuries in the plant in the preceding ten years, only one or possibly two occurred because of leaks in the pipeline. *Colson v. Standard Oil*, 60 Cal. App. 3d 913 (1976).

After reviewing these facts, do you think punitive damages are justified?

ASSESSMENT OF DAMAGES

From a practical perspective, the evaluation of damages is a critical aspect of a plaintiff's case and of a defendant's response to a claim. What follows is a list of the types of questions plaintiffs' attorneys frequently ask when considering the value of a case:

Medical Expenses

1. What type of treatment was received?
2. For how long was the treatment received?
3. Was the treatment recognized in the medical community?
4. Who performed the treatment (e.g., a medical doctor, osteopath, chiropractor, physician's assistant, physical therapist, etc.)?
5. Was the treatment excessive considering the nature of the injuries?
6. Was the plaintiff hospitalized? If so, for how long?
7. Did the plaintiff have to be removed from the scene of the accident by an ambulance?
8. Was the plaintiff treated in the emergency room?
9. What percentage of medical expenses was devoted to diagnostics and what percentage to treatment?
10. Did the plaintiff suffer any permanent injuries, such as scarring, a limp, loss or impairment of a limb or organ? How serious are these injuries?
11. To what extent will these permanent injuries impair the plaintiff's ability to work, to exercise, to enjoy hobbies, and to otherwise enjoy life?
12. Did the plaintiff suffer any loss of mental function or emotional trauma, and to what extent has this compromised her life?
13. To what extent will the plaintiff be prevented from pursuing interests or opportunities she had but had not yet pursued?
14. What is the nature and extent of rehabilitation the plaintiff has required?
15. What medical supplies and equipment, drugs, and nursing services has the plaintiff required?
16. In what ways have the plaintiff's injuries created a substantial impact on the plaintiff's family?
17. Is there a loss of consortium claim?
18. Will the plaintiff be a credible witness?
19. Has the plaintiff had prior claims? If so, what were they for?

Lost Wages

1. How much money would the plaintiff have earned but for being injured?
2. How much work has the plaintiff lost as a result of being injured, including vacation and sick time that was taken while recovering from the injuries?
3. Is the number of lost work hours reasonable in light of the nature and extent of the injuries sustained?
4. Has the plaintiff lost potential pay increases (e.g., promotions or bonuses) as a result of lost work?

Property Damage

1. What is the cost of repairing damaged property?
2. If a vehicle had to be rented while the plaintiff's vehicle was being repaired, what is the cost of that rental?
3. What personal items were lost or destroyed as a result of the defendant's actions and what is the cost of replacing those items based on their fair market value?
4. What is the fair market value of any items that cannot be replaced (i.e., heirlooms, paintings)?
5. How much did the plaintiff expend in sales taxes in replacing or repairing property?

Pain and Suffering

1. What is the nature and extent of injuries?
2. To what extent is the plaintiff incapacitated by permanent injuries or disfigurement?
3. To what extent are the plaintiff's daily activities curtailed or made more difficult as a result of being injured?
4. What kinds of recoveries have been awarded in cases involving injuries of comparable nature and degree?

To answer last question, attorneys consider their own experience as well as the experiences of other litigators, which they can do by accessing the following:

a. trial reporters (or jury reporters), which are issued weekly or biweekly and list the verdicts received in jury trials, arbitrations, mediations, non-jury trials, and other dispute resolution mechanisms, such as summary trials.

b. compendiums, which are compilations of all dispute resolution mechanisms involving specific injuries for a designated period of time. Compilation can also be requested for verdicts and settlements for particular doctors, attorneys, firms, or judges.

c. personal injury valuation programs, which are software programs that allow attorneys to input the data from their cases and help them compute the value of their case.

d. journals published by the American Trial Lawyers Association, state trial lawyers' associations, and defense organizations that list the verdicts for cases that went to trial or were settled. Attorneys can also place personal ads soliciting information from other attorneys who have tried or settled cases involving injuries similar to those implicated in the case the attorney is litigating.

e. websites on the Internet that provide access to forums, discussion groups, bulletin boards, and research tools, all of which can be used in evaluating cases.

To evaluate future medical expenses, attorneys usually consult with medical doctors to help assess what kinds of medical treatment and rehabilitation will be required in the future and to what extent that treatment will temporarily incapacitate the plaintiff. If, for example, the doctor projects that in twenty years the plaintiff will need another hip replacement, the attorney needs to know how much time the plaintiff will spend in the hospital and undergoing rehabilitation before being restored to relatively normal functioning. To assess future lost wages attorneys rely on the expertise of economists and vocational rehabilitation counselors, who help predict what the plaintiff will be able to do, whether special schooling will be required, and how much that schooling will cost. Less tangible factors that attorneys consider in evaluating cases are the experience and reputation of opposing counsel and the adjustor, as well as the policies and reputation of the insurance company against which they have a claim.

WRONGFUL-DEATH AND SURVIVAL ACTIONS

Under the common law, when a plaintiff died as a consequence of injuries inflicted on him by the defendant, his tort action died along with him.

At that point his spouse and children also lost any right to recovery. The reasoning behind this rule was that it was immoral to put a monetary value on a human life. Unfortunately, this rule increased the likelihood that defendants would kill their plaintiffs, as it was cheaper for the defendant if the plaintiff died.

Lord Campbell's Act, passed in England in 1846 and after which most modern statutes are patterned, allowed recovery to families of individuals killed by tortious conduct. In accord with this act all states have passed statutes allowing some kind of **survival action** so that the injured party's claim survives his death (see Exhibit 7–3). In most states the cause of death is irrelevant, but in a few states if the death resulted from the defendant's tort, a wrongful-death action and not a survival claim must be filed. All survival statutes provide that a cause of action for injury to tangible property survives the death of the plaintiff. The majority allows personal injury actions to survive as well. A few states permit claims pertaining to intangible interests, such as infliction of emotional distress and defamation, to survive. Most allow a tort action to be maintained or even initiated after the defendant's death as well. Similarly, statutes allowing **wrongful-death** actions have also been passed, so that third persons, usually the decedent's spouse and children, can recover for losses they sustained as a result of the decedent's death.

The issue of wrongful death is unique in the field of tort law because it centers around the interpretation of statutes. Litigants in this area are forced to engage in statutory construction and determination of legislative intent. This is often onerous because most of the statutes were written more than 100 years ago.

EXHIBIT 7–3 *Comparison of Survival Statutes and Wrongful-Death Statutes*

SURVIVAL STATUTES	WRONGFUL-DEATH STATUTES
• Injured party's claim survives his death. • Damages awarded to deceased's estate.	• Third parties can recover for losses they sustain as a result of victim's death. • Proceeds go to spouses, parents, or children of deceased.

Types of Recovery Allowed

When a survival action is filed separately from a wrongful-death action, the possibility of double recovery exists. To prevent this from happening, many states limit survivor actions to those losses occurring prior to the decedent's death. Damages are restricted, therefore, to the decedent's medical expenses, lost earnings prior to death, and pain and suffering. Consequently, in such states, if the death is instantaneous no survival action exists at all because no damages occurred prior to death (see *Restatement [Second]) of Torts* § 926, cmt. a).

LOCAL LINKS

In your state what damages can be recovered in a survival action?

Under Lord Campbell's Act and the wrongful death legislation patterned after that act, damages were to be limited to pecuniary or economic losses caused by the decedent's death. Typically, the loss is measured in terms of the monetary contributions that the decedent would have made during her lifetime to the plaintiff beneficiary. In more recent years a pecuniary value has been attached to the companionship, sexual relationship, and moral guidance provided by the decedent. Furthermore, several states allow recovery for grief and other mental suffering of the survivors. Some of those states have imposed a cap on those damages, however, to protect against runaway awards.

LOCAL LINKS

In your state can survivors recover for their grief and suffering? Also, can survivors recover for the loss of companionship, sexual relationship, and guidance provided by the decedent?

Recovery in this area becomes particularly problematic when parents bring a wrongful-death action for a child's death. Most wrongful-death statutes require that the child be born alive in order to recover damages for the child's wrongful death. The, issue of whether or not a wrongful death action for a fetus is a viable claim has been the subject of considerable litigation. Technology has extended the debate to include the question of whether a claim for wrongful death for a fetus is appropriate and/or against public policy. Determining damages for the wrongful death of child is complicated since the expense of raising a child usually far surpasses any earnings the child can be expected to bring home. Many courts allow recovery of a substantial reward for loss of companionship of the child. Other courts have allowed consideration of what the decedent child might have brought to his parents in terms of support in their old age. In one case, for example, $100,000 was allowed for loss of a very intelligent seven-year-old who exhibited talent as a cartoonist (*Haumerson v. Ford Motor Co.*, 257 N.W.2d 7 [Iowa 1977]).

LOCAL LINKS

In your state can parents recover for the loss of companionship of a child?

Disclosure of Remarriage

Another issue that arises in wrongful-death and survival actions is whether a surviving spouse who remarries is entitled to keep this information from the jury. The concern is that a jury in particular may be inclined to give a lower verdict if it learns of the remarriage. Of course, defendants are eager to disclose this information during voir dire and argue that they need to do so in case prospective jurors are acquainted with the new spouse. Most courts, however, refuse to allow evidence of remarriage even if used for this limited purpose.

LOCAL LINKS

Do the courts in your state allow evidence of remarriage during voir dire?

Who Recovers?

Survival actions are usually brought by the executor or administrator of an estate. Recovery becomes an asset of that estate and may be reached by creditors. It is often distributed in accordance with state testacy and intestacy laws. Some argue that survival actions may result in a windfall to distant relatives who had little or no contact with the decedent. In contrast, relatives who were not named beneficiaries in a wrongful-death action may be able to recover in a survival action. Recovery for pain and suffering in survival actions is allowed only if the decedent was conscious of pain. Courtroom battles often revolve, therefore, around the issue of the decedent's consciousness, particularly if he survived only a few seconds or minutes after being injured (such as in a mid-air collision of an aircraft).

Defenses

Although any defenses that could have been raised against the decedent are still available to the defendant in a survival action, considerable disagreement exists as to which defenses should be allowed in a wrongful-death action. Most states resolve this by allowing the defendant to assert any defenses she would have been able to use against the decedent if the decedent were still alive. In such cases, for example, the defendant may argue that the decedent was contributorily negligent or that he assumed the risk.

Statutes of limitations are another concern in wrongful death and survival actions. Suppose, for example, the decedent failed to file an action until after the statute of limitations had run. Would a wrongful death or survival action be barred? Most courts have answered no and indicate that the death action begins to run from the date of death.

Remember that survival actions and wrongful-death actions are statutory creatures and are therefore subject to statutory construction. Be sure to examine the statutory scheme in your state dealing with these types of claims.

DISCOUNTING FUTURE DAMAGES

A plaintiff, in a sense, receives a windfall by collecting in the present for future losses. The rationale is that a lump sum paid now for future loss is worth more to the recipient than future payments, because a lump sum has the potential of creating more money through investment. In practical terms, having $10,000 in the bank now, invested at a modest rate of return, is more advantageous than having $10,000 ten years from now. To illustrate, the **present value** (defined as the current value of money that is to be paid in the future) of $1.00 payable at 5 percent compound interest in one year is $0.95, whereas the present value of $1.00 in ten years is $0.61, and the present value of $1.00 payable in twenty years is $0.38. Recognition of the earning power of money has resulted in many courts requiring juries to reduce, or discount, awards to the present value of lost future earnings. **Discounting an award** prevents the plaintiff from realizing an unwarranted windfall and reduces losses to the defendant.

Life expectancy tables, annuity tables, and work expectancy tables are used for determining earning expectancy. The present value of anticipated earnings can be computed by calculating a dollar at the current

PUTTING IT INTO PRACTICE 7:4

After buying a used vehicle that proved to be defective, Garcia returned the vehicle to the seller and refused to make further payments. After several unsuccessful attempts by a collection agency to collect payments, sheriff's deputies are sent to execute a writ of attachment on Garcia's mobile home. When they arrive Garcia kills one of the deputies and then engages in a shootout with the other deputy, resulting in the death of both Garcia and the deputy. A wrongful-death action is filed alleging that the wrongful acts of the collection agency drove Garcia insane, and that while insane he engaged in a gunfight with the deputies that was tantamount to suicide.

Consult the wrongful-death and survival statutes in your states to determine who could bring this claim. What kinds of damages could be claimed? What would be the statute of limitations for this claim?

rate of interest and multiplying that by the average monthly earnings for the designated period of time. The present value, for example, of twenty-five annual payments of $10,000 per year ($250,000 total) would be $127,833 if an interest rate of 6 percent is assumed. As you can see, the defendant receives a type of "interest" on the advance payment when the plaintiff is awarded the present value of the losses (*Restatement [Second] of Torts* § 913A). See "Practice Pointers" at the end of this chapter for more details on the calculation of present values.

Some attorneys have argued that inflation offsets the discounting of present-value awards. The argument is that claiming future damage for present value does not fully compensate the victim, as the upward movement of prices can generally be anticipated. In one case, for example, the court concluded that inflation and present value canceled each other out (*Pierce v. New York Central Rail Co.*, 304 F. Supp. 44 [W.D. Mich. 1969]). The court noted that a dollar invested that would earn 5 percent per year now would increase in value to $2.30 after twenty-six years. However, if the purchasing power of that same dollar was reduced 5 percent per year, then in twenty-six years it would take $2.30 to purchase what it presently cost a dollar to buy. Other courts have rejected this argument as being too speculative.

STRUCTURED SETTLEMENTS

Traditionally under the common law past and future damages were paid in a single lump sum. More recently, large future damages have been paid using a periodic-payment settlement, often referred to as a **structured settlement**. Three reasons are generally given for the use of a structured settlement. First, the plaintiff does not have the responsibility of making arrangements to invest the money if he receives periodic payments over a long period of time. Money will be available to cover basic human needs. Second, a large amount of the money will be prudently invested and will not be squandered through ignorance, bad advice, or frivolity. Third, the income tax that the plaintiff has to pay is usually minimized using a structured settlement. Although tax need not be paid on

a lump-sum amount, it does have to be paid on any income resulting from an investment of a lump-sum damage award.

The downside of these settlements from the plaintiff's perspective is the inability to freely spend the monies; the uncertainty of the real present cash value of the settlement (because the negotiated figure is in the hands of the defendant); the fixed nature of the payments, which cannot be modified over time; the possibility that the death of the recipient may terminate some payments; and the possibility of insolvency of the company responsible for the payments.

The structured settlement is widely used in product liability cases (such as in the cases involving thalidomide, the drug that was shown to cause severe birth defects) and can bridge the gap between a plaintiff's final settlement demand and a defendant's final offer. To illustrate the incentive for defendants to enter into such agreements, benefits worth $3 million over time could actually cost a defendant $2 million if made through a structured settlement. These settlements can also reduce defense costs by avoiding trial and appeal and can provide defense counsel more flexibility in the negotiating process. Agreements may provide for an up-front fixed payment, including an amount covering attorney's fees, and then guaranteeing specified payments over time. Payments for medical, hospital, nursing, therapy, prescription drugs, medical equipment, and supply needs can also be added. Structured settlements are limited only by the imagination and ingenuity of the parties and the rules and regulations imposed by the Internal Revenue Service.

We will not explore any of the intricacies involved in structuring such a settlement. Suffice it to say that federal tax law is crucial in shaping the form of a settlement. Some attorneys, however, feel that the advantages of structured settlements are illusory and that such arrangements better serve the interests of the insurance company than they do that of the plaintiff. (See A. Fuchsberg, "Pitfalls in Structured Settlements," *Trial* 42 [Sept. 1989].) Structured settlements are required by statute under certain circumstances in some states and are generally supported by the defense bar.

NET NEWS

For information about structured settlements and their value, go to the web page for the National Structured Settlements Trade Association at **http://www.nssta.com**.

MITIGATION OF DAMAGES

The duty to mitigate damages required under contract law is also required under tort law. Under this rule, also referred to as the **avoidable-consequences rule**, a plaintiff cannot recover for any damages she could reasonably have avoided. Recovery will not be allowed, for example, for the additional medical expenses necessary to treat an infection incurred by the plaintiff's failure to seek prompt medical care for a wound caused by the defendant's negligence. The burden would be on the defendant, however, to prove that the plaintiff could have avoided the harm.

Although this rule is usually applied to the plaintiff's conduct after the accident, in some states it has been used to argue that the plaintiff should have taken certain safety precautions before the accident. In states mandating the wearing of seat belts or motorcycle helmets, the argument has been made that the plaintiff suffered injuries that he would not have sustained had he taken the precautions required by statute. The defendant's argument in such cases is that passage of such statutes represents legislative recognition of the capacity to avoid injuries by the wearing of seat belts or motorcycle helmets. In other states, failure to take such safety precautions is considered contributory negligence.

MENTAL SUFFERING

A plaintiff need not show that he suffered some kind of physical harm to recover for mental suffering Where there is physical injury, damages from mental suffering are often called **parasitic damages** because they attach to the physical injury.

When the plaintiff sustains no physical injury, the courts are reluctant to permit recovery for emotional suffering because of a fear that the suffering may be feigned. Suppose a woman eats cottage cheese containing broken glass. She is not cut or in any way physically injured, but she is frightened at the prospect of possibly having swallowed some glass. She is slightly nauseated and unable to sleep that evening. The vast majority of courts will deny her recovery if she is unable to point to any non-transitory (ongoing) physical symptoms of her emotional distress. The theory is that the lack of objective physical symptoms greatly increases the risk of fraudulent claims and therefore recovery is denied (*Restatement [Second] of Torts* § 436A, cmts. b and c, illus. 1.).

Many courts have allowed an exception to this general rule in cases involving the negligent mishandling of corpses (such as the misplacement or dismemberment of a corpse) or in cases involving the negligent transmission of an erroneous message regarding the death of a family member. Such cases are thought by their very nature to cause actual suffering and therefore minimize the risk of fake claims.

A small minority of courts follow the *impact rule*, predicating recovery for mental suffering on the plaintiff experiencing some type of physical "impact." An impact could be an electric shock, a slight jarring, inhalation of smoke, dust in the eye, or any contact even of a trivial nature. Impact was achieved in a particularly novel way in one case in which a circus horse defecated in the plaintiff's lap (*Christy Bros. Circus v. Turnage*, 144 S.E. 680 [1928]). The vast majority of courts have abandoned the impact rule in favor of requiring the plaintiff to exhibit some physical manifestation if she is to recover for mental disturbances.

Attempts to Circumvent the Physical-Harm Requirement

If the defendant's conduct was intentional or willful, the courts have been much more willing to allow recovery for pure emotional distress. If the plaintiff suffers emotional distress that subsequently manifests in the form of physical consequences, the vast majority of courts also allow recovery even if the manifestation of physical consequences is not immediate.

Some states have abandoned the rule altogether when the facts are such that one could readily believe there could have been actual mental distress. In one notable case a plaintiff was allowed to recover against the defendant doctors and hospital who had mistakenly told his wife that she had syphilis (*Molien v. Kaiser Foundation Hospitals*, 616 P.2d 813 [Cal. 1980]). As a result of this disclosure the plaintiff's wife became suspicious that the plaintiff was having an extramarital affair and their marriage broke up. The court rejected the artificial physical harm requirement for two reasons:

> First, the classification is both over inclusive and under inclusive when viewed in the light of its purported purpose of screening false claims. It is over inclusive in permitting recovery for emotional distress when the suffering accompanies or results in any physical injury whatever, no matter how trivial. If physical injury, however slight, provides

the ticket for admission to the courthouse, it is difficult for advocates of the "floodgates" premonition to deny that the doors are already wide open. . . . More significantly, the classification is under inclusive because it mechanically denies court access to claims that may well be valid and could be proved if the plaintiffs were permitted to go to trial.

The second defect in the requirement of physical injury is that it encourages extravagant pleading and distorted testimony. Thus it has been urged that the law should provide a remedy for serious invasions of emotional tranquility, "otherwise the tendency would be for the victim to exaggerate symptoms of sick headaches, nausea, insomnia, etc., to make out a technical basis for bodily injury, upon which to predicate a parasitic recovery for the more grievous disturbance, the mental and emotional disturbance she endured."

The court concluded that the jurors were in the best position to determine whether the defendants' conduct could have caused emotional distress.

Some courts presented with the physical-harm problem in the context of a plaintiff who has seen injury occur to others have taken the *Palsgraf* "zone of danger" approach. They have held that a plaintiff who is not within the "zone of danger" and who is therefore not endangered by the defendant's conduct is owed no duty. Such a plaintiff cannot recover for emotional distress as a result of another's injury even if this distress leads to physical harm.

A growing number of states have, however, begun to abandon the physical-harm requirement if the plaintiff was near the scene of the accident, personally observed it, and was closely related to the victim. In one such case a young girl and her brother were passengers in an automobile that was involved in a traffic accident (*Shipley v. Williams* 14 Misc.3d 682 [N.Y. 2006]). The sister sought damages for emotional distress because she had observed her brother's death. The court, in allowing the sister to recover, noted that the sister was in the zone of danger along with her brother at the time of impact.

Although modern courts have relaxed restrictions around physical harm requirements, most have restricted liability to experiences of serious emotional harm, such as neuroses, psychoses, chronic depression, phobia, or shock, and have refused to extend liability to plaintiffs who have experienced only transitory states of fright, disappointment, regret, nausea, grief, or humiliation.

APPLICATION

Although neither Teddy nor Mr. Goodright would be entitled to recover for punitive damages, as the Baxters' negligence did not rise to the level of recklessness, they would both be entitled to compensatory damages if the Baxters were found liable. Both could certainly recover for their medical expenses and for their pain and suffering, both past and future. Proof of their past medical expenses would probably be relatively straightforward, but future medical expenses might be more difficult to quantify. Teddy, for example, might require ongoing psychiatric care as a result of his phobic disorder. Because estimating the length and cost of such treatment would be difficult, a concrete dollar figure would also be difficult to calculate. If Mr. Goodright might have to endure future operations, the expenses of those operations, along with all other future medical expenses, would have to be estimated. Remember, too, that Mr. Goodright's

---

PUTTING IT INTO PRACTICE 7:5

1. A mother watches from the front porch of her home as her son is killed by a negligent motorist. Does she have grounds for a claim of negligent infliction of emotional distress?

2. After being told that her child has been involved in an accident, a mother arrives moments later at the scene and sees her child's body in the street. Does she have grounds for a claim of negligent infliction of emotional distress?

3. A doctor incorrectly advises a patient that she has tested positive for AIDS when in fact her test results are negative. Does she have a claim against the doctor for negligent infliction of emotional distress?

spouse and Teddy's parents could also file claims for loss of consortium.

The pain and suffering endured by this duo, though less tangible than their physical injuries, would be a crucial element in their recoveries. Teddy's attorney would want to point to the physical trauma that Teddy experienced as well as the ongoing psychological pain he could be expected to suffer for the remainder of his life in relationship to his fear of dogs. His attorney would want to paint a vivid picture of the limitations stemming from this emotional trauma. If Teddy were unable to secure a job as a paper carrier as a result of his phobia, or if he became so chronically anxious that his social life were disrupted, his attorney would point to this as evidence of the long-term effects of Gertrude's attack. Mr. Goodright's attorney, in contrast, would focus more on the life-changing consequences of Gertrude's actions in bringing Mr. Goodright's concert pianist career to an abrupt end. Again, the challenge in this case would be in converting the intangible but real suffering of a human being into a dollar figure. Both parties would also be able to recover for any permanent disfigurement, such as scarring, that they sustained.

At a more tangible level, Mr. Goodright's attorney would have to project Mr. Goodright's loss of income resulting from the termination of his career. Obviously, one could anticipate conflict between counsel in reference to the relative values of a concert pianist's career and a piano teacher's career. Both counsels would have to dig out as many facts as possible to substantiate their positions. This is what makes litigation so challenging! Any other limitations that Mr. Goodright suffered as a result of his disabled hand would also have to be quantified. Specific, concrete evidence illustrating such disability would be necessary.

The Baxters might argue that the plaintiffs in this case failed to mitigate their damages if, for example, they failed to seek immediate medical treatment. They would also want to minimize the pain and suffering experienced by the plaintiffs and would want to do everything in their power to present evidence that the plaintiffs had magnified their damages. They would argue that any recoveries by the plaintiffs should be discounted to present values and would likely push for some form of structured settlement.

SUMMARY

Damages can be divided into three categories: compensatory, punitive, and nominal. Compensatory damages are further divided into two categories: general and special.

The difficulty in awarding damages for pain and suffering is in the assignment of a numerical value. Some attorneys, in an effort to quantify suffering, have used a per diem technique. Attempts to compensate plaintiffs for pain and suffering have been subject to criticism.

Plaintiffs may be compensated for loss of future earning capacity. In calculating these damages jurors are expected to project the anticipated life span of the plaintiff. Generally plaintiffs are not directly compensated for their shortened life expectancy. Under the collateral-source rule, plaintiffs are entitled to recover for damages for which they have been reimbursed by a collateral source, such as an insurance company. Plaintiffs are not entitled to compensation for the expenses of litigation, although some have suggested that, as a practical matter, punitive damages and awards for pain and suffering in effect provide for such compensation.

Damages for physical harm to property are tied to the fair market value of the property. Fair market value is considered the highest price one seeking to sell the property could have realized and not the lowest price at which a sale could have been made.

Punitive damages are reserved for defendants who have acted in a particularly egregious manner. These damages have been criticized as constituting undue compensation to the plaintiff and as having the potential of bankrupting defendants, especially in product liability cases.

Spouses can recover for loss of consortium, which is considered a derivative claim. Parents are also entitled to recover for the lost services and earnings of their minor children. Some courts have allowed minor children to recover for loss of consortium when a parent on whom they were dependent dies or is seriously injured.

Survival statutes allow an injured party's claim to be sustained after her death. Wrongful-death statutes allow third persons, usually a decedent's spouse and children, to recover for losses they sustained as a result of the decedent's death. Survival actions are typically brought by the executor or administrator of an estate and recovery becomes an asset of the estate, which may be reached by creditors. Although at one time wrongful-death actions were limited to economic losses caused by the decedent's death, in more recent times they have been extended to the loss of companionship of the decedent. Most states have ruled that wrongful-death and survival actions begin to run from the date of the decedent's death. Both survival and wrongful-death actions are subject to statutory construction.

To prevent plaintiffs who recover for future losses from receiving a windfall, many courts require juries to discount awards to a present value. Some have argued that the discounting of awards is unfair to plaintiffs because inflation offsets the discounting of present-value awards. Large future damages are frequently paid using a periodic-payment settlement called a structured settlement. Arguably, this type of settlement relieves the plaintiff of the responsibility of making arrangements to

invest the money and minimizes the amount of income tax required.

Under the avoidable-consequences rule, a plaintiff has a duty to mitigate his damages by avoiding any harm that reasonably could have been avoided. This rule has been used as a defense in seat belt and motorcycle helmet cases.

A plaintiff in a negligence claim must typically show that she suffered some kind of physical harm or, in a few states, some kind of impact. Some courts have abandoned this rule in circumstances where one could readily believe the plaintiff actually suffered mental distress. Some courts have denied compensation for emotional distress to any plaintiff not within the zone of danger, whereas others have allowed recovery when the plaintiff was near the scene of the accident, personally observed it, and was closely related to the victim.

KEY TERMS

additur
When the trial court increases a jury award or orders a new trial because the jury's award of damages is inadequate

avoidable-consequences rule
Obligation of a plaintiff to minimize (mitigate) her damages

collateral-source rule
The collateral-source rule precludes the admission of evidence to the jury regarding payment of benefits such as Social Security, Medicare, pension payments and vacation and/or sick pay to the injured party from a source other than the tortfeasor. The rule gives the plaintiff the ability to recover twice for damages.

compensatory damages
Damages designed to compensate the plaintiff; consist of both general and special damages

derivative claim
Claim derived from underlying claim (e.g., loss of consortium)

discounting an award
Reducing an award to its present value

exemplary damages
Damages designed to punish the defendant and to deter similarly situated wrongdoers (also known as punitive damages)

fair market value
Amount property could be sold for on the open market

general damages
Damages that generally result from conduct engaged in by the defendant

loss of consortium
Loss of services, including companionship, sex, and earnings outside of the home

nominal damages
Damages awarded when liability is shown but no actual damages are proved

parasitic damages
Damages attached to physical injury, e.g., mental suffering

present value
Value of money paid now to compensate for future earnings, based on the assumption that money received today is worth more than money received in the future because of the investment potential of money

punitive damages
Damages designed to punish the defendant (also known as exemplary damages) and to deter others from engaging in reckless or egregious misconduct

remitted
When the trial court lowers the jury's award of damages or orders a new trial because the damages awarded were excessive

special damages
Damages that are unique to the plaintiff

structured settlement
Agreement to pay damages in installments rather than a lump sum

subrogation
Right of party making payment on plaintiff's behalf to be reimbursed out of judgment plaintiff receives

survival action
Action that remains available after the decedent's death

wrongful-death action
Action brought by third parties to recover for losses they suffered as a result of the decedent's death

REVIEW QUESTIONS

1. What is the difference between general and special damages?

2. When is it appropriate to award nominal damages, and when is it appropriate to award punitive damages?

3. What is the problem with awarding damages for pain and suffering?
   a. How do day-in-the-life videos assist jurors?
   b. How does the per diem technique assist attorneys in making their arguments regarding awards for pain and suffering?

4. What criticisms have been raised against the awarding of damages for pain and suffering?

5. What is the problem with proving loss of future earnings?

6. Why are courts reluctant to allow recovery for shortened life expectancy?

7. What does the collateral-source rule prevent defense attorneys from doing?
   a. What is the rationale for this rule?
   b. What is subrogation, and how does it relate to this rule?

8. Why are most personal injury cases handled on a contingency-fee basis?

9. Why are contingency fees criticized?

10. How is the fair market value of property determined?

11. What do courts do when plaintiffs cannot be fairly compensated based on a fair market value because of personal value the property has to the plaintiff?

12. What is the purpose in awarding punitive damages?
   a. What must plaintiff prove to justify punitive damages?
   b. On what grounds are punitive damage awards criticized?
   c. Why did the Grimshaw court believe that the punitive-damages award was not excessive?

13. What does recovery for loss of consortium include?
   a. Why is it considered a derivative claim?
   b. How can double recovery for spouses arise, and how is it prevented?
   c. Can parents recover for loss of consortium in reference to a child?
   d. Can children recover for loss of companionship of a parent?

14. What sources can an attorney consult when evaluating the value of a case?

15. What is the difference between a wrongful-death and a survival action?
   a. What can be recovered in a survival action? In a wrongful-death action?
   b. What defenses can be raised in each?
   c. Can the remarriage of a spouse be brought up during a case or during voir dire in a wrongful-death action?
   d. How are survival actions and wrongful-death actions unique in tort law?

16. Why might it be to a defendant's advantage to discount an award of future damages?

17. What information is needed to calculate the present value of a future award?

18. What is the avoidable-consequences (or "duty to mitigate") rule?

19. Why are courts reluctant to award damages when a plaintiff has suffered emotional injuries but not physical injuries?
   a. Why are damages from mental suffering considered parasitic?
   b. In what situations are courts more likely to bypass the physical harm requirement?
   c. What is the "impact" rule?
   d. Why have some courts abandoned the physical-harm requirement?
   e. How do courts deal with plaintiffs who witness injury to others?
   f. With what types of emotional injury are courts likely to award damages?

PRACTICE EXAM

Students should complete the practice exam after studying each chapter. The answers are in Appendix A. If you score lower than 80%, you should re-read the materials.

True-False

1. General damages are unique to the plaintiff.
2. Punitive damages are designed to make a plaintiff whole.
3. Nominal damages cannot be awarded in intentional tort and strict liability cases but can be awarded in negligence cases.
4. Day-in-the-life videos are generally inadmissible because they unfairly appeal to jurors' sympathies.
5. Some argue that compensation of those suffering pain serves to reinforce and therefore increase their pain.
6. Studies show that compensation of pain and suffering is not necessarily equitable.
7. Losses for impaired earning capacity include recovery for both past earnings and future losses.
8. A plaintiff's impairment need not be permanent in order for her to recover for future losses.
9. In determining future losses jurors must determine how long a plaintiff is expected to live.
10. Losses for shortened life expectancy were denied under the common law and by most courts today.
11. If a plaintiff receives services from friends or family members, she can recover the reasonable value of those services.
12. In most courts evidenced of collateral benefits is inadmissible.
13. In the United States the winning party is entitled to recover for his expenses of litigation, including attorney's fees.
14. Arguably punitive damages and awards for pain and suffering allow plaintiffs to pay attorney's fees and still be compensated for their losses.
15. If the market value of property does not provide adequate compensation because property has personal value to the plaintiff, the courts will look at the original cost of the property and the condition of the property.

16. Punitive damages are criticized because they can bankrupt defendants.
17. Punitive damages are in essence criminal fines that arguably should be paid to the state.
18. Employers cannot be held liable for punitive damages resulting from torts committed by their employees.
19. The *Grimshaw* court concluded that high punitive-damage awards were not necessary because governmental sanctions are effective deterrents to manufacturers who make defective products.
20. Loss of consortium was available only to the husband under the common law.
21. Loss of consortium is available to spouses but not to parents.
22. Many states require that spouses sue only once for injuries resulting from a single accident or event.
23. In most jurisdictions loss of companionship can be recovered in reference to a minor child but lost services and earnings cannot.
24. Some courts allow recovery when the child is a minor who is still dependent on the parent.
25. In assessing the expected recovery in a case, attorneys consult trial reporters and professional journals.
26. Under the common law a plaintiff's complaint survived his death.
27. Double recovery is possible even if a case is filed under both a wrongful-death and survival statute.
28. In some states survival actions are limited to losses occurring prior to a decedent's death and are not allowed if a decedent's death is instantaneous.
29. The problem with wrongful-death actions involving the death of a child is that the cost of raising a child usually far surpasses any earnings the child might be expected to bring home.

30. Knowledge of the remarriage of a surviving spouse is information jurors are usually given, at least during voir dire to ensure that no juror knows the new spouse.

31. Defendants in wrongful-death actions are not allowed to raise the defenses they could have raised against the decedent.

32. Inflation clearly has no effect on the discounting of present-value awards.

33. Structured settlements minimize the income tax a plaintiff has to pay.

34. Structured settlements are favored by the defense bar.

35. Structured settlements are severely restricted in how they can be structured.

36. A plaintiff who fails to wear a seat belt may be seen as having failed to mitigate her damages.

37. When a plaintiff suffers no physical injury, courts are reluctant to award damages for emotional suffering because of a fear of fraudulent claims.

38. Courts will award damages for emotional suffering even if there is no physical suffering when there is a negligent mishandling of a corpse or transmission of an erroneous message about the death of a family member.

39. Courts are sometimes willing to abandon the physical-harm requirement when the facts are such that one could readily believe that the plaintiff suffered mental distress.

40. A growing number of courts have allowed recovery for pure emotional distress if the plaintiff was near the scene of the accident, observed it, and was related to the victim.

41. When confronted with a plaintiff who has seen injury occur to others, courts have rejected the use of the *Palsgraf* "zone of danger" test.

42. In cases in which there is no physical harm, most courts restrict liability to emotional suffering that is serious.

Matching

GROUP 1

_____ 1. Punish tortfeasors
_____ 2. No actual damages
_____ 3. Pain and suffering
_____ 4. Restore plaintiff
_____ 5. Medical expenses; lost wages

a. compensatory damages
b. general damages
c. special damages
d. punitive damages
e. nominal damages

GROUP 2

_____ 1. Defendant should not benefit from plaintiff's investments
_____ 2. Insurance company's right of reimbursement
_____ 3. Create potential conflict of interest between attorneys and clients
_____ 4. Voluntary sale by leisurely seller and willing buyer
_____ 5. Compensation for lost services

a. contingency fees
b. collateral source
c. fair market value
d. loss of consortium
e. subrogation

GROUP 3

_____ 1. Difference between value of property before and after tort occurred
_____ 2. Value of property at time and place tort occurred
_____ 3. Value of use of property

a. plaintiff is deprived of use of property
b. property destroyed
c. property damaged

GROUP 4

_____ 1. Brought by survivors of decedent

_____ 2. Brought by decedent's estate

_____ 3. Initiated by defendant to reduce payment

_____ 4. Duty of plaintiff

_____ 5. Eliminate plaintiff's need to invest

a. present value

b. structured settlement

c. survival action

d. wrongful-death action

e. mitigate damages

Fill-in-the-Blanks

1. _____ _____ _____ damages must be specially pleaded in a complaint.

2. _____ damages are reserved for those defendants who act recklessly or with an "evil mind."

3. The _____ technique assigns a numerical value to suffering on a daily or hourly basis.

4. Under the _____ _____ rule a plaintiff can recover for medical expenses from the defendant even if she has been reimbursed for those expenses by her insurance carrier.

5. _____ _____ arrangements are the most commonly used fee arrangements in personal injury cases.

6. _____ _____ value refers to the amount property can be sold for on the open market.

7. If a plaintiff can raise the issue of _____ damages, he can show the wealth of the defendant.

8. Loss of consortium is considered a(n) _____ claim because it is based on another person's underlying claim.

9. _____ _____ programs are software programs that help attorneys evaluate the value of their case, whereas _____ are compilations of verdicts and settlements pertaining to specific injuries, doctors, attorneys, and so forth.

10. In assessing future lost wages, attorneys consult with _____ _____ _____ counselors who help predict what the plaintiff will be able to do and how much schooling will be required.

11. _____ _____ statutes allow spouses and children to recover for losses they sustained as a result of the decedent's death.

12. A(n) _____ _____ results in periodic payments to the plaintiff.

13. The duty to mitigate damages is also known as the _____ _____ rule.

14. In cases involving physical injury, mental suffering is considered _____ because it attaches to the physical injury.

Multiple-Choice

1. Punitive damages
   a. cannot be awarded for intentional torts.
   b. cannot be used to compensate plaintiffs for the expenses of litigation.
   c. are considered a windfall to plaintiffs.
   d. all of the above.

2. Some people believe punitive damages
   a. punish defendants without the benefit of the constitutional safeguards available under the criminal law.
   b. place a social-policy decision in the hands of those who lack the necessary information to make an informed decision.
   c. deter future tortfeasors from engaging in conduct that is potentially dangerous to others.
   d. all of the above.

3. The _Grimshaw_ court
   a. concluded that the management team was unaware of the defect when it gave permission to manufacture the Pinto.
   b. considered the reprehensibility of the defendant's conduct and the deterrent effect of the award in deciding whether the punitive damage award was excessive.
   c. concluded that the punitive damages represented a disproportionate share of Ford's income.
   d. all of the above.

4. In assessing the value of a case, an attorney
   a. may consult trial reporters and professional journals.
   b. generally ignores the reputation of opposing counsel and the adjustor.
   c. must set aside any conceptions he has about the policies and reputation of the insurance company.
   d. all of the above.

5. Survival statutes allow
   a. third parties to recover for losses they sustained as a result of the decedent's death.
   b. claims pertaining to intangible interests to survive the decedent's death.
   c. claims pertaining to damage to tangible property to survive the decedent's death.
   d. all of the above.

6. In some states plaintiffs who file a wrongful-death action can recover for
   a. loss of companionship and sexual relationship.
   b. monetary contributions the decedent would have made during his lifetime to the plaintiff beneficiary.
   c. loss of moral guidance.
   d. all of the above.

7. Survival actions
   a. result in recovery that cannot be reached by creditors.
   b. can result in a windfall to distant relatives.
   c. are barred if the decedent failed to file an action until after the statute of limitations had run.
   d. all of the above.

8. Discounting of awards
   a. prevents the plaintiff from receiving a windfall.
   b. requires use of annuity and life expectancy tables.
   c. involves calculations involving the present value of a dollar.
   d. all of the above.

9. Structured settlements
   a. prevent the plaintiff from freely spending her money.
   b. can have payments that are modified over time.
   c. require the plaintiff to be involved in the investment process.
   d. all of the above.

10. Some courts have abandoned the physical-harm requirement
    a. because they believe it mechanically excludes cases that are probably valid.
    b. because it encourages plaintiffs to engage in exaggerated pleading and distorted testimony.
    c. in the cases of intentional torts.
    d. all of the above.

PRACTICE POINTERS

As a paralegal you may be called on to provide the evidence necessary to prove or disprove a claim for damages (see Exhibit 7–4). Here we will consider the practical implications of proving past and future medical expenses, loss of earning capacity, and pain and suffering.

Past Medical Expenses

In terms of proving past medical expenses, the plaintiff has the burden of proving the amount of the expenses and that the expenses were necessary and reasonable. The best way to prove past expenses is, of course, through the use of bills that reflect the charges made. Alternatively, the plaintiff can testify to the amount of the bill or have a doctor or the person who prepared the bill testify as to the amount of the charge made. It is important to keep a running account of all bills. These bills should be tabulated on a monthly basis and may be submitted to the insurance company and to defense counsel on an ongoing basis. Some plaintiffs' counsel feel that the continual amassing of medical expenses into an ever-burgeoning file has a psychological impact on the defendant. Defense counsel, for obvious reasons, deny this.

In most jurisdictions proof of medical bills plus proof of payment raises the presumption that the bill was necessary and reasonable. In some states, however, testimony from a doctor, druggist, or other expert is required. The reasonableness and necessity of treatment become particularly problematic when dealing with preexisting conditions. If the plaintiff was not suffering from the preexisting condition at the time of the injury, the expenses will probably be recoverable. If, however, the plaintiff was under treatment for that condition at the time of the injury, she will have difficulty proving which expenses were necessitated by

EXHIBIT 7–4 *Proving Damages*

TYPES OF DAMAGES	EVIDENCE USED TO PROVE
PAST MEDICAL EXPENSES	• Bills from doctors, hospitals, radiology, etc. • Testimony from expert showing necessity of treatment
FUTURE MEDICAL EXPENSES	• Expert testimony • Award is discounted to present value
LOSS OF EARNING CAPACITY	• Plaintiff's work record showing hours lost due to injuries • Wage stubs, W-4 forms, or IRS records (showing value of lost earnings) • Evidence of lost profits and loss of fringe benefits • Extent of plaintiff's education and training (showing earning potential)
PAIN AND SUFFERING	• Plaintiff's testimony • Testimony of those who have observed plaintiff's suffering; day-in-the-life video

© Cengage Learning 2012

the aggravation caused by the defendant's negligence and which expenses stemmed from the preexisting condition. The plaintiff may therefore be unable to recover any of the medical expenses.

Future Medical Expenses

Future medical expenses are much less subject to quantification. No doctor can state with absolute certainty how long future treatment will be needed nor what exact amount of future medical expenses will be incurred. Courts are aware of this ambiguity and do not require the same degree of mathematical proof that they do for past expenses. In some jurisdictions future medical expenses are left for the jury to determine based on the amount of past medical expenses, the nature of the plaintiff's injuries, and the condition of the plaintiff at the time of trial. Other jurisdictions require medical testimony regarding a dollar amount and do not allow a jury to award more than the amount supported by testimony.

As was noted in the text of this chapter, future awards are often discounted to present value. Discounting is based on the idea that a dollar today is worth more than a dollar ten years from now because of the investment potential of that dollar. Present-value tables, an example of which is shown in this section, allow one to calculate the present value of future awards.

Let us use a hypothetical scenario to illustrate the use of these tables. Suppose $1,000 is to be awarded the plaintiff in year 1, $2,000 in year 2, and $3,000 in year 3. Using an interest rate of 10 percent, what would be the present value of that award? Locate 10 percent on the table. Notice that next to year 1 in the third column is the number 0.90909, which indicates that the value of a dollar received a year from now, is worth $.90909 now. Therefore, $1,000 a year from now would be worth $909.09 today. By the same token $2,000 in year 2 would be worth $2,000 3 .82645 or $1,652.90; $3,000 in year 3 would be worth $3,000 3 .75132 or $2,253.96. Therefore, the total present value would be $4,815.95:

PRESENT VALUE OF $1

Paid at End of Year	8%	9%	10%	11%	12%
1	0.92593	0.91743	0.90909	0.90090	0.89286
2	0.85734	0.84168	0.82645	0.81162	0.79719
3	0.79383	0.77219	0.75132	0.73119	0.71178
4	0.73503	0.70843	0.68302	0.65873	0.63552
5	0.68058	0.64993	0.62092	0.59345	0.56743
6	0.63027	0.59627	0.56448	0.53464	0.50663
7	0.58349	0.54704	0.51316	0.48166	0.45235
8	0.54027	0.50187	0.46651	0.43393	0.40388
9	0.50025	0.46043	0.42410	0.39093	0.36061

10	0.46319	0.42241	0.38555	0.35219	0.32197
15	0.31524	0.27454	0.23939	0.20901	0.18270
20	0.21455	0.17843	0.14865	0.12404	0.10367
25	0.14602	0.11597	0.09230	0.07361	0.05882
30	0.09938	0.07537	0.05731	0.04368	0.03338
35	0.06764	0.04899	0.03559	0.02592	0.01894
40	0.04603	0.03184	0.02210	0.01539	0.01075

$1,000 × .90909 = $ 909.09
$2,000 × .82645 = $1,652.90
$3,000 × .75132 = $2,253.96
Total Present Value = 5 $4,815.95

Loss of Earning Capacity

To prove loss of earning capacity, you must first prove that the injuries creating the plaintiff's physical disability impaired his ability to work and earn money. Second, you must prove the value of that incapacity. To prove the latter you must obtain copies of the plaintiff's wage stubs, W-4 forms, and/or IRS records (not admissible in some states). The defense will want to show that the plaintiff's work record was sporadic, that the earnings for the years at issue were unusually high, or that for some reason the plaintiff would not have been able to earn comparable wages in the years ahead for reasons other than the disability sustained.

Proof of earning capacity becomes more problematic if the plaintiff was temporarily disabled prior to the injuries or was for some reason not able to work before sustaining the injuries. In such cases the jury will be left to determine the value of the lost earning capacity based on their own common sense and sense of fair play.

Proof of lost earning capacity can also be difficult when the plaintiff was self-employed. In such cases a difference in profits prior to and after the plaintiff's injuries is not considered a measure of damages because factors other than the plaintiff's incapacity, such as changes in the market, could account for the decrease in profits. The plaintiff is obligated to prove that it was inability to work rather than other economic factors that caused the loss of business income.

Other types of evidence you might want to consider using to show a plaintiff's earning potential would be evidence of education and on-the-job training, as well as evidence of fringe benefits, such as bonuses, insurance programs, tips, and pensions. Prospective earnings from reasonably anticipated promotions or advancements may also be submitted, as well as evidence that the plaintiff was studying or in other ways taking steps to advance into better paying work.

Evidence of income that the plaintiff receives that is unrelated to work is inadmissible. The fact that the plaintiff receives Social Security benefits, workers' compensation benefits, welfare benefits, dividends from stocks, or monies from other investments is irrelevant and therefore inadmissible unless used to impeach the plaintiff.

Pain and Suffering

Damages for pain and suffering are by their very nature not amenable to quantification. Therefore, all a plaintiff can do is prove that the physical pain and mental anguish were in fact experienced. The most direct evidence of pain and suffering is testimony by the plaintiff as to objective symptoms, such as the actual injuries received, and subjective symptoms, such as headaches. Mental anguish may take the form of fear, worry, depression, or humiliation.

Elicit detailed descriptions from the plaintiff, complete with specific incidents that illustrate the nature and depth of the pain and anguish and the limitations such suffering imposed on his lifestyle. In major personal injury lawsuits, plaintiffs' attorneys frequently use "day-in-the-life" videotapes to illustrate graphically to the jury the full extent of the plaintiff's injuries. Such videos chronicle in a simple but poignant way the everyday suffering of the plaintiff and those who care for her. If your firm is without such resources, the attorney must create vivid word pictures in the jurors' minds through the process of direct examination. In preparing the plaintiff for such testimony you must draw his attention to all those events in the course of a day that are rendered more difficult as a result of the injuries.

Doctors as well as others who are familiar with the plaintiff can testify regarding their observations that are indicative of pain and suffering. In working with these potential witnesses it is important to strive for detailed information that can be used to create a visual picture for the jury. Generalizations and vague statements are not helpful and will not create the kind of jury empathy plaintiff's counsel desires.

The defendant will want to rebut the plaintiff's claim of physical and mental anguish by presenting evidence that the plaintiff is pain-free and relatively happy or, alternatively, that the plaintiff's suffering is caused by factors other than the injuries. The courts are reluctant, however, to admit evidence of collateral events causing the plaintiff's suffering because such evidence may be highly prejudicial to the plaintiff. Therefore, a defendant who wants to introduce such evidence must show that the connection between the collateral event and the plaintiff's suffering is not purely conjectural.

TORT TEASERS

1. Suppose your firm represents Mr. Goodright and you have been asked to interview him to ascertain the full extent of his damages. Write down a list of the questions that you would want to ask him in reference to his medical expenses, lost income, lost future income, and pain and suffering.

2. If your firm were representing Teddy, what information would you want to elicit from the medical doctors and psychologists who treated Teddy?

3. Your client is injured in an automobile accident and as a result suffers a fractured dislocation of his right ankle. He is determined to have a remaining work life of twenty-nine years. Medical testimony indicates that he will be unable to work from one to five years at anything other than a sedentary type of job that would require no prolonged walking, running, or heavy lifting. Your client receives a medical discharge from the Air Force after the accident, receiving a 60 percent disability compensation, 40 percent of which is attributed to his ankle and the remaining 20 percent to other medical problems not related to the accident. *Beaulieu v. Elliott*, 434 P.2d 665 (Alaska 1967).

   a. What types of damages would you attempt to recover in this case?

   b. How would you go about determining a monetary value for each of these damages?

   c. What arguments do you anticipate your opponents will make in reference to the payment of damages?

4. A twenty-one-year-old college student dies allegedly as a result of improper diagnosis and care as well as the administration of unsafe drugs. Her parents bring a claim under the wrongful-death statute on their behalf and under the survival statute on behalf of their daughter's estate. *Warner v. McCaughan*, 460 P.2d 272 (Wash. 1969).

   a. What problems would you anticipate with the parents filing a wrongful death action?

   b. What damages would you attempt to recover under the survival statute?

   c. What arguments would you want to make if you were the defense in this case as to why the parents should not be able to recover for their daughter's pain and suffering?

5. An internationally known singer and recording artist, Connie Francis, is sexually assaulted in her motel room. After the assault she suffers from depression, social and sexual withdrawal, and traumatic phobia. Psychiatrists testify that she will probably have difficulty resuming her professional career for at least the next ten years, and she testifies she is unable to perform because of her shame and humiliation. She sues the motel owner for pain and suffering, mental anguish, humiliation, and loss of earnings; her husband sues for loss of consortium. How would you go about determining the amount of their damages? *Garzilli v. Howard Johnson's Motor Lodges*, 419 F. Supp. 1210 (E.D.N.Y. 1976).

6. A driver with a blood alcohol level of approximately 0.155% (state law presumes intoxication in anyone with over 0.10%) rear ends the plaintiff, who is on a motorcycle waiting to make a left-hand turn. The defendant, who had consumed at least ten 12- ounce beers and 20 milligrams of Valium (a tranquilizer) prior to the accident, is speeding and driving recklessly according to witnesses. Do you think the plaintiff is entitled to an award of punitive damages? *Olson v. Walker*, 162 P. 2d 174 (Ariz. App. 1989).

7. Former church member filed lawsuit against church after several church members physically restrained her in an effort to excise demons from her body. What types of damages would you seek for Plaintiff? *Pleasant Glade Assembly of God v. Schubert*, 264 S.W.3d 1 (Tex. 2008).

INTERNET INQUIRIES

The evaluation of a case requires an objective assessment of the projected value of that case if brought before a jury. In conducting this assessment, attorneys often find it helpful to know what juries in that jurisdiction have awarded plaintiffs in similar cases. All states have some kind of trial reporting system that catalogs cases according to types of cases, attorneys, judges, and other criteria. Such trial reporters allow attorneys to project the probable range of verdicts they can expect if they take their case to trial. Some trial reporters also report on settled cases as well as those that actually go to trial. Because the settlement value of a case can vary widely from one jurisdiction to another, attorneys generally focus on the trials reported in their own states, but if they are facing litigation that is novel in their area, they may need to look at reported cases in other states.

The following are online sources of jury verdicts and settlements:

- Morelaw.com (http://www.morelaw.com) provides nationwide jury verdict and settlement reports and headlines of important cases that have been litigated or settled.

- National Association of State Jury Verdict Publishers (http://www.juryverdicts.com) offers off-line jury-verdict summaries for each state prepared from information provided directly by the attorneys trying the cases.

For assistance in doing jury verdict research, consult the following online articles:

- "Putting a Price on It: Researching Jury Verdicts and Settlements" by J. Bissett and M. Heinen at http://www.llrx.com by entering "Putting a Price on it" as your search term.

- "Jury Verdict Research Using the Internet" by R. Ambrogi at http://www.legaline.com by entering "Jury Verdict Research" as your search term (although this is a 1997 article, it is still considered one of the best overviews of researching jury verdicts and settlements online).

Read these articles and summarize the resources you find available in your state to locate jury verdicts and settlements.

PRACTICAL PONDERABLES

Your firm has been contacted by parents whose only daughter was allegedly murdered. The murder trial of the accused resulted in a hung jury. Frustrated by the results of the criminal trial, the parents have come to your firm seeking to file a wrongful-death action against the alleged murderer, who is an influential and wealthy businessman. Two years and two days have elapsed since the daughter's body was found.

1. Find the wrongful-death statute in your state. (You can go to http://www.law.cornell.edu to find the statutes in your state.) What does it provide?

2. Can the parents of an adult child bring a wrongful-death action in your state?

3. What is the statute of limitations for wrongful-death actions in your state?

4. What kinds of damages can the parents recover?

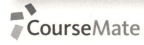 CourseMate   Access an interactive eBook, chapter-specific learning tools, including flashcards, quizzes, and more in your Paralegal CourseMate, accessed through www.CengageBrain.com.

CHAPTER 8

Negligence: Defenses

© Cengage Learning 2012

CHAPTER OBJECTIVES

After completing the chapter, you should be able to

- Identify the elements of contributory negligence, comparative negligence, and assumption of risk.
- Recognize the exceptions to the contributory-negligence rule.
- Recognize the problems that arise in the administration of a comparative-negligence system.
- Differentiate between contributory negligence and assumption of risk.
- Identify situations in which immunity can be raised as a defense.
- Recognize the purpose behind the problems inherent in a statute-of-limitations defense.

If Teddy and Mr. Goodright are able to prove their claims of negligence against the Baxters, the Baxters will certainly want to raise some form of defense (see Exhibit 8–1). The three defenses they will consider are **contributory negligence**, **comparative negligence**, and **assumption of risk**. If Teddy and Mr. Goodright were contributorily negligent—if they contributed in some way to their own injuries—they would be totally barred from recovery. If the state in which the suit is filed has adopted a system of comparative negligence rather than contributory negligence, their recovery will be reduced in direct proportion to their own degree of negligence. For example, suppose Teddy suffered damages of $10,000 and was shown to be 20 percent negligent. His recovery would be reduced to $8,000, i.e., $10,000–$2,000 (20 percent of $10,000). Under the doctrine of assumption of risk, if it can be shown that Teddy and Mr. Goodright voluntarily consented to take the chance that harm would occur, they might, at the worst, be precluded from recovery and, at best, have their recovery reduced.

Before diving into this chapter, be aware of two things. First, the area of defenses is largely controlled by statute. Therefore, this chapter is merely a general description of the subject and an overview of approaches followed across the United States; to be knowledgeable about defenses as they are applied in your jurisdiction, you must consult the relevant statutes and case law in your state.

LOCAL LINKS

Does your state use a contributory-negligence or comparative-negligence system?

CONTRIBUTORY NEGLIGENCE

The defense of contributory negligence in essence shifts the loss from the defendant to the plaintiff by completely barring the negligent plaintiff from recovery. The plaintiff is barred even though the defendant was negligent and, in most cases, was more negligent than the plaintiff.

The rationale for this judge-created rule stems from the notion that negligent plaintiffs should be punished for failing to protect their own safety. Additionally, some courts have argued that the plaintiff's negligence becomes the proximate cause of her injuries, thus removing the defendant as the proximate cause. This argument does not hold water, however, in light of the principles of proximate cause discussed in Chapter 6. Remember that if several events contribute to the plaintiff's injuries, each of them will be considered a distinct proximate cause. A more practical explanation of the judicial creation of contributory negligence lies in judges' historical distrust of juries and their fear that, given free rein, juries would hamper the growth of industry by awarding huge awards to injured plaintiffs.

Exceptions to Contributory-Negligence Rule

The results rendered by the rule of contributory negligence are often harsh and unjust. Worthy plaintiffs are often denied recovery and blameworthy defendants go unscathed. As a result the courts have developed various escape mechanisms by which plaintiffs can avoid this rule. One way, which has been adopted in every jurisdiction that adheres to the contributory-negligence system, is the requirement

EXHIBIT 8–1 *Defenses to Negligence*

CONTRIBUTORY NEGLIGENCE	Plaintiff barred from recovery.
COMPARATIVE NEGLIGENCE	Plaintiff's recovery reduced.
ASSUMPTION OF RISK	Plaintiff either barred from recovery or recovery is reduced.
IMMUNITY	Plaintiff barred from recovery.
STATUTE OF LIMITATIONS AND STATUTE OF REPOSE	Plaintiff barred from recovery.

© Cengage Learning 2012

that contributory negligence be proved and specifically pleaded by the defendant. Additionally, in most jurisdictions the question of contributory negligence is left to the jury. Arguably, juries have an opportunity to apply a comparative-negligence standard in those cases in which application of a contributory-negligence standard would lead to unfair results.

Most states require that the plaintiff's negligence meet the standards of the but-for or substantial-factor test of actual causation in order to be barred from recovering. A few courts, however, bar the plaintiff's recovery if her negligence contributed in any way to the result, no matter how slight that contribution might have been.

In most cases, the same rules that apply in determining proximate cause in terms of the defendant's conduct also apply to the plaintiff. In one instance, however, proximate cause is construed more narrowly in the case of contributory negligence than it is in the case of the defendant's negligence. If the harm that is likely to occur as a result of the plaintiff's negligence occurs in some unforeseen manner, the plaintiff's conduct is usually held not to be the proximate cause of the harm. Suppose a pedestrian crosses a street without looking and is injured, not by an oncoming vehicle, but by an explosion that occurs when a truck carrying dynamite strikes an automobile. In such a case the plaintiff's negligence would not be considered the proximate cause of the injuries because the injury came about as a result of an unforeseen risk (an explosion) and not the foreseeable risk of being run over. Because the harm that occurred came about in a different way than the harm that was threatened, the plaintiff would not be barred from recovery (*Restatement [Second] of Torts* § 468).

Last-Clear-Chance Doctrine

The most significant way in which the contributory negligence defense has been limited has been through the use of the **last-clear-chance doctrine**. Under this doctrine, if the defendant has an opportunity that is unavailable to the plaintiff to prevent the harm that occurs and does not take advantage of it, the defendant will remain liable despite the plaintiff's contributory negligence. In essence the defendant's failure to take advantage of an opportunity to prevent the harm negates, or wipes out, the plaintiff's contributory negligence. Although the courts have used various explanations to rationalize this doctrine, it most likely stems from an attempt to mitigate the harshness of the contributory-negligence defense.

The last-clear-chance doctrine, which is essentially a defense of the plaintiff, was first utilized in the case of *Davies v. Mann*, 152 Eng. Rep. 588 (1842), in which the plaintiff had chained up his donkey and left it blocking the roadway; the defendant ran his wagon into the animal. Because the defendant could have taken measures to avoid the collision, and the plaintiff was at a loss to do anything at the time of the accident, the defendant was held liable.

The courts have struggled with the variations to this last-clear-chance doctrine (see Exhibit 8–2). In all the variations, the courts are unanimous in holding the defendant liable if the plaintiff is unable to avoid the predicament and if the defendant is aware of but negligently fails to circumvent the harm. Less consensus exists, however, if the plaintiff is helpless and the defendant negligently fails to discover the plaintiff's situation because the defendant is inattentive. Suppose the plaintiff negligently turns her vehicle in front of the defendant, and the defendant, who could have avoided the accident had he been paying attention instead of talking with his passenger, is unable to avoid the plaintiff by the time he sees her. Most, but not all, courts would apply the last-clear-chance doctrine, thereby holding the defendant liable.

Suppose the plaintiff is inattentive rather than helpless and negligently fails to extricate himself from the danger. If the defendant discovers the plaintiff's predicament but negligently fails to respond to it, most courts will adhere to the last-clear-chance doctrine. A train engineer, for example, may be liable if she fails to blow the train's whistle a second time or slow the train down once she becomes aware that a person standing on the track has not heard or has disregarded the first blow of the whistle (*Restatement [Second] of Torts* § 480, cmt. b).

WHEN LAST-CLEAR-CHANCE DOCTRINE IS NOT APPLICABLE: If both the defendant and the plaintiff are inattentive so that neither discovers the danger, the last-clear-chance doctrine is not applicable. Also, if the defendant discovers the plaintiff's peril but cannot avoid it because of the defendant's earlier negligence, the majority of courts will not allow the last-clear-chance doctrine to be applied. Suppose the defendant is driving a car with defective brakes, and as a result, although he sees the plaintiff turning in front of him, he cannot stop in time. Should the last-clear-chance doctrine be applied? Most courts have refused to apply the doctrine in this so-called "first clear chance" case. The general rule is that the last-clear-chance doctrine is

EXHIBIT 8-2 *Last-Clear-Chance Doctrine Variations*

PLAINTIFF IS HELPLESS AND:	1. Defendant discovers danger but negligently fails to avoid it.	Plaintiff can recover in all courts.
	2. Defendant fails to discover danger because he is inattentive.	Plaintiff can recover in most courts.
PLAINTIFF IS INATTENTIVE BUT NOT HELPLESS AND:	1. Defendant discovers danger but negligently fails to avoid it.	Plaintiff can recover in most courts.
	2. Defendant fails to discover danger because he is inattentive.	Plaintiff cannot recover.
DEFENDANT IS UNABLE TO AVOID HARMING PLAINTIFF	(even though he is aware of danger) because of defendant's earlier negligence ("first-clear-chance doctrine").	Plaintiff cannot recover in most courts.

© Cengage Learning 2012

inapplicable when the defendant's original act of negligence precludes her from avoiding the accident after she discovers the plaintiff's peril (*Restatement [Second] of Torts* § 479, illus. 3).

In other words, if because of his prior negligence (such as driving with defective brakes) the defendant does not have an opportunity to avoid the accident, the plaintiff cannot allege that the defendant had the last clear chance to avert that accident. That opportunity was not in fact available to the defendant.

When Contributory Negligence is not a Defense

Contributory negligence is not a defense to an intentional tort (see Exhibit 8–3). A defendant in a battery case cannot, for example, argue that the plaintiff was negligent in failing to duck. Similarly, contributory negligence is not allowed as a defense if the defendant's conduct was "willful and wanton" or "reckless" unless the plaintiff's conduct was also willful and wanton or reckless. The rationale for these rules is that defendants who intentionally or recklessly harm others should not be able to escape liability simply because those whom they harmed are negligent.

A defendant who is negligent per se might not be able to raise the defense of contributory negligence. If the statute upon which the defendant's negligence is based was enacted for the sole purpose of protecting a class of persons of which the plaintiff was a member, and if the statute's intent was to place sole responsibility upon the defendant, contributory negligence is not a viable defense. Such a statute is one prohibiting the sale of liquor to minors.

EXHIBIT 8-3 *Exceptions to Contributory Negligence Rule*

- Plaintiff's negligence does not meet standards of but-for or substantial-factor tests.
- Harm likely to occur as a result of plaintiff's negligence occurs in unforeseen manner.
- Last-clear-chance doctrine—defendant did not take advantage of opportunity to avoid accident and plaintiff had no such opportunity. (Not applicable if neither plaintiff nor defendant discovers danger due to inattentiveness or if defendant's original act of negligence made it impossible for him to avoid accident.)
- Defendant committed an intentional tort.
- Defendant was "willful and wanton" or "reckless."
- Defendant was negligent per se. (If statute's intent was to place sole responsibility on defendant and was enacted to protect class of people to which plaintiff belongs.)

© Cengage Learning 2012

PUTTING IT INTO PRACTICE 8:1

Assume that contributory negligence is the rule in each of the following questions.

1. Jeff is speeding down the highway when Josie, who is putting on her makeup at the time, crosses slightly over the center line, scraping the side of Jeff's car. As a result, Jeff loses control of his car and careens into a ditch. Expert testimony shows that Jeff's excessive speed did not contribute to the collision but did contribute to his losing control of his car. Can Jeff recover for the damage to his vehicle and for his personal injuries?

2. Because of her negligent driving, Geraldine gets involved in a collision and her car is thrown to the opposite side of the road. Corinne, who is approaching the scene in her vehicle, sees Geraldine's car and unreasonably believes she can cut around it. She is wrong and ends up overturning Geraldine's car, causing Geraldine to fracture her back. Is Corinne liable to Geraldine for the fractured back?

   a. Would your answer change if Corinne had tried to stop but in her confusion hit the accelerator rather than the brake?

   b. Would your answer change if Corinne had tried to stop but could not do so because her brakes were not operating properly?

3. Margaret's car becomes disabled. She pulls over to the side of the road but negligently fails to put her lights on so that other drivers can see her vehicle. The headlights on Christy's vehicle go out, but she decides to drive home anyway. Because of her lack of headlights she is unable to detect Margaret's car in time and runs into the vehicle. Can Margaret recover for the damage to her vehicle?

Finally, some kinds of contributory negligence are not considered defenses in strict liability actions. A consumer, for example, who fails to inspect a defective product before using it and is injured as a result, will not be prevented from recovering damages even though he was contributorily negligent. (See Chapter 12, "Product Liability," for further discussion of this topic.) Some statutes explicitly abolish the defense of contributory negligence, and others do so implicitly by imposing a strict liability standard.

COMPARATIVE NEGLIGENCE

Comparative negligence was created as an alternative to the all-or-nothing approach of the contributory negligence system (see Exhibit 8–4). In one of the more famous cases in which a court adopted the

EXHIBIT 8–4 Comparative Negligence

TYPES OF COMPARATIVE NEGLIGENCE	PROBLEMS RELATED TO COMPARATIVE NEGLIGENCE
• Pure • 50% Approach 1. Not as great as 2. Not greater than	• How is fault assigned, especially where there are multiple defendants? • Is the last-clear-chance doctrine applicable? • Should a negligent plaintiff's recovery be reduced if the defendant was negligent per se?

doctrine of comparative negligence (*Li v. Yellow Cab Co.*, 532 P.2d 1226 [Cal. 1975]), the court explained why it felt that use of the contributory-negligence rule undermined confidence in the jury system:

> It is unnecessary for us to catalogue the enormous amount of critical comment that has been directed over the years against the "all-or-nothing" approach of the doctrine of contributory negligence. The essence of that criticism has been constant and clear: the doctrine is inequitable in its operation because it fails to distribute responsibility in proportion to fault.[1] Against this have been raised several arguments in justification, but none have proved even remotely adequate to the task. The

basic objection to the doctrine—grounded in the primal concept that in a system in which liability is based on fault, the extent of fault should govern the extent of liability—remains irresistible to reason and all intelligent notions of fairness.

For a more in-depth discussion of the reasons supporting the adoption of comparative negligence, read *McIntyre v. Balentine*, 833 S.W.2d 52 (Tenn. 1992). Contained within the original opinion was a listing of the states that have adopted comparative negligence along with the applicable statutes in those that have done so by legislative action. The appendix to the opinion contains sample jury instructions and a verdict form that you might find interesting.

NET NEWS

To read about the development of comparative negligence, go to **http://www.thelockeinstitute.org** and enter "comparative negligence" as your search term.

CASE — *McIntyre v. Balentine*
833 S.W.2d 52 (Tenn. 1992)

DROWOTO, Justice.

In this personal injury action, we granted Plaintiff's application for permission to appeal in order to decide whether to adopt a system of comparative fault in Tennessee. We are also asked to determine whether the criminal presumption of intoxication is admissible evidence in a civil case. We now replace the common law defense of contributory negligence with a system of comparative fault. Additionally, we hold that the criminal presumption of intoxication established by T.C.A. § 55-10-408(b) (1988) is admissible evidence in a civil case.

In the early morning darkness of November 2, 1986, Plaintiff Harry Douglas McIntyre and Defendant Clifford Balentine were involved in a motor vehicle accident resulting in severe injuries to Plaintiff. The accident occurred in the vicinity of Smith's Truck Stop in Savannah, Tennessee. As Defendant Balentine was traveling south on Highway 69, Plaintiff entered the highway (also traveling south) from the truck stop parking lot. Shortly after Plaintiff entered the highway, his pickup truck was struck by Defendant's Peterbilt tractor. At trial, the parties disputed the

(continues)

---

1. Dean Prosser states the kernel of critical comment in these terms: "It [the rule] places upon one party the entire burden of a loss for which two are, by hypothesis, responsible." [cite omitted] Harper and James express the same basic idea: "[T]here is no justification—in either policy or doctrine—for the rule of contributory negligence, except for the feeling that if one man is to be held liable because of his fault, then the fault of him who seeks to enforce that liability should also be considered. But this notion does not require the all-or-nothing rule, which would exonerate a very negligent defendant for even the slight fault of his victim. The logical corollary of the fault principle would be a rule of comparative or proportional negligence, not

the present rule." [cite omitted] . . . "[P]ractical experience with the application by juries of the doctrine of contributory negligence has added its weight to analyses of its inherent shortcomings: "Every trial lawyer is well aware that juries often do in fact allow recovery in cases of contributory negligence, and that the compromise in the jury room does result in some diminution of the damages because of the plaintiff's fault. But the process is at best a haphazard and most unsatisfactory one." [cite omitted] It is manifest that this state of affairs, viewed from the standpoint of the health and vitality of the legal process, can only detract from public confidence in the ability of law and legal institutions to assign liability on a just and consistent basis.

exact chronology of events immediately preceding the accident.

Both men had consumed alcohol the evening of the accident. After the accident, Plaintiff's blood alcohol level was measured at .17 percent by weight. Testimony suggested that Defendant was traveling in excess of the posted speed limit.

Plaintiff brought a negligence action against Defendant Balentine and Defendant East-West Motor Freight, Inc. . . . Defendants answered that Plaintiff was contributorily negligent, in part due to operating his vehicle while intoxicated. After trial, the jury returned a verdict stating: "We, the jury, find the plaintiff and the defendant equally at fault in this accident; therefore, we rule in favor of the defendant."

After judgment was entered for Defendants, Plaintiff brought an appeal alleging the trial court erred by (1) refusing to instruct the jury regarding the doctrine of comparative negligence, and (2) instructing the jury that a blood alcohol level greater than. 10 percent creates an inference of intoxication. The Court of Appeals affirmed, holding that (1) comparative negligence is not the law in Tennessee, and (2) the presumption of intoxication provided by T.C.A. § 55-10-408(b) (1988) is admissible evidence in a civil case.

I.

The common law contributory negligence doctrine has traditionally been traced to Lord Ellenborough's opinion in *Butterfield v. Forrester*, 11 East 60, 103 Eng. Rep. 926 (1809). There, plaintiff, "riding as fast as his horse would go," was injured after running into an obstruction defendant had placed in the road. Stating as the rule that "[o]ne person being in fault will not dispense with another's using ordinary care," plaintiff was denied recovery on the basis that he did not use ordinary care to avoid the obstruction. . . .

The contributory negligence bar was soon brought to America as part of the common law . . . and proceeded to spread throughout the states. . . . This strict bar may have been a direct outgrowth of the common law system of issue pleading; issue pleading posed questions to be answered "yes" or "no," leaving common law courts, the theory goes, no choice but to award all or nothing. . . . A number of other rationalizations have been advanced in the attempt to justify the harshness of the "all-or-nothing" bar. Among these: the plaintiff should be penalized for his misconduct; the plaintiff should be deterred from injuring himself; and the plaintiff's negligence supersedes the defendant's so as to render defendant's negligence no longer proximate. . . .

In Tennessee, the rule as initially stated was that "if a party, by his own gross negligence, brings an injury upon himself, or contributes to such injury, he cannot recover;" for, in such cases, the party "must be regarded as the author of his own misfortune." In subsequent decisions, we have continued to follow the general rule that a plaintiff's contributory negligence completely bars recovery. . . .

Equally entrenched in Tennessee jurisprudence are exceptions to the general all-or-nothing rule: contributory negligence does not absolutely bar recovery where a defendant's conduct was intentional; where defendant's conduct was "grossly" negligent; where defendant had the "last clear chance" with which, through the exercise of ordinary care, to avoid plaintiff's injury; or where plaintiff's negligence may be classified as "remote."

In contrast, comparative fault has long been the federal rule in cases involving injured employees of interstate railroad carriers and injured seamen. . . .

Similarly, by the early 1900s, many states, including Tennessee, had statutes providing for the apportionment of damages in railroad injury cases. . . . While Tennessee's railroad statute did not expressly sanction damage apportionment, it was soon given that judicial construction. In 1856, the statute was passed in an effort to prevent railroad accidents; it imposed certain obligations and liabilities on railroads "for all damages accruing or resulting from a failure to perform said dut[ies]." . . . Apparently this strict liability was deemed necessary because "the consequences of carelessness and want of due skill [in the operation of railroads at speeds previously unknown] . . . are so frightful and appalling that the most strict and rigid rules of accountability must be applied." The statute was then judicially construed to permit the jury to consider "[n]egligence of the person injured, which caused, or contributed to cause the accident . . . in determining the amount of damages proper to be given for the injury." This system of comparative fault was utilized for almost a century until 1959 when, trains no longer unique in their "astonishing speeds," the statute was overhauled, its strict liability provision being replaced by negligence per se and the common law contributory negligence bar. . . .

Between 1920 and 1969, a few states began utilizing the principles of comparative fault in all tort litigation. . . . Then, between 1969 and 1984, comparative fault replaced contributory negligence in 37 additional states. . . . In 1991, South Carolina became the 45th state to adopt comparative fault . . . leaving Alabama, Maryland, North Carolina, Virginia, and Tennessee as the only remaining common law contributory negligence jurisdictions.

(continues)

Eleven states have judicially adopted comparative fault.[2] Thirty-four states have legislatively adopted comparative fault.[3]

II.

Over 15 years ago, we stated, when asked to adopt a system of comparative fault: "We do not deem it appropriate to consider making such a change unless and until a case reaches us wherein the pleadings and proof present an issue of contributory negligence accompanied by advocacy that the ends of justice will be served by adopting the rule of comparative negligence. . . ." Such a case is now before us. After exhaustive deliberation that was facilitated by extensive briefing and argument by the parties, amicus curiae, and Tennessee's scholastic community, we conclude that it is time to abandon the outmoded and unjust common law doctrine of contributory negligence and adopt in its place a system of comparative fault. Justice simply will not permit our continued adherence to a rule that, in the face of a judicial determination that others bear primary responsibility, nevertheless completely denies injured litigants recompense for their damages.

We recognize that this action could be taken by our General Assembly. However, legislative inaction has never prevented judicial abolition of obsolete common law doctrines, especially those, such as contributory negligence, conceived in the judicial womb. . . . Indeed, our abstinence would sanction "a mutual state of inaction in which the court awaits action by the legislature and the legislature awaits guidance from the court," thereby prejudicing the equitable resolution of legal conflicts.

Nor do we today abandon our commitment to stare decisis. While "[c]onfidence in our courts is to a great extent dependent on the uniformity and consistency engendered by allegiance to stare decisis, . . . mindless obedience to this precept can confound the truth and foster an attitude of contempt." . . .

III.

Two basic forms of comparative fault are utilized by 45 of our sister jurisdictions, these variants being commonly referred to as either "pure" or "modified." In the "pure" form,[4] a plaintiff's damages are reduced in proportion to the percentage negligence attributed to him; for example, a plaintiff responsible for 90 percent of the negligence that caused his injuries nevertheless may recover 10 percent of his damages. In the "modified" form,[5] plaintiffs recover as in pure jurisdictions, but only if the plaintiff's negligence either (1) does not exceed ("50 percent" jurisdictions) or (2) is less than ("49 percent" jurisdictions) the defendant's negligence.

Although we conclude that the all-or-nothing rule of contributory negligence must be replaced, we nevertheless decline to abandon totally our fault-based tort system. We do not agree that a party should necessarily be able to recover in tort even though he may be 80, 90, or 95 percent at fault. We therefore reject the pure form of comparative fault.

We recognize that modified comparative fault systems have been criticized as merely shifting the arbitrary contributory negligence bar to a new ground. . . . However, we feel the "49 percent rule" ameliorates the harshness of the common law rule while remaining compatible with a fault-based tort system. . . . Therefore we hold that so long as a plaintiff's negligence remains less than the defendant's negligence the plaintiff may recover; in such a case, plaintiff's damages are to be reduced in proportion to the percentage of the total negligence attributable to the plaintiff.

In all trials where the issue of comparative fault is before a jury, the trial court shall instruct the jury on the effect of the jury's finding as to the percentage of

2. In the order of their adoption, these states are Florida, California, Alaska, Michigan, West Virginia, New Mexico, Illinois, Iowa, Missouri, Kentucky, and South Carolina. Nine courts adopted pure comparative fault. . . . In two of these states, legislatures subsequently enacted a modified form. . . . Two courts adopted a modified form of comparative fault. . . . The "pure" and "modified" forms are discussed in Part III infra.
3. Six states have legislatively adopted pure comparative fault: Mississippi, Rhode Island, Washington, New York, Louisiana, and Arizona; eight legislatures have enacted the modified "49 percent" rule (plaintiff may recover if plaintiff's negligence is less than defendant's): Georgia, Arkansas, Maine, Colorado, Idaho, North Dakota, Utah, and Kansas; eighteen legislatures have enacted the modified "50 percent" rule (plaintiff may recover so long as plaintiff's negligence is not greater than defendant's): Wisconsin, Hawaii, Massachusetts, Minnesota, New Hampshire, Vermont, Oregon, Connecticut, Nevada, New Jersey, Oklahoma, Texas, Wyoming, Montana, Pennsylvania, Ohio, Indiana, and Delaware; two legislatures have enacted statutes that allow a plaintiff to recover if plaintiff's negligence is slight when compared to defendant's gross negligence: Nebraska and South Dakota.

4. The 13 states utilizing pure comparative fault are Alaska, Arizona, California, Florida, Kentucky, Louisiana, Mississippi, Missouri, Michigan, New Mexico, New York, Rhode Island, and Washington.
5. The 21 states using the "50 percent" modified form: Connecticut, Delaware, Hawaii, Illinois, Indiana, Iowa, Massachusetts, Minnesota, Montana, Nevada, New Hampshire, New Jersey, Ohio, Oklahoma, Oregon, Pennsylvania, South Carolina, Texas, Vermont, Wisconsin, and Wyoming. The 9 states using the "49 percent" form: Arkansas, Colorado, Georgia, Idaho, Kansas, Maine, North Dakota, Utah, and West Virginia. Two states, Nebraska and South Dakota, use a slight-gross system of comparative fault.

(continues)

negligence as between the plaintiff or plaintiffs and the defendant or defendants. . . . The attorneys for each party shall be allowed to argue how this instruction affects a plaintiff's ability to recover.

IV.

Turning to the case at bar, the jury found that "the plaintiff and defendant [were] equally at fault." Because the jury, without the benefit of proper instructions by the trial court, made a gratuitous apportionment of fault, we find that their "equal" apportionment is not sufficiently trustworthy to form the basis of a final determination between these parties. Therefore, the case is remanded for a new trial in accordance with the dictates of this opinion.

V.

We recognize that today's decision affects numerous legal principles surrounding tort litigation. For the most part, harmonizing these principles with comparative fault must await another day. However, we feel compelled to provide some guidance to the trial courts charged with implementing this new system.

First, and most obviously, the new rule makes the doctrines of remote contributory negligence and last clear chance obsolete. The circumstances formerly taken into account by those two doctrines will henceforth be addressed when assessing relative degrees of fault.

Second, in cases of multiple tortfeasors, plaintiff will be entitled to recover so long as plaintiff's fault is less than the combined fault of all tortfeasors. . . .

Further, because a particular defendant will henceforth be liable only for the percentage of a plaintiff's damages occasioned by that defendant's negligence, situations where a defendant has paid more than his "share" of a judgment will no longer arise, and therefore the Uniform Contribution Among Tortfeasors Act, T.C.A. §§ 29-11-101 to 106 (1980), will no longer determine the apportionment of liability between codefendants.

Fourth, fairness and efficiency require that defendants called upon to answer allegations in negligence be permitted to allege, as an affirmative defense, that a non-party caused or contributed to the injury or damage for which recovery is sought. In cases where such a defense is raised, the trial court shall instruct the jury to assign this nonparty the percentage of the total negligence for which he is responsible. However, in order for a plaintiff to recover a judgment against such additional person, the plaintiff must have made a timely amendment to his complaint and caused process to be served on such additional person. Thereafter, the additional party will be required to

answer the amended complaint. The procedures shall be in accordance with the Tennessee Rules of Civil Procedure.

Fifth, until such time as the Tennessee Judicial Conference Committee on Civil Pattern Jury Instructions promulgates new standard jury instructions, we direct trial courts' attention to the suggested instructions and special verdict form set forth in the appendix to this opinion. . . .

SUGGESTED JURY INSTRUCTIONS

[The following instructions should be preceded by instructions on negligence, proximate cause, damages, etc.]

1. If you find that defendant was not negligent or that defendant's negligence was not a proximate cause of plaintiff's injury, you will find for defendant.

2. If you find that defendant was negligent and that defendant's negligence was a proximate cause of plaintiff's injury, you must then determine whether plaintiff was also negligent and whether plaintiff's negligence was a proximate cause of his/her injury.

3. In this state, negligence on the part of a plaintiff has an impact on a plaintiff's right to recover damages. Accordingly, if you find that each party was negligent and that the negligence of each party was a proximate cause of plaintiff's damages, then you must determine the degree of such negligence, expressed as a percentage, attributable to each party.

4. If you find from all the evidence that the percentage of negligence attributable to plaintiff was equal to, or greater than, the percentage of negligence attributable to defendant, then you are instructed that plaintiff will not be entitled to recover any damages for his/her injuries. If, on the other hand, you determine from the evidence that the percentage of negligence attributable to plaintiff was less than the percentage of negligence attributable to defendant, then plaintiff will be entitled to recover that portion of his/her damages not caused by plaintiff's own negligence.

5. The court will provide you with a special verdict form that will assist you in your duties. This is the form on which you will record, if appropriate, the percentage of negligence assigned to each party and plaintiff's total damages. The court will then take your findings and either (1) enter judgment for defendant if you have found that defendant was not negligent or that plaintiff's own negligence accounted for 50 percent or more of the

(continues)

total negligence proximately causing his/her injuries or (2) enter judgment against defendant in accordance with defendant's percentage of negligence.

SPECIAL VERDICT FORM

We, the jury, make the following answers to the questions submitted by the court:

1. Was the defendant negligent?
   Answer: _____ (Yes or No)
   (If your answer is "No," do not answer any further questions. Sign this form and return it to the court.)

2. Was the defendant's negligence a proximate cause of injury or damage to the plaintiff?
   Answer: _____ (Yes or No)
   (If your answer is "No," do not answer any further questions. Sign this form and return it to the court.)

3. Did the plaintiff's own negligence account for 50 percent or more of the total negligence that proximately caused his/her injuries or damages?
   Answer: _____ (Yes or No)
   (If your answer is "Yes," do not answer any further questions. Sign this form and return it to the court.)

4. What is the total amount of plaintiff's damages, determined without reference to the amount of plaintiff's negligence?
   Amount in dollars: $_____

5. Using 100 percent as the total combined negligence, which proximately caused the injuries or damages to the plaintiff, what are the percentages of such negligence to be allocated to the plaintiff and defendant?
   Plaintiff _____%
   Defendant _____%
   (Total must equal 100%)

_____

Signature of Foreman

PUTTING IT INTO PRACTICE 8:2

1. Why did the appellate court accept this case for review?

2. Why was the plaintiff contributorily negligent?

3. What reasons have been used to justify the harshness of the contributory-negligence rule?

4. In what federal cases has comparative negligence long been the rule?

5. Check footnotes 3–5 to see what rules your state has adopted.

6. Why does this court adopt comparative negligence?

7. How does the court respond to the arguments that this decision is a legislative one and that the court is bound by the principle of stare decisis?

8. Why does the court adopt the "49 percent" rule rather than the pure comparative-negligence standard?

9. In accord with this decision,
   a. what happens to the last-clear-chance doctrine?
   b. under what conditions can a negligent plaintiff recover when there are multiple defendants?
   c. will jurors be allowed to assign a percentage of negligence to nonparties?
   d. what assistance does the court offer trial courts?

Under the comparative-negligence doctrine, the plaintiff's recovery is reduced in direct proportion to her degree of negligent contribution to her own injuries. Therefore, if a plaintiff is found to be responsible for 20 percent of her injuries and suffers damages of $1,000,000, her recovery will be reduced by 20 percent of the $1,000,000, or $200,000. Today all but four states have adopted a comparative-negligence system by statute or through a state court decision.

The states that have adopted comparative negligence have, for the most part, adopted either a pure comparative-negligence standard or a 50 percent approach. (See the listing of these states in part III of the *McIntyre* opinion.) Under the pure system the plaintiff can recover no matter how extensive his negligence. For example, if the plaintiff is found to be 80 percent negligent by the jury, under a pure comparative-negligence system he can still recover 20 percent of his damages. Contrast this with the 50 percent approach, in which such a plaintiff would be precluded from recovering because he was more than 50 percent responsible for his own injuries.

Two subsystems of the 50 percent approach have been developed: the "not as great as" and the "not greater than" (referred to as "49 percent rule" in the *McIntyre* decision) approaches. Although subtle in terms of language, the differences in these two systems can have a profound impact on the plaintiff. Under the "not as great as" approach the plaintiff's claim is barred as soon as her negligence is as great as the defendant's negligence; under the "not greater than" approach the plaintiff is barred only when her negligence is greater than the defendant's. The reason this subtle distinction can give rise to tremendous differences in outcome results from juries' tendency to assign a 50:50 apportionment in terms of blame. In a 50:50 apportionment the plaintiff would be barred under the "not as great as" approach (because her negligence would be as great as the defendant's) but would not be barred under the "not greater than" approach (because her negligence would not be greater than the defendant's).

LOCAL LINKS

§ Does your state follow a pure comparative-negligence approach or a 50 percent approach? If your state follows a 50 percent approach, does it use a "not as great as" or "not greater than" approach?

Administrative Problems

The administration of the comparative-fault system creates some practical problems. For example, how should the percentage of fault be assigned to the plaintiff and defendant? Should fault be based on the extent that the party's conduct contributed to the resulting harm, as suggested by the Uniform Comparative Fault Act? Or should fault be based on the extent to which the plaintiff's conduct deviated from a reasonable standard of care? Both methods are used and can lead to different outcomes.

What if some persons are not parties to an action? Should fault be assigned to their actions? How is negligence assigned if there are more parties than just the plaintiff and defendant? Under a pure comparative-negligence system the answer is simple: the negligence of all parties will be considered and the plaintiff will be allowed to recover in direct proportion to the negligence of those parties.

Suppose, for example, the jury determines the damages to be $100,000 and allocates the fault as follows:

Plaintiff	25%
Defendant 1	20%
Defendant 2	30%
Nonparty	25%

The plaintiff would receive a judgment of $50,000, for which defendant 1 would be liable for $20,000 and defendant 2 would be liable for $30,000. (This allocation is based on the assumption that the jury determined that the plaintiff's fault should be applied to reduce the plaintiff's damages.)

A problem arises, however, in jurisdictions where the plaintiff may recover only if her negligence is less than that of the defendants. Should such a plaintiff be allowed to recover if her negligence is less than that of all the defendants combined but greater than that of a particular defendant? Suppose, for example, the plaintiff is responsible for 40 percent of her injuries, Defendant A is 30 percent responsible, Defendant B is 20 percent responsible, and Defendant C is 10 percent responsible. Should the plaintiff be able to recover when her negligence exceeds that of each individual defendant, even though she is less negligent than all of the defendants combined? Most state statutes do not answer this question.

on liability is buried in fine print where the plaintiff is unlikely to see it, it will not be binding on him. The plaintiff must also voluntarily accept the risk given the time, knowledge, and experience such that he can make an intelligent choice to engage in the risk. If there are no other reasonable alternatives to avoid the injury or to exercise or protect a right or privilege the plaintiff cannot have voluntarily assumed the risk. A plaintiff that subjects himself to the injury despite reasonable alternatives has assumed the risk of the injury.

The defendant's failure to establish any one of the three elements of the defense will not prevail on the defense of assumption of risk. Under the common law a plaintiff who was found to have assumed the risk was completely barred from recovery. Most courts today have discontinued that practice but do take into account the plaintiff's assumption of risk when determining how to apportion damages.

Expressed Assumption of Risk

A plaintiff can either expressly or impliedly assume the risk. A plaintiff who signs a release in which she agrees to assume all risk of injury to herself and her property has expressly assumed the risk. Even an express agreement, however, may not be enforced by the courts if the defendant has unusual bargaining power, if she is the sole or unique provider of a service, and if she uses her power to compel the plaintiff to waive liability.

By the same token, agreements involving common carriers, public utilities, or other regulated industries are unlikely to be enforced. The courts usually feel that such entities are obligated to provide reasonable service and will not allow them to escape their responsibility through the use of waivers.

Additionally, waivers of liability are valid only in reference to the defendant's negligence and not for his intentional tortious acts nor for his gross or willful and wanton negligence. One area in which the courts are unwilling to uphold a waiver, no matter how well informed that waiver is, is in the field of medical care. Agreements, for example, in which patients waive potential malpractice claims in exchange for reduced fees are unenforceable.

A release must be expressed in clear, unequivocal language. To see how the enforceability of releases is generally viewed, consider *Cahill v. Ski Liberty Operating Corp.*, 2006 (Pa. Com. Pl.), in which the plaintiff signed a release prior to snow skiing at defendant's resort:

Notice of **Risk**

I understand and accept the fact that snowsports (skiing. . .) in their various forms, including the use of lifts are dangerous with inherent and other **risks**. These **risks** include but are not limited to . . . ice and icy conditions . . . All of the inherent and other **risks** of snowsports present the risk of permanent catastrophic injury or death.

Assumption of **Risk**

Understand and agreeing that snowsports are hazardous, I voluntarily and expressly assume for myself the **risk** of injury while participating in these sports.

Release From Liability

In consideration of the use of the ski area's facilities, I AGREE NOT TO SUE Ski Liberty Operating Corp., Whitetail Mountain Operating Corp., and / or Ski Roundtop Operating Corp., their owners, agents and employees, if injured while using the facilities, regardless of any negligence on the part of the Ski Area or its employees. . . .

Acknowledgement

In consideration of being permitted to use the facilities at Liberty Mountain Resort, Whitetail Mountain Resort and Ski Roundtop, I expressly acknowledge:

(1) I have read and understand the 'Notice of **Risk**,' '**Assumption** of **Risk**,' '**Release** from **Liability**,' 'Be aware, Ski with Care,' and 'Your Responsibility Code.' . . .

(3) I voluntarily assume for myself all the **risks** involved in snow-sports. (emphasis in original)

The *Cahill* court noted that releases such as the release signed by Cahill were in furtherance of the public policy that there are inherent risks in the sport of downhill skiing and to the policy to enforce the doctrine of assumption of risk against those who knowingly engage in downhill skiing. The court found that the releases executed by plaintiff were ambiguous in both their language and intent. For a release to be enforceable, the court said it must be expressed in "unmistakable language," and it must be plainly and precisely apparent that "the limitation of liability extends to negligence or other fault of the party attempting to shed his ordinary responsibility." Although the term "negligence" need not be used, words conveying a similar meaning must appear. The court found the quoted release to be unenforceable because its "opaque terminology" did not reveal that plaintiff released defendant from liability for injury that might result from defendant's failure to use due care.

Implied Assumption of Risk

A plaintiff is said to have impliedly assumed the risk when her conduct shows that she was aware of the risk in question and voluntarily agreed to bear that risk herself. Suppose a plaintiff watches as her friend mounts the defendant's horse and is subsequently bucked off. If the plaintiff then climbs aboard the same horse, she will have impliedly assumed the risk for any injuries she sustains.

For this principle to be applicable the plaintiff must actually be aware of the particular risk in question. It is not enough that the plaintiff merely should have known of the risk involved. The plaintiff must also voluntarily consent to the risk. Consent is not voluntary if the plaintiff had no reasonable choice but to confront a danger.

The consent principle is colorfully illustrated in a case in which the plaintiff, who was a tenant of the defendant, fell through a hole in the outhouse floor when she submitted to a "call of nature." The court held that the plaintiff did not voluntarily assume the risk, even though she was aware of the defective floor, because she had no choice but to use the facilities at her disposal. The court concluded that she was under no legal obligation to seek other facilities (*Rush v. Commercial Realty Co.*, 145 A. 476 [N.J. 1929]). If the plaintiff in this case had had a reasonable alternative, such as another intact outhouse on the same property, she might have been held to have assumed the risk.

In sports and recreation the inherent risks involved are known by the parties, who are free to either engage in the activity or not. Those who sponsor or organize such activities are obligated to use reasonable care to make conditions as safe as they appear. In some jurisdictions but as long as the risks are fully understood or perfectly obvious, the plaintiff will be deemed to have assumed the risk. Furthermore, professional athletes are assumed to be more cognizant of the risks and more willing to accept them (because of the monies involved) than amateurs. Therefore, when

a professional jockey was severely injured when his horse tripped over the heels of another horse, causing the jockey to be thrown, the court concluded that the jockey had assumed the risk and did not allow him to recover from the jockey of the other horse or the track owner. The court found that the jockey was aware of the dangers of speeding horses changing position and bumping each other during a race and of the track conditions and the dangers associated with them, especially as he had participated in three prior races at the track on the day of the accident (*Turcotte v. Fell*, 502 N.E.2d 964 [N.Y. 1986]). A court declined to apply the assumption of risk doctrine when a softball catcher who suffered a knee injury as a result of a collision with a base runner. The court explained that it could find no reason to immunize sports participants from liability for negligent conduct (*Crown v. Campo*, 630 A.2d 368 [N.J. 1993]).

What if a plaintiff protests against being asked to assume a risk but ultimately agrees to take that risk? In most cases the courts will hold that he waived his objection and assumed the risk. Even if the risk the plaintiff is exposed to is not created by the defendant, he is still considered to have voluntarily accepted the risk. For example, a plaintiff who is badly injured in an accident and who requests that the defendant drive him to the hospital, despite his knowledge that the defendant's car has bad brakes, assumes the risk of injury caused by the defective brakes. Although the risk involved is not due to the defendant's wrongdoing, the plaintiff is still deemed to have assumed the risk (*Restatement [Second] of Torts* § 496E, illus. 1).

Comparison to Contributory Negligence

Some states have in effect abolished the doctrine and consider assumption of risk to be a form of contributory negligence. The justification behind this merger is that often a plaintiff who has assumed the risk has also been contributorily negligent. A plaintiff who voluntarily but unreasonably decides to take a risk can also be said to have behaved in a negligent manner.

In some situations, however, a plaintiff is not negligent simply because he has assumed the risk. If the plaintiff's decision to entertain a risk is reasonable in light of the circumstances, he will not be considered negligent, particularly if few options are available to him other than engaging in risky behavior. Suppose a father uses a car with defective brakes because it is the only car available to him and he must use it to get his seriously injured child to the hospital. He has assumed the risk even though he has not acted negligently. In situations such as this, the defense of assumption of risk can be raised even though the defense of contributory negligence cannot.

Differences between Assumption of Risk and Contributory Negligence

Some states have extended assumption of risk to any situation in which the plaintiff voluntarily exposes herself to a known risk. The definition of voluntary exposure goes beyond the concept of consenting to a risk and further blurs the distinction between assumption of risk and contributory negligence (see Exhibit 8–5). To get around this ambiguity some courts have characterized contributory negligence as "carelessness" and assumption of risk as "adventurousness." A plaintiff who deliberately walks down defective steps when others, only slightly more inconvenient, are available may voluntarily assume the risk of confronting a known hazard, even though she exercises due care on the stairs. Such a plaintiff is said to assume the risk but not to be contributorily negligent if assumption of risk is defined as adventurousness (*Hunn v. Windsor Hotel Co.*, 193 S.E. 57 [W.Va. 1937]).

If the plaintiff's conduct constitutes both assumption of risk and contributory negligence, the defendant can choose to assert either defense or, in some

jurisdictions, both. In deciding which of the defenses to raise, the defendant should consider the standards used to assess the plaintiff's conduct. An objective standard is used to assess the reasonableness of the plaintiff's conduct in the case of contributory negligence. A subjective standard is used in cases involving assumption of risk. It requires that the plaintiff actually have understood the risk that he undertook and not merely that a reasonable person would have understood.

Contributory negligence cannot be raised as a defense if the defendant is reckless and cannot generally be used as a defense in strict liability cases. Conversely, assumption of risk can be used as a defense of reckless conduct and in strict liability cases.

LOCAL LINKS

- Has your state abolished sovereign immunity?
- Does your state have some kind of state tort claims act? If so, what are the provisions of that act?

Comparative Negligence and Assumption of Risk

Those states that have adopted comparative-negligence statutes have, for all intents and purposes, removed assumption of risk as a separate defense and have

PUTTING IT INTO PRACTICE 8:4

Your client, a motorcyclist, was involved in a motor vehicle accident in which he was seriously injured. He was not wearing a helmet at the time of the accident.

1. Under the laws of your state, could he recover damages if he was found to be contributorily negligent?

2. Could he recover if a jury found him to be 50 percent responsible for his injuries?

3. If another vehicle were involved as well, could your client recover if a jury found him to be 40 percent responsible and the other two defendants each 30 percent responsible for his injuries?

4. How would the jury be instructed if a nonparty was partially responsible for your client's injuries?

5. Will the jury be instructed that your client's contribution should be determined on the basis of how much his conduct contributed to his injuries or on the basis of how much his conduct deviated from a reasonable standard of care?

6. Could the defendant claim comparative negligence if his lack of care in driving was considered willful and wanton?

7. Could your client use the last-clear-chance doctrine?

merged it, in part at least, into the defense of comparative negligence. Therefore, a plaintiff who unreasonably places himself in danger is considered negligent and his recovery is reduced although not barred completely. If his conduct in exposing himself to the danger is reasonable, he is not considered negligent at all.

PUTTING IT INTO PRACTICE 8:5

1. Why are the waivers on the back of event tickets generally not enforceable?

2. A tennis umpire is struck on the head by a ball during a match. A wrongful-death suit is filed alleging that the rules required the umpire to stand in a position of danger and thereby increased his risk of being injured. Did the umpire assume the risk?

3. Do you think someone who flails around in the mosh pit (an area in the front of the stage where concert attendees engage in various types of wild activities, such as body slamming) should be able to recover for his injuries, or has he assumed the risk of injury?

4. In 1993 several former waitresses at the restaurant called Hooters sued the chain for sexual harassment, alleging that Hooters established a work environment in which its customers felt free to make sexual comments and advances to the waitresses. Examples of the offensive nature of the work environment included the name of the restaurant (Hooters, a slang term for women's breasts) as well as the sexually provocative uniforms the waitresses were required to wear. Do you think assumption of risk should be allowed as a defense to hostile work environment sexual-harassment claims such as these?

CASE

Goepfert v. Brookings Hospital
1997 SD 56, 563 NW2d 140
Supreme Court of South Dakota.

KONENKAMP, Justice.

Michael Goepfert lost his life shortly after he jumped from a moving car. His parents sued the driver and others, and the circuit court granted summary judgment for the driver. Ordinarily, assumption of the risk is a question of fact for a jury, but under these circumstances, can it be decided as a matter of law? Because he voluntarily alighted from a moving vehicle without warning, we conclude Goepfert assumed the risk, and thus we uphold the summary judgment.

FACTS

On Friday evening, October 29, 1993, several friends, including Chris Stethem and Michael Goepfert, began celebrating the annual "Hobo Day" homecoming at South Dakota State University in Brookings. After dinner and a few beers at a friend's home, the group of six left for downtown. Stethem drove. Goepfert was in the front passenger seat, another man sat between them, and the remaining three were in the backseat. As they neared their destination, the Chevy Lounge on Main Street, they approached an intersection with a red traffic light. Stethem slowed, but never stopped. About fifty feet from the intersection, a passenger in the back told Stethem, "Let us out. Let us out right here." Goepfert said nothing, but others joined in, wanting to be dropped off near the bar, so they would not have to walk back from where they would park. Stethem replied, "No, we'll all walk up there." One passenger persisted, and Stethem said, "If you want to get out, get out." They were still moving at approximately 10 to 15 miles per hour when the light turned green. Stethem began to accelerate normally. According to everyone in the car, at the moment of acceleration, Goepfert simultaneously, without a word, opened the car door and jumped out. When his feet hit the roadway, he flipped over backwards, causing his head to strike the pavement. He came to rest in the crosswalk where the car entered the intersection. Stethem pulled over on the other side, and all ran back to help their friend.

Goepfert was unconscious. He was taken by ambulance to Brookings Hospital, treated and released. Concerned friends watched him through the night to monitor his condition. In the morning, they took him

(continues)

back to the hospital when he became unresponsive. Doctors then discovered a skull fracture and intracranial hemorrhaging. Goepfert was rushed by air ambulance to a hospital in Sioux Falls, where he died the next day. His parents brought a wrongful death action against Stethem and certain medical providers. The malpractice claims are not part of this appeal. Stethem moved for summary judgment. Concluding as a matter of law Goepfert assumed the risk of injury by exiting a moving car, negating any duty Stethem owed to him, the circuit judge granted the motion.

STANDARD OF REVIEW

The framework for determining summary judgment questions is set forth in SDCL 15-6-56(c): "The judgment sought shall be rendered forthwith if the pleadings, depositions, answers to interrogatories, and admissions on file, together with the affidavits, if any, show that there is no genuine issue of material fact and that the moving party is entitled to a judgment as a matter of law." Id. (reproduced in part); *Ward v. Lange*, 1996 SD 113, 10, 553 N.W.2d 246, 249. We will affirm only when the legal questions have been correctly decided and there is no genuine issue of material fact. *142 *Koeniguer v. Eckrich*, 422 N.W.2d 600, 601 (S.D.1988); *Bego v. Gordon*, 407 N.W.2d 801, 804 (S.D.1987). As the moving party has the burden of proof, the "evidence must be viewed most favorably to the nonmoving party and reasonable doubts should be resolved against the moving party." *Rumpza v. Larsen*, 1996 SD 87, § 9, 551 N.W.2d 810, 812 (citations omitted); *Pickering v. Pickering*, 434 N.W.2d 758, 760 (S.D.1989). If any legal basis exists to support the circuit court's ruling, affirmance is proper. *Petersen v. Dacy*, 1996 SD 72, § 5, 550 N.W.2d 91, 92 (citations omitted).

ANALYSIS AND DECISION

The circuit court ruled from the bench:

[I]n looking at everything in the light most favorable to the plaintiff here, the scenario I get is that the driver of the car was driving by the Chevy Lounge, the passengers were saying, "Let us out here and so we don't have to walk all the way back to the Chevy Lounge after you find a place to park." The driver of the car said, "No," and then because he was getting badgered about it, he says, "Well, if you want to get out, get out now," but the car had not stopped; that is undisputed. It was going slow, but it had not stopped, and even looking at it from the perspective of the decedent here, that the defendant was slowing down and that he took the defendant's statement seriously, that "If you want to get out, get out now," that that was permission to exit the car, no reasonable person exits a moving car until it is stopped.

I think that anytime somebody exits a moving vehicle, he is assuming a known risk. He is assuming there is a good chance that he is going to get injured. He has got to wait until it stops. And so to me, as a matter of law, I conclude that there was assumption of the risk here.

To learn whether the judge decided correctly, we now examine the concept of assumption of the risk with the facts viewed in a light most favorable to Goepfert. We review this question under the de novo standard. *Boever v. South Dakota Board of Accountancy*, 526 N.W.2d 747, 749 (S.D.1995) (Boever I).

Assumption of the risk embodies three elements. It must be shown that Goepfert: (1) had actual or constructive knowledge of the risk; (2) appreciated its character; and (3) voluntarily accepted the risk, with the time, knowledge, and experience to make an intelligent choice. *Bauman v. Auch*, 539 N.W.2d 320, 326 (S.D.1995); *Bell v. East River Electric Power Co-op., Inc.*, 535 N.W.2d 750, 754 (S.D.1995); *Nelson v. Nelson Cattle Co.*, 513 N.W.2d 900, 904 (S.D.1994); *Wolf v. Graber*, 303 N.W.2d 364, 368 (S.D.1981). Failure to establish any one element negates the defense. *Westover v. East River Elec. Power Co-op., Inc.*, 488 N.W.2d 892, 901 (S.D.1992). We recently stated in *Mack v. Kranz Farms, Inc.*, 1996 SD 63, § 8, 548 N.W.2d 812, 814:

"Ordinarily, questions of negligence, contributory negligence and assumption of risk are for the jury, provided there is evidence to support them." *Stenholtz v. Modica*, 264 N.W.2d 514, 517 (S.D.1978); see also *Lovell v. Oahe Elec. Co-op.*, 382 N.W.2d 396, 399 (S.D.1986); *Myers v. Lennox Co-op. Ass'n*, 307 N.W.2d 863, 864 (S.D.1981); *Wolf v. Graber*, 303 N.W.2d 364, 368 (S.D.1981).

Though assumption of the risk is most often an issue for the jury, we have occasionally held summary judgment appropriate. "It is only where the essential elements are conclusively established that the plaintiff may be charged with assumption of the risk as a matter of law." *Smith v. Community Co-op. Ass'n of Murdo*, 87 S.D. 440, 443, 209 N.W.2d 891, 892 (1973). See *Westover*, 488 N.W.2d at 896 ("In the absence of a factual dispute, where the evidence warrants, the circuit court and this court can find assumption of the risk as a matter of law."). In *Myers v. Lennox Co-op. Ass'n*, 307 N.W.2d 863 (S.D.1981), for example, we affirmed summary judgment on assumption of the risk against a plaintiff who was injured after stepping on an unstable pile of lumber while loading a garbage truck. No facts were in dispute; he had reasonable alternatives to stepping on the lumber; and reasonable persons could not differ over the risk the plaintiff assumed. "His decision to walk on the lumber was made under such circumstance *143 that he must be held to have made an intelligent choice to

(continues)

encounter the risk presented by that course of action." Id. at 865. Has each required element been satisfied in this case?

First, to assume a risk, one must have actual or constructive knowledge of the peril involved. Constructive knowledge will be imputed if the risk is so plainly observable that "anyone of competent faculties [could be] charged with knowledge of it." *Westover*, 488 N.W.2d at 901 (internal citations omitted). Risk is intrinsic to some acts. Considering these facts and exercising ordinary common sense, reasonable minds cannot differ on the jeopardy involved in stepping from a moving vehicle. See *Nix v. Williams*, 35 A.D.2d 188, 316 N.Y.S.2d 321, 324 (1970)(passenger who suddenly and unexpectedly jumped out of moving vehicle without saying anything barred from recovery as a matter of law); *Groshek v. Groshek*, 263 Wis. 515, 57 N.W.2d 704, 706 (1953)(where plaintiff driver allowed a passenger to drive while he reached into the backseat, it cannot be reasonably said that plaintiff did not know the danger in such activity).

Next, an individual will be held to have appreciated the danger undertaken if it was "a risk that no adult person of average intelligence can deny." *Bell*, 535 N.W.2d at 754; *Nelson*, 513 N.W.2d at 905. Obviously, "there are some risks to which no adult will be believed if he says he did not understand them." Staats by *Staats v. Lawrence*, 576 A.2d 663, 668 (Del.Super.Ct. 1990), aff'd, 582 A.2d 936 (Del.1990). Michael Goepfert, a twenty-two year old college student, had to know and appreciate the hazard he faced in leaping from a moving car. "[One] may not close his eyes to obvious dangers, and cannot recover where he was in possession of facts from which he would be legally charged with appreciation of the danger." *Herod v. Grant*, 262 So.2d 781, 783 (Miss.1972)(quoting 57 AmJur2d Negligence § 282 (1971)). No testimony from anyone in the car suggests Goepfert was unaware of what he was doing or that he misperceived the car was moving.

Finally, assumption of the risk requires voluntarily acceptance, having had the time, knowledge, and experience to make an intelligent choice. Bauman, supra. As he leapt from the car, Goepfert may not have known the light had turned green and Stethem was just then accelerating. One passenger testified:

Q. After Chris said, "If you want to get out, get out," did you expect Chris to accelerate?

A. No.

Q. Then if you did not expect Chris to accelerate, would it not be reasonable that Mike would not have expected him to accelerate, too?

A. But Mike's focus wasn't on the green light is what I'm getting at. Chris was watching the road.

He was focused on the green light. Mike's focus was thinking that if he stops, I'm going to jump out and get up there before everybody else does.

Consistent with the others, this same witness testified:

Q. "Were you surprised that Mike jumped out of the vehicle?"

A. "Yeah, I was very much so."

Everyone in the car felt Stethem spoke in jest or was acting the "smart aleck" when he said, "If you want to get out, get out." Even if Goepfert took this comment seriously, he still gave no sign of his intent, other than, as one passenger said, to glance at his friends in the backseat: "It was like he was joking like he was going to. Kind of acting like he was going to do it and then not really do it. Then he went ahead and did it." Automobile passengers have a duty of care for their own safety. *Glandon v. Fiala*, 261 Iowa 750, 156 N.W.2d 327, 331 (1968); *Atwood v. Holland*, 267 N.C. 722, 148 S.E.2d 851, 854 (N.C.1966) ("A gratuitous passenger in an automobile is required to use that care for his own safety that a reasonably prudent person would employ under the same or similar circumstances."); *Rutz v. Iacono*, 229 Minn. 591, 40 N.W.2d 892, 895 (1949); *White v. Huffmaster*, 326 Mich. 108, 40 N.W.2d 87, 89 (1949).* Goepfert's decision surpassed mere negligence.

Acceptance of risk necessarily connotes attention to reasonable alternatives. *Mack*, 1996 SD 63, §§ 15-17, 548 N.W.2d at 814-15. Here "reasonable" refers to whether one had a fair opportunity to elect whether to subject oneself to danger. *Berg v. Sukup Mfg. Co.*, 355 N.W.2d 833, 835 (S.D.1984) (Berg II). Acceptance is not voluntary if another's tortious conduct leaves no reasonable alternative to avert harm or to exercise or protect a right or privilege, which another has no right to deny. *Mack*, 1996 SD 63, § 15, 548 N.W.2d at 815 (quoting Restatement of Law (Second) Torts, § 496E, p 576 (1965)).

---

* Compare cases involving passengers engaged in horseplay in and around moving vehicles. See, e.g., *Brown v. Derry*, 10 Wash.App. 459, 518 P.2d 251, 253 (1974)(considering sixteen-year-old who rode on the trunk of a car, "The risk of harm in attempting to ride on the exterior of an automobile for even a short distance in such a fashion is plainly a foreseeable risk, and reasonable minds could not differ with respect to it"); *Miller v. General Accident Fire & Life Assur. Corp.*, Ltd., 280 So.2d 280, 282 (La.Ct.App.1973)(man riding on a car fender, "The general rule when one is an outrider on a vehicle is that he only assumes such risks as are ordinarily incident to his position"); *Vaughn v. Cortez*, 180 So.2d 796 (La.Ct.App.1965)("playing cowboy" while riding on the front of a moving car is so dangerous, a risk is assumed); *Irwin v. Klaeren*, 4 Ill.App.2d 114, 123 N.E.2d 743, 744 (1954)(holding as a matter of law and noting that "it is hard to conceive of a more reckless disregard for his own safety" than a man who holds his head and shoulders outside of the window of a moving car).

(continues)

Everyone agreed Stethem drove normally. The car may have been moving faster than Goepfert anticipated when he jumped, but that cannot erase the reality that he still elected to jump while the car was moving. On this point the evidence is unrefuted. Goepfert's only reasonable alternative was to stay in the car until it reached a complete stop. No one's wrongful conduct forced him to make his fateful choice.

As a matter of law, Goepfert assumed the risk. We see no genuine issues of material fact for trial. By jumping from the car, Goepfert voluntarily and unfortunately accepted the peril inherent in such act, and, to the sorrow of his family and friends, his decision ended in tragedy.

Affirmed.

MILLER, C.J., and SABERS, AMUNDSON and GILBERTSON, JJ., concur.

IMMUNITIES

Immunity is a complete defense to tort liability in that it completely absolves the defendant of all liability. It is granted to those entities that bear a particular relationship to the plaintiff, such as a spouse, or who occupy a status, such as that of a governmental or charitable entity (see Exhibit 8–6).

Governmental Immunity

Federal Government

Under the common law the immunity of the king was based on the precept that "the king can do no wrong." American courts applied this adage early by adopting the principle that the United States government could not be sued without its consent. To get around this principle Congress passed private bills authorizing particular plaintiffs to sue on certain claims. Obviously this process created considerable inconvenience for Congress. The fear of being inundated by thousands of private bills upon the return of servicemen after World War II prompted Congress in 1946 to pass the Federal Tort Claims Act (FTCA).

In general the FTCA provides that money damages can be recovered against the United States "for injury or loss of property or personal injury or death caused by the negligent or wrongful act or omission of any employee of the government while acting within the scope of his office or employment, under circumstances where the United States, if a private

EXHIBIT 8–6 *Immunities*

GOVERNMENTAL IMMUNITIES	PARENT-CHILD IMMUNITY
• Federal government immunity (limited by Federal Tort Claims Act) • State government immunity • Local government immunity (for governmental but not proprietary functions) • Public official immunity	• Abolished in majority of states and limited in others today

INTERSPOUSAL IMMUNITY	CHARITABLE IMMUNITY
• Abolished by majority of states today	• Abolished in some states and limited in others today

© Cengage Learning 2012

person, would be liable to the claimant" (28 U.S.C. § 1346[B]). Thousands of claims are filed against the federal government each year, more than half of which arise out of automobile accidents.

Several exceptions limit the scope of the FTCA. The United States is not liable, for example, for intentional torts such as assault, battery, false imprisonment, false arrest, abuse of process, or malicious prosecution except when they are committed by federal law enforcement officials. Questions regarding interpretation often arise in determining what types of claims should and should not be permitted

NET NEWS

For an overview of the Federal Tort Claims Act, including preconditions to suit, exceptions to the FTCA, and limitations on damages, go to **http://opencrs.com** and enter " Federal Tort Claims Act" as the search term.

under the FTCA. In one case, a lawsuit alleging an Army recruiter sexually assaulted the plaintiff was dismissed because intentional torts are excluded under the FTCA (*Olsen v. United States*, 144 Fed. App. 727 [Oak. 2005]).

One of the most troubling exclusions to the FTCA pertains to a federal agency's or federal employee's exercise or failure to exercise a **discretionary function** or duty. No liability exists when a discretionary function is involved, even if that discretion is abused (28 U.S.C. § 2680[A]). Deciding what constitutes a discretionary function has caused the courts considerable grief. The United States Supreme Court has provided some guidance by indicating that discretion is involved "where there is room for policy judgment and decision" (*Dalehite v. United States*, 346 U.S. 15, 34–36 [1953]).

Furthermore, discretionary functions occur at the planning stages. In *Dalehite* an explosion occurred at a fertilizer exportation program run by the government. The Court held that decisions about how fertilizer was to be bagged and how the bags were to be labeled and transported were made at the planning level. Therefore, those who did the planning could have been found liable for negligence, but the underlings who carried out the plans could not.

State Government

Traditionally, state governments enjoyed sovereign immunity as well, but today most of them have abolished it to some extent, either by statute or judicial decision. Many courts that have abolished governmental immunity have done so because of the availability of public liability insurance. Some have viewed taking responsibility for the torts of public employees as being part of the cost of administering a government. Regardless of the state's stance toward immunity, judges and legislators are almost never liable for their acts. Similarly, the making of "basic policy decisions" rarely results in liability (*Restatement [Second] of Torts* § 895B[3]).

States usually replace complete sovereign immunity with a statutory form of immunity, through some form of state tort claims act. Statutory limits are often placed on damages, thereby limiting plaintiffs' recovery. Many statutes require any person claiming to have been injured as a result of tortious conduct by a public entity or employee to file a written notice of the claim within a designated time period after the date of discovering the injury. Failure to comply with such notice requirements may forever bar any claim.

Local Government

Local governmental entities, such as police and fire departments, school systems, and public hospitals, have traditionally enjoyed at least partial immunity. The key legal argument that arises in the context of local government is whether the function being performed is a **governmental function** or a **proprietary function**. A proprietary function is one that could be performed as well by a private corporation as by the government. This type of function is usually being performed in activities that produce revenue for the government, such as those carried out by gas and water utilities and city airports. Police and fire departments and school systems, in contrast, are almost exclusively involved in governmental functions.

Governmental functions are subject to immunity whereas proprietary functions are not. To date, many courts have abolished local government immunity or have allowed suit when liability insurance is available. Administrative policy decisions, as well as judicial and legislative actions, still enjoy immunity.

Public Officials

Legislators and judges, as well as some other public officials, receive complete immunity so long as the act complained of is within the scope of their duties. The rationale for this immunity is that a public official must be given free rein to carry out the difficult tasks of her office unfettered by fear of being sued. Furthermore, by granting immunity, the government ensures that competent people are not deterred from seeking public office out of fear of being sued. This protection extends even to those officials who are obviously operating out of a sense of greed or malice toward the plaintiff. Exception is made only when the official's act is outside the jurisdiction of the office.

NET NEWS

An in-depth analysis in support of the doctrine of sovereign immunity can be found at **http://www.bc.edu** by entering "sovereign immunity" as your search term.

To illustrate the extremes to which this doctrine can be taken, consider the Supreme Court decision involving a judge who ordered a fifteen-year-old plaintiff to be sterilized. The order was given as a result of a petition by the plaintiff's mother. No notice was given to the plaintiff, nor did any statutory authorization exist for such a judicial order. Nevertheless, the court held that the judge did not act wholly beyond his jurisdiction and he was therefore immune from suit (*Stump v. Sparkman*, 435 U.S. 349 [1978]).

LOCAL LINKS

- Has your state abolished the defense of assumption of risk?
- If your state has this defense, how does it define assumption of risk?
- In your state, can a defendant raise the defense of contributory negligence as well as the defense of assumption of risk?

In some states high-ranking administrative officials receive the same complete immunity that legislators and judges do. In others they have limited immunity, which protects them only if they do not act in bad faith.

A public official's immunity is separate from governmental immunity. Therefore, if governmental immunity is abolished, the public official may still be protected by her own immunity. In contrast, even if the government is immune, the public official may still be liable. To illustrate, consider the amendments made by Congress to the Federal Tort Claims Act, making it the exclusive remedy for plaintiffs alleging torts committed by federal officers and employees, including those in the legislative and judicial branches, acting within the scope of their employment. Under these provisions plaintiffs must file suit against the United States only and not the employees individually, thus effectively rendering the employees immune from suit. Although these provisions do not prevent plaintiffs from suing, they substantially limit any chance of recovery because of the United States' immunity for "discretionary" functions.

Another provision of the Federal Tort Claims Act that limits recovery is one that limits liability of the government (and renders the employee immune) for any injuries arising out of a federal employee's operation of a motor vehicle. However, a very important act that *promotes* recovery when individuals' civil rights have been violated is the Civil Rights Act of 1871 (42 U.S.C. § 1983). Under this so-called *1983*

action, anyone who "under color of any statute, ordinance, regulation . . . of any state" violates the federal civil rights of any person "shall be liable to the party injured in an action at law." An inmate of a correctional institution, for example, may file a 1983 action against the state government, the correctional institution, and its employees if he is not provided adequate medical care while institutionalized. He must show that the employees were acting "under the color of state law," that they violated his constitutional right (in this case, the right to be protected from cruel and unusual punishment under the Eighth Amendment), that he suffered damages as a result of the employees' actions, and that the employees were not immune. Such 1983 actions are often relied upon when suing governmental officials like police officers and correctional officers.

The subject of immunity is a crucial one when deciding whom to sue. It is imperative before filing suit that you review applicable state or federal statutes as well as any case decisions pertaining to immunity. A case involving the state as a defendant that looks particularly appealing under the "deep pocket" theory (the theory that one should go after the defendant with the most money) can take on a different light when the issue of immunity is considered.

LOCAL LINKS

In your state what kind of immunity do high-ranking administrative officials receive?

Interspousal Immunity

Under the common law, spouses were immune from suit by their spouses, and parents were immune from suit by their children. Spousal immunity arose out of the precept that a husband and wife were one entity and could not therefore sue each other. Consequently, a wife, for example, could not sue her husband if she was injured while a passenger in a car that he negligently drove.

The majority of states have now abolished interspousal immunity, rejecting the common law notion of the unity of the husband and wife as well as the arguments that allowing such suits would create family discord and encourage fraud. The claim that abolition of this immunity would result in a flood of litigation has not materialized. Some fraudulent cases have arisen in which the defendant spouse has failed to fully litigate a claim against him or her so that the other spouse could collect the insurance. But most courts have chosen to weed out those claims from the meritorious claims rather than bar all interspousal cases.

Even those states that have not completely abolished interspousal immunity have applied certain limitations. Some, for example, have abolished immunity in reference to automobile accidents or when the tort committed was intentional.

Parent-Child Immunity

Some of the same reasons given to justify interspousal immunity were also given under the common law to bar suits by children against their parents and vice versa. Briefly, the fear was that such suits would breed disharmony in the family, encourage collusion and fraud among family members, and create a flood of litigation.

Some states have chosen to abolish this immunity, particularly in cases involving motor vehicle accidents. The reason commonly given is that most suits are between a family and its insurance company and not between individual members of a family. Even in those states that have not abolished such immunity, many have allowed suit when the tort was intentional, when it involved loss of property or other pecuniary loss, when the injury occurred in the course of a business activity, when the child was legally emancipated or was a stepchild of the defendant, or when the parent-child relationship was terminated by the death of one of the parties prior to the suit. No immunity exists between siblings or in other family relationships.

One of the problems that can arise in the context of parent-child suits is the matter of negligent supervision. Consider the case of a child left unsupervised by her mother and who, as a result of this lack of supervision, is run over by the defendant. Should the defendant be allowed to bring a third-party claim against the plaintiff's mother for negligent failure to supervise the child? Some courts have said no, arguing that permitting such claims would in effect reduce the child's compensation by allowing the defendant to obtain contribution from the parent. Others have allowed such claims and have created a "reasonable parent" standard in determining the duty of supervision owed to a child.

Charitable Immunity

Charitable organizations, including educational and religious organizations, received immunity under the common law in nine states. The purpose of such immunity was to protect charitable institutions from tort claims and thereby promote their existence. Some courts have argued that the beneficiaries of charitable organizations impliedly waive their right to sue when they accept the benefits offered by that organization. Other courts have characterized this so-called *implied-waiver theory* as a legal fiction that

PUTTING IT INTO PRACTICE 8:6

1. The coaches of a school athletics program are alleged to be negligent in causing injury and death to some football players as a result of heat prostration during team practice. The school charges admission to football games, but the program has been operating at a net loss for the past five years. Can negligence actions be filed against the school district and the coaches?

2. An indigent defendant believes that his public defender failed to adequately represent him and that because of this lack of competent representation he was convicted. Can he sue the public defender under a § 1983 claim or, alternatively, under a theory of negligence (malpractice)?

3. An action is brought against the Archdiocese of Newark for the reckless and negligent hiring of a priest who forced a child to engage in sexual conduct with him while attending a camp sponsored by the church. The child ultimately commits suicide, and his brother, who attended the same camp, suffers medical problems as a result of feeling responsible for his brother's death. Can the parents recover for their damages and their children's damages?

4. A minor suffers mental and emotional harm as a result of being sexually assaulted by his father. Can he sue his father?

has no relevance in emergency situations, such as the receipt of emergency aid from a charitable hospital.

The other rationale used to justify charitable immunity is sometimes referred to as the *trust-fund theory*. This theory is based on the premise that funds given for charitable purposes should not be used to pay judgments resulting from tort claims. The refutation of this argument is that the trust-fund theory refers to how a judgment should be satisfied and not to the root question of whether an individual has a right to bring an action. In short, the argument goes, the question of liability should not be based on the charity's ability to satisfy a judgment.

The majority of states have abolished charitable immunity altogether; others have abolished it only in reference to charitable hospitals. Some, in deference to the trust-fund theory, have allowed liability when liability insurance is available but have denied it when a judgment would have to be paid out of trust funds. Still others, relying on the rationale of the implied-waiver theory, have allowed those who are not beneficiaries of the charity, such as employees or visitors, to sue.

LOCAL LINKS

What is the status of the following immunities in your state?
1. Interspousal immunity
2. Parent-child immunity
3. Charitable immunity

STATUTES OF LIMITATIONS AND STATUTES OF REPOSE

A **statute of limitations**, as the name indicates, is a statute limiting the time in which an action can be brought. Any action not commenced within that time period is barred. The purpose of such statutes is to protect individuals from having to defend stale claims. They also allow people to have some measure of stability and predictability in their lives by limiting the time frame in which they can anticipate being sued.

Because most statutes of limitations begin to run when a cause of action accrues, the question is when **accrual** takes place. Most courts have held that accrual occurs when there has been an actual injury to the plaintiff's person or property. Problems arise, however, when the plaintiff could not reasonably have discovered her injury until after the statute had run. Suppose, for example, that the statute of limitations on medical malpractice claims is five years but that the plaintiff did not begin to suffer complications from

the medical procedures she underwent until six years later. By the time she discovered she had a cause of action she would be barred from pursuing it.

To mitigate the harshness of a statute that precludes recovery in a case such as this, many courts have created the so-called *discovery doctrine*, which provides that the statute does not begin to run until the injury is, or should have been, discovered. Many states apply this rule to all surgical cases, but some have limited it to claims that an object was left in the patient's body. Still others have held that the statute begins to run when the doctor-patient relationship terminates, regardless of whether the plaintiff has discovered her injury at that time.

Some have argued that the discovery doctrine contributes to the rising cost of medical malpractice insurance. Many policies cover a physician's conduct during a particular year even though a claim based on that conduct may not arise for several years. As a result of the actuarial projections necessitated by this type of policy, premiums are very high. Arguably, premiums could be reduced if policies were issued on a claims-made basis so that only those claims filed against the physician that year, regardless of when the act of malpractice occurred, would be covered. Alternatively, some argue that a maximum time limit should be set for discovery under the discovery doctrine.

A similar issue arises in the case of malpractice by lawyers and other professionals. When should the statute of limitations begin to run when a lawyer negligently prepares a will? What if a latent construction defect does not show up until many years after the completion of construction? In some states the discovery doctrine has been applied.

It is important to consult the statutes in your state to determine the applicable statute of limitations and to ascertain when a cause of action accrues. This is one of the first questions that an attorney must answer when deciding whether to take a case. Failure to determine the appropriate statute of limitations could be grounds for malpractice.

Whereas the statute of limitations begins to run at the time of injury, a **statute of repose** begins to run at the date of sale of a product. Such statutes are designed to limit a manufacturer's liability, to lower insurance costs for manufacturers, and to introduce a sense of certainty in the area of product liability litigation. Most statutes of repose are five to twelve years and in some cases may bar suit even before injury occurs. As a practical matter, however, few suits are

PUTTING IT INTO PRACTICE 8:7

1. Pam consults with an attorney after she is severely injured in an automobile accident. The attorney convinces her to settle out of court for $100,000. Ten years later, when she is having her will done by another attorney, she mentions her personal injury case and the name of the attorney who represented her. She discovers that the attorney was subsequently disbarred for unethical conduct, specifically relating to his collusive agreements with a particular insurance company. She also finds out that the actual value of her case was probably closer to $1 million. Under the statute of limitations in your state, can she sue her former attorney and the firm for which he worked?

2. John buys a defective air gun and is injured. He does not realize until ten years later that he has a claim against the manufacturer. Under the laws of your state, can he still sue?

actually prevented, as few plaintiffs are injured by old, defective products. The effects are devastating, however, to certain victims, such as those who were injured by DES or asbestos or by some kinds of long-lasting machinery. Some courts have found statutes of repose to be constitutionally impermissible.

APPLICATION

The Baxters will likely claim that Teddy and Mr. Goodright were contributorily negligent. If they prevail in this claim and they live in a contributory-negligence state, both Teddy and Mr. Goodright will be precluded from recovering. If, however, they live in a comparative-negligence state, their recoveries will be reduced in direct proportion to their percentage of negligence. Whereas Teddy would likely be found negligent, Mr. Goodright would probably not be found negligent as long as he acted reasonably in rescuing Teddy. The last-clear-chance doctrine is inapplicable because the Baxters were not present during the time of the attack on Teddy, and Mr. Baxter did everything he could to rescue Mr. Goodright when he became aware of Gertrude's attack.

Arguably, Teddy impliedly assumed the risk by going into the Baxters's backyard, as he was aware of Gertrude's presence and of her propensity to attack. The defendants will have to prove, however, that Teddy actually knew that there was a risk and not merely that he ought to have known. Again, because of his classification as a rescuer, Mr. Goodright will probably be successful in rebutting any claim that he assumed the risk.

As a result of the consideration of the defenses that can be raised in this case, it is likely that Teddy's attorney will opt for a strict liability claim if at all possible. Remember that contributory negligence is generally not a defense to strict liability, although assumption of risk will usually be a complete defense. Nevertheless, assumption of risk requires subjective proof, putting the burden on the Baxters to show that Teddy knew the risk that he was confronting. The Baxters' task in proving assumption of risk would be more difficult than proving contributory negligence, in which an objective standard would be used to evaluate Teddy's conduct.

LOCAL LINKS

Does your state have a statute of repose? If so, what is the time period in which suits must be filed? Has your state created some kind of discovery doctrine?

Although no immunities could be raised as defenses, consideration of the applicable statute of limitations would be important. If Teddy and Mr. Goodright "sat" on their cases for a considerable period of time, their attorneys would be required to conduct their initial investigations expeditiously and file immediately before the statute of limitations ran. If the attorneys failed to file in a timely manner and their clients were consequently precluded from filing due to the statute of limitations, the attorneys would be subject to malpractice claims.

SUMMARY

The three defenses most commonly raised in negligence cases are contributory negligence, comparative negligence, and assumption of risk. Because the contributory-negligence rule is sometimes viewed as harsh and unjust, courts have developed various escape mechanisms by which plaintiffs can avoid this rule. The most significant exception to the contributory-negligence defense is the last-clear-chance doctrine. This doctrine does not apply if neither the defendant nor the plaintiff discovers the danger as a result of their inattentiveness. The doctrine is also inapplicable if the defendant's act of negligence precedes the plaintiff's predicament and precludes him or her from avoiding the accident after discovering the plaintiff's peril.

Contributory negligence cannot be used as a defense against an intentional tort. Nor is it allowed if the defendant's conduct was willful and wanton or reckless unless the plaintiff's conduct was also willful and wanton or reckless. Contributory negligence can be raised in the case of negligence per se unless the statute on which the defendant's negligence is based was enacted solely to protect a class of persons of which the plaintiff is a member and if the statute's intent was to place sole responsibility on the defendant.

All but a few states have adopted a comparative-negligence system. Under a pure comparative-negligence system the plaintiff recovers regardless of the extent of his or her negligence. Under the 50 percent approach, a plaintiff's claim is barred if his negligence is either as great as or not greater than the defendant's negligence. Difficulty is often encountered in assigning fault to the parties, particularly when there are more parties involved than just the plaintiff and defendant.

As with contributory negligence, comparative negligence cannot be raised as a defense to an intentional tort. It can be raised if the defendant's conduct was willful and wanton, reckless, or negligent per se. Some jurisdictions continue to apply the last-clear-chance doctrine, although the Uniform Comparative Fault Act expressly rejects its use in a comparative-negligence system.

The distinction between contributory negligence and assumption of risk is often blurred. Contributory negligence is sometimes characterized as "carelessness" whereas assumption of risk is sometimes perceived as "adventurousness." In the defense of contributory negligence, an objective standard is used; in assumption of risk a subjective standard is relied on. Assumption of risk, unlike contributory negligence, can be used as a defense to reckless conduct and in a case of strict liability.

A plaintiff can either expressly or impliedly assume the risk. An express waiver will not be enforced if the defendant has unusual bargaining power or if the plaintiff is unaware of the risk. In terms of implied consent the plaintiff will not be considered to have acted voluntarily if she had no reasonable choice but to confront the danger. Those states that have adopted comparative negligence have, to some degree, removed assumption of risk as a separate defense.

Immunity is a complete defense to tort liability. Immunity of federal government officials has been curtailed by the Federal Tort Claims Act. Federal officials performing discretionary functions are immune from suit. State governments traditionally enjoyed sovereign immunity although most states have abolished it to some extent. Local governmental entities have enjoyed at least partial immunity. Immunity is typically granted for governmental functions but not allowed for proprietary functions. Legislators, judges, and some other public officials receive complete immunity as long as they are acting within the scope of their duties.

The majority of states have now abolished interspousal immunity, or at the least have imposed various limitations on such immunity. Similarly, some states have chosen to abolish parent-child immunity. Charitable immunity has been abolished altogether in the majority of states. Some courts have adhered to the trust-fund theory and have denied liability if the judgment would have to be paid out of trust funds. Still other courts have adhered to the implied-waiver theory and have allowed recovery only to those who are not beneficiaries of the charity.

Statutes of limitations and statutes of repose prevent the bringing of stale claims and allow some measure of stability and predictability in people's lives. The key question that arises in reference to these statutes is the question of accrual. Under the discovery doctrine a statute does not begin to run until the injury is or should have been discovered. A statute of repose begins to run at the date of sale of a product.

KEY TERMS

accrual
Time at which a statute of limitations begins to run, usually at the time the plaintiff is injured

assumption of risk
Defense that the plaintiff voluntarily consented to take the chance that harm would occur if he engaged in certain conduct

comparative negligence
Defense that the plaintiff's recovery should be reduced in direct proportion to the plaintiff's percentage of contribution to her own injuries

contributory negligence
Defense that the plaintiff contributed to his own injuries and should therefore be barred from recovery

discretionary function
Act of a government employee requiring the use of judgment

governmental function
Tasks typically performed by a governmental entity

immunity
Absolute defense derived from the defendant's status (e.g., a government official) or relationship to the plaintiff (e.g., spouse of the plaintiff)

last-clear-chance doctrine
Doctrine that allows the plaintiff to recover in a contributory-negligence system despite the plaintiff's negligence

proprietary function
Function performed by the government that could just as easily be performed by a private entity

statute of limitations
Statute that limits the time period in which a claim can be filed

statute of repose
Statute of limitations in product liability cases that limits the time period during which suit can be filed

REVIEW QUESTIONS

1. What is the difference between contributory negligence, comparative negligence, and assumption of risk?

2. What is the rationale for contributory negligence?

3. What have some courts done to mitigate the harshness of the contributory negligence doctrine?

4. What is the last-clear-chance doctrine?

   a. What variations to this doctrine exist?
   b. What is the first-clear-chance doctrine?
   c. When is the last-clear-chance doctrine not applicable?

5. When is contributory negligence not a defense?

6. What is the justification for the development of the comparative-negligence standard?

7. What is the difference between pure comparative negligence and the 50 percent approach?

   a. What is the difference between the "not greater than" and "not as great as" approach?
   b. Why is this difference significant?

8. What administrative problems arise in the context of comparative negligence?

9. How have states that have adopted comparative negligence treated the last-clear-chance doctrine?

10. Are contributory negligence and comparative negligence a defense to

    a. intentional torts?
    b. reckless or willful and wanton conduct?
    c. negligence per se?

11. How does assumption of risk compare to contributory negligence?

12. How have courts that have adopted comparative negligence treated assumption of risk?

13. Under what conditions are courts unlikely to enforce a release in which the plaintiff expressly assumes the risk?

14. What is required for a release to be enforceable?

15. What must be shown before a plaintiff will be considered to have impliedly assumed the risk?

16. How do the courts treat professional and amateur athletes differently when it comes to impliedly assuming the risk?

17. In what respect is immunity a complete defense?

18. What is the rationale underlying sovereign immunity?

19. Why was the Federal Tort Claims Act (FTCA) passed?

    a. What does this act provide?
    b. What exceptions limit the scope of this act?
    c. What is the significance of a discretionary function for purposes of this act?

20. For what reasons have many states abolished state sovereign immunity?

    a. What immunities do states typically preserve?
    b. What kind of statutory immunity is often created by states, and what are the basic provisions of these statutes?

21. What kinds of functions of local government are usually protected by immunity?

22. Give an example of a function that is usually protected by immunity and of one that generally is not.

23. Which officials are granted immunity, and under what conditions is this immunity granted?

24. How does a public official's immunity relate to governmental immunity?

25. What is a 1983 action?

26. Why was interspousal immunity created, and what is its status today?

27. Why was parent-child immunity created, and what is its status today?

28. What are the justifications for charitable immunity, and what is its status today?

29. What is the purpose of a statute of limitations?
    a. When does a statute accrue?
    b. What is the discovery doctrine, what is its purpose, and why is it sometimes criticized?
    c. What is a statute of repose, and what is a potential problem with this statute?

PRACTICE EXAM

Students should complete the practice exam after studying each chapter. The answers are in Appendix A. If you score lower than 80%, you should reread the materials.

True-False

1. Tort defenses are largely controlled by statute.

2. Contributory negligence prevents a negligent plaintiff from recovering unless the defendant is more negligent than the plaintiff.

3. The rationale for one reason for the judicial creation of contributory negligence is that judges distrust jurors and are afraid that they might harm industry by giving large awards to injured plaintiffs.

4. In those states that have adopted a contributory-negligence system, the defendant is required to prove and specifically plead contributory negligence in order to use it as a defense.

5. Without exception, the rules that govern proximate cause in relation to a defendant's conduct also apply to a plaintiff's conduct in determining contributory negligence.

6. To recover under the last-clear-chance doctrine, plaintiffs must prove only that the defendant failed to take advantage of an opportunity to prevent harm to the plaintiff.

7. Contributory negligence is not a defense to intentional torts or to claims of negligence per se.

8. Comparative negligence is an easier system to administer than contributory negligence.

9. In assigning a percentage of fault to a plaintiff's conduct, one considers the extent to which that conduct contributed to the resulting harm or the extent to which it deviated from a reasonable standard of care.

10. When a pure comparative-negligence standard is used, the negligence of everyone is considered, even nonparties.

11. Plaintiffs are not allowed to recover if their negligence is less than all of the defendants combined but greater than that of each individual defendant.

12. The last-clear-chance doctrine has been retained in most states that have adopted comparative negligence.

13. Comparative negligence can be used to reduce a plaintiff's recovery if the defendant is reckless or willful and wanton.

14. In some states that have adopted comparative negligence, apportionment of fault is not allowed if the defendant violated a statute that is designed to protect members of the plaintiff's class and if that statute places sole responsibility on the defendant.

15. Assumption of risk completely bars the plaintiff from recovery in most modern courts.

16. Assumption of risk can be raised as a defense in strict liability cases and can be used in defense of reckless conduct.

17. Those states that have adopted comparative negligence have either abolished assumption of risk as a separate defense or have merged it into the defense of comparative negligence.

18. When sports are involved, those who participate have assumed the risks as long as the risks are understood or completely obvious.

19. Professional athletes are assumed to be more cognizant of the risks than amateurs.

20. If a plaintiff protests against assuming a risk but ultimately agrees to assume it, his consent will be considered voluntary.

21. Most states have retained complete sovereign immunity and also provide complete immunity for judges and legislators.

22. State tort claims acts usually require that written notice of a claim be given during a designated time period after the discovery of the injury.

23. Many courts have abolished local governmental immunity.

24. Immunity is granted to legislators, judges, and other public officials so that they can carry out the difficult tasks of their office without fear of being sued, but that immunity does not extend to those who act out of greed or malice toward a plaintiff.

25. High-ranking administrative officials receive no immunity.

26. If the government is immune, a public official is also immune.

27. Under the FTCA the United States government and its employees are liable for any injuries arising out of a federal employee's operation of a motor vehicle.

28. A 1983 action occurs when a defendant acts under color of a state statute, ordinance, or regulation and violates a plaintiff's civil rights.

29. Under the common law a husband and wife were considered one entity.

30. Under the common law a wife could not sue her husband for injuries she sustained as a passenger when he was driving, but a husband could sue his wife.

31. Some courts bypass parent-child immunity when an intentional tort or business activity is involved.

32. Some courts disallow negligent supervision suits because they reduce the child's compensation.

33. In response to the argument that beneficiaries of a charitable organization should not be able to sue, opponents of charitable immunity argue that this justification should not apply in emergency situations.

34. Some states allow suit against charitable organizations when liability insurance is available.

Matching

GROUP 1

_____ 1. Defendant fails to take advantage of opportunity to avoid harm to plaintiff

_____ 2. Because of earlier negligence defendant cannot take advantage of opportunity to prevent harm to plaintiff

_____ 3. Punishes negligent plaintiffs

_____ 4. The 49 percent rule

_____ 5. Punishes adventurous plaintiffs

a. assumption of risk
b. comparative negligence
c. contributory negligence
d. first clear chance
e. last clear chance

GROUP 2

_____ 1. King can do no wrong
_____ 2. Abolished in some states
_____ 3. Abolished in most states
_____ 4. A 1983 action
_____ 5. Allows United States government to be sued for negligence of employees

a. interspousal immunity
b. parent-child immunity
c. sovereign immunity
d. Federal Tort Claims Act
e. Civil Rights Act

GROUP 3

_____ 1. What happens when injury occurs
_____ 2. Mitigates harshness of statute of limitations
_____ 3. Prevents stale claims
_____ 4. Begin to run when product is sold

a. statute of limitations
b. statutes of repose
c. accrues
d. discovery doctrine

Fill-in-the-Blanks

1. Most states have adopted some form of a _____ negligence standard.

2. Under the _____ _____ _____ doctrine the defendant remains liable because of a failure to take advantage of an opportunity to prevent harm to the plaintiff.

3. Under a comparative-negligence defense, a plaintiff who was awarded $1,000,000 and who was found to be 30 percent negligent would receive an award of _____.

4. A plaintiff who is 50 percent negligent cannot recover in a state that adopted a _____ approach.

5. In assessing a plaintiff's conduct who has allegedly assumed the risk, a(n) _____ standard is used, whereas in assessing a plaintiff's conduct who was allegedly negligent, a(n) _____ standard is used.

6. _____ is a complete defense to tort liability because it completely absolves the defendant of liability.

7. Local governments can often claim immunity when a(n) _____ function is involved.

8. Activities carried out by water and gas utilities are considered _____ functions of a local government.

9. _____ immunity was instituted to protect charitable institutions from tort claims.

10. Under the _____ _____ theory, beneficiaries of charitable organizations waive their right to sue when they accept the benefits of a charitable organization.

11. Under the _____ _____ theory, funds given for charitable purpose should not be used to pay judgments.

12. The purpose of _____ is to limit the time frame in which individuals can be sued.

13. A cause of action _____ when an actual injury occurs to the plaintiff's person or property.

14. Under the _____ doctrine, an action does not begin until an injury is or should have been discovered.

Multiple-Choice

1. Under the doctrine of contributory negligence,
   a. worthy plaintiffs are protected.
   b. the question of negligence is left up to the judge.
   c. the rationale is that negligent plaintiffs should be punished for failing to protect their own safety.
   d. all of the above.

2. The last-clear-chance doctrine
   a. mitigates the harshness of the contributory negligence defense.
   b. prevents the plaintiff from recovering if both the plaintiff and defendant are inattentive and the defendant fails to discover the danger to the plaintiff because of his inattentiveness.
   c. prevents the plaintiff from recovering if the defendant is unable to avoid harming the plaintiff because of the defendant's earlier negligence.
   d. all of the above.

3. A plaintiff who assumes the risk
   a. is necessarily negligent.
   b. can be considered negligent as well.
   c. cannot be considered negligent.
   d. involuntarily exposes herself to a risk.

4. Express agreements to accept the risk will usually be enforced
   a. if they are prepared by common carriers, public utilities, or other regulated industries.
   b. even if the defendant is the sole or unique provider of a service.
   c. even if the defendant has unusual bargaining power.
   d. none of the above.

5. A waiver of liability will not be enforced
   a. for intentional torts but will be enforced for willful and wanton or gross negligence.
   b. unless it is expressed in language that is clear and unequivocal.
   c. if it does not contain the word "negligence."
   d. all of the above.

6. For a plaintiff to impliedly assume a risk,
   a. she must be aware of the risk.
   b. she must voluntarily assume the risk.
   c. she must have a reasonable choice to do something other than accept the risk.
   d. all of the above.

7. The FTCA applies to
   a. intentional torts committed by law enforcement officials.
   b. a federal employee's acts that are considered discretionary.
   c. a federal employee's acts that are part of a planning process.
   d. all of the above.

8. When sovereign immunity is abolished,
   a. it is done because courts believe being responsible for the torts of employees is one of the costs of administering a government.
   b. it is done even though public insurance is not available.
   c. state tort claims are usually abolished simultaneously.
   d. all of the above.

9. Interspousal immunity and parent-child immunity were instituted
   a. to prevent a flood of litigation.
   b. out of a concern that allowing such suits would encourage family discord.
   c. out of a fear of fraudulent suits.
   d. all of the above.

10. Statutes of repose
   a. are usually one to five years long.
   b. have been found to be constitutionally impermissible.
   c. tend to increase insurance costs for manufacturers.
   d. all of the above.

PRACTICE POINTERS

PREPARING A DEFENSE

Paralegals often participate in the discovery process, which (if you represent the defendant) involves gathering information that supports your client's defense. This process includes

- sending out interrogatories and requests for production of documents.
- setting up depositions.
- interviewing witnesses.
- requesting the plaintiff to sign medical release authorizations (which allow the release of medical records by doctors and other medical providers).
- checking with the county recorder's office and the clerk's office to determine if the plaintiff has been involved in other suits.
- checking Motor Vehicle Department records (to determine vehicle ownership, for example).

Once the requested records are assembled, medical records, accident reports, repair records, and the records of the major medical insurance carrier must be reviewed to determine the

- nature, type, and extent of the plaintiff's injuries.
- existence of preexisting injuries and any claims relating to those injuries.
- names, addresses, and phone numbers of potential witnesses.
- treatments the plaintiff has received and the prognosis for recovery.

Medical Records

To secure medical records and the records of the plaintiff's medical insurance carrier, interrogatories must be sent out to identify the plaintiff's treating physicians both before and after the accident (see Chapter 6). These doctors are then contacted to find out if any advance fees are required before the records will be copied. Medical authorization requests are sent to the plaintiff's attorney with a request to have the plaintiff sign them. If the plaintiff complies, these forms are submitted to the appropriate physicians. If the plaintiff refuses to sign the medical authorization requests and the procedural rules permit such a refusal, the records are subpoenaed using a subpoena duces tecum and a notice of deposition, which are sent to the custodian of the medical records. A notice of deposition follows, along with a letter stating that if the custodian voluntarily agrees to submit the records, he need not appear at the deposition. The custodian must sign an affidavit affirming that all of the requested records have been sent and must return the affidavit along with the records (all of which must be returned before the date of the deposition).

Police Records and Other Official Records

To obtain accident reports, you must send a written request to the law enforcement agency and enclose any required fees. Many agencies require forms to be filled out, and some require that a need be established before the records will be provided, because the records may not be available to the public. A similar process must often be followed to secure death certificates (usually from a department of health services), motor vehicle registration records, and driver's license information.

County Recorder's Office and Court Clerk's Office

Become familiar with the location, procedures, and personnel in the county recorder's office and the court clerk's office. Paralegals often are asked to obtain records and file documents with these offices. Find out if the records in these offices are available online and whether this service is free or subscription-based.

TORT TEASERS

1. The so-called "seat belt defense" is used by defense counsel to argue that the plaintiff was contributorily negligent or negligent per se in his failure to wear a seat belt. Assume you are representing a defendant in a motor vehicle accident case and argue (a) the plaintiff was contributorily negligent; (b) the plaintiff was comparatively negligent; (c) the plaintiff assumed the risk; (d) the plaintiff failed to mitigate his damages; and (e) the plaintiff was negligent per se. Be as specific as possible in terms of the type of legal argument you would want to make and the type of evidence that you would want to introduce. Would you rather argue that the plaintiff contributed to his own injuries or that he assumed the risk? Why? Now assume you are representing the plaintiff and want to argue that the seat belt defense is inappropriate. In your arguments consider whether the plaintiff has a duty to use a seat belt and whether his failure to do so constitutes the proximate cause of the accident. Furthermore, you might want to consider when the plaintiff's duty to mitigate his damages arises.

2. Police officer left a handcuffed prisoner in the back seat of his police cruiser. The back seat was separated from the front seat by a Plexiglas shield. On the way to the jail, the officer stopped and exited the cruiser to assist with traffic control and left the keys in the ignition with the engine and emergency lights on. The prisoner somehow maneuvered into the front seat and drove away at a very high rate of speed, crashing head on into a vehicle and causing the death of both the driver of the other vehicle and himself. Should immunity be extended to the police officer and the City for the officer's gross negligence? *Pile v. City of Brandenburg*, 215 S.W.3d 36 (Ky. 2006).

3. The plaintiff, a participant in a "National Lap Sitting Contest" promoting wrinkle-free slacks, is injured when the chair in which he is sitting collapses because he was holding fourteen girls on his lap. What defenses do you think should be raised in this case, and why? *Wyly v. Burlington Industries*, 452 F.2d 807 (5th Cir. 1971).

4. A woman purchases doughnuts sealed in their original package. She opens the package in her automobile and in the course of driving consumes several pieces of one doughnut by breaking them off with her fingers and popping them into her mouth. Because of an abscessed tooth and sore jaw, she sips milk through a straw, allowing the doughnut to dissolve in her mouth, rather than chewing the doughnuts. It is the dissolving nature of the doughnut that prompts her to buy this particular product. Shortly after beginning to consume the doughnut, she feels something stick in her throat and immediately suffers ingestion. It is discovered through x-rays the same day that the woman had consumed a piece of doughnut containing a metal wire and causing her subsequent injury. Do you think the manufacturer is justified in claiming contributory or comparative negligence? *Coulter v. American Bakers Co.*, 530 So.2d 1009 (Florida 1988).

5. Prisoner is detained seven days beyond his sentence due to a clerical error. The Department of Corrections argues that it has immunity and the lawsuit should be dismissed. Do you agree? *Kingman v. State Dept. of Corrections* 129 P.3d 887 (Alaska 2006).

6. A college student is raped while on campus. She wants to sue the college for its failure to maintain adequate security in the classrooms. Why do you think she may have a difficult time recovering for her injuries? What arguments would you make to support her being able to recover? *Kleisch v. Cleveland State University*, 2005 WC 663214 (Ohio Ct. Ct. 2005)

7. A woman is injured while riding an ATV (all-terrain vehicle) she borrowed from a friend. She is hospitalized for her injuries, during which time she requires near constant narcotic pain medication and is often unaware of what is going on around her. A year after she is injured she files suit against the manufacturer of the ATV. This date is ten years and thirteen days after her friend purchased the ATV. The state has a ten-year statute of repose. The plaintiff argues that statute of repose was tolled by the legal-disability statute during the twenty days that she remained mentally incapacitated in the hospital. What information would you need about the statute of repose and the disability statute to evaluate her argument? What will happen to her suit if she is not successful in making this argument? *Penley v. Honda Motor Co.*, 31 S.W.3d 181 (Tenn 2000).

8. Maurice saw defendant hit his friend, Kevin, over the head with a broken beer bottle. Maurice was stabbed in the neck with the broken beer bottle when he attempted to break up the fight between Kevin and defendant. What defenses should the defendant raise in the lawsuit filed by Kevin and Maurice? Explain what defenses you believe defendant should raise, and why? *Duda v. Phatly McGees, Inc.*, 758 N.W.2d 754 (S.D. 2008).

INTERNET INQUIRIES

In states that participate in the VitalChek program, qualified individuals can obtain certified copies of vital records, including birth and death certificates, via a request by phone, mail, fax, or the Internet. Visit VitalChek's site at http://www.vitalchek.com. Guidelines about ordering vital records from most states are available at Vital Records Info at http://www.vitalrec.com. Go to the website for VitalChek and find out if your state is a participant. If it is, answer the following questions:

a. Can you order birth and death certificates by fax? Online?

b. What is the cost of ordering a birth certificate? A death certificate?

c. What information must you provide to get a copy of a birth certificate?

d. What information must you provide to get a copy of a death certificate?

e. Who is entitled to get a death certificate?

PRACTICAL PONDERABLES

Your firm has been asked by the state court to represent an inmate in one of your state prisons who was severely injured when he was electrocuted as a result of reaching up and screwing in a light bulb above his bed. He was in solitary confinement at the time and had repeatedly requested that this light bulb be repaired as it had bare wires hanging down from the ceiling. The inmate had to stand on his bed in order to reach the light. This was the only light in his room, and without it he was in total darkness.

Before deciding whether to represent this inmate in a negligence suit against the prison, your supervising attorney asks you to do some preliminary research as follows:

1. She wants you to read the immunity statutes in your state regarding state institutions. What do you discover? Can the prison be sued? Can the individual guards be sued?

2. She is concerned that the inmate was negligent himself. What will you need to do to determine if he was negligent?

3. The inmate has been trying to find someone to represent him for about a year. He was hospitalized for his injuries thirteen months ago. What is the statute of limitations in your state for a negligence action? Is this statute tolled while a plaintiff is incarcerated?

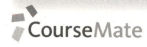

CourseMate Access an interactive eBook, chapter-specific learning tools, including flashcards, quizzes, and more in your Paralegal CourseMate, accessed through www.CengageBrain.com.

CHAPTER 9

© Cengage Learning 2012

Malpractice

CHAPTER OBJECTIVES

After completing the chapter, you should be able to

- Explain the standard of care to which a professional is held.

- Identify ways in which professional negligence is committed.

- Explain the informed-consent doctrine.

- Recognize defenses that can be raised in response to a professional negligence claim.

- Appreciate the reasons for the increase in professional negligence claims.

The attorney by whom you have just been hired is a recent law school graduate. Early in his career, he discovers, through personal experience, many of the legal land mines on which an attorney can step. First, he advises a woman who was injured in an automobile accident that she has no viable cause of action. Two days after the statute of limitations runs out, she consults with another attorney on a separate matter. This attorney advises her that she did indeed have a good cause of action for which she probably could have netted a considerable recovery.

Next, unaware of the malpractice noose now dangling over his head, your attorney blithely decides not to relay a settlement offer to another client because in his opinion the client should not accept the offer. When the case goes to trial the client is awarded less than he would have received under the terms of the offer. The client is most displeased when he discovers that the terms of the settlement offer were never relayed to him.

Finally, you forget to file a list of exhibits and witnesses on the date it is due. As a result, the judge refuses to allow your key witness to testify, and the case is lost when it goes to trial. What will clients in each of these cases have to prove if they allege professional negligence? What might the attorney argue in his defense?

WHAT IS REASONABLE CARE?

As we discussed in Chapter 5, the duty of care required of professionals is one of reasonableness. A professional is required to have the skill and learning commonly possessed by members in good standing within that profession. The question that frequently arises is whether professionals should be required to meet national or local standards. For example, should a physician who practices in a rural area be held to the same standard of care as one who practices in an urban, high-tech office? In the medical area many states have opted for a local standard, apparently with an implicit acknowledgment that expectations of reasonableness are dependent on locale. Some courts, however, influenced by the elevated expectations of professionals resulting from enhanced communications, have discarded the "locality rule" in favor of a national standard.

LOCAL LINKS

What standard do the courts in your jurisdiction use to determine what must be disclosed to a patient?

Negligence is not necessarily equated with unfavorable outcome. Simply because a course of action ultimately yields undesirable results does not make it negligent. Hindsight, as we all know, is perfect, but reasonable foresight is all that is required of a professional. A veterinarian, for instance, may recommend surgery for an ailing dog, but if the dog dies from complications, the veterinarian is not necessarily negligent even though the outcome proves the prognosis incorrect. The veterinarian's recommendation need only be reasonable, not accurate.

In many instances several possible options are available to the professional. The rule of reasonable care does not require that all other professionals would have chosen the same course of action as that decided upon by the defendant professional. The fact that other dentists, for example, might testify that they personally would have opted for a different procedure than that used by the defendant does not necessarily make the defendant's conduct negligent. If, however, only one recognized method of treatment is used by dentists in good standing in the profession and the defendant dentist chooses another course of action, the choice will likely be considered negligent.

HOW NEGLIGENCE CAN OCCUR

Professional negligence, like any other type of negligence, can occur in a number of ways (see Exhibit 9–1). A professional may lack the requisite training to perform a given task. He may fail to ask for the information necessary to make an informed recommendation to the plaintiff, or may fail to refer his client to a specialist when the situation dictates such a referral. An attorney in general practice with no training or experience in securities fraud, for example, could be negligent if she represented a client in a securities fraud case to the detriment of that client.

Even if a professional chooses an appropriate course of conduct, he may be negligent if he fails to use due diligence and care. Professionals who resort to unorthodox procedures are more likely to be found negligent if the client ultimately suffers some kind of damage than professionals who rely on more

EXHIBIT 9-1 *What Constitutes Professional Negligence*

- Failure to have skills and learning commonly possessed by members in good standing within a profession
- Failure to use good judgment in choosing course of action, to the extent that the action chosen constitutes a deviation from the standard of care reasonably expected of professionals in the field
- Failure to ask for essential information from client
- Failure to make referrals when appropriate
- Failure to keep abreast of changes in profession
- Failure to follow up on client's progress, condition, or status
- Failure to adhere to specialist's standard of care when appropriate
- Failure to provide informed consent.

© Cengage Learning 2012

conventional techniques. The degree of innovation that will be considered legally acceptable will be determined largely by the seriousness of the situation. If a physician uses a method unknown or disapproved of by her peers when dealing with a critically ill patient, she is more likely to be found negligent than if she is dealing with someone suffering a minor illness. In extremely difficult cases the professional may be expected to consult with someone else in the field. A general physician, for example, who identifies a condition that he is ill equipped to handle has an obligation to consult with a specialist.

A professional is obligated to keep abreast of new developments in the field. Accountants are expected to be aware of recent changes in tax law. Physicians are expected to be aware of innovations in medications and procedures.

Professionals are obligated to pay attention to their clients' complaints and feedback. A physician who fails to remain apprised of her patient's change in condition may be negligent. In one case a fifteen-year-old boy was voluntarily admitted to the psychiatric unit. He had a history of substance abuse, suicidal thoughts, and had attempted suicide by placing a gun in his mouth. He survived because the gun misfired. The psychiatrists failed to speak with the boy and

failed to review his chart prior to releasing him. The chart contained notations regarding the boy's constant thoughts of suicide. The boy committed suicide less than two months after his release. The doctor's motion for summary judgment arguing no proximate cause was denied (*Purcell v. Breese,* 552 S.E.2d 865 [GA. App. 2001]). Doctors may also commit malpractice by prescribing medications to patients without first examining the patient. The Washington Department of Health revoked a doctor's license to practice medicine after he wrote prescriptions to patients he never personally examined. The court held that the doctor was not able to safeguard against improper diagnosis, or identify adverse reactions to the prescribed drugs (*Ancier v. State Dept. of Health,* 2007 WL 2473472 [Wash. App. 2007]).

The elements of a malpractice claim are set forth in *Ang v. Martin* 114 P.3d 637 (Wash. 2005). Notice that even when the defendant professional is negligent, if the plaintiff cannot prove that the negligence was the proximate cause of his injuries, no malpractice claim exists. Furthermore, in *Ang,* because the legal malpractice claim arose out of a criminal case, the plaintiff bore the burden of proving that they were actually innocent of the criminal charges that were filed against them.

CASE

Ang v. Martin
114 P.3d 637 (Wash. 2005)

OWENS, J.

We are asked to determine whether plaintiffs in a malpractice action against their former criminal defense attorneys were properly required to prove by

a preponderance of the evidence that they were actually innocent of the underlying criminal charges. The Court of Appeals concluded that, as an element of their negligence claim, plaintiffs were required "to prove

(continues)

innocence *in fact* and not merely to present evidence of the government's inability to prove guilt." *Ang v. Martin*, 118 Wash.App. 553, 558, 76 P.3d 787 (2003). We affirm the Court of Appeals.

FACTS

Psychiatrist Jessy Ang and his wife Editha jointly owned Evergreen Medical Panel, Inc., a company that provided the Washington State Department of Labor and Industries with independent medical examinations of injured workers. As a result of Dr. Ang's contact with a target of a governmental task force investigating social security fraud, Dr. Ang himself became a person of interest. In February 1994, the task force executed a search warrant on Dr. Ang's office and seized copies of two sets of signed tax returns that reported conflicting amounts of income. The Angs were arrested in April 1996, following the execution of a search warrant at their residence. A year later, the Angs were indicted on 18 criminal counts, including conspiracy to defraud the United States, bank and tax fraud, and filing false statements.

The Angs retained defendants Richard Hansen and Michael G. Martin for flat fees of $225,000 and $100,000, respectively. Attorneys Hansen and Martin engaged in a round of plea negotiations prior to trial, but the Angs rejected the plea bargain. The case proceeded to a jury trial before Judge Tanner in federal district court in December 1997. On the fifth day of trial, just prior to the conclusion of the government's case, Hansen and Martin recommended that the Angs accept another proffered plea, one that the Angs viewed as the least attractive of any agreement previously presented. After Dr. Ang was allegedly told that Mrs. Ang could face sexual assault in prison, the Angs agreed to plead guilty to two of the 18 counts.

The Angs then engaged attorney Monte Hester to review the plea discussions and provide a second opinion. Hester concluded that the government had not met its burden of proof and that the plea agreement provided the Angs with no material benefit. Retaining Hester and Keith A. MacFie to represent them, the Angs successfully moved to withdraw the pleas, which Judge Tanner had never formally accepted. In September 1999, the matter again proceeded to trial before Judge Tanner, with the Angs waiving their right to a jury. Although the government offered another plea bargain prior to trial, one requiring no plea on Dr. Ang's part, a misdemeanor or felony for Mrs. Ang, and a $500,000 fine, the Angs rejected the plea and were acquitted on all 18 counts.

The Angs, along with Evergreen Medical, filed the present legal malpractice action against Hansen and Martin in May 2000 in Pierce County Superior Court. The complaint stated claims for legal malpractice and for violations of the Washington Consumer Protection Act, chapter 19.86 RCW. The trial court denied the defendants' motion for summary judgment, and a jury trial began in November 2001. The trial court instructed the jury that the Angs had to prove by a preponderance of the evidence that they were innocent of the underlying criminal charges. On January 11, 2002, responding to the initial two questions on a special verdict form, the jury found that the Angs had not "proven by a preponderance of the evidence [they were] innocent of all the criminal charges against [them]." Clerk's Papers at 1663–64. As to the verdict form's third question, asking whether "any of the defendants [had been] negligent," the jury made a finding of negligence against Martin only. *Id*. at 1664.

The plaintiffs appealed, but the Court of Appeals affirmed. This court granted the plaintiffs' petition for review.

ISSUES

(1) Where a legal malpractice suit stems from the representation of clients in a criminal prosecution, must plaintiffs who were acquitted of the criminal charges prove their actual innocence of the crimes, or does their acquittal satisfy the innocence element of their malpractice action? (2) Did the Angs properly request review of jury instruction 13, which directed the jury to determine the Angs' innocence of the criminal charges but provided no legal definitions of the named crimes, relying instead on the jury's access to the proposed instructions from the criminal trial?

ANALYSIS

Standard of Review. The Angs contend that the trial court erred in requiring them to prove, in their malpractice suit against former defense counsel, their actual innocence of the underlying criminal charges. They also assert that the court inadequately instructed the jury on the definitions of those charges. As with all questions of law, the issues presented here are reviewed de novo. *Kommavongsa v. Haskell*, 149 Wash.2d 288, 295, 67 P.3d 1068 (2003).

10 Essential Elements of Legal Malpractice Claims against Criminal Defense Counsel. A plaintiff claiming negligent representation by an attorney in a civil matter

(continues)

bears the burden of proving four elements by a preponderance of the evidence:

(1) The existence of an attorney-client relationship
which gives rise to a duty of care on the part of the
attorney to the client; (2) an act or omission by the
attorney in breach of the duty of care; (3) damage to
the client; and (4) proximate causation between the
attorney's breach of the duty and the damage incurred.

Hizey v. Carpenter, 119 Wash.2d 251, 260–61,
830 P.2d 646 (1992); *Bowman v. John Doe Two,*
104 Wash.2d 181, 185, 704 P.2d 140 (1985) (noting that, in legal malpractice suits, proof of attorney-
client relationship is grafted onto customary elements
of negligence claim). The fourth element, proximate
causation, includes "[c]ause in fact and legal causation." *Hartley v. State,* 103 Wash.2d 768, 777, 698 P.2d
77 (1985). Cause in fact, or "but for" causation, refers
to "the physical connection between an act and an
injury." *Id.* at 778, 698 P.2d 77. In a legal malpractice
trial, the "trier of fact will be asked to decide what a
reasonable jury or fact finder [in the underlying trial
or 'trial within the trial'] would have done but for the
attorney's negligence." *Daugert v. Pappas,* 104 Wash.2d
254, 258, 704 P.2d 600 (1985) (emphasis added).
Legal causation, however, presents a question of law:
"It involves a determination of whether liability should
attach as a matter of law given the existence of cause
in fact." *Hartley,* 103 Wash.2d at 779, 698 P.2d 77. To
determine whether the cause in fact of a plaintiff's harm
should also be deemed the legal cause of that harm,
a court may consider, among other things, the public
policy implications of holding the defendant liable. *Id.*
In "criminal malpractice" suits,[1] two elements related
to proximate causation have been added. In *Falkner
v. Foshaug,* 108 Wash.App. 113, 29 P.3d 771 (2001),
the Court of Appeals "conclude[d] that postconviction
relief is a prerequisite to maintaining [a criminal mal-
practice] suit and proof of innocence is an additional
element a criminal defendant/malpractice plaintiff must
prove to prevail at trial in his legal malpractice action."
Id. at 124, 29 P.3d 771 (emphasis added); *see also id.*
at 123, 29 P.3d 771 (referring to "an actual innocence
requirement").

The trial court in the present case thus instructed
the jury as follows on the elements of the Angs criminal
malpractice claims:

To prove their legal malpractice claims, the plaintiffs
bear the burden of proving by a preponderance of the
evidence each of the following:

First, that there is an attorney-client relationship giving rise to a duty owed by a defendant to a plaintiff;

Second, *that plaintiffs have obtained a successful challenge to their convictions* based on their attorneys failure to adequately defend them;

Third, that *plaintiff was innocent of the crimes charged;*

Fourth, that there is an act of omission by a defendant that breached the duty of care of an attorney;

Fifth, that a plaintiff was damaged; and

Sixth, that a breach of duty by a defendant is a proximate cause of a plaintiff's damages. . . .[2]

The Angs assigned error to this instruction, contending that their undisputed acquittal of the criminal
charges met not only the additional element of postconviction relief but also the innocence requirement.

By successfully withdrawing their guilty pleas and
receiving an acquittal on all charges, the Angs unquestionably received the equivalent of postconviction
relief,[3] but contrary to their contention, they did not
thereby satisfy the *Falkner* courts innocence requirement. The Angs mistakenly claim that, under *Falkner,*
they were simply required to prove legal innocence, not
actual innocence. *See Shaw v. State,* 861 P.2d 566, 570 n.
3 (Alaska 1993) (*Shaw* II) (noting that "[l]egal guilt or
innocence is that determination made by the trier of fact
in a criminal trial," whereas "[a]ctual guilt is intended
to refer to a determination in a civil trial, by a preponderance of the evidence, that the defendant engaged
in the conduct he was accused of in the prior criminal
proceeding"). But the *Falkner* court referred explicitly
to the "*actual* innocence requirement" and at no point

---

1. The phrase "criminal malpractice" has been widely adopted to
denote "legal malpractice in the course of defending a client accused
of crime." Otto M. Kaus & Ronald E. Mallen, *The Misguiding Hand of
Counsel-Reflections on "Criminal Malpractice,"* 21 UCLA L.Rev. 1191,
1191 n. 2 (1974).

2. Jury Instruction 12, Br. of Appellants, App. 3 (emphasis added). The
jury instructions were not included among the clerk's papers.

3. A number of jurisdictions "have imposed appellate, post conviction, or habeas relief, dependent upon attorney error, as a predicate to
recovery in a criminal malpractice action, when the claim is based on an
alleged deficiency for which appellate, post conviction, or habeas relief
would be available." *Berringer v. Steele,* 133 Md.App. 442, 758 A.2d 574,
597 (2000). *See, e.g., Shaw v. State,* 816 P.2d 1358, 1360 (Alaska 1991)
(*Shaw* I); *Stevens v. Bispham,* 316 Or. 221, 851 P.2d 556, 566 (1993);
Heck v. Humphrey, 512 U.S. 477, 486–87, 114 S.Ct. 2364, 129 L.Ed.2d
383 (1994); *Morgano v. Smith,* 110 Nev. 1025, 879 P.2d 735, 737 (1994);
Peeler v. Hughes Luce, 38 Tex. Sup.Ct. J. 1117, 909 S.W.2d 494, 495 (1995);
Adkins v. Dixon, 253 Va. 275, 482 S.E.2d 797, 801 (1997); *Steele v. Kehoe,*
24 Fla. L. Weekly S237, 747 So.2d 931, 933 (1999); *Coscia v. McKenna
Cuneo,* 25 Cal.4th 1194, 108 Cal.Rptr.2d 471, 25 P.3d 670, 674–75
(2001); *Canaan v. Bartee,* 276 Kan. 116, 72 P.3d 911, 916–21, *cert. denied,*
540 U.S. 1090, 124 S.Ct. 962, 157 L.Ed.2d 795 (2003).

(continues)

equated the innocence requirement with *legal* innocence.[4] Plainly, a requirement of legal innocence would have been redundant alongside the additional, unchallenged requirement of postconviction relief and would have necessitated a confusing overlay of standards of proof, requiring the malpractice jury to consider whether the Angs had proved by a preponderance of the evidence that they would not have been found guilty beyond a reasonable doubt in the underlying criminal trial. *See Wiley v. County of San Diego,* 19 Cal.4th 532, 79 Cal.Rptr.2d 672, 966 P.2d 983, 990 (1998) (observing that, as to dual standards of proof, "mental gymnastics required to reach an intelligent verdict would be difficult to comprehend much less execute").

Moreover, proving actual innocence, not simply legal innocence, is essential to proving proximate causation, both cause in fact and legal causation. *Falkner,* 108 Wash.App. at 115, 29 P.3d 771 (noting that criminal malpractice plaintiff must prove that "deficient representation, not his illegal acts, . . . [was] the proximate cause" of harm). Unless criminal malpractice plaintiffs can prove by a preponderance of the evidence their actual innocence of the charges, their own bad acts, not the alleged negligence of defense counsel, should be regarded as the cause in fact of their harm. Likewise, if criminal malpractice plaintiffs cannot prove their actual innocence under the civil standard, they will be unable to establish, in light of significant public policy considerations, that the alleged negligence of their defense counsel was the legal cause of their harm. Summarizing the policy concerns, the *Falkner* court observed that, "[r]equiring a defendant to prove by a preponderance of the evidence that he is innocent of the charges against him will prohibit criminals from benefiting from their own bad acts, maintain respect for our criminal justice systems procedural protections, remove the harmful chilling effect on the defense bar, prevent suits from criminals who may be guilty, [but] could have gotten a better deal, and prevent a flood of nuisance litigation."

---

4. *Falkner,* 108 Wash.App. at 123, 29 P.3d 771 (emphasis added). Many jurisdictions have imposed an actual innocence requirement. *See, e.g., State ex rel. O'Blennis v. Adolf,* 691 S.W.2d 498, 503 (Mo. App.1985); *Carmel v. Lunney,* 70 N.Y.2d 169, 518 N.Y.S.2d 605, 511 N.E.2d 1126, 1128 (1987); *Glenn v. Aiken,* 409 Mass. 699, 569 N.E.2d 783, 785–88 (1991); *Shaw* II, 861 P.2d at 572; *Bailey v. Tucker,* 533 Pa. 237, 621 A.2d 108, 113 (1993); *Wiley,* 79 Cal.Rptr.2d 672, 966 P.2d at 991; *Mahoney v. Shaheen, Cappiello, Stein Gordon, P.A.,* 143 N.H. 491, 727 A.2d 996, 998–99 (1999); *Rodriguez v. Nielsen,* 259 Neb. 264, 609 N.W.2d 368, 374–75 (2000); *Griffin v. Goldenhersh,* 323 Ill.App.3d 398, 257 Ill.Dec. 52, 752 N.E.2d 1232, 1238 (2001); *Schreiber v. Rowe,* 27 Fla. L. Weekly S248, 814 So.2d 396, 399 (2002); *Hicks v. Nunnery,* 253 Wis.2d 721, 643 N.W.2d 809, 823 (2002).

108 Wash.App. at 123–24, 29 P.3d 771 (footnotes omitted) (quoting *Stevens v. Bispham,* 316 Or. 221, 851 P.2d 556, 565 (1993)).

In the alternative, the Angs argue that, if a plaintiffs actual guilt or innocence has any place in a criminal malpractice suit, the issue should be raised as an affirmative defense, not as an element of the plaintiffs cause of action. The Angs find support in *Shaw* II, the only decision adopting the actual innocence requirement and shifting to the criminal malpractice defendant "the burden of proof by a preponderance of the evidence as to the actual guilt of the plaintiff." 861 P.2d at 572. As respondent Martin explained, however, "[t]he criminal defendant/malpractice plaintiff is in a far better position to bear the burden of establishing innocence," since, unlike his defense attorney, he "knows if he is actually innocent," "was, presumably, present or involved in the underlying events which led to the criminal charges," "has unlimited access to the information about his own acts necessary to prove innocence," "would know what, if any, inculpatory facts he withheld from his lawyer," and would have the "opportunity to accept a plea, potentially an *Alford* plea which could preserve his malpractice claim, before all facts and witness testimony have been developed or are known to his or her attorney." Suppl. Br. of Respt Martin at 13. We find this practical analysis persuasive and thus decline to adopt the minority position of *Shaw* II.

In sum, we conclude that the Angs were properly required to prove by a preponderance of the evidence that they were actually innocent of the underlying criminal charges. We therefore affirm the Court of Appeals.

Plaintiffs Challenge to Adequacy of Jury Instructions on Underlying Criminal Charges. Instructing the jury that the Angs were required to prove their innocence of the criminal charges, the court identified those charges as "Tax Fraud, Bank Fraud, False Statement, and Conspiracy." Jury Instruction 13, Br. of Appellants, App. 3. When the jury interrupted its deliberations to ask the court for the legal definitions of the charges, the court, in concert with counsel, advised the jury to "review carefully this Court's instructions and the evidence (testimony and exhibits) admitted into evidence." 27 Verbatim Report of Proceedings at 3822–30. (Among the exhibits admitted into evidence were the government's and plaintiffs' proposed jury instructions in the underlying criminal case.) Although the Angs counsel "readily agree[d]" to the courts response to the jurors question, the Angs now contend that the trial court should have instructed the jury on the elements of each of the charged crimes. *Id.* at 3823.

This issue was not adequately raised. In their opening brief below, none of the Angs' six assignments of

(continues)

error mentioned this alleged deficiency in the jury instructions, nor did any of their seven "issues pertaining to the assignments of error" address the trial court's failure to instruct the jury on the elements of the underlying criminal charges. RAP 10.3(a)(3). While the Angs' fifth issue was whether it was "error in the legal malpractice trial to give the jury no instructions as to how to determine the plaintiffs' 'innocence,'" the issue was tied to the first two assignments of error and therefore pertained to the definition of the innocence requirement in *Falkner* (that is, whether "innocence" meant actual or legal innocence). Br. of Appellants at 3. In any case, the Angs' brief contained no argument or citation to authority on the question of whether, in light of the jury's access to the proposed instructions from the criminal trial, jury instruction 13 was adequate. *See State v. Olson,* 126 Wash.2d 315, 321, 893 P.2d 629 (1995) (approving "proposition that when an appellant fails to raise an issue in the assignments of error, in violation of RAP 10.3(a)(3), *and* fails to present any argument on the issue or provide any legal

citation, an appellate court will not consider the merits of that issue"). The Angs incidental allusion (in a footnote in their opening brief) to the absence of "standard criminal law instructions" is inadequate to satisfy RAP 10.3(a)(3). *See* Br. of Appellants at 29 n. 5.

CONCLUSION

We conclude that, as plaintiffs in a criminal malpractice action, the Angs were properly required to prove by a preponderance of the evidence that they were actually innocent of the underlying criminal charges. We find no persuasive reasons for this court to follow the minority position and shift the burden to the defendant attorneys to prove that their former clients were actually guilty of the charged crimes. Finally, in light of RAP 10.3(a)(3) and prior precedent, which require an appellant to make "separate concise" assignments of error, tie those errors to legal issues, and argue those issues with some citation to authority, we decline to review the Angs' challenge to jury instruction 13. We affirm the Court of Appeals.

PUTTING IT INTO PRACTICE 9:1

1. Why did the clients pursue a claim against the lawyers that initially represented them?

2. What was the Plaintiff's burden of proof for a claim of negligent representation?

3. Was there sufficient evidence in the record to show that but for Hansen and Martin's alleged negligence, the clients would not have been damaged?

4. What damages did the clients suffer?

PUTTING IT INTO PRACTICE 9:2

1. Before, during, and after her mastectomy, Helen is transfused with blood. Some of the blood with which she is transfused is drawn from someone who is HIV-positive. As a result, Helen contracts and eventually succumbs to AIDS. Her estate sues the surgeon and her attending physician for negligence. The following is an excerpt from the testimony of the medical expert who testifies regarding the care of Helen's attending physician:

    To review, it is my opinion that Dr. Eck did not meet the standard of care for a family physician in the treatment of his patient, Helen Perpinka, from the time that she was discovered to be HTLV III (HIV) positive to the time that she was referred to an infectious disease specialist.... It is my opinion that because he chose not to refer Mrs. Perpinka to an infectious disease specialist that he undertook these awesome responsibilities on his own and he was ill-prepared to carry them out. This in all likelihood delayed the

(continues)

PUTTING IT INTO PRACTICE 9:2 (continued)

administration of anti-viral medication, which may have hastened the onset of opportunistic disease in Mrs. Perpinka and caused her illness to progress sooner than it might have.

Does Helen's estate have a viable claim for medical malpractice based on this testimony?

2. Following surgery for an enlarged prostate, Herman suffers from abdominal myoclonus, which results in violent, jerking abdominal contractions. His medical malpractice claim is dismissed because his attorney fails to make proper service of process. Herman is prepared to introduce expert medical testimony that the anesthesiologist's failure to wait for more than ten minutes before administering a second dose of anesthetic deviated from accepted practice and that the resulting overdose of anesthetic was the proximate cause of Herman's myoclonus. His medical expert will admit, however, that he has never previously seen a case of abdominal myoclonus, that he does not know of any reported cases of abdominal myoclonus caused by the spinal anesthetic used in this case, and that the studies he will rely upon (involving 65,000 cases) report only one or two cases of myoclonus, but only in the legs rather than in the abdomen. The doctor will also testify that abdominal myoclonus can occur spontaneously, without any drugs, trauma, or evidence of disease.

Do you think Herman will be able to prevail in a legal malpractice claim against the attorney, based on the failure to make proper service of process? (To answer this question you must decide whether the underlying medical malpractice claim is viable.)

NET NEWS

Links to several articles relating to the evaluation of medical malpractice cases and to working with medical experts are available at **http://www.lectlaw.com**.

SPECIALISTS

Specialists are held to a higher standard of care than generalists. They must adhere to the standard of the "reasonably careful and prudent specialist" in that field. Therefore, a neurosurgeon is held to the standard of care of the average neurosurgeon rather than the average physician. As a result, a specialist may be found negligent in a situation in which a general practitioner doing the same thing might not.

Specialists are typically required to adhere to a national standard of care in their field rather than a local one. The reasoning is that clients particularly seek out a specialist because they want someone who is aware of advances in the field. A pediatrician, for example, who failed to make a standard PKU test on a newborn was found negligent even though the hospitals in his community did not use such a test. Because these tests were in general use by pediatricians throughout the rest of the country, the defendant's conduct was held against the national standard of care and he was found negligent (*Naccarato v. Grob*, 180 N.W.2d 788 [Mich.1970]).

Attorneys are held to a general standard of care unless they present themselves as certified specialists. Those who advertise themselves as certified specialists are held to the standard of care of a specialist.

INFORMED CONSENT

Professionals have a **fiduciary relationship** with their clients in that the relationship is one of trust and confidence. Therefore, they have an obligation to disclose all relevant facts to their clients so that the clients can make informed decisions. The principle of autonomy underlying the doctrine of **informed consent** requires clients to be given ultimate dominion over their bodies and those events that affect their lives.

Particularly in the area of medical treatment, the issue of consent is very important. Certainly every human being has a right to determine what is to be done with her body, and no physician may force unwanted treatment on anyone. Under the doctrine of informed consent a physician has a duty to warn patients of possible hazards, complications, and expected and unexpected results of treatment, as well as risks of any alternative treatments. Particularly if a therapy is new or experimental, the physician has a duty to warn the patient that all side effects of the treatment are not completely known. The duty to warn increases as the probability or severity of risk to the patient increases. Any patient who is unaware of the inherent risk of a proposed procedure cannot voluntarily consent to that procedure.

If alternative treatments exist, a physician is obligated to advise a patient about those alternatives. Failure to explain an alternative may in itself constitute negligence. If a physician does not think that an alternative would work in a particular patient's case, however, she has no obligation to suggest that alternative. In emergency situations, when a patient is unconscious or so ill that he is unable to comprehend what is being said, the physician has a right to render treatment without informing the patient of the risks involved.

In determining what should and should not be disclosed to a patient, some courts look to the expectations of a reasonable layperson and ask what a patient in that position would reasonably need to know to make an informed decision. In the words of one court, informed consent should be judged by

whether the physician disclosed all those facts, risks and alternatives that a reasonable man in the situation which the physician knew or should have known to be the plaintiff's would deem significant in making a decision to undergo the recommended treatment. This gives maximum effect to the patient's right to be the arbiter of the medical treatment he will undergo without either requiring the physician to be a mindreader into the patient's most subjective thoughts or requiring that he disclose every risk lest he be liable. . . . The physician is bound to disclose only those risks which a reasonable man would consider material to his decision whether or not to undergo treatment. This standard creates no unreasonable burden for the physician. . . . This formulation has been described as the "prudent patient" standard. It attempts to reconcile the tension between the patient's right to self-determination and the physician's responsibility to exercise sound medical judgment. (*Cooper v. Roberts*, 286 A.2d 647 [Pa. 1971])

Under this standard the question boils down to whether a reasonable patient in that situation would

---

PUTTING IT INTO PRACTICE 9:3

1. Leslie has a CT scan under his doctor's orders. Prior to the test, he is given no information about the risks of the procedure, which include the injection of a contrast dye. He does answer routine questions by the hospital staff regarding allergies, illnesses, medications, and previous reactions to contrast materials. Later he develops thrombophlebitis at the site of the injection. Does Leslie have a valid claim based on lack of informed consent?

2. Hazel has a heart valve replacement. Before the surgery her doctor tells her that mechanical valves (like the Beall valve which is to be implanted in her) outlast natural-tissue valves. She is not told about the danger of the development of thromboemboli and strokes, nor about the need for a lifelong regimen of anticoagulants. After the surgery, Hazel suffers multiple episodes of thromboemboli, leaving her with severe, permanent brain damage. Later, a natural-tissue implant is used to replace the Beall valve. Does Hazel have a valid claim based on lack of informed consent?

have submitted to the procedure had she been advised of the risks involved.

Other courts rely on the "professional" standard, under which a physician must disclose only those risks and alternatives that the reasonable medical practitioner in the community would disclose under similar circumstances. Some consider this a paternalistic standard that leaves the choice to the medical community, rather than the patient, whose life is most intimately affected by the choices made.

Nature of Risk Involved

A physician must balance the need to provide information against the effect such information will have on the patient's morale. Studies show a close connection between a patient's mental state and his response to treatment, so physicians naturally want to avoid doing anything to jeopardize the healing process. If a risk is highly improbable, and if advising the patient of this risk would, in the physician's opinion, induce the patient to forego necessary treatment or would severely reduce the efficacy of any treatment, the physician is not required to disclose this information. If the probability of the risk is statistically high, however, the patient should be informed regardless of the effect it might have on his morale. Even if the probability of the risk is statistically low but the consequence is extremely severe, the patient should be informed. If the probability of harm is statistically low and its severity is relatively minor, the physician can tailor the warning to avoid unnecessarily exciting the patient.

BATTERY VERSUS NEGLIGENCE

Plaintiffs alleging lack of consent may sue on a theory of either battery or negligence (based on lack of informed consent). If a patient is in total ignorance of what is to be done, or if the physician obtains consent for one procedure and then performs another, an action for battery will lie. In the more typical case, however, the patient is aware of the procedure and in fact signs a consent form but does not clearly understand some of the risks inherent in the procedure. In this case a more appropriate cause of action is negligence. Today negligence has for the most part displaced battery as a basis for liability. The practical difference between the two theories is that if battery is alleged, lay witness testimony is sufficient. In cases of negligence, however, expert witnesses are required to testify to the standard of care and the fact that it was breached. Also, the statute of limitations for battery is typically longer than the statute for negligence.

If the cause of action is for negligence, the primary issue is whether the risks that were not disclosed were material risks. In determining what is and is not material, the courts consider the severity of the consequences and the probability of their occurrence, as well as the feasibility of any alternatives. The plaintiff is also required to prove that the outcome was a foreseeable risk and not an unpredictable consequence. If the risk pertaining to that outcome is remote, recovery will not be allowed.

CASE / **McQuitty v. Spangler**
976 A.2d 1020 (Md. 2009).

BATTAGLIA, J.

In this case we explore the boundaries of the doctrine of informed consent in the context of a healthcare provider's treatment of a patient. Petitioner, Peggy McQuitty, mother of Dylan McQuitty, who was born on May 8, 1995 with severe cerebral palsy, sued Dr. Donald Spangler in the Circuit Court for Baltimore County. In addition to alleging medical malpractice, Ms. McQuitty alleged that he breached his duty to obtain her informed consent to treatment, when he failed to inform her, after she consented to hospitalization and treatment

for a partial-placental-abruption,[1] of risks and available alternative treatments related to material changes in

1. A placental abruption has been described as follows:
The placenta is a structure that develops in the uterus during pregnancy to nourish the growing baby. If the placenta peels away from the inner wall of the uterus before delivery-either partially or completely-it's known as placental abruption. Placental abruption can deprive the baby of oxygen and nutrients and cause heavy bleeding in the mother. Left untreated, placental abruption puts both mother and baby in jeopardy.
Placental Abruption-Mayo Clinic.com, http:// www. mayo clinic. com/ health/placental-abruption/ DS 00623 (last visited July 16, 2009).

(continues)

her pregnancy, those being a second partial-placental-abruption, oligohydramnios,[2] and intrauterine growth restriction.[3]

During a trial in April of 2004, a jury returned a verdict in favor of Dr. Spangler on the medical malpractice claim, but could not reach a verdict on the informed consent claim. A second trial, only addressing the informed consent issue, took place in September of 2006, and the jury awarded the McQuittys $13,078,515.00 in damages. Dr. Spangler moved for judgment notwithstanding the verdict, which the trial judge granted, holding that, "it is well established in Maryland that the doctrine of informed consent pertains only to affirmative violations of the patient's physical integrity." The McQuittys appealed to the Court of Special Appeals, which, in an unpublished opinion, affirmed, on the same basis as that relied upon by the trial judge. The McQuittys petitioned this Court for certiorari, which we granted, *McQuitty v. Spangler*, 406 Md. 744, 962 A.2d 370 (2008), to address two questions, which we have reordered:

I.   Does an informed consent claim exist under Maryland law in the absence of damages caused by a battery committed by the physician?

II.   Does an informed consent claim exist under Maryland law where a physician withholds material information from his patient about changes in her medical status, which would have negated her consent to further delay in operative treatment, causing harm?[4]

---

2. At trial, oligohydramnios was identified as a condition describing significantly low levels of amniotic fluid that can lead to abnormal compression of the umbilical cord, resulting in harm to the fetus. The condition has been described accordingly:

Oligohydramnios is the condition of having too little amniotic fluid. Doctors can measure the amount of fluid through a few different methods, most commonly through amniotic fluid index (AFI) evaluation or deep pocket measurements. If an AFI shows a fluid level of less than 5 centimeters (or less than the 5th percentile), the absence of a fluid pocket 2–3 cm in depth, or a fluid volume of less than 500mL at 32–36 weeks gestation, then a diagnosis of oligohydramnios would be suspected. About 8% of pregnant women can have low levels of amniotic fluid, with about 4% being diagnosed with oligohydramnios. It can occur at any time during pregnancy, but it is most common during the last trimester. If a woman is past her due date by two weeks or more, she may be at risk for low amniotic fluid levels since fluids can decrease by half once she reaches 42 weeks gestation. Oligohydramnios can cause complications in about 12% of pregnancies that go past 41 weeks.

Low Amniotic Fluid Levels: Oligohydramnios: American Pregnancy Association, http://www.americanpregnancy.org/pregnancycomplications/lowamnioticfluidoligohydramnios.htm (last visited July 16, 2009).

3. At trial, testimony was elicited explaining that intrauterine growth restriction is a condition by which the fetus's growth is inhibited.

4. Because we conclude that an informed consent claim involves the duty to provide a patient with information material to a decision about whether to undergo or continue a treatment or procedure, including those involving a violation of the patient's physical integrity, we need not address the second question.

We shall hold that an informed consent claim may be asserted by a patient in the absence of a battery or affirmative violation of the patient's physical integrity, because it is the duty of a health care provider to inform a patient of material information, or information that a practitioner "knows or ought to know would be significant to a reasonable person in the patient's position in deciding whether or not to submit to a particular medical treatment or procedure." *Sard v. Hardy*, 281 Md. 432, 444, 379 A.2d 1014, 1022 (1977).

I. FACTS

We adopt the facts set forth by the Court of Special Appeals in its unreported opinion:

Peggy McQuitty was twenty-eight weeks pregnant when admitted to Franklin Square Hospital Center on March 30, 1995. While she was a patient at Franklin Square Hospital, Dr. Spangler, an obstetrician, was her primary attending physician. The physical complaint which brought her to the hospital was vaginal bleeding. Dr. Spangler ordered that an ultrasound be performed. That ultrasound revealed a partial placental abruption, which is a premature separation of the placenta from the uterus. This condition is irreversible and can lead to fetal death. There is no cure or treatment that will restore the function of that tissue once it has become detached from the uterus. And, the greater the extent or degree of placental separation, the greater the reduction of the perfusion of oxygen and nutrients to the fetus and the greater the risk of fetal morbidity.

Given Mrs. McQuitty's prior history of having delivered another child by Cesarean section, coupled with the presence of the partial abruption, Dr. Spangler concluded that Mrs. McQuitty could not safely deliver her child vaginally. He believed that for her to deliver a child at that stage would entail too great a risk that the placenta could separate completely from the uterus during labor, which would cause fetal death. Because Mrs. McQuitty had experienced only a partial abruption and as a consequence a portion of the placenta remained attached to the uterus and was functioning as of March 30, 1995, Dr. Spangler developed a plan to deliver the baby by Cesarean section at a later date. As part of his plan, Mrs. McQuitty was kept at the hospital from March 30, 1995, until Dylan was delivered thirty-nine days later on May 8, 1995.

The management plan adopted by Dr. Spangler included physically invasive actions, such as establishing intravenous access for the administration of intravenous fluids and medications; serial injections of Betamethasone, a corticosteroid, and other medications; the insertion of a

(continues)

urethral foley catheter for urine collection and analysis; and the performance of serial blood extractions for hematologic studies. After Dr. Spangler formulated the aforementioned plan, the only question was when the delivery would be performed.

The timing of the Cesarean section delivery, and the circumstances under which it would be performed, affected the relative risk to the unborn infant. Delaying an operative Cesarean section increased the risk of further separation of the placenta from the uterine wall, which was not predicable and, according to expert testimony introduced by the plaintiffs, "could occur at any time." Further, abruption of the placenta would leave the fetus with diminished oxygen, and a complete abruption would leave the fetus without a source of oxygen at all, and would lead to almost immediate death.

On the other hand, an immediate delivery by Cesarean section on March 30, 1995, posed a risk of fetal morbidity due to fetal lung immaturity. The risk associated with prematurity, however, would necessarily decrease over time, as the baby matured and as appropriate medical interventions were implemented. In addition, Mrs. McQuitty's pre-existing hypertension, coupled with the partial placental abruption, would tend to "stress" the fetus and accelerate the natural production of fetal surfactant, which over time would reduce the risk of respiratory difficulties associated with prematurity.

Dr. Spangler met with Mr. and Mrs. McQuitty after he diagnosed the partial placental abruption on March 30, 1995, and informed them that if the placenta continued to separate from the uterus, then the baby would have to be immediately delivered by Cesarean section. Based upon this information from Dr. Spangler, Mr. And Mrs. McQuitty understood that if their son were delivered by immediate Cesarean section on March 30, 1995, he would not likely survive.

The next day, Mrs. McQuitty's condition stabilized with a substantial decrease in the amount of vaginal bleeding. Based upon the information previously provided to her by Dr. Spangler, Mrs. McQuitty consented to Dr. Spangler's management and treatment plan, which was to delay the Cesarean section and otherwise to permit continued administration of intravenous fluids, medicines, etc.

Over the next few weeks, Mrs. McQuitty told Dr. Spangler that she wanted to return home. Dr. Spangler persuaded her not to leave because "there was a very slight possibility that what happened [on March 30, 1995] could happen again," and in light of the fact that the McQuittys lived fifty minutes away, it was important that she stay at the hospital. Mrs. McQuitty was under

the impression "that if something happened-even though it wasn't very likely-I was better off being in the hospital because that would-right off the bat they wouldn't have to wait for me to get there for fifty minutes." The plan, according to Mrs. McQuitty, was "barring any emergent situation," they would wait until she was thirty-six weeks along and test to see if Dylan's lungs were mature and then decide what to do.

On April 12, 1995, an ultrasound examination revealed evidence of a new and significant abruption. Although the medical records show that Mrs. McQuitty was informed of the abruption, she testified that she did not remember receiving such information. She testified that she would have remembered being told if she had been advised as to this type of problem with her pregnancy.

On April 28, 1995, another ultrasound revealed the development of an intrauterine growth restriction ("IUGR"). An IUGR develops as a direct result of the decreased perfusion of nutrients to the developing fetus resulting from an abruption. Fetuses that develop IUGR are at an increased risk for intrauterine fetal death, resulting from inadequate nutrition. The ultrasound examination also revealed that the infant's estimated fetal weight had fallen below the 10th percentile for his gestational age. Mrs. McQuitty acknowledged at trial that Dr. Spangler informed her of the IUGR. She claimed, however, that the explanation provided by Dr. Spangler was inadequate because it left her with the mistaken impression that the test simply revealed that her baby would be small. Accordingly, she believed that she simply needed to eat more and drink milk shakes. Even in light of the latest ultrasound findings Dr. Spangler did not offer Mrs. McQuitty the option of having an immediate Cesarean section on April 28, 1995.

On May 3, 1995, an ultrasound examination revealed a significantly low level of amniotic fluid, a condition known as oligohydramnios. Because amniotic fluids act as a buffer against incidental or abnormal compression of the umbilical cord, a significantly low level of amniotic fluid presents the risk of harm to the fetus. Mrs. McQuitty alleges that Dr. Spangler only told her that the test revealed that the baby was not doing well and that it would be necessary to take her to labor and delivery immediately. Shortly thereafter, however, Dr. Spangler told Mrs. McQuitty that the baby would not be delivered that day and that she was to return to her room and drink plenty of water because her fluid level was low. Mrs. McQuitty asked Dr. Spangler "can't we please just get this baby out?" She then told her doctor, "I have been here for four or five weeks. Everything is apparently fine. I am

(continues)

tired of being here. I want to go home. I want to be with my husband and my daughter. Please take this baby." Dr. Spangler replied that the longer that she could keep the baby, the better off the infant would be.

Mrs. McQuitty experienced a complete abruption on May 8, 1995, requiring an immediate emergency Cesarean section. . . .

The doctrine of informed consent, which we shall apply here, follows logically from the universally recognized rule that a physician, treating a mentally competent adult under non-emergency circumstances, cannot properly undertake to perform surgery or administer other therapy without the prior consent of his patient.

Id. at 438–39, 379 A.2d at 1019. We recognized that the obligation to obtain consent evolved over the course of the twentieth century into an obligation to obtain "informed" consent, primarily to enable the patient to make an informed choice about a particular therapy or procedure so that healthcare providers did not substitute their own judgment for that of the patient's:

> The law does not allow a physician to substitute his judgment for that of the patient in the matter of consent to treatment.

See *Sard*, at 340, 379 A.2d at 1020, citing *Collins v. Itoh*, 160 Mont. 461, 503 P.2d 36, 40 (1972) ("The law will not allow a physician to substitute his own judgment, no matter how well founded, for that of his patient."). Thus, we recognized that personal autonomy and personal choice were the primary foundations of the informed consent doctrine.

In explicating the boundaries of the duty of informed consent, we began with the doctrine's "general principles." Importantly, we acknowledged that the duty to provide information extended not only to a patient's ailment or condition, but also to "the nature of the proposed treatment, the probability of success of the contemplated therapy and its alternatives, and the risk of unfortunate consequences associated with such treatment":

> Simply stated, the doctrine of informed consent imposes on a physician, before he subjects his patient to medical treatment, the duty to explain the procedure to the patient and to warn him of any material risks or dangers inherent in or collateral to the therapy, so as to enable the patient to make an intelligent and informed choice about whether or not to undergo such treatment. *Salgo v. Leland Stanford Jr. Univ. Bd. of Trustees*, 154 Cal.App.2d 560, 317 P.2d

170, 181 (1957); *Bang v. Charles T. Miller Hospital*, 251 Minn. 427, 88 N.W.2d 186, 190 (1958); *Scaria v. St. Paul Fire & Marine Ins. Co.*, 68 Wis.2d 1, 227 N.W.2d 647, 654 (1975).

This duty to disclose is said to require a physician to reveal to his patient the nature of the ailment, the nature of the proposed treatment, the probability of success of the contemplated therapy and its alternatives, and the risk of unfortunate consequences associated with such treatment. *Natanson v. Kline*, 186 Kan. 393, 350 P.2d 1093, 1106, rehearing denied, 187 Kan. 186, 354 P.2d 670 (1960); *Scaria v. St. Paul Fire & Marine Ins. Co.*, 227 N.W.2d at 653; 2 D. Louisell & H. Williams, Medical Malpractice § 22.01 (1973).

Id. at 439–40, 379 A.2d at 1020 (emphasis added). We admonished, however, that a healthcare provider "is not burdened with the duty of divulging all risks, but only those which are material to the intelligent decision of a reasonably prudent patient." Id. at 444, 379 A.2d at 1022 (emphasis in original). In so stating, we adopted a "general or lay standard of reasonableness," under which "the scope of the physician's duty to inform is to be measured by the materiality of the information to the decision of the patient." Id. We defined material information as information "which a physician knows or ought to know would be significant to a reasonable person in the patient's position in deciding whether or not to submit to a particular medical treatment or procedure." Id. We explained that the "materiality test" was the best measure of a healthcare provider's duty to provide information, because, "[b]y focusing on the patient's need to obtain information . . . the materiality test promotes the paramount purpose of the informed consent doctrine- to vindicate the patient's right to determine what shall be done with his own body and when." Id. (emphasis added). Applying these standards, we ultimately held that Mrs. Sard had stated a viable cause of action for breach of informed consent, and that it was for the jury to determine whether a two-percent risk of a failed sterilization procedure was a material risk.

The gravamen of an informed consent claim, therefore, is a healthcare provider's duty to communicate information to enable a patient to make an intelligent and informed choice, after full and frank disclosure of material risk information and the benefit of data regarding a proposed course of medical treatment. Sard did not limit a healthcare provider's duty to disclose material information to the type of proposed treatment: i.e., whether the proposed treatment or therapy was or was not surgical or physically invasive in nature. See

(continues)

id. at 440, 379 A.2d at 1020 ("This duty [of informed consent] is said to require a physician to reveal to his patient the nature of the ailment, the nature of the proposed treatment, the probability of success of the contemplated therapy and its alternatives, and the risk of unfortunate consequences associated with such treatment.").

What has confused the understanding of the doctrine of informed consent, nevertheless, is the apparent introduction of a physical invasion requirement in *Reed*, 332 Md. at 242–43, 630 A.2d at 1153. In that case, when attempting to distinguish a failure to recommend or instruct about a diagnostic procedure from a failure to obtain informed consent, we cited the New York case of *Karlsons v. Guerinot*, 57 A.D.2d 73, 394 N.Y.S.2d 933 (N.Y.App.Div.1977). In so doing, we shifted the focus of the doctrine of informed consent from a healthcare provider's duty to divulge material information to a patient to the act undertaken by the provider.

In *Reed*, a mother brought wrongful birth and breach of informed consent actions against her physician in federal district court, alleging that her physician failed to diagnose the possibility of neural tube defects in utero, which are genetically caused; that her child was born with deformities as a result of the defects; and that she would have had an abortion had she known of the in utero condition. Two certified questions were forwarded to us,[7] the second of which pertained to informed consent:[8]

> "ii. Whether the continuation of a pregnancy is a decision requiring the informed consent of the patient which can give rise to a Maryland tort cause of action for lack of informed consent when the allegedly negligent course of treatment is the

defendant physician's failure to inform a pregnant patient about the availability, risks and benefits of diagnostic testing which might reveal birth defects, and failure to inform the patient about the benefits and risks associated with aborting a severely deformed fetus."

Id. at 228, 630 A.2d at 1146, quoting *Reed v. Campagnolo*, 810 F.Supp. 167, 172–73 (D.Md.1993). We answered that "informed consent must be to some treatment," and that because here, "the defendants never proposed that the tests be done," the "defendants . . . duty to offer or recommend the tests [had to be] analyzed in relation to the professional standard of care." Id. at 241, 630 A.2d at 1152.

In attempting to elucidate the distinction between informing a patient about a proposed treatment, implicating the doctrine of informed consent, and failing to recommend a diagnostic test, implicating a medical malpractice claim, we cited *Karlsons*, 57 A.D.2d at 73, 394 N.Y.S.2d 933, in which the New York intermediate appellate court stated that an informed consent claim could not lie absent "an affirmative violation of the patient's physical integrity":

> "[A] cause of action based upon [the doctrine of informed consent] exists only where the injury suffered arises from an affirmative violation of the patient's physical integrity and, where nondisclosure of risks is concerned, these risks are directly related to such affirmative treatment. Here, the resultant harm did not arise out of any affirmative violation of the mother's physical integrity. Furthermore, the alleged undisclosed risks did not relate to any affirmative treatment but rather to the condition of pregnancy itself. Allegations such as these have traditionally formed the basis of actions in medical malpractice and not informed consent."

Id. at 242–43, 630 A.2d at 1153, quoting *Karlsons*, 57 A.D.2d at 82, 394 N.Y.S.2d 933 (internal citations omitted). *Karlsons'* articulation of an affirmative physical invasion requirement was premised upon the understanding that an informed consent claim sounded in assault or battery, rather than negligence:

> The cause of action is not based on any theory of negligence but is an offshoot of the law of assault and battery. Any nonconsensual touching of a patient's body, absent an emergency, is a battery and the theory is that an uninformed consent to surgery obtained from a patient lacking knowledge of the dangers inherent in the procedure is no consent at all.

---

7. The certified questions were reviewed pursuant to Sections 12–601 through 12–609 of the Courts and Judicial Proceedings Article, Maryland Code (1974, 1989 Repl.Vol.), under the Maryland Uniform Certification of Questions of Law Act.

8. The Reeds specifically alleged that Dr. Campagnolo failed to inform them about possible diagnostic tests that were available to them: "[D]efendants failed in the course of pre-natal care to 'inform plaintiffs of the existence or need for routine [a-fetoprotein] ("AFP") testing of maternal serum to detect serious birth defects such as spina bifida and imperforate anus.' Had they been informed about AFP testing they would have requested it. Had such testing been done, it would have revealed elevated protein levels, indicative of an abnormal fetus, which would have led plaintiffs to request amniocentesis. Amniocentesis, claim plaintiffs, would have revealed the extent of the fetus's defects and plaintiffs ultimately would have chosen to terminate the pregnancy."
Reed v. Campagnolo, 332 Md. 226, 229, 630 A.2d at 1146 (1993), quoting *Reed v. Campagnolo*, 810 F.Supp. 167, 169 (D.Md.1993).

(continues)

Karlsons, 57 A.D.2d at 81–82, 394 N.Y.S.2d 933.[9]

In *Reed,* however, we ultimately concluded, after citing, but not relying on Karlsons, that a failure to offer or recommend diagnostic tests should be analyzed under a healthcare provider's duty to provide an acceptable standard of care, not under a duty to obtain informed consent:

> Whether the defendants had a duty to offer or recommend the tests is analyzed in relation to the professional standard of care. Application of that standard may or may not produce a result identical with the informed consent criterion of what reasonable persons, in the same circumstances as the Reeds, would want to know.

Id. at 241, 630 A.2d at 1152–53. Physical invasion was not articulated as a basis.

---

9. Within three years of the decision in Karlsons, the same New York appellate court, without referring to Karlsons, held that an informed consent claim is predicated on negligence rather than on battery or assault. In *Dries v. Gregor,* 72 A.D.2d 231, 234–36, 424 N.Y.S.2d 561 (N.Y.App.Div.1980), the court acknowledged that consent actions at common law could lie both in battery (trespass vi et armis) and in negligence (trespass on the case), and that modern claims involving informed consent, absent the performance of an invasive procedure wholly without a patient's consent, are actions sounding in negligence:

The theory of lack of informed consent in medical malpractice actions presents conceptual difficulties arising from the awkward mixture of assault and battery in a suit based upon negligence. A brief look at their ancestry clarifies their differences. Assault and battery is a descendant of the early English common-law action of trespass. Negligence, on the other hand, traces its ancestry back to another ancient common-law writ titled an action of trespass on the case. Originally they were related to each other. The older action of trespass developed new variations which became separate forms of action. One variety was "upon a special case" or, later, simply "trespass on the case." (Plucknett, A Concise History of the Common Law [2d ed], pp 335, 336.). Trespass was the remedy for direct injuries and trespass on the case for indirect injuries. These common-law actions have now been abandoned in modern practice, particularly the artificial classification of injuries as direct or indirect. The law today looks instead to the intent of the wrongdoer or to his negligence. In their evolution the action of trespass remained as the remedy for all intentional wrongs and action on the case was extended to include injuries which were not intended but were merely negligently inflicted (Prosser, Law of Torts [4th ed], § 7, p 28). Trespass on the case . . . had become distinct from trespass by 1390, and as early as the 16th century had evolved as the remedy for libel and slander, negligence and deceit (Plucknett, A Concise History of the Common Law [2d ed], p 336). Battery remains by definition an intentional tort, just as its progenitor trespass.

Negligence as the direct descendant of trespass on the case has a different conceptual basis than battery because negligence includes those unintended wrongs which one actor causes to another.

From a practical standpoint, the conduct of the parties should be measured by a negligence analysis in both "informed consent" and "negligent" malpractice actions.

Id. at 234–36, 424 N.Y.S.2d 561.

Recently, the New York intermediate appellate court seemingly permitted an informed consent claim to be pursued that was not premised on a surgical procedure. See *Cicione v. Meyer,* 33 A.D.3d 646, 823 N.Y.S.2d 173 (N.Y.App.Div.2006).

Our citation to Karlsons in *Reed* has been viewed as introducing an element of affirmative physical invasion or battery into an informed consent doctrine predicated on negligence in a few subsequent decisions. See, e.g., *Landon,* 389 Md. at 230–31, 884 A.2d at 156 (holding that trial judge properly denied a request for a jury instruction on informed consent, because prescribing a CAT scan did not involve an affirmative violation of the patient's physical integrity); *Arrabal v. Crew-Taylor,* 159 Md.App. 668, 862 A.2d 431 (2004) (applying the physical invasion standard when holding that an informed consent action could not lie).

Viewed with the benefit of hindsight, our reference to Karlsons deviated from our common law roots, as well as from cases in which we have explicitly stated that an allegation of lack of informed consent sounds in negligence, as opposed to battery or assault, in direct contravention to Karlsons. In this regard, the case of *Slater v. Baker & Stapleton,* 95 Eng. Reports 860 (K.B.1767), which has been incorporated into the common law of this state under Article V of the Maryland Constitution Declaration of Rights,[10] illustrates that, as early as 1767, an action for lack of consent could be pled on the case, the precursor to negligence, as opposed to trespass vi et armis or battery.[11] See Black's Law Dictionary 1542

---

10. Article V of the Maryland Declaration of Rights, states, in pertinent part that, "the Inhabitants of Maryland are entitled to the Common Law of England . . . according to the course of that Law, and to the benefit of such of the English statutes as existed on the Fourth day of July, seventeen hundred and seventy-six."

11. We recently discussed the historical change from pleading in form to fact-based pleading in *Khalifa v. Shannon,* 404 Md. 107, 128–29, 945 A.2d 1244, 1256–57 (2008) ("When pleading was by form rather than by fact, a cause of action had to be alleged within the narrow constructs of predefined pleadings forms."), and *Ver Brycke v. Ver Brycke,* 379 Md. 669, 696, 843 A.2d 758, 773 (2004) ("We repeatedly have stated that the strictures of common law pleading, whereby the causes of action pled define the action, have been replaced by fact-based pleading so that remedies sought serve to delineate the type of action, whether it be in law or equity.").

In Khalifa, 404 Md. at 128–29, 945 A.2d at 1256–57 (2008), we also distinguished actions on the case from actions trespass vi et armis, quoting the following passage from 1 John P. Poe, Pleading and Practice in Courts of Common Law 115 (5th ed.1925) (italics in original):

Trespass [vi et armis] lies to recover damages for an injury committed with force, either actual or implied by law, where the injury is direct and immediate, and where it is committed either upon the person of the plaintiff, or upon his tangible and corporeal property, whether real or personal. Case, on the other hand, lies to recover damages for any wrong or cause of complaint to which covenant, assumpsit or trespass will not apply. Or to adopt another definition, more sharply contrasting it with trespass, it lies generally to recover damages for torts not committed with force, actual or implied; or, if committed with force, where the injury is not immediate but consequential; or, where the matter effected is not tangible. . . . An injury is considered immediate where it is occasioned by the act complained of itself, and not merely by a consequence of that act. In all other cases it is consequential.

(continues)

(18th ed. 2004) (Trespass on the case "was the precursor to a variety of modern-day tort claims, including negligence. . . ."); 1 John P. Poe, Pleading and Practice in Courts of Common Law 154–55 (3rd ed. 1897); see also Paul Mark Sandler & James K. Archibald, Pleading Causes of Action in Maryland, at Prologue xx (3rd ed.2004) (same). In *Slater,* Slater brought an action against Baker, the surgeon, and Stapleton, the apothecary, as a special action upon the case, alleging that they treated his broken leg with an experimental device, to which he did not consent. After Slater was awarded damages by a jury, Baker and Stapleton argued before the King's Bench that Slater's award of damages could not stand because Slater had not pled his action correctly: i.e., he should have pled it as a trespass vi et armis or battery rather than as a special action on the case or negligence. In a per curiam opinion, the King's Bench disagreed, holding that a lack of consent claim could be brought as a special action upon the case. In so holding, the court recognized that the gravamen of a lack of consent claim is a physician's duty, according to the "law of surgeons," to obtain a patient's consent to treatment:

> 2dly, it was objected that the evidence given does not apply to this action . . . the evidence is, that the callous of the leg was broke without the plaintiff's consent; but there is no evidence of ignorance or want of skill, and therefore the action ought to have been trespass vi & armis for breaking the plaintiff's leg without his consent. All the surgeons said they never do any thing of this kind without consent,
>
> In answer to this, it appears from the evidence of the surgeons that it was improper to disunite the callous without consent; this is the usage and law of surgeons: then it was ignorance and unskilfulness in that very particular, to do contrary to the rule of the profession, what no surgeon ought to have done; and indeed it is reasonable that a patient should be told what is about to be done to him, that he may take courage and put himself in such a situation as to enable him to undergo the operation. It was objected, this verdict and recovery cannot be pleaded in [case] to an action of trespass vi & armis to be brought for the same damage; but we are clear of opinion it may be pleaded in [case].

Id. at 862 (emphasis added). Thus, Slater was permitted to pursue his lack of consent action against Baker and Stapleton as a special action upon the case.

In *Sard* and its progeny, moreover, we repeatedly and explicitly have held that lack of informed consent sounds in "negligence, as opposed to battery or assault." *Sard,* 281 Md. at 440 n. 4, 379 A.2d at 1020 n. 4 ("We note in passing our approval of the prevailing view that a cause of

action under the informed consent doctrine is properly cast as a tort action for negligence, as opposed to battery or assault."). See, e.g., *Goldberg v. Boone,* 396 Md. 94, 122–27, 912 A.2d 698, 714–17 (2006) (holding that a trial judge was correct to permit a lack of informed consent instruction to go to the jury when evidence was produced that the physician failed in his duty to inform patient that there were other more experienced surgeons that could perform the necessary procedure); *Mole v. Jutton,* 381 Md. 27, 47, 846 A.2d 1035, 1046–47 (2004); *Dingle v. Belin,* 358 Md. 354, 359, 749 A.2d 157, 159 (2000) (recognizing, in a case where a patient alleged that she did not consent to performance of gall bladder surgery by a resident physician, that a lack of informed consent action is negligence-based); *Wright v. Johns Hopkins Health Sys. Corp.,* 353 Md. 568, 595 n. 16, 728 A.2d 166, 179 n. 16 (1999) ("Wright's parents' cause of action for lack of informed consent is properly a cause of action for negligence."); *Faya,* 329 Md. at 435, 620 A.2d at 327.

In our recent case, *Mole v. Jutton,* 381 Md. at 45, 47, 846 A.2d at 1046–47, a patient brought an informed consent action against her surgeon, alleging negligence and battery, when her surgeon cut her milk ducts when removing two cysts in her breast. At the close of evidence, the trial judge instructed the jury regarding negligence, related to the doctor's failure to inform Ms. Mole of the risk of cutting the ducts, but refused to instruct on battery. The jury awarded Ms. Mole $22,500 in actual damages, but she, nevertheless, appealed, arguing that it was error for the trial judge to refuse to instruct on battery. We granted certiorari prior to any proceedings in the intermediate appellate court and affirmed. In so doing, we reemphasized that an informed consent action sounds in negligence, rather than in battery, and that a battery action is limited to certain circumstances:

> A claim under the informed consent doctrine must be pled as a tort action for negligence, rather than as one for battery or assault.
>
> "The battery theory should be reserved for those circumstances when a doctor performs an operation to which the patient has not consented. . . . However, when the patient consents to certain treatment and the doctor performs that treatment but an undisclosed inherent complication with a low probability occurs, no intentional deviation from the consent given appears. . . . In that situation the action should be pleaded in negligence."

Id., 381 Md. at 39, 47, 846 A.2d at 1042, 1046–47, quoting *Cobbs v. Grant,* 8 Cal.3d 229, 104 Cal.Rptr. 505, 502 P.2d 1, 8 (1972) (citations omitted).

In *Faya v. Almaraz,* 329 Md. at 435, 620 A.2d at 327, moreover, we elucidated that information provided to

(continues)

(or withheld from) a patient is the crux of an informed consent action and that the action is to be analyzed using the negligence rubric. In that case, Dr. Almaraz was infected with the AIDS virus and operated on numerous patients, including Ms. Faya, without disclosing that he was infected with the disease. Upon learning of Almaraz's condition, patients sued, alleging breach of informed consent, but the trial judge dismissed for failure to state a claim upon which relief could be granted. The patients appealed, and we granted certiorari prior to any proceedings in the Court of Special Appeals and reversed, holding that the patients had alleged sufficient facts to support a claim of negligence. In reaching this conclusion, we applied each element of the negligence four-part rubric to the plaintiffs' actions, id. at 448, 620 A.2d at 333 ("To state a cause of action in negligence, a plaintiff must allege that the defendant had a duty of care which he breached, and that the breach proximately caused legally cognizable injury"), and held that the patients validly had alleged facts to support a cause of action for breach of informed consent because they had asserted that Dr. Almaraz withheld information that was material to their assessments of the risks and benefits prior to his engaging in a treatment or a procedure. See id. at 450, 620 A.2d at 334. In so holding, we relied on Sard and were explicit that the patients' complaint was not that Dr. Almaraz had acted negligently when performing the operation, but that he was negligent in failing to provide them with information material to an effective risk-benefit analysis:

> Thus, in evaluating the well-pleaded allegations of the complaints with respect to the duty component of the tort of negligence, we cannot conclude that they are legally insufficient to survive the appellees' motions to dismiss; in other words, we cannot say as a matter of law that no duty was imposed upon Dr. Almaraz to warn the appellants of his infected condition or refrain from operating upon them.[6]

The cause of action for lack of informed consent is one in tort for negligence, as opposed to battery or assault. Id. at 440 n. 4, 379 A.2d 1014. Id. at 450 & n. 6, 620 A.2d at 334 & n. 6. Thus, the development of our jurisprudence has elucidated that a lack of informed consent claim is clearly predicated on negligence and the gravamen is the healthcare provider's duty to provide information, rather than battery or the provider's physical act.

Finally, requiring a physical invasion to sustain an informed consent claim contravenes the very foundation of the informed consent doctrine-to promote a patient's choice. In Sard we emphasized that, "the paramount purpose of the doctrine of informed consent [is] to vindicate the patient's right to determine what shall be done with [her] body and when," Sard, 281 Md. at 444, 379 A.2d at 1022, and that a healthcare provider's duty to obtain a patient's informed consent is "to enable . . . the choice about whether or not to undergo . . . treatment." Id. at 440, 379 A.2d at 1020 (emphasis added). When describing the scope of that duty, we held that a healthcare provider has a duty to inform of those risks "which are material to the intelligent decision of a reasonably prudent patient." Id. at 444, 379 A.2d at 1022. In other contexts, we have spoken of a patient's right to withdraw her consent to treatment at any time. See Wright, 353 Md. at 572, 728 A.2d at 168 ("Under Maryland common law, a competent adult has the right to refuse medical treatment and to withdraw consent to medical treatment once begun. . . . This right is a corollary to the common law doctrine of informed consent."). An affirmative physical invasion requirement countermands a patient's choice by permitting the healthcare provider to make treatment decisions, in lieu of patient involvement in the healthcare choice. This rationale also has been articulated by a New Jersey appellate court, when, in an informed consent case, it stated:

> Conventional medical judgments during the course of treatment remain for the physician to make, subject to ordinary malpractice controls. But determinations bearing upon which course of treatment to adopt are the capable patient's prerogative, assisted by as much information and advice as the physician may reasonably be able to furnish. This is especially so not only where considerations of medical risk and benefit are involved in the choice of treatment, but also where lifestyle choices and other considerations of personal autonomy are implicated. To the extent the physician has a view as to which of the reasonably available alternative courses of treatment is the best in the circumstances as a matter of medical judgment, the physician must also give the patient the benefit of a recommendation. There is no

---

6. We noted in *Sard v. Hardy*, 281 Md. 432, 379 A.2d 1014 (1977), that a surgeon has a legal duty, except in emergency circumstances, to obtain the "informed consent" of the patient before undertaking the surgical procedure. We said that the surgeon's duty is "to explain the procedure to the patient and to warn him of any material risks or dangers inherent in or collateral to the therapy, so as to enable the patient to make an intelligent and informed choice about whether or not to undergo such treatment." Id. at 439, 379 A.2d 1014. We further said that the proper test for measuring a physician's duty to disclose risk information is whether such data would be material to the patient's decision. Id. at 443, 379 A.2d 1014. In this regard, we explained that "[a] material risk is one which a physician knows or ought to know would be significant to a reasonable person in the patient's position in deciding whether or not to submit to a particular medical treatment or procedure." Id. at 444, 379 A.2d 1014.

(continues)

reasonable basis for the apprehension, as expressed by defendant in argument before the trial judge, that the physician will ever be required to perform surgery or administer any other course of treatment that he or she believes to be contraindicated. If the patient selects a course, even from among reasonable alternatives, which the physician regards as inappropriate or disagreeable, the physician is free to refuse to participate and to withdraw from the case upon providing reasonable assurances that basic treatment and care will continue. In such circumstances, there can be no liability for the refusal.

Matthies v. Mastromonaco, 310 N.J.Super. 572, 709 A.2d 238, 253 (1998).

In the present case, we are reviewing the grant of judgment notwithstanding the verdict premised upon the requirement of a physical invasion. We hold today that this is not a requirement to sustain an informed consent claim. As a result, the case will be remanded to the trial court for consideration of the remittitur motion filed by Dr. Spangler, which was not decided.

JUDGMENT OF THE COURT OF SPECIAL APPEALS REVERSED. CASE REMANDED TO THAT COURT WITH INSTRUCTIONS TO REVERSE THE JUDGMENT OF THE CIRCUIT COURT FOR BALTIMORE COUNTY AND TO REMAND THE CASE TO THE CIRCUIT COURT FOR PROCEEDINGS NOT INCONSISTENT WITH THIS OPINION. COSTS IN THIS COURT AND IN THE COURT OF SPECIAL APPEALS TO BE PAID BY RESPONDENT.

Judge GREENE joins in the judgment only.

PUTTING IT INTO PRACTICE   9:4

Patricia is under the care of a doctor for the treatment of trichomonas vaginitis, an infection of the female reproductive tract. She is admitted to the hospital and treated intravenously with the antibiotic Flagyl. She develops peripheral neuropathy as a result of the Flagyl treatment and argues that her doctor failed to inform her of the risks of this antibiotic. Does the doctrine of informed consent apply to the intravenous administration of a therapeutic drug in a state that has a battery standard rather than a negligence standard for informed consent?

DEFENSES TO PROFESSIONAL NEGLIGENCE

A plaintiff attempting to prove professional negligence must prove both the standard of care expected within the profession and the defendant's deviation from that standard. To do this requires expert testimony, which is usually provided by a professional in that same area of practice. If the defendant is a specialist, the expert is typically a specialist in the same area. The expert witness must also be familiar with the procedures or techniques used in the case, although she need not follow the same practices. In courts that follow the locality rule, the expert must be familiar with the standard of care in the relevant community or similar communities. The plaintiff also has the burden of proving that his injuries, more probably than not, resulted from the negligence of the professional.

The professional can then choose either to refute the plaintiff's factual allegations of negligence or to raise the affirmative defenses of contributory negligence, comparative negligence, or assumption of risk. To allege contributory negligence, the defendant must show that the plaintiff's negligence was concurrent with his own. If the plaintiff's negligence merely added to the effects of the defendant's negligence, the defendant will not be relieved of liability. The damages awarded to the plaintiff, however, may be reduced. Exhibit 9–2 lists defenses to the charge of professional negligence.

EXHIBIT 9–2   Defenses to Professional Negligence

- Rebut plaintiff's factual allegations.
- Prove plaintiff was negligent and that plaintiff's negligence was concurrent with professional's.
- Prove plaintiff assumed the risk by knowingly and voluntarily consenting to risks involved in treatment.
- Prove state of emergency (in medical situations).

Contributory Negligence

Typically, when the defense of contributory negligence is raised, the defendant argues that the client refused to comply with her instructions or was otherwise uncooperative. If a client lies to his attorney about the facts of the case, he cannot later claim that the attorney was negligent, because the attorney relied on the client's veracity in making strategic decisions. If, however, the client's negligence merely compounded the attorney's negligence, the attorney will remain liable and the plaintiff's damages will simply be reduced. In the medical arena, a physician may argue that the patient contributed to her injuries by delaying so long in seeking medical attention that the condition became untreatable. The physician would then have to prove that the untoward effects suffered by the patient were the sole result of the patient's procrastination and that the physician was not in any way negligent himself.

Assumption of Risk

Related to the issue of informed consent is the doctrine of assumption of risk. A patient who understands the risk involved in treatment and knowingly consents to that treatment can be said to have assumed the risk. Of course, if those risks are not carefully explained or the plaintiff does not clearly understand them, this defense is inapplicable. No client can assume the risk of negligent care. For example, a physician who advises a patient regarding the risk involved if given improper care and then provides improper care cannot claim that the patient assumed the risk.

Emergency Situations

In medical situations the defense of emergency can also be used. Treatment given during a life-and-death emergency is not required to be of the same level of care as that provided under less stressful circumstances. If death is imminent and treatment is absolutely necessary for the patient's protection, the defense of emergency may be a viable defense to a claim of negligent treatment. A patient who suffers brain damage subsequent to being treated for a cardiac arrest, for example, may file a negligence claim for her damages, but will most likely meet with the defense of emergency. However, if the emergency is caused by the physician's negligence, he cannot use it as a defense. The physician in such cases bears the burden of proving that an emergency in fact existed and that it was not due to any fault of his.

What constitutes adequate care in an emergency depends on the circumstances in which the emergency occurs. A doctor intent on treating a severe head injury who fails to notice a fractured arm may or may not be considered negligent for her failure to diagnose the fracture. Such a question would be submitted to the jury for its determination of whether the doctor's conduct conformed to the expectations for a reasonable doctor working under those conditions.

MAINTAINING ADEQUATE RECORDS

Maintenance of adequate records on a client's case may be of critical importance in proving that no negligence occurred. Professionals should therefore allocate time for the completion of such records even though it may seem a frivolous expenditure of valuable time when being done. The passage of time weakens our memories. Therefore, a professional confronted with a lawsuit one, two, or more years after he has last seen the client may not remember anything about the case. He will be grateful in that circumstance if he can locate records that can be used to refresh his recollection and that he can use to establish his defense. Of course, such records can also be used to build the plaintiff's case.

Acquiring medical records may present a problem, because the physical record itself is considered the property of the health care provider. The content of the record, however, is usually considered to be the patient's property, so if the patient will waive the physician-patient privilege, most state laws require that the record be released to her. Trial courts have uniformly ordered the release of such records. In a personal injury case in which the plaintiff has made her medical problems the subject of litigation, all relevant medical records are subject to subpoena by the defendant. If the defendant professional, for example, claims that the plaintiff's injuries preceded the damages the plaintiff alleges were caused by the defendant, the defendant has a right to subpoena the records of physicians who previously treated the plaintiff for related complaints.

UNDERLYING CAUSES OF PROFESSIONAL NEGLIGENCE SUITS

Professional negligence claims appear to be on the rise, particularly those involving attorneys. Mandatory continuing legal education programs in almost every state and the increasing cost of malpractice insurance premiums attest to the increased incidence of professional negligence suits against attorneys.

As of 1992, malpractice claims cost lawyers and their insurers over $4 billion each year, and these costs were projected to increase, according to Robert O'Malley of Attorneys' Liability Assurance Society, the nation's largest malpractice insurance carrier. The annual claims for doctors is on par with that for attorneys, although the per-capita amount paid for malpractice claims is significantly higher for lawyers than doctors (because at least 40 percent of the nation's lawyers are uninsured). Although much press has been devoted to exorbitant jury awards, legal malpractice costs are greater than what is collected annually from punitive and compensatory damages awarded by juries nationwide (in 1992 about $5.8 billion was awarded in total damages by juries, of which approximately $580 million was due to punitive damages). The reported number of malpractice claims represents only the tip of the iceberg; it is estimated that only 10 percent of legal malpractice ever becomes an insurance claim. (For references to the statistics cited here and for further reading, see Manuel Ramos, "Legal Malpractice: Reforming Lawyers and Law Professors," 70 *Tulane L. Rev.* 2583 [June 1996].)

The ABA Standing Committee on Lawyers' Professional Liability, after conducting a study for the years 1996–1999, concluded that the frequency and severity of claims against lawyers increase as there is a downturn in the economy. Mirroring the stable economy of the late 1990s the claims against lawyers remained very stable. (To see the actual statistics arising out of this study, you can review the book *Profiles of Legal Malpractice Claims: 1996–1999* from the American Bar Association.) Interestingly, this same study found that nearly 68 percent of the malpractice claims filed against lawyers resulted in no payment at all to the claimant, and that only a little more than 1 percent of the cases resulted in a judgment for the plaintiff. (For references to the statistics cited here and for further reference, see Steven Berenson, "Is It Time for Lawyer Profiles?" 70 *Fordham L.Rev.* 675 [December 2001].)

Today's lawyer can anticipate having three or more claims filed against her before she finishes her career. The attorney most likely to be sued is the litigator. The statistics from about 30,000 legal malpractice claims gathered by the American Bar Association's Standing Committee on Lawyers' Professional Liability show that plaintiffs' personal injury lawyers account for about 25 percent of all claims nationwide and as high as 31 percent in California (taken from a 1986 study conducted by the ABA National Data Center for Malpractice). When claims against lawyers arising out of litigation in other areas of law—such as business, property, and family law—are included, the allegations against litigation attorneys account for almost 50 percent of all claims.

Furthermore, these same statistics document that the greatest number of errors committed by litigators are administrative errors. Interestingly, such errors are 100 percent greater for plaintiffs' personal injury lawyers than for lawyers in general. (Administrative errors constitute 26 percent of all claims in general and 50 percent of all claims against plaintiffs' personal injury lawyers.) Forty percent of the administrative errors involve failure to file actions in a timely manner, usually because of missed statutes of limitation. Surprisingly, experienced lawyers account for a disproportionate number of these claims.

Although the public has become more sophisticated in terms of its legal rights, the primary culprit behind many malpractice claims is a breakdown in communication. Poor client relations is probably the single most important factor contributing to these claims. The most common complaint levied against attorneys, according to most state bar organizations, is lack of communication. Many attorneys are notoriously bad about returning telephone calls to clients or advising clients about the status of their case. The failure of lawyers to communicate with their clients has resulted in so many disciplinary and civil complaints that the American Bar Association's Model Rules of Professional Conduct now include Rule 1.4, which requires clients to be kept "reasonably informed about the status" of the case and lawyers to promptly respond to reasonable requests for information. Failure to return phone calls when there are overt requests for help or information is considered particularly egregious and may be grounds for a negligence claim.

Professionals can maintain a good rapport with their clients by talking openly with clients about their problems, listening to their complaints, and behaving in a manner that indicates they respect their clients. Those who do so are far less likely to be sued for negligence, even when they make mistakes, than are those who treat clients in a paternalistic, disdainful manner.

Another possible explanation for the increase in malpractice claims is the unreasonable expectations many plaintiffs have as a result of what they hear from friends and what they learn from the media. The media tends to glamorize personal injury cases, for example, by heavily publicizing large jury awards and then only casually mentioning when those awards are reduced or the verdicts are overturned. People compare these multimillion-dollar awards to their own claims and unrealistically extrapolate what their damages should be. Those watching television shows about life in the medical and legal fields may expect the professionals they deal with to have the same charismatic persona and demonstrate the same infallibility they see depicted on television. When reality does not conform to their expectations, some seek recourse by filing suit.

HOW TO PREVENT PROFESSIONAL NEGLIGENCE SUITS

Although professionals can do little to counteract this sort of publicity, they can take several steps to improve client relations (see Exhibit 9–3). First, they

EXHIBIT 9–3 *Ways to Avoid Malpractice Exposure*

- Maintain a reasonable workload
- Calendar deadlines; maintain a back-up calendar
- Maintain client confidences
- Be alert to client dissatisfaction
- Keep clients well informed
- Return client phone calls and respond to client correspondence in a timely fashion
- Keep client files well organized
- Use management techniques and devices that enhance efficiency
- Allocate the time necessary to complete tasks completely
- Bill periodically and in detail; monitor accounts receivable on a regular basis.

© Cengage Learning 2012

can ensure that their workload does not exceed their capacity to perform. Many professionals, fearful of experiencing a dearth of clients in the future, take on more clients than they can possibly handle at one time. Juggling an unrealistic workload forces them to cut corners, and the first corner usually cut is client communication. Therefore, professionals should accept no more clients than they can reasonably handle.

Second, professionals need to learn how to manage their businesses. Most have dedicated many years of their lives to honing their technical skills, but few have allocated much time or attention to consideration of the management of their practices. Simple, inexpensive management devices that would make them more efficient and less likely to commit silly errors of omission are often overlooked.

Third, professionals must be willing to dedicate the amount of time necessary to handle a client's problem competently. Consequently, if research should be done or if other practitioners should be consulted, the professional must be willing to expend the time and money necessary to do this. Professionals who constantly take shortcuts in this area are flirting with the specter of malpractice claims.

Role of Legal Assistants

Confidentiality

One way to prevent malpractice claims is to ensure that client confidences are maintained. In accordance with the attorney-client privilege, confidential information between an individual and his attorney cannot be disclosed unless the individual consents to the disclosure. Any information exchanged between a client and his attorney that is not disclosed to a third person is considered confidential. Disclosure to a third person does not waive the privilege if the person to whom the information is disclosed receives it for the purpose of furthering the client's interest or the disclosure is necessary for the communication of information. If, for example, an attorney writes a letter to a private investigator outlining the case so that the investigator has sufficient information to begin work, the letter is considered privileged because the information is intended to further the client's interest. Once a privilege is lost it cannot be regained. Therefore, a legal assistant must never do anything that could jeopardize the attorney-client privilege.

This privilege may be claimed by the individual, her attorney, or anyone authorized to claim the privilege on behalf of the individual, such as a representative of the client's estate. All employees of an attorney or law firm are subject to any prohibitions regarding disclosure and must not disclose privileged information to spouses or anyone else. As the intermediary between support staff and lawyers, the legal assistant is often in the best position to ensure that client confidences are maintained. Therefore, it is often up to the legal assistant to make sure that faxes, electronic mail (e-mail) and other computer-generated information are reviewed periodically to ensure confidentiality and that client conferences are conducted in places where privacy is protected.

Unauthorized Practice of Law

One of the axioms by which the paralegal profession operates is that legal assistants cannot give legal advice. Doing so constitutes the unauthorized practice of law and can be the basis of a malpractice claim. The question, however, is, what constitutes legal advice? Does suggesting to a client that she might want to consider filing a particular motion constitute legal advice? What about conducting research to determine the meaning of a particular statute? Case law is generally not helpful in answering these types of questions. You may find it more enlightening to consult attorney general and ethics committee opinions rendered in your state.

Most importantly, consult with your attorney as to what tasks you should perform. Clarify, for example, what your role should be in dealing with clients. Determine what types of questions you should answer yourself and which ones you should refer to the attorney.

Most attorneys are careful about supervising the work of their legal assistants because they are aware that the ultimate responsibility for any work product lies with them. Nevertheless, some attorneys, because of their workload or outright carelessness, are less than diligent in carrying out their supervisorial tasks. In some cases you may have to insist that an attorney review your work. If an attorney should ever gloss over his refusal to carry out his review responsibilities by assuring you of his implicit trust in you, do not be unduly flattered. For the protection of all concerned, it is imperative that you work under the auspices of an attorney.

The question regarding the appropriate scope of duties of legal assistants is further complicated by the close working relationship legal assistants often establish with clients. Some clients have more contact with the legal assistant than with the attorney, so these clients may naturally turn to the legal assistant for legal advice. Even though the legal assistant may know the answer, she must confirm the answer with an attorney. Failure to do so can result in problems for the attorney, the legal assistant, and the client. Furthermore, incorrect advice may lead to a malpractice claim against the attorney and the firm, and an ethics complaint against the attorney who allowed the legal assistant to engage in the unauthorized practice of law.

Client Relations

Despite the caveat against giving legal advice, legal assistants can do their part to prevent professional negligence claims by improving client relations. A legal assistant can maintain close contact with clients, informing them of the progress of their cases, listening to their concerns, and answering their questions. By doing these things he can shield the attorney from some of the time-consuming interpersonal tasks that make for good rapport with clients but are often avoided by attorneys because of their limited time.

Making clients aware of the strengths and weaknesses of their case and keeping them apprised as to the status of their case minimizes exposure to malpractice claims. Additionally, regular communication helps create realistic expectations on the part of the client and reassures the client that her case is important to the firm.

Maintenance of Documents and Files

Because legal assistants often bear the responsibility for maintaining documents and files, they can make sure files are well organized so that information can be easily retrieved. Having information but not being able to access it is almost as bad as not having the information at all. Client relations suffer when a client comes to the office to discuss her case and the attorney cannot locate relevant documents in the file. All files should be reviewed periodically to ensure that all necessary documents are included and that they are organized logically. Although document control has been made more efficient with computer technology, the legal assistant should still back up all information in the computer so that data is not lost if the computer malfunctions.

Legal assistants must also ensure that information requested on behalf of a client is received in a timely manner. If, for example, medical records are requested from health care providers, the legal assistant should track these records to make sure they have been received and appropriately filed.

Trust Accounts

Although attorneys cannot delegate ultimate responsibility for client trust accounts to anyone, legal assistants can make sure that the trust account can be quickly and accurately reviewed by the attorney each month. Legal assistants must exhibit great care in dealing with clients' money and remember that they are doing so on behalf of the client and under the direction of the attorney. Courts show no mercy when discrepancies concerning trust accounts arise, even when the attorney was merely sloppy.

Filing and Court Date

Legal assistants can also assume responsibility for meeting filing dates. By using management tools, such as "tickler" systems, to alert them to upcoming deadlines, they can minimize the chances of missing important filing and court dates (including trial dates, trial setting conferences, depositions, and brief due dates). Because legal assistants must be intimately familiar with the procedural rules and customs of the courts in their jurisdiction, you should pay special attention to procedural law courses in your program of study.

MEDICAL MALPRACTICE CRISIS

In the late 1950s, medical malpractice lawsuits were filed against one out of seven doctors. In 1969, after a hearing on the issue, Congress determined that the so-called medical malpractice crisis did not exist. Most doctors did not carry medical malpractice insurance prior to 1970 (Ann Louis Zarwick, "Damages Deferred: Determining When A Cause of Action Begins to Accrue for A Cancer Misdiagnosis Claim," *U. Tol. L. Review*, 445 [Winter 2010]). By the mid 1970s a medical malpractice crisis was declared because of the increase in the amount of litigation since the 1960s, the size of the judgments sometimes awarded, and the concomitant increase in the cost of medical malpractice insurance.

Studies, however, indicate a leveling off of claims since 1985. In 1994 the American Medical Association reported that since the large increases of the early 1980s, the number of claims against hospitals and physicians dropped at an average rate of 1.9 percent per year (Martin L. Gonzalez, *Socioeconomic Characteristics of Medical Practice* 41 [1994]). Some attribute this decrease to the high procedural cost associated with filing a medical malpractice claim, which includes outlays for medical reports, second opinions, and expert witnesses.

A multidisciplinary team from Harvard examined more than 100,000 medical, legal, and insurance claim records from New York, Utah, and Colorado and interviewed thousands of doctors and patients over more than a decade in its evaluation of malpractice liability's impact on the health care system. It concluded that approximately 1 percent of hospitalized patients are victims of medical malpractice, with consequences ranging from complete recovery in less than one month (46 percent of those negligently injured) to death (25 percent of those negligently injured). If these figures are extrapolated to the entire nation, medical negligence accounts for 120,000 deaths each year. Only approximately 2 percent of those who were negligently injured filed a claim, but a substantial majority of claims were filed in cases in which there was no negligence. However, for every invalid claim filed against a doctor or hospital, seven valid claims go unfiled. (For references to the statistics cited here and for further reference, see David Hyman, "Medical Malpractice and the Tort System: What Do We Know and What (If Anything) Should We Do About It?" 80 *Tex. L. Rev.* 1639 [June 2002].)

There is emerging scholarly consensus "that the core problem is one of patient safety" as opposed to malpractice litigation (Abigal R. Moncrieff, "Federalization Snowballs: The Need for National Action in Medical Malpractice Reform," 109 *Colum. L. Rev.* 844 [2009]). In 1999, the Institute of Medicine reported that 98,000 medical error related deaths occurred every years, making medical errors the eighth leading cause of death in the United States (The Institute of Medicine, *To Err is Human: Building A Safer Health Care System*, National Academy Press [2000]).

Legislators attempting to slay the "malpractice dragon" have enacted legislation resulting in modification of the informed-consent doctrine, the burden of proof, evidentiary rules, shortening statutes of limitation, the awarding of punitive damages, the setting of the standard of care, mandating medical review panels or hearings prior to filing a lawsuit, and imposing a statutory cap on damages. You would be prudent, therefore, to consult the statutes in your state when getting involved in a medical malpractice case.

Some statutes imposing limitations on the damages recoverable in medical malpractice cases have been challenged as a denial of equal protection and held invalid. One court, for example, concluded that a limitation on recovery not only created an arbitrary classification between malpractice victims and denied full recovery to the most seriously injured malpractice victims, but also constituted special legislation that violated the equal protection provision of the state's constitution. Caps, it is argued, are not necessary, as excessive jury awards can be reduced by judges through their remittitur powers.

Some states require pretrial review panels to hear malpractice claims, providing that these claims must be submitted to a panel for findings on the issues of liability or damages or both before proceeding to trial. Some of these statutory provisions, which are designed to encourage settlement, have been attacked as a denial of the constitutional right of access to the courts.

A few states have enacted legislation called *practice guidelines*, which define the standard of care to be used in certain clinical situations. The standardization of minimal actions necessary for care protects physicians from malpractice suits and discourages physicians from practicing defensive medicine (e.g., ordering additional and arguably unnecessary tests and procedures to minimize the chances of being sued for malpractice). Under this system, doctors need only demonstrate that they have complied with the guidelines to avoid litigation. How much weight at trial is given to these guidelines, however, is up to the trier of fact.

LOCAL LINKS

What legislation has been passed in your state in response to the perceived medical malpractice crisis?

NET NEWS

To read more about statutes passed in reaction to the perceived medical malpractice crisis, go to http://www.lectlaw.com and enter "special medical malpractice statutes" as your search term.

SUMMARY

Professionals are held to a reasonable standard of care, in that they are required to have the skill and learning commonly possessed by members in good standing within their profession. Choosing a course of action that other professionals might not have chosen or that results in an undesirable outcome does not necessarily make a professional negligent. Lack of proper training, failure to refer to a specialist when necessary, failure to stay abreast of new discoveries, and failure to follow up on a client's progress may all constitute negligence. Specialists are held to the standard of care of a "reasonably careful and prudent specialist." Unlike generalists, specialists must adhere to a national standard of care rather than a local one.

The doctrine of informed consent requires that a physician warn patients of possible hazards, complications, and expected and unexpected results of treatment as well as possible risks of alternative treatments. This duty increases as the probability or severity of risk to the patient increases. How much information must be disclosed to the patient depends on the situation, but sufficient information must be given so that the patient can make an informed decision. If no information is disclosed, or if the physician obtains consent for one procedure and then opts to perform another, the patient may sue for battery. If, however, the patient is simply uninformed as to the nature of the risks involved, he may sue for negligence. With the latter cause of action, the key question is whether the risks that were not disclosed were material risks. Adequate records should always be maintained so that the professional's memory can be refreshed in the event of a lawsuit.

KEY TERMS

fiduciary relationship
Relationship based on trust and confidence that imposes an obligation to act in good faith; an example is the attorney-client relationship

informed consent
Knowledgeable consent based on disclosure of all relevant facts that allows one to make an informed decision

REVIEW QUESTIONS

1. Are professionals held to a local or national standard of care?

2. Is a professional negligent by definition if the client experiences a negative outcome?

3. Is a professional negligent if she chooses a course of action that is different from the one that many other professionals would have chosen?

4. List at least five ways that a professional can commit malpractice.

5. To what standard of care is a specialist held?

6. What does the informed-consent doctrine require doctors to disclose?

7. What is the difference between a negligence and a battery cause of action based on failure to inform?

8. What is a plaintiff alleging malpractice required to prove?

9. Must a plaintiff's negligence add to or be concurrent with a defendant professional's negligence for the defendant to be relieved of liability?

10. What does a professional who decides to allege contributory negligence usually argue?

11. Under what conditions can a patient be said to have assumed the risk?

12. When is the defense of emergency a viable defense to a claim of negligence? When is it not?

13. Why is it important for professionals to maintain adequate records?

14. To whom do medical records belong? When do defendants have a right to these records?

15. Are professional negligence suits increasing or decreasing?

    a. What percentage of legal malpractice claims become insurance claims?

    b. How many claims are filed against most attorneys?

    c. Do most of these claims result in recovery of damages?

    d. What kind of attorney is most likely to be sued, and what type of error does this attorney typically commit?

16. What are the primary reasons for most legal malpractice claims?

17. What can attorneys do to prevent professional negligence suits?

18. What communications does the attorney-client privilege protect?

    a. How is this privilege waived?

    b. Who is subject to this privilege?

    c. What should legal assistants do to preserve this privilege?

19. What types of activities constitute the unauthorized practice of law?

    a. Why is it important that attorneys review all of the work produced by their legal assistants?

    b. How does the relationship legal assistants have with clients complicate the issue of unauthorized practice of law?

20. Why is it important for legal assistants

    a. to promote good client relations?

    b. to create well-organized files?

    c. to handle client monies carefully?

    d. to meet all filing dates?

21. Are medical malpractice claims increasing or decreasing?

22. What have some states done in an effort to reduce the number of medical malpractice claims?

PRACTICE EXAM

Students should complete the practice exam after studying each chapter. The answers are in Appendix A. If you score lower than 80%, you should reread the materials.

True-False

1. A professional who engages in conduct that results in a negative outcome for her client is by definition negligent.

2. A professional can be found negligent if he fails to use due diligence and care even if he chooses an appropriate course of action.

3. A plaintiff who is suing for malpractice will be successful if she can prove that the defendant professional was negligent even if she cannot prove that this negligence was the proximate cause of her injuries.

4. Specialists are generally held to a national standard of care.

5. Attorneys are held to a general standard of care even if they are certified specialists.

6. A doctor's duty to warn increases as the probability and severity of risk to the patient increase.

7. A physician has a legal obligation to inform a patient about an alternative treatment even if he does not think the alternative treatment will work in the patient's case.

8. In an emergency situation in which the patient is comatose or too ill to comprehend what is being said, the doctor can render treatment without informing the patient of the risks involved.

9. The primary question in a negligence cause of action based on lack of informed consent is whether the risks that are not disclosed were material risks.

10. Treatment provided in an emergency must be of the same quality of care as that provided under less stressful circumstances.

11. What constitutes reasonable care in an emergency depends on the circumstances in which the emergency occurs.

12. Maintaining client records is a frivolous expenditure of valuable time.

13. In a personal injury case in which the plaintiff has made her medical problems the subject of litigation, all of her medical records are subject to subpoena by the defendant.

14. Professional negligence claims appear to be diminishing.

15. Annual malpractice claims for doctors are much higher than they are for attorneys.

16. Attorneys who talk openly with their clients are less likely to be sued for negligence when they make mistakes than attorneys who treat their clients in a paternalistic manner.

17. One reason some clients file malpractice claims against their attorney is that they have unrealistic expectations about their case.

18. The attorney-client privilege prevents employees of an attorney from disclosing confidential information to anyone except their spouses.

19. Legal assistants should make sure that client conferences are conducted in places where privacy is assured.

20. A legal assistant can answer a client's question about a legal issue as long as she is sure she knows the answer.

21. Legal assistants are often responsible for helping to make sure that filing dates are met.

22. The number of medical malpractice claims has escalated sharply since the late 1980s.

Fill-in-the-Blanks

1. Professionals have a(n) _____ relationship with their clients, meaning that the relationship is built on trust and confidence.

2. Under the _____ _____ doctrine, clients have the right to ultimate dominion over their bodies and events that affect their lives.

3. Today _____ has for the most part replaced _____ as a basis for liability in lack of informed-consent cases.

4. A patient who understands the risks involved in treatment and consents to that treatment is said to have _____.

Multiple-Choice

1. In deciding whether a professional is negligent, courts use
   a. a local standard.
   b. a national standard.
   c. both a local and national standard.
   d. neither a local nor national standard.

2. A defendant will likely be considered negligent if
   a. she chooses a course of action that is different from what most other professionals would have selected.
   b. she chooses a course of action different from the only recognized course of action by members of good standing in the profession.
   c. neither of the above.
   d. both of the above.

3. A professional commits malpractice by
   a. performing a task for which he lacks the requisite skills.
   b. failing to refer a client to a specialist when the situation dictates.
   c. failing to ask for the information necessary to make a recommendation to a client.
   d. all of the above.

4. Which of the following is true?
   a. Physicians who use unorthodox methods of treatment are less likely to be found negligent than those who use conventional treatment.
   b. Physicians who use unorthodox treatments with patients who are critically ill are less likely to be found negligent than if they use unorthodox treatments with those suffering from minor ailments.
   c. The degree of innovation that a physician uses that is legally acceptable depends on the seriousness of the situation.
   d. all of the above.

5. A professional is obligated to
   a. keep abreast of changes in his field.
   b. follow up on a client's condition or status.
   c. make referrals when appropriate.
   d. all of the above.

6. A neurosurgeon
   a. is held to the standard of care of a reasonably careful and prudent neurosurgeon.
   b. is held to the standard of care of a reasonably careful and prudent physician.
   c. cannot be held liable for doing something for which a physician doing the same thing would not be liable.
   d. all of the above.

7. Under the informed-consent doctrine
   a. a doctor is obligated to warn a patient about possible hazards of a form of treatment but is never obligated to advise a patient about alternative treatments.
   b. a doctor has a duty to warn a patient that all the side effects of new or experimental treatment are not known.
   c. a doctor can, under some circumstances, force a treatment on an unwilling adult patient.
   d. all of the above.

8. In deciding what should be disclosed to a patient, some courts
   a. consider the expectations of a reasonable layperson.
   b. use a "prudent patient" standard, which requires a doctor to disclose those risks that a reasonable person would consider material to her decision to undergo treatment or not.
   c. use a professional standard that requires doctors to disclose only those risks that other reasonable doctors in the community would have disclosed.
   d. all of the above.

9. A doctor will not necessarily have to disclose a risk if
   a. the risk is highly improbable and the doctor believes that disclosing it would severely reduce the effectiveness of the treatment.
   b. the risk is high but the doctor believes that disclosing it would severely reduce the effectiveness of the treatment.
   c. the risk is highly improbable but the consequence is severe.
   d. none of the above.

10. In negligence causes of action based on lack of informed consent
    a. lay-witness testimony is all that is needed.
    b. the statute of limitations is generally longer than it is for battery.
    c. a patient typically signs a consent form but does not understand some of the risks involved.
    d. all of the above.

11. A risk is considered a material risk if
    a. the consequences of the risk are severe.
    b. the occurrence of the risk is highly probable.
    c. there are feasible alternatives.
    d. all of the above.

12. To prove malpractice, a plaintiff must show
    a. the standard of care expected within the profession.
    b. the defendant's deviation from the standard of care within the profession.
    c. that her injuries more probably than not resulted from the actions of the professional.
    d. all of the above.

13. An expert witness in a malpractice case must
    a. be familiar with the techniques and procedures used in the case.
    b. use the same techniques and procedures as those used in the case.
    c. be familiar with the standard of care in the community whether a local or national standard is used.
    d. all of the above.

14. To be relieved of liability a defendant must show that the plaintiff's negligence
    a. added to his own.
    b. was concurrent with his own.
    c. either added to or was concurrent with his own.
    d. none of the above.

15. A client could be considered contributorily negligent if she
    a. fails to follow a doctor's instructions.
    b. lies to her attorney.
    c. delays seeking medical attention.
    d. all of the above.

16. The defense of assumption of risk
    a. is applicable even if the client does not understand the risks involved.
    b. is inapplicable if the risks are not clearly explained.
    c. is applicable even if the defendant provides negligent care.
    d. all of the above.

17. Emergency is a defense
    a. if death is imminent and treatment is absolutely necessary for the patient's survival.
    b. only if an emergency actually exists.
    c. as long as the emergency was not created by the doctor's negligence.
    d. all of the above.

18. Maintaining adequate client records
    a. may later help a defendant professional refresh his memory about a client's case.
    b. has little relevance to building a defendant's defense against a malpractice claim.
    c. is generally a frivolous expenditure of valuable time.
    d. none of the above.

19. In regard to medical records,
    a. the physical record is considered the property of the patient.
    b. the content of the record is considered the property of the health care provider.
    c. most state laws require that the records be released to the patient as long as the patient will waive the physician-patient privilege.
    d. all of the above.

20. Which of the following is true?
    a. The type of attorney most likely to be sued is the litigator.
    b. Most attorneys can expect to have only one malpractice claim filed against them during the course of their career.
    c. The greatest number of errors committed by litigators are ones involving strategy.
    d. all of the above.

21. Poor communication is
    a. the most common cause of client complaints against attorneys.
    b. the primary cause of malpractice claims against attorneys.
    c. the primary reason for attorneys having poor client relations.
    d. all of the above.

22. Failure to return client phone calls or to keep clients reasonably informed about their case
    a. can be grounds for an ethical violation.
    b. is not by itself grounds for negligence.
    c. is grounds for negligence but is not covered by the Model Rules of Professional Conduct.
    d. none of the above.

23. Attorneys can avoid malpractice claims by
    a. taking no more clients than they have time to handle.
    b. spending the amount of time necessary to competently handle their clients' cases.
    c. more efficiently managing their office.
    d. all of the above.

24. Which of the following is true about the attorney-client privilege?
    a. The privilege pertains to any information exchanged between an attorney and client even if that information is disclosed to a third person.
    b. Confidential communications between an attorney and client cannot be disclosed unless the client consents.
    c. Even if the privilege is lost, it can, under some circumstances, be regained.
    d. all of the above.

25. Because legal assistants are not allowed to practice law, they should
    a. not answer any questions from a client.
    b. not talk with clients.
    c. insist that an attorney review their work.
    d. all of the above.

26. If a legal assistant provides incorrect legal advice to a client it may result in
    a. a malpractice claim against the attorney and firm.
    b. an ethics charge against the attorney supervising the legal assistant.
    c. disastrous results for the client.
    d. all of the above.

27. Legal assistants
    a. should never discuss the status of a client's case.
    b. can shield attorneys from some of the interpersonal tasks with clients that are time-consuming.
    c. can listen to clients' concerns but should never answer any of their questions.
    d. all of the above.

28. Legal malpractice claims can be minimized by
    a. making sure clients know the strengths and weakness of their case.
    b. keeping clients apprised of the status of their case.
    c. reassuring clients that their case is important to the firm.
    d. all of the above.

29. Client files
    a. should be well organized so that information can be retrieved quickly and easily.
    b. should be organized logically so that they never have to be reviewed.
    c. are the sole province of the legal secretary.
    d. all of the above.

30. Legal assistants
    a. are often delegated responsibility for client trust accounts.
    b. are not allowed to do anything in relation to client trust accounts.
    c. should make sure that client trust accounts can be easily reviewed by the attorney.
    d. none of the above.

31. A medical malpractice crisis has arisen
    a. despite the decrease in litigation since the 1960s.
    b. even though the size of judgments has diminished.
    c. because of the increase in the cost of malpractice insurance.
    d. all of the above.

32. Some states have dealt with medical malpractice by
    a. passing statutes that limit the amount of recovery in medical malpractice cases.
    b. requiring pretrial review panels to hear malpractice claims.
    c. enacting practice guidelines that define the standard of care in certain situations.
    d. all of the above.

33. In an effort to reduce the number of malpractice cases, some legislatures have modified
    a. the informed-consent doctrine.
    b. statute of limitations and evidentiary rules.
    c. rules regarding burden of proof and standard of care.
    d. all of the above.

PRACTICE POINTERS

The defendant in a malpractice case may request that the plaintiff submit to an independent physical or mental examination to verify injuries claimed and to justify expenses and suffering alleged. In most jurisdictions, however, the plaintiff is required to submit to only one examination. The examination cannot take place at a location unduly far from the plaintiff's residence and must not include any procedure that is particularly painful or intrusive. Physical examinations must be conducted by a licensed physician or health care professional, and mental examinations must be conducted by a licensed physician or clinical psychiatrist.

Typically, the defendant submits a written demand for physical examination to the plaintiff. Such a demand must include the time and location that the examination is to take place, the identity and specialty of the examining physician, and a description of the conditions, scope, and nature of the examination. This demand is served on all other parties to the action but is not filed with the court. The plaintiff must then file a response to the demand indicating whether she will comply with the terms of the demand. Alternatively, the plaintiff can insist that certain modifications be made, such as a change in the time or location of the examination. If the defendant then concludes that the plaintiff's request for changes or refusal to appear is unwarranted, she may move the court for an order compelling compliance with the demand.

If a physical examination of someone other than the plaintiff is requested, or if a mental examination of any person is demanded, a court order must be obtained unless all other parties stipulate to allowing an examination. A motion for medical examination must include the same elements as a demand for physical examination. Additionally, it must contain a declaration showing that the parties have attempted to resolve the issue by stipulation. If an examination is held a long way from the plaintiff's residence (more than seventy-five miles, according to federal rules), a court will order attendance only if the requesting party can show good cause for requesting an examination at this distance and if the moving party agrees to advance travel expenses. If a party seeking recovery for personal injuries stipulates that no claim is being made for mental or emotional distress (other than that normally anticipated to arise from a physical injury) and that no expert testimony will be used to show unusual mental and emotional distress, a court may not order a psychological examination.

Most states prohibit the presence of anyone other than the examinee at a psychological examination. In many cases, however, the examiner or the examinee may tape-record a mental examination. An attorney for the examinee does, however, have a right to attend a physical examination as well as to tape-record that examination. The attorney has a right to suspend the examination if, in his opinion, the physician uses tests or procedures that were not included in the order for physical examination. Either the physician or the attorney may suspend an examination if either believes it necessary to secure a protective order.

After submitting to a medical examination, the party may, by written demand, obtain a written report setting forth the findings of the examiner. This report should include the examiner's conclusion, the results of all tests, and copies of any previous reports prepared by the examiner in reference to the examinee. If the demanding party fails to receive these reports in a timely manner, it may move the court for an order compelling delivery. If a party fails to comply with this court order, the court must exclude the testimony of the examiner whose report was not delivered. By the same token, the party who conducts the examination, at the time it serves the demanded report, is entitled to any reports prepared as a result of an examination of the same condition. Additionally, that party is entitled to the identity of any physician who conducts an examination but does not prepare a report, as well as the identification of any physician who later examines the patient.

Demand for Physical Examination

Bridgewater and Boyle
1620 Blissful Lane
Suite 6200
Carefree, Arizona 85254
(555) 897–1334
Mason Bridgewater
Steven Boyle
Attorneys for the Defendants
    Superior Court for the State of _____
    For the County of _____

CASE NUMBER C 6096-ABC

THEODORE JONES, et al.,

    Plaintiffs

    v.

STEVEN AND MILDRED BAXTER,
husband and wife
    Defendants

DEMAND FOR PHYSICAL
EXAMINATION

TO ALL PARTIES AND TO THEIR ATTORNEYS OF RECORD HEREIN:
    A demand is hereby made upon Plaintiff THEODORE JONES to submit to a physical examination. The examination will take place on April 4, 20___ at 10:30 am at the office of Dr. Bryon Happytimes, Do It Now Medical Center, 4700 Harmony Lane, Suite 200, Scottsdale, Arizona.
    The examination will be conducted by Dr. Lee Richard Wiley, a board certified dermatologist.
February 22, 2008

        Bridgewater and Boyle

        Mason Bridgewater

        Attorney for Defendants

TORT TEASERS

1. Review the hypothetical scenario at the beginning of this chapter. Has professional negligence been committed? What defenses can be raised?

2. An attorney in general practice tries but fails to create a trust that would have given his client a tax advantage. Though conceding his inexperience, the attorney argues that he did a fair job of working on the matter and that he did not have a duty to refer the client to a tax specialist. Do you think the attorney should be found negligent for his failure to seek assistance? *Horne v. Peckham*, 158 Cal. Rptr. 714 (Ct. App. 1979).

3. The father of a small child takes the child to an emergency room and tells the attendants that the child has ingested a large quantity of aspirin. The attendants specifically tell the father to advise the physician of this fact but the father fails to make mention of it. The physician diagnoses the child as having the flu. The child dies shortly thereafter and the parents sue the physician for negligence. Should the parents be able to recover? What defense might the physician raise? *Hudson v. St. Paul Mercury Insurance Co.*, 219 So. 2d 524 (La. 1969).

4. A patient goes to his surgeon for a vasectomy. The surgeon amputates the patient's testicle. On what theory should the patient base his cause of action and why? *Whittington v. Mason* 906 So. 2d 10 (Miss.App. 2004).

5. A troubled twenty-four-year-old man consults the head pastor of a church and several of its pastoral counsel. Severely depressed, he tells them he has contemplated suicide. Defendants advise him that suicide is an acceptable alternative in some cases. Defendants visit him in the hospital after he unsuccessfully attempts suicide, and he tells them that he will reattempt suicide when he is released. Defendants do not advise the doctors or the young man's

family about this conversation. Two weeks after he is released from the hospital, the young man commits suicide. Plaintiffs, the parents of the young man, sue for wrongful death, alleging, among other things, "clergy malpractice." How would you go about determining whether Defendants were negligent? *Nally v. Grace Community Church*, 763 P.2d 948 (Cal.), *cert. denied*, 109 S. Ct. 1644 (1989).

INTERNET INQUIRIES

Legal assistants are frequently assigned the task of locating and reviewing medical records. Several online resources are available to assist in the reviewing process. If you come across terms you do not understand, two online medical dictionaries you can consult are MedicineNet.com (select "MedTerms Dictionary") and National Institute of Health's MedLinePlus (http://www.nih.gov). To use the medical dictionary in MedlinePlus, select "MedlinePlus" and then enter the medical term in the search box. If you want to get some anatomical information, in English or Spanish, "MEDtropolis" (http://www.medtropolis.com) is one possible source. Select "Virtual Body" and move your cursor over the parts of the body you want to identify and then get a close-up lateral view of those parts you want magnified. You can also receive a narrative tour of body organs and systems.

MedicineNet.com and MedEngine! provide links to a great many other medical resources dealing with diseases and conditions, procedures and tests, drugs, medical associations, medical publications and references, and a host of other topics. Another excellent source of medical information is Martindale's Health Science Guide, which can be found at http://www.martindalecenter.com. In addition to offering general medical information, dictionaries, and diagnostic and treatment information, it has tutorials on anatomy. Medscape.com (http://www.medscape.com) has direct links to clinical medical articles, a physician's directory, drug information, and MedLine (references and abstracts from medical journals). You must register before you can access this site.

The *Merck Manual of Diagnosis and Therapy* (17th edition) full text is now available online for no charge at http://www.merck.com, by selecting "Merck Manuals" link. Considered the physician's "bible," it is a seminal source of information regarding clinical procedures, diagnosis, pharmacology, and contemporary therapy for almost all disorders. The *Merck Manual of Medical Information—Home Edition* is also available online.

Using the online medical resources just described, find out the following:

1. What is an anterior cruciate ligament?
2. Where is it located, and what function does it serve in the body?
3. How is a torn ACL repaired?

PRACTICAL PONDERABLES

Your attorney has recently interviewed Dr. Willard Smith, who suffered an anaphylactic reaction to a dye that was used when administering a diagnostic test designed to test his pulmonary capacity. Because he temporarily stopped breathing but was not treated for about ten minutes (it took that long for the paramedics to get to him), he became comatose for several weeks, and it was believed he was going to die. He regained consciousness and was in physical therapy for almost a year, regaining about 60 percent of the mobility and 40 percent of the manual dexterity he had before the incident. He is no longer able to work as a veterinarian and has sustained substantial financial as well as emotional losses as a result.

Dr. Smith wants to sue the hospital where the test was administered. Your supervising attorney has asked you to do some preliminary research before she decides whether to accept this case. What information do you think the attorney will need before she can make an informed choice about whether to take on Dr. Smith as a client?

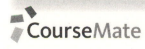
CourseMate Access an interactive eBook, chapter-specific learning tools, including flashcards, quizzes, and more in your Paralegal CourseMate, accessed through www.CengageBrain.com.

© Cengage Learning 2012

CHAPTER 10

Misrepresentation, Nuisance, and Other Torts

CHAPTER OBJECTIVES

After completing the chapter, you should be able to

- Distinguish among intentional, negligent, and innocent misrepresentation and identify the elements of each.
- Identify situations in which one is entitled to rely on the representations of another.
- Identify the two ways in which a plaintiff's damages can be measured.
- Distinguish between public and private nuisance and identify the elements of both.
- Identify the elements of the torts involving interference with business relations.
- Distinguish among the torts involving misuse of legal process and identify the elements of each.

After meeting your sister's fiancé, you suspect that he is not all he pretends to be. You ask a friend of yours, who is a private investigator, to conduct a background check on him. You discover, among other things, that your prospective brother-in-law had an affair with a woman who was married to a prominent businessman. When the husband discovered their relationship and terminated their affair, your sister's boyfriend sought revenge. First he went to the attorney general's office and tried to convince an attorney to prosecute the husband for price fixing, even though he was aware that such claims were utterly false. In a further act of petulance, he sent the husband materials advertising a get-rich-quick scheme that your future relation knew was bogus and included several fake endorsements by well-known people, in an effort to capture the husband's interest. Not being one to forgive and forget, your brother-in-law-to-be is currently trying to purchase property next to the husband's business. He plans to open a bookstore that features pornographic materials. Because the husband operates a religious bookstore, he is confident that this will, at the very least, have a detrimental effect on the husband's business and, more likely, he hopes, contribute to its demise.

What torts has this potential bane of your existence committed? Has he committed nuisance, interference with business relations, misrepresentation, or misuse of legal process? Let us see.

DEVELOPMENT OF MISREPRESENTATION AND ITS RELATIONSHIP TO OTHER TORTS

Misrepresentation (which is basically the making of false representations) can be found interwoven among other types of tortious behavior. A conversion, for example, can be committed by making false representations. A battery can be committed by a person who uses deceit to induce the plaintiff to consent to physical contact. A claim for intentional infliction of emotional distress may arise out of a maliciously spread lie.

Misrepresentation as a distinct cause of action arose out of the common law action of **deceit**. Typically, in a case of deceit the plaintiff lost money or property as a result of reliance on the defendant's representations. Today, however, the law of misrepresentation is broader than an action for deceit. Although deceit was usually based on intent to deceive, misrepresentation can be based not only on intentional deception, but also on negligent deception or innocent deception (strict liability).

INTENTIONAL MISREPRESENTATION

Intentional misrepresentation corresponds to what was known as "deceit" or "fraud" under the common law. The elements of intentional misrepresentation are as follows (see Exhibit 10–1):

- The defendant misrepresents something with the intent of inducing the plaintiff's reliance on that misrepresentation.
- The defendant knows that the representation is false or acts with reckless indifference to the truth.
- The plaintiff justifiably relies on the defendant's misrepresentation.
- The plaintiff suffers damages stemming from this reliance.

What Constitutes a Misrepresentation?

A defendant commits misrepresentation by affirmatively making a false statement. Alternatively, he may intentionally conceal a fact from the plaintiff. A seller of a house, for example, who deliberately paints the ceiling to conceal from the plaintiff-buyer the fact that the roof is leaking commits misrepresentation.

EXHIBIT 10–1 Elements of Intentional Misrepresentation

- Defendant makes a misrepresentation with intent of inducing plaintiff's reliance.
- Defendant knows the misrepresentation is false or acts with reckless indifference to truth or falsity of representation.
- Plaintiff justifiably relies on misrepresentation.
- Plaintiff suffers damages as a result of reliance.

Actions alone may constitute misrepresentation. The seller of a car who turns back the odometer misrepresents the mileage on that car even though he says nothing (*Restatement [Second] of Torts* § 525, illus. 1).

Under the common law, mere failure to disclose a material fact (as opposed to deliberate concealment) was not considered a misrepresentation. Until the 1950s, the doctrine of *caveat emptor* ("let the buyer beware") reigned, and sellers of real estate had virtually no duty to disclose what they knew about the condition of their property to potential purchasers. Courts premised this doctrine on the idea that buyers and sellers of comparable power, skill, and experience were conscious of the risks they assumed and could protect themselves against those risks. In the modern view, however, nondisclosure may be considered concealment under certain circumstances, especially when the defect is a **latent defect** (not visible to the buyer). A **patent defect** is one that is visible or readily discoverable. A duty to disclose, for example, is frequently set forth in the so-called "termite" cases, in which the homeowner fails to tell the purchaser that the house has been infested with termites.

Similarly, liability may be imposed if a defendant presents a "half-truth," a statement that although literally true tends to be misleading. A statement such as "We have no termites in this house" is a half-truth if the termites have been long-term residents up until a month before the statement was made. If a **fiduciary relationship** exists between the parties, such as that between parent and child or attorney and client, the law imposes a more demanding obligation to disclose than if a transaction occurs at *arm's length* (i.e., no special relationship exists between the parties). For example, a businessman selling property to his business partner (assuming they have a fiduciary relationship for purposes of the transaction involved) has an obligation to disclose information that he would not be required to disclose if he were conducting an arm's-length transaction with a stranger.

The courts are more likely to find misrepresentation if a nondisclosed fact is essential to the transaction. If a seller of land fails to disclose to a buyer that nothing can be grown on the land even though she is aware that the buyer intends to use the land to grow crops, she is likely to be found liable for misrepresentation. Even if a plaintiff is unable to recover damages for nondisclosure, he can get rescission (which results in the canceling of the contract) if the nondisclosed fact is a material one.

Today a small but rapidly growing number of states have enacted legislation or created regulations that require sellers of residential property to disclose certain aspects of the property's physical condition to potential purchasers. A copy of the mandatory disclosure form used in Ohio is shown in Exhibit 10–2.

LOCAL LINKS

Has your state enacted legislation requiring sellers of property to disclose information about the property's physical condition to prospective purchasers?

To Whom Must the Misrepresentation Be Made?

Under the traditional common law, a defendant was liable only to those persons whom he intended to influence by the misrepresentation. A debtor, for example, who misrepresented his credit record to a creditor and then failed to make payments was not liable to a party who bought the debtor's note from the creditor. The requirement has been relaxed in recent times. Presently a plaintiff can recover if she is a member of a class whom the defendant could reasonably expect to learn of and rely on the misrepresentation.

Additionally, the plaintiff's reliance must occur in the "type of transaction" the defendant could reasonably expect the plaintiff to engage in as a result of the reliance (*Restatement [Second] of Torts* §§ 531 and 533). Suppose an architect supplies erroneous specifications to a builder, who in turn subcontracts the electrical work. If the subcontractor suffers pecuniary (monetary) damages because of the faulty specifications, he will be allowed to recover from the architect. Recovery will be allowed even if the architect is unaware of the identity of the subcontractor when he gives the specifications to the builder (*Restatement [Second] of Torts* § 531, illus. 5).

Another exception to the rule requiring intent to induce reliance occurs in the context of commercial documents. Those who incorporate misstatements into commercial documents are liable to persons who suffer as a result of their justifiable reliance on the truth of those statements. A company that markets clover seed intentionally mislabeled as alfalfa seed is liable to those who plant the seeds in reliance on the label and consequently suffer a loss. Again, it does not matter whether the seed company intended to make

EXHIBIT 10—2 Residential Property Disclosure Form (Ohio)

DEPARTMENT OF COMMERCE
RESIDENTIAL PROPERTY DISCLOSURE FORM

Pursuant to Ohio Revised Code Section 5302.30

To Be Completed by Owner (Please Print)

Property Address:

Owners Name(s):

Date: , 20___

Owner ( ) is   ( ) is not occupying the property. If owner is occupying the property, since what date.

Purpose of Disclosure Form: This is a statement of the condition of the property and of information concerning the property actually known by the owner as required by Ohio Revised Code Section 5302.30. Unless otherwise advised in writing by the owner, the owner, other than having lived at or owning the property, possesses no greater knowledge than that which could be obtained by a careful inspection of the property by a potential purchaser. Unless otherwise advised, owner has not conducted any inspection of generally inaccessible areas of the property. THIS STATEMENT IS NOT A WARRANTY OF ANY KIND BY THE OWNER OR BY ANY AGENT OR SUBAGENT REPRESENTING THE OWNER OF THE PROPERTY. THIS STATEMENT IS NOT A SUBSTITUTE FOR ANY INSPECTIONS. POTENTIAL PURCHASERS ARE ENCOURAGED TO OBTAIN THEIR OWN PROFESSIONAL INSPECTION.

Owner's Statement: The representations contained on this form are made by the owner and are not the representations of the owner's agent or subagent. This form and the representations contained in it are provided by the owner exclusively to potential purchasers in a transfer made by the owner, and are not made to purchasers in any subsequent transfers. The information contained in this disclosure form does not limit the obligation of the owner to disclose an item of information that is required by any other statute or law to be disclosed in the transfer of residential real estate.

Instructions to Owner: (1) Answer ALL questions. (2) Identify any material matters in the property that are actually known. (3) Attach additional pages with your signature if additional space is needed. (4) Complete this form yourself. (5) If some items do not apply to your property, write NA (not applicable). If the item to be disclosed is not within your actual knowledge, indicate Unknown.

THE FOLLOWING STATEMENTS OF THE OWNER ARE BASED ON OWNER'S ACTUAL KNOWLEDGE

A) WATER SUPPLY: The source of water supply to the property is (check appropriate boxes):

( ) Public Water Service   ( ) Private Water   ( ) Well Service   ( ) Holding Tank

( ) Cistern   ( ) Spring   ( ) Pond   ( ) Unknown   ( ) Other

If owner knows of any current leaks, backups or other material problems with the water supply system or quality of the water, please describe:

B) SEWER SYSTEM: The nature of the sanitary sewer system servicing the property is (check appropriate boxes):

( ) Public Sewer   ( ) Private Sewer   ( ) Septic Tank   ( ) Leach Field

( ) Aeration Tank   ( ) Filtration Bed   ( ) Unknown   ( ) Other

If not a public or private sewer, date of last inspection.

If owner knows of any current leaks, backups or other material problems with the sewer system servicing the property, please describe:

C) ROOF: Do you know of any current leaks or other material problems with the roof or rain gutters?
( ) Yes   ( ) No

If "Yes," please describe:

(continues)

EXHIBIT 10–2 *Residential Property Disclosure Form (Ohio)* *(continued)*

If owner knows of any leaks or other material problems with the roof or rain gutters since owning the property (but not longer than the past 5 years), please describe and indicate any repairs completed:

D) BASEMENT/CRAWL SPACE: Do you know of any current water leakage, water accumulation, excess dampness or other defects with the basement/crawl space?   ( ) Yes   ( ) No

If "Yes," please describe:

If owner knows of any repairs, alterations or modifications to the property or other attempts to control any water or dampness problems in the basement or crawl space since owning the property (but not longer than the past 5 years), please describe:

E) STRUCTURAL COMPONENTS (FOUNDATIONS, FLOORS, INTERIOR AND EXTERIOR WALLS): Do you know of any movement, shifting, deterioration, material cracks (other than visible minor cracks or blemishes) or other material problems with the foundation, floors, or interior/exterior walls?   ( ) Yes   ( ) No

If "Yes," please describe:

If you know of any repairs, alterations or modifications to control the cause or effect of any problem identified above, since owning the property (but not longer than the past 5 years), please describe:

F) MECHANICAL SYSTEMS: Do you know of any current problems or defects with the mechanical systems?
( ) Yes   ( ) No

If "Yes," please describe:

For purposes of this section, mechanical systems include electrical, plumbing (pipes), central heating and air conditioning, sump pump, fireplace/chimney, lawn sprinkler, water softener, security system, central vacuum, or other mechanical systems that exist on the property.

G) WOOD BORING INSECTS/TERMITES: Do you know of the presence of any wood boring insects/termites in or on the property or any existing damage to the property caused by wood boring insects/termites?
( ) Yes   ( ) No

If "Yes," please describe:

If owner knows of any inspection or treatment for wood boring insects/termites, since owning the property (but not longer than the past 5 years), please describe:

H) PRESENCE OF HAZARDOUS MATERIALS: Do you have actual knowledge of the presence of any of the below identified hazardous materials on the property?

	Yes	No	Unknown
1) Lead-Based Paint	( )	( )	( )
2) Asbestos	( )	( )	( )
3) Urea-Formaldehyde Foam Insulation	( )	( )	( )
4) Radon Gas	( )	( )	( )
4a) If Yes, indicate level of gas if known			
5) Other toxic substances	( )	( )	( )

If the answer to any of the above questions is "Yes," please describe:

I) DRAINAGE: Do you know of any current flooding, drainage, settling or grading problems affecting the property?   ( ) Yes   ( ) No

If "Yes," please describe:

If owner knows of any repairs, modifications or alterations to the property or other attempts to control any flooding, drainage, settling or grading problems since owning the property (but not longer than the past 5 years), please describe:

(continues)

EXHIBIT 10–2 **Residential Property Disclosure Form (Ohio) (continued)**

J) CODE VIOLATIONS: Have you received notice of any building or housing code violations currently affecting the use of the property? ( ) Yes ( ) No

If "Yes," please describe:

K) UNDERGROUND STORAGE TANKS/WELLS: Do you know of any underground storage tanks, oil or natural gas wells (plugged or unplugged), or abandoned water wells on the property? ( ) Yes ( ) No

If "Yes," please describe:

L) OTHER KNOWN MATERIAL DEFECTS: The following are other known material defects currently in or on the property:

For purposes of this section, material defects would include any non-observable physical condition existing on the property that could be dangerous to anyone occupying the property or any non-observable physical conditions that would inhibit a person's use of the property.

Owner represents that the statements contained in this form are made in good faith based on his/her actual knowledge as of the date signed by the Owner.

OWNER: DATE:

OWNER: DATE:

RECEIPT AND ACKNOWLEDGEMENT OF POTENTIAL PURCHASERS

Potential purchasers are advised that the owner has no obligation to update this form but may do so according to Revised Code Section 5302.30(G). Pursuant to Ohio Revised Code Section 5302.30(K), if this form is not provided to you prior to the time you enter into a purchase contract for the property, you may rescind the purchase contract by delivering a signed and dated document of rescission to Owner or Owner's agent, provided the document of rescission is delivered prior to all three of the following dates: 1) the date of closing; 2) 30 days after the Owner accepted your offer; and 3) within 3 business days following your receipt or your agent's receipt of this form or an amendment of this form.

I/WE ACKNOWLEDGE RECEIPT OF A COPY OF THIS DISCLOSURE FORM AND UNDERSTAND THAT THE STATEMENTS ARE MADE BASED ON THE OWNER'S ACTUAL KNOWLEDGE AS OF THE DATE SIGNED BY THE OWNER.

My/Our Signature below does not constitute approval of any disclosed condition as represented herein by the owner.

PURCHASER: DATE:

PURCHASER: DATE:

contact with those buyers (*Restatement [Second] of Torts* § 532, illus. 2).

Required State of Mind

Proof of intentional misrepresentation also requires showing that the defendant knew of the falsity of the statement or acted with reckless disregard to the truth. A defendant who lacks grounds for his representation or confidence in its accuracy possesses the state of mind required for intentional misrepresentation. State of mind is what distinguishes intentional misrepresentation from negligent misrepresentation.

A defendant is also culpable if he makes a statement that is merely a belief but represents it as being actual knowledge. In one case the officers of a corporation told one of the company's creditors that the company was making money. They also sent him some erroneous financial statements. In reliance on the officers' statements, the plaintiff refrained from collecting his debt. In truth, the company was losing money, and when the plaintiff finally sought reimbursement he was unable to collect the monies owed him. The defendant officers were found liable in this case, not because their statements were false but because they had made statements regarding the solvency of the company without knowing whether the company was making money or not. Their culpability lay in their representation of belief as knowledge (*Sovereign Pocohontas Co. v. Bond,* 120 F.2d 39 [D.C. Cir. 1941]).

Reliance on the Misrepresentation

A plaintiff must also show that she relied on the defendant's misrepresentation. The question that commonly arises is whether the plaintiff made any independent investigation of her own and whether her reliance was on the misrepresentation, her investigation, or both. Suppose the seller of a horse fraudulently misrepresents the breeding potential of the horse, and the plaintiff, wishing to confirm these representations, checks with other experienced horse breeders. If the plaintiff relies totally or almost totally on his own investigation, he will be deemed not to have relied on the seller's misrepresentation. If, however, the seller's misrepresentation is a substantial factor in inducing the plaintiff's reliance, the reliance requirement will be fulfilled and the seller will be found liable.

Was the Reliance Justifiable?

A related question is whether the plaintiff's reliance was justifiable. Is a plaintiff entitled to rely on an opinion offered by the defendant? Traditionally, courts have been reluctant to allow plaintiffs to recover on the basis of any of the defendant's statements that could be characterized as opinion.

In some circumstances, however, such reliance may be justified. If a defendant and plaintiff have a fiduciary relationship, or if the defendant has worked to secure the confidence of the plaintiff, the plaintiff may be justified in relying on the defendant's opinion. Also, if the defendant purports to have special knowledge that the plaintiff does not have, the plaintiff may be justified in relying on the defendant. Similarly, if the defendant is aware that the plaintiff is particularly gullible or unintelligent and will be easily misled by any kind of opinion, a justifiable reliance will more likely be found. A horse trader, for example, who tells an ignorant investor that a particular horse is worth $500,000 may be found liable for misrepresentation if, in fact, any knowledgeable investor would recognize that figure as being wholly unrealistic (*Restatement [Second] of Torts* § 542). Following

are some examples of when reliance may or not be justifiable.

"Puffing"

Mere "puffing" is not actionable. A used car dealer who tells a customer that this car is "the best deal you will ever make" is not liable for the statement even though the dealer does not actually believe that the car is a particularly good deal (*Restatement [Second] of Torts* § 542, cmt. e).

As Justice Learned Hand once commented, "Such statements, like the claims of campaign managers before election, are rather designed to allay the suspicion which would attend their absence than to be understood as having any relation to objective truth" (*Vulcan Metals Co. v. Simmons Manufacturing Co.,* 248 F. 853, 856 [2d Cir. 1918]).

Opinion of Disinterested Party

The result may be different if the plaintiff reasonably perceives that the opinion is being expressed by a "disinterested" party, meaning a neutral one, someone who will receive no benefit. In that case the plaintiff's reliance is more likely to be considered reasonable. If a consumer advocacy group indicates that a particular brand of off-road vehicle is safe and the plaintiff is injured in that vehicle, the consumer group's argument that its endorsement was merely an opinion is likely to fail. By holding itself out as a disinterested party that examined and ultimately endorsed the product, the group likely will be deemed as possessing special information upon which the public was reasonably justified in relying.

Opinion Implying Facts

If a defendant renders an opinion implying that no facts incompatible with that opinion exist, the plaintiff may be able to recover if she can show that the defendant was aware of such incompatible facts. For example, a corporation president who, in an effort to sell stock, represents his company as being a "gold mine" when in fact he knows the company to be losing money may be found liable for misrepresentation (*Ragsdale v. Kennedy,* 209 S.E.2d 494 [N.C. 1974]).

Remember that the line between fact and opinion is a tenuous one at best—but if the defendant crosses over that line by making a statement of fact that she knows to be false, she can be found liable. A statement of value that would normally be considered opinion may become a factual statement because of the context in which it is expressed. A defendant who says, "The land across the street sold for $10,000 an acre last year," has made a statement of fact for which he will be liable if he is aware that the land actually sold for much less.

Predictions

A prediction that a certain event is bound to happen will almost always be regarded as an opinion. If, however, the defendant knows of facts inconsistent with that prediction, he may still be found liable for misrepresentation. A landowner who predicts that the value of her land will increase 10 percent a year for the next five years could be held liable if the plaintiff could show that the landowner was aware that the property was about to be condemned.

Statement of Intentions

If a defendant makes a statement as to her own intentions, a plaintiff's reliance on that statement will frequently be considered justifiable. If a party to a contract is unable to sue for breach of contract because the opposing party can raise a contract defense, such as the Statute of Frauds, the party wanting to sue may be able to claim misrepresentation if she relied on the defendant's statements. Suppose a defendant promises to buy the plaintiff's house for $50,000, but at the time she makes this promise she actually has no intention of buying the house. When the plaintiff sues for breach of contract, if the defendant raises a statute-of-frauds defense (because the contract was not in writing), the plaintiff can sue on the basis of misrepresentation, arguing that the defendant never intended to keep her contract. If the plaintiff can prove this was the defendant's intent, most courts will not allow the defendant to raise the statute of frauds, the parol evidence rule, lack of consideration, or any other contract defense to bar liability.

Proximate Cause

The plaintiff in a suit for misrepresentation must prove that he sustained actual damages that were proximately caused by the defendant's misrepresentation. In other words, the loss must be a "reasonably foreseeable" result of the misrepresentation.

Suppose, for example, the plaintiff purchases stock in reliance on the defendant's misrepresentation. If the market value of the stock declines due to causes unrelated to those misrepresentations, the defendant will not be considered the proximate cause of the plaintiff's losses (*Restatement [Second] of Torts* § 548A, illus. 1).

Damages

Damages for misrepresentation may be measured in two ways. First, the plaintiff may be asked to be put in the position she was in before the misrepresentation (referred to as the *reliance measure*). Alternatively, the plaintiff may be asked to be put in the position she would have been had the misrepresented facts been true (referred to as the *benefits-of-the-bargain measure*). The majority of courts use the latter measure of damages.

To exemplify these approaches, suppose that a plaintiff pays $20,000 for a horse that is actually worth $10,000. If the horse would have been worth $50,000 if the misrepresentation about the horse had actually been true, under the benefits-of-the-bargain approach the plaintiff will receive $40,000 (the difference between the actual value of the horse, $10,000, and what it would have been worth if it had been as it was represented, $50,000). Under the reliance method of measurement the plaintiff will recover $10,000 (the difference between the actual value of the horse, $10,000, and what the plaintiff paid, $20,000). Note that in assessing damages, the fact that the plaintiff would have made a bad bargain even if the defendant had made no misrepresentations is irrelevant.

Exhibit 10–3 lists the aspects of misrepresentation we have been discussing.

NEGLIGENT MISREPRESENTATION

Although historically recovery for negligent misrepresentation was not permitted, today most American courts allow such a claim. Other than intent, the requirements for an action of negligent misrepresentation are essentially the same as those for intentional misrepresentation.

The courts are most inclined to allow recovery for negligent misrepresentation when the defendant makes false statements during the course of her business or profession or has a pecuniary interest in the

EXHIBIT 10–3 **Misrepresentation**

WHAT IS A MISREPRESENTATION?

- False statement.
- Concealment by actions.
- Failure to disclose material fact that is essential to transaction.
- Telling of half-truth.

TO WHOM MUST MISREPRESENTATION BE MADE?

- Plaintiff belongs to class of persons that defendant could reasonably expect to learn of and rely on misrepresentation.
- Plaintiff is involved in the type of transaction defendant could reasonably expect plaintiff to engage in as a result of reliance.
- Defendant incorporates misstatements into commercial documents.

DEFENDANT'S STATE OF MIND

- Is aware of falsity of representation.
- Acts with reckless disregard for truth or falsity of representation.
- Has mere belief but acts as if she has actual knowledge.

WHAT IS JUSTIFIABLE RELIANCE?

Defendant offers an opinion and:
- Defendant and plaintiff have fiduciary relationship.
- Defendant has worked to gain plaintiff's confidence.
- Defendant is aware plaintiff is gullible or unintelligent.
- Plaintiff is likely to perceive that opinion is offered by "disinterested" party.
- Defendant suggests no facts incompatible with opinion exist when he is aware such facts exist.
- Defendant makes prediction and is aware of facts inconsistent with prediction.
- Defendant states what his intentions are, knowing the actual intentions are different.

HOW ARE DAMAGES PROVED?

Reliance: Putting plaintiff in position she was in prior to misrepresentation.
Benefit of the bargain: Putting plaintiff in position she would have been in had the misrepresented facts been true.

PUTTING IT INTO PRACTICE 10:1

1. Lucille, a blackjack dealer in Lake Tahoe, has a "tummy tuck" operation to lower the scar from a previous tummy tuck. She says the surgeon assured her there were no risks involved, that her skin "would be as smooth as a baby's," and that she would be pleased with the results. After the operation Lucille's scar is lowered, but her skin blisters and she experiences severe pain in an area above the stitches. The doctor promises either to resolve the problem himself or to pay for another doctor to do so. He continues to treat Lucille and never refuses to answer her questions or respond to her requests for treatment.

    Lucille decides to consult with other physicians and then hires an attorney to litigate her grievance.

(continues)

At trial, Lucille's expert witness speculates that the blisters could be due to a chemical or "cast" burn, a minor injury, or, as the defense expert testifies, due to liquid silicone that had been injected into Lucille's breast years earlier and that had migrated to the abdomen.

Do you think Lucille has a cause of action for misrepresentation based on any of the doctor's representations to her?

2. Barbara files suit for misrepresentation after suffering an ectopic pregnancy resulting from intercourse with her attorney (who is representing her in a domestic relations matter). The attorney vowed to her that "I can't possibly get anyone pregnant." Does she have a viable claim?

Suppose Barbara had delivered a healthy child after falsely telling the attorney before they engaged in intercourse that she was on birth control pills. If she had sued him for child support, would the attorney have a viable claim for misrepresentation?

3. Maria and Martin are Polish prisoners of war who meet in a displaced persons camp. He proposes to her, and she signs what she believes to be an application for a marriage certificate but later discovers she has entered into a civil marriage. Martin promises her a church marriage. Because she refuses to have marital relations with him until they are properly married, Martin locks her in a room and rapes her. After several days of confinement she escapes, but he induces her to return, again promising a church marriage. Once again she escapes, only to return reluctantly when Martin promises her they will be married in the church.

Should Maria be granted an annulment on the basis of Martin's false representation? Is her reliance on Martin's promises justifiable?

4. Peter claims that the school district he attended for twelve years and from which he graduated deprived him of basic academic skills in reading and writing. Part of his complaint alleges that the district "allowed him 'to pass and advance from a course or grade level' with knowledge that he had not achieved either its completion or the skills 'necessary for him to succeed or benefit from subsequent courses,' . . . assigned him to classes in which the instructors were unqualified or which were not 'geared' to his reading level, and . . . permitted him to graduate from high school although he was 'unable to read above the eighth grade level.'" Peter claims that as a result of the district's and its employees' fraudulent representations that he was "performing at or near grade level in basic academic skills," he has suffered a loss of earning capacity. Should Peter be allowed to recover for intentional misrepresentation?

5. Florence brings suit against Kaiser Health Plan for malpractice because of the delay of her husband's doctor in ordering a biopsy in the diagnosis of her husband's condition. Florence maintains that when Kaiser represented that it would provide "high standards" of medical service, it promised a "standard higher than nonnegligence." She also points out that although Kaiser claimed to be a "nonprofit" organization, it was actually built around a system that encouraged doctors to be conservative in ordering tests and treatments. Because she and her husband were not told about Kaiser's policies, she alleges that they were fraudulently led to believe they would receive "the best quality of care and treatment." Do you think Florence has a viable claim for misrepresentation?

transaction at hand. A real estate broker, for example, may be liable for negligent misrepresentation by failing to use reasonable care in ascertaining the truth of a representation made by a seller, even if the broker honestly believes it to be true.

The defendant is not required to receive compensation directly. If a prospective client comes to an attorney's office and the attorney negligently gives him incorrect advice as part of a "free first consultation," the defendant attorney is still liable for the misrepresentation (*Restatement [Second] of Torts* § 552, cmt. d).

One who negligently misrepresents something, however, is liable to a narrower class of third persons than is one who intentionally misrepresents something. One who makes an *intentional* misrepresentation is liable to anyone whom he reasonably expects to learn about the statement (under the modern view). One who makes a *negligent* misrepresentation is liable only to those whom he intends to reach with the information or those he knows the recipient of the information intends to reach.

Nevertheless, as long as the defendant is aware that a negligent misrepresentation will be passed on to a limited number of people, she will be liable even if unaware of their precise identity. Suppose a surveyor negligently provides a landowner with an erroneous description of her land. If the surveyor is aware that the owner is planning to sell her land, he will be liable to the purchaser for his errors even though he does not know the name of the purchaser. By the same token, a lawyer who negligently drafts a will may be liable to the beneficiaries even though he may be unaware of the identity of those beneficiaries.

The courts deny recovery, however, when the class of people intended to be reached by the negligent misrepresentation is not limited. Suppose a stock ticker service negligently reports information to its customer brokers. The plaintiff, a stock owner, reads the news at his broker's office and immediately sells his stock because he expects stock prices to fall. The stock ticker service is not liable because the plaintiff did not subscribe directly to its service; therefore, the "limited number of persons" requirement is not met (*Jaillet v. Cashman*, 139 N.E. 714 [N.Y. 1923]).

To see an interesting application of the law regarding intentional and negligent misrepresentation in the context of adoptions, read *Gibbs v. Ernst*, 647 A.2d 882 (Pa. 1994). Notice how, and for what social policy reasons, the court allows the common law tort of misrepresentation to be applied to an area of law that is wholly created by statute. Note, too, how courts are more reluctant to hold adoption agencies liable for their negligent misrepresentations than for their intentional misrepresentations, out of a fear that imposing too heavy a burden on adoption agencies will unduly hamper their ability to place children in homes.

PUTTING IT INTO PRACTICE 10:2

William has an ankle replacement after fracturing his right ankle. Before the surgery he is told by his physician that the physician has performed three successful ankle replacements. When William asked the doctor what would happen if the ankle replacement did not work, the doctor responded, "The worst that could happen is that we will just take that out and fuse it." The doctor also assures him that amputation is "not a problem" and "not something to worry about." Based on the doctor's representations, Williams agrees to the ankle replacement. After the surgery, the ankle becomes infected; the infection does not respond to antibiotics, and William's leg has to be amputated below the knee by another doctor. At trial the doctor testifies that he had never personally performed an ankle replacement, although members of his medical group had.

Do you think William has a claim for negligent misrepresentation? Are there any other grounds upon which William might be able to sue?

CASE / *Gibbs v. Ernst*
647 A.2d 882 (Pa.1994)

MONTEMURO, Justice.

This is an appeal by Concern Professional Services for Children and Youth; Concern's Director, Paul Ernst; Concern Adoption Specialist, Marsha S. Hiester (hereinafter collectively Concern); and Northhampton County Children and Youth; its Executive Director, R. Nancy Haley; and its Caseworker, Brenda Messa (hereinafter collectively Children and Youth) from an Order of the Commonwealth Court reversing the trial court's grant of demurrers to counts of Wrongful Adoption and Negligent Placement of Adoptive Child in the complaint filed by appellees Frank A. and Jayne Gibbs, and Michael J. Gibbs.

Appellees initiated this action in the Court of Common Pleas of Bucks County against Concern and Children and Youth arising out of the adoption of Michael J. Gibbs on October 21, 1985. Children and Youth is an agency of the Commonwealth of Pennsylvania and, pursuant to law, is responsible for placing children who are wards of the Commonwealth with agencies for the purposes of adoption. Concern is a private child placement agency, licensed by the Commonwealth.

The sole issue presented before this Court is whether the law of the Commonwealth recognizes as causes of action Wrongful Adoption and Negligent Placement of Adoptive Child. For the reasons set forth below, we affirm in part the decision of the Commonwealth Court and hold that traditional common law causes of action sounding in fraud and negligence apply in the adoption context.

The Complaint alleges the following facts: in early 1983, appellees Jayne and Frank Gibbs, who were already foster parents, inquired of Concern about the availability of a healthy Caucasian infant for adoption, and were informed that there was a two year waiting list for healthy Caucasian infants. Appellees were actively encouraged by agency representatives to apply for the adoption of an older child, and were told that it would be easier to adopt a "hard to adopt due to age" child, and that if the child had been physically or sexually abused, Concern would disclose fully the history of these occurrences. Appellees were invited to look through a book containing photographs of older children available for adoption, along with brief positive descriptions of the children.

In May of 1983, appellees submitted a dual application for adoption of a healthy Caucasian infant and a "hard to adopt due to age" child. After a home-study by Marsha Hiester, Concern's adoption specialist, appellees reviewed the book of waiting children approximately twice a month at Concern's offices. On each occasion they completed a form for the child they wanted to adopt, and on each occasion they specifically requested a child who was "hard to place due to age," but who had no history of sexual or physical abuse or any mental or emotional problems.

In late August or early September 1984, appellees were informed by Concern that they had been chosen to adopt Michael, a five year old boy from Northhampton County.[1] In addition to his age, appellees were told by Concern that Michael was presently repeating kindergarten, that he was Caucasian, and that he had been in foster care, but for only two years and only with one family. Appellees were further informed by Concern that Michael was hyperactive, behind in his school work, had been verbally abused by his mother, and that the major problem was neglect by his mother. Concern specifically denied any history of physical or sexual abuse. In October of 1984, appellees were introduced to Michael and his caseworkers at Concern. They were given information about Michael's foster family, and were once again informed by Concern that there was no history of sexual or physical abuse. Later that same afternoon, appellees met with Brenda Messa, a caseworker at Children and Youth's offices in Easton, Pennsylvania where they requested a more detailed social and medical history of Michael.

During the first weekend of November, 1984, Michael was placed for adoption with appellees who filed a Report of Intention to Adopt with the Orphan's Court of Berks County. Shortly thereafter, Concern forwarded certain documents identified as Michael's medical file, consisting of records of Michael's birth and the medical history of his natural mother. Appellees once again requested more information about Michael's psychological and emotional history.

Concern supervised Michael's placement with appellees and although he had educational problems, Michael seemed much calmer and passed first grade. In September of 1985, Concern consented to the finalization of the adoption. Prior to finalization, appellees met with Concern and specifically asked whether there was anything in Concern's file that had not been disclosed to them. They were assured by Concern that they had been given everything Children and Youth had provided to Concern; but were told that Children and Youth had "promised additional information," and that there was a "communication problem" with Children and Youth. Concern agreed to check all records to make sure everything was made available to appellees prior to the finalization of the adoption.

---

1. We note that Michael was born on May 21, 1977, making him, in fact, more than seven years old in August/September of 1984.

(continues)

On October 21, 1985, a final order was entered in the Court of Common Pleas of Berks County granting the adoption of Michael J. Gibbs. Immediately thereafter, Michael began experiencing severe emotional problems. He became violent and aggressive toward younger children, attempting to amputate the arm of a five year old; attempting to suffocate his younger cousin; attempting to kill another cousin by hitting him over the head with a lead pipe; deliberately placing Clorox in a cleaning solution, causing Ms. Gibbs to burn her hands badly; and starting a fire which seriously injured a younger cousin.

After Michael's admission and evaluation at the Philadelphia Child Guidance Center, appellees were advised that little chance existed of any change in his violent behavior. Michael's conduct deteriorated further, and he was admitted to a special program for adopted children at the Northwestern Institute where he remained until he was transferred by court order to the Eastern State School and Hospital. On or about September 15, 1989, Michael was declared dependent by the Family Division of the Philadelphia Court of Common Pleas, and was placed in the custody of the Department of Human Resources.

In September of 1989, a caseworker from the Department of Human Services informed appellees for the first time that Michael had been severely abused, both physically and sexually, as a young child. Records in the possession of Northwestern Institute revealed that Michael had been in ten different foster placements before he was freed for adoption; that during his first six years Michael's mother repeatedly placed him in and then removed him from foster care; that there was a long, serious history of abuse, both physical and sexual, by his biological parents; that Michael had been neglected by his biological mother; that Michael had an extensive history of aggressiveness and hostility towards other children; and that Michael's mother at one time attempted to cut off his penis. At no time prior to the finalization of the adoption did Concern or Children and Youth disclose this information although it was in their possession and had been requested.

In April of 1990, appellees commenced this action in the Court of Common Pleas of Bucks County, setting forth in Count I of their complaint a cause of action for Wrongful Adoption and in Count II a cause of action for Negligent Placement of Adoptive Child. Appellants, Concern and Children and Youth, filed preliminary objections in the nature of a demurrer to these counts which the trial court granted. The Commonwealth Court reversed, *Gibbs v. Concern Professional Services*, 150 Pa. Commw. 154, 160, 615 A.2d 851, 854 (1991), and in June of 1993, we granted allocatur on the sole question of whether the Commonwealth Court was correct in its conclusion that appellees could maintain their action for Wrongful Adoption and Negligent Placement of Adoptive Child.

The Commonwealth Court's standard of review in assessing the propriety of a common pleas court decision is limited to a determination of whether constitutional rights have been violated or whether the common pleas court abused its discretion or committed an error of law. . . . We agree with the Commonwealth Court that the Court of Common Pleas erred in sustaining appellants' demurrer.

In examining appellees' claims, we do not believe that we are considering novel theories of recovery, since the terms employed by appellees are somewhat of a misnomer. The proper focus of this case is whether longstanding common law causes of action should be applied to the adoption context.

Most authorities have recognized that causes of action for wrongful adoption are no more than an extension of common law principles to the adoption setting. . . .

In determining whether these traditional common law causes of action should be applied to the adoption context in our Commonwealth, we are well aware of the competing interests involved. On one side is the interest of prospective parents in obtaining as much information as possible about the child they are to adopt. Adoption experts are virtually unanimous in the belief that complete and accurate medical and social information should be communicated to adopting patents. Providing full and complete information is crucial because the consequences of non-disclosure can be catastrophic; ignorance of medical or psychological history can prevent the adopting parents and their doctors from providing effective treatment, or any treatment at all. Moreover, full and accurate disclosure ensures that the adopting parents are emotionally and financially equipped to raise a child with special needs. Failure to provide adequate background information can result in the placement of children with families unable or unwilling to cope with physical or mental problems, leading to failed adoptions.[6] . . .

---

6. It can be argued that adoptive parents are entitled to no notice of medical problems, since natural parents receive no advance warning of a child's special needs. However, the risks assumed by adoptive parents are, in truth, very different from those of [natural] parents. Biological parents, theoretically at least, are aware of their medical histories and can decide to have a child with knowledge of, e.g., an increased risk of genetic abnormality. Adoptive parents, without full and accurate information, have no way of knowing if the adoptee has a risk of a genetic problem. This Court is also mindful that adoptive parents are performing a valuable social service in providing a family to otherwise unwanted children. In light of this contribution to society, it is only equitable to conclude that adoptive parents should not be asked to assume unwittingly the same risks as natural parents. For these reasons, a policy in favor of full and accurate disclosure of a child's medical history improves the chances of a successful placement and promotes public confidence in the institution of adoption.

(continues)

On the other side of the ledger, adoption agencies and intermediaries are justifiably concerned lest any undue burden placed upon them should ultimately reduce the number of successful adoptions. In deciding to apply traditional common law causes of action to the adoption context, we have paid particular attention to the obligations placed upon adoption agencies so as not to diminish their effectiveness in placing children. We are convinced that the vast majority of adoption agencies in this Commonwealth conduct the adoption process with the utmost professionalism. However, we are also convinced that agencies, on occasion, do fail to provide prospective parents with complete and accurate information, and worse, occasionally supply information which is both false and misleading.[8] Mindful of the seriousness of this problem and its potentially devastating consequences, we hold that the traditional common law causes of action grounded in fraud and negligence to apply to the adoption setting.

The Adoption Act of 1970, codified at 23 Pa.C.S. §§ 2101–2901, sets forth the steps which must be taken to realize an adoption, and the responsibilities and duties of adoption intermediaries in the process. Any person intending to adopt a child must file a Report of Intention to Adopt, 23 Pa.C.S. § 2531, within six months of which the intermediary must respond by reporting to the court information specifically required by 23 Pa.C.S. § 2533. Under Section 2533 (b) (12), the intermediary must include as part of its report "[a] statement that medical history was obtained and if not obtained, a statement of the reason therefore." Medical history information is defined as:

> [m]edical records and other information concerning an adoptee or an adoptee's natural family which is relevant to the adoptee's present or future health care or medical treatment. The term includes otherwise confidential or privileged information providing that identifying contents have been removed pursuant to section 2909 (relating to medical history information). 23 Pa.C.S. § 2102.

Section 2909 sets forth medical history requirements and states in pertinent part that "[m]edical history information shall, where practicable, be delivered by the attending physician or other designated person to the intermediary who shall deliver such information to the adopting parents or their physician." 23 Pa.C.S. § 2909(a).

Appellants argue that the Commonwealth Court exceeded its authority and encroached upon the province of the legislature in recognizing appellees' action for Wrongful Adoption and Negligent Placement of Adoptive Child because they are not mentioned in the Adoption Act. Although the Act, . . . sets forth the duties of an adoption intermediary with regard to providing the medical history of an adoptive child, it provides no sanction against an intermediary who fails to meet that obligation.

Appellants correctly assert that adoption is a statutorily created mechanism, unknown at common law. It is also true that the Adoption Act must be strictly construed . . . and that exceptions to the Act may not be judicially created. However, we find nothing in the Act to be inconsistent with the application of traditional common law principles to the adoption setting.

In *Roe v. Catholic Charities*, the Illinois Appellate Court considered precisely the question of whether common law causes of action were disallowed where the adoption statute did not provide for them. There, the court analogized adoption to corporations, which are also creatures of statute, but which are bound by both statutory and common law. After noting that, for example, a corporation may be sued in tort, the court concluded that "[p]rivate adoption agencies and agencies of not-for-profit corporations in particular, are bound by all the law . . . both statute and common law."

We are in full accord with the reasoning of the court in *Roe*. The Adoption Act establishes the procedures that govern the adoption process, and the cases cited by appellants properly stand for the notion that these procedures are to be strictly construed. However, the Act is silent on whether adoption intermediaries are liable for the commission of torts. It is our opinion that this silence evidences the legislature's intention that adoption agencies be liable under the long-established common law of Pennsylvania. Had the legislature intended for the Adoption Act to provide intermediaries with immunity from common law sanctions, it would have said so explicitly. The causes of action we address today are so well established that we find affirmative action by the legislature, rather than silence, would be necessary to prevent their application in the adoption context. Until such legislative action is forthcoming, we hold that adoption intermediaries are subject to all the law of this Commonwealth, both statutory and common law.

The complaint suggests several common law theories of recovery. The first such cause of action is intentional misrepresentation or fraud, which contains the following elements: (1) a representation; (2) which is material to the transaction at hand; (3) made falsely, with knowledge of its falsity or recklessness as to whether it is true or false; (4) with the intent of misleading another into relying on it; (5) justifiable reliance on

---

8. Research reveals that one third of the parents who had adopted physically abused children, and one half of those adopting sexually abused children were not informed of the abuse.

(continues)

the misrepresentation; and (6) the resulting injury was proximately caused by the reliance.[12]

Our sister states have unanimously applied the theory of intentional misrepresentation to the adoption context. . . . In *Burr*, the adopting parents were told that the adoptee was born in a hospital to an eighteen year old unwed mother who gave up the child to move to Texas in search of a better job. The agency stated that the child was a "nice, big, healthy, baby boy." The child later developed severe medical problems requiring twenty-four hour nursing care, and was eventually institutionalized for the remainder of his life. The adopting parents later learned that the child had, in fact, been born in a mental institution to a mentally retarded woman and had previously been placed with several foster families. The adoption agency was well aware of these facts and that the child was developing slowly, but provided the adopting parents a fictional story about the child's medical history. The parents sued the adoption agency for intentional misrepresentation, and the Ohio Supreme Court upheld an award of damages, concluding that "[i]t would be a travesty of justice and a distortion of the truth to conclude that deceitful placement of this infant, known by [the adoption agency] to be at risk, was not actionable when the tragic, but hidden realities of the child's infirmities finally came to light."

The law of this Commonwealth has long recognized fraud or intentional misrepresentation as actionable conduct in other settings. . . . We now hold, in accord with the unanimous decisions of our sister jurisdictions, that the cause of action for intentional misrepresentation is equally applicable in the adoption context. Such application will further the goal of providing prospective parents with full and accurate information about the child, and, at the same time will inhibit adoption agencies from providing false information. Adopting parents will then be able to make informed choices about adoption, ensuring that they have the emotional and financial resources to care properly for the child they have consented to adopt. This truthfulness in the adoption process will, thus, result in fewer failed adoptions and enhance public confidence in the process. We, like the court in Burr, believe that it would be a "travesty of justice" to allow adoption agencies to engage in deceitful and fraudulent conduct with impunity. . . . Few would argue that the knowing provision of false information by adoption intermediaries to prospective parents so as to induce them to accept a particular child is not reprehensible and blameworthy conduct. Still, we have carefully considered the interests of adoption intermediaries so as not to place an undue burden on them. We find that the only burden placed upon agencies arising from the application of this tort is the obligation to refrain from fraudulent and deceitful tactics. We require no less from every other business or non-profit organization in this Commonwealth, and see no valid reason to release adoption intermediaries from the burden of truth in their daily operations. Indeed, we find it particularly apposite in this context because of the potentially devastating consequences that can result from fraudulent conduct here.

Upon review of the complaint, we find that appellees clearly plead the elements of intentional misrepresentation . . ., and we hold that they should be able to proceed to trial on this cause of action.

The complaint also suggests that negligent misrepresentation provides grounds for recovery. The elements which must be proven for such a wrong to be shown are: (1) a misrepresentation of a material fact; (2) the representor must either know of the misrepresentation, must make the misrepresentation without knowledge as to its truth or falsity or must make the representation under circumstances in which he ought to have known of its falsity; (3) the representor must intend the representation to induce another to act on it; and (4) injury must result to the party acting in justifiable reliance on the misrepresentation. . . . Thus, negligent misrepresentation differs from intentional misrepresentation in that to commit the former, the speaker need not know his or her words are untrue, but must have failed to make reasonable investigation of the truth of those words.

Several of our sister states have recognized the tort of negligent misrepresentation in the adoption context. . . .

Any action in negligence is premised on the existence of a duty owed by one party to another. . . . In a claim for negligent misrepresentation, the adoption agency has assumed a duty to tell the truth when it volunteers information to prospective parents, but has failed to perform that duty. . . . In *Meracle*, the adoption agency

---

12. The tort of intentional non-disclosure has the same elements as the tort of intentional misrepresentation except that in a case of intentional non-disclosure the party intentionally conceals a material fact rather than making an affirmative misrepresentation. . . . The tort of intentional non-disclosure has been recognized in the adoption setting by other state courts. We have recognized that concealment or non-disclosure is an actionable tort in this Commonwealth. . . . Such fraud arises where there is an intentional concealment calculated to deceive. . . . We need not decide whether actions for the closely related tort of intentional non-disclosure or concealment should be allowed in the adoption setting, since close examination of appellees' complaint reveals that they have not pleaded such a cause of action.

(continues)

informed the prospective parents that the adoptee's paternal grandmother had died from Huntington's Disease. The parents asserted that the agency told them that the child's natural father had tested negative for the disease, and that, therefore, the child had no greater chance of developing the illness than any other child. The parents later learned that, in fact, there was no test to determine whether the father had inherited Huntington's. When the child developed the disease, the adopting parents sued the agency for negligently misrepresenting to them the father's condition. The court concluded that the parents' claim was not barred by public policy, and that "[s]uch a conclusion does not expose adoption agencies to potentially unlimited liability nor does it make such agencies the guarantors of the health of adoptive children. To avoid liability agencies simply refrain from making affirmative representations about a child's health."

In *Caritas*, the adopting parents were told that a slight possibility of incest in the child's background existed, but that the child was otherwise in good health. When serious behavioral and emotional problems developed after adoption, the child's psychologists contacted the agency for more information regarding the child's genetic background. The agency provided a document revealing that the child's biological parents were a 17-year-old boy and his 13-year-old sister, and that the father was hyperactive with a history of psychological problems. The parents sued the agency maintaining that it had made negligent misrepresentations about the child's background. The court held that public policy did not preclude a negligent misrepresentation action against an adoption agency, finding instead that "our decision will give potential parents more confidence in the adoption process and in the accuracy of the information they receive. Such confidence would be eroded if we were to immunize agencies from liability for false statements made during the adoption process."

Pennsylvania has long recognized the common law tort of negligent representation . . . and there is no reason why this cause of action should not be recognized in the adoption context.

We are fully aware that application of the tort of negligent misrepresentation presents more of a burden on adoption agencies than the tort of intentional misrepresentation, which requires only that adoption agencies refrain from fraudulent and deceitful conduct. Negligent misrepresentation, however, requires that the adoption agency make reasonable efforts to determine whether its representations are true. . . . Nevertheless, we believe that this admittedly heavier burden is tempered in several ways. First, agencies are only under the obligation to make reasonable efforts to determine if their statements are true. Thus, adoption agencies need not offer warranties or guarantees as to the information they provide. Second, as aptly stated by the court in *Meracle*, agencies may refrain from making any representations at all if they find that the burden of reasonable investigation is too harsh. While we adopt the traditional common-law cause of action of negligent misrepresentation in the adoption setting today, we in no way imply that adoption agencies are insurors or warrantors of a child's health. The tort we now recognize is not similar to, nor can it be compared with products liability or contractual warranties. Adoption agencies must merely use reasonable care to insure that the information they communicate is accurate, and the parents must show that any negligently communicated information is causally related to their damages. We believe that this tort is sufficiently restricted by the common law notion of foreseeability as found in the concepts of duty and proximate cause to prevent it from becoming in any way a guarantee or warranty of a child's future health.

An important element of duty is foreseeability; thus, the liability of adoption agencies is limited to those conditions reasonably predictable at the time of placement. . . . As the court in Foster held, "[a] duty does not exist if the defendant could not reasonably foresee any injury as the result of his acts or if his conduct was reasonable in light of what he could anticipate—no one is expected to guard against events which are not reasonably to be anticipated or that are so unlikely that the risks would be commonly disregarded." Accordingly, under the traditional principles of negligence, the duty of adoption agencies for the purposes of negligent misrepresentation will only apply where the condition of the child was foreseeable at the time of placement so that the agency is blameworthy in making a misrepresentation. . . .

Upon reviewing appellees' complaint we find that they have pleaded a cause of action for negligent misrepresentation. In Count I, 53, they aver that appellants "should have known" the statements and representations they made were false. Thus, 52–59 state a cause of action for negligent misrepresentation as well as intentional misrepresentation. We therefore hold that appellees should be able to proceed to trial on the theory of negligent misrepresentation. . . .

For the reasons set forth above, we affirm the order of the Commonwealth Court to the extent that it allows appellees to proceed to trial on claims of intentional misrepresentation [and] negligent misrepresentation.

PUTTING IT INTO PRACTICE 10:3

1. What is the issue in *Gibbs*?

2. What are the competing interests implicated in deciding how much information should be revealed to prospective adoptive parents?

3. Does an adoption intermediary have an obligation under the Adoption Act of 1970 to provide prospective parents with the medical history of adoptees and their natural family?

4. Is adoption a statutorily created mechanism that was unknown under the common law? Does this mean that common law principles cannot be applied to the adoption setting?

5. What does the Adoption Act indicate about whether adoption intermediaries can be held liable for the commission of a tort? What does the court believe the legislature would have to do to indicate that common tort law is not applicable in the adoption context?

6. How does the tort of intentional nondisclosure differ from intentional misrepresentation?

7. How have other states treated the issue of intentional misrepresentation in the context of adoption? How have they treated negligent misrepresentation?

8. What does the court hold in reference to whether the parents in this case should be able to proceed to trial on the intentional-misrepresentation claim? What about the negligent-misrepresentation claim?

9. Why does the court believe that the additional burden imposed on adoption agencies by allowing suit for negligent misrepresentation is not unreasonable?

INNOCENT MISREPRESENTATION

Until relatively recently, the courts have been unwilling to impose liability for innocent misrepresentations, which are, in effect, representations for which a defendant is strictly liable. At least two circumstances exist, however, in which many courts are now willing to allow recovery (see Exhibit 10–4). If a party involved in a sale, rental, or exchange transaction makes a material misrepresentation to the other in an effort to close a deal, he will be liable even if the misrepresentation is innocent (*Restatement [Second] of Torts* § 552C (1)). If a seller of land, for example, represents in good faith that he is selling property that he in fact does not own, he will be liable to the purchaser for his misrepresentation even though it is perfectly innocent. The sale, rental, or exchange must be directly between the plaintiff and the defendant. Suppose a manufacturer makes a representation to a retailer, who in turn passes it on to the plaintiff to induce her to buy the product.

In that case strict liability does not apply (*Restatement [Second] of Torts* § 552C).

Cases involving innocent misrepresentations can also be brought on the basis of an implied or express warranty theory. The plaintiff may opt for the strict liability theory because certain contract defenses that can be raised in a warranty suit are inapplicable in a strict liability suit. The parol evidence rule, for example, which precludes the admission of oral and written evidence external to a contract, is inapplicable in a strict liability suit but is certainly appropriate in a warranty suit.

Innocent misrepresentation also arises in the context of product liability. Similar to the "express warranty" provisions of the Uniform Commercial Code (UCC), a seller of goods that makes misrepresentations on a label or through public advertising is strictly liable for any physical injury that results from such misinformation. Even if the plaintiff does not buy the product from the defendant, the defendant remains liable. (See discussion on warranty in Chapter 12.)

EXHIBIT 10–4 *Recovery for Negligent and Innocent Misrepresentation*

WHEN IS RECOVERY ALLOWED FOR NEGLIGENT MISREPRESENTATION?	WHEN IS RECOVERY ALLOWED FOR INNOCENT MISREPRESENTATION?
• Misrepresentation is made during course of defendant's business or profession. • Misrepresentation is made during transaction in which defendant has a pecuniary interest. • Plaintiff is someone defendant intends to reach with representation or knows recipient of representation intends to reach. • Defendant is aware that misrepresentation will be passed on to limited number of persons although he does not know their identities.	• Defendant makes misrepresentation during course of sale, rental, or exchange in effort to close the deal. • Defendant makes misstatement on product label or in course of public advertising.

© Cengage Learning 2012

PUTTING IT INTO PRACTICE 10:4

The Ballards are interested in buying a lot with an unfinished dwelling and a well. The sellers' listing mentions a 100-foot well, and their real estate broker, believing the well to be good based on representations made to him by the sellers, tells the Ballards the well is adequate. Based on their belief in the sufficiency of the well, the Ballards buy the property. They are forced, however, to haul water when the well fails to provide sufficient water and then have to deepen the well so that its water production is adequate. Do the Ballards have a claim of innocent misrepresentation against the broker?

NUISANCE

A precise definition of the term **nuisance** has eluded the courts for centuries. In fact, one of the foremost scholars of tort law, William Prosser, refers to nuisance as "a sort of legal garbage can." The most that can be said is that a defendant's interference with a plaintiff's interest constitutes nuisance. A nuisance can be either a public nuisance or a private nuisance. The essence of a *public nuisance* is an interference with "a right common to the general public" (*Restatement [Second] of Torts* § 821B [1]). A *private nuisance*, in contrast, is an unreasonable interference with the plaintiff's use and enjoyment of his or her land (*Restatement [Second] of Torts* § 822). The key to private nuisance is the need for the plaintiff to have an interest in the land that has been affected by the defendant's activities. The maintenance of a feedlot or a house of prostitution in close proximity to a residential area is an example of a public nuisance; the playing of extremely loud music at 2:00 a.m. in a residential area exemplifies a private nuisance. Exhibit 10–5 defines the aspects of public and private nuisances.

EXHIBIT 10–5 *Nuisance*

PUBLIC NUISANCE	PRIVATE NUISANCE
• Substantial interference • Affects right common to general public • Public must be injured or exposed to injury • Plaintiff need not have interest in land • Plaintiff must suffer damages peculiar to him.	• Substantial interference • Affects plaintiff's use and enjoyment of land • Plaintiff must suffer substantial interference with use or enjoyment of land • Plaintiff must have interest in land.

© Cengage Learning 2012

Public Nuisance

To sustain a claim for public nuisance, the plaintiff must show that the public at large was actually injured or was exposed to the possibility of injury. It is not sufficient if only the plaintiff is injured, even if she is injured in a public place. Furthermore, the harm must be a substantial one. Under the common law, only conduct that constituted a crime met the requirement of a public nuisance. Most modern courts no longer require conduct to be criminal, although such conduct is still more likely to be deemed a public nuisance than conduct that is not.

The plaintiff must also show that he suffered damage peculiar to him that was not shared by the rest of the public. Suffering the same inconvenience or being exposed to the same threat as everyone else in the community is not sufficient. The rationale for this rule is that wrongs to the community as a whole should be redressed by the community's representatives to avoid duplication of legal actions. The government, however, can bring an action on behalf of the public without this showing. This special-injury element requires that the injuries of a private plaintiff be "different in kind" from the injuries suffered by the general community, but that they be incurred in the plaintiff's exercise of the common right enjoyed by the community. This special-injury requirement has raised a barrier to potential private plaintiffs bringing nuisance claims relating to environmental hazards.

The courts, however, have struggled with this notion of "particular damage." Some have allowed recovery if the plaintiff suffered greater economic loss than others in the community; others have denied recovery in similar cases. If the plaintiff's pecuniary loss precludes him from performing on a contract or causes him additional expense in his performance, many courts have allowed the plaintiff to recover. Similarly, if the defendant has interfered with the plaintiff's commercial use of his land, many courts allow recovery for public nuisance. Commercial fisheries, for example, have been allowed to recover for losses due to pollution even though ordinary citizens who used the polluted waters could not recover.

A legislature can, by virtue of its police power, declare uses of property or conduct that are detrimental to the health, morals, peace, or general welfare of its citizens to be a nuisance. Because neighbors are more likely to spot nuisances in their community than are local officials, some states have set up administrative systems in which citizens can alert government officials about a nuisance property in their neighborhood. A Texas statute, for example, allows the district

attorney to call public meetings to identify public nuisances after receiving a request for such a meeting by a certain percentage of the registered voters in the area. At the meeting, neighbors may, in front of the property owner, voice their complaints about the alleged nuisance. After the meeting, the district attorney may elect to take legal action if she determines that sufficient evidence exists. Florida law provides for the creation of local administrative boards that receive neighbors' complaints and conduct hearings regarding alleged public nuisances. These boards have the authority to declare a property to be a public nuisance, to prohibit further operation of the premises for one year, and/or to seek court injunctions.

LOCAL LINKS

Has your state set up some kind of administrative procedure whereby citizens can notify government officials of potential nuisances?

Private Nuisance

The key to suing on the basis of private nuisance, as mentioned earlier, is the plaintiff's ability to show that she has an interest in the affected land. Tenants, as well as family members of an owner or tenant, are considered to have such an interest. The plaintiff must prove that the use and enjoyment of her land was substantially interfered with and that the defendant's conduct was either negligent, intentional, or abnormally dangerous.

Nuisance versus Trespass

The difference between a private nuisance and trespass is subtle. A trespass consists of an interference with the plaintiff's right to *possession* of her property; nuisance consists of an interference with the plaintiff's right to *enjoy* and *use* her property. Nuisance can occur, therefore, even if nothing physically enters the plaintiff's property. Furthermore, the fact that the interference must be substantial also differentiates nuisance from trespass. Recall that a plaintiff may recover for trespass even though suffering no substantial harm,

NET NEWS

Discussion of an Illinois appellate court decision finding gun makers liable for public nuisance by distributing weapons in such a way that criminals and juveniles could easily access them is available at **http://www.state.il.us/court/**. Select "Opinions" from either the Supreme Court or the Appellate Court. On the new page, select "Archive table." Enter "1-00-3541" in the search box.

as the tort requires only an intentional invasion of the plaintiff's property. Most conduct that constitutes a trespass typically meets the criteria for a nuisance as well. Blasting activities in the vicinity of the plaintiff's land, for example, obviously create a nuisance in light of the noise and vibrations that are produced. But if rocks and other debris are cast on the plaintiff's land, a trespass is also committed.

What Constitutes Substantial Interference

Substantial interference undoubtedly occurs when the plaintiff is injured or her property is damaged. The interference may also be substantial if the plaintiff is inconvenienced or subjected to unpleasant sensory awarenesses, such as obnoxious odors or blaring sounds. The plaintiff must show that a person of normal sensitivity would be seriously bothered by the defendant's conduct. An abnormally sensitive plaintiff, therefore, will be precluded from recovery. What constitutes substantial interference will, of necessity, hinge on the type of neighborhood in which the activity occurs. Activities that constitute a nuisance in a quiet suburban area might not qualify as a nuisance in a densely populated urban area.

Intentional and Unreasonable Interference

Although a defendant's conduct can be either negligent, intentional, or abnormally dangerous, most private-nuisance claims arise out of intentional conduct. A defendant must, in other words, know with substantial certainty that interference will occur even if he has no desire to interfere with the plaintiff's use and enjoyment of his land.

If the defendant's interference is intentional, the plaintiff must also prove that such interference is unreasonable. To determine whether interference is unreasonable, some courts have balanced the utility of the defendant's conduct against the plaintiff's harm. In accordance with this test, a plaintiff may be barred from recovery, even though she suffered substantial harm, if the utility of the defendant's conduct exceeds the harm the plaintiff suffered.

The *Restatement (Second)* has rejected this balancing test for reasonableness and deemed that interference is unreasonable if one of two things is true: (1) the plaintiff's harm outweighs the utility of the defendant's conduct or (2) the harm caused by the conduct is substantial and greater than anything any individual should be required to bear without compensation (*Restatement [Second] of Torts* § 829A).

Under this criterion, even if the defendant's activity is socially useful he will be required to compensate the plaintiff, unless so many people are affected by the defendant's conduct that requiring the defendant to pay damages would make it impossible for him to continue the activity.

In one case a coal-burning electric generating plant emitted 90 tons of sulphur-dioxide gas into the atmosphere each day, causing extensive crop damage and other harm. The defendant claimed it had used due care in constructing and operating the plant. Nevertheless, the emissions from the plant were determined to be a nuisance. Even though the economic and social utility of the plant outweighed the harm to the farmers, the court required the plant to compensate the farmers for their damages (*Jost v. Dairy Cooperative*, 172 N.W.2d 647 [Wis. 1970]).

Remedies

A plaintiff alleging private nuisance may seek either compensatory damages or an injunction. If the nuisance is likely to be permanent, she can recover for both past and prospective damages in the same action. However, if it is unclear whether the harm will be an ongoing one, she can recover only for those damages sustained at the time of suit and must bring future actions for subsequent harm.

If damages would be an insufficient remedy, the plaintiff may be entitled to an injunction. If she seeks an injunction, she must prove that the harm to her outweighs the utility of the defendant's conduct. Compare this to the *Restatement* approach discussed earlier, in which a plaintiff can recover damages even if the harm to her does not outweigh the utility of the defendant's conduct as long as it would be unfair to deprive her of payment.

Defenses

Both contributory negligence and assumption of risk can be raised as defenses in private-nuisance claims. One way a plaintiff can assume the risk is if he "comes to the nuisance" by purchasing property while having advance notice that the nuisance exists. A plaintiff who purchases a home adjacent to an industrial plant that is in full operation and spewing gases and waste into the environment is said to have come to the nuisance. Although at one time the courts treated coming to the nuisance as an absolute defense, modern courts look at that fact as merely one of many factors to be considered in deciding whether the plaintiff should be allowed to recover. To bar recovery to all plaintiffs who come to the nuisance would allow defendants, in essence, to condemn the land in their vicinity so that the land would become valueless to others. The courts expect defendants to contemplate the possibility that others will eventually want to settle in the area and to anticipate that nuisance claims may arise in the future.

This point is illustrated in one interesting case involving a defendant cattle feedlot that produced "over a million pounds of wet manure per day" in a rural area outside of Phoenix. The plaintiff developer constructed a retirement development, "Sun City," one portion of which adjoined the feedlot. The plaintiff alleged that the flies and odor from the feedlot rendered this portion of the development unhealthy and virtually uninhabitable. The court concluded that the plaintiff had indeed "come to the nuisance" in its building of a subdivision in the vicinity of an already existing feedlot. Nevertheless, the court enjoined the defendant from operating the feedlot because the rights of innocent third parties, the residents of Sun City, were also involved. Because the plaintiff had come to the nuisance, however, the court required the plaintiff to indemnify the defendant for its moving costs (*Spur Industries, Inc. v. Del E. Webb Development Co.,* 494 P.2d 700 [Ariz. 1972]).

Environmental Law

Currently, nuisance law is enjoying a resurgence, especially in environmental law. Most claims for money damages for pollution brought under state common law include a claim for nuisance. Nuisance laws are resorted to because of some of the advantages they have over statutory remedies. Public-nuisance claims provide environmental plaintiffs with a cause of action that is both flexible and powerful.

At one time plaintiffs rarely prevailed in hazardous waste cases, because they could not prove that the harm hazardous waste sites caused was greater than the necessity and utility of most of the polluting activities. Today most courts find polluters' conduct to be unreasonable because they conclude that hazardous waste contamination interferes with the use

and enjoyment of land and in most cases causes substantial harm (see discussion in *Wood v. Picillo*).

In 1986 Congress passed the Comprehensive Environmental Response, Compensation and Liability Act (CERCLA), which authorizes the Environmental Protection Agency to clean up sites contaminated by toxic wastes. When Congress passed CERCLA, many observers anticipated that nuisance law would become outmoded. Instead, common law actions have emerged as potent weapons for recovering damages caused by hazardous wastes.

Plaintiffs have found several advantages in pursuing nuisance claims instead of filing actions under CERCLA: they can recover more in damages, resulting in significantly higher awards; they can obtain injunctions more easily; and they enjoy the common law's broader parameters of liability. For example, CERCLA excludes petroleum and petroleum by-products in its definition of "hazardous substances" and exempts the normal application of fertilizer and the release of nuclear materials from its definition of "release." These products are not exempted under nuisance law. Furthermore, under traditional public-nuisance law there is no statute of limitations, and the plaintiff need not show that his property was physically harmed.

Defendants also enjoy advantages under the common law tort of nuisance. First, under nuisance law, defendants are liable only for the contamination they cause. Thus, if a defendant is responsible for 70 percent of a site's contamination, she need pay for only 70 percent of cleanup costs, whereas she might have to pay for 100 percent under CERCLA. Second, the original owner of a contaminated site can, under nuisance law, defeat liability claims by subsequent owners by asserting caveat emptor ("buyer beware") as a defense. In contrast, under CERCLA, the original parties remain liable for cleanup costs to those who buy the site at a later date. Third, common law defendants can avoid long-term cleanup costs by arguing that a site is "permanently contaminated," thereby being required to pay only the difference between the original land value and the current value

NET NEWS

To read more about environmental law issues, go to the website for the Center for International Environmental Law at **http://www.ciel.org**. A guide to electronic resources for environmental law can be found at the site for the American Society of International Law, **http://www.asil.org**; enter "ASIL Guide to Electronic Resources for International Law" in the search box and select "Electronic Research Tools."

of the contaminated land. Such cleanup can be very expensive and take decades. Fourth, remedies under nuisance law are contingent on balancing the costs and benefits of the nuisance, whereas remedies under CERCLA can require defendants to carry heavy burdens regardless of the costs or benefits.

Despite the advantages to both plaintiffs and defendants, common law actions are not a panacea. Designing and monitoring cleanup is easier under CERCLA; also, because the outcome of litigation is more predictable with CERCLA, settlement is more likely with CERCLA than with nuisance claims. Furthermore, relying on state-by-state adjudication inhibits efforts to create a uniform national campaign to clean up hazardous wastes. Also, common law actions require a plaintiff to file a lawsuit, whereas under CERCLA the Environmental Protection Agency may initiate an enforcement action any time there is "a release, or threatened release" of a hazardous substance. If individual injuries are slight and large numbers of people are affected by a hazardous waste, individuals have little incentive to file nuisance suits.

An illustration of litigation involving a hazardous waste site is *Wood v. Picillo*, 443 A.2d 1244 (R.I. 1982). This case chronicles the evolution of nuisance law in the context of environmental concerns. Notice how the court acknowledges and conforms to changes in societal attitudes and scientific knowledge.

NET NEWS

CERCLA was amended by the Superfund Amendments and Reauthorization Act ("SARA"). An overview of SARA can be found at **http://www.epa.gov** by entering "SARA" as your search term.

CASE   *Wood v. Picillo*
443 A.2d 1244 (R.I. 1982)

WEISBERGER, Justice

This is an appeal from a judgment of the Superior Court entered after trial without the intervention of a jury. Finding that the defendants created a public and private nuisance in maintaining a hazardous waste dump site on their Coventry farm, the trial justice enjoined further chemical disposal operations at the defendants' property and ordered the defendants to finance cleanup and removal of the toxic wastes. The defendants now contend that the trial justice erred in finding the disposal operation to be a public and private nuisance. We strongly disagree. Accordingly, the judgment of the Superior Court is affirmed.

This testimony elicited during the extensive hearings conducted on this case revealed the following dramatic events. On September 30, 1977, an enormous explosion erupted into fifty-foot flames in a trench on defendants' Coventry property. Firefighters responded to the blaze but could not extinguish the flames. As the fire raged within the trench, additional explosions resounded. From the conflagration billowed clouds of thick black smoke that extended "as far as the eye could see on the Eastern horizon."

Not unexpectedly, the extraordinary blaze aroused the interest of various state officials. The state fire marshal declared the dump site a fire hazard and ordered defendants to cease disposal activity and to remove all flammable wastes. Personnel from the Department of Environmental Management (DEM) also investigated the dumping operation, conducting soil, water, chemical, and topographical analyses of defendants' property and adjacent areas. Despite the fire marshal's order and the ongoing official investigations, the dumping and burying of chemical wastes continued.

A general description of the Picillo property and adjacent lands is helpful in evaluating the evidence. According to the testimony of various witnesses, the Picillos owned acreage on Piggy Hill Lane in Coventry, Rhode Island. Piggy Hill Lane, which serves only the Picillos' property, is a winding dirt road running from Perry Hill Road. Near the entrance to the property defendants maintain pigs, and two houses are located in this general area. A three- to five-acre clearing in once-wooded land lies approximately 800 feet uphill from the two homes. It is this clearing that houses the chemical dump site. About 600 feet downhill to the north-northwest of the clearing is a marshy wetland. The wetland is part of the Quinabog River Basin; the wetland waters drain in a gradual southwesterly flow into the Quinabog River, Wickford Pond, the Roaring

(continues)

Brook, and Arnold Pond. These fish-inhabited waters are utilized both by the general public and by a commercial cranberry grower.

The dump site proper might best be described in the succinct expression of the trial justice as "a chemical nightmare." John Quinn, Jr., chief of the DEM's solid-waste management program, visited defendants' property on October 13, 1977 and testified to what he saw. Quinn stated that at one side of the clearing lay a huge trench which he estimated to be 200 feet long, 15 to 30 feet wide, and 15 to 20 feet deep. A viscous layer of pungent, vari-colored liquid covered the trench bottom to a depth of six inches at its shallowest point. Along the periphery of the pit lay more than 100 fifty-five gallon drum-type and five-gallon pail-type containers. Some of the containers were upright and sealed, some tipped, and some partially buried; some were full, some partially full, and some empty. An official from the state fire marshal's office also visited the dump site. He testified that on October 15, 1977, he observed a truck marked "Combustible" offloading barrels of chemical wastes. The truck operator knocked the barrels off the truck's tailgate directly onto the earth below, and chemicals poured freely from the damaged barrels into the trench. In 1979 state officials discovered a second dump site when "sink holes" emitting chemical odors opened in the earth at some distance from the previously described pit.

Several witnesses testified at trial to the immediate and future effects of the chemical presence. Neighbors of the Picillos reported that in the year preceding the fire, tractor-trailer traffic to and from defendants' property greatly increased. According to the testimony many of the trucks bore "Flammable" warnings and the name of a chemical company. The neighbors also testified that on several occasions during the summer of 1977 pungent odors forced them to remain inside their homes. The odors were described variously as "sickening," "heavy," "sweet," "musky," "terrible," and like "plastic burning." One neighbor testified that the odors induced in her severe nausea and headaches, while another stated that on one occasion fumes from the Picillo property caused her to cough severely and to suffer a sore throat that lasted several days.

At trial expert witnesses developed a scientific connection between the neighbors' experiences and the Picillos' operations. Laboratory analyses of samples taken from the trench, monitoring wells, and adjacent waters revealed the presence of five chemicals: toluene, xylene, chloroform, III trichloroethane, and trichloro-ethylene.[2] Doctor Nelson Fausto, a professor of medical sciences in the pathology division of the Department of Biological and Medical Sciences at Brown University, described the toxic effects of the five discovered chemicals. Doctor Fausto testified that chloroform is a narcotic and an anesthetic that will induce vomiting, dizziness, and headaches in some persons exposed to it. Trichloroethane and trichloroethylene, according to Dr. Fausto, are similar to chloroform in chemical structure and in toxic effect. Toluene and xylene are also toxins, Dr. Fausto testified, that may cause irritation of the mucous membranes in the upper respiratory tract.

Doctor Fausto explained that the chemicals in question also exert chronic or long-term effects on animals and humans. According to the professor, chloroform, trichloroethane, and trichloroethylene are strong carcinogens that cause cirrhosis (cell death) of the liver and hepatoma (cancer of the liver). Doctor Fausto asserted that there is no safe level of human or animal exposure to these chemicals. Regarding toluene and xylene, Dr. Fausto testified that neither is as yet known to be carcinogenic, but both exert a toxic effect on bone marrow, causing anemia in susceptible persons. Additionally, Dr. Fausto stated, the presence of chloroform in areas where it might be heated presents further potential danger. Heated to sixty-eight degrees Fahrenheit, chloroform converts to phosgene gas, a nerve gas of the type utilized in World War I. Doctor Fausto stated that direct sunlight would provide sufficient heat to turn chloroform present in surface water into phosgene.

According to the experts, the chemicals present on defendants' property and in the marsh, left unchecked, would eventually threaten wildlife and humans well down-stream from the dump site. Mr. Frank Stevenson, the principal sanitary engineer for the DEM, and Dr. William Kelly, an Associate Professor of civil and environmental engineering at the University of Rhode Island, testified as experts in soil mechanics and groundwater hydrology. The experts established that the soil at the dump site consisted of an unstratified composition of sand, gravel, and silt of varying sizes. The permeable nature of this soil would allow any liquid or chemical in or on it to percolate down to the water table and to travel with the groundwater in a northerly flow. The opinion of the experts was buttressed by the documented presence of toluene, xylene, chloroform, trichloroethane, and trichloroethylene in the northern marsh and in several monitoring wells.[3] The only possible source of the pollutants, according to Dr. Kelly, was the Picillo dump site.

2. These were the only chemicals for which tests were conducted.

3. The chemicals were detectable not only through laboratory processes but also by gross visual inspection. Experts reported a reddish discoloration and an oily surface in one section of the wetland, along with a pungent chemical odor. Doctor Kelly stated also that at one location chemicals seeped out of the ground as if from a spring.

(continues)

Expert testimony further revealed that the chemicals had traveled and would continue to travel from the dump site into the marsh at the rate of about one foot per day. From the marsh, predicted the experts, the chemicals would flow in a southwesterly direction into the Quinabog River and its tributaries Moosup River and Roaring Brook, and Wickford Pond. These waters are inhabited by fish and used by humans for recreational and agricultural purposes.

On these and other facts the trial justice determined the dump site to be a public and private nuisance. He found also that the current danger to the public health and safety posed by the chemical presence would worsen unless effective remedial action was quickly taken. The trial judge thus permanently enjoined disposal operations on defendants' property and ordered that all chemicals and contaminated earth be removed to a licensed disposal facility. Because defendants had in the past displayed an unwillingness or inability to remedy the danger, the Superior Court justice authorized plaintiffs to effectuate cleanup of defendants' property at defendants' expense.

The defendants contend that the evidence adduced at trial was insufficient to support a finding of public and private nuisance. The defendants point to two alleged evidentiary inadequacies: (1) that plaintiffs failed to establish any significant injury to persons or to natural wildlife and (2) that plaintiffs failed to meet their obligation to show that defendants acted negligently in disposing chemical wastes on their property. We find both assertions to be without merit.

The essential element of an actionable nuisance is that persons have suffered harm or are threatened with injuries that they ought not have to bear. . . . Distinguished from negligence liability, liability in nuisance is predicated upon unreasonable injury rather than upon unreasonable conduct. . . . Thus, plaintiffs may recover in nuisance despite the otherwise nontortious nature of the conduct which creates the injury.

In his brief defendant has accurately stated that the injury produced by an actionable nuisance "must be real and not fanciful or imaginary." . . . The defendant next suggests that the injuries in the case at bar are of the insubstantial, unactionable type. It is this statement, however, rather than the purported injuries, that is fanciful. The testimony to which reference is made in this opinion clearly establishes that defendants' dumping operations have already caused substantial injury to defendants' neighbors and threaten to cause incalculable damage to the general public. The Picillos' neighbors have displayed physical symptoms of exposure to toxic chemicals and have been restricted in the reasonable use of their property. Moreover, expert testimony showed that the chemical presence on defendants' property threatens both aquatic wildlife and human beings with possible death, cancer, and liver disease. Thus, there was ample evidence at trial to support the finding of substantial injury implicit in the trial justice's finding of public and private nuisance.

The defendants' remaining contention is that Rhode Island case law requires plaintiffs to prove negligence as an element of the nuisance case and that plaintiffs failed to do so. Generally, this court has not required plaintiffs to establish negligence in nuisance actions. . . . In one case, however, the Rhode Island Supreme Court refused to impose nuisance liability upon an oil refining company absent proof of negligence. The defendant asserts that the *Rose* case is apposite to and controls the case at bar. We disagree.

Whether or not a nuisance is actionable absent proof of negligence depends upon the nature of the nuisance and the facts of the particular case. . . .

The facts of *Rose* are somewhat similar to the facts of the present case. The plaintiff, Manuel Rose, owned a fifty-seven-acre farm in East Providence, Rhode Island, on which he maintained a piggery and hennery. Rose drew drinking water for his family and for the hens from a fresh-water well dug on the property, and the pigs drank from a stream that traversed the farm. The well and the stream were fed by waters that percolated from an underground source.

The defendant in *Rose* was the owner of a large oil refinery and several storage tanks situated directly across the street from the plaintiff's farm. The refinery and the storage tanks discharged and leaked petroleum, gasoline, and waste products into basins, streams, and ponds on the defendant's property. These substances, however, did not remain in their natural repositories. Rather, the oil products percolated through the soil into the groundwater and discharged into the plaintiff's well and stream. The pollutants contaminated the plaintiff's drinking water, killing 700 hens and 75 breeding sows. The plaintiff instituted suit against Socony-Vacuum, alleging private nuisance but not negligence.

The Superior Court sustained defendant's demurrer. On appeal, the Supreme Court framed the issue in the following terms:

> "While the defendant could appropriate to its own use the percolating waters under its soil—providing that in so doing it was not actuated by an improper motive and was not negligent—can it, by the use to which it puts its land, deprive the plaintiffs of such waters by rendering them unfit for plaintiffs' use by contamination?" 54 R.I. at 418–19, 173 A. at 630.

(continues)

The court held that the defendant could with inpunity contaminate the plaintiff's drinking water if the defendant polluted nonnegligently.... The court reasoned that because "courses of subterranean waters are ... indefinite and obscure," rights to them are less easily definable than riparian rights to surface streams. Suggesting that it might be unjust to subject landowners to liability for the unforeseeable consequences of legitimate land uses, the court looked to the teaching of other courts that had considered the issue. Examination of the cases disclosed a split of authority; jurisdictions with primarily agricultural economies imposed nuisance liability without proof of negligence, whereas jurisdictions with primarily industrial economies required a negligence showing. The *Rose* court determined that petroleum products were vital to the highly developed industrial economy of the local area, and held as a matter of policy that injury of the type occasioned by the defendant's percolating pollutants was, absent negligence, "damnum absque injuria."

Since this court decided *Rose v. Socony-Vacuum* in 1934, the science of groundwater hydrology as well as societal concern for environmental protection has developed dramatically. As a matter of scientific fact the courses of subterranean waters are no longer obscure and mysterious. The testimony of the scientific experts in this case clearly illustrates the accuracy with which scientists can determine the paths of groundwater flow. Moreover, decades of unrestricted emptying of industrial effluent into the earth's atmosphere and waterways has rendered oceans, lakes, and rivers unfit for swimming and fishing, rain acidic, and air unhealthy. Concern for the preservation of an often precarious ecological balance, impelled by the spectre of "a silent spring," has today reached a zenith of intense significance. Thus, the scientific and policy considerations that impelled the Rose result are no longer valid. We now hold that negligence is not a necessary element of a nuisance case involving contamination of public or private waters by pollutants percolating through the soil and traveling underground routes. For the reasons stated, the defendants' appeal is denied and dismissed. The judgment of the Superior Court is affirmed.

PUTTING IT INTO PRACTICE 10:5

1. What facts support a finding that the defendants' dump site constitutes a nuisance?

2. How does a negligence claim differ from a nuisance claim?

3. What facts support the plaintiffs' contention that they were injured by the chemical wastes harbored by the defendants?

4. On what basis does the court distinguish Rose?

5. Must negligence be shown in a nuisance case involving contamination of public or private waters by pollutants percolating through soil and traveling underground?

PUTTING IT INTO PRACTICE 10:6

1. Seventy-five neighbors of an apartment complex sue the landlords of the complex for failure to combat a drug-dealing operation on the property. The neighbors assert they have been confronted by drug dealers, drug customers, and prostitutes, and that such confrontations, along with the sounds of gunshots, fighting, and yelling, have made them fear for their lives. Neither the dealers, their customers, nor the neighbors are tenants of the landlords. Do the neighbors have grounds for a nuisance action?

(continues)

> ## PUTTING IT INTO PRACTICE 10:6 *(continued)*
>
> 2. A local health club employs females, who under the ruse of being massage therapists and while completely nude, provide body massages consisting of genital stimulation. Do the neighbors of this "health club" have grounds for a public nuisance suit?
>
> 3. Property owners whose properties are not subject to groundwater contamination emanating from the defendants' property argue that even though no contaminants had reached their properties, the defendant should be held liable "for any loss in property values due to public concern about the contaminants in the general area." Do the property owners have grounds for a private nuisance claim?
>
> 4. Jet noise from an airport is described by residents as being comparable to the "noise of a riveting machine or steam hammer." The noise interrupts residents' sleep, makes it difficult for them to converse on the phone, and causes their windows to vibrate and plaster to fall. What relief, if any, are the residents entitled to?

INTERFERENCE WITH BUSINESS RELATIONS

Two tort actions specifically protect business interests: (1) interference with existing contractual relations and (2) interference with prospective contractual relations.

Interference with Existing Contractual Relations

One commits interference with existing contractual relations by inducing another to breach a contract with the plaintiff. The defendant's interference must be intentional (negligence is not sufficient) and improper. Several factors are taken into consideration when deciding if a tort has been committed. They include the purpose and motive of the defendant, the means used to create the interference, and the type of interest with which the defendant interferes, as well as the social interest involved in protecting both the defendant's freedom of action and the contractual interest of the plaintiff (*Restatement [Second] of Torts* §§ 766 and 767).

One of the first and certainly most famous decisions imposing liability for intentional inducement of a breach of contract was *Lumley v. Gye*, 118 Eng. Rep. 749 (Q.B. 1853). In *Lumley*, the plaintiff's theater entered into a contract with an opera singer in which she agreed she would not perform for anyone else during a period of time. The defendant deliberately enticed the singer to refuse to perform and was held liable for improper interference with a contractual relationship.

In more modern times, liability for contractual interference was found in a case in which an attorney, after terminating his employment with a law firm, actively engaged in an attempt to procure business for his new law firm. He contacted some of the first firm's clients with whom he had been working and advised them that he was leaving the firm and that they could choose to be represented by him, the firm, or any other firm or attorney. Additionally, he mailed these clients form letters that could be used to discharge the firm as counsel and create a contingency-fee agreement between him and the client. The court reasoned that the attorney had used his position of trust and responsibility to unfairly prejudice the firm. The court also concluded that no public interest was served in allowing such use of confidential information (*Adler, Barish, Daniels, Levin & Creskoff v. Epstein*, 393 A.2d 1175 [Pa. 1978]).

A more modern case involving two major oil companies, Texaco and Pennzoil, aptly illustrates the tort of interference with contractual relations. In this case Pennzoil agreed to purchase Getty Oil for $110 per share. Although the companies entered into no formal agreement, they both issued a press release indicating their "agreement in principle." Subsequently Texaco offered to buy Getty Oil for $125 per share, after which Getty withdrew from its agreement with Pennzoil and agreed to merge with Texaco. Pennzoil sued for interference with contractual relations, and a jury found Texaco liable, assessing damages at $7.3 billion and

NET NEWS

An article entitled "Tortious Interference with Business Relations in the Employment Context in Georgia" is available at **http://www.rkmc.com**. Enter "tortious interference" as your search term.

awarding punitive damages of $3 billion. Although at trial Texaco denied having any knowledge of the agreement between Pennzoil and Getty, both the jury and the appeals courts found sufficient evidence to conclude that Texaco had actively sought to acquire Getty by inducing its breach with Pennzoil. After the court of appeals affirmed the jury's verdict, Texaco and Pennzoil agreed to settle for $3 billion, (*Texaco, Inc. v. Pennzoil Co.*, 729 S.W.2d 768 [Tex. Ct. App. 1987]).

Active Interference

The defendant must actively interfere with the contract. Merely offering a better price to a third person, knowing that this might cause the third person to breach his contract with the plaintiff, is not sufficient. However, suppose the defendant says, "I'll give you a better price than the plaintiff is offering, and if you accept my offer you'll save enough money to afford to break your contract with the plaintiff and still come out ahead." By this statement the defendant actively induces a breach of contract (*Restatement [Second] of Torts* § 766, illus. 3).

Kind of Contract Involved

Some kinds of contracts cannot serve as a basis for this tort. The plaintiff cannot recover if a contract that is illegal or contrary to public policy is breached. Similarly, most courts will not hold the defendant liable if she induces the breach of a contract that is terminable at will. An **at-will employee** is one who, because of the employment agreement into which he entered with his employer, can be discharged at any time for any reason. The *Restatement (Second)* and a growing number of courts, however, do consider the inducing of a breach of an at-will contract to be contractual interference. The reasoning behind this approach is that a plaintiff has a right to expect that the contract will not be tampered with until it is in fact terminated. Contracts that are unenforceable for other reasons, such as lack of consideration or because they are not in conformance with the statute of frauds, can serve as a basis for contractual interference.

Remedies

The plaintiff may certainly recover for pecuniary losses he sustains as a result of the interference and also, according to some courts, may be allowed to recover for emotional harm. The plaintiff can recover for breach of contract against the person the defendant induced to breach the contract.

In one case, the plaintiffs, a black family who had contracted to buy a house in a white neighborhood, were allowed to recover for mental suffering from the defendants, their would-be neighbors, who induced the owner not to go through with the sale. They were also allowed to seek specific performance from the seller as well as incidental expenses they incurred as a result of the breach. The plaintiffs were not, however, entitled to recover twice for the same damages. They could not, for example, recover from the seller the interest they had to pay while waiting for their suit and then recover that sum again from the defendants who induced the breach (*Duff v. Engelberg*, 47 Cal. Rptr. 114 [Ct. App. 1965]).

The following excerpts from *PM Group, Inc. v. Stewart* demonstrates interference with contractual relations and negligent misrepresentation claims in the entertainment industry.

CASE

PM Group, Inc. v. Stewart
154 Cal.App.4th 55, (Cal.App. 2007).

KLEIN, P.J.

The plaintiffs in this case are concert promoter Howard Pollack, dba PM Group, and two subpromoters, Achilles Sojo dba AKE Music and Richard Leon Velarde dba Boulevard CIE. The defendants are singer Rod Stewart, his company Stewart Annoyances, Ltd., his manager Annie Challis of Stiefel Entertainment, his attorney Barry Tyerman of the then Armstrong Hirsch

(continues)

**CASE
(CONTINUED)**

Jackoway Tyerman & Wertheimer (AH), and his agent Steve Levine of International Creative Management (ICM).

The plaintiffs sued for the return of $780,000 deposited toward a concert tour by Stewart that did not materialize and for interference with contract and prospective economic advantage. Stewart cross-complained for $2.1 million, the full amount he would have been paid for the tour.

In a special verdict, the jury found the parties never entered into a binding contract for Stewart's services. The jury awarded the plaintiffs $780,000 on theories of money had and received and negligent misrepresentation by Challis and Levine. The jury also found the defendants Tyerman and Levine intentionally interfered with subcontracts for concert performances by Stewart, which the plaintiffs had interest into with various third parties, resulting in damages of $1.6 million. The jury found in favor of the defendants on the cause of action for intentional interference with prospective economic advantage.

We conclude the failure of the parties to enter into a contract for the proposed concert tour precluded performance of the subcontracts. Thus, the defendants, as a matter of law, did not interfere with the performance of the subcontracts. Additionally, Stewart and his representatives cannot interfere with subcontracts that contemplate concert performances by Stewart. Accordingly, we reverse the judgment on the cause of action for intentional interference with contract. In all other respects, the judgment is affirmed.

FACTUAL AND PROCEDURAL BACKGROUND

1. *Initial negotiations.*
In October of 2001, Pollack began negotiations with Stewart's agent, Steve Levine at ICM, for a concert tour of South and Latin America by Stewart. Pollack had partners/subpromoters in each of the cities the proposed tour would visit. On October 19, 2001, one of these subpromotors, plaintiff Achilles Sojo of Argentina, arranged for $100,000 to be deposited into ICM's trust account to demonstrate good faith. Pollack thereafter agreed with Levine and Stewart's manager, Annie Challis, on a 9 city, 18-day concert tour commencing February 20, 2002, for $2.1 million, half of which was due on signing of a formal contract.

2. *Tyerman becomes involved.*
On November 15, 2001, Challis sent Stewart's attorney, Barry Tyerman at AH, an email outlining the terms of the tour and instructing Tyerman to prepare

a contract and collect the deposit. Tyerman enclosed the first draft of the contract to Pollack in a letter dated November 20, 2002. The letter directed Pollack to sign and return the contract and arrange for wire transfer of the balance of the first payment, $950,000, to the AH trust account.

The first draft of the contract required Pollack to pay all air fare and cargo, even though Pollack had negotiated a "delivered" deal. The next draft omitted a *force majeure* clause Pollack wanted because of unrest in Argentina. Tyerman mailed the fourth draft of the contract to Pollack on December 20, 2001. It provided the first payment of $1,050,000 was due on January 2, 2002, and the balance was due on February 4, 2002.

While drafts of the contract were being exchanged, the subpromoters made additional deposits toward the first payment. By January 3, 2002, $350,000 had been deposited into the ICM trust account and $180,000 had been deposited into the AH trust account. There was talk of Sojo paying Stewart's $300,000 cargo bill in Argentina, in lieu of $300,000 of the deposit, in order to avoid restrictions on international transfers of money from Argentina.

Tyerman sent emails to Pollack on December 28, 2001, and January 4 and 7, 2002, asking for the signed contract and the balance of the first payment. Tyerman threatened to terminate plans for the tour and retain the deposits.

3. *Pollack releases funds from the ICM trust account.*
On January 9, 2002, Challis asked Levine to transfer $460,000 that had been deposited into the ICM trust account to the AH trust account. From there it would be transferred to one of Stewart's companies to permit Challis to pay expenses related to the tour. Before Pollack signed the release of the funds, he spoke to Challis and Levine by telephone and specifically asked if they were "setting him up" for a cancellation. Each assured him the tour would go forward and, in fact, he had to release the funds for that to happen.

Pollack discussed the release of the funds with Sojo and, after Pollack signed the release, Sojo commenced ticket sales in Argentina. Sojo testified it is customary to sell tickets after money is released to the artist. After Pollack signed the release, $460,000 was transferred from the ICM trust account to the AH trust account.

4. *The negotiations continue and eventually unravel.*
At some point, Pollack changed the due date for the first payment of the deposit in the fourth draft of the contract from January 2 to January 15, 2002, initialed the change and returned the draft to Tyerman. On January 11, 2002, Pollack advised Tyerman by email the promoters had agreed to pay approximately $50,000 for in-ear monitors

(continues)

at the concert venues, thus concluding the last deal point in dispute. A formal contract was never signed. However, witnesses on both sides of the dispute agreed concert tours frequently proceed in the absence of a signed contract and, in some cases, the contract is signed after the tour is completed.

On January 14, 2002, $640,000 was transferred from the AH trust account to Stewart's company.

On January 15, 2002, Challis learned that tickets for the concert in Argentina had gone on sale, even though she had not yet authorized ticket sales and the first payment had not yet been made. Challis, Levine and Tyerman conferred and decided to cancel the tour. Tyerman wrote Pollack a letter that day informing him of their decision to terminate the contract and retain the deposits.[1]

On January 16, 2002, $100,000 was deposited into the ICM account by Telefonica Italiano Mobile (TIM) for the concert date in Peru. ICM retained this deposit as a credit against fees owed ICM by Stewart. This deposit brought the total amount deposited toward the first payment to $780,000.

On January 18, 2002, Pollack tried to salvage the deal and proposed a 10-city tour for $2.2 million, with an additional $400,000 to be deposited the next day, but the deposit was never made.

By letters dated January 22, 2002, Tyerman advised the six subpromoters who were working with Pollack that "PM Group has no contractual or other relationship with [Stewart], is not authorized to furnish the services or rights of Mr. Stewart or otherwise bind our clients in any way and no concert by our client will be performed."

5. *Litigation.*

The plaintiffs sued for return of the $780,000 deposited toward the first payment on counts of unjust enrichment

and money had and received. Pollack and PM Group also sought to recover these deposits based on negligent misrepresentation by Challis and Levin. The plaintiffs further alleged intentional and negligent interference with their contracts with the subpromoters and interference with prospective economic advantage based on the plaintiffs' loss of the opportunity to promote concert tours by other entertainers with whom they already were in negotiations. Finally, the plaintiffs sought punitive damages.

Stewart cross complained for $2.1 million which he claimed was due under the fourth draft of the contract, initialed by Pollack.

6. *Post evidentiary motions, verdict and post verdict motions.*

Following presentation of the evidence to the jury, the trial court granted nonsuit on the plaintiffs' claim for punitive damages finding there was insufficient evidence of malice, fraud or oppression.

The matter went to the jury with a 26-question special verdict form. In response to the first question, the jury found Pollack and Stewart never entered into a contract. The jury found in favor of the plaintiffs on the claim of money had and received in the amount of $780,000, assigning $280,000, $270,000, and $230,000, to Pollack, Sojo, and Velarde, respectively. The jury also found Challis and Levine made negligent misrepresentations to Pollack in connection with the January 9 release of the funds from the ICM trust account resulting in damages in the amount of $780,000.

On the claim of intentional interference with contract, the jury found Tyerman and Levine knowingly and intentionally disrupted the performance of the six subpromoter contracts involved in the transaction and that, as a result, plaintiffs were damaged in the total amount of $1.6 million, consisting of $350,000 to PM Group (Pollack), $450,000 to AKE Music (Sojo) and $800,000 to Boulevard EIRL (Velarde).[2]

The jury found against the plaintiffs on their claim of intentional interference with prospective economic advantage and found the manager's privilege did not apply to Tyerman, Challis, or Levine.

On the equitable claim of unjust enrichment, the trial court, sitting without a jury, found in favor of the plaintiffs in the amount of $780,000. The trial court also found the defendants Levine, ICM, Tyerman, AH, Challis and Stiefel Entertainment were agents of Stewart and the agents of each other. Thus, any recovery on

---

1. Tyerman's letter to Pollack dated January 15, 2002, stated Pollack and PM Group were in "material breach" of their obligations to Stewart in that Pollack had:

> "1. Failed to execute and return the fully negotiated document confirming the details of the agreement with respect to the concert tour;
>
> "2. Failed to make payment of the agreed upon sum of $1,050,000 due from you to our client on or before January 2, 2002; and
>
> "3. Apparently caused or permitted the public sale of tickets to one or more of the proposed concerts, notwithstanding specific written notice from our clients' agents, acknowledged and agreed to by you, that no such sales for any of the concerts would take place unless and until your various breaches had been cured and you were specifically authorized by our clients to proceed."

Tyerman concluded by indicating Stewart would retain the money already deposited and might seek "payment of the balance of the guaranteed fee. . . ."

---

2. The subcontracts were between: (1) PM Group and AKE Music, (2) PM Group and CIE Brasil, (3) PM Group and Jose Dueno, (4) AKE Music and Rafael Fernandez, (5) AKE Music and Multimusica, and (6) Ricardo Leon Velarde and Grand Entertainment.

(continues)

the negligent misrepresentation claim would reduce the unjust enrichment and the money had and received claims.

The trial court denied the defendants' motions for judgment notwithstanding the verdict and awarded the plaintiffs attorney fees in the amount of $472,216 pursuant to Civil Code section 1717 because they prevailed on Stewart's contract based cross-complaint for $2.1 million.

CONTENTIONS

The defendants contend the trial court should have excluded the testimony of the plaintiffs' expert and the $1.6 million awarded for intentional interference with contract must be set aside. With respect to the award of $780,000, the defendants contend any negligent misrepresentation related to the written release of the funds was harmless, the plaintiffs lacked standing to recover any money deposited by entities who were not plaintiffs, and no misrepresentations were made to Pollack. Finally, the defendants contend the award of attorney fees must be reversed because the plaintiffs recovered in quasi-contract.

On cross-appeal, the plaintiffs contend the trial court erred in not allowing the jury to decide their claim for punitive damages.

DISCUSSION

2. *The judgment on the count of intentional interference with contract must be reversed*

The jury found the defendants interfered with subcontracts among: (1) PM Group and AKE Music; (2) PM Group and CIE Brasil; (3) PM Group and Jose Dueno; (4) AKE Music and Rafael Fernandez; (5) AKE Music and Multimusica; and (6) Velarde and Grand Entertainment. Each of these subcontracts contemplated a concert performance by Stewart at one or more of the venues on the proposed tour.

However, as a matter of law, Stewart and his agents could not have interfered with the performance of these subcontracts. The tort of intentional interference with contractual relations is committed only by "strangers-interlopers who have no legitimate interest in the scope or course of the contract's performance." (*Applied Equipment Corp. v. Litton Saudi Arabia Ltd.* (1994) 7 Cal.4th 503, 514, 28 Cal.Rptr.2d 475, 869 P.2d 454.) Consequently, a contracting party is incapable of interfering with the performance of his or her own contract and cannot be held liable in tort for conspiracy to interfere with his or her own contract. (*Ibid.; Weinbaum v. Goldfarb, Whitman & Cohen* (1996) 46 Cal.App.4th 1310, 1316–1317, 54 Cal.Rptr.2d 462.) Because the subcontracts at issue here provided for Stewart's performance, neither Stewart nor his agents can be liable for the tort of interfering with the subcontracts.

Additionally, the jury concluded Stewart and PM Group never entered into a binding contract for Stewart's performance. Thus, none of the subcontracts among the plaintiffs and the subpromoters could have been performed. Accordingly, the defendants cannot be said to have caused the failure of the subcontracts and therefore cannot be liable for intentional interference with contract. (*Franklin v. Dynamic Details,* Inc. (2004) 116 Cal.App.4th 375, 391, 10 Cal.Rptr.3d 429 [interference with contractual relations requires proof the defendant's conduct was a substantial factor in bringing about an injury, damage, loss or harm]; *Service by Medallion, Inc. v. Clorox Co.* (1996) 44 Cal.App.4th 1807, 1818, 52 Cal.Rptr.2d 650.)

For both of the foregoing reasons, the cause of action for intentional interference with contract fails.

3. *The damages awarded by the jury on the count of money had and received and by the trial court on the count of unjust enrichment need not be reduced*

The defendants contend the damages for money had and received must be reduced because only $100,000 of the $780,000 deposited belonged to plaintiffs. The defendants note Velarde deposited $70,000 and Sojo deposited $30,000 and the rest of the deposits came from entities who were not parties to the lawsuit. Thus, the plaintiffs lack standing to recover more than $100,000. (Code Civ. Proc., § 367.) The defendants argue that allowing the plaintiffs to recover deposits made by third parties on a theory of money had and received creates the possibility of multiple lawsuits seeking duplicative recoveries against the same defendant. *Keru Investments, Inc. v. Cube Co.* (1998) 63 Cal.App.4th 1412, 1424, 74 Cal.Rptr.2d 744.) The defendants conclude the judgment on the count for money had and received should be reduced to $100,000.

On a similar theory, the defendants claim the trial court's ruling on the unjust enrichment claim must be reduced to $100,000, the value of the benefit the plaintiffs themselves conferred on the defendants. The defendants also argue the money deposited by entities who were not plaintiffs was for the use and benefit of Stewart as it was paid toward the guaranteed compensation he was to receive for the concert tour. *First Nationwide Savings v. Perry* (1992) 11 Cal.App.4th 1657, 1662, 15 Cal. Rptr.2d 173.) Thus, the claim of unjust enrichment fails.

We do not find these arguments persuasive. The evidence showed the plaintiffs either personally made or orchestrated the deposits pursuant to what amounted to a joint venture among the plaintiffs, the subpromoters, and the entities that deposited money to secure Stewart's performance at the various venues. The jury and the trial court reasonably could conclude the plaintiffs were entitled to demand the return of the money deposited

(continues)

on behalf of the entities each plaintiff brought to the venture. Indeed, given the unusual circumstances presented, no danger of multiple lawsuits seeking duplicative recoveries appears.

Moreover, the defendants obtained reversal of the $1.6 million awarded for intentional interference with contract, essentially, because the facts underlying this dispute showed a single, interrelated negotiation among the plaintiffs, the subpromoters, and the entities that deposited money for concert performances by Stewart. Thus, the defendants could not, as a matter of law, interfere with the subcontracts for Stewart's performance. It would be inequitable to permit the defendants now to splinter the joint venture into its constituent parts in order to avoid the negligent misrepresentation award. Accordingly, these claims fail.

4. *Sufficiency of the evidence to support the cause of action for negligent misrepresentation*

a. *The negligent misrepresentations*

ICM and Levine (Levine) contend the judgment on the claim of negligent misrepresentation must be reversed because the evidence demonstrates Levine made no misrepresentation to PM Group.[3] Levine notes both he and Pollack testified Levine did not represent the tour would go forward if Pollack signed the release and also said PM Group needed to pay the full deposit. Levine argues this testimony contrasts with Pollack's testimony that Challis "assured me that they weren't canceling. She assured me that they were in . . . too deep." Levine concludes that because the evidence does not demonstrate a misrepresentation on his part, the cause of action for negligent misrepresentation must fail. (*Goehring v. Chapman University* (2004) 121 Cal. App.4th 353, 364, 17 Cal.Rptr.3d 39.)

However, as the trial court observed in its post trial rulings, each defendant was the agent of Stewart and the agent of each other. This being the case, Challis and Levine were agents of Stewart and agents of each other. Based on Pollack's testimony that each denied they were "setting him up" for a cancellation before Pollack signed the release, the jury reasonably could conclude Challis and Levine each had sufficient involvement in the negligent misrepresentation to warrant imposition of liability. Consequently, this contention amounts to little more than a request to reweigh the evidence on appeal.

b. *The evidence adequately demonstrates causation*

The defendants contend any misrepresentation by Challis or Levine was harmless in that, even if Pollack

had not signed the release, the $470,000 in ICM's client trust account on January 9, 2002 would not have been returned to the plaintiffs. Rather, the funds would have been treated the same as the $130,000 that remained in the ICM client trust account and the $180,000 that went directly to the AH trust account. Because release of the funds had no impact on the plaintiffs' damages, there was no harm caused by any misrepresentation. (*Goehring v. Chapman University, supra,* 121 Cal.App.4th at p. 364, 17 Cal.Rptr.3d 39; *Service by Medallion, Inc. v. Clorox Co., supra,* 44 Cal. App.4th at p. 1818, 52 Cal.Rptr.2d 650 [tort recovery requires proof of "detriment proximately caused" by the defendant's tortious conduct].)

Defendants next urge there is no proximate causation with respect to the $30,000 deposited by Grand Entertainment Group on January 9, or the $100,000 deposited by Telephono Italiano Mobile (TIM) on January 16, 2002, because those Peruvian entities were unaware of any misrepresentation made to Pollack in connection with the release. Thus, these entities could not have relied thereon. The defendants assert that, because the plaintiffs failed to demonstrate a link between the alleged misrepresentations to Pollack on January 9 and any reliance on those statements by either Grand Entertainment Group or TIM, there was no evidence the alleged misrepresentation played any part in the deposit of these additional funds.(*Cadlo v. Owens-Illinois, Inc.*(2004) 125 Cal.App.4th 513, 520, 23 Cal. Rptr.3d 1.) The defendants conclude Pollack and PM group, the only plaintiffs on the negligent misrepresentation claim, failed to show they were damaged and, because none of the $130,000 came from PM group or Pollack, they did not suffer damages. (*Weinbaum v. Goldfarb, Whitman & Cohen, supra,* 46 Cal.App.4th at p. 1315, fn. 6, 54 Cal.Rptr.2d 462.)

We disagree with the defendants' view of the case. It appears the jury found the written release extracted from Pollack by the defendants acting in concert caused a fundamental change in the bargaining positions of the parties and thus had an impact on the deal in its entirety, including all the funds deposited in anticipation of the concert tour. Consequently, the attack on the sufficiency of the evidence to demonstrate causation fails. . . .

DISPOSITION

The judgment in favor of the plaintiffs on the cause of action for intentional interference with contract is reversed. In all other respects, the judgment is affirmed.

The plaintiffs are awarded costs on appeal.

We concur: CROSKEY, and ALDRICH, JJ.

---

3. Challis and Stiefel join in ICM's brief on this point and the causation argument that follows.

Privileges

If a defendant merely tries to protect his own existing contractual rights, he will be privileged to induce a breach as long as his motive is not to gain business for himself. If a buyer is aware, for example, that a manufacturer of goods has promised to deliver goods to both himself and another buyer, he can ask that the manufacturer fulfill his contract even if he is aware that the manufacturer will be unable to fulfill both contracts.

If an individual induces a breach for the purpose of promoting social interests, she will also be privileged. One unusual case illustrating this point involved a burlesque troupe known as the Wu Tut Tut Revue, whose manager so underpaid the performers that they were forced to eke out an existence by resorting to prostitution. The defendant persuaded the theater owners with whom the troupe had contracted to perform to cancel the contract unless higher wages were paid to the performers. The defendant's action was considered justified and therefore not tortious (*Brimelow v. Casson*, 1 Ch. 302 [1924]).

Interference with Prospective Contractual Relations

Essentially the same rules apply to interference with prospective contractual relations as to interference with existing contractual relations, except for one major difference. Because no contract actually exists, the defendant is given greater leeway as to what he can do to interfere. Although a defendant cannot interfere with an existing contract for the purpose of obtaining business for himself, he is privileged to do so when only a potential contract is involved. He is even privileged to drive a plaintiff out of business, as long as he does not use unlawful means such as price fixing or monopolization. But if he acts out of sheer malice, his conduct will not be privileged.

Interference with a plaintiff's non-business expectations of financial gain can be the basis for this tort. If the defendant induces a testator to leave the plaintiff out of her will, he can be held liable. Interference with a plaintiff's potential legal claim can also be tortious. A defendant may be liable if he tampers with medical records or conceals facts from the plaintiff that if known would reveal a cause of action.

NET NEWS

A definition of interference with prospective contractual relations and a comparison to interference with contractual relations can be found at **http://www.lectlaw.com** by entering "interference with prospective contractual relations" as your search term.

PUTTING IT INTO PRACTICE 10:7

1. Pro-Image and University Graphics are business competitors. Pro-Image has leased space from a commercial landlord when it discovers that University Graphics is negotiating to rent space in the same location. Representatives for Pro-Image express their concern about the landlord renting space to their "fierce competitor;" the landlord decides not to lease space to University Graphics to avoid conflict between tenants. Does University Graphics have grounds for a claim of interference with existing contractual relations against Pro-Image? Does it have grounds for a claim of interference with prospective contractual relations?

2. An attorney represents a proprietary court-reporting school student who is being sued by the school to collect unpaid fees. The student counterclaims for fraud and misrepresentation. In the course of representing the student, the attorney contacts several students at the school and discovers that many of them are dissatisfied with the court-reporting program. Some of the students approach the attorney and indicate that they might be interested in suing the school. The attorney takes the names of the students and contacts them when the collection case is settled. The attorney holds three meetings in his office with the students. After the third meeting, approximately thirty-five students withdraw from the program. The school files a claim for interference with contractual relations against the attorney. Does the school have a viable claim?

NET NEWS

Malicious prosecution is defined and explained at **http://www.lectlaw.com**. Enter "malicious prosecution" as your search term.

MISUSE OF LEGAL PROCESS

A plaintiff who has been subjected to unwarranted judicial proceedings may sue on the basis of malicious prosecution, wrongful institution of civil proceedings, or abuse of process (see Exhibit 10–6). Notice that the plaintiff in these cases was originally the defendant in the cause of action leading to the suit involving the misuse of legal process. Suppose an individual became the target of a criminal investigation that resulted in his becoming the defendant in a criminal trial. If the individual believed the prosecutor's chief witness fabricated the story involving the defendant and actively sought to bring criminal proceedings against the defendant out of vengeance because of a squabble the two had had years earlier, the defendant in the criminal action could sue the prosecutor's witness, who would become the defendant in the malicious prosecution suit.

Malicious Prosecution

A defendant whose motives are for some purpose other than bringing the plaintiff to justice and who, without probable cause, institutes criminal proceedings against another commits *malicious prosecution* (*Restatement [Second] of Torts* § 653). For the plaintiff to recover, the proceedings must conclude in the plaintiff's favor and the defendant must actively participate in instigating the prosecution. A defendant who leaves the decision in the hands of the prosecutor is not considered to have actively participated in the prosecution. Rather, the defendant must have lied to the prosecutor or attempted in some way to influence his decision to prosecute. The proceedings are deemed to have concluded in favor of the plaintiff if the prosecutor decides not to prosecute, the grand jury refuses to indict, or the case is dismissed because of the weakness of the case. A plaintiff's plea of guilty in acceptance of a plea bargain is not considered a favorable conclusion for the plaintiff.

The most difficult hurdle for plaintiffs to overcome in malicious prosecution cases is the probable-cause requirement. If a defendant reasonably believes that the plaintiff committed certain acts, he will be deemed to have probable cause. If it turns out that the defendant's belief is mistaken, his mistake will not constitute lack of probable cause as long as the mistake is a reasonable one. An acquittal does not necessarily indicate a lack of probable cause, because an acquittal may occur on the basis of reasonable doubt rather than lack of probable cause. Therefore, even if the plaintiff is acquitted, the defendant has a right to, in essence, retry the plaintiff. If he can show by a preponderance of the evidence that the plaintiff was guilty, he can establish the existence of probable cause.

In showing improper purpose, the plaintiff must show that the defendant acted out of malice or for some reason other than seeing justice done. A creditor, for example, who uses the criminal process to compel a debtor to pay her debt has an improper purpose (*Restatement [Second] of Torts* § 668, cmt. g).

Prosecutors are almost always immune from malicious prosecution suits. Immunity is also generally

EXHIBIT 10–6 Misuse of Legal Process

MALICIOUS PROSECUTION	WRONGFUL INSTITUTION OF CIVIL PROCEEDINGS
Defendant institutes criminal proceedings against plaintiff but has no probable cause and acts out of motives other than a sense of bringing plaintiff to justice.	Defendant institutes civil proceedings against plaintiff but has no probable cause and acts out of motives other than seeking compensation for wrong suffered.

ABUSE OF PROCESS
Defendant uses litigation devices for improper purposes.

given to police officers as long as they are acting within the general scope of their duties.

Wrongful Institution of Civil Proceedings

Although the tort of malicious prosecution normally applies to criminal proceedings, most states allow similar actions for *wrongful institution of civil proceedings*. The elements are essentially the same as for malicious prosecution, although civil proceedings may encompass administrative proceedings, bankruptcy proceedings, and insanity proceedings as well as ordinary civil lawsuits. Proving lack of probable cause in a civil case is more difficult than in a criminal case because one can initiate civil proceedings with far less certainty of the facts than in a criminal proceeding. A suit brought merely to harass an opponent or to extort a settlement when the defendant is aware there is no real chance of succeeding exemplifies wrongful institution of civil proceedings. A counterclaim brought solely for the purpose of delaying proceedings is another example.

Abuse of Process

If an individual initiates a criminal or civil proceeding based on probable cause and on the basis of permissible motives, he may still be liable for **abuse of process** if he uses certain litigation devices for improper purposes. Using a subpoena, for example, to harass someone or to induce her to settle rather than for its practical purpose of obtaining testimony could be considered abuse of process (*Restatement [Second] of Torts* § 682, illus. 3). As long as the primary purpose for the proceeding is justified, the fact that the defendant has an ulterior motive or that the proceedings may be of some incidental benefit to her is irrelevant. If the instigation of bankruptcy proceedings is justified, it does not become abuse of process merely because the instigator of those proceedings hopes she will gain some benefit from the closing down of her competitor's business. Typically, abuse of process involves situations in which a party puts undue pressure on another to induce her to engage in or refrain from a particular action.

NET NEWS

To read about a trial court's characterization of tactics employed by Allstate Insurance Company as abuse of process, go to **http://www.chiroweb.com** and enter "Allstate abuse of process" as your search term.

PUTTING IT INTO PRACTICE 10:8

1. Robert, a freelance reporter and owner of a helicopter news service, films a night-time air hoist rescue of a stranded fisherman. One of the firefighters involved in the rescue claims that Robert shone a bright spotlight from his helicopter during the rescue, causing the firefighter to momentarily lose control of the hoist, thereby endangering his crew and the fisherman. The firefighter brings his complaint to the Federal Aviation Administration (FAA), which exonerates Robert after an investigation. The firefighter then goes to the city attorney's office. The prosecutor brings charges against Robert but drops them after learning of the FAA adjudication and the exonerating evidence presented. Robert files a claim for malicious prosecution. Do you think a court would uphold his claim?

2. Rosemary is dismissed from her job at Nursefinders. Later she returns to Nursefinders to discuss vacation pay she thought might be due her and tells her former supervisor that she has been contacted by someone from Norrell Health Care Services regarding potential employment there. After consulting with an attorney, who tries to contact Rosemary numerous times without success, Nursefinders seeks and obtains a temporary restraining order. The order prevents Rosemary from accepting employment from any of Nursefinders' competitors, in conformance with a two-year noncompetition clause in her contract with Nursefinders. After a hearing, the trial court dissolves the temporary restraining order and denies the request for a preliminary injunction. Rosemary then files suit, claiming malicious prosecution and abuse of process. Does she have a viable suit?

SUMMARY

Misrepresentation arose out of the common law action of deceit. Intentional misrepresentation, corresponding to fraud under the common law, requires that (1) the defendant makes a misrepresentation with the intent of inducing the plaintiff's reliance on that misrepresentation, (2) the defendant knows the representation is false or acts with reckless indifference to the truth, (3) the plaintiff justifiably relies on the defendant's misrepresentation, and (4) the plaintiff suffers damages stemming from her reliance.

A misrepresentation may consist of a false statement or an intentional concealment of a fact or an action by itself. Under modern law, mere failure to disclose a material fact may be considered concealment under certain circumstances.

A plaintiff can recover if he is a member of the class whom the defendant can reasonably expect to learn of and rely on the misrepresentation. The plaintiff must also show that her reliance occurred in the type of transaction the defendant could reasonably expect the plaintiff to engage in as a result of the reliance. A defendant must know that his statement is false or act with reckless disregard to the truth or falsity of the statement. In reference to the issue of reliance, the question is whether the plaintiff made any independent investigation of her own, and whether reliance was on the misrepresentation, the investigation, or both.

The plaintiff is not usually entitled to rely on an opinion offered by the defendant. If, however, the defendant and plaintiff have a fiduciary relationship, or if the defendant has worked to secure the plaintiff's confidence or purports to have special knowledge, the plaintiff may be justified. Mere "puffing" is not actionable unless the plaintiff reasonably perceives that the opinion being offered is being made by a disinterested party. Predictions are almost always considered opinion unless the defendant is aware of facts inconsistent with that opinion.

To recover for misrepresentation, the plaintiff must show that the losses suffered were the reasonably foreseeable results of the misrepresentation. A plaintiff may ask either to be put into the position she was in before the misrepresentation (reliance measure) or to be put in the position she would have been in had the misrepresented facts been true (benefit of the bargain measure).

Most courts today allow a claim for negligent misrepresentation. Recovery is most likely to be allowed when a defendant makes false statements during the course of his business or profession or has a pecuniary interest in the transaction in which he is involved. One who makes a negligent misrepresentation is liable only to those he intends to reach with his information or whom he knows the recipient of his information intends to reach.

Recovery for innocent misrepresentation is allowed if a party makes an innocent but material misrepresentation in the course of a sale, rental, or exchange transaction. The seller of goods who makes misrepresentations on a label or through public advertisement is also liable for any innocent misrepresentations resulting in physical injury.

A public nuisance requires interference with a right common to the general public; a private nuisance is an unreasonable interference with the plaintiff's use and enjoyment of her own land. To prove public nuisance a plaintiff must show that the public at large was injured or exposed to the possibility of injury, and the harm must be a substantial one. The harm suffered by the plaintiff must be peculiar to her and not shared by the rest of the public. Some courts allow recovery, however, if the plaintiff suffers greater economic loss than others in the community.

Private nuisance, in contrast, requires only that the plaintiff's use and enjoyment of his land be substantially interfered with and that the defendant's conduct be negligent, intentional, or abnormally dangerous. Interference is considered substantial if the plaintiff is inconvenienced or subjected to unpleasant sensory awarenesses. A plaintiff may seek either compensatory damages or an injunction. If he seeks an injunction, however, he must prove that his harm outweighs the utility of the defendant's conduct. Contributory negligence and assumption of risk can be raised as defenses in private nuisance claims.

Two tort actions that specifically protect business interests are interference with existing contractual relations and interference with prospective contractual relations. Intentionally and actively inducing another to breach a contract with the plaintiff constitutes interference with existing contractual relations. When deciding if this tort has been committed, the courts will consider the defendant's motive and purpose, the means he uses to create the interference, the type of interest with which he interferes, and the social interest involved in protecting both the defendant's freedom of action and the contractual interest of the plaintiff. Greater latitude is allowed defendants charged with interference with prospective contractual relations.

Anyone subjected to unwarranted judicial proceedings may recover on the basis of malicious prosecution, wrongful institution of civil proceedings, or abuse of process. Malicious prosecution occurs when a defendant actively participates in instituting criminal proceedings against another, lacks probable cause, and has motives other than bringing the plaintiff to justice. Wrongful institution of civil proceedings is comparable to malicious prosecution except that it involves the initiation of civil proceedings. Abuse of process occurs when an individual institutes criminal or civil proceedings on the basis of permissible motives and with probable cause but uses litigation devices for improper purposes.

KEY TERMS

abuse of process
Use of litigation devices for improper purposes
at-will employee
Employee who, because of the nature of his employment contract, can be discharged at any time for any reason
deceit
Common law cause of action equated with intentional misrepresentation; also referred to as fraud
fiduciary relationship
Relationship based on trust and confidence imposing an obligation to act in good faith

latent defect
Defect that is invisible or not readily discoverable
nuisance
Substantial and unreasonable interference with a plaintiff's interest; includes public and private nuisance
patent defect
Defect that is visible or readily discoverable

REVIEW QUESTIONS

1. What is the relationship between deceit and misrepresentation?

2. What are the basic elements of misrepresentation?

3. How does intentional misrepresentation differ from negligent and innocent misrepresentation?

4. Is nondisclosure grounds for misrepresentation? If yes, under what circumstances?

5. Is making a statement that is a half-truth grounds for misrepresentation?

6. How do the courts treat transactions involving parties having a fiduciary relationship differently than transactions that are done at "arm's length"?

7. To what group of persons is a defendant liable if he makes a misrepresentation?

8. What state of mind is required for intentional misrepresentation?

9. Is a defendant liable if a plaintiff relies on the defendant's misrepresentation but also conducts an investigation of her own?

10. Under what circumstances is a plaintiff justified in relying on a defendant's opinion?

11. How do courts treat statements by defendants that could be characterized as
    a. puffing?
    b. opinion by a disinterested party?
    c. opinion implying facts?
    d. prediction?
    e. statement of intentions?

12. What do plaintiffs have to prove in terms of causation?

13. What is the difference between a reliance measure of damages and a benefits-of-the-bargain measure?

14. In what ways do the courts treat negligent misrepresentation differently than they do intentional misrepresentation?

15. Under what circumstances are today's courts willing to allow recovery for innocent misrepresentation?

16. Why is nuisance referred to as the "legal garbage can"?

17. What is the difference between private and public nuisance?

18. What are the elements of public nuisance?
    a. Why must the plaintiff prove that he suffered damages peculiar to him?
    b. In what way have the courts struggled with the concept of "particular damage"?

19. What are the elements of private nuisance?
    a. How does private nuisance differ from trespass?
    b. What is considered "substantial interference"?
    c. Must the defendant's conduct be intentional?
    d. What is considered when determining if a defendant's conduct is unreasonable?
    e. What remedies are available to a plaintiff?
    f. What defenses can be raised?

20. Why has nuisance enjoyed a resurgence?
    a. What is CERCLA?
    b. What advantages over CERCLA does a nuisance claim offer a plaintiff?
    c. What advantages over CERCLA does a nuisance claim offer a defendant?
    d. What advantages does CERCLA offer over a nuisance claim?
21. What are the elements of interference with existing contractual relations?
    a. Is this tort committed by offering a third person a better price, knowing that doing so could induce this person to breach his contract with the plaintiff?
    b. What kinds of contracts cannot serve as a basis for this tort?

    c. What can a plaintiff recover?
    d. When is a defendant privileged to induce a breach of contract?
22. How does interference with prospective contractual relations differ from the tort of interference with existing contractual relations?
23. What are the elements of malicious prosecution?
    a. Which is the most difficult element to prove, and why?
    b. Why are prosecutors and police officers rarely sued for this tort?
24. How does the tort of wrongful institution of civil proceedings differ from malicious prosecution?
25. Under what circumstances is someone liable for abuse of process?

PRACTICE EXAM

Students should complete the practice exam after studying each chapter. The answers are in Appendix A. If you score lower than 80%, you should reread the materials.

True-False

1. The common law action of deceit required that the plaintiff lose money or property as a result of relying on the defendant's representation.
2. To recover for intentional misrepresentation a plaintiff must prove that the defendant knew the misrepresentation was false or acted with reckless indifference to the truth.
3. Misrepresentation cannot consist of actions alone or just of concealing a fact.
4. A defendant cannot be found liable for misrepresentation if he makes a statement that is a half-truth.
5. Courts are more willing to find misrepresentation if the defendant has a fiduciary relationship with the plaintiff than if a transaction occurs at arm's length between the parties.
6. Defendants who incorporate misstatements into commercial documents are liable to those who suffer as a result of their reliance on the truth of those statements even if the defendants never intended to make contact with those persons.
7. A defendant possesses the requisite state of mind for intentional misrepresentation if he

makes a statement that is merely a belief but represents it as actual knowledge.
8. The defendant is still liable even if the plaintiff relied mainly on her own investigation rather than the defendant's misrepresentation.
9. "Puffing" is an actionable form of misrepresentation.
10. A plaintiff may be able to recover if a defendant expresses an opinion implying that no facts incompatible with that opinion exist.
11. A defendant can be found liable for a prediction if he knows of facts inconsistent with that prediction.
12. If a defendant promises to buy the plaintiff's house for $100,000 but actually has no intention of doing so, and the plaintiff sues for breach of contract, the defendant will probably not be allowed to raise the statute-of-frauds defense just because the contract was not in writing.
13. Negligent misrepresentation has different elements than intentional misrepresentation.
14. A plaintiff is most likely to recover for negligent misrepresentation when the defendant has a

pecuniary interest in or makes false statements during a business transaction.

15. A defendant who is aware that a negligent misrepresentation will be passed on to a limited number of people will be liable even she is unaware of their precise identity.

16. Modern courts generally allow recovery for innocent misrepresentation under the same circumstances as they would allow recovery for intentional or negligent misrepresentation.

17. Innocent misrepresentation is a viable cause of action in product liability cases even when the plaintiff does not buy the product directly from the defendant.

18. To sustain a claim for private nuisance the plaintiff must have an interest in the land that has been affected by the defendant's activities.

19. Recovery for public nuisance is allowed even if only the plaintiff is injured, as long as that injury occurs in a public place.

20. A legislature does not have the right to declare conduct that is detrimental to the welfare of its citizens to be a public nuisance.

21. To prove private nuisance a plaintiff must show that the defendant's conduct was intentional, negligent, or abnormally dangerous.

22. A plaintiff can recover for public nuisance only if something physical enters the plaintiff's property and causes a substantial interference.

23. Interference is considered "substantial" for purposes of public nuisance if the plaintiff is inconvenienced or is exposed to an unpleasant sensory experience.

24. To recover on a private-nuisance claim a plaintiff must prove that the defendant intended to interfere with the plaintiff's use and enjoyment of her land.

25. Even if a defendant intentionally interfered with the plaintiff's use of his land, some courts require that the plaintiff prove that the harm he suffered was greater than the utility of the defendant's conduct.

26. A plaintiff suing for private nuisance can always seek to recover compensatory damages or to obtain an injunction.

27. Nuisance law has some advantage over statutory remedies.

28. Nuisance claims have the advantage over CERCLA claims in that they allow plaintiffs to recover more in damages and to more easily obtain injunctions.

29. Under CERCLA, defendants are liable only for the contamination they actually cause.

30. Remedies under nuisance law are contingent on balancing the costs and benefits of the nuisance, but such balancing is not required under CERCLA.

31. Under CERCLA, designing and monitoring cleanup of hazardous waste is easier than with nuisance claims.

32. In deciding whether the tort of interference with existing contractual relations has been committed, courts consider the purpose and motive of the defendant as well as the social interests involved in protecting the defendant's freedom of action and the plaintiff's contractual interests.

33. Offering a better price to a third person, knowing that this could induce this person to breach his contract with the plaintiff, does not constitute interference with contractual relations.

34. A plaintiff in a breach of existing contractual relations claims can recover for pecuniary losses but not for emotional harm.

35. A plaintiff in a breach of existing contractual relations claims cannot recover for breach of contract against the person the defendant induced to breach the contract.

36. A defendant is not considered to have interfered with prospective contractual relations if he drives a plaintiff out of business, as long as he does not act in malice or do something illegal.

37. A defendant is given more leeway with what he can do to interfere with a prospective contract than with an existing contract.

38. The plaintiff in a misuse-of-legal-process case was originally the defendant in the cause of action leading up to the misuse-of-legal-process case.

39. To recover for the tort of malicious prosecution, the proceedings must be concluded in the plaintiff's favor.

40. Proceedings are not deemed to have concluded in favor of the plaintiff for the purpose of malicious prosecution if the prosecutor declines not to prosecute.

41. Proving lack of probable cause is usually the easiest part of a plaintiff's malicious prosecution case and is easier to prove in these cases than in cases of wrongful institution of civil proceedings.

42. Proving lack of probable cause in a malicious-prosecution case is automatic if the plaintiff is acquitted.

43. To prove improper purpose in a malicious-prosecution case the plaintiff must show that the defendant acted with malice or for some reason other than seeing that justice would be done.

44. Prosecutors and police officers are the most frequent defendants in malicious-prosecution suits.

45. Wrongful institution of civil proceedings cannot arise out of administrative or bankruptcy proceedings.

46. Abuse of process does not occur if the primary purpose of the proceedings is justified, even if the defendant has some ulterior motive.

Matching

GROUP 1

_____ 1. nuisance
_____ 2. private nuisance
_____ 3. public nuisance
_____ 4. CERCLA
_____ 5. come to the nuisance

a. advance notice about nuisance
b. statutory remedy for toxic wastes
c. loud music in evening in residential area
d. feedlot next to residential area
e. legal garbage can

GROUP 2

_____ 1. interference with existing
_____ 2. interference with prospective
_____ 3. malicious prosecution
_____ 4. wrongful institution of
_____ 5. abuse-of-processa.

a. filing suit solely to harass plaintiff contractual relations
b. defendant lies to prosecutor contractual relations
c. breach of at-will contract
d. use of subpoena to induce civil proceedings settlement
e. interference with potential legal claim

Fill-in-the-Blanks

1. The tort of _____ refers to a plaintiff's right to possess his property, whereas the tort of _____ refers to a plaintiff's right to use and enjoy his property.

2. For a plaintiff to recover for public nuisance, the harm caused by the defendant's conduct must be _____.

3. The _____ _____ element of private nuisance requires that the plaintiff suffer an injury different in kind from that suffered by the rest of the community.

4. A defendant in a nuisance action can argue that the plaintiff _____ _____ _____ _____ in that the nuisance existed before the plaintiff purchased her property.

5. _____ _____ _____ occurs when a defendant intentionally or negligently induces someone to breach a contract with the plaintiff.

6. To recover for the tort of _____ _____ the plaintiff must prove that the defendant instituted criminal proceedings without probable cause and for purposes other than bringing the plaintiff to justice.

7. Filing a counterclaim solely for the purpose of delaying proceedings is an example of _____ _____ _____ _____ _____.

8. _____ _____ _____ occurs when a person misuses a litigation device.

Multiple-Choice

1. Deceit
   a. is broader than the tort of misrepresentation.
   b. is the origin of the tort of misrepresentation.
   c. can be based on a mental state of intentional or innocent misrepresentation.
   d. all of the above.

2. Failure to disclose a material fact
   a. constituted misrepresentation under the common law.
   b. is not considered misrepresentation today because of the doctrine of caveat emptor.
   c. is more likely to be considered misrepresentation when a latent fact is involved.
   d. none of the above.

3. A defendant is liable
   a. even if the plaintiff's reliance did not occur in the type of transaction the defendant could reasonably expect the plaintiff to engage in as a result of the reliance.
   b. only to those persons he intended to influence with his misrepresentation.
   c. only if the plaintiff's reliance occurred in the type of transaction the defendant could reasonably expect the plaintiff to engage in as a result of the reliance.
   d. all of the above.

4. A plaintiff
   a. is never entitled to rely on a defendant's opinion.
   b. is entitled to rely on a defendant's opinion if the defendant purports to have special knowledge that the plaintiff does not have.
   c. need not have justification for relying on a defendant's misrepresentation.
   d. is not entitled to rely on a defendant's opinion even if the defendant worked to secure the confidence of the plaintiff.

5. In a case of misrepresentation,
   a. a plaintiff's losses may be measured by using either a reliance or benefits-of-the-bargain measure.
   b. the plaintiff does not have to prove that she suffered actual damages.
   c. the plaintiff's damages need not be proximately caused by the defendant's conduct.
   d. all of the above.

6. A defendant
   a. is not liable for negligent misrepresentation if she does not receive compensation directly from the plaintiff.
   b. is liable to those whom she intends to reach with the information.
   c. is liable to anyone she reasonably expects to learn about the statement.
   d. all of the above.

7. The "special-injury" requirement for private nuisance
   a. operates as a barrier to many plaintiffs who want to bring claims as a result of environmental hazards.
   b. can be met by a showing that the plaintiff suffered greater economic loss than others in the community.
   c. can be met by a showing that the defendant interfered with the plaintiff's commercial use of her land.
   d. all of the above.

8. A defendant
   a. will not be considered to have committed a breach of existing contractual relations if he is merely trying to protect his own interests.
   b. is not privileged to induce a breach of contract if the purpose of the breach is to promote a social interest.
   c. is privileged to induce a breach of his own existing contractual rights even if his motive is to gain business for himself.
   d. all of the above.

TORT TEASERS

1. Answer the questions posed in the hypothetical scenario given at the beginning of this chapter.

2. A law firm writes an opinion letter for its client in which it indicates that the client is a general partnership. In fact, some of the members claim to be limited partners and are therefore not subject to full liability. Does the law firm have a duty to disclose this information to Plaintiff, who is contemplating making loans to the partnership? *Roberts v. Ball, Hunt, Hart & Barerwitz*, 57 Cal. App. 3d 104, 128 Cal. Rptr. 901 (1976).

3. An attorney negligently gives erroneous "curbstone advice" to his client. Can he be held liable for misrepresentation? *Buttersworth v. Swint*, 186 S.E. 77 (Va. 1936).

4. Plaintiff, who is interested in buying a boiler, requests that Defendant inspect the boiler. Defendant negligently provides Plaintiff with a report that the boiler is in good condition when in fact it is not. Defendant is aware that his report is to be passed on to the seller, who can be expected to rely on the report in giving warranties. When the seller does sell the boiler, it proves to be defective, and the seller suffers pecuniary loss when he incurs liability for breach of warranty. Is Defendant liable for misrepresentation? *Du Rite Laundry v. Washington Electric Co.*, 263 A.D. 396, 33 N.Y.S.2d 925 (1942).

5. Plaintiff is a strong believer in spiritualism. She receives a "Spanish prisoner" letter from Mexico, which states that the writer is unjustly imprisoned and that he has a draft for $20,000 that he has been unable to cash, located in a New York bank. He promises Plaintiff that this draft will be turned over to her if she will deliver $8,500 to a designated agent of the writer. Plaintiff consults Defendant, a spiritualist medium, who tells Plaintiff that the letter is legitimate. Relying on this assurance, Plaintiff mortgages her house, pays the $8,500, and loses it. Should Plaintiff be allowed to recover from Defendant? *Hyma v. Lee*, 60 N.W.2d 920 (Mich. 1953).

6. A violin expert tries to sell an instrument purported to be a genuine Stradivarius to a purchaser who is also a violin expert. Should the seller be liable for his misrepresentation? *Banner v. Lyon & Healy Co.*, 249 A.D. 569, 293 N.Y.S. 236 (1937).

   Decide which tort you think would be appropriate to allege in each of the following cases.

7. Defendant purchases a home in a residential area and uses it to operate a funeral home. *Williams v. Montgomery*, 186 So. 302 (Miss. 1939).

8. A bitter dispute arises between Plaintiff school district and Defendant teachers' association. The teachers' association subpoenas eighty-seven teachers and refuses to stagger their appearances, thereby requiring the school district to hire substitutes to avoid a total shutdown of the schools. *Board of Education v. Farmingdale Classroom Teachers' Ass'n, Inc.*, 343 N.E.2d 278 (N.Y. 1975).

9. The Virginia Department of Social Services (DSS) opened up bidding for its proposal to privatize the two child support offices. Maximus, Inc. and Lockheed Management Information Systems were the only two bidders. To evaluate the bids, DSS created a selection panel composed of five state employees. The panel heard oral testimony, reviewed and scored the proposals, and issued a Notice of Intent to Award the contract to Maximus. Subsequently, Lockheed filed a formal protest of DSS's decision to award the contract to Maximus. In its protest, Lockheed alleged that two members of the evaluation panel had undisclosed conflicts of interest that compromised the integrity of the evaluation process. State officials conducted an investigation and canceled the Notice of Intent to Award the contract to Maximus. Maximus filed an action against Lockheed claiming that Lockheed knew, or had reason to know, that the allegations in its formal protest were false, that the false allegations were intentionally presented to create an appearance of impropriety, and that the protest was calculated to wrongfully interfere with Maximus' contractual relationship with DSS. Lockheed responded by asserting in part that it filed its protest pursuant to a statutory right and was therefore protected by privilege. What would you have to know to decide which company should prevail? *Maximus, Inc. v. Lockheed Information Management Systems, Inc.*, 493 S.E.2d 375 (Va. 1997).

INTERNET INQUIRIES

At the federal level, requests for information sometimes require going through the Freedom of Information Act (FOIA). This act applies to agencies of the executive branch, including cabinet departments, military departments, government corporations, and independent regulatory agencies. The FOIA does not apply to elected officials of the federal government (e.g., president, vice president, Congress), the federal courts, the White House staff, state agencies, schools, or private organizations and businesses.

The FOIA requires federal agencies to make available to the public records relating to such issues as consumer product safety, environmental hazards, public health, labor relations, and government spending. Individuals can also request that they be provided any records that the government has regarding them. Federal agencies can refuse to release certain types of exempted information: trade secrets, defense and foreign policy secrets, personnel and medical files, confidential financial information, geological information, internal agency rules and government memos, and investigative reports prepared for law enforcement purposes.

If you are not sure which agency has the records you want, go to the library and check the *United States Government Manual* (available online at http://www .access.gpo.gov), or call the local office of your representative in Congress. The manual has a complete list of all federal agencies, a description of their functions, and the address of each agency. Your request should be in writing and you should

- reasonably describe the records you want with sufficient specificity that an employee of the agency familiar with the records can locate them in a reasonable amount of time and without undue effort.
- restrict your request to the records you really want rather than asking for "all the files relating to. . .".
- address your request to a specific agency and send it to the agency's FOIA officer or the head of the agency.
- state the request is being made under the FOIA.

- provide identifying information such as social security number, date of birth, and address, if requesting personal records.
- specify the purpose for which the records are requested and your status in requesting these records (this is done so that the appropriate fees can be assessed).
- mark your envelope "Attention: Freedom of Information Act."
- keep a copy of the request letter and related correspondence until the request has been finally resolved.

The Department of Justice Office of Information and Privacy provides information regarding access to public records through electronic reading rooms, FOIA web sites and FOIA updates at http://www.usdoj.gov. Select the link titled "FOIA."

For assistance in writing an FOIA letter to a federal agency, go to http://www.thefirstamendment.org and select the "Resources" link. The American Civil Liberties Union provides FOIA request letters at its site, http:// www.aclu.org. Enter "FOIA request" as your search term. If you want to prepare a draft by simply filling in the blanks (e.g., name of the agency you are requesting documents from, your name, documents requested, etc.), you can go to the National Freedom of Information Coalition at http://www.nfoic.org. This site will do form letters for both federal and state agencies, provide you with links to state open-meeting and open-records laws, and give you the names and addresses of individuals and agencies helpful in getting information from a state or federal agency. Finally, a citizen's guide to making requests under both the FOIA and the Privacy Act of 1974 is available at http://www.tncrimlaw.com. This site provides links to FOIA sites and explains in some detail the provisions of the FOIA and its exemptions and the Privacy Act.

Go to the preceding websites and then prepare a form letter that you can keep on file in the event you are asked to prepare an FOIA request in the future.

PRACTICAL PONDERABLES

Watch the movie *The Insider*, which is based on a true story involving Dr. Jeffrey Wigand, a senior research chemist for Brown and Williamson, who was asked after he was fired by the company to be interviewed by Mike Wallace on *60 Minutes*. When the tobacco company learned about the interview, it threatened to sue CBS for interference with contractual relations on the grounds that doing the interview induced Wigand to breach his confidentiality agreement with the company.

After watching the movie, answer the following questions.

1. Review the case law in your state, and determine what Brown and Williamson would have had to prove to recover for interference with contractual relations.
2. What defenses do you think CBS could have raised?
3. Who do you think would have prevailed if this case had gone to trial?

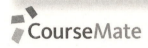 CourseMate   Access an interactive eBook, chapter-specific learning tools, including flashcards, quizzes, and more in your Paralegal CourseMate, accessed through www.CengageBrain.com.

CHAPTER 11

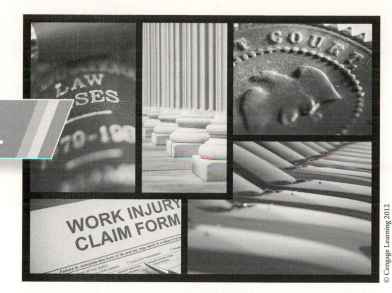

© Cengage Learning 2012

Strict Liability

CHAPTER OBJECTIVES

After completing the chapter, you should be able to

- Identify those circumstances in which animal owners are held strictly liable for damages caused by their animals.
- Describe abnormally dangerous activities.
- Describe the defenses that can be raised in response to a strict liability claim.

In this high-tech era of powerful but potentially dangerous sources of energy, we are now faced with the problem of waste disposal. We are just beginning to awaken to the horrendous potential posed by hazardous chemicals and are taking our first faltering steps toward safeguarding future generations. But some in our society have already begun to experience the repercussions of our ignorance. Suppose a woman comes to your supervising attorney and claims she has contracted cancer as a result of the leakage of toxic chemicals into her home. She wants to sue the city for approving the construction of the housing development in which she lives. She tells you that fifteen years before the land was developed into a residential area, it was used as a disposal site for chemical wastes. Is the city liable for the residents' injuries, even if those who allowed the dumping of wastes were, at the time, completely unaware of the potential medical dangers posed by such wastes?

OVERVIEW OF STRICT LIABILITY

In such a case your attorney might choose a theory of strict liability as an alternative to a negligence theory. **Strict liability** is applicable even when a defendant is neither negligent nor has any intent of wrongdoing (see Exhibit 11–1). It is a particularly useful theory in situations involving **abnormally dangerous** activities. Injuries involving defective products and dangerous animals are two other areas in which strict liability is imposed. An in-depth discussion of product liability is presented in Chapter 12, including further discussion of strict liability, the subject of this chapter.

In cases involving strict liability, defendants who engage in particularly dangerous kinds of activities must pay for any damage that results even if they carry out those activities in the most careful manner possible. Liability is imposed even though a defendant is not at fault. This lack of fault is what distinguishes strict liability from negligence.

Some courts refer to strict liability as "absolute liability." The latter description, however, is somewhat misleading because defenses to strict liability actions can be raised; therefore, liability is not absolute. Others refer to strict liability as "liability without fault." This term is also a misnomer because liability without fault exists under an intentional-tort basis of liability. Therefore, we use the term *strict liability* throughout this text rather than the alternate terms.

NET NEWS

A description of the development of strict liability under the common law can be found at **http://www .thelockeinstitute.org**; enter "strict liability" as your search term.

EXHIBIT 11–1 *Strict Liability*

ANIMALS	• Trespassing • Wild
PRODUCT LIABILITY	
ABNORMALLY DANGEROUS ACTIVITIES*	Abnormally Dangerous /Acts • Crop dusting • Storage of flammable liquids (urban areas) • Toxic waste disposal • Use of poisonous gas exterminators • Testing of rocket fuel Not Abnormally Dangerous Acts • Airplane flight (except ground damage) • Defective electrical wiring • Water damage from burst dam • Defective plumbing • Household use of gas, water, or electricity

© Cengage Learning 2012

*The courts do not agree on what does or does not constitute an abnormally dangerous activity. The examples given are representative of the majority position but should not be considered definitive.

Remember that the key distinction between negligence and strict liability lies in the area of fault. In a strict liability cause of action, a defendant may be liable even if he did not intentionally injure the plaintiff and in fact adhered to an objective standard of reasonable care.

STRICT LIABILITY FOR HARM CAUSED BY ANIMALS

Trespassing Animals

Under the English common law, owners of animals were liable for property damage caused when animals trespassed on another's land. Owners could not escape liability even if they used the utmost care to prevent their animals from escaping. Luckily for animal owners, the rule applied only to animals likely to roam, such as cattle, horses, sheep, and goats, and not to household animals such as dogs and cats.

Most American jurisdictions follow the English rule of strict liability in reference to trespassing animals. Historically, the Western states, whose economic base relied on cattle that were customarily allowed to graze at large on open range, rejected the common law rule. Many of these states have, however, adopted "fencing in" statutes, which provide that an owner is not strictly liable if she attempts to fence in the animals but is strictly liable if she does not. Under "fencing out" statutes, property owners who properly fence their land have a strict liability claim against those whose animals trespass onto their land.

LOCAL LINKS

What is the rule in your state regarding liability for damage caused by trespassing animals?

Nontrespassing Animals

One who keeps "dangerous animals" is strictly liable for the harm done by those animals. The definition of the term depends on whether the animal is considered wild or domesticated. A domesticated animal, according to the *Restatement (Second) of Torts* § 506(2), "is by custom devoted to the service of mankind." Under this definition, the courts have generally held that bulls and stallions, though often very dangerous, are domesticated. The apparent reasoning is that ownership of animals serves a valid social purpose and should not be discouraged.

According to the *Restatement (Second) of Torts*, people who keep wild animals are strictly liable for all damage caused by such animals if the damage results from a "dangerous propensity" typical of that particular species (*Restatement [Second] of Torts* § 507). Javelinas and foxes are examples of animals that are considered wild. Liability also exists when the damage stems from a dangerous tendency of the particular animal in question of which the owner is or should be aware. Some courts have moved away from a strict liability standard to a negligence standard when dealing with those who display wild animals to the public (as in a zoo, for example).

Strict liability is imposed in the case of domestic animals when the owner knows or has reason to know that the animal has vicious propensities. If an animal has unsuccessfully attempted to bite someone in the past or in general has a vicious temperament, the owner will be deemed to have reason to know of the pet's dangerous tendencies and will be held liable for any damage caused. The oft-repeated phrase, "Every dog is entitled to one free bite," is an illusion and should not be relied on to evade liability. Note, too, that the common law regarding liability for dog bites has been changed by statute in many states. Furthermore, statutory provisions, such as those requiring dogs to be leashed or muzzled, may also affect liability. Failure to comply with such statutes may render an owner negligent per se.

LOCAL LINKS

Under what conditions are dog owners in your state strictly liable for damages resulting from their dog biting someone?

CASE

Bard v. Jahnke
6 N.Y.3d 592, 848
N.E.2d 463 (N.Y., 2006)

READ, J.

The accident underlying this litigation occurred on September 27, 2001 at Hemlock Valley Farms in Otsego County, a dairy farm owned and operated by defendant Reinhardt Jahnke and his wife in partnership with their two sons. At roughly 8:00 A.M., plaintiff Larry Bard, a self-employed carpenter, arrived at the farm to meet defendant John Timer, another self-employed carpenter. One of Jahnke's sons had asked Timer to repair ripped cow mattresses in a certain section-called the "low cow district"-of the farm's free-stall dairy barn. This large barn, which was divided into several sections, housed approximately 400 cows at the time, 130 of them in the low cow district. The repair work involved chiseling off the bolts fastening the damaged mattresses to the concrete base of a stall, stretching the mattresses and then refastening the bolts. Timer had asked Bard the day before if he would be interested in helping him carry out this task, and Bard had replied that he would.

Timer, who had performed carpentry and odd jobs on the farm for about four or five years, walked Bard through the dairy barn, pointing out some of the projects that he had completed and where the milking parlor was. Timer took Bard to the barn's low cow district, told him how to start the mattress repairs, and then left to complete another chore, planning to return shortly. Neither Timer nor Bard saw a bull; Bard testified that he saw no farm animals at all in the barn when he walked through it with Timer. From his previous work at the farm, Timer knew there was a bull at another barn about a quarter-mile distant from the dairy barn. Prior to Bard's accident, he did not know that at all times there was a bull present in the dairy barn's low cow district.

Bard retrieved some tools from his truck and started to work at about 8:30 A.M. He testified that a number of cows wandered into the area as he was working. Further, he was "familiar with working in and around cows," which would "come up, drool on you, lick on you and everything else," and that he didn't "usually pay much attention to them." At about 9:00 A.M., as Bard was down on his knees removing bolts, he first noticed a bull "[w]hen he stepped in behind him" and "bellered" within a distance of two to three feet. Bard testified that he "slowly kind of looked around, and didn't know what to do at that point." As he "went to stand up," the bull "took [him] in the chest. [The bull] charged [him] then [and] proceeded to start slamming [him] into the pipes" in the stall. No one else was present in the low cow district at the time. Neither Jahnke nor anyone else associated with the farm knew ahead of time that Timer planned to repair the mattresses that

day, or that Bard would be working for Timer to carry out this task.

Bard pulled himself outdoors through an opening at the bottom of the barn, and crawled over to his truck, where he lay for "quite awhile to get some wind and establish what was going on." He caught the attention of someone working in the field, whom he asked to call an ambulance. Bard's injuries included fractured ribs, a lacerated liver and exacerbation of a preexisting cervical spine condition.

The hornless dairy bull who injured Bard was named Fred. He was about 1 1/2 years old, and had been the resident "cleanup" bull at the farm for at least six months prior to September 27, 2001. The cows and heifers on the farm are bred by artificial insemination. Fred was housed and roamed freely in the low cow district of the dairy barn so that he might impregnate cows stabled there who had failed to conceive by artificial insemination. Before this accident, Fred had concededly never threatened or injured any other farm animal or human being. As was the case with all the dairy bulls ever owned by Jahnke, a longtime dairy farmer, Fred was never chained, caged or barricaded within the barn. Prior to September 27, 2001, none of the bulls on any of the farms worked on or owned by Jahnke had ever acted aggressively toward, or injured, another farm animal or human being.

Bard, with his wife suing derivatively, commenced an action against both Jahnke and Timer to recover damages for his personal injuries, alleging causes of action sounding in strict liability and negligence. Plaintiffs subsequently moved for summary judgment on liability, and defendants cross-moved for summary judgment dismissing the complaint. Ruling on defendant's cross motion,[1] Supreme Court first observed that New York's appellate courts had been "markedly consistent" in applying the common-law vicious propensity rule to decide whether owners of dogs and cats were liable for injuries caused by their animals. Citing Restatement (Second) of Torts § 518 and prior cases in the Appellate Division, however, the court concluded that a different rule applied to owners of domestic animals other than dogs and cats. According to Supreme Court, these owners are subject to "some duty of enhanced care" to restrain or confine the animal or to warn a human being who might come into contact with it. Applying this rule to the facts,

---

1. Plaintiffs withdrew their motion for summary judgment at oral argument.

(continues)

Supreme Court granted defendants' motions for summary judgment because Jahnke did not know that Bard would be at his farm or working in the dairy barn, and Timer was unaware of the cleanup bull's presence in the barn.

The Appellate Division affirmed, but on a different basis altogether. Noting that a bull is a domestic animal as defined in Agriculture and Markets Law § 108(7) and citing our recent decision in *Collier v. Zambito*, 1 N.Y.3d 444, 775 N.Y.S.2d 205, 807 N.E.2d 254 [2004], the Court concluded that Jahnke was not liable for Bard's injuries unless he knew or should have known of the bull's vicious or violent propensities. The Court noted that the record contained no evidence of this, and "[t]o the contrary, it contains competent evidence establishing that, prior to [Bard's] accident, the subject bull had never injured another person or animal or behaved in a hostile or threatening manner" (16 A.D.3d 896, 897, 791 N.Y.S.2d 694 [3d Dept.2005]).

Bard had submitted the affidavit of a professor of animal science, who opined that "bulls, in particular breeding bulls, are generally dangerous and vicious animals," and that therefore Jahnke should have restrained the bull or warned Bard of its presence (*id.*). The Court found this affidavit unavailing, especially in light of its "consistent[ ], and recently[ ] reiterated" view that "the particular type or breed of domestic animal alone is insufficient to raise a question of fact as to vicious propensities" (*id.* [internal quotation marks and citations omitted]).

Finally, with respect to Bard's negligence claim, the Appellate Division noted that it had "considered and decline[d] to adopt the enhanced duty rule espoused under certain limited circumstances by the First and Second Departments" (*id.* at 898, 791 N.Y.S.2d 694). Bard subsequently sought to appeal so much of the Court's order as affirmed the grant of summary judgment to Jahnke. We granted him leave to appeal, and now affirm on the ground adduced by the Appellate Division.

Only two years ago, in *Collier*, we restated our longstanding rule

"that the owner of a domestic animal who either knows or should have known of that animal's vicious propensities will be held liable for the harm the animal causes as a result of those propensities. Vicious propensities include the propensity to do any act that might endanger the safety of the persons and property of others in a given situation" (*Collier*, 1 N.Y.3d at 446, 775 N.Y.S.2d 205, 807 N.E.2d 254 [internal quotation marks and citations omitted]; *see also* N.Y. PJI 2:220 [2006]).

Once this knowledge is established, the owner faces strict liability [2]. We made two additional points in *Collier*, which bear repeating.

First, while knowledge of vicious propensities "may of course be established by proof of prior acts of a similar kind of which the owner had notice," a triable issue of fact as to whether the owner knew or should have known that its animal harbored vicious propensities may be raised by proof of something less (*Collier*, 1 N.Y.3d at 446, 775 N.Y.S.2d 205, 807 N.E.2d 254). In Collier, a case in which a dog bit a child, we gave the example of evidence that a dog had, for example, "been known to growl, snap or bare its teeth," or that "the owner chose to restrain the dog, and the manner in which the dog was restrained" (*id.* at 447, 775 N.Y.S.2d 205, 807 N.E.2d 254).

"In addition, an animal that behaves in a manner that would not necessarily be considered dangerous or ferocious, but nevertheless reflects a proclivity to act in a way that puts others at risk of harm, can be found to have vicious propensities-albeit only when such proclivity results in the injury giving rise to the lawsuit" (*id.*).

Here, Fred had never attacked any farm animal or human being before September 27, 2001. He had always moved unrestrained within the limits of the barn's low cow district, regularly coming into contact with other farm animals, farm workers and members of the Jahnke family without incident or hint of hostility. He had never acted in a way that put others at risk of harm. As a result, Bard cannot recover under our traditional rule.

Bard therefore argues alternatively that he can recover under a common-law cause of action for negligence, as expressed in Restatement (Second) of Torts § 518, Comments *g* and *h*. This common-law cause of action is, he claims, separate and apart from and in addition to our traditional rule.

Section 518 provides generally that the owner of a domestic animal, which the owner does not know or have reason to know to be abnormally dangerous, is nonetheless liable if he intentionally causes the animal to do harm, or is negligent in failing to prevent harm. Comment *g*, "*Knowledge of normal characteristics*" provides that

"[i]n determining the care that the keeper of a not abnormally dangerous domestic animal is required to

---

2. Our rule is virtually identical to Restatement (Second) of Torts § 509(1) (1977): "A possessor of a domestic animal that he knows or has reason to know has dangerous propensities abnormal to its class, is subject to liability for harm done by the animal to another, although he has exercised the utmost care to prevent it from doing the harm."

(continues)

exercise to keep it under control, the characteristics that are normal to its class are decisive, and one who keeps the animal is required to know the characteristics. Thus the keeper of a bull or stallion is required to take greater precautions to confine it to the land on which it is kept and to keep it under effective control when it is taken from the land than would be required of the keeper of a cow or gelding."

Comment *h*, "*Animals dangerous under particular circumstances*" states that

"[o]ne who keeps a domestic animal that possesses only those dangerous propensities that are normal to its class is required to know its normal habits and tendencies. He is therefore required to realize that even ordinarily gentle animals are likely to be dangerous under particular circumstances and to exercise reasonable care to prevent foreseeable harm. Thus the keeper of even a gentle bull must take into account the tendencies of bulls as a class to attack moving objects and must exercise greater precautions to keep his bull under complete control if he drives it upon a public highway. So, too, the keeper of an ordinarily gentle bitch or cat is required to know that while caring for her puppies or kittens she is likely to attack other animals and human beings."

Building on these provisions and their specific references to bulls, Bard contends that because Fred was not only a bull, but a breeding bull housed with the herd over whom he exercised dominance, Jahnke was negligent in failing to restrain Fred,[3] or to warn non-farm personnel of his presence. But this is no different from

arguing that Jahnke was negligent in that he *should have known* of Fred's vicious propensities because—as plaintiffs' expert put it—"bulls, in particular breeding bulls, are generally dangerous and vicious animals." (16 A.D.3d at 897, 791 N.Y.S.2d 694.)

As already noted, an animal's propensity to cause injury may be proven by something other than prior comparably vicious acts. As a result, a common shorthand name for our traditional rule—the "one-bite rule"—is a misnomer. We have never, however, held that particular breeds or kinds of domestic animals are dangerous, and therefore when an individual animal of the breed or kind causes harm, its owner is charged with knowledge of vicious propensities. Similarly, we have never held that male domestic animals kept for breeding or female domestic animals caring for their young are dangerous as a class. We decline to do so now, or otherwise to dilute our traditional rule under the guise of a companion common-law cause of action for negligence. In sum, when harm is caused by a domestic animal, its owner's liability is determined solely by application of the rule articulated in *Collier*.

Accordingly, the order of Appellate Division should be affirmed, with costs.
Order affirmed, with costs.
[Dissenting opinion omitted.]

---

3. Fred was, of course, restricted to the low cow district of the barn. He was not, in any sense, "loose": he neither escaped nor was he taken from the confines within which he was normally kept, and he was not driven upon a public highway, the specific situations referenced in Comments g and h, respectively.

PUTTING IT INTO PRACTICE 11:1

1. Two-year-old Jessica is bitten by Smokey, a seventy-five-pound German shepherd, when he tries to get away from her hugging him and she will not let go. She has bites under and over one eye and over her lip. Smokey has played with other children with no problems, but did bite one man who had kicked him on three occasions. Should Smokey's owner be held strictly liable for Jessica's $20,000 in medical care?

2. Evelyn, a Jehovah's Witness, is going house to house to discuss the Bible with those who might be interested. When she passes by one house, Bandit, a sixty-five-pound pit bull, runs toward her, jumps on her, and causes her to break her hip. Bandit is restrained by a 100-foot chain at the time but has access to the driveway, where Evelyn walked toward the house. Bandit has never bitten anyone and is generally considered a well-behaved dog, but does have a tendency to jump on people. Is Bandit's owner strictly liable for Evelyn's injuries?

ABNORMALLY DANGEROUS ACTIVITIES

Doctrine of *Rylands v. Fletcher*

The path to strict liability for abnormally dangerous activities was paved in the English case of *Rylands v. Fletcher*, L.R. 3 H.L. 330 (1868). In *Rylands* the defendants hired an engineer and contractors to plan and construct a reservoir to supply their mill with water. When the defendants filled the reservoir, the water broke through into some abandoned mine shafts and then flooded adjacent mine shafts owned by the plaintiffs. An arbitrator found that although the defendants themselves were not guilty of any negligence, the engineer and contractors were negligent in their failure to use proper care. The case reached the House of Lords, the final appellate tribunal in England. The court, in finding for the plaintiff, established the rule that "the person who for his own purposes brings on his lands and collects and keeps there any thing likely to do mischief if it escapes, must keep it in at his peril, and if he does not do so, is prima facie answerable for all the damage which is the natural consequence of its escape."

The majority of American courts, along with the *Second Restatement*, have adopted the rationale of *Rylands* and imposed strict liability in cases involving abnormally dangerous activities. *Restatement (Second) of Torts* § 520 suggests consideration of six factors in determining whether an activity is abnormally dangerous:

- high degree of risk: "high degree of risk of some harm to the person, land or chattel of others"
- risk of serious harm: "likelihood that the harm that results from it will be great"
- cannot be eliminated even by due care: "inability to eliminate the risk by the exercise of reasonable care"
- not a matter of common usage: "extent to which the activity is not a matter of common usage"
- inappropriateness: "inappropriateness of the activity to the place where it is carried on"
- value: "extent to which its value to the community is outweighed by its dangerous attributes"

In determining whether strict liability should be imposed, the courts consider all of these factors (see Exhibit 11–2). Read *Yukon Equipment, Inc. v. Fireman's Fund Insurance Co.* to see an application of the six-factor test (although observe that the court ultimately rejects this test). Any one factor alone is generally not sufficient to warrant strict liability; however, all of the factors need not be present to find strict liability. The essential question is whether the risk created is so unusual (either because of its magnitude or because of the circumstances surrounding it) to justify strict liability even though the activity was carried out with all reasonable care. An example of such an activity is the transportation of nuclear materials. This activity necessarily involves a major risk of harm to others no matter how carefully it is carried out. (Note: Federal statutes impose a ceiling on liability for any nuclear mishaps.)

Be aware that the following examples of activities the courts have or have not considered abnormally dangerous are highly fact-specific. In other words, if the fact pattern had varied slightly in any of these cases, the court could have arrived at a different conclusion. Therefore, do not categorize certain activities as being either abnormally dangerous or not. Rather, look at these cases as illustrative of the courts' reasoning in the context of specific fact patterns.

EXHIBIT 11–2 **Six-Factor Test for Abnormally Dangerous Activity** (Restatement [Second] of Torts)

- Is there a high degree of risk of harm to person or property?
- Is any harm that results from the activity likely to be serious?
- Can the risk of harm be eliminated by exercising reasonable care?
- Is the activity a matter of common usage?
- Is the activity inappropriate in reference to the place where it is carried on?
- Is the value of the activity to the community outweighed by its dangerousness?

CASE 7

Yukon Equipment, Inc. v. Fireman's Fund Insurance Co.
585 P.2d 1206 (Alaska 1978)

MATTHEWS, Justice.

A large explosion occurred at 2:47 A.M. on December 7, 1973, in the suburbs north of the city of Anchorage. The explosion originated at a storage magazine for explosives under lease from the federal government to petitioner E. I. du Pont de Nemours and Company, which was operated by petitioner Yukon Equipment, Inc. The storage magazine is located on a 1,870 acre tract of federal land which had been withdrawn by the Department of the Interior for the use of the Alaska Railroad for explosive storage purposes by separate orders in 1950 and 1961. The magazine which exploded was located 3,820 feet from the nearest building not used to store explosives and 4,330 feet from the nearest public highway. At the time of the explosion it contained approximately 80,000 pounds of explosives. The blast damaged dwellings and other buildings within a two-mile radius of the magazine and, in some instances, beyond a two-mile radius. The ground concussion it caused registered 1.8 on the Richter scale at the earthquake observation station in Palmer, some 30 miles away.

The explosion was caused by thieves. Four young men had driven onto the tract where the magazine was located, broken into the storage magazine, set a prepared charge, and fled. They apparently did so in an effort to conceal the fact that they had stolen explosives from the site a day or two earlier.

This consolidated lawsuit was brought to recover for property damage caused by the explosion. Cross-motions for partial summary judgment were filed, and summary judgment on the issue of liability was granted in favor of the respondents. Respondents presented alternative theories of liability based on negligence, nuisance, absolute liability, and trespass. The court's order granting partial summary judgment did not specify the theory on which the liability was based.

Petitioners contend that none of the theories may be utilized to fix liability on them by summary judgment and further that the intentional detonation of the magazine is a superseding cause relieving them of liability under any theory. Respondents argue that the summary judgment is sustainable under the theory of absolute liability and that the intentional nature of the explosion is not a defense. We agree with respondents and affirm.

I.

The leading case on liability for the storage of explosives is *Exner v. Sherman Power Constr. Co.*, 54 F.2d 510 (2d Cir. 1931). There dynamite stored by the defendant exploded causing personal injury and property damage to the plaintiffs who resided some 935 feet away from the storage site. A distinguished panel of the Circuit Court of Appeals for the Second Circuit held the defendant liable regardless of fault:

> Dynamite is of the class of elements which one who stores or uses in such a locality, or under such circumstances as to cause likelihood of risk to others, stores or uses at his peril. He is an insurer, and is absolutely liable if damage results to third persons, either from the direct impact of rocks thrown out by the explosion (which would be a common law trespass) or from concussion.

Id. at 512–13. The court pointed out that while the general principle of absolute liability expressed in the English case of *Rylands v. Fletcher* had been accorded a mixed reception at best in United States courts, there had been no such reluctance to impose absolute liability in blasting cases. The court then noted that some authorities had made a distinction between damage done by rocks or debris hurled by an explosion, as to which there would be absolute liability, and damage caused by a concussion, as to which a negligence standard applied. The court concluded that such a distinction was without a logical basis and rejected it. *Id.* at 514. The court also determined that there was no reason for attaching different legal consequences to the results of an explosion "whether the dynamite explodes when stored or when employed in blasting." The court expressed the policy behind the rule of absolute liability as follows:

> The extent to which one man in the lawful conduct of his business is liable for injuries to another involves an adjustment of conflicting interests. . . . When, as here, the defendant, though without fault, has engaged in the perilous activity of storing large quantities of a dangerous explosive for use in his business, we think there is no justification for relieving it of liability, and that the owner of the business, rather than a third party who has no relation to the explosion, other than that of injury, should bear the loss.

Id. at 514. *Exner* has been widely followed, and was based on many earlier authorities imposing absolute liability for explosions. . . .

> The storage and transportation of explosive substances are ultra-hazardous activities because no precautions and care can make it reasonably certain that they will not explode and because the harm resulting from their explosion is almost certain to be serious.

(continues)

Comment (e) addresses the question of common usage, stating:

> While blasting is recognized as a proper means of clearing woodlands for cultivating and of excavating for building purposes, the conditions which require its use are usually of brief duration. It is generally required because of the peculiar character of the land and it is not a part of the customary processes of farming or of building operations. Likewise, the manufacture, storage, transportation and use of high explosives, although necessary to the construction of many public and private works, are carried on by a comparatively small number of persons and, therefore, are not matters of common usage.

Thus the particular rule of *Exner*, absolute liability for damage caused by the storage of explosives, was preserved by the *Restatement* and a general rule, inferred from *Exner* and the authorities on which it was based, and from *Rylands v. Fletcher* and its antecedents, was stated which imposed absolute liability on any other activity which met the definition of ultra-hazardous.

The *Restatement (Second) of Torts* (1977), adopted by the ALI after the explosion in this case, does not reflect a per se rule of liability for the storage of explosives. Instead it lists six factors to be considered in determining whether an activity is "abnormally dangerous" and therefore subject to the rule of absolute liability. The factors are:

(a) existence of a high degree of risk of some harm to the person, land or chattels of others;

(b) likelihood that the harm that results from it will be great;

(c) inability to eliminate the risk by the exercise of reasonable care;

(d) extent to which the activity is not a matter of common usage;

(e) inappropriateness of the activity to the place where it is carried on; and

(f) extent to which its value to the community is outweighed by its dangerous attributes.

Id. § 520.

Based in large part on the *Restatement (Second)*, petitioners argue that their use was not abnormally dangerous. Specifically they contend that their use of the magazine for the storage of explosives was a normal and appropriate use of the area in question since the storage magazine was situated on lands set aside by the United States for such purposes and was apparently located in compliance with applicable federal regulations. They point out that the storage served a legitimate community need for an accessible source of explosives for various purposes. They contend that before absolute liability can be imposed in any circumstance a preliminary finding must be made as to whether or not the defendant's activity is abnormally dangerous, that such a determination involves the weighing of the six factors set out in section 520 of the *Restatement (Second) of Torts*, and that an evaluation of those factors in this case could not appropriately be done on motion for summary judgment.

If we were to apply the *Restatement (Second)*'s six-factor test to the storage of explosives in this case we would be inclined to conclude that the use involved here was an abnormally dangerous one. Comment (f) to section 520 makes it clear that all of the factors need not be present for an activity to be considered abnormally dangerous:

> In determining whether the danger is abnormal, the factors listed in clauses (a) to (f) of this Section are all to be considered, and are all of importance. Any one of them is not necessarily sufficient to itself in a particular case, and ordinarily several of them will be required for strict liability. On the other hand it is not necessary that each of them be present, especially if others weigh heavily.

The first three factors, involving the degree of risk, harm, and difficulty of eliminating the risk, are obviously present in the storage of 80,000 pounds of explosives in a suburban area. The fourth factor, that the activity not be a matter of common usage, is also met. Comment (i) states:

> Likewise the manufacture, storage, transportation, and use of high explosives, although necessary to the construction of many public and private works, are carried on by only a comparatively small number of persons and therefore are not matters of common usage.

The fifth factor, inappropriateness of the activity, is arguably not present, for the storage did take place on land designated by the United States government for that purpose. However, the designation took place at a time when the area was less densely populated than it was at the time of the explosion. Likewise, the storage reserve was not entirely appropriate to the quantity of explosives stored because the explosion caused damage well beyond the boundaries of the reserve. The sixth factor, value to the community relates primarily to situations where the dangerous activity is the primary economic activity of the community in question. Thus comment (k) states that such factor applies

> particularly when the community is largely devoted to the dangerous enterprise and its prosperity largely

(continues)

depends upon it. Thus the interests of a particular town whose livelihood depends upon such an activity as manufacturing cement may be such that cement plants will be regarded as a normal activity for that community notwithstanding the risk of serious harm from the emission of cement dust.

The comment further states that

> in Texas and Oklahoma, a properly conducted oil or gas well, at least in a rural area, is not regarded as abnormally dangerous, while a different conclusion has been reached in Kansas and Indiana. California, whose oil industry is far from insignificant, has concluded that an oil well drilled in a thickly settled residential area in the City of Los Angeles is a matter of strict liability.

Since five of the six factors required by section 520 of the *Restatement (Second)* are met and the sixth is debatable, we would impose absolute liability here if we were to use that approach.

However, we do not believe that the *Restatement (Second)* approach should be used in cases involving the use or storage of explosives. Instead, we adhere to the rule of *Exner v. Sherman Power Constr. Co.* and its progeny imposing absolute liability in such cases. The *Restatement (Second)* approach requires an analysis of degrees of risk and harm, difficulty of eliminating risk, and appropriateness of place, before absolute liability may be imposed. Such factors suggest a negligence standard.[1] The six-factor analysis may well be necessary where damage is caused by unique hazards and the question is whether the general rule of absolute liability applies, but in cases involving the storage and use of explosives we take that question to have been resolved by more than a century of judicial decisions.

The reasons for imposing absolute liability on those who have created a grave risk of harm to others by storing or using explosives are largely independent of considerations of locational appropriateness. We see no reason for making a distinction between the right of a homesteader to recover when his property has been damaged by a blast set off in a remote corner of the state, and the right to compensation of an urban resident whose home is destroyed by an explosion originating in a settled area. In each case, the loss is properly to be regarded as a cost of the business of storing or using explosives. Every incentive remains to conduct such activities in locations which are as safe as possible, because there the damages resulting from an accident will be kept to a minimum.

II.

The next question is whether the intentional detonation of the storage magazine was a superseding cause relieving petitioners from liability. In *Sharp v. Fairbanks North Star Borough*, 569 P.2d 178 (Alaska 1977), a negligence case, we stated that a superseding cause exists where "after the event and looking back from the harm to the actor's negligent conduct, it appears to the court highly extraordinary that it should have brought about the harm." We further explained in *Sharp*,

> [w]here the defendant's conduct threatens a particular kind of result which will injure the plaintiff and an intervening cause which could not have been anticipated changes the situation but produces the same result as originally threatened, such a result is within the scope of the defendant's negligence.

Id. at 183 n. 9. The considerations which impel cutting off liability where there is a superseding cause in negligence cases also apply to cases of absolute liability.

Prior to the explosion in question the petitioners' magazines had been illegally broken into at least six times. Most of these entries involved the theft of explosives. Petitioners had knowledge of all of this.

Applying the standards set forth in *Sharp, supra,* to these facts we find there to have been no superseding cause. The incendiary destruction of premises by thieves to cover evidence of theft is not so uncommon an occurrence that it can be regarded as highly extraordinary. Moreover, the particular kind of result threatened by the defendant's conduct, the storage of explosives, was an explosion at the storage site. Since the threatened result occurred it would not be consistent with the principles stated in *Sharp* to hold there to have been a superseding cause. Absolute liability is imposed on those who store or use explosives because they have created an unusual risk to others. As between those who have created the risk for the benefit of their own enterprise and those whose only connection with the enterprise is to have suffered damage because of it, the law places the risk of loss on the former. When the risk created causes damage in fact, insistence that the precise details of the intervening cause be foreseeable would subvert the purpose of that rule of law.

---

1. In the analogous area of strict liability for defective products we have rejected the approach of § 402(a) of the Restatement (Second) of Torts which requires proof that a product is "unreasonably dangerous." "It represents a step backwards in the development of products liability cases. The purpose of strict liability is to overcome the difficulty of proof inherent in negligent and warranty theories, thereby insuring that the costs of physical injuries are borne by those who market defective products." *Butaud v. Suburban Marine* & Sporting Goods, Inc., 543 P.2d 209, 214 (Alaska 1975).

(continues)

The partial summary judgment is AFFIRMED. RABINOWITZ, Justice, concurring.

Although I concur in the result reached by the court, I disagree with its adoption of the approach of *Exner v. Sherman Power Construction Co.*, 54 F.2d 510 (2d Cir. 1931), which imposes absolute or strict liability in all cases involving the use or storage of explosives. I am persuaded that sections 519 and 520 of the *Restatement (Second) of Torts* (1977) embody a sounder rule of law. On balance, I think it is preferable that the court, in making the determination whether an activity

is "abnormally dangerous" and therefore subject to absolute liability, employ the criteria articulated in section 520 to analyze the particular acts and circumstances of the case. In my view, consideration of these criteria offers a rational solution to the problem of determining whether a particular activity is abnormally dangerous.

Despite the foregoing, I can agree with the court's overall disposition of this appeal since application of section 520 to the facts of the case leads to the conclusion that the activity in question was abnormally dangerous. Thus absolute liability was properly imposed.

PUTTING IT INTO PRACTICE 11:2

1. Why was suit brought in this case?
2. What was the cause of the explosion?
3. Who are the petitioners, and on what basis do they argue that they should not be held liable for damages resulting from the explosion?
4. What factors listed in the *Restatement (Second)* in reference to abnormally dangerous activities do the petitioners argue do not exist in this case?
5. What factors outlined in the *Restatement* does the court believe are present in this case?
6. Why does the court decide not to follow the *Restatement*? What standard does it use instead?
7. Does the court apply a strict liability standard?
8. What does the court conclude in reference to the superseding-cause argument, and why?

Examples of Activities Some Courts Have Considered Abnormally Dangerous

Crop Dusting

The plaintiffs were organic farmers who used no non-organic fertilizers, insecticides, or herbicides in their farming; they sold their produce to organic food buyers. The defendant, a crop duster, while spraying land adjoining the plaintiffs' land, during one spraying pass began spraying while over the plaintiffs' property. The residue rendered the plaintiffs' produce unfit to sell to buyers of organic food. The court, considering each of the six factors set forth in the *Second Restatement*, held that the defendant was strictly liable for the damage caused by his aerial spraying. The court emphasized

that the risk of harm was accentuated by the fact that the drift of chemicals in aerial spraying is particularly unpredictable. The court also noted that the likelihood that harm would result was dependent upon what adjoining property owners did with their land. In balancing the risk of harm versus the utility of the activity, the court concluded that an equitable balancing of social interests could be attained only if the defendants were made to pay for the consequences of their acts (*Langan v. Valicopters, Inc.*, 567 P.2d 218 [Wash. 1977]).

Poisonous Gases

In an effort to kill cockroaches, the defendant, an exterminator, put hydrocyanic acid gas in the basement of a commercial building one evening while the building was unoccupied. The next morning the plaintiff was almost fatally poisoned because he was unable to smell the fumes (due to having a cold) and because he was unaware of the defendant's nocturnal activities. The court found that the defendant had engaged in an ultra hazardous activity that was likely to cause injury even though the utmost care was used. The court also concluded that the defendant knew or should have known injury might result and that the use of gas in this case was not "common usage;" even though the gas was commonly used by fumigators, it was not used generally by the public (*Luthringer v. Moore*, 190 P.2d 1 [Cal. 1948]).

Other activities the courts have held subject to strict liability include the following:

- storage of flammable liquids in urban areas
- disposal of hazardous waste
- testing of rocket fuel

Examples of Activities Some Courts Have Considered Not Abnormally Dangerous

Airline Crash

An airline crash resulted in fire damage to a nearby apartment building. The court held for the defendant after concluding that flying is not an abnormally dangerous activity and that there was no intent to crash and no control over the plane after the midair collision preceding the crash (*Wood v. United Air Lines, Inc.*, 223 N.Y.S.2d 692, *aff'd*, 226 N.Y.S.2d 1022, *appeal dismissed*, 230 N.Y.S. 207 [1961]).

In the early days of commercial aviation, airlines were held to a strict liability standard. Modern safety records no longer warrant classifying flying as an abnormally dangerous activity, and most courts have retreated to a negligence standard in this area. In many states, strict liability continues to apply to ground damage caused by an airline crash, although an increasing number of states appear to be abandoning that position.

Irrigation Dam

A saboteur ruptured the defendant's irrigation dam, causing damage to the plaintiff's property. The appellate court held that reservoir owners are not absolutely liable for damage to the property of others caused by escaping waters if the breach is caused by an "act of God," a public enemy, or the malicious act of a third person. The court noted that in a semi-arid climate, an irrigation reservoir does not qualify as an uncommon usage or an ultrahazardous activity (*Wheatland Irrigation District v. McGuire*, 537 P.2d 1128, *reh'g granted in part*, 552 P.2d 1115, *reh'g*, 562 P.2d 287 [Wyo. 1975]).

Falling Tree

The plaintiff, a motorist, was injured when his automobile was struck by a falling tree. The plaintiff alleged that the defendant's construction of an irrigation canal was abnormally dangerous conduct that caused the roots of the tree to weaken. The court held that the defendant's acts were not abnormally dangerous because building an irrigation canal was not an uncommon activity in a rural area and did not involve an abnormally high degree of risk (*Stroda v. State Highway Commission*, 539 P.2d 1147 [Or. Ct. App. 1975]).

Other activities that the courts have concluded are not abnormally dangerous include:

- a defective lawn sprinkler that resulted in an automobile crash.
- defective plumbing that caused damage to plaintiff's lower floor apartment.
- defective electric wiring that resulted in property damage.

The courts do not agree as to what does or does not constitute an abnormally dangerous activity. Public policy appears to influence that determination; an overview of the cases in several jurisdictions indicates that courts are more likely to classify an activity as abnormally dangerous if the activity occurs in a highly populated area and less likely to do so if the activity occurs in an isolated area. Courts are more likely, for example, to hold strictly liable those who store flammable liquids or explosives in densely populated areas than they are those who store these materials in rural areas. By the same token, courts appear reluctant to classify the household use of gas, water, or electricity as an abnormally dangerous activity.

NET NEWS

Links to numerous sites providing information about specific toxic tort issues, such as lead poisoning, fen-phen, industrial solvents, and tobacco are available at **http://www.megalaw.com/** under the "Legal Research" link. Select "Legal Topic Index", then select "Toxic Torts Center."

PUTTING IT INTO PRACTICE 11:3

1. A hotel guest is burned while watching a fire-eating act. He sues the hotel owner and the travel service that had arranged the "mystery tour" on the basis of strict liability, claiming that the act was an abnormally dangerous activity. Should he be allowed to recover?

2. Mr. Warner is seriously injured when the truck in which he is a passenger is struck by a locomotive. He sues the railway on the basis of strict liability, arguing that the operation of a railway is an abnormally dangerous activity. Should he be able to recover on that basis?

3. The Tenneco Corporation operates a natural gas pipeline that includes 16,000 miles of pipe extending from Texas to New England. Compressor stations, which are necessary to compress and push the gas, are located at intervals along the pipeline. Since an air line explosion at compressor station 106, caused by the use of lubricants that lacked fire retardants, Tenneco began using a fire-retardant lubricant called Pydraul AC, which contains a polychlorinated biphenyl (PCB) called Aroclor 1254. In the late 1960s or early 1970s, Tenneco discontinued the use of Pydraul AC in favor of another non-PCB-containing lubricant. The use of PCBs was banned in 1976 by the Toxic Substances Control Act. Tenneco alleges it only recently discovered that PCBs were dumped directly onto the ground surrounding station 106 or into the station's drainage system.

   The Fletchers own a farm adjacent to station 106. PCBs have been detected in the soil of their property, in the water that drains onto their property, in their beef cattle, and in the blood of some members of the Fletcher family. Tenneco admits that its use of Pydraul AC is a source of the Fletchers' PCB contamination.

   Should Tenneco be held strictly liable for the Fletchers' injuries, even though it was unaware of the dangerousness of PCBs at the time it installed the compressor stations? Are there other torts the Fletchers might rely on to recover?

4. Danny's clothing is set on fire and he suffers facial burns and serious injury to his eyes when a shell from a firework display explodes nearby the crowd of onlookers of which Danny is a part. Should the company that is putting on the display be held strictly liable for Danny's injuries?

5. A service station owner sues the oil company for damage resulting from the leakage of gasoline from underground storage tanks. The tanks are in a state of preventable disrepair at the time of the leakage. Is the storage and removal of gasoline in underground storage tanks an abnormally dangerous activity for which the oil company should be strictly liable?

PRODUCT LIABILITY

The rationale underlying strict liability in the area of product liability is that it is easier for the defendant to bear the risk of loss than for the plaintiff. Advocates of strict liability reason that merchants and manufacturers have the ability to internalize the costs of accidental losses and can distribute such losses among the consumers who purchase their products.

Another reason given for imposing strict liability is that product safety is better promoted by a strict liability theory than by traditional negligence theory. Once courts render decisions imposing strict liability on defendants even though they were not negligent, defendants arguably have a strong incentive to prevent the occurrence of future harm. Preventing future harm is a primary goal for those who advocate strict liability. This theory of liability is discussed at length in Chapter 12.

NET NEWS

To read a paper called "Accidents Waiting to Happen: Liability Policy and Toxic Pollution Releases" which analyzes the effects on strict liability on polluters releasing toxins into the environment, go to **http://www .rff.org/** and enter "accidents waiting to happen" as your search term.

LIMITATIONS ON STRICT LIABILITY

A defendant can raise either of two defenses in a strict liability case. First, a defendant can argue lack of proximate cause, i.e., that the damage that occurred was not the result of the kind of risk that made the activity abnormally dangerous. Second, a defendant can argue that a plaintiff who has "assumed the risk" should be barred from recovery.

Proximate Cause

A defendant is strictly liable only for damages that result from the kind of risk that made the activity abnormally dangerous. The *Restatement (Second) of Torts* illustrates this point using an example of a pedestrian run over by a truck transporting dynamite. Although transporting dynamite is an abnormally dangerous activity, the plaintiff will not be able to sue on the basis of strict liability because the risk of hitting pedestrians is not one of the things that make such transportation abnormally dangerous.

A related rule is that a defendant will not be strictly liable if the harm occurred only because the plaintiff was conducting an "abnormally sensitive" activity. The case commonly used to illustrate this point is one in which the plaintiff's female minks killed their young as a result of being frightened by the defendant's blasting operation being conducted more than two miles from the plaintiff's mink ranch (*Foster v. Preston Mills Co.,* 268 P.2d 645 [Wash. 1954]). The court reasoned that blasting operations are unusually dangerous because of "the risk that property or persons may be damaged or injured by coming into direct contact with flying debris, or by being directly affected by vibrations of the earth or concussions of the air." Here, because the minks were harmed only because of their "exceedingly nervous disposition," the court held that the defendant was not strictly liable. Strict liability does not protect against "harms incident to the plaintiff's extraordinary and unusual use of land."

Some courts will also relieve defendants of liability if the harm occurred in an unforeseeable manner.

An "act of God," for example, is often enough to relieve a defendant of strict liability. Although the *Restatement (Second) of Torts* rejects the "act of God" exception, many courts have been reluctant to impose liability when the harm that occurred was clearly out of the control of the defendant. Courts have refused to impose strict liability, for example, when extraordinary rainfall washed out a dam or when a hurricane caused water to overflow from a hydroelectric plant, resulting in flood damage.

Although the courts are not uniform in where they draw the line on strict liability, most courts impose liability for a narrower range of harm in cases involving strict liability than in cases involving negligence. That is, a court is more likely to find proximate cause in a negligence case than in a strict liability case. Likewise, a court is more likely to deny liability if there is an unforeseen, intervening cause in a strict liability case than in a negligence case. This willingness to curtail liability in strict liability cases is most likely due to the fact that the defendant is without fault.

Assumption of Risk

A plaintiff who knowingly, voluntarily, and either reasonably or unreasonably subjects himself to danger is barred from recovering on the basis of strict liability. For example, a plaintiff who insists on driving through an area where blasting is being done, after seeing warning signs and being detained by a flagman, assumes the risk if he is injured by the blasting (*Restatement [Second] of Torts* § 523, illus. 2). Note, however, that contributory negligence usually will not bar a plaintiff from recovery. In the preceding example, if the driver had been merely inattentive and had missed the warning signs, this contributory negligence would not have barred him from recovery. Even though the driver in that situation did not discover a risk he should have discovered, full responsibility would lie with the party who created the abnormal risk (*Restatement [Second] of Torts* § 524, cmt. a).

PUTTING IT INTO PRACTICE 11:4

1. The owner of a food store sues an electric cooperative for a loss of food and equipment suffered as a result of a power outage. An expert for the defendant testifies that the power outage was due to the failure of an electrical transformer, which was caused by an excessive load, lightning, or an internal problem. In the expert's opinion, the most likely cause was lightning. The food store owner sues under a theory of strict liability. Is he likely to recover?

2. Kramer, a forklift driver, brings a strict liability action against a forklift manufacturer after he is injured in an accident involving the forklift. At the time of the accident, Kramer failed to look in the direction of travel and to keep his foot inside the operator's compartment (contrary to written warnings). Both of these actions may have contributed to the accident. The forklift is defective in that it lacks a guard on the operator's compartment; this defect makes the forklift dangerous. What defenses might the forklift manufacturer raise? Are these defenses likely to be successful?

3. Martin accepts a job hauling nitroglycerine. Because of the danger involved he is paid more than for hauling other types of loads. He is involved in a two-vehicle crash and is killed. Can his estate recover on the basis of strict liability?

4. Lynn tries to pass a truck on a narrow road. The truck is clearly marked "Danger, Dynamite," but Lynne, intent on passing the truck, fails to read the sign. She negligently runs into the truck and is killed in the ensuing explosion. Will her estate be barred from recovering if suit is filed on the basis of strict liability?

SUMMARY

Strict liability is a cause of action that can be used in cases involving abnormally dangerous activities, dangerous animals, and product liability. A plaintiff can recover damages even if the defendant acted without fault. The rationale underlying strict liability is that persons who engage in unusually dangerous activities must be responsible for any damages resulting from those activities.

Animal owners who are or should be aware of the vicious propensities of their domesticated pets are strictly liable for damages caused by those pets. Under the common law, owners were liable for property damage created by trespassing animals if those animals were likely to roam. This rule was modified by the "fencing in" and "fencing out" statutes adopted by many Western states.

Abnormally dangerous activities are those activities involving a high degree of risk of serious harm that cannot be eliminated with due care. Furthermore, the activity must not be a matter of common usage, must be inappropriate to the place where it is carried out, and its value to the community must be outweighed by its dangerous attributes. Crop dusting and the storage of flammable liquids are both examples of abnormally dangerous activities. Public policy concerns appear to affect the courts' classification of activities as being abnormally dangerous.

A defendant can be absolved of liability if the plaintiff assumes the risk by voluntarily and knowingly exposing herself to the danger created by the defendant. If proximate cause is lacking, in that the damage that occurred did not result from the kind of risk making the activity abnormally dangerous, the defendant is not liable.

KEY TERMS

abnormally dangerous activity
Activity for which a defendant is strictly liable if someone is injured; characterized as an activity having a high degree of risk of serious harm that cannot be eliminated with due care and whose value is outweighed by its dangerous attributes

strict liability
Liability imposed without a showing of intent or negligence

REVIEW QUESTIONS

1. In what types of cases is strict liability an appropriate theory of recovery?

2. Is strict liability synonymous with absolute liability or liability without fault?

3. What is the general rule regarding liability for damage caused by trespassing animals?

4. What do the "fencing in" and "fencing out" statutes provide?

5. Under what conditions are animal owners strictly liable for damage caused by non-trespassing animals?

6. What are the six factors considered in accordance with the *Restatement* to determine if a particular activity is abnormally dangerous?

7. Give examples of two activities that courts have classified as abnormally dangerous, and explain why they were considered to be so.

8. Give examples of two activities that courts have classified as not being abnormally dangerous, and explain why they were not considered to be so.

9. What is the rationale underlying strict liability for defective products?

10. What are the possible defenses that can be raised in response to a strict liability claim?

PRACTICE EXAM

Students should complete the practice exam after studying each chapter. The answers are in Appendix A. If you score lower than 80%, you should reread the materials.

True-False

1. Strict liability is synonymous with absolute liability.

2. Strict liability is applicable to defendants who carry out their activities with the utmost of care.

3. With strict liability, a defendant can be found liable even if she adhered to an objective standard of care.

4. Under the English common law, which has been adopted in all states, owners of animals were strictly liable for property damage caused by their animals when they trespassed on another's land.

5. Bulls and stallions are considered domesticated even though they are often dangerous.

6. Dog owners are strictly liable for damage caused when their dog bites someone if they know or have reason to know that the dog has vicious propensities; however, under the law of most states, dogs are allowed one "free bite."

7. The rationale for the decision in *Rylands v. Fletcher* has been adopted by the majority of American courts and the *Restatement (Second) of Torts*.

8. Courts hold manufacturers of defective products strictly liable because they believe that manufacturers can internalize the costs of accidental losses.

9. A defendant is not strictly liable for harm that occurs as a result of a risk that is not the kind of risk that makes the activity dangerous.

10. A defendant is strictly liable even if it is only because the plaintiff is conducting an abnormally sensitive activity.

11. Courts are more likely to find proximate cause in a strict liability case than in a negligence case and to deny liability if there is an unforeseen, intervening cause in a negligence case than in a strict liability case.

Fill-in-the-Blanks

1. A defendant can be _____
   _____even though he has no intent of
   wrongdoing and is not negligent.

2. Under _____ _____
   statutes, owners of animals are not strictly liable
   for property damage caused by their trespassing animals as long as they attempt to fence the
   animals in, whereas under _____
   _____ statutes, property owners
   who fence in their land have a strict liability
   claim against those whose animals trespass on
   their land.

3. The owner of a _____ animal is
   strictly liable for any damage resulting from a
   dangerous propensity typical of that particular
   species.

Multiple-Choice

1. In deciding whether an activity is abnormally
   dangerous, courts consider whether the activity
   a. is a matter of common usage.
   b. creates a high degree of risk of harm to others.
   c. creates a risk of harm that could be eliminated
      by due care.
   d. all of the above.

2. In deciding whether an activity is abnormally
   dangerous,
   a. courts consider the value of the activity to the
      community.

   b. courts generally ignore the appropriateness of
      the activity for the place in which it is being
      carried out.
   c. a court is unlikely to conclude that an activity
      is abnormally dangerous unless all six factors
      are present.
   d. a court is likely to conclude that an activity is
      abnormally dangerous even if only one factor
      is present.

3. The activity a court is least likely to characterize
   as abnormally dangerous is
   a. crop dusting.
   b. storage of flammable liquids.
   c. an airline flight.
   d. all of the above.

4. Which of the following situations or activities is a court likely to find to be abnormally
   dangerous?
   a. damage caused by escaping waters from an
      irrigation dam.
   b. testing of rocket fuel.
   c. defective plumbing or electrical wiring.
   d. none of the above.

5. A defendant sued for strict liability can raise the
   defense of
   a. assumption of risk.
   b. proximate cause.
   c. contributory negligence.
   d. all of the above.

PRACTICE POINTERS

Evidence Collection and Preservation

Litigation in strict liability cases, as with negligence, is often
fact-intensive—and though attorneys may be the masters of
the law, legal assistants are the masters of the facts. Therefore, from the inception of a lawsuit until its resolution, a
legal assistant can be invaluable to an attorney in performing factual research. Factual research involves interaction
with such entities as governmental agencies, courts, corporations, fact witnesses, expert witnesses, other law firms,
and computer database resources to obtain documentary
evidence and witness statements.

In product liability cases, for example, product information and research data is essential and can be obtained
from the governing organization for that product. The

United States Patent Office is also an excellent source of
documentary evidence. Patents usually contain detailed dia-
grams along with explanations of how the product works.
Patents can be located using the patent number, which usually appears in the manufacturer's literature. Advertisements
should also be consulted to determine claims made about
the product, and the original product should be obtained
along with any instructions, warranties, and warnings.

Other examples of documents that may be helpful
in a case include telephone records (which can be subpoenaed) and records produced by city, county, and state street
and highway departments. The latter show road conditions
and construction projects, road maintenance, traffic signal
sequence and pedestrian light timing, and, in some cases,

histories of traffic accidents and traffic impact studies that record vehicle counts at a particular location. Before attempting to secure documents relevant to a case, you must determine the procedures and fees involved in obtaining records from a particular agency.

Witness Statements

Having interviewed a witness, you may decide that you want to take his statement. Several means can be used to do that. You may, with the permission of the witness, tape-record his statement. Alternatively, you may ask him to write out his statement, although it is rare that individuals do an adequate job. Frequently, investigators write out the person's statement and have the witness sign it. The obvious drawback to this procedure is that the witness can later deny having made the statement or can say she signed it without being given an opportunity to read it. In such cases the statement may be inadmissible and the investigator may be forced to take the stand to testify as to the witness's statement. Putting the statement in the words of the witness makes it more difficult for him later to deny having made the statement. In addition to having the witness sign the statement, have him initial each page, as well as sign a statement attesting to the truth and accuracy of the foregoing statement.

Although expensive, another alternative is the use of a court reporter. This method virtually precludes the witness from denying that she made the statement, but if she does, the court reporter, who is a disinterested third party, can be called to testify to the truth.

Statements should be as specific as possible. Detailed, specific information rather than abstract generalizations are the goal. Be sure to get the witness's actual observations and not his opinions, because opinions of lay witnesses are generally not admissible.

Witness statements can also be made from recorded telephone statements. When taking a statement over the telephone, identify yourself, the purpose of the phone call, the name of the person being interviewed, the date and time of the call, the telephone number of each party, and the fact that the conversation is being recorded and that the witness gave permission to record the statement. The witness should then be asked to give his full name, date of birth, address, driver's license number, and social security number. Having all of this information facilitates location of the witness two or three years later if the case ultimately goes to trial. This same identifying information should be obtained when recording a statement in person. During the conversation, be careful to avoid making extraneous comments or speaking while the witness is speaking. After the statement has been recorded, the tape should be labeled with the case name, witness name, and date of interview and should be transcribed as soon as possible after the interview.

If a witness is unwilling to be recorded or to sign an affirmative statement, she may be willing to sign a written "negative" statement. Such a statement denies any knowledge on the part of the witness (e.g., I did not see anything happen at location X at time Y). Having this statement in writing precludes the witness from coming back at a later date with new recollections.

Photographs

Photographs are extremely helpful in relating a story to a jury. Careful attention must be given to the photographic process. Keep in mind that the purpose of photographing evidence is evidentiary, not aesthetic. Therefore, black-and-white film rather than color film should be used in certain instances, because black-and-white produces sharper details. Always try to fill the frame as much as possible, blocking out any distracting background. Lighting is especially crucial. When photographing shoe prints or tire impressions, oblique (low-angle) lighting is essential to bring out the unique characteristics of the evidence.

Also, make sure that the photographs accurately reflect the scene as it occurred. Distortions are easily created through the use of photography, so the attorneys who cross-examine you will be interested in finding out the precise manner in which you took each photograph. To help jog your memory, record details, such as camera speed, lighting conditions, and camera location for each photograph. Never alter any evidence in photographing it; such alterations will render the photograph inadmissible.

Sometimes a series of photographs will be necessary. For example, if the plaintiff has been bruised, the discoloration will not appear for a while, and the bruises will have to be photographed over time. Accident scenes should also be photographed in a series of shots, recreating the scene from the viewpoint of the drivers. Begin shooting from the direction of your client's vehicle about 500 feet from the point of impact and move progressively closer to the point of impact. Repeat this sequence from the viewpoint of the other driver. Take these photographs at the eye level of the driver so that they represent the scene from the driver's vantage point.

Remember that a photograph is indeed "worth a thousand words." Never skimp on film to save a little money. Photograph every square inch of an accident scene from every conceivable angle. Take several photographs of damaged areas of vehicles, including less visible damages such as scratches or paint scrapings. A piece of evidence that may at the time seem trivial to you may be the very evidence upon which the whole case hinges at trial. Taking photographs in the investigative process is an exacting science. If possible, you should consider taking courses or at least reading extensively in this area to enhance your expertise.

Aerial photographs can be helpful in orienting jurors to the conditions existing at a particular location, especially when presenting accident cases involving freeways, complicated intersections, or remote areas. Such photographs can often be obtained from the highway department, the United States Department of Agriculture, or the United States Army Corps of Engineers. Private companies also do aerial photographs and they are helpful in having photographs enlarged to scale.

In this era of television and movies, jurors are accustomed to seeing moving visual displays and often benefit from seeing videos. A video of how a product is made, how it works, and what it does, for example, can help focus jurors on key factual issues in a product liability case. Videos should be prepared professionally and should be done with a clear sense of purpose and direction.

TORT TEASERS

1. Remembering the hypothetical scenario presented at the beginning of the chapter, what arguments would you make if you wanted to allege that those who dispose of hazardous wastes, such as toxic chemicals, are strictly liable for the consequences of their dumping? Analogize to the cases in this chapter, arguing that your case is most like those cases used to illustrate abnormally dangerous activities and unlike those cases used to illustrate activities that are not abnormally dangerous.

2. Plaintiff, while employed by defendants to look after their children, is startled by defendants' pet bird when it alights on her face. In trying to avoid the bird she steps back, falls, and fractures her hip. Defendants often let the bird out of its cage and do not lock the cage. Should defendants be held strictly liable? *Neagle v. Morgan*, 277 N.E.2d 483 (Mass. 1971).

3. Plaintiff boards his mare in a pasture with other horses. One day while trying to feed his mare, Plaintiff leads the mare away from the other horses in the pasture. Defendant's colt approaches him in a menacing manner and Plaintiff, who is aware of the colt's vicious propensities, drives the colt away and returns to feeding his mare. The colt waits and then stealthily comes up behind Plaintiff and kicks him in the behind. Do you think this is a case of strict liability? What defenses might be raised and why? *Sandy v. Bushey*, 128 A. 513 (Me. 1925).

4. The court's synopsis of the facts in this particular case certainly bears repeating. "On September 14, 1907, the plaintiff was the owner of a thoroughbred Holstein-Friesian heifer, which was born on January 9, 1906, and had been thereafter duly christened 'Martha Pietertje Pauline.' The name is neither euphonious nor musical, but there is not much in a name anyway. Notwithstanding any handicap she may have had in the way of a cognomen, Martha Pietertje Pauline was a genuine 'highbrow,' having a pedigree as long and at least as well authenticated as that of the ordinary scion of effete European nobility who breaks into this land of democracy and equality, and offers his title to the highest bidder at the matrimonial bargaining counter. The defendant was the owner of a bull about one year old, lowly born and nameless as far as the record discloses. This plebeian, having aspirations beyond his humble station in life, wandered beyond the confines of his own pastures, and sought the society of the adolescent and unsophisticated Martha, contrary to the provisions of Sec. 1482, . . . As a result of this somewhat morganatic mesalliance, a calf was born July 5, 1908." What would a court consider in deciding whether Defendant should be held strictly liable for Plaintiff's damages? *Kopplin v. Quade*, 130 N.W. 511 (Wis. 1911).

5. Plaintiff, a fireman, suffers severe chemical bronchitis as the result of inhaling antimony pentachloride gas when he responds to a call to give assistance to two men trapped in a tank. When Plaintiff arrives at the scene, he is told that the men have been extricated and that he should return to the station. While at the scene he encounters gas in the form of a haze or fog coming from an unknown source. Plaintiff never puts on a face mask to protect himself. Although Plaintiff experiences some irritation resulting from his contact with the gas, he is unaware of the potential danger created by exposure to the gas. Should Plaintiff be able to recover on the basis of strict liability? *Langlois v. Allied Chemical Corp.*, 249 So. 2d 133 (La. 1971).

6. Defendants' gasoline trailer breaks away from the truck towing it, leaves the highway, and falls onto a road below. Thousands of gallons of gasoline spill onto the road, and a motorist driving across the road is killed when the gas explodes and his car is engulfed in flames. Plaintiff brings a wrongful-death action against Defendants, one of whom is the owner of the truck and the other of whom is the driver. Do you think strict liability should be imposed? *Siegler v. Kuhlman*, 502 P.2d 1181 (Wash. 1973).

7. Gerald is injured by a stray bullet that is fired by a group of target shooters who are practicing at a nearby firing range. Is the firing range strictly liable for Gerald's damages? *Miller v. Civil Constructors, Inc.*, 651 N.E.2d 239 (Ill. App. 1995).

INTERNET INQUIRIES

Virtual Gumshoe (http://www.virtualgumshoe.com), formerly Webgator, is an outstanding source of online investigative resources for anyone conducting a civil or criminal investigation. At this one site, you can link directly to statutes in any state, to federal and state records, to state government sites, newspapers, property records, court records, libraries, government directories—and more! The scope of this site is virtually overwhelming, and it is updated on a regular basis.

PRACTICAL PONDERABLES

Suppose Jack Major, one of your firm's clients, owns a Rottweiler dog by the name of Misty, who recently bit a door-to-door salesman who came to their home. Jack is concerned that he will be sued and has come to your firm for legal advice. Jack assures you that Misty is generally a good-natured animal and that she has never bitten anyone before. He observed the salesman behaving in what he perceived as a threatening manner toward Misty and believes he provoked her into biting him.

To discourage trespassing on his property, Jack has posted several warning signs indicating that a guard dog is on the premises. He admits that Misty is not much of a guard dog and that he has never encouraged her to be aggressive but believes that her imposing presence would intimidate most would-be trespassers. Your supervising attorney asks you to do some preliminary research to answer the following questions.

1. What statutes in your state relate to dog bites, and what do they provide?
2. Under what conditions is a dog owner strictly liable for injuries caused by his dog biting someone?
3. What can Jack argue, and what evidence will he need to present in his defense if he is sued on the basis of strict liability?

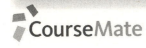 Access an interactive eBook, chapter-specific learning tools, including flashcards, quizzes, and more in your Paralegal CourseMate, accessed through www.CengageBrain.com.

CHAPTER 12

Product Liability

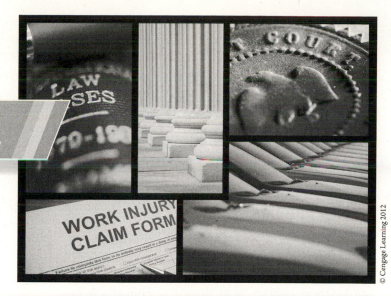

© Cengage Learning 2012

CHAPTER OBJECTIVES

After completing the chapter, you should be able to

- Differentiate among negligence, warranty, and strict liability causes of action.
- Appreciate the importance of classifying losses as personal injury losses, property damage, or economic losses.
- Identify characteristics and examples of manufacturing defects, design defects, and defective warnings.
- Recognize when it is appropriate to sue on the basis of negligence, strict liability, and breach of warranty.
- Identify the characteristics of express and implied warranties.
- Explain the rationale behind strict liability.
- Outline the elements of a strict liability claim.
- Identify the defenses that can be raised in negligence, strict liability, and warranty causes of action.
- Explain what a class action is, what its benefits are, and the requirements of its certification.

Having spent several years desperately trying to have children, Tom and Susan go to Dr. Payne to determine the reason for Susan's inability to conceive. After running several tests, Dr. Payne concludes that Tom's sperm count is so low that he probably will never be able to impregnate Susan. Dr. Payne suggests that they might be able to impregnate Susan using semen from a sperm bank. After studying in depth the procedures used in artificial insemination, Tom and Susan opt for this technique. Based on a list that Tom and Susan prepare as to the traits they wish their child to have, Dr. Payne selects a specific anonymous donor. Susan becomes pregnant as a result of the artificial insemination and delivers a boy. Unfortunately, when the child is quite young, it is discovered that he has a serious congenital birth defect. Tom and Susan sue Dr. Payne for the harm caused to their child.

Are Dr. Payne and the sperm bank negligent in supplying a defective product, i.e., sperm that contains faulty genetic coding? Did they breach any implied warranties? Should they be held strictly liable for the injuries sustained by the child? Can the child as well as the parents sue for his damages? What defenses can Dr. Payne and the sperm bank raise?

OVERVIEW OF PRODUCT LIABILITY

Product liability refers to the liability of a manufacturer, seller, or other supplier of a chattel which, because of a defect, causes injury to a consumer, a user, or in some cases a bystander.

THEORIES OF RECOVERY

Liability can be based on any of three theories of recovery: (1) negligence, (2) warranty, or (3) strict liability.

Negligence

Anyone who negligently manufactures a product is liable for any personal injuries proximately caused by her negligence. A manufacturer may be negligent in (1) the way it designs or manufactures its product, (2) its failure to conduct a reasonable inspection or test of its finished products, or (3) its failure to package and ship its products in a reasonably safe manner.

Users and Makers of Component Parts

The manufacturer of a component part, no less than the manufacturer of the completed product, may be liable for failure to use reasonable care. Additionally, a manufacturer that uses defective components prepared by others may be liable if it did not take reasonable care to obtain them from a reliable source or did not make a reasonable inspection of the components before incorporating them. Thus, an automobile manufacturer who assembles a chassis using components prepared by other manufacturers is liable for any malfunctions that result from a defect in the component parts if the manufacturer does not make a reasonable inspection of those components before incorporating them.

Retailers

A manufacturer is liable if a retailer fails to make an inspection that it is under an obligation to make. If, however, the retailer learns of the defect, either by inspection or through some other means, and fails to warn the customer, many courts have found the chain of causation to be broken and have absolved the manufacturer of any liability.

Retailers as well as manufacturers may be found negligent, but suits against retailers on the basis of negligence are often unsuccessful. The sale of a negligently manufactured or designed product is not enough by itself to show negligence. Generally, a retailer has no duty to inspect goods unless it has reason to believe they may be dangerous, because even if it did inspect, it would have no chance of finding the defect. A retailer selling microwave ovens, for example, has no duty to break open the boxes in which the ovens are packaged to inspect the ovens.

A majority of courts have, however, imposed a duty to make at least a superficial examination, especially when the retailer is a car dealer. The consequences of a defect in a car are likely to be severe, and the retailer is much more able than the buyer to discover any defects. If a retailer knows or should know that a product is unreasonably dangerous, it is negligent if it does not at least warn customers. Generally, plaintiffs suing retailers opt for warranty or strict liability theories for reasons we will discuss later in this chapter.

Lessors, Real Estate Agents, and Sellers of Services

Lessors of goods may also be liable in negligence for failing to discover defects. Rental car companies that lease defective cars, for example, may be found negligent. The sellers of real estate as well as suppliers of services (e.g., the providers of blood transfusions) may also be found negligent.

Privity

Formerly, a plaintiff in a negligence action was required to contract directly with the defendant. This so-called **privity** requirement was abolished in *MacPherson v. Buick Motor Co.*, 111 N.E. 1050 (N.Y. 1916), allowing a plaintiff who buys a product from a retailer and not directly from the defendant manufacturer to recover. Therefore, a plaintiff can sue the manufacturer, the retailer, or the lessor of a product. Users of products who do not purchase the products can also recover under a negligence theory if they are "reasonably foreseeable" plaintiffs. (See *Palsgraf* in Chapter 6 for a discussion of foreseeability.)

Damages in Negligence Cases

Although plaintiffs generally seek to recover damages resulting from personal injuries, they can also recover for property damage. Suppose a defendant fails to use due care in manufacturing a television set, and the defect in the electrical wiring in the television causes it to catch fire and burn down the plaintiff's house. The plaintiff can recover for the resulting property damage.

Plaintiffs in negligence actions generally have a hard time recovering for pure economic loss. Breach of warranty, rather than negligence, is the preferred theory for use in recovering for economic damages. Also, the distinction between property damage and economic loss is not always clear. Is the destruction of the plaintiff's property or of the product itself considered property damage or economic loss? Similarly, does the fact that the product no longer works or is now worthless because of the defect constitute property damage or economic loss? Consult the case law in your state to see how the courts in your jurisdiction have resolved these issues.

Warranty

Combination of Tort and Contract Law

A cause of action based on breach of warranty is a hybrid one, containing characteristics of both tort and contract law. Originally the action was deemed a form of misrepresentation and was therefore considered a tort. But because most warranties arose under the common law in situations involving a contract of sale, contract law was also applicable. Today this amalgamated form of law is made even more confusing by the efforts of the Uniform Commercial Code (UCC) to deal with warranties on a statutory basis.

Pay particular attention to the fact that the public policy justifications underlying tort law and contract law are quite different. Tort remedies are designed to protect the public from dangerous products. The purpose of strict liability is to protect consumers and allocate the risk to manufacturers, who are better able than consumers to bear the risk of loss. Contract remedies, in contrast, are designed to compensate parties for the loss of the benefit of their bargain. Under the UCC the free flow of commerce is encouraged (see UCC § 1–102, Official Comment 2), and commercial parties of equal bargaining power are allowed to allocate the risk of loss between themselves. A party to a commercial contract may, for example, choose to forgo a remedy in exchange for a lower purchase price. Presumably, merchants are better able to protect themselves from economic loss than are consumers.

In deciding whether to apply contract law or tort law, a court must consider the nature of the defect in the product and the type of loss for which the plaintiff seeks compensation. In a tort claim, for example, the plaintiff might allege that she has been exposed by means of a hazardous product to an unreasonable risk of injury. In a contract case, however, she would allege that the product failed to perform in accordance with the expectations one would have for a product of a particular quality and fit for ordinary use. Tort law, then, is reserved for defects that result in an unreasonably dangerous product. Contract remedies are more appropriate when the defect involves only the quality of the product and presents no unreasonable danger to persons or property.

The type of loss—personal injury, property damage, or economic loss—also determines whether the plaintiff will select a contract or tort claim. Although a majority of jurisdictions restrict contract liability to recovery for commercial or economic loss and restrict tort liability to recovery for damage to persons or property, this distinction has been challenged

NET NEWS

Links to information regarding various products liability suits can be found at **http://www .classactionlitigation.com/litig.htm**.

by several modern courts. Some, such as the Arizona courts, have reasoned that if the plaintiff's only loss is an economic one, the parties are best left to their commercial remedies. If the plaintiff's economic loss is accompanied by some physical damage to a person or other property, the party's interests are best protected via tort liability. Consult the case law in your state to determine how the courts in your jurisdiction have analyzed this issue.

Express Warranty

There are two types of warranties: express and implied. With an **express warranty** a seller expressly represents that the goods possess certain qualities. A description of a windshield by a manufacturer as being "shatterproof" is an example of an express warranty. If the purchaser can later show that the product does not possess such qualities (if, for example, the windshield shatters after being hit by a stone), she may sue for breach of warranty. An express warranty may be made in one of three ways:

- as an "affirmation of fact or promise" regarding the goods, or
- a description of the goods, or
- by use of a sample or model of the goods (UCC § 2–313).

LOCAL LINKS

Do the courts in your state restrict contract liability to recovery for economic loss and tort liability to recovery for damage to property and persons?

A seller might describe goods as being water-resistant, for example, or might use a model to demonstrate how the product works, thus suggesting to consumers that the product they buy is similar in nature.

WHO MAY RECOVER? In a sense, breach of express warranty is a type of strict liability claim. The plaintiff need not show that she believed the seller's representations to be true nor, in most cases, that she was even aware of the express warranty. All the plaintiff need show is that the representation was in fact false.

A drug company that produced a drug it believed to be nonaddictive and that it advertised as such was found liable when a consumer became addicted to the drug and ultimately died from his addiction (*Crocker v. Winthrop Laboratories*, 514 S.W.2d 429 [Tex. 1974]). The court discounted the reasonableness of the company's belief in the no addictiveness of the drug. It focused on the falsity of the company's representations and the disastrous results of the physician's misplaced reliance on such representations.

Plaintiffs may recover for breach of express warranty even when they are not in privity with the seller, in that they did not purchase directly from the seller. According to some courts, a plaintiff who is a user and not a purchaser of a product must show that he is a member of the general class of the public that the manufacturer expected or should have expected to be reached by the warranty. In many cases express warranties, such as the warranty of shatterproofness, would be considered to be addressed to the public at large. Therefore, a remote buyer, user, or even bystander would probably be held to be part of the general class to which the warranty was addressed.

WHAT MAY BE RECOVERED? A plaintiff whose damages are solely economic, such as lost profits, can recover the difference between what the product would have been worth had it been as it was warranted and what it was in fact worth with its defect (UCC § 2–714[2]).

The buyer can also recover for incidental and consequential damages (UCC § 2–715). As in the case of negligence, plaintiffs can certainly recover for property damage and personal injuries resulting from the defective product.

Implied Warranty

A seller also makes an **implied warranty** by virtue of offering a product for sale. The two most common types of implied warranties are the warranty of merchantability and the warranty of fitness for a particular purpose.

A **warranty of merchantability** is implied in a contract for the sale of goods if the seller is a merchant in the regular business of selling the kind of goods in question. According to UCC § 2–314, for goods to be merchantable they must (among other things),

- be "fit for the ordinary purposes for which such goods are used"
- be "within the variations permitted by the agreement, of even kind, quality, and quantity within each unit and among all units involved"
- be "adequately contained, packaged, and labeled as the agreement may require"
- "conform to the promises or affirmations of fact made on the container or label, if any."

The courts have consistently held that retailers impliedly warrant the merchantability of their products. A few courts, however, have created what is known as the "sealed container" doctrine, which absolves retailers who sell sealed containers of any liability. Under the UCC, the merchantability warranty is applicable to the sale of food or drink. The code does not apply, however, to services and to real estate transactions, although some courts have creatively applied warranty theory to such transactions. Some courts, for example, have utilized an "implied warranty of habitability" in finding liability on the part of builders of homes when purchasers of the homes suffered injuries. The courts are in disagreement as to whether an implied warranty of merchantability exists for sellers dealing in used goods.

LOCAL LINKS

- Have the courts in your state adopted a "sealed container" doctrine?
- Does an implied "warranty of habitability" exist in your state?
- Does an implied warranty for sellers of used goods exist in your state?

An implied **warranty of fitness for a particular purpose** is created when a seller who knows that a buyer wants goods for a particular (noncustomary) purpose makes a recommendation on which the buyer relies (UCC § 2–315). Suppose, for example, a consumer asks advice from a salesman at the hardware store regarding what type of lumber he should purchase for a particular construction project. If the type of lumber he purchases turns out to be unsuitable for such use, the consumer can sue the hardware store on the basis of breach of implied warranty.

WHAT CAN BE RECOVERED? A direct purchaser, i.e., one who buys directly from the defendant, can certainly recover on the basis of breach of implied

warranty for personal injury and property damage resulting from the product, and also for solely economic damages such as lost profits. As with express warranties, a direct purchaser can recover the difference between what the product would have been worth had it been as warranted and what it is worth with its defect. The direct buyer can also recover for incidental and consequential damages.

A purchaser can recover for personal injury on the basis of implied warranty even though he bought the product from a dealer and not the defendant manufacturer. Some states allow such remote purchasers to recover for property damage alone on the basis of breach of implied warranty. A remote purchaser, however, probably would not be able to recover for purely economic damages, such as lost profits. According to the majority position, a nonprivity plaintiff should instead sue the immediate seller for economic damages resulting from a breach of an implied warranty. Many states permit a nonpurchaser (user), such as an employee of a purchaser, whose use of the product was foreseeable, to recover for personal injuries from the manufacturer or others in the distributive chain.

There is a great deal of variation among states regarding privity requirements in reference to implied warranties. The UCC itself suggests three alternatives for dealing with privity requirements. Therefore, it is important that you check the case law and statutes in your state pertaining to recovery by remote purchasers and nonpurchasers.

WHO CAN BE HELD LIABLE? Breach of warranty actions can be brought against manufacturers, retail dealers, and component manufacturers (those who manufacture components that are incorporated into a larger product). Considerable controversy exists as to whether warranty liability can be imposed on the sellers of used goods, but by analogizing to the UCC, the courts do allow recovery on the basis of implied warranty in cases involving lessors of goods, sellers of real estate, and sellers of services. A mass producer of homes, for example, can be held liable for breach of an implied warranty of habitability for having installed faulty plumbing.

LOCAL LINKS

Does your state have a privity requirement for implied warranties?

COMPARISON WITH STRICT LIABILITY CLAIMS: Many plaintiffs opt for strict liability over warranty claims because strict liability is easier to prove than breach of warranty and in many respects is virtually identical to warranty claims. In a few instances, however, the plaintiff may have an advantage in suing on a warranty theory. A plaintiff who is the direct purchaser and whose damages are solely economic will likely sue for breach of warranty rather than for strict liability or negligence because of the generosity of the UCC in providing for damages. Remember that under the UCC, whether a warranty is express or implied, a direct purchaser can recover the difference between what the product would have been worth had it been as warranted and what it is worth with its defect. The buyer can also recover for incidental and consequential damages. Under the UCC a remote purchaser who has suffered only economic harm may recover on the basis of breach of express warranty, whereas she would be precluded from doing so on the basis of strict liability or negligence. Furthermore, in many states the statute of limitations used in warranty actions is the contract statute of limitations, which is typically longer than the tort statute of limitations used in strict liability claims.

PUTTING IT INTO PRACTICE 12:1

1. Elite Professionals, Inc., a trucking company, sues Carrier Corporation for damages arising out of a truck refrigeration unit malfunction that resulted in the spoilage of a cargo of meat. Elite had bought the unit from Carrier. The incident giving rise to Elite's claim occurs when Elite is transporting a twenty-three-ton load of frozen hog sides from Vermont to California. The first evidence of a refrigeration problem is discovered by the driver when he stops in New Mexico to check out the truck. The "T-ticker" gauge on the outside of the refrigeration unit shows that the temperature inside the reefer is three to five degrees above zero (the temperature must be maintained at 0 degrees to preserve the meat). The driver turns the temperature control down and telephones Elite's headquarters to report the situation to Elite's president, who tells the driver to proceed and call back later. A few hours later the driver reports that the temperature has risen to 20 degrees. The president instructs the driver to continue, thinking this to be the most expedient decision and hoping that making a direct run to California will result in getting the cargo transported more quickly than getting assistance at a Carrier service facility. Unfortunately, when the refrigerator is opened the next morning, the temperature has risen to 60 degrees and the hog sides have spoiled. The truck is immediately taken to Carrier, whose mechanics identify and replace a defective solenoid coil.

   The printed warranty and disclaimer that Elite received upon purchasing the refrigeration unit reads in part:

MANUFACTURER'S WARRANTY TRUCK/ TRAILER REFRIGERATION UNITS

Carrier . . . through its dealer organization shall, at their facility, during normal working hours, repair or replace with a new or remanufactured part, any parts or components of the [refrigeration unit] . . . which . . . malfunction as a result of defects in material or workmanship. . . .

THE FOREGOING OBLIGATION IS EXPRESSLY GIVEN IN LIEU OF ANY OTHER WARRANTIES, EXPRESSED OR IMPLIED, INCLUDING ANY IMPLIED WARRANTY OF MERCHANTABILITY OR FITNESS FOR PARTICULAR PURPOSE, WHICH EXCEEDS THE RESPONSIBILITIES SET FORTH HEREIN.

LIMITATION OF LIABILITY

Carrier . . . expressly disclaims and denies all liability for SPECIAL, INCIDENTAL, OR CONSEQUENTIAL DAMAGES or losses of a commercial nature arising out of a malfunctioning product or its parts or components thereof, as a result of defects in material or workmanship. THE OWNER'S SOLE AND

(continues)

PUTTING IT INTO PRACTICE 12:1 *(continued)*

EXCLUSIVE REMEDY AND [CARRIER'S] SOLE AND EXCLUSIVE LIABILITY SHALL BE LIMITED TO THE REPAIR OR REPLACEMENT OF PARTS OR COMPONENTS CONTAINED IN THE [REFRIGERATION UNIT] ... WHICH ... MALFUNCTION AS A RESULT OF DEFECTS IN MATERIAL OR WORKMANSHIP IN ACCORDANCE WITH THE APPLICABLE PROVISIONS AND LIMITATIONS STATED ABOVE.

Carrier argues that by replacing the defective solenoid coil it has satisfied its "repair or replace" obligation under the warranty. Elite responds that the remedy provided in the warranty failed and that under the UCC if "circumstances cause an exclusive or limited remedy to fail of its essential purpose, remedy may be had as provided in [the Uniform Commercial Code]."

    a. Is the warranty at issue express or implied?

    b. Did Carrier satisfy the requirements of the warranty?

2. Women whose mothers took DES (diethylstilbestrol) to prevent miscarriages are suing the manufacturers of the drug for injuries they have suffered. On what grounds might they sue under a theory of warranty?

3. A widower files a product liability action against some tobacco companies on the grounds that statements made by the companies about smoking and health were express warranties. These statements were made in a 1954 report entitled "Frank Statement to the Public by the Makers of Cigarettes" and "A Statement About Tobacco and Health."

    Do you think representations by tobacco companies that cigarettes are safe to use constitute express warranties as to their safety? Does the fact that the plaintiff cannot show that his wife actually read these reports necessarily preclude his claim?

Strict Liability

Rationale Justifying Strict Liability

Strict liability theories now constitute the primary basis for liability for manufacturers of products. Three basic reasons are given to support the premise that manufacturers should be held strictly liable for defects in their products. Foremost is the idea that sellers of defective products, rather than consumers, should bear the cost of compensating tort victims for the injuries they sustain from defective products. Proponents argue that manufacturers are in a better economic position than consumers to bear such costs.

Second, some feel that sellers should be made to internalize the cost of any injuries their products inflict, forcing them to incorporate the cost of liability into the product itself and thereby raising the market price of the product. The reasoning is that consumers, when faced with the higher costs of such products, will purchase cheaper and presumably safer products.

The third argument is that the sophistication of modern products precludes the average consumer from pinpointing the act of negligence responsible for her injuries. When some of the evidentiary obstacles to recovery found under negligence analysis are removed, more consumers are able to recover under a strict liability theory and manufacturers are deterred from producing unsafe products.

Many courts and commentators refute these arguments, however. Some have pointed out that empirical evidence of strict liability's effect on product safety is lacking. Some feel that the pendulum has swung too far in favor of consumer protection and should reach a more moderate position, so that manufacturers will not be unduly hampered in their efforts to meet consumer demands.

Section 402A of the Restatement

One of the first decisions dealing with strict liability was rendered by Justice Traynor, who was disenchanted with the warranty theory. In *Greenman v. Yuba Power Products, Inc.*, 377 P.2d 897 (Cal. 1963), Justice Traynor held that the plaintiff's failure to give timely notice of breach of warranty to the defendant, as required by California law, did not bar his recovery, because the defendant was strictly liable. (In *Greenman* the plaintiff was injured by a piece of wood that flew off a lathe he was using.) Traynor noted that "a manufacturer is strictly liable in tort when an article he places on the market, knowing that it is to be used without inspection for defects, proves to have a defect which causes injury to a human being." Traynor reasoned that manufacturers who put defective products on the market should bear the cost of injuries resulting from such defective products rather than the injured parties who, he believed, were powerless to protect themselves. Consumers, he concluded, were better protected under a strict liability theory than under a warranty theory.

Traynor's opinion laid the foundation for § 402A of the *Restatement (Second) of Torts*, which has been adopted by the majority of American jurisdictions. Section 402A reads as follows:

Section 402A. Special liability of seller of product for physical harm to user or consumer.

1. One who sells any product in a defective condition unreasonably dangerous to the user or consumer or to his property is subject to liability for physical harm thereby caused to the ultimate user or consumer, or to his property, if

   a. the seller is engaged in the business of selling such a product, and

   b. it is expected to and does reach the user or consumer without substantial change in the condition in which it is sold.

2. The rule stated in subsection (1) applies although

   a. the seller has exercised all possible care in the preparation and sale of his product, and

   b. the user or consumer has not bought the product from or entered into any contractual relation with the seller.

Under § 402A, as interpreted by most courts, the plaintiff must prove five elements.

- a product was sold
- the product was defective
- the defective product was the cause in fact and proximate cause of the plaintiff's injuries
- the defect existed at the time the product left the defendant's hands
- the item was manufactured or sold by the defendant

Unlike the plaintiff proving negligence, the plaintiff who has opted for a strict liability claim need not prove that the manufacturer or seller failed to use due care. In other words, the defendant in a strict liability case is liable even if he was not at fault (see Exhibit 12–1).

SALE OF A PRODUCT: Section 402A applies only to the sale of products and not to the provision of services. A typical sale of a carpet, for example, involves a sales-service transaction. The actual sale of the carpet involves the sale of a product, but the installation involves a service. The seller need not be engaged solely in the business of selling products. The owner of a theater who sells popcorn and candy to patrons is engaged in the sale of products even though the sales are incidental to his primary business (*Restatement [Second] of Torts* § 402A, cmt. f.) In one case a patient sued the surgeon who had implanted his mandibular prosthesis, which later was found to be defective. The court refused to hold the doctor strictly liable because it found that the doctor was not a "seller" of a product. Refusing to analogize to the movie theater example in the *Restatement*, the court explained that although the "implant was incidental to the surgical

---

EXHIBIT 12–1 Elements of Strict Liability Claim

- Was a product sold (as opposed to a service)?
- Was the product defective (in a "defective condition unreasonably dangerous")?
- Was the defective product the proximate cause and cause in fact of the plaintiff's injuries?
- Did the defect exist at the time the product left the defendant's hands?
- Was the product manufactured or sold by the defendant?

procedure . . . it was a necessary adjunct to the treatment administered, as were the scalpel used to make the incision, and any other material objects involved in performing the operation, all of which fulfill a particular role in provision of medical service, the primary activity" (*Cafazzo v. Central Medical Health Services*, 668 A.2d 521 [Pa. 1995]).

This sales-service dichotomy also used to be a point of contention, for example, in the so-called "bad blood" cases in which the plaintiffs contract a disease after receiving contaminated blood in the form of transfusions. The question is whether a transfusion involves the sale of a product (blood) or is part of the package of services provided by a hospital and is therefore not a sale but a service. (The same issue arises in the context of warranty cases, because the UCC applies only to goods sold and not to services rendered.) Now most states have statutes protecting blood banks from being held strictly liable for "bad blood," so this issue is moot in most instances.

DEFECTIVE CONDITIONS: What constitutes a defective condition for purposes of strict liability? In most strict liability cases the courts focus on whether the product is in "a defective condition unreasonably dangerous." According to *Restatement (Second) of Torts* § 402A, cmt. i, a product is in a *defective condition unreasonably dangerous* if it is "dangerous to an extent beyond that which would be contemplated by the ordinary consumer who purchases it, with the ordinary knowledge common to the community as to its characteristics." Good whiskey, therefore, is not considered unreasonably dangerous merely because some people will become drunk and injure themselves. Bad whiskey containing a dangerous amount of isopropyl alcohol, however, is considered in a defective condition unreasonably dangerous. The phrase *defective condition unreasonably dangerous* is a legal term and so the words "defective condition" should not be separated from the words "unreasonably dangerous."

Some courts look at the acts of a reasonable consumer, using the consumer-expectation test, to determine whether a product is in a defective condition unreasonably dangerous. Others look at the acts of a reasonable defendant, using what is commonly referred to as the risk-utility test. Under this test, the court imputes knowledge of a defective condition of the product to the defendant. The core inquiry is whether a reasonable person would conclude that the perceived risks created by the design and marketing of the product outweigh the benefits. Would the defendant, as a reasonable person, have put the product into the stream of commerce if she had knowledge of its defective condition? This test was used in *Mikolajczyk v. Ford Motor Co.*, 870 N.E.2d 885 (Ill. App. 2007), to determine whether Ford Motor Company's design of the Escort's seat was defective.

A defective condition unreasonably dangerous can arise not only from the characteristics of the product itself but also from foreign objects contained in the product, from decay or deterioration before sale, or from the way in which the product was prepared or packaged. A carbonated beverage that is bottled under excessive pressure and explodes upon being opened, or a beverage that contains bits of glass, is in a defective condition unreasonably dangerous.

UNAVOIDABLY UNSAFE PRODUCTS: Unavoidably unsafe products are those products that are incapable of being made safe for their intended and ordinary use. If the benefits of such products outweigh their risks, the courts will not hold their manufacturers strictly liable for harm coming to the consumers. Experimental drugs exemplify unavoidably unsafe products. Their absolute safety cannot be assured because of insufficient research data and lack of medical experience. Those who sell these drugs are not held strictly liable for any untoward consequences resulting from their use as long as they prepare and market the drugs properly and give adequate warnings to consumers (§ 402A, cmt. k). Note, however, that if a manufacturer is negligent in failing to make adequate tests before selling the drugs, a plaintiff can recover for negligence.

Many courts have classified blood as an unavoidably unsafe product. Additionally, many states have precluded by statute strict liability suits by those receiving "bad" blood. In one case in which the plaintiff contracted serum hepatitis as a result of receiving a blood transfusion, the court held that neither the hospital nor the blood bank was strictly liable (*Bourque v. Louisiana Health System Corp.*, 956 So2d 60 [La.App.2007]). No technology existed at the time to determine whether a particular specimen was infected with hepatitis, even though blood banks were aware that a percentage of all specimens would be infected with hepatitis. The court concluded "in 1975, the risk of contracting Hepatitis C from blood transfusion was unavoidably safe." The court rejected what it called the Plaintiff's last ditch argument that the blood was not properly prepared and they were not properly warned reasoning that "one cannot properly prepare or market, nor properly warn against something that is unknown."

Plaintiffs generally cannot introduce evidence that the defendant redesigned the product to make it safer. Such evidence is, however, admissible for the limited purpose of rebutting the defendant's argument that the product is unavoidably unsafe because of the extreme cost involved in removing the defect.

CAUSATION: The plaintiff must also show that the product was the cause in fact and proximate cause of his injuries. Suppose, for example, that the plaintiff eats a food product manufactured by the defendant and becomes ill several hours later. He must establish that it was the defendant's product and not some other factor that caused his illness.

Frequently, defendants will argue that intervening events were the proximate cause of the plaintiff's injuries or that other factors were the sole cause in fact of the accident. Remember from our discussion on strict liability in Chapter 11 that the courts are more likely to find a superseding cause in a strict liability cause of action than in a negligence case. Generally, if the act was reasonably foreseeable, it will not be considered a superseding act. If the act was unforeseeable but caused the same type of harm that made the product dangerous, then once again the act will not be considered superseding.

Unique causation problems have been raised in the diethylstilbestrol (DES) litigation. In one of the first DES cases, *Sindell v. Abbott Laboratories*, 26 Cal. 3d 588, 607 P.2d 924, *cert. denied*, 101 S. Ct. 285 (1980), the plaintiff was unable to identify the manufacturer responsible for making the DES taken by her mother while the plaintiff was in utero. Sympathizing with the plaintiff's plight, the court determined that because the plaintiff had sued five of the manufacturers of DES, whom she asserted produced 90 percent of the DES marketed, the burden of proof shifted to the defendants to demonstrate that they could not have supplied the DES that caused the plaintiff's injuries. Furthermore, the court reasoned that each defendant that failed to make such a showing would be held liable for the proportion of the judgment represented by its share of the DES market.

The theory of *alternate liability* (see Chapter 6 for further discussion), adopted by *Restatement (Second) of Torts* § 433B(3), preceded the market-share liability

theory of *Sindell*. It has been used by at least one AIDS victim (a hemophiliac), who could not identify the manufacturer that made the blood product from which he contracted AIDS (*Poole v. Alpha Therapeutic Corp.*, 696 F.Supp. 351 (N.D. Ill. 1988)). Under this theory, if two or more persons have committed a tortious act and it can be proven that the harm done to the plaintiff was done by only one of them, but there is uncertainty as to which one did the harm, the burden is on each defendant to prove that she did not cause the harm. Any defendant that cannot prove her actions did not cause the plaintiff's injuries will be found liable. In *Poole*, once the plaintiff was able to identify all of the defendants that could possibly have caused him to contract AIDS, the burden of proof shifted to the defendants to prove that they were not responsible for the plaintiff's injuries.

WHEN DEFECT EXISTED: Finally, the plaintiff must show that the defect existed at the time the product left the hands of the defendant manufacturer. If it is just as likely that the defect developed while the product was in the hands of an intermediate dealer, the plaintiff cannot sustain her burden of proof against the manufacturer. Proof of this is exacerbated in cases in which the product passed through several intermediaries before it was used by the plaintiff. Most courts, however, are fairly liberal in allowing the plaintiff to at least get to the jury on this issue.

Strictly speaking, res ipsa loquitur is not applicable in a strict liability case, but some of the inferences made under that doctrine are applicable. The fact that a product malfunctioned and no one else tampered with it may give rise to a permissible inference that the product was defective and that the defect existed when it left the hands of the defendant. The principles of res ipsa loquitur were successfully used in one strict liability case in which shortening exploded when the user drained it from a fryer into a can. In light of the fact that the plaintiff had properly handled and used the shortening, there was no possible explanation for the explosion other than a defect in the shortening, as shortening does not normally explode (*Franks v. National Dairy Products Corp.*, 414 F.2d 682 [5th Cir. 1969]).

Who May Be a Defendant?

Strict liability applies to anyone in the business of selling goods, whether or not he is the manufacturer. A retail dealer in the business of selling goods is therefore strictly liable for the sale of any defective goods even if the sale is not a predominant part of the business. An owner of a movie theater, for example, is strictly liable for any defective popcorn or candies he sells even though such sales are presumably a by-product of his main business. In contrast, a private individual who sells her furniture is not strictly liable, because she is not in the business of furniture selling. Component manufacturers are usually held to a standard of strict liability if the plaintiff can show that the defect existed at the time the component left the manufacturer's shop. Many courts have been willing to impose strict liability on lessors of defective goods (when the lessor is in the business of leasing) as well as sellers of real estate and sellers of services. Those who sell used goods, however, generally are not held to a standard of strict liability unless the plaintiff can show that the defects were created by the seller.

Who May Be a Plaintiff?

Strict liability allows recovery for anyone who is the "ultimate user or consumer." Consumers include those who prepare a product for consumption (such as the husband who opens a bottle of beer for his wife to drink), those who passively enjoy the benefit of a product (such as passengers in an airplane), and those who use the product for the purpose of doing work on it (such as a serviceperson making repairs on an automobile) (*Restatement [Second] of Torts* § 402A, cmt. l.)

Many courts have been willing to extend strict liability protection to bystanders whose presence was reasonably foreseeable. One court reasoned that bystanders are entitled to greater protection than consumers or users because they do not have the same opportunity to inspect products for defects that consumers and users do (*Elmore v. American Motors Corp.*, 451 P.2d 84 [Cal. 1969]). But the courts have struggled with where to draw the line in reference to the protection of bystanders. Should a father, for example, be able to sue a manufacturer of birth control pills on behalf of his twin Down's syndrome daughters, one of whom is living and one of whom is deceased, on the theory that the pills altered the mother's chromosome structure, causing the resultant birth defects (*Jorgensen v. Meade Johnson Laboratories, Inc.*, 483

F.2d 237 (10th Cir. 1973))? The *Jorgensen* court held that the plaintiffs' claim for pain and suffering, mental retardation, and deformity, all of which were prenatal injuries, could be maintained because the children were born alive. While recognizing the father's right to bring this cause of action, the circuit court saw the key problem as being one of causation, i.e., presenting sufficient medical evidence to prove that the contraceptives did in fact cause the Down's syndrome.

The extension of strict liability to bystanders includes businesses. For example, one court ruled that the owner of a water company could bring a strict liability action against a gasoline refiner despite the fact that the water company was not the ultimate user or consumer of gasoline. The water company claimed damages for leakage of additive methyl tertiary butyl (MTBE) from the gas station into the bystander Plaintiff's water system. The court reasoned that the leak occurred from a foreseeable use of gasoline such as "storing it at a gas station, transferring it through gas pumps into a vehicle and storing it in a vehicle's tank before it is burned as fuel," *Nelson v. Superior Court*, 50 Cal.Rptr.3d 684 (2006).

Damages

Plaintiffs suing under a strict liability cause of action may recover for property damage as well as damages resulting from personal injuries. Lost profits and other intangible economic harm are generally not recoverable under a strict liability theory unless the plaintiff can show that she also suffered injury or property damage.

A prime example of a case in which the court classified the plaintiff's losses as economic and therefore unrecoverable involved the purchase of property that was contaminated by lead paint. The homeowners argued that damages consisted of paying for an abatement program to identify and remove the lead paint. They also sought expenses to inspect and test for lead and to demolish and refurbish their property (*County of Santa Clara v. Atlantic Richfield Co.*, 40 Cal. Rptr.3d 313 (2006). The court rejected the Plaintiff's arguments holding that recovery in strict liability is limited to physical harm to person or property. Lead contamination did not constitute such harm.

NET NEWS

A variety of useful websites for legal assistants doing work in the product liability area are available in the "Resources" section at **http://www.paralegals.org**.

PUTTING IT INTO PRACTICE   12:2

1. If someone experiences serious and damaging consequences from being injected with a rabies vaccine, is the manufacturer strictly liable?

2. The parents of a child injured in a go-cart accident bring a strict liability action against the amusement park owner. They allege that the go-cart was defective because it inadequately absorbed the energy of rear-end collisions and inadequately protected the driver's neck in rear-end collisions. The owner claims he was providing a service and therefore could not be subject to a strict liability claim. Do you think strict liability is an appropriate theory of recovery? What public policy reasons support a strict liability claim?

3. The parents of a child bring a strict liability suit against the manufacturer of Bic lighters after their child is seriously injured as a result of a fire ignited with the lighter by an older child. The parents argue that the lighter was defective because it was not designed to be "childproof." The manufacturer argues that it should not be held strictly liable because children were not the intended users of the lighter and that a product is defective only if it is unreasonably dangerous to its intended users. The parents claim that Bic designed a lighter unreasonably dangerous to foreseeable users, to whom the lighters were attractive and by whom they were easily lit. They are prepared to introduce evidence that thousands of children have been killed or seriously injured in childplay fires in the past twenty years. Based on this evidence they argue that Bic knew or should have known that a safer, child-resistant lighter design was feasible and should have been employed.

   Which side do you think has the better argument? Should the manufacturer be held liable under a theory of negligence even if it is not strictly liable?

4. The parents of a child who chokes to death on a toy building block sue the manufacturer and retailer for strict liability. The manufacturer argues that because the child was fifteen months old and that the box containing the blocks indicated that the blocks were for "Ages 1 ½–5," the child was not an intended user. Based on the results in the case in question 3, do you think the strict liability claim is likely to stand?

5. The manufacturers of DES (diethylstilbestrol), a drug used to prevent miscarriages, are sued under the theory of strict liability by the daughters of the women who ingested the drug. The plaintiffs argue that the drug is in a "defective condition unreasonably dangerous." How would their claim be analyzed on a consumer-expectation standard versus a risk-utility test? For what public policy reasons might a court consider not applying a strict liability standard to a prescription drug like DES?

6. What considerations should a plaintiff make when deciding what theory of recovery to rely upon in a product liability case? Use Exhibit 12–2 to help you decide when you should sue under a theory of

   a. strict liability

   b. warranty

   c. negligence

EXHIBIT 12–2 *Considerations for Theories of Recovery*

WHO CAN SUE?	
NEGLIGENCE	Direct purchaser Remote purchaser User (if reasonably foreseeable)
EXPRESS WARRANTY	Direct purchaser Remote purchaser User (if member of general class expected to be reached by warranty)
IMPLIED WARRANTY	Direct purchaser Remote purchaser User (some courts)
STRICT LIABILITY	Direct purchaser Remote purchaser User Bystanders (some courts)

WHO CAN BE SUED?	
NEGLIGENCE	Manufacturer User or manufacturer of component part Retailer (difficult to prove) Lessor Seller of real estate Supplier of service
EXPRESS WARRANTY	Manufacturer User or manufacturer of component part Retailer Lessor Seller of real estate Supplier of service
IMPLIED WARRANTY	Manufacturer User or manufacturer of component part Retailer (except for sealed containers [in some courts]) Lessor Seller of real estate (in some courts) Seller of service (in some courts)
STRICT LIABILITY	Manufacturer User or manufacturer of component part Retailer Lessor Seller of real estate Supplier of service

WHAT CAN PLAINTIFF RECOVER?	
NEGLIGENCE	Personal injuries Property damage Economic loss (although pure economic loss is difficult to recover)

(continues)

EXHIBIT 12–2   *Considerations for Theories of Recovery (continued)*

	WHAT CAN PLAINTIFF RECOVER?
EXPRESS WARRANTY	Personal injuries Property damage Pure economic loss Incidental and consequential damages
IMPLIED WARRANTY	Personal injuries Property damage Pure economic loss Incidental and consequential damages (direct purchaser only)
STRICT LIABILITY	Personal injuries Property damage Economic loss if accompanied by personal injury or property damage

© Cengage Learning 2012

TYPES OF LOSSES

Defective products can cause three types of losses: personal injury, property damage, and economic loss. Injury to a person resulting from a defective product is, logically enough, referred to as *personal injury*, whereas physical injury to property is referred to as *property damage*. **Economic loss** is defined as a diminution in the value of the product and includes such items as the cost of repairs, the cost of replacement, and the loss of profits.

For example, if a computer in a car malfunctions, resulting in an explosion and ensuing fire, any damage to the car is classified as property damage, whereas any injuries to the driver of the car are considered personal injuries. If the computer malfunction results in the driver of the car being late for work and thereby losing his job, such loss is deemed an economic loss.

Most courts do not allow recovery under a strict liability theory for purely economic loss in the absence of personal injury or property damage. However, the method for categorizing a loss as either economic loss or property damage varies tremendously among the states. Some courts consider damage to the product itself as property damage; others consider such damage economic loss. If the computer malfunction mentioned earlier results in damage only to the computer and not to any other part of the car, the question is whether that constitutes property damage or economic loss. A claim classified as an economic loss in one state (and therefore not recoverable) may be

PUTTING IT INTO PRACTICE 12:3

1. Review "Putting It Into Practice" exercise 12:1 in this chapter referring to the litigation between Elite and Carrier. What kind of damages is Elite seeking if it wants to recover for the loss of the meat in accordance with the preincident value of the meat?

2. A commercial chicken and egg producer loses more than 140,000 chickens who suffocate when a power failure interrupts the power supply to the ventilation system in the chicken houses. Is the loss of the chickens an economic loss?

3. A law firm is forced to close its offices because of a power failure. The firm sues the power company for its loss in billable hours, lost rental value, and lost use of parking facilities. The firm does not allege actual physical harm to persons or property but contends that "impairment of their opportunity to practice law, to provide time and advice for a fee, is tantamount to physical harm to property." Will the firm be allowed to recover under a theory of negligence?

classified as property damage (and therefore recoverable) in another state. Because the classification of economic loss is an unsettled area of the law, you should consult the case law in your state when dealing with damages of an economic nature.

LOCAL LINKS

How do the courts in your state distinguish between economic losses and property damage?

TYPES OF DEFECTS

Most product liability causes of action involve products that are defective in some way. The three major defects plaintiffs typically allege are (1) manufacturing defects, (2) design defects, and (3) defective warnings (see Exhibit 12–3). A **manufacturing defect** results from a deviation in the manufacturing process that causes the item that injures the plaintiff to be different from others manufactured by the defendant. In a **design defect** case, all products manufactured by the defendant are the same but possess a feature that is unreasonably dangerous; thus the defect arises from the design. **Defective warning** cases involve a failure to give adequate warnings or directions for use.

The definition of *defective* lies at the core of all product liability cases, so we will examine the three categories of defects in some detail.

Manufacturing Defects

A classic example of a manufacturing defect is found in the landmark case of *MacPherson v. Buick Motor Co.*, 111 N.E. 1050 (N.Y. 1916). Buick Motor Company made a car that it sold to a retail dealer, who in turn sold it to the plaintiff. One of the wheels was made of defective wood and its spokes crumbled into fragments, causing injury to the plaintiff when the car suddenly collapsed. The defendant manufacturer was found liable even though it had not manufactured the wheel. The court reasoned that the manufacturer could have discovered this defect by reasonable inspection and that its failure to do so constituted a breach of its duty of care. Notice that what was at issue here was the faulty construction of one of the wheels and not the design of the wheel.

Whereas *MacPherson* was based on a theory of negligence, the famous case of *Henningsen v. Bloomfield Motors, Inc.*, 161 A.2d 69 (N.J. 1960), was based on a breach of warranty. In *Henningsen*, defendant Chrysler Corporation produced a car with a defective steering mechanism. One of its dealers, defendant Bloomfield Motors, sold the car to Mr. Henningsen, who gave it to his wife. While Mrs. Henningsen was driving the car the steering mechanism failed, causing the car to veer sharply to the right and into a wall, resulting in her injury. The court held that Mrs. Henningsen could recover from Chrysler for breach of implied warranty of merchantability. As in *MacPherson*, the defect was peculiar to this particular car and was not inherent in the design of the car.

Manufacturing defects are not restricted to manmade products. They can also be found in food that is improperly produced, processed, or stored. A manufacturer or retailer, for example, can be found liable for a manufacturing defect if a consumer contracts botulism as a result of purchasing a can of improperly stored food.

Design Defects

The key issue in a design defect case is whether the defendant chose a design that posed an unreasonable danger to the plaintiff in light of the availability of some other design. For instance, a sanding machine that contains no guards or shields to protect the operator of the machine might be found defective if the manufacturer, with little cost or inconvenience, could have created a design that had a shield or guard.

Design defect claims can be cast in terms of a negligence or strict liability standard. The key issue in a negligence case is the reasonableness of the manufacturer in placing the product on the market. Is the product an essential item? Is it likely to cause injury and is any such injury likely to be serious? These

EXHIBIT 12–3   What Is a Defect?

MANUFACTURING DEFECT	Results from deviation in manufacturing process
DESIGN DEFECT	Feature in design of product is unreasonably dangerous Structural Safety feature Misuse of product
DEFECTIVE WARNING	Failure to give adequate warnings or directions

questions are representative of the types of questions a court will contemplate in determining whether a manufacturer acted in a reasonable manner.

The key issue in a strict liability case is the consumer's expectations, i.e., whether the product performed as safely as an ordinary consumer would expect. A court will consider how much the consumer paid for the product in determining what the reasonable expectations should be. Use by the consumer extends to any reasonably foreseeable use even if it is not the use intended by the manufacturer. Whether phrased in negligence or strict liability terms, the key element in a design defect case is whether the defendant chose a design that posed an unreasonable danger to the plaintiff in light of the availability of affordable, safer alternative designs.

Defendants will often raise the "state-of-the-art" defense, in which they argue that the level of technology existing at the time they made the product precluded them from utilizing a safer design. Although courts generally allow such a defense, defendants relying on this argument will not necessarily be absolved of liability. A jury could conclude, for example, that even though no reasonable alternative design existed at the time, the risk created by producing such an item outweighed its utility.

In defective-design cases the plaintiff will frequently try to bring out the fact that the defendant redesigned the product to make it safer after the plaintiff received injuries. Such evidence is generally inadmissible to prove defectiveness. The rationale underlying this rule is that the admission of this evidence would inhibit manufacturers from redesigning products to make them safer.

If the plaintiff does recommend an alternative design, the burden rests on him to show that the alternative is practicable. Plaintiffs must, in other words, conduct a type of cost-benefit analysis in which they produce evidence that their alternative design is an economically viable one.

Any design defect alleged by a plaintiff must fall into one of three categories: (1) structural defect; (2) absence of safety features; or (3) misuse of product.

Structural Defects

A *structural defect* exists when the defendant's choice of materials results in a structural weakness, causing the product to be dangerous. A stepladder that collapses when anyone of more than average weight steps on it might, for example, be structurally defective. Defendants are not, however, obliged to provide the most durable design. Nor are they expected to make products that last forever. Their only obligation is to make products that are *reasonably* safe.

Safety Features

In determining whether a *safety feature* must be installed, one must consider the expense of installation of the feature in comparison with the cost of the product and the magnitude of the danger that exists without such a safety feature. If the expense is relatively minimal, any design not incorporating the safety feature is likely to be considered defective.

Defendants often claim that their product is as safe as that of the competition. Although often successful, such a defense is unpersuasive in situations in which the entire industry has been negligent in the installation of safety devices.

A defendant may also argue that the danger was so obvious that the plaintiff could have protected herself even in the absence of any safety device. Even though the obviousness of the danger is considered when determining the degree of dangerousness, most courts will not automatically dismiss the need for protective devices just because the defect is obvious. A manufacturer could, for example, be found liable for failing to provide protective guard rails for a machine even though the potential danger inherent in getting too close to the machine might be patently obvious.

Foreseeable Misuse

One of the most common design defect arguments is that the product, though not dangerous when used in the manner intended by the manufacturer, becomes dangerous when put to some other use. If such misuse is reasonably foreseeable by the manufacturer, most courts will require the manufacturer to employ reasonable design precautions to protect the plaintiff from the danger resulting from that misuse.

The most common foreseeable-misuse cases center around the production of "crashworthy" vehicles. Plaintiffs reason that manufacturers should protect vehicle occupants involved in "second collisions," the collisions that occur inside the vehicle following the initial accident. Most modern courts have found that secondary collisions are clearly foreseeable and that manufacturers have an obligation to take reasonable precautions to make their cars reasonably safe in the event of an accident.

CASE

Turner v. General Motors Corp.
514 S.W.2d 497 (Tex. Civ. App. 1974)

COULSON, Justice.

This is an appeal from an order sustaining a plea of privilege in a products liability case. Appellant Robert Turner sued General Motors Corporation, appellee, and Raymond Kliesing d/b/a Kliesing Motor Company in strict liability in tort for personal injuries received when his car rolled over in an accident. . . . Turner sued General Motors and Kliesing in strict liability in tort for a defectively designed roof on his automobile which enhanced his injuries, but did not cause the accident. The trial judge, in his findings of fact, found all the facts necessary for this alleged cause of action, if such a cause of action does exist; the sustaining of a plea of privilege was, in effect, a holding that no such cause of action exists in Texas.

The question here is whether a manufacturer and retailer may be held strictly liable in tort for a defectively designed automobile which enhances the injuries of plaintiff, but does not cause the accident.

At the plea of privilege hearing, Turner testified that in April of 1971 he was driving on a two-lane farm-to-market road in his 1969 four-door, Chevrolet Impala, hardtop sedan with a center post. He was following a truck, which started to pull onto the right shoulder. Turner accelerated to fifty or sixty miles per hour to pass the truck, but the truck attempted to make a left-hand turn when Turner came up to it. Turner pulled to the right to avoid a collision and left the road. When he attempted to return to the road, he overturned and the car landed on its top. Turner estimated his speed immediately before the roll-over at twenty to thirty miles per hour. Turner's seat belt was buckled, but the right-front portion of the roof collapsed and came into contact with his head. This contact paralyzed Turner's hands and legs.

Mr. James Barron, called as an expert witness by Turner, stated that he had worked as a design engineer for the Chevrolet Division of General Motors from 1963 to 1965, and had then worked in the same capacity for American Motors for over five years. Barron testified that General Motors designed for future production five years in advance and that he was involved in the design of the 1969 Impala. Barron informed his superiors at General Motors of the desirability of putting a roll bar in the roof of their cars, and Barron worked on a roll bar program. He testified that a roll bar would be expensive as an option, but relatively inexpensive if put on all cars at their birth on the assembly line. The roll bar program was discontinued, and Barron was told this was due "primarily [to] cost reasons and cost in conjunction with the fact that the consumer could not see what he was paying for." His supervisor told him that "it is difficult to pass on something to the consumer and charge him money for it if he cannot see it."

Barron testified that it would be impossible to design a crash proof car. He defined the term "crashworthiness" as the ability of a car "to withstand normal hazard conditions." Crashworthiness was broken down into the following categories: the structural integrity of the car's shell; the elimination of sharp or protruding objects in the interior; passenger restraint devices; and the elimination of post-crash fire. Barron estimated that, in the context of all possible types of accidents, roll-overs occur in twenty percent of all accidents involving "principal" injuries.

Barron drew a diagram of the Impala's roof structure and termed the roof "cosmetic," in that it provided protection from sun and rain, but it would not provide adequate protection in an overturn regardless of the speed. He categorized the roof as definitely defective, "uncommonly dangerous," and "unreasonably dangerous." The design of the Impala's roof was called perhaps the weakest way to design a roof, and Barron said that all of the roof structure in this Impala had collapsed. There was nothing in the roof of the car which would support the car in an overturn.

Barron suggested that there were many alternative ways to design a roof more safely and specifically proposed the roll bar or roll cage (the latter is, in effect, a connected double roll bar forming a rectangle with a bar at each corner attaching the frame to the body of the car). Roll bars and roll cages had been known to Barron since 1952, and he stated that General Motors put them on test cars and racing cars. In Mr. Barron's opinion, roll bars would greatly minimize roll-over injuries. Barron admitted that no mass-produced automobile in the United States had ever come equipped with a roll bar or roll cage and conceded that the Impala's roof was no more dangerous than the roof in any other car produced at that time. He frankly stated that he considered the roofs on all American cars defectively designed, including those currently manufactured (West Germany's Porsche Targa was the only production car cited by Barron as being equipped with a roll bar).

Raymond Kliesing, the defendant dealer, testified that, based upon his forty-five years of sales experience, the average consumer believes that a sedan vehicle will be a reasonably safe product in a roll-over.

The trial judge sustained General Motors' plea of privilege and filed findings of fact and conclusions of law. The trial judge found that Kliesing was an authorized General Motors dealer, that Turner's roof

(continues)

collapsed and injured him in the accident, and that the auto immediately before the accident was in substantially the same condition it was in when sold. The court's crucial finding is that the car was

> defectively designed in that the roof was not a sufficient structural support to prevent the roof from collapsing and thereby injuriously encroaching into the passenger compartment in the event of an overturn of the automobile and this defective design rendered the automobile unreasonably dangerous to the user or consumer, i.e., dangerous to an extent beyond that which would be contemplated by the ordinary user or consumer with the knowledge available to him as to the characteristics of a 1969 Chevrolet four-door sedan with a center post.

The defect was found by the trial judge to be a proximate and producing cause of the injuries, and the possibility of overturn accidents was held to be clearly foreseeable by General Motors.

The trial judge's sustaining of General Motor's plea of privilege was a ruling, in effect, that Turner had failed to prove a bona fide claim against Kliesing. In light of the trial judge's findings of fact, it is clear that his implicit conclusion of law was that strict tort liability in Texas does not encompass the liability of a manufacturer or retailer of a defective product when the defect enhances the injuries of a plaintiff, but plays no role in causing the accident. The question thus presented is one of first impression in Texas.

The genesis of this issue can be found in *Evans v. General Motors Corporation*. . . . There the plaintiff sued under general negligence, strict liability, and implied warranty principles with the argument that the manufacturer of his automobile should be liable for his enhanced injuries due to the "X" frame without side rails on his car, despite the fact that this defect had not caused the collision. The Seventh Circuit held that the manufacturer owed no duty to design or make an accident-proof or foolproof car. The court also said that the intended purpose of a car does not include its participation in collisions. In *Larsen v. General Motors Corporation*, . . . the plaintiff claimed under negligence principles that his car was defectively designed in that the steering shaft protruded in front of the axle so that his injuries were enhanced when his car was struck in the left front. The Eighth Circuit said that an auto manufacturer has a duty to design and construct its product to be reasonably fit for its intended use and free of hidden defects which would render it unsafe for that use. The court found that the real issue was one of intended use and said that the intended use of an automobile necessarily entails the risk of injury-producing accidents; such injuries are foreseeable as an incident to the normal and expected use of a car. Since *Evans* and *Larsen*, more than twenty jurisdictions have addressed the issue of crashworthiness and have split evenly. . . . We are persuaded by the logic of *Larsen*. . . .

Before addressing the merits of the *Evans-Larsen* controversy, it is necessary to discuss several Texas cases which General Motors feels have implicitly rejected the doctrine of crashworthiness. In *Muncy v. General Motors Corp.*, . . . an automobile was alleged to be negligently designed because the key could be removed from the ignition while the car was in gear and the engine was running. The court held that the appellant "was not using the car in the manner and for the purpose for which it was intended—at least appellants have failed to prove that the car was being so used." *Kahn v. Chrysler Corporation* . . . involved an allegation of negligent design in regard to sharp, protruding tailfins on a car. The plaintiff was a boy who had ridden his bicycle into a fin. The court, relying heavily on *Muncy*, held that the "duty of the automobile manufacturer extends to the ordinary use of the vehicle . . . But the manufacturer has no obligation to so design his automobile that it will be safe for a child to ride his bicycle into it while the car is parked." . . . Because of the Supreme Court's decision in *Otis Elevator Company v. Wood*, we believe that both these decisions have taken an overly narrow and restrictive view of the standard of "intended use." General Motors also cites *Kerby v. Abilene Christian College*, . . . which involved a finding of contributory negligence on the part of the plaintiff in failing to close the sliding door of his van; this act had substantially increased the plaintiff's injuries but had played no part in causing the accident. The court held:

> We draw a sharp distinction between negligence contributing to the accident and negligence contributing to the damages sustained. Contributory negligence must have the causal connection with the accident that but for the conduct the accident would not have happened. Negligence that merely increases or adds to the extent of the loss or injury occasioned by another's negligence is not such contributory negligence as will defeat recovery.

This holding explicitly restricts the basic scope of contributory negligence, does not deal with actionable primary negligence, and we think, simply expresses the Court's rejection of the harsh doctrine of denying a plaintiff any recovery because of an omission playing no part in causing the accident from which his injuries flow. General Motors would construe *Kerby* to stand for the general proposition that pre-existing negligence which causes injury is not actionable if another's intervening

(continues)

negligence specifically sparks the accident. This is not the law of Texas. . . .

General Motors cites one case applying Texas law which does deal with the issue of defective design and crashworthiness. In *Willis v. Chrysler Corporation*, . . . plaintiff was traveling at seventy miles per hour and was struck head-on by another car moving at an undetermined but extremely high rate of speed. The plaintiff's auto broke completely in two, directly behind the front seat, and suit was brought for breach of the manufacturer's warranty. The court held that a manufacturer has "no duty to design an automobile that could withstand a high speed collision and maintain its structural integrity." The court then agreed with *Evans* that the intended purpose of a car does not include its participation in collisions. While we simply disagree with the court's acceptance of *Evans* as the law of Texas, we do not believe that *Larsen* imposes a duty to design an automobile which will withstand the type of high-speed, head-on collision described in *Willis*.

We find pertinent and agree with *South Austin Drive-In Theatre v. Thomison*. . . . In that case, the driver of a riding lawn mower backed the vehicle into a child and knocked him down. The driver attempted to pull the boy away, but found him pinned by the machine. The boy lost a leg. The court rejected the manufacturer's arguments of foreseeability, misuse, and industry custom. The manufacturer was held to have negligently designed the mower in failing to have a guard over the drive chain and gear sprocket, despite the fact that this design had not caused the accident. The court said, . . .

> We believe it is a correct statement of the law to say that [the manufacturer] owed a duty to use reasonable care in the design and manufacture of its power mower to prevent injury to the user and to persons [the manufacturer] should reasonably expect to be in the vicinity of the mower's probable use.

Preliminary to a discussion of the question of crashworthiness, it must be noted that the issues and arguments pertinent to the question are essentially the same whether suit is brought under general negligence or under strict tort liability. Most of the decisions from other jurisdictions involving crashworthiness were brought under negligence, but they are nevertheless applicable here. The issue of a manufacturer's exercise of due care under negligence becomes the issue of whether he has put an unreasonably dangerous product into the stream of commerce under strict liability, and the issues of foreseeability and intended use under negligence are transformed into the issue of normal use under strict liability.

General Motors concedes that it could foresee that its products would be involved in accidents of an infinite variety, including roll-overs. Its argument is that foreseeability cannot be equated with duty. General Motors characterizes the *Larsen* argument as being that, since car accidents can be foreseen, there is a duty to design cars to reduce the injuries from these accidents. If duty were commensurate with foreseeability, then an automobile manufacturer would be an insurer. . . . However, duty has never properly been defined solely by foreseeability. . . . This argument was expressed by the Seventh Circuit in *Evans* as follows:

> The intended purpose of an automobile does not include its participation in collisions with other objects, despite the manufacturer's ability to foresee the possibility that such collisions may occur. As defendant argues, the defendant also knows that its automobiles may be driven into bodies of water, but it is not suggested that defendant has a duty to equip them with pontoons.

We agree that foreseeability alone cannot define an automobile manufacturer's duty; this would create the duty to design a crash-proof car. However, *Larsen* seeks merely to hold the manufacturer to the duty of designing a crashworthy vehicle. While all agree that there is no duty to design a crash-proof car, one court has termed it a "non sequitur" to use this truism as a basis for thus saying there is no duty to design a crashworthy car. . . . The rule of *Larsen* is not grounded upon foreseeability, but upon the *unreasonable risk* of injury in the event of a collision. Under strict liability the question of liability in each case turns upon whether the product is in a defective condition which is "unreasonably dangerous."

The controlling issue in the crashworthiness inquiry is not foreseeability, but intended use. General Motors argues that the normal and proper use of an automobile does not include its participation in collisions. The *Evans* court said that collisions are not an intended purpose of the automobile even though the manufacturer may foresee the "possibility" of collisions. The *Larsen* court terms collisions a "probability;" the court stated that between one-fourth and two-thirds of all automobiles are involved during their life in a collision producing injury or death. . . . It is irrelevant whether the occurrence of an accident involving a particular car is a possibility or a probability. What is germane is the fact that collisions are so frequent and common that they must be considered an unavoidable incidence of the normal and proper use of automobiles. Misuse of an automobile may occur, such as the intentional use of a car as a bulldozer. However, the normal use of an

(continues)

automobile is to transport people safely over the public roads. It cannot be argued that a manufacturer should not be liable for a defect which causes an accident, and no logical distinction can be drawn between that situation and one in which a defect causes injury in a foreseeable accident. We hold that an automobile manufacturer may be held strictly liable for a defective design which produces injuries, but not the accident. . . .

The doctrine of crashworthiness does not make insurers of automobile manufacturers. The Fourth Circuit, in adopting *Larsen*, noted that the question of whether a manufacturer had created an unreasonable risk of injury involves a traditional balancing of the gravity and likelihood of harm against the burden of precautions to avoid the harm. *Dreisonstock v. Volkswagenwerk.* . . . The court stated that the burden of taking precautions included a consideration of the particular purpose of the vehicle, the style or aesthetic appeal of the model, and the cost of the change and of the vehicle. So viewed, it is obvious that manufacturers are not required to produce the safest possible car, but only a reasonably safe one. For instance, if a change in design would add little to safety, render the vehicle ugly or inappropriate for its particular purpose, and add a small fortune to the purchase price, then a court should rule as a matter of law that the manufacturer had not created an unreasonable risk of harm.

The same type of balancing of factors takes place under strict liability. Section 402A states that a manufacturer is strictly liable for a product in a defective condition "unreasonably dangerous" to the user or consumer. Comment I to § 402A defines "unreasonably dangerous" as "dangerous to an extent beyond that which would be contemplated by the ordinary consumer who purchases it, with the ordinary knowledge common to the community as to its characteristics." . . .

When Comment I is applied to crashworthiness, *Dreisonstok's* balancing test for negligence governs characteristics of a product which lie within the ordinary knowledge of the community. . . . This approach would reply to the *Evans'* pontoon argument that, while the average consumer as a matter of law does not expect his car to float, he may well expect the roof of that car to maintain its structural integrity in a roll-over accident.

The moderate approach of *Dreisonstok* to the issue of crashworthiness should dispel General Motors' fears of absolute liability. This approach may be contrasted with that of *Cronin v. J. B. E. Olson Corporation.* . . . There, a clasp holding bread trays on a delivery truck failed to hold the trays in a collision, sending the driver through the windshield. The plaintiff recovered under his allegation of defective design in strict liability. The court adopted *Larsen* and then stated that it was not necessary for a plaintiff to establish that the product was unreasonably dangerous after he had shown a defect and causation, because such a requirement would place too onerous a burden upon plaintiffs. Such an approach to crashworthiness does indeed make insurers of manufacturers.

The courts adopting *Evans* often say that safety standards must be left to Congress, because courts lack the expertise for dealing with such complex matters, because sporadic and ad hoc court decisions will result in wrong and even contradictory standards, and because Congress had already proceeded to set safety standards. In 1966 (eighteen months before *Larsen*), Congress enacted the National Traffic and Motor Vehicle Safety Act, 15 U.S.C.A. §§ 1381–1431. Section 1392 instructs the Secretary of Transportation to establish motor vehicle safety standards.[1] Section 1397(a) prohibits the manufacture of vehicles not in compliance with these standards. However, § 1397(c) provides: "Compliance with any Federal motor vehicle safety standard issued under this subchapter does not exempt any person from any liability under common law." It is obvious from this language that the federal standards were meant to supplement rather than obviate the law of negligence and products liability. It has been suggested that, while the federal regulations propounded by the Secretary do not preempt the common law, they may serve as strong evidence of negligence, if not negligence per se, in regard to vehicles before the effective date of each regulation. . . . The question of whether safety standards should be left to federal regulation presents a separate question from that of congressional intent. However, we are not aware that the argument of the necessity of federal regulation has been made in regard to design defects which cause accidents, and we cannot see any reason why design defects which cause injuries are any more in need of federal control. The danger that juries will arrive at conflicting conclusions is a hazard every manufacturer who distributes nationally runs. The complex, technical questions facing juries, aided by expert testimony, cannot be more difficult than the questions in such fields as medical malpractice. Finally, the argument that a single jury verdict may have profound consequences disrupting an essential industry has been characterized as contending that the desirability of immunity from liability is directly proportional to the magnitude of the risk created. . . .

Assuming the existence of liability for a design defect causing injuries, but not the accident, General Motors

---

1. The Secretary's Standard No. 216 ("roof crush resistance—passenger cars") provides that a force equal to one and one-half the weight of the vehicle or 5,000 pounds, whichever is less, applied to the corner of the roof must not move the roof more than five inches. 49 C.F.R. § 571.216 (1973).

(continues)

argues that the trial judge's finding of defective design is supported by no evidence, insufficient evidence, or is contrary to the great weight and preponderance of the evidence. The expert witness below admitted that no mass-produced automobile had ever been manufactured in the United States with a roll bar or roll cage, and he agreed that the roof of Turner's vehicle was no more unsafe than the roof on other vehicles of the same manufacturing era.

General Motors relies principally upon two cases for these evidence point. *Dyson v. General Motors Corporation* . . . involved roof deformation in the roll-over accident of a hardtop. General Motors argued that to require roofs which would be perfectly safe in a roll-over would be to declare convertibles unreasonably dangerous per se. The court adopted *Larsen* and said . . .,

[T]he manufacturer was not necessarily under an obligation to provide a hardtop model which would be as resistant to roll-over damage as a four-door sedan; but the defendant was required, in my view, to provide a hardtop automobile which was a reasonably safe version of such model, and which was not substantially less safe than other hardtop models.

In *Dreisonstok*, a 1968 Volkswagen van was involved in a front-end collision. Such a vehicle does not have the engine in front, but plaintiff's experts declared the van to be defectively designed by comparing it to a 1966 midsized Ford passenger car. The Fourth Circuit, amplifying upon *Dyson*, held that this was impermissible; vehicles of the same type must be compared in order to determine defective design. These two cases do not stand for the proposition that defective design must be shown by comparing plaintiff's vehicle to similar vehicles. The expert below indicted the entire industry, a possibility which *Dreisonstok* does not foreclose. This is in accord with the law of Texas that, while conformance to industry custom is admissible on the question of negligence, the custom itself may be shown to be negligent. . . . We think the expert's condemnation of the industry for its failure to install roll bars constitutes a sufficient showing that the custom itself was unreasonably dangerous. General Motors' evidence points are overruled.

The judgment of the trial court is reversed, and judgment here rendered that General Motors' plea of privilege is overruled.

PUTTING IT INTO PRACTICE 12:4

1. What is the question in this case?

2. What is the alleged defect in the Impala's design?

3. What is the *Evans-Larsen* controversy?

4. Can the analysis regarding crashworthiness in the context of negligence be applied in the context of strict liability?

5. Does foreseeability alone define a manufacturer's duty? Does a manufacturer have a duty to design a crash-proof car?

6. Is the rule of *Larsen* grounded on foreseeabilty? If not, what is it grounded on?

7. What is the issue in a crashworthiness inquiry?

8. Is a manufacturer strictly liable for a design that produces injuries even if it does not cause accidents?

9. Can the average consumer be expected to anticipate that the roof of a car will maintain its structural integrity in a rollover accident?

10. What reasons do the courts that have adopted *Evans* give for leaving the safety standards up to Congress?

11. At the time of this decision, had any mass-produced automobiles been manufactured with a roll bar or roll cage? What was the court's response to GMC's argument that it had conformed to the industry standard?

Turner v. General Motors Corp. contains an interesting analysis of the doctrine of crashworthiness. Note the court's conclusion that automobile manufacturers have an obligation to make cars reasonably safe in a collision. In arriving at this conclusion the court advocates the use of a balancing test in which the gravity and likelihood of harm resulting from a particular design are weighed against the burden of precautions necessary to avoid the harm. It is noteworthy that the *Turner* court found the General Motors car to be unreasonably unsafe even though no American car had ever been manufactured with the roll bar recommended by the design engineer. Clearly, industry custom itself may be found to be negligent.

The issue of crashworthiness has also arisen in the relatively new area of litigation surrounding airbags. Because automobile manufacturers have a duty to build reasonably safe cars based on state-of-the-art technology and feasibility considerations, the question exists as to whether manufacturers who have failed to install airbags have fully complied with that duty. The controversy centers around the question of whether airbags are necessary to make a car reasonably safe in case of an accident. Airbag proponents argue that airbag systems are within the realm of state-of-the-art protection; automobile manufacturers assert that airbags have not been proven to be reliable and might even be potentially hazardous to car occupants (as evidenced by improperly deployed airbags that have caused accidents). Consumer advocates and representatives of the automobile industry also clash over the potential cost of airbag systems as well as the public's desire to have such systems.

To prevail at trial, a plaintiff must prove that the manufacturer's failure to install airbags rendered the vehicle's design defective. She proves this by showing that (1) an alternative, safer design (a design with airbags) was practicable and existed at the time of the accident; (2) the plaintiff's injuries would not have been as severe if the manufacturer had installed airbags; and (3) the extent of the enhanced injuries is attributable to the lack of airbags.

Airbag cases are not easy to win. Besides having to establish that a vehicle without an airbag is defective or unreasonably dangerous, plaintiffs have to show the technological and economic feasibility of airbags at the time the vehicle was manufactured. With earlier models this may be a difficult burden to bear. Furthermore, most jurisdictions require proof that the design defect enhanced the plaintiff's injuries, a rule that in effect shifts the burden of proof to the defendant to prove which portion of the injuries was due to the absence of the airbag. In a few states, however, plaintiffs must distinguish the injuries that would have occurred despite an airbag from those than an airbag would have prevented. Finally, manufacturers can avail themselves of certain fact-specific defenses. They can argue, for example, that a plaintiff's failure to wear a lap belt or shoulder harness constituted contributory or comparative negligence.

Defective Warnings

The absence of a warning regarding the possible dangers of a product may also lay the groundwork for a defective product claim. A seller may be required to give directions or warnings on a container to keep the product from being deemed unreasonably dangerous. In determining what warnings or instructions will suffice, a court looks at the likely number and severity of accidents that could be avoided by having a warning or instruction. The court then weighs these factors against the difficulty of providing such warnings or instructions.

In cases involving the manufacture of drugs, courts look at whether the warnings clearly convey the nature, gravity, and likelihood of the known or knowable risks of the drugs. An advertising or publicity campaign for a drug, however, may dilute the warning to the point that it becomes inadequate. For example, a warning that a drug for heartburn could cause adverse cardiac effects was diluted by other marketing materials in which Defendants touted the drugs efficacy (*Smith v. Johnson and Johnson Co.,* 800 N.Y. S.2d 357 [2004]).

If the defendant can show that it neither knew nor should have known of the danger at the time of the sale of the product, most courts have held that the defendant has no duty to warn. Manufacturers are not to be the insurers of their products. So if a drug manufacturer can show that it had subjected a drug to reasonable testing procedures and did not discover any adverse side effects, it would escape liability for injuries to consumers resulting from long-term side effects not known to either the manufacturer or researchers at the time the drug was produced. In some rare cases, however, such as those involving asbestos, the defense of ignorance has failed. The courts have held asbestos manufacturers liable even if they were unaware of the danger, essentially holding them to a strict liability standard.

Obviousness of danger is a factor that is considered in determining the defendant's obligation to warn. But obviousness of danger alone does not preclude a duty to warn. Indeed, a product may be so dangerous that it should not be marketed at all. A light fixture with exposed (noninsulated) wiring, for example, is dangerous with or without a warning attached advising consumers of the danger. In such a case giving a warning would not protect the defendant from liability.

The manufacturer may have a postsale duty to warn if it discovers that a product is hazardous after it is sold. Manufacturers that receive complaints of injuries or adverse reactions to their products have been found liable for failure to warn consumers of the potential for injury or adverse reactions (*Patton v. Hutchinson Wil-rish Mfg. Co.*, 861 P.2d 1299 [Kan. 1993]).

PUTTING IT INTO PRACTICE 12:5

1. A man commits suicide shortly after he begins taking Xanax, a prescription tranquilizer. His estate sues the drug manufacturer.

   a. Under what theories of recovery might the estate sue?

   b. What types of defects might the estate claim?

   c. Should the question of defect be analyzed using a reasonable-consumer-expectation or a reasonable-doctor-expectation standard?

   d. Given the social policy questions at stake, do you think the manufacturer should be held strictly liable? How would you use the Learned Hand formula to answer this question?

2. Review the facts in question 4 of "Putting It into Practice" exercise 12.2. What defense might the manufacturer raise in response to a defective warning claim?

3. Wilma sues the manufacturer of Halcion for the injuries she has sustained as a result of having been prescribed this drug between 1987 and 1992. Her claim includes an allegation that the manufacturer failed to "warn of the dangerous propensities of Halcion." If the same court that heard the DES case described in question 5 of "Putting It into Practice" exercise 12.2 hears this case, do you think Wilma will be allowed to recover?

4. The estate of a man who is alleged to have died as a result of being exposed to an herbicide sues the manufacturer of the herbicide. If the manufacturer were unaware of the potential dangers of the herbicide, what defense might it raise to avoid being held strictly liable?

5. The parents of children injured by blasting caps bring an action against several explosives manufacturers and their trade association. The manufacturers argue that under the "intended use" doctrine, they had a duty to exercise reasonable care only toward "those who use [the product] for a purpose for which the manufacturer should expect it to be used and . . . those whom [the manufacturer] should expect to be endangered by its probable use." How might the plaintiffs rebut this argument?

6. A widower sues a tobacco company after his wife dies from a cigarette-induced illness. He alleges a design defect and introduces a report issued by the Surgeon General of the United States that concludes that smoking lower-yield cigarettes seems to reduce the risk of lung cancer. This report was issued more than ten years after his wife had quit smoking. What additional evidence will the plaintiff have to muster to rebut a defense motion for summary judgment?

DEFENSES

Negligence

The plaintiff's contributory negligence, comparative negligence, or assumption of risk are defenses to product liability claims based on a theory of negligence (see Exhibit 12–4). For a complete discussion of those defenses, see Chapter 8.

Warranty

The rules pertaining to contributory negligence are generally applicable to cases involving warranty claims. If a buyer discovers that a good is defective and uses it anyway, his action rather than the breach of warranty may be considered the proximate cause of the injuries. The buyer's unreasonable failure to examine goods before using them may also constitute a defense to a breach-of-warranty claim. The courts tend to be more lenient, however, with consumers than with merchants in terms of the obligation to examine goods.

If the plaintiff's negligence is due to her misuse or abnormal use of the product, many courts will analyze the warranty action as involving a proximate cause or duty problem rather than as involving an affirmative defense. If a plaintiff, for example, misuses a bottle in attempting to remove its cap, a court might hold that the defendant had no duty to produce a bottle that could withstand unreasonable handling or, alternatively, that the makeup of the bottle was not the proximate cause of the plaintiff's injuries. The only real significance in this difference in analysis lies in the burden of proof. If the court uses a duty or proximate-cause analysis, then the burden of proof lies with the plaintiff. If, however, the court treats the misuse as an affirmative defense, then the burden of proving that misuse lies with the defendant.

In addition to contributory negligence, assumption of risk is also generally a valid defense in warranty actions.

Disclaimers

Under the UCC a seller can *disclaim* both implied and express warranties. To disclaim a warranty of merchantability the UCC requires that the seller use language that is conspicuous and that specifically mentions merchantability (UCC § 2–316). Alternatively, an implied warranty of merchantability is disclaimed if the product is sold "as is" or if the buyer has an opportunity to examine the goods but refuses to do so. Federal law (under the Magnuson-Moss Federal Trade Commission Improvement Act, 15 U.S.C. § 2301 *et seq.*) precludes any manufacturer that provides a consumer with a written warranty from disclaiming any implied warranty. Any written warranty provided by a manufacturer must therefore include the implied warranty of merchantability.

Limitations of Remedies

Sellers sometimes try to limit the remedies available to plaintiffs for breach of implied warranties by providing that they (sellers) will not be liable for consequential damages. "[L]imitation of consequential damages for injury to the person in the case of consumer goods is prima facie unconscionable" (UCC § 2–719[3]). Therefore, provisions limiting the seller's liability to repair or replacement of goods will not be enforced in cases involving personal injuries resulting from defects in products designed for personal use. Limitation of damages is not unconscionable, however, when the loss is commercial, i.e., involving intangible economic loss (UCC § 2–719[3]).

EXHIBIT 12–4 *Defenses in Product Liability Claims*

NEGLIGENCE	WARRANTY	STRICT LIABILITY
• Contributory negligence • Comparative negligence • Assumption of risk • Statute of limitations/ Statute of repose	• Contributory negligence • Comparative negligence • Assumption of risk • Disclaimer of warranty • Limitation of remedies • Failure to discover breach in reasonable time • Statute of limitations/ Statute of repose	• Contributory negligence (only if plaintiff misused product or used it in abnormal fashion) • Comparative negligence (subject to much controversy) • Assumption of risk • Statute of limitations/ Statute of repose

Time Limits

A seller can also argue that a buyer must "within a reasonable time after he discovers or should have discovered any breach" notify the seller of the breach (UCC § 2–607[3]). Courts frequently refuse to enforce this requirement when the plaintiff is not in privity with the defendant.

Strict Liability

A plaintiff's contributory negligence is not a defense to a strict liability claim if the plaintiff fails to discover the defect or to guard against the possibility of its existence. A valid defense may exist, however, if the plaintiff misuses the product or uses it in an abnormal fashion. Examples of the misuse or abnormal use of a product include knocking a bottled beverage against a radiator to remove the cap and overeating a product to the point of becoming ill (*Restatement [Second] of Torts* § 402A, cmt. h). However, if the abuse or misuse is reasonably foreseeable, the manufacturer has a duty to anticipate such misuse and to make the product safe against it. Drivers inadvertently trying to start their vehicles from the "drive" position might, for example, be foreseeable. In that case manufacturers would have a duty to protect consumers from the consequences of their negligence. As discussed in the section on defenses to warranty actions, cases of misuse or abnormal use can be phrased in terms of a duty or proximate cause analysis rather than as an affirmative defense.

Suppose the manufacturing defect is not the sole proximate cause of the plaintiff's injuries, but, in fact, the plaintiff's own negligence is an additional proximate cause. The plaintiff can still recover if she can show that the acts were not so unforeseeable that they should be considered superseding acts.

In comparative-negligence jurisdictions, considerable controversy exists as to whether a plaintiff suing on the basis of strict liability should have recovery reduced in proportion to her own negligence. Some courts have construed their comparative-negligence statutes so as to find them applicable to strict liability situations, in effect reducing the plaintiff's recovery. The Uniform Comparative Fault Act suggests that the plaintiff's strict liability recovery should be reduced in proportion to the degree of fault.

Assumption of risk is basically treated in the same fashion in strict liability cases as it is in negligence cases. A plaintiff who discovers a defect and voluntarily and unreasonably proceeds to use the product is barred from recovery.

Statute of Limitations

A defendant must look at the plaintiff's pleadings to determine the appropriate statute of limitations. The general tort statutes, which are usually relatively short, are applicable to negligence claims. The UCC's statute of limitations (§ 2–725) usually applies to breach-of-warranty actions and gives the plaintiff four years from the time of sale of the product in which to sue. In strict liability cases the courts are in disagreement as to whether the UCC or the general tort statutes are applicable.

Some states have adopted **statutes of repose**, which provide a fixed period of time from the date of the original sale during which a product liability suit can be brought. Unlike a statute of limitations, which begins to run at the time of injury, a statute of repose begins to run at the date of sale. Consequently, some product liability suits may be barred by a statute of repose before the injury even occurs. Victims of DES or AIDS, whose injuries become apparent years after the initial exposure, will often be precluded from filing suit if a statute of repose exists. Because the majority of bodily injuries occur within five years of purchase, however, statutes of repose have little effect on most claims.

PREEMPTION

A state common law tort action cannot be brought if a federal statute expressly or impliedly **preempts** (prohibits) such an action. The roots of the federal preemption doctrine can be traced back to the framers of the Constitution, who foresaw the potential for conflict between the two separate lawmaking bodies of federal and state government. They addressed this problem by mandating within the Constitution that the laws of the United States "shall be the Supreme Law of the Land." Preemption, however, goes beyond the concept of supremacy. Under the supremacy doctrine, states are free to act as long as their laws do not conflict with federal law; under the rules of preemption, states lose their power to act at all, regardless of any conflict with federal law.

Federal preemption of state law can either be express or implied. Under *express preemption* Congress explicitly states the extent to which its enactments preempt state law. To illustrate, the Public Health Cigarette Smoking Act (15 U.S.C. §§ 1331–1340) specifically states "[n]o statement relating to smoking and health, other than the statement required by [the act] . . . shall be required on any cigarette package [or on advertising of labeled cigarettes]." In *Cipollone v. Liggett*, 112 S. Ct. 2608 (1992) (a suit against cigarette manufacturers based on design defect, failure to warn, express warranty, fraud, and conspiracy to defraud claims), the United States Supreme Court held that this preemption clause preempted state law claims based on failure to warn, but not claims based on breach of warranty, product liability, or intentional fraud, because Congress had expressly limited the scope of preemption.

Implied preemption can occur in one of two ways—field preemption or conflict preemption. *Field preemption* occurs when a statute is in a field that Congress intended the federal government to occupy exclusively. In *Cipollone*, for example, a plurality of the Supreme Court reasoned that because Congress had expressly preempted failure-to-warn claims against cigarette manufacturers, preemption could not be implied with respect to the breach-of-warranty or fraud claims. In a later decision (*Myrick v. Freightliner*, 115 S. Ct. 1483 [1995]), the Court clarified that express preemption did not necessarily foreclose the possibility of implied preemption, although it did support an inference of implied preemption.

Under *conflict preemption* a state law is preempted to the extent that it actually conflicts with federal law. Such a conflict may arise when compliance with both state and federal law is impossible or when the purpose and objectives of Congress would be blocked by the state law.

To understand the impact of preemption on product liability cases, consider *Cipollone*, the much publicized case involving a suit against the tobacco industry. *Cipollone* was initiated by Rose Cipollone and her husband against three cigarette manufacturers; they both died during the course of this protracted litigation and her son then represented their estate. Their suit alleged the following: cigarettes are defective because manufacturers failed to use a safer alternative design and because the dangers of cigarettes outweighed their social value; the manufacturers failed to provide adequate warnings of the health consequences of smoking; the manufacturers expressly warranted that smoking did not present

any significant health risk (express warranty); the manufacturers tried to neutralize the warning labels through their advertising (fraudulent misrepresentation); and the manufacturers conspired to deprive the public of medical and scientific data (conspiracy to defraud).

The manufacturers claimed, among other things, that the Federal Cigarette Labeling and Advertising Act (1965) and its successor, the Public Health Cigarette Smoking Act of 1969, protected them from any liability based on their conduct after 1965. The district court ruled that the statutes did not preempt common law actions. The court of appeals reversed, the United States Supreme Court denied a petition for certiorari, and the case was remanded to the district court for trial. Complying with the court of appeals' mandate, the district court held that the failure-to-warn, express-warranty, fraudulent-misrepresentation, and conspiracy-to-defraud claims were barred to the extent that they relied on the manufacturers' advertising, promotional, and public relations activities after January 1, 1966 (the effective date of the 1965 act). The court also ruled that the design-defect claims were not preempted by federal law but were barred on other grounds. Following a four-month trial, the jury rejected the misrepresentation and conspiracy claims, but found that Liggett had breached its duty to warn in its express warranties before 1966. It found, however, that Rose Cipollone had "'voluntarily and unreasonably encounter[ed] a known danger by smoking cigarettes'" and that 80 percent of the responsibility for her injuries was attributable to her. The jury awarded $400,000 to Rose Cipollone's husband for losses attributed to the manufacturers' breach of warranty but awarded no damages to her estate. On cross-appeals from the final judgment, the court of appeals affirmed the district court's preemption rulings but remanded for a new trial on other issues. The preemption issue was then taken before the United States Supreme Court, whereupon the Court ruled that Congress had intended to preempt the failure-to-warn claims but not the other claims.

The Court's rulings in *Cipollone* muddied the waters concerning preemption, creating a patchwork of rulings among the lower courts. One area that has

NET NEWS

Articles on preemption can be found at **http://www.law.umkc.edu**. Enter "preemption" in the search box.

NET NEWS

You can read *Cipollone* online by going to **http://www.law.umkc.edu.** Enter "Cipollone" as your search term.

NET NEWS

Deposition testimony of senior research scientist Dr. Jeffrey Wigand, whose story of courage in the face of intimidation by a major tobacco company is told in the movie, *The Insider*, can be found at **http://www.tobaccofreekids.org** by using "Wigand deposition" as your search term. His testimony revealed the extent to which the tobacco industry not only knew of the addictive nature of nicotine but strove to enhance its addictive qualities.

been affected by the uncertainty about preemption is airbag litigation. In a typical airbag case, the automaker alleges that the National Traffic and Motor Safety Act of 1966 preempts the plaintiff's claim because the vehicle complies with Federal Motor Vehicle Safety Standard Act (Standard 208), which covers occupant crash protection. The defendant specifies that between 1973 and 1986, Standard 208 gave a manufacturer three options for protecting front-seat automobile occupants, and that compliance with any one satisfied the federal standard. In accordance with this standard, the manufacturer chose to install manual seat belts rather than airbags. Defense contends that imposing liability for failure to select one particular option undermines the legislative purpose of providing manufacturers the flexibility to choose among alternatives. The counterargument to this position is that the Safety Act expressly preserves common law tort claims, by virtue of a savings clause in the act stating,

> Compliance with any Federal motor vehicle safety standard issued under this subchapter does not exempt any person from liability under common law.

Prior to *Cipollone*, courts that were inclined to find preemption relied on the concept of conflict preemption by finding that a tort claim was in conflict with the Safety Act. The courts began their analysis by acknowledging that the savings clause explicitly preserved liability under the common law and that the preemption clause was silent on the issue (hence no express preemption). The courts then found a conflict between the options of Standard 208 and the implications of a common law judgment for the plaintiff. Upon finding a conflict, the courts ruled that common law actions were impliedly preempted because state common law cannot prevent the exercise of a federally granted option. Because the preemption defense eliminates cases before plaintiffs can argue the merits of their cases, car manufacturers have frequently resorted to this defense.

A clear application of *Cipollone* has eluded the lower courts, even after the Supreme Court tried to clarify its *Cipollone* holding by revisiting the preemption issue (see *Myrick v. Freightliner*, 115 S. Ct. 1483 [1995]). Therefore, predicting how a court will resolve preemptive issues in the context of airbag cases or any other kind of product liability claim has become increasingly difficult. An in-depth discussion of preemption goes beyond the scope of this text, but the foregoing analysis, albeit superficial, reveals the pitfalls that preemption poses for plaintiffs in the realm of product liability.

PUTTING IT INTO PRACTICE 12:6

1. Your firm represents a manufacturer of blasting caps. This manufacturer is one of six manufacturers being sued by parents of children who were injured in blasting cap accidents. The blasting caps contained no warning labels and could easily be detonated by children. The plaintiffs are unable to prove which

(continues)

PUTTING IT INTO PRACTICE 12:6 *(continued)*

manufacturer made the caps that injured their children. They allege, however, that their children's injuries stemmed from the manufacturers' failure to warn and failure to design caps that were less easily detonated by children. They further allege that the manufacturers had actual knowledge of how frequently children were injured by blasting caps. What defenses should your firm suggest the manufacturer raise?

2. The parent of a teenager who was killed while using a shredder sues the manufacturer on the basis of strict liability. What defenses might the manufacturer consider raising?

3. Consider the facts in question 1 of "Putting It into Practice" exercise 12.1, involving the dispute between Elite and Carrier. What defenses might Carrier raise?

4. Joseph brings a product liability action against cigarette manufacturers, which move for summary judgment based on the statute of limitations. Joseph began smoking when he was thirteen or fifteen; he began experiencing breathing problems and a chronic cough in the early 1970s; his condition deteriorated through the 1980s; he was diagnosed with chronic obstructive pulmonary disease (COPD) in 1988. During this time, physicians repeatedly warned Joseph of the dangers of smoking, and when he was diagnosed with COPD, his doctors told him that his illness was caused by smoking. Joseph filed his action in July 1995. Joseph contends that his cause of action accrued when he discovered or should have discovered the "wrongful conduct" of the tobacco companies, such as their denial of the addictive nature of nicotine despite their internal research that proved otherwise and their manipulation of nicotine levels in cigarettes to increase their addictiveness. His complaint is based on strict liability, negligence, failure to warn, and defendants' willful misrepresentation of the true nature of the health risks associated with cigarette use.

    When do you think his cause of action accrued? Joseph argues that his injury includes not only his COPD but also his addiction and that his addiction is due to the misconduct of the defendants in enhancing the addictive effects of nicotine. He maintains that his claim did not accrue until he knew the true cause of his addiction and that he could not have known that until November 1995, when a former tobacco research chief "let the cat out of the bag" while being deposed in another case. Are you persuaded by this argument?

5. The Federal Insecticide, Fungicide and Rodenticide Act (7 U.S.C. §§ 136–136y) expressly bars state labeling requirements additional to federal requirements. What defense can a manufacturer that complies with the federal regulations set forth in this act raise if sued by a consumer for improper labeling?

CLASS ACTIONS

When a large number of people are injured as a result of a widely distributed product (examples include tobacco, breast implants, the weight-reduction drug fen-phen, and asbestos), they may opt to bring one **class action** suit rather than many individual suits. A class action is a suit in which representative members of a class sue on behalf of other members of the class. The representative parties act on behalf of everyone that was injured, eliminating the need for each one of those to file an individual suit or be personally involved in the courtroom process. Class actions prevent the court system from being overwhelmed by a myriad of suits. They also allow individuals to be represented whose minimal recovery might have otherwise precluded them from finding an attorney. Attorneys who cannot justify accepting individual personal injury claims usually find class actions worth their expenditure of time and effort.

Before a class action can be brought, a court must provide **certification of a class,** allowing one or more members of the class to serve as representatives for the other members of the class. Certification requirements are usually stringent, requiring proof (1) that there is a common issue of law or fact among members of the class, (2) that the claims and defenses alleged by the proposed representative are typical of the claims and defenses of the other members of the class, (3) that there are so many potential claimants it would be impractical to join them in one action as plaintiffs, (4) that the proposed representative party will fairly and adequately represent every member of the class, and (5) that adequate notice will be given to all potential members of the class (usually done by placing ads in newspapers and establishing websites).

In recent years class actions have been brought successfully against tobacco companies, who for years previously had thwarted efforts by smokers to sue them. In 1996 Liggett settled a class action brought in the Alabama courts on behalf of a nationwide class of smokers. Liggett conceded that nicotine is addictive and that certain health problems are associated with smoking. It also agreed to cooperate in lawsuits filed against other tobacco companies. The following year forty states and tobacco companies reached a settlement requiring that the companies would pay $368.5 billion to cover the cost of Medicare claims for treating smokers who had become ill. Although the settlement fell apart because Congress failed to act, the provisions of the settlement were astonishing. Among other things, the tobacco companies agreed to give the Food and Drug Administration (FDA) expanded authority to regulate nicotine levels in cigarettes, to stop all outdoor advertising, and to be subject to severe surcharges if the number of underage smokers did not decline dramatically in the next decade. Subsequently, several states pursued actions on their own against the tobacco companies and reached settlements. In 1998 forty-four states reached a settlement requiring payment of $206 billion over twenty-five years for smoking-related health care costs that the states had paid out for smoking-related diseases. Because the claimants in this case were the states, class actions or individual suits brought on behalf of smokers were not precluded. Recently a Florida jury returned a punitive-damages award of $144 billion in a class action against five of the largest tobacco manufacturers. In 2001 a jury rendered a landmark $3 billion punitive-damages award against Philip Morris on behalf of an individual smoker. Although the punitive damages were reduced to $100 million by the trial judge, and the award is being appealed by the defendant, this trend bespeaks a grim future for tobacco manufacturers, who once appeared invincible.

A class action suit was also filed against American Home Products (now Wyeth), manufacturer of the diet drugs fenfluramine and phentermine (commonly referred to as fen-phen), both of which have been associated with a number of medical problems, including heart valve damage and pulmonary hypertension. As a result of a Mayo Clinic 1997 report that 30 percent of users experienced some kind of heart valve problem, the manufacturer agreed, under pressure from the FDA, to take Pondimin (fenfluramine) and Redux (dexfenfluramine) off the market (phentermine was not removed). In December of 1997 all federal lawsuits were transferred to the district court for the Eastern District of Pennsylvania. Plaintiffs' counsel selected by the judge spent two years gathering and reviewing documents, conducting depositions of senior executives of the manufacturers, and preparing their clients' cases for trial. In 2002 final approval of a landmark $3.75 billion settlement was given in relationship only to fen-phen users who had experienced heart valve disease, not to those with pulmonary hypertension. A trust fund was established, and as of June 2002, the trust has paid out more than $900 million to former Redux and Pondimin users. Subsequently, Wyeth agreed to contribute an additional $1.4 billion to pay users' claims.

Claimants who took Pondimin or Redux for more than sixty days could recover their prescription costs and, if they had an echocardiogram that shows a sufficiently high level of heart valve regurgitation, could recover either $6,000 in cash or $10,000 worth of additional medical care. Those who had taken either of these drugs for less than sixty days could recover lesser amounts of money. Any claimant who suffered from serious heart disease could qualify for additional benefits, up to $1,485,000.

NET NEWS

Key litigation documents pertaining to the settlement reached by the attorneys general of forty-four states against the tobacco companies can be viewed at **http://www.library.ucsf.edu**. Enter "tobacco" in the search window, then select "Tobacco Litigation Documents".

SUMMARY

Product liability cases can be based on theories of negligence, breach of warranty, or strict liability. All three types of actions involve products in a defective condition, which can involve manufacturing defects, design defects, or defective warnings. Design defects include structural defects, absence of safety features, and misuse of a product if the misuse is reasonably foreseeable.

Plaintiffs recovering on the basis of negligence can sue the manufacturer, retailer, or lessor of a product whose defect was the proximate cause of their injuries. They can recover for personal injuries and property damage but will have difficulty recovering for pure economic loss.

Warranty actions, which are a hybrid of contract and tort law, can be based on breach of an express or implied warranty. The most common implied warranties are warranties of merchantability and warranties of fitness for a particular purpose. A plaintiff who is a direct purchaser will, because of the generosity of the UCC, likely opt for a warranty theory over a negligence or strict liability theory if the damages are solely economic. Privity requirements, which vary from state to state, dictate who may and may not be sued.

Strict liability is the most commonly used cause of action in product liability cases. Plaintiffs must prove that the product was in a "defective condition unreasonably dangerous," that the defect was the cause in fact and proximate cause of the plaintiff's injuries, that the defect existed at the time the product left the defendant's hands, and that the product was manufactured or sold by the defendant. Strict liability extends to the ultimate user or consumer of a product, including, for many courts, bystanders whose presence was reasonably foreseeable. Anyone

in the business of selling goods, including manufacturers, retailers, and lessors, can be held strictly liable for the defective products they pass on to others.

Contributory and comparative negligence and assumption of risk are defenses to negligence and warranty claims. With certain restrictions, warranties can be disclaimed under the UCC, and sellers can limit the remedies available in the event of a breach. Contributory negligence is not a defense in a strict liability case unless the plaintiff abused the product in an unforeseeable way. Assumption of risk is generally a defense to strict liability. Plaintiffs must determine the appropriate statute of limitations and must consider any statute of repose when filing claims. Some claims are preempted (expressly or impliedly) by actions of Congress.

Class actions allow representative parties to act on behalf of every party that was injured, eliminating the need for each one to file an individual suit or be personally involved in the courtroom process. Not only do class actions prevent the court system from being overwhelmed, but they also allow individuals to be represented who might have otherwise been denied. To certify a class, a court must find that there is a common issue of law or fact among members of the class, that the representatives' claims and defenses are typical of the claims and defenses of the other members of the class, that there are so many potential claimants it would be impractical to join them in one action, that the proposed representative party will fairly and adequately represent every member of the class, and that adequate notice will be given to all potential members of the class. Class action suits that have made the news lately are those involving the stock brokers and financial institutions.

KEY TERMS

certification of a class
Court's agreement to allow one or more members of the class to serve as representatives for the other members of the class

class action
Suit in which representative members of a class sue on behalf of other members of the class

defective warning
Defect arising out of a manufacturer's failure to give adequate warnings or directions for use. In other words, it is the warning that is defective rather than the product

design defect
Defect arising out of a manufacturer's use of an unreasonably dangerous design

economic loss
Diminution in the value of a product

express warranty
Express representation by a seller that a product possesses certain qualities

implied warranty
Representations as to a product's qualities that are implied by virtue of the product being offered for sale

manufacturing defect
Defect arising out of a deviation in the manufacturing process

preempts
Prohibits a state tort law claim due to a federal enactment

privity
Requirement that the plaintiff must contract directly with the defendant in order to recover for losses

product liability

The liability of a manufacturer, seller, or other supplier of a chattel which, because of a defect, causes injury to a consumer, a user, or in some cases a bystander. Liability can be based on any of three theories of recovery: (1) negligence, (2) warranty, or (3) strict liability

statutes of repose

Statutes of limitations in reference to sale of products

unavoidably unsafe products

Products incapable of being made safe for their ordinary and intended use

warranty of fitness for a particular purpose

Implied warranty that goods are suitable to be used for a particular (noncustomary) purpose

warranty of merchantability

Implied warranty that goods are fit for the ordinary purpose for which they are used

REVIEW QUESTIONS

1. Under what circumstances can the following be found negligent when a plaintiff is injured by a defective product?
   a. manufacturer
   b. maker of component part
   c. user of component part
   d. retailer

2. Can lessors, real estate agents, and providers of service be found liable on the basis of negligence?

3. What is privity, and what is its status today?

4. What damages can be recovered in a product liability case based on negligence?

5. What are the differences between tort remedies and contract remedies based on a breach-of-warranty claim?

6. What is an express warranty, and how is it created?
   a. Who may recover on the basis of breach of express warranty?
   b. What can be recovered?

7. What is the difference between an implied warranty of merchantability and a warranty of fitness for a particular purpose?
   a. What can be recovered when suing on the basis of breach of an implied warranty?
   b. Who can be held liable?
   c. What is the "sealed container" doctrine?

8. When is it to a plaintiff's advantage to sue on the basis of strict liability, and when is it to her advantage to sue on the basis of breach of warranty?

9. What is the justification for strict liability in product liability cases? Why are some courts critical of strict liability?

10. What does section 402A of the *Restatement* provide, and how did it evolve?

11. What must be proved in a strict liability case?
   a. What is the difference between a consumer-expectation test and a risk-utility test?
   b. What is an unavoidably unsafe product?
   c. What unique causation problems exist with strict liability, and how have the courts dealt with these problems?
   d. Is res ipsa loquitur applicable to strict liability cases?
   e. Who can be sued on the basis of strict liability?
   f. Who can sue on the basis of strict liability?
   g. What can be recovered in a strict liability case?

12. How does a manufacturing defect differ from a design defect?

13. What are the three types of design defects?
   a. How does a design-defect case brought on the basis of negligence differ from one brought on the basis of strict liability?
   b. What is a state-of-the-art defense?
   c. Why is a plaintiff not allowed to introduce evidence that a defendant redesigned a product after the plaintiff was injured?
   d. Give an example of a structural defect.
   e. What determines whether a safety feature must be installed?
   f. Give an example of a foreseeable-misuse case, and explain why the manufacturer would be liable even though the plaintiff misused the product.
   g. What must a plaintiff prove in an airbag case, and why are such cases difficult to prove?
   h. Under what conditions will a manufacturer's warnings be considered defective?

14. What defenses can be raised in a warranty case?
    a. How can a defendant disclaim a warranty?
    b. Can a seller limit his consequential remedies?

15. What defenses can be raised in a strict liability case?

16. What issues arise in the context of statutes of limitations and statutes of repose in product liability cases?

17. What is preemption, and how did it arise?
    a. What is the difference between implied and express preemption?
    b. What is the difference between field preemption and conflict preemption?
    c. Why has preemption been such a significant issue in tobacco and airbag cases?

18. What is a class action, and what are its advantages?

19. What must be shown before a court will agree to certify a class action?

PRACTICE EXAM

Students should complete the practice exam after studying each chapter. The answers are in Appendix A. If you score lower than 80%, you should reread the materials.

True-False

1. Retailers have no duty to inspect goods unless they believe they may be dangerous.

2. Retailers have no duty to make superficial inspection of cars they sell.

3. Suppliers of services can be found negligent, but sellers of real estate cannot.

4. Plaintiffs in negligence actions cannot recover if they are only users of a product but did not purchase it.

5. The distinction between property damage and economic loss is not always clear.

6. Most courts restrict contract recovery to economic losses and tort recovery to damages to property or persons.

7. A description of a windshield as being "shatter-proof" allows a plaintiff to recover if the windshield shatters after being hit by a rock.

8. Courts uniformly agree that implied warranties of merchantability apply to sales of food and drink, services, and real estate transactions.

9. Those who argue that manufacturers should be strictly liable for damages resulting from the sale of their products justify their position on the basis that the modern sophistication of products precludes consumers from being able to pinpoint the acts of negligence responsible for their injuries.

10. An argument against strict liability is that manufacturers are unduly hampered in trying to meet consumer demands by the threat of strict liability suits.

11. If a plaintiff contracts a disease as a result of receiving a blood transfusion, the question that a court must answer is whether the provision of blood involves the sale of a service or product.

12. In most cases plaintiffs are allowed to introduce evidence of a defendant's redesign of a product.

13. In *Sindell v. Abbott Laboratories* the court held that each defendant that could not prove it did not supply DES to the manufacturers was liable for a proportion of the judgment representing its share of the market.

14. The alternate theory of liability allows a defendant to be found liable if he cannot prove that he did not cause the plaintiff's injuries.

15. Strict liability is applicable to private individuals who sell defective goods and to sellers of used goods.

16. Plaintiffs suing on the basis of strict liability can always recover for purely economic losses.

17. Economic loss includes damage to a product.

18. In a design-defect case the question is whether the defendant chose a design that posed an unreasonable danger to the plaintiff.

19. In a design-defect case the availability of other designs is not considered.

20. Manufacturers are obligated to use the most durable design possible.

21. In determining whether a safety feature must be installed, courts consider the cost of the product and the magnitude of the danger without the safety feature.

22. An industry as a whole may be determined to be negligent.

23. If a plaintiff misuses a product, most courts will not allow the plaintiff to recover.

24. In *Turner v. General Motors Corp.* the court found General Motors not liable because no car manufacturer at that time had ever made a car with a roll bar.

25. An adequate warning of a drug must convey the nature, gravity, and likelihood of the risks involved in taking the drug.

26. An advertising campaign for a drug can dilute a warning to the extent it becomes inadequate.

27. Manufacturers have a duty to warn even if they neither knew nor should have known of the dangers of the sale of the product at the time it was sold.

28. Obviousness of danger precludes an obligation to warn.

29. In a warranty action defendants can claim that the plaintiff knew the product was defective and used it anyway.

30. A seller cannot disclaim an express warranty.

31. An implied warranty of merchantability can be disclaimed if the buyer has an opportunity to examine the goods and refuses to do so.

32. Under federal law, manufacturers who provide a written warranty can still disclaim any implied warranties.

33. A seller cannot limit her consequential damages when personal injuries result from a defective product.

34. A buyer has an unlimited time in which he can notify a seller of a breach of warranty.

35. It is a valid defense to a strict liability claim that the plaintiff misused the product or used it in an abnormal fashion unless the misuse or abuse was reasonably foreseeable.

36. UCC statutes of limitations are shorter than general tort statutes of limitations.

37. UCC statutes of limitations apply to warranty actions.

38. Statutes of repose begin to run at the time of injury.

39. The federal preemption doctrine allows states to act as they please as long as they do not conflict with federal law.

40. In *Cipollone* the plaintiff sued three tobacco companies on the basis of breach of express warranty, defective design, and failure to warn.

41. *Cipollone* muddied the waters for the lower courts with regard to preemption.

42. In airbag cases manufacturers often contend that allowing a lawsuit conflicts with the National Traffic and Motor Safety Act of 1966, which gave manufacturers three options in choosing how to protect front-seat occupants.

43. Before a class action can be certified, the party requesting certification must prove that adequate notice will be given to all potential members of the class.

44. Class actions have been allowed in cases involving such drugs as fen-phen but disallowed in tobacco cases.

Matching

GROUP 1

_____ 1. Requires direct contact between plaintiff and defendant

_____ 2. Protects public from dangerous products

_____ 3. Compensates parties for loss of benefit of bargain

_____ 4. Description of windshield as shatterproof

_____ 5. Warranty of merchantability

a. express warranty

b. implied warranty

c. contract remedies

d. tort remedies

e. privity

GROUP 2

_____ 1. Defect that causes product to injure plaintiff is missing in other such products manufactured by defendant

_____ 2. Defect in a feature that makes product unreasonably dangerous

_____ 3. Lack of adequate instructions

_____ 4. Diminution in value of product

_____ 5. Crashworthy vehicle

a. foreseeable misuse
b. economic loss
c. design defect
d. manufacturing defect
e. defective warning misuse

GROUP 3

_____ 1. Statute that blocks purpose and objectives of Congress

_____ 2. Statutes that make it impossible to obey both federal and state laws

_____ 3. Statute that is in area under Congress's exclusive control

_____ 4. Representatives act on behalf of others

_____ 5. Requires common issue of law or fact

a. conflict preemption
b. field preemption
c. implied preemption
d. certification
e. class action

Fill-in-the-Blanks

1. For goods to be _____ they must be fit for the ordinary purpose for which such goods are used.

2. The _____ _____ doctrine absolves retailers of liability when a sealed container is involved.

3. One of the arguments supporting _____ _____ is that manufacturers should be forced to internalize the cost of injuries their products inflict, which they can do by raising the market price of the product.

4. Courts will not hold manufacturers of experimental drugs strictly liable because they are _____ _____.

5. A _____ _____ _____ _____ defense is a defense that argues that the level of technology available at the time the product was made precluded a safer design.

6. A _____ defect occurs when a defendant chooses materials that result in the product having a structural weakness that makes it dangerous.

7. In defective-warning cases courts consider the _____ and _____ of accidents likely to occur without adequate warnings or instructions.

8. An implied warranty of merchantability can be disclaimed by selling the product _____ _____.

9. _____ _____ _____ provide a fixed period of time in which a product liability suit can be brought.

10. The federal _____ doctrine can be traced back to the framers of the Constitution, who foresaw potential conflicts between the federal and state legislatures.

11. "No statement related to smoking and health, other than the one required by this act, shall be required on any cigarette package" is an example of a (an) _____ preemption.

Multiple-Choice

1. A manufacturer
   a. can be found negligent in its failure to inspect or test its finished product but not for its failure to package and ship its products in a reasonably safe manner.
   b. who uses component parts is exempt from negligence for failure to use reasonable care in obtaining them.

c. is always liable for a retailer's failure to conduct an inspection it is obligated to make.

d. none of the above.

2. Plaintiffs in negligence actions
   a. cannot recover if they are only users of a product but did not purchase it.
   b. can recover from the manufacturer even if they bought the product from a retailer.
   c. can always recover for property damage and pure economic loss.
   d. all of the above.

3. In warranty causes of action,
   a. aspects of both contract and tort remedies are involved.
   b. a contract remedy is more appropriate when the defect in the product involves only the quality of the product.
   c. a tort remedy is more appropriate when the product is hazardous.
   d. all of the above.

4. In an express warranty case, a plaintiff
   a. may not be able to recover unless she can show that she is not only a user but also a member of the general class of public that the manufacturer knew or should have known would have been reached by the warranty.
   b. must show that she believed the seller's representations.
   c. can recover for property damage and personal injuries but not consequential and incidental damages.
   d. all of the above.

5. An express warranty can be made by
   a. describing the good being warranted.
   b. affirming a fact or promise relating to the good.
   c. using a sample or model of the good in advertising.
   d. all of the above.

6. Bystanders probably cannot recover
   a. in an express-warranty case even if they can show they were a member of the general class of public that the manufacturer knew or should have known would have been reached by the warranty.
   b. in strict liability cases.
   c. in implied-warranty cases.
   d. all of the above.

7. A seller must know that the buyer wants to buy a good for a particular purpose and must make a recommendation to the buyer that the buyer relies on to create
   a. an express warranty.
   b. an implied warranty of merchantability.
   c. an implied warranty of fitness for a particular purpose.
   d. none of the above.

8. A direct purchaser suing based on an implied warranty can recover for
   a. property damage and personal injury.
   b. incidental and consequential damages.
   c. the difference between what the product would have been worth had it been as warranted and what it is worth with the defect.
   d. all of the above.

9. Breach-of-implied-warranty actions
   a. do not allow nonpurchasers to recover anything.
   b. can be brought against sellers of services and real estate.
   c. always allow remote purchasers to recover for pure economic loss.
   d. all of the above.

10. A warranty cause of action
    a. is easier to prove than strict liability.
    b. offers more generous damages to those whose damages are solely economic than a strict liability cause of action does.
    c. uses a tort statute of limitations.
    d. all of the above.

11. The provisions of section 402A of the *Restatement*
    a. have been adopted by very few courts.
    b. apply only to the sale of services.
    c. can be traced back to Judge Traynor's decision in *Greenman v. Yuba Products*.
    d. all of the above.

12. In strict liability cases
    a. the courts focus on whether the product is in a defective condition unreasonably dangerous.
    b. use both the consumer-expectation and risk-utility test.
    c. a product may be considered defective if it contains foreign objects.
    d. all of the above.

13. In a strict liability case
    a. a plaintiff is not required to prove cause in fact or proximate cause.
    b. an act will not be considered a superseding cause of the plaintiff's injury if the act was foreseeable.
    c. an act will be considered a superseding cause of the plaintiff's injury if the act was unforeseeable even if it caused the same type of harm that made the product dangerous.
    d. all of the above.

14. In strict liability cases
    a. courts are fairly liberal about letting plaintiffs pose the question to the jury on the issue of whether a defect existed at the time it left the manufacturer.
    b. the principles of res ipsa loquitur are inapplicable.
    c. consumers cannot sue if they have been injured while repairing or passively enjoying a product.
    d. all of the above.

15. Economic loss includes
    a. the cost of repairs.
    b. the cost of replacement.
    c. lost profits.
    d. all of the above.

16. The key issue in a design-defect case based on a strict liability standard
    a. is the reasonableness of the manufacturer in placing the product on the market.
    b. the expectations of the consumer.
    c. whether the plaintiff used the product in a way not intended by the manufacturer.
    d. all of the above.

17. In airbag cases
    a. the question is whether airbags are necessary to make cars safe in the event of an accident.
    b. consumer advocates and representatives of the auto manufacturers clash over the reliability and safety of airbags.
    c. the plaintiff must prove that the lack of airbags enhanced the severity and extent of the plaintiff's injuries.
    d. all of the above.

18. If a plaintiff injures himself while misusing a hammer, a court could
    a. conclude that the manufacturer had no duty to produce a hammer that could withstand this type of misuse.
    b. conclude that the plaintiff's actions were the proximate cause of his injuries.
    c. require that the defendant raise the plaintiff's misuse of the hammer as an affirmative defense.
    d. all of the above.

19. Assumption of risk is a defense in a
    a. warranty action.
    b. strict liability action.
    c. negligence action.
    d. all of the above.

20. A class action suit prevents
    a. the court system from being overloaded.
    b. some individual members from representing other members of the same class.
    c. plaintiffs with minimal recovery from being able to sue.
    d. all of the above.

PRACTICE POINTERS

Expert witnesses are an integral part of product liability suits because such suits are often complex and technical. At trial, experts can offer their opinions on relevant issues (e.g., the defectiveness of the product) and can educate jurors on technical matters. Before trial they are even more invaluable, for they can

- investigate facts, including
  - review medical and accident records.
  - inspect the product.
  - review records relating to the product's design or warnings.
  - analyze literature relating to injuries sustained using the product.
  - research industry standards.
  - conduct experiments.
- determine and evaluate alternate theories of defect or defenses.
- identify sources of facts, experts, and references.
- assist in preparation of and response to discovery.
- review documents produced by the opponent.

- assist in preparing for their own depositions as well as the depositions of witnesses called by the opposition.
- attend depositions of opposing experts.
- assist in attacking the credentials and methodology of the opposition's experts.
- provide the factual basis for motions for summary judgment and motions to dismiss.
- assist in preparing for cross-examination of the opposition's experts at trial.
- assist in cross-examination of the opposition's experts at trial.
- assist in preparing demonstrative evidence to be used at trial.

Legal assistants can help attorneys select and prepare experts. First, they can help the attorney identify a potential pool of experts by consulting trade journals, university rosters, client recommendations and recommendations from others in the profession or industry, and computer databases. The legal assistant can then review résumés and/or curricula vitae of candidates and weed out those who are unable to address the relevant issues. From this preliminary research, the legal assistant can recommend a list of potential candidates.

The legal assistant can also locate articles, case law, testimony from other lawsuits dealing with similar issues, and information about the opposition's expert witnesses. Once the expert has been retained, the legal assistant can compile relevant case materials on which the expert witness will base his or her opinion. Legal assistants can also help prepare the experts for their own depositions as well as for depositions of the opposition's expert witnesses.

The legal assistant should prepare a witness file in advance of trial. This file contains everything necessary to prepare the witness for testimony and to guide the attorney in examining the witness at trial. It should include the trial subpoena, deposition transcript and summary, attorney notes and memoranda of interviews, signed statements or affidavits, transcripts of deposition or trial testimony taken in other cases, and a memorandum that identifies the objectives of the examination and that arranges the areas within that examination in a logical sequence. This memorandum gives the attorney a starting point from which to prepare her examination of a witness and for her to prepare the witness for cross-examination by opposing counsel. An outline format enables the attorney to quickly read and grasp the key components of the examination.

To prepare the witness file, you need to outline the areas of inquiry during examination of the witness and attach the documents that are relevant to those areas. The headings of this outline should be succinct and should indicate the subjects and objectives of examination. Under each heading, list the subparts in their appropriate sequence and identify the exhibits (in sequence) by exhibit number and a brief description. Highlight critical passages in the documents, indicate the admissions and acknowledgments expected to be elicited on examination, and write a succinct description of the importance of the witness's statement. At the top of the page, identify the event to which the document relates or show the relationship between the document and preceding or subsequent exhibits. When preparing a file for a witness who is to be cross-examined include, for impeachment purposes, extracts from the witness's prior testimony.

TORT TEASERS

What type of defect would you argue exists in each of the following cases?

1. Plaintiff, a twenty-six-year-old woman, is given a prescription for oral contraceptives by her physician. The pill dispenser she receives is labeled with the warning "Oral contraceptives are powerful and effective drugs which can cause side effects in some users and should not be used at all by some women," and that "[t]he most serious known side effect is abnormal blood clotting which can be fatal." The warning also refers Plaintiff to a booklet that contains detailed information about the medication, including the increased risk to vital organs. The booklet specifically notes the possibility of the brain being damaged by abnormal blood clotting. The word "stroke" does not appear on the dispenser warning or in the booklet. Three years after commencing use of the pills, Plaintiff suffers a

disabling stroke. *MacDonald v. Ortho Pharmaceutical Corp.*, 475 N.E.2d 65 (Mass. 1985).

2. The petcock in the undercarriage of a bus is unprotected from debris on the road. One night while Plaintiff is driving his heavily overloaded bus down the highway, the petcock becomes disengaged by the debris, allowing the brakes to drain. The resultant brake failure causes an accident. *Carpini v. Pittsburgh & Weirton Bus Co.*, 216 F.2d 404 (3d Cir. 1954).

3. Plaintiff passenger suffered an injury to her right eye as the result of the deployment of an airbag during an accident. Plaintiff alleged that the airbag erroneously deployed in a low speed collision with excessive and dangerous force. *Gonzalez v. Autoliv ASP Inc.*, 154 Cal.App.4 780 (Cal.App. 2007).

In each of the following cases, which of the three theories of recovery (negligence, breach of warranty, or strict liability) would you use as a basis for recovery and why?

4. The District of Colombia and nine individuals who were wounded or represent decedents shot and killed by persons unlawfully using firearms filed suit against the manufacturer and distribution of firearms. Plaintiffs allege that Defendants have distributed firearms without adequate self-regulation to increase sales, while supplying the unlawful flow of firearms into the district. *District of Colombia v. Beretta, U.S.A., Corp.* 872 A.2d 633 (D.C. 2005).

5. After selling a plastic molding press to Company A, a manufacturer learns that the press has a dangerous tendency to crush the hands of people using it and that it violates state safety laws. When Company A sells the machine to Company B, the manufacturer learns of this transaction through repair records and offers Company B a safety device for the machine for $500. Company B declines this offer, and Plaintiff, one of its employees, gets her hand crushed. *Balido v. Improved Machinery, Inc.,* 105 Cal. Rptr. 890 (Ct. App. 1973).

6. Farmers who fed calves a non-medicated milk substitute filed a lawsuit against the manufacturer and distributor of milk substitute. The farmers alleged that the milk substitute damaged the calves' immune systems, resulting in poor growth and higher mortality. *Grams v. Milk Products, Inc.,* 699 NW 2d 167 (Wis. 2005).

What would you argue as the defendant in the following cases? How would you, as the plaintiff, respond to the defendant's arguments?

7. Plaintiff buys a car with a defective seat belt from Defendant. When Plaintiff brings the car back for a new belt Defendant tells him that nothing can be done until a new one is received from the factory. While waiting for the new belt, Plaintiff drives without a belt and is involved in an accident. *DeVaney v. Sarno,* 311 A.2d 208 (N.J. 1973).

8. A strict liability claim is brought against the manufacturer of the Opel automobile on behalf of a driver who is killed as a result of an alleged defect in the door latch. The evidence shows that the driver was not using a shoulder harness, did not lock the door, and was intoxicated at the time of the accident. *Daly v. General Motors Corp.,* 575 P.2d 1172 (Cal. 1978).

9. Plaintiff alleges she developed a debilitating and incurable neurological condition due to consumption of a generic prescription drug. Plaintiff filed a lawsuit against the manufacturer and several of its generic manufacturer competitors asserting that the manufacturer's product warnings failed to warn consumers of the long-term use of the drug. *Conte v. Wyeth, Inc.,* 85 Cal.Rptr.3d 299 (2008).

10. Recall the hypothetical problem posed at the beginning of this chapter, and answer these questions:

a. Which of the three theories of recovery would you use if you decided to sue the doctor and the sperm bank? What would be the reasoning underlying your choice?

b. Outline the elements you would have to prove if you decided to sue on the basis of negligence. Then do the same for warranty and strict liability.

c. Develop a list of questions you would want to ask your potential clients, Tom and Susan, at the initial interview.

d. Draft some interrogatories that you would want to submit to the sperm bank.

e. Compile a list of questions you would want to submit to a doctor you are thinking about using as an expert witness.

f. Prepare a list of the documents and correspondence you would want to request during discovery from Dr. Payne and the sperm bank.

INTERNET INQUIRIES

Expert witnesses have become an essential part of today's litigation practice. They are used as both consultants to assist attorneys in preparing for trial and as witnesses at the trial itself. Although the actual selection of experts is the responsibility of the attorney, paralegals are often given the task of finding potential experts for the attorney to interview.

Organizations like the American Association for Justice (AAJ) (http://www.atlanet.org), which is an organization

for plaintiffs' attorneys, and the Defense Research Institute (DRI) (http://www.dri.org/), which is an organization for defense counsel, maintain lists of experts. Additionally, they provide links to state and local organizations that are also able to identify experts. Two of the best known private companies that facilitate the location of experts are Technical Advisory Service for Attorneys (better known as TASA—http://www.tasanet.com) and Technical Assistance Bureau (TAB—http://www.tabexperts.com), which locates medical experts. Both companies charge a fee for finding an appropriate expert.

Internet resources abound for finding expert testimony. Some of these sites provide free access to experts while others require a fee. One way to find recommended sites is to go to the Web page for your local bar association. On this page you can usually find law-related links that will take you to any number of sites for expert witnesses. The National Federation of Paralegal Associations (NFPA) also has a link to directories for experts on its Web page (http://www.paralegals.org).

1. Use the Internet to find experts in your area in reference to school violence. You will want to focus on the topic of psychology, being especially alert for psychologists who specialize in the areas that relate to violence in the schools. First go to the web page for your local bar association and look for links to sites for finding expert witnesses. Now visit at least five different links and look for experts in reference to violence in schools. Then answer the following questions:

a. For which sites did you find the names and contact information for experts on school violence?

b. For which sites did you have to pay or have a password to get the names of experts on school violence?

c. For which sites were you able to link to a web page for the experts in whom you were interested?

d. After reviewing these sites, write down the names and web addresses of the ones you think would be most helpful in finding expert witnesses. After the name of each site, write a brief summary of the information available on that site.

2. Go to the web page for NOCALL (Northern Association of California Law Libraries) at http://www.nocall.org/ and select "Internet Resources," then "Expert Witnesses." Go to at least three of the links listed. Find the names of three experts in school violence that are available in your state or in a nearby state. Summarize the information you are able to gather about each of these experts.

PRACTICAL PONDERABLES

Your firm has a client, Ken, who purchased an Arabian stallion from Ellie Arabians. His intent was to use the stallion to enhance his breeding program, but in the first year that he used the stallion, only one of the mares "settled" (got pregnant) and in the second only two of ten mares settled. Ken had the stallion's sperm analyzed and discovered that it has an abnormally low sperm count. In essence, the stallion is not fit for breeding purposes. Ken wants to sue Ellie Arabians and recover his losses.

1. What theories of recovery do you think should be used, and why? What research will need to be done to answer this question?

2. What kind of defect do you think should be alleged?

3. What defenses do you anticipate Ellie Arabians will raise?

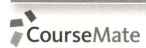 **CourseMate** Access an interactive eBook, chapter-specific learning tools, including flashcards, quizzes, and more in your Paralegal CourseMate, accessed through www. CengageBrain.com.

CHAPTER 13

Defamation and Related Torts

© Cengage Learning 2012

CHAPTER TOPICS

Libel versus Slander

What Is a Defamatory Statement?

Privileges

Defamation on the Web

Invasion of Privacy

Injurious Falsehood

CHAPTER OBJECTIVES

After completing the chapter, you should be able to

- Distinguish between libel and slander.
- Identify the elements of defamation and the damages that can be recovered.
- Recognize the importance of distinguishing between private and public figures.
- Distinguish between absolute and qualified privileges of defendants.
- Distinguish among the four torts that are considered an invasion of privacy and identify the elements of each.
- Identify the tort of injurious falsehood and distinguish between slander of title and trade libel.

The headlines of the *National Snoop* proclaim that the current "heartthrob" of a daytime soap opera has impregnated his costar. In reality, the young lady is indeed pregnant. Further adding fuel to this story is the fact that in real life the couple has been seen together on several occasions. The actor, however, vehemently denies that he is the father of the child. What would he have to show if he wanted to claim libel? Suppose that stories of his purported fatherhood circulate around the studio but are never published. Will he have any more difficulty proving slander than he will proving libel? Let us consider the elements of defamation and the distinction between libel and slander as we attempt to answer these questions.

LIBEL VERSUS SLANDER

Defamation, which is defined as an invasion of the reputation of a person or group resulting from libel or slander (as defined in the following pages), is a complex tort. Some of its complexity stems from the courts' struggle to balance freedom of expression against protection of the individual's reputation. Before the key case in this area, *New York Times Co. v. Sullivan*, 376 U.S. 254 (1964), the United States Supreme Court had held that defamatory statements were outside the protection of the First Amendment and that defamation was primarily a matter of state law. In limiting states' power to establish their own defamation laws, *New York Times* dramatically shifted the course of defamation law and, in the opinion of some critics, struck a balance that gives too much latitude to media defendants.

The *New York Times* court found "a profound national commitment to the principle that debate on public issues should be uninhibited, robust, and wide-open, and that it may well include vehement, caustic, and sometimes unpleasantly sharp attacks on government and public officials." Consequently, the Court created a federal rule that required public officials to prove that defamatory statements made relating to their official conduct were made with **actual malice**—reckless disregard for the truth or with knowledge that the statement is false. (Actual malice is discussed further later on in this chapter.) Under the common law plaintiffs could essentially prove defamation if they could show that the defendant's statements were false. The Court's concern was that such a "rule compelling the critic of official conduct to guarantee the truth of all his factual assertions—and to do so in face of libel judgments virtually unlimited in amount—leads to 'self-censorship.'"

Today the key features that shape defamation law are the status of the plaintiff (public official or public figure versus private individual) and the subject matter of the statement (public issue versus private). These features determine which standard of proof a plaintiff must meet to recover damages.

Keep in mind, however, that no matter how much controversy swirls around this area of the law, defamation is extremely difficult to prove and does not warrant litigation unless the damages are substantial. Few cases are actually litigated, and of those that are, especially those against media defendants, many are lost. In fact, the number of libel suits involving the media has declined in recent years, and the rate of defense wins at trial has risen since 1990. (According to the *Libel Defense Resource Center Bulletin*, Jan. 31, 1994, media defendants won 26.3 percent of jury trials in the 1980s and 45.5 percent of jury trials in 1992–1993.) Although the media are concerned about what they perceive as the chilling effects of defamation reform, because they contend such reform will result in less aggressive reporting and the avoidance of controversial topics, the average American is unlikely ever to be involved in a defamation suit.

Defamation encompasses the two related torts of libel and slander (see Exhibit 13–1). **Libel** refers

EXHIBIT 13–1   Libel versus Slander

LIBEL	SLANDER
• Statements are written (including records, computer tapes, dictation by stenographer). • No need to prove special harm. • Presumed damages awarded if (a) actual malice is shown in matter of public concern or (b) matter is a private concern, even if no actual malice is shown.	• Statements are oral. • Must prove special harm unless slander per se. • Presumed damages not awarded.

to written defamatory statements; **slander** refers to oral statements. Libel encompasses communications occurring in "physical form" (according to many modern courts and the *Restatement [Second]*). Under this definition defamatory statements on records and computer tapes are considered libel rather than slander. Spoken words that are intended to be written down, such as words dictated to a stenographer, are also categorized as libel. A radio or television program that originates from a written script is considered libel, but the courts do not agree about how to classify a program that is "ad-libbed."

Special Harm

The distinction between libel and slander is sometimes blurred, but it is a significant one. To prove slander a plaintiff must establish that she suffered some kind of **special harm**, meaning harm of a **pecuniary** (monetary) nature. Loss of friendship and emotional upset are not generally considered to have pecuniary value. However, if a plaintiff is able to prove pecuniary loss, she can attach emotional damages to her pecuniary loss.

Special harm need not necessarily be proved in the case of libel.

Four exceptions to the special-harm requirement for slander exist. In these four cases of **slander per se** pecuniary harm can be assumed. The four categories encompass statements alleging (1) that the plaintiff engaged in criminal behavior; (2) that the plaintiff suffers from some type of venereal or otherwise loathsome and communicable disease; (3) that the plaintiff is unfit to conduct his or her business, trade, or profession; and (4) that the plaintiff has engaged in sexual misconduct.

Under the common law, special harm did not have to be proved, and damages were presumed in cases of libel in which the defamatory nature of the statement was obvious. **Presumed damages** are those damages that ordinarily flow from defamation, thereby precluding the necessity of the plaintiff proving actual harm. If damages are presumed, a plaintiff can recover an amount that approximates the damages that normally result from a defamatory statement like the one made by the defendant. Recovery is allowed even though the plaintiff produces no evidence of any actual harm, such as loss of business or friends.

Supreme Court decisions, however, have substantially limited the courts in their right to award presumed damages. In cases involving matters of public concern, a plaintiff cannot be awarded presumed damages if he is unable to prove "actual malice" (*Gertz v. Robert Welch, Inc.*, 418 U.S. 323 [1974]). A defendant who acts with actual malice either knows the falsity of his statement or acts with reckless disregard in reference to the truth or falsity of his statement. If the plaintiff is able to prove actual malice, then presumed damages may be awarded. In matters involving purely private concerns, the plaintiff can recover presumed damages even without a showing of actual malice.

WHAT IS A DEFAMATORY STATEMENT?

The *Restatement (Second) of Torts* defines a statement as being defamatory if it tends to harm one's reputation, thereby lowering her in the estimation of the community or deterring others from associating with her (see Exhibit 13–2). Defamation requires proof that the defendant's statement was defamatory and that it was *published*, that is, communicated to someone other than the plaintiff. Furthermore, the defendant must, at the very least, act negligently (although a greater degree of fault is required under certain circumstances).

PUTTING IT INTO PRACTICE 13:1

1 A news broadcaster falsely announces that a famous actor has AIDS. Has the actor been libeled or slandered?

2 A wax figure representing Sam is displayed in a "Chamber of Horrors" that depicts figures of several famous murderers. The exhibition is shown for several months. Has Sam been libeled or slandered?

3 Louis makes a gesture at Andrew indicating that Shari carries the "evil eye," which is highly disparaged in their community. Has Louis libeled or slandered Shari?

© Cengage Learning 2012

EXHIBIT 13-2 *Elements of Defamation*

- Plaintiff's reputation is harmed or tended to be harmed.
- Statement is reasonably interpreted by at least one person as referring to plaintiff.
- At least one interpretation of statement could reasonably be considered defamatory.
- Statement is false.
- Statement is seen or heard by someone other than plaintiff (publication).
- Defendant acts with actual malice (if plaintiff is a public official or public figure).

Harm to Reputation

To be considered defamatory, a statement must have a tendency to harm the reputation of the plaintiff (*Restatement [Second] of Torts* § 559). The plaintiff's reputation need not actually be injured. A statement is sufficiently harmful if the plaintiff's reputation would have been injured if those who heard the statement had believed it. Therefore, even if everyone who hears a defamatory statement believes it to be false, this statement can still be considered defamatory.

A plaintiff may recover even if his reputation is tarnished in the eyes of only a certain segment of a community, as long as the segment consists of a significant and "respectable" minority of people. In one case, for example, the defendant mistakenly published the plaintiff's picture next to a testimonial signed by a nurse praising the medicinal merits of Duffy's pure malt whiskey. As Judge Holmes noted, "If the advertisement obviously would hurt the plaintiff in the estimation of an important and respectable part of the community, liability is not a question of majority vote" (*Peck v. Tribune Co.*, 214 U.S. 185, 190 [1909]). Nonetheless, the statement must contain some element of "disgrace." Although referring to a Democrat as a Libertarian, for example, might engender some feelings of hostility, such a statement could not be construed as defamatory.

Reasonable Interpretation

The plaintiff must also prove that the statement was reasonably understood by at least one person as referring to the plaintiff. The defendant need not refer to the plaintiff, but someone must interpret the statement as pertaining to the plaintiff. Furthermore, the defendant need not refer to the plaintiff by name as long as it is reasonably understood to whom the defendant is referring. A plaintiff will often have a difficult time recovering if the defendant's statement is made in reference to a group to which the plaintiff belongs. The statement probably will not be considered defamatory unless the group is a relatively small one.

Burden of Proving Truth

Statements can often be interpreted in several different ways. The plaintiff must show that the statement is defamatory in accordance with at least one interpretation that a reasonable person might make, and must also prove that at least one person interpreted it in a defamatory way. Before the jury can declare a statement defamatory, a judge must first determine that the statement is subject to at least one reasonable interpretation that is defamatory.

To illustrate this point, consider the case involving the famous attorney Melvin Belli, in which a newspaper alleged that, while on an expense-paid appearance before the Florida bar, Belli "took" the bar by charging hundreds of dollars' worth of clothing to his hotel bill. The trial judge ruled that the statement was not defamatory and refused to submit the case to the jury. The appellate court, however, held that the statement had a clear defamatory meaning (indicating Belli was dishonest) as well as a nondefamatory meaning (indicating Belli was clever) and that the case should have been submitted to the jury (*Belli v. Orlando Daily Newspapers, Inc.*, 389 F.2d 579 [5th Cir. 1967]).

Contrast *Belli* with a case involving the ex-wife of Jerry Solomon, who later married Nancy Kerrigan, the well-known figure skater. The *National Enquirer* published an article entitled "Nancy Kerrigan in Love Nest with Married Man." The paper attributed the following quotation to the plaintiff: "Nancy Kerrigan stole my husband! She's a home-wrecker—a witch who deserves to burn in hell!" The plaintiff contended that the statements in the *Enquirer* portrayed her as a "woman who is so hateful, contemptuous, and bitter that she would blasphemously call forth damnation

NET NEWS

A copy of an article regarding the impact of The Communication Decency Act on online student publications is located at **http://www.splc.org**. Enter "Know Your Cybershield" as your search term.

PUTTING IT INTO PRACTICE 13:2

The *National Enquirer* publishes an article with the headline "Night That Turned Mom Into Killer." The article pertains to Susan Smith, the young mother who publicly maintained that her two young sons had been abducted and later admitted that she had drowned them by allowing her vehicle to roll down into a lake with her children strapped inside. A smaller headline reads "Shocking scene in bar with her lover just hours before she drowned her babies." A photo of the plaintiff appears above type that reads "BAR MANAGER Lorinda Robins says she knew something was wrong."

The article describes Smith's visit to the local bar where Lorinda was working, telling how Tom Findlay, Smith's former lover, had kidded with Lorinda in Smith's presence about a prior affair he and Lorinda had had. Lorinda is quoted as saying, "We were just cutting up. But I guess maybe Susan misunderstood. She abruptly got up and walked out." In the article Lorinda speculates that "when I think about that night, I'm convinced that's what pushed her over the edge." Two psychiatrists quoted in the article agree that the episode in the bar could have contributed to Smith's murder of her children the following day.

Lorinda argues that the article implicates her as being at least partially responsible for the deaths of Susan Smith's children. Do you think Lorinda has been defamed?

---

on another person." The court found the plaintiff's contention "far-fetched to say the least," noting that "it strains credulity to believe that others in the community would read the article as literally as Plaintiff apparently has." The court denied the plaintiff's claim, finding her interpretation of the published statement to be unreasonable as a matter of law (*Solomon v. National Enquirer*, 1996 WL 635384 [D. Md. 1996]).

Sometimes the defamatory content of a statement may not be recognizable unless certain extrinsic facts are known. A birth announcement, for example, may not be defamatory on its face, but if the recipient of that announcement is made aware that the plaintiff has been married for only six months then the defamatory implications become clearer. The plaintiff must specifically show in his pleadings the **innuendo**, which refers to the way in which the extrinsic facts convey a defamatory meaning. The plaintiff in the case pertaining to the birth announcement would be required to allege that because of the fact that the plaintiff had been married

for only six months, the birth announcement created a false impression that the plaintiff had been unchaste prior to marriage.

A statement must be obviously false to be considered defamatory. A statement that is substantially true—even though it may not be literally true in all respects—is considered a true statement. Under the common law the defendant had the burden of proving the truth of her statement. Supreme Court decisions, however, have limited a state's ability to require the defendant to bear such a burden. Today the plaintiff bears the burden of proving that a statement was false if the statement involves a matter of "public interest" and the defendant is a media defendant (*Philadelphia Newspapers v. Hepps*, 106 U.S. 1558 [1986]). Even plaintiffs who are private figures must bear this burden of proof. Whether a defendant may be required to bear the burden of proving the truth of the statements if the statements are not of public interest and the plaintiff is a private figure is not clear.

NET NEWS

An article about defamation in the workplace titled "Are You a Victim of Workplace Defamation" can be found at http://www.faceintel.com. Select Defamation, Libel, Slander.

Who Can Be Defamed?

Only living persons can be defamed. Therefore, survivors of the deceased cannot sue for defamation because of statements made against the deceased. If the words defame a living person by implication, however, recovery is allowed. For example, a statement that the deceased was unwed when she gave birth to her child tends to defame that child. A corporation, partnership, or association can be defamed only if the statement "tends to prejudge it in the course of its business or to deter others from dealing with it" (*Restatement [Second] of Torts* §§ 561 and 562).

Opinion

Under the common law an opinion could be defamatory unless it fell under the privilege of "fair comment" i.e., the expression was an opinion on a matter of public concern. Supreme Court decisions point to the conclusion that a pure expression of opinion cannot be defamatory (*Restatement [Second] of Torts* § 566 cmt. c). A statement that implies factual matters, however, can be considered defamatory.

The difference between fact and opinion is not always clear, but the courts look at a number of factors in making that distinction. The more precise a statement is, the more likely a court will consider it a fact. A statement that is almost impossible to verify is likely to be considered an opinion. The literary context in which the statement is made is also considered. Readers are generally assumed to understand, for example, that statements made by reviewers constitute opinion rather than objectively verifiable facts. Statements implying undisclosed facts may be actionable even though they are opinions. A statement such as, "I think George is an alcoholic" may be defamatory even though the declarant is apparently expressing an opinion. The implication from the statement is that the declarant knows or has factual information about George's alcohol consumption that would justify rendering an opinion as to George's alcoholic condition (*Restatement [Second] of Torts* § 566, illus. 3).

Suppose, however, someone says, "George has lived in this house for a year. Every night I see him with a drink in his hand. I think he must be an alcoholic." This statement offers facts upon which the opinion is based and does not imply other facts. Because the facts are not defamatory, the statement is not defamatory (*Restatement [Second] of Torts* § 566, illus. 4).

Publication

The term **publication**, when used in the context of defamation, is a term of art requiring that the statement be seen or heard by someone other than the plaintiff. The publication may be intentional or negligent. Merely overhearing a statement made by the defendant to the plaintiff does not constitute publication. The publication must also be understood by the person who hears it. A defamatory statement made in a language not understood to the person hearing it does not meet the requirement of publication.

Repetition of a defamatory statement is considered publication. One who repeats a statement is just as liable as if he were the first person to make the statement, even if the one repeating the statement does not believe it to be true (*Restatement [Second] of Torts* § 578 cmt. e). Those who distribute or sell defamatory matter, such as news dealers and libraries, are not liable if they can show they had no reason to believe that the materials were defamatory. Under the *single-publication rule* most courts hold that an entire edition of a book or periodical should be treated as one publication. Therefore, even if several copies of a book are sold, only one defamation can be alleged.

Intent

Under the common law, defamation was essentially a strict liability tort, because defendants could be liable even if they had every reason to believe that a statement they made was true. That situation has changed, however, with United States Supreme Court decisions. In the Court's first landmark decision in this area, *New York Times Co. v. Sullivan*, 376 U.S. 254 (1964), discussed earlier in this chapter, it held that if a plaintiff is a public official, she can recover only by showing that the defendant acted with actual malice. *Actual malice*, also discussed earlier, is defined as having the knowledge that a statement is false or acting with "reckless disregard" for the truth or falsity of the statement. Note that this definition differs from the lay meaning of the term, which normally implies some type of ill will. *Reckless disregard* has been defined as evidence indicating that the defendant in fact "entertained serious doubts" as to the truth of her statements (*St. Amant v. Thompson*, 390 U.S. 727 [1969]).

The actual-malice requirement was extended to public figures in a later case. The Supreme Court defined a **public figure** as "one who has achieved pervasive fame or notoriety" or who "voluntarily injects himself or

PUTTING IT INTO PRACTICE 13:3

Melba Moore, an entertainer, goes on the Maury Povich show and engages in a lively discussion with members of the panel (a divorce attorney, a marital counselor, and members of the studio audience). Povich introduces her by saying that she has recently come out of an acrimonious divorce and that she is now destitute and applying for welfare. The subject of the show is divorce and its financial aftermath. Some of the dialogue is as follows:

"(1) MAURY POVITCH: Or you have applied for welfare, I don't know..."

MELBA MOORE: I've, I've applied for welfare and I have been accepted and I just came from the Human Resources Office, where I put in a petition for child support enforcement, because my husband is, he's only been required to pay two hundred dollars a week, and it's very erratic. But I got to this position because my husband was my manager, we had a company called Hush Productions, and he got a fraudulent, secret divorce from me....

* * *

(8) MELBA MOORE: Extremely well. My husband is a multi-millionaire.

MAURY POVICH: How do you know that?

MELBA MOORE: Well, I can't prove that, but we lived down the street from each other because he wasn't able to get me out of my apartment. We have a multi-million dollar building at 231 West 58th Street. That's just one asset.

MAURY POVICH: And that's supposed to be part of... that's supposed to be... are, are you on the deed for that, too... on the title for that?

MELBA MOORE: Well, as part of the, of the partnership, I should share in something...

MAURY POVICH: And you feel you're sharing in nothing?

Moore's husband sues her for defamation. Based on the preceding statements only, do you think he has a cause of action against her?

---

is drawn into a particular public controversy" (*Gertz v. Robert Welch, Inc.*, 418 U.S. 323 [1974]). In *Gertz* the plaintiff was a locally well-known lawyer who represented the family of a young man killed by a policeman. The defendant, publisher of a John Birch Society magazine, falsely accused the plaintiff of being a criminal and a Communist. The court held that a person does not become a public figure merely because he becomes involved in a controversy of public interest. Therefore, the plaintiff in *Gertz* was not a public figure merely because the newspapers took an interest in the lawsuit. The *Gertz* court's reasoning for giving less protection to public figures was that those in the public eye "usually enjoy significantly greater access to the channels of effective communication and hence have a more realistic

opportunity to counteract false statements than private individuals normally enjoy." Whether *New York Times* and *Gertz* apply to nonmedia defendants is not clear.

The public-figure issue arose when Robert Jewell, a security guard in Atlanta, sued the *Atlanta Journal-Constitution* for defamation after becoming a suspect in the bombing that occurred at the Olympic Games (*Atlanta Journal-Constitution v. Jewell*, 555 S.E.2d 175 [Ga. Ct. App. 2001]). Initially, Jewell assisted law enforcement in evacuating buildings after he spotted a suspicious-looking package. Following the explosion Jewell granted one photo shoot and ten interviews, most of them to prominent members of the national press. He was in demand enough to require the assistance of a media handler to coordinate his appearances.

Jewell claims he gave interviews only to accommodate his employer and that he never intended to influence the outcome of the controversy. Whether an individual has voluntarily injected himself into a public controversy cannot be determined solely by reference to his subjective motives, however. The question is whether a reasonable person would have concluded that Jewell would play or was seeking to play a major role in affecting the outcome of the controversy. The appellate court concluded that, viewed objectively, the evidence was sufficient to support the trial court's finding that Jewell was a public figure. His repeated comments regarding the appropriateness of law enforcement's response to the bombing and his attempts to improve the public's perception of security at the park could realistically be expected to have an impact on the controversy's resolution. The court observed that people can become involved in public controversies and affairs without their consent. Jewell, by virtue of being in the vicinity of a tragedy, had the misfortune of being just such a person.

The public-figure issue is discussed at length in *Street v. National Broadcasting Co.*, a historically interesting case that emanates from the famous "Scottsboro Boys" case involving the alleged rape of two white women by nine black youths. Once the *Street* court concludes that the plaintiff is a public figure, it is faced with the question of how long she retains that status. Pay particular attention to the court's public policy arguments, and note its application of the actual-malice standard.

If a plaintiff is neither a public official nor a public figure, the Constitution does not require that he prove actual malice. Strict liability, however, is not sufficient. The plaintiff must, at the very least, prove that the defendant acted negligently.

CASE

Street v. National Broadcasting Co.
645 F.2d 1227 (6th Cir. 1981)

MERRITT, Circuit Judge.

This is a Tennessee diversity case against the National Broadcasting Company for libel and invasion of privacy. The plaintiff-appellant, Victoria Price Street, was the prosecutrix and main witness in the famous rape trials of the Scottsboro boys, which occurred in Alabama more than forty years ago. NBC televised a play or historical drama entitled "Judge Horton and the Scottsboro Boys," dramatizing the role of the local presiding judge in one of those trials.

The movie portrays Judge Horton as a courageous and tragic figure struggling to bring justice in a tense community gripped by racial prejudice and intent on vengeance against nine blacks accused of raping two white women. In the movie Judge Horton sets aside a jury verdict of guilty because he believes that the evidence shows that the prosecutrix—plaintiff in this action—falsely accused the Scottsboro defendants. The play portrays the plaintiff in the derogatory light that Judge Horton apparently viewed her: as a woman attempting to send nine innocent blacks to the electric chair for a rape they did not commit.

This case presents the question of what tort and First Amendment principles apply to an historical drama that allegedly defames a living person who participated in the historical events portrayed. The plaintiff's case is based on principles of libel law and "false light" invasion of privacy[1] arising from the derogatory portrayal.

At the end of all the proof, District Judge Neese directed a verdict for defendant on the ground that even though plaintiff was not a public figure at the time of publication the defamatory matter was not negligently published. We affirm for the reason that the historical events and persons portrayed are "public" and distinguished from "private." A malice standard applies to public figures under the First Amendment, and there is no evidence that the play was published with malice.

I. STATEMENT OF FACTS
A. Historical Context

In April 1931, nine black youths were accused of raping two young white women while riding a freight train between Chattanooga, Tennessee, and Huntsville, Alabama. The case was widely discussed in the local, national, and foreign press. The youths were quickly tried in Scottsboro, Alabama, and all were found

---

1. False light invasion of privacy is one of four generally recognized forms of the tort of invasion of privacy. It differs from the other three forms in that falsity is one of its essential elements.

(continues)

guilty and sentenced to death. The Alabama Supreme Court affirmed the convictions.... The United States Supreme Court reversed all convictions on the ground that the defendants were denied the right to counsel guaranteed by the Sixth Amendment. *Powell v. Alabama*, 287 U.S. 45, 53 S.Ct. 55, 77 L.Ed. 158 (1932). The defendants were retried separately after a change of venue from Scottsboro to Decatur, Alabama. Patterson was the first defendant retried, and this trial was the subject of the NBC production. In a jury trial before Judge Horton, he was tried, convicted, and sentenced to death. Judge Horton set the verdict aside on the ground that the evidence was insufficient. Patterson and one other defendant, Norris, were then tried before another judge on essentially the same evidence, convicted, and sentenced to death. The judge let the verdicts stand, and the convictions were affirmed by the Alabama Supreme Court.... The United States Supreme Court again reversed, this time because blacks were systematically excluded from grand and petit juries.... At his fourth retrial, Patterson was convicted and sentenced to seventy-five years in prison.... Defendants Weems and Andrew Wright were also convicted on retrial and sentenced to a term of years. Defendant Norris was convicted and his death sentence was commuted to life imprisonment by the Alabama governor. Defendants Montgomery, Roberson, Williams, and Leroy Wright were released without retrial. Powell pled guilty to assault allegedly committed during an attempted escape. The last Scottsboro defendant was paroled in 1950.

The Scottsboro case aroused strong passions and conflicting opinions in the 1930s throughout the nation. Several all white juries convicted the Scottsboro defendants of rape. Two trial judges and the Alabama Supreme Court, at times by divided vote, let these verdicts stand. Judge Horton was the sole trial judge to find the facts in favor of the defendants. Liberal opinion supported Judge Horton's conclusions that the Scottsboro defendants had been falsely accused.

During the lengthy course of the Scottsboro trials, newspapers frequently wrote about Victoria Price. She gave some interviews to the press. Thereafter, she disappeared from public view. The Scottsboro trials and her role in them continued to be the subject of public discussion, but there is no evidence that Mrs. Street sought publicity. NBC incorrectly stated in the movie that she was no longer living. After the first showing of "Judge Horton and the Scottsboro Boys," plaintiff notified NBC that she was living, and shortly thereafter she filed suit. Soon after plaintiff filed suit, NBC rebroadcast the dramatization omitting the statement that plaintiff was no longer living.

B. The Dramatization

The script for "Judge Horton and the Scottsboro Boys" was based on one chapter of a book by Dr. Daniel Carter, an historian, entitled *Scottsboro: A Tragedy of the American South* (Louisiana State University Press, 1969). The movie is based almost entirely on the information in Dr. Carter's book, which, in turn, was based on Judge Horton's findings at the 1933 trial, the transcript of the trial, contemporaneous newspaper reports of the trial, and interviews with Judge Horton and others. NBC purchased the movie from an independent producer.

Plaintiff's major libel and invasion of privacy claims are based on nine scenes in the movie in which she is portrayed in a derogatory light. The essential facts concerning these claims are as follows:

1. After an opening prologue, black and white youths are shown fighting on a train. The train is halted, and the blacks are arrested. The next scene shows plaintiff standing next to Ruby Bates at the tracks. Plaintiff claims that this scene, in effect, makes her a perjurer because she testified at the 1933 trial and in this case that she fainted while alighting from the train and did not regain consciousness until she was taken to a local grocery store. Judge Horton, in his opinion sustaining the motion for a new trial, found that the observations of other witnesses and the testimony of the examining doctor contradicted her testimony in this respect. Horton concluded that it was unlikely that Victoria Price had fainted.

2. As plaintiff and Ruby Bates are led away from the tracks by the sheriff and his men, the sheriff in the play calls the two women a "couple of bums." There is no indication in Judge Horton's opinion, in the 1933 trial transcript, or in Dr. Carter's book that this comment was actually made.

3. In a pretrial conversation between two lawyers representing the defendant, the play portrays one of them as advising restraint in the cross-examination of plaintiff Price. He says to the other defense lawyer: "The Scottsboro transcripts are really clear.... The defense at the last trial made one thing very clear, Victoria was a whore, and they got it in the neck for it...." (Emphasis added.) There is no evidence that this specific conversation between the two defense lawyers actually occurred. Dr. Carter does state in his book that one of the purposes of the defense in cross-examining plaintiff was to discredit her testimony by introducing evidence that she was a common prostitute....

4. Plaintiff in this action contends that the movie falsely portrays her as defensive and evasive during her direct and cross-examination. Judge Horton found

(continues)

in his 1933 opinion granting a new trial that plaintiff was not a cooperative witness: "Her manner of testifying and her demeanor on the stand militate against her. Her testimony was contradictory, often evasive, and time and again she refused to answer pertinent questions."

5. Plaintiff claims that the last question put to her on cross-examination in the play is inaccurate. In the movie the defense attorney asks: "One more question: have you ever heard of a white woman being arrested for perjury when she was the complaining witness against Negroes in the entire history of the state of Alabama?" According to the 1933 trial transcript, the actual question was, "I want to ask you if you have ever heard of any single white woman ever being locked up in jail when she is the complaining witness against Negroes in the history of the state of Alabama?" Plaintiff objects to the insertion of the word "perjury" in the play.

6. In the play, Dr. Marvin Lynch, one of the doctors who examined plaintiff after she alighted from the train, approaches Judge Horton outside the courtroom and confides that he does not believe that the two women were raped by the Scottsboro boys. Dr. Lynch refuses to go on the witness stand and so testify, however. Plaintiff argues that this scene is improper because it is not supported in the 1933 trial record. This is true. Neither the 1933 trial transcript nor Judge Horton's opinion make reference to this incident. The Carter book does state, however, that Judge Horton told the author in a later interview that this incident occurred. . . .

7. The play portrays events leading up to plaintiff's trip to Chattanooga with her friend, Ruby Bates. It was on the return trip to Alabama that the rape alleged occurred. Lester Carter, a defense witness in the play, testifies that he had intercourse with Ruby Bates on the night before the trip to Chattanooga and the plaintiff had intercourse with Jack Tiller. During the testimony there is a flashback that shows an exchange in a boxcar in which Ruby Bates suggests that they all go to Chattanooga and plaintiff says, "[m]aybe Ruby and me could hustle there while you two [Carter and Tiller] got some kind of fill-in work. What do you say?" This is an accurate abridgement of the substance of the actual testimony of Lester Carter at the 1933 trial, although Price denied, both at the 1933 trial and in the defamation trial below, that she had had intercourse with Tiller. Judge Horton specifically found that she did not tell the truth. The dramatization quoted or closely paraphrased substantial portions of Judge Horton's 1933 opinion. Judge Horton concluded that the testimony of Victoria Price "is not only uncorroborated, but is contradicted by other evidence," evidence that "greatly preponderates in favor of the defendant":

When we consider, as the facts hereafter detailed will show, that this woman had slept side by side with a man the night before [the alleged rape] in Chattanooga, and had intercourse at Huntsville with Tiller on the night before she went to Chattanooga. . . . the conclusion becomes clearer and clearer that this woman was not forced into intercourse with all of these Negroes upon the train, but that her condition [the presence of dead sperm in her vagina] was clearly due to the intercourse that she had on the nights previous in this time.

8. Lester Carter also testifies in the play that plaintiff urged him to say that he had seen her raped. The 1933 trial transcript reveals that Carter actually testified that he overheard plaintiff tell another white youth that "if you don't testify according to what I testify I will see that you are took off the witness stand. . . ." Judge Horton in his opinion observed that there was evidence presented at the trial showing that Price encouraged others to support her version of what had happened.

9. Another witness in the play, Dallas Ramsey, testifies that he saw plaintiff and Ruby Bates in a "hobo jungle" near the train tracks in Chattanooga the night before the train trip back to Alabama. Ramsey testifies that plaintiff states that she and her husband were looking for work and that "her old man" was uptown scrounging for food. The play dramatizes Ramsey's testimony while he is on the stand by a flashback to the scene at the "hobo jungle." The flashback gives the impression that plaintiff is perhaps inviting sexual advances from Ramsey, although the words used do not state this specifically. The substance of Ramsey's testimony, as portrayed in the play, is found in the 1933 trial transcript. The record provides no basis for the suggestive flashback.

The facts recited above illustrate that the play does cast plaintiff in an extremely derogatory light. She is portrayed as a perjurer, a woman of bad character, a woman who falsely accused the Scottsboro boys of rape knowing that the result would likely be the electric chair. The play is a gripping and effective portrayal of its point of view about her, the Scottsboro boys, and Judge Horton. As an effective dramatic production, the play has won many awards, including the George Foster Peabody Award for playwriting and awards from the Screenwriters' Guild and the American Bar Association. . . .

III. THE FIRST AMENDMENT DEFENSES
A. Plaintiff was a Public Figure During the Scottsboro Trials

Since common law defenses do not support the directed verdict for NBC, we must reach the constitutional issues, particularly the question whether plaintiff should

(continues)

be characterized as a "public figure." In *Gertz*, the Supreme Court held that one characterized as a "public figure," as distinguished from a private individual, "may recover for injury to reputation *only on clear and convincing proof* that the defamatory falsehood was made with *knowledge of its falsity or with reckless disregard for the truth*." ... (emphasis added). In balancing the need to protect "private personality" and reputation against the need "to assure to the freedoms of speech and press that 'breathing space' essential to their free exercise," the Supreme Court has developed a general test to determine public figure status.

Gertz establishes a two-step analysis to determine if an individual is a public figure. First, does a "public controversy" exist? Second, what is "the nature and extent of [the] individual's participation" in that public controversy? ... Three factors determine the "nature and extent" of an individual's involvement: the extent to which participation in the controversy is voluntary, the extent to which there is access to channels of effective communication in order to counter-act false statements, and the prominence of the role played in the public controversy....

The Supreme Court has not clearly defined the elements of a "public controversy." It is evident that it is not simply any controversy of general or public interest. Not all judicial proceedings are public controversies. For example, "dissolution of a marriage through judicial proceedings is not the sort of 'public controversy' referred to in *Gertz*." *Time, Inc. v. Firestone* ... (1976). Several factors, however, lead to the conclusion that the Scottsboro case is the kind of public controversy referred to in *Gertz*. The Scottsboro trials were the focus of major public debate over the ability of our courts to render even-handed justice. It generated widespread press and attracted public attention for several years. It was also a contributing factor in changing public attitudes about the right of black citizens to equal treatment under law and in changing constitutional principles governing the right to counsel and the exclusion of blacks from the jury.

The first factor in determining the nature and extent of plaintiff's participation is the prominence of her role in the public controversy. She was the only alleged victim, and she was the major witness for the State in the prosecution of the nine black youths. Ruby Bates, the other young woman who earlier had testified against the defendants, later recanted her incriminating testimony. Plaintiff was left as the sole prosecutrix. Therefore, she played a prominent role in the public controversy.

The second part of the test of public figure status is also met. Plaintiff had "access to the channels of effective communication and hence ... a ... realistic

opportunity to counteract false statements." ... The evidence indicates that plaintiff recognized her importance to the criminal trials and the interest of the public in her as a personality. The press clamored to interview her. She clearly had access to the media and was able to broadcast her view of the events.

The most troublesome issue is whether plaintiff "voluntarily thrust" herself to the forefront of this public controversy. It cannot be said that a rape victim "voluntarily" injects herself into a criminal prosecution for rape.... In such an instance, voluntariness in the legal sense is closely bound to the issue of truth. If she was raped, her participation in the initial legal proceedings was involuntary for the purpose of determining her public figure status; if she falsely accused the defendants, her participation in this controversy was "voluntary." But legal standards in libel cases should not be drawn so that either the courts or the press must first determine the issue of truth before they can determine whether an individual should be treated as a public or a private figure. The principle of libel law should not be drawn in such a way that it forces the press, in an uncertain public controversy, to guess correctly about a woman's chastity.

When the issue of truth and the issue of voluntariness are the same, it is necessary to determine the public figure status of the individual without regard to whether she "voluntarily" thrust herself in the forefront of the public controversy. If there were no evidence of voluntariness other than that turning on the issue of truth, we would not consider the fact of voluntariness. In such a case, the other factors—prominence and access to media—alone would determine public figure status. But in this case, there is evidence of voluntariness not bound up with the issue of truth. Plaintiff gave press interviews and aggressively promoted her version of the case outside of her actual courtroom testimony. In the context of a widely reported, intense public controversy concerning the fairness of our criminal justice system, plaintiff was a public figure under *Gertz* because she played a major role, had effective access to the media and encouraged public interest in herself.

B. Plaintiff Remains a Public Figure for Purposes of Later Discussion of the Scottsboro Case

The Supreme Court has explicitly reserved the question of "whether or when an individual who was once a public figure may lose that status by the passage of time." *Wolston v. Reader's Digest Ass'n, Inc.*, 443 U.S. 157 (1979). In *Wolston* the District of Columbia Circuit found that plaintiff was a public figure and retained that status for the purpose of later discussion of the espionage case in which he was called as a witness. The Supreme Court found that the plaintiff's role

(continues)

in the original public controversy was so minor that he was not a public figure. It therefore reserved the question of whether a person retains his public figure status.

Plaintiff argues that even if she was a public figure at the time of the 1930s trial, she lost her public figure status over the intervening forty years. We reject this argument and hold that once a person becomes a public figure in connection with a particular controversy, that person remains a public figure thereafter for purposes of later commentary or treatment of *that controversy*. This rule finds support in both case law and analysis of the constitutional malice standard.

On this issue the Fifth Circuit has reached the same conclusion as the District of Columbia Circuit in *Wolston*. In *Brewer v. Memphis Publishing Co., Inc.,* 626 F.2d 1238 (5th Cir. 1980), plaintiff sued when a newspaper implied that she was reviving a long-dormant romantic relationship with Elvis Presley. The Fifth Circuit concluded that although the passage of time might narrow the range of topics protected by a malice standard, plaintiff remained a public figure when the defendant commented on her romantic relationship. The court noted that plaintiff's name continued to be connected with Presley even after her retirement from show business....

Our analytical view of the matter is based on the fact that the Supreme Court developed the public figure doctrine in order that the press might have sufficient breathing room to compose the first rough draft of history. It is no less important to allow the historian the same leeway when he writes the second or the third draft.

Our nation depends on "robust debate" to determine the best answer to public controversies of this sort. The public figure doctrine makes it possible for publishers to provide information on such issues to the debating public, undeterred by the threat of liability except in cases of actual malice. Developed in the context of contemporaneous reporting, the doctrine promotes a forceful exchange of views.

Considerations that underlie the public figure doctrine in the context of contemporaneous reporting also apply to later historical or dramatic treatment of the same events. Past public figures who now live in obscurity do not lose their access to channels of communication if they choose to comment on their role in the past public controversy. And although the publisher of history does not operate under journalistic deadlines it generally makes little difference in terms of accuracy and verifiability that the events on which a publisher is reporting occurred decades ago. Although information may come to light over the course of time, the distance of years does not necessarily make more data available

to a reporter: memories fade; witnesses forget; sources disappear.

There is no reason for the debate to be any less vigorous when events that are the subject of current discussion occurred several years earlier. The mere passage of time does not automatically diminish the significance of events or the public's need for information. A nation that prizes its heritage need have no illusions about its past. It is no more fitting for the Court to constrain the analysis of past events than to stem the tide of current news. From Alfred Dreyfus to Alger Hiss, famous cases have been debated and reinterpreted by commentators and historians. A contrary rule would tend to restrain efforts to shed new light on historical events and reconsideration of past errors.

The plaintiff was the pivotal character in the most famous rape case of the twentieth century. It became a political controversy as well as a legal dispute. As the white prosecutrix of nine black youths during an era of racial prejudice in the South, she aroused the attention of the nation. The prosecutions were among the first to focus on the conscience of the nation on the question of the ability of our system of justice to provide fair trials to blacks in the South. The question persists today. As long as the question remains, the Scottsboro boys case will not be relegated to the dusty pages of the scholarly treatise. It will remain a living controversy.

C. Evidence Insufficient to Support Malice[6]
A plaintiff may not recover under the malice standard unless there is "clear and convincing proof" that the defamation was published "with knowledge of its falsity or with reckless disregard for the truth." There is no evidence that NBC had knowledge that its portrayal of Victoria Price was false or that NBC recklessly disregarded the truth. The derogatory portrayal of Price in the movie is based in all material respects on the detailed findings of Judge Horton at the trial and Dr. Carter in his book. When the truth is uncertain and seems undiscoverable through further investigation, reliance on these two sources is not unreasonable.

---

6. The District Court found that even if plaintiff was a public figure forty years ago, she no longer was a public figure at the time of publication. The court then directed a verdict for NBC on grounds that there was no evidence of negligence. The evidence indicates, however, that there is arguably some proof of negligence by NBC. NBC was notified between the first and second showings of the film that not only was plaintiff alive but that she objected to her characterization in the movie. NBC made no attempt to verify the factual presentation in the movie thereafter. This arguably presents a jury-submissible case of negligence, as Judge Peck's dissent points out.

(continues)

We gain perspective on this question when we put to ourselves another case. Dr. Carter, in his book, persuasively argues, based on the evidence, that the Communist Party financed and controlled the defense of the Scottsboro boys. A different playwright might choose to portray Judge Horton as some Southern newspapers portrayed him at the time—as an evil judge who associated himself with a Communist cause and gave his approval to interracial rape in order to curry favor with the eastern press. The problem would be similar had Judge Horton—for many years before his death an obscure private citizen—sued the publisher for libel.

Some controversial historical events like the Scottsboro trials become symbolic and take on an overlay of political meaning. Speech about such events becomes in part political speech. The hypothetical case and the actual case before us illustrate that an individual's social philosophy and political leanings color his historical perspective. His political opinions cause him to draw different lessons from history and to see historical events and facts in a different light. He believes the historical evidence he wants to believe and casts aside other evidence to the contrary. So long as there is no evidence of bad faith or conscious or extreme disregard of the truth, the speaker in such a situation does not violate the malice standard. His version of history may be wrong, but the law does not punish him for being a bad historian.

The malice standard is flexible and encourages diverse political opinions and robust debate about social issues. It tolerates silly arguments and strange ways of yoking facts together in unusual patterns. But it is not infinitely expandable. It does not abolish all the common law of libel even in the political context. It still protects us against the "big political lie," the conscious or reckless falsehood. We do not have that in this case.

Accordingly, the judgment of the District Court is affirmed.

PUTTING IT INTO PRACTICE 13:4

1. What is the issue in this case?

2. For what reason did the court conclude that no libel had been committed?

3. How was the plaintiff portrayed in the drama?

4. Under *Gertz*, what two factors determine whether an individual is a public figure?

5. Was the Scottsboro trial a "public controversy"?

6. How does the plaintiff meet the requirements of the three factors that determine the nature and extent of her participation in the controversy?

7. Why does the plaintiff remain a public figure fifty years after the trial?

8. Why is the malice standard not satisfied in this case?

PUTTING IT INTO PRACTICE 13:5

1. Halle Berry decides to sue the *National Enquirer* for what she alleges are defamatory headlines and articles appearing about her in the magazine. What intent on the part of the *Enquirer* will she have to prove, and why?

(continues)

PUTTING IT INTO PRACTICE 13:5 *(continued)*

2. Charlotte White is employed by "Native America, Inc." as an organizer and promoter of Native American pow-wows across the country. An article is published referring to her first pow-wow in Florida regarding how Ms. White left "a trail of bad checks" and was "briefly jailed on charges of fraud." The article states that "White is in hiding because of money she owes to Native American entertainers who came to Florida in January after being guaranteed up to $75,000 in fees" and that she left $10,000 in unpaid hotel expenses. Although she admits that rain hindered the success of the Florida pow-wow, she denies all the allegations made in the article.

   Ms. White sues for defamation; the publication argues that she is a public figure because she appeared at a city council meeting requesting that the City of Manchester run additional water lines to the proposed pow-wow site. It maintains that this request for $10,000 in public funds to run the water lines satisfies the public controversy requirement for public figures. Should Ms. White be classified as a public figure?

3. Gerry Spence, a well-known attorney, represents a client (an activist engaged in a fight against pornography) in an action against *Hustler* magazine. In response to the litigation, Larry Flynt, owner of *Hustler*, refers to Spence as a "parasitic scum-sucker," a "reeking rectum," a "vermin-infected turd dispenser," a "hemorrhoidal type," and "Asshole of the Month for July." Some statements by Flynt are apparently false; he says, for example, that Spence stands to "fatten his wallet" by his litigation against *Hustler* when in fact Spence has assigned all of his proceeds to a charitable organization. Spence sues *Hustler* for defamation. Is he a public figure for purposes of this suit? If he is a public figure, can he recover damages for the statements that are clearly false?

Damages

A plaintiff who successfully proves defamation can recover for pecuniary as well as nonpecuniary losses, such as lost friendship, illness, and humiliation. As a constitutional matter, punitive damages may not be awarded to private figures in suits involving matters of public interest unless the plaintiff is able to prove that the defendant acted with actual malice (*Dun & Bradstreet, Inc. v. Greenmoss Builders, Inc.*, 472 U.S. 749 [1985]). Punitive damages may still be awarded, however, in matters pertaining to issues of merely private concern when only negligence is shown.

Recall that under the common law, presumed damages were allowed in most cases of libel and in cases involving slander per se. Thus, the plaintiff could recover even if she could not prove that she suffered any actual harm, because she could recover for the harm that "ordinarily" stems from a defamatory statement. United States Supreme Court decisions, however, cut back on this allowance by requiring the plaintiff to prove that the defendant acted at least

with reckless disregard of the truth if she is to recover presumed damages. Therefore, in those states requiring plaintiffs to prove mere negligence, plaintiffs are constitutionally precluded from recovering presumed damages. If a matter is not one of public interest, however, presumed damages may be awarded even if the plaintiff proves only mere negligence.

Even though a plaintiff suffers no quantifiable loss he may still be motivated to go to court in an effort to clear his name. Such a plaintiff is often willing to accept only nominal damages just to be given the opportunity to have his day in court.

The majority of states, in an effort to discourage defamation suits, have enacted *retraction statutes*. These statutes essentially bar a plaintiff from recovery if a defendant retracts a defamatory statement within a certain time period. Other statutes merely require the defendant to provide the plaintiff with response time and do not bar the plaintiff's recovery.

To illustrate how such statutes function, consider the Uniform Correction or Clarification of Defamation

Act, which serves as a model for states to enact. This act requires that either the plaintiff request a correction or clarification from the defendant within ninety days after learning of the publication or that the defendant voluntarily make a correction or clarification. Plaintiffs requesting a correction after the ninety-day period are limited to recovering economic losses only and cannot recover for pain, suffering, embarrassment, humiliation, or loss of reputation. Under this act the media can act with intentional or reckless disregard toward the truth, immunizing itself from all but economic damages, as long as it prints a timely retraction. Nevertheless, plaintiffs are afforded public correction even when they are unable to prove actual malice, when case law requires such a showing.

Exhibit 13–3 summarizes the essential points of defamation law.

EXHIBIT 13–3 Summary of Defamation Law

1. Plaintiffs who are public figures or public officials must prove actual malice.
2. Plaintiffs who are private figures need not prove actual malice, but must prove falsity and establish fault when suing a media defendant over speech involving matters of public concern.
3. If the statement involves a public matter, plaintiffs must prove at least negligence and cannot recover presumed or punitive damages unless they can show actual malice.
4. If the challenged statement involves a private matter, private plaintiffs need not prove actual malice to recover presumed or punitive damages.

© Cengage Learning 2012

LOCAL LINKS

Does your state have some kind of retraction statute? If so, what does this statute provide?

PRIVILEGES

A plaintiff may lose even if she proves defamation if the defendant can establish that he was privileged. Privileges can either be **absolute privileges**, in which instance they apply regardless of the defendant's motives, or **qualified privileges**, in which case they apply only when the defendant acts on the basis of certain well-defined purposes (see Exhibit 13–4).

Absolute Privileges

Absolute privileges emanate largely from the nature of the defendant's job or function. Judges, lawyers, parties, and witnesses enjoy an absolute privilege for the statements they make during judicial proceedings, regardless of the motives for their statements. Such statements must, however, bear some relation to the matter at issue (*Restatement [Second] of Torts* §§ 585–589). Similarly, legislators acting in furtherance of their legislative function during a legislative hearing enjoy an absolute privilege. Witnesses testifying before the legislature are also absolutely privileged. All federal officials, governors, and high-ranking state officials have absolute immunity while acting in their official capacities. The states are in disagreement, however, as to whether absolute immunity extends to lower-ranking officials, such as police officers. Note that no privilege applies to statements issued outside the course and furtherance of the defendant's job.

EXHIBIT 13–4 Privileges

ABSOLUTE PRIVILEGES

- Judges, lawyers, parties, and witnesses during judicial proceedings
- Legislators acting in furtherance of legislative function
- Witnesses testifying before legislature
- Federal officials, governors, and high-ranking state officials acting in official capacity
- Husband-wife communications

QUALIFIED PRIVILEGES

- Reports of public proceedings (e.g., judicial and legislative hearings)
- Statement made to someone with capacity to act in the public interest
- Statement made to protect one's own interests as long as not for the purpose of obtaining a competitive advantage

© Cengage Learning 2012

PUTTING IT INTO PRACTICE 13:6

The November 1983 issue of *Hustler* Magazine features an "ad" in which Jerry Falwell (a well-known minister) says that his "first time" was with his mother in an outhouse. The ad is a "parody" of a liquor advertisement that featured interviews with celebrities about their "first times." Small print at the bottom of the page contains the disclaimer, "ad parody—not to be taken seriously." The magazine's table of contents lists the ad as "Fiction; Ad and Personality Parody."

1. Is this a potential slander or libel claim?
2. Is Falwell a public figure for purposes of this case?
3. Is the parody defamatory?

Absolute immunity can also evolve out of a relationship. Husband-wife communications, for example, are absolutely privileged. If, however, the defamation originates with a third person and is relayed from one spouse to another, the repetition will still be considered a publication and the third person will be liable for the privileged repetition of his defamatory statement. Any publication to which a plaintiff consents is considered absolutely privileged.

LOCAL LINKS

Do police officers in your state have absolute immunity from defamation claims?

Qualified Privileges

Reports pertaining to public proceedings, such as court cases and legislative hearings, enjoy a qualified privilege of immunity. Because of *Sullivan* and *Gerst* the privilege is no longer necessary in those cases involving public officials or public figures unless the plaintiff can prove the defendant acted with actual malice. If the report involves a private figure, the actual-malice requirement is not applicable and the press is limited to a right to comment accurately on a public proceeding.

A statement made to one who has the capacity to act in the public interest, such as a public official, is subject to a qualified privilege. An accusation to a prosecutor about purported criminal activity, for example, is privileged unless the person making the accusation makes it recklessly. A defendant is also privileged in protecting her own interests as long as

those interests are sufficiently important and the defamation is directly related to those interests. A defendant who protects his property, for example, by telling the police about his suspicions that the plaintiff stole his property is privileged.

Making a defamatory statement for the purpose of gaining a competitive advantage is not privileged, such as telling potential customers about the poor workmanship of the competition. A defendant may be qualifiedly privileged to act for the protection of the recipient of her statement if the recipient is someone to whom making such a statement would be considered "within the generally accepted standards of decent conduct" (*Restatement [Second] of Torts* § 595 [1][b]). Statements made within the parameters of "decent conduct" must be made in response to a request and within the context of a close personal or business relationship. Credit-reporting agencies, for example, enjoy a qualified privilege in many states in giving their subscribers creditworthiness reports on potential customers (*Restatement [Second] of Torts* § 595, cmt. h).

A qualified privilege can be lost if it is abused. For example, a defendant who makes a statement knowing it to be false or who acts in reckless disregard as to the truth or falsity of the statement will lose the privilege. If the primary purpose behind the defendant's statement is something other than protecting the interest for which the privilege was originally granted, the privilege will be lost. Suppose an employee's former employer informs his new employer about the employee's alleged dishonesty. These allegations will not be privileged if the primary motivation is

---

PUTTING IT INTO PRACTICE 13:7

1. The state attorney general issues a press release explaining why his office has been delayed in prosecuting certain cases. In the release he accuses Geraldine of suppressing evidence. Can the attorney general be found liable for defamation? Would your answer change if a local district attorney has made the announcement?

2. In his opening remarks to the jury, a prosecuting attorney makes statements about the defendant that he knows are false. Can the defendant sue him for defamation?

3. Pam overhears a conversation in which she thinks a plot is being conceived to kill Connie. She calls the police and tells them Mary Sue is planning to kill Connie. The police arrest Mary Sue. Is Pam liable for defamation if it turns out there was no plot to kill Connie?

---

preventing the employee from leaving his employment rather than warning the new employer. A privilege is also considered abused if a statement is made to more people than is reasonably necessary to protect the interest in question. In the same vein, the privilege is abused if more damaging information is added than is reasonably necessary. A defendant who reports her suspicion to the police that the plaintiff has stolen her property will probably lose the privilege if she adds her belief that the plaintiff is promiscuous (*Restatement [Second] of Torts* § 605).

DEFAMATION ON THE WEB

In August 2000 a disgruntled employee of an Internet news organization issued a phony news release purportedly originating from the Emulex Corporation, a network equipment-maker, announcing that Emulex had restated its earnings, resulting in the immediate resignation of its CEO. Within minutes, several Internet news organizations picked up the bogus story and disseminated it throughout the investment community, resulting in a temporary loss of $2.5 billion in Emulex's market value and causing private investors to suffer serious financial losses.

This incident graphically illustrates the power of the Internet and the potentially damning effects defamatory statements can have on the community. Nevertheless, in light of legislation enacted by Congress, it has become increasingly difficult for those damaged by defamatory statements to recover against Internet Service Providers (ISPs), and the anonymity of the Internet makes it almost impossible to recover against individuals.

The Internet makes the risk of defamation more likely because it is a global media that is highly accessible. Messages can be sent via e-mail, published on home pages, or posted in chat rooms or newsgroups. Furthermore, anyone can publish on the Internet at little or no cost. Unlike other forms of media that routinely credit their sources, the Internet promotes anonymity. Content on the Internet is, for the most part, unregulated, further enhancing the chances of defamation. Not surprisingly, anonymity encourages some to be cavalier with the truth. Corporations and individuals increasingly find themselves defamed on the Net by anonymous users—who may include disgruntled investors or employees, unethical competitors, or even ex-lovers.

Knowing that people rely on the Internet as a medium for political and educational discourse, Congress has done its best to promote its development. One significant act it enacted to protect ISPs from defamation claims was the Communications Decency Act (CDA) of 1996. This legislation was passed in response to *Stratton Oakmont, Inc. v. Prodigy Services Co.*, 23 Media L. Rep. (BNA) 1794 (N.Y. Sup. Ct. 1995), the decision of a New York state trial court in which ISP Prodigy Services was found liable for defamatory Internet statements, mainly because it retained editorial control over the content of the site. Prodigy operated a bulletin board called "Money Talk." An anonymous user posted a message on "Money Talk" claiming that one of Stratton Oakment's securities offerings was a fraud, that the president of Stratton Oakmont was a criminal, and that Stratton employed brokers who either lied for a living or got fired. Stratton Oakmont, a securities investment banking firm, sued Prodigy for defamation, asserting that Prodigy was a publisher of allegedly libelous statements. In *Prodigy* the New York Supreme Court held that the ISP was a publisher, not a distributor.

The CDA directly overruled *Prodigy* by removing liability for ISPs and other providers when they act in good faith to regulate objectionable content. Section 230(c)(1) of Title V states that "no provider or user of an interactive computer service shall be treated as the publisher or speaker of any information provided by another information content provider." This section overrules *Stratton Oakmont v. Prodigy*. Consequently, when Internet providers implement software-screening programs designed to filter out distasteful material, they are not treated as making editorial decisions. The impact of the CDA is to virtually eliminate all liability in defamation actions in which the plaintiff alleges that the online company is a publisher. Moreover, since ISPs are not treated as publishers, it becomes impossible to satisfy the publication element of defamation claims.

While nothing in the CDA prohibits recovery from ISPs as "distributors" of defamatory statements that they did not themselves author, the 4th Circuit, in *Zeran v. America Online, Inc.*, 958 F. Supp. 1124 (E.D. Va.), aff'd, 129 F.3d 327 (4th Cir. 1997), *cert. denied*, 118 S.Ct. 2341 (1998), foreclosed that possibility by extending the CDA's publisher immunization to content distributors. Zeran alleged that he was defamed by an anonymous America Online (AOL) subscriber who posted several times on AOL's bulletin-board services advertising that Zeran was selling T-shirts with tasteless slogans related to the Oklahoma City bombing. The postings listed Zeran's home telephone number, a number from which Zeran actually did run a legitimate home-based business. As a result of the postings, Zeran was inundated with telephone complaints and death threats, at some times receiving telephone calls every two minutes. He immediately requested that AOL remove the postings, which AOL agreed to do, but AOL refused Zeran's request to post a retraction. Following the removal of the original posting, subsequent postings by an unknown user appeared that continued to advertise offensive products associated with Zeran's name. Zeran repeatedly contacted AOL and was told that the account of the anonymous user who had been posting the advertisements would soon be shut down.

Zeran sued AOL, arguing not that AOL was liable as a publisher (in view of section 230 of the CDA) but that AOL had negligently distributed and delayed the removal of the defamatory postings and failed to screen similar future postings. The 4th Circuit held in favor of AOL, ruling that section 230 of the CDA immunizes interactive computer services from claims based on information posted by a third party. The court concluded that ISPs should not be liable for the exercise of a publisher's traditional editorial functions, such as deciding whether to publish, withdraw, or alter content. According to the court of appeals, holding AOL liable would frustrate the policy of section 230, which is to encourage service providers to regulate the dissemination of offensive materials and to minimize government interference.

Although defamation plaintiffs would rather reach the relatively deep pockets of ISPs, they can at least sue the individual who posted the defamatory materials. But getting behind the anonymity of Internet messages can be extremely difficult. The first step in unmasking an anonymous online author is to determine which ISP has a record of that person's name and address. ISPs generally will not disclose subscriber information without a subpoena. In determining whether to issue a subpoena against an ISP, courts balance the interests of the plaintiff against the First Amendment rights of the author. They consider whether the plaintiff has exhausted good-faith, traditional avenues for identifying a defendant, has identified the anonymous defendant specifically enough that the court can determine whether jurisdiction exists, and has set forth a prima facie cause of action against the anonymous defendant.

In October 2000 a Virginia federal jury awarded the first known verdict for defamation on the Internet against an anonymous author (*Graham v. Oppenheimer*, No. 3:00-CV-57 [E.D. Va. Oct. 2000] [unpub]). An individual calling himself "fbiinformant" defamed the plaintiff, Dr. Sam Graham Jr., by posting statements on a Yahoo! message board claiming that Graham had been forced to resign as chairman of a medical school's urology department because he had been discovered taking kickbacks from UroCor, a uropathology laboratory. After issuing subpoenas to Yahoo! and others for several months, plaintiff's counsel determined that "fbiinformant" was another doctor who had been fired by UroCor and, using a variety of aliases, regularly attacked the laboratory on the message board. The defendant did not personally know Graham and had made no independent effort to verify the statements before posting them on the Internet. Even after others told the defendant that his statements were false, "fbiinformant" did not remove his defamatory statements until after Graham discovered his identity and filed suit. The jury awarded substantial damages to Graham for injury to his reputation and intentional infliction of emotional damages, as well as the maximum amount of punitive damages permitted by Virginia law. The case settled while on appeal.

INVASION OF PRIVACY

The right to privacy, sometimes referred to as "the right to be let alone," has a unique origin. Prior to 1890 such a tort had never been recognized by the English or American courts. But in that year Samuel Warren and Lewis Brandeis, fueled by their perception that individuals needed protection from what they viewed as an increasingly invasive press, authored a *Harvard Law Review* article proposing the creation of a new tort. Their proposal was the subject of extensive academic debate and was accepted as a basis of recovery in some lower courts. The New York Court of Appeals generated a storm of public disapproval when it denied recovery to a plaintiff whose picture had been used to advertise flour without her consent. The New York legislature went on to pass a statute allowing recovery in such cases. Today every state except Rhode Island has recognized the right to privacy in some form or another.

Invasion of privacy actually comprises four distinct torts, dissimilar in every respect except that they all protect the plaintiff from unreasonable interference with his privacy. These four torts are appropriation, unreasonable intrusion, public disclosure of private facts, and false light (see Exhibit 13–5).

Appropriation

If the value of a plaintiff's name or picture is used by a defendant for his own financial gain, the plaintiff can sue for this **appropriation**. Note that the *value* of the plaintiff's name must be appropriated, not just the name itself. In other words, the mere use of a name the same as that of the plaintiff's does not impose liability. The purpose for the appropriation, however, typically may be for either commercial or noncommercial purposes, although some state statutes limit recovery to commercial appropriations. The unauthorized use of an actress's photograph for the purposes of advertising could give rise to a cause of action for appropriation. Notice that appropriation was one of the allegations made by Robyn Douglass in *Douglass v. Hustler Magazine, Inc.*

EXHIBIT 13–5 Invasion of Privacy

APPROPRIATION	UNREASONABLE INTRUSION
Value of plaintiff's name or picture is used by defendant for financial gain.	Defendant intentionally intrudes upon seclusion of plaintiff in a way that would be highly offensive to a reasonable person.

PUBLIC DISCLOSURE OF PRIVATE ACTS	FALSE LIGHT
Defendant publicizes details of plaintiff's private life that would be highly offensive to a reasonable person.	Defendant puts plaintiff before public in false light that would be highly offensive to a reasonable person.

CASE

Douglass v. Hustler Magazine, Inc.
769 F.2d 1128 (7th Cir. 1985)

POSNER, Circuit Judge.

Robyn Douglass, the actress and model, obtained $600,000 in damages in this diversity suit against the corporation that publishes *Hustler* magazine, for invasion of her right of privacy.... *Hustler* (as we shall call the magazine and its publisher interchangeably) has appealed, raising questions of tort law, freedom of the press, and trial procedure; Douglass has cross-appealed, complaining about the judge's action in reducing the punitive damages awarded by the jury.

Robyn Douglass moved to Chicago in 1974 and began a career as an actress and model. That year she posed nude together with another woman for the freelance photographer Augustin Gregory, a codefendant with *Hustler* in the district court. The photographs were intended for a forthcoming feature in *Playboy* magazine, the "Ripped-Off" pictorial. Gregory testified that he required all his photographic models to sign releases allowing him to do with the photographs whatever he wanted. Robyn Douglass testified (and the jury was entitled to believe) that all she signed was a release authorizing *Playboy* to publish or otherwise use the photographs "for any lawful purpose whatsoever, without restrictions." The release does not refer to sale as such; but in granting rights not only to *Playboy* but to its "assigns and licensees," Douglass in effect gave *Playboy* carte blanche to dispose of the photos in any lawful way it wanted. Some of the photographs were published in *Playboy* in March 1975 as planned. Gregory had in 1974 also taken nude photographs of Douglass for a "Water and Sex" pictorial, also intended for *Playboy*; and there is a similar conflict over the release.

Douglass's career throve in the following years. She appeared eight times nude in *Playboy* but also made television commercials for Chicago advertising agencies and appeared in television dramas and in movies—notably "Breaking Away," where she had a starring role. Meanwhile in 1980 Gregory had become the photography editor of *Hustler*. This move was not unconnected with his earlier photographing of Douglass. The magazine wanted to publish nude photos of celebrities, and in negotiations over becoming *Hustler*'s photography editor, Gregory had shown management some of his photographs of Douglass. After he was hired, management asked Gregory for releases authorizing publication of these photographs. He testified that he couldn't find the releases at first but that eventually he submitted to *Hustler* two releases signed by Douglass, one for the photo session for the "Ripped-Off" pictorial, the other for the "Water and Sex" pictorial. At trial *Hustler* was

able to produce only photostats of the releases allegedly signed by Douglass. The parties stipulated that, if called as a witness, a handwriting expert would testify that Douglass's signature had been forged on one of the releases and that the photostat of the other was too poor to allow the authenticity of the signature to be determined.

Douglass heard that there was to be a photo feature on her in the January 1981 issue of *Hustler* (an acquaintance had seen an announcement of it in a previous issue). She complained to the magazine that it had no authority to publish any photos of her. It responded with photostatic copies of the alleged releases, which within two or three days she denounced to *Hustler* as forgeries. The issue containing the feature had already been printed and distributed to retailers; and though it had not yet appeared on newsstands or been mailed to subscribers, *Hustler* made no effort to recall the issue, and it was widely sold. The feature, entitled "Robyn Douglass Nude," contained nude photographs from the two photo sessions for *Playboy* and stills (not nude) from two of her movies. The magazine paid Gregory a fee, over and above his regular salary, for the photographs he had supplied.

This suit charges that Gregory and *Hustler* invaded Douglass's right to privacy under the common law of Illinois by publishing "Robyn Douglass Nude." The feature, she charged, invaded her right of privacy in two ways: it cast her in a "false light," and it appropriated valuable commercial rights that belong to her. At trial she presented evidence that the publication of the feature had caused her emotional distress, and had killed her career of making commercials in Chicago because advertisers thought she had voluntarily appeared in what they considered an extremely vulgar magazine. An economist testified that the present value of her lost earnings was $716,565 at the time of trial (1983).

The judge gave the jury a verdict form with a blank beside each defendant's name for the amount of compensatory damages if the jury found either defendant liable, and a separate blank beside each name for punitive damages. The jury found both defendants liable and awarded the plaintiff $500,000 in compensatory damages against each defendant and $1,500,000 in punitive damages against *Hustler*. The judge remitted all but $100,000 of the punitive damages and Douglass accepted the remittitur. The award of compensatory damages against Gregory was not executed because on the eve of the trial he had made an agreement with Douglass that if he testified truthfully, and consistently

(continues)

with his deposition, she would not execute any judgment against him. Hence the real judgment was only $600,000. Gregory has not filed an appearance in this court.

Hustler argues that the facts, even when viewed favorably to the plaintiff, do not make out a cause of action under the Illinois common law of privacy, so that the judgment should be reversed with directions to dismiss the complaint; or that if they do, still the complaint must be dismissed because the plaintiff failed to prove "actual malice" by clear and convincing evidence, as required by the Constitution. Alternatively it argues that a new trial should be ordered because of errors in the instructions to the jury, and other trial errors.

First of all, *Hustler* denies that Illinois even recognizes the "false light" tort. Illinois' substantive law governs this suit, apart from the defendants' First Amendment defense; and no Illinois court has ever found liability for such a tort, ... In cases in which that tort has been charged, albeit unsuccessfully, the Illinois courts have proceeded as if it existed in Illinois. In *Leopold v. Levin*, the only false-light case decided by the Illinois Supreme Court, Leopold, the surviving defendant in the Leopold and Loeb murder case, brought suit against the author of a book about the case, charging that the book (*Compulsion*) placed Leopold in a false light. The Illinois Supreme Court held that Leopold had no cause of action. He had forfeited any right of privacy by the notoriety of his crime; the book was represented to the public as a fictionalized rather than literal account; Leopold was a public figure; and to award tort damages would have unduly limited freedom of expression. These points would have been unnecessary to make if the court had thought that the false-light tort was not part of the common law of Illinois.... Incidentally, we do not read *Leopold v. Levin* to deny the protection of the tort to any and all public figures (Robyn Douglass, as we shall see, is a public figure). Leopold's status as a public figure was relevant to but not, as we read the opinion, conclusive on whether his rights had been violated.

Like every other division of the tort law of privacy, the "false light" tort ... can be criticized, especially for overlapping with the tort of defamation.... Why should a plaintiff be able to circumvent the technical limitations with which the tort of defamation is hedged about by calling his suit one for placing him in a false light? Several answers are possible, however:

1. Some of those limitations seem not to reflect considered policy, but instead to be fossil remnants of the tort's prehistory in the discredited practices of

Star Chamber and the discredited concept of seditious libel.... If they are gotten around by allowing a plaintiff to plead invasion of privacy, there is no great loss.

2. The principal limitations concern the requirement of proving special damages in some cases.... Since Robyn Douglass proved special damages (i.e., a pecuniary loss), these limitations would not have impeded her even if she had brought this suit as one for defamation. As for the other limitations in the law of defamation, *Hustler* has not shown how any of them, either, would have posed an embarrassment for Douglass on the facts of this case. And if she had sued for defamation she would not have had to prove (though it was not difficult to prove) that the offending materials had been widely publicized, an element of invasion of privacy that has no counterpart in the law of defamation.

3. Part of Douglass's claim is that *Hustler* insinuated that she is a lesbian; and such a claim could of course be the basis for an action for defamation. But the rest of her claim fits more comfortably into the category of offensive rather than defamatory publicity. The difference is illustrated by *Time, Inc. v. Hill*, 385 U.S. 374, 87 S.Ct. 534, 17 L.E.2d 456 (1967). Life magazine had presented as true a fictionalized account of the ordeal of a family held hostage by escaped convicts. The members of the family were shown being subjected to various indignities that had not actually occurred. The article did not defame the family members in the sense of accusing them of immoral, improper, or other bad conduct, and yet many people would be upset to think that the whole world thought them victims of such mistreatment. The false-light tort, to the extent distinct from the tort of defamation (but there is indeed considerable overlap), rests on an awareness that people who are made to seem pathetic or ridiculous may be shunned, and not just people who are thought to be dishonest or incompetent or immoral. We grant, though, that the distinction is blurred by the fact that a false statement that a woman was raped is actionable as defamation, ... though in such a case the plaintiff is represented to be a victim of wrongdoing rather than a wrongdoer herself.

At all events, the criticisms of the false-light tort have to our knowledge persuaded the courts of only one state that recognizes a tort of invasion of privacy to withhold recognition of this subtype of the tort— North Carolina.... Almost all signs point to Illinois' recognizing it when a suitable case arises. A more difficult question is whether the facts of this case make out a false-light tort. We must decide in what light *Hustler* may be said to have cast Robyn Douglass, and

(continues)

(by comparison with her activities as a *Playboy* model) in what if any sense the light could have been found to be a false one. To answer these questions we shall have to enter imaginatively into a world that is not the natural habitat of judges—the world of nude modeling and (as they are called in the trade) "provocative" magazines.

The feature "Robyn Douglass Nude" in the January 1981 issue of *Hustler* occupies three full pages about a third of the way from the end of the magazine. The first page is dominated by a picture of Douglass, shown from the front, rain-splattered, wearing only an open raincoat. This is one of the photos that had been taken for the "Water and Sex" pictorial. Her mouth is open and her eyes closed. The text on the page reads:

> She played Katherine, the Midwestern coed in the film *Breaking Away*, and Jamie, the shapely newspaper reporter in the TV series *Galactica 1980* (below). But in HUSTLER seductive young actress Robyn Douglass plays herself. In these never-before-published photos this hot new star strips away her screen image to reveal the flesh of a real woman. An accomplished stage performer and TV-commercial model (Orbit gum, Gatorade and United Airlines), Robyn has been trained to use her body as a tool of her trade. These photos show just how well she's learned to use that tool.

The "below" reference is to an innocuous still photo from the television series.

The second page of the feature is given over to four more photographs of Douglass, two from "Water and Sex," and two from the "Ripped-Off" pictorial. (To be precise, these and the other nude photos in "Robyn Douglass Nude" were photos that had been taken for the two *Playboy* pictorials but, apparently, had not actually been published.) The photographs from "Water and Sex" again show Douglass from the front with the raincoat playing out behind her. In one picture her mouth is open while in the other she seems to be looking abstractedly at herself. In the two photos from "Ripped-Off," Douglass, now wearing a slip rather than a raincoat, appears to be engaged in erotic play with the other woman in the pictorial.

The last page of the feature has the following text beneath a picture of Douglass, fully clothed, on a motorcycle:

> When asked to audition for the role of Katherine in *Breaking Away* (above), Robyn sought out the character's most emotional scene to read for director Peter Yates. "You only have a short time to prepare; so I went through the script to try to find the climactic

moments for Katherine." From the looks of Robyn (who's blond in the photos of her and a female friend), she's never had difficulty finding climactic moments.

The rest of the page is given over to two photographs from the "Ripped-Off" pictorial. The underwear visible in the other two photographs from this session has indeed been ripped off; the two women are naked. Douglass is straddling the other woman and the two appear to be engaged in sexual activity.

Douglass argues that the *Hustler* feature casts her in a false light in two respects. First, it insinuates that she is a lesbian, which (all agree) she is not. Second, it insinuates that she is the kind of person willing to be shown naked in *Hustler*. Nothing in the feature itself suggests that the nude photographs of her are appearing without her permission and against her will, and readers might well assume that she had cooperated in the preparation of the feature in order to stimulate interest in her films. Moreover, she had been described in a previous issue of *Hustler* as a forthcoming "*Hustler* celebrity-exclusive," and in another issue *Hustler*'s chairman, Larry Flynt, had announced in an editorial column that he does not publish photographs of women without their consent. It is (or so a jury could find) as if *Hustler* had said, "Robyn Douglass is proud to pose nude for *Hustler* magazine." To complete this part of her argument Douglass asserts that voluntary association with *Hustler* as a nude model is degrading.

We would not ourselves think that *Hustler* was seriously insinuating—or that its readership would think—that Robyn Douglass is a lesbian. *Hustler* is a magazine for men. Few men are interested in lesbians. The purpose of showing two women in apparent sexual embrace is to display the charms of two women. Moreover, the photos obviously are posed rather than candid shots; they show what the photographer wanted the women to do, not necessarily what the women wanted to do. Nevertheless we cannot say that a reasonable jury seeing the pictures and reading the accompanying text with its references to "climactic moments" and "female friend" could not infer that Douglass was being represented to be a lesbian.

The question whether she was also being depicted in a degrading association with *Hustler* invites attention to the difference between libel and false light. It would have been difficult for Douglass to state this claim as one for libel. For what exactly is the imputation of saying (or here, implying) of a person that she agreed to have pictures of herself appear in a vulgar and offensive magazine? That she is immoral? This would be too strong a characterization in today's moral climate. That

(continues)

she lacks good taste? This would not be defamatory.... The point is, rather, that to be shown nude in such a setting before millions of people—the readers of the magazine—is degrading in much the same way that to be shown beaten up by criminals is degrading (although not libelous, despite the analogy to being reported to have been raped), though of course if Douglass consented to appear nude in this setting she is responsible for her own debasement and can get no judicial redress.

That the setting is indeed a degrading one requires only a glance through the issue of *Hustler* in which "Robyn Douglass Nude" was published to confirm. The cover shows a naked woman straddling and embracing a giant peppermint stick. The titles of several articles in the issue are printed on the cover, next to the picture, including, along with some titles that are not related to sex, "New Discovery: How to Give Women Vaginal Orgasms." This is directly below "Nude Celebrity: Robyn Douglass, Star of Galactica and Breaking Away." The inside cover is a full page of advertisements for pornographic video cassettes. On page 5 there is the "publisher's [Larry Flynt's] statement"—a call to tax the churches. This sounds another theme of *Hustler*: "irreverence," which has the practical meaning in *Hustler* of hostility to or contempt for racial, ethnic, and religious minorities. Then there is a "World News Roundup"—the news is all concerned with sex—and a page of coarse advice to readers who have sexual problems. Between these two features is a full-page advertisement entitled "Get Any Girl *Within 5 Minutes* or YOU PAY NOTHING!" with subtitles such as "Turn Women Into Putty." The issue contains many similar sexual advertisements, some with obscene pictures and text....

We shall leave off here, ... having sufficiently indicated the character of the magazine. To be depicted as *voluntarily* associated with such a sheet ... is unquestionably degrading to a normal person, especially if the depiction is erotic ... for although the magazine is offensive on several planes, the sexual is the one most emphasized. These features of the case help to distinguish *Ann-Margret v. High Society Magazine, Inc.*, 498 F.Supp. 401, 404–06 (S.D.N.Y. 1980), where a semi-nude still of an actress was published without her authorization in a magazine (*High Society Celebrity Skin*) described by the judge merely as "tacky," *McCabe v. Village Voice, Inc.*, 550 F.Supp. 525, 529 (E.D.Pa. 1982), a case like *Ann-Margret* except that the magazine was completely inoffensive; and *Brewer v. Hustler Magazine, Inc.*, 749 F.2d 527, 530 (9th Cir. 1984), where a previously published photograph was republished in a "sexually explicit" magazine—none other than *Hustler* itself—but apparently the plaintiff did not argue that the magazine was degrading, as distinct from merely explicit. And the

photograph was of Brewer pretending to shoot himself in the head (for unexplained reasons, he had this photograph printed on his business cards); he was not associated with the magazine's view of sex. More important, in none of these cases was it argued that the subject was being represented as appearing voluntarily in the magazine, and (except in *McCabe*) the photographs had previously been published elsewhere. These points are related. If a photograph has been published previously the implied representation that its present publication is with the consent of the subject is weakened; the first publication may have put the photograph in the public domain. But the nude photographs of Robyn Douglass that *Hustler* published had not been published before.

Hustler argues that publication of "Robyn Douglass Nude" could not be degrading to one who had posed nude for *Playboy*. This fact distinguishes the case from the two cases that give the most support to Douglass's false-light claim: *Wood v. Hustler Magazine, Inc.*, 736 F.2d 1084 (5th Cir. 1984), where the plaintiff was not a model or actress and her nude photo (taken by her husband) had not been published previously and had not been intended to be published; and *Braun v. Flynt*, 726 F.2d 245 (5th Cir. 1984), where the photo of the plaintiff that was published on the same page with offensive matter in another "provocative" magazine published by Flynt (*Chic*) was not a nude photo; the plaintiff was wearing a bathing suit.... (It should be apparent by now that this little niche of the law of privacy is dominated by Larry Flynt's publications.)

To evaluate *Hustler*'s contention required the jury to compare the two magazines. We shall use for comparison the issue of *Playboy* in which the "Ripped-Off" pictorial appeared, though the jury had other issues of *Playboy* to peruse as well. The cover shows a young woman with partially naked buttocks and thighs but otherwise clothed. The only (other) suggestion of sex on the cover is the words "Ripped Off! A Torrid Nine-Page Pictorial," which by its position on the cover appears to be a reference to the cover girl. The inside cover is a conventional advertisement for Scotch whisky. Besides advertisements (none sexual), the issue contains fiction, a column of sexual advice (more refined than its *Hustler* counterpart), book reviews (only one of a book on sex), and articles. None of the stories or articles is obscene, though one story is erotic (a "Ribald Classic") and there are many bawdy cartoons and jokes (but not vicious ones, like many of those in *Hustler*) and four nude pictorials. In one of the pictorials a woman is doing exercises and being massaged; some of the frames contain an erotic suggestion of a mild sort. Two of the other pictorials show nude women in various poses but there is no suggestion that they are engaged in erotic

(continues)

activity. The last nude pictorial is "Ripped-Off," which turns out to consist of photographs of nude women (some in erotic poses) by different photographers. Two of the photographs are by Gregory, and one of them is of Robyn Douglass, though she is not identified by name. Although she is shown removing the slip of the other woman, as in the *Hustler* pictures, the text beneath the picture weakens any inference of lesbianism: "How long since you've seen a girl—let alone two—in lingerie like this? 'I pick very feminine, almost outdated slips for the girls to wear in this scene,' says photographer Gregory. 'To me, that made it more of a fantasy, more of a turn-on.' " Among other pictures in "Ripped-Off," one could be taken to be an (obviously simulated) photograph of sexual intercourse.

Although many people find *Playboy*, with its emphasis on sex and nudity, offensive, the differences between it and *Hustler* are palpable. *Playboy*, like *Hustler*, contains nude pictorials, but the erotic theme is generally muted, though there are occasional photographs that an earlier generation would have considered definitely obscene. And unlike *Hustler*, *Playboy* does not carry sexual advertisements, does not ridicule racial or religious groups, and avoids repulsive photographs—though most of the jokes and cartoons have sex as their theme, and not all are in good taste. We cannot say that it would be irrational for a jury to find that in the highly permissive moral and cultural climate prevailing in late twentieth-century America, posing nude for *Playboy* is consistent with respectability for a model and actress but that posing nude in *Hustler* is not (not yet, anyway), so that to portray Robyn Douglass as voluntarily posing nude for *Hustler* could be thought to place her in a false light even though she had voluntarily posed nude for *Playboy*. Apart from the evidence of the magazines themselves, Douglass presented evidence that advertising agencies in Chicago were afraid of their clients' reactions if she appeared in commercials after her appearance in *Hustler*, but cared nothing about her appearing nude in *Playboy*. And of course the issue for us is not whether the jury was right but whether a reasonable jury could have found a false-light tort on the facts of this case.

However, since Douglass gave a general release to *Playboy*, it can be argued that she consented to have her photographs appear in any lawful setting; and there is no contention that "Robyn Douglass Nude," or the issue of *Hustler* in which it appeared, could lawfully have been suppressed on obscenity or other grounds. The jury could find, however, that only Douglass or *Playboy* could give consent to the publication of the photographs and that neither had done so. True, by giving *Playboy* a general release Douglass took a risk that her nude photographs would end up in an offensive setting that would damage her career as a model for television commercials, and it might seem that someone who takes such a risk cannot have a high regard for her privacy. But the risk she took and the risk that materialized were not the same. She took what may have seemed a trivial risk that *Playboy* would resell her photographs to a competitor, not the risk that the competitor would steal them. *Playboy* has an interest, on which Douglass could reasonably rely in executing a release to *Playboy*, is not degrading its models and in maintaining exclusive rights to its photos of them. The woman in the Wood case assumed the risk that her husband would sell *Hustler* the nude photograph that he took of her, but this did not deprive her of the right to sue for invasion of privacy when *Hustler* published the photograph having gotten it from someone who had broken into her house and stolen it.

We conclude that Robyn Douglass has a cause of action against *Hustler* for portraying her in a false light. Further, we think the jury did not exceed the bounds of reason in finding that *Hustler* also violated her rights under the commercial-appropriation branch of the right of privacy—what is sometimes called the "right of publicity," which *Hustler* concedes is a part of the common law of Illinois. This is the right to prevent others from using one's name or picture for commercial purposes without consent. Although originally the forbidden use was putting one's name or picture into an advertisement, it is apparent from *Zacchini v. Scripps-Howard Broadcasting Co.*, 433 U.S. 562 (1977), that the right can extend to publication in the nonadvertising portions of a magazine or broadcast. This extension is closely related to copyright.... Zacchini had perfected a "human cannonball" act that lasted about 15 seconds. A television station broadcast the whole act as part of a news program. The station argued that the act was newsworthy; in copyright terms this would make the broadcasting of it a "fair use." *Hustler* makes a similar argument here—Robyn Douglass is newsworthy and "Robyn Douglass Nude" was fair comment on her career. But the station could have done a story on Zacchini without showing his entire act; and showing the whole act was likely to shrink the paying audience for it—people could see it on television for nothing. Thus there was an invasion of Zacchini's rights, analogous to copyright, under state tort law. Similarly, Robyn Douglass or her agents must have control over the dissemination of her nude photographs if their value is to be maximized. *Hustler* can run a story on her and use any photographs that are in the public domain or that it can buy but it cannot use photographs made by others for commercial purposes and (temporarily) withheld from public distribution....

(continues)

The unauthorized publication did impair the commercial exploitation of Douglass's talents, though probably not as much as she asserts and mainly because of where they were published. But an important aspect of the "right of publicity" is being able to control the places as well as time and number of one's public appearances; for example, no celebrity sells his name or likeness for advertising purposes to all comers. In any event, Douglass was not paid by *Hustler* for the right to publish nude photos of her.

Of course the issue in *Zacchini* was not whether the common law created a right of action against the television station—let alone the common law of Illinois (the case came from Ohio)—but whether the Constitution barred such a right of action if it existed in state law. There are not Illinois cases like *Zacchini*. But forced to guess, we guess that Illinois would recognize a "right of publicity" on the facts of *Zacchini* and the analogous facts of the present case. Indeed, this may be an easier case than *Zacchini*, where the performance had been in public, though in a different medium. This case approaches very closely to a violation of common law copyright, as in the theft and unauthorized publication of an author's manuscript. Of course Douglass would have no claim if Gregory had gotten a general release from her. But by executing only a limited release, she retained a right in the photos he took of her that, if not quite a property right, is nevertheless given legal protection under the (misleading) rubric of privacy.

But it was error to allow the jury to find an invasion of Douglass's right of publicity in the fact that *Hustler* published stills from her movie and television shows—whether reversible error we need not decide (for reasons to appear). Apparently these stills were in the public domain, for they had been published and *Hustler* is not accused of copyright infringement in republishing them. Republishing previously published, uncopyrighted photographs of a celebrity is a fair use justified by the news-worthiness of celebrities, and it therefore does not violate the right of publicity.... To forbid *Hustler* to publish any photographs of people without their consent, merely because it is an offensive, though apparently a lawful, magazine, would pretty much put *Hustler* out of the news business, would probably violate the First Amendment, and would in any event cross outside the accepted boundaries of the right of publicity. But as noted earlier the nude photographs of Douglass that *Hustler* published had not been published before. They were, in a sense that tort law recognizes, part of her portfolio. She had a legally protected interest in deciding at least their first place of publication, provided *Playboy* did not exercise its rights to publish

them or to license their publication to others, a right for which Douglass had been compensated in executing the release to *Playboy*.

Although we reject *Hustler*'s argument that Douglass failed to prove an invasion of her right of privacy, we must also consider among other issues whether a reasonable jury could have found "actual malice" by *Hustler*. For failure to show actual malice would (possibly subject to qualification, as we shall see) be a defense, based on the First Amendment, to her tort suit. As the term is used in relation to the limitations that the First Amendment has been held to place on suits for defamation and "false light" invasion of privacy, it means knowledge of falsity or reckless disregard for truth....

As *Hustler* does not so much as argue that it ever believed that Douglass was a lesbian, it was at the very least reckless in representing her as one, which we said a reasonable jury could have found it had done in "Robyn Douglass Nude." With regard to "actual malice" in representing her as voluntarily associating with the magazine, the only question is whether *Hustler* knew it was acting without authorization—knew, in other words, that Douglass was not voluntarily associating herself with the magazine—or didn't care. *Hustler* argues that it relied on Gregory to supply authentic releases and cannot be found to have acted with actual malice if he submitted forged ones. The absence of any release from the other woman in the "Ripped-Off" pictorial undermines this claim; but a more important point is that Gregory was *Hustler*'s photography editor, acting within the scope of his employment, so that his knowledge of the falsity of the releases was the corporation's knowledge. It makes no difference whether in submitting the photographs he was acting as an independent contractor, as *Hustler* argues, or as an employee. As photography editor, which is to say in his capacity as an employee, he had some—it does not matter precisely how much—responsibility for the provenance of the photographs that were published. If someone had submitted nude photographs of Robyn Douglass to him without a release and he had told his superiors there was a release, he would have been acting within the scope of his employment. It makes no difference that in fact he was the seller as well as the buying agent. The doctrine of respondeat superior is fully applicable to suits for defamation and invasion of privacy, notwithstanding the limitations that the First Amendment has been held to place on these torts....

Although there is no basis for ordering the complaint dismissed, there were a number of trial errors which together persuade us that there must be a new trial. The first relates to the judge's failure to instruct the jury that it must find actual malice by "clear and

(continues)

convincing" evidence. This is one of the requirements that the Supreme Court has imposed in the name of freedom of the press on suits for defamation...and we can think of no reason why it might be inapplicable to suits against the press for invasions of privacy, at least when the invasion takes the form of casting the plaintiff in a false light—a form of invasion of privacy that, as we have seen, overlaps the tort of defamation. Courts have assumed as a matter of course that the requirement of proving actual malice by clear and convincing evidence indeed applies to the false-light tort....

The judge here said that his error did not matter because the evidence of actual malice was clear and convincing. It may have been, but that did not make the error harmless. Douglass was not entitled to a directed verdict. Therefore the error in the instruction on burden of proof was not harmless....

All of this assumes of course that actual malice must be proved regarding even so mundane a question as whether consent was obtained to publish some photographs, which is the only question on which *Hustler*'s knowledge is a matter of fair debate. As an original matter we would have our doubts. The purpose of requiring proof of knowledge of falsity, or reckless disregard for the truth, is to lighten the investigative burdens on the press of determining the truth of what it writes. It is no great burden to determine whether a release has been executed; it is not like ascertaining the truth about allegations that a government official took a bribe or engaged in insider trading or fudged casualty statistics. A requirement that the plaintiff prove that the defendant was negligent in mistaking the existence of the release might be quite enough to protect the press from having to make costly investigations. The contrary argument is that the law under the First Amendment is complicated enough without attempting to make distinctions among the types of fact as to which actual malice is required in torts so closely related as defamation and false light. The qualification, however, and the analogy to copyright which supports Douglass's right-of-publicity claim, suggest that knowledge or even care is irrelevant at least to that claim; for it is no defense to copyright infringement that the infringer reasonably but mistakenly thought he had a license....

Fortunately we need not try to unravel this tangled skein. The plaintiff does not argue that she was excused from having to prove actual malice because of the nature of her claim or the nature of *Hustler*'s falsity in regard to her. She does argue that she was excused from having to prove actual malice because she is not a public figure. But a successful actress and model who has appeared nude many times in *Playboy*

magazine cannot be called a "private person"; she is a public figure in a literal sense. The lifting of the burden of proving actual malice in defamation cases from the shoulders of plaintiffs who are not public figures reflects two things: the fact that people who do not thrust themselves into the public eye have on average a greater sense of privacy than those who do; and the difficulty that obscure people have, compared to celebrities, in commanding the media's attention to efforts to rebut innuendoes about them (whether defamatory, or merely offensive in a false-light sense).... But not only is Robyn Douglass no shrinking violet; she is a budding celebrity eager to be seen in the nude by millions of people—she had been seen in the nude by millions of people, the readers of *Playboy*, before *Hustler* got hold of her photographs. She is not like the plaintiff in *Braun v. Flynt, supra,* who did not become a public figure merely because her job in a local amusement park included feeding "Ralph, the Diving Pig" from a bottle of milk while treading water.

As an original matter one might want to confine the class of public figures to government officials and other politicians; freedom of political speech, and in particular freedom to criticize government officials and aspirants to public office, was the original concern of the First Amendment. But it is too late in the day to make such a distinction, at least at this judicial level. Art, even of the questionable sort represented by erotic photographs in "provocative" magazines—even of the artless sort represented by "topless" dancing—today enjoys extensive protection in the name of the First Amendment.... And so with news about art and entertainment. Entertainers can therefore be public figures for purposes of a publisher's or a broadcaster's First Amendment defense to a charge of false-light invasion of privacy.... Robyn Douglass clearly is one.

There is, incidentally, some question whether a plaintiff in a false-light case, merely because he (or she) is not a public figure, is relieved from having to prove actual malice, as would be true in a defamation case. The question was left open in *Cantrell v. Forest City Publishing Co.,* 419 U.S. at 250–51, 95 S.Ct. at 469. An argument can be made that the injury that being cast in a false light creates is less serious than that created by being defamed, and therefore the plaintiff should have a tougher row to hoe. We need not resolve the question here, but mention it lest our discussion of whether Robyn Douglass is a public figure be taken to have resolved it implicitly....

The judgment is reversed and the case remanded for a new trial. No costs in this court.

Reversed and remanded.

PUTTING IT INTO PRACTICE 13:8

1. In what two ways did Robyn Douglass claim her right to privacy had been invaded?

2. Why did the court think the plaintiff should be able to "circumvent the technical limitations" of defamation by claiming invasion of privacy?

3. On what grounds did Douglass claim that *Hustler* placed her in a false light?

4. Could a reasonable jury have concluded that Douglass was being represented as a lesbian?

5. Could voluntary association with *Hustler* by allowing one's nude photographs to be published therein be considered degrading?

6. Could a portrayal of Douglass as voluntarily agreeing to pose nude for *Hustler* place her in a false light even though she had voluntarily posed nude for *Playboy*?

7. Why did the court conclude that Douglass had a false-light claim even though she had consented to being photographed nude by *Playboy*?

8. On what basis did Douglass have a commercial appropriation (or "right of publicity") claim against *Hustler*?

9. Why was publication of stills from Douglass's movies and TV shows not an invasion of privacy?

Unreasonable Intrusion

A defendant who intentionally intrudes upon the seclusion of another is liable for invasion of privacy if his intrusion would be considered "highly offensive to a reasonable person" (*Restatement [Second] of Torts* § 652B). Physical intrusion includes the use of mechanical devices, such as binoculars or wiretaps. A private detective, for example, who in the process of seeking evidence for a lawsuit rents a room in a house adjoining the plaintiff's residence and monitors the plaintiff's activities for a period of time using a telescope will be considered to have invaded the plaintiff's privacy. Unreasonable intrusion may also be committed by opening the plaintiff's private mail, searching her purse, or examining her private bank account.

When consumer advocate Ralph Nader planned to publish a book attacking the safety of automobiles manufactured by General Motors, the company attempted to harass Nader by making threatening telephone calls, interviewing his acquaintances, tapping his phone, eavesdropping on him using electronic equipment, using women to make illicit proposals to him, and conducting surveillance on him in public places. The court held that Nader had a cause of action for invasion of privacy because of the wiretapping and electronic eavesdropping. The other activities, however, did not constitute invasion of privacy because the court did not consider them unreasonably intrusive (*Nader v. General Motors Corp*, 255 N.E.2d 765 [N.Y. 1970]).

Public Disclosure of Private Facts

By the same token, publicizing the details of the plaintiff's private life may also constitute invasion of privacy. The matter publicized must be of the type that would be "highly offensive to a reasonable person" and must "not be of legitimate concern to the public" (*Restatement [Second] of Torts* § 652D). For example, a disgruntled creditor who posts a notice in the window of his store saying that the plaintiff owes him money invades the plaintiff's privacy (*Restatement [Second] of Torts* § 652D, illus. 2).

NET NEWS

The Reading Room section of The Reporters Committee for Freedom of the Press contains several articles regarding privacy law and other First Amendment issues at **http://www.rcfp.org**.

No invasion of privacy exists if the details publicized are contained in a public record. If the name of a deceased rape victim is broadcast on television, the victim's parents have no claim for invasion of privacy because the victim's name would be available in an indictment, which would be available for public inspection at the suspect's trial (*Cox Broadcasting Corp. v. Cohn*, 420 U.S. 469 [1975]). Similarly, a murder suspect whose past history and daily life are recorded in the newspaper cannot claim invasion of privacy, because his activities would be considered matters of legitimate concern to the public (*Restatement [Second] of Torts* § 652D, illus. 13).

False Light

A plaintiff put before the public eye in a **false light** that would be highly offensive to a reasonable person can also sue for invasion of privacy (*Restatement [Second] of Torts* § 652E). Suppose that a newspaper publishes an article about local taxi drivers cheating on their fares and uses the plaintiff's photograph to illustrate the article. If the photograph clearly implies that the plaintiff resorts to such practices (and in fact he does not), the plaintiff may recover for invasion of privacy. Such "false light" actions can be brought only if the plaintiff can show that the defendant deliberately portrayed the plaintiff in a false light or acted in reckless disregard of the issue (*Time, Inc. v. Hill*, 385 U.S. 374 [1967]).

A false-light case may or may not be considered grounds for defamation. The *Douglass* court considers the similarities and dissimilarities between false light and defamation and discusses why a plaintiff may opt for a false-light claim rather than a defamation claim. In addition to being easier to prove in some respects than defamation, the court points out, the tort of false-light allows recovery for offensive publicity (depicting a plaintiff as pathetic or ridiculous) and not just defamatory publicity (depicting the plaintiff as immoral or dishonest).

Suppose a movie that is made about a war hero's life includes fictitious details about a nonexistent romance. Even if the moviemaker is aware of the falsity of some of the portrayal, the plaintiff cannot sue for defamation as long as the movie did not tend to harm the plaintiff's reputation. He could, however, sue for invasion of privacy if the presentation would be considered "highly offensive to a reasonable person" (*Restatement [Second] of Torts* § 652E, illus. 5).

NET NEWS

A brief summary of a California Court of Appeals case involving plaintiffs who sued Time Warner for invasion of privacy because of pictures published in relationship to a child molestation case can be read at **http://www.techlawjournal.com.** Enter "Time Warner Invasion of Privacy" as your search term.

PUTTING IT INTO PRACTICE 13:9

1. A 1982 edition of the *National Enquirer* details Clint Eastwood's romantic involvement with singer Tanya Tucker and actress Sondra Locke. Eastwood alleges in part that the offending article falsely states

   a. that Eastwood "loves" Tucker and that Tucker means a lot to him.

   b. that Eastwood was, in late February 1982, swept off his feet and immediately smitten by Tucker; that Tucker makes his head spin; that Tucker used her charms to get what she wanted from Eastwood; and that Eastwood now daydreams about their supposedly enchanted evenings together.

   c. that Eastwood and Tucker, in late February 1982, shared ten fun-filled romantic evenings together; were constantly, during that period, in each other's arms; publicly "cuddled" and publicly gazed romantically at one another; and publicly kissed and hugged.

(continues)

PUTTING IT INTO PRACTICE   13:9 *(continued)*

d. that Eastwood is locked in a romantic triangle involving Tucker and Sondra Locke ("Locke"); is torn between Locke and Tucker; can't decide between Locke and Tucker; is involved in a romantic tug-of-war involving Locke and Tucker; that Locke and Tucker are dueling over him; that Tucker is battling Locke for his affections; and that when he is with Locke, Tucker is constantly on his mind.

e. that, in or about late February of 1982, there were serious problems in Eastwood's relationship with Locke; that he and Locke at that time had a huge argument over marriage; that he and Locke had a nasty fight; and that Locke stormed out of his presence.

f. that after his supposed romantic interlude with Tucker, Locke camped at his doorstep and, while on hands and knees, begged Eastwood to "keep her," vowing that she wouldn't pressure him into marriage; but that Eastwood acted oblivious to her pleas.

Does Eastwood have a viable false light claim? If the *Enquirer* featured Eastwood's name and photograph along with the subject of the article in a telecast advertisement, would he have a claim for appropriation?

2. June, who is hospitalized with a rare disease, is approached by a reporter who requests an interview over the phone, which June refuses. The reporter then comes to the hospital and photographs June, over her objection. What, if any, tort has the reporter committed?

3. Marie is told she will have to have a cesarean operation. A doctor asks if he can videotape the operation to show to medical students for educational purposes. Marie agrees. Later the doctor shows the video to the public in a commercial theater. What tort, if any, has the doctor committed?

4. Jean Valjean, who had served time for robbery, has changed his name, concealed his identity, and led an exemplary life in another city for twenty years. A reporter discovers Valjean's criminal history and publishes an article in which Valjean's true identity is revealed. Valjean's life and career are ruined. What, if any, tort has been committed?

5. A young child is photographed after being hit by a car. A few years later her photo is included in an article on the negligence of children with the caption "They Ask to Be Killed." What, if any, tort has been committed?

INJURIOUS FALSEHOOD

Injurious falsehood protects plaintiffs against false statements made against their business, product, or property rights. If the plaintiff's goods or business are falsely disparaged, the tort committed is typically referred to as **trade libel**, but if the disparagement refers to property rights of the plaintiff, the tort is usually referred to as **slander of title**.

Trade Libel

To recover for trade libel, the plaintiff must show that the defendant made a false statement clearly referring to the plaintiff's goods or business and disparaging those goods or business. A defendant who falsely claims during an interview on national television that his company is the only one of its kind may be liable for disparaging a plaintiff's business that is identical to his.

Note that trade libel differs from defamation in that the false statement need not ridicule or disgrace the plaintiff. As with defamation, however, the plaintiff must show the statement was published and that he suffered some kind of pecuniary harm. The defendant must also either know his statement is false, act with reckless disregard for the truth or falsity of his statement, or (according to some courts) act out of spite toward the plaintiff.

The same defenses that are applicable to defamation are applicable to trade libel. A defendant is also privileged to fairly compete with a plaintiff by making general comparisons between his product and the plaintiff's. A competitor is in fact permitted to "puff" even if he is aware that his statements are false and are made for the purpose of taking business away from the plaintiff. The defendant is not privileged, however, if he makes specific false allegations about the plaintiff's product.

Slander of Title

If a defendant falsely disparages the property right of another, he commits slander of title. For example, if he interferes with the plaintiff's right to hold or dispose of property by filing a false document, such as a mortgage or levy of execution, he commits slander of title. Leases, mineral rights, trademarks, copyrights, and patents may all be subjected to slander of title. The same intent, defenses, and privileges applicable to trade libel apply to slander of title. Additionally, a defendant has a qualified privilege to protect his own interest by asserting a bona fide claim to property. An assertion of infringement on a patent right is privileged as long as the assertion is made in good faith and in the absence of any motive of a desire to do harm.

PUTTING IT INTO PRACTICE 13:10

The CBS news program *60 Minutes* airs a story based on a report published by the Natural Resources Defense Council discussing the detrimental effects of pesticide use by farmers. The program highlights the effects of the herbicide Alar, which is used by apple growers to stimulate growth and enhance apple appearance. As a result of the program some consumers boycott apples and apple products. Do apple growers have a viable cause of action against CBS and the Natural Resources Defense Council?

SUMMARY

Defamation consists of the related torts of libel and slander. A statement is defamatory if it tends to harm the reputation of another in such a way as to lower him in the estimation of the community or deter others from associating with him. In addition to proving that a statement is defamatory, a plaintiff must also prove publication and, at the very least, negligence.

Slander requires proof of suffering of some kind of special harm except in cases of slander per se. Under the common law, special harm did not have to be proved because damages were presumed. Under Supreme Court decisions in cases involving matters of public concern, however, a plaintiff cannot be awarded presumed damages unless she can prove actual malice.

A defamatory statement must have a tendency to harm the reputation of the plaintiff even though the plaintiff's reputation is not in fact injured. If the statement involves a matter of public interest and the defendant is a media defendant, the plaintiff must prove that the statement was false. At least one person must reasonably interpret the statement as being defamatory even if the statement could be interpreted in several different ways. If the defamatory content of the statement is not recognizable unless certain extrinsic facts are known, the plaintiff must specifically show the innuendo in her pleadings. Expressions of opinion generally are not considered defamatory.

Defamation requires publication. Mere repetition of a defamatory statement is considered publication even if the person repeating the statement does not believe it. An entire edition of a book or periodical is treated as one publication under the single publication rule.

Under *New York Times Co. v. Sullivan*, public officials and public figures are required to prove actual malice. A public figure is one who has achieved "pervasive fame or notoriety" or who "voluntarily injects himself or is drawn into a particular public controversy."

A successful plaintiff can recover for compensatory damages, including such nonpecuniary losses as loss of friendship, illness, and humiliation. Punitive damages can be recovered in matters of public interest if the plaintiff is able to prove the defendant acted with actual malice and in matters of private concern when only negligence is shown.

In certain circumstances defendants may be able to claim an absolute or qualified privilege of immunity. Judges, lawyers, parties, and witnesses, for example, have absolute immunity for the statements they make during judicial proceedings. Reports pertaining to public proceedings, as well as statements made to those having the capacity to act in the public interest, are subject to a qualified privilege. Qualified privileges can be lost if they are abused.

The Internet makes the risk of defamation more likely because it is a global media that is highly accessible and that promotes anonymity. Nevertheless, since the Communications Decency Act (CDA) of 1966, it has become increasingly difficult for those damaged by defamatory statements to recover against Internet Service Providers (ISPs). This act virtually eliminates all liability in defamation actions in which the plaintiff alleges that the online company is a publisher. If defamation plaintiffs cannot recover from ISPs, they can still sue the individual who posted the defamatory materials, but getting behind the anonymity of Internet messages can be extremely difficult.

The right to privacy consists of four separate torts: appropriation, unreasonable intrusion, public disclosure of private facts, and false light. Appropriation consists of the use of the value of the plaintiff's name or picture for the defendant's financial gain. Unreasonable intrusion occurs when the defendant intentionally intrudes upon the seclusion of another if that intrusion would be considered highly offensive to a reasonable person. Publicizing details of the plaintiff's private life that would be highly offensive to a reasonable person and would not be of legitimate concern to the public constitutes public disclosure of private facts. If the details publicized are contained in a public record, no tort is committed. The so-called "false light" cases occur when the plaintiff is put in the public eye in a false light that would be highly offensive to a reasonable person.

A false statement made against a plaintiff's business, product, or property opens one to a claim of injurious falsehood. A false statement made in reference to the plaintiff's goods or business is usually referred to as trade libel, but a false statement in reference to the property rights of the plaintiff is referred to as slander of title.

KEY TERMS

absolute privileges
Absolute defense to defamation, regardless of defendant's motives

actual malice
Acting with knowledge of the falsity of one's statement or with reckless disregard as to the truth or falsity of one's statement

appropriation
Use of the value of plaintiff's name or picture for defendant's financial gain

defamation
Statement that tends to harm the reputation of another, encompassing both libel and slander

false light
Representing the plaintiff to the public in a way that would be highly offensive to a reasonable person

injurious falsehood
False disparagement of a plaintiff's business, product, or property rights

innuendo
Use of extrinsic facts to convey the defamatory meaning of a statement

libel
Written defamatory statements

pecuniary
Monetary; that which can be valued in terms of money

presumed damages
Damages that ordinarily stem from a defamatory statement and that do not require the showing of actual harm

publication
Hearing or seeing of a defamatory statement by someone other than the plaintiff

public figure
One who has achieved persuasive fame or notoriety or who becomes involved in a public controversy

qualified privileges
Privilege that applies only when a defendant acts on the basis of certain well-defined purposes

slander
Oral defamatory statements

slander of title
False disparagement of the plaintiff's property rights

slander per se
Slander in which pecuniary harm can be assumed

special harm
Harm of a pecuniary nature

trade libel
False disparagement of the plaintiff's goods or business

REVIEW QUESTIONS

1. Why is defamation a complex tort?
2. How did *New York Times v. Sullivan* change the face of defamation?
3. Why is defamation seldom litigated?
4. What is the difference between libel and slander?
5. What is the special-harm requirement?
   a. In what four cases does special harm not have to be proved?
   b. What are presumed damages, and what is their relationship to special harm?
   c. What limitations has the United States Supreme Court put on presumed damages?
6. What must a plaintiff prove to recover for defamation?
7. Must a plaintiff's reputation actually be injured for her to recover for defamation? Must her reputation be tarnished in the eyes of the majority to the community?
8. How many people must reasonably understand that the defendant's statement is referring to the plaintiff in order for defamation to be proved?
   a. Must the defendant refer to the plaintiff?
   b. Must the defendant refer to the plaintiff by name?
   c. Can the plaintiff recover if the defendant's statement is made in reference to a group to which the plaintiff belongs?
9. What must a judge determine before a jury can determine that a statement is defamatory?
10. When must a plaintiff show in his pleadings the innuendo of the defendant's statement?
11. Who has the burden of proving the truth or falsity of the defendant's statement?
12. Can the survivors of a deceased person sue for defamation based on statements made about the deceased?
13. Can an expression of pure opinion be defamatory?
    a. What if the opinion implies factual matters?
    b. What do the courts consider in deciding if a statement is an opinion?

14. What is publication?
    a. What is required for a publication to occur?
    b. Does repetition of a defamatory statement constitute publication?
15. Why was defamation considered a strict liability tort under the common law?
    a. How did *New York Times v. Sullivan* change that situation?
    b. What is the definition of actual malice, and when must it be proved?
    c. Who is considered a public figure, and why are public figures given less protection than private individuals?
16. What damages can a plaintiff recover in a defamation case?
    a. Can punitive damages be awarded?
    b. Can presumed damages be awarded?
17. What are retraction statutes, and how do they operate?
18. What is the difference between an absolute and qualified privilege?
    a. Who enjoys an absolute privilege?
    b. Under what circumstances is a defendant protected by a qualified privilege?
    c. How can a qualified privilege be lost?
19. How was the tort of invasion of privacy created?
20. What four torts constitute invasion of privacy, and how are they all related?
21. Define and give an example of each of the following:
    a. appropriation
    b. unreasonable intrusion
    c. public disclosure of private facts
    d. false light
22. What is injurious falsehood?
    a. What is the difference between trade libel and slander of title?
    b. How does trade libel differ from defamation?

PRACTICE EXAM

Students should complete the practice exam after studying each chapter. The answers are in Appendix A. If you score lower than 80%, you should reread the materials.

True-False

1. Defamation involves the courts' attempt to balance freedom of expression against protection of individuals' reputation.

2. Many defamation cases are litigated, and most of those are won, especially against media defendants.

3. Libel includes statements on records and computer tapes but does not include words dictated to a stenographer.

4. In cases of slander, pecuniary losses are not necessary.

5. Under contemporary court decisions, presumed damages can never be awarded unless the plaintiff can prove actual malice.

6. A defamation plaintiff must prove that the defendant's statement is defamatory in accord with at least one interpretation a reasonable person might make.

7. A statement that is substantially true, even if it is not true in all respects, is considered a true statement.

8. Under today's United States Supreme Court decisions a defendant has the burden of proving that his statement is true.

9. Survivors of a deceased person can sue for defamation because of statements made against that person.

10. A partnership or corporation can be defamed.

11. Statements are more likely to be considered opinion if they are precise and easily verifiable.

12. A statement implying undisclosed facts may not be defamatory if it is an opinion.

13. One who repeats a defamatory statement is liable even if he does not believe it to be true.

14. Those who distribute or sell defamatory materials are liable even if they can show they had no reason to believe the materials were defamatory.

15. Defamation is essentially a strict liability tort.

16. A person can become a public figure merely by becoming involved in a controversy of public interest.

17. Unless the matter is not one of public interest, United States Supreme Court decisions require plaintiffs to prove that the defendant acted with reckless disregard at the very least if they are to recover presumed damages.

18. A defamation plaintiff who suffers no quantifiable damages cannot go to trial.

19. Absolute privileges are enjoyed by judges, lawyers, parties, and witnesses during judicial proceedings unless their motive is defamation.

20. Absolute immunity applies to husband-wife communications.

21. An individual may be qualifiedly privileged to act for the protection of the recipient of statement if the statement is made within the parameters of the generally accepted standards of decent conduct and is in the context of a close personal or business relationship.

22. A privilege can be lost if the statement is made to more people than necessary to protect the interest in question or if more damaging information is disclosed than is reasonably necessary.

23. Invasion of privacy originated as the result of a *Law Review* article.

24. Appropriation occurs when a defendant uses the plaintiff's name or picture for his own financial gain.

25. The tort of unreasonable intrusion requires proof that the defendant negligently intruded upon the seclusion of another and that the intrusion was disturbing to the plaintiff.

26. The physical intrusion required in a claim of unreasonable intrusion can involve the use of mechanical devices.

27. Public disclosure of private facts occurs when private details are published about the plaintiff's life that would be highly offensive to a reasonable person.

28. Public disclosure of private facts is a viable claim even if the details published are contained in a public record.

29. A false-light claim can also be considered grounds for defamation.

30. A false-light claim is easier in some respects to prove than defamation.

31. To recover for trade libel a plaintiff must show that the defendant made a false statement that ridiculed or disgraced the plaintiff's good or business.

32. A competitor is not privileged to "puff" if he knows his statements are false and he intends to take business away from the plaintiff.

33. The same intent, defenses, and privileges applicable to trade libel apply to slander of title.

Matching

GROUP 1

_____ 1. Radio program derived from written script

_____ 2. Requires proof of special harm

_____ 3. Required when extrinsic facts are needed to prove defamation

_____ 4. Made by a reviewer

_____ 5. Requirement that statement be seen or heard by someone other than plaintiff

a. innuendo
b. opinion
c. publication
d. slander
e. libel

GROUP 2

_____ 1. Reckless disregard for truth or falsity of statement

_____ 2. Achieved pervasive fame or notoriety

_____ 3. Discourage defamation suits

_____ 4. Enjoyed by federal and high-ranking state officials

_____ 5. Protects records from court cases and legislative hearing

a. absolute privilege
b. qualified privilege
c. public figure
d. retraction statutes
e. actual malice

GROUP 3

_____ 1. Use of value of plaintiff's name for financial gain

_____ 2. Examining the plaintiff's private bank account

_____ 3. Offensive publicity

_____ 4. False disparagement of product

_____ 5. False information about patent or copyright

a. false light
b. unreasonable intrusion
c. appropriation
d. slander of title
e. trade libel

Fill-in-the-Blanks

1. In today's defamation law, the standard of proof a plaintiff must meet is determined by the _____ of the plaintiff and the _____ involved.

2. _____ refers to defamation involving written words, whereas _____ refers to defamation involving oral words.

3. Under the common law, damages were _____ in cases of libel if the defamatory nature of the statement was obvious.

4. Under the _____ _____ rule, each copy of a book is considered a separate defamation.

5. If a plaintiff is a public official or public figure, she can recover for defamation only if she can show that the defendant acted with _____ _____.

6. A(n) _____ _____ is one who voluntarily injects himself into or is drawn into a public controversy.

7. _____ statutes may bar a plaintiff's recovery if the defendant withdraws a defamatory statement within a given time period.

8. A privilege can be lost if it is _____.

Multiple-Choice

1. Defamation
    a. is a fairly simple tort.
    b. is, under the common law, outside the protection of the First Amendment.
    c. is, after *New York Times v. Sullivan*, outside the protection of the First Amendment.
    d. all of the above.

2. The *New York Times v. Sullivan* court
    a. encouraged robust debate that may include sharp attacks on government and public officials.
    b. agreed with the common law rule that defamation plaintiffs could recover if they could show that the defendant's remarks were false.
    c. believed that defamation was a matter of state law.
    d. all of the above.

3. Special harm need not be proved in cases of slander in which it is alleged that the plaintiff
    a. has engaged in criminal conduct.
    b. has a venereal disease.
    c. is unfit to conduct her business, trade, or profession.
    d. all of the above.

4. To be considered defamatory, a statement
    a. must actually injure the plaintiff's reputation.
    b. the plaintiff must prove that at least one person understood it to refer to the plaintiff.

    c. the plaintiff's reputation must be tarnished in the eyes of the majority of the community.
    d. all of the above.

5. An opinion
    a. was considered defamatory under the common law unless it fell under the privilege of fair comment.
    b. is not considered defamatory by the United States Supreme Court if it is a pure expression of opinion.
    c. can be defamatory if it implies factual matters.
    d. all of the above.

6. Publication
    a. does not occur if the statement is not understood by the person hearing it.
    b. occurs when someone overhears the defendant make a statement about the plaintiff.
    c. must be intentional.
    d. all of the above.

7. A private figure
    a. must prove actual malice.
    b. who successfully proves defamation can recover pecuniary losses but not nonpecuniary ones.
    c. who successfully proves defamation can never recover punitive damages.
    d. all of the above.

8. A qualified privilege protects
    a. those who have the capacity to act in the public interest, such as prosecutors, when they make defamatory statements.
    b. someone who makes a defamatory statement for the purpose of gaining a competitive advantage.
    c. those who make defamatory statements to protect their own interests, no matter how insignificant those interests are, as long as they are sufficiently important and the defamation is directly related to those elements.
    d. all of the above.

9. False-light claims require proof that
    a. the plaintiff is put before the public in a false light that would be highly offensive to a reasonable person.
    b. the defendant deliberately portrayed the plaintiff in a false light.
    c. the publicity was defamatory.
    d. all of the above.

PRACTICE POINTERS

Suppose your attorney asked you to find out what happened when the Gerry Spence case was remanded to the trial court. Was Spence awarded damages against *Hustler*? If so, in what amount? How would you go about getting this information given that the lower court decision was never published?

You could contact Gerry Spence's law office and talk to his staff about the case. But how would you get the telephone number? First you would look at the appellate decision to find the name of the city and state in which Spence's attorney is practicing. Knowing the probable location of Spence's practice, you could look in the *Martindale-Hubbell Law Directory*, a compilation of the names of attorneys, their areas of practice, and personal data, including phone number, fax number, address, e-mail, and website.

Alternatively, you could go to the trial court to which the case was remanded and, using the court's indexing system, pull the court file. If you went to the court clerk's office, you could ask for the plaintiff or defendant's index and look under Spence or *Hustler*. In this file you might find, in addition to information about the disposition of the *Spence* matter, a gold mine of information, including copies of interrogatories, requests for production, and various motions that may be well researched and even well written. If the case is recent enough, you might use the jury instructions to assist in drafting jury instructions for similar cases. Once the file is reviewed, copies of exemplary documents should be copied. If the case is particularly instructive, don't be afraid to ask the attorneys or their staff questions or to see their files. Remember that imitation is the sincerest form of flattery.

On remand, the *Spence* case might have been assigned to another judge. If that were so, you could contact the original judge, whose name would be included in the appellate decision. The judge or his staff would probably be glad to find out who the assigned judge was.

Most appellate decisions are not published, and memorandum decisions are often not readily available. To get a copy of a memorandum decision, you may have to go to the clerk of the appellate court and look in an index that is similar to that used by the trial courts. Once again, you might want to look in these files at briefs to take advantage of the research done in preparing them. You might also look for transcripts of the oral arguments, which may upon request of the clerk's office be available on audiotape.

TORT TEASERS

1. Review the hypothetical scenario at the beginning of this chapter. What will the "heartthrob" have to prove if he sues for defamation? Are there any elements you anticipate he will have difficulty proving? Do you think he would be considered a public figure? Would it be difficult for him to prove libel or slander? Why?

What must the plaintiff prove in the following cases?

2. *Time Magazine* publishes a report that Plaintiff and her husband, both of whom are wealthy socialites, were granted a divorce based on adultery when in fact the divorce was granted on other grounds. The court's final judgment reads (in part): According to certain testimony in behalf of the defendant, extramarital escapades of the plaintiff were bizarre and of an amatory nature which would have made Dr. Freud's hair curl. Other testimony, in plaintiff's behalf, would indicate that defendant was guilty of bounding from one bed-partner to another with the erotic zest of a satyr. The court is inclined to discount much of this testimony as unreliable. Nevertheless, it is the conclusion and finding of the court that neither party is domesticated, within the meaning of that term as used the Supreme Court of Florida…. In the present case, it is abundantly clear from the evidence of marital discord that neither of the parties has shown the least susceptibility to domestication, and that the marriage should be dissolved.

Time's article reads as follows:

Divorced. By Russell A. Firestone Jr., 41, heir to the tire fortune: Mary Alice Sullivan Firestone, 32, his third wife; a onetime Palm Beach schoolteacher, on grounds of extreme cruelty and adultery; after six years of marriage, one son; in West Palm Beach, Fla. The 17-month intermittent trial produced enough testimony of extramarital adventures on both sides, said the judge, "to make Dr. Freud's hair curl." *Time, Inc. v. Firestone*, 424 U.S. 448 (1976).

3. The manager of Defendant's motel sends a certified letter to Plaintiff, who had been a guest at the motel. In the letter he alleges that Plaintiff left without making payment and "accidentally

packed" several items of motel property. The letter is received by Plaintiff's maid and read by Plaintiff's wife. Defendant is unaware that the Plaintiff is married. *Barnes v. Clayton House Motel*, 435 S.W.2d 616 (Tex. 1968).

4. Defendants author a book in which they claim that the models at Neiman-Marcus are "call girls" and that most of the salesmen are "fairies." Fifteen of the total of twenty-five salesmen sue on their own behalf and on behalf of the others, and all nine models sue for defamation. *Neiman-Marcus v. Lait*, 13 F.R.D. 311 (S.D.N.Y. 1952).

5. What might the defendants want to argue in the following case? Defendants file a letter with the grievance committee of the Association of the Bar of the City of New York alleging that Plaintiff has been fraudulent and dishonest in his practice as an attorney. Plaintiff claims that such allegations are defamatory. *Wiener v. Weintraub*, 239 N.E.2d 540 (N.Y. 1968).

6. Robertson, an African American, filed an action against Southwest Bell and three of her co-workers, Smithee, Graf, and Walsh, for slander and libel concerning a telephone conversation that was inadvertently recorded on the employer's voicemail system. During the conversation the co-workers blamed Southwest Bell's poor stock performance on "incompetent employees." Smithee, inferring that minorities were incompetent, stated that a "white girl" dealt with issues related to his home service from Southwest Bell. Walsh began complaining about "quotas."

Smithee: They'll never go away in Dallas. They can't get a job anywhere else. Five dollar employees that we're paying $40,000 a year for.

Graf: (inaudible) He said, yeah, if I had to take something down to the third floor to somebody like [Plaintiff], I'd just put it in her box and run

Walsh: Yeah

Was Plaintiff slandered by her co-workers' comments? *Robertson v. Southwestern Bell Yellow Pages, Inc.*, 190 S.W.3d 899 (Tex.App. 2006).

7. Philip and Barbara, high school teachers, filed a lawsuit against the school district and its principal for slander based on statements made by the principal during a meeting with Philip and Barbara. The principal accused the two of adultery after they were discovered in a locked bathroom. The principal also told them that they were subject of rumors by the staff and students who had observed them spending time together including the incident in the bathroom. Can the plaintiffs prove that they were slandered? *Williams v. Lancaster County School District*, 369 S.C. 293 S.E.2d 286 (S.C.App. 2006).

8. Plaintiff, a manufacturer of loudspeaker systems and other audio equipment, claims that the Defendant, a consumer product-testing organization, published false statements in its review of Plaintiff's loudspeakers. What claim might Plaintiff file in addition to a defamation claim? *Bose Corp. v. Consumers Union*, 508 F. Supp. 1249 (C.D. Mass. 1981).

INTERNET INQUIRIES

When locating an attorney in or outside your state, you can often do your searching online. Martindale-Hubbell has an online directory (http://www.martindale.com), as do most state bar associations. Several other online resources are available, including

West Lawyer Directory
(http://www.lawoffice.com)

Legal Industry Directory
(http://www.lawinfo.com)

1. Go to the Martindale-Hubbell online directory and find the listing for the law firm to which Gerry Spence belongs.

   a. What is the name of the law firm?

   b. When was the firm initiated?

   c. What areas of practice is the firm involved in other than those in which Mr. Spence is active?

   d. Where does the firm have offices?

2. Go to the online West Lawyer Directory (at the Web address given before question 1), and look for Gerry Spence. What additional information do you find about him that you did not find at Martindale-Hubbell?

3. Go to the Legal Industry Directory and USA Law Attorney Directory (at the Web addresses given before question 1) and look up one of the areas in which Gerry Spence practices. In which of these directories do you find a listing for Mr. Spence under his area of practice?

PRACTICAL PONDERABLES

You have been called in by your supervisor to do some preliminary work on a potential defamation case involving Ramona, a medical technician who was the victim of a vicious smear campaign conducted by members of the medical organization where she worked after it was discovered that she was about to publicly reveal their unethical billing practices. Although ultimately it became unnecessary for Ramona to testify against the medical group (because prosecutors discovered another source of the same information), Ramona believes that her name has been irreparably damaged. She has been accused by her employer of lying, of stealing monies, and of being involved in other unethical practices, all of which Ramona vehemently denies.

What will she need to prove in order to recover for defamation, and what evidence will you need to gather to support her claim?

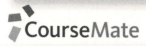 CourseMate   Access an interactive eBook, chapter-specific learning tools, including flashcards, quizzes, and more in your Paralegal CourseMate, accessed through www.CengageBrain.com.

PART III

Whom to Sue

© Cengage Learning 2012

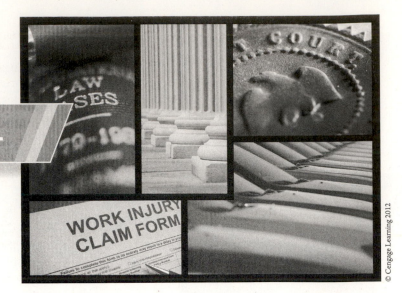
© Cengage Learning 2012

CHAPTER 14

Vicarious Liability

CHAPTER OBJECTIVES

After completing the chapter, you should be able to

- Identify the circumstances in which an employer is vicariously liable for the acts of an employee or an independent contractor.

- Distinguish between an employer-employee relationship and an employer–independent contractor relationship.

- Identify the exceptions to the bailor-nonliability rule as applied to the owners of automobiles.

- Recognize situations in which contributory negligence is imputed.

- Identify the circumstances in which parents are vicariously liable for the acts of their children.

Let us take a brief excursion into the not-too-distant future when you have completed your program of study and have assumed a position as a legal assistant. Suppose you are asked by your supervising attorney to draft a contract, and the attorney, who is called out of town on a personal emergency, never reviews the contract. As he dashes out of the office he yells back at you to be sure that the contract is signed by the parties within the week. Before you can utter a word of protest he is gone. Can he be held liable for any provisions in the contract that eventually prove detrimental to the client?

Suppose that your attorney asks you to do a research project in the library. While en route to the library you happen to pass a very elite clothing store, which you know is having an outrageous one-day only sale. Knowing that this is your only chance to take advantage of these bargains, you stop by the store for a few minutes. You put your briefcase on the floor so your hands are free to do some serious shopping. Another customer fails to notice your briefcase, catches her heel on its handles, and falls to the ground. The tumble she takes is a bad one and paramedics have to be called. Will this woman be able to sue your employer, as you were engaged in your shopping diversion during your work time?

Now suppose that, unnerved by the incident at the clothing store, you rush off to the library. Once there you immerse yourself in the task at hand. Suddenly whose face appears among the book stacks but your ex-spouse's? Because you have only recently escaped the chains of matrimony, within thirty seconds the two of you are engaged in a full-scale verbal war. Without warning, some demonic urge possesses you and you find yourself using your briefcase (the same one that just wreaked havoc on the customer) as a weapon. Will your ex be able to recover from your employer for the injuries sustained as a result of your pugilistic activities? These and other related questions are explored in this chapter.

OVERVIEW OF VICARIOUS LIABILITY

Under the doctrine of **vicarious liability**, an individual is held liable for the tortious acts of another. These acts are imputed to him because of the special relationship he holds to the tortfeasor. The most common relationship is the one between employer and employee, in which the employer is held vicariously

EXHIBIT 14–1   Examples of Vicarious Liability

Employers–Employees.
Employers–Independent Contractors.
Members of Joint Enterprise.
Automotive Consent Statutes.
Family Purpose Doctrine.

© Cengage Learning 2012

liable for the tortious acts of her employee. Vicarious liability may also arise in relationships between employers and independent contractors and in activities involving joint enterprises. Furthermore, automobile-consent statutes and the family-purpose doctrine contain elements of vicarious liability (see Exhibit 14–1).

EMPLOYER-EMPLOYEE RELATIONSHIP

An employer is vicariously liable for the acts of an employee under the doctrine of **respondeat superior**, which translates as "let the person higher up answer." This doctrine applies to negligent torts, intentional torts, and strict liability actions (see Exhibit 14–2). The rationale most commonly used to justify this doctrine is that employers should consider the expense of reimbursing those injured by their employees as part of the cost of doing business. As a practical matter, keep in mind that typically the employee is judgment-proof, whereas the employer is the proverbial "deep pocket."

For the doctrine to be applicable the employee must be acting "within the scope and furtherance of his employment" (*Restatement [Second] of Agency* § 229). An employee will be considered to be doing this as long as he is intending to further his employer's business purpose. Even if the means he chooses are indirect or foolish or if his intent is a combination of serving his employer and meeting his personal needs, he will be viewed as acting "within the scope and furtherance of his employment." Travel to and from work, however, is generally not included as falling within the scope of employment.

Intentional Torts

What if an employee intentionally injures another? The employer will still be liable as long as the tort is reasonably connected to the employee's job.

EXHIBIT 14−2 *Employer-Employee Liability (Respondeat Superior)*

EMPLOYER IS LIABLE	EMPLOYER IS NOT LIABLE
• Employee is acting within the scope and furtherance of employment. • Employee commits intentional tort reasonably connected to job. • Employee's deviation from business purpose is reasonably foreseeable. • Employee commits acts expressly forbidden by employer but within scope of employment. • Employee negligently delegates his or her rights and authority to another without the employer's authorization.	• Employee goes on "frolic" or "detour." • Employee is traveling to or from work.

A company may be liable, for example, for false imprisonment committed by an overzealous security guard who unreasonably detains a customer she suspects of shoplifting or for assault and battery committed by an employee who resorts to Rambo-style techniques in trying to collect a debt for the company. The employer will not be liable if the employee's acts are driven by some purely personal motive, such as vengeance.

Frolics and Detours

An employer is not vicariously liable when an employee goes on a "frolic" or "detour" of his own. Suppose an employee of a pizza parlor, having completed his deliveries, drives twenty miles out of his way for a little rendezvous with his girlfriend. His twenty-mile side trip would likely be considered a "frolic" or "detour" and, under the traditional view, his employer would not be vicariously liable for any acts of negligence he might commit. However, if the employee became involved in an accident while en route back to the pizza parlor, the employer would once again become vicariously liable because once he got back on track, the employee would be acting within the scope of his employment.

Under the more modern view, the employee would be seen as acting within the scope of her employment if her deviation from her business purpose was "reasonably foreseeable." Under this approach an employee whose deviation is slight in terms of time and distance is considered acting within the scope of her employment even when she is on a personal errand. The reasoning underlying this approach is that

employers should be liable for those things that can generally be anticipated as one of the risks of doing business.

Forbidden Acts

Is the employer liable even if she explicitly forbids the employee to engage in certain acts and the employee does so anyway? Yes, as long as the acts are done within the scope and furtherance of employment. Suppose a store expressly forbids its employees from using physical force to detain someone suspected of shoplifting. The store will nevertheless be vicariously liable for the negligence of its employees who countermand those orders, and wrestle to the ground and hogtie an uncooperative customer whom they suspect of shoplifting.

Delegation of Authority or Rights

Vicarious liability may or may not exist when an employee delegates his authority or rights to another without the employer's authorization. What if an employee hires someone without the employer's permission? Or what if he allows an unauthorized person to use the employer's property, such as the company car, and that person commits a tort? In both cases vicarious liability will exist if the employee acted negligently. If the employee knew or should have known that the individual lacked skills and would be unable to safely complete the job, the employer will be vicariously liable. Notice that the issue of vicarious liability hinges on the employee's negligence and not the third party's negligence, because vicarious liability is based on the link existing between the employer and the employee.

CASE

State v. Schallock
189 Ariz. 250, 941 P.2d 1275 (1997)

FELDMAN, Justice.

The state filed an action seeking a declaration that it had no duty to defend or indemnify Allen Heinze, the former executive director of the Arizona Prosecuting Attorneys Advisory Council, in two cases seeking damages for sexual harassment. The state argued indemnification was not available in either case because Heinze's acts were not in the course and scope of employment. On cross-motions for summary judgment, the trial court ruled that the state must indemnify Heinze. The court of appeals reversed, granting summary judgment in favor of the state. *See State v. Schallock*, 185 Ariz. 214, 914 P.2d 1306 (App.1995).

We granted review to decide two issues of statewide importance: first, whether collateral estoppel applies and, second, whether Heinze's actions were within the terms of the state's insurance coverage. We have jurisdiction**1277 *252 pursuant to Ariz. Const. art. VI, § 5(3) and Ariz.R.Civ.App. 23.

FACTS AND PROCEDURAL HISTORY
A. Background

Colleen Schallock, a 23-year-old law student, clerked during the summer of 1988 with the Arizona Prosecuting Attorneys Advisory Council (APAAC). Bertha Saunders was a secretary at APAAC. Allen Heinze was the executive director of APAAC and answerable only to its members, a collection of county attorneys and other government officials who meet quarterly to coordinate the training of and assistance to prosecutors.[1] Schallock and Saunders both filed lawsuits against Heinze and APAAC seeking damages for sexual harassment.

Given the procedural posture of this action, we view the facts in the light most favorable to Schallock and Saunders. Over a period spanning almost a decade, Heinze often made off-color comments, vulgar gestures, and sexual jokes, and inappropriately touched the women in the office. Work conditions were such that women employees would not work late unless a male

staff attorney was also there. One former APAAC staff member described Heinze's treatment of women employees as "like his personal harem." Between June 1984 and fall 1990, Heinze "engaged in multiple acts of sexual misconduct, including touching Saunders' crotch, buttocks, and breasts, running his hands over her arms, shoulders and the top of her chest, placing his arms around her in an attempt to force her to kiss him, unzipping his pants, unfastening his belt, and simulating sexual intercourse from behind." While both were attending a seminar in June 1984, Heinze entered Saunders' hotel room, made sexual comments, and asked her to engage in sexual intercourse. He then forced himself upon Saunders, pressing against her.

Similarly, Heinze at least twice touched Schallock's breasts and put his hand down her skirt. At a conference in Sedona in the summer of 1988, Heinze propositioned Schallock, telling her he would help her get a job in Phoenix and at the same time placing his hand on her thigh under a table. Schallock told him that was not the way she wanted to get a job. Later in the evening in a hotel room, Heinze raped Schallock. Afterward he told her he would give her a job at any amount of money she wanted. In December 1988, when Schallock was no longer working at APAAC, Heinze insisted she have lunch with him. He assaulted her again after the lunch. When she threatened to reveal the rape, he told her he was a powerful political figure and would "take her down with him."

B. Schallock's Tort Action

In her complaint, Schallock alleged (1) Heinze personally and APAAC vicariously were liable for a public policy tort (sexual harassment); (2) APAAC independently was liable for damages on the theory of negligent retention; and (3) Heinze personally and APAAC independently and vicariously were liable for intentional infliction of emotional distress. Heinze believed he would be indemnified by state insurance for any judgment against him and his wife. The state, however, reserved its rights if a court subsequently determined that Heinze's acts were outside the coverage or indemnity provided by A.R.S. § 41–621.[2] Asserting his Fifth Amendment rights, Heinze refused to give evidence in Schallock's tort case.

A. The department of administration shall obtain insurance against loss, to the extent it is determined

---

1. See A.R.S. § 41–1830 et seq., creating and defining the functions of APAAC. Title 41 of the Arizona Revised Statutes covers "State Government." APAAC was created pursuant to § 1830 of the title. APAAC is a council consisting of county attorneys, the Attorney General or his designee, one of the state's two law school deans, the chief prosecutor for a city larger than 250,000 people, one full-time prosecutor appointed by the Governor to represent smaller cities, and the Chief Justice of the Supreme Court or his designee. The Council meets quarterly to coordinate the state's prosecutors, formulate rules for prosecution, and assist prosecutors by providing various research and training programs. The Director of the Administrative Office of the Courts is the Chief Justice's present designee to APAAC.

2. § 41–621 Purchase of insurance; coverage; limitations; exclusions; definition

(continues)

necessary and in the best interests of the state as provided in subsection E of this section, on the following:

* * *

3. The state and its departments, agencies, boards and commissions and all officers, agents and employees thereof ... against liability for acts or omissions of any nature while acting in authorized governmental or proprietary capacities and in the course and scope of employment or authorization except as prescribed by this chapter.

* * *

D. The department of administration may determine, in the best interests of the state, that state self-insurance is necessary or desirable and, if that decision is made, shall provide for state self-insurance for losses arising out of state property, liability or worker's compensation claims prescribed by subsection A of this section. If the department of administration provides state self-insurance, such coverage shall be excess over any other valid and collectible insurance. (Emphasis added.) The department evidently obtained insurance from Fireman's Fund under subsection (A), but the policy was apparently exhausted and the state became a self-insurer under subsection (D).

**1278 *253 After trial, the jury returned three verdicts for Schallock and against APAAC and Heinze. In the first verdict, the jury found Heinze liable for "intentional or reckless infliction of emotional distress, and/or sexual harassment in the workplace, and ... the full damages to be $1,476,535.50."[3] In its second verdict (form 3), the jury stated APAAC was liable " for intentional infliction of emotional distress, and/or sexual harassment in the workplace and ... the full damages to be $908,446.50." In its third verdict (form 6), the jury found APAAC liable for "negligent hiring and full damages to be $908,446.50." Given the jury's answer to the accompanying interrogatory, we interpret this verdict as finding APAAC directly liable for negligent hiring, supervision, and retention of Heinze based on evidence that (1) Heinze had been dismissed from previous employment with a law enforcement agency because of charges of sexual impropriety, a fact allegedly known to one or more APAAC members when Heinze was hired; and (2) Heinze's aberrant sexual activities with APAAC's employees extended over almost a decade and were known or should have been known to APAAC's members. The jury also wrote a note: "We want it to

be clear that we have divided the liability in the following manner: Mr. Heinze $1,476,553.50 and APAAC $908,446.50 and total liability is $2,385,000."

VERDICT FORM 1: Jury to use this form if the jurors answered either or both of the following questions in the affirmative. The jurors answered both affirmatively.
1. Was Heinze liable to Schallock for intentional or reckless infliction of emotional distress?
2. Was Heinze liable to Schallock for sexual harassment in the work place?
VERDICT: Jury found for Schallock and against Heinze for intentional or reckless infliction of emotional distress, and/or sexual harassment in the workplace. Full damages: $1,476,553.50 (handwritten in is "total $2,389,000").

VERDICT FORM 3: Jury to use this form if the jurors answered either of the following questions in the affirmative. The jurors answered both affirmatively.
1. Was APAAC liable for intentional or reckless infliction of emotional distress?
2. Was APAAC liable for sexual harassment in the work place?
VERDICT: Jury found for Schallock and against APAAC for intentional infliction of emotional distress, and/or sexual harassment in the workplace. Full damages: $908,446.50.

VERDICT FORM 6: Jury to use this form if the jurors answered the following question in the affirmative. The jurors answered affirmatively.
1. Was APAAC at fault for negligently hiring, supervising, and retaining Heinze?
VERDICT: Jury found for Schallock and against APAAC on the negligent hiring, retention, and supervision claim. Full damages: $908,446.50.

Before trial, the state and Schallock made a "high-low" agreement, providing a formula for a guaranteed payment to Schallock; in return, if a verdict were returned against APAAC, Schallock agreed to dismiss the action against it. Therefore, although verdicts 3 and 6 were returned on the claims presumably establishing APAAC's direct and vicarious liability, judgment was never entered on those verdicts. Instead, complying with the settlement agreement, Fireman's Fund, the state's insurer, paid Schallock $725,000 in full settlement of the $908,000 verdict against APAAC. We assume the $1.4 million verdict against Heinze, which was eventually reduced to judgment, remains unpaid.

C. The State's Declaratory Judgment Action
During the course of the tort litigation, the state filed this declaratory judgment action **1279 *254 claiming it

---

3. The jury was given various verdict forms and interrogatories to answer. The verdict form used depended on the answers to the interrogatories. The verdicts returned by the jury were:

(continues)

could not indemnify Heinze for Saunders' and Schallock's claims because his acts were outside the course and scope of his employment. In Schallock's trial, the judge directed a verdict on the vicarious liability issue, finding no factual support for the state's contention that Heinze's actions were not in the course and scope of his authority as APAAC's director. However, because the verdict was never reduced to judgment, the order directing a verdict on course and scope was never merged in a final judgment or appealable order.

Because there was no judgment entered, the state claims there is no collateral estoppel on the issue of course and scope and the directed verdict therefore cannot be used to establish course and scope for insurance purposes under A.R.S. § 41–621(A)(3). On cross-motions for summary judgment, the trial judge in the declaratory judgment action relied on the doctrine of collateral estoppel flowing from the directed verdict in the tort case and concluded that under § 41–621 the state was required to indemnify Heinze.

D. The Court of Appeals' Opinion

Putting aside as irrelevant the issue of APAAC's direct liability, the court of appeals characterized the question as whether the state must indemnify a state employee against his personal liability for sexual harassment. The court of appeals held there was no collateral estoppel on the issue of course and scope because the directed verdict was never reduced to judgment. It then concluded as a matter of law that Heinze's "tortious acts were not in the course and scope of his employment" and therefore A.R.S. § 41–621 "does not extend Heinze indemnity for his conduct." Schallock, 185 Ariz. at 218, 914 P.2d at 1310. The court vacated the summary judgment granted in favor of Schallock and ordered the trial judge to enter judgment in favor of the state, in effect granting its motion for summary judgment.

We granted review to consider only two questions:

1. Whether collateral estoppel applies where a party has fully litigated the issue to a verdict but a judgment has not been entered because of a settlement between the parties.
2. Whether Heinze's actions were within the terms of the coverage provided by the state insurance pursuant to A.R.S. § 41–621.

DISCUSSION

1. What was decided on course and scope
A review of the trial court record in this action reveals ample evidence that at least some APAAC members knew of Heinze's improper conduct. Relevant portions of the transcripts and depositions taken in the tort case were part of the declaratory judgment action record. In those depositions, APAAC staff attorneys admitted having seen Heinze fondle female employees and force them to kiss him at holiday parties, and heard him use crude and sexually explicit language. Likewise, some Council members heard Heinze use rough, sexually explicit language and had received complaints from outside attorneys about Heinze's use of pejoratives of a sexual nature. Finally, at a conference in May 1988, a former clerk spoke with a Council member and a former APAAC employee about Heinze's propensity to treat women employees as his harem. The clerk had also complained to the staff attorneys about the unwanted attention from Heinze, to no avail. Thus, as the court of appeals acknowledges, there was evidence in the tort case from which the judge could have found as a matter of law that Heinze's actions were or should have been known to some Council members. Schallock, 185 Ariz. at 218, 914 P.2d at 1310. However, because the entire evidentiary record from the tort case is not before us, it is impossible to fully ascertain the grounds on which the judge based his directed verdict ruling.

B. Course and Scope for Purposes of Indemnification

The second issue on which we granted review was whether the state must indemnify Heinze because his actions were within the course and scope of his employment. This does not quite state the issue briefed and argued. Because Heinze was found liable in the tort action and the state has satisfied its direct liability to Schallock under the settlement agreement, the correct issue in the declaratory judgment action is whether the state must indemnify Heinze for the judgment against him. At this point, the state is evidently a self-insurer providing coverage under A.R.S. § 41–621(D), which provides for "self-insurance for losses arising out of state … liability … [as] prescribed by subsection A of this section."

As both the trial judge and court of appeals correctly saw it, the central issue is whether Heinze's conduct was within the coverage extended by subsection A, which provides indemnity for an officer acting within "the course and scope of employment or authorization." Of course, when the officer acts in that manner, the state ordinarily will be vicariously liable. See Restatement (Second) of Agency Y (hereinafter Restatement) § 219 et seq. The insurance statute thus understandably provides coverage for the officer in those situations in which the state itself could be held liable.

1. Interpreting course, scope, and authorization
We turn, as did the court of appeals and trial court, to the nature of Heinze's actions. On this issue, the trial judge in the tort case instructed the jury as follows:

If you find that Defendant Heinze intentionally inflicted emotional distress upon Plaintiff, then you must determine if Defendant APAAC is responsible for his actions.

(continues)

1. Defendant APAAC is subject to liability for the actions of Defendant Heinze committed while acting in the scope of his employment. To hold an employer liable, an employee must:

    a. have acted within the scope of his employment;

    b. be subject to the employer's control or right of control;

    c. have acted in furtherance of the employer's business.

An employee's conduct is within the scope of employment if and only if;

    a. it is the kind he is employed to perform;

    b. it occurs substantially within authorized time and space limits; and

    c. it is motivated, at least in part, by a purpose to serve the employer.

2. Defendant APAAC is subject to liability for the actions of Heinze acting outside the scope of his employment, if;

    a. Defendant APAAC intended the conduct or the consequences; or

    b. Defendant APAAC was negligent or reckless; or

    c. Defendant Heinze purported to act or speak on behalf of Defendant APAAC and he was aided in accomplishing his misconduct by the existence of the agency relationship.

(Emphasis added.) The instruction, taken almost verbatim from *Restatement* § 219, contains two separate theories of vicarious liability. Part 2(c) paraphrases the words of § 219(2)(d), which, as we shall see later, deals with the master's vicarious liability for torts a servant was empowered to commit because of the master's delegation of authority.

The court of appeals noted the "state correctly asserts that 'Heinze is provided coverage [by the statute] only if his acts were performed . . . in the course and scope of employment or authorization.' Schallock and Saunders respond that 'so long as the tort complained of was caused incidental to the exercise of the supervisory power, Heinze must be deemed as acting within the course and scope of his employment.' " *Schallock*, 185 Ariz. at 219, 914 P.2d at 1310.

In concluding that Schallock's position was incorrect, the court of appeals relied on its prior decision in *Smith v. American Express Travel Related Services Co.*, which held the employer was not vicariously liable for a supervisor's harassment and sexual assaults on an employee because the supervisor's acts were not expressly or impliedly authorized by the employer or in furtherance of its business. 179 Ariz. 131, 136, 876 P.2d 1166, 1171 (1994). The language of Smith, standing alone, would mean that an employer is never vicariously liable for an intentional tort. We believe this sweeps much too

broadly. In addition, we note that in Smith the evidence did not establish the employer's actual or constructive knowledge of the supervisor's conduct. Thus, even if correctly decided, Smith is much different than the case before us, as can be seen from the court's language:

[N]o evidence exists from which a reasonable juror could conclude that [the employer] knew about [the supervisor's] sexual misconduct and ratified it. . . . Finally, no evidence exists in this record from which a reasonable juror could conclude that [the employer] knew or should have known that [the supervisor] had created a sexually offensive working environment and thus was capable of sexual assault.

Id. at 137, 876 P.2d at 1172. We do not believe Smith is applicable here and turn therefore to an analysis of agency law.

2. Law of agency-factors peculiar to supervisory sexual harassment cases

In *Schallock* the court of appeals stated, "[f]ollowing Smith and the *Restatement (Second) of Agency*, we hold that Heinze did not act in the course and scope of employment. . . . Though Heinze used his broad supervisory authority as a license for sexually predatory acts, these acts were not intended to serve APAAC but himself." *Schallock*, 185 Ariz. at 218, 914 P.2d at 1310. The court then rejected Schallock's contrary argument because it "confuses elements of independent **1282 *257 and vicarious liability[4] and obscures the traditional lines of course and scope." Id.

We disagree with the court of appeals on several grounds. First, given the facts of this case, we do not believe it can be said as a matter of law that Heinze was outside the course and scope of authority with regard to many or most of the incidents alleged by Saunders and Schallock. Second, the court has overlooked entirely the question of authorization: the statute grants indemnity for acts done within "course and scope or authorization." A.R.S. § 41–621(A)(3) (emphasis added). Finally, the court has conflated principles required to establish a master's direct liability in tort with those necessary to find vicarious liability.

Before addressing these issues, it is important to note four special factual and legal considerations in cases of the present type. First, this case involves claims of a managing officer's sexual harassment of subordinate employees over whom he had power to hire and fire, promote and demote, instruct and control. This distinguishes the case from the great majority of cases involving torts committed by a servant against either a

---

4. But see *Restatement* § 213, cmt. h, "In a given case the Employer may be liable both on the ground that he was personally negligent and because the servant's conduct was within the scope of employment."

(continues)

non-employee or co-employee. Language used in such cases is sometimes inapplicable to cases involving a managing officer's harassment of a subordinate. See David Benjamin Oppenheimer, Exacerbating the Exasperating: Title VII Liability of Employers for Sexual Harassment Committed by Their Supervisors, 81 Cornell L.Rev. 66, 71 (1995). Second, the law of agency governs both commercial relations and master-servant relations. We must be careful to apply only those rules that pertain to the latter situation. Id. Third, phrases such as "course and scope of employment" and "scope of authority" carry the gloss of historical meaning and policy considerations much more complex than the words themselves indicate. See *Doe v. Samaritan Counseling Center*, 791 P.2d 344, 349 (Alaska 1990) (quoting *Fruit v. Schreiner*, 502 P.2d 133, 140–41 (Alaska 1972)). Finally, in determining course and scope in a sexual harassment case, we must realize that employers never adopt resolutions authorizing sexual harassment. Nor do they grant such authority in job descriptions or employment manuals. *Oppenheimer*, supra, 81 Cornell L.Rev. at 84; *Faragher v. City of Boca Raton*, 111 F.3d 1530, 1541 (11th Cir.1997) (Barkett, J., concurring in part, dissenting in part). In the absence of written controls, a firm's policies set the limits both on what is tolerated or permitted and on the authority given its supervisors.

With these considerations in mind, we address the specifics of the present case.

3. The *Restatement* rule
We believe the court of appeals erred in concluding the *Restatement* compelled them to grant summary judgment to the state. The principles expressed by the *Restatement* do not permit judgment for the state as a matter of law. Conduct within the scope of employment may be either of the same nature as that authorized or incidental to that authorized. *Restatement* § 229(1). Many factors are to be considered in determining whether conduct not expressly authorized is so incidental as to be within course and scope, including time and place of the conduct. Id. § 229(2)(b). Almost all of Heinze's improper acts took place at APAAC's office or a related location, such as a seminar site or training session, and were within or incidental to business hours or sessions.

Another factor is the previous relation between master and servant. Id. § 229(2)(c). Taking Schallock's case at its strongest, as we must on summary judgment, APAAC was aware for close to a decade that Heinze, the person managing its affairs, was engaged in egregious improprieties and did little or nothing to call a halt. A jury might well choose not to believe claims that these acts were unauthorized and outside the course of employment when the employer permitted them to occur and recur over a long period at its place of business and during**1283 *258 business hours. In addition to evidence of Council members' actual knowledge, there is considerable evidence that the abusive working conditions created by Heinze were so pervasive that a jury could infer APAAC was aware of the way Heinze ran its business and by permitting such conditions to continue authorized his abusive acts. See *Faragher*, 111 F.3d at 1538, and cases cited.

A third relevant factor is whether "the master has reason to expect that such an act will be done." *Restatement* § 219(2)(b). One can hardly be surprised when sexual harassment that has occurred for years continues. A jury might well find that if APAAC was aware of the work environment Heinze created, it should have anticipated even the final sexual assaults and rapes with which Heinze is charged in these cases.

Some aspects of this case seemingly favor a finding that Heinze's actions were not in the scope and course of employment. One is the purpose of the acts: to be within the course and scope, the act must be, at least in part, motivated by a purpose to serve the master rather than solely to serve personal motives unconnected to the master's business. *Restatement* § 235. But here again, and particularly in a sexual harassment case, the act in question is not the ultimate tortious act but rather conduct related to the tort. In fondling the file clerks and offering advancement for sex, Heinze was both serving the master by running the office—a task he was explicitly authorized to do—and serving his personal desires. That his motives were mixed is of consequence, but the mixed motives cut both ways. See *Restatement* §§ 235 & 236. In Doe, the Alaska Supreme Court reviewed the cases and concluded that an improper sexual relationship initiated by a pastoral counselor during therapy sessions with a patient satisfied the "motivation to serve" test because it was incidental to the servant's legitimate work activity-therapy. 791 P.2d at 347–48; see also *Perez v. Van Groningen & Sons*, 41 Cal.3d 962, 227 Cal.Rptr. 106, 719 P.2d 676 (Cal.1986) (while driving master's equipment, servant gave plaintiff ride for personal reasons); *Samuels v. Southern Baptist Hospital*, 594 So.2d 571, 573–74 (La.App.1992) (rape of patient by nursing assistant); *Oppenheimer*, supra, 81 Cornell L.Rev. at 66, 82–84. The relevant purpose to be ascertained is not whether Heinze had authority to harass—no supervisor has that authority—but whether he had authority to run and was running APAAC's business. See *Restatement* § 235, cmt. b.

This principle has been recognized in Arizona. In *State v. Pima County Adult Probation Department*, several probation officers sought coverage under *A.R.S.*

(continues)

§ 41–621(A)(3) against a damage claim asserted because a probationer under the department's supervision had been allowed contact with juveniles, in direct violation of the superior court's order. The state argued that because the probation officers intentionally violated the court's express instructions, they were not acting within the course and scope of employment and thus were not entitled to coverage. The court of appeals rejected that claim, holding that in supervising the probationer, the officers acted in the course and scope of their employment because the act of supervision was their employer's business. The fact that they violated express instructions was an element to be considered but not conclusive on the question of course and scope. 147 Ariz. 146, 149, 708 P.2d 1337, 1340 (App.1985). So long as the officers were subject to the department's control or right of control and were in general acting in furtherance of the department's business, they were within the course and scope. Id. at 149–50, 708 P.2d at 1340–41. See *Faragher*, 111 F.3d at 1536 (If "the act was the agent's way of accomplishing some authorized purpose, then the master cannot avoid liability even if he has given specific, detailed and emphatic instructions to the contrary.");[5] W. Page Keeton,**1284 *259 et al., Prosser & Keeton on the *Law of Torts* § 70, at 507 (5th ed.1984) (describing "tendency" in later cases to find course and scope when the "employment has provided a peculiar opportunity and even incentive" for servant's intentional tort).

[A principal] is held liable to third persons in a civil suit for the frauds, deceits, concealments, misrepresentations, torts, negligences, and other malfeasances, or misfeasances, and omissions of duty, of his agent, in the course of his employment, although the principal did not authorize, or justify, or participate in, or, indeed, know of such misconduct, or even if he forbade the acts, or disapproved of them.

111 F.3d at 1541 (quoting Joseph Story, *Commentaries on the Law of Agency* § 452, at 536–37 (5th ed. 1857)).

Other factors to be considered include the seriously criminal nature of the acts and extent of departure from normal methods of operation. See *Restatement* § 229(2) (i) & (j). But acts may be found in the scope even if "forbidden or done in a forbidden manner," and even if consciously criminal or tortious. *Restatement* §§ 230 and 231.

[10] The acts complained of here were part of or incidental to Heinze's employment by APAAC, even though done to satisfy Heinze's aberrant desires. Heinze was in complete charge of APAAC's day-to-day operation. Conduct done "with no intention to perform it as part of a service for which the servant is employed"

is ordinarily outside the scope. *Restatement* § 235. Heinze's conduct, however, was incidental to his position and authority as APAAC's executive director.

We therefore conclude that the court of appeals' reliance on the *Restatement of Agency* to support summary judgment on the issue of course and scope was misplaced. Under *Restatement* principles, the *Restatement* factors that apply to the facts of this case create a jury question. But we do not rely on the *Restatement* alone. We believe analysis of case law dealing with similar situations leads to the same conclusion.

4. **Federal cases on course and scope in sexual harassment cases**

In Smith, the court of appeals discounted the federal cases, reasoning that liability under cases dealing with Title VII[6] "is much broader than common law tort liability." *Smith*, 179 Ariz. at 135, 876 P.2d at 1170. We again disagree with Smith, believing the United States Supreme Court's decision in *Meritor Savings Bank v. Vinson* instructed federal courts to take agency law as a guide in determining employer liability for a supervisor's acts of sexual harassment when deciding a Title VII case. 477 U.S. 57, 71–72, 106 S.Ct. 2399, 2408, 91 L.Ed.2d 49 (1986).

Chief Justice Rehnquist, writing for the Court, proclaimed no unique rule for determining vicarious liability in cases dealing with a supervisor's sexual harassment. Instead, the Court rejected the administrative agency's view that an employer is absolutely or strictly liable for a supervisor's actions and directed the district courts as follows:

Congress wanted courts to look to agency principles for guidance in this area. While such common law principles may not be transferrable in all their particulars to Title VII, Congress' decision to define employer to include any "agent" of an employer, ... surely evinces an intent to place some limits on the acts of employees for which employers under Title VII are to be held responsible. For this reason, we hold that the court of appeals erred in concluding that employers are always automatically liable for sexual harassment by their supervisors. See generally *Restatement (Second) of Agency* § 219–237 (1958). For the same reason, absence of notice to an employer does not necessarily insulate that employer from liability.

Id. at 72, 106 S.Ct. at 2408. Following Meritor, most if not all circuit court decisions dealing with Title VII sexual harassment actions have applied the common law of agency to determine the employer's vicarious liability. See Katherine Philippakis, Comment, When Employers

---

5. This is not a new principle. Judge Barkett's opinion relies on Justice Story's 1857 Commentaries on the Law of Agency:

6. We use "Title VII" to describe the Civil Rights Act of 1964, 42 U.S.C. §§ 2000e-17 (1988).

(continues)

Should be Liable for Supervisory Personnel: Applying Agency Principles to Hostile-Environment Sexual Harassment Cases, 28 Ariz. St. L.J. 1275, 1279 (1997). For that reason, we believe post- Meritor Title VII cases apply common-law agency principles and should be considered.

The federal cases cover both quid pro quo and hostile work environment situations. A quid pro quo claim is one in which the offender conditions job benefits or advancements on the employee's performance **1285 *260 of sexual favors, while a hostile-environment claim is one in which the offender creates a sexually "hostile or offensive working environment." Id. at 1276; *Meritor*, 477 U.S. at 65, 106 S.Ct. at 2404. Given these definitions, both types of claims are raised by the facts here.

In quid pro quo cases, applying traditional agency principles, many courts have hold an employer liable because a quid pro quo harasser is able to grant such job benefits or detriments only because he has actual or apparent authority to do so delegated to him by his employer.... Under traditional agency principles the exercise of such actual or apparent authority gives rise to liability on the part of the employer under a theory of respondeat superior. See *Restatement (Second) of Agency* § 219(2)(d) (1958).

Nichols v. Frank, 42 F.3d 503, 514 (9th Cir.1994) (collecting cases).

Some hostile environment cases have found a jury question with regard to vicarious liability. In a case similar to ours, the plaintiff had both hostile environment and quid pro quo claims. The harasser was not only her immediate supervisor but the corporate vice president in charge of managing the hotel property where the plaintiff worked. He had full authority to determine employee benefits and to hire, fire, promote, and discipline the employees. *Martin v. Cavalier Hotel Corp.*, 48 F.3d 1343, 1348 (4th Cir.1995). The circuit court affirmed judgment against the employer, stating that it was following Meritor and applying the common law of agency in determining the question of vicarious liability. Id. at 1350. In applying those "principles in the context of this case," the court stated:

[W]hether an employee's acts are within the scope of his employment requires an examination of when the act took place, where it took place, and whether it was foreseeable. See generally *Restatement (Second) of Agency* §§ 210 to 245 (1958). (Emphasis in original.) An employer may be liable for an employee's acts even if the employee's motive is not to benefit the employer, to advance his self interest rather than the interest of his employer.... A forbidden or even consciously criminal or tortious act may still be within the scope of employment.... Indeed an employer may be liable for its employee's unauthorized use of force

if such use was foreseeable in view of the employee's duties.... The test of the liability of the employer for the tortious act of the employee is not whether the tortious act itself is a transaction within the ordinary course of the business of the employer or within the scope of the employee's authority, but whether the service itself in which the tortious act was done was within the ordinary course of such business or within the scope of such authority....

Here Bachelor's assaults took place in the work place, during working hours, on an employee whom he had authority to hire, fire, promote, and discipline. There is no question that such sexual assaults were foreseeable;.... Thus, under common law agency principles Bachelor was acting within the scope of his employment with Cavalier and so Cavalier is liable for Bachelor's assaults on Martin. To be sure, ... Bachelor's assaults on Martin were "outrageous and violative of his employer's rules." Nonetheless, those assaults arose out of Bachelor's management of the hotel,.... At the very least, because Bachelor's "willful and malicious acts were committed while he was performing his employment duties" there is here ... sufficient evidence to present "a jury issue" as to whether Bachelor was acting "within the scope of his employment" with Cavalier.

Id. at 1351–52 (citations omitted, emphasis added) (quoting *Commercial Business Systems, Inc. v. Bellsouth Services, Inc.*, 249 Va. 39, 453 S.E.2d 261, 266 (Va.1995)); see also *Fields v. Sanders*, 29 Cal.2d 834, 180 P.2d 684 (1947); *Philappakis*, supra, 28 Ariz. State L.J. at 1288 (any other interpretation of motive to serve the employer would be unduly constrained and antithetical to the *Restatement* position).

Many other federal cases have reached the same conclusion on more or less the same analysis, applying the *Restatement* and common law agency cases in both quid pro **1286 *261 quo and hostile environment cases. See, e.g., *Kauffman v. Allied Signal, Inc.*, 970 F.2d 178, 183–84 (6th Cir.1992) (court should look at "when the act took place, where it took place, and whether it was foreseeable" to determine whether supervisor's harassment occurred within course and scope of employment). Kauffman holds the employer is relieved of liability if the company learns of the hostile work environment created by its supervisor and takes prompt remedial action. Id. at 184. This part of the decision has been cogently criticized on the ground that prompt remedial action could insulate against direct liability for negligence and against punitive damage claims, but not against vicarious liability. *Oppenheimer*, supra, 81 Cornell L.RevV. at 132. We need not concern ourselves with this issue because the present record contains no evidence of remedial action prior to Schallock's filing her damage action.

(continues)

Some federal cases have rejected employer course and scope liability absent evidence that the employer also knew or should have known of the hostile work environment created by the supervisor. See, e.g., *Nichols*, 42 F.3d at 508; *Henson v. City of Dundee*, 682 F.2d 897, 905 (11th Cir.1982). These cases have also been cogently criticized as confusing elements necessary for a finding of direct liability with those required for vicarious, course and scope responsibility. See *Phillipakis*, supra, 28 Ariz. State L.J. at 1285; *Oppenheimer*, supra, 81 Cornell L.Rev. at 133–35 (citing cases). Again, though the criticism seems logical, we need not solve this problem because the partial record of the tort case indicates quite clearly that APAAC had either actual knowledge of the hostile work environment or at worst constructive knowledge because the conditions were so widespread and prevalent. See *Faragher*, 111 F.3d at 1538; *E.E.O.C. v. Mitsubishi Motor Mfg. of Am. Inc.*, 102 F.3d 869, 870 (7th Cir.1996) (where hostile work environment is pervasive, employer's knowledge may be imputed or inferred).

Notwithstanding the confusion and debate among the federal circuits, we conclude APAAC is not entitled to summary judgment on the course and scope issue in Schallock's and Saunders' hostile environment claims. The court of appeals thus erred in instructing the trial court to enter judgment for the state.

C. Authorization

We believe the court of appeals also erred in overlooking the word "authorization" as used in *A.R.S.* § 41–621(A)(3), which provides coverage for officers acting in "course and scope of employment or authorization." (Emphasis added.)

We note first that authorization must mean something other than the idea that the tortious act was authorized. If the act itself was authorized, then the conduct would have been in the course and scope. We believe, therefore, that authorization as used in the statute applies to vicarious liability found outside course and scope of employment.

That liability is described in *Restatement* § 219(2) and may be imposed because of the authority or power the master has given a servant, especially one in a supervisorial position. Under common-law principles of agency a master is vicariously liable outside of course and scope of employment for torts committed by a servant when the servant purports to "act or speak on behalf of" the master and "was aided in accomplishing the tort by the existence of the agency relationship." *Restatement* § 219(2)(d).

Heinze spoke and acted for APAAC. It put him in a position to control and run its business, evidently investing him with power to run its office and control its employees.

It did this arguably knowing or having reason to know of his aberrant propensities. It kept him in that position for nearly a decade, again arguably knowing the manner in which he conducted himself. From this record, it appears APAAC did not adopt either a formal policy against sexual harassment or a grievance procedure for employees. As a result, complaints about sexually harassing incidents presumably were to be resolved by Heinze, the perpetrator. Given these factors, we cannot say as a matter of law that the master has no vicarious liability for acts outside the scope of employment. The comment**1287 *262 to *Restatement* § 219 puts it in the following words:

This Subsection enumerates the situations in which a master may be liable for torts of servants acting solely for their own purposes and hence not in the scope of employment.... Clause (d) includes primarily situations in which the principal's liability is based upon conduct which is within the apparent authority of a servant, as where one purports to speak for his employer in defaming another or interfering with another's business. Apparent authority may also be the basis of an action of deceit, and even physical harm. In other situations, the servant may be able to cause harm because of his position as agent, as where a telegraph operator sends false messages purporting to come from third persons. Again the manager of a store operated by him for an undisclosed principal is enabled to cheat the customers because of his position. The enumeration of such situations is not exhaustive, and is intended only to indicate the area within which a master may be subjected to liability for acts of his servants not in scope of employment.

Restatement § 219(2), cmt. e (citations omitted) (emphasis added). We believe *Restatement* § 219(2)(d) deals with a supervisor's authority and that employer liability in factual situations such as this is well recognized both in agency case law and in Title VII cases. See, e.g., *Faragher*, 111 F.3d at 1536; see also *Oppenheimer*, supra, 81 Cornell L. Rev. at 88–90 and nn. 110–113 (analyzing both common law and Title VII cases). Oppenheimer concludes that such "liability is properly viewed as vicarious, not direct, since it [may be] imposed without considering the fault of the employer." Id. at 88.

Many of the federal cases have found vicarious liability properly imposed under *Restatement* § 219(2)(d) under facts similar to those before us. See, e.g., *Harrison v. Eddy Potash, Inc.*, 112 F.3d 1437, 1445–46 (10th Cir.1997); *Karibian v. Columbia University*, 14 F.3d 773, 780 (2d Cir.1994).

Application of the authority concept to supervisorial sexual harassment cases has been described in the following manner:

Moreover, under common law agency principles an employer is also liable for an employee's wrongful acts,

(continues)

even if those acts are not committed within the actual scope of his employment, if the employee uses his apparent authority to accomplish the wrongful acts and so is acting within the "apparent scope" of his employment.

Martin, 48 F.3d at 1352 (citations omitted) (emphasis in original).

Under the common law of agency a supervisor's use of the actual or apparent authority of his position-power conferred by the employer-"gives rise to [the employer's] liability under a theory of respondeat superior." Nichols, 42 F.3d at 514, citing *Restatement* § 219(2)(d) and cases; see also *Harrison*, 112 F.3d at 1450.

Heinze's sexually abusive acts were thus within his authorization if it is found that APAAC gave Heinze the power and authority with which to create and maintain a sexually abusive work environment or to establish a quid pro quo position over APAAC employees. We believe the record in this case, including the authority given Heinze, his methods of operating the office, APAAC's

tolerance of those methods, and the lack or presence of sexual harassment policies or grievance procedures are factors that prohibit summary judgment in favor of the state on this issue also. See *Harrison*, 112 F.3d at 1444.

CONCLUSION

The trial judge erred in granting summary judgment on the basis of collateral estoppel. That doctrine is inapplicable to this case, in which no judgment was entered against the party sought to be estopped. Accordingly, we vacate the trial court's judgment in favor of Schallock.

The court of appeals erred in directing judgment in favor of the state. The present record does not establish as a matter of law that Heinze's acts were not within the course and scope or authorization of his employment. Accordingly, we vacate the court of appeals' opinion.

Because this court did not accept review of all the issues raised on appeal, we remand the case to the court of appeals for further proceedings consistent with this opinion.

PUTTING IT INTO PRACTICE 14:1

1. Mr. Stone, a car salesman, is involved in a fatal accident on the way to pick up Mr. Urban, a customer. Is the car dealership liable for the injuries Stone caused, considering that no one at the dealership authorized or even knew about his trip? What factors would you consider in answering this question?

2. Richard, an employee of Staggs-Bilt Homes, is hired to patrol several subdivisions that are under construction. He is instructed to observe and report suspicious behavior but not to get involved. While filling up a Staggs truck at a service station, Richard pulls his gun from his holster, either in horseplay or to show Rex, the service station attendant. The gun accidentally discharges, injuring Rex. Is Staggs-Bilt Homes vicariously liable for Richard's negligence?

3. A janitor negligently starts a trash fire when he burns the refuse. He was specifically ordered not to dispose of trash by burning it. Is his employer vicariously liable?

4. Contrary to his employer's instructions not to let anyone drive the truck or even ride in it, a truck driver allows a thirteen-year-old to drive the truck. If they are involved in an accident while the teenager is driving, under what conditions will the employer be liable to the injured party?

5. Tena, a cocktail waitress, is involved in an accident while she is en route to the assistant manager's house immediately following her shift. At the request of a band member, she is picking up a microphone part, which the band needs to complete its performance. The band has been hired by the restaurant to draw people into the restaurant. Members of the band are staying at the assistant manager's house. Should the restaurant be held liable for the accident Tena caused?

6. In accordance with directions by his employer, a clerk takes home papers to work on. He is involved in an accident on his way back to work. Should his employer be held vicariously liable?

EMPLOYERS–INDEPENDENT CONTRACTORS

Generally, one who hires an independent contractor will not be held vicariously liable for the tortious acts of that person. Exceptions exist, but before dealing with those exceptions, let us first distinguish between an employee and an independent contractor. An employee is typically viewed as someone under the control of the person who hired him; an **independent contractor**, although hired to produce certain results, is considered her own boss. An independent contractor works at her own pace, in her own way, under her own supervision.

Under this definition, would a newspaper carrier be considered an employee or an independent contractor? *Santiago v. Phoenix Newspapers, Inc.*(794 p2d 138 (Ariz. 1990) raises this question. The court considers a number of factors, including the amount of control exercised by the employer over the carrier's work, the nature of the carrier's work, the length of employment, the method of payment, and so on. Read *Santiago* and notice that the language in the parties' contract does not determine the nature of their relationship.

CASE

Juarez et al, Plaintiffs v. CC Services, Inc.
434 F.Supp.2d 755 (D.Ariz.,2006)

SILVER, District Judge.

Both Plaintiffs and Defendants have filed a Motion for Summary Judgment. For the following reasons, Plaintiffs' motion will be denied and Defendants' motion will be granted.[1]

BACKGROUND

Between 1997 and 2002, Plaintiff Guillermo Juarez ("Juarez") worked at residential home construction sites operated and controlled by Westarz Homes, L.L.C. (Id. § 9) (Defendants' Statement of Facts "DSOF" Exhibit 5) Kim Westberg was the principal of Westarz. (Id. § 9) He hired or contracted with Travis Bever ("Bever") "to act as a superintendent" at various construction sites operated by Westarz. (Id. § 9) Bever's responsibilities at those sites included supervising sub-contractors, overseeing the progress of construction, and hauling trash from the sites to local landfills. (DSOF § 14, Bever Depo. 31) Westarz provided a dump truck for Mr. Bever to haul the trash. (Id.) This truck belonged to Mr. Westberg and it was insured by an automobile insurance policy with Defendant Country Mutual Insurance Company ("Country"). (Bever Depo. 31, DSOF § 5)

On January 31, 2002, Juarez and Bever were working at a Westarz operated construction site in Phoenix. (DSOF Ex. 5) While backing the dump truck down a driveway, Bever struck Juarez, crushing his left arm and shoulder. (DSOF Ex. 5) As a result of that accident, Juarez was unable to work and he filed for worker's compensation benefits. (Id.) After filing for benefits, Juarez learned that Westarz did not have workers' compensation insurance. Westarz justified this failure by claiming that it did not have any employees. (DSOF Ex. 6) In light of Westarz's lack of insurance, Juarez requested compensation from the Special Fund.[2] (DSOF Ex. 6) The Special Fund concluded that Juarez was entitled to benefits. (DSOF Ex. 7) Westarz sought review of the Special Fund's decision, arguing that Juarez had not been an employee and was there-fore*757 not entitled to compensation from the Special Fund. In responding to the request for review of the Special Fund's decision, Juarez set forth that he was an employee of Westarz. Juarez argued when "determining whether a person is an independent contractor or an employee, the [Special Fund] should consider the various indicia of control, which include the duration of the Applicant's employment, the method of payment, the right to hire and fire, who furnishes equipment, whether the work was performed in the usual and regular course of the employer's business, and the extent to which the employer may exercise control over the details of the work." (DSOF Ex. 10) Juarez claimed that all of these factors were in his favor because he "had worked for [Westarz] for a long period of time," he had worked at multiple construction sites run by Westarz, he was paid a "set weekly salary," "[h]e did not pay for any of the costs of the business," his work was "performed in the

---

1. The Court did not set oral argument because the parties submitted memoranda thoroughly discussing the law and evidence in support of their positions, and oral argument would not have aided the Court's decision. See *Mahon v. Credit Bur. of Placer County, Inc.*, 171 F.3d 1197, 1200 (9th Cir.1999).

2. Employees working for an uninsured "employer" may seek compensation from a "Special Fund" established by statute. See *Uzoh v. Indus. Comm'n of Ariz.*, 158 Ariz. 313, 762 P.2d 600, 601 (1988) (stating that when injured employee learned his employer was uninsured he could either file suit in superior court or seek compensation from the Special Fund).

(continues)

usual and regular course of [Westarz's] business," and his activities were controlled by Westarz. The Special Fund's decision was sustained and Juarez received benefits. As of September 2004, Juarez had received over $52,000 from the Special Fund. (DSOF Ex. 9)

On January 27, 2003, Juarez and his wife Olivia Juarez filed suit against Bever and his construction company, T. Bever Construction, L.L.C. (DSOF Ex. 8) Juarez alleged that Bever's negligence in operating the dump truck caused Juarez's injury. Juarez sought "special damages and losses" as well as "general damages" to both Juarez and his wife. Bever believed that the insurance policy for the dump truck issued by Country was applicable. Thus, Bever tendered the defense to Country. (PSOF Ex. 3) Country responded in writing, stating that coverage did not exist under the policy. Specifically, Country believed that two policy exclusions applied to Juarez's claim. The policy exclusions cited by Country stated that no coverage existed for

1. "bodily injury to anyone eligible to receive benefits which you [Westarz] either provide or are required to provide under any workers' compensation, disability benefits, or any similar law;" and

2. "bodily injury sustained by your [Westarz's] employee in the course of employment for you."

Country claimed that once Juarez was determined to be an employee and workers' compensation coverage became available, the first exclusion applied. Also, "because Mr. Juarez was an employee in the course of employment for Westarz, exclusion number [two]" precluded coverage. (PSOF Ex. 4) According to Country, "[w]hether Bever [was] an employee of Westarz is an open question, but not relevant to the question of liability coverage … under the Westarz policy."

Bever obtained independent counsel and answered the complaint. In his answer, Bever asserted that he was a co-employee of Juarez and Juarez's "exclusive remedy [was] under the Workers Compensation laws of the State of Arizona." (PSOF Ex. 4) Bever and Juarez eventually entered into an agreement pursuant to *Damron v. Sledge*, 105 Ariz. 151, 460 P.2d 997 (1969). Judgment was entered against Bever for the amount of $600,000 and Bever assigned his claims against Country to Juarez. Juarez later instituted this declaratory judgment action against Country, alleging breach of contract and failure to defend (bad faith).

ANALYSIS
I. Jurisdiction

Juarez and his wife are residents of Arizona. Country is a corporation with its principal place of business and state of incorporation is Illinois. (Doc. 1) The amount in controversy exceeds $75,000. *758 (Id.) The Court has jurisdiction pursuant to 28 U.S.C. 1332(a) (diversity jurisdiction).

II. Applicable Law

"[F]ederal courts sitting in diversity jurisdiction apply state substantive law and federal procedural law." *Freund v. Nycomed Amersham*, 347 F.3d 752, 761 (9th Cir.2003). The parties agree that Arizona law applies to Plaintiff's claims. Thus, the Court will use Arizona law where appropriate.

III. Summary Judgment Standard

A court must grant summary judgment if the pleadings and supporting documents, viewed in the light most favorable to the non-moving party, "show that there is no genuine issue as to any material fact and that the moving party is entitled to a judgment as a matter of law." Fed.R.Civ.P. 56(c); see *Celotex Corp. v. Catrett*, 477 U.S. 317, 322-23, 106 S.Ct. 2548, 91 L.Ed.2d 265 (1986). Substantive law determines which facts are material, and "[o]nly disputes over facts that might affect the outcome of the suit under the governing law will properly preclude the entry of summary judgment." *Anderson v. Liberty Lobby, Inc.*, 477 U.S. 242, 248, 106 S.Ct. 2505, 91 L.Ed.2d 202 (1986). In addition, the dispute must be genuine, that is, "the evidence is such that a reasonable jury could return a verdict for the nonmoving party." *Anderson*, 477 U.S. at 248, 106 S.Ct. 2505.

Furthermore, the party opposing summary judgment "may not rest upon the mere allegations or denials of [the party's] pleading, but … must set forth specific facts showing that there is a genuine issue for trial." Fed.R.Civ.P. 56(e); see *Matsushita Elec. Indus. Co., Ltd. v. Zenith Radio Corp.*, 475 U.S. 574, 586–87, 106 S.Ct. 1348, 89 L.Ed.2d 538 (1986). There is no issue for trial unless there is sufficient evidence favoring the non-moving party; "[i]f the evidence is merely colorable, or is not significantly probative, summary judgment may be granted." *Anderson*, 477 U.S. at 249–50, 106 S.Ct. 2505 (citations omitted). However, "[c]redibility determinations, the weighing of the evidence, and the drawing of legitimate inferences from the facts are jury functions, not those of a judge." Id. at 255, 106 S.Ct. 2505. Therefore, "[t]he evidence of the non-movant is to be believed, and all justifiable inferences are to be drawn in his favor" at the summary judgment stage. Id.

IV. Collateral Estoppel

A crucial issue is the employment status of Bever. If Bever were an employee of Westarz at the time of the accident the workers' compensation statutes and perhaps certain policy exclusions would prevent Juarez

(continues)

from recovering from Bever.[3] If, however, Bever was not an employee of Westarz, the workers' compensation statutes would not prevent Juarez' recovery and the Court would have to determine if the policy exclusions are valid and enforceable. A.R.S. § 23-1023 ("If an employee entitled to [workers' compensation] is injured*759 . . . by the negligence or wrong of another not in the same employ, such injured employee . . . may pursue his remedy against such other person."). Juarez believes that the state court judgment could not have been entered if Bever were an employee of Westarz because of the statutory preclusion of suits between co-employees. A.R.S. § 23-1022. Thus, Juarez argues that the state court's judgment contains an implicit finding that Bever was not an employee of Westarz and collateral estoppel prevents Country from challenging that finding now. Country responds that collateral estoppel does not apply because there was a conflict of interest between Bever and Country at the time the state court judgment was entered. The Court agrees with Country.

Generally, if an "insurance company refuses to defend an action under circumstances where it has a duty to defend, it is bound under the doctrine of collateral estoppel by the facts determined in the trial of such action which are essential to the judgment of tort liability." *Farmers Ins. Co. of Ariz. v. Vagnozzi*, 138 Ariz. 443, 675 P.2d 703, 705 (1983). But collateral estoppel "is predicated upon an assumed identity of interests" between the insured and insurer. Id. at 706. And "where there is a conflict of interest between an insured and his insurer, the parties will not be estopped from litigating in a subsequent proceeding those issues as to which there was a conflict of interest, whether or not the insurer defended in the original tort claim." Id. at 708.

The Arizona Supreme Court relies on the *Restatement (Second) of Judgments* for the definition of a conflict of interest. Id. That definition states a conflict of interest "exists when the injured person's claim against the [insured] is such that it could be sustained on

different grounds, one of which is within the [insurer's] obligation to indemnify and another of which is not." Id. (quoting *Restatement (Second) of Judgments* § 58(2) (1982)) (emphasis added). Pursuant to this definition, a conflict of interest existed between Bever and Country. Country's obligation to indemnify depended on Bever's employment status. If Bever were an employee of Westarz, the workers' compensation statutes, and possibly the policy exclusions, would preclude any recovery by Juarez. If, however, Bever were found not to be an employee, the workers' compensation statutes would not bar the suit and the parties would have to litigate the enforceability of the policy exclusions. If those policy exclusions were found enforceable, Country would not have to indemnify Bever; but if the policy exclusions were found unenforceable, Country would have to indemnify. Thus, Bever had an incentive to stipulate that he was not an employee and allow judgment be taken against him. By doing so, Bever prevented the possible outcome of a court determining he was not a co-employee, ruling the policy exclusions enforceable, and finding he was personally liable to Juarez for his injuries. See *Vagnozzi*, 675 P.2d at 708 (finding insurer was not collaterally estopped from asserting a policy exclusion for intentional torts when insured had consented to judgment that he had been negligent); *United Services Auto. Ass'n v. Morris*, 154 Ariz. 113, 741 P.2d 246, 253 (1987) ("[A]ny stipulation of facts essential to establishing coverage would be worthless."). By agreeing to the judgment, Bever ensured that Juarez would not pursue his personal assets but would ask Country to satisfy the judgment.[4] Because of the conflict of interest *760 between Bever and Country, the state court judgment cannot act as a bar on Country litigating the employment status of Bever.

V. Employment Status

Country wishes to establish Bever and Juarez were co-employees because the workers' compensation statutes bar Juarez from recovering anything from a co-employee, A.R.S. 23-1024. Both parties have moved for summary judgment on the employment status of Bever. Summary judgment on the issue of employment status is "appropriate only '[i]f the inference . . . is clear that [a] master-servant relationship exist[ed].'" *Mitchell v. Gamble*, 207 Ariz. 364, 86 P.3d 944, 949 (2004) (quoting *Santiago v. Phoenix Newspapers, Inc.*, 164 Ariz. 505, 794 P.2d 138, 141 (1990)). The parties agree on the factors relevant to the determination of Bever's employment status pursuant

---

3. A combination of a number of workers' compensation statutes would prevent Juarez' suit. See A.R.S. § 23-1022 (stating that workers' compensation "is the exclusive remedy against the employer or any co-employee acting in the scope of his employment"); A.R.S. § 23-907(B) (stating employee that works for an uninsured employer may either file suit or seek compensation from the Special Fund); A.R.S. § 23-1024 (providing that injured employee who accepts workers' compensation waives his right to institute other proceedings). Also, certain policy exclusions might apply if Juarez and Bever were co-employees. See DSOF ex. 2 p. 5 (stating that insurance policy did not provide coverage for employee subject to workers' compensation or for "bodily injury sustained by [Westarz'] employee in the course of employment for [Westarz]").

---

4. Juarez stated in his complaint that Bever entered into the Damron agreement "to protect [his] personal assets." (Doc. 1)

(continues)

to the workers' compensation statutes. (Doc. 15 p. 6, Doc. 20 p. 6) Those factors include

1. The extent of control exercised by the master over details of the work and the degree of supervision;
2. The distinct nature of the worker's business;
3. Specialization or skilled occupation;
4. Materials and place of work;
5. Duration of employment;
6. Method of payment;
7. Relationship of work done to the regular business of the employer;
8. Belief of the parties.

Santiago, 794 P.2d at 142.[5] "No one factor is in itself controlling," *Ringling Bros. & Barnum & Bailey Combined Shows, Inc. v. Superior Court*, 140 Ariz. 38, 680 P.2d 174, 178 (1984), so a court must "consider the totality of the circumstances." *Mitchell v. Gamble*, 207 Ariz. 364, 86 P.3d 944, 948 (2004). Also, "[n]either the presence nor the absence of a written contract controls the resolution of whether the claimant is an employee." *Swichtenberg v. Brimer*, 171 Ariz. 77, 828 P.2d 1218, 1224 (1991). Evaluating the facts in this case in light of the relevant factors leads to the conclusion that Bever was an employee of Westarz.

A. *Extent of Control*
A strong indication of control is an employer's power to give specific instructions with the expectation that they will be followed." *Santiago*, 794 P.2d at 142–43. Bever and Westberg both stated in their depositions that Westberg retained ultimate control over the job sites. (DSOF § 11) Bever's deposition contains the following exchange.

Question: If Mr. Westberg would have given you some instructions to do something specific, would you have done them?
Bever: Yes.
Question: Why is that?
Bever: Because it's his project. He's the boss …
Westberg had the authority to give specific instructions and Bever understood that he had to follow such

instructions. This was recognized by Juarez before the Industrial Commission. According to a document filed by Juarez, "Mr. Westberg may not *761 have been at every job site, every hour of every day, [but] he clearly had the right to control the details of all the workers' activities and any final decisions as to the details of the work were ultimately his." (DSOF ex. 10 p. 4) This factor weighs in favor of finding Bever was an employee.

B. *Distinct Occupation*
"Whether the worker's tasks [were] efforts to promote his own independent enterprise or to further his employer's business" helps determine if an employer-employee relationship existed. Id. at 143. Bever's efforts were aimed at furthering Westarz' business of building homes. This weighs in favor of finding Bever was an employee.

C. *Skilled Occupation*
An employer-employee relationship is more likely present when "the work does not require the services of one highly educated or skilled." Id. Bever had extensive experience in the construction business. (DSOF § 21) The parties did not, however, point to evidence in the record establishing that Bever possessed or did not possess skills especially important to his job. This factor does not favor either party.

D. *Materials and Place of Work*
"If an employer supplies tools, and employment is over a specific area … a master-servant relationship is indicated." Id. at 144. Bever worked at a variety of Westarz job sites and used his own vehicle to travel between sites. (DSOF § 24) Bever also used his own phone at the job sites. (Id.) Westarz provided blueprints and building materials. (DSOF § 25) Westarz also provided the truck that was involved in the accident and Westarz would reimburse Bever if he had to pay for an item out-of-pocket related to the job sites. (DSOF §§ 26, 28) Because the job sites were dictated by Westarz and Westarz provided materials Bever used at the sites, this factor weighs in favor of finding Bever was an employee.

E. *Duration of Employment*
"Whether the employer seeks a worker's services as a one-time, discrete job or as part of a continuous working relationship may indicate that the employer-employee relationship exists." Id. Also, "the employer's right to terminate may indicate control and therefore an employer-employee relationship." Id. In fact, "[t]he 'right to fire' is considered one of the most effective methods of control." Id. Bever began his working relationship with Westberg in 1998. (DSOF § 9, ex. 4 p. 13) The relationship continued until 2002. (DSOF § 29) During this time period,

---

5. Another court has emphasized a test premised on four factors. "[E]mployment can often be solidly demonstrated on the strength of one of four factors: (1) evidence of actual control exercised by the 'employer' and submitted to by the 'employee;' (2) the method of payment, whether on a time, piecework or commission basis, or on a completed project basis; (3) whether the 'employer' furnishes the 'employee' with valuable equipment; and (4) whether the 'employer' has the right to terminate the relationship without liability." *Swichtenberg v. Brimer*, 171 Ariz. 77, 828 P.2d 1218, 1224 (1991). Because the two tests substantially overlap, the Court uses the test set out in Ringling Bros., 680 P.2d at 178-79.

(continues)

Bever would work on any Westarz job site that needed him and he did not work for anyone other than Westarz. (DSOF ex. 4 p. 15, 19) Also, both Bever and Westberg believed that Westberg could fire Bever at any time. (DSOF § 15) In fact, Westberg fired Bever when he could no longer afford to pay him. (DSOF ex. 4 p. 22) The duration of Bever's relationship with Westarz favors finding Bever was an employee.

F. *Method of Payment*

"Payment on a time basis is a strong indication of the status of employment. Payment on a completed project basis is indicative of independent contractor status. Payment on a piece-work or commission basis is consistent with either status." Arthur Larson & Lex K. Larson, Larson's Workers' Compensation Law § 61.06 (2005).[6] Bever was paid a set salary every *762 Friday. (DSOF ex. 4 p. 17) Payment was issued to T. Bever Construction, L.L.C. and Westarz did not withhold any taxes. (DSOF ex. 4 p. 18) Bever's L.L.C. was set up at the request of Westberg for "tax purposes." (DSOF ex. 4 p. 38) The regular payment of a set salary weighs in favor of an employer-employee relationship but Westarz' failure to withhold taxes weighs in favor of the opposite conclusion. The payment method, however, was apparently devised for tax purposes rather than an attempt to reflect a true independent contractor relationship. Thus, this is another factor in favor of finding Bever was an employee.

G. *Regular Business of Employer*

"A court is more likely to find a worker an employee if the work is part of the employer's regular business." *Santiago*, 794 P.2d at 144. There is no dispute that Westarz and Westberg were in the business of building homes. Bever's duties included "overseeing what's going on [at the sites], checking on everything, checking on the progress, [and] changing things." (DSOF ex. 4 p. 24) Thus, Bever's activities were "an integral part of [Westarz'] business." *Anton v. Indus. Comm'n of Ariz.*, 141 Ariz. 566, 688 P.2d 192, 199 (1984). This weighs in favor of finding Bever was an employee.

H. *Parties' Belief*

Arizona courts have provided somewhat inconsistent statements regarding the impact of the parties' beliefs. In *Swichtenberg v. Brimer*, 171 Ariz. 77,

828 P.2d 1218, 1224 (1991), the court observed that "[t]he parties' own subjective beliefs or opinions concerning the nature of their relationship are immaterial." But in *Santiago*, 794 P.2d at 145, the Arizona Supreme Court quoted the *Restatement of Agency's* formulation that the parties' beliefs are not "determinative" but may be helpful. The formulation in Santiago controls. See *Gravquick A/S v. Trimble Navigation Intern. Ltd.*, 323 F.3d 1219, 1222 (9th Cir.2003) ("A federal court applying California law must apply the law as it believes the California Supreme Court would apply it."). In this case, the parties expressed the belief that an employer-employee relationship had not been established. (PSOF 1) Bever also stated, however, that he was a "co-employee" of Juarez. (DSOF ex. 4 p. 43) Because of Juarez's and Bever's statements in this case that they are not co-employees, a credibility issue exists which precludes a finding as a matter of law in favor of either party on this issue.

In light of all these factors, "the inference ... is clear that [a] master-servant relationship exist[ed]." *Mitchell v. Gamble*, 207 Ariz. 364, 86 P.3d 944, 949 (2004) (quoting *Santiago*, 794 P.2d at 141). Westberg exercised ultimate control over all of Bever's activities, Bever's activities were meant to further the interests of Westarz, Westarz provided materials necessary for Bever's job, Westarz dictated where Bever would work, Bever and Westarz had a four-year exclusive relationship, Bever was paid a set amount each week, and Bever provided a vital service to Westarz' business. These facts are very similar to the facts Juarez argued to the Special Fund when he sought to obtain workers' compensation benefits. (DSOF Ex. 10) Thus, just as Juarez was found to be an employee, Bever was also an employee at the time of the accident.

Juarez and Bever were co-employees and Juarez has already sought workers' compensation benefits for his injury. Accordingly, Arizona law precluded Juarez from bringing suit against Bever for additional compensation. A.R.S. § 23-1022. The fact that Bever eventually allowed judgment be taken against him does not control here. Country's policy was not implicated by the accident and the Court *763 need not address the viability of the policy exclusions.

Therefore,

IT IS ORDERED Defendant's Motion for Summary Judgment (Doc. 15) is GRANTED.

IT IS FURTHER ORDERED Plaintiff's Motion for Summary Judgment (Doc. 16) is DENIED.

---

6. Arizona courts often rely on Larson's when addressing workers' compensation issues. See, e.g., *Grammatico v. Indus. Comm'n*, 211 Ariz. 67, 117 P.3d 786, 790 (2005) (citing to Larson's); *Hypl v. Industrial Comm'n*, 210 Ariz. 381, 111 P.3d 423, 427 (2005) (same) (Ariz.App. Div.2,2005).

PUTTING IT INTO PRACTICE 14:2

1. Why did Westarz request review of the decision of the Special Fund?

2. What is the question before the court?

3. Why does the insurance company seek to prove that Bever is an employee of Westarz?

4. What factors does the court consider in determining whether an employer-employee relationship exists?

5. What factor is a strong indication of control, according to the court? What facts indicate that Westarz had control over Bever?

6. Does the court find Bever's business to be distinct from his responsibilities to Westarz? What facts support this conclusion?

7. Does the court find Bever's job to be specialized?

8. Did Westarz supply "tools" or "materials" to Bever?

9. Which is more likely an indication of an employer-employee relationship: a one-time, discrete job or a continuous working relationship? What effect does the right to terminate have on this classification? What factors does the court consider in reference to duration of employment in the context of the Westarz-Bever relationship?

10. Is a court more likely to find a worker to be an employee if his work is part of the employer's regular business? Were Bever's job duties part of Westarz's regular business?

11. Did Bever believe he was an employee? What is the effect of Bever's belief on the court's analysis of whether he was an independent contractor?

The mere fact that an employer refers to someone as an independent contractor is not dispositive in classifying the relationship. The nature of the relationship and not the label that is attached to the relationship determines its classification. Therefore, an employer cannot evade liability simply by casting the label of independent contractor on an employee.

Exceptions to Nonliability Rule for Independent Contractors

Several exceptions to the nonliability rule for independent contractors exist. First, if the employer himself is negligent in dealing with an independent contractor, he can be found liable. For example, if the employer hires someone that he knows will not perform the work safely (such as an individual who has a poor safety record), or if he fails to inspect work after it is done, the employer can be liable even if the injuries stem from the contractor's negligence (see Exhibit 14–3).

EXHIBIT 14–3 *Employer–Independent Contractors*

GENERAL RULE:
- Employers are not vicariously liable for torts of independent contractors.

EXCEPTIONS TO NONLIABILITY RULE:
- Employer is negligent in dealing with independent contractor.
- Employer delegates nondelegable duty to independent contractor.
- Employer hires independent contractor to conduct an activity involving unusual risks that are recognizable in advance.
- Employer contracts for performance of an illegal act.
- Doctors are liable for negligent acts of those under their control (this doctrine has been abolished in some jurisdictions and limited in others).

© Cengage Learning 2012

Nondelegable Duties

Some duties of care are so important that they are nondelegable. A city that hires a private contractor to work on its streets cannot delegate to the company its duty to keep its streets in good repair. For this same reason the owner of a shopping mall can be held vicariously liable for damages resulting from an independent contractor's negligent repair of its roof. The courts have not clearly defined what is and is not a "delegable" duty, but their decisions are generally motivated by a desire to prevent employers from avoiding liability by hiring independent contractors to carry out their responsibilities.

One of the most litigated exceptions to the independent contractor nonliability rule is the "retained control" exception, adopted from the *Restatement (Second) of Torts* § 414, which provides the following:

> One who entrusts work to an independent contractor, but who retains control of any part of the work, is subject to liability for physical harm to others whose safety the employer owes a duty to exercise reasonable care, which is caused by his failure to exercise his control with reasonable care.

Comment c to § 414 provides:

> It is not enough that [the employer] has merely a general right to order the work stopped or resumed, to inspect its progress or receive reports, to make suggestions or recommendations which need not necessarily be followed, or to prescribe alterations and deviations. Such a general right is usually reserved to employers, but it does not mean that the contractor is controlled as to his methods of work, or as to operative detail. There must be such a retention of a right of supervision that the contractor is not entirely free to do the work in his own way.

For this section to apply to a situation, the control exercised by the employer must go beyond retaining control over the premises; the control must relate to the actual manner in which the work performed by the contractor is done. Supervising the sequence of the work is not enough; the employer must have actual control over the details of how the work is done.

In one case, for example, a general contractor hired an independent contractor to install a pipe from a water main to a building that was under construction. Plaintiff, who was employed by the independent contractor, was injured while working in a trench that collapsed on him. The court found that the general contractor had insufficient control over the contractor to come within the retained control exception (*Downs v. Steel & Craft Builders, Inc.*, 831 N.E.2d 92 [Ill.App 2 Dist. 2005]). Although the general contractor retained control over scheduling, change orders and hiring approval the general contractor relied on the subcontractor for compliance with safety issues and regulations.

Extraordinary Risks

Employers continue to be vicariously liable if they hire independent contractors to carry out activities involving risks that require more than ordinary precautions. If an employer hires an independent contractor to relocate date palm trees, for example, special precautions obviously would have to be taken in securing the trees to ensure that transportation along public highways was done without endangering others. In the case of an accident the employer would be vicariously liable. This special rule of liability applies only to unusual risks and not to risks arising out of ordinary forms of negligence. Suppose the contractor were asked to transport common shrubs in an enclosed truck rather than freestanding palm trees. In that case the employer would not be liable if the contractor drove negligently, because the risk involved in hauling shrubs is not an unusual one.

Employers will not be liable if the risks involved are not recognizable in advance. If a family hires a lawn-care service to tend their lawn while they are on vacation and one of the caretakers decides to add water to the pool and forgets to shut it off, the family will not be vicariously liable for the flood damage to their adjoining neighbor's property. The risk of overfilling the pool would not be considered an inherent or foreseeable risk of lawn care.

Illegal Acts

Another exception to the nonliability of employers for the acts of independent contractors is in the area of illegal acts. If an employer contracts for the performance of an illegal activity, she will be vicariously liable for any damage caused by the contractor.

Physicians

Historically, physicians were exceptions to the nonliability rule. A physician was vicariously liable for the negligence of nurses, other physicians, paramedical personnel, and hospital administrators who, although not under her employ, were for legal purposes considered to be under the physician's control. The courts reasoned that a physician acting in a supervisory role over other medical personnel was the "captain of the ship" and thus should be held vicariously liable for their negligent acts. The impetus behind this doctrine probably lay in the court's attempt to circumvent charitable immunity and find a solvent defendant. With the demise of charitable immunity, this doctrine has been abolished in many places and in other jurisdictions has been strictly limited to acts committed during surgery. This same rationale has been used, however, by plaintiffs to recover from hospitals that hire private franchises to carry out special functions in the hospital, such as radiology and serology.

PUTTING IT INTO PRACTICE 14:3

1. After being cited for speeding, Faustino appears before Justice of the Peace Phares and pays a fine. Due to a clerical or administrative error, the receipt of Faustino's payment is not noted; during a subsequent review of his file, Phares determines that the fine has not been paid and issues a bench warrant for Faustino. Later Faustino is stopped for a minor traffic violation and is arrested and incarcerated overnight because of the outstanding bench warrant. Faustino appears before Phares, and the clerical error is discovered and corrected. Apologies are made and Faustino is released. Later Faustino sues Phares and the county that employs Phares. Is the county vicariously liable for Phares's actions?

2. A motion picture company employs an independent contractor to provide a circus act using performing lions. While the picture is being made, one of the lions escapes and injures an actor. Is the motion picture company vicariously liable for the injuries sustained by the actor?

3. The van that a hotel uses to convey passengers to the airport is damaged in a collision. The hotel contracts with a rental company to use one of its vans to take hotel guests to the airport. The only driver available is inexperienced, and while driving the passengers from the hotel he is involved in an accident because he inadvertently hits the accelerator instead of the brake. Is the hotel liable to the driver of the other vehicle involved in the accident? Would your answer change if the driver had been experienced but had been talking to one of the passengers and not watching where he was going when he ran into the other vehicle?

4. Fisher is a member of a chicken-catching crew that was assembled by Reid, a weighmaster who was working for Townsends, a chicken-processing business. Fisher is injured while he is riding in a vehicle driven by Reid. At the time Reid is driving he is working for Townsends.

   Reid has worked for Townsends for five years exclusively. Their relationship began with oral understandings; shortly before the accident Townsends presented Reid with a written Catching Crew Agreement. This agreement, which indicates that Reid is an independent contractor, was not intended to change their oral agreement. The parties disagree about whether the Catching Crew Agreement was executed prior to Reid's accident.

   Townsends supplies Reid with Daily Movement Sheets that identify the farm where the day's work is to be done, the birds that are to be removed, which crew is to be assigned to a job, and the time the crew is to report. Townsends owns and supplies the trucks, forklifts, cages, and stools that are used to catch chickens, as well as the paper masks and disposable gloves worn by the catchers. Townsends' manager visits the farms periodically to see if the weighmasters, truck drivers, or forklift operators are experiencing problems. Townsends requires its weighmasters to keep two-way radios in the vehicles they use to

(continues)

transport their crews. Townsends supplies Reid with these radios, which allows Townsends to keep Reid advised of changes in work sites and work orders and enables him to communicate with Townsends' processing plant, truck drivers, and forklift operators regarding work-related problems.

Apply the criteria set forth in *Santiago v. PNI* to decide how you would characterize the relationship between Townsends and Reid.

5. In celebration of Japan Week, Jetro and Chamber contract with Marutamaya to provide a fireworks display. Marutamaya then contracts with R. Borgman Sales Co. to conduct the display. During the display two of the shells explode prematurely, injuring two of the operators, both of whom are employees of Borgman and are experienced, licensed pyrotechnic operators. Should Jetro and Chamber be held liable for the operators' injuries, or did they delegate their responsibility to Marutamaya by hiring the company as an independent contractor?

6. A workman is killed in a dirt slide while performing an excavation on a site owned by a mining company, Kennecott Copper Company. The company was in the process of expanding its facilities and had contracted with the employer of the deceased workman to do the job. Under its contract with the contractor, Kennecott maintained control over employee selection and over salaries to be paid to key employees. Kennecott could discharge any employee on the job and had to approve drawings detailing how work was to be performed. Should Kennecott be held liable for the death of the employee of its contractor?

BAILMENTS

If a party temporarily entrusts goods to the care of another, the party who hands over the goods is referred to as a **bailor**; the person who receives custody of the goods is a **bailee**. When you take your car in for repair, you are the bailor and the service station is the bailee. The question in terms of vicarious liability is whether a bailor should be liable for the negligence of a bailee.

Under the common law majority rule, a bailor is not vicariously liable for the acts of a bailee (see Exhibit 14–4). Thus, if someone rents a car from a rental agency and negligently injures a plaintiff while driving such a car, the rental agency (bailor) is not vicariously liable for the acts of the individual who rented the car (bailee). The bailor may be liable for his own negligence if he entrusts control of his property to a person that he knows or reasonably should know is likely to endanger others. Therefore, if the rental agency in this example was aware that the driver was intoxicated or otherwise unable to control the vehicle, it could be held vicariously liable for the driver's negligent acts.

Exceptions to Bailor Nonliability

The courts, for the most part, have been dissatisfied with the nonliability rule regarding bailors when that rule is applied to owners of automobiles who allow others to drive. They have adopted a number of strategies by which vicarious liability can be placed on the owners of vehicles. The implicit reasoning behind the notion of owner liability is that owners are more likely to be able to pay for damages than those to whom they loan their vehicles and that owners, not drivers, are expected to carry insurance.

In some courts the mere presence of the owner in the car creates the presumption that the owner had control over the driving. As a result the owner is considered vicariously liable for the acts of the driver. Some courts have retreated from this position by making the presumption a rebuttable one. Others have negated the presumption altogether and treat the nondriving owner as if she were a guest in her own car. The courts will not, however, impute the driver's negligence to the owner if the owner is not present.

EXHIBIT 14–4   Bailments

GENERAL RULE:
- Bailors are not vicariously liable for the acts of a bailee.

EXCEPTIONS TO NONLIABILITY RULE:
- Bailor negligently entrusts property to one he knows or should know will endanger others.
- In some states, mere presence of owner in vehicle makes owner vicariously liable for acts of driver.
- Family Purpose Doctrine—driver (nonowner) is presumed to be carrying out family purpose, making owner vicariously liable.
- Automobile Consent Statutes—owner is vicariously liable for negligent acts committed by anyone using the vehicle with the owner's permission.
- Joint Enterprise Doctrine—owner is vicariously liable for negligent acts committed by joint venture.

© Cengage Learning 2012

LOCAL LINKS

In your state does the presence of an owner in a vehicle create the presumption that the owner is in control of the vehicle?

Family-Purpose Doctrine

In their struggle to circumvent the nonliability rule for absent owners, some courts created a legal fiction called the *family-purpose doctrine*. Under this doctrine the assumption is made that the driver is carrying out a "family purpose," making the family head, typically the most financially responsible person in the family, vicariously liable. This doctrine is maintained even though, typically, the driver is using the vehicle on his own behalf. So long as the driver is a member of the family's household and has permission to use the car, the head of the family is vicariously liable for the driver's negligent acts.

The family-purpose doctrine is in effect in less than half the states today and is complicated by a host of exceptions. It arises most often in cases in which a minor is relegated to driving a particular vehicle. Usually parents provide only as much insurance on a vehicle driven by a minor as mandated by law, but provide more extensive coverage on the vehicles they themselves drive. Anyone injured by the minor will find little compensation in the minor's coverage and will often be motivated to turn to the parents for relief. If the plaintiff can meet the requirements of the family-purpose doctrine, she can recover from the parents instead of the minor.

Automobile Consent Statutes

Dissatisfaction with the rule of nonliability of bailors led several state legislatures to adopt *automobile-consent statutes*. These statutes make the owner vicariously liable for negligent acts committed by anyone using the car with the owner's permission. If the borrower (bailee) of the car exceeds the scope of the owner's consent, the owner (bailor) is generally not vicariously liable unless the deviation is a relatively minor one. If the bailee in turn lends the car to a third person, the courts are divided in terms of the owner's liability. In one case a rental agency explicitly forbade customers from allowing anyone else to drive the car. The court found that the agency was deemed to have impliedly given consent and held the agency liable when its customer allowed a third person to drive who subsequently caused a collision (*Shuck v. Means*, 226 N.W.2d 285 [Minn. 1974]). Not all courts agree with this case, however, and such courts are less likely to find liability when the bailee is not in the vehicle at the time of the accident.

The *omnibus clause* in most automobile liability insurance policies has substantially reduced the need for automobile-consent statutes. Such clauses extend insurance coverage to members of the insured's household and to any person using the automobile with the insured's permission as long as the use falls within the scope of the permission given. Consequently, plaintiffs have no incentive to find liability on the part of the owner, at least up to the policy limits.

Joint Enterprises

Another court-created doctrine designed to make the owner of an automobile vicariously liable is the *joint-enterprise doctrine* (see Exhibit 14–5). A **joint enterprise** consists of four elements:

1. an express or implied agreement among members of a group
2. a common purpose or goal to be carried out by the group
3. a common pecuniary interest in the purpose or goal
4. an equal right of each member to control the direction of the enterprise. (*Restatement [Second] of Torts* § 491, cmt. c.)

EXHIBIT 14–5 *Joint Enterprise*

> **GENERAL RULE:**
> • All joint venturers are vicariously liable for the negligent acts of other joint venturers.
>
> **ELEMENTS OF JOINT ENTERPRISE:**
> • Express or implied agreement.
> • Common purpose or goal.
> • Common pecuniary interest.
> • Equal right to control direction of enterprise.

© Cengage Learning 2012

LOCAL LINKS

Does your state have an automobile-consent statute in effect?

A social trip is not a joint enterprise because it involves no sharing of a pecuniary interest. The mere sharing of expenses is not enough by itself to establish a pecuniary interest. Furthermore, the courts frequently find that a passenger on a social trip has no right of control over the driver. For this doctrine to be applicable, each of the joint venturers must have some say in how the car is to be driven. Each person need not have a right to arbitrarily steer the car at any time, but each must have an equal say in what route will be followed, how fast the car will travel, and so on. Two partners in a law firm, for example, who carpool together would be considered members of a joint enterprise.

Once the joint-enterprise requirements are met, each of the joint venturers is vicariously liable for the negligence of the others. This doctrine almost always arises in the context of automobile cases. Typically the plaintiff is a passenger in another car and wishes to recover against a passenger (usually the "deep pocket") in the joint venturer's vehicle. By imputing the negligence of the driver to the passenger, the plaintiff is allowed to recover.

IMPUTED CONTRIBUTORY NEGLIGENCE

Suppose the driver of an automobile and a truck driver for Company X negligently collide with each other. Should the truck driver's negligence be imputed to—that is, charged against or attributed to—Company X, making Company X contributorily negligent and thus barring it from suing the automobile driver, who was also negligent? Under traditional common law, the answer to that question was yes. The negligence of a driver was imputed to the passengers. Because of the contributory negligence imputed to him, an injured passenger could not sue the other driver. Similarly, a few courts have actually used **imputed negligence** to preclude a passenger from suing the driver of the vehicle in which she was riding when the driver and passenger are joint venturers. The driver's negligence is imputed to the passenger, who is then considered contributorily negligent and thus barred from recovering from the driver.

Under the modern rule, however, contributory negligence is imputed only if the relationship is such that the plaintiff would be vicariously liable if she were a defendant (*Restatement [Second] of Torts* § 485). In the earlier example of the passenger wanting to sue the driver of the vehicle with which he collided, the passenger would not be vicariously liable for the negligence of the driver of the vehicle in which he was a passenger. Therefore, no negligence would be imputed to the passenger and he could recover for his injuries (see Exhibit 14–6).

The rationale for not imputing a driver's negligence to a passenger is that a passenger basically has no control over the acts of the driver of the vehicle in which he is riding. The passenger should not, therefore, be saddled with responsibility for the driver's negligence. In other words, contributory negligence should not be imputed unless negligence can also be imputed.

In the case of the truck driver, because the employer (Company X) would be vicariously liable for the truck driver's acts, the truck driver's negligence would be imputed to the employer and the employer would be prevented from suing the other driver. Because the employer bears responsibility for the acts of his employees, imputing the negligence of employees to their employer seems neither illogical nor unfair, according to the prevailing reasoning of the courts. The negligence of the employee is not imputed to the employer, however, if the employer is suing the employee rather than a third party.

The rule regarding the imputation of negligence is in general disfavor today. In most states the negligence of one spouse is not imputed to the other (except in some community-property states where recovered damages are treated as community property), nor are parents or children barred from recovery because of the

EXHIBIT 14–6 *Imputation of Negligence*

NEGLIGENCE NOT IMPUTED

Negligence of D2 is *not* imputed to P2

Driver 1 (D1)   Driver 2 (D2)   Passenger 2 (P2)

P2 can sue D1

NEGLIGENCE IMPUTED

Negligence of D1 imputed to ER

Employer (ER)   Driver 1 (D1)   Driver 2 (D2)

ER cannot sue D2, because of ER's imputed contributory negligence

© Cengage Learning 2012

PARENTAL LIABILITY

Some states, in an effort to curb juvenile delinquency, have enacted statutes that hold parents liable for the tortious acts of their children. These torts can involve either personal injury or property damage, but they must be intentional torts. Most such statutes have damage ceilings, which can be as high as several thousand dollars. A Georgia statute that provided no such ceiling was held void under the due-process clause (*Corley v. Lewless*, 182 S.E.2d 766 [Ga. 1971]).

Although lawsuits based on negligent supervision are generally rare, they become more visible in the wake of the shootings at Columbine High School in Littleton, Colorado. Several families of the students who were killed or wounded filed lawsuits against the parents of the two teenage shooters, Harris and Klebold, for failure to supervise their children. The defendant parents claimed to have no awareness of their sons' activities, but the plaintiffs argued that it would have been hard for them to have no knowledge of their sons' year-long building and exploding of bombs. At the time this book went to press, the families have recovered more than $2 million in insurance money.

In the aftermath of Columbine many states have reexamined their parental-responsibility laws. New York passed a statute allowing schools and local governments to recover thousands of dollars from students who make phony bomb threats. Many states have considered statutes that would hold parents criminally responsible if their children commit crimes using firearms.

A parent may also be vicariously liable if she encourages the commission of a tortious act or accepts benefits from it. Similarly, a parent who negligently entrusts a dangerous object to a child or who fails to protect others from dangerous tendencies of the child will be held liable. In one case the parents of a fifteen-year-old boy were held liable for the injuries suffered by a five-year-old girl he molested while babysitting. The boy's parents were aware of his history of molestation of young girls (*Schurk v. Christensen*, 497 P.2d 937 [Wash. 1972]).

negligence of the other. Under the modern rule the contributory negligence of a bailee is generally not imputed to the bailor, even when the bailor would be liable as a defendant pursuant to an automobile-consent statute.

In derivative claims, such as wrongful-death actions and loss-of-consortium claims, the contributory negligence of the injured party is imputed to the plaintiff. Because the plaintiff's claim is derived from and dependent on another person's injury, the imputed-negligence doctrine is applicable. Therefore, if a driver is killed in a collision and her family sues the other driver in a wrongful-death action, any negligence on the part of the decedent will be imputed to the family.

LOCAL LINKS

In what situations do the courts in your state impute negligence?

LOCAL LINKS

What do the statutes in your state provide in terms of parental liability?

PUTTING IT INTO PRACTICE 14:4

1. Steven, who is twenty years old, is involved in a motor vehicle accident. The driver of the other vehicle seeks grounds upon which he can sue Steven's father, because Steven is financially insolvent. The driver discovers the following: Steven paid for the car and liability insurance himself; his father co-signed for the car so that the financing agency would loan Steven the money; the car was registered in the father's name; Steven exercised exclusive control of the car, and his father drove the car only a couple of times. Do you think the injured driver will be able to recover from Steven's father under the family-purpose doctrine?

2. The owner of a vehicle specifically instructs her teenage daughter not to let anyone else drive her vehicle. One day she allows her daughter to drive to a friend's house on an errand but insists that the daughter return immediately after performing the errand. Instead of returning directly home, the daughter picks up some teenage friends and drives to the outskirts of town. One of the girls takes over the wheel and, while driving at high speed, runs into two boys on a bicycle. Is the owner of the vehicle liable for the injuries to the boys if an automobile-consent statute is in effect?

3. A group of hikers is crossing a rock slide area when one of the hikers accidentally knocks rocks down to the road below. A driver coming down the roadway is unable to avoid all of the rocks and is forced to drive over one of them, causing damage to his vehicle. The insurer of the company brings suit against the leader of the hikers under a theory of joint enterprise. Do you think the insurer is likely to be successful?

4. Is the negligence of one spouse imputed to the other spouse under the laws of your jurisdiction?

5. Are parents liable for the tortious acts of their children under the laws of your jurisdiction?

SUMMARY

The doctrine of vicarious liability provides that an individual is liable for the tortious acts of another if she shares a special relationship with the tortfeasor. Examples of such special relationships are those between employers and employees, employers and independent contractors, parents and children, and parties involved in a joint enterprise. Both the family-purpose doctrine and automobile-consent statutes involve elements of vicarious liability.

The doctrine of respondeat superior is applicable if an employee is acting "within the scope and furtherance of his employment" but not if an employee goes on a "frolic" or "detour" of his or her own. Even if an employee engages in conduct specifically prohibited by the employer, the employer remains liable as long as the acts are done within the scope and furtherance of the employment. An employer also retains liability if an employee negligently delegates his authority or rights to a third party without the employer's authorization and the third party commits a tort.

In general, one who hires an independent contractor is not vicariously liable for the tortious acts of that individual.

Exceptions to the nonliability rule for independent contractors exist. An employer who is negligent in dealing with an independent contractor can be found liable, as can an employer who contracts for the performance of an illegal activity. Some duties of care cannot be delegated; thus, in some cases at least, employers will be prevented from evading liability by hiring an independent contractor. Employers will be vicariously liable if they hire independent contractors to carry out activities that involve risks requiring more than ordinary precautions, but they will not be liable if those risks are not recognizable in advance.

Under the majority rule, bailors are not vicariously liable for the acts of bailees unless they negligently entrust control of their property to a person they know or reasonably should know is likely to endanger others. Dissatisfaction with this rule as applied to owners of automobiles led some courts to create the presumption that an owner's mere presence in the car establishes his control over the driving, making him vicariously liable.

In accordance with the court-created family-purpose doctrine, a driver is assumed to be carrying out a "family purpose" as long as she is a member of the owner's household and has permission to use the car. Along similar lines, many state legislatures have adopted automobile-consent statutes, which make an owner vicariously liable for the negligent acts committed by anyone using the car with the owner's permission unless the bailee exceeds the scope of the owner's consent. The joint-enterprise doctrine, also created by the courts, renders the owner of an automobile vicariously liable for the negligence of the driver if the two are involved in a joint enterprise.

Modern courts generally impute contributory negligence only if the relationship is such that the plaintiff would be vicariously liable if he were a defendant. Under this rule an employee's negligence is imputed to the employer, which prevents the employer from suing any other third party who is negligent as well.

KEY TERMS

bailee
One who is temporarily entrusted with the custody of goods

bailor
One who entrusts her goods to the temporary custody of another

imputed negligence
Negligence that is charged or attributed to another

independent contractor
Someone hired to do a job who works at his own pace, in his own way, under his own supervision

joint enterprise
Two or more persons who agree to a common goal or purpose, share a common pecuniary interest, and have an equal right to control the direction of the enterprise

respondeat superior
Doctrine establishing the vicarious liability of employers for the acts of their employees

vicarious liability
Liability for the tortious acts of another

REVIEW QUESTIONS

1. What is the doctrine of respondeat superior, and what is its rationale?

2. Under what conditions does respondeat superior apply, and when does it not apply?

3. What criteria are used to distinguish an employee from an independent contractor?
   a. What is the significance of this difference?
   b. Under what conditions can an employer be held liable for the negligence of an independent contractor?

4. Give an example of a bailor-bailee relationship.
   a. Identify the bailor and the bailee in this relationship.
   b. Is a bailor generally liable for the negligence of a bailee?

5. What have courts and legislatures done to avoid the bailor-nonliability rule?
   a. Describe the family-purpose doctrine.
   b. What is an automobile-consent statute?
   c. What is an omnibus clause, and how has it affected automobile-consent statutes?

6. What is a joint enterprise?
   a. What is the purpose of the joint-enterprise doctrine?
   b. What elements must be present for a joint enterprise to exist?

7. Give an example of a situation in which negligence would be imputed.
   a. Give an example of a situation in which negligence would not be imputed.
   b. What is the general rule today regarding the imputing of contributory negligence?

8. In what circumstances can parents be held liable for the tortious acts of their children?

PRACTICE EXAM

Students should complete the practice exam after studying each chapter. The answers are in Appendix A. If you score lower than 80%, you should reread the materials.

True-False

1. Under the doctrine of vicarious liability the acts of a tortfeasor are imputed to another even though there is no special relationship between the tortfeasor and the individual held liable.

2. The doctrine of respondeat superior applies to negligent torts but not intentional torts or strict liability actions.

3. An employer is vicariously liable for negligent acts engaged in by an employee while traveling to and from work.

4. If an employee hires a third party without the employer's authorization, the employer is not vicariously liable for the negligence of the third party under any circumstances.

5. The language of two parties' contract is not dispositive of whether they have created an employer-employee or employer–independent contractor relationship.

6. An employer cannot be held liable for the negligence of an independent contractor even if he is negligent in hiring that person or fails to inspect the work of that person.

7. An employer who hires an independent contractor but who retains control over any part of the work can be held liable for the negligence of that contractor.

8. Under the "retained control" exception to the nonliability rule for independent contractors, an employer is considered to have retained control if the employer maintains control over the premises or supervises the sequence of the contractor's work.

9. Under the common law majority rule, a bailor is not vicariously liable for the acts of a bailee unless the bailor is negligent in entrusting his goods into the care of a bailee he reasonably should know will endanger others.

10. The courts hold owners liable for the negligence of those to whom they loan their vehicles because they believe owners are usually better able to pay for damages and are more likely to carry insurance than the drivers to whom they loan their vehicles.

11. The family-purpose doctrine has been adopted in almost every state.

12. If the borrower of a vehicle loans it to a third person, the courts are divided as to whether the owner of the vehicle should be liable for the negligence of the third party.

13. The omnibus clause of most insurance policies has increased the need for automobile-consent statutes.

14. Under the modern view of imputing negligence, contributory negligence is imputed only if the relationship between the parties is such that the plaintiff would have been vicariously liable if he had been the defendant.

15. Parents can be held liable for any tortious acts of their children.

Matching

_____ 1. Employer liable for negligence
_____ 2. Employer not liable for negligence
_____ 3. Insurance that covers extended family and borrowers of vehicle
_____ 4. Allows plaintiff to sue parents of underin-sured teenager
_____ 5. Bypasses bailor nonliability rule for defendant who is underinsured borrower of vehicle
_____ 6. Liable for the negligence of one another

a. family-purpose doctrine
b. automobile-consent statute
c. respondeat superior
d. independent contractor
e. joint venturers
f. omnibus clause

Fill-in-the-Blanks

1. Under the doctrine of _____ _____, an individual is held liable for the tortious acts of another.

2. _____ _____ means "let the person higher up answer."

3. A(n) _____ _____ is considered her own boss and works at her own pace in her own way.

4. A person who entrusts goods into the care of another is referred to as a(n) _____, whereas the person who agrees to accept custody of the goods is referred to as a _____.

5. The _____ _____ doctrine assumes that the head of the family is the most financially responsible person in the family.

6. _____ _____ statutes make the owner of a vehicle liable for the negligence of anyone using his car with his permission.

7. A company whose driver is negligent cannot sue the driver of the other automobile who is also negligent because the negligence of its driver is _____ to the company.

Multiple-Choice

1. The doctrine of respondeat superior does not apply if an employee is
   a. acting outside the scope and furtherance of his employment.
   b. serving his employer and meeting his personal needs.
   c. intending to further his employer's business by doing something foolish.
   d. all of the above.

2. An employer can be held liable
   a. if an employee intentionally injures someone.
   b. for the negligence of an employee who goes on a frolic or detour if the employee's deviation is reasonably foreseeable.
   c. if she expressly forbids an employee to do something and he does it anyway.
   d. all of the above.

3. An employer can be held liable for the negligence of an independent contractor
   a. if the employer tries to delegate a nondelegable duty to that independent contractor.
   b. if the employer hires the contractor to carry out an activity that is the slightest bit risky.
   c. unless the activity the independent contractor is to carry out is illegal.
   d. all of the above.

4. Under the majority law today, doctors are
   a. vicariously liable for the negligence of nurses, paramedics, and other personnel they supervise.
   b. perceived as the "captain of the ship" for legal purposes as a means of circumventing the charitable-immunity rule.
   c. not held vicariously liable for the acts of those they supervise except, in some states, when they are performing surgery.
   d. none of the above.

5. A joint enterprise
   a. requires that each member of the group have an equal right to control the direction of the enterprise.
   b. is created when people go on a social trip.
   c. is created any time there is a sharing of expenses on a trip.
   d. all of the above.

6. Under the modern rule, negligence is usually imputed
   a. to spouses.
   b. to the plaintiff in wrongful-death actions.
   c. to bailors.
   d. all of the above.

PRACTICE POINTERS

One of the easiest ways to gain information about an employer's relationship to a worker is through the use of interrogatories. In comparison to depositions, interrogatories are relatively inexpensive to prepare. They do not, however, provide the same type of information that depositions do.

Depositions give attorneys an opportunity to see how an individual reacts to pressure and allows them, in general, to assess the individual's probable performance on the witness stand. Additionally, depositions allow attorneys to follow up immediately on questions and to pursue a line of questioning aggressively without giving the individual an opportunity to collect her thoughts. Although depositions are typically a more helpful discovery device, their expense precludes extensive use. Therefore, law firms spend considerable time preparing and answering interrogatories.

Interrogatories give more insight into the attorney's thoughts than to the client's. This is because attorneys assist clients in responding to interrogatories and, in some cases, actually prepare the answers for the client's signature. Generally, attorneys strive to avoid answering any questions they do not absolutely have to, and they try to reveal no more information than is ethically required.

Because attorneys often delegate the task of drafting interrogatories to their legal assistants, you should become familiar with this process. Interrogatories should be as specific and narrow as possible. General questions promote general answers. If you want to know how the plaintiff was injured, do not ask broad questions such as, "How did the accident occur?" Use questions that call for specific information. Divide the accident into relatively short time sequences, and ask questions pertaining to each sequence. Ask, for example, what the defendant was doing immediately preceding the accident, which direction he was headed in, what time of day it was, what the lighting conditions were, what intersection the accident occurred at, when the defendant first observed the plaintiff, and so on.

Avoid asking questions that can be truthfully answered with a simple "yes" or "no" unless you intend to follow up with detail-seeking questions. Include specific requests for names, addresses, and titles of witnesses. Ask whom the other side intends to call as witnesses and what their anticipated testimony will be. Also ask about the documentation and exhibits opposing counsel intends to use at trial.

Phrase questions carefully to prevent opposing counsel from having an excuse for evading any question. Questions that violate any privileges (such as the privilege against self-incrimination, the attorney-client privilege, or the attorney work-product rule) should be avoided, as

should questions that are irrelevant or overly burdensome for opposing counsel to respond to.

When formulating questions it is often helpful to mentally walk through the chain of events that led up to the plaintiff's injury and that ultimately culminated in the plaintiff?'s seeking legal assistance. The sequence of your questions should follow that same chronological order. Imagine that you are photographing the scene as it unfolds and that now, as you ask your questions, you have slowed down the camera speed so that you can see one frame at a time. Try to ask at least one question for each frame of action. Even when this proves impractical, the frame-by-frame approach will encourage you to ask extremely narrow questions.

When you review your questions, check to see that they are straightforward and concise. Confusing, convoluted questions often beget confusing, convoluted answers. Simplicity and precision are the key to effective interrogatories.

Sample Interrogatories

1. How long has Laura Huxley been associated with your company?
2. What was the original purpose of the association?
   a. Has that purpose changed? If yes, what is the current purpose of her association?
3. Has Laura Huxley ever signed a contract or agreement with your company?
   a. If so, please attach a copy of any such documents if you will do so without a subpoena.
4. List the specific duties Laura Huxley was assigned when she was first associated with your company.
   a. Have those duties changed? If yes, specify the duties she is currently assigned.
5. What was Laura Huxley's title when she was first associated with your company?
   a. What titles has she held since that time?
   b. What is her current title?
6. How did you first learn that Laura Huxley was or might be available to provide services for your company?
7. Did Laura Huxley in the past, or does she currently, have her own office outside of your company?
8. Did Laura Huxley in the past, or does she currently, advertise her services to others?
9. Did Laura Huxley in the past, or does she currently, have her own equipment?
10. Do you exercise any control over who Laura Huxley can hire or work with on projects for your company?
11. Is Laura Huxley covered by any insurance policies owned or paid for by your company?
    a. If so, list each such policy.

TORT TEASERS

1. Review the three hypothetical questions posed at the beginning of this chapter, and determine if the attorney in each case would be liable for the acts of his employee (you).

2. At a Christmas office party Defendant (an employee) becomes drunk and while driving home negligently causes the Plaintiff injury. What would you need to know to determine if Defendant was acting within the scope of his employment? *O' Conner v. Gaspar*, 2005 WL 914441 (Mass. Super. 2005).

3. Plaintiff is involved in a car accident that he contends was caused by Defendant's negligent repair of his brakes fifteen months prior to the accident. Should Defendant be held liable? *Nguyen v. Good Chevrolet, Inc.*, 2005 WL 762624 (Wash.App. Div1 2005).

4. A sergeant for the Los Angeles Police Department (LAPD) stops a woman for erratic driving and asks her to perform a field sobriety test to determine if she is intoxicated. She does poorly on the test and begins to cry and plead with the officer not to take her to jail. The sergeant is on duty as a field supervisor, assigned to supervise and train police officers patrolling the streets. He orders the woman to get in the front seat of the police car but does not handcuff her. He then drives to her home and tells her he expects "payment" for taking her home instead of to jail. Once there he rapes her. Is the LAPD vicariously liable for the acts of its sergeant, or is his conduct so "unusual," as the police department argues, that he cannot be considered to be acting within the scope of his employment? *Mary M. v. City of Los Angeles*, 814 P.2d 1241 (Cal. 1991).

5. Employee, entrusted with a vehicle by Employer, suffers an epileptic seizure and causes an accident that results in the death of one person. Employer hired Employee six weeks before the accident. Three weeks before the accident Employee suffered dizzy spells and had minor accidents on three separate occasions, two of which were brought to the attention of Employer. Employer arranged to have Employee examined by a physician, who found nothing wrong with Employee. Should Employer be held vicariously liable in a wrongful-death action? *Syah v. Johnson*, 55 Cal. Rptr. 741 (Ct. App. 1966).

6. The owner of a vehicle brings his car to a car wash. It is attached to a tow line and towed without its operator through the car wash. When it emerges from the wash it rolls down an incline and strikes Plaintiff's automobile. Is the car wash liable for the damages to Plaintiff's car?

   Assume that the motor vehicle code of that state provides that the negligence of one who uses or operates a vehicle with the owner's express or implied permission is imputed to the owner of the vehicle. In accordance with this statute, should the vehicle owner be held liable for the property damage to Plaintiff's vehicle? *Allcity Insurance Co. v. Old Greenwich Delicatessen*, 349 N.Y.S.2d 240 (Civ. Ct. 1973).

7. Defendant driver collides with a school bus while acting as a chauffeur for the owner of the vehicle he is driving. Defendant is driving with the owner's permission for the purpose of keeping the car running in good shape. If Defendant was contributorily negligent, can the owner sue the driver and owner of the school bus for the damages sustained by his vehicle? Can the two passengers in the vehicle at the time of the accident recover for their injuries? Can the driver's wife recover for her injuries (assume this is a community-property state)? *Muhammad v. United States*, 366 F.2d 298 (9th Cir.), *cert. denied*, 386 U.S. 959 (1966).

8. Plaintiff files suit against Defendant gasoline station alleging its employees negligently sold gasoline to drunk driver who was visibly intoxicated and could not push the correct button to activate the gas pump. Defendant's employees testified that they could smell the alcohol on drunk driver. Drunk driver exited the gasoline station without turning on the lights to his car and drove away on the wrong side of the road and struck Plaintiff's car. Should the gasoline station be held liable for the accident? *West v. East Tennessee Pioneer Oil Co.*, 172 S.W.3d 545 (Tenn. 2005).

INTERNET INQUIRIES

One of the many gateways to legal information is http://www.katsuey.com. Do not let the unusual name deceive you (it is named after the creator's cat)—this site is chock full of useful information and links to a number of legal resources. If you are doing research and are not sure where to look, spend a few minutes on this site to see if you can find some key places to start.

Go to this site and find a link that provides

1. abbreviations and acronyms for medical and pharmaceutical terms.
2. links that will assist you in conducting medical research.
3. information about forensic sciences.
4. links to federal public records.
5. an article on finding experts.

PRACTICAL PONDERABLES

Your firm has recently accepted Maria Conseulas as a client. Maria was seriously injured when she fell off a horse while jumping it at a horse show. The horse caught its foot when going over a difficult jump and fell, crushing Maria under its body. A couple of trainers who observed the accident commented to Maria's parents that they believed the horse she was riding was being asked to jump at a level it was not physically able to do and that Maria's trainer should not have entered Maria in this event. Maria's parents would like to sue the horse trainer, but some preliminary research indicates that the trainer is essentially judgment-proof. The trainer does, however, work for a large ranch, Escondido Farms.

What will your firm need to ascertain before it can decide whether Escondido Farms can be sued in this case? What questions should be asked in making this determination?

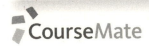 **CourseMate** Access an interactive eBook, chapter-specific learning tools, including flashcards, quizzes, and more in your Paralegal CourseMate, accessed through www.CengageBrain.com.

CHAPTER 15

© Cengage Learning 2012

Joint Liability

CHAPTER OBJECTIVES

After completing the chapter, you should be able to

- Identify situations in which tortfeasors are jointly and severally liable for their acts.
- Apply the concepts of contribution, satisfaction, and indemnification.
- Distinguish between releases and covenants not to sue.
- Recognize the problems associated with releases in light of contribution.

Y ou and a friend go out west for a week's vacation. While there you decide to take in the local scene by going on a trail ride through the desert. The ostentatious resort where you are staying sponsors these rides, which are designed for "dudes" such as yourself. It is advertised as a peaceful, scenic ride that allows you to enjoy the panoramic vistas of the desert. When you arrive at the stable, you tell the trail hands, Tex and Rex, of your ignorance about horses. Tex and Rex, engaging in a little cowboy humor, put you on Molly, a mare noted for her impulsive urges to return to her stablemates without giving any notice to her rider. Unfortunately, Molly succumbs to this urge while you are a passenger. She dumps you unceremoniously on the rocky ground, never demonstrating the least bit of remorse as she gallops back to the stable.

You suffer several broken bones and a concussion as a result of this little adventure and decide to sue Tex and Rex, the stable that employed them, and the resort that promoted the trail ride. Assuming you are able to prove liability on behalf of all the defendants, can you elect to recover your damages only from the resort, even though Tex and Rex were primarily responsible for your injuries? Can the resort then turn around and seek reimbursement from the stable for its portion of the damages? If the stable is held liable only because the negligence of Tex and Rex is imputed to it, can the stable seek reimbursement from Tex and Rex? If Tex comes to you and says that the whole scheme was Rex's idea, can you agree to absolve Tex from all liability in exchange for securing his testimony against Rex? See if you can answer these questions after reading this chapter.

JOINT AND SEVERAL LIABILITY

Two or more persons who act in concert to produce a negligent or intentional tort are called **joint tortfeasors**. Joint tortfeasors are jointly and severally liable, in that they are totally liable for the entire loss suffered by the plaintiff if that loss is indivisible. A loss that cannot be apportioned among the defendants is considered *indivisible*. The rule of joint liability also applies to **concurrent tortfeasors**, those whose independent acts concur (combine) to cause the plaintiff's injury. Notice that joint tortfeasors act together whereas concurrent tortfeasors act independently, but their combined acts cause the plaintiff's injuries.

Under the rule of **joint and several liability**, each defendant can be held responsible for the entire harm or any designated portion of the harm (see Exhibit 15–1). Although a plaintiff may recover from one or all of the joint tortfeasors, she can recover only once for the total damages. As a result of this rule, one defendant can be held responsible for payment of all damages even though his contribution to the plaintiff's injuries was relatively minor. Therefore, if the plaintiff suffered damages in the amount of $10,000, and five defendants acted together to cause the injuries, the plaintiff could recover $2,000 from each defendant, $10,000 from one defendant, or $1,000 from four of the defendants and $6,000 from one of the defendants, and so on.

If the plaintiff dies as a result of the independent or concerted acts of the defendants, each defendant will be held liable for the plaintiff's death because death is not apportionable. Similarly, if the plaintiff's

EXHIBIT 15–1 Joint and Several Liability

JOINT LIABILITY	SATISFACTION	CONTRIBUTION
Each tortfeasor is liable for entire loss if loss is indivisible.	Plaintiff is entitled to only one satisfaction (payment) of judgment.	A defendant who pays more than his pro rata share of damages is entitled to contribution (partial reimbursement) from other defendants.

RELEASE	INDEMNIFICATION
A plaintiff who agrees to release a defendant absolves that defendant of all liability.	A tortfeasor who agrees to indemnify another tortfeasor accepts all financial responsibility on behalf of that tortfeasor.

property is destroyed, the harm is considered indivisible and nonapportionable.

Even if one of the defendants directly causes the plaintiff's injuries, all the defendants will be held liable if a court concludes that they acted in concert. Suppose two young men are drag-racing down a public street and one of them collides with the plaintiff's car. Both will be held liable even though only one of them actually came in contact with the car. The reasoning is that the tortious conduct of one encouraged the tortious behavior of the other and the combination led to the harm caused. (See, for example, *Bierczynski v. Rogers*, 234 A.2d 218 [Del. 1968].)

Harm That Cannot Be Apportioned

The rule of joint and several liability does not apply if the harm can be apportioned. In other words, if 60 percent of the harm was caused by defendant A and the remainder by defendants B and C, defendant A will be responsible for 60 percent of the damages and defendants B and C will be responsible for the other 40 percent. As discussed in Chapter 7 on damages, if the harm can be apportioned but can be done so only with great difficulty, the burden of allocating harm will shift to the defendants. If the defendants are unable to satisfactorily prove who was responsible for each percentage of the damages, all the defendants will be held jointly and severally liable.

Status of Joint and Several Liability

Joint and several liability has been abolished in some states, primarily because of the concern that the doctrine is used to go after the "deep pocket" defendant, who may actually be responsible for only a minimal portion of the harm. A corporation, for example, whose negligence contributed to only 10 percent of the plaintiff's harm may be held totally responsible for the plaintiff's damages under the rule of joint and several liability simply because the more blameworthy defendant is penniless.

Pared to its essentials, the question of whether to retain joint and several liability is a matter of social policy—where society wants to assign the burden when a liable party cannot pay damages. Without joint and several liability, the injured plaintiff bears the loss. Although society pays less, some plaintiffs will not be fully compensated. If joint and several liability is in effect, the loss is assigned to other liable defendants, who routinely pass on their added costs to society as a whole.

LOCAL LINKS

What is the status of joint and several liability in your state?

Many criticisms of joint and several liability center on the risks and costs it forces on defendants. Critics maintain that defendants should not be required to shoulder the burden for harm caused by others. Others argue that joint and several liability hurts industry because even if a business can pass on its tort-related costs to society as a whole through higher prices, those higher prices hurt the business. Using business to provide "insurance" only encourages plaintiffs to find wealthy business defendants to sue, resulting in a tort system that is no longer grounded in moral obligation and that serves up defendants as scapegoats.

One well-publicized case that illustrates the policy questions posed by the doctrine of joint and several liability involves a sympathetic plaintiff and a nominally negligent defendant. In this case a husband and wife, Gene and Cynthia Ellwood, and Cynthia's four children from a previous marriage were crowded inside a van Gene was driving. Gene failed to notice a stop sign as he headed into a busy intersection at forty miles per hour, and went directly into the path of a school bus loaded with a soccer team. The officer at the scene said there was nothing the bus driver could have done to avoid the accident. The impact killed Cynthia's ten-year-old son and left Cynthia in a coma from which the doctors said she would never recover. She will require constant care in a nursing home as long as she lives, at a total cost of $1 million or more.

Gene was insured for $100,000; beyond that he had few if any assets. His insurance company paid immediately, but the $100,000 barely covered the medical bills for the first month after the crash.

The bus driver admitted during a deposition that she never saw the Ellwood car approaching the intersection. The side road on which the Ellwoods were traveling joined the highway at a slant from the bus driver's left. Nothing blocked vision in the area between the roads. Based on this testimony the attorney representing the bus company estimated the bus driver's negligence at under 10 percent. The attorney representing Cynthia estimated the worth of the case as somewhere between $4 and $5 million.

Fifteen months after the accident, and just days before trial was to begin, the insurance carrier paid $1.9 million on its $2 million policy and the case was dismissed. The attorney for the insurance carrier says he settled out of court because "we just couldn't risk going to trial" and facing responsibility under joint and several liability for a verdict greater than $2 million.

The ultimate question in this case was, "Who should pay?" If the bus company's insurance had not provided $2 million for Cynthia's expenses, she would have had no one to take care of her except Social Security. Joint and several liability thus tapped a minimally negligent defendant to provide a safety net for Cynthia. However, because of this doctrine a defendant that was only nominally responsible was forced to pay large damages.

This case was the topic of heated debate and during legislative hearings was used to illustrate the abuses countenanced by a doctrine that most jurisdictions have since abolished or modified. Some states, for example, limit the liability of tortfeasors whose contribution to the plaintiff's damages falls below a certain percentage; such tortfeasors are liable only for their equitable share of the damages. For a more in-depth discussion of joint and several liability as it relates to the broader topic of tort reform, see Chapter 16.

CASE

Hall v. E.I. DuPont de Nemours & Co.
345 F. Supp. 353 (E.D.N.Y. 1971)
Memorandum And Order

WEINSTEIN, District Judge.

These two cases arise out of eighteen separate accidents scattered across the nation in which children were injured by blasting caps. Damages are sought from manufacturers and their trade association, the Institute of Makers of Explosives (I.M.E.). The basic allegation is that the practice of the explosives industry during the 1950's—continuing until 1965—of not placing any warning upon individual blasting caps and of failing to take other safety measures created an unreasonable risk of harm resulting in plaintiffs' injuries.

In most instances the manufacturer of the cap is unknown. The question posed is whether a group of manufacturers and their trade association, comprising virtually the entire blasting cap industry of the United States, can be held jointly liable for injuries caused by their product. Our answer is that there are circumstances, illustrated by this litigation, in which an entire industry may be liable for harm caused by its operations.

While the cases are closely linked in their litigation history and underlying legal theory, they differ in several crucial respects. See *Hall v. E.I. DuPont de Nemours & Co.*, 312 F. Supp. 358 (E.D.N.Y. 1970) for an earlier phase of the litigation. In *Chance*, the name of the manufacturer who actually produced the cap causing a particular injury is apparently unknown. In *Hall* it is, plaintiffs allege, known. We turn to *Chance* first since it presents the more difficult legal problems.

I. The *Chance* Case
A. Facts and Proceedings

Thirteen children were allegedly injured by blasting caps in twelve unrelated accidents between 1955 and 1959. The injuries occurred in the states of Alabama, California, Maryland, Montana, Nevada, North Carolina, Tennessee, Texas, Washington and West Virginia.

Plaintiffs are citizens of the states in which their injuries occurred. They are now claiming damages against six manufacturers of blasting caps and the I.M.E. on the grounds of negligence, common law conspiracy, assault, and strict liability in tort. In addition, two parents sue for medical expenses. Federal jurisdiction is based on diversity of citizenship. 28 U.S.C. § 1332.

While the plaintiffs' injuries occurred at widely varied times and places, the complaint alleges certain features common to them all. Each plaintiff, according to the complaint, "came into possession" of a dynamite blasting cap which was not labeled or marked with a warning of danger, and which could be easily detonated by a child. In each instance an injurious explosion occurred.

The complaint does not identify a particular manufacturer of the cap which caused a particular injury. It alleges that each cap in question was designed and manufactured jointly or severally by the six corporate defendants or by other unnamed manufacturers, and by their trade association, the I.M.E.

Plaintiffs' central contention is that injuries were caused by the defendants' failure to place a warning on the blasting caps, and to manufacture caps which would have been less easily detonated. This failure, according to the plaintiffs, was not the result of defendants' ignorance of the dangerousness of their product to children. The complaint states that the defendants had actual knowledge that children were frequently injured by blasting caps, and, through the trade association, kept statistics and other information regarding these accidents. Recognizing the dangerousness of their product to children, the defendants, through the trade association, used various means—such as placards and printed notices—to warn users of the caps and the general public. These measures were allegedly inadequate in light of the known risks of injury. Moreover, defendants are said to have jointly

(continues)

explicitly considered the possibility of labeling the caps, to have rejected this possibility, and to have engaged in lobbying activities against legislation which would have required such labeling. The long-standing industry practice of not placing a warning message on individual blasting caps was, it is urged, the result of a conscious agreement among the defendants, in the light of known dangers, with regard to this aspect of their product.

* * *

B. Issues Presented

* * *

(1) The Elements of Joint Liability

Joint liability has historically been imposed in four distinguishable kinds of situations:

(1) the actors knowingly join in the performance of the tortious act or acts; (2) the actors fail to perform a common duty owed to the plaintiff; (3) there is a special relationship between the parties (e.g., master and servant or joint entrepreneurs); (4) although there is no concerted action nevertheless the independent acts of several actors concur to produce indivisible harmful consequences...

These categories reflect three overlapping but distinguishable problems with which the law of joint liability has been concerned. The first is the problem of joint or group control of risk: the need to deter hazardous behavior by groups or multiple defendants as well as by individuals. The second is the problem of enterprise liability: the policy of assigning the foreseeable costs of an activity to those in the most strategic position to reduce them. The third is the problem of fairness with respect to burden of proof: the desire to avoid denying recovery to an innocent injured plaintiff because proof of causation may be within defendants' control or entirely unavailable. The complaint and defendants' motion to dismiss raise all three problems for consideration. [The discussion of causation has been omitted here.]

(2) Joint Control of Risk

The problem of joint control of risk was early posed in a case of group assault. In imposing joint liability, [one] court reasoned that "[with] all coming to do an unlawful act, and of one party, the act of one is the act of all".... Even in its earliest form the doctrine of joint liability for concerted action contained all the elements necessary for its future development: (1) causing harm (2) by cooperative or concerted activities (3) which violated a legal standard of care.

American courts have imposed joint liability for concerted action in cases involving a complex interaction of the three elements of the doctrine. "Cooperation" or "concert" has been found in various business and property relationships, group activities such as automobile racing, cooperative efforts in medical care or railroad work, and concurrent water pollution. "Express agreement is not necessary; all that is required is that there shall be a common design or understanding."...

The standard of care to which defendants have been jointly held has ranged from assault and reckless driving to negligence in building maintenance, brush burning, water pollution, and manufacture of explosives....

These diverse cases impose joint liability on groups whose actions create unreasonable hazards of risks of harm, even though only one member of the group may have been the "direct" or physical cause of the injury. Where courts perceive a clear joint control of risk—typically the racing and assault cases, as well as those involving common duties or joint enterprise—the issue of who "caused" the injury is distinctly secondary to the fact that the group engaged in joint hazardous conduct.

This rationale was recognized in the nineteenth century. In a case involving a horse race in a crowded street, a New York court noted that the collision was "not willful or intentional on the part of the defendants," but it upheld a jury determination that the negligent racing of the defendants was the joint cause of injury. Imposing liability on the defendant not involved in the actual collision, the court stated that "these defendants were acting together and in concert in this race. It was the race that created the condition that resulted in the accident."... By participating in a joint creation of negligent risk, both defendants were held liable for the consequences.... Analogous language focusing on the joint creation of risk can be found in the "common duty" cases, as when several defendants neglect to maintain a party wall....

Joint control of risk can also arise through business relations or joint enterprise.... The opinions frequently refer to the defendants' violations of a common duty of care not only in terms of joint control of risk, but also as concurrent causes which combine to produce injury....

Defendants argue that their participation in the I.M.E. safety program, and their cooperative or parallel activities regarding the safety features of blasting caps do not give them joint control over the risks of injury for purposes of tort liability. Joint control of risk and consequent joint responsibility arises, in their view, only when manufacturers enter into a conspiracy to commit intentional harm, or into a partnership or joint venture. The key to a joint venture, they assert, is an agreement to share profits and to pursue a limited number of business objectives over a short period of time. Since the defendants' membership in their trade association involves neither profit-sharing nor a limited time-span,

(continues)

they contend that no joint responsibility arises from the association and its members' activities.

The problem with this argument is that the elements of joint control of risk do not coincide with those in the formal doctrine of joint venture.

* * *

[A] joint venture exists when there is "an agreement between the parties under which they have . . . a joint interest, in a common business undertaking, and understanding as to the sharing of profits and losses, and a right of joint control."

* * *

The lesson is clear that joint control of risk can exist among actors who are not bound in a profit-sharing joint venture. This point is thoroughly confirmed by cases imposing joint liability on "joint enterprises," which are distinguished from "joint ventures" as being "non profit undertaking[s] for the mutual benefit or pleasure of the parties" . . . and on which joint liability is imposed because of the parties' effective joint control of the risk.

Joint control may be shown in one of three ways. First, plaintiffs can prove the existence of an explicit agreement and joint action among the defendants with regard to warnings and other safety features—the classic "concert of action." Second, plaintiffs can submit evidence of defendants' parallel behavior sufficient to support an inference of tacit agreement or cooperation. Such cooperation has the same effects as overt joint action, and is subject to joint liability for the same reasons. . . .

Third, plaintiffs can submit evidence that defendants, acting independently, adhered to an industry-wide standard or custom with regard to the safety features of blasting caps. Regardless of whether such evidence is sufficient to support an inference of tacit agreement, it is still relevant to the question of joint control of risk. The dynamics of market competition frequently result in explicit or implicit safety standards, codes, and practices which are widely adhered to in an entire industry. . . . Where such standards or practices exist, the industry operates as a collective unit in the double sense of stabilizing the production costs of safety features and in establishing an industry-wide custom which influences, but does not conclusively determine, the applicable standard of care. . . . As our decision in *Hall* below indicates, the existence of industry-wide standards or practices alone will not support, in all circumstances, the imposition of joint liability. But where, as here . . ., individual defendant-manufacturers cannot be identified, the existence of industry-wide standards or practices could support a finding of joint control of risk and a shift of the burden of proving causation to the defendants. . . .

In view of the allegations of explicit cooperation among members of the industry, it is apparent that plaintiffs have chosen the fist of the above three alternative theories. We have set forth the other two lines of possible proof only to suggest the a fortiori position presented in the instant case.

There is thus no support for defendants' argument that to establish joint control of risk, plaintiffs must demonstrate that the explosives industry was "rigidly controlled" through the trade association with regard to blasting cap design, manufacture, and labeling, and that the object of such control was some particularly reprehensible breach of duty. The variety of business and property relationships in which joint control of risk has been found demonstrates the flexibility of the doctrine. Liability is not limited to particular formal modes of cooperation, nor to illegal or grossly negligent activities.

Two recent cases provide examples under both strict liability and negligence standards. In *Vandermark v. Ford Motor Co.*, 61 Cal.2d 256, 37 Cal.Rptr. 896, 391 P.2d 168 (1964), . . . [h]olding the retailer strictly liable was . . . justified on the grounds that "in some cases the retailer may be the only member of [the] enterprise reasonably available to the injured plaintiff." . . . Joint liability "affords maximum protection to the injured plaintiff and works no injustice to the defendants, for they can adjust the costs of such protection between them in the course of their continuing business relationship." . . .

In the *Vandermark* case, the factors considered relevant to the issue of joint liability were (1) the standard of care—itself a function of the foreseeability and gravity of risk and the capacity of avoiding it; (2) the participants' capabilities of promoting the requisite safety in the risk-creating process; (3) the need to protect the consumer, both in terms of ascertaining responsible parties and providing compensation; and (4) the participants' ability to adjust the costs of liability among themselves in a continuing business relationship.

The Fifth Circuit looked to similar considerations in a case involving the question of joint control of risk in the context of res ipsa loquitur. The plaintiff in *Dement v. Olin-Mathieson Chemical Corp.*, 282 F.2d 76 (5th Cir. 1960), had been injured while working with an explosive charge containing three component parts. Evidence indicated that two of the components—the blasting cap and the dynamite—might have caused the accident. One of the defendant-manufacturers argued that the plaintiff was not entitled to the aid of res ipsa, since only one of the components had been under its exclusive control.

This "musical chairs argument" was rejected on the grounds it was not necessary that in order for res ipsa

(continues)

to apply one particular force must be severed out, identified and held as a matter of law to be the cause of the premature explosion. The various components were manufactured to be a part of one combination.... Even in cases in which there is no combination as there obviously is here, the Texas courts recognize joint liability against actors completely independent and unrelated to each other in circumstances where their conduct has caused indivisible injury which cannot be accurately apportioned and identified by the plaintiff.

Like the Supreme Court of California in *Vandermark*, the Fifth Circuit emphasized the defendant-manufacturers' high duty of care to guard against defects in explosives, the defendants' control over the products at the critical stage when care was needed, the necessity of not imposing impenetrable procedural and burden of proof requirements on injured plaintiffs, and the possibility of cost-adjustment among the defendants....

Plaintiffs' allegations in this case raise genuine issues under these criteria. As discussed in detail above, the allegation that defendants had actual knowledge of risks to children and of feasible safety measures provides a basis for finding an applicable duty of care under negligence and strict liability principles. Plaintiffs further allege that the defendant manufacturers obtained this knowledge through a jointly-sponsored trade association; the manufacturers delegated, in effect, at least some functions of safety investigation and design (such as labeling) to an industry-wide entity. Whether defendants collected and shared this knowledge as a group, and made joint or cooperative decisions on the basis of the known risks, are critical issues which require full factual development.

Factors which must be explored to determine both the existence of joint control of risk and appropriate remedies (if any) include the size and composition of the trade association's membership, its announced and actual objectives in the field of safety, its internal procedures of decision-making on this issue, the nature of its information-gathering system with regard to accidents, the safety program and its implementation by the association and member manufacturers, and any other activities by the association and its members (such as legislative lobbying) with regard to safety during the time period in question....

(3) Enterprise Liability

Joint liability has been traditionally imposed on multiple defendants who exercise actual collective control over a particular risk-creating product or activity. In a related but distinguishable fashion, joint or vicarious liability has been imposed on the most strategically placed participants in a risk-creating process, even though

injuries are caused "directly" or partially by other participants under their general supervision....

A similar principle of enterprise liability is embedded in the doctrine of respondeat superior—an employer's vicarious liability to third parties for employees' wrongs committed "in the scope of their employment." In the pure vicarious liability case, an employer is not charged himself with violating a standard of care—such as failing to properly supervise the inspection or labeling of a product. Rather, the employer is held liable because, despite reasonable precautions, his employee has violated the applicable standard of care.... The employer may be held liable even though the employee's acts (or failure to act) were forbidden or intentionally wrongful....

The rationale for an employer's vicarious liability to third parties has been analyzed as being very close to the enterprise liability basis of workmen's compensation. In both types of cases

[w]e are not ... looking for the master's fault but rather for risks that may fairly be regarded as typical of or broadly incidental to the enterprise he has undertaken.... [O]ne of the purposes for such a quest is to mark out in a broad way the extent of tort liability (as a cost item) that it is fair and expedient to require people to expect when they engage in such an enterprise, so there can be some reasonable basis for calculating this cost.... What is reasonably foreseeable in this context, however, is quite a different thing from the foreseeably unreasonable risk of harm that spells negligence. In the first place, we are no longer dealing with specific conduct but with the broad scope of a whole enterprise. Further, we are not looking for that which can and should reasonably be avoided, but with the more or less inevitable toll of a lawful enterprise. The foresight that should impel the prudent man to take precautions is not the same measure as that by which he should perceive the harm likely to flow from his long-run activity in spite of all reasonable precautions on his own part. The proper test here bears far more resemblance to that which limits liability for workmen's compensation than to the test for negligence. The employer should be held to expect risks, to the public also, which arise "out of and in the course of" his employment of labor....

Enterprise liability is also apparent in the long line of cases imposing joint and vicarious liability on owners, employers and manufacturers for breach of "non-delegable duties", or for miscarriage of "inherently dangerous activities" by their contractors, employees, and distributors....

A review of the cases demonstrates that the range of non-delegable duties is very broad; Dean Prosser

(continues)

suggests that the only unifying criterion is "the conclusion of the courts that the responsibility is so important to the community that the employer [—in the broad sense of one who utilizes the services of another—] should not be permitted to transfer it to another." The list of "inherently dangerous activities" is also long, running from classic categories such as the keeping of vicious animals or blasting to any activity "in which there is a high degree of risk in relation to the particular surroundings" and which thus requires definite or special precautions....

This body of precedent, whether couched in the language of non-delegable duty or inherently dangerous activity or both, is addressed essentially to the problem of when it is justifiable for an owner, employer, or manufacturer to rely on the services of another to guard against known or foreseeable risks ... The factors which must be considered in deciding whether such reliance is justifiable include

> the competence and reliability of the person upon whom reliance is placed, his understanding of the situation, the seriousness of the danger and the number of persons likely to be affected, the length of time elapsed, and above all the likelihood that proper care will not be used, and the ease with which the actor himself may take precautions.

In many instances the most strategic point of foresight, precaution and risk distribution may be the individual manufacturer, supplier, or employer. In other situations—typically water or air pollution by multiple emitters—the only feasible method of ascertaining risks, imposing safeguards and spreading costs is through joint liability or other methods of joint risk control.... The point is not only that the damage is caused by multiple actors, but that the sole feasible way of anticipating costs or damages and devising practical remedies is to consider the activities of a group. We do not, of course, suggest that private actions are the best way to meet these problems but only that in the absence of preemptive legislation, tort principles will support a remedy....

The allegations in this case suggest that the entire blasting cap industry and its trade association provide the logical locus at which precautions should be taken and liability imposed. It is unlikely that individual manufacturers would collect information about the nationwide incidence and circumstances of blasting-cap accidents involving children, and it is entirely reasonable that the manufacturers should delegate this function to a jointly-sponsored and jointly-financed association.

In the event that the evidence warrants it, the imposition of joint liability on the trade association and its members should in no way be interpreted as "punishment" for the establishment of industry-wide institutions. Such liability would represent rather the law's traditional function of reviewing the risk and cost decisions inherent in industry-wide safety practices, whether organized or unorganized....

To establish that the explosives industry should be held jointly liable on enterprise liability grounds, plaintiffs, pursuant to their pleading, will have to demonstrate defendants' joint awareness of the risks at issue in this case and their joint capacity to reduce or affect those risks. By noting these requirements we wish to emphasize their special applicability to industries composed of a small number of units. What would be fair and feasible with regard to an industry of five or ten producers might be manifestly unreasonable if applied to a decentralized industry composed of thousands of small producers....

PUTTING IT INTO PRACTICE 15:1

1. How many separate accidents are represented in this case?

2. Who are the defendants? What is the basic allegation against them?

3. How does the case involving Hall differ from that involving Chance?

4. What kinds of joint activities are the defendants alleged to have engaged in?

5. What is the question before the court in regard to joint liability?

6. What three problems with respect to joint liability does the court examine?

(continues)

PUTTING IT INTO PRACTICE 15:1 *(continued)*

7. What is the defendants' argument regarding joint control? What problem does the court find with this argument?

8. In what three ways does the court indicate that joint control can be shown? Which of these theories did the plaintiffs rely on?

9. Must the plaintiffs prove that the explosives industry was "rigidly controlled" or that the object of the control was some illegal or grossly negligent activity?

10. What factors does the court indicate must be explored to determine if the defendants exerted joint control?

11. What is enterprise liability?

12. What must the plaintiffs show if they are to hold the manufacturers jointly liable on the grounds of enterprise liability? Would these requirements be the same if thousands of producers were involved rather than five or ten?

PUTTING IT INTO PRACTICE 15:2

1. A psychiatric patient goes to a general practitioner, complaining of certain pains; the patient is hospitalized and rehospitalized. The first physician calls in a psychiatrist, who diagnoses the patient as suffering from chronic anxiety reaction and continues to treat her. After her discharge from the hospital, the psychiatrist prescribes drugs that the patient believes caused her to have an automobile accident. The first physician never sees the patient after she is discharged from the hospital, and the psychiatrist treats her until she is involved in the accident.

   The patient alleges that the two physicians are jointly liable, on the grounds that (1) one prescribed an excessive quantity of dangerous drugs and failed to inform her of the risks of driving while taking the drugs and (2) the other failed to inform her that the physician to whom he had referred her was a psychiatrist and gave her insufficient information to enable her to decide whether to accept the recommended treatment. Are the physicians jointly liable if they independently diagnosed and treated the patient?

2. Two pediatricians negligently fail to diagnose phenylketonuria (a rare childhood disease that begins at birth and results in progressive mental retardation) in a timely manner. A jury returns a verdict in favor of the plaintiff for $80,000. Should both of the physicians be jointly and severally liable for the $80,000 if the second physician began treating the plaintiff after the first physician had already initiated treatment?

3. A young woman is injured when the bumper car she is driving on a ride at Disney World is struck by a bumper car driven by her fiancé. At trial the jury apportions 14 percent of the fault to the young woman, 85 percent to her fiancé, and 1 percent to Disney World. The plaintiff does not join the fiancé as a defendant to the action. Can Disney World be held liable for 86 percent of the damages?

4. A university sues a manufacturer, a contractor, an engineer, and a subcontractor for negligently failing to complete a project for football practice fields. Is each of the parties individually and collectively responsible for the damages suffered by the university?

SATISFACTION

If tortfeasors A, B, and C are jointly and severally liable for a $10,000 judgment and the plaintiff recovers the full amount from A, she cannot collect anything from B and C. Additional recovery is not allowed because the plaintiff is entitled to only one **satisfaction** (payment) of the claim. Although she can collect from all the tortfeasors, she can collect on her judgment only once.

CONTRIBUTION

Tortfeasor A may, however, be entitled to **contribution** from B and C. In other words, A may turn to B and C for partial reimbursement because he paid more than his pro rata share of the damages. Early American courts denied contribution to intentional tortfeasors and eventually denied it to all joint tortfeasors. That common law rule was severely criticized and has today been changed by statute or judicial decision. Under the majority rule, today contribution is permitted to some extent. Although typically allowed for negligent tortfeasors, contribution is often denied for intentional tortfeasors. The justification underlying contribution is that one tortfeasor should not be saddled with all the damages while others are allowed to escape without any responsibility.

The courts disagree about the division of damages in the context of contribution. In some jurisdictions each defendant is required to pay an equal share of the damages. In those states that have adopted comparative negligence, the damages are generally divided in proportion to each defendant's contribution to the plaintiff's harm. A defendant to whom a jury assigns 25 percent fault but who pays the entire judgment can collect 75 percent of that amount from the other defendants in a comparative negligence state.

Contribution hinges on joint liability. If a defendant can raise a defense, such as immunity, that would bar recovery by the plaintiff, then the other defendants cannot seek contribution from him. Similarly, contribution cannot be sought against an employer if a workers' compensation statute prevents the plaintiff employee from suing the employer. This is because under workers' compensation statutes, employees can recover from insurance carried by their employers for any work-related injury, regardless of who was at fault. Employees who recover under these statutes are therefore barred from suing their employers in tort.

LOCAL LINKS

In your state how are damages divided in the context of contribution?

RELEASE

Contribution becomes particularly problematic when a **release**, a document absolving a defendant of all liability, is given to one defendant. Under the common law, a plaintiff had a single, indivisible cause of action against all joint tortfeasors. Therefore, a release of one tortfeasor released all tortfeasors. To avoid the restrictive results of a release, a plaintiff who settled with one defendant would enter into a **covenant not to sue**, in which she promised not to sue that particular defendant but continued to hold all other defendants liable.

According to *Restatement (Second) of Torts* § 885, which reflects the majority rule, all tortfeasors are released if the release is silent regarding their continuing liability. To illustrate this point, suppose the plaintiff is injured by defendant A and seeks medical treatment from defendant B, who aggravates the injury through negligent treatment. If the plaintiff receives payment from defendant A and signs a release that does not mention defendant B, defendant B can later point to the common law rule regarding releases and escape all liability.

A plaintiff may preserve her rights against other tortfeasors by specifically including a provision to that effect in the release. A desire to reserve one's right to sue may be proved by external evidence, such as verbal statements. This evidentiary rule was promulgated out of a desire to protect those who enter into such

NET NEWS

An article titled "Damages: Apportionment Among Joint Tortfeasors" reviews the history of the development of joint and several liability and contribution and can be found at **http://www.dcba.org**. Select "Brief Magazine", enter "October 1997" in the search window, select Vol. 10 (1997–98), then select "Damages: Apportionment Among Joint Tortfeasors."

Differences between a Release and a Covenant Not to Sue

Note the distinction between a release and a covenant not to sue: a plaintiff who enters into a release surrenders her claim; a plaintiff who enters into a covenant not to sue does not surrender her claim but agrees that she will not sue on it. If the plaintiff later reneges on a covenant not to sue and decides to sue, the defendant with whom she entered into the covenant will have a counterclaim for breach of contract.

Plaintiffs should be cautioned against entering into releases prematurely. If a plaintiff's injuries turn out to be more extensive than originally realized, the release may have to be set aside on the grounds of fraud or mistake. Litigation regarding the validity of releases can be avoided by simply refraining from entering into releases until the full extent of the plaintiff's injuries is known.

Problems with Releases in Light of Contribution

Problems arise in the context of contribution when one defendant is granted a release and the other defendants are not (see Exhibit 15–2). Suppose the plaintiff accepts $2,000 from defendant A and releases him and then sues defendant B and obtains a judgment for $20,000. Can B obtain contribution from A? Under the traditional majority rule the answer is yes. Unfortunately, this rule discourages defendants from settling because they know they may be subject to contribution at a later time.

To prevent this problem some courts disallow contribution but reduce the plaintiff's claim against the nonreleased defendant on a pro rata basis. Suppose that, as in the previous example, the plaintiff releases defendant A and is later awarded damages in a jury trial against defendant B for $20,000. The plaintiff will be allowed to recover only $10,000 from defendant B because, by settling with defendant A, she liquidated half of her total right to recovery. Defendant B, however, would not be allowed to obtain contribution from defendant A. This rule is also problematic in that it discourages plaintiffs from settling as much as the previous rule discouraged defendants from settling.

To encourage settlement, therefore, some courts relieve the settling defendant from contribution liability altogether. Both the plaintiff and the settling defendant must reach settlement in "good faith." They must also show they did not act in collusion with each other. The issue of good faith often ends up being litigated under this approach.

LOCAL LINKS

How do the courts in your state deal with contribution when one defendant has been released?

EXHIBIT 15–2 *Three Approaches to the Problem of Releases in the Context of Contribution*

APPROACH A	APPROACH B	APPROACH C
Nonreleased defendant can seek contribution from released defendant. *Problem Associated with Approach A:* Discourages defendants from settling.	Nonreleased defendant cannot seek contribution, but plaintiff's claim against nonreleased defendant is reduced. *Problem Associated with Approach B:* Discourages plaintiffs from settling.	Nonreleased defendant cannot seek contribution, and plaintiff's claim is unaffected by release as long as parties negotiate in good faith. *Problem Associated with Approach C:* Leads to litigation regarding issue of good faith.

© Cengage Learning 2012

Gulfstream Park Racing Association, Inc. v. Gold Spur Stable, Inc.
820 So.2d 957 (D.Ct., Fla. 2002)

TAYLOR, J.

Gulfstream Park Racing Association, Inc. (Gulfstream) appeals a trial court order granting summary judgment in favor of third-party defendant and appellee, John C. Kimmel (Dr. Kimmel). This appeal arises from an incident wherein a thoroughbred horse, named Devil's Cup, fractured a bone in his right front leg while racing on the turf course at Gulfstream Park. After several months of medical care, the horse was put down. The owner of the horse, Gold Spur Stable, Inc. (Gold Spur), sued Gulfstream, alleging negligence in the design, maintenance, and operation of the track and failure to warn Gold Spur of any dangerous conditions.

Gulfstream denied any negligence and affirmatively asserted that Gold Spur was comparatively negligent. It further claimed that the negligence of third parties, including the horse's veterinarian and trainer, Dr. Kimmel, contributed to Gold Spur's damages. Gulfstream filed a third-party complaint against Dr. Kimmel for contribution and contractual indemnification. Gulfstream's contribution count was predicated on a duty of care that Dr. Kimmel, as trainer, allegedly owed to Gold Spur to protect the horse from unreasonably dangerous conditions. Specifically, Gulfstream alleged that Dr. Kimmel knew or should have known of the "soft" and wet conditions of the track, yet, despite having discretion to withhold Devil's Cup from the race, allowed the horse to run on the turf track that day. Gulfstream's second count, contractual indemnity, was based upon release and assumption of risk provisions contained in documents executed by Dr. Kimmel, as agent for Gold Spur.

In response to Gulfstream's requests for admissions and in his deposition, Dr. Kimmel acknowledged that he was responsible for the care, safety, and well-being of the horse. He testified that on the day of the race, he knew that the turf was soft because there had been a significant amount of rain. He did not walk the course to examine the track before the race.[1] He admitted that he was uncertain how Devil's Cup would handle the soft turf because the horse had never raced on soft turf before. Further, he was aware that Devil's Cup had undergone surgery for a synovial cyst in a hind leg when he was two years old.

Dr. Kimmel acknowledged that as the trainer, he was advisor to the horse's owner and had authority to withdraw or scratch the horse from the race for any reason, up until the time that the horse entered the starting gate. Dr. Kimmel and Alan Quartucci, the racing manager for Gold Spur, discussed the turf course conditions that day, and both expressed concern about whether Devil's Cup should run in the race. Despite their concerns, they allowed the horse to race.

Several witnesses were deposed concerning a trainer's duties and obligations to the owner of the horse. These witnesses, mostly horse trainers, said that trainers have a duty to assess the track before deciding whether to run their horses and that they can scratch a horse from a race if they feel that a track is unsafe. They noted that some trainers routinely walk the turf course before every race; they agreed that every trainer should inspect the course if they have safety concerns.

Doug Donn, the president and chief executive officer of Gulfstream, gave similar testimony regarding a trainer's duties and responsibilities. However, in his opinion, the turf was not a factor in Devil's Cup's injury, since no other horses in the turf races suffered any injury. Another witness opined that Devil's Cup broke down because the horse was lame going into the race and had been sore through training.

Dr. Kimmel moved for summary judgment against Gulfstream on the contribution and indemnification counts. He argued that the only negligence alleged by Gold Spur was the negligence of Gulfstream for maintenance, design and operation of the race track, for which he had no joint liability. As to indemnification, Dr. Kimmel argued that the indemnity clause in the Stall Agreement[2] does not clearly and unequivocally state that he must indemnify Gulfstream for its own negligence, but only allows indemnification for Dr. Kimmel's negligence. After determining that there were no disputed facts on these issues, the trial court granted summary judgment in favor of Dr. Kimmel.

A party moving for summary judgment must conclusively demonstrate the absence of any genuine issue of material fact and the moving party's entitlement to judgment as a matter of law.... Summary judgments are reviewed de novo on appeal.... On review, the court must indulge every possible inference in favor of the party against whom summary judgment was granted...

---

1. Dr. Kimmel testified that he could have walked the track, but that he rarely walks a course before a race because the turf course is inside the dirt course, and on a muddy or sloppy day it is impossible to get there without getting covered in mud

2. The Stall Agreement was titled "Application for Stall Space; Conditions to Stabling, Entry in Races, Release and Indemnification Agreement."

(continues)

Moreover, in negligence cases, summary judgment should be cautiously granted.... The issue of negligence, and more specifically, the determination of proximate cause, is ordinarily a question that should be left for a jury ... Further, "[u]nless a movant can show unequivocally that there was no negligence, or that plaintiff's negligence was the sole proximate cause of the injury, courts will not be disposed to granting summary judgment in his favor." ... As the movant, Dr. Kimmel had the burden to prove to the trial court that no genuine issue of material fact existed with regard to Gulfstream's claims for contribution and indemnification and that he was entitled to judgment as a matter of law on both counts.

Contribution

In its third party complaint against Dr. Kimmel, Gulfstream alleged that if it were found negligent, Dr. Kimmel's negligence may have contributed to the horse's injury. Gulfstream's claim for contribution was based upon the Uniform Contribution Among Joint Tortfeasors Act. § 768.31, Fla. Stat. (1997). This act provides, in pertinent part:

> Except as otherwise provided in this act, when two or more persons become jointly or severally liable in tort for the same injury to person or property, or for the same wrongful death, there is a right of contribution among them even though judgment has not been recovered against all or any of them. § 768.31(2)(a).

As long as the parties share a common liability, a right to contribution exists, even where the liability of the parties rests on different grounds ... The " 'essence of the action for contribution is *common liability* to the injured person, not liability for *common negligence*, or *similar* negligence, or *like* negligence.' " ... Common liability means that " 'each party, by reason of his wrongful act, is made legally liable to respond in damages to the injured party.' "*Id.*

In this case, whether Dr. Kimmel was negligent and whether his negligence combined with Gulfstream's alleged negligence to cause Devil's Cup's injury were questions for the jury. Based on the record, there are genuine issues of fact regarding whether Dr. Kimmel breached his duties to Gold Spur by negligently failing to scratch Devil's Cup from the race, thereby contributing to the horse's injuries. To prevail on his motion for summary judgment, Dr. Kimmel had to conclusively disprove these allegations against him. The record evidence, as recounted above, demonstrates that there is, at a minimum, a reasonable inference that Dr. Kimmel was negligent in allowing the horse to race under conditions which he feared might compromise its safety. As such, the trial court erred in granting summary judgment on this count.

Dr. Kimmel argues that Gulfstream's third-party complaint for contribution is impermissible under Rule 1.180, Florida Rules of Civil Procedure, because the two claims do not arise out of the same transaction or occurrence as is required by the rule. We reject this argument. Pursuant to Rule 1.180(a):

> At any time after commencement of the action a defendant may have a summons and complaint served on a person not a party to the action who is or may be liable to the defendant for all or part of the plaintiff's claim against the defendant, and may also assert any other claim that arises out of the transaction or occurrence that is the subject matter of the plaintiff's claim.

Here, the evidence demonstrates that Gulfstream's claim arose out of the same transaction or occurrence—the race. Gold Spur's claim is based upon Gulfstream's negligence in failing to provide a safe track for the horses to run. In turn, Gulfstream's claim against Dr. Kimmel is based upon his negligence in allowing the horse to run on an unstable track. Both of these claims arise out of the accident wherein Devil's Cup broke his leg. Further, the third-party complaint is proper because of allegations that Gulfstream and Dr. Kimmel may share a common liability for injury to Devil's Cup.

Indemnification

Gulfstream also argues that the trial court erred in granting summary judgment to Dr. Kimmel on the indemnification count. Gulfstream's claim for indemnification was based on the Stall Agreement signed by Dr. Kimmel as Gold Spur's agent. The relevant portions of the Stall Agreement provide:

> 6.B.(1) Trainer hereby agrees to indemnify, hold harmless and defent [sic] Gulfstream and its officers, directors, agents, representatives, employees, successors and assigns from any claims, losses, liabilities or demands whatsoever, including claims [sic] for medical and hospital bills, resulting from or arising directly or indirectly from the acts or omissions of Trainer and its agents, servants, employees, owners or invitees, in whole or in part, from or ou [sic] of or in connection with Trainer's activities at Gulfstream Park.

* * *

(continues)

6.B.(2) This indemnification provision shall not be effective as to any loss attributsble [sic] exclusively to the negligence or willful act or omission of Gulfstream.

* * *

6.D. Trainer assumes full responsibility for the safety and well-being of all horses under his care, custody and control while stabled at Gulfstream Park or while otherwise on Gulfstream's property utilizing the facilities.... Accordingly, Trainer agrees to take all reasonable measures for the protection of such horses, including providing adequate supervision of such horses while utilizing Gulfstream's facilities ... Furthermore, the undersigned acknowledges that Gulfstream has no obligation to remedy any condition at Gulfstream Park, including the racing surfaces, unless Gulfstream has prior written notice of the existence of such condition and has a reasonable opportunity to repair such condition.

Dr. Kimmel argues that the indemnity clause in the Stall Agreement does not require him to indemnify Gulfstream for its own negligence, but only allows indemnification for Dr. Kimmel's negligence. He relies on *Univ. Plaza Shopping Ctr. v. Stewart*, 272 So.2d 507 (Fla.1973). There, the supreme court reviewed an agreement purporting to indemnify a landlord for consequences arising solely from its own negligence. The court held that the general terms " 'indemnify ... against any and all claims' [did] not disclose an intention to indemnify for consequences arising solely from the negligence of the indemnitee." *Id.* at 511. After reviewing conflicting decisions in Florida on indemnity provisions, the court announced that a contract which attempts to relieve a party of its own negligence will be upheld only if it expresses such intent in clear and unequivocal terms. *Id.* at 509.

Here, Dr. Kimmel argues that because there is no language in the Stall Agreement specifically stating that he would indemnify Gulfstream for acts of Gulfstream's own negligence, the agreement falls short of the "clear and unequivocal" standard enunciated in *Univ. Plaza*. Therefore the trial court correctly granted him summary judgment as a matter of law. Gulfstream counters that the Stall Agreement does not provide for indemnification for its sole negligence; it provides that Dr. Kimmel must indemnify Gulfstream if Gulfstream and Dr. Kimmel are jointly negligent and it does so in clear and unambiguous terms. Gulfstream contends that the test for upholding such an agreement is not whether the contract actually contains the phrase "its

own negligence" but whether its language is so clear and understandable that an ordinary party will know what he is contracting away ...

In *Leonard L. Farber Co.*, a shopping mall patron sued the lessor and lessee of a shopping mall for injuries she sustained when she slipped on a piece of sausage lying on a common walkway within the mall. The indemnity provision contained in the contract between the lessor and lessee stated:

> Lessee shall indemnify Lessor and save it harmless from suits, actions, damages, liability and expense in connection with loss of life, bodily or personal injury or property damage arising from or out of any occurrence in, upon or at or from the Demised Premises or any part thereof, or occasioned wholly or in part by any act or omission of Lessee, . . .

We determined that the language "occasioned wholly or in part by any act or omission of Lessee" was sufficiently clear and unequivocal so as to make the Lessee liable for the joint negligence of the Lessor and the Lessee ...

Similarly, in *Marino v. Weiner*, 415 So.2d 149 (Fla. 4th DCA 1982), we found that the phrase "occasioned wholly or in part by an act or omission of [l]essee ..." manifested the unequivocal intent to indemnify the lessor where joint negligence existed? ...

In this case, the language of the Stall Agreement is in line with the above cases. The language of 6.B.(1), which states that Kimmel will indemnify Gulfstream for any "claims, losses, liabilities or demands whatsoever ... resulting from or arising directly or indirectly from the acts or omissions of Trainer ... in whole or in part ... 458." is consistent with the holdings of *Leonard L. Farber Co.* and *Marino*. The language of 6.B.(2), which states that the provision "shall not be effective as to any loss [attributable] exclusively to the negligence or willful act or omission of Gulfstream" is consistent with the holding of *Mitchell Maint. Sys.*

We conclude that the Stall Agreement clearly and unequivocally provides that Dr. Kimmel must indemnify Gulfstream except where it is determined that Gulfstream was exclusively or solely negligent. Because genuine issues of material fact exist as to Dr. Kimmel's negligence, the trial court erred in granting Dr. Kimmel's motion for summary judgment on the indemnification count. Accordingly, we reverse the order granting final summary judgment and remand this case for further proceedings. REVERSED and REMANDED.

PUTTING IT INTO PRACTICE 15:3

1. Why did Gold Spur sue Gulfstream?

2. On what basis did Gulfstream bring in Dr. Kimmel as a third-party defendant?

3. What were Dr. Kimmel's duties as a trainer? Did he have a duty to inspect the track?

4. On what basis did Kimmel move for summary judgment against Gulfstream?

5. On what basis does the court indicate the Gulfstream has a right to contribution from Kimmel?

   a. On what basis does Kimmel argue that Gulfstream does not have a right to contribution?

   b. Why does the court conclude that Gulfstream's claim for contribution is permissible?

6. On what basis is Gulfstream's claim for indemnification based?

   a. What is Kimmel's argument regarding indemnification?

   b. What is Gulfstream's counterargument?

   c. What does the court decide and why?

"MARY CARTER" OR "GALLAGHER" AGREEMENTS

Plaintiffs and defendants sometimes enter into agreements known as "Mary Carter" or "Gallagher" agreements. Mary Carter agreements have been so designated because of *Booth v. Mary Carter Paint Co.*, 202 So. 2d 8 (Fla. Dist. Ct. App. 1967) in which such an agreement was first reviewed by the appellate courts. Under these agreements a defendant (or some of the defendants) agrees to guarantee the plaintiff a certain amount of money if the plaintiff loses or recovers less than a stated amount. In return, the plaintiff agrees to refund part of the defendant's payment in the event of a verdict against the defendant in excess of a stated amount. Funds may actually change hands prior to trial or may be transferred on paper alone. Numerous variations on this theme exist, but the important feature is that the contracting defendant, although still a party in the case and usually a participant at the trial, benefits by the size of the judgments against the other defendants.

A typical agreement may also prohibit the plaintiff from settling with nonagreeing defendants for an amount less than the guaranteed amount without the agreeing defendant's consent, and might require that the parties conceal the agreement not only from the jury but also from the court and other parties. The terms of Gallagher agreements are fully disclosed, thereby distinguishing them from Mary Carter agreements, which are cloaked in secrecy.

Plaintiffs benefit from such arrangements because they pressure settling defendants, who have a substantial interest in a sizeable plaintiff's recovery, to cooperate with the plaintiff in discovery, peremptory challenges, trial tactics, witness examination, and influencing the jury. By having the settling defendants remain at trial, the plaintiff is relieved of dealing with the "empty chair" defense. Besides obtaining security by being guaranteed payment, the plaintiff is able to present a more streamlined, simplified case merely by reducing the number of defendants. She may also profit from disputes that break out during trial between the settling and nonsettling defendants as they maneuver to establish the other's liability.

Likewise, settling defendants benefit by eliminating the risk of paying more than the amount agreed on. The cost of litigation is reduced because the need for an aggressive defense is no longer warranted. Most importantly, the settling defendant has in effect purchased part of the plaintiff's claim, giving him a chance to recover all or part of what it has paid or agreed to pay. If the parties to a Mary Carter or Gallagher agreement succeed in their attack on the remaining defendants, the settling defendants may end up paying nothing—even if the jury finds substantial fault on their part.

The vast majority of courts tolerate these agreements even though the secrecy of their terms is subject to great controversy. A few states, however, have found that such agreements violate public policy. In a case that illustrates the structure and potential abuses of these agreements, the Texas court struck down Mary Carter agreements as being contrary to public policy (*Elbaor v. Smith*, 845 S.W.2d 240 [Tex. 1992]). In *Elbaor* the plaintiff, Carole, received emergency treatment for her ankle at the Dallas/Fort Worth Medical Center-Grand Prairie by Dr. Syrquin after being severely injured in a motor vehicle accident. Subsequent to this treatment she was transferred to Arlington Community Hospital, where she received treatment from a team of physicians including Dr. Elbaor, an orthopedic surgeon, as well as a plastic surgeon and an infectious disease specialist. Later she was operated on twice as a result of complications from her ankle injury. Ultimately Carole brought a medical malpractice suit against Dallas/Fort Worth Medical Center-Grand Prairie, Arlington Community Hospital, Drs. Elbaor and Syrquin, and other doctors. Prior to trial, Carole entered into Mary Carter agreements with Dr. Syrquin, Arlington Community Hospital, and another doctor. She then settled with Dallas/Fort Worth Medical Center-Grand Prairie, releasing them from the suit. Dr. Elbaor, who filed cross-claims against the other doctors and Arlington Community Hospital for contribution in the event he was found liable, remained as the sole nonsettling defendant.

LOCAL LINKS

Do the courts in your state permit Mary Carter or Gallagher agreements? If so, what restrictions do they put on these agreements?

Under the terms of her Mary Carter agreement with Dr. Syrquin, Carole accepted $350,000; under the terms of her agreement with Arlington Community Hospital she accepted $75,000. Both defendants retained a financial stake in the lawsuit and were required to participate at trial. The jury found that Carole's damages totaled $2,253,237.07, of which Dr. Elbaor was responsible for 88 percent, and Dr. Syrquin for 12 percent. After deducting all credits for Dr. Syrquin's percentage of causation, and Carole's settlements with other defendants, the trial court rendered judgment against Dr. Elbaor for $1,872,848.62.

In finding Mary Carter agreements contrary to public policy, the court characterized Mary Carter agreements as agreements that skew the trial process, mislead the jury, promote collusion among adversaries, and create the likelihood that a less culpable defendant will be held liable for the full judgment. The court balanced the public policy of judicial integrity against judicial economy and found that the need for fair trials outweighed the desirability of Mary Carter agreements as partial settlement tools.

The court pointed to specific evidence of abuses that occurred during this trial. For example, even though Carole's own experts testified that Dr. Syrquin committed malpractice, her attorney stated during both voir dire and opening statements that Dr. Syrquin's conduct was "heroic" and that it was Dr. Elbaor's negligence that caused Carole's damages. The attorneys for the settling defendants characterized Carole's damages as "devastating," "astoundingly high," and "astronomical." On cross-examination, they elicited testimony from Carole that was favorable to her case and requested recovery for pain and mental anguish.

As the facts of *Elbaor* demonstrate, these agreements may promote settlement, but they can also be abusive to nonsettling defendants, who may be faced with a lower chance of resolving the dispute as well as an increased exposure for damages. Although most courts now require the disclosure of such agreements, at least to the court and the nonsettling parties, these agreements continue to affect trials covertly. They skew the litigation process by hiding from the jury the full extent of the allegiance between the plaintiff and the settling defendant and by distracting the parties and the court from the merits of the case. As can be seen by the events in *Elbaor*, these agreements may force attorneys into questionable ethical situations and can encourage settling defendants to share with the plaintiff information obtained from other defendants during joint defense efforts.

In effect these agreements allow parties relief from any no-contribution rule. If the no-contribution rule is in effect and a plaintiff executes a judgment against a "deep pocket" defendant, that defendant will be unable to limit his liability by seeking relief from the other joint tortfeasors. Mary Carter and Gallagher agreements, however, allow defendants to limit their liability, in essence circumventing rules prohibiting contribution.

CASE

Hodesh v. Korelitz
123 Ohio Ar.3d 72, 914 N.E.2d 186, (Ohio 2009)

The sole legal issue in this case is whether an agreement between appellant, Michael Hodesh, and one of the defendants in Hodesh's medical-malpractice action, Jewish Hospital of Cincinnati, should have been disclosed to the jury. For the reasons that follow, we conclude that the trial court did not abuse its discretion by not requiring disclosure of the agreement.

Facts and Procedural History

[§ 2] Michael Hodesh filed a medical-malpractice action against appellee Dr. Joel Korelitz and the Jewish Hospital of Cincinnati, among others, alleging that Korelitz and the hospital staff had left a towel in his abdomen following a surgery for diverticulitis. Two and a half weeks before the trial, Hodesh and the hospital entered into a "Contingency Agreement," which contained, among other provisions, a series of provisions that collectively limited the hospital's exposure to $250,000 and ensured that Hodesh would receive at least $175,000.

[§ 3] On the first day of trial, Korelitz requested disclosure of any agreements between Hodesh and the hospital. The court ordered Hodesh to submit to the court any existing agreements between him and the hospital. Hodesh submitted the agreement, which the judge did not read before placing it under seal. The judge stated that there was no evidence of collusion and, based on Hodesh's declaration that the agreement was a high/low agreement, concluded that the agreement did not need to be disclosed to the jury. The jury found Korelitz negligent and returned a verdict in favor of Hodesh, awarding him $775,000. The jury also found that the hospital was not liable. After the verdict, the court provided a copy of the agreement to Korelitz.

[§ 4] Korelitz appealed on several grounds. The only issue he raised that is relevant to this case is whether the trial court erred by not compelling disclosure of the agreement. The court of appeals held that the trial court committed reversible error by not disclosing the agreement to the jury. We accepted Hodesh's discretionary appeal.

Settlement Agreements

Settlement agreements are valid when "there is no evidence of collusion, in bad faith, to the detriment of other, non-settling parties." *Krischbaum v. Dillion* (1991), 58 Ohio St.3d 58, 69–70, 567 N.E.2d 1291 Although settlement agreement are as varied as the cases in which they are used, they fall into general categories. In a typical settlement agreement, "a settling defendant is withdrawn from the case and released from liability." In a typical "high-low settlement agreement * * *, the settling defendant remain [s] in the case and the extent of her liability [is] predicated on the amount of the verdict." *Id.* There is another species of settlement agreement, called a Mary Carter agreement, *see Booth v. Mary Carter Paint Co.,* 202 So.2d 8 (Fla.App. 1967), which we have defined as "a contract between a plaintiff and one defendant allying them against another defendant at trial." *Vogel v. Wells* (1991), 57 Ohio St.3d 91, 93, 566 N.E.2d 154. *See Saleeby v. Rocky Elson Constr., Inc. (Fla.2009), 3 So.3d 1078, fn 3*(a Mary Carter agreement is "a contract by which one co-defendant secretly agrees with the plaintiff that, if such defendant will proceed to defend himself in court, his own maximum liability will be diminished proportionally by increasing the liability of the other co-defendants"). The court of appeals in this case determined that the agreement between Hodesh and the hospital was a Mary Carter agreement, and that determination is why it held that the agreement should have been disclosed.

Mary Carter agreements are per se invalid in some states. *See,* e.g., *Dosdourian v. Carsten* (Fla. 1993), 624 So. 2d 241, 246; *Cox v. Kelsey-Hayes Co.* (1978), 1978 OK 148, 594 P.2d 354, 360; *Elbaor v. Smith* (Tex.1992), 845 S.W.2d 240, 250. We mentioned this minority view in *Ziegler v. Wendel Poutry Servs., Inc.* (1993), 67 Ohio St.3d 10, 16, 615 N.E.2d 1022, overruled on other grounds by *Fidelholtz v. Peller* (1998), 81 Ohio St.3d 197, 690 N.E.2d 502. We did not adopt the minority position then, nor do we now. Instead, we are persuaded that the majority approach, which requires Mary Carter agreements to be disclosed to codefendants and the jury, is more reasonable and compatible with Ohio's approach to settlement agreements. *Monti,* 287 Conn. At 124, 947 A.2d 261. *Soria v. Sierra Pacific Airlines, Inc.* (1986), 111 Idaho 594, 604, 726 P.2d 706 (disclosure exposes a settling defendant's incentive to increase plaintiff's damages).

We have considered agreements alleged to be Mary Carter agreements on two separate occasions; both times we determined that the agreement was valid and did not need to be disclosed to the jury. *Vogel,* 57 Ohio St. 3d at 93–94, 566 N.E.2d 154; Ziegler, 67 Ohio St.3d at 17, 615 N.E.2d 1022. In *Vogel,* a defendant/appellant alleged that another defendant and the plaintiff had entered into a collusive agreement akin to a Mary Carter agreement and that the trial court had erred in refusing to disclose the existence of the agreement to the jury. *Vogel,* 57 Ohio St. 3d at 93–94, 566 N.E.2d 154. We noted that Mary Carter agreements typically have three basic provisions: a guarantee of a minimum payment

(continues)

to the plaintiff, an agreement that the plaintiff will not enforce a court judgment against the settling defendant, and an agreement that the settling defendant will remain a party in the trial but his monetary exposure is reduced in proportion to an increase in the liability of nonsettling codefendants. *Id.* at 93, 455 N.E.2d 154, fn. 1. We concluded that the agreement at issue was not collusive, after examining the trial court's decision under an abuse-of-discretion standard. *Id.* at 94, 566 N.E.2d 154.

In Ziegler, we concluded that the agreement between the plaintiff and one of the defendants was not a Mary Carter agreement, primarily because "[t]he amount of damages assessed against [the nonsettling defendant] had no impact on the amount [the settling defendant] would pay to [the plaintiff]. There was no built-in incentive on [the settling defendant's] part to increase [the plaintiff's] damages." *Ziegler,* 67 Ohio St.3d at 16–17, 615 N.E.2d 1022. We also stated that "[o]ne of the major dangers of Mary Carter agreements lies in the distortion of the relationship between the settling defendant and the plaintiff, which allows the settling defendant to remain nominally a defendant to the action while secretly conspiring to aid the plaintiff's case." *Id.* at 17, 615 N.E.2d 1022. *See Vermont Union School Dist. No. 21 v. H.P. Cummings Constr. Co.* (1983), 143 Vt. 416, 427, 469 A.2d 742.

Although the advent of complex contingent agreements has complicated the matter, we remain committed to facilitating the settlement of legal controversies, even contingent agreements that do not preclude the necessity of a trial. *Krischbaum,* 58 Ohio St.3d at 69–70, 567 N.E.2d 1291. All settlement agreements in Ohio must be free from collusion, regardless of whether they fall under the category of Mary Carter agreements. When reviewing a settlement agreements to determine whether it is collusive, we are guided by the typical Mary Carter agreements provisions; specifically, we look for a provision that decreases the settling defendant's liability in proportion to an increase in the nonsettling defendant's liability. *Vogel,* 57 Ohio St.3d at 93, 566 N.E.2d 154, fn. 1 (setting forth the basic Mary Carter agreement provisions). *See Hoops v. Watermelon City Trucking Inc.* (C.A.10, 1988), 846 F.2d 637, 640. We are concerned that such an arrangement provides an inducement for the settling defendant to "secretly conspir[e] to aid the plaintiff's case." *Ziegler,* 67 Ohio St.3d at 17, 615 N.E.2d 1022. This collusive purpose is obviated when the settling defendant " 'remain[s] at risk of liability in a significant amount.' " *Id.,* quoting the court of appeals opinion (Dec. 31, 1991), 3d Dist. Nos. 3-90-31 and 3-90-44, 1991 WL 280029.

The Agreement between Hodesh and the Hospital

As a preliminary matter, we note that "[i]n construing the terms of any contract, the principal objective is to determine the intention of the parties." *Hamilton Ins. Servs., Inc. v. Nationwide Ins. Cos.* (1999), 86 Ohio St.3d 270, 273, 714 N.E.2d 898.

The agreement between Hodesh and the hospital contains 16 numbered paragraphs. When read in pari materia, they evince an intention to ensure that Hodesh receives at least $175,000 and that the hospital's liability be capped at $250,000. This is apparent from paragraph 7 of the agreement, which states, "In any contingency that has not been addressed specifically by this Agreement, [the hospital] guarantees [Hodesh] a total payment of at least $175,000.00 with a cap of $250,000.00. In no event, will [the hospital] be required to pay Hodesh more than $250,000.00." The most problematic contingency for Hodesh is paragraph 3, which includes, among other things, this provision: "In the event there is a verdict against Korelitz and not [the hospital] for more than $250,000.00, Hodesh will not look to [the hospital] for any payment and will recover all from Korelitz."

This provision appears to provide an incentive for the hospital to increase the damages against Korelitz. *See Ziegler,* 67 Ohio St.3d at 16–17, 615 N.E.2d 1022. But three factors prevent us from reaching that conclusion. First, there are several contingency clauses under which the hospital will pay less if the damages are less. The lower the verdict, the greater the likelihood that the hospital would be required to pay $175,000 and the less the likelihood that it would be required to pay $250,000. Thus, the hospital had a financial interest in a lower verdict. *See Ziegler* at 17, 615 N.E.2d 1022.

Second, paragraph 3 requires the hospital to pay $175,000, even if the verdict against Korelitz exceeded $250,000, if Korelitz or his insurance company does not pay within 30 days. An appeal by Korelitz would delay payment past 30 days, triggering this provision, and the higher the verdict, the more likely it would be that Korelitz would appeal.

Third, the trial judge saw no signs of collusion during the trial. Even though the judge had not read the agreement, he knew that Hodesh and the hospital had an agreement and that Korelitz was concerned that the agreement was collusive. Thus, he was on alert for any trial tactics that appeared collusive.

A better course of action would have been for the judge to read the agreement prior to sealing it. But after the trial, when the document was disclosed to Korelitz and he moved for a new trial, the judge determined that the agreement was not collusive and denied the motion.

(continues)

After reading the agreement and reviewing the record, we also are convinced that the parties to the agreement were not in collusion.

The court of appeals read much into the hospital's decision to oppose bifurcation of the trial, which would have separated the issue of negligence from the issue of intentional destruction of evidence, and the hospital's decision to excuse a juror who was potentially sympathetic to the defendants. Although it is always possible to second-guess trial tactics, the trial court was in a better position than the court of appeals to determine the motives of counsel and whether collusion was behind their decisions, because he observed counsel and witnesses while the court of appeals reviewed a cold record. In denying Hodesh's posttrial motions to revoke the agreement and to grant a new trial, the trial court wrote, "[T]here was no evidence that [the hospital] remained as only a nominal Defendant which conspired with [Hodesh] to the detriment of Dr. Korelitz. The positions of [Hodesh] and the hospital remained adversarial at all times."

Other Considerations

A fact that must be considered whenever one defendant makes an allegation of collusion between his codefendant and the plaintiff is that codefendants often attempt to blame each other. Part of the defense for both the hospital and Korelitz in this case is that the other defendant was to blame for the towel having been left in Hodesh's abdomen. That the hospital attempted to show that Korelitz was responsible was no more evidence of collusion than Korelitz's attempt to convince the jury that the hospital staff was to blame. The legal positions of codefendants are often antithetical and adversarial. Plaintiffs benefit when codefendants attempt to blame each other; that, standing alone, is not evidence of collusion.

Conclusion

For all the reasons above, we conclude that the agreement between Hodesh and the hospital was not collusive and that the trial court did not abuse its discretion in refusing to disclose the agreement to the jury. We reverse the judgment of the court of appeals on this issue. Several issues that were raised in the court of appeals were mooted by that court when it determined that the agreement should have been disclosed. Those issues now need to be addressed. Accordingly, we remand the cause to the court of appeals with instructions to consider those issues.

Judgment reversed and cause remanded.

INDEMNIFICATION

When one tortfeasor accepts total financial responsibility for another tortfeasor, he is said to have indemnified that other tortfeasor. The party against whom **indemnification** is sought is referred to as an *indemnitor* and the party seeking to be indemnified is an *indemnitee*. Indemnification can be distinguished from contribution in that contribution involves a sharing of liability, whereas indemnification involves a shift of liability from one tortfeasor to another. A discussion of the rules of both contribution and indemnity is found in *Gulfstream v. Gold Spur*, excerpted earlier in this chapter. The most frequent way indemnification arises is by contractual agreement in which one party promises to indemnify another, as is often the case in contracts between general contractors and their subcontractors.

The right to indemnity also arises out of the law's attempt to avoid unjust enrichment of tortfeasors, as in cases involving vicarious liability. The unjust enrichment occurs when a tortfeasor is not required to reimburse a tortfeasor who pays the claim, resulting in the discharge of them both. An employer, for example, pays a judgment incurred by one of its employees only because it is vicariously liable for the torts of its employees. The courts reason that if the employer was not then indemnified by its employee so that it could recover the full amount of what it paid in damages, the employee would be unjustly enriched by being allowed to shirk his responsibility to pay for damages he caused. Because employers and employees are generally covered under a single insurance policy, however, liability of both parties is satisfied by the insurance company's payment of the claim, and so indemnification is rarely sought.

In addition to situations involving vicarious liability, indemnity also applies to defendants who are liable only because they failed to discover or prevent another's misconduct. A retailer, for example, who innocently fails to discover a defect in goods that he sells, will be indemnified by the manufacturer of the defective goods. If, however, the retailer knows of the defect, the manufacturer will not be obligated to indemnify him. Some courts also deny indemnity if the retailer acts negligently.

The issue of indemnification sometimes arises when an individual follows the directions of another and reasonably believes the directions to be lawful. Typically this occurs in the context of a principal-agent relationship in which the agent acts under the direction of the principal. But it can also take place when a sheriff is instructed to seize someone's property and no lawful basis for such seizure exists. As long as the sheriff reasonably believes that the orders are lawful and engages in no deliberate wrongdoing, he will be indemnified by the governmental agency for which he works.

Indemnity is sometimes allowed in cases in which the plaintiff's injuries were aggravated by negligent treatment. If a driver, for example, pays for the total damages incurred by the plaintiff whom she injured,

she can be indemnified by the doctor who aggravates the plaintiff's injuries by negligent medical care. The driver would be entitled to indemnification for that portion of the plaintiff's damages that were attributed to the negligent treatment.

Traditionally indemnity was an all-or-nothing situation, requiring that the indemnitor pay the indemnitee the full amount that the indemnitee paid the plaintiff. Under the doctrine of *equitable indemnity*, the amount of indemnity is dependent on the relative fault of the tortfeasors. Therefore, a tortfeasor may conceivably be indemnified for only part of the total damages she paid. Suppose a judgment is paid in full by an individual because the other defendants are penniless. In accordance with the doctrine of equitable indemnity, if that individual were to be indemnified by her principal, she would be indemnified only to the extent that she was actually responsible for the plaintiff's damages. The doctrine of equitable indemnity is inapplicable in cases in which the indemnitee's liability is purely vicarious.

NET NEWS

Writers and composers are often required to sign indemnification agreements. An explanation of these agreements, and suggestions for those who are required to sign them, can be found at **http://www.asja .org**. Go to "For Writers: Free Resouces" and select "How to Deal With Indemnification Clauses" under the "Position Papers" section.

PUTTING IT INTO PRACTICE 15:4

1. A subcontractor's employee is injured when he falls from a ladder at a construction site. He obtains a judgment against the owner and the general contractor for his injuries. On what basis might the owner and general contractor recover from the subcontractor?

2. Ms. Hall sues Stich, a psychologist, claiming that he engaged in sexual improprieties while treating her. She also sues Dr. Schulte, from whom Stich is renting office space, and the Schulte Institute for Psychotherapy and Human Sexuality. During the trial Stich agrees to pay Ms. Hall $500,000 in exchange for the following agreement:

   Hall covenants not to enforce or execute on any judgment entered against Stich, expressly reserving the right to proceed against James and Marjorie Schulte and the Schulte Institute on all of Hall's claims against Schulte including, but not limited to, the respondeat superior, implied agency, ostensible agency and apparent authority claims based upon the acts of Stich.

   Is this agreement a release or a covenant not to sue?

(continues)

PUTTING IT INTO PRACTICE   15:4 *(continued)*

3. Students, parents, and teachers bring a product liability action against the manufacturer of chlordane after alleging injury from exposure to this termiticide. The plaintiffs and manufacturer reach a settlement. If the board of education and other companies in the chain of distribution are sued by the plaintiffs, what is their recourse? What effect will the settlement between the plaintiff and the manufacturer have on their options?

4. One of the defendants in a case in which a jury verdict for $1.5 million is rendered agrees to settle with the plaintiff for $5,000, in the hope that the defendant who had to pay the remainder of the judgment will be barred from obtaining contribution against the settling defendant. The settling defendant is a relative of the plaintiff. Will the nonsettling defendant be barred from contribution?

5. Jill and Jose are involved in a motor vehicle accident with a tractor-trailer driven by Richard. The cause of the accident is in dispute. Jill, who was seriously injured, sues Jose and Richard as well as Richard's employer and the employer's insurance carrier. Prior to trial Jose's insurance company and Jill enter into a compromise settlement of her claim against Richard. On the morning of trial, the defendants and the trial court are advised of the settlement, but not of its terms. Richard remains in the suit as a named defendant at trial. The other defendants demand that the settlement agreement be produced at trial and admitted into evidence. Do you think they will be successful?

SUMMARY

Joint tortfeasors are those who act together to produce a negligent or intentional tort. If the harm created is indivisible, each tortfeasor is jointly and severally liable for the harm suffered by the plaintiff. If all the defendants acted in concert, all will be held liable even though only one of the defendants directly caused the plaintiff's injuries. If the harm can be apportioned (divided), the rule of joint and several liability is inapplicable. Joint and several liability has been abolished in some states and limited in others.

A plaintiff is entitled to only one satisfaction of his claim. A defendant who has paid more than his pro rata share may, however, turn to the other defendants for contribution. Although contribution was denied under the common law, it is allowed in most states for negligent torts. The courts are not in agreement as to how damages should be divided in the context of contribution.

Contribution becomes particularly problematic when a release is given to one defendant. The rules created by the courts to deal with contribution when a release has been granted have discouraged either plaintiffs or defendants from settling. Under the common law, a release of one tortfeasor was a release of all tortfeasors. Under the *Restatement*, however, those defendants not parties to a release are absolved of liability only if the release is silent regarding their continuing liability.

Plaintiffs and defendants sometimes enter into Mary Carter or Gallagher agreements. In such agreements, one (or more) of the defendants agrees to guarantee the plaintiff a certain amount of money regardless of the outcome of the case and the plaintiff agrees to reimburse the defendant if the verdict exceeds a stated amount.

Indemnification involves one tortfeasor's acceptance of total financial responsibility for another. An employer that is vicariously liable for the torts of its employee may be indemnified by that employee, in that it can recover the full amount of what it paid in damages. Defendants who are liable only because they failed to discover or prevent another's misconduct may also be indemnified. The doctrine of equitable indemnity, which has been adopted by some courts, allows indemnity to be based on the relative fault of the tortfeasors.

KEY TERMS

concurrent tortfeasors
Tortfeasors who independently cause the plaintiff injury

contribution
Partial reimbursement of a tortfeasor who has paid more than her pro rata share of the damages

covenant not to sue
Promise by a plaintiff not to sue a particular defendant

indemnification
Total acceptance of financial responsibility by one tortfeasor for another

joint and several liability
Liability for an entire loss if the loss is indivisible

joint tortfeasors
Those who act together to cause the plaintiff's injury

release
Agreement to absolve a defendant of all liability

satisfaction
Payment of a judgment

REVIEW QUESTIONS

1. What is joint and several liability?

2. When is the doctrine of joint and several liability applicable, and when is it not?

3. What is the status of joint and several liability today?

4. What social policy underlies joint and several liability?

5. Why is the doctrine of joint and several liability criticized?

6. Define the following:
   a. satisfaction
   b. contribution
   c. indemnification
   d. release
   e. covenant not to sue

7. What was the common law rule regarding contribution, and what is the majority rule today?

8. What is the justification for contribution?

9. What problems arise in reference to contribution when the plaintiff releases a defendant?

10. How have courts dealt with the problem of contribution when a release is given, and what consequences arise out of each solution the courts have devised?

11. What should a plaintiff do before agreeing to release a defendant?

12. What do Mary Carter agreements typically provide, and how do they differ from Gallagher agreements?

13. How do plaintiffs and defendants benefit from Mary Carter and Gallagher agreements?

14. Why are some courts critical of Mary Carter and Gallagher agreements?

15. How do Mary Carter and Gallagher agreements affect contribution?

16. Who is the indemnitor and who is the indemnitee in an indemnification agreement?

17. How does indemnification usually arise?

18. What is the doctrine of equitable indemnity?

PRACTICE EXAM

Students should complete the practice exam after studying each chapter. The answers are in Appendix A. If you score lower than 80%, you should reread the materials.

True-False

1. Concurrent tortfeasors cannot be jointly and severally liable.

2. Under the rule of joint and several liability a defendant can be held responsible for all of the damages even though his contribution to the plaintiff's injuries was relatively minor.

3. Joint tortfeasors can each be held jointly and severally liable if the harm can be apportioned.

4. The question of whether to retain joint and several liability depends on where society wants to place the burden when a liable defendant cannot pay damages.

5. When joint and several liability is abolished, plaintiffs must bear the loss if liable defendants are unable to pay a judgment.

6. Critics of joint and several liability argue that this doctrine hurts business because it leads to an increase prices to compensate for tort-related expenses.

7. In some states defendants whose contribution to the plaintiff's injuries falls below a designated percentage are liable only for their equitable share of the damages.

8. In the context of contribution, tortfeasors need not necessarily pay an equal share of the damages.

9. If a plaintiff reneges on a covenant not to sue, the defendant cannot later sue for breach of contract.

10. Plaintiffs should enter into releases as soon as the defendant offers to settle the case.

11. Defendants are discouraged from settling when nonreleased defendants cannot seek contribution from released defendants.

12. The contracting defendant to a Mary Carter agreement does not participate at trial and is no longer considered a party to the case.

13. Plaintiffs benefit from Mary Carter and Gallagher agreements because these agreements pressure the defendant into cooperating with the plaintiff during discovery and at trial, but they are a disadvantage to plaintiffs in that they make the trial more complicated and cause plaintiffs to deal with the "empty chair" defense.

14. Defendants benefit from Mary Carter and Gallagher agreements because they can recover some or even all of what they have agreed to pay the plaintiff and they can reduce the cost of litigation.

15. Some courts object to Mary Carter and Gallagher agreements because they believe such agreements promote collusion among adversaries and mislead the jury.

16. Indemnification can arise out of a contractual agreement.

17. Indemnification of a retailer by a manufacturer is required when a retailer innocently fails to discover a defect in a product but is not required if the retailer is negligent or knows of a defect in a product but sells the product anyway.

18. The doctrine of equitable indemnity provides that the indemnitor must pay the indemnitee the full amount that the indemnitee paid the plaintiff.

Matching

GROUP 1

____	1. Surrender of claim	a. indemnification
____	2. Agreement not to sue	b. contribution
____	3. Only one of these for plaintiff	c. release
____	4. Sharing of liability	d. covenant not to sue
____	5. Shifting of liability	e. satisfaction

GROUP 2

____	1. Party seeking indemnification	a. Mary Carter agreement
____	2. Party against whom indemnification is sought	b. Gallagher agreement
____	3. Terms of agreement that are secret	c. equitable indemnity
____	4. Terms of agreement that are disclosed	d. indemnitor
____	5. Indemnity dependent on relative fault of tortfeasors	e. indemnitee

Fill-in-the-Blanks

1. Joint tortfeasors are jointly and severally liable for any harm that is _____.

2. _____ tortfeasors act together, whereas as _____ tortfeasors act independently.

3. Joint and several liability has been abolished in some states out of a concern that it is unfair to hold _____ _____ defendants fully liable when they were only marginally responsible for the plaintiff's injuries.

4. Although the plaintiff can collect from any or all defendants under the doctrine of joint and several liability, she is entitled to only one _____ of her claim.

5. With a(n) _____ _____ agreement the defendant agrees to guarantee the plaintiff a certain amount of money if the plaintiff loses or receives less than a designated amount. The terms of this agreement are usually cloaked in secrecy, but in _____ agreements the terms of the agreement are usually disclosed to the court and jury.

Multiple-Choice

1. Joint tortfeasors
   a. will be considered jointly and severally liable even if the defendants can prove who was responsible for each percentage of the damages.
   b. cannot each be held liable for the death of the plaintiff or destruction of the plaintiff's property.
   c. can each be held liable even if only one defendant directly caused the plaintiff's injuries.
   d. all of the above.

2. Contribution
   a. was allowed to all tortfeasors under the common law.
   b. is allowed for intentional tortfeasors.
   c. is justified on the basis that some defendants should not be saddled with all of the damage while other defendants escape responsibility.
   d. all of the above.

3. Contribution can be sought
   a. only when defendants are jointly liable.
   b. can be sought from a defendant who has a valid defense.

   c. can be sought from an employer if workers' compensation statutes prevent the plaintiff from suing the employer.
   d. all of the above.

4. If a plaintiff releases one tortfeasor,
   a. under the common law, all of the tortfeasors were released.
   b. and wants to reserve her right to sue the other tortfeasors, she can enter into a covenant not to sue with a particular defendant.
   c. and wants to reserve her right to sue the other tortfeasors, she can make verbal statements indicating her intention to reserve her right to sue the remaining defendants.
   d. all of the above.

5. In some courts a nonreleased defendant
   a. can seek contribution from a released defendant.
   b. cannot seek contribution, but the plaintiff's claim against the nonreleased defendant can be reduced.
   c. cannot seek contribution as long as the released defendant negotiated with the plaintiff in good faith.
   d. all of the above.

6. A typical Mary Carter agreement
   a. involves no exchange of funds, even on paper, before trial.
   b. provides that the plaintiff cannot agree to settle with the nonagreeing defendant for an amount less than the guaranteed amount without the agreeing defendant's consent.
   c. reveals the terms of the agreement to the jury, the court, and the other parties.
   d. all of the above.

7. Mary Carter and Gallagher agreements
   a. create the likelihood that a less culpable defendant will be held liable for the full judgment.
   b. help defendants avoid the no-contribution rule but are not particularly effective settlement tools.
   c. tend to focus parties on the merit of the case.
   d. all of the above.

8. Indemnification sometimes arises out of
   a. the law's attempt to avoid unjust enrichment of a tortfeasor.
   b. a contractual agreement.
   c. a relationship in which one party is vicariously liable for the torts of another.
   d. all of the above.

9. Indemnification
   a. is often needed when an employer pays an employee's claim.
   b. will be allowed if an agent follows the directions of her principal, reasonably believing the directions to be lawful, even though the orders are subsequently shown to be unlawful.
   c. will not be allowed if a doctor aggravates the injuries sustained by the plaintiff in an automobile accident and the driver who injured the plaintiff pays the entire judgment.
   d. all of the above.

PRACTICE POINTERS

Legal assistants are sometimes asked to draft releases, which are typically prepared by defense counsel or the defendant's insurance carrier. They are accompanied either by a draft of the agreed-to settlement terms or a letter stating that such draft will be provided upon return of the executed release agreement by the plaintiff.

When preparing a release, you should consider doing the following where appropriate:

- designate the capacities and authorities of the releasors and the released parties.
- include reference to all officers, directors, agents, and employees.
- identify the consideration for the release and the time and manner of making payment as consideration.
- disclose all legal rights and obligations of parties without a release.
- identify the common law, statutory, constitutional, administrative, and contractual rights of action and recovery affected.
- identify the effect of the release on heirs, successors, or assigns of parties.
- describe the claim or liability released.
- describe the scope of the release and exceptions to or limitations on the release.
- identify the rights and obligations not affected by the release.
- explain how the release is affected by matters unknown and unknowable by parties at the time of execution.
- explain how the release is affected by criminal acts; intentional torts; illegal acts; malicious, reckless, or wanton misconduct; or grossly negligent acts or omissions.
- explain how the release is affected by the conduct of agents, officers, or employees acting beyond the scope of duty, authority, agency, or employment.
- explain how the release is affected by damage or injury to the releasor.
- identify the duration of the release.
- identify the grounds for and manner of terminating or invalidating the release.

- include the releasor's acknowledgment of understanding the terms, conditions, and effect of the release; a statement of the releasor's capacity to understand and execute; and the releasor's acknowledgment of delivery and acceptance of consideration and release.
- identify the date and place of execution and the signatures of the parties.
- designate representative capacities and authority.
- notarize signatures.

The following is a sample release, which contains some, but not all, of the provisions just listed.

Mutual Release Agreement (Sample)

THIS AGREEMENT is entered into by and between James T. Smith, a single man (hereinafter referred to as "Smith"), and ABC Insurance Corporation, a Delaware corporation (hereinafter referred to as "ABC").

FOR AND IN CONSIDERATION of the entering into of this Agreement, and other good and valuable consideration, the receipt of which is hereby acknowledged, Smith does hereby remise, release, and forever discharge ABC, its subsidiaries and the other affiliates, and their respective officers, directors, employees, and agents, and ABC does hereby remise, release, and forever discharge Smith from any and all actions, claims, liabilities, promises, and demands whatsoever which they now have or may hereafter have on account of or arising out of or otherwise associated with, or assertable in, that certain litigation instituted by Smith against ABC entitled "James T. Smith, plaintiff, vs. ABC Insurance Corporation, a Delaware corporation, Defendant," bearing Cause No. CV 99–12345 in the Alpha County Superior Court (the "Lawsuit").

Smith/ABC
Mutual Release
Page 1 of 2

As additional consideration for this Release, Smith shall cause the Litigation to be dismissed forthwith with prejudice. Upon receipt of the fully executed Notice of

Dismissal with Prejudice, and this fully executed release, ABC shall pay to Smith the sum of Thirty-three Thousand Dollars ($33,000.00).

It is expressly understood that this Release includes any consequences which may hereinafter develop as well as those that have already developed and are not apparent as the result of the dealings between the parties relating to the issues or facts involved in the Lawsuit. This Release includes all claims, known and unknown.

As further consideration for the execution of this Agreement, the parties hereto warrant that (1) no promises or agreements not herein expressed have been made to or by them; (2) in executing this Release they are not relying upon any statements or representations made by any party, their agents, servants, or attorneys concerning the nature, extent, or duration of the damages, if any, or other thing or matter, but they are relying solely upon their own judgment; (3) the above-referenced consideration is received by each party in full settlement and satisfaction of all the claims that were or could have been asserted in the Lawsuit, known or unknown, or that otherwise arise out of the facts relating to the issues in the Lawsuit; (4) they are over the age of eighteen (18) years and legally competent to execute this Release; and (5) before signing this Release they have fully informed themselves of its contents and of the meanings thereof and have executed the same with full knowledge and advice of their attorneys.

It is further agreed and understood by the parties that this is a compromise settlement and is not in any way to be considered as an admission of liability on the part of either party hereto.

IN WITNESS WHEREOF, the parties hereto have executed this Mutual Release on this day of August, 1999.

Smith:

_____

James T. Smith, a single man

ABC:
ABC INSURANCE CORPORATION, a
Delaware corporation,
By _____

_____

Its Duly Authorized Representative

Smith/ABC
Mutual Release
Page 2 of 2

TORT TEASERS

1. Discuss the questions raised at the beginning of this chapter. What additional information would you need to fully answer these questions?

2. A is injured as a result of the combined negligence of B and C. A settles with B for $2,000 and releases him. A then sues C and obtains a judgment for $30,000. If C pays $30,000, can he obtain contribution from B?

3. An automobile passenger injured in a one-vehicle accident enters into an agreement with his host driver to limit the amount of liability the driver will be exposed to, regardless of the verdict in the passenger's action against the city. Assuming there is no evidence of unethical conduct or collusion, is such an agreement in violation of public policy? *City of Glendale v. Bradshaw*, 493 P.2d 515 (Ariz. 1972).

4. HOVIC enters into a contract with Beloit in which Beloit agrees to supply certain equipment for installation at the HOVIC refinery. HOVIC then contracts with Litwin for the installation of the equipment HOVIC purchased from Beloit. A Litwin employee is seriously injured while installing the Beloit equipment at the HOVIC refinery. The employee brings an action against Beloit, and a jury finds Beloit liable. Beloit subsequently brings an action against HOVIC for contractual indemnity based on the contract of sale between Beloit and HOVIC. Defendant HOVIC then impleads Litwin as a third-party defendant, arguing that if HOVIC owes anything to Beloit, then through the operation of an indemnity provision in HOVIC's contract with Litwin, Litwin is required to indemnify HOVIC.

   The law of the state in which these actions take place requires that an indemnification clause must state in clear and unambiguous terms that a party may be subject to indemnification. Under these guidelines do you think the following clause (drafted by Beloit) should be enforceable against HOVIC?

   N. *Warranty*
   Under no circumstances shall the seller have any liability for liquidated damages or for collateral, consequential or special damages or for loss of profits or for actual losses, or for loss of production or progress of construction, whether resulting from delays in

delivery or performance, breach of warranty, claims of or negligent manufacture or otherwise. The aggregate total liability of the seller under this contract, whether for breach of warranty or otherwise, shall in no event exceed the contract price. Buyer agrees to indemnify and hold harmless seller from all claims by third parties which extend beyond the foregoing limitations on seller's liability.

Do you think the following indemnity clause should be enforceable by HOVIC against Litwin?

VI. INDEMNITY AND INSURANCE
A. From date of Contract until Ready for Charge date, CONTRACTOR shall indemnify and hold HOVIC harmless from and against any and all loss, damage, injury liability and claims thereof, including claims for personal injuries, death and property damage and loss, unless caused by the sole negligence of HOVIC....

Beloit Power Systems, Inc. v. Hess Oil Virgin Islands Corp., 561 F.Supp. 279 (Virgin Islands, 1983) and 757 F.2d 1427 (3d Cir. 1984).

5. Plaintiffs are injured when the car in which they are passengers collides with a taxicab. Plaintiffs sue the owner of the taxicab but not the owner of the car in which they were riding. What are the options of the taxicab owner? *Knell v. Feltman,* 174 F.2d 662 (D.C. Cir. 1949).

INTERNET INQUIRIES

In deciding whom to sue, an attorney must assess the assets of each potential defendant. If a potential defendant is not insured and has no assets that can be collected if a judgment is won, initiating a lawsuit may be an exercise in futility. After all, a lawsuit is only as viable as the solvency of the defendant against whom the lawsuit is directed.

Legal assistants are often asked to assist in the process of asset evaluation. Some of the information they can use to assess an individual's or company's financial status includes

- property records
- tax liens
- recorded judgments
- pending litigation
- credit reports (credit reports for individuals can be accessed only for specific purposes).

We will focus on recorded judgments in this exercise. The trial phase of litigation ends when a judgment is entered. In federal court, entry occurs when a judgment is signed by the court and filed in the clerk's *docket* (list of cases on the court's calendar). In state courts, the procedure may vary, but in all courts judgments are ultimately filed. In most instances, the judgment is recorded with the county recorder's office. This recorded judgment is a public record that can be accessed by anyone willing to take the time to find it and is most often considered as constructive notice to the world of the existence of the judgment. Most states also recognize that a recorded judgment is a *lien* (a legal claim against real or personal property) on all property owned by the judgment debtor in the county where the judgment is recorded.

Judgments can be found by going to the county recorder's office, the clerk's office of the court where the judgment was rendered, or by having a private company find the judgment. Courts maintain a judgment docket (also called an *abstract of judgment index*), which is prepared by the court clerk or the judge who issued the judgment. The judgment docket indicates:

- judgment debtor (the party against whom the judgment was entered)
- judgment creditor (the party in whose favor the judgment was entered)
- amount of the judgment
- date the judgment was entered
- case number (number of the action)
- whether the judgment has been satisfied.

Using a name provided by your instructor (or the name of someone you know to be a judgment debtor), go to the web page for your local county recorder (which you can find by going to http://www.lexisone.com). If more than one judgment exists, use only one to answer the following questions. (If your county recorder is not online, go to the Maricopa County's home page at http://www.maricopa.gov and follow the appropriate steps to find judgments for the judgment debtor, Michael P. Welty.)

1. What is the judgment creditor's name?
2. What is the amount of the judgment?
3. When was the judgment entered?
4. Has the judgment been satisfied?
5. Describe the process you must follow to bring up a judgment record for this individual.

6. For what time period are these records available online?
7. What is the telephone number and address of your local recorder's office?

PRACTICAL PONDERABLES

Assume the same facts as given in the "Practical Ponderables" feature for Chapter 14, except assume that the trainer is an employee of Escondido Farms and has substantial assets of his own. Further assume that Maria's injuries were compounded by negligent treatment in the emergency room and that her parents decide to sue Mercy Hospital and the doctor who treated her, Dr. Martin, for negligence.

1. In your state, can Maria recover her entire judgment from Escondido Farms even if a jury decides that it was only 10 percent responsible for her injuries?

2. What options does Escondido Farms have if Maria decides to recover her entire judgment from this defendant alone?
3. Go on the Internet and find a sample release you think could be modified for use in this case if Maria decided to release the trainer.
4. In your state could Escondido Farms seek contribution from the trainer if he were released?
5. In your state could your firm enter into a Mary Carter or Gallagher agreement with the trainer? What limitations would be put on this agreement?

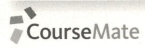 Access an interactive eBook, chapter-specific learning tools, including flashcards, quizzes, and more in your Paralegal CourseMate, accessed through www.CengageBrain.com.

PART IV

Torts in Practice

© Cengage Learning 2012

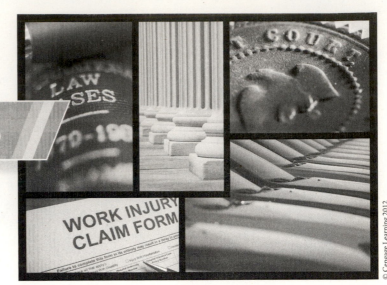

© Cengage Learning 2012

CHAPTER 16

Tort Reform

CHAPTER OBJECTIVES

After completing the chapter, you should be able to

- Identify the goals of the tort system.
- Identify the historical roots of tort reform.
- Describe the primary issues that drive the tort reform movement today.
- Critique the measures being proposed to reform the tort system in reference to punitive damages, joint and several liability, collateral-source payments, and frivolous lawsuits.

A burglar falls through a skylight during a robbery. A jury grants him a lifetime award of $206,000 with a monthly award of $1,500 a month. These are the "facts" as represented by an American Tort Reform Association publicity pamphlet. But is this what really happened? Actually, there was no jury award, because the case was settled. The plaintiff was a teenager who had climbed up on the school roof to take a floodlight. The skylight was painted over and the boy was rendered paraplegic as a result of his fall. A similar accident had resulted in a death at another school eight months earlier, and school officials had contracted to board over the skylights to resolve maintenance and safety problems.

GOALS OF THE TORT SYSTEM

What are these goals? First, the tort system is designed to compensate victims. Not only are victims served by this compensation, but society also benefits because tort victims who are compensated are less likely to become public charges, thereby alleviating some of the stress on an overburdened social welfare system. Second, tort law serves a deterrent function, providing individuals with an incentive to act in socially responsible ways. Over time, both individuals and businesses learn to consider the social consequences of their actions. Third, tort law spreads the risk of injury among members of society. By incorporating the costs of this social "insurance" into the costs of goods and services, all are protected from the expenses of catastrophic loss. Fourth, justice is served when victims are made whole. Restoring victims to the positions in which they would have been but for the defendant's wrong serves the collective conscience. Fifth, tort

EXHIBIT 16–1 Goals of the Tort System

- Compensation
- Deterrence
- Cost-spreading
- Restoration
- Exposure

© Cengage Learning 2012

law exposes corruption, incompetence, and a variety of other forms of misconduct. Behaviors that might otherwise have escaped public attention are brought into the limelight of public scrutiny and rectified. (See Exhibit 16–1.)

Two key questions that should be uppermost in the minds of tort reformers are (1) are these viable goals, and (2) if they are, is the tort system as presently structured effectively meeting these goals? For example, *should* the tort system serve a deterrent function, or is that function better left within the purview of the criminal justice system? And if deterrence is a viable goal, do punitive damages, for example, actually accomplish that goal? Broad policy questions such as these must be addressed before a meaningful discussion about specific issues is possible.

HISTORICAL ROOTS OF TORT REFORM

A brief review of the historical roots of tort reform illustrates the consequences of changes in goals. After World War I, in the Progressive Era of tort reform, legal commentators were primarily concerned with plaintiffs being adequately compensated.

NET NEWS

Numerous articles relating to tort reform and the effects on consumers can be found at **http://www .citizen.org** and entering "tort reform" as your search term.

Because at the time the tort system tended to protect defendants' interests, reformers opted for changes in the law that were plaintiff-oriented, such as workers' compensation and strict liability. Seeing the role of the tort system as something of a "karmic adjustor," through which the wrongs of society could be righted by means of a type of social engineering, they advocated no-fault approaches that helped the plaintiff at the defendant's expense.

From the 1960s through the 1980s, a series of social phenomena influenced the evolution of tort law. In the late 1960s medical costs rose sharply, according to health care providers, because more patients filed negligence claims. In the late 1970s manufacturers experienced rising liability insurance premiums. In the late 1980s insurance companies, which complained of continuing financial losses, cancelled or refused to reissue policies held by high-risk policyholders. The public assigned the tort system primary blame for these perceived crises and began to associate lawsuits with the shackling of business.

The legal community also became disenchanted with the focus on plaintiff compensation and sought to correct what it saw as the excesses of the Progressive Era. Focusing on the goal of deterrence, the classical tort reformers sought the repeal of any rules that were not aimed at deterring potential tortfeasors from engaging in risky behavior. In particular, they sought to eliminate any rules they viewed as being particularly harsh toward defendants.

What specific changes occurred as a result of the classical reform movement? In the 1970s, responding to the medical crisis of the 1960s, at least forty-three states passed legislation that limited the potential malpractice liability of health care providers. The second wave of classical reforms resulted in many states eliminating joint and several liability and imposing caps on non-economic damages, particularly punitive damages. Several states reestablished sovereign-immunity doctrines; others allowed defendants to pay awards periodically rather than in lump sums; some penalized plaintiffs who brought frivolous lawsuits; still others mandated some form of alternative dispute resolution. By 1991 nearly all states had enacted some form of tort reform. (See Exhibit 16–2.)

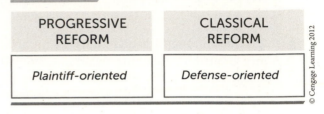

EXHIBIT 16–2   *Pendulum Swing of Tort Reform*

PROGRESSIVE REFORM	CLASSICAL REFORM
Plaintiff-oriented	*Defense-oriented*

© Cengage Learning 2012

FOCUS OF TODAY'S REFORMERS

What is the rallying cry of today's reformers? Most have focused on the law's plaintiff orientation, the litigiousness of society, the excessiveness of jury verdicts, and the inhibition of medical and business practices (see Exhibit 16–3). The insurance industry in particular has accused the plaintiff orientation of the tort system of making it nearly impossible to predict risks and set prices.

Before considering the alleged plaintiff orientation of the tort system, we should evaluate insurance industry claims that the tort system is to blame for its financial woes. There is evidence to indicate that the crisis proclaimed by the insurance industry in the mid-1980s was actually caused by a cyclical downturn combined with questionable underwriting practices and a drop in interest rates, not by an increase in lawsuits (Eliot M. Blake, "Rumors of Crisis: Considering the Insurance Crisis and Tort Reform in an Information Vacuum," 37 *Emory L.J.* 401, 411–12 [1988]). This conclusion is consistent with a 1986 report on the insurance industry by the National Association of Attorneys General, which declared that the causes of the insurance crisis lay within the insurance industry itself (Kenneth S. Abraham, "The Causes of

EXHIBIT 16–3   *Focus of Today's Reformers*

- Plaintiff orientation
  - No-fault
  - Causation requirements
  - Comparative negligence
  - Privity
- Litigiousness
- Runaway verdicts
- Inhibition of medical practice and business

© Cengage Learning 2012

the Insurance Crisis," in *New Directions in Liability* [New York: Academy of Political Science, 1988], p. 54). Furthermore, the tort reforms advocated by the insurance industry have not resulted in lower insurance costs. A study based on data from the Insurance Services Office concluded that tort reform laws that limit damage awards and lawsuits have done nothing to lower insurance costs. In some states, premiums have risen more in states that have implemented tort reform laws than those that have not (Lawrence Messina, "Tort Reforms Not Affecting Insurance Rates, Study Says," *WV Gazette*, July 18, 1999, p. 2A). In the area of medical liability, heath economist and independent legal experts argue that "medical liability costs are a small fraction of the spiraling costs of the U.S. heath care system, and that the medical errors that malpractice liability tries to prevent are themselves a huge costs—both to the injured patients and to the health care system as a whole" (Daphne Eviatar, "Tort Reform Unlikely to Cut Health Care Costs," *The Washington Independent,* August 18, 2009).

Plaintiff Orientation

Specific examples of plaintiff orientation singled out for blame are the expansion of liability to include no-fault liability, the relaxation of causation requirements, the adoption of comparative negligence, and the abolition of privity.

No-Fault

No-fault (strict liability) for defective design, manufacture, and warnings is the primary example raised to illustrate the unbridled expansion of tort liability. One of the most noteworthy examples of no-fault involves *Restatement (Second) of Torts* § 402A. To review, this section shifts the costs of injuries resulting from unreasonably dangerous products to manufacturers, who, the drafters of the *Restatement* reasoned, are better able to absorb the costs of injuries into their overall business expense. Expansive interpretations of this *Restatement* section (which was widely adopted by state legislatures) have allowed escalated claims against manufacturers and prompted calls for reform.

Causation Requirements

Relaxed causation requirements have also fueled the debate about the permissiveness of contemporary tort law. The case most often pointed to in this regard is *Sindell v. Abbott Laboratories,* 607 P.2d 924 (Cal. 1980) (see Chapter 6). Recall that in this class action, a group of women whose mothers had received DES during pregnancy to prevent miscarriage sued when the drug was later linked to the daughters' cancer. In what some perceive as a radical liberalization of the rules concerning proof of causation, the California Supreme Court found each defendant manufacturer of DES liable for its market share of the damages to the plaintiff class, even though the plaintiffs were unable to prove which companies had actually supplied DES to their mothers. This waiver of proof as to who actually caused the plaintiffs' injuries dramatically altered causation principles, despite this doctrine's limitation to certain factual situations.

Comparative Negligence

Comparative negligence has allowed recovery by plaintiffs who would have been excluded by the restrictive parameters of contributory negligence (see Chapter 8).

Privity

By the same token, abolition of privity has allowed plaintiffs who did not buy directly from the manufacturer to sue the manufacturer as well as the retailer. Recall that privity requires a plaintiff suing in negligence to have direct contact with the defendant. This liberalization of the scope of suit further expanded the realm of tort liability and opened up the universe of potential defendants.

Litigiousness

Today's reformers diagnose society as suffering from the pangs of overlitigiousness. In *The Litigation Explosion: What Happened When America Unleashed the Lawsuit* (New York: Truman Talley Books, 1991), Walter Olson accused lawyers of inciting businesspeople to sue rather than negotiate and of encouraging individuals to pursue claims and defend rights they might otherwise ignore. Although the book certainly fueled the debate on tort reform, the author provided little in the way of empirical evidence to support his claims. To the contrary, a Rand Institute for Civil Justice study revealed that in 1989 only one in ten Americans who were injured sought compensation from someone involved in the accident. Most of these were auto accidents. In non-auto, non-work accidents, the attempted claim rate was only three out of one hundred (Hensler et al., *Rand Survey of Compensation for Accidental Injuries in the United States* [Santa Monica, CA: The RAND Corporation, 1990]).

NET NEWS

Findings regarding tort cases in large counties can be found at **http://www.lectlaw.com** by using "tort cases in large counties" as your search term.

State Courts

Much of the emphasis by those urging reform is on data from the federal courts; however, 98 percent of all civil litigation takes place in state courts (Galanter, "The Day After the Litigation Explosion," 46 *Md. L. Rev.* 3, 5 [1986]).

In 2007 civil cases accounted for 17.5 percent of the 18 million civil cases filed in the state courts an increase of about 800,000 cases (4.6%) from the previous year. Contract and small claims cases typically account for 70 percent of civil caseloads ("Examining the Work of State Courts: An Analysis of 2007 State Court Caseloads," National Center for State Courts).

Federal Courts

The federal courts have experienced a 9 percent increase in overall filings in the five-year period between 2005 and 2009. Most of the increase involved litigation related to asbestos, consumer credit, contract insurance, and marine contracts. Tort cases accounted for 63,631 of the 258,535 civil cases filed in federal courts in 2009 (Judicial Business of the U.S. Courts, 2009 Annual Report).

What Do the Statistics Mean?

When assessing claims of litigiousness, several questions should be raised. Is the increase in the number of lawsuits filed commensurate with increases in population? Although more lawsuits are being filed today, the question is whether any increase in litigation *per capita* has occurred. Are Americans more litigious than citizens of other countries? Some studies show that American litigation rates are not significantly higher than those in other industrialized countries. Although many countries have much lower rates of litigation, per capita use of the courts in Canada, Australia, New Zealand, England, Denmark, and Israel appears to be within the same range as that of the United States (Galanter, "Reading the Landscape of Disputes: What We Know and Don't Know [and Think We Know] About Our Allegedly Contentious and Litigious Society," 31 *UCLA L. Rev.* 4, 53 [1983]). How do litigation rates today compare with those of 100 years ago? Several studies document higher per capita rates of civil litigation in nineteenth- and early twentieth-century America, as well as in colonial times (McIntosh, "150 Years of Litigation and Dispute Settlement: A Court Tale," 15 *Law & Soc'y Rev.* 823 [1980–81]). Furthermore, the 1930s and 1940s, which form the baseline for many comparisons, were a historic low point for litigation (Seacat, "The Problem of Decreasing Litigation," 8 *U. Kan. City L. Rev.* 135 [1940]).

Even a finding that filings have increased, however, does not necessarily mean that society has become more litigious. An increase might not mean that plaintiffs are more litigious but that defendants are more resistant to resolving disputes outside of litigation. In the interest of tort reform many large corporations have adopted a fight at all costs strategy to send a message to plaintiff's lawyers to think twice before filing a tort lawsuit. Daimler Chrysler AG spent over $250,000 to defend an $8,700 case which it lost. As the prevailing party the plaintiff was awarded almost $150,000 in attorney's fees (Corporate Wolves in Victims' Clothing. Trial 36–37, July 2006). Increased filing can also result from an increase in the number of transactions between parties. If doctors, for example, are having more doctor-patient contacts, and thereby providing more medical care, more injuries and consequently more complaints could be anticipated.

To summarize, empirical evidence is needed to substantiate claims of overly litigious behavior. Once the evidence is amassed, it must be carefully analyzed before any relevant conclusions can be drawn regarding American attitudes toward litigation.

Runaway Verdicts

The issue of runaway jury verdicts is also subject to dispute. According to the Jury Verdict Research (JVR) organization in Horsham, Pennsylvania, the national median for jury awards in personal injury cases is increasing. JVR maintains a nationwide database of verdicts and settlements for personal injury claims, receiving verdicts from every state.

Although JVR data are frequently cited by tort reformers, the organization is not considered a reliable source because it does not conduct systematic and representative sampling and, in fact, does not include defense verdicts or take-nothing verdicts in its calculations. It also relies on reporting by lawyers, on word of mouth, and on media reports but does no original research into actual verdicts. JVR's chairman is on record as stating that the organization has not asserted or published any conclusions to the effect that the average size of jury verdicts has recently skyrocketed. The chairman maintains that JVR statistics have been grossly misstated (Daniel J. Capra, "Playing the Psychiatric Odds: Can We Protect the Public by Predicting Dangerous?" 20 *Pace L. Rev.* 339 [2000]).

Rather than permitting plaintiffs to ransack defendants' coffers, the evidence indicates that juries are generally cautious about awarding plaintiffs substantial awards. To begin with, plaintiffs prevail in fewer than half (48 percent) of the cases that juries hear (press release, Citizens for Corporate Accountability & Individual Rights, *New Government Study Disputed Myths About Out of Control Civil Juries*, June 13, 2000). Moreover, the average jury award is generally less than the actual losses suffered by plaintiffs (W. Kip Viscusi, "Towards a Diminished Role for Tort Liability: Social Insurance, Government Regulation, and Contemporary Risks to Health and Society," 6 *Yale J. on Reg.* 65, 95–97 [1989]). When juries do make large awards, it is usually in business litigation and not tort cases (Center for Justice & Democracy, *Punitive Damages in California: Myth vs. Reality*, cited in B. Tassoni, D. O'Fallon, and B. Finzen, "Tort Reform: Perception versus Reality," *Minnesota Trial Lawyer*, Winter 2003, footnote 6). In fact, scholars investigating jury verdicts have noticed a marked underpayment when plaintiffs suffer major damages, as illustrated by an insurance industry study that concluded that claimants with more than $1 million of legitimate economic loss were awarded an average of only fifty-eight cents on the dollar by juries (Lawrence W. Soular, *A Study of Large Product Liability Claims Closed in 1985* [Downers Grove, IL: Alliance of American Insurers, 1986], p. 18; confirmed by Deborah Jones Merritt and Kathryn Ann Barry, "Is the Tort System in Crisis? New Empirical Evidence," 60 *Ohio St. L.J.* 315, 397 [1999]). Furthermore, more than 90 percent of tort actions settle out of court, and on average tort claims settle for 74 percent of their potential recovery (Patricia M. Danzon, "Malpractice Liability: Is the Grass on the Other Side Greener?" in *Tort Law and the Public Interest*, edited by P. H. Schuck [New York: Norton, 1991], p. 30).

Interpreting the Statistics

Interpreting these results is another matter, say those at JVR. Because the tracking organization does not poll jurors, it does not know jurors' rationales. Furthermore, the statistics may simply reflect a random fluctuation rather than a statistical trend. Some argue that statistical trends are unimportant anyway and that individual excessive awards are the primary indicia of a dysfunctional system. The American Tort Reform Association often uses specific cases to illustrate its premise that jury awards are sometimes irrational. Caution must be used, however, in evaluating these claims, because sometimes not all of the facts are included in the case summaries (as illustrated in the opening of this chapter).

When evaluating statistics for median jury awards, researchers are likely to make adjustments for inflation of health care costs—but what about the costs of rehabilitation? Because medicine is better able to prolong life and to rescue people who just a few years ago would have died, jurors are more likely now to factor the cost of round-the-clock medical care and rehabilitation into their awards. If plaintiffs live longer and receive more treatment, jury awards should be expected to reflect those increases in longevity.

Alternatively, increases in jury awards may reflect the types of cases attorneys are bringing into the courts. If more people are bringing their claims to attorneys and attorneys consequently have a higher quality pool of cases from which to select, they are likely to choose those cases with large potential recoveries.

Consequently, even if jury awards are on the increase, the reasons behind this increase must be explored before one can conclude that the system is out of control. Given that one of the goals of the tort system is restoring the victim to wholeness, does an increase in awards reflect a cultural value that should be nurtured or misguided philanthropy that should be brought into balance? If jurors today tend to place a higher value on human life and health, should that trend be discouraged or encouraged?

Along the same line, another criticism of the tort system is that all of society bears the brunt of an increase in jury awards ("we all pay"). In light of the cost-spreading goal of the tort system, should we accept increased costs as part of the social price of security, or should we reevaluate the wisdom of this goal? After all, if the system is designed to remove some of the burden of accidents from the individual and shift it to the larger society, redesigning the system so that individuals bear the brunt of their misfortune is a fundamental social change. This change has widespread implications that, apart from the monetary ramifications, should be examined.

Inhibition of Medical and Business Communities

Finally, supporters of tort reform claim that increased tort liability has obstructed product development and created the practice of *defensive medicine* (the conservative practice of medicine aimed at the avoidance of potential lawsuits rather than the furtherance of patient needs). Essentially, tort reformers maintain that excessive tort liability has hampered business, resulting in higher prices and fewer new products. In medicine, the tort system has allegedly thwarted the practice of good medicine by increasing prices, encouraging unnecessary tests, and making doctors reluctant to perform high-risk procedures.

As evidence to the contrary, the American Medical Association reported that by 1994, the number of claims against doctors and hospitals had dropped at an average rate of 1.9 percent per year since the large increases of the 1980s (Martin Gonzalez, *Socioeconomic Characteristics of Medical Practice* [Chicago: AMA, 1994], pp. 41–45). Nevertheless, the 1992 claims rate of 8.9 percent was the highest since 1985, when the claims rate was 10.2 percent (*id.*). Some attribute the decrease in claims to the high procedural cost of filing a malpractice claim (costs for medical reports, expert witnesses, second opinions, etc.) (Physician Payment Review Commission, *Annual Report to Congress* 291 [1994]).

To determine whether doctors actually use unnecessary procedures because of fear of liability, the Office of Technology Assessment (OTA) analyzed existing studies and then did a national survey of cardiologists, surgeons, and obstetrician/gynecologists. The OTA did not find substantial levels of defensive medicine, even though it set up scenarios that were specifically designed to elicit a defensive response (Office of Technology Assessment, *Defensive Medicine and Medical Malpractice*, 103d Cong. 56 [1994]: 43–46). In an extensive study of medical practices, respected researcher Patricia M. Danzon concluded that malpractice claims have not induced an increase in laboratory tests and X-rays (primary forms of defensive medicine) (Patricia M. Danzon, "Malpractice Liability: Is the Grass on the Other Side Greener?" in *Tort Law and the*

Public Interest edited by Schuck [New York: Norton, 1991]).

In fact, some believe that the crisis in the medical arena and business community is not that so many needless and capricious claims are being filed but that so many wrongs are going unredressed. A Harvard Medical Practice Study revealed that in New York State, eight times as many patients are injured from medical negligence as there are malpractice claims. Only about half of claimants receive compensation. Consequently, there are about sixteen times as many patients who suffer from medical negligence as those who receive compensation through the tort system (Harvard Medical Practice Study, *Patients, Doctors and Lawyers: Medical Injury, Malpractice Litigation, and Patient Compensation in New York* [Cambridge, MA: The President and Fellows of Harvard College, 1990]). If this study is representative of what is transpiring in the larger health care system, then consideration might be given to enhancing incentives to bringing suit rather than reducing them.

Interestingly, plaintiffs prevail in a smaller fraction of malpractice cases that go to trial than in any other category of litigation (M. Peterson and G. Priest, *The Civil Jury: Trends in Trials and Verdicts, Cook County, Illinois, 1960–1979* [Santa Monica, CA: *Institute for Civil Justice*, 1982], table 3, p. 19). This relatively small rate of recovery may indicate that juries tend to give health care practitioners the benefit of the doubt. If, as some data indicate, the fraction of plaintiff verdicts is increasing (*id.*, p. 17), perhaps the increase can be attributed to a change in jury attitudes or a change in the quality of cases being brought to trial.

On a more positive note, evidence indicates that products are safer as a result of tort litigation. In *Wyeth v. Levine*, 129 S.Ct. 1187, 1202 (2009) the Supreme Court noted that "State tort suits uncover unknown drug hazards and provide incentives for drug manufacturers to disclose safety risks promptly. They serve a distinct compensatory function that may motivate injured persons to come forward with information." More than 75 percent of defendants subject to punitive damages in product liability cases surveyed between 1969 and 1990 took some safety steps in the wake of litigation, including removing products from the market or redesigning them (Michael Rustad, *Demystifying Punitive Damages in Products Liability Cases: A Survey of a Quarter Century of Trial Verdicts* [Washington, DC: The Roscoe Pound Foundation, 1991]). Managers say products have become safer,

NET NEWS

The American Osteopathic Association maintains a list of proposed and enacted tort reform bills that can be found at http://www.aoa-net.org by entering "tort reform" as your search term.

manufacturing procedures have been improved, and instructions have become more explicit (N. Weber, "Product Liability: The Corporate Response," *The Conference Board*, Report No. 893 [1987]). One scholar has suggested that the tort system is now so unwieldy and costly that only a select few can maneuver through its obstacles. Those few may receive awards that exceed their just compensation. Although such recoveries could represent only a tiny fraction of the real costs of injury, they may serve as an effective deterrent that is out of proportion to their actual costs to defendants and insurers. Such a system would create an image of unfairness to the public because of the few plaintiffs who received large awards, while the unfairness to the many plaintiffs who are uncompensated would remain invisible (Michael Saks, "If There Be a Crisis, How Shall We Know It?," 46 *Md. L. Rev.* 63, 67 [1986]).

Contrary to industry claims that businesses are being overwhelmed by lawsuits, one study reveals that liability costs for corporations decreased 37 percent from 1992 to 1997 (Ernst & Young LLP and Risk & Insurance Management Society, Inc., *RIMS Benchmark Survey*, 1998). A study by the Office of Technology Assessment (OTA) found that the greatest influence on corporate competitiveness with foreign corporations is capital costs. Its report did not even mention liability laws as a factor (Office of Technology Assessment, *Competing Economies: America, Europe, and the Pacific Rim*, 1991, pp. 3–7). Moreover, studies show that jurors tend to be generally favorable toward business, more skeptical about the profit motives of individual plaintiffs than of business defendants, and committed to holding down awards (Valerie Hans and William Lofquist, "Jurors' Judgments of Business Liability in Tort Cases: Implications for the Litigation Explosion Debate," 26 *Law & Soc'y Rev.* 85, 94–95 [1992].

Judicious Use of Statistics

Discerning trends and making comparisons is important in gaining an understanding of litigation in relationship to the business and medical world, but statistics must be used and evaluated with care. A case in point involves an oft-cited statistic that the

average verdict in product liability cases is over $1 million. This claim can be traced to a report by JVR in 1984 indicating that the average award in product liability cases was $1,021,956 (Jury Verdict Research, *Injury Valuation: Current Award Trends IV*, No. 304 [1986], p. 19).

Several points should be made regarding this statistical claim. First, this average was computed on the basis of plaintiffs' verdicts alone—and yet less than half of product liability cases tried by a jury result in a plaintiff verdict (*id.* p. 20). Second, this average is based on a small sample of product liability verdicts (the 1984 average was derived from only 337 plaintiff verdicts), which represents only a small portion of the universe of product liability verdicts (*id.* p. 19). Third, the sampling of JVR includes only "significant" or "important" verdicts, not typical ones (*id.* p. 12). Therefore, these averages are weighted toward the high end of the range.

Can Tort Reform Benefit the Business Community?

Is there any evidence that tort reform could actually benefit the business world? Tort reformers can now point to a study released by the National Bureau of Economic Research in Cambridge, Massachusetts, that suggests a possible link between the adoption of tort reform and increases in employment and productivity. The study uses economic data from 1969 to 1990 and looks at eight legal reforms: punitive damage reform, limits on damage awards, elimination of joint and several liability, caps on contingency fees, elimination of the collateral-source rule, adoption of comparative negligence, institution of periodic rather than lump-sum payments, and required payment of prejudgment interest. The study showed that the adoption of plaintiff-friendly doctrines, such as comparative negligence, led to declines in employment and productivity, whereas adoption of defendant-oriented reforms led to increased employment and productivity.

The authors of the study are quick to point out that these gains may have been due to other state policies, such as lower taxation. Also, they note, capital may flow from high-liability to low-liability states. Or

NET NEWS

Ralph Nader's position on tort reform can be found at **http://www.lectlaw.com** by entering "Ralph Nader On Tort Reform" as your search term.

companies in low-liability states may have lower costs simply because they are not bearing the true costs of production (as reflected in states where companies are more likely to be sued). Although the results do not support any definitive conclusions, they certainly provide fodder for additional research, and they support tort reformers' claims that expansive tort liability is bad for business.

IS THERE REALLY A PROBLEM?

Many of the allegations about the "system gone berserk" are unsubstantiated by empirical evidence, or the evidence is subject to debate (see Exhibit 16–4). Nevertheless, some very real problems do exist. Insurance premiums keep going up, insurance coverage is getting more difficult to obtain, and the insurance industry appears to be losing money. The caseload of the courts is growing, even if that growth is simply proportional to population growth. Some plaintiffs are overcompensated for their injuries while others are either undercompensated or receive nothing at all.

How do we set about constructively remodeling the system? Do we search for empirical evidence, or is the controversy more ideological in nature? Consider a $150 million verdict against General Motors in *Hardy v. General Motors Corp.*, CV-93–56 (Ala. Cir. Ct., Lowndes County, verdict June 3, 1996). To some the verdict ($50 million in compensatory damages and $100 million in punitive damages) for a thirty-eight-year-old driver who was rendered paraplegic illustrates the chaos and lack of control in the tort

EXHIBIT 16–4 *Questioning the Criticisms of the Tort System*

Criticism: Americans have become too litigious.
- Is increase in lawsuits commensurate with population growth?
- Do most Americans sue when injured?
- Are increases in litigation at the state or federal level?
- Have plaintiffs become more litigious, or are defendants more resistant to suit?
- In areas of law that have experienced increases in litigation, has there been a concomitant increase in the number of transactions?
- Are Americans more litigious than citizens of other nations?
- Are Americans more litigious today than they were 100 years ago?

Criticism: Jury awards are out of control.
- Has there been a substantial increase in median jury awards?
- Are increases in jury awards due to random fluctuation, or do they represent a change in jurors' thinking?
- When analyzing this issue, should we focus on statistical trends or individual cases?
- Do increases in some types of awards reflect increases in longevity and the resulting costs of long-term care?
- Are attorneys bringing better cases to trial today?
- Are jurors today placing a higher value on health and life?
- Should we reexamine the cost-spreading goal of the tort system?
- If the frequency in both small and large awards has increased (as some data would indicate), is this increase due to the use of smaller juries?

Criticism: The increase in tort liability has hampered the business and medical communities.
- Are more claims being filed against doctors and hospitals today?
- Are there significant numbers of patients who are injured but never compensated?
- Do medical malpractice claims so often fail because they are meritless, or because jurors tend to give health care practitioners the benefit of the doubt?
- If the percentage of plaintiff verdicts is increasing, is this increase due to a change in juror attitudes or to the better quality of cases being brought to trial?

system. For others, the verdict exemplifies the need for deterrence of indifferent corporate behavior and confirms that this is the role that punitive damages should play. In this case the driver argued that he was injured when he was ejected through a driver-side door that opened because of a defective door latch. GM had allegedly been informed of the defective latch by its engineers but had made no efforts to remedy it. GM claimed that the driver, who had admitted to not wearing a seat belt, and who GM claimed had been drinking, was ejected through the windshield and that the driver-side door had never opened.

What can we glean from this case? Does it serve as evidence of a tort system run amuck, or it is an aberration? Was the award reasonable in the context of all the evidence presented? Should we use individual cases like this one as the impetus to remodel the system, or do these cases simply further polarize opponents? If individual cases are insufficient, what data should we be collecting? Once we have data, how do we determine its relevance before assigning cause-and-effect relationships? As you can see, revamping the tort system is a bit more complex than it might appear at first glance.

TORT REFORM IN PRACTICE

Operating from the assumption that society is overly litigious and that jury awards are excessive, the primary objectives of today's tort reformers are to curb what are perceived as unduly high damage awards and to reduce the number of claims filed. Several avenues have been pursued to fulfill these objectives (see Exhibit 16–5). Caps have been proposed on damage awards, particularly punitive damages; joint and several liability and the collateral-source rules have been modified; efforts have been made to discourage frivolous lawsuits. Other reform measures being considered that are not discussed in this chapter relate to statutes of repose, rules of discovery, alternative dispute resolution, workers' compensation immunity, auto insurance, periodic payments, sovereign immunity, and limits on attorney fees.

The Common Sense Reform bills illustrate these proposals. When the Republican Party gained control

EXHIBIT 16–5   Objectives of Today's Tort Reform

- Damage award caps
- Modification of joint and several liability
- Modification of collateral-source rule
- Discouragement of frivolous lawsuits
- Statutes of repose
- Rules of discovery
- Alternative dispute resolution
- Workers' compensation immunity
- Automobile insurance
- Periodic payments
- Sovereign immunity
- Attorney fee limitations

© Cengage Learning 2012

of Congress in 1994, the momentum of tort reform shifted from the state to the federal level. Tenet 9 of their Contract with America called for a variety of tort reforms, including punitive-damage limitations, reformation of product liability rules, and institution of the British rule of fee-shifting (see section later in this chapter on frivolous lawsuits). In the first 100 days of office, the party introduced four Common Sense Reform bills. Several of the bills precluded a plaintiff from recovering punitive damages unless she could show by clear and convincing evidence that the defendant had acted with conscious indifference to the plaintiff's safety (actual malice). Most of the bills limited punitive damages to the greater of $250,000 or three times the plaintiff's economic injury. They also eliminated joint and several liability and reduced the liability of a manufacturer for a plaintiff who misused a defective product to a proportion equal to the percentage of harm caused by the misuse. All of the bills sought to deter frivolous lawsuits.

Damage Caps

Let us examine each of these measures individually, beginning with a topic that most state legislatures have tackled: damage caps. Why is the limitation of damages such a concern? Assigning a precise numerical value to a physical injury is virtually impossible. For this reason, jury verdicts for compensation for bodily harm are always unpredictable.

NET NEWS

The effects of California tort reform medical malpractice caps on injured children can be seen at **http://www.lectlaw.com** by entering "malpractice caps injured children" as your search term.

Responding to this unpredictability, most states have passed some kind of legislation aimed at regulating damage awards. The American Bar Association, in contrast, has criticized these reforms as depriving those who are most seriously injured of their due compensation.

The courts' responses to these caps have varied depending on whether the damage award involved economic damages, non-economic damages, or punitive damages. Restrictions on economic damages have not generally been favored by the courts. For example, an Ohio statute restricting general damages to $200,000 was found to violate the equal protection clause because it unfairly burdened those plaintiffs least able to pay their medical and legal expenses. The court observed that "the legislative scheme of shifting responsibility for loss from one of the most affluent segments of society to those who are most unable to sustain that burden, i.e., horribly injured or maimed individuals, is not only inconceivable, but shocking to this court's conscience" (*Duren v. Suburban Community Hospital*, 495 N.E.2d 51, 58 [Ohio 1985]).

A Wisconsin statute that placed a $350,000 ceiling on non-economic damages in medical malpractice cases was striken as unconstitutional, The court found that the statute created classes of victims; those that are fully compensated and those that are partially compensated (Ferdon ex rel. *Petrucelli v. Wisconsin Patients Compensation Fund* 701 N.W. 2d 440.

Another variation on limiting damages are efforts to penalize plaintiffs if they reject settlement. One such statute was overturned as violating the Georgia constitution's guarantee of access to the courts and the equal protection clause; and as undermining the jury's function. The statute required plaintiffs in tort cases to pay the defendant's attorney fees and costs if the plaintiff received a jury verdict less than 25 percent higher that a previous settlement offer by the defendant.

When non-economic rather than economic damages are restricted, the courts have been more willing to uphold the regulating statute. In so doing, courts either defer to rational legislative objectives or they uphold across-the-board limitations that they see as fair, consistent, and promoting settlement. Some courts have pointed out that excessive awards can be prevented by trial courts' use of *remittur*.

Punitive Damages

PURPOSE OF PUNITIVE DAMAGE: In the debate over the capping of damages, the lion's share of attention has gone to punitive damages. The primary purpose of punitive damages is to deter undesirable behavior and to punish those who engage in such behavior. In one decision, the Alabama Supreme Court opined that often the only recourse for victims of fraud is litigation and that punitive damages have historically served as part of the remedy for those victims (*Life Insurance Co. v. Johnson,* 1996 WL 202543 [Ala.]). The court quoted an author who explained that punitive damages have been used "to help equalize the playing field between the powerful and the powerless—whether between king and subject, railroad and passenger, or corporation and consumer" (Jonathon Massey, "Why Tradition Supports Punitive Damages: And How the Defense Bar Misreads History," *Trial*, September 1995, p. 19). The court reviewed the historical use of punitive damages in England against the crown and the aristocracy, and in nineteenth-century America against the railroads and robber barons. It then concluded that the consumer plaintiff suing the corporate defendant falls within the historical legacy of using punitive damages to redress imbalances in relationships.

Some question whether caps on punitive damages might encourage companies to let defective products go without recall or improvement. They are concerned that some companies will see it as cost-effective to bypass safety measures. In *Grimshaw v. Ford Motor Company*, 174 Cal. Rptr. 348 (Ct. App. 1981), the company deliberately decided against including safety measures it knew would save human lives because those measures were not considered cost-effective. Punitive damages put such manufacturers on notice that indifference to human life is not acceptable and will be subject to severe sanctions. A cap on punitive damages, in contrast, arguably enhances the probability that they will weigh the costs of manufacturing against the highest possible damage award and choose the more profitable action even at the expense of consumer safety.

CRITICISMS OF PUNITIVE DAMAGES: Critics have warned that punitive damages either do not deter at all or lead to overdeterrence, as in the case of manufacturers who are overly cautious to avoid liability and thus fail to develop new and useful products for fear of potential litigation. Critics have also charged that punitive damages lead to excessive litigation by plaintiffs who hope that defendants wishing to avoid the expense and risk of litigation will settle. Some further argue that plaintiffs unfairly benefit from a windfall of monies intended to punish tortfeasors. This windfall encourages even more litigious behavior. Finally, punitive damages have been criticized for hampering business by increasing the cost of insurance. Specifically, in the medical arena, critics claim that punitive damages victimize doctors serving socially useful functions (particularly in such high-risk areas as obstetrics) and inhibit doctors as a group from taking risks. (See Exhibit 16–6.)

In the context of product liability specifically, the doctrine of punitive damages is criticized because punitive damages (1) against corporations punish shareholders of defendant corporations rather than the actual wrongdoers; (2) do not serve the goals of punishment and deterrence associated with such awards; (3) are not necessary to achieve optimal product safety; (4) are incompatible with the fault-free theories of strict liability and breach of warranty; (5) cause overpunishment, which leads to adverse social and economic consequences; and (6) cause cases to be overvalued because punitive damages are a wild card in the sense that they make it difficult for corporations to predict damages.

Do punitive damages actually wreak havoc on the system? A study by the RAND Institute for Civil Justice indicated that the frequency and magnitude of punitive-damage awards changed little from 1962 to 1987 (William Landes and Richard Posner, *The Economic Structure of Tort Law* [Cambridge, MA: Harvard University Press, 1987], p. 15). Furthermore, the General Accounting Office examined data from five states from 1983 to 1985 and concluded that punitive-damage awards were neither excessive nor frequent (General Accounting Office, *Report to the Chairman, Subcommittee on Commerce, Consumer Protection, and Competitiveness*, GAO/HRD-88–89, [September 1989], p. 2).

Studies conducted by the Bureau of Justice Statistics and the National Center for State Courts in the nation's seventy-five largest counties concluded that punitive damages are awarded in only 3.3 percent of all cases and that judges were more likely than juries to award them. (Judges awarded punitive damages 7.9 percent of the time while juries awarded them 2.5 percent of the time. The median damage awarded by judges was $75,000; the median jury award was $27,000 (National Council for State Courts, *Litigation Dimensions: Torts and Contracts in Large Urban Areas* [1995]; Bureau of Justice Statistics, *Civil Jury Cases and Verdicts in Large Counties* [July 1995]). A review of nine empirical studies on punitive damages reveals the following: (1) punitive damages are awarded most frequently in intentional-tort cases and business and contract disputes rather than in personal injury litigation; (2) roughly half of all punitive-damage awards are reversed or reduced in the post-verdict period, with the largest awards having the highest post-verdict mortality rate; (3) the South accounts for more than 50 percent and the Western states for about 20 percent of non-asbestos punitive-damage awards; (4) between 1965 and 1990 Texas led the nation with fifty-one punitive damages verdicts, whereas six states (Louisiana, Michigan, Nebraska, New Hampshire, North Dakota, and South Dakota) awarded no punitive damages in any personal injury or product liability case during that same time period; (5) punitive damages peaked in most jurisdictions between 1981 and 1985; (6) juries award punitive damages infrequently (in only about 5 percent of cases), and the amounts are usually modest; and (7) five states account for almost half of all punitive damages awarded in medical malpractice litigation, whereas eleven states did not have a single punitive-damage verdict in a medical malpractice case from 1963 to 1993 (Michael Rustad, "Unraveling Punitive Damages: Current Data and Further Inquiry," 1998 *Wis. L. Rev.* 15 [1998]).

No case has generated more furor about punitive damages than the so-called "hot coffee" case in which McDonald's was sued when one of its patrons was severely burned by scalding coffee. This case is

EXHIBIT 16–6 *Criticisms of Punitive Damages*

- Product development inhibited
- Excessive litigation fostered
- Windfalls given to plaintiffs
- Medical practice inhibited

© Cengage Learning 2012

often the poster child for campaigns that assert the tort system has spun out of control. Stella Liebeck was seventy-nine years old at the time she purchased a cup of coffee from McDonald's drive-through window. Liebeck, a passenger in her grandson's parked automobile, attempted to secure the Styrofoam coffee cup, by placing it between her legs and removing the lid to put sugar and cream in the cup. The cup tipped over spilling hot coffee on her inner thigh, perineum, buttocks, genital and groin areas resulting in third degree burns. She was hospitalized for eight days and required whirlpool treatment for debridement of her wounds and skin grafting. She was disabled for two years and had permanent scarring. She filed the lawsuit after McDonald's refused to pay her medical bills of approximately $20,000.00.

The jury heard evidence that the temperature of the coffee was mandated by McDonald's corporate office to be 180–190 degrees Fahrenheit which is hot enough to cause third-degree burns in two to seven seconds. From 1982 to 1992 McDonald's had over 700 reported claims and lawsuits regarding the temperature of the coffee. McDonald's quality control manager testified McDonald's enforces a requirement that the coffee be maintained at 185 degrees, plus or minus five degrees, and that McDonald's did not intend to reduce the temperature. McDonald's' human-factors engineer told the jury that the issue of hot coffee burns was statistically insignificant when compared to the billion cups of coffee that McDonald's sells each year. The jurors regarded this testimony to be saying that the graphic photos of Liebeck's burns didn't matter.

The jury awarded Liebeck $200,000.00 in compensatory damages, reduced by 20 percent for her negligence and $2.7 million in punitive damages. The judge reduced the damages to $480,000.00 and the parties settled for an undisclosed lesser amount before the appeal was decided. Revenue from McDonald's coffee sales was $1.3 million a day, which meant that the company would lose slightly more than two days revenue by paying the $2.7 million punitive-damage award.

REFORMS BEING IMPLEMENTED: Despite the lack of data supporting the notion of a punitive-damage crisis, reform in this area is now burgeoning. In 1995 alone, nine state legislatures enacted reform measures addressing punitive damages (Illinois, Indiana, New Jersey, North Carolina, North Dakota, Oklahoma, Oregon, Texas, and Wisconsin). To illustrate, under Indiana's new laws, punitive damages are capped at the greater of $50,000 or three times the compensatory damages. New Jersey's cap is the greater of $350,000 or five times the compensatory damages, except for particularly abhorrent offenses such as drunk driving or child molestation. The American College of Trial Lawyers itself has recommended that the recovery of punitive damage awards be limited to the greater of twice the amount of compensatory damages or $250,000.

Oklahoma's new Tort Reform Law provides an interesting example of punitive-damage reform. Under this law, such awards are divided into three categories: In Category I, the plaintiff must prove by clear and convincing evidence that the defendant acted with reckless disregard for the rights of others (the prior statute required a preponderance of the evidence). Having done that, the plaintiff may recover punitive damages in the amount of the actual damages or $100,000, whichever is greater. In Category II, if the plaintiff proves that the defendant acted intentionally and with malice toward others, she may recover the greater of $500,000, twice the amount of actual damages, or the increased financial benefit that the defendant derived as a direct result of its misconduct. This last measure is subject to reduction by the amount that the defendant has already paid in punitive damages in Oklahoma state court actions to other plaintiffs based on the same conduct. In Category III, no limits are placed on punitive damages, but the plaintiff must prove that the defendant acted intentionally and with malice toward others and also engaged in life-threatening conduct toward humans.

The decision of how to classify an action (Category I, II, or III) now falls to the jury rather than the judge, and the jury must make these findings under a clear-and-convincing-evidence standard. (Both the jury and judge must decide if a case comes under Category III.) The determination of the appropriate category is made separately from the determination of the amount of the award. Because the defendant's financial condition is not relevant to determining the defendant's liability, evidence of the defendant's net worth is not admissible until after actual damages have been awarded and the jury has selected the appropriate category for the defendant's conduct.

Some states have created specific defenses to punitive damages. In North Dakota, for example, punitive damages cannot be awarded against a manufacturer when the product complied with federal or administrative regulations or was certified by a federal agency.

A few states have responded to those who feel that punitive damages represent an undeserved windfall to plaintiffs. They have followed the lead of Chief Justice Rehnquist, who recommended that punitive damages be awarded "to the State, not to the plaintiff—who by hypothesis is fully compensated" (*Smith v. Wade*, 461 U.S. 30, 59 [1983]). The Alabama Supreme Court, for example, implemented a new procedure for trying punitive-damage claims. In *Life Insurance Co. v. Johnson*, 1996 (Ala.), the court required half of any punitive damage award to be distributed to the state after attorney fees were paid. Although Alabama was the first state to impose an award-sharing requirement by court order, other states, such as Illinois and Iowa, have adopted this requirement by statute.

The bifurcated procedure for determining punitive damages established by the Alabama court is interesting. After determining liability and compensatory damages, the jury must decide by special verdict whether the evidence supports the imposition of punitive damages. If the jury answers in the affirmative, a second trial is held in which the jury determines the amount of punitive damages it finds appropriate.

Other states have limited punitive damages to a given multiple of compensatory damages or to a percentage of the defendant's profits. Such caps have been criticized, however, as irrational and contrary to the goals of punitive damages. Some critics have argued that punitive-damage liability should be decided by judges rather than by juries because juries are arguably not competent to decide whether punitive damages are appropriate. The rationale for allowing the judge to set the dollar value is that awards would be more predictable, which would further the goal of deterrence. Some argue that the burden of proof should be heightened when determining punitive damages because more proof of culpability should be required when the intent is to punish the tortfeasor. Still other reformers assert that juries are not given enough guidance for determining punitive-damage awards and that jury instructions should be altered. Whether the wealth of the defendant should be considered by the jury when deciding punitive-damage awards is also a point of contention. Some states do not allow evidence of the defendant's wealth to be admitted because they do not consider it relevant evidence.

When Are Punitive Damage Awards Excessive?

Read the Supreme Court decision, *State Farm Mut. Auto Ins. Co. v. Campbell*, 123 S.Ct. 1513 (2003) (Chapter 7) where the Court applied the standards established seven years earlier for awarding punitive damages in *BMW of North America, Inc. v. Gore*, 116 S. Ct. 1589 (1996). The Court rejected defendant's argument that a manufacturer's "good faith" compliance with government regulation or industry standards creates an irrebuttable presumption that its actions were reasonable as opposed to reprehensible and therefore punitive damages were inappropriate.

Are Punitive-Damage Caps Effective?

Do the caps being proposed by such bills as the Common Sense Reform bills protect businesses? The Common Sense Product Liability Legal Reform Act of 1996 (which was vetoed by President Clinton on the ground that it would harm consumers more than it would correct the injustices of the legal system) was designed to establish a nationwide ceiling for punitive-damage awards in product liability cases. The act would have limited such awards to the greater of $250,000 or twice the plaintiff's total economic and noneconomic damages (pain and suffering, emotional distress, and loss of companionship). This act would not protect small businesses, which would be devastated by a $250,000 verdict. Even large companies would face insolvency if the plaintiff's damages were high, as they are in a typical toxic tort case.

One way to assess the viability of proposed damage caps in preventing runaway awards is to apply the legislation to an actual jury award. Applying the provisions of the Product Liability Legal Reform Act to the $150 million verdict against General Motors in *Hardy* would have had no effect on that verdict. The jury in that case awarded $40 million in compensatory damages to the plaintiff, $10 million to the plaintiff's wife, and $100 million in punitive damages. Therefore, the $100 million punitive-damage award was within the acceptable range of twice the compensatory damage award of $50 million.

Alternatives to Punitive-Damage Caps

Some scholars suggest (as some states, such as Alabama, are already doing) that plaintiffs should be required to relinquish punitive-damage awards to a third party, such as the state. Medical malpractice awards, for example, could be allocated toward improving the quality of medical care, thereby deterring physician misconduct. Doing so would discourage plaintiffs from bringing meritless suits. Also, because plaintiffs would not be the beneficiaries of such awards, relinquishment would address the criticism that punitive damages are a windfall to plaintiffs. Such claims would presumably be pressed by state-appointed attorneys who would pursue defendants with an eye for deterrence.

Others have suggested that guidelines could be structured for punitive damages around such factors as the actual harm the plaintiff suffered, the harm not covered by compensatory damages, the likelihood that plaintiffs will sue, and the chances that the defendant will escape detection. Having uniform guidelines would protect against excessive awards when deep-pocket defendants are involved and would still deter defendants whose actions resulted in social harm.

Punitive Damages: A Summary

Although punitive damages may serve a socially useful service of punishing tortfeasors, their deterrence value, their effects on plaintiffs' decisions to sue, and their potential inhibition of the medical and business communities are questionable. The Supreme Court concluded that punitive awards can violate the due process clause if they are "grossly excessive," but the *BMW* decision will probably have little effect on the majority of cases involving punitive damages. Many states have imposed punitive-damage caps, but these caps would not affect many cases, even those involving very large punitive-damage awards.

Alternatives to damage caps have also been proposed, but two questions remain despite the efforts to curb punitive damages. First, are excessive punitive damages really a primary problem facing the tort system? Second, will any of the legislative reforms being proposed or currently enacted actually change litigant behavior and jury outcomes? Or will they open the doorway for potential misconduct, particularly in the business and medical world?

Joint and Several Liability

Historically, the Progressive Era reformers heralded joint and several liability because it dispersed losses among defendants rather than plaintiffs and provided plaintiffs with full compensation for their injuries. They believed it was more important to compensate a victim of negligence than to protect a negligent tortfeasor from disproportionate liability.

Classical reformers labeled joint and several liability the "deep-pocket" theory, meaning that it allowed plaintiffs to go after defendants with maximum financial resources even if they had minimal culpability and claimed that this practice was patently unfair. They also reasoned that plaintiffs should bear the risk of insolvent defendants in multiple-defendant actions just as they bore the risk of an insolvent defendant in a single-defendant action. (See Exhibit 16–7.) As one court noted, "Between one plaintiff and one defendant, the plaintiff bears the risk of the defendant being insolvent; on what basis does the risk shift if there are two defendants, and one is insolvent?" (*Bartlett v. New Mexico Welding Supply, Inc.*, 646 P.2d 579, 585 [N.M. Ct. App. 1982]). Further, they argued that this practice increased insurance costs because it precluded insurance companies from being able to accurately predict potential liability. Their reasoning was that anything that interfered with the insurer's predictive capacities led to increased costs. Some advocates of joint and several liability argue

EXHIBIT 16–7 *Criticisms of Joint and Several Liability*

- It is unfair to defendants.
- Plaintiff, not defendant, should bear risk of insolvency.
- It increases insurance costs.
- Under comparative negligence, joint and several liability is no longer necessary.
- It causes increased taxes and reduced services by municipalities.

© Cengage Learning 2012

PUTTING IT INTO PRACTICE 16:1

Assume you represent State Farm in *State Farm Mut. Auto Ins. Co. v. Campbell* (Chapter 7). What arguments would you make on appeal to support your contention that the punitive-damage award was excessive? What arguments do you think the plaintiff would make in rebuttal?

that elimination of this doctrine could lead to increased insurance rates because nonjoint liability would require more proceedings and longer court delays as more plaintiffs sued defendants individually (for strategic reasons).

The doctrine of joint and several liability was originally warmly embraced; by 1973, it was found in every state. Some studies, however, show that in actual practice joint and several liability is seldom relied upon. One Wisconsin study, for example, showed that joint and several liability played a role in only 1.6 percent of 834 personal injury jury verdicts (Paul Bargen, "Comment, Joint and Several Liability: Protection for Plaintiffs," 1994 *Wis. L. Rev.* 453 [1994]).

Two conflicting objectives thus dominate the discussion of joint and several liability. The first objective is to hold defendants liable only for their proportionate share of fault. The second objective is to compensate plaintiffs fully for their injuries. When joint and several liability was originally instituted, the doctrine of contributory negligence prevailed. Under that doctrine, usually only wholly innocent plaintiffs could recover. Therefore, when the innocent plaintiff was compared to the tortfeasor, fairness dictated that the guilty party bear the damages for other insolvent, unreachable, or unknown defendants.

Comparative negligence, however, changed this equation. Most states that adopted comparative negligence modified joint liability so that only defendants whose fault was relatively large in comparison to the plaintiff were jointly liable. In the words of one court,

> Previously when the plaintiff had to be totally without negligence to recover and the defendants had to be merely negligent to incur an obligation to pay, an argument could be made that justified putting the burden of seeking contribution on the defendants. Such an argument is no longer compelling because of the purpose and intent behind the adoption of the comparative negligence statute. It appears more reasonable for the legislature to have intended to relate duty to pay to the degree of fault. Any other interpretation [of the statute] destroys the fundamental conceptual basis for the abandonment of contributory negligence. (*Brown v. Keill*, 580 P.2d 867, 874 [Kan. 1978])

To see the inequities that can still result when joint and several liability coexists with comparative negligence, consider the case of a husband and wife who, while riding on a motorcycle, ran into an automobile.

A jury determined that the husband was 99 percent negligent and that the driver of the automobile was 1 percent negligent. Although the husband was precluded from recovering, the defendant driver had to compensate the wife for the entire amount of her injuries because her husband was immune from suit (*Dunham v. Kampman*, 547 P.2d 263 [Colo. Ct. App.], aff'd en banc, 560 P.2d 291 [Colo. 1977]).

The drive to modify joint and several liability has stemmed from injustices such as this. Local governments also complained of being deep pockets even when their comparative fault was relatively low, and argued that such liability resulted in increased taxes and reduced services. At least thirty-five states responded by either abolishing or modifying the joint and several liability rule. Some states have abolished or modified joint and several liability except for certain types of torts (for example, those involving hazardous wastes) or when the plaintiff is fault-free (in which case joint and several liability applies). In other states, the doctrine applies only to certain types of damages (as in California, where joint and several liability was retained for economic damages but abolished for non-economic damages), or its application depends on the percentage of the defendant's fault (as in Iowa, where joint and several liability applies unless a tortfeasor's fault is less than 50 percent of the total fault assigned to all parties).

To resolve the inequities of this doctrine, some have suggested that if a plaintiff is unable to collect from a defendant, the remaining parties, whether defendant or plaintiff, should be held accountable for that uncollected share, based on their individual fault percentage (assigned by the jury). This suggestion resolves the issue of unfairly burdening defendants who have committed minimal wrongs and, at the same time, ensures that joint tortfeasors are made to internalize costs created by an insolvent tortfeasor.

Empirical research on litigation trends in those states that have repealed joint and several liability showed an increase in tort litigation (Hans-Duck Lee et al., "How Does Joint and Several Tort Reform Affect the Rate of Tort Filings? Evidence from the State Courts," *J. Risk & Ins.* 61 (1994): 295). Scholars attribute this increase in part to the fact that the repeal of joint and several liability reduced incentives for defendant safety because they were exposed to a lesser risk of payment. Another reason is that plaintiffs must bring separate actions against each tortfeasor to collect the value of all harm suffered, which

PUTTING IT INTO PRACTICE | 16:2

Do you think joint and several liability should be maintained in a comparative-negligence jurisdiction? Why or why not?

---

means that insurers end up defending policy holders in more cases.

LOCAL LINKS

What is the status of joint and several liability in your state?

LOCAL LINKS

What is the status of the collateral-source rule in your state?

Frivolous Lawsuits

In the Progressive Era, the notion of frivolous lawsuits was foreign to legal scholars, because the common law rules tended to be pro-defendant. Pretrial screening mechanisms made it unlikely that non-meritorious claims would survive. As reforms led to the liberalization of tort rules, classical reformers observed that some plaintiffs were filing claims with the primary intent of inducing defendants to settle in order to avoid the costs of litigation or the possibility of a large award. Because of this, insurance claims—and hence insurance premiums—escalated.

Reformers looked first to Rule 11 of the *Federal Rules of Civil Procedure*, which allows sanctions to be issued against parties who file frivolous lawsuits. Although this rule was at first used infrequently by the courts, amendments to it have eroded courts' reluctance to impose sanctions and encouraged them to use it as a tool to discourage frivolous lawsuits. More recently, however, the Common Sense Reform bills propose adoption of the British rule, which requires that losers in a lawsuit pay all or part of the winner's attorney fees. This rule is clearly intended to discourage plaintiffs from bringing claims they are likely to lose and to discourage defendants from settling frivolous claims to avoid the costs of trial, as those costs will be borne by the losing party.

Some argue that the British rule may actually increase administrative costs of the judicial system. When both parties believe they are going to win, they are less likely to settle under this rule, because the amount they estimate they will save by settling is unimportant if they believe their litigation costs will be covered. If fewer cases settle under this rule, administrative costs will rise.

A one-way fee-shifting rule has also been proposed by some scholars. Fee-shifting rewards plaintiffs who are successful by reducing their litigation costs but does not penalize plaintiffs who lose. Although such a rule encourages potential tortfeasors' compliance with the law, it does not discourage plaintiffs from suing. Therefore, it does nothing to curb frivolous lawsuits and is unlikely to be given serious consideration in today's political climate.

SUMMARY

Before a comprehensive reform of the tort system is attempted, a careful review of the goals of the system should be undertaken to determine if the goals are still viable and if they are being achieved by the current system. A historical review of the Progressive Era and classical reform movements illustrates how changes in goals have resulted in changes in tort law.

The deficiencies that today's reformers perceive in the tort system are that it is too plaintiff-oriented, that it encourages overly litigious behavior, that it promotes excessive jury awards, and that it inhibits the business and medical communities. Examples of plaintiff-oriented changes that reformers point to are the development of no-fault doctrines, the relaxation of causation requirements, the evolution of comparative negligence, and the abolition of privity. Claims of over-litigiousness, excessive jury awards, and inhibition of business and medical practices lack the support of unequivocal empirical evidence. Before these claims can be intelligently addressed, their validity must be verified and claims of cause-and-effect relationships must be carefully studied.

The primary objectives of tort reformers today are curbing damage awards and reducing the number of claims filed. Toward those ends, legislation has been proposed at the federal level and enacted at the state level that implements damage caps, that abolishes or modifies joint and several liability and the collateral-source rule, and that discourages frivolous lawsuits. Although little evidence supports the contention that punitive-damage awards are out of control, the bulk of reform measures has been directed at punitive damages. Whether the reforms that have been implemented actually solve the problems they are intended to address remains in question. In reviewing large punitive-damage awards, the United States Supreme Court refused to apply the fines clause of the Eighth Amendment, but used the due process clause to overturn an award that it found to be grossly excessive.

Since the introduction of comparative negligence, most states have abolished or modified the doctrine of joint and several liability in order to avoid unfairness to wealthy defendants. By the same token, many states have modified the collateral-source rule to limit some of the duplication that arises when the plaintiff is compensated by multiple sources. Federal Rule of Civil Procedure 11 has been amended, and some have recommended adoption of the British rule of fee-shifting as a means of discouraging frivolous lawsuits.

One scholar, Dr. John Hasnas, suggests that the litigation explosion should come as no surprise if the purpose of the tort system is to vindicate wrongs suffered by victims of torts. He suggests that we allow the system to self-correct through a natural evolutionary process rather than trying to change the system artificially.

REVIEW QUESTIONS

1. What are the goals of the tort system, and why is it important to understand these goals when contemplating tort reform?

2. What changes did the Progressive Era reformers bring to the tort system, and why?

3. What changes did the classical tort reformers bring to the tort system, and why?

4. What is the focus of today's tort reformers?

5. In what respects is our tort system arguably plaintiff-oriented?

6. Is today's American society an unduly litigious society?

7. Are jury verdicts out of control?

8. What factors should be considered when assessing statistics?

9. What effects has the tort system had on the medical community?

10. What effects has the tort system had on the business community?

11. Has the business community benefited from tort reform?

12. Why have some states instituted caps on damages, and how have the courts responded to these caps?

13. What is the purpose of punitive damages?
    a. Why are punitive damages criticized?
    b. Have punitive-damage awards wreaked havoc on the tort system?
    c. What reforms have been instituted with regard to punitive damages?
    d. Under what conditions can a punitive-damage award violate the Constitution?
    e. Are punitive-damage caps effective?
    f. What alternatives to damage caps are available?

14. How do the Progressive Era reformers and the classical reformers view joint and several liability?
    a. What are the conflicting objectives that dominate any discussion of joint and several liability?
    b. What inequities can this doctrine create, and how have those inequities been resolved by some states?
    c. What has been the consequence in some states of repealing joint and several liability?

15. Why have some states limited or eliminated the collateral-source rule?

16. What steps have been taken to prevent the filing of frivolous lawsuits?

17. What is Dr. Hasnas's view of tort reform, and what does he consider the best way to bring about reform?

PRACTICE EXAM

Students should complete the practice exam after studying each chapter. The answers are in Appendix A. If you score lower than 80%, you should re-read the materials.

True-False

1. The Progressive Era of tort reform favored reforms that benefited defendants.

2. The classical reformers eliminated sovereign immunity.

3. Those who maintain that the tort system is too plaintiff-oriented point to the expansion of strict liability and the adoption of comparative negligence.

4. Most Americans who are injured in an accident seek compensation from the individual or entity that caused the accident.

5. Most of the data used by those advocating tort reform come from the federal courts, and are therefore misleading because most tort claims are litigated in state courts.

6. In the federal courts the greatest overall increase in filings was due to an increase in filings by the federal government.

7. In assessing the litigiousness of American society the question is not whether there has been an increase in tort filings but whether there has been an increase in litigation per capita.

8. An increase in tort filings points to a clear increase in litigiousness.

9. The national median for jury awards has steadily increased since 1990.

10. Both smaller and larger jury awards are more frequent than they were twenty years ago because of the failure to use small juries.

11. Jury Verdict Research is reluctant to interpret trends in jury awards because they do not poll juries and do not know jurors' reasoning.

12. Although individual cases may point to a dysfunctional system they may be misleading when not all of the facts are known.

13. In most medical malpractice cases, either the claims are meritless or the jury tends to give doctors the benefit of the doubt.

14. The oft-cited statistic that the average verdict in product liability cases is $1 million is misleading because it was based on typical defendants' verdicts.

15. It appears that plaintiff-friendly reform increases employment and promotes productivity.

16. The problems of the tort system cannot be resolved by simply gathering empirical evidence.

17. Plaintiffs are almost always overcompensated.

18. Punitive-damage awards are frequent and commonly excessive.

19. Courts are generally willing to uphold legislation imposing limits both on economic damages and noneconomic damages.

20. One criticism of punitive damages is that they lead to excessive litigation by plaintiffs who hope to intimidate defendants into settling.

21. Some states have required some part of punitive-damage awards to be distributed to the state.

22. The excessive-fines clause of the Eighth Amendment does not apply to punitive damages, but the due process clause does.

23. In *State Farm v. Campbell* the Court found the punitive-damage award grossly excessive because the ratio between the compensatory damages and punitive damage was unreasonable.

24. Tort reform legislation does not necessarily prevent runaway verdicts.

25. When plaintiffs are required to relinquish their awards to the state, their claims are pursued by state-appointed attorneys.

26. Progressive Era reformers advocated the adoption of joint and several liability because they thought it was important to protect negligent tortfeasors from disproportionate liability.

27. Classical reformers disliked joint and several liability because they believed that plaintiffs should bear the risk of insolvent multiple defendants just as they did when there was only one defendant.

28. After adopting comparative negligence some states abolished joint and several liability or modified it so that only defendants whose fault was large in comparison to the plaintiff could be jointly liable.

29. Under the collateral-source rule a plaintiff might not be fully compensated for all of her injuries.

30. The collateral-source rule has been abolished in some states because allowing the admission of evidence of supplemental benefits helps ensure that liability is divided among tortfeasors in accord with their respective degrees of culpability.

31. Rule 11 of the *Federal Rules of Civil Procedure* is used infrequently.

32. The British rule may increase administrative costs of the judicial system.

33. Dr. John Hasnas attributes the decline in jury verdicts to jurors' awareness of the effects that large awards in automobile cases can have on their insurance premiums.

Matching

GROUP 1

_____ 1. No-fault approaches
_____ 2. Eliminated joint and several liability
_____ 3. Abolition of privity
_____ 4. Increase in health care costs
_____ 5. Common Sense Reform bill

a. limits punitive damages
b. increase in jury awards
c. plaintiff orientation
d. Progressive Era reform
e. classical reform

GROUP 2

_____ 1. Redresses imbalances in relationships
_____ 2. Companies produce defective products
_____ 3. Windfall to plaintiffs
_____ 4. Requires proof of actual malice
_____ 5. Classification of punitive damages
_____ 6. Bifurcated procedure to determine punitive damages

a. Common Sense Reform bill
b. Criticism of punitive damages
c. Consequence of cap on punitive damages
d. Purpose of punitive damages
e. Alabama
f. Oklahoma

GROUP 3

_____ 1. Filed to induce defendants to settle
_____ 2. Sanctions against attorneys
_____ 3. Winner pays attorney fees
_____ 4. Applies to punitive damages
_____ 5. Does not apply to punitive damages

a. Eighth Amendment
b. Due process clause
c. Rule 11
d. frivolous lawsuits
e. British rule

Fill-in-the-Blanks

1. The goal of classical reformers was to create rules in the tort system that favored _____, while the goal of reformers in the Progressive Era was to create rules favoring _____.

2. Proponents of tort reform argue that increased tort liability has increased the practice of _____ medicine.

3. Under the _____ _____ the tortfeasor is prevented from benefiting from insurance protection the plaintiff has obtained.

Multiple-Choice

1. Tort law
   a. has a function of compensation but not deterrence.
   b. prevents the risk of injury from being spread among all members of society.
   c. exposes incompetence, corruption, and other forms of misconduct.
   d. all of the above.

2. Personal injury claims
   a. make up the majority of civil cases.
   b. have experienced little or no increase since 1986.
   c. are usually litigated in federal courts.
   d. all of the above.

3. Litigation rates
   a. are not significantly higher in the United States than they are in other industrialized countries.
   b. are higher now than they were in the nineteenth century and early twentieth century.
   c. were at their highest in the 1930s and 1940s, and those rates are used as a baseline for many comparisons of litigation.
   d. all of the above.

4. Tort reformers claim that
   a. Americans are too litigious.
   b. the insurance industry finds it impossible to predict risks and set prices because the tort system is too defendant-oriented.
   c. the median for jury awards is relatively stable.
   d. all of the above.

5. One of the greatest problems in the medical system is that
   a. claims against doctors and hospitals have steadily increased since the 1980s.
   b. many wrongs are going unredressed.
   c. more plaintiffs that go to trial prevail than in other categories of litigation.
   d. all of the above.

6. Joint and several liability
   a. is frequently relied upon by plaintiffs.
   b. was originally introduced when the doctrine of contributory negligence prevailed.
   c. seems to reduce insurance costs.
   d. all of the above.

7. The collateral-source rule
   a. has been abolished in some states because allowing the admission of evidence of supplemental benefits helps ensure that liability is divided among tortfeasors in accord with their respective degrees of culpability.
   b. prevents plaintiffs from being fully compensated.
   c. prevents or limits duplication in awards from multiple sources.
   d. all of the above.

8. Dr. John Hasnas believes that
   a. the perceived litigation explosion is an aberration.
   b. we are better off with the dynamic but imperfect system of the common law.
   c. tinkering with the tort system by means of reform is the best way to correct the flaws in the tort system.
   d. the tort system is hopelessly flawed.

TORT TEASERS

1. What reform measures have been instituted in your state in regard to damage caps, joint and several liability, the collateral-source rule, and frivolous lawsuits? How effective have they been? What reform measures are currently proposed?

2. How would you answer this question: "Are the benefits that parties and attorneys reap by fighting in the courts worth the cost to the rest of society?" Explain your answer.

3. What is the essence of the debate surrounding joint and several liability? Summarize the arguments made for its retention and for its abolition. Do you think joint and several liability should be retained, abolished, or modified? Why?

4. Critique the Punitive Damages Act of New Jersey, which provides a cap on punitive damages of the greater of $350,000 or five times the defendant's liability for compensatory damages. The cap does not apply to certain "abhorrent offenses." The plaintiff must prove that the defendant acted with "actual malice" or "wanton or willful disregard" of injury to possible plaintiffs

by clear and convincing evidence (the old law required a preponderance of the evidence). Punitive damages cannot be awarded for negligent or grossly negligent conduct. In what ways does this statute satisfy the criticisms levied against punitive damages? What problems does it not resolve?

5. Do you think the punitive-damage award against McDonald's by Stella Liebeck was a reasonable one in light of the facts? Why or why not? Does the award satisfy the purpose of punitive damages? Does it illustrate any of the criticisms levied against punitive damages? If you think the award was unreasonable, propose a workable alternative.

INTERNET INQUIRIES

Washburn University Law Library has an easily referenced index that takes you to everything from full-text court opinions and law journal articles to legal dictionaries and zip code directories. This is one of the most complete sources of practical and research law-related information you can find on the Web. Go to http://www.washlaw.edu to find the following:

1. Select "Law Library Catalogs" and find a law library in your state. Select its Web page. What must you do to get books online from this library?

2. Select "Legal Forms" and scroll down until you find state forms. What forms from your state are linked to this site?

3. Select your state. What links come up?

PRACTICAL PONDERABLES

Choose one topic of reform discussed in this chapter and prepare a paper explaining (in your own words) what the problems in this area of the law are, what proposals have been suggested and why, and which proposal you think is best and why. Find at least two cases and/or articles that are not cited in the text in writing this paper. You can do this on the Internet simply by going to http://www.google.com and typing in the topic of interest.

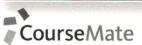 Access an interactive eBook, chapter-specific learning tools, including flashcards, quizzes, and more in your Paralegal CourseMate, accessed through www.CengageBrain.com.

CHAPTER 17

Automobile Insurance

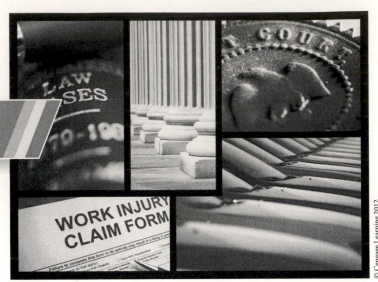

© Cengage Learning 2012

CHAPTER OBJECTIVES

After completing the chapter, you should be able to

- List the characteristics of medical payment, collision, comprehensive, UM, UIM, and umbrella coverage.
- Recognize an insurer's subrogation and termination rights.
- Recognize when reformation of policies is appropriate.
- Describe the arbitration process used to resolve disputes.
- List the characteristics of no-fault automobile insurance.

As Pauline and Perry are leaving their local fast-food restaurant, Perry prepares to make a left turn across traffic on a four-lane street immediately in front of the restaurant. Upon pulling out into traffic, Pauline and Perry's 1990 Chevrolet, a one-half-ton pickup, is broadsided in the second lane of traffic by Denise, who is driving a 1963 Chrysler. Her fourteen-year-old brother, David, is a passenger. Perry, who is not wearing a seat belt, is critically injured in the accident and dies ten days later. Pauline, who is wearing her seat belt, is also seriously injured. She suffers a broken shoulder, a concussion, extensive scarring to the side of her face, and severe soft tissue injuries, including cervical strain and sprain.

Neither Denise, a sixteen-year-old unlicensed driver, nor David is wearing a seat belt. Denise's injuries require only minor medical treatment. David, however, is catapulted from the front seat through the windshield of the Chrysler and suffers severe facial injuries as well as nerve damage that renders him a paraplegic.

Pauline and Perry's automobile insurance policy for the pickup, set forth in Appendix D, provides $100,000/$300,000 liability coverage, $10,000 medical payments coverage, $50,000 property damage coverage, and $15,000/$30,000 in both UM (uninsured motorist) coverage and UIM (underinsured motorist) coverage. They also have a $500 deductible collision coverage and a zero deductible comprehensive provision. The Chrysler that Denise is driving, which she took without her parent's permission, has no applicable insurance. Her father had purchased the car five months earlier and was in the process of restoring it.

At the time of the accident Denise was driving with her headlights off. Pauline tells the investigating officers that she was looking to the left when her husband was making his turn and did not see the Chrysler coming. Wilma, a registered nurse who was immediately behind Pauline and Perry at the restaurant exit, tells the investigating officer that she saw the Chrysler approaching even without seeing its headlights. Warren, a construction worker driving a van, tells the investigating officers that he was approximately fifty yards behind Denise at the time of the accident and that Denise was driving at the speed limit but never applied her brakes prior to impact with Perry's pickup. Warren also states that the Chrysler did not have illuminated taillights. In fact, he says, he almost ran into Denise's car earlier because the car, being dark green and unilluminated, was difficult to see at night.

Denise's father is an assembler at a local electronics plant, where he works the night shift from 4 to 12 P.M. Her mother has been hospitalized for two weeks with a serious illness, which has severely strapped the family's financial resources. Because her mother was hospitalized and her father was working, Denise had the responsibility of watching out for David. For this reason she had access to the keys to the Chrysler. Prior to this joy riding incident Denise had always been a very responsible teenager and was an honor student at her high school. We will use this scenario in the "Tort Teasers" section at the end of the chapter to apply the concepts presented throughout this chapter.

OVERVIEW OF AUTOMOBILE INSURANCE

As mentioned in Chapter 16, more litigation arises out of the automobile insurance contract than any other type of insurance. The horrendous number of automobile accidents, coupled with the mandatory insurance legislation in most states, has created this proliferation of lawsuits. Failure to obtain and maintain the minimal insurance coverage required by state law can prevent an automobile owner from either registering or driving a vehicle. Additionally, in most states either civil or criminal sanctions await those who unlawfully drive without mandatory insurance coverage.

The types of automobile insurance coverage available vary, depending on whether the state requires **fault insurance** or **no-fault insurance**. No-fault insurance is based on the concept that the insured's carrier should pay for the insured's damages regardless of who is at fault.

AUTOMOBILE LIABILITY COVERAGE

The primary purpose of automobile insurance is to provide liability coverage to the insured for the bodily injury or property damage he causes while operating an automobile (see Exhibit 17–1). An example of the terms and conditions of liability and property damage

EXHIBIT 17–1   *Characteristics of Automobile Policies*

- Single-limit versus split-limits coverage
- Coordination-of-benefits provisions
- Primary versus secondary coverage
- Subrogation rights
- Arbitration rights

coverage is set forth in coverage N (Section III) of the insurance policy in Appendix D. This coverage provides either split limits or single-limit coverage. With **split-limits coverage**, each individual may recover a set amount of damages, with an aggregate amount available for damages independent of the total number of individuals injured. A **single-limit coverage** amount for property damage resulting from the insured's negligence is usually provided.

An example of split-limits coverage is the minimum limits set by many states, in which $15,000 must be available for each person injured, and $30,000 must be available as an aggregate amount for all individuals injured. If a minimum of $10,000 were required to cover property damage, the liability limits of such a policy would be described as $15,000/$30,000/$10,000.

Exhibit 17–2 lists types of automobile insurance coverage, each of which will be discussed in detail.

Umbrella Policy

The total limits of liability available for bodily injury and property damage are as high as the maximum amount provided by the carrier issuing the policy. As a practical matter, however, bodily injury limits in excess of $250,000 to $500,000 and property damage in excess of $100,000 generally are not covered by the automobile policy itself but by a separate policy called an **umbrella policy**. The umbrella policy may be written by the same carrier issuing the automobile insurance policy or by a different carrier. Such a policy is usually subject to a large deductible.

The umbrella carrier is liable only after the first insurer pays the full limits of its coverage. If, for example, a primary insurer pays $500,000 to the person injured by the insured for bodily injuries but the individual actually sustains $750,000 in damages for bodily injuries, the umbrella carrier would pay the additional $250,000 (or the amount up to the limits of the insured's umbrella policy).

Reformation of Policy

If an insurance carrier attempts to issue a policy with limits less than those required by the statute, the courts will call for **reformation of the policy** by construing it to provide the minimum statutory coverage. In some instances the insurance policy itself provides terms and conditions to conform the policy to state law in the event the cancellation or nonrenewal provisions are contrary to the laws of the state.

Subrogation

If an insurer pays its insured, the insurer is then subrogated to the rights of the insured, meaning it can institute suit against the responsible person, in the name of the insured, to collect the amounts paid by the insurer to the insured. **Subrogation** is universally allowed with respect to uninsured motorist, collision, and comprehensive payments made by the insurer. If subrogation is allowed, the insured has an obligation to cooperate with his insurer in the subrogation claim. Cooperation could include assisting the insurer at trial and in the discovery process.

An example of a subrogation provision is shown in the policy in Appendix D in coverage P (Section III), paragraph 6, and endorsement 303 (Section III), paragraph 6. A subrogation provision called a trust agreement provides that the insured will take no action that would cause the insurer to lose any of its rights of recovery against either the uninsured or underinsured motorist. In many states there is no right of subrogation for underinsured motorist claims.

EXHIBIT 17–2 Types of Coverage

LIABILITY	Coverage for losses caused by the insured while operating a motor vehicle.
MEDICAL PAYMENT	Reimbursement of medical expenses incurred when injured in vehicle covered by policy.
COMPREHENSIVE	Coverage for losses resulting from something other than collision.
COLLISION	Reimbursement for repair or replacement of damaged vehicle.
ACCESSORY	Emergency road service. Car rental. Death and disability.
UNINSURED MOTORIST	Coverage for losses caused by uninsured motorist.
UNDERINSURED MOTORIST	Coverage for losses caused by motorist whose liability insurance is insufficient to cover the insured's losses.

NET NEWS

Answers to FAQs regarding automobile insurance, practical advice about what to consider when buying insurance, and a list of state-by-state minimums for liability insurance can be found at **http://www.insure .com** under "Car Insurance Basics."

PUTTING IT INTO PRACTICE / 17:1

1. A single-limit policy provides for $300,000 in bodily injury coverage and $50,000 in property damage coverage. How would you shorthand the coverage available?

2. An umbrella policy can also provide extended protection for any uninsured motorist (UM) or under-insured motorist (UIM). Check with your insurance agent to determine the additional cost of UM and UIM coverage in an umbrella policy.

MEDICAL PAYMENT COVERAGE

Medical payment coverage provides for reimbursement of all reasonable medical expenses incurred by an insured while occupying a covered vehicle or when the insured, as a pedestrian, is struck by a different vehicle. In some states medical payment coverage is referred to as *personal injury protection* (PIP). If the insured is injured in a motor vehicle owned by someone other than the insured, the owner's medical payment coverage will be **primary coverage**. In other words, the automobile owner's medical payment coverage will be primarily responsible for payment of the insured's medical expenses up to the limits of the owner's medical payment coverage.

If the insured's medical expenses exceed the owner's limits, the **secondary coverage** available to the insured under her own medical payment coverage will come into effect. Suppose an automobile owner's medical payment coverage is $5,000 and the individual injured has medical payment coverage of his own for $10,000. If the individual incurs reasonable medical expenses of $20,000, the first $5,000 will be paid by the owner's policy, the next $10,000 by the injured person's medical payments carrier, and the balance of $5,000 by the injured party or his own health insurance policy, assuming no third party is liable for the injuries.

Most medical payment policies provide that benefits are payable only for those medical expenses incurred within a fixed time period after the date of the accident. Typically, these time periods range from one to three years after the accident. If medical expenses are incurred after this time has elapsed, the insurer is not responsible for payment.

In most instances, an injured party may receive benefits under medical payment coverage in addition to any benefits received under any of her other medical policies. Some policies have a **coordination of benefits provision**, which precludes payment if other insurance is available. If neither the medical payments nor the health insurance coverage has this provision, the injured party can lawfully recover twice for medical expenses. Such recovery is, of course, subject to any deductible or co-insurance limit in the health insurance policy. This double recovery, allowed under the so-called collateral-source rule (see Chapter 7 on damages), is premised on the idea that the insured, who is paying a separate premium for each type of coverage, should be able to reap the benefits of his investment.

Many medical payment plans also provide for benefits in the event of the insured's death. Death benefits are usually fixed at a certain dollar amount and are intended, in part at least, to cover burial expenses. Medical expenses incurred by the deceased up to the date of death are also covered.

The terms and conditions of a typical medical payment provision are listed in coverage Q (Section III) of the insurance policy in Appendix D. Be aware that the exclusions are applicable to all coverage in Section III of the policy.

NET NEWS

The Kelley Blue Book is available online at **http://www.kbb.com**. You can find market values for both new and used vehicles there.

COMPREHENSIVE COVERAGE

Comprehensive automobile insurance provides coverage for loss to the insured vehicle and, in some cases, to a nonowned automobile for losses other than those resulting from collision. Coverage for property damage and loss caused by fire, theft, windstorm, and hail is included. Losses typically recovered under comprehensive coverage are from a shattered windshield, from the theft of valuables from a vehicle, and from the loss of a vehicle and its contents due to fire or theft. Reimbursement for a lost or damaged item is determined by its *actual cash value* (purchase price less depreciation) or its *replacement cost*. Many policies require physical signs of forced entry before the insured can be reimbursed for stolen property. Some policies are subject to a deductible, which is the responsibility of the insured to pay.

State insurance departments do not require comprehensive coverage to be part of the standard automobile insurance contract. However, if a vehicle is being financed through some kind of financing institution, the insured may be required to maintain comprehensive as well as collision coverage. Typical provisions providing comprehensive coverage are shown in Appendix D under coverages R and S (Section III).

COLLISION INSURANCE

Collision insurance reimburses the insured if he must repair or replace a damaged vehicle. Like medical payment insurance, collision insurance provides coverage irrespective of who is to blame for the damages. In the case of a negligent motorist, the carrier is subrogated to the rights of the insured and can seek reimbursement from the motorist for any expenses it incurs in repairing the insured vehicle. If the damage is caused by the insured's own negligence, the insurer has no right to seek payment from the insured. Most collision policies are issued subject to a deductible. Typical examples of the protection provided by having collision coverage are also set forth in the policy in Appendix D under coverage T (Section III).

MISCELLANEOUS COVERAGE

The automobile insurance contract can also include coverage for emergency road service, which pays for towing and any other emergency services occurring on the road, up to a maximum amount (often $25). Its primary purpose is to pay for towing a disabled vehicle to the nearest service station. Other available coverages include death and disability insurance and car rental insurance. Most provisions of this type establish the absolute maximum amount for which the insurer is liable as well as the maximum per diem expense that will be paid.

Care should be taken in selecting these accessory coverages. Make sure the premium for the risk to be covered is in proportion to the premiums and risk covered in a regular disability or accidental death policy. The latter may provide coverage whether or not the incident triggering coverage resulted from the use of an automobile.

These types of "miscellaneous" coverage provisions are shown in Appendix D as endorsements 323, 334, 335, and 368 (Section III).

UNINSURED MOTORIST COVERAGE

Next to liability insurance, the most important coverage available under the standard automobile insurance contract is uninsured motorist (UM) coverage, which provides coverage only for injuries caused by an uninsured motorist. The percentage of uninsured motorists on the road is alarmingly high, especially in those states requiring automobile insurance coverage but not requiring written proof of such insurance when one registers a motor vehicle. Because many uninsured motorists are financially incapable of paying any substantial award for damages they inflict, UM coverage ensures that funds are available to compensate the injured insured. This coverage guarantees compensation up to the limits of the insured person's policy, by her own insurer to the extent that a third party (the uninsured motorist) is responsible for her injuries.

An *uninsured motorist* is typically defined as a motorist having no applicable automobile insurance policy for the vehicle being driven or having an applicable policy with an insolvent insurance carrier. In some policies a hit-and-run driver may be considered an uninsured motorist.

Most states require that UM coverage be provided with the issuance of a liability policy. The minimum limits of this coverage are generally set by statute and are often the same as the minimum-coverage limits required for liability insurance coverage. Uninsured motorist coverage typically does not provide for any deductible to be paid by the insured. In most states the insured's carrier can reduce the amount of damages paid to its insured in proportion to the insured's own negligence.

LOCAL LINKS

Does your state require UM coverage with the issuance of a liability policy? If so, what are statutory limits of this coverage?

If payment is made to the insured, the UM carrier is subrogated to the rights of its insured and can bring an action in the name of its insured against the responsible party. Subrogation relieves the insured of having to chase the uninsured motorist to either obtain or collect a judgment.

An insurance company cannot, for the most part, attempt to offset monies paid under a medical payment policy against the amount otherwise due the insured under a UM policy, especially if the policy is the minimal amount allowed by law. Suppose an insured has $10,000 in medical payment coverage and $15,000 in UM coverage (the statutory minimum). The carrier cannot credit monies paid under medical payments to the amount otherwise due the insured under her UM coverage. That credit might, however, be allowed if the insured has UM coverage in excess of the statutory minimum.

Primary versus Secondary Coverage

Most UM policies provide coverage regardless of whether the insured was driving the automobile specifically referred to in the policy or a different vehicle. If the insured was driving a different vehicle, the UM coverage will be coordinated with the coverage that would otherwise be available on the vehicle being driven. Most policies designate the coverage provided with the vehicle being driven as primary and the policy covering the driver (the insured in this case) as secondary. The primary carrier is liable for all damages up to the limits of its policy. At that point the secondary carrier is liable for any damages sustained by the insured above the limits of the primary policy up to the amount of the insured's loss or the limits of the excess policy, whichever is less.

Coordination of Benefits

If an insured has applicable insurance in addition to that provided by her automobile policy, the coordination of benefits provision (mentioned earlier) of most policies will require the insurance carrier to be responsible for its pro rata share of the damages, as long as the insured is driving her own vehicle. A carrier's pro rata share is determined by the proportion of its coverage to the total amount of available insurance. Suppose the insured has UM coverage of $50,000 per person and an additional $100,000 of coverage under a different but applicable policy. The UM insurance carrier would be responsible for no more than one-third of the damages ($50,000/$150,000), up to a total maximum liability of $50,000. Because the carrier that provided $100,000 of coverage probably has a comparable coordination of benefits provision, litigation between the two carriers would likely be necessary to determine their respective obligations. Coordination of benefits provisions also apply to underinsured coverage (discussed next).

Typical provisions contained in a policy providing UM coverage are set forth in coverage P (Section III) of Appendix D.

LOCAL LINKS

Is stacking of UM and UIM coverage allowed in your state?

UNDERINSURED MOTORIST COVERAGE

Underinsured motorist (UIM) coverage protects the insured who is injured by a motorist whose liability coverage is insufficient to fully compensate the insured for his injuries. UIM coverage is applicable, for example, when the insured sustains $50,000 in damages but

PUTTING IT INTO PRACTICE 17:2

1. To reduce premiums, some companies are now providing medical payment coverages that have deductible and co-insurance provisions. What would be the advantage of having medical payment insurance if you had your own non-automotive medical insurance?

2. Refer to the scenario at the beginning of this chapter. Assuming that Denise's vehicle had an applicable liability policy for property damage, why might Pauline have her vehicle repaired under her own collision coverage, even with its $500 deductible?

3. A comprehensive coverage loss is usually evaluated on the basis of actual cash value. Why might it be worth the additional premium expense to purchase replacement cost coverage?

the responsible party has only $15,000 worth of liability coverage. In that case the responsible party's insurance carrier will pay $15,000 and the insured's UIM policy will compensate the insured for the remaining $35,000, assuming the UIM coverage limit is $35,000 or greater. UIM coverage typically does not provide for any deductible to be paid by the insured.

Most states prohibit **stacking of policies** for UM and UIM coverage. In other words, UM and UIM are not available to the insured for the same accident. Therefore, an uninsured motorist who is the responsible party cannot be alleged by the insured to be both uninsured for the purposes of UM coverage and underinsured for purposes of UIM coverage. In multi-vehicle accidents, however, UM coverage may be applicable to one joint tortfeasor and UIM coverage may be applicable to another.

Typical provisions contained in a policy providing UIM coverage are set forth in endorsement 303 (Section III) of Appendix D.

ARBITRATION

Most policies require arbitration for disputes arising out of medical payment, UM, or UIM coverage with respect to the amount of damages sustained by the insured. As most states favor the use of arbitration to resolve contractual disputes, these policy provisions are generally enforceable. Both the insured and the carrier are usually required to select and pay for an arbiter of their choosing. The two arbiters then select a third arbiter, whose compensation is split evenly by the insured and the insurer.

In a hearing before the three arbiters, local evidentiary rules are often applied; a decision rendered by two of the arbiters is binding on both parties. Often, however, the arbitration clause provides that if an award is entered in excess of the statutory minimal limits for bodily injury, the arbitration award will not be binding. If either party contests an award, a trial de novo, in which the issue of damages is relitigated without regard to the arbiters' findings, is held. An arbiter's findings with respect to the insured's damages are not admissible at trial.

The current trend is away from three-arbitrator panels. Many insurers require that they and the insured agree on a single arbitrator to hear the dispute instead. The use of a single arbitrator greatly reduces the cost of arbitration. As a practical matter, it was usually the third arbitrator in the three-arbitrator panels who controlled the outcome.

NET NEWS

The American Arbitration Association (AAA) is a private, nonprofit organization that provides rules for parties to follow in private arbitrations. It also maintains a list of qualified arbitrators with knowledge in specific areas. For information about the AAA, go to **http://www.adr.org**. At this site you will find publications pertaining to arbitration, get information about the rules and procedures governing arbitration, and see a roster of arbitrators.

A typical arbitration requirement is shown in Appendix D in paragraph 5 of coverage P (Section III). These arbitration provisions relate only to uninsured and underinsured motorist coverage claims. However, many policies also require that disputes with respect to medical payments be arbitrated.

TERMINATION

An automobile insurance contract can be terminated at the request of the insured or due to the acts of the insured. If the insured chooses to terminate his policy, the termination is effective on the date notice is given, usually to the insured's agent. The insured is then entitled to a return, usually pro rata, of any advance premiums paid.

Voluntary termination has been complicated in some states by mandatory insurance requirements. In certain circumstances termination can result in the insured forfeiting her registration rights to the vehicle unless another policy that meets state requirements is taken out. Statutes and case law should be carefully researched to determine the implications of voluntary termination.

If the insurer initiates termination, it must comply with the policy's notification requirements as well as the terms and conditions upon which termination is permitted in that state. Termination is always an option for an insurer if an insured fails to pay the premiums. In most instances termination for non-payment becomes effective only after a designated time period following the giving of written notice. The insurer can also terminate a policy if an insured or driver who lives with the insured has her license suspended or revoked. In accord with current societal attitudes about intoxication, most policies allow termination if an insured is convicted of driving while intoxicated.

LOCAL LINKS

In your state what must an insurer do before terminating an automobile insurance policy?

NO-FAULT INSURANCE

No-fault automobile insurance was created in response to what was perceived as a crisis in the automobile insurance industry—a crisis caused by the increasing volume of tort claims for automobile accidents. In concept, no-fault insurance was to result in prompt payment to injured insureds for economic damages and in reduced automobile insurance premiums. Neither goal has been attained.

In a pure no-fault jurisdiction the insured gives up her right to sue in tort for damages sustained as a result of a third party's negligence. The injured insured's own carrier pays for the damages she sustains, up to the limits of her own policy. The ability to recover for pain and suffering is relinquished in exchange for a promised reward of lower premiums and prompt payment for economic loss. But of the more than twenty states that have adopted no-fault statutes, none is "pure" no-fault.

In all no-fault states, the right to sue for tort damages is retained for intentional injuries inflicted with an automobile and for injuries caused by intoxicated drivers. Many no-fault states have set limits above which the injured party may sue the responsible party for tort damages. In Colorado, for example, the injured insured cannot sue in tort until her

PUTTING IT INTO PRACTICE 17:3

If you had a small claim that was subject to arbitration, would the prospect of having to pay for arbitrators to have it evaluated affect your position on settlement?

NET NEWS

Articles on the basic elements and purpose of no-fault insurance are available at **http://www.kiplinger .com** by entering "no-fault insurance" as your search term.

NET NEWS
A table showing no-fault restrictions on pain-and-suffering lawsuits can be examined at **http://www .insure.com** by entering "no-fault restrictions" as your search term.

medical expenses exceed $2,500. (Legislators are constantly tinkering with the no-fault figures, so this number may have already changed by the time you read this.)

These thresholds are generally tied to an injured person's medical expenses. They begin as low as $200 (New Jersey) and go as high as $5,600 (Hawaii). Some states, such as New York ($50,000), have higher thresholds but are not tied to medical expenses alone. Other no-fault states allow tort damage claims if the injured person suffers a permanent disability or disfigurement.

States also vary greatly in the minimum amount of benefits they require insureds to purchase. These benefits, often called *personal injury protection*, vary from a few thousand dollars to an unlimited amount. Separate limits may be set for various types of damages; for example, medical expenses, lost wages, and rehabilitation may all have different limits. Alternatively, an aggregate limit, such as $50,000, may be set for all economic damages sustained in an accident.

The no-fault experiment has not been particularly successful. In many states, such as New Jersey, the threshold for suing in tort is so low that the no-fault benefits are merely add-on costs for the typical tort suit that follows. The existence of a threshold amount also appears to have increased treatment expenses in no-fault states. To illustrate, when one no-fault state raised its threshold amount, the average cost of treatment expenses went up by an equal amount. In that same state the average number of chiropractic visits per automobile accident went from ten to thirty, and the total payout for chiropractic services increased 320 percent.

LOCAL LINKS
Has your state adopted some form of no-fault insurance? If so, how is it structured?

In some ways the no-fault system closely parallels the workers' compensation acts discussed in Chapter 19. In a no-fault system the right to sue is relinquished; medical expenses are paid; and, after a prescribed waiting period, lost wages are paid for a preset percentage of the insured's average monthly wage. Unlike workers' compensation, no-fault medical and rehabilitation expenses are limited by the amount of coverage purchased, as is the amount of lost wages.

Ideas currently under discussion include prohibiting uninsured motorists from suing for damages they sustain, based on the fact that they have not contributed to the insurance pool. A less punitive approach is to prohibit uninsureds from suing for pain and suffering but to allow them to claim economic losses.

No-fault is a relatively new concept, and one that has been implemented fairly recently in many states. Changes occur with great frequency in almost every no-fault jurisdiction. The applicable limits for the various required coverages and the threshold levels for suit are constantly being adjusted. No jurisdiction has yet allowed no-fault and traditional tort remedies to co-exist. The possibility of such coexistence now appears more likely, however, as neither system has lived up to the expectations of its proponents. One stumbling block to greater experimentation with no-fault is the states' constitutions, many of which have provisions prohibiting interference with citizens' right to sue.

NET NEWS
To read about the effects of no-fault insurance on driving behavior as well as the results of other studies conducted by the RAND Institute with regard to automobile insurance, go to **http://www.rand.org**, and enter "effect of no-fault automobile insurance" as your search term.

SUMMARY

The primary purpose of automobile insurance is to protect the insured for expenses incurred as a result of bodily injury or property damage caused while the insured is operating her automobile. Both single-limit and split-limits coverage are available. Umbrella policies are available as a secondary source of coverage when the full limits of the primary coverage are exceeded. Courts will reform policies in which the policy limits are less than those required by statute.

The insurer is subrogated to the rights of the insured, which allows the insurer to institute suit against the responsible person in the name of the insured. Many states prohibit subrogation with respect to UIM claims. An insured has an obligation to cooperate with his insurer in subrogation claims.

Medical payment coverage reimburses the insured for all reasonable medical expenses incurred while occupying a covered vehicle or when, as a pedestrian, she is struck by a different vehicle. If an insured is injured in a motor vehicle owned by someone other than the insured, the automobile owner's medical payment coverage is primarily responsible for payment of the insured's medical expenses up to the limits of the owner's medical payment coverage. Once that limit is exceeded, the insured's own medical payment coverage takes effect. If the medical payment coverage has a coordination-of-benefits provision, the injured is not allowed to recover twice for her medical expenses.

Other types of automobile insurance coverages include comprehensive, collision, and "accessory" coverages such as towing, car rental, and death and disability insurance. Comprehensive coverage applies to property damage and losses caused by fire, theft, windstorm, and hail. Collision insurance provides coverage regardless of who is to blame for the damages.

Most states require uninsured motorist (UM) coverage. A carrier cannot credit monies paid under a medical payment policy to the amount due the insured under his UM coverage unless the insured has UM coverage in excess of the statutory minimum. Most UM policies provide coverage regardless of whether the insured was driving the automobile referred to in the policy or a different vehicle. Underinsured motorist (UIM) coverage protects an insured who is injured by a motorist whose liability coverage is insufficient to fully compensate the insured for the injuries sustained. Most states prohibit stacking of UM and UIM coverage.

Arbitration is usually required as a means of resolving disputes that arise with respect to coverage. An arbitration award is often not binding if it exceeds the statutory minimum limits for bodily injury.

An insured can voluntarily terminate her automobile insurance contract by giving notice to the agent. Likewise, an insurer can terminate the contract for nonpayment of premiums, or because the insured's license is suspended or revoked, or if the insured is convicted of driving while intoxicated.

No-fault insurance is an alternative to the tort system for dealing with automobile accident cases. In no-fault the insured gives up the right to sue for pain and suffering (in varying degrees) for promised prompt payment of economic losses and reductions in automobile insurance premiums. This relatively new concept is in the experimental stage, but the results to date have not met its proponents' expectations.

KEY TERMS

coordination of benefits provision
Policy provision that precludes payment to the insured if the insured has other insurance available

fault insurance
Automobile insurance coverage where the insurance carrier of the vehicle pays for damages to the vehicle's occupants and others only if the driver of the vehicle was responsible for the injuries sustained

no-fault insurance
Automobile insurance coverage where the insurance carrier of the vehicle pays for damages to the vehicle's occupants irrespective of whether or not the driver of the vehicle was responsible for the injuries sustained

primary coverage
Insurance providing initial coverage for all damages up to the limits of the policy

reformation of a policy
Construing a policy to provide the minimum coverage required by statute

secondary coverage
Insurance that provides coverage for damages incurred but that does not do so until the limits of the primary policy have been exhausted

single-limit coverage
Insurance coverage providing a single amount of recovery that is available for damages

split-limits coverage
Insurance coverage that sets forth a maximum amount an individual can recover for damages and an aggregate amount available for damages independent of the total claims involved

stacking of policies
Using one or more policies to provide coverage for the same incident

subrogation
The right of an insurer to institute suit in the name of the insured against the responsible party to collect for monies paid by the insurer to the insured

umbrella policy
Policy that provides a secondary source of coverage after the deductible has been paid, usually coordinated with the limits of the underlying policy

REVIEW QUESTIONS

1. What is the primary purpose of automobile insurance coverage?

2. What is the difference between split-limits and single-limit coverage? Give an example of each.

3. What is an umbrella policy?

4. Under what circumstances will a court reform an insured's policy?

5. What does subrogation allow an insurer to do?

6. What do each of the following coverages provide?
   a. medical payment
   b. comprehensive
   c. collision
   d. uninsured motorist
   e. underinsured motorist

7. If an insured is injured while driving a motor vehicle owned by someone other than the insured, whose coverage is considered primary and whose coverage is considered secondary?

8. What is a coordination-of-benefits provision?

9. How is the value of damaged property determined for purposes of reimbursement by means of comprehensive coverage?

10. What precautions should be taken when purchasing miscellaneous coverage?

11. Why is buying uninsured motorist (UM) coverage so important?

12. Who is considered an uninsured motorist (UIM)?

13. Is UM coverage required in most states?

14. Can an insurer offset monies paid under a medical payment coverage against an amount due under a UM policy?

15. Can UM and UIM coverage be stacked?

16. In what types of disputes involving insurance is arbitration typically used?

17. Describe the arbitration process followed when resolving a typical dispute pertaining to insurance coverage.

18. On what grounds can an insurance contract be terminated?
    a. What has complicated voluntary termination?
    b. What steps must an insurer take to terminate an insured's policy?

19. What is the purpose of no-fault insurance?
    a. What can and cannot be recovered with no-fault insurance?
    b. What limits are often established with no-fault insurance, and on what are these limits based?
    c. Is no-fault insurance generally considered a successful experiment?
    d. How does no-fault insurance compare with workers' compensation?
    e. What suggestions have been made to improve the no-fault system?

PRACTICE EXAM

Students should complete the practice exam after studying each chapter. The answers are in Appendix A. If you score lower than 80%, you should reread the materials.

True-False

1. An umbrella policy must be issued by the same carrier that provides the automobile policy.

2. Subrogation is always allowed with respect to collision, comprehensive, and UIM coverage.

3. Insureds have no obligation to cooperate with their insurer in the subrogation claim.

4. Medical payment coverage does not apply to damages sustained by an insured when he is injured as a pedestrian.

5. If an insured is injured while in a vehicle owned by someone else, the insured's coverage will be used to pay her medical expenses up to the limits of her coverage.

6. Most medical payment policies provide for a fixed period time after the accident that payments for medical expenses will be allowed.

7. Death benefits under medical payment coverage are usually fixed at a certain dollar amount.

8. Under the terms of a collision insurance policy, coverage is dependent on who is at fault.

9. Under the terms of a collision insurance policy, the insurer can seek payment from the insured if the insured is responsible for the damage to the vehicle.

10. Coverage for such services as emergency services is almost always cost-effective and should be routinely purchased.

11. Uninsured motorists do not include motorists who have a policy with an insolvent insurer or hit-and-run drivers.

12. In most states the insurer can reduce the damages paid to the insured in proportion to the insured's negligence.

13. An insurance company cannot offset monies paid under a medical payment plan against the amount due the insured under his UM coverage.

14. Under a coordination-of-benefits provision, an insurer is responsible for its pro rata share of the damages as long as the insured was driving her own vehicle.

15. Arbitration is usually required in most policies in the event of a dispute regarding the amount of the insured's damages with respect to UM, UIM, and medical payment coverage.

16. In most policies parties must agree on and jointly pay for the services of a single arbitrator who hears the case.

17. Most policies provide that a decision by two of three arbitrators is binding on the parties and cannot be appealed.

18. If a party appeals an arbitration award, the issue of damages can be relitigated in consideration of the arbitrator's findings.

19. An insurer cannot terminate a contract on the basis of the insured being convicted of driving while intoxicated.

20. No-fault insurance was created to result in prompt payment for insureds for economic damages and to reduce automobile insurance premiums.

21. In a pure no-fault system the insured gives up her right to sue for damages sustained as a result of a third party's negligence and also for pain and suffering.

22. None of the states that have adopted no-fault have a pure no-fault system.

23. States vary in the minimum amount of benefits they require insureds to buy.

24. In a no-fault system, lost wages are paid immediately in the amount actually lost by the injured party.

25. Some have suggested that uninsured motorists in no-fault states should not be allowed to recover for their damages.

26. Changes are rare in no-fault jurisdictions.

27. Several jurisdictions allow no-fault and tort remedies to coexist.

Matching

GROUP 1

_____ 1. Individual and aggregate amounts of recovery

_____ 2. One limit for recovery

_____ 3. Prevents double recovery

_____ 4. Allows insurer to file suit against responsible person

_____ 5. Augments standard policy

a. single limit

b. split limits

c. umbrella

d. coordination of benefits

e. subrogation

GROUP 2

_____ 1. Personal injury protection

_____ 2. Cover burial expenses

_____ 3. Losses to vehicle

_____ 4. Repair of damaged vehicle

_____ 5. Car rental

a. miscellaneous

b. collision

c. death benefits

d. comprehensive

e. medical payment

Fill-in-the-Blanks

1. Courts can _____ a policy if an insurance carrier provides limits less than those required by statute.

2. If an insured is injured while in a vehicle owned by someone else, the insured's coverage will be considered _____ and the coverage for the vehicle will be considered _____.

3. Reimbursement for a lost or damaged item is determined by its _____ value or its _____ _____ value.

4. _____ _____ coverage provides for when an uninsured motorist is unable to pay substantial damages.

5. If a party appeals an arbitration award, a trial _____ _____ is held.

Multiple-Choice

1. Termination of an insurance contract
   a. does not entitle an insured to a return of advance premiums.
   b. can result in the insured forfeiting her registration rights to a vehicle.
   c. for nonpayment is always an option even if no notice is given.
   d. all of the above.

2. In a no-fault state
   a. an injured party cannot sue for intentional injuries inflicted with an automobile.
   b. an injured party cannot sue for injuries caused by an intoxicated driver.
   c. thresholds for recovery may be tied to a party's medical expenses.
   d. all of the above.

3. No-fault
   a. has resulted in the lowering of treatment expenses.
   b. allows an injured party to retain the right to sue.
   c. allows an injured party to recover for his actual medical and rehabilitation expenses and lost wages.
   d. none of the above.

4. UM coverage
   a. is not required in most states with the issuance of a liability policy.
   b. can be stacked with UIM coverage.
   c. may be allowed in multi-vehicle accidents for one vehicle and UIM coverage for another.
   d. all of the above.

5. Comprehensive insurance coverage
   a. does not apply to the shattering of a windshield or to the theft of valuables.
   b. must always be part of any standard automobile contract.
   c. often requires proof of forced entry before the insured will be reimbursed for stolen property.
   d. all of the above.

PRACTICE POINTERS

Once your law firm has been retained (and sometimes before), you will want to review the client's automobile insurance policy. In many cases the client has been with the same insurer for some time and may not be able to find his policy; or he may not be able to find all the various endorsements and amendments that have been made a part of the original policy. Make sure that you are aware of all insurance policies that might provide coverage for the accident. An injured passenger, for example, might have his own medical payment coverage, which might be available to him if the medical payment coverage on the vehicle in which he is injured is insufficient to pay for all his medical expenses.

If your client cannot find a current policy, or if you think that the documents provided are not complete, have the client contact her insurance agent and request a copy of the policy that was in effect on the date of the accident. Most of the relevant facts regarding the policy can be found on the declarations page of the policy. Many companies make the declarations page a part of their annual or semiannual billing. On policies that are paid monthly, the declarations page is generally not included with the monthly invoice.

In the online companion to this book there is a declaration page for Pauline's policy. It provides bodily injury coverage of $100,000 per person, $300,000 per accident and $50,000 for property damage (a $100,000/$300,000/$50,000 liability policy). Medical payment coverage is $10,000 per person and $30,000 per accident. UM and UIM motorist coverage are the same: $15,000 per person, $30,000 per accident. There is no provision showing either collision or comprehensive coverage. The bells and whistles for towing, car rental, etc. are not shown and should not be a part of the policy.

After reviewing the policy for the types of coverage and their dollar limits, discuss the results with the client. It is not unusual for a client to think he had coverage not shown on the declarations page (and/or not to know of coverage he *does* have). Any questions raised should be thoroughly investigated.

In many policies, accessory coverages like towing, car rental, additional living expenses, etc., are not detailed on the declarations page. Often they are shown only by a notation such as "additional coverage (or additional endorsements)–323, 324, 368." Some companies use letters rather than numbers to designate additional coverage. What is important, as shown in endorsements 323, 324, and 368 above, and which are set forth in detail in the Appendix D, Endorsements Applicable to Section III, are the details and amount of coverage specified in the policy. With the new insurance coverages and provisions (such as having a deductible and coinsurance with medical payment coverage) being offered, each policy must be thoroughly examined.

Your supervising attorney should direct you on how to proceed after coverage is decided. Some firms assist in filing related claims for towing, car rental, and so on. Others bring such matters to the client's attention so that he can institute the procedures and paperwork for reimbursement with the insurer.

While you are identifying and reviewing all applicable automobile insurance policies, also examine the client's medical insurance policies. It may be that the client can legally submit his medical expenses to both the automobile insurer and the medical insurer. It is also possible that his medical insurer is an ERISA plan, which is governed by the federal law. ERISA plans provide for reimbursement from the insured for any medical expenses incurred as a result of the acts of third parties if the insured is paid damages by the third party. The client's medical policy may also have provisions that the client should be reminded of, such as the deductible (if any), co-insurance, dollar limits on chiropractic or other treatment, exclusion of certain types of treatment from coverage, and so forth. Make sure that you and the client know about any insurer that may make a claim on any portion of the proceeds from settlement or trial, as well as the amount of the claim.

TORT TEASERS

Reread the introductory scenario at the beginning of this chapter and use the insurance policy in Appendix D when necessary to answer the following questions.

1. Pauline seeks legal advice to determine her rights in reference to the medical expenses incurred by her and her late husband, the damages she sustained, and Perry's wrongful death. Denise and David also see an attorney, who says that she cannot represent both Denise and David because David may have a claim against Denise. She then refers Denise to another attorney.

If the parties sustain the following damages, the questions before us are who has a claim against whom and what portions of Pauline and Perry's insurance policy are applicable.

- Perry—medical expenses of $6,000, funeral expenses of $4,000.
- Pauline–medical expenses of $15,000, personal damages of $90,000, wrongful-death claim with respect to Perry of $250,000, property damage claim of $16,000.

- Denise—medical expenses of $500, personal damages of $3,500.
- David—medical expenses of $24,000, future medical expenses of $76,000, personal damages of $2.5 million.
- Denise's father—property damage claim of $840.

    Use this scenario to review the concepts you have learned. To resolve issues of damages you will first need to assess the liability of the parties and determine any defenses they can raise. To assist in doing this you might want to review Chapters 4–8, 14–15.

2. How much, if any, would Perry and Pauline's insurance carrier have to pay of Pauline's medical expenses of $15,000, the $6,000 in medical expenses incurred by Perry prior to his death, and Perry's funeral expenses of $4,000?

3. Does Pauline have a claim against Denise that should be compensated by the UM coverage of Perry's policy?

4. If Pauline pursues a wrongful-death claim, who will be the appropriate party to sue? Can Pauline look to any coverage under her own policy for payment of all or a portion of the claim?

5. How much will Pauline's insurer have to pay of her property damage claim of $16,000?

6. Does Denise have a potential recovery claim for her medical expenses and personal damages? If so, against whom should the claim be made? What defenses to her claim could be alleged?

7. Against whom does David have a claim?

8. Can Denise's negligence be imputed to David? Did David assume the risk by voluntarily going with Denise?

9. Do you think Pauline's insurance carrier will offer to settle David's claim for the policy limits of $100,000? Why or why not?

10. Does Denise's father have a claim against Perry? If so, how would you evaluate Denise's father's claim?

11. In terms of potential recovery, which of the following claims would you rather be representing? Explain why. What defenses might be raised in each case?
    a. Pauline's wrongful-death claim
    b. Pauline's personal injury claim
    c. Perry's damages claim
    d. Denise's damages claim
    e. David's damages claim
    f. Denise's father's claim

12. Is the interspousal-immunity doctrine in effect in your state? If so, does that change any of your answers to the previous question? Why or why not?

13. Is any claim by Denise barred because of her wrongful use of the family vehicle and lack of a driver's license?

14. Will Pauline's wrongful-death claim be affected by the fact that Perry was not wearing his seat belt at the time of the accident? Assume that an accident reconstructionist will testify that although Perry would have suffered serious injuries, he would not have been killed had he been wearing a seat belt.

INTERNET INQUIRIES

Your supervising attorney has asked you to find a list of possible arbitrators that could be used to arbitrate a motor vehicle accident case. Go to the Internet to find sources of arbitrators. Summarize what you find; include web addresses of relevant sites.

PRACTICAL PONDERABLES

Review your own automobile insurance policy. Check the types of coverage you have purchased and make a record of the premium (and the coverage period—monthly, quarterly, semi-annual, etc.) as well as the coverage limits for each. Note the type of vehicle and where it is located. Compare the costs of coverage with the other students in the class. See if you can determine why the costs vary so much.

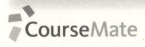 Access an interactive eBook, chapter-specific learning tools, including flashcards, quizzes, and more in your Paralegal CourseMate, accessed through www.CengageBrain.com.

CHAPTER 18

© Cengage Learning 2012

Bad Faith

CHAPTER OBJECTIVES

After completing the chapter, you should be able to

- Identify the elements of a bad faith claim.
- Recognize the rationale behind the development of bad faith actions.
- Distinguish between first-party and third-party claims for purposes of bad faith, and recognize the importance of that distinction.

On a Labor Day weekend Jerry and a number of his fraternity brothers and sorority sisters decide to spend their three-day holiday near a place called Rocky Point on the Gulf of California in Mexico. The entire group has to wait in line to enter the gate that allows vehicles to enter Sandy Beach. Jerry steps up on the back bumper of a Jeep driven by Dick when Dick suddenly accelerates his Jeep to move up in line. The sudden movement catches Jerry unaware, and he is thrown backward, striking his head on the hard-packed sand. He is knocked unconscious for a few minutes, and when he comes to his fraternity brothers put him in the back of a van to recuperate. After a few hours it becomes apparent that Jerry has suffered a serious injury, so he is taken to a hospital. He is hospitalized for two weeks and is ultimately forced to withdraw from the first semester of his sophomore year at the university. He suffers short-term memory loss with respect to the accident and has some longer-term problems with his speech, reading abilities, and memory retention.

Both Dick and Jerry are insured by the same automobile insurance carrier, and each of their policies provides liability coverage for any accident that occurs in Mexico as long as the accident takes place within fifty miles of the United States border. Dick's policy was issued in Colorado, a no-fault state. It does not provide medical payment coverage (called personal injury protection in Colorado) on Dick's Jeep when it is outside the United States. Jerry's policy does provide medical payment coverage in Mexico if the accident occurs within fifty miles of the United States border.

Your attorney, who represents Jerry, submits Jerry's medical expenses to his insurance carrier, but the carrier neither accepts nor rejects the claim. After eight months of insurer inaction, your attorney files suit against the carrier for breach of contract and bad faith. After the suit is filed the carrier hires a professor who analyzes information obtained from various witnesses (whom the carrier had not interviewed prior to the filing of the bad faith action). The professor concludes that the accident occurred somewhere between 51 and 51.5 miles outside the United States border. Your attorney hires an expert who determines that the accident occurred between 49.63 and 51 statute miles from the United States border.

The key issue is whether the accident occurred outside the 50-mile geographical limitation of Jerry's policy. The policy does not define a mile as being a statute mile (5,280 feet) or a nautical mile (6,080.1 feet). Unquestionably, if nautical miles are used the accident occurred within the 50-mile limit. The insurance carrier provides many of its insureds with maps indicating that the area of the accident is not more than 48 statute miles from the United States border. Keep this fact pattern in mind as you read about bad faith as a cause of action.

HOW BAD FAITH IS COMMITTED

Bad faith is considered an intentional tort; mere negligence on the part of the insurance carrier is not actionable. Bad faith can occur if (1) the insurance carrier unreasonably delays payment on a policy, (2) the carrier acts unconscionably toward its insured, or (3) the carrier engages in unfair claims practices (see Exhibit 18–1).

HISTORICAL DEVELOPMENT OF BAD FAITH CONCEPT

Historically courts held that insurance carriers have an implied covenant of good faith and fair dealing in reference to their insureds. Courts classified some insurance contracts as adhesion contracts. An **adhesion contract** is a standardized contract commonly used in business (an example of which is the contract signed by consumers when financing a car). Adhesion contracts are characterized by the courts as those contracts in which the party drafting the contract has superior bargaining power and the other party is typically unfamiliar with the terms of the contract and also has no real opportunity to negotiate what those terms will be.

EXHIBIT 18–1   What Constitutes Bad Faith

- Insurer unreasonably delays payment.
- Insurer acts unconscionably toward insured.
- Insurer engages in unfair claims practices.

© Cengage Learning 2012

Focusing on the unequal bargaining power between insureds and insurers, as well as the public interest in insurance contracts, the courts scrutinized insurance contracts more carefully than many other contracts in which the parties were assumed to know and understand the terms of the contracts they signed. The courts also realized that insureds rely heavily on their insurance carriers to protect their interests. Therefore, the courts created various mechanisms to protect insureds' contract rights as well as their "reasonable expectations" regarding policy provisions.

In accordance with their vision of insurance contracts as adhesion contracts, courts held that certain policy provisions could not necessarily be utilized against an insured and that the insured was not presumed to understand all the terms of the insurance contract. Courts later developed a rule of law requiring contracts to be interpreted in favor of the nondrafter (the insured) so that any "ambiguities" in a contract would be construed against the carrier and in favor of the insured. This rule was propagated in the hope that insureds would be protected from complex insurance contracts and that the insurance industry would be pressured into drafting contracts comprehensible to those who read them.

Interpreting contracts in favor of the nondrafter eventually evolved into the modern-day rule generally referred to as the *reasonable expectations doctrine*. This doctrine protects the insured's reasonable expectation that coverage will be provided and not defeated by provisions that would be unanticipated by the ordinary insured and that were never negotiated between the insured and the carrier. The court will reform the contract to the reasonable expectations of the insured even though a detailed review of the contract itself does not support those expectations.

An insurance policy is a contract between the insured and the insurance company. Traditionally, when the insurance company breaches the policy the remedy provided by contract law was expectancy damages. Expectancy damages permit the non-breaching party to recover what was bargained for in the contract, no more or less. The nonbreaching party is then placed in the exact economic position he expected to be in if the contract were performed as agreed by the parties. Therefore, if George's garages enter into a contract to repair the engine in Matthew's car for $500 and fail to provide the repairs, Matthew's remedy under contract law is to rescind or void the contract. He can also ask the court to enforce the contract so that he will receive the benefit of the contract or the expectancy damages. In this case expectancy damages constitute repair of the car. Most jurisdictions also award the prevailing party in a contract dispute their attorney's fees and costs. Under contract law Matthew is not entitled to receive payment for the inconvenience and emotional distress he suffered as a result of the delay in repairing his car.

In their efforts to curb the sometimes misused discretion of insurance carriers, courts have looked for remedies beyond those found in contract law, because such remedies impose a relatively small penalty on overreaching carriers. Because insurance companies know that, at the worst, they will have to perform their obligations under the contract and pay only a minor penalty for their indiscretions, they can afford to be rather cavalier in their actions toward their insureds. Accordingly, insurers have little incentive to be concerned about the majority of their insureds, who can ill afford the tremendous expense involved in litigating with a major company.

Some courts have found a fiduciary duty between the insurance carrier and the insured. Objectionable acts of a carrier as well as objectionable terms of an insurance contract are then found to be a breach of the fiduciary duty owed the insured. As a result, objectionable terms can be eliminated from the contract.

Some states have restricted the strict interpretation of contracts by providing the insured with standard tort remedies. For example, recovery for intentional infliction of mental distress has been allowed when an insurance company has committed especially egregious acts. In many cases, however, the physical complications required for this cause of action cannot be shown in the context of an insurer-insured relationship.

NET NEWS

The website for Fight Bad Faith Insurance Companies (FBIC) at **http://www.badfaithinsurance.org** has a listing of attorneys who take bad faith cases and a FAQ section regarding bad faith. There are numerous links to other sites as well. FBIC is strictly an insured's organization. It lists the best and worst "bad faith" insurance companies.

NET NEWS

Go to http://www.mcgeorge.edu and enter "jury verdicts in bad-faith cases" as your search term for a historical review of the development of the concept of bad faith and an economic analysis of over a hundred California bad faith cases from 1991 to 1999.

OVERVIEW OF BAD FAITH

There is an inherent conflict of interest in the insurer's promise to provide benefits to its policy holders while at the same time it seeks to maximize profits by paying as few claims as possible. All contracts have an implied covenant of good faith and fair dealing that requires the parties to fulfill their obligations under the contract honestly, fairly, reasonably, and in good faith. Courts have held in some circumstances where there is a special relationship between the parties that breach of the covenant of good faith and fair dealing is a tort called bad faith, which can be pursued by the nonbreaching party. Damages for bad faith go beyond the expectancy damages awarded in contract law. Bad faith damages include the full range of tort damages including punitive damages and damages for emotional distress and loss of consortium.

As can be seen from this brief historical review, the concept of bad faith evolved as a means of providing relief to the insured. Bad faith is a question of fact for the jury. Only when the court determines that no reasonable person could conclude that bad faith has occurred can the court take the case from the jury.

Initially, bad faith applied only to *third-party claims* (claims in which the insured paid damages to a third party). Most jurisdictions now recognize the tort of bad faith in cases of *first-party claims* (claims in which an insured demands payment from his insurer in his own right).

Bad faith cases also involve a breach of contract claim as well. Some jurisdictions, however, recognize that bad faith can occur even when the contract is not breached. A bad faith claim can occur without a breach of the insurance contract when the insurer unreasonably denies a claim. The unreasonable denial of the claim can support a cause of action for bad faith even when a court subsequently determines that the insurer had no contractual obligation to provide coverage for the claim. An insurance carrier might, for example, deny coverage without a proper investigation of the claim and later, after being sued, discover evidence that supported its original denial of coverage.

Such a discovery would not, however, diminish the carrier's initial failure to act in good faith.

Suing the Insured

Although theoretically possible, an insurance carrier rarely sues an insured for bad faith. The duty of good faith is an unconditional and independent contractual obligation of the insurer, and most states provide relief even when the insured has not fulfilled all of his contractual duties. Those courts that have recognized bad faith claims against insureds have allowed the insurers to recover contractual damages only. Tort damages as well as punitive damages have been denied. Conceivably, however, comparative negligence could be used to reduce an insured's award of damages if an insured acted in bad faith.

LOCAL LINKS

Does your state recognize the tort of bad faith? When was the cause of action first approved?

FIRST-PARTY VERSUS THIRD-PARTY CLAIMS

In first-party cases the plaintiff (insured) and defendant (insurer) are easily defined. The insured, pursuant to a contractual right emanating from her insurance contract, sues the insurer. As previously mentioned, most bad faith claims include a breach of contract claim and, if supported by the insurer's acts, a claim for punitive damages. Although the requisite conduct for punitive damages varies, the trend is to award punitive damages only when an "evil mind guides the evil hand."

Third-party suits follow a more circuitous route to the courthouse. Most states do not allow those who have been injured by the insured and then damaged by the insurer's actions toward its insured to file suit directly against the insurance company, because injured parties are not in privity of contract with the insurance company. A third-party case usually reaches trial in the name of the insured only after the insured "cuts a deal" with the injured party and assigns the bad faith claim to the third party. The assignment permits the third party claimant to stand in the shoes of the insured and pursue the bad faith claim.

LOCAL LINKS

Does your state recognize the tort of bad faith for both first-party and third-party claims?

Resolution of Third-Party Claims

A third-party action often arises after the insurer refuses to settle the injured party's claim against the insured for an amount less than or equal to the policy limits. Bad faith can occur when the insured is required to pay an **excess judgment** (a judgment for more than the policy limits), because the insurer is regarded as having gambled with its insured's money by rejecting a reasonable settlement offer within the policy limits. Consider the case where an automobile accident is covered by a $50,000 auto liability policy and the insurer rejects a $50,000 demand to pay the insured party's bodily injury claim, which has a value of $500,000. If the injured party subsequently recovers a judgment against the negligent insured for $500,000, the insurance company is obligated under the insurance policy to pay the policy limits of $50,000 and no more. The insured would therefore have to pay the excess judgment of $450,000. The insured can file a lawsuit against the insurer for bad faith because of the unreasonable exposure to the excess judgment. Alternatively, the insured can assign the bad faith claim to the injured party, which will permit the injured party to pursue the bad faith claim. Although many states prohibit the assignment of "pure" personal injury claims, most allow the assignment of contract rights. Because a bad faith claim arises out of contract, the insurance policy, and therefore is not considered a pure tort, most courts allow its assignment. Some states also allow the assignment of any right the insured might have to punitive damages.

Once the assignment is made, the injured party then pursues the insurer in the name of the insured. Because the lawsuit is filed in the insured's name, as part of the assignment the insured must cooperate in the action against the insurer. The lawsuit will in fact be orchestrated by the injured party.

The insured may also assign her rights to the injured party when the insurer denies coverage for the injured party's claim and/or agrees to defend the insured only under a reservation of rights. An insurance carrier that defends its insured under a reservation of rights initially tells its insured it will provide a defense to the claim. At the same time, however, the carrier reserves its rights to later deny that coverage exists, in which case it can withdraw the defense previously offered. In most cases the insurance carrier's reservation of rights letter will advise the insured to consider employing his own counsel.

Insured's Option When Denied Coverage

An insured's remedies upon being denied coverage are often based on whether coverage was denied outright or whether his position was compromised as a result of a reservation of rights. If coverage is flatly denied, the insured has no chance of indemnity for any judgment rendered against him, and no opportunity to mount a defense except from his own pocket.

LOCAL LINKS

Does your state have any statutes regulating the contents of a reservation of rights letter?

Because of the vulnerability of an insured that has been denied coverage, some courts allow the insured to enter into an agreement with the injured party, stipulating the amount of the judgment to be entered in favor of the injured party. The injured party must still present evidence to substantiate the damages claimed, but with no adversary attempting to exclude evidence the injured party usually has little difficulty obtaining a large judgment. Once the judgment is entered, the insured assigns all rights under the insurance policy to the injured party. Then, once again in the name of the insured, the injured party sues the insurance carrier, seeking indemnity for the amount of the judgment entered, or garnishes the insurer.

When this procedure is allowed, an insurance carrier's liability usually does not exceed the policy limits unless the carrier has denied coverage in bad faith. In that case the injured party can recover the amount of the judgment obtained (up to the policy limits) for breach of contract and can also pursue an independent bad faith claim against the insurance carrier.

Insured's Option When Insurer Defends under a Reservation of Rights

If an insurer defends under a reservation of rights, the insured is not left completely naked. The insurer, in essence, loans him a "coat" but at the same time advises the insured that the "coat" may be recalled at any time. Under these circumstances some courts have allowed the insured to enter into an agreement with the injured party that basically protects the insured if the insurer subsequently denies coverage. Entering into such an agreement is not considered a violation of the *cooperation clause*, found in most insurance contracts, that mandates the insured's cooperation with the insurer.

In a typical reservation of rights case the insured enters into negotiations with the injured party to protect the insured from being exposed to an uninsured judgment. Any agreement normally provides for a judgment to be entered based on evidence presented to the court, usually without objection from the insured. Care must be taken to ensure that no fraud is perpetrated on the court when such an agreement is entered into. After judgment is entered the insured assigns all rights under her insurance contract to the injured party.

In a reservation of rights case an insured must usually advise the insurer of the terms and conditions of the agreement prior to entering into any agreement. The insurer then has one last opportunity to withdraw its reservation of rights and provide an unconditional defense to the insured.

The reservation of rights case is resolved when the injured party files suit against the insurer in the name of the insured. Alternatively, the injured party can garnish the insurer. Suit is considerably different from the trial of a denial of coverage case. The injured party must prove that the insurance policy issued to the insured covers the claim and that the agreement between the insured and the injured party was not a fraud on the court. He must also show that the judgment entered by the court was not fraudulent but was fair and reasonable considering the issue of liability, the facts relating to actual damages, the advantages and risks of going to trial, and the risks of the insurer not being liable under the policy. Under this scenario the jury must be told the terms and conditions of the agreement and the fact that the insured was released from liability. The jury would also be advised, however, that the insurer had reserved the right to deny coverage and that it was the concern of noncoverage

that motivated the insured to enter into its agreement with the injured party.

This "trial within a trial" allows the insurer to introduce all relevant evidence that counters any of the positions taken by the plaintiff (the injured party, who is acting in the name of the insured). If the jury determines that no coverage exists, it will enter a judgment for the defendant (insurer). If the jury determines that the judgment obtained in accordance with the agreement between the insured and the injured party was excessive, it can award damages in a lesser amount.

Failure to Settle Claim

The insurer can be subjected to bad faith even when it acknowledges coverage and provides a complete defense. This type of bad faith occurs when the insurance carrier has a reasonable opportunity to settle the injured party's claim within the policy limits. If the insurer refuses to settle, the insured can be liable for the amount of the judgment in excess of the policy limits.

Of particular concern to the insured are areas of liability in which the potential damages are extremely large. In those instances the insurer might be tempted to "roll the dice" by going to the jury in the hope of getting a defense verdict. Because the insurer's liability does not exceed the insured's policy limits, the insurer has nothing to lose by going to trial. The insurer, after entry of an excess judgment, can pay the amount of its policy limits and leave the insured to deal with the injured party. The insured would then have a potential bad faith claim against the insurance carrier for its failure to settle the claim within the policy limits. As the insured would probably be very happy to be relieved from having to pay the injured party, she would likely assign to that party any rights she might have against the insurer. The injured party would then proceed, in the name of the insured, in a bad faith claim against the insurer.

Some have questioned whether an insured who knows the insurer has refused to settle within the policy limits is in a position to strike a deal with the injured party before an excess judgment has actually

---

NET NEWS

Interesting articles on bad faith cases can be found at **http://www.appellate.net** in the "Articles and Treatises" section under the "1999 Term" articles.

been entered. Most courts have held that an insured in this situation is bound to cooperate with the insurer and may not enter into an agreement with the injured party until after judgment is entered. The courts reason that the insured, having selected the limits of coverage, cannot shift her responsibility to adequately insure herself to her insurer when those limits turn out to be too low to cover the risk that actually occurred.

Underpayment of Claims

Bad faith can occur when an insurance company underpays (lowballs) claims with full knowledge of the full value of the claim. *Republic Insurance Company v. Hires*, 810 P.2d 790 (Nev.1991) reveals the lowballing tactics of an insurance company that underpaid claims of its lower income clients and used other tactics to undermine the ability of its policy holders to recover full value for property damage claims.

CASE

Republic Insurance Company v. Hires
810 p.2d 790 (Nev.1991)

PRIOR HISTORY: Appeal from judgment awarding compensatory and punitive damages. Second Judicial District Court, Washoe County; Robert L. Schouweiler, Judge.

DISPOSITION: Affirmed; punitive damage award reduced from $22.5 million to $5 million.

OPINION BY: YOUNG

OPINION

A jury awarded Jack A. Hires $ 22.5 million in punitive damages because of the manner in which Republic Insurance Company treated Hires in connection with payment of an insurance claim.

FACTS

Before leaving on a weekend trip to California, Hires secured his home in Sparks and asked his neighbor, Doug France, to maintain the swimming pool. Soon after reaching his destination, Hires received a telephone call from France who told him that his house had been "robbed." Hires immediately returned to Sparks. He found extensive damage to the residence and furniture; in addition, several items had been stolen.

Hires notified Republic Insurance Company of the loss. The homeowner's coverage with Republic was a basic homeowner's policy with a replacement cost endorsement for an additional cost.

On Monday, Terry Hunt, an independent insurance adjuster hired by Republic, went to the house to inspect damages. After reviewing the damage, Hunt told Hires that a contractor would take care of it. Hunt recommended that Hires contact UTE Construction Company regarding repairs.

The following night, Gary Schizler from UTE went to the Hires home and told Hires to replace the damaged furniture. Relying on the instructions of Hunt and Schizler, Hires threw away the damaged furniture and bought new replacement furniture, partially with cash and on credit. Hires gave the receipts to Hunt, who indicated that he would take care of it.

Two weeks later, Hunt informed Hires that Republic would not reimburse Hires the full $2,242.82 for the new furniture, but that Republic would pay only $400, which is what Republic estimated it would cost to reupholster the furniture. Republic finally paid Hires only sixty-five percent of the $400 because Republic claimed Hires lacked documentation, even though there had been no question raised as to Hires' ownership of the furniture.

The next problem Hires encountered was with regard to his bedroom furniture. Hires estimated that it would cost $580 to replace the furniture. Republic estimated a replacement cost of $300 and offered to pay only sixty-five percent of the $300. Republic's excuse for the across-the-board thirty-five percent reduction in payments to Hires was that Hires did not have sufficient documentation to establish price and ownership on some items. Even the items for which there was sufficient documentation were paid for by Republic at sixty-five percent of replacement value. According to Republic claims adjuster Trisha Funk, it was customary for Republic to begin negotiations at a reduced figure, leaving the policyholder with the obligation of arguing for a larger amount.

Moreover, Republic refused to pay any amount to Hires until four months after the burglary. Hires testified this created financial difficulties. Hires also testified that he experienced marital difficulties before the experience with Republic and that Republic's treatment of him and the ensuing financial difficulties finally resulted in his divorce.

In November 1986, four months after the burglary, Hires contacted legal counsel who sent a letter to Terry Hunt demanding payment of the claim. Republic continued its refusal to pay. By Christmas, Hires had experienced major financial difficulties because of the payments due on replacement furniture that he had purchased and the repairs which he had paid.

Finally, on December 30, 1986, Republic gave Hunt authority to settle a claim for damage for loss of

(continues)

contents in the amount of $7,238 which was $5,800 under the demand by Hires. Hires accepted payment while reserving his right to contest the amount paid.

Republic's conduct with regard to its investigation of the burglary was also an issue at trial. Officer Schmidt of the Sparks Police Department investigated the burglary and concluded that, because of the large amount of vandalism associated with the burglary, the perpetrator might have been a member of the Hires family or someone with a great dislike for the family. When Officer Schmidt's suspicions were satisfied, the police investigation was closed.

Republic apparently did not agree with Officer Schmidt's conclusion and conducted a full neighborhood investigation into Hires' possible involvement in the burglary. Part of the investigation concerned Mrs. Hires' alleged extramarital activities and possible involvement in the burglary. Hires testified that, prior to the investigation, he enjoyed a very close relationship with people in the neighborhood. After the investigation, he perceived a change in his neighbors' attitude toward him and his family.

Hires stated that his children mentioned remarks by their friends indicating that the Hires family had been involved in the burglary. Republic finally concluded that the family had no involvement in the burglary. Terry Hunt, who performed the investigation for Republic, testified that ordinarily he would not have conducted such a thorough investigation, but that Republic was usually more willing than other companies to investigate the background of its own insureds. The investigation apparently ended in November 1986.

About eighteen months after the burglary and after the lawsuit was filed, Republic again investigated the incident. An investigator employed by Republic's attorney contacted Doug France and asked if France had collaborated with the Hires family in committing the burglary. The investigator asked France if he had been involved in a relationship with Mrs. Hires. France interpreted this question as referring to a sexual relationship. This investigation was conducted throughout the neighborhood. In December 1987, pursuant to the investigator's request, the Sparks Police Department reopened the investigation, but closed it again upon verification of information previously received.

Hires brought suit against Republic based on breach of contract, misrepresentation, bad faith, negligence and invasion of privacy. The jury awarded Hires $410,000 in compensatory damages and $22.5 million in punitive damages.

On appeal, Republic raises a number of claims of procedural error. We conclude that these claims were either not properly preserved for review or that, if objection was properly made, there was no abuse of discretion by the trial judge. Moreover, we have reviewed the record and conclude that evidence supported the award of compensatory damages. We will now address the question of punitive damages.

Republic raises a constitutional argument regarding punitive damages, but we reject this argument because the availability of punitive damages is accepted as settled law by nearly all state and federal courts. *Pacific Mutual Life Ins. Company v. Haslip, U.S.,* 59 U.S.L.W. 4157 (March 4, 1991). Our court has stated that punitive damages provide a benefit to society by punishing undesirable conduct not punishable by the criminal law. *Ace Truck v. Kahn, 103 Nev. 503, 746 P.2d 132 (1987).*

NRS 42.005 authorizes an award of punitive damages where the defendant has been guilty of oppression, fraud or malice. If we read the record in the light most favorable to Hires and least favorable to Republic, we conclude evidence indicates Republic was guilty of oppressive conduct. *K Mart Corp. v. Ponsock, 103 Nev. 39, 732 P.2d 1364 (1987).*

After hearing all the evidence in the case, the trial judge summarized the case as follows:

> This claim was not one in the gray area, but rather was one that reasonable persons would agree *should* [emphasis in original] be paid.... Republic insisted on an across the board reduction of the claim. Furthermore, the testimony of Terry Hunt, by way of his first deposition, established that this *conduct was the unqualified policy of Republic, particularly with regard to lower and middle income policyholders, who are less likely to dispute Republic's position.* This conscious wrongdoing on the part of Republic, along with the malicious intent, is what the jury sought to punish. *And the jury knew that a substantial sum was necessary to deter further conduct by a wealthy, powerful and impersonal corporation.* (Our emphasis.)

From the above comments by the court and the record, it is clear that Republic was guilty of oppressive behavior. Evidence showed that the net worth of Republic was approximately $172 million. We conclude that $22.5 million is a larger sum than is necessary in this case to serve as a deterrent. Although we are reluctant to substitute our judgment for that of the trier of fact on punitive damages, we conclude that the amount awarded by the jury is clearly disproportionate to the blameworthiness and harmfulness in the conduct of Republic under the circumstances of this case. *Ace Truck, 103 Nev. at 509, 746 P.2d at 136–37.*

Based on the standards established in *Ace Truck* and after considering all of the factors enumerated therein,

(continues)

we conclude that in this case any punitive damage award in excess of $5 million would be unreasonable and disproportionate to the behavior of Republic. An award of more than $5 million would be more than is necessary to deter Republic and others from engaging in this kind of oppressive behavior.

We affirm the judgment of the trial court in all respects except for the award of punitive damages. The judgment for punitive damages is reduced from $22.5 million to $5 million.

CONCUR BY: SPRINGER
CONCUR
Springer, J., concurring in the judgment:

Although I am willing to join with the other members of the court in ordering a reduced $5 million punitive damage judgment in favor of Hires, I am unwilling to sign the majority opinion because I do not think that it accurately portrays the magnitude of the oppressive conduct engaged in by Republic Insurance Company.[1] The majority opinion as it now reads does not in my view justify a punitive award of even $5 million; it is for this reason that I file a separate, concurring opinion.

While the family was out of town they received a phone call from a neighbor, Doug France, advising that the family home had been "robbed." Hires returned immediately to his Sparks home. Upon arriving at the house he found extensive damage to the residence and furniture. Several items had been stolen, the waterbed had been punctured, and other pieces of furniture and portions of the house had been vandalized.

Hires notified his homeowner's insurance carrier, Republic Insurance Company, about the loss. The homeowner's coverage which Hires had with Republic was a basic homeowner's policy with a replacement cost endorsement made available by Republic for an additional cost.

On Monday, Terry Hunt, the independent insurance adjuster hired by Republic, went to the house and observed the damages. After Hunt made a review of the damage to the house and its contents, Hires asked Hunt what to do about the furniture. Hunt told him to leave it for the contractor to take care of. Hunt recommended that Hires contact UTE Construction Company about the repairs.

The next night, Gary Schizler from UTE went to the Hires' home and told Hires to replace the damaged furniture. Based on the instructions of Hunt and Schizler, Hires threw away the damaged furniture and bought

new replacement furniture partially with cash and the rest on credit. Hires gave the receipts to Hunt, and Hunt indicated that he would take care of it. After approximately two weeks, however, Hunt informed Hires that Republic would not reimburse him the full $2,242.82 for the new furniture, but that Republic would pay only $400.00, which is what Republic estimated it would cost to reupholster the furniture. Republic finally paid Hires only sixty-five percent of the $400.00 because Republic claimed Hires lacked documentation, even though there had been no question concerning Hires' ownership of the furniture.

The next problem Hires encountered was with regard to his bedroom furniture. Hires estimated that it would cost $580.00 to replace the furniture while Republic estimated a replacement cost of $300.00, but Republic would pay only sixty-five percent of the $300.00. Republic's excuse for the across-the-board thirty-five percent reduction in payments to Hires was that Hires allegedly did not have sufficient documentation to establish price and ownership on some items. Even the items for which there was sufficient documentation were paid for by Republic at sixty-five percent of their replacement value. According to Republic claims adjuster Trisha Funk, it was customary for Republic to begin negotiations with an insured at a reduced figure, leaving the policyholder with the obligation of arguing for a larger amount. At trial, Hires contended that Republic had refused to pay, in all, about $5,800.00 which was due him under the policy.

Republic refused to pay any amount to Hires until almost four months after the burglary. Hires testified that this caused him financial difficulties. Hires also testified that he had marital difficulties before the experiences with Republic and that Republic's treatment of him and the ensuing financial difficulties finally resulted in his divorce.

Hires contacted legal counsel in November 1986, four months after the burglary, and counsel sent a letter to Terry Hunt demanding payment of the claim. While Hunt realized that Republic should pay the claim and requested Republic to do so, Republic continued in its refusal. By Christmas, Hires had experienced major financial difficulties because of the payments due on the replacement furniture he had bought and the repairs he had paid for.

Finally, on December 30, 1986, Republic gave Hunt authority to settle for $7,238.00, which was well under the demand made by Hires. Republic indicated to Hires, through Terry Hunt, that the $7,238.00 was a take-it-or-leave-it offer. Hires accepted payment while preserving his right to contest the amount paid.

Republic's conduct with regard to its investigation of the burglary also was an issue at trial. Officer Schmidt of

---

1. Rather than state the facts in detail in the body of this concurring opinion I will summarize the facts in this note because I think the reader may get a better grasp of Republic's blameworthiness upon reading of the way in which the company treated the Hires family.

(continues)

the Sparks Police Department investigated the burglary and concluded that, because of the large amount of vandalism associated with the burglary, the perpetrator might have been a member of the Hires family or someone with a great dislike for the family. Officer Schmidt's suspicions were satisfied, however, when he found out that Hires had been out of town when the burglary took place.

Republic apparently did not agree with Officer Schmidt's conclusion, though, and conducted a full neighborhood investigation into Hires' possible involvement in the burglary. Part of the investigation involved Mrs. Hires' alleged extramarital activities and her potential involvement in the burglary. Hires testified that prior to the investigation he had a very close relationship with the people in the neighborhood, but after the investigation he perceived a change in his neighbors' attitude toward him and his family. He stated that his children mentioned remarks by their friends that the family had been involved in the burglary. Republic finally concluded that the Hires family had no involvement in the burglary. Terry Hunt, who conducted the investigation for Republic, testified that he would not have done such a thorough investigation except that Republic was usually more willing to investigate the background of its own insureds than other companies. This investigation apparently ended in November 1986.

Republic again investigated the burglary about eighteen months after the burglary and after the lawsuit in this case had been filed. An investigator contacted Doug France and asked if France had collaborated with the Hires family in committing the burglary. The investigator asked France if he had a relationship with Mrs. Hires, which France interpreted as meaning a sexual relationship. This investigation was conducted throughout the neighborhood. In December 1987, the investigator requested that the Sparks Police Department reopen the criminal investigation. The police department did reopen the case but closed it again upon verification of the information that it had previously received.

Hires brought suit against Republic based on breach of contract, misrepresentation, bad faith, negligence, and invasion of privacy. The jury awarded Hires $410,000.00 in compensatory damages and $22.5 million in punitive damages. This award equals approximately thirteen percent of Republic's $172 million net worth.

I do not think that the majority opinion accurately portrays, as it should, how awful Republic really was in its dealings with Hires and its other insurance policyholders. As the trial court concluded, Republic was guilty of "conscious wrongdoing" and "malicious intent"; but what aggravates the wrongdoing in this case

is the massive oppression engaged in by Republic and Republic's focus on defeating the legitimate claims of its low income, relatively powerless clientele. What the company was doing was to underpay its claimants on an "across the board" basis by starting "negotiations" with claimants at sixty-five percent of the true value of the claim as assessed by the company itself, and then negotiating downward from there.[2] Shortchanging its policyholders was, according to the trial judge, "the unqualified policy of Republic, particularly with regard to lower and middle income policyholders, who are less likely to dispute Republic's position." There is evidence to support the conclusion that this oppressive policy was employed in over one million claims per year.[3] The amount "shaved" off (to use a term coined by one of the witnesses) of Hires' legitimate claim was around $5,800.00. If, for example, only a trifling $100.00 were shaved from each of a million claims each year, we would have a staggering fraud on the company's policyholders of $100 million per year. This kind of fraud, this kind of oppression is indeed deserving of punishment. The trial court properly observed that policyholders should not have to "be confronted with the unreasonable and outrageous behavior of an insurance company." The trial court specifically concluded that the jury was justified under the circumstances in awarding $22.5 million as being "necessary to punish the tortfeasor and to deter others from similar misconduct." Perhaps, as my colleagues conclude, $5 million (which is less than three percent of Republic's net worth) is enough to punish Republic and to deter other insurance companies from similar fraudulent and oppressive misconduct; but I am not willing to concur in such a judgment without at least putting on the record a more detailed account of the abominable misconduct of which this insurance company was guilty in this case. A business practice more

2. This course of conduct was revealed by Republic's own employees. One of Republic's insurance agents testified that Republic deliberately treated its customers differently depending on their socio-economic status. In addition, one of Republic's claims adjusters explained that it was *customary* for Republic to begin negotiations with an insured with a reduced figure, leaving the policyholder with the obligation of arguing for a larger amount.

3. Prior to trial, Hires requested that Republic produce all of its complaints that were "similar in nature to the allegations in this litigation," or "reasonably related to the allegations in this litigation." In response to this discovery request, Republic presented Hires with a large box of complaints. Over 100 of these specific complaints were admitted into evidence at trial. These 100 claims provide a rough sample of cases similar to the case before us. We can readily see from these complaints what Republic was doing, but we cannot tell how much money was bilked from its insurance claimants. Hires' counsel suggested a minimum of $20 million, but this sum is low when we consider that over one million claims a year are presented to the company.

(continues)

reprehensible than that practiced here would be hard to imagine. It is difficult to envision in the business world anything more repugnant that the picture of a group of corporate executives charged with the management of a giant insurance company sitting down to plan how the company can prosper by refusing to pay legitimate claims. Imagine: "First, we will take every claim and reduce it to sixty-five percent of what we think the claim is actually worth. Then, by delay, harassment, and intimidation we will force claimants to accept an amount lower than sixty-five percent of the claim's true value, if possible. This scheme will work particularly well in cases where claimants are short of money and must accept inadequate compensation in order to survive."

The ugly spectacle of Republic's behavior in systematically depriving the powerless of their legitimate indemnification claims is, to say the least, troubling. Such conduct exemplifies in the extreme the oppressive behavior contemplated by *NRS 42.005* as warranting the award of punitive damages.[4] The hallmark of this case is *oppression*, the use of massive economic and social power to trample on the rights of the "little guy." The concept is well captured in the first paragraph of Hires' brief:

This case is about David and Goliath. One party is a financially weak UPS deliveryman who paid insurance premiums in order to obtain protection for his family, and whose life was shattered when his home was burglarized and vandalized. The other party is a large national insurance corporation which has millions of dollars in assets, which is a subsidiary of an even larger insurance conglomerate, and which flexed its enormous muscles in order to reduce its policyholder's claim and increase its profit.

The failure to bring into judicial cognizance the true nature of oppression as a basis for punitive damages was recognized in *Farr v. Transamerica Occidental Life Ins. Co., 699 P.2d 376, 384 (Ariz.Ct.App. 1985)*, in which the courts' common failure to define adequately oppressive conduct was noted. The Arizona court stated: "The cases fail to define what is meant by oppressive conduct, but a good example would encompass the situation where the insured's loss has made him desperate to settle, and the insurer is specifically aware of this vulnerability and plays upon it while recklessly failing to investigate, process or pay a claim." *699 P.2d at 384*. In the case now before us, we are not dealing with a company's mere failure to investigate, process or pay a claim but, rather, with an intentional, conscious company policy to avoid paying lawful claims, thus inflicting on weak and vulnerable policy holders a "cruel and unjust hardship." *United Fire, 105 Nev. at 512–13, 780 P.2d at 198; Ainsworth, 104 Nev. at 590, 763 P.2d at 675*.

Further aggravating the oppressive actions of this insurance company is its inexplicable failure to acknowledge, even during the appellate process, that it has done anything wrong. This remorseless attitude, combined with the contemptible conduct detailed above, sufficiently supports the lower court's firm and unequivocal declaration that Republic was deserving of very severe punishment.

I do have some concern in this case about the "windfall" of $22.5 million that would be enjoyed by Hires if this punitive award were affirmed; and this influences my decision to join with the majority's reduction of the punitive award. Also, I am concerned about just who is actually being punished by the punitive award. As noted in the margin, those actually responsible for the oppressive behavior exhibited by Republic as a corporation may go entirely unpunished.[5]

Some commentators argue that this kind of punitive damage award punishes the innocent shareholder and does not have a deterrent effect on the corporate

---

4. I believe that the majority should have placed more emphasis on the oppressiveness of Republic's behavior. Oppression was defined for the jury in terms of Republic's "conscious disregard for the rights of others." This definition, however, and the definition of oppression given in our past cases falls short of capturing the true essence of oppression. This court has defined oppression as "a conscious disregard for the rights of others which constitutes an act of subjecting plaintiffs to cruel and unjust hardship." *United Fire Insurance Co. v. McClelland, 105 Nev. 504, 512–13, 780 P.2d 193, 198 (1989), reh'g denied (Nov. 11, 1989); see also Ainsworth v. Combined Ins. Co., 104 Nev. 587, 590, 763 P.2d 673, 675 (1988)*. This description covers Republic's behavior in this case, but it does not in my opinion adequately cover the most important, most essential element of true oppression, namely, the power differential between the oppressor and the oppressed. The etymological root of the word oppressed is the pressing or crushing denotation, the sense of the stronger party pressing down on and crushing the weaker. Webster defines oppression as the "[u]njust or cruel exercise of authority or power." Webster's New Int'l Dictionary 1710 (7th ed. 1961) (unabridged). The real gist of oppression, then, (appreciated, it would seem, by the jury in this case) is the abuse of power by the stronger over the weaker. Incorporating this idea of crushing by superior power into the language of our past cases, I would define oppression as the unjust abuse of power by one who is stronger and who, in the exercise of that greater power, consciously disregards the rights of one who is weaker, thereby causing injury by subjecting the weaker party to cruel and unjust hardship.

5. Republic is a large subsidiary company with assets of about $172 million. If this were a personal, not a corporate, defendant, one might not be concerned with a punishment that took $5 million, or even $22.5 million, from a rich and powerful person who preyed upon the weak and was guilty of an unjust and cruel abuse of power. In a case like this, however, it is, to some degree, the innocent, at least relatively innocent, stockholders who suffer loss for the evil doings of corporate management.

(continues)

managers who actually committed the wrongful acts. They argue that if, say, as here, three percent of the net worth of a company were to be awarded to the plaintiff it would take three cents from every dollar's worth of the stock belonging to the shareholders, while the wages and salaries of the employees and officers of the corporation would remain untouched. *See Roginsky v. Richardson-Merrell, Inc.*, 378 F.2d 832, 841 (2d Cir. 1967).

Opponents of the "innocent shareholder" theory state that loss or decline in value of an investment is a risk that investors must assume. They argue that the shareholders should not be allowed to enjoy "ill-gotten" gains. In addition, they state that punitive damages cutting into the shareholders' pocketbooks will encourage the shareholders to exercise closer control over corporate operations. 1 J. Ghiardi & J. Kircher, *Punitive Damages Law and Practice*, § 6.10 (1988). The assertion that shareholders could be motivated to exercise close control over the corporation seems to ignore the reality, whether good or bad, that the modern multi-million dollar corporation is ruled by its directors and officers and that the individual shareholders who own just a few shares each and are not acquainted with any of the other shareholders have and want little or nothing to say concerning corporate management. It appears in this record that the principal stockholder of Republic is another corporation, and the innocent stockholder argument may not obtain here; still, it is worth noting that attention should be given to the desirability of punishing those who are really at fault.

Under the tort theory of recovery here employed, the contracting party, the company, is the only party liable in tort for breach of the implied covenant of good faith and fair dealing. There is, however, no reason why stockholders should not, in these kinds of bad faith cases, be able to pursue a recoupment of their losses. The record before us fails to identify which agents of the corporation brought about the oppressive treatment of Mr. Hires in this case. No doubt a class stockholders' action could get to the bottom of this mystery and perhaps recover the stockholders' losses from the guilty parties. A class action by defrauded claimants might also be in order in this case.

I have decided to join my brothers in the judgment in this case, but I admit to a certain "reluctance to substitute [my] judgment for that of the trier of fact on the issue of damages." *Automatic Merchandisers, Inc. v. Ward*, 98 Nev. 282, 284, 646 P.2d 553, 555 (1982). Nevertheless, even in the face of the massive corporate oppression generated by the management of Republic Insurance Company, I am willing to join with my colleagues in reducing the $22.5 million punitive award to $5 million.

Damages—Third-Party Claims

The amount of damages to be awarded in third-party cases is based on four factors: (1) the amount of judgment entered against the insured in excess of the policy limits (i.e., the amount the insured must pay out of his own pocket); (2) the legal fees the insured has incurred in pursuing the claim against the insurer; (3) the emotional distress, if any, suffered by the insured; and (4) any other monetary loss or damage to the insured's credit or reputation (see Exhibit 18–2).

If the insurer's actions have been sufficiently egregious, punitive damages might also be available. Punitive damages are intended to prevent similar misconduct in the future rather than to compensate the plaintiff. Therefore, the amount of punitive damages to be awarded is based on the financial condition of the insurer and the degree of its misconduct rather than the impact of its misconduct on the insured. Because the insurance business is often very lucrative, a plaintiff asking for relatively small actual damages may seek punitive damages in the millions of dollars range.

EXHIBIT 18–2 *Damage Factors—Third-Party Claim*

- Amount of judgment entered against insured in excess of insured's policy limits
- Legal fees incurred by insured
- Emotional distress suffered by insured
- Monetary loss or damaged credit reputation of insured

© Cengage Learning 2012

Resolution of First-Party Claims

A first-party bad faith case is more straightforward than a third-party case because only two parties are involved. In a first-party bad faith case the insured is denied the benefits of her contract with her insurer due to the insurer's failure to deal with her fairly and in good faith. An insurer acts in bad faith by either failing to investigate a claim made by the insured or by inadequately investigating a claim. If coverage is denied as a result, or if an unreasonably low evaluation of the damages is made, a claim for bad faith will lie.

NET NEWS

An interesting article on third-party bad faith cases can be found at http://www.darlaw.com in the "Articles" section. The article debunks attempts to reinstitute the case law of *Royal-Globe* by statute in California (*Royal Globe* allowed third parties to sue the insurer directly for bad faith; it was subsequently overturned by the California Supreme Court).

An insurance carrier's delay tactics in investigating and evaluating a claim can also lead to bad faith. A carrier obviously benefits financially by delaying payment of a claim as long as possible. Such a delay allows the carrier to obtain the maximum benefits of its investment of the insured's premium.

Because an insurer is obligated to properly investigate its insured's claim, many courts refuse to allow information obtained after the filing of a bad faith lawsuit to be used by the insurer to justify its prior actions. Suppose an insurer denies coverage but never investigates the claim. That insurer usually cannot later submit evidence supporting its denial of coverage if it finds this evidence by virtue of an investigation conducted after the insured files a bad faith suit.

An additional basis for bad faith in first-party cases involves fraudulent or harassing practices by the carrier. In some states violation of state statutes governing unfair claim-settlement procedures can result in claims for bad faith.

Damages—First-Party Claims

Determining the amount to be paid in first-party cases entails consideration of elements similar to those used in third-party claims (see Exhibit 18–3). The major difference is that first-party claims involve the loss of unpaid benefits, whereas third-party claims involve an excess judgment. Unpaid benefits include the insured's loss of the benefit of the bargain, any resulting consequential damages, and lost interest on the unpaid amount due the insured.

In many cases, such as those involving health or disability insurance claims, wrongful denial results in not only the insured's inability to pay bills but also the loss of his and his family's credit rating. If such losses can be proved to stem from the wrongful acts of the insurer they can also be recovered. Care must be taken, however, in evaluating losses alleged to have occurred as a result of the insurer's bad faith. Asking a jury to stretch its concept of proximate cause may result in a backlash against the insured, if he is perceived as overreaching.

Standards Used to Determine Bad Faith

An insured is often exposed to lesser risk in first-party bad faith cases than in third-party matters. In first-party cases the insurer does not have sole control of litigation relating to the insured's potential liability, which it has in third-party cases. Additionally, in first-party cases the insured makes her claim directly in her own name and does not face losses in excess of her policy limits.

Because of these differences, many courts use a different standard in a first-party case than in a third-party case to determine whether bad faith has been committed. In first-party situations the standard is based on the reasonableness of the insurer's position. Some courts consider denial of a claim reasonable (and therefore not in bad faith) if the claim is "fairly debatable." Some courts require a showing of more than mere negligent conduct before they will find that an insurer acted in bad faith. For those courts an unintentional mistake, oversight, or carelessness of an insurer's employee does not constitute bad faith even though a jury, with hindsight, could objectively determine that the carrier's actions were unreasonable.

EXHIBIT 18–3 *Damage Factors—First Party Claim*

- Unpaid benefits of policy
- Legal fees incurred by insured
- Lost interest on unpaid amount due insured
- Emotional distress suffered by insured
- Any other financial losses of insured caused as a result of insurer's bad faith

© Cengage Learning 2012

LOCAL LINKS

What are the standards used by the courts of your state to determine if bad faith has occurred?

Because in third-party situations the insured has almost no control over the processing of the claim against her, most courts have held the insurer to a higher standard of care. The courts go beyond asking whether an insurer's position was fairly debatable. Many inquire whether the insurer gave as much consideration to its insured's interests as it did to its own (the "equal consideration" test).

LOCAL LINKS

What is the difference in the standard for bad faith in a first-party action versus in a third-party action in your state?

PUTTING IT INTO PRACTICE 18:1

Refer to the hypothetical scenario at the beginning of this chapter in answering these questions.

1. Does Jerry have a third-party claim? Against whom?

2. Does Jerry have a first-party claim? What portions of his automobile insurance policy would it be covered under?

3. Why might Dick's carrier initially defend him from any claim by Jerry under a reservation of rights? Could a bad faith claim be made if an insurer sent out a reservation of rights letter to an insured without first investigating the claim?

4. Assume the insurer alleges that it investigated the accident but was unable to determine its exact location, because all of the witnesses had been drinking and the accident occurred in the evening. Would that change your opinion about the viability of a breach of contract claim? Bad faith?

5. Does the existence of a map, distributed by the insurer, affect your analysis?

6. How reasonable would it be for Dick's attorney to argue that nautical rather than statute miles should be used to determine the extent of coverage?

CASE

Shobe v. Kelly and Allstate Insurance Company
279 S.W.3d 203, (Mo.App. W.D.,2009)

THOMAS H. NEWTON, Chief Judge.

Allstate Insurance Company (Allstate) and Roxanne Kelly, an Allstate insurance adjuster, appeal from a denial of their motion for judgment notwithstanding the verdict (JNOV), or in the alternative for a new trial. The jury found for Quinlock Shobe, an Allstate insured, on her claim for bad faith failure to settle and awarded her actual and punitive damages. We reverse in part and affirm in part.

FACTUAL AND PROCEDURAL BACKGROUND

We give deference to the jury's role and state the facts most favorable to its verdict. *Overcast v. Billings Mut. Ins. Co.*, 11 S.W.3d 62, 64 n. 2 (Mo. banc 2000). Ms. Shobe had an auto insurance policy with Allstate. Because she worked as a personal care attendant for the elderly and sometimes drove her clients' vehicles, she

had sought a policy providing liability coverage when she drove a client's car. Her Allstate policy provided liability coverage on "non-owned" vehicles. Ms. Shobe began having mechanical trouble with her Dodge van. In late December 1997, L.C. Harris offered to sell her a 1992 Aerostar van. Ms. Shobe gave Mr. Harris $500 as a down payment, and he allowed her to keep the van for a test drive.

Before she had finalized the transaction, Ms. Shobe called her Allstate agent, told him she was considering buying the Aerostar, and inquired about the premium cost. The agent explained that there was a problem with the identification number on the paperwork and asked her for the VIN number, but Ms. Shobe could not locate it on the van. Ms. Shobe told the agent she would ask Mr. Harris to explain the discrepancy. While still trying

(continues)

to locate Mr. Harris, in January of 1998 Ms. Shobe had an accident while driving the Aerostar. The accident injured three pedestrians: Altha Lott and her two children (the Lotts).

Ms. Shobe reported the accident to Allstate. Ms. Kelly was assigned to the claim. She contacted Ms. Shobe and took a recorded statement. In the statement, Ms. Kelly did not tell Ms. Shobe that there were any concerns with coverage of the accident. In the beginning of March, Ms. Kelly sent a letter to a claimant stating, "We do not have coverage for this accident." At the end of March, Ms. Kelly noted in her claims activity log that she had contacted in-house counsel and advised she did not feel the accident should be covered. In April, Ms. Kelly sent a letter to counsel for Truman Medical Center stating that there was no coverage for the accident, but she was still investigating. In her subsequent deposition, Ms. Kelly admitted that she presumed Ms. Shobe had no coverage. She testified that she made a conclusive determination that there was no coverage prior to speaking with a lawyer. Ms. Kelly also admitted she did not consider Ms. Shobe's financial interests.

Subsequently, Ms. Kelly contacted an attorney whom Allstate used as outside counsel. She sent him the file, including her claim log with her findings on coverage. In May, outside counsel gave Allstate a letter opining that Ms. Shobe's accident was not covered by her policy. He promised a "more formal report" after an examination of Ms. Shobe under oath and noted that if Ms. Shobe did not cooperate, this would be "an additional basis for denial of coverage." No legal citations or references were included in the letter. In July, Ms. Kelly noted "[c]overage will remain denied." In October, after examining Ms. Shobe under oath without counsel, outside counsel gave Allstate a second letter stating his opinion that the accident was not covered. He noted that Ms. Shobe was a 53-year-old African-American woman who had lived in Kansas City all her life, had ten children, and worked as a nurse. This second opinion letter also included no legal citation or reference other than discussion of the policy.[1] In November, Allstate informed Ms. Shobe that it would not cover the accident.

The Lotts subsequently filed suit against Ms. Shobe for their injuries. In February of 1999, Allstate made a decision to defend the suit under a reservation of rights and to file an action for a declaratory judgment; it later retracted this decision. In June of 2000, the Lotts sent

a letter offering to settle their claims for Ms. Shobe's policy limit of $50,000. The next day, Allstate's outside counsel replied to the Lotts that Allstate's policy did not cover the accident and Allstate would not settle the case. Allstate's counsel later testified that he gave no regard for Ms. Shobe's financial interests because "it was not a proper factor." Judgment was subsequently entered for the Lotts against Ms. Shobe for $138,339.20.

The Lotts filed an equitable garnishment action to collect the underlying $50,000 policy limit from Allstate. The circuit court found Ms. Shobe's liability for the accident was covered under her Allstate policy because the Aerostar was a "non-owned" vehicle. Allstate appealed. This court also held that Ms. Shobe's accident was covered under her Allstate policy. *Lott v. Allstate Ins. Co.*, 131 S.W.3d 439 (Mo.App. W.D.2004). Thereafter, Allstate paid the policy limit of $50,000 and accumulated interest to the Lotts. However, $124,341.03 was still owed on the Lotts' claim, with interest accumulating at nine percent.[2] Ms. Shobe became concerned about losing her home and having her wages garnished; she went to speak to a bankruptcy attorney. The bankruptcy attorney testified that Ms. Shobe did not understand the circumstances that led to the judgment, and he took her to see a plaintiff's attorney.

In 2005, Ms. Shobe filed suit against Allstate and Ms. Kelly, alleging a bad faith failure to settle in violation of their fiduciary duty to Ms. Shobe as an insured. At trial, Ms. Shobe offered an insurance claims adjuster as an expert witness. He stated that Ms. Kelly's claims diary showed a preconceived intent to deny coverage before fully investigating the claim. Making a "no coverage" decision before investigating the claim, he asserted, destroyed the relationship of trust and protection between an insured and an insurer. He further stated that there was no rational basis for Allstate's attorney to reference Ms. Shobe's race, gender, and the number of her children in his coverage opinion. He explained standard options for insurance companies where policy coverage was in doubt were to provide a defense under a reservation of rights or to file a declaratory judgment action. He testified further that Allstate's failure to consider Ms. Shobe's financial interests deviated significantly from industry standards.

A trial attorney who had represented insurers and insureds also testified as an expert witness for Ms. Shobe. He asserted that an insurer starts with a presumption of coverage and that there is a fiduciary relationship between an insurer and an insured. From his review of the files, the attorney asserted that Ms. Kelly made a

---

1. In the letter, counsel opined the accident was not covered because Ms. Shobe was not driving the vehicle listed on her declarations page, and he believed the Aerostar did not fit the policy definition of a "replacement auto, additional auto, substitute auto, or non-owned auto."

2. At trial the outstanding amount with interest was $160,338.86.

(continues)

determination of no coverage before she ever consulted with counsel, and then she communicated that conclusion to counsel. He did not believe there had been any reasonable basis for denying coverage to Ms. Shobe and that Ms. Kelly sought legal advice only to justify her preconceived opinion.

A mortgage banker, also testifying as an expert witness, explained that Ms. Shobe had perfect credit but that the judgment placed her in a subprime loan category and, paid or unpaid, would affect her credit history for ten years. Ms. Shobe's mortgage and auto loans were being charged interest at almost twice the market rate. He also testified to the effect of a judgment on insurance premiums and the ability to obtain insurance, as well as on the ability to obtain financing. Ms. Shobe then offered evidence that Allstate's net profit for 2006 was $4.9 billion and its net worth was $21.8 billion.

Allstate and Ms. Kelly did not offer rebuttal experts at trial. Allstate's outside counsel testified that his firm sought unsuccessfully to find Mr. Harris, thinking that his insurance on the Aerostar might provide coverage. He also testified that Allstate was a repeat client, that he was interested in keeping its business, and that Allstate liked to have advice of counsel documented so there would not be criticism when a claim was paid. Ms. Kelly testified to her involvement in the case.

The jury found for Ms. Shobe on all claims and awarded $500,000 in actual damages and $500,000 in punitive damages. Allstate and Ms. Kelly moved for JNOV or, in the alternative, for a new trial. The motion was denied and this appeal followed.

STANDARD OF REVIEW

Allstate and Ms. Kelly assert five points on appeal assigning error to the trial court's denial of their posttrial motion and entry of judgment on the jury's verdict. Whether Ms. Shobe made a submissible case is a question of law we review de novo. *Rinehart v. Shelter Gen. Ins. Co.,* 261 S.W.3d 583, 595 (Mo.App. W.D.2008). We accept the plaintiff's evidence as true, disregard the defendants' contradictory evidence, and draw all inferences in favor of the plaintiff's case. Id. We also review de novo whether evidence is substantial and whether inferences drawn from it are reasonable. *Johnson v. Allstate Ins. Co.,* 262 S.W.3d 655, 661–62 (Mo.App. W.D.2008). We reverse the jury's verdict for insufficient evidence only where there was a complete lack of probative fact to support its conclusion. Id. at 662.

LEGAL ANALYSIS

In their first point on appeal, Ms. Kelly and Allstate contend that no cause of action for the tort of bad faith failure to settle (BFFS) lies against an insurance claims

adjuster. The parties acknowledge no case is dispositive on whether Missouri recognizes a cause of action against an insurance claims adjuster, as opposed to an insurance company, for the tort of BFFS. Ms. Kelly and Allstate assert that because the adjuster is not in privity of contract with the insured, there can be no fiduciary duty implied in tort. Ms. Shobe contends that the fiduciary duty arises from the relationship of trust, not the contract.

The tort of BFFS was initially recognized by the Missouri Supreme Court in *Zumwalt v. Utilities Insurance Co.,* 360 Mo. 362, 228 S.W.2d 750 (1950). An insurer under a liability policy has a fiduciary duty to its insured to evaluate and negotiate third-party claims in good faith. *Duncan v. Andrew County Mut. Ins. Co.,* 665 S.W.2d 13, 18 (Mo.App. W.D.1983). Where it wrongfully breaches this duty and refuses to settle within policy limits, the insurer may be held liable for resulting losses to the insured. *Id.* The tort presupposes that the tortfeasor is the insurer and has the power to settle the claim.

Our review of the record shows that to the extent Ms. Kelly had an opportunity to settle the claims through her employment with Allstate, she was acting as Allstate's agent, not as a principal. Ms. Kelly did not personally control the settlement, she did not have the individual capacity to settle the claims, nor did she represent that she had such capacity. Any settlement monies were not her funds; she was functioning solely as an agent of her employer. Thus, she cannot be held personally liable in this case. Point one is granted, and the order denying JNOV against Ms. Kelly is reversed.

Bad Faith Failure to Settle

In its second point, Allstate argues that the tort of BFFS requires four discrete elements and that Ms. Shobe failed to satisfy two of them. At the trial level, Allstate made this same argument when objecting to the verdict director. The instruction premised Allstate's liability on a finding that Allstate: (1) had the opportunity to settle within policy limits, (2) acted in bad faith through its refusal to do so, and (3) such failure caused damage to Ms. Shobe.

In responding to Allstate's objection, the trial court noted that the enumerated elements argued by Allstate appeared to emerge in Dyer, a first-party disability insurance case, which was factually distinct from Ms. Shobe's case. See *Dyer v. Gen. Am. Life Ins. Co.,* 541 S.W.2d 702, 705 (Mo.App.1976); see also *Duncan,* 665 S.W.2d at 19 (BFFS is not a cause of action in a first-party insurance case because there is no fiduciary relationship). After reviewing cases offered by the parties, the trial court found it was obligated to follow Missouri Supreme Court

(continues)

and Western District cases, which had not limited the tort to these four discrete elements.

In Dyer, while determining that BFFS did not apply to first-party claims, the court stated without citation:

The elements of the tort appear to be that: (1) the liability insurer has assumed control over negotiation, settlement, and legal proceedings brought against the insured; (2) the insured has demanded that the insurer settle the claim brought against the insured; (3) the insurer refuses to settle the claim within the liability limits of the policy; and (4) in so refusing, the insurer acts in bad faith, rather than negligently.

541 S.W.2d at 704 (emphasis added). Allstate argues that Ms. Shobe failed to show that it assumed control of the proceedings or that Ms. Shobe made a demand on Allstate to settle the claim.

What Allstate fails to recognize is that in this case, Allstate never provided a defense to Ms. Shobe, even under a reservation of rights. We cannot reward Allstate's refusal to provide a defense by insulating it from a BFFS claim.[3] Also, as to the demand that the insurer settle the claim, here Allstate had full knowledge of the Lotts' demand to settle within the policy limits. Allstate argues that it was entitled also to a demand letter from Ms. Shobe or her attorney, but Allstate had rejected all responsibility toward Ms. Shobe, informed her that it was providing no coverage for the accident, and thus was in no position to criticize her failure to reiterate the demand of which Allstate was already aware.

When our Supreme Court recognized BFFS, it found that the wrong committed was the insurer's intentional disregard of the duty it owed to its insured. *See Zumwalt*, 228 S.W.2d at 754. "The insurance company incurs liability exposure…when the company refuses to settle a claim within the policy limits and the insured is subjected to a judgment in excess of the policy limits as a result of the company's bad faith in disregarding the interests of its insured in hopes of escaping its responsibility under the liability policy." *Overcast*, 11 S.W.3d at 67–68. Whether an insurer acted in bad faith is determined in each case "upon its particular state of facts." *Zumwalt*, 228 S.W.2d at 754; *see Johnson*, 262 S.W.3d at 662 (discussing *Zumwalt* and listing circumstances which may show bad faith); *Truck Ins. Exch. v. Prairie Framing, LLC*, 162 S.W.3d 64, 94 (Mo.App. W.D.2005) (the "obligation to act in good faith regarding settlement

continues even if an insurer denies coverage and refuses to defend the insured").

The tort creates liability in order to compensate an insured where she has been wrongly subjected to an excess judgment, and to deter insurance companies from failing to fulfill fiduciary duties to their insureds. *See Truck Ins. Exch.,* 162 S.W.3d at 93. Allstate's position requires liability to be premised on procedural steps-the assumption of control of legal proceedings by the insurer, the making of a demand by the insured-which are not likely to occur where the insurer completely rejects its fiduciary duties. If an insurer wrongly denies coverage, denies even a defense under a reservation of rights, and then completely refuses to engage in settlement negotiations, it cannot avoid liability by its wrongful refusal to assume control of the proceedings. Similarly, if an insurer wrongly denies any responsibility for a claim, it cannot avoid liability because the insured fails to make a futile demand that the insurer provide funds for a settlement offer of which it is already aware. Given Allstate's blanket rejection of responsibility to its insured, we cannot find that the trial court erred in denying Allstate's post-trial motions on this issue. Consequently, Allstate's second point is denied.

Showing of Bad Faith

In its third point, Allstate asserts that bad faith was not proven by sufficient and substantial evidence because, it argues, it acted in good faith by performing an adequate investigation and seeking outside legal opinion. Even if its actions were in error, it contends, it was at most negligent.

An insurer's bad faith is a state of mind. *Johnson*, 262 S.W.3d at 662. The jury may find bad faith on direct evidence, or it may infer bad faith from circumstantial evidence. *Rinehart*, 261 S.W.3d at 595. Examples of bad faith include: failing to fully investigate a third-party claimant's injuries or recognize their severity, ignoring that a verdict could exceed policy limits, refusing to consider a settlement offer, and not keeping an insured informed of settlement offers or the risks of an excess judgment. *Johnson*, 262 S.W.3d at 662. Limiting an investigation to the question of coverage, then standing on a denial without considering the interests of an insured also shows bad faith. *Landie v. Century Indem. Co.*, 390 S.W.2d 558, 566 (Mo.App.1965).

Ms. Shobe offered evidence for the jury to infer that Allstate: (1) concluded that Ms. Shobe had no coverage before investigating, while at the same time Ms. Kelly admitted knowing of cases requiring coverage on similar facts, as well as admitted that she started with a presumption of no coverage and that for the insurer do so is to act in bad faith; (2) denied coverage to persons

---

3. Had Allstate defended under a reservation of rights, it would have preserved more opportunity to protect against a BFFS claim. The duty to defend is broader than the duty to indemnify. *Am. States Ins. Co. v. Herman C. Kempker Const. Co.*, 71 S.W.3d 232, 236 (Mo. App. W.D.2002).

(continues)

injured in the accident before full investigation;
(3) accepted legal conclusions from outside counsel
that Ms. Shobe had no coverage without legal citation
or reference; (4) ignored Ms. Shobe's financial interests
and made no inquiry as to the extent of the plaintiffs'
injuries or the risk Ms. Shobe would be subjected to if a
suit were carried forward; and (5) rejected a settlement
offer within policy limits without consulting Ms. Shobe
or considering the damage to her interests—even while
considering defending under a reservation of rights,
thus implying that coverage was in doubt. The jury also
heard evidence that where an insurer has a good faith
question as to its obligations, seeking a declaratory
judgment is an "adequate remedy." *See id.* at 567. From
these facts, the jury could conclude that Allstate acted
in bad faith by seeking to avoid payment of the policy
rather than honoring its duty to its insured.

Allstate correctly asserts that bad faith requires more
than an erroneous denial of coverage. At trial, Allstate
argued that it made a mistake, only an error in opinion,
where reasonable minds could differ. "Of course if that
was their honest opinion, then that would be a good
defense," our Supreme Court wrote in *Zumwalt*, "but
that would be a question for the jury." 228 S.W.2d at
754. Consequently, Allstate's third point is denied.

ACTUAL DAMAGES AWARD

In its fourth point on appeal, Allstate argues that the trial
court erred in denying its post-trial motion because the
actual damages awarded by the jury were excessive.[4] It
asserts that the damages on a BFFS claim are limited to
the amount an insured was forced to pay on the unsettled
claim. Second, while Allstate concedes that the unsat-
isfied amount of the excess judgment—approximately
$160,000[5]—as well as Ms. Shobe's attorney fees in the
underlying case with the Lotts—$1,500—were both recov-
erable and proven with sufficient evidence, it contends
that the actual damages award of $500,000 was excessive
because it goes beyond these amounts and was not supported by substantial evidence.

We do not agree with Allstate that damages for BFFS
are limited to the amount due on the unsettled third-
party claim. No case cited by Allstate states such a rule.
BFFS is a tort action based on the insurer's failure to
protect the interests of its insured, not an action on the
insurance contract. *See Overcast*, 11 S.W.3d at 67. In
tort, the insurer is liable for the damages proximately
caused by its bad faith. *Landie*, 390 S.W.2d at 565–66.
The insured is entitled to be made whole and damages

should "put the insured into the same position as if
the company had performed its obligations under the
policy." *Truck Ins. Exch.*, 162 S.W.3d at 93.

Second, the assessment of damages is in the province
of the jury. *Knifong v. Caterpillar, Inc.*, 199 S.W.3d 922,
927 (Mo.App. W.D.2006). We interfere only if "the
verdict is so grossly excessive that it shocks the conscience." *Harrell v. Cochran*, 233 S.W.3d 254, 258
(Mo.App. W.D.2007) (internal quotation marks and
citation omitted). Thus, our interference is "with hesi-
tation and only when the verdict is manifestly unjust."
McCormack v. Capital Elec. Constr. Co., 159 S.W.3d 387,
395 (Mo.App. W.D.2004). Each case is considered on
its own facts. *Id.* at 395. Considerations may include
pecuniary losses, the nature and extent of a plaintiff's
injuries, awards in comparable cases, the jury and trial
court's superior opportunity to evaluate damages, and
intangibles that do not lend themselves to easy calculation. *Id.* Here, given the ten years of litigation Ms. Shobe
has undergone; her fears of bankruptcy; her economic
losses in credit, interest rates, and insurance; as well as
other "intangibles" not easily calculated, we do not find
that the jury's award was manifestly unjust. As a result,
Allstate's fourth point is denied.

PUNITIVE DAMAGES AWARD

In its final point, Allstate contests the jury's award of
punitive damages, asserting that Ms. Shobe failed to
make the required showing. A punitive damages award
requires more than the showing for bad faith. *Zumwalt*,
228 S.W.2d at 756. The plaintiff must present "clear
and convincing evidence that the defendant's conduct
was outrageous because of evil motive or reckless indifference." *Rinehart*, 261 S.W.3d at 596–97. Clear and
convincing evidence establishes the character of the
defendant's actions to a "high probability." *Id.* at 597.

We find that the evidence Ms. Shobe offered to show
Allstate's bad faith was also sufficient to carry this higher
burden for punitive damages. Punitive damages are justified where the evidence supports an inference that the
insurer acted with reckless indifference to the interests
of its insured. *Johnson*, 262 S.W.3d at 666. Ms. Kelly
testified that Allstate did not consider Ms. Shobe's interests as its insured; it was irrelevant to the company's
coverage decision. Ms. Shobe also offered evidence that
the "no coverage decision" was made before investigation, confirmed without adequate investigation, and
was made contrary to existing law—leaving Ms. Shobe
wrongly exposed to a judgment far in excess of her policy limits. These facts were sufficient for the jury to infer
reckless indifference. *See id.*

In addition, Ms. Shobe offered evidence of Allstate's
correspondence about her age, race, the number of her

---

4. Appellants did not seek remittitur at the trial court.

5. This amount continues to accrue interest at the rate of nine percent.

(continues)

CASE (CONTINUED)

children, and her occupation. At trial, Ms. Shobe asked the jury to infer that Allstate denied coverage because it presumed she did not have the resources to challenge its decision. In closing, plaintiff's counsel argued:

And about [Allstate's attorney], who remember, is not writing his coverage letter for Ms. Kelly; he's writing his letter for the bigwigs at Allstate....And he says he's just describing Ms. Shobe, and she's a 50- or 60-year-old woman and she has ten children and he tells about her race and she says, she says that she's working as a CNA.

What is he telling Allstate? What is he telling people in the management? It's Allstate code for she won't have

the resources to fight the denial. That's what that was about.

The jury had a basis to find that Allstate acted with reckless indifference to Ms. Shobe's interests as its insured. We see no reason to disturb its verdict. Allstate's fifth point is denied.

CONCLUSION

We reverse the portion of the trial court's order denying JNOV for Ms. Kelly and otherwise affirm the decision.

JAMES M. SMART, JR., and VICTOR C. HOWARD, JJ., concur.

Although the equal-consideration test varies somewhat from jurisdiction to jurisdiction, the concept is illustrated in *General Accident Fire & Life Assurance Corp. v. Little*, 443 P.2d 690 (Ariz. 1968). Eight factors deemed important to the Little court in determining whether the insurer had given equal consideration to its insured were (also see Exhibit 18–4):

1. The relative strength of the injured party's claim in reference to the issues of liability and damages against the insured.

2. The insurer's failure to properly investigate the claim so as to determine the availability of relevant evidence.

3. The insurer's failure to advise its insured of an offer to settle within policy limits.

4. The insurer's failure to follow the advice of its own attorney or agent.

5. The extent of the financial risk to its insured if the insurer refused to settle.

6. Any attempt by the insurer to get the insured to contribute to the settlement.

7. Any action by the insured that might have influenced the insurer to reject any compromise settlement offers.

8. Any other factors that might support or disprove bad faith on the part of the insurer.

A third-party bad faith claim does not have to have elements of each of these considerations.

Read the *Little* case before you do Putting It Into Practice 18–2.

DECLARATORY JUDGMENT ACTIONS

Insurance carriers will often institute a declaratory judgment action to determine if coverage exists. In a **declaratory judgment action** the court renders an opinion with respect to a matter of law or with regard to the rights of the parties, but orders no action to be taken. Such an action can serve both defensive as well as offensive purposes. Offensively, a declaratory judgment action can serve to determine that no coverage exists and that the insurer need not defend or

EXHIBIT 18–4 Equal-Consideration Factors for Third-Party Claims

- Relative strength of injured party's claims in reference to issues of liability and damages against insured
- Insurer's failure to properly investigate claim so as to determine availability of relevant evidence
- Insurer's failure to advise insured of offer to settle within policy limits
- Insurer's failure to follow advice of its attorney or agent
- Extent of financial risk to insured if insurer refused to settle
- Attempt by insurer to get insured to contribute to settlement
- Action by insured that might have influenced insurer to reject any compromise settlement offers
- Any other factors that might support or disprove bad faith on the party of insurer

PUTTING IT INTO PRACTICE 18:2

1. Does the *Little* court appear, at first, to favor the position of the insurer?

2. At the time *Little* was decided, contributory negligence was a complete defense; comparative negligence was not in existence. Do you believe that the insurer really thought that there was only a 40 percent chance for a plaintiff's verdict? (The insurer admitted that the plaintiff could make out a prima facie case.)

3. What was the court really saying when it stated, "General and its attorney were being less than realistic when they estimated a potential verdict at a low of $3,000 and a high of $10,000"?

4. Does the outcome of *Little* turn on the court's perception of the credibility of the insurer and its attorney in evaluating the case? If so, is mere negligence, in this case, grounds for a finding of bad faith?

compensate its insured. Defensively, such an action allows a carrier to dispute coverage, as well as to go before a court hoping that the potential for a bad faith claim will be minimized by its efforts to obtain a judicial determination of its position.

LOCAL LINKS

Where are the rules for declaratory actions found in your state? Are they statutory, rules of procedure, or both?

UNINSURED AND UNDERINSURED MOTORIST COVERAGE

Uninsured motorist (UM) and underinsured motorist (UIM) coverage has characteristics of both first-party and third-party claims. One first-party characteristic is that the insurer is obligated to make payment directly to the insured. A third-party characteristic is that the insurer stands in the shoes of the allegedly responsible party. As such the insurer can assert any defense that the responsible party might have, including comparative or contributory negligence, assumption of risk, and denial of liability.

LOCAL LINKS

Are UM and UIM claims treated as first-party claims in your state?

Most UM and UIM policies prohibit the insured from suing her carrier over the issue of damages. If an insurer and its insured cannot reach agreement with respect to damages, the matter is submitted to arbitration. The issue of coverage, however, is not subject to arbitration in most UM and UIM policies. Coverage is determined in a separate lawsuit.

Because many states require automobile policies to provide UM and UIM coverage, some argue that carriers should have to meet the standard appropriate for third-party claims. Most courts, however, view UM and UIM claims as first-party claims. As first-party claims, the maximum benefit due an insured as a result of an insurer's breach of its contractual

PUTTING IT INTO PRACTICE 18:3

1. Why might Dick's and Jerry's insurer want to file a declaratory judgment action and seek a court ruling finding no coverage for the accident?

2. Would the value of the declaratory judgment action be the same if the insurer waited until after Jerry filed suit against it or Dick?

3. The insurer has the burden of proof in a declaratory judgment action. Does that burden affect your analysis of whether the insurer should file such an action? On its timing?

obligations is the policy limits. If a UM or UIM claim is fairly debatable, most courts hold that the insurer is not liable to its insured on the basis of bad faith.

UM and UIM carriers have tried to convince the courts that because they stand in the shoes of the allegedly responsible party, an adversarial relationship exists between them and their insureds. This argument, for the most part, has been rejected. The courts have, however, reasoned that bad faith has not occurred if the liability of the allegedly responsible party is reasonably in question and the amount of damages that must be paid the insured is reasonably disputed.

PUTTING IT INTO PRACTICE   18:4

1. Does Jerry have a first-party claim? More than one?

2. If Dick is denied coverage, most states (and insurance policies) would deem him an uninsured motorist. Does that fact influence how the insurer would react to a claim by Jerry (i.e., denial of coverage, defend under a reservation of rights, or tender an unconditional defense)?

3. If Jerry eventually went to trial and it was determined that Dick's policy provided coverage for the accident, could Jerry then make an underinsured motorist claim?

SUMMARY

Bad faith is an intentional tort that occurs when a party to an insurance contract breaches its implied covenant of good faith and fair dealing. Most cases of bad faith involve allegations against the insurance carrier. Bad faith arises when the insurer (1) wrongly refuses to provide coverage for a client, (2) fails to adequately investigate a claim before making its decision to deny coverage or pay only a portion of the insured's claim, or (3) unreasonably refuses to settle a third-party claim within the limits of the insured's policy.

In most jurisdictions the standard of care owed to an insured by the insurer depends on whether the case is a first- or third-party claim. In first-party claims, some jurisdictions use the "fairly debatable" standard. Under that standard, if a claim submitted by an insured is fairly debatable the insurer's actions in refusing to pay the claim will not constitute bad faith. For third-party claims, most courts impose a higher duty on the insurer. This higher duty, sometimes referred to as an "equality of consideration" standard, requires the insurer to give the same consideration to the insured's interests as it does to its own.

In most jurisdictions something more than mere negligence is required before the courts will find that the insurer has violated its implied covenant of good faith and fair dealing.

The position of an insured varies depending on whether the insurer denies coverage or defends the insured under a reservation of rights. The insured is able to negotiate an agreement more freely with an injured party when coverage of the claim is denied. He may still be able to work out an agreement with the injured party when the insurer is defending him under a reservation of rights. The insured does, however, have greater obligations to the insurer, including a duty to advise the insurer of the agreement so that the insurer can withdraw its reservation of rights before the agreement becomes effective.

UM and UIM coverage has aspects of both first- and third-party claims. Most jurisdictions treat UM and UIM claims as first-party claims. UM and UIM policies generally prohibit suit over the issue of damages, but the issue of coverage is often resolved in a declaratory judgment action.

KEY TERMS

adhesion contract
   Standardized contract characterized by the unequal bargaining power of the parties and the lack of negotiation regarding the terms of the contract

declaratory judgment action
   Action in which the court renders an opinion as to a matter of law or in reference to the rights of the parties but does not order any action to be taken

excess judgment
   Judgment for more than the insured's policy limits

REVIEW QUESTIONS

1. How is bad faith committed?
2. What are the characteristics of an adhesion contract?
3. What are the two types of bad faith, and how do they differ?
4. What part of an excess judgment is the insured liable for?
5. What is a reservation of rights?
6. What might an insured do to protect herself from an excess judgment?
7. What damages can be awarded in a third-party bad faith action?
8. What damages can be awarded in a first-party bad faith action?
9. "Fairly debatable" is a standard in what type of bad faith action?
10. "Equal consideration" is a standard in what type of bad faith action?
11. When and for what purpose would an insurer file a declaratory judgment action against its insured?
12. Are UM and UIM actions considered first-party or third-party actions?

PRACTICE EXAM

Students should complete the practice exam after studying each chapter. The answers are in Appendix A. If you score lower than 80%, you should reread the materials.

True-False

1. The tort of bad faith is an intentional tort.
2. The tort of bad faith is always based on a breach of a contract.
3. An adhesion contract results from uneven bargaining power between the parties concerning specific, negotiated, provisions.
4. In response to contracts of adhesion the courts developed a rule of law that the contract be interpreted in favor of the party that did not draft the contract.
5. A contract provision that can be reasonably be interpreted in more than one way is considered "ambiguous."
6. A third-party claim occurs when there are at least three plaintiffs.
7. A first-party claim involves only the one plaintiff and one defendant.
8. An excess judgment occurs when the jury awards too much money to the plaintiff.
9. A defendant against whom an excess judgment has been awarded often assigns his rights against his insurer to the plaintiff.
10. The insurer is held to a higher standard of care in third-party cases than in first-party cases.

Fill-in-the-Blanks

1. A(n) _____ _____ is characterized by uneven bargaining power and lack of negotiation of terms.
2. An insurer will file a(n) _____ _____ action to have the court determine if there is coverage under an insurance contract.
3. When an injured party obtains a verdict that is more than the insured's policy limits, it is called a(n) _____ _____.

Multiple Choice

1. Which of the following are acts constituting of the tort of bad faith?
   a. the insurance carrier unreasonably delays payment.
   b. the insurance carrier act unconscionably toward its insured.
   c. the insurance carrier engages in unfair claims practices.
   d. all of the above.
2. Under the "reasonable expectations" doctrine,
   a. the court expects both parties to be reasonable.
   b. the court will reform the contract to meet the reasonable expectation of the nondrafter of the contract.

c. the court will interpret the contract to give the nondrafter what he expected he was getting.

d. none of the above.

3. An action in which the insured is seeking payment from her insurer is called
   a. a class action suit.
   b. a first-party claim.
   c. a bad faith claim.
   d. a breach of contract action.

4. An action in which an injured party makes a claim against an insured for damages covered by the insured's policy is called
   a. a first-party claim.
   b. a bad faith claim.
   c. a breach of contract action.
   d. none of the above.

5. A reservation of rights is
   a. found in the Fourteenth Amendment to the United States Constitution.
   b. the act of an insured in first-party claim.
   c. the act of an insurer in initially providing a defense to its insured but advising the insured it may withdraw the defense at a later time.
   d. none of the above.

6. Bad faith can occur even if an insurer acknowledges coverage and provides a defense if
   a. it refuses to settle for policy limits.
   b. it evaluates the case as having a value above policy limits but refuses to settle and then will not pay the excess judgment.
   c. it requires the insured to allow a deposition to be taken and demands the insured's presence at trial.
   d. none of the above.

7. Damages in third-party cases include
   a. the amount of the judgment in excess of policy limits.
   b. the legal fees incurred by the third-party in the name of the insured.
   c. other, provable, monetary losses that caused the insurer's actions.
   d. all of the above.

8. Damages in first-party cases include
   a. the amount of the judgment in excess of policy limits.
   b. the legal fees incurred by the third-party making the claim.
   c. unpaid benefits provided in the contract.
   d. all of the above.

9. The general standard of care in third-party cases is that
   a. the claim must be "fairly debatable."
   b. the insurer must give equal consideration to its insured.
   c. the insurer must give greater consideration to its insured than to its own self-interest.
   d. none of the above.

10. In a declaratory judgment action, the court
    a. determines what the amount of the judgment should be.
    b. declares judgment for or against a third party.
    c. in the insurance context makes a determination as to whether there is or is not coverage.
    d. none of the above.

11. An uninsured motorist coverage claim is generally treated as a
    a. first-party claim.
    b. third-party claim.
    c. second-party claim.
    d. none of the above.

12. Uninsured and underinsured motorist claims are usually
    a. mediated.
    b. litigated in court.
    c. arbitrated.
    d. none of the above.

PRACTICE POINTERS

Bad faith cases are very fact-intensive. What the insurer did, and when it did it, is as important as what the insurer knew at the time it took action. Most insurers maintain what is known as a *claims file*. The claims file should contain all notes and memoranda prepared by the adjuster, along with copies of all correspondence and attachments. Care must be taken when documents are requested from an insurer. Because each company has its own way of handling claims, merely requesting the claims file may not result in the production of all of the documents you want. If, for example, an adjuster's case evaluation and the amount of reserve set aside for a claim is maintained in a special file, a request for the claims file, and its subsequent production, will not contain all relevant information.

Another fertile area of dispute is trial preparation materials. Because an insurance carrier is often involved in litigation, it can and often does argue that everything

it does in handling a claim is in preparation for trial. That argument has not been completely successful. Because the insurance business deals, to a great extent, with handling claims, the courts have rejected the position that all acts in adjusting a claim are in preparation for trial. Once it becomes clear that litigation will result, subsequent documents may not be subject to discovery. If your jurisdiction follows the *Federal Rules of Civil Procedure*, review Rule 26.

Review some of the reported bad faith cases for the past few years in your jurisdiction. Try to find a case that refers to a discovery dispute relating to trial preparation or attorney-client materials. Go to the trial court file and review the arguments submitted by each side. There will probably be a motion for a protective order or a motion to compel discovery. The documents that were requested, and that created the dispute, should be set out in the pleadings.

TORT TEASERS

Review the hypothetical scenario at the beginning of this chapter and answer the following questions.

1. What is the significance of the insurer providing its insureds with maps showing that the Rocky Point area is within forty-eight statute miles of the United States border?

2. Can Jerry use these maps to prevent the insurer from alleging that the accident occurred more than fifty statute miles from the United States border?

3. Would your answer to the preceding question be different if Jerry testified that not only was he unaware of the maps issued by his insurer, but he was also unaware at the time of the accident that he had coverage for medical payment expenses and UM in Mexico?

4. How do the insurer's actions in obtaining an expert to determine the location of the accident affect your analysis of whether bad faith has been committed?

5. If the insurer hires experts and denies coverage prior to a bad faith suit being instituted, does that change your evaluation of Jerry's claim?

6. If the insurer institutes a declaratory judgment action before Jerry files his bad faith action, does that affect your opinion as to whether the insurer acted in bad faith?

7. The insurer argues that because it neither accepted nor denied Jerry's claim, it cannot be found to have acted in bad faith. How would you respond?

8. The insurer has determined that the accident occurred more than fifty statute miles from the United States border, so it has denied liability coverage to Dick and UM coverage to Jerry. Suppose Dick loses his coverage argument in the suit he institutes in the Colorado courts against his insurer. Is it possible that at the same time Jerry could win his case in the Arizona courts regarding his UM benefits?

9. What type of agreement could Dick enter into with Jerry upon denial by Dick's insurer that he had liability coverage for the accident?

10. With respect to each of the possible claims that Jerry and Dick may have, determine what type of coverage the claim would be made under and whether it would be a first- or third-party claim.

INTERNET INQUIRIES

The Meta-Index for United States Legal Research (http://gsulaw.gsu.edu/, select "MetaIndex" for U.S. Legal Research) allows you to search for United States Supreme Court and circuit court decisions, federal legislation, federal regulations, *Law Review* articles, and law professionals all at the same site. This site, which is hosted by the Georgia State University of Law, does more than provide links; it actually does searches for you. Because the Meta-Index uses a different index for each type of search, it provides a sample request with each index that allows you to see how that particular index works. This is probably as close to one-stop searching as you will ever get. Go to the Meta-Index and answer the following questions:

1. How many circuit court cases can you find in your jurisdiction relating to bad faith of insurance companies?

2. Find *Law Review* articles relating to bad faith, and give the citation of one that you find.

3. Find federal legislation relating to medical malpractice. Give the title and bill number of one of the bills you find as well as the date it was introduced.

PRACTICAL PONDERABLES

Your firm has agreed to represent Scott, an insured of XYZ Insurance Company. Scott was sued by a person injured in an automobile accident that Scott was responsible for. Scott's policy limits were $15,000 per person, $30,000 per accident. The jury returned a verdict against Scott for $50,000. XYZ paid for the defense of the suit and paid the plaintiff $15,000 after the verdict was entered. Scott wants to know what options he has. He will have to file for bankruptcy if he has to pay the excess judgment of $35,000. Your supervising attorneys want to find out if XYZ committed bad faith in not settling Scott's case.

1. What will you have to prove to show XYZ acted in bad faith?

2. Is an excess judgment always caused by bad faith?

3. What evidence will need to be presented if you are going to establish a cause of action for bad faith?

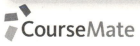

Access an interactive eBook, chapter-specific learning tools, including flashcards, quizzes, and more in your Paralegal CourseMate, accessed through www.CengageBrain.com.

CHAPTER 19

Workers' Compensation

© Cengage Learning 2012

CHAPTER OBJECTIVES

After completing the chapter, you should be able to

- Explain the historical basis for the workers' compensation system.

- Explain the statutory and administrative procedures followed in workers' compensation cases.

- Identify the requirements for filing a workers' compensation claim.

- Identify current workers' compensation issues.

Juan Lopez was a farm worker. While he was operating a small farm tractor in a cotton field near Phoenix, Arizona, a rock became lodged in a piece of equipment he was towing. Juan got off the tractor and attempted to dislodge the rock. He was unsuccessful in doing so manually and asked a co-worker to back the tractor a few inches. The co-worker, who was not familiar with the tractor, pulled forward, causing Juan's right foot to be run over by a tire on the equipment being pulled.

Juan was a sixty-five-year-old diabetic who had returned to work only five weeks prior to the accident. He had been out of work for seven months while recovering from a vascular bypass in his right leg, necessitated by his diabetes. The accident occurred at the height of the harvest season when Juan was working eighty to ninety hours per week (at $5.00 per hour).

The accident occurred late Sunday evening; on Monday Juan went to a doctor recommended by his employer and was treated for a swollen foot and minor abrasions. On Tuesday the foot became very painful and Juan went to the emergency room. On Friday Juan had the toenail removed from the big toe on his right foot. Four weeks later his big toe was amputated. Two months after that, his right leg was amputated just below the knee.

Juan's medical expenses totaled $84,000. His postoperative care, including prosthesis, came to $28,000. The initial physician charged $45 for the office visit and billed Juan's employer's workers' compensation carrier. Because Juan did not know what workers' compensation was, or that he had sustained an employment-related injury, his hospital and related expenses were charged to, and paid by, his personal medical insurer.

Juan was denied workers' compensation benefits for the loss of his leg. The carrier took the position that it was his diabetes, not the accident, that caused the loss of his leg. Juan's unfortunate experience affords us an opportunity to explore the intricate functioning of the workers' compensation system.

WHAT IS WORKERS' COMPENSATION?

Workers' compensation is a relatively new concept conceived to circumvent certain problems of the tort system and to protect workers who are injured, whether or not due to their own negligence. It also relieves employers from tort responsibility for on-the-job injuries to their employees. Workers' compensation systems were intended to provide fast and efficient relief to injured workers without regard to fault. In theory, an injured worker gave up her right to sue her employer (and the right to a jury) in return for the implied promise that her reasonable medical expenses would be taken care of and that she would be compensated for the wages she lost as a result of the injury.

What has actually evolved is a system that rivals the entire tort system in cost and has become so complicated that many states recognize workers' compensation as a legal specialty. Just as tort reform preoccupies legislative bodies on a regular (if not continuous) basis, rarely does a year go by that legislators do not tinker with workers' compensation statutes.

HISTORICAL BACKGROUND

Workers' compensation systems arose out of the industrial revolution of the nineteenth century. Hard physical labor with machines and equipment designed to perform tasks without regard for the protection of operators resulted in numerous injuries. The tort system of the time was ill-equipped, from the employee's standpoint at least, to handle the medical expenses and lost wages of injured workers. Several common law defenses were available to the employer, such as contributory negligence, assumption of risk, and the **fellow-servant rule** (which rendered an employer nonliable for an injury inflicted upon an employee through the negligence of a fellow employee, but made every employee liable to his fellow workers for his own negligence). Because of these defenses and the employer's superior financial position, injured workers had little chance to obtain compensation through the courts.

Even when the courts began to relax enforcement of the common law defenses, the injured worker, with no income and mounting medical expenses (if he was able to get treatment), stood in such an inferior financial position to his employer as to preclude an effective legal remedy. Employees (including those injured) were not eager to testify against their employers and face potential unemployment.

Beginning in Germany in the mid-1800s, in response to a growing public outcry about the way workers were treated, a system began to develop to take the issue of fault out of the workplace and provide benefits for injured workers. England adopted a "fault-less" system in the late 1800s and the United States,

PUTTING IT INTO PRACTICE 19:1

1. Would Juan be deemed to have opted in to the workers' compensation system in your state?

2. Does your state have voluntary or compulsory coverage?

beginning in the early 1900s, followed suit. Although the new concept initially faced, and lost, constitutional challenges, the issue was resolved in favor of a new, noncompulsory system by the United States Supreme Court in *New York Central Railroad v. White*, 243 U.S. 219 (1917). An earlier, compulsory version had been held to violate due process. Shortly thereafter, the vast majority of states adopted their own doctrines of workers' compensation. Today all states have a workers' compensation system.

The two major types of workers' compensation are mandatory coverage and voluntary coverage. In mandatory-coverage jurisdictions, the employee has no alternative other than to accept the benefits and restrictions imposed by the statutory framework adopted in her state. In voluntary-coverage jurisdictions, the employee may opt out of the system and retain her right to sue the employer in state court. Because most workers are unaware of what the system does or how it actually works, voluntary opting out is more illusory than real. Additionally, in most states if one accepts *any* benefits (medical expenses or lost wages), one is conclusively deemed to have opted in.

 LOCAL LINKS

In your state is the workers' compensation system mandatory or voluntary?

THE STATUTORY FRAMEWORK

What appears to be a straightforward goal—compensation of injured workers without regard to fault—has not been easily implemented. To process disputed or questioned claims outside of the court system, an entire administrative hierarchy had to be created. Judges and juries were replaced with administrative law judges or hearing officers. The rules of civil procedure were replaced and/or supplemented by administrative rules and regulations.

Exceptions to coverage for intentional or self-inflicted injuries and those caused by intoxication were grafted onto the framework. For example, in *Coleman*

v. Wyoming Workers' Compensation Division, 915 P.2d 595 (Wyo. 1996), the deceased worker's family was denied benefits based on the finding that his intoxication *contributed* to the accident, even though the decedent's inexperience in driving the vehicle actually caused the accident. Wyoming has a statute, similar to those of many other states, that prohibits recovery if intoxication of the worker is involved.

 LOCAL LINKS

In your state does voluntary intoxication act as a complete bar to recovery under the workers' compensation statutes?

Workers' compensation also has required that different types of injuries be scheduled and a fixed method of determining the amount of compensation to the worker be devised. In many states injuries such as loss of an eye, total blindness, or loss of an appendage are classified as **scheduled injuries**, that is, a fixed benefit (usually a set number of months' compensation) is paid for the injury without regard to lost wages or medical expenses. Some injuries, such as back injuries, produce varying types of symptoms and could not be scheduled as easily as, for example, the loss of an eye or a limb. New rules for these unscheduled injuries had to be created. Notice requirements and specialized forms were devised, and failure to use them (or to use them correctly) had potentially drastic implications for both the employer and the employee.

A new insurance industry was created to allow the employer to spread the risk of the new system. Employers who chose not to be insured (rules and regulations determined who could and could not self-insure) risked the loss of their businesses, as they became personally liable for the costs to which injured workers would become entitled. To cover that situation, most jurisdictions developed a fund that stepped in to cover the worker when his employer lacked insurance or the funds (or willingness) to pay the statutory sums due or when the employer's insurance carrier became insolvent.

NET NEWS

The workers' compensation laws, together with administrative rules and forms for the fifty states and the District of Columbia, as well as for federal employees, are available at **http://www.workerscompensation .com**.

PUTTING IT INTO PRACTICE / 19:2

How would your state treat Juan's injuries? Would the loss of his leg be scheduled?

TODAY'S SYSTEMS

A typical constitutional and statutory scheme for workers' compensation is found in Arizona. The state constitutional provision enabling the workers' compensation statutes is article XVIII, § 8, which states,

> The Legislature shall enact a Workers' Compensation Law applicable to workmen engaged in manual or mechanical labor in all public employment whether of the State, or any political subdivision or municipality thereof as may be defined by law and in such private employments as the Legislature may prescribe by which compensation shall be required to be paid to any such workman, in case of his injury and to his dependents, as defined by law, in case of his death, by his employer, if in the course of such employment personal injury to or death of any such workman from any accident arising out of and in the course of, such employment, is caused in whole, or in part, or is contributed to, by a necessary risk or danger of such employment, or a necessary risk or danger inherent in the nature thereof, or by failure of such employer, or any of his or its agents or employee or employees to exercise due care, or to comply with any law affecting such employment; provided that it shall be optional with any employee engaged in any such private employment to settle for such compensation, or to retain the right to sue said employer or any person employed by said employer, acting in the scope of his employment, as provided by this Constitution; and, provided further, in order to assure and make certain a just and humane compensation law in the State of Arizona, for the relief and protection of such workmen, their widows, children or dependents, as defined by law, from the burdensome, expensive and litigious remedies for injuries to or death of such workmen, now existing in the State of Arizona, and producing uncertain and unequal compensation therefore, such employee, engaged in such private employment, may exercise the option to settle for compensation by failing to reject the provisions of such Workmen's Compensation Law prior to the injury, except that if the injury is the result of an act done by the employer or a person employed by the employer knowingly and purposely with the direct object of injuring another, and the act indicates a willful disregard of the life, limb or bodily safety of employees, then such employee may, after the injury, exercise the option to accept compensation or to retain the right to sue the person who injured him.
>
> The percentages and amounts of compensation provided in House Bill No. 227 enacted by the Seventh Legislature of the State of Arizona, shall never be reduced nor any industry included within the provision of said House Bill No. 227 eliminated except by initiated or referred measure as provided by this Constitution.

The United States Supreme Court has held that workers' compensation statutes do not violate the due process clause. Nevertheless, each state has had to look to its own constitution to determine if a constitutional amendment was necessary to allow implementation. In Arizona an original constitutional provision prohibited abrogation of the right to sue. If the workers' compensation provision had not been a part of the original state constitution, a constitutional amendment to legalize the workers' compensation statutes would have been required.

In most jurisdictions, a governmental entity was created to administer the new laws. The Arizona Industrial Commission, for example, administers the workers' compensation system in Arizona. To date it has enacted sixty-four rules of procedure for workers' compensation hearings (Ariz. Admin. Code §§ R20-5-101 through R20-5-164). These rules, which supplement the statutory framework, must be followed by employee and employer alike. Failure to follow the rules often results in the loss of benefits or the right to contest the award. Some of the rules modify the normal procedure for obtaining witnesses (R20-5-141), the use of interrogatories (R20-5-144), and independent medical examinations (R20-5-144).

To get a feel for the complexity of the statutory framework and the morass of rules promulgated in workers' compensation statutes, go to http://www.workerscompensation.com and select your state. Review the statutes and rules regulating your workers' compensation system.

Is Workers' Compensation a Fair Deal?

The theoretical benefits anticipated by advocates of workers' compensation have not always been realized. Many of the roadblocks that existed in the early 1900s are no longer part of the American legal system. Unsafe working conditions, machinery without safety devices, and an employer-friendly tort system are not prevalent problems in today's workplace.

The bureaucracy that was birthed to solve the problems of the injured worker has created many new problems. To illustrate, state legislatures control the benefits to be paid and how they are to be calculated. Therefore, today's employers may have as much control over their employees as they did before the onset of workers' compensation. Although outdated wage scales and artificial maximum benefits may spur injured employees to return to work as soon as possible, they do not necessarily provide adequate compensation for injured employees with valid claims. Furthermore, fraud is rampant amongst employees, and insurance carriers have resorted to "hardball" tactics to counteract this deception. Such responses to workers' compensation have created a climate of fear and distrust between employees and employers.

The system does not always fairly compensate injured employees. An injured worker is generally not entitled, for example, to continued employer contributions for retirement benefits while she is off work because of an injury. Furthermore, she may lose her job, seniority, and/or job advancement opportunities. The compensation she is paid is almost always less than her earnings prior to the accident even though the employer remains liable for her medical expenses.

What is the maximum wage benefit paid to an injured worker in your state?

Most states limit employees' compensation by putting a cap on the monthly wage they can be paid. The injured employee is paid only a percentage of what his average monthly wage was before the accident. In Arizona, for example, the injured worker who cannot return to work is paid 66.7 percent of his average monthly wage at the time of the accident. Because no state or federal taxes (including Social Security and Medicare) are withheld from payments made to the injured worker, a reduction of one-third of the employee's gross wage appears reasonable on the surface. For wage earners with a family, however, whose state and federal tax rate is very low or nonexistent, the reduction results in a real loss of disposable income of as much as 25 percent.

Many major injuries are scheduled. Loss of an arm or leg is worth so many months' compensation, in addition to payments received for being unable to return to work due to an accident. In Arizona, loss of the dominant arm is worth an additional sixty months' compensation; loss of a leg is worth fifty months' compensation (compensation is at 55 percent of the injured worker's average monthly wage).

For example, a secretary making $7.50 per hour would earn $1,300 per month, calculated as follows:

$$\begin{array}{r} \$7.50 \text{ per hour} \\ \times\, 40\, \text{hours} \\ \times\, 4.33\, \text{weeks} \\ \hline \$1,300 \text{ per month} \end{array}$$

If she lost her leg due to a work-related accident, she would receive an additional benefit of 55 percent of her average monthly wage ($715) for fifty months. That monthly benefit would be paid for the prescribed period (fifty months) in addition to any other benefits to which she might be entitled (which would be a maximum of $866.67 per month, 66.7 percent of $1,300). For an executive secretary earning $3,000 per month, the respective benefits would be $880 (loss of leg at 55 percent) for fifty months and $1,600 (66.7 percent of maximum monthly wage of $2,400) while she was temporarily permanently disabled. The $1,600 monthly payment, but not the $880 for the loss of her leg, will cease when she can return to work.

If the loss of her leg resulted in her being unable to earn the same amount of income after recovering from the injury, she would be entitled (in Arizona) to payments equal to 66.7 percent of the difference between her post-injury earning capacity and her pre-injury average monthly income. She would also be entitled to post-injury training and rehabilitation.

In most jurisdictions, the statutory monthly wage is not tied to the cost of living index or the state's actual average monthly wage. It is changed, if at all, only by legislative action. In Arizona the maximum average wage was recently changed to $2,400 from the $2,100-per-month level set in June of 1991. The previous maximum was $1,800.

The elaborate statutory framework and rules associated with workers' compensation have not gone unchallenged. In Arizona, over 2,000 reported cases (not including memorandum decisions) have made it to the appellate courts. Note that a workers' compensation case can be appealed, in Arizona, only after a final decision by an administrative law judge. To appeal to an appellate court, a petition to review the decision must be made to the Industrial Commission.

 LOCAL LINKS

How is the maximum wage benefit determined (i.e., maximum allowed wage and percentage multiplier) in your state?

The Adversarial Part of "No Fault"

All workers' compensation systems provide for resolution of disputed claims. The employer's premium is based on its claims history. It is, therefore, in the employer's best interest to minimize the number of claims and get the injured worker stabilized and back to work (or able to get back to work) as soon as possible. The employer's insurance carrier acts as a watchdog, monitoring the claims it processes to check for and weed out malingerers and frauds.

This adversarial aspect of the system causes the greatest delays in claims resolution. The employer, usually acting through its insurance carrier, can require the injured employee to submit to an independent medical examination (IME) by a doctor of the employer's choosing. (An IME is sometimes not allowed in states where the employer can require the employee to be treated by an approved workers' compensation physician.) When disputes occur they are heard by administrative law judges. The hearings are often bifurcated to allow the physicians to testify at times convenient for them. These procedural requirements slow down the resolution process.

If the employee wants to get a second opinion regarding his condition, he must usually pay for it. The procedures for getting a new treating physician vary but usually require the acquiescence of the employer or an order from the agency overseeing the workers' compensation system.

Employees have caused many of the problems with a system designed to ensure fast and efficient resolution of claims. Outright fraud and attempts to continue receiving benefits after recovery are widespread. In California, for example, it is estimated that 10 percent of all claims and 25 percent of all payments are the result of fraud (G.T. Schwartz, "Waste, Fraud, and Abuse in Workers' Compensation: The Recent California Experience," *Md. L. Rev.* 52 [1993]: 983, 988.) Surveillance of claimants to catch them performing physical acts of which they are supposedly incapable, is commonplace. The results appear to justify the money spent on such surveillance.

Employees' attempts to circumvent the system rarely result in criminal prosecution. The most the employee stands to lose is benefits to which he is not entitled. Hardball insurance carriers also have little fear of predatory practices. Bad faith claims in workers' compensation cases are difficult to prove. Many states have statutes protecting insurers from liability for their actions in workers' compensation cases.

PUTTING IT INTO PRACTICE 19:3

1. How would you calculate Juan's average wage for benefit purposes? If Juan worked only eight months a year, would that make a difference?

2. What is the average monthly wage for a legal assistant who is paid $12 per hour for a forty-hour work week? In your state, what is the dollar value for the loss of her dominant arm?

Many of those activities, if they occurred in other contexts, such as with homeowners or automobile insurance claims, could subject the carrier to general tort damages, including punitive damages.

In most states employers are not permitted to ask their employees to waive their rights to workers' compensation or to require their employees to pay any part of the insurance premium. With limited exceptions agreements to waive workers compensation claims or that the employees will pay any portion of the workers' compensation insurance premium are void.

FILING A WORKERS' COMPENSATION CLAIM

The first requirement for filing a workers' compensation claim is that the employee be injured "on the job." Whether an employee was on the job is the subject of many of the reported cases. The answer is not as easy as it might first appear. For example, is an employee on the job when she is on her way to work? When she is parking her car in the employee parking lot? Leaving the parking lot to go home? On a personal errand but on company time? Dropping off a package for her boss on her way to lunch?

Once an on-the-job accident has occurred, the employer and employee have independent obligations to report it. The employee must report to the employer, and the employer must notify the agency overseeing the workers' compensation system (and the employer's insurance carrier). Depending on the nature of the accident and the amount of time lost by the injured employee, the system reacts in different ways. A minor injury might result in no medical expenses and little or no lost time for the employee. The amount of lost time is important because compensation is usually not paid for the first few days (generally five to seven days) that the employee misses work. Medical expenses are paid from the time of the accident. The treating physician is usually required to give notice if the physician believes the injury to be job-related.

 LOCAL LINKS

In your state what is the longest time period a worker can wait after an industrial injury to make a claim before it is barred?

If the injury results in lost work time greater than the minimum time period prescribed, the employer will normally submit information to the agency to establish the employee's average monthly wage. The rules and procedures (and case law) in this area are quite complicated. Rules vary, for example, depending on whether the claimant is a new hire who has just received a raise. To illustrate, imagine the difficulty in computing the average monthly wage for a felon just recently released from prison after three years, who had been on the job for only a week before the accident.

In most cases the average monthly wage is determined by the prior year's income. Separation from employment for illness or family emergency confuses the issue. A recent increase in pay may be averaged in with the prior year's income. Such a computation effectively reduces the average monthly income to less than that actually being earned by the employee at the time of the accident.

Once the monthly wage for benefit purposes has been established, the payments to the employee are generally made on a monthly basis. When the injury has stabilized, a decision is made regarding the permanency of the injury and whether the employee has suffered a loss of earning capacity. The rules for payment of permanent partial disability vary but are usually based on a percentage of the difference between an employee's preinjury earning capacity and his postinjury earning capacity (which requires a whole category of expert testimony). Compensation is not allowed for permanent impairment that does not affect job ability. For example, an employee with a permanent limp will not be compensated if the limp does not affect earning capacity. The same is usually true for nonvisible scarring.

If an injury is caused by a co-employee, no claim can be made by the injured worker. If a third party caused the injury on the job, the employee can assert any tort claims she may have against the third party. The laws of most jurisdictions, however, provide that the employer (or its insurance carrier) has subrogation rights to the extent of any medical or wage payments made to the employee. In many states the claim is actually assigned by operation of law to the employer or its carrier if the employee does not assert her rights against the responsible party.

The subrogation claim that might have to be paid from the settlement or litigation of any lawsuit against a third party could be an impediment to the employee asserting his rights. In the third-party context, the employee would be subject to all tort defenses, including contributory negligence, comparative negligence,

PUTTING IT INTO PRACTICE 19:4

1. What ethical problems might arise for those representing the employer in pursuing an employee's third-party claim?

2. If Juan did not know he had a claim, would the system get notice of his accident without his input?

3. How long do benefits get paid in your state? Is there an offset for social security benefits? What if the worker lives to be ninety-five? What if he retires and draws a pension and social security?

assumption of risk, etc. Most attorneys would not take an employee's tort claim if, due to the amount of the carrier's lien, only the attorney and the insurer would get paid. In states where the employee's third-party rights are transferred to the employer, the employer could pursue the employee's claim against the responsible third party in the name of the employee.

LOCAL LINKS

Does your state have an automatic subrogation of the injured worker's third-party claim to the workers' compensation carrier? How long after the accident is it reassigned to the carrier by law?

CURRENT ISSUES IN WORKERS' COMPENSATION

Just as society has grappled with workplace issues such as sexual harassment, creation of a hostile environment, AIDS, and employee rage, so too has the workers' compensation system. Many systems are still groping for the appropriate ways to handle issues supposedly addressed by federal and state legislation.

For example, is potential exposure to AIDS a compensable injury if the worker does not become infected? Do the psychological stresses caused by the fear of possibly contracting AIDS, which could result in a person's being unable to work, constitute a work-related injury? Psychological incapacity due to sexual harassment and/or hostile work environments must also be addressed. Many systems are having problems as well in dealing with purely psychological injuries that have no physical cause.

In one case, the New York Court of Appeals held that the psychological injury caused to a secretary by the psychic trauma of finding her boss's body right after he had committed suicide was compensable to the same extent as any physical injury (*Wolfe v. Sibley,*

Lindsay & Curr Co., 330 N.E.2d 603 [N.Y. 1975]). The dissent in *Wolfe* expressed concern about allowing compensation for "pure" psychological injuries arising out of an occurrence in which the claimant was not a participant. Would you, for example, approve of a Social Security system that provided benefits when an individual experienced everyday mental trauma, such as the loss of a family member?

Furthermore, the Americans with Disabilities Act of 1990, 42 U.S.C. § 12101 *et seq.* (ADA), has created some potential problems. In the past most states did not require an employer to keep an injured worker on as an employee after she recovered from her injury. The ADA may affect what an employer can do if an employee suffers a recognized disability as a result of an industrial accident.

Telecommuting has also raised new issues regarding workers' compensation. Generally workers' compensation statutes provide compensation for injuries that "arise out of" and "in the course of" employment. Some jurisdictions have held that employees can be compensated for injuries that occurred while performing work required by the employer at home. In at least one case, compensation was awarded when the employee was injured at home as a result of work-related fatigue. In *Schwindt v. Red Roof Delivery, Inc.,* a restaurant manager was injured when she fell down the stairway in her home at 4:30 A.M. after falling asleep while working on employee work schedules.

LOCAL LINKS

Does your state have specific rules regarding HIV and how those claims are to be made?

LOCAL LINKS

Does your state allow compensation for purely psychological injuries?

NET NEWS

At http://www.workerscompresources.com you can find sites to various reports and upcoming seminars, including reports comparing workers' compensation provisions in the fifty states, the District of Columbia, and American territories, as well as for federal employees, to the most recent recommendations of the National Commission on State Workmen's Compensation Laws.

PUTTING IT INTO PRACTICE 19:5

1. Does your state's workers' compensation law allow recovery for purely psychological injuries, such as those in *Wolfe*?

2. How does your state deal with AIDS? Does it have a statute addressing the issue?

3. Etta worked in a munitions factory. She was constantly harassed by fellow employees, who would throw things at her and make noises like a bomb exploding. She had a son who had been injured in training during the Persian Gulf War. Her co-employees would put depictions of dead and mutilated soldiers on her workstation. She twice attempted suicide as a result of the harassment and insults she faced at work. Shortly after her second discharge from a hospital's psychiatric unit, she filed a claim for benefits for psychiatric impairment. Should her claim be allowed?

SUMMARY

Workers' compensation is a system that was statutorily implemented in the early 1900s to protect injured workers from poverty. The employer agreed to be responsible for all work-related injuries and the employee gave up his right to sue and to a jury trial. Today's systems are either mandatory or voluntary. Many of the reasons underlying establishment of workers' compensation no longer exist.

With today's artificially low payments and aggressive claims handling, the injured worker can easily fall below today's poverty level if she becomes unable to return to work due to a job-related injury. Increases in benefits can be obtained only through legislative action. Worker fraud is prevalent as well and provides support for both aggressive claims-handling processes and payment of benefits that do not return the injured worker to her preinjury financial condition.

AIDS, psychological impairment, and the ADA have generated difficult questions for the workers' compensation system. The adversarial nature of the system, the delay in processing claims, and the current disputes regarding compensable and noncompensable injuries, as well as the continued viability of workers' compensation, remain issues that must be addressed.

KEY TERMS

fellow-servant rule
Doctrine that shields employers from liability for damages incurred for injuries to an employee due to the negligence of a co-worker

scheduled injuries
Injuries, such as loss of sight or of an appendage, for which stated benefits are paid

REVIEW QUESTIONS

1. What was the cause for the creation of workers' compensation laws?

2. What types of injuries are exempt from compensation?

3. How do scheduled injuries differ from unscheduled injuries?

4. What types of benefits are generally not compensated for in workers' compensation systems?

5. How is the amount of compensation to be paid to an injured worker limited?

6. How are appeals often governed in workers' compensation laws?

7. What is the name of the judicial figure that often presides over workers' compensation hearings?

8. What effect does subrogation have on an employee asserting a claim against a third party?

9. How might the ADA affect workers' compensation laws?

PRACTICE EXAM

Students should complete the practice exam after studying each chapter. The answers are in Appendix A. If you score lower than 80%, you should reread the materials.

True-False

1. Workers' compensation is often thought of as a no-fault system.

2. The underpinnings of workers' compensation as we now know it began to take shape in the nineteenth century.

3. Britain was the European country where the underpinnings of workers' compensation as we now know it began to take shape.

4. An IME is an independent medical examination.

5. For an injured worker to receive compensation she must be injured while working at the place of her employment.

6. An injured worker's compensation is always based on his income at the time of the injury.

7. Permanent scarring is always, by itself, a basis for an award of compensation.

8. Psychological damages, without physical injury, are always subject to a compensation award.

9. The Americans with Disabilities Act is often referred to as the ADA.

10. For an injured worker to get an independent medical evaluation from a doctor of his choosing, he must usually pay for it or get permission from the agency overseeing workers' compensation.

Fill-in-the-Blanks

1. The _____ _____ rule protects employers from suit by employees injured by coworkers.

2. Injures that provide a fixed sum for compensation based on a workers' monthly wage are called _____ injuries.

Multiple Choice

1. The fellow-servant rule helped protect employers from claims from their employees by
   a. preventing lawsuits against fellow workers.
   b. making the responsible employee solely liable for damages caused a fellow worker.
   c. prohibiting all servants from filing suit.
   d. none of the above.

2. The primary difference between voluntary and mandatory workers' compensation systems is that
   a. in mandatory systems the employee must accept the benefits.
   b. in voluntary systems the employee may retain the right to sue the employer.
   c. a and b.
   d. none of the above.

3. The name of the United States Supreme Court case that upheld noncompulsory workers' compensation systems in 1917 was
   a. *Miranda v. Arizona.*
   b. *Roe v. Wade.*
   c. *New York Central Railroad v. White.*
   d. *Brown v. Board of Education.*

4. The difference between a scheduled and an unscheduled injury is that
   a. a scheduled injury provides a fixed amount of compensation.
   b. an unscheduled injury provides a fixed amount of compensation.
   c. a scheduled injury provides for more compensation.
   d. none of the above.

5. States limit the amount of compensation paid to injured workers by
   a. fixing a maximum wage on which compensation is paid.
   b. providing for payment of a percentage of the maximum monthly wage.
   c. not indexing the maximum monthly wage to an inflationary index.
   d. all of the above.

6. The injured workers' rights against a liable third party are subrogated to
   a. the party causing the injury.
   b. the employer or its insurer.
   c. the employee.
   d. none of the above.

7. In the early 1900s the factors that led to adoption of workers' compensation laws were
   a. unsafe working conditions.
   b. the fellow-servant rule.
   c. an employer-friendly tort system.
   d. all of the above.

PRACTICE POINTERS

In many workers' compensation cases it will be the legal assistant's duty to review the file. Most states have an administrative body (such as Arizona's Industrial Commission) that maintains the file. The administrative body where the transcript of proceedings and all filings must be made is the official repository.

As in the court system, documents filed at the central repository can usually be reviewed without court order. The administrative body often contracts with court reporters, so it may not be possible to make copies of all of the documents in the file. If you want a copy of the transcript for review, you may have to contact the reporter who was present at that proceeding and pay for the copy.

All medical records, billings, doctors' reports, and notices that were sent to the employer, employee, or treating physician are in the file. Many states require the treating physician to file regular progress reports. Notices of any change in status are in the file, such as termination-of-benefits notices, return-to-work notices, and the like. The calculation of the monthly wage is also in the file.

Due to the volume of workers' compensation cases, many states maintain a paper file for only a short period of time, after which the documents are transferred to microfiche or electronic storage. It is important to understand and be able to search the storage media, to ensure that all important documents you need to review can be found and that any relevant documents that you may not know about will not be overlooked.

Review some of the reported workers' compensation cases from the past five years in your jurisdiction. You want to find a case that refers to documents that should be in the file and, preferably, a case that refers to a transcript, perhaps the testimony of a doctor. Once you have reviewed and briefed the case, go to the depository of the file. Your task will be to locate all documents referred to in the reported case.

If the case you choose is in paper form and your jurisdiction uses other storage media for older cases, review one of those case files to see how the documents are handled. In some jurisdictions the filings are copied chronologically, some with and some without an index. If electronic media are used, check to see the type, if any, of indexing that is used. What kind of searches can be made? If the electronic storage is graphic rather than text-based, you need to be sure that you do not miss an important document during your review of the file. Without an index or the ability to search the database, you will have to physically review each document in the file, much like the procedure with court files.

TORT TEASERS

1. If Juan came to your office for advice, what additional, factual information would you need to give your supervising attorney in order for her to make a decision regarding representation of Juan?

2. Review the statutory framework for your state's workers' compensation system. How does it compare with Arizona's?

3. How would you argue that Juan's seven-month break in employment should not be considered in determining his average monthly wage?

4. Calculate Juan's average monthly wage according to the laws of your state, assuming that Juan usually works forty-five hours per week (six months of the year) and overtime (eighty to ninety hours per week) for two months of the year. Also assume Juan has never worked more than eight months a year.

PRACTICAL PONDERABLES

Julie was a courier for a law firm in your state carrying workers' compensation insurance. While in the scope and course of her employment she was hit, head-on, by a negligent driver. Julie lost part of her right leg, below the knee, as a result of her injuries. She was salaried, making $18,000 per year at the time of the accident. Julie has come to your office (her office said it would be a conflict of interest for them to represent her) for legal advice. Your supervising attorney has requested that you calculate the following:

1. Julie's maximum monthly benefit.
2. The amount of compensation she will receive solely as a result of losing part of her right leg.
3. Julie's vocational rehabilitation benefits if she cannot return to her position as a courier.
4. The amount of benefits paid to Julie that would have to be repaid from any legal action against the driver of the vehicle that caused her injuries.

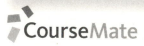

APPENDIX A

Suggested Responses to "Putting It into Practice" Exercises and Answers to Practice Exams

Putting It into Practice

CHAPTER 3

3:1 Assault/Battery

If Tyson believes the fan's intent is to contact Tyson's body with his fists, and if the fan has an apparent ability to carry out the threatened contact, an assault has been committed even if Tyson is unafraid of being injured.

3:2 False Imprisonment

These facts are based on an actual case, *May Department Stores Co., Inc. v. Devercelli*, 314 A.2d 767 (D.C. 1974). The jury concluded that the officer lacked probable cause to apprehend the plaintiff, and the majority found that the evidence supported their conclusion. The dissent, in contrast, believed that probable cause existed as a matter of law and that despite the conflicting testimony no disagreement existed regarding the material facts.

3:3 Intentional Infliction of Emotional Distress

These are the facts of *Tandy Corp. v. Bone*, 678 S.W.2d 312 (Ark. 1984). The court held that the manager's reaction to stress and his request for Valium put his employer on notice that he was not someone of "ordinary temperament" and that he would probably not be able to endure the stressful situation to which he had been subjected. This notice to the employer provided the basis for a jury question of extreme outrage.

3:4 Trespass

In *Copeland v. Hubbard Broadcasting, Inc.*, 526 N.W.2d 402 (Minn. 1995), from which these facts were taken, the court found that a claim for trespass could exist. The district court concluded that the television station was entitled to summary judgment because the student did not exceed the boundaries of the Copelands' consent—they did not expressly limit their consent to her educational goals. The appellate court, however, recognized trespass as a remedy when secret cameras are used for gathering news and held that newsgathering does not create a license to trespass into a private home. The court remanded the case to the jury to determine the nature of the Copelands' consent to the student.

3:5 Trespass to Chattels/Conversion

These hypotheticals are taken from the *Restatement (Second) of Torts* § 222A, illus. 5, 6, 12, 25, and 26. No conversion is committed when Matthew puts the furniture in storage and changes the locks, but Matthew does convert John's property when he moves it to a distant warehouse that greatly inconveniences John. John does not convert Matthew's car when he drives the extra ten miles, but he does convert it when he gets into an accident.

3:6 Consent

In *Berthiaume v. Pratt*, 365 A.2d 792 (Me. 1976), the court found no grounds for consent. The surgeon argued that the medical importance of the photographs overrode any apparent objections of the patient, but the court refused to create any medical exception to the rules surrounding consent.

3:7 Self-Defense

Some facts are lacking, such as the man's distance from George and Sandy, but as long as a reasonable person in George's situation would have believed deadly force was immediately necessary to protect himself and another, George would be justified in defending himself and Sandy. Because the man is threatening with deadly force (a knife), George would be justified in responding with deadly force. The fact that the man is mentally ill does not change the answer unless his mental illness and the harmlessness of the knife would have been apparent to a reasonable person in that situation.

3:8 *Katko v. Briney*

1. Frustrated by a series of trespassings and burglaries to an abandoned house on their property, the Brineys installed a spring gun that was aimed at an intruder's legs. The plaintiff broke into the house, which he believed to be abandoned, to take some bottles and fruit jars. When he entered the bedroom, the spring gun went off, shooting him in the leg, causing serious physical injury.

2. The value of human life outweighs property rights if there is a threat to personal safety.

3. If the law prohibits the use of deadly force by someone who is present, that same degree of force is prohibited in that person's absence.

4. The infliction of serious bodily injury cannot be used to prevent trespassing.

5. Yes.

3:9 Regaining Possession of Chattel

The officers did appear to exceed their authority in detaining the man for more than an hour, in their attempts at intimidation (refusing his request to make phone calls and slapping the gun), and in their use of duress to induce him to sign a release. The court found that the officers lacked probable cause to arrest the man and should have kept him under surveillance longer before detaining him for questioning.

3:10 Private/Public Necessity

These hypotheticals are taken from the *Restatement (Second) of Torts* § 262, illus. 1, and § 263, illus. 1. Both the fireman and Liz are privileged. The fireman is not liable for damages to Maryann's car, but Liz is liable for damages to the scarf.

CHAPTER 4

4:1 Attractive-Nuisance Doctrine

1. A subjective standard is used with this doctrine, because the age, intelligence, and experience of the plaintiff are taken into consideration.

2. According to the *Restatement (Second) of Torts* § 339(i), illus. 5, the company is not liable, because the attractive-nuisance doctrine does not apply when the defendant is maintaining "normal, necessary and usual implements" that are essential to a business and that "reckless children can use to their harm in a spirit of bravado or to gratify some other childish desire" with full perception of the risks involved. The fact that Jed accepted the dare indicates that he was aware of the risk.

3. The second hypothetical is taken from illustrations 6 and 7 in § 339(i) of the *Restatement*. The pond owner owes a duty to Marie if she is three but not if she is ten, because the ten-year-old is expected to be aware of the dangers of the pond whereas the three-year-old is not. If Marie was not able to appreciate the dangers of drowning because of some unique mental or physical disability, the owner could owe her a duty even if she was ten.

4. The third hypothetical is taken from illustration 9 of § 339(i) of the *Restatement*. The railroad company could be liable if it could have easily installed a locking device, but would not be liable if the locking device would have seriously interfered with its business. The difference in answers arises out of a balancing test—balancing the risk to the children against the utility of the dangerous condition (the turntable). The company would probably not be liable, however, if Micki had been forewarned about the dangers of the turntable (illustration 8), because he was aware of the risks involved and chose to ignore those risks out of recklessness or bravado.

4:2 Invitees/Licensees/Trespassers

1. According to the *Restatement (Second) of Torts* § 332, from which these examples were taken, the appropriate classifications are

    a. licensee (comment b).

    b. licensee (comment d).

c. invitee (comment d).

d. invitee (comment e).

e. loses invitee status when she goes behind counter where she does not have permission to go; becomes a trespasser (comment l).

f. licensee.

2. Because the child is a licensee (a social guest), the homeowners owe her a duty to warn her of hidden danger. The court in this case grappled with whether a pool was a hidden peril to a nineteen-month-old child and decided that it was a matter of fact for the jury to determine. The court noted that even if the homeowners made the parents aware of the pool, they did not necessarily fulfill their duty to the child. *Shaw v. Peterson*, 821 P.2d 220 (Ariz. Ct. App. 1991).

3. The store has a duty to inspect the premises for hidden dangers. The store owner might reasonably expect that customers' attention will be diverted by the displays and that they will not discover what is obvious, the owner has a duty to take reasonable steps to protect customers from what is otherwise an obvious condition. *Restatement (Second) of Torts* § 343A, illus. 2.

4:3 *Walls v. Oxford Management Co., Inc.*

1. The plaintiff was sexually assaulted in her vehicle at the apartment complex where she lived. Violent crimes had been occurring at the apartment complex over the two-year period preceding the assault. The plaintiff claimed that the owner of the apartment complex had a duty to provide reasonable security measures for the protection of the residents of the apartment. The plaintiff also claimed that the landlord had a duty to warn them of the numerous criminal activities that had occurred at the property.

2. a. Does a landlord have a duty to protect tenants from foreseeable criminal attacks committed by third parties?

   b. Does a landlord have a duty to warn residents of a lack of security?

   c. Does a landlord have a duty to warn residents of criminal activities that have occurred at the property?

3. Private persons have no duty, but innkeepers do. The difference in duty is due to the nature of the innkeeper-guest relationship. Guests' entrustment of their safety to the innkeeper entitles guests to expect innkeepers to use reasonable care to protect them from attack.

4:4 *New York v. Riss*

1. "Because we owe a duty to everybody, we owe it to nobody."

2. Holding the state liable will result in a financial disaster for New York City, because every time a crime is committed, inadequate police protection will be claimed and the city will be sued.

3. No municipality has gone bankrupt because it was held liable for negligent police actions. The burden on the city's budget for tort claims in other areas has not been burdensome. Under a negligence standard the police are held to a standard of reasonableness, not perfection. In the instant case the plaintiff would not have been able to recover under a negligence standard if she had been attacked after her first visits to the police station. The police were negligent only after failing to provide her protection after verifying her claims that her life was in danger.

4. This case had nothing to do with a decision regarding the allocation of resources or manpower. Furthermore, courts frequently review administrative practices in other types of tort claims involving municipalities and in so doing they routinely apply the principles of vicarious liability. If an injury is a result of failure to allocate sufficient funds, agencies can opt either to improve their administrative practices or to accept the cost of compensating those who have been injured.

5. The real costs of negligent police protection have been hidden by charging those costs to those who have been injured rather than to the community, which had the power to prevent those injuries.

6. It establishes the standard of conduct that should be followed and the penalties for failing to follow those standards.

4:5 Duty to Protect

The court in this case (*Figueroa v. North Park College*, 879 F.2d 1427 [Ill. 1998]) concluded that the plaintiff was not an invitee. The court used a three-part test:

1. Did she enter the premises by express or implied invitation?

2. Was her entry connected with an activity the owner conducted or permitted to be conducted on the land?

3. Was there a mutuality of benefit or a benefit to the owner?

The court determined that the first two parts of the test could be subject to reasonable dispute but concluded that as a matter of law the plaintiff failed to meet the third part of the test, finding that any "public relations benefit" to the defendant was "too remote to confer invitee status."

The court also used a voluntary-undertaking analysis and found that North Park had voluntarily undertaken to provide security measures and that it had an obligation to provide reasonable protection to the plaintiff. The court further found that North Park had not been negligent in preventing the crime against the plaintiff, as the plaintiff had failed to prove that the assault against her had been foreseeable.

CHAPTER 5

5:1 *Eimann v. Soldier of Fortune Magazine*

1. Nine. Extortion; jailbreaks.

2. No.

3. The average subscriber would understand that certain phrases were solicitations for illegal activities based on the context of those ads (e.g., the presence of other classified ads as well as display ads). No, he could not distinguish ads.

4. SOF did not have a duty to refrain from publishing a facially innocuous classified ad whose context made its message ambiguous.

5. They have used it to determine whether a defendant has an obligation to act as a reasonable person would under the circumstances at issue and what standard of conduct would satisfy that obligation. Under this test a risk becomes unreasonable when its magnitude outweighs the social utility of the act or omission that creates it.

6. Yes.

7. Yes. As many as nine ads had served as links in criminal plots, ranging from extortion to jailbreaks. SOF staff had participated in at least two police investigations in which these ads had played a role.

8. To recognize and refrain from publishing ads that " 'reasonably could be interpreted as an offer to engage in illegal activity' based on their words or 'context.' " This burden was too heavy based on the ambiguity of the Hearn ad and the pervasiveness of advertising in our culture.

9. The serious harm created by these ads combined with the gravity of that harm does not outweigh the onerous burden of requiring publishers to reject all ads for products or services that might pose a threat of harm.

5:2 Using the *Restatement* to Determine Reasonableness of Conduct

The utility of the state's inaction must be weighed against the risk to those who might be harmed by diving into shallow waters. Although the state's failure to warn could certainly result in harm to those unaware of the dangers of shallow water, the question is "the extent of harm likely to be caused," the chance that such harm would occur, and "the number of persons whose interests are likely to be invaded if the risk takes effect in harm." The utility to the state pertains to the feasibility of the state inspecting the terrain of the park for hidden dangers, considering the size and nature of the park. In balancing the risk against the utility of the state's conduct one would have to consider (1) the size of the park, (2) the extent of use of the lake and of the cove in question, (3) the accessibility of the cove, (4) the extent to which the park was and could reasonably be patrolled, (5) the time and resources that would have to be expended in taking the requisite precautions, and (6) the obviousness of the danger the cove presented. After weighing the magnitude of the risk of the cove against the utility of the state's conduct, one might expect the state to inspect locations such as the cove for hidden dangers and either remove them or post warnings regarding their existence, or one might find such an inspection impracticable; or, alternatively, that inspections were unreasonable but that reasonable care required posting signs prohibiting diving. For the court's analysis of this case, see *Markowitz v. Arizona Parks Board*, 706 P.2d 364 (Ariz. 1985).

5:3 What the Reasonable Person is Expected to Know

1. Yes. The dangerous nature of icy roads is common knowledge in the community. *Restatement (Second) of Torts* § 290, illus. 4.

2. Yes. The danger of explosion is common knowledge in the community. *Restatement (Second) of Torts* § 290, illus. 3.

3. Yes. Susan is charged with knowledge of the ordinance and should expect the trolley to stop. *Restatement (Second) of Torts* § 290, illus. 7.

4. The court in *Dolezal v. Carbrey*, 778 P.2d 1261 (Ariz. 1989) concluded that reasonable minds could differ as to whether it was "foreseeable that an otherwise gentle horse might bolt in reaction to out-of-the-ordinary cues" from an inexperienced rider. The questions the court believes should be considered in assessing the reasonableness of Frank's conduct are whether Frank should have let an inexperienced rider ride an animal accustomed to proper and subtle cues, whether he sufficiently instructed Carole before she rode, and whether he adequately supervised her riding and dismount.

5:4 Standard of Care in Special Circumstances

1. In *Breunig v. American Family Insurance Co.*, 713 N.W.2d 619 (Wis. 1970), the court did not allow the defendant to claim insanity as a defense. The court noted, however, that if the defendant had not experienced similar delusions previously, it would have allowed the insanity defense, because if insanity strikes suddenly with no forewarning, individuals cannot do anything to avoid liability.

2. The minor could be held to an adult standard of care if a court concluded that hunting is a dangerous activity engaged in by adults and not children. But if a court concluded that minors commonly hunt, the minor would be held to the standard of care of a child of the defendant's age, intelligence, and experience.

3. If the driver had never experienced a seizure previously, he would not, as a reasonable person, be expected to take any precautions to prevent an accident. But having been treated for epilepsy, he would be held to the standard of a reasonable epileptic. According to the *Restatement (Second) of Torts* § 283C, cmt. c, it might be negligence for such a person to drive at all, although the fact that the driver had been seizure-free for more than ten years makes that unlikely.

5:5 Negligent Per Se

1. According to the *Restatement (Second) of Torts* § 286 illus. 5, the statute establishes the standard of conduct for the cow hit by the train but not for the poisoned cow.

2. The purpose of the statute is to protect the public from incompetent physicians. The defendant's violation of the statute does not by itself establish negligence; the plaintiff must prove that the defendant was incompetent (that he fell below the standard of care of a reasonable physician). *Brown v. Shyne*, 151 N.E. 197 (N.Y. 1926).

3. Marjorie can, but Helena cannot, because the statute was designed to protect employees, not visitors. *Restatement (Second) of Torts* § 286, illus. 1.

4. The court says the statutory "standard established was to prevent the police from being injured but not to prevent the plaintiff from being injured." *Good v. City of Glendale*, 722 P.2d 386 (Ariz. 1986).

CHAPTER 6

6:1 *Palsgraf v. Long Island Rail Co.*

1. The question is whether proximate cause can be inferred from the facts of the case.

2. "But-for" causation exists in those cases in which the plaintiff most likely would have survived but for the negligence of the doctor.

3. Because the plaintiff can show only that even when all of the tortfeasors are taken together, their negligence *might* have caused the death of the plaintiff's husband.

4. No. A lost-chance-of-recovery allegation.

5. It allows plaintiffs to recover even though they can show only a lost chance to recover rather than that the death in question was due to the defendant's negligence.

6:2 Actual Causation

1. No. Although the plaintiff may argue that but for the misrepresentation, she would not have bought the condo (and she can certainly claim damages for that misrepresentation), she cannot apply the but-for test to the broken pipes because the representation by the broker made no reference to the plumbing. Therefore, there is no causal link between the broken pipes and the misrepresentation.

2. No, the court found no causal connection between the association's sponsorship and the plaintiff's loss. According to the court, "The only connection between the conduct of [Ford] and plaintiff's injury was an aura of legitimacy given to the race by the participation of a nationally-known sponsor." *McCulloch v. Ford Dealers Advertising Ass'n*, 234 Cal. App. 3d 1385 (1991).

3. Because most diseases can be tied to a number of causal factors, they will have difficulty proving with a reasonable degree of medical certainty that Agent Orange was in fact the precipitating cause of the plaintiffs' injuries. The defendant will scrutinize the medical histories of the plaintiffs, looking for signs of cigarette smoking, alcohol abuse, drug use (prescription and nonprescription), family history, exposure to other toxic chemicals and to pathogens (such as bacteria and parasites), and any other factors connected with the diseases in question. The plaintiffs will have to present strong expert testimony and epidemiological evidence (and to a lesser degree animal studies) to establish causation.

6:3 *Palsgraf* Again

1. Yes. No.

2. A duty.

3. She must show a "wrong to herself, i.e., a violation of her own right." It is defined in "terms of the natural or probable."

4. When "it results in the commission of a wrong, and the commission of a wrong imports the violation of a right."

5. No, the negligence must be in relation to the plaintiff.

6. A duty to "protect society from unnecessary danger, not to protect A, B, or C alone."

7. To "refrain from those acts that may unreasonably threaten the safety of others." No.

8. "Because of convenience, of public policy, of a rough sense of justice, the law arbitrarily declines to trace a series of events beyond a certain point." Practical politics. It is a matter of expediency.

9. Because the chauffeur's negligence was not the proximate cause of their injuries, because a prudent person would not have foreseen these consequences. Because he should be responsible for what might reasonably be expected to follow from an explosion.

10. No. A question of judgment.

11. Yes.

6:4 Actual Cause versus Proximate Cause

The *Markowitz* court found that reasonable people could find the state's failure to post warning signs to be the cause of David's injuries because they could have concluded that David would have avoided diving if an adequate warning had been given. The question of actual causation revolves around whether the state's inaction in fact caused David's injury, i.e., can it be argued that but for the state's failure to warn, David would not have been injured, or that the state's inactivity was a substantial factor leading up to David's injury? The question of proximate cause is a question of foreseeability: was David's injury a reasonably foreseeable consequence of the failure to post warning signs, or was the connection too remote to find proximate cause?

6:5 Exceptions to Cardozo Rule

1. Yes, according to the court in *In re Kinsman Transit Co.*, 338 F.2d 708 (2d Cir. 1964). All of the riverbank landowners were members of the general class as to which there was a general foreseeability of harm, because loose ships and failure to raise a drawbridge pose a danger to riverbank property owners in general. Even though the precise way the accident occurred was not foreseeable, a general, foreseeable risk existed that a loose ship and an unraised drawbridge would damage adjoining property. The harm suffered by the landowners was of the same general type that made the defendants' conduct negligent.

2. Yes. Under the "eggshell skull" rule, even if a normal person in Helen's position would have recovered after leaving the plant, Helen's psychological vulnerability would not break the chain of causation. In fact, the court (in what the appellate court refers to as the case of the "dynamite heart") found that Helen failed to prove actual causation and denied her recovery for her hypochondriacal injuries on that basis. *Stoleson v. United States*, 708 F.2d 1227 (7th Cir. 1983).

6:6 *Ontiveros v. Borak*

1. Tavern owners were not liable for injuries caused by an intoxicated patron even if their negligence in serving the patron contributed to the cause of the accident.

2. The "terrible toll" in personal injuries and property damage caused by those who drink and drive.

3. The court reasoned that the drinking of alcohol and not the serving of it was the cause of injury.

4. Yes.

5. The patron's drinking.

6. The court reasons that it was foreseeable that someone served thirty beers in five to six hours would get involved in an accident if he drove.

7. Because it will be difficult to sort out cause and effect if the patron was already intoxicated and might have been involved in an accident even without the "help" of the tavern owner.

8. A person of ordinary prudence would know enough not to serve liquor to someone obviously so intoxicated he should not be allowed to drive.

9. Those cases are overruled.

6:7 Intervening versus Superseding Causes

1. Yes, as long as Lucinda was being reasonably careful in learning to use her crutches. Her behavior in walking across the narrow walkway was probably unreasonable and would be considered an abnormal consequence of the original broken leg, making her actions a superseding cause. *Restatement (Second) of Torts* § 460, illus. 1 and 2.

2. The court found that the driver was an intervening cause and that the defendants' negligence exposed Charles to the type of harm that might foreseeably have occurred even though the intervening act occurred in an unforeseeable manner. *Bigbee v. Western Electric*, 93 Cal. App. 3d 451 (1979).

3. No, because the extraordinary and gross negligence of the ship's captain would be considered a superseding cause. The trial court found that the "captain's failure to plot fixes . . . was entirely independent of the fact of breakout." *Exxon Co. v. Sofec, Inc.*, 116 S. Ct. 1813 (1996).

CHAPTER 7

7:1 Damages in Case of VA Patient

These facts are taken from *Christopher v. United States*, 237 F. Supp. 787 (E.D. Pa. 1965). The plaintiff was awarded damages for lost wages, future lost earnings (reduced to present value), future medical expenses, and pain and suffering. He received no compensation for past medical expenses because those had been paid for by the government. The court deducted past disability payments from his award because the government had already paid these sums to the plaintiff and under the servicemen's benefit laws he could not recover twice for the same injury.

The court looked at the plaintiff's past salary, the wages he had lost since his operation, the projected salaries he would have earned had he been able to work until he was sixty-five (his proven earning ability along with his prospects for future employment), the operations he would probably need, and the rehabilitation and counseling he would need. In assessing his pain-and-suffering award the court considered the daily humiliation he endured, his physical pain, his depression, his loss of sexual powers, and his disfigurement and anxiety, as well as the ongoing mental and physical distress he would continue to suffer. A "day in the life" video would be helpful in such a case and, in fact, in considering pain-and-suffering damages, the court alluded to one incident that required the plaintiff to be "washed down with a hose" after having an involuntary bowel movement while on an outing with friends.

7.2 *Campbell v. State Farm*

1. State Farm's Performance, Planning and Review policy was a major factor.

2. Evidence pertaining to the PP & R policy concerned State Farm's business practices for over 20 years in numerous states. Most of these practices bore no relation to third-party automobile insurance claims, the type of claim underlying the Campbells' complaint against the company.

3. State Farm argued during phase II that its decision to take the case to trial was an 'honest mistake' that did not warrant punitive damages.

4. It said courts must ensure that the measure of punishment is both reasonable and proportionate to the amount of harm to the plaintiff and to the general damages recovered. In the context of this case, we have no doubt that there is a

presumption against an award that has a 145-to-1 ratio. An application of the *Gore* guideposts to the facts of this case, especially in light of the substantial compensatory damages awarded (a portion of which contained a punitive element), likely would justify a punitive damages award at or near the amount of compensatory damages. The punitive award of $145 million, therefore, was neither reasonable nor proportionate to the wrong committed, and it was an irrational and arbitrary deprivation of the property of the defendant.

7:3 Punitive Damages

1. Punitive damages are not justified according to this court in this case. *Woolstrum v. Maillioux*, 141 Cal. App. 3d Supp. 1 (1983). The defendants were negligent, not willful and wanton. The evidence did not show that the "defendant knew his fence was dangerously weak . . . and that he consciously disregarded the probability (not possibility) that a cow would lean against it and that, if it did, the cows would escape and probably (not possibly) cause a serious accident."

2. The court held that as a "matter of law the evidence of the plaintiff fell far short of showing a wanton disregard by defendant of a probable" injury.

7:4 Wrongful-Death/Survival Claims

These facts are taken from *Bendalin v. Valley National Bank*, 540 P.2d 194 (Ariz. 1975).

7:5 Damages for Mental Suffering

1. In *Sinn v. Burd*, 404 A.2d 672 (Pa. 1979), the court allowed a claim of infliction of emotional distress because the plaintiff was "located near the scene of the accident, the shock resulted from a direct emotional impact upon the plaintiff from the sensory and contemporaneous observance of the accident, and the plaintiff and victim were closely related."

2. In *Mazzagatti v. Everingham*, 516 A.2d 672 (Pa. 1986), the court reasoned that "where the close relative is not present at the scene of the accident, but instead learns of the accident from a third party, the close relative's prior knowledge of the injury to the victim serves as a buffer against the full impact of observing the accident scene. By contrast the relative who contemporaneously observes the tortious conduct has no time in which to brace his or her emotional system."

3. In allowing the emotional-distress claim, the court in *Chizmar v. Mackie*, 896 P.2d 196 (Alaska 1995), held "that the emotional distress resulting from a misdiagnosis of AIDS is foreseeable and that such distress is serious or severe. . . . The significance of a false imputation of AIDS is unquestionable."

CHAPTER 8

8:1 Contributory Negligence

1. Jeff can recover for the initial damages to his car because his negligence in speeding did not cause the accident, but because his negligence did result in his losing control of his car, he cannot recover for his personal injuries or the damages resulting from going into the ditch. *Restatement (Second) of Torts* § 465, illus. 1.

2. Yes, under the last-clear-chance doctrine.

    a. The last-clear-chance doctrine still applies.

    b. The last-clear-chance doctrine does not apply because Corinne's negligence preceded her encounter with Geraldine. Therefore, she did not have a "last clear chance" to avoid the accident. *Restatement (Second) of Torts* § 479, illus. 1–3.

3. No, because the last-clear-chance doctrine does not apply. Christy's prior negligence prevented her from discovering Margaret's car. *Restatement (Second) of Torts* § 479, illus. 4.

8:2 *McIntyre v. Balentine*

1. To decide whether to adopt a comparative-negligence system.

2. Because he drove while intoxicated.

3. The plaintiff should be penalized for his misconduct, he should be deterred from engaging in misconduct, and no proximate cause exists because the plaintiff's negligence exceeds the defendant's negligence.

4. In cases involving injured employees of interstate railroads and involving seamen.

5. Answers will vary.

6. Because the court concludes, after extensive research, that justice demands this adoption.

7. The court indicates that legislative inaction does not preclude the courts from abolishing an obsolete doctrine. The court also observes that mindless adherence to stare decisis can "confound" the truth and create a sense of "contempt."

8. Because it feels that it is unfair to award damages to a plaintiff who is primarily responsible for his own injuries, and it believes that the "49 percent" rule eliminates the harshness of the contributory-negligence standard while maintaining consistency with a fault-based system.

9. a. It is abolished.

   b. The plaintiff cannot recover unless his negligence is less than the combined fault of all of the tortfeasors.

   c. Yes, as long as the defendant alleges that a non-party caused or contributed to the plaintiff's injuries.

   d. Provides sample jury instructions and a special verdict form.

8:3 *Yi v. Yellow Cab Co.*

1. The problems addressed are

   a. how to assess fault when there are multiple parties and not all of them are brought before the court.

   b. how to assign percentages of fault to each party.

   c. what to do with the last-clear-chance doctrine and the defense of assumption of risk.

   d. how to treat willful misconduct.

2. The issues regarding multiple parties and willful misconduct.

3. The court abolishes both because it believes there is no longer a need for the last-clear-chance doctrine and that assumption of risk (which it considers to overlap with the defense of contributory negligence) is subsumed under the general process of assessing liability in proportion to fault.

4. Because it believes the trial courts are in a better position to resolve practical problems than is the appellate court.

5. The court believes that the "49 percent" rule is unfair because it merely lowers the bar of contributory negligence, allowing a plaintiff who is found 49 percent negligent to recover but preventing a plaintiff who is 50 percent negligent from recovering. The court also looks at the experience of Wisconsin, the leading exponent of the "50 percent" system, and concludes that the numerous appeals regarding that system have led to a fractured system that this court wishes to avoid.

8:4 Contributory Negligence, State Law

[Answers depend on the laws of your state.]

8:5 Assumption of Risk

1. The ticket holder might not read the waiver and thus may claim lack of notice; because the printing is so small, notice of the waiver is unlikely. No signature is required, so any agreement on the part of the ticket holder is hard to prove.

2. Yes, according to the court in *Wertheim v. United States Tennis Ass'n*, 150 A.D.2d 157 (N.Y. 1989), which held as a matter of law that being hit by a tennis ball is a risk normally associated with the sport.

   Did public policy influence your opinion?

   For an interesting review of this question, read K. Cahill, "Should There Be an Assumption of Risk Defense to Some Hostile Work Environment Sexual Harassment Claims?," 49 *Vand. L. Rev.* 1107 (1995), in which the author concludes that assumption of risk should be allowed in some form.

8:6 Immunity

1. No, according to the court in *Lovitt v. Concord School District*, 228 N.W.2d 479 (Mich. 1975), because the program was a governmental rather than proprietary function. The fact that the school charged admission to football games did not influence the court's analysis. However, in reference to the claims against the coaches, the court found that the "liability of the teachers is not based upon negligence imputed to them as public functionaries, but rather it arises from their individual conduct. . . . [E]ven if it is assumed that the teachers. . . could be considered 'public officers' otherwise sharing in the protection of governmental immunity, they would still be subject to liability because they invaded the rights of specific persons."

2. The United States Supreme Court has prohibited section 1983 claims against public

defenders by ruling that they do not act "under color of state law." Most courts have refused to grant immunity to public defenders in malpractice claims, arguing that the public defender is not like a judge or prosecuting attorney, but rather like a private attorney whose only duty is to the client, and that it would be unfair to deprive indigent defendants of this remedy. Others have granted immunity relying on policy arguments regarding the limited funds and heavy caseloads that face public defenders, the possible "chilling effect" that liability would have on the public defender's defense strategies, and the problems that liability would have on recruiting attorneys to work as public defenders. They distinguish public defenders and private attorneys on the basis that public defenders cannot decline clients, even those with meritless cases. *Barner v. Julie Leeds*, 13 P.3d 704 (Ca. 2002).

3. In *Schultz v. Roman Catholic Archdiocese*, 472 A.2d 531 (N.J. 1984), the court held that the Charitable Immunity Act prevented a charity from being found liable for negligence. The dissent, however, argued that statutory charitable immunity does not apply to intentional torts and that the "negligent hiring, supervision and retention of potentially harmful employees by the entity constitutes an exception to the rule of charitable immunity."

4. Not if the state in which he resides has adopted, by statute or judicial decision, parent-child immunity. For an exemplary case, see *Richards v. Richards*, 604 So. 2d 487 (Fla. 1992).

8:7 Statutes of Limitations

[Consult the applicable statutes in your state.]

CHAPTER 9

9:1 *Ang*

1. To recover the $325,000 they paid.

2. The Plaintiff's were required to prove that they were actually innocent of the underlying criminal charges.

3. There is no causation between Hansen and Martin's conduct and the charges filed against the Plaintiffs, the harm to their reputation or the money lost by the Plaintiffs.

9:2 Malpractice Claim

1. The court found that the estate had failed to establish a prima facie case of malpractice because the medical expert's testimony failed to express the requisite degree of medical certainty. "An expert fails this standard of certainty if he testifies 'that the alleged cause "possibly," or "could have" led to the result, that it "could very probably account" for the result, or even that it was "very highly probable" that it caused the result.'" *Hoffman v. Brandywine Hospital*, 661 A.2d 397 (Pa. 1995).

2. The appellate court concluded that the expert testimony failed to establish a causal link between the anesthesiologist's actions and Herman's myoclonus. The court characterized the expert's conclusion regarding proximate cause as "mere speculation." Because Herman was unable to prove the underlying medical malpractice claim, his legal malpractice claim must fail. *Stanski v. Ezersky*, 644 N.Y.S.3d 220 (N.Y. 1996).

9:3 Informed Consent

1. The court found a lack of informed consent in that the hospital's silence as to the risks "amounted to an assurance that there were none whereas its own questions to patients regarding reactions to this specific procedure demonstrate[d] that [it] . . . recognized the substantial possibility of complications." *Keel v. St. Elizabeth Medical Center*, 842 S.W.2d 860 (Ky. 1992).

2. The court found a lack of informed consent because the doctors failed to describe the advantages and disadvantages of the various replacement valves and to disclose the recognized risks of the Beall valve. The court explained that doctors must discuss alternative valves when they "represent medically recognized alternatives." *Stover v. Association of Thoracic & Cardiovascular Surgeons*, 635 A.2d 1047 (Pa. 1993).

9:4 Battery versus Negligence

Because Patricia is claiming that she was harmed by the drug, not by the insertion of the needle, the court refused to find a battery. The fact that the doctor or nurse had to touch Patricia in order to insert the needle was not sufficient to invoke the battery doctrine.

The court agreed with the plaintiff, however, that it was time to adopt a negligence standard, because "[a] patient's decision to undergo drug therapy should be no less informed than a decision to undergo surgery." *Wu v. Spence*, 605 A.2d 395 (Pa. 1992).

CHAPTER 10

10:1 Intentional Misrepresentation

1. The doctor's representations regarding the results of the operation are not fraudulent. Lucille's scar was in fact lowered, and the surgery, except for the blistering, accomplished the results she expected. His promises to fix the problem were not misrepresentations in that he did continue to treat her and never refused to see her. Lucille opted to consult other doctors, so she did not rely on the doctor's representations and suffered no damages as a result of these postsurgical promises. *Stone v. Foster*, 164 Cal. Rptr. 901 (Ct. App. 1980).

2. The court allowed the claim of misrepresentation in *Barbara A. v. John G.*, 193 Cal. Rptr. 422 (Ct. App. 1983). The court refused to allow recovery in a "wrongful birth" case, however, for social-policy reasons (invasions of privacy and concern for the welfare of the child). The court distinguished the cases based on the damages: damage to a woman's body caused by an ectopic pregnancy versus the "damage" of an unexpected child accompanied by support obligations.

3. An annulment was granted. Although the trial court opined that "if there were false representations, the plaintiff condoned them," the appellate court concluded that Maria's actions had to be considered in light of her background and the atmosphere in which she was living and that she "was no more capable of 'condoning' defendant's false representations than would be an infant or one of unsound mind." *Zmyslinski v. Zmyslinski*, 151 N.Y.S.2d 774 (App. Div. 1956).

4. The court refused to allow Peter to recover because he failed to prove the element of reliance, noting that the plaintiff had "elected to stand upon [the complaint] without exercising his leave to amend." *Peter W. v. San Francisco Unified School District*, 131 Cal. Rptr. 854 (Ct. App. 1976).

5. The court found no misrepresentation. The court saw no more in Kaiser's literature than a "generalized puffing" to the effect that the foundation's doctors would exercise good judgment in their care. The court also concluded that the "incentive" plan used by Kaiser was recommended by professional organizations as a means of reducing unnecessary medical costs and that it was not evidence that any doctors had acted negligently or that they had refrained from recommending necessary diagnostic procedures or treatments. *Pulvers v. Kaiser Foundation Health Plan*, 160 Cal. Rptr. 392 (Ct. App. 1980).

10:2 Negligent Misrepresentation

The court concluded that William had a claim for negligent misrepresentation because he relied (to his detriment) on the doctor's misrepresentations regarding his experience as well as the lack of risk of amputation. The court suggested that William had a viable claim for lack of informed consent as well. *Bloskas v. Murray*, 646 P.2d 907 (Colo. 1982).

10:3 *Gibbs v. Ernst*

1. Whether common law fraud can be applied in the adoption context.

2. The need for prospective parents to be given as much information as possible to ensure a successful placement with parents who are emotionally and financially able to care for the children they adopt versus the concern that an undue burden placed on adoption agencies would diminish the number of children being successfully placed in homes.

3. Yes.

4. Yes. No.

5. The act is silent. The legislature would need to take affirmative steps to indicate it did not want tort law to be applicable.

6. Intentional nondisclosure involves an intentional concealment of a material fact rather than the making of an affirmative misrepresentation.

7. They have all allowed intentional misrepresentation, and several have recognized negligent misrepresentation.

8. The court allows them to proceed on both claims.

9. Because the agencies are not required to guarantee that the information they provide is accurate; they are required only to use reasonable care in their investigations.

10:4 Innocent Misrepresentation

The court affirmed a judgment for the Ballards against the broker on the grounds that brokers have a duty to know about the property they are selling and that as professionals possessing superior knowledge buyers should be expected to rely on their representations. Brokers, the court suggested, could protect themselves "by investigating the owner's statements, or by disclaiming knowledge, by requiring the seller to sign at the time of listing a statement setting forth representations which will be made, certifying that they are true and providing for indemnification if they are not." The facts supported a misrepresentation claim, in that the listing, which mentioned a 100-foot well, would reasonably lead buyers to assume the well was good; the listing misrepresented the well; and the Ballards relied on that misrepresentation. *Bevins v. Ballard*, 655 P.2d 757 (Alaska 1982).

10:5 *Wood v. Picillo*

1. The odors of chemicals were obvious, as was visual evidence of chemicals in a trench and chemicals flowing from barrels. Trucks from chemical companies were seen entering the property. Soil samples were tested and found to contain a number of toxic chemicals. Testimony showed that the chemicals were traveling from the dump site to waters inhabited by fish and used by humans.

2. Nuisance requires a showing of unreasonable injury rather than unreasonable conduct.

3. The neighbors showed signs of exposure to toxic chemicals, and testimony showed that the chemicals found on the defendants' property threatened wildlife and human life with possible death, cancer, and liver disease.

4. The science of hydrology has grown since 1934, when *Rose* was decided, and societal concern for environmental protection has grown considerably since that time, so that the scientific and societal considerations that governed *Rose* no longer apply.

5. No.

10:6 Nuisance

1. Yes; the court found that the landlords had not acted reasonably in dealing with the problem. *Lew v. Superior Court*, 25 Cal. Rptr. 2d 42 (Ct. App. 1993).

2. Yes. The court observed that public nuisance is not confined to physical injury to the senses and that a public nuisance can be a condition or use of property that offends public morals or decency. *Bensenville v. Botu, Inc.*, 350 N.E.2d 239 (Ill. 1976).

3. No. The court refused to find a private nuisance on the basis that publicity concerning the contamination of groundwater in the area (not the plaintiffs' groundwater) had caused a diminution in property value. The court observed that "negative publicity resulting in unfounded fear about dangers in the vicinity of the property does not constitute a significant interference with the use and enjoyment of land." Although property depreciation is an element of damages in a nuisance action, such an allegation by itself does not establish a claim of private nuisance. *Adkins v. Thomas Solvent Co.*, 487 N.W.2d 715 (Mich. 1992).

4. Damages for injuries resulting from the noise, according to the court in *Griggs v. Allegheny County*, 369 U.S. 84 (1962).

10:7 Interference with Business Relations

1. The court granted summary judgment to Pro-Image on the interference with existing contractual relations claim because the evidence showed that Pro-Image was acting to protect its own legitimate business interests rather than to harm University Graphics. The court also granted summary judgment on the prospective contractual relations claims, noting that when a "defendant acts at least in part for the purpose of protecting some legitimate interest which conflicts with that of the plaintiff, a line must be drawn and the interests evaluated" and that interferences that "are sanctioned by the 'rules of the game' which society has adopted" are regarded as privileged. Pro-Image's expression of its concerns regarding University Graphics "falls within the 'rules of the game' permitted by society" and was justified as a means of protecting its own interests. *University Graphics, Inc. v. Pro-Image Corp.*, 913 F. Supp. 338 (C.D. Pa. 1996).

2. The court granted summary judgment to the attorney, because as a legal adviser to the students, he was privileged to advise them to breach their

contracts with the school. As an attorney, he "was required to make a full and complete investigation of his clients' allegations"; he was also justified in contacting witnesses and in giving legal advice regarding the enforceability of contracts. The court noted that "an attorney who in good faith counsels a client to breach a contract with a third party must not be hindered or impeded by fear of retaliatory lawsuits." *Brown Mackie College v. Graham*, 768 F. Supp. 1457 (D. Kan. 1991).

10:8 Misuse of Process

1. A jury found the defendant firefighter liable and awarded Robert $500,000 in damages, but the appellate court reversed because it found the defendants, who were public employees acting within the scope of their employment, to be immune. *Tur v. City of Los Angeles*, 59 Cal. Rptr. 2d 470 (Ct. App. 1997).

2. The court found that Nursefinders had probable cause for requesting a restraining order and injunction on the ground that the facts showed evidence of a threatened breach of contract by Rosemary. Numerous efforts by Nursefinders' attorney to contact Rosemary were unsuccessful, thereby precluding any possibility of resolution of their conflict. The court affirmed summary judgment in favor of Nursefinders on both the malicious prosecution and abuse of process claims. *McLain v. Nursefinders of Mobile, Inc.*, 598 So. 2d 853 (Ala. 1992).

CHAPTER 11

11:1 Animals

1. The court refused to instruct the jury that Smokey had unmistakable vicious propensities based on Smokey's having bitten the man who kicked him. The jury found for the defendant. *Deardorff v. Burger*, 606 A.2d 489 (Pa. 1992).

2. The jury concluded that Bandit did not have a dangerous or vicious propensity. *Drake v. Dean*, 19 Cal. Rptr. 325 (Ct. App. 1993).

11:2 *Yukon Equipment Inc. v. Fireman's Fund Ins. Co.*

1. To recover for property damage resulting from an explosion of a storage magazine for explosives.

2. It was caused by thieves.

3. Yukon Equipment and E.I. DuPont de Nemours & Co. are the petitioners. They argue that the intentional nature of the detonation was a superseding cause and that they are not liable under any theory of liability.

4. They argue that the storage of explosives was normal and appropriate for the area and that such storage met a community need.

5. The court believes there is a high degree of risk of harm that is great and difficult to eliminate, that storage of explosives is not a matter of common usage, and the value to the community is outweighed by its dangerousness.

6. Because the court sees no reason to turn to the *Restatement* when a long line of cases already deal with the storage of explosives.

7. Yes.

8. The court concludes that the thieves are an intervening, not a superseding, cause because it concludes that incendiary destruction by thieves is not so unusual as to be considered an extraordinary event.

11:3 Abnormally Dangerous Activities

1. The court found fire-eating acts to be "foolhardy" but not abnormally dangerous, noting that fire-eating acts are performed throughout the world without incident. *Thomalen v. Marriott Corp.*, 880 F. Supp. 74 (C.D. Mass. 1995).

2. Based on the *Restatement of Torts*, Virginia case law, and case law from other jurisdictions, the court found that the operation of a railway is not an abnormally dangerous activity. *Warner v. Norfolk & Western Railway Co.*, 758 F. Supp. 370 (Va. 1991).

3. The court found that the contamination of the Fletchers' property created a high degree of risk of great harm, that disposal of PCB-laden waste by dumping it onto land or into a drainage system was not a matter of common usage, that it was inappropriate in any location, and that it was not essential to Tenneco's gas transmission and thus was of no value to the community. The Fletchers also sued on the basis of nuisance and trespass. *Fletcher v. Tenneco, Inc.*, 1993 (E.D. Ky. 1993).

4. The court held that setting off public fireworks is an abnormally dangerous activity that is not of common usage and that presents an "ineliminably

high risk of serious bodily injury or property damage." *Klein v. Pyrodyne Corp.*, 810 P.2d 917 (Wash. 1991).

5. The court found strict liability inapplicable because it considered the storing and removing of gasoline from commercial underground gasoline storage tanks to be widespread and routine and noted that having service stations in residential areas was appropriate because they provide a necessary resource for residents. In this case the tanks were dangerous only because they were in a defective condition and not because they were dangerous in their "normal or nondefective state." If the risk of harm can be avoided by reasonable care, the court observed that negligence is the appropriate remedy. *Arlington Forest Ass'n. v. Exxon Corp.*, 774 F. Supp. 387 (C.D. Va. 1991).

11:4 Defenses

1. The trial judge accepted the defense expert's opinion that the damage to the transformer was incurred as an act of nature (lightning), precluding the plaintiff from recovering. *Boyd v. Washington-St. Tammany Electric Cooperative*, 618 So. 2d 982 (La. 1993).

2. The manufacturer could (and did) raise the defense of assumption of risk and argued that the plaintiff's conduct was the proximate cause of his injuries. In refusing to admit evidence of Kramer's conduct, the court noted that although his conduct was a but-for cause of his injuries, such evidence had little probative value; "the fact that Kramer's conduct was a 'but for' cause [did] not give the jury reason to conclude that the forklift defect—also a 'but for' cause—was not a proximate cause of Kramer's injuries." Such evidence did, however, have a "significant potential to mislead the jury into thinking that Kramer should not recover if he was negligent." Because the manufacturer failed to show that Kramer was aware of the forklift defect, the court ruled as a matter of law that Kramer had not assumed the risk. *Kramer v. Raymond Corp.*, 840 F. Supp. 333 (C.D. Pa. 1993).

3. No; because Martin was obviously aware of the danger, he assumed the risk. *Restatement (Second) of Torts* § 523, cmt. d.

4. No, Lynn's negligence does not bar her estate from recovering under strict liability. *Restatement (Second) of Torts* § 524A, illus. 1.

CHAPTER 12

12:1 Warranty

1. a. Express warranty.

   b. The court remanded the case to the trial court to determine whether "the time and place availability to Elite of normal working hours services at a Carrier facility" provisions of the warranty were met. If a jury found that Carrier were unavailable to Elite in a meaningful way prior to Elite's arrival in California, the essential purpose of the remedy accorded by the warranty would have failed. *Elite Professional, Inc. v. Carrier Corp.*, 827 P.2d 1195 (Kan. 1992).

2. They might argue breach of implied warranty on the ground that the drug was not "fit for the ordinary purposes" for which it was intended. If the manufacturer made any claims about the medication, the plaintiffs might argue breach of express warranty and submit proof that the drug did not conform to those promises.

3. No. The court said statements made by the companies could not be "considered warranties against adverse health effects since the dangers of cigarette smoking ha[d] long been known to the community." No, although the court never reached this question because of its finding that the statements were not express warranties. *Marks v. R.J. Reynolds Tobacco Co.*, 1997 (W.D. La.).

12:2 Strict Liability

1. No, as long as the vaccine is properly prepared and is accompanied by proper directions and warning. It is considered an unavoidably unsafe product.

2. The court held that selling tickets to the public for go-cart usage constituted providing access to a product, not a service. The court suggested several public policy reasons to support a strict liability claim: the owner of the go-cart was in a better position to bear the cost of the injury; because the go-cart owner profited from the public's use of the go-cart, the cost of injury should be imposed on him; placing liability on the owner would ensure that he would use care in selecting responsible go-cart manufacturers to minimize his risks of operation. *Golt v. Sports Complex, Inc.*, 644 A.2d 989 (Del. 1994).

3. The court agreed with the manufacturer and found that "foreseeability . . . plays no part in the initial determination of defect in strict liability." In analyzing the negligence issue, the court observed that even though "foreseeability is an integral part of the duty analysis in negligence," it is not in strict liability; thus, "holding 'no duty' in strict liability does not per se eliminate consideration of the duty factor in negligence law." In applying a risk-utility analysis to the facts presented, the court concluded that failure to childproof the lighter was unreasonable if "the high social value placed on the safety of people and property threatened by childplay fires, the high gravity of risk, the considerable probability of risk, and the likelihood of a reasonably available alternative . . . outweigh[ed] BIC's interest in producing its lighters without childproofing features." *Griggs v. BIC Corp.*, 981 F.2d 1429 (3d Cir. 1993).

4. The court contrasted the facts of *Griggs* with this case and concluded that it was not clear from the record whether the intended user recommendation on the box pertained to children who were chronologically one-and-one-half to five years old or to those who were developmentally within that age range. Noting that "although foreseeability is not a term that should be associated with strict liability, the concept, to the extent it implies an objective test, is not entirely foreign to a strict liability analysis, although it is applied in a more narrow sense than in negligence law." The court explained that "unless the use giving rise to a strict liability cause of action is a reasonably obvious misuse, or the user a reasonably obvious unintended user, as was the case in *Griggs*, or unless the particular use or user is clearly warned against, the manufacturer is not obviously exonerated." The court concluded that the "intended user" should be determined in the "context of the knowledge and assumptions of the ordinary consumer in the relevant community." *Metzgar v. Playskool, Inc.*, 30 F.3d 459 (3d Cir. 1994).

5. Under the consumer-expectation standard, the question is whether the reasonable consumer would consider DES defective. The defendants in this case argued that the "consumer" was the physician, not the person who purchased the drug, because the manufacturer's warnings were directed to physicians.

The risk-utility test balances the risks and benefits of having such a drug. The defendants argued that this test could not be applied to prescription drugs, because they could not be "redesigned" but instead are created in accordance with a scientific formula. The court disagreed because it believed that the plaintiff might be able to demonstrate that the drug could be reformulated to be safer or that other, less harmful drugs were available to prevent miscarriages, and the benefit of such alternate drugs could be weighed against the advantages of DES.

The court declined to apply a strict liability standard to prescription drugs because "public policy favors the development and marketing of beneficial new drugs, even though some risks, perhaps serious ones, might accompany their introduction, because drugs can save lives and reduce pain and suffering." Being subject to strict liability, the court explained, could intimidate drug manufacturers and deter them from developing new drugs or distributing existing drugs, and could elevate prices to the point that drugs were no longer affordable to some consumers. In support of this argument, the court cited drugs and vaccines that manufacturers refused to market because of fear of anticipated lawsuits, pointing out that only two vaccine manufacturers remain in the market. To illustrate, the court cited the cost of one vaccine as having risen from 11 cents in 1982 to $11.40 in 1986, $8 of which was for an insurance reserve, with the price increase paralleling the increase in lawsuits from one in 1978 to 219 in 1985. *Brown v. Abbott Laboratories*, 751 P.2d 470 (Cal. 1988).

6. Consider (a) who you can sue, (b) what damages you can recover, and (c) whether you are in a position to sue. Strict liability is generally the easiest to prove and includes the broadest range of plaintiffs (extending to bystanders in some cases). Warranty has the broadest range of damages and is the theory of choice when economic losses are unaccompanied by personal injury or property damage. Negligence is harder to prove than strict liability and is less liberal than the UCC as far as damages, but should still be pleaded whenever possible, especially when the court for policy reasons is likely to deny a claim for strict liability. Of course, plead all three theories if possible.

12:3 Losses

1. Because Elite did not seek to recover for the refrigeration unit itself, the court characterized the loss of meat as property damage. It defined

"pure economic losses" as those "including loss of use of the defective product, cost of replacing the product, loss of profits to plaintiff's business, or damage to plaintiff's business reputation from use of the product." *Elite Professionals, Inc. v. Carrier Corp.*, 827 P.2d 1195 (Kan. 1992).

2. No, they are a property loss.

3. No, because the firm's losses are solely economic. The court was unimpressed with the firm's argument that the economic loss rule is an "anachronism" and concluded that without being able to show injury to persons or property, the firm could not recover. *Bamberger & Feibleman v. Indianapolis Power & Light Co.*, 665 N.E.2d 933 (Ind. 1996).

12:4 *Turner v. GMC*

1. Can a manufacturer and retailer be held strictly liable for a defectively designed vehicle that enhances injuries but does not cause accidents?

2. A roof structure that provides inadequate protection to occupants in the event of a rollover.

3. The issue of crashworthiness.

4. Yes.

5. No. No.

6. No. Unreasonable risk of injury in the event of a collision.

7. Intended use.

8. Yes.

9. Yes.

10. Courts lack the expertise to deal with such complex matters; sporadic court decisions will result in wrong and contradictory standards; Congress has already begun to set safety standards.

11. No. The industry custom was unreasonably dangerous.

12:5 Defects

1. a. Negligence, warranty, and strict liability (being in a defective condition, unreasonably dangerous).

   b. Defective design, failure to warn.

   c. The court relies on the doctor's expectations rather than the consumer's.

   d. The court, in opposition to the Brown court (discussed in "Putting It into Practice" 13:2),

finds "it consistent with the purposes underlying strict products liability that manufacturers should be deterred from marketing certain products and that the cost of the defense of strict products liability litigation and any resulting judgments should be borne by the manufacturer who is able to spread the cost through insurance and by charging more for its products." In applying a "risk/benefit" analysis to the facts at hand, the court explained that the fact finder should consider "the seriousness of the side effects or reactions posed by the drug, the likelihood that such side effects or reactions would occur, the feasibility of an alternative design which would eliminate or reduce the side effects or reactions without affecting the efficacy of the drug, and the harm to the consumer in terms of reduced efficacy and any new side effects or reactions that would result from an alternative design" and balance those factors against "the seriousness of the condition for which the drug is indicated." *Shanks v. Upjohn Co.*, 835 P.2d 1189 (Alaska 1992).

2. Obviousness of danger. The district court reasoned that the risk of a small child choking on one of Playskool's smaller blocks was so objectively obvious as to preclude the necessity of a warning, but the appellate court remanded the issue for jury deliberation. *Metzgar v. Playskool, Inc.*, 30 F.3d 459 (3d Cir. 1994).

3. The court allows Wilma's claim to stand; it finds the reasoning in *Brown* to be inapplicable because "unlike strict liability for design defects, strict liability for failure to warn does not potentially subject drug manufacturers to liability for flaws in their products that they have not, and could not have, discovered. Drug manufacturers need only warn of risks that are actually known or reasonably scientifically knowable." *Carlin v. Upjohn Co.*, 920 P.2d 1347 (Cal. 1996).

4. State-of-the-art defense. *Sternhagen v. Dow Co.*, 935 P.2d 1139 (Mont. 1997).

5. Argue foreseeable misuse. The court found that injuries to children were a foreseeable risk and that this risk was known or should have been known to the manufacturers. *Hall v. E.I. DuPont de Nemours & Co.*, 345 F. Supp. 353 (E.D.N.Y. 1972).

6. The court granted the defense motion because the plaintiff failed to introduce expert testimony to show that a feasible alternative cigarette design existed at the time the plaintiff's wife was smoking, that she would have availed herself of this design, that this design would have prevented her illness, and that such a design would have been reasonable under a risk-benefit test. *Marks v. R.J. Reynolds Tobacco Co.*, 1997 (W.D. La.)

12:6 Defenses

1. Causation (failure to prove who the manufacturers of the blasting caps that caused injury were and failure to prove that the lack of warnings caused the children's injuries); no duty to children (unforeseeable users; unreasonable cost of taking precautions [cost/benefit analysis]); misuse of product. Check statute of limitations also.

2. Assumption of risk; contributory negligence; comparative negligence.

3. Disclaimer; limited remedy.

4. The court held that the action accrued when Joseph knew or reasonably should have known of his illness and a possible causal connection between his illness and his use of cigarettes, in this case no later than 1988, when he was diagnosed with COPD. The court was not persuaded by his argument, because the discovery about the research came in November 1995, four months after the complaint was filed (July 1995), and because Joseph knew in 1988 that he was addicted to and had been injured by cigarettes and was thereby in possession of sufficient information to commence an action. *Arnold v. R.J. Reynolds Tobacco Co.*, 956 F. Supp. 110 (D.R.I. 1997).

5. Express preemption.

CHAPTER 13

13:1 Libel or Slander

1. Libel. *Restatement (Second) of Torts* § 568A.

2. Libel. *Restatement (Second) of Torts* § 568, illus. 3.

3. Slander. *Restatement (Second) of Torts* § 568, illus. 4.

13:2 Defamatory Statements

In *Robins v. National Enquirer*, 1995 (D.S.C. 1995), the court noted that Lorinda did not allege that the statements made in the article were false and that although "the article, in hindsight, may have made her seem insensitive . . . [the] quotes have no bearing upon Plaintiff's integrity or reputation."

13:3 Opinion

In *Huggins v. Povitch*, 1996 (N.Y. Sup. Ct. 1996), the court considered the context in which the statements were made (on a talk show organized around controversial topics and designed to encourage public debate) and concluded that reasonable listeners would know they were listening to the "subjective opinion of Ms. Moore upon the emotionally charged topic of her divorce and its financial consequences." The court pointed out that "both the host and other guests repeatedly pointed out, and Moore confirmed, that her statements were her own personal views and that her ex-husband denies her 'charges' or 'allegations.'"

In examining the quoted excerpts the court found that the statements were "vague and contain[ed] loose figurative language that [did] not refer to verifiable acts of criminal conduct." The court explained that her belief that she "should share in" property does not mean her husband committed a crime but "merely expresses her dissatisfaction with the distribution approved by the court." Moore used the fact that her ex-husband failed to share partnership assets to support her opinion about him and "[o]pinions, false or not, are constitutionally protected if the facts supporting them are set forth."

13:4 *Street v. National Broadcasting Co.*

1. Did a historical drama defame the plaintiff or place her in a false light by depicting her as one who falsely accused others of raping her?

2. Because the historical events portrayed were considered public events, requiring the plaintiff to prove malice, which the evidence did not support.

3. As a perjurer, a woman of bad character, and a woman who falsely accused the Scottsboro boys of raping her.

4. a. Was there a public controversy?

   b. What was the "nature and extent" of the plaintiff's participation in the public controversy?

5. Yes.

6. As the only prosecutrix, she played a prominent role in the controversy; she had ample access to the media; she thrust herself voluntarily into the controversy by granting interviews and aggressively promoting her version of the events outside of the courtroom.

7. The question raised by the trial was whether the justice system could provide fair trials to blacks in the South, and that remains a "living controversy."

8. Because no evidence was presented to show bad faith or extreme disregard of the truth.

13:5 Public Figure

1. She will have to prove actual malice, because she is considered a public figure.

2. The court in *White v. Manchester Enterprise, Inc.,* 871 F. Supp. 934 (E.D. Ky. 1994) refused to classify White as a public figure, explaining that "public concern about wasteful public expenditures is not sufficient unless the individual is surrounded by a specific controversy." The court cited *Hutchinson v. Proxmire,* 443 U.S. 111, 99 S. Ct. 2675, 61 L. Ed. 2d 411 (1979), in which a federal research-grant recipient who reported on Senator Proxmire's Golden Fleece Award for wasteful public spending was not given public figure status even though the recipient had sufficient access to the media to rebut attacks on the value of his research: "Clearly, those charged with defamation cannot, by their own conduct, create their own defense by making a claimant a public figure."

3. In *Spence v. Flynt,* 816 P.2d 771 (Wyo. 1991), *Hustler* argues that in taking on the fight against pornography, Spence thrust himself into a public controversy, thereby casting himself as a public figure. Alternatively, *Hustler* argues that by virtue of writing about his case against *Hustler* he became a public figure. The court points out that Spence's book was published after his litigation involving *Hustler* and so he was not a public figure on that basis for purposes of this litigation. The court also notes that a "professional person, who may be a 'public figure' for some purposes, should be free to offer his services to a client as a private professional without being subjected to public-figure defamation. To hold otherwise would have a chilling effect upon attorneys who undertake to represent clients in difficult,

unpopular, high profile, or sensational types of cases. . . . Free speech cannot equate with the freedom to intimidate, destroy and defame an advocate seeking to represent a client."

13:6 Review of Defamation

1. Libel.

2. Yes.

3. In this case, *Hustler Magazine v. Falwell,* 485 U.S. 46 (1988), the jury found against Falwell, deciding that the parody could not "reasonably be understood as describing actual facts about [Falwell] or actual events in which [he] participated."

13:7 Privileges

1. The attorney general enjoys an absolute privilege; the privilege of the district attorney is qualified even if the press release is within the scope of his official duties. *Restatement (Second) of Torts* § 591, illus. 3–4.

2. No. *Restatement (Second) of Torts* § 586.

3. Not as long as she did not make the allegation recklessly.

13:8 *Douglass v. Hustler*

1. By placing her in a false light and appropriating a commercial right.

2. The tort allows plaintiffs to get around some of the outdated historical limitations of defamation; in this case the limitations of defamation would not have impeded the plaintiff's case; her claim is better classified as "offensive" than defamatory.

3. By insinuating that she was a lesbian and that she was the type of person willing to appear nude in *Hustler.*

4. Yes.

5. Yes.

6. Yes.

7. Because the jury could reasonably conclude that only Douglass or *Playboy* could have consented to the publication of those photos.

8. Because *Hustler* used photos that were made by others for commercial purposes.

9. Because they were in the public domain.

13:9 Invasion of Privacy

1. The *Enquirer* did not contest the false-light claim. In finding that the *Enquirer* had commercially exploited Eastwood's name, the court observed that the magazine had used Eastwood's fame and personality to its commercial advantage and "to generate maximum curiosity and the necessary motivation to purchase the newspaper." *Eastwood v. National Enquirer*, 198 Cal. Rptr. 342 (Ct. App. 1983).

2. Unreasonable intrusion. *Restatement (Second) of Torts* § 652B, illus. 1.

3. Public disclosure of private facts. *Restatement (Second) of Torts* § 652D, illus. 11.

4. Although disclosure of a crime is generally not a tort, when the disclosure is made several years later and the revelation destroys the life of a reformed criminal, the tort of public disclosure of private facts may have been committed. *Restatement (Second) of Torts* § 652D, illus. 26.

5. False light. *Restatement (Second) of Torts* § 652E, illus. 8.

13:10 Injurious Falsehood

The court dismissed the case (and the appellate court affirmed the dismissal) on the ground that the growers failed to prove that the claims were "verifiably false." In response the growers in several states introduced the so-called "veggie libel laws," which authorize damages for "the disparagement of any perishable agricultural product." *Auvil v. CBS "60 Minutes,"* 800 F. Supp. 941 (E.D. Wash. 1992), *aff'd*, 67 F.3d 816 (9th Cir. 1995).

CHAPTER 14

14:1 Scope of Liability of Employer

1. Yes. The court observed that picking up customers to try to sell them cars, even on off-hours, was considered commonplace for salesmen; Mr. Stone had done business with Mr. Urban on previous occasions; the route Mr. Stone had taken was the route to Mr. Urban's house. *Ray Korte Chevrolet v. Simmons*, 571 P.2d 699 (Ariz. Ct. App. 1977).

2. No. Although the accident occurred during Richard's hours of employment and at a place where he was authorized to be, his display of his gun was not related in any way to his employment. *Olson v. Staggs-Bilt Homes*, 534 P.2d 1073 (Ariz. Ct. App. 1975).

3. Yes, because the employer had an obligation to control the janitor's behavior. *Restatement (Second) of Agency* § 230, illus. 2.

4. If the truck driver was negligent in entrusting the driving to the thirteen-year-old or was negligent in supervising the teenager's driving.

5. Yes. An employer is vicariously liable "for the conduct of an employee engaged in a special errand for the employer, even though the errand may be different from the type of work usually performed for the employer." *Love v. Liberty Mutual Insurance Co.*, 760 P.2d 1085 (Ariz. Ct. App. 1988).

6. No. The court explained that his possession of his employer's papers was merely incidental and did not, in itself, convert his travel to work into a part of his employment. *S.&W. Construction Co. v. Bugge*, 13 So. 2d 645 (Miss. 1943).

14:2 *Juarez v. CC Services, Inc.,*

1. Because it wanted a finding that Juarez was an independent contractor. Westarz would then not be responsible for Juarez's injuries.

2. Is the relationship between Bever and Westarz that of employer-employee or employer–independent contractor?

3. So it (Country) would not be responsible for the judgment Juarez obtained against Bever.

4. Extent of control exercised by the employer and the degree of supervision; distinct nature of the worker's business; degree of specialization of worker's occupation; materials provided by employer; duration of employment; method of payment; relationship of worker's work done to the regular business of the employer; belief of the parties.

5. Employer's power to give specific instructions with the expectation that they will be followed. Westarz selected the time and place and area for the work to be done, as well as the manner in which it was to be completed.

6. No. He had no delivery business distinct from his work with Westarz.

7. No, there was no evidence on this question.

8. Yes.

9. A continuous working relationship. A right to terminate indicates control and thus an employer-employee relationship. Bever could be terminated with cause at any time.

10. Yes. Yes.

11. Yes. Yes.

14:3 Independent Contractors

1. No. A justice of the peace is not an employee or agent of the county; the independence of judges is "based on the constitutional doctrine of the separation of powers and the lack of a principal-agent relationship between elected officials and other governmental bodies." *Hernandez v. Maricopa County*, 673 P.2d 341 (Ariz. 1983).

2. Yes, because the lions are inherently dangerous. *Restatement (Second) of Torts* § 427A, illus. 1.

3. Yes, because the hotel was aware of the driver's lack of experience. Yes; the hotel would not be liable if the accident was due to unforeseen negligence on the part of the driver. *Restatement (Second) of Torts* § 411, illus. 3 and 4.

4. The court said that the determination is a factual one and remanded the case to the trial court for a jury's deliberation. *Fisher v. Townsends*, 695 A.2d 53 (Del. 1997).

5. Yes. Jetro and Chamber were not entitled to delegate their responsibility to exercise care when dealing with a product that created a grave risk of serious bodily harm. They were the ones that primarily benefited from the fireworks display, and they could protect themselves from liability by selecting a qualified independent contractor. *Ramsey v. Marutamaya Ogatsu Fireworks Co.*, 140 Cal. Rptr. 247 (Ct. App. 1977).

6. Yes. The court found Kennecott liable under the retained control exception of section 414 of the *Restatement*. *Welker v. Kennecott Copper Co.*, 403 P.2d 330 (Ariz. Ct. App. 1965).

14:4 Bailments

1. No. The family-purpose doctrine is inapplicable because the father had not furnished the vehicle for general family use and did not exercise control over the car. "Mere ownership demonstrated by record titleholder status is not conclusive on the issue of liability under the family purpose doctrine." *Madrid v. Shyrock*, 745 P.2d 375 (N.M. 1987).

2. Yes. The court reasoned that "parents cannot blind themselves to the realities of youthful behavior, the universal proclivity of young people for joyriding, and the inclination of young people to permit friends to drive their automobiles." *Granley v. Crandall*, 180 N.W.2d 190 (Minn. 1970).

3. No, because no pecuniary interest existed on the part of the hikers. *Farmers Insurance Exchange v. Parker*, 936 P.2d 1088 (Utah 1997).

4. [Consult the applicable law in your state.]

5. [Consult the applicable law in your state.]

CHAPTER 15

15:1 *Hall v. DuPont*

1. Eighteen.

2. Explosives manufacturers and their trade association (IME). The practice of not placing warnings on individual blasting caps and of failing to follow other safety measures created an unreasonable risk of harm that resulted in the plaintiffs' injuries.

3. In *Hall* the plaintiffs know the name of the manufacturer that produced the cap causing the plaintiff's injury; in *Chance* the identity is unknown.

4. They designed and manufactured blasting caps, they considered and rejected the possibility of labeling caps, and they lobbied to prevent such labeling.

5. Do the parallel safety practices of the defendants form a basis for joint liability?

6. Joint control of risk; enterprise liability; proof of causation.

7. They did not have joint control over the risks of injury because they did not enter into a conspiracy to commit intentional harm or into a partnership or joint venture. The elements of joint control of risks differ from those of joint venture.

8. By showing an explicit agreement or joint action; by presenting evidence that supports an inference of a tacit agreement or cooperation; by showing evidence of an industry-wide standard or custom. The first one.

9. No.

10. The size and composition of the trade association, its announced and actual objectives in reference to safety, its internal procedures and decision-making process in relationship to safety, the nature of its information-gathering system regarding accidents, the design and implementation of a safety program, and the nature of any

other activities (such as lobbying) relating to safety.

11. Assigning of foreseeable costs of an activity to those in the best position to reduce those costs.

12. Joint awareness of the risks involved and joint capacity to reduce or affect those risks. No.

15:2 Joint and Several Liability

1. No, because a physician who calls in another physician is not liable for the other's malpractice if there are no concerted actions by the two physicians. *Stovall v. Harms*, 522 P.2d 353 (Kan. 1974).

2. No. The first physician should be liable for the full amount of the plaintiff's damages and the second physician should be liable for only that portion of damages that occurred after his treatment of the plaintiff began. In this case the jury held both physicians jointly and severally liable for $20,000 and the first physician individually liable for the remaining $60,000. *Naccarato v. Grob*, 180 N.W.2d 788 (Mich. 1970).

3. Yes, if this jurisdiction has adopted the doctrine of joint and several liability. *Walt Disney World v. Wood*, 515 So. 2d 198 (Fla. 1987).

4. Yes, because the parties performed separate acts that combined to produce a single, indivisible economic injury. *University of Miami v. All-Pro Athletic Surfaces, Inc.*, 619 So. 2d 1034 (Fla. Dist. Ct. App. 1993).

15:3 *Gulfstream v. Gold Spur*

1. Gold Spur sued Gulfstream for negligence in designing, maintaining, and operating its race track and for failure to warn of a dangerous condition on the track.

2. Gulfstream brought Kimmel in on the basis that his negligence contributed to Gold Spur's damages. Gulfstream requested contribution from Kimmel and contractual indemnification.

3. He was responsible for the care, well-being, and safety of the horse. He had a duty to inspect the track to make sure it was safe.

4. Kimmel alleged that Gulfstream had been sued for negligence in creating, maintaining, and operating the track and he was not jointly liable for those activities. He also argued that his contractual agreement with Gulfstream allowed

indemnification for his negligence but did not require him to indemnify Gulfstream for its own negligence.

5. The court says Gulfstream has a right to contribution because it and Kimmel share a common liability.

    a. Kimmel argues he does not have a right to contribution because his liability and the liability of Gulfstream rest on different grounds.

    b. The court says that sufficient evidence exists to support a reasonable inference that Kimmel was negligent in allowing the horse to race.

6. Gulstream's claim for indemnification is based on a stall agreement signed by Kimmel as Gold Spur's agent.

    a. Kimmel argues that the indemnification clause does not unequivocally require him to indemnify Gulfstream for its own negligence.

    b. Gulfstream counters that the clause clearly and unambiguously provides that Kimmel must indemnify Gulfstream if they are jointly negligent, not if Gulfstream is solely negligent.

    c. The court agrees with Gulfstream, arriving at its conclusion by comparing the language in the indemnification clause in this case with those in previous cases. It concludes that the language clearly indicates that Kimmel is to indemnify Gulfstream if both Gulfstream and Kimmel are jointly negligent.

15:4 Contribution, Releases, and Indemnification

1. They could seek contribution and indemnification (both contractual and based on the employer-employee relationship).

2. A covenant not to sue. *Hall v. Schulte*, 836 P.2d 989 (Ariz. 1992).

3. They can seek contribution and indemnification. The court concluded that as long as the settlement was in "good faith," the non-settling defendants were barred from contribution but not from indemnification. *Dunn v. Kanawha County Board of Education*, 459 S.E.2d 151 (W. Va. 1995).

4. No, because the agreement is collusive and therefore not in "good faith." *International Action Sports, Inc. v. Sabellico*, 573 So. 2d 928 (Fla. 1991).

5. The court adopted this rule in reference to Mary Carter agreements:

When a settlement agreement is entered into between the plaintiff and one or more, but not all, alleged defendant tortfeasors, the parties entering into such agreement shall promptly inform the court in which the action is pending and the other parties to the action of the existence of the agreement and its terms. If the action is tried to a jury and a defendant who is a party to the agreement is a witness, the court shall, upon motion of a party, disclose the existence and content of the agreement to the jury unless the court finds in its discretion such disclosure to the jury will create substantial danger of undue prejudice, of confusing the issues, or of misleading the jury. (*Ratterree v. Bartlett*, 717 P.2d 1063 [Kan. 1985])

CHAPTER 16

16:1 *State Farm Mut. Auto Ins. Co. v. Campbell*

Argument: Defendant's conduct did not justify punitive damages; award was windfall to plaintiff; award will encourage others to sue.

Rebuttal: Defendant's greed and callous indifference towards its policyholders warranted punitive damages; award will offset costs of litigation for plaintiff; awards like these deter businesses from engaging in similar conduct.

16:2 Joint and Several Liability

Consider reasons for adopting joint and several liability and whether those needs still exist when comparative negligence is operative.

CHAPTER 17

17:1 Subrogation

1. $300,000/$50,000.
2. [Answer will vary; fact-specific.]

17:2 Underinsured Motorist Coverage

1. It could pay your deductible and co-insurance costs.
2. If there is a question of liability, Denise's carrier may refuse to pay to repair the vehicle until after judgment. It is often easier to deal with your own insurer and pay the deductible than to deal with the other party's carrier. Because there is a right of subrogation, if your insurer pays and it is determined the other party was responsible, your insurer will pay you back the deductible when it collects from the other insurance company. If you do not prevail on liability, your insurer may treat the accident as your fault.
3. Replacement-cost coverage means that there will be sufficient proceeds to buy a new item rather than a used item. Many items depreciate very quickly (cars, computers, clothes, etc.). If there is a deductible, the money received from an actual cash-value policy may be insufficient.

17:3 Termination

It should. Most arbitrators are attorneys. The hourly charges for arbitrators can quickly exceed the total value of a small claim. You may also have your own attorney's costs in addition to those for the arbitrators.

The policy provision in Appendix D regarding arbitration provides that local rules of law regarding arbitration apply. Does your jurisdiction have applicable arbitration statutes? Does your court have rules of mandatory arbitration for lawsuits?

CHAPTER 18

18:1 First-Party versus Third-Party Claims

1. Yes, he has a liability claim against Dick.
2. Yes, he can make a claim under his medical payments coverage.
3. When a carrier defends under a reservation of rights while it investigates the claim, the insured is not left without a defense. Because the insurer is providing a defense (but might refuse to indemnify), even though the defense may be withdrawn, the chances of the insurer's being subjected to a bad faith claim are substantially lessened. An insurer that denies coverage and refuses to provide a defense faces tremendous exposure if it is later determined that there is coverage.

Insurers are in the business of investigating and settling claims. The failure of an insurer to investigate a claim before sending a reservation of rights letter is almost per se bad faith.

4. It is the insured's duty to prove that the policy was in effect at the time of the accident. It is the

insurer's obligation to prove lack of coverage. If it does not have sufficient evidence to deny coverage, it must either provide coverage or do an investigation that is thorough enough to show where the accident occurred.

5. The map may be important to show that the insurer had no reasonable basis to deny coverage or defend under a reservation of right. The fact that the company sent out the map does not necessarily bind it to any errors in the map.

6. Although the argument has some initial appeal, it is unlikely that nautical miles would win out. If we look at the reasonable expectations of the parties, it is hard to argue that nautical miles (that most people do not even know exist) were expected. If it is alleged that the lack of specificity creates an ambiguity that must be resolved in favor of the insured, it will still be difficult to argue that a term that is foreign to most insureds (and insurers) should be used rather than the commonly used statute mile.

18:2 Resolution of First-Party Claims

1. Yes. Not until late in the opinion does the court state that the insurer's evaluation of the case was "less than realistic."

2. Contributory negligence was a complete defense that, if found by the jury, would bar any recovery by the plaintiff. The defense of contributory negligence was seldom the basis of a jury verdict.

3. The court did not believe that the attorney or his client could legitimately value the life of a seventeen-year-old boy so low.

4. It appears that it does. It also appears that the court did not look at the unrealistically low evaluation of the case as mere negligence. Rather, it appears that the court did not believe that the values stated were the true values as determined by the attorney or the insurer.

18:3 Declaratory-Judgment Actions

1. If the insurer truly believes that there is no coverage for the accident, a declaratory-judgment action would confirm the lack of coverage. Seeking prompt declaratory-judgment relief would also save the insurer the majority of the cost of defending the claims, even if a defense was tendered under a reservation of rights. A court ruling that there was no coverage would also greatly reduce the possibility of a bad faith action being filed.

2. Possibly. Until suit is filed, technically there is no duty to defend. However, most claims are settled before suit is filed. The insurer could be in a very poor position if it handled the claim as though there were coverage (i.e., negotiated with Jerry or his attorney) and then later claimed there was no coverage.

3. Yes. If the insurer cannot prove that the accident is excluded from coverage, a declaratory-judgment action would result in a finding for the insured. Although there may not be a finding of coverage, the judgment would show that the insurer does not have sufficient evidence to deny coverage.

Timing would be very important. Until the claim had been investigated and evidence found that there is a basis for a filing of no coverage, any court action would be to the insurer's detriment.

18:4 Uninsured and Underinsured Motorist Coverage

1. Jerry has his claim for medical payments under his automobile insurance policy. If his insurer denied coverage for Dick, Jerry could also put in a claim under his uninsured motorist coverage. If his insurer did not deny coverage for Dick, Jerry may have a claim under his underinsured motorist coverage.

2. Yes. Because denial of coverage to Dick would almost have to result in coverage for Jerry, it would be prudent for the insurer to file a declaratory-judgment action. The insurer would have to have completed its investigation before filing suit.

3. Yes, if his damages were greater than Dick's liability coverage.

CHAPTER 19

19:1 Historical Background

1. [Use your state's statutes and rules to determine if Juan is deemed to have opted in.]

2. [Use your state's statutes and rules to determine if your state has voluntary or compulsory coverage.]

19:2 The Statutory Framework

[Answer will vary by state.]

In Arizona the employer takes the employee as he is (i.e., the eggshell plaintiff). If the industrial injury contributed to Juan's hospitalization and subsequent treatment, the injuries would be compensable. Juan's loss of his leg would be compensable under Ariz. Rev. Stat. § 23-1044(B)(15) for fifty months compensation at 55 percent of his average monthly wage.

19:3 Is Workers' Compensation a Fair Deal?

1. [Use your state's statutes and rules in determining Juan's average wage.] In Arizona, Ariz. Rev. Stat. § 23-1041 provides that the monthly wage is the average wage paid during and over the month in which the injury occurs. If the injured worker has not been employed for a month, different methods of determining the average wage are used. Because Juan had been working for five weeks, his average wage would be: $5.00 per hour × 85 hours per week × 4.33 weeks per month = $1,840.25 per month. Seasonal employment may be taken into account, as well as unusual, nonrepetitive wages (such as overtime).

[Use your state's statutes and rules in determining Juan's average wage if he works only eight months per year.] In Arizona his average wage, excluding the overtime issue, would be 8/12 of $1,840.25 or $1,226.83.

2. $12.00 per hour × 40 hours per week × 4.33 weeks per month = $2,078.40 per month. [Use your state's statutes and rules to calculate this answer.] In Arizona, loss of a dominant arm is scheduled at 55 percent for sixty months for a total of $68,587.20 (.55 × $2,078.40 per month × 60 months).

19:4 Filing a Workers' Compensation Claim

1. Who would the real client be? What obligations would there be to maximize recovery if your "true" client wanted to get back only the benefits that were paid? How would you deal with the injured employee? Would there be a conflict of interest between what the employer wants and what the employee would want? In the standard case, the attorney would attempt to negotiate a lower payment to the employer (if representing the employee). Would you have to advise the employee that it would be in her best interest to retain an attorney to pursue her claim? What would happen if the claim had already been assigned to the employer by operation of law?

2. [Use your state's statutes and rules to determine who is required to give notice of an industrial injury.] In Arizona, Ariz. Rev. Stat. § 23-908(A) requires that the employer (if it learns of the accident) and the treating physician must file a report with the Arizona Industrial commission. Paragraph D of that statute requires that the injured employee report the accident to the employer.

3. [Use your state's statutes and rules in determining how long benefits are paid.] In Arizona, Ariz. Rev. Stat. § 23-1045 provides that permanent total disability payments shall continue for the life of the injured person. Ariz. Rev. Stat. § 23-1044 provides that temporary partial disability payments shall continue so long as there is a reduction in earning capacity of the worker due to the accident. In Arizona there is no offset for Social Security benefits nor any age limitation. Arizona also allows an injured worker to draw retirement benefits without penalty.

19:5 Current Issues in Workers' Compensation

1. [Use your state's statutes and rules in determining if purely psychological injuries are compensable.] In Arizona, Ariz. Rev. Stat. § 23-1043.01 provides that some unexpected, unusual, or extraordinary stress related to employment must be a substantial contributing factor for benefits to be paid.

2. [Use your state's statutes and rules in determining how AIDS is dealt with.] Ariz. Rev. Stat. § 23-1043.02 provides specific steps for testing employees who may have been exposed during the course of employment.

3. Etta's claim was allowed in *Conley v. Workers' Compensation Division*, 483 S.E.2d 542 (W. Va. 1997). The law was changed after she filed her claim (in 1991) to preclude any claims based on injuries that were caused by nonphysical means and did not involve any physical injury.

Practice Exams

CHAPTER 1

True-False

1. T
2. T
3. T
4. F
5. T
6. T
7. F
8. T
9. F
10. F
11. F
12. T
13. F
14. F
15. F
16. T
17. T
18. T
19. T
20. F
21. T
22. T
23. F
24. T

Fill-in-the-Blanks

1. public policy
2. slippery-slope
3. crime; tort
4. preponderance of the evidence
5. blood feud; moot
6. action in trespass; trespass on the case

Multiple-Choice

1. a
2. b
3. d
4. b
5. c
6. a
7. c
8. c

CHAPTER 2

True-False

1. T
2. F
3. F
4. T
5. F
6. F
7. T
8. T
9. F
10. F
11. T
12. T
13. T
14. F
15. T

Matching

Group 1: 1 with d, 2 with b, 3 with a, 4 with c

Group 2: 1 with c, 2 with e, 3 with d, 4 with b, 5 with a, 6 with f

Group 3: 1 with c, 2 with d, 3 with b, 4 with a, 5 with e

Group 4: 1 with d, 2 with e, 3 with a, 4 with b, 5 with c

Fill-in-the-Blanks

1. demand
2. verification
3. default judgment
4. affirmative defense
5. motion
6. interrogatories
7. deposition
8. request for production of documents
9. request for medical examination
10. disclosure statement

11. motion for summary judgment
12. motion in limine
13. factual; legal; bench
14. voir dire
15. challenge for cause; peremptory challenge
16. overrules
17. charge
18. general; special
19. judgment notwithstanding the verdict
20. appeal; cross-appeal
21. res judicata

Multiple-Choice

1. d
2. d
3. a
4. c
5. a
6. d
7. b
8. c
9. b
10. a
11. a
12. a
13. c

CHAPTER 3

True-False

1. F
2. F
3. T
4. F
5. T
6. F
7. F
8. F
9. T
10. T
11. F
12. T
13. T
14. F
15. T
16. F
17. T
18. T
19. F
20. T
21. T
22. F
23. T
24. T
25. T
26. F
27. T
28. T
29. F
30. T
31. F
32. T
33. F
34. F
35. T
36. T
37. T
38. F
39. F
40. F
41. T
42. T
43. F
44. F
45. F
46. F
47. T
48. T
49. F
50. F
51. T
52. F
53. F

54. F
55. T
56. T
57. T
58. F
59. T

Matching

1 with e, 2 with d, 3 with b, 4 with a, 5 with c, 6 with e

Fill-in-the-Blanks

1. transferred intent
2. battery
3. extreme; outrageous
4. trespass
5. conversion
6. private necessity; public necessity
7. severity; likelihood

Multiple-Choice

1. b
2. d
3. c
4. c
5. d
6. c
7. a
8. b
9. b
10. d
11. b

CHAPTER 4

True-False

1. T
2. F
3. F
4. T
5. F
6. T
7. T
8. F
9. T
10. T
11. T
12. F
13. T
14. T
15. F
16. T
17. T
18. T
19. F
20. T
21. F
22. T
23. F
24. T
25. T
26. F
27. F
28. F
29. F
30. T
31. F
32. F

Matching

Group 1: 1 with b, 2 with c, 3 with d, 4 with a, 5 with e

Group 2: 1 with c, 2 with b, 3 with c, 4 with b, 5 with a, 6 with a

Fill-in-the-Blanks

1. licensee; invitee
2. attractive nuisance
3. voluntary undertaking
4. family purpose
5. vicariously

Multiple-Choice

1. a
2. c
3. b

4. b
5. c
6. a
7. d

CHAPTER 5

True-False

1. T
2. F
3. F
4. F
5. T
6. T
7. T
8. F
9. F
10. F
11. T
12. F
13. F
14. T
15. F
16. T
17. F
18. T
19. T
20. T
21. T
22. T
23. T
24. T
25. T
26. T
27. T
28. F

Fill-in-the-Blanks

1. gravity; probability (likelihood)
2. age, experience, intelligence
3. higher
4. automobile guest
5. res ipsa loquitur

Multiple-Choice

1. a
2. c
3. b
4. b
5. c
6. a

CHAPTER 6

True-False

1. F
2. T
3. T
4. F
5. F
6. T
7. F
8. T
9. T
10. T
11. T
12. F
13. T
14. F

Matching

Group 1: 1 with e, 2 with d, 3 with a, 4 with b, 5 with f, 6 with c

Group 2: 1 with b, 2 with a, 3 with b, 4 with b, 5 with b, 6 with a

Group 3: 1 with d, 2 with d, 3 with b, 4 with a

Fill-in-the-Blanks

1. but-for
2. market share liability
3. concerted action
4. foreseeability
5. duty
6. direct
7. eggshell skull
8. intervening; superseding

Multiple-Choice

1. a
2. d
3. c
4. c
5. a

CHAPTER 7

True-False

1. F
2. F
3. F
4. F
5. T
6. T
7. T
8. F
9. T
10. T
11. T
12. T
13. F
14. T
15. T
16. T
17. T
18. F
19. F
20. T
21. F
22. T
23. F
24. T
25. T
26. F
27. T
28. T
29. T
30. F
31. F
32. F
33. T
34. T
35. F
36. T
37. T
38. T
39. T
40. T
41. F
42. T

Matching

Group 1: 1 with d, 2 with e, 3 with b, 4 with a, 5 with c

Group 2: 1 with b, 2 with e, 3 with a, 4 with c, 5 with d

Group 3: 1 with c, 2 with b, 3 with a

Group 4: 1 with d, 2 with c, 3 with a, 4 with e, 5 with b

Fill-in-the-Blanks

1. special
2. punitive
3. per diem
4. collateral source
5. contingency fee
6. fair market
7. punitive
8. derivative
9. personal valuation; compendiums
10. vocational rehabilitation
11. wrongful death
12. structured settlement
13. unavoidable consequences
14. parasitic

Multiple-Choice

1. c
2. d
3. b
4. a
5. c
6. d
7. b

8. d
9. a
10. d

CHAPTER 8

True-False

1. T
2. F
3. T
4. T
5. F
6. F
7. F
8. F
9. T
10. T
11. F
12. F
13. T
14. T
15. F
16. T
17. T
18. T
19. T
20. T
21. F
22. T
23. T
24. F
25. F
26. F
27. F
28. T
29. T
30. F
31. T
32. T
33. T
34. T

Matching

Group 1: 1 with e, 2 with d, 3 with c, 4 with b, 5 with a

Group 2: 1 with c, 2 with b, 3 with a, 4 with e, 5 with d

Group 3: 1 with c, 2 with d, 3 with a, 4 with b

Fill-in-the-Blanks

1. comparative
2. last clear chance
3. 70 percent
4. not as great as
5. subjective; objective
6. immunity
7. governmental
8. proprietary
9. charitable
10. implied waiver
11. trust fund
12. statute of limitations
13. accrues
14. discovery

Multiple-Choice

1. c
2. d
3. b
4. d
5. b
6. d
7. a
8. a
9. d
10. b

CHAPTER 9

True-False

1. F
2. T
3. F
4. T
5. F
6. T

7. F
8. T
9. T
10. F
11. T
12. F
13. T
14. F
15. F
16. T
17. T
18. F
19. T
20. F
21. T
22. F

Fill-in-the-Blanks

1. fiduciary
2. informed consent
3. negligence; battery
4. assumed the risk

Multiple-Choice

1. c
2. b
3. d
4. c
5. d
6. a
7. b
8. d
9. a
10. c
11. d
12. d
13. a
14. b
15. d
16. b
17. d
18. a

19. c
20. a
21. d
22. a
23. d
24. b
25. c
26. d
27. b
28. d
29. a
30. c
31. c
32. d
33. d

CHAPTER 10

True-False

1. T
2. T
3. F
4. F
5. T
6. T
7. T
8. F
9. F
10. T
11. T
12. T
13. F
14. T
15. T
16. F
17. T
18. T
19. F
20. F
21. T
22. F
23. T

24. F
25. T
26. T
27. T
28. T
29. F
30. T
31. T
32. T
33. T
34. F
35. F
36. F
37. T
38. T
39. T
40. T
41. F
42. F
43. F
44. T
45. F
46. T

Matching

Group 1: 1 with e, 2 with c, 3 with d, 4 with b, 5 with a

Group 2: 1 with c, 2 with e, 3 with b, 4 with a, 5 with d

Fill-in-the-Blanks

1. trespass; nuisance
2. substantial
3. special injury
4. came to the nuisance
5. interference with existing contractual relations
6. malicious prosecution
7. wrongful institution of civil proceedings
8. abuse of process

Multiple-Choice

1. b
2. c
3. c

4. b
5. a
6. b
7. d
8. a

CHAPTER 11

True-False

1. F
2. T
3. T
4. F
5. T
6. F
7. T
8. T
9. T
10. F
11. F

Fill-in-the-Blanks

1. strictly liable
2. fencing in; fencing out
3. wild

Multiple-Choice

1. d
2. a
3. c
4. b
5. a

CHAPTER 12

True-False

1. T
2. F
3. F
4. F
5. T
6. T
7. T

8. F
9. T
10. T
11. T
12. F
13. T
14. T
15. F
16. F
17. F
18. T
19. F
20. F
21. T
22. T
23. F
24. F
25. T
26. T
27. T
28. F
29. T
30. F
31. T
32. F
33. T
34. F
35. T
36. F
37. T
38. F
39. F
40. T
41. T
42. T
43. T
44. F

Matching

Group 1: 1 with e, 2 with d, 3 with c, 4 with a, 5 with b

Group 2: 1 with d, 2 with c, 3 with e, 4 with b, 5 with a

Group 3: 1 with c, 2 with a, 3 with b, 4 with e, 5 with d

Fill-in-the-Blanks

1. merchantable
2. sealed container
3. strict liability
4. unavoidably unsafe
5. state of the art
6. structural
7. number; severity
8. as is
9. statutes of repose
10. preemption
11. express

Multiple-Choice

1. d
2. b
3. d
4. a
5. d
6. c
7. c
8. d
9. b
10. b
11. c
12. d
13. b
14. a
15. d
16. b
17. d
18. d
19. d
20. a

CHAPTER 13

True-False

1. T
2. F
3. F
4. F

5. F
6. T
7. T
8. F
9. F
10. T
11. F
12. F
13. T
14. F
15. F
16. F
17. T
18. F
19. F
20. T
21. T
22. T
23. T
24. F
25. F
26. T
27. T
28. F
29. T
30. T
31. F
32. F
33. T

Matching

Group 1: 1 with e, 2 with d, 3 with a, 4 with b, 5 with c

Group 2: 1 with e, 2 with c, 3 with d, 4 with a, 5 with b

Group 3: 1 with c, 2 with b, 3 with a, 4 with e, 5 with d

Fill-in-the-Blanks

1. status; subject matter
2. libel; slander
3. presumed
4. single publication
5. actual malice

6. public figure
7. retraction
8. abused

Multiple-Choice

1. b
2. a
3. d
4. b
5. d
6. a
7. c
8. d
9. a

CHAPTER 14

True-False

1. F
2. F
3. F
4. F
5. T
6. F
7. T
8. F
9. T
10. T
11. F
12. T
13. F
14. T
15. F

Matching

1 with c, 2 with d, 3 with f, 4 with a, 5 with b, 6 with e

Fill-in-the-Blanks

1. vicarious liability
2. respondeat superior
3. independent contractor
4. bailor; bailee

5. family purpose
6. automobile consent
7. imputed

Multiple-Choice

1. a
2. d
3. a
4. c
5. a
6. b

CHAPTER 15

True-False

1. F
2. T
3. F
4. T
5. T
6. T
7. T
8. T
9. F
10. F
11. F
12. F
13. F
14. F
15. T
16. T
17. T
18. F

Matching

Group 1: 1 with c, 2 with d, 3 with e, 4 with b, 5 with a

Group 2: 1 with e, 2 with d, 3 with a, 4 with b, 5 with c

Fill-in-the-Blanks

1. indivisible
2. joint; concurrent
3. deep pocket

4. satisfaction
5. Mary Carter; Gallagher

Multiple-Choice

1. c
2. c
3. a
4. d
5. d
6. b
7. a
8. d
9. b

CHAPTER 16

True-False

1. F
2. F
3. T
4. F
5. T
6. T
7. F
8. F
9. F
10. F
11. T
12. T
13. T
14. F
15. F
16. T
17. F
18. F
19. F
20. T
21. T
22. T
23. T
24. T
25. T

26. F
27. T
28. T
29. F
30. T
31. F
32. T
33. T

Matching

Group 1: 1 with d, 2 with e, 3 with c, 4 with b, 5 with a

Group 2: 1 with d, 2 with c, 3 with c, 4 with a, 5 with f, 6 with e

Group 3: 1 with d, 2 with c, 3 with e, 4 with b, 5 with a

Fill-in-the-Blanks

1. defendants; plaintiffs
2. defensive
3. collateral source

Multiple-Choice

1. c
2. b
3. a
4. a
5. b
6. b
7. a
8. b

CHAPTER 17

True-False

1. F
2. F
3. F
4. F
5. F
6. T
7. T
8. F
9. F

10. F
11. F
12. T
13. T
14. T
15. F
16. F
17. F
18. F
19. F
20. T
21. T
22. T
23. T
24. F
25. T
26. F
27. F

Matching

Group 1: 1 with b, 2 with a, 3 with d, 4 with e, 5 with c

Group 2: 1 with e, 2 with c, 3 with d, 4 with b, 5 with a

Fill-in-the-Blanks

1. reform
2. secondary; primary
3. replacement; actual cash
4. uninsured motorist
5. de novo

Multiple-Choice

1. b
2. c
3. d
4. c
5. c

CHAPTER 18

True-False

1. T
2. F
3. T

4. T
5. T
6. F
7. F
8. F
9. T
10. T

Fill-in-the-Blanks

1. adhesion contract
2. declaratory judgment
3. excess judgment

Multiple-Choice

1. d
2. b
3. b
4. d
5. c
6. b
7. d
8. c
9. b
10. c
11. a
12. c

CHAPTER 19

True-False

1. T
2. T
3. F
4. T
5. F
6. F
7. F
8. F
9. T
10. T

Fill-in-the-Blanks

1. fellow; servant
2. scheduled

Multiple-Choice

1. b
2. c
3. c
4. a
5. d
6. b
7. d

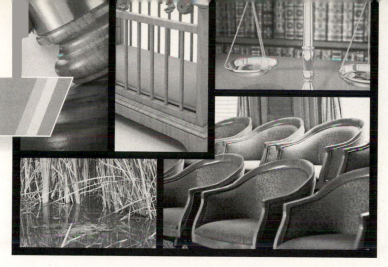

Interviewing

Johnny and Susie are lovers. Johnny has just bought a new red Corvette and, of course, he wants to impress Susie with his acquisition, so he picks her up at her house to take her to a very expensive French restaurant. While en route he enters the intersection at Seventh Avenue and Primrose Lane at the same time that Harriet, driving to the weekly meeting of the local Library Preservation Society in her fourteen-year-old Chrysler, turns in front of him. Neither sees the other vehicle until a few split seconds before impact. No one is permanently injured, but the Corvette suffers extensive damage, and Harriet's car, although relatively unscathed, needs minor repairs. Within a month of the accident Johnny comes into your office with Susie in tow. Your supervising attorney asks you to interview them. What do you do?

POTENTIAL CONFLICT OF INTEREST

Suppose that as you escort Johnny and Susie into your office, Johnny impulsively blurts out that the investigating officer and two of the witnesses are liars and are out to get him. In this spontaneous diatribe he further alleges that Harriet was drunk and that three witnesses will testify that the other two witnesses are lying when they said Johnny ran a red light. Without taking a breath he assures you that the witnesses are also prepared to testify that the officer was incorrect when he concluded that Johnny was speeding at the time of the accident.

Having heard this capsulized version of Johnny's defense, you are now alerted to the potential conflict that may exist between Johnny and Susie. Susie, if she was injured, may have to name Johnny in her suit, as he may have been wholly or partially to blame for her injuries. Caution and conservatism are now your best attributes. You should either get assistance from your supervising attorney to guide you according to your

firm's policy or take the risk that further investigation of this potential conflict may preclude the firm from representing either Johnny or Susie.

Be forewarned that Susie is likely to protest that she could never consider suing Johnny because it was all Harriet's fault. Also, Susie herself saw that the light was green and that Johnny was not speeding. Do not be pacified by this assertion. Before getting any information from Susie or even discussing the case further with the two of them together, you must determine whether Susie's claim is so inconsistent with Johnny's that they need separate representation.

If you conclude that Susie's and Johnny's claims are so at odds that they cannot be represented by the same attorney, you must advise Susie accordingly and then ask her to wait in the reception area. Note that Susie and not Johnny is asked to leave because it is Johnny who made statements to you with respect to the case. Because Susie has said nothing at this point,

EXHIBIT B-1 *Diagram of Accident*

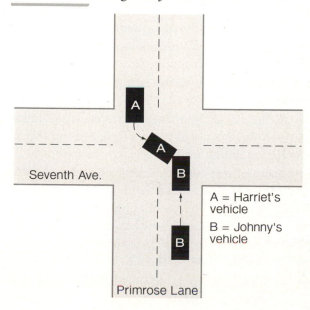

your firm can still represent Johnny. Susie, however, needs to seek alternate counsel.

SETTING THE STAGE

Typically your first contact with Johnny will be after he has spoken with the attorney who will handle the case. Interviewing Johnny will be far easier if he has already met with the attorney, because the basic cause(s) of action already will have been determined by the attorney and you can narrow your questions to those particular claims. Your role as a legal assistant in this case will have been explained by your attorney prior to your meeting with Johnny. Nevertheless, it is imperative that Johnny understand from the outset what your duties and limitations are.

If you are the first person to talk with Johnny, remember that in the opening moments of your conversation you will establish the tenor of his relationship with your firm. His decision on whether to use the firm may be determined by this initial contact. Furthermore, you must not only obtain essential biographical and background information but also ascertain the potential claims he may have. You need to glean sufficient information so that the attorney can decide whether Johnny has a cause of action, whether the claim is the type your firm would pursue, and, if not, to whom Johnny might be referred. You may also be expected to field some of Johnny's questions regarding his case.

Before you start asking questions, you should try to establish a rapport with Johnny so that he will feel free to speak openly and frankly to you about his case. Remember that you may need to ask very personal questions about, for example, injuries sustained, emotional damage, sexual dysfunction, and scarring. Such information is not easily revealed to friends, let alone complete strangers, so you must put Johnny at ease if you are going to elicit such sensitive disclosures.

At the outset, you should impress upon Johnny that anything he says to you is privileged and that this privilege is just as applicable to conversations he has with you as it is to conversations he has with the attorney. Also advise him that the privilege is applicable even if he and the firm do not enter into a contractual relationship. Try to interview him in the privacy of an office or relatively small room. Your assurances regarding the confidentiality of the information he gives you will have little meaning if strangers pass through while you are interviewing him.

You can help create a relaxed environment by the way in which you arrange the furniture. Relegating Johnny to a low-backed reception chair while you stare at him from behind a palatial desk, seated in an imposing high-backed chair, will not promote trusting, uninhibited communication. You can appear more approachable if you position your chair alongside his. Be careful, however, that you do not get so close that you make him feel uncomfortable by "invading his space."

You can also offer him a cup of coffee, glass of water, or some soda to help break the ice. Devoting a few minutes to small talk will give him an opportunity to get used to you and his surroundings. Taking time to create a comfortable setting will be time well spent and will certainly reap more benefits than immediately bombarding him with questions.

HOW TO ASK AND HOW TO LISTEN

Once you have succeeded in relaxing Johnny, you should try to determine as soon as possible why he came to the office. Although he may be unable to articulate the precise legal basis of his concern, he can probably convey the general nature of his claim, i.e., personal injury, trespass, nuisance, slander, and so on. Of course, regardless of what he believes the claim to be, the facts as they unfold may not support his claim as he perceives it, or may support additional claims that will become apparent when subject to appropriate legal analysis.

Rather than asking for directed responses at the beginning of an interview, allowing a client to give a free-flowing narrative of his version of what happened is often better. Therefore, you might start by letting Johnny tell his side of the story. Then you can follow up with more directed questions to fill in the gaps and clarify any points of confusion you might have. You might consider structuring these follow-up questions using the five Ws demanded of a good journalist—who, what, where, when, and why. Who are the key actors involved? What did they do? Where and when did they do it? Why did they do it? Making sure you can answer these key questions will minimize your chances of forgetting to ask relevant questions.

Using notes and prepared questions to organize your thinking will be helpful if you know in general what you will be discussing with Johnny. You can use your notes to refresh your memory about key points you want to explore. Do not, however, become so dependent on your notes that you are unable to deviate in any way. Be flexible; adapt your questions to Johnny's statements. Do not fail to hear what Johnny is telling you. Free yourself of any preconceived notions, and be willing to explore avenues that you had not previously considered.

Most importantly, listen carefully to Johnny. Pay attention to the details. Note any omissions in his story. Be aware of his body language and the pace, volume, and pitch of his speech. These subtle clues may reveal more than his verbal communication. When you think you have gathered all the pertinent information, summarize to him what you think he has said. You may be surprised at how many discrepancies exist between what you think you heard and what he thinks he said.

An awareness of basic human nature comes in handy when conducting interviews. Some people will provide you with only the sketchiest of details. They will treat each piece of information you extract from them as if it were some kind of valuable ore. Others will inundate you with details, digressing into so many subplots of their story that you will begin to lose sight of their central theme. Some will re-experience the emotional trauma of the events and become so distraught that they will be unable to recount what happened to them.

Although you must distance yourself emotionally enough to be objective regarding the legal claims, you must remain sensitive to the emotional needs and psychological defenses of those you interview. A certain amount of detachment is necessary to do your job, but divorcing yourself from your own humanity is neither necessary nor desirable. You must develop your own means of cajoling information from the reclusive, channeling the storytellers, and reassuring the distressed. And you must do this as you are clinically evaluating their potential causes of action—a formidable task!

Remember that interviewing is a two-way street. Just as you are assessing Johnny, so he is assessing you. Be conscious of the messages you are sending. Are you acting bored? Incredulous? Impatient? Condescending? You must communicate a sense of receptivity and warmth if you want him to trust you and cooperate with you fully.

GATHERING BACKGROUND INFORMATION

In almost all cases you need to obtain relatively detailed background information. For example, suppose a minor is involved in the case. The non-client parent may be the primary custodial parent and the one who has actual authority to institute litigation on behalf of the minor. If a shared custody agreement exists providing that the parents are jointly responsible for decisions made on behalf of the child, one parent alone may be unable to select the child's attorney. You may find yourself in an embarrassing situation if you involve your employer in litigation only to find out that your client is not authorized to institute the suit. Consequently, you should obtain relatively detailed background information, including residential address, marriages, children, employment history, medical history, and the like. In any tort case, but especially in a personal injury case such as Johnny's, this information is essential.

Any tort case also requires that a complete insurance profile be constructed. First, determine if Johnny has automobile insurance for the vehicle and, if so, whether it provides medical-payment and collision coverage. If he has such coverage, assure Johnny that, except for the deductible, the collision coverage will repair his new Corvette. The medical-payment coverage, as you should point out, will help pay for his medical expenses as well as Susie's, even if she subsequently submits a claim against him. Note that if Johnny had been a pedestrian or a bicyclist who had been injured in an accident involving a motor vehicle, some coverage would be available from his homeowner's policy.

Review any applicable insurance policies very, very thoroughly in the context of state statutes and court decisions. Be particularly concerned with the enforceability of clauses in the policies. The mere fact that an insurance policy appears to deny coverage does not mean that that provision is necessarily enforceable. (We discuss this problem in Chapter 18.)

Obtain basic information from Johnny, such as his date of birth, Social Security number, the addresses of his residence and place of employment, the identity of his insurance carrier, and, to the extent known, his coverage and its limits. Then ask for detailed information regarding the nature and extent of his injuries. If his injuries could potentially interfere with his relationships with third parties, such as parents, children, and perhaps even brothers and sisters, consider the possibility of filing a separate loss-of-consortium claim against Harriet.

Inquire about Johnny's prior medical history. Who is his family physician? What injuries or diseases has he had? What physical examinations has he had, including those for obtaining employment, for school attendance, or for other activities? This information is important because Johnny's medical history prior to the accident may have a significant impact on the amount of damages he will be entitled to receive.

Find out if Johnny was taken to an emergency room and, if so, whether he was taken by ambulance or if he drove himself. Identify Johnny's treating physicians, if any, since the accident, and find out how many times he has seen them and for what reasons. Note whether Johnny has been unable to work or has been able to do only those jobs characterized as "light duty." In many instances, an injury does not prevent the client from working but may preclude him from working in certain activities or force him to forgo certain benefits, such as overtime.

You also need to determine the nature and extent of the damages to Johnny's vehicle. Depending on your firm's policy, you might become involved in assisting Johnny with his property-damage claim.

SCENE OF THE ACCIDENT

When you first ask Johnny to describe the accident he may want to relate what happened in a conclusory fashion. He may say, for example, "I was obeying the law, and this drunk turned in front of me on a green light." Let him ventilate. Once he has done that, you need to piece together the chain of events leading up to the accident and to verify the validity of what he has given you. Suppose, for example, that Johnny tells you that the accident occurred at 8:00 p.m. on Saturday evening, April 9, one month ago. You need to confirm that April 9 was a Saturday. Later, if your firm accepts this case, you will need to ascertain the weather and road conditions at the time of the accident. For example, was there any construction? Was the road made of dirt, granite, asphalt, or concrete? How many lanes of traffic were there in each direction?

In piecing together the events that preceded the accident you will need to take Johnny back to the time he woke up that morning. What time did he get up? Where had he been the night before? Did he have breakfast? What did he do prior to the accident? Did he have lunch? Did he have anything to drink during the afternoon? Was he with friends who could confirm his whereabouts and activities? Did he have a good night's sleep, or was he overtired? Did he have dinner Saturday evening? Did he go to Susie's to pick her up, or was she with him to begin with? Do they live together? Did he have anything to drink prior to the accident?

You will also want to question Johnny regarding his new Corvette. Had he had it for a long time? Was he accustomed to driving it? Had he had prior traffic violations? Were his headlights on? Was the car functioning properly? What was he doing prior to the accident? Was he talking to Susie? Was he looking forward or to the left or right? Did he see Harriet before she made the turn? Did he see Harriet making the turn? What evasive actions did either Johnny or Harriet make prior to the collision? You will want to find out how much traffic was on Primrose Lane and on Seventh Avenue that night at 8:00 p.m. How well lit was the intersection? Were Harriet's headlights on? Had Harriet turned on her turn signal? Did Harriet appear to hesitate and then speed up, or did she make the left-hand turn as though there were no oncoming traffic? Were Johnny and Susie wearing seat belts? Was Harriet wearing a seat belt?

Then you need to zero in on what happened at the scene of the accident. Does Johnny recall slamming on the brakes and hearing any sounds associated with skidding tires? Did the brakes of the Corvette lock up? Where exactly was the point of impact? Could Johnny or Susie get out of the vehicle immediately after the accident? Were they coherent? Was anyone cut? Was blood evident anywhere? Did the vehicle itself remain secure, i.e., did the seats break their mountings or did the backs collapse? How much damage was done to Harriet's old Chrysler? Who was the first person on the scene? Did Johnny, Susie, or Harriet speak to that person? Did Johnny or Susie speak to Harriet? Did they speak to any of the other witnesses? Where were the other witnesses at the time of the accident? Did any of them almost collide with Harriet or Johnny? Did any of them actually collide with either? Did any other accidents occur as a result of the collision between Harriet and Johnny?

Johnny indicated that an officer eventually came to the scene, so you should determine what law enforcement agency the officer worked for. Did Johnny speak to the officer? What was the nature of their conversation? What was Johnny's attitude at the time, i.e., was he angry, subdued, crying, in pain? Did the officer speak with Susie or Harriet? Does Johnny know whether the officer spoke with any of the other witnesses and, if so, which ones? Did the officer make any measurements at the scene of the accident that Johnny is aware of?

Johnny made several allegations during his earlier soliloquy. Now you need to follow up on those. Johnny indicated to you that Harriet was drunk. How does he know that? Did he speak with Harriet or smell her breath? Did the officer indicate that he was citing Harriet for driving under the influence? Johnny said that the officer cited him for speeding. Did the officer tell him the basis for making that determination? Johnny also stated that other witnesses said he ran a red light. Was he cited for running a red light? Where were those alleged witnesses when they saw Johnny run the red light? In which direction were they facing?

DISCOVERING THE WEAKNESSES

As you conduct the interview do not become so wrapped up in the tale that is being told that you fail to notice any time gaps or apparently inconsistent statements. The appropriate time to discover any problems with your case is when you first become involved, not after a great deal of time, money, and effort have been expended in pursuit of the claim. Remember that not everyone who is involved in an automobile accident is entitled to compensation, and even if a victim is entitled to compensation it may well be that problems with respect to liability (i.e., who was at fault and to what extent), will discourage the firm from representing that person. Someone with $100,000 worth of injuries, for example, who is 99 percent responsible for those injuries, has a $1,000 case, not a $100,000 case (in a comparative-negligence state). The recoverable damages would not justify a firm's investment in such a case.

STATUTE-OF-LIMITATIONS PROBLEMS

Clients often "sit" on their claims for some time before acting on them, and when they do finally get around to pursuing their claims they may be barred because the statute of limitations has expired. Be aware of the appropriate statute, and act in a timely fashion both to protect the client's claim and to protect your firm from being sued for malpractice for inadequate representation. If the expiration of the statutory time period were imminent in Johnny's case, the attorney might opt to draft a bare-bones complaint naming Johnny as his own attorney. This would prevent the attorney from having to evaluate the case too hastily and would still protect the interests of all involved. If the client serves as her own attorney, no paperwork will have to be filled out for substitution of attorney if your firm decides to decline representation.

INVESTIGATING OFFICER INTERVIEW

Having determined Johnny's side of the story, you must now interview the third parties involved to find out their recollections of the events. The first person to start with is the investigating officer. Although in most cases the officer has no personal firsthand information other than the measurements taken, she may have talked to some of the witnesses. In some states the actual investigation with respect to skid marks, point of impact, estimated speed of travel, and so forth is left to civilian employees of the police department. Therefore, you must determine which individuals actually investigated the accident scene and what their training, job classification, and responsibilities were.

Should your jurisdiction be one of those in which the police officer does the actual investigation, including making measurements and interviewing witnesses, interview the officer as soon as possible. The notion that police officers can recall specific details of every investigation they conduct by simply reviewing their notes is erroneous. Remember, they are involved in numerous incidents on a daily basis, and substantial time has usually passed between the accident in question and your interview. Nothing is as important as fresh, firsthand information.

Any attempt to interview the investigating officer should begin with the Police Liaison Unit. This unit, which exists in one form or another in most jurisdictions, is primarily involved in ensuring that the officers involved in a criminal case are aware of the events that are occurring and the times when they must appear in court. You can also use this unit to make arrangements to interview the officer about the strictly civil portions of an incident. It is often possible for the officers to be paid for the time involved in meeting and discussing the case with you, so it is imperative, at the outset at least, to work with the Police Liaison's office. Certainly officers will be far happier talking with you if they know they are getting paid or being given release time for the time spent with you, rather than receiving only the standard jurisdictional witness fee.

Additionally, because police officers frequently encounter attorneys in an adversarial context, they are often prepared to do battle. Therefore, make sure you are well prepared for the interview. Do not create the impression of wasting the officer's time with irrelevant or nonsensical questions. When you interview a police officer you should have a detailed outline of your questions.

Prior to interviewing the officer, mentally retrace the events leading up to, during, and after the accident in as much detail as possible, noting the names of any witnesses that you are aware of. Using precise questions will not only enhance your credibility with the officer but will also greatly reduce the amount of time necessary to complete the interview.

If departmental procedures allow it and the officer has no objections, tape-record the interview. Transcribe the interview as soon as possible and send it to the officer, asking him to make appropriate corrections. Let the officer know about this procedure at the beginning of the interview if you intend to tape it.

Never "talk down" to an officer or try to contradict her. Establishing a good rapport will serve you well later in the case, whereas being patronizing will result in an adversarial rather than a cooperative relationship. You should maintain control of the interview and strive to earn the officer's respect, but you must do so without sacrificing his ego. You will undoubtedly encounter the arrogant officer who will test your capacity to control your tongue. Before you succumb to the temptation to engage in verbal repartee, remember that an officer who dislikes your style of questioning could become a liability rather than an asset to your case. Prudence is often the wisest course of action.

All basic background information, such as time on the force, experience in accident investigation, and training, is important. Focus, however, on the information contained in the report the officer prepared. Determine what information in the report came from the officer's firsthand observations at the accident scene, which information came from witnesses the officer deemed credible, and which information the officer rejected because she thought the witnesses were not credible.

The officer writing the report may not have interviewed some of the witnesses, so you need to ascertain which officers spoke to which witnesses and, if necessary, interview each of those officers. You need to find out, for example, if there was a backup unit that assisted the investigating officer and if those officers talked to witnesses, if statements were taken by any other officers, and if measurements were made by a different officer or by a civilian accident investigator. You need to get the names of these individuals and establish the relevance of the information they may have to offer to determine if you should also interview them.

At this juncture you must determine whether the officer has any independent recollection of the accident. Then you must distinguish what the officer knows by virtue of independent recollection versus what he remembers by reviewing the police report and other documents that you brought to the interview. Knowing when and where to give information to the officer comes from experience and intuition. What you should do will vary on a case-by-case and officer-by-officer basis.

LAY WITNESS INTERVIEWS

As soon as possible after the incident and, with luck, before they are spoken to by the adverse party, contact all lay witnesses. Many people are very concerned about the perceived hazards of having to testify in court, and you should do everything possible to allay their fears. It is not unusual for someone to "not recall" an event to ensure that her testimony will not be required. Meeting the person at his home after work or for lunch can make a reluctant witness feel more comfortable and less "put out" than requesting that he come to your office.

Once you know whether the witness will either support or negate your client's position, you will need to decide whether to tape-record the interview, assuming the witness will allow it. If the witness's recollections are supportive of your client's position, you might want to provide a copy of the tape to opposing counsel in the hope of speeding up settlement. Note, however, that the presence of a tape recorder makes many people very uncomfortable and may therefore be counterproductive. If you opt to record the interview, be sure the witness feels comfortable and at ease before starting. Be forewarned that several evidentiary obstacles must be overcome before tape-recorded statements can be used in court, even for impeachment purposes.

Once again, you must explain, at the beginning of an interview, who you are, why you want to talk to the witness, and what the potential ramifications of talking with you could be. You should also advise witnesses that the opposing parties' attorney or legal assistant may also want to interview them. Any attempts to influence the testimony of witnesses or to discourage them from speaking with opposing counsel could, and should, result in your being fired. Such overt attempts to influence witnesses could also, in many jurisdictions, result in criminal charges being filed against you.

Typically one begins questioning by allowing the witness to give a free-flowing narrative of the events he observed. Note that the ability to make these observations depends on conditions at the time of the incident. For example, the witness may be wearing glasses at the time of the interview, but that does not mean that he had his glasses on as she observed the events. Her observations may therefore be suspect.

Try to pinpoint the exact location of the witness at the time the events occurred to determine whether the observation was possible. It is not uncommon for witnesses to make materially false statements and be honestly unaware of their falsity. For example, a driver who was behind a vehicle that was involved in an accident may state that he saw the driver of the other vehicle lose physical control of the automobile. In reality, all he could see was the back of the other driver's head. If later he saw paramedics remove somebody from the driver's seat of the vehicle, he would assume, quite logically, that the person he observed being removed from the driver's side of the car was the person he had observed driving the car, which is not necessarily true. Consequently, his statement regarding the driver's identity could be honest but false.

What if the witness is hostile and alleges, for example, that the accident was all your client's fault and that he should be punished for what he did? In such a case you will have to summon all of your interpersonal skills to get an in-depth and accurate interview. Pin down a hostile witness with as many specific facts and details as possible. You need to find out exactly where the witness was standing, what she was doing, who was at the scene, what they were wearing, who was doing what to whom, and so on. If nothing else, by restricting the witness to exacting factual details, she may be more easily impeached at a later date should other witnesses or physical evidence conflict with her statements.

Witnesses may ask to review the transcription of the tape recording, obtain a copy of the tape, or review your notes. Be aware of your firm's policy in this regard. In most instances there would be no problem in allowing a witness to review the transcribed interview or taking a copy of the actual tape recording itself. Problems arise, however, if the tape recording or its transcription is discoverable when in the hands of the witness but not discoverable when in the possession of one of the party's attorneys. It may be prudent to advise witnesses that the tape recording or its transcription is available for review at the attorney's office but that legal procedural rules prohibit a copy being given to them.

Do not assume that only personal, firsthand information is of any value. A witness may be able to provide you with useful information that leads to legally admissible evidence. She may, for example, advise you that a photographer from one of the local newspapers took photographs of the scene, that other individuals in the vicinity observed the accident, or that she was accompanied by friends whose names are not on the police report. This information might allow you to obtain additional collaborative evidence to support your client's story or to impeach the recollections of a hostile witness.

Finally, and most importantly, always be gracious. An interview is not the place for aggressive, hard-hitting questions. Witnesses do not have to talk to you. If you irritate them, they may terminate the interview. You cannot afford to burn bridges at the initial stages of an investigation only to find out later that the witness you alienated is the one you most need.

APPENDIX C

Overview of Insurance

TYPES OF INSURANCE COVERAGE AVAILABLE

Learning about all the different types of insurance coverage would be too time-consuming to be of practical value. Suffice it to say that for the required premium the occurrence of almost any contingency can be insured. Those contingencies that are not insurable generally are due to public policy concerns that allowing certain events to be insured would encourage wrongful behavior. A brief synopsis of the more common types of insurance coverage is set forth in Exhibit C–1.

SPECIFIC TYPES OF INSURANCE

The types of insurance available are many and varied. Some policies are designed for business (commercial lines) and some for individuals (personal lines).

In many cases the coverage overlaps. One of the most prevalent types of insurance is fire insurance.

Fire Insurance

Fire insurance may be found in different types of policies but is most often encountered in the standard homeowners' policy. The 1943 New York Standard Policy provides the pattern for the standard coverage in today's homeowners' policies. This insurance prototype has been extensively reviewed by the courts, and its contents are familiar to insurance regulators in all states.

One of the important provisions of the 1943 policy is the right given to the insurer to rebuild the damaged structure, repair it, or if necessary replace it. An insurer will obviously select the most economical option available. These options, which are similar to those available to the insurer under automobile

---

EXHIBIT C–1 *Overview of Types of Insurance Coverage Available*

FIRE INSURANCE	Covers rebuilding, repair, and replacement of property damaged by fire.
ACCIDENT INSURANCE	Provides fixed benefits in event of accidental injury.
HEALTH INSURANCE	Reimbursement for expenses resulting from sickness or accidental injury.
HOMEOWNERS' INSURANCE	Reimbursement for losses related to damage to one's residence (excludes losses stemming from use of automobile).
LIABILITY INSURANCE	Reimbursement for losses for which insured is liable (usually excluding intentional and criminal acts).
LIFE INSURANCE	Payments to insured's estate or beneficiaries in event of insured's death.
MARINE INSURANCE	Reimbursement for losses incurred in shipping of goods.
MALPRACTICE INSURANCE	Reimbursement for losses stemming from professional negligence.
PRODUCT LIABILITY INSURANCE	Reimbursement for losses stemming from defective products.
PROPERTY INSURANCE	Reimbursement for losses sustained to property.
TITLE INSURANCE	Coverage for losses resulting from defective title to property.
AUTOMOBILE INSURANCE	Coverage relating to the use of an automobile.

collision coverage, often result in disputes between the insured and the insurer as to whether the option selected by the insurer was appropriate. Quite possibly, for example, a residence that is rebuilt because of severe fire damage may have a stigma attached to it that results in a substantial reduction of its fair market value. One vital prerequisite to recovery under any fire insurance policy is that the insured must not have intentionally caused the damage or conspired with another to intentionally cause the damage.

Irrespective of the amount of fire insurance obtained by an insured on a particular piece of property, the amount to be paid by the insurer will not be greater than the property's fair market value or replacement cost, depending on the type of insurance purchased. The mere fact that an insured purchases fire insurance for $100,000 on a building worth only $50,000 does not allow her to collect $100,000 in the event of the total loss of the structure.

Accident Insurance

Accident insurance is designed to provide the insured with specified coverage in the event of an accidental injury. A policy might provide a fixed amount for the loss of one eye, a greater amount for the loss of both eyes, a fixed sum for the loss of a leg, and so on. Often the accident insurance policy provides a fixed benefit in the case of an accidental death. Accident insurance, unlike health insurance, does not reimburse the insured for expenses incurred as the result of an accident. Rather, it provides an agreed-upon payment if an accidental injury covered by the policy should occur.

Health Insurance

Health insurance is designed to provide reimbursement for medical expenses incurred by the insured as a result of sickness or accidental injury. Most health insurance policies provide for a deductible that must be paid by the insured before benefits become payable.

In addition, most health insurance policies require the insured to be responsible for a percentage of the medical expenses incurred above the deductible, up to what is called the co-insurance limit. Above the co-insurance limit the insurer is totally responsible for payment of expenses. Suppose the insurer is responsible for 80 percent of the medical expenses incurred above the deductible of $1,000, to a total of $5,000 above the deductible (the co-insurance limit). If $10,000 in medical expenses were sustained, the insured would have to pay the deductible of $1,000 plus 20 percent of $5,000 ($1,000). The insurer would then be totally responsible for the remainder of the expenses ($4,000) and would have to pay 80 percent of the $5,000 above the deductible, for a total of $8,000.

Most health insurance policies have a maximum figure for which the insurer will be responsible for medical expenses as the result of any one claim. Once the policy limits are met by the insurer, the insured is responsible for the payment of any shortfall. Depending on the policy, that maximum might be reinstated if the insured were to sustain medical expenses as a result of a different cause. Some policies also have lifetime maximums that will be paid irrespective of the number of claims.

The standard health insurance policy provision requires that the insured remain treatment-free as a result of any preexisting conditions for a fixed period of time after the policy is issued. A preexisting condition is any medical condition suffered by the insured prior to securing a policy from the insurer. The time period required varies from policy to policy but can be as short as ninety days or as long as two years. Any medical expenses incurred or treatment begun prior to expiration of the period set forth in the policy will not be covered. The insurer may also provide specific exclusions for preexisting conditions. For example, a policy could contain an exclusion precluding payment for expenses relating to any injury to the insured's knee. Such an exclusion would be required by the insurance carrier because of prior problems with or treatment of the insured's knee.

One problem that often arises in health insurance policies is an allegation by the insurer that the insured failed to give a full and complete disclosure of a prior medical condition on the health insurance application. How the courts deal with such nondisclosure varies, but most policies allow for cancellation if the insurer refunds the premiums paid. If an insured can show that the insurer would have issued a policy with only an exclusion for the type of injury that was not disclosed and that the injury he sustained was not related to any misrepresentation on the application, some courts will require the insurer to pay the expenses despite the misrepresentation. Other courts look to the material misrepresentation and allow the insurer to avoid its contractual obligations, even though the misrepresentation was unrelated to the injury or sickness actually sustained by the insured.

Homeowners' Insurance

Homeowners' insurance policies have been designed for the owner-occupant of a single-family residence. These policies may provide either basic or extended coverage. Basic coverage provides for protection against loss due to fire, lightning, windstorm, or hail. Extended coverage provides personal liability protection as well as "all risk" coverage, which is coverage for all risk of physical loss to insured property except for exclusions specifically listed in the policy. Most lenders require, at the minimum, that a homeowner/insured maintain coverage for fire, windstorm, hail, vandalism, and malicious mischief. The purpose of this requirement is to ensure that any losses sustained that might affect the security of the lender will be reimbursed by the homeowner's insurance carrier.

The standard homeowners' policy specifically excludes any liability that might be imposed on the insured arising out of the operation of a motor vehicle. It may, however, provide liability coverage for the insured and the insured's family for acts that occur at locations other than the residence insured under the policy. One fertile field of litigation with respect to the standard homeowners' policy is the issue of liability for the death of minor children in a homeowner's swimming pool. Injuries caused to others by the insured or members of her family are also hotly litigated. If, for example, the insured's son injures his friend while engaging in unreasonably rough horseplay while on the premises, or if the insured's dog bites a guest, the insured's homeowners' policy should provide coverage.

Many homeowners' insurance policies provide for medical payment insurance. They also frequently require that the insured specifically list (and pay an extra premium for) items of unusual value such as works of art, musical instruments, jewelry, excessive cash, and weapons.

Liability Insurance

Liability insurance is one of the more comprehensive types of insurance available. Under this policy the insurer must reimburse (indemnify) the insured for any loss covered by the policy for which the insured may be responsible. Liability insurance covers damages the insured may be required to pay as a result of bodily injury or property damage caused by the insured's negligence.

Illegal or intentional acts of the insured are not covered in a standard liability policy. Most policies, either by their specific language or by court interpretation, do not provide coverage for punitive damages.

Liability insurance is written either in single-limit or split-limits coverage. Under the single-limit approach, a set amount is all that is available to injured third parties, irrespective of the total amount of the injuries they sustain. For example, a $300,000 single-limit policy provides coverage for damages up to a maximum of $300,000 no matter how many claimants apply and no matter how great their actual losses are. Potentially, one claimant could recover $300,000 and the other claimants could be left with nothing under this type of policy.

Under split-limits coverage a fixed amount is set for each individual claim, along with a different fixed amount for the total of all claims arising out of the same incident. The split-limits coverage of a $100,000/$300,000 policy, for example, would allow a maximum recovery of $100,000 for each person injured and a maximum recovery of $300,000 for all persons injured. This type of coverage would prevent one claimant from usurping all of the $300,000 by putting a $100,000 cap on individual recovery.

As mentioned previously, liability insurance is a standard part of the homeowners' insurance policy. In most cases it is also a required part of the automobile insurance policy.

Life Insurance

Unlike the other types of insurance we have discussed, life insurance does not indemnify the insured for any losses sustained. In essence, a life insurance contract is an agreement by the insurance carrier to pay the insured's estate or the named beneficiary a fixed amount upon the insured's death. Unlike liability insurance or, for that matter, most other forms of insurance, the event insured against (death) is certain to happen.

Life insurance carriers have devised a variety of life insurance plans because of the perceived diverse needs of the American public (see Exhibit C–2). They have also attempted to capitalize on the tax benefits that have been granted to the life insurance industry. These tax benefits, which arguably stem from Congress's perception of life insurance as a type of savings, have provided life insurance carriers with sales pitches unavailable to other types of insurers. For example, insurers can offer policies that allow the insured to accumulate tax-free interest during the term of the policy and to pay taxes only upon actually receiving the funds. When the monies are received the insured is typically

EXHIBIT C–2 Types of Life Insurance

ORDINARY	TERM
Insured pays fixed premium with benefits paid to estate or beneficiaries in event of insured's death.	Insured pays fixed premiums with benefits paid to estate or beneficiaries in event of insured's death.

JOINT	SURVIVORSHIP
Benefits payable upon death of one or more insureds.	Benefits payable only to survivors of two or more insureds.

© Cengage Learning 2012

in a much lower tax bracket, according to the insurance carrier, usually as a result of retirement. Individual life insurance premiums are not tax deductible, and the face amount of the policy paid to the beneficiary upon the insured's death is generally not taxable.

The most common types of life insurance now available are ordinary life, term life, joint life, and survivorship insurance.

Ordinary Life Insurance

An ordinary life insurance policy has a fixed monthly or yearly premium based on the age of the insured at the time the policy is taken out. This premium is paid during the life of the insured in consideration of the payment (based on the face amount of the policy) guaranteed to be paid his estate or beneficiary at the insured's death. Some ordinary life insurance policies are set up so that premiums are prorated through a certain age such as sixty, sixty-five, or seventy-five, at which time the policy is considered fully paid.

Typically the ordinary life insurance policy provides for the building of a cash value, which occurs after the first few years. Initially the payments provide the means for the agent to be paid a commission. As a result, the insurer pays the insured the cash value of the policy if the policy is canceled prior to her death. Alternatively, the insurer could loan the insured monies in an amount equal to the loan value of the policy, as determined by the insurance contract. The loan value of a policy varies depending on the number of years the policy has been in effect and the internal rate of return of the insured. If the insured takes a loan on the policy, the policy stays in effect as long as premiums and loan payments are paid on a timely basis.

Term Insurance

Term insurance has a fixed term, usually a year, and provides for payment only if the insured dies during that term. Unlike ordinary life insurance, the rates of term insurance vary on a periodic basis, depending on the age of the insured at the time the policy is taken out. Term insurance is more like other types of insurance in that the risk insured against (death during the term of the policy) is not certain to occur. Term insurance is often the insurance of choice for younger couples who want to provide for their dependents in the event of their own demise but who are unable to afford the higher premiums demanded by ordinary life insurance. Some term policies, while allowing the premium to vary with the age of the insured, guarantee insurability to the insured. Many waive the need for a physical examination as long as the insured renews the policy prior to the expiration of every term, so that no break in the coverage occurs.

Joint Life Insurance

With joint life insurance the benefits become payable upon the death of one of the insureds covered by the policy. Joint life insurance requires at least two insureds, although a limitless number of insureds could theoretically be covered.

Joint life insurance is particularly advantageous when a small group of individuals, each of whom is vital to the group, begins a joint enterprise. Because the death of any group member could adversely affect the success of the endeavor, a joint life policy provides a fund from which the survivors can be compensated for the loss of one of their members. Term insurance, taken in the name of each individual, can result in premiums that exceed the enterprise's ability to pay. Joint life insurance, in contrast, provides reimbursement to the enterprise at a minimal cost. Subsequent to the death of one of the group members, the survivors could obtain a second policy covering the survivors.

Survivorship Insurance

A survivorship policy is the mirror image of a joint life policy. Joint life insurance provides benefits when one of the insureds dies; survivorship insurance provides benefits when all but one of the insureds has died (i.e., it pays the last survivor). Survivorship insurance might be preferable to term insurance for a married couple when one spouse is considerably older than the other. Although a survivorship policy would cost more than a term policy issued on the eldest spouse, it would cost less than purchasing term policies for both of them. This type of policy might also be advantageous to a group in which the efforts of individual deceased members could be duplicated but a lone survivor would be unable to carry on the enterprise.

Marine Insurance

Marine insurance, the oldest form of insurance, protects against losses incurred in shipping goods. It covers the loss itself as well as lost profits. Modern-day marine insurance traces its beginning to the emergence of England as a maritime power in the sixteenth century. The preeminent insurer in this area, Lloyds of London, issues the industry standard, called the "English Lloyds policy."

Malpractice Insurance

Malpractice insurance is analogous to the errors and omissions policy used to protect officers and directors of major corporations. Malpractice insurance applies to professionals, who are held to the standard of care reasonably expected of similar professionals in the geographic area in which they practice. The major distinction between errors and omissions insurance and malpractice insurance lies in the standard of care. As previously noted, negligence is measured in terms of the standard of care of a "reasonable person." The standard of care for malpractice, however, is based on the expectations of a reasonable professional in a particular field and geographic area. Malpractice insurance is available for medical and dental practitioners, including pharmacists, hospitals, and nurses, as well as for lawyers, psychologists, veterinarians, and other professionals.

One of the factors that differentiates malpractice insurance from errors and omissions insurance is that malpractice insurance requires state licensure, whereas errors and omissions generally does not. Licensing is one of the first things to consider when determining what type of insurance might be available, although it is not a consistent requirement. Most real estate salespeople, for example, are required to be licensed, and yet their coverages are still considered errors and omissions policies rather than malpractice policies.

One fairly recent change in malpractice policies lowers the amount of coverage available to a claimant by including the cost of his defense as part of the insurance coverage. Including defense costs is an illusory attempt to lower premiums while maintaining the same face value of coverage. In the past the cost of defending a lawsuit was not considered part of the policy. Under these terms, a claimant could avail himself or herself of a sum equal to the face value of the policy minus the deductible. Under the new policy the amount available to the claimant is the face value of the policy minus the malpractice carrier's cost of defending the insured.

Product Liability Insurance

Product liability insurance is a creation of the twentieth century. Manufacturers and producers of goods obtain product liability insurance to protect themselves against claims by the ultimate users and/or handlers of their products. Because most product liability cases are based on strict liability, the potential for loss is very high. In some industries, such as the airline industry, a single incident can result in numerous multimillion-dollar claims.

Because of this exposure, product liability insurance is very expensive but, from a practical standpoint, necessary to any entity that either manufactures or produces products. Problems arise when the cost of product liability insurance results in the production or manufacture of the product no longer being economical. At that point the maker of the goods must decide whether to go uninsured and hope that no claims are made, or to discontinue manufacturing the product altogether.

Testing of new products and modification of old products is often required by providers of product liability insurance. Underwriters Laboratory's "seal of approval," for example, allows manufacturers promotional advantages by being able to prominently display the "UL" symbol. But, more importantly, testing may be a prerequisite to the obtaining of product liability insurance.

In the marketplace the cost of product liability insurance unquestionably inhibits the introduction of new products. Many hope this cost will spur manufacturers to exhibit greater concern for consumers, but the cost/benefit ratio is still difficult to determine. The question remains whether the high cost of admission to the marketplace has created artificial barriers to the introduction of new and innovative concepts.

Property Insurance

Property insurance is an agreement by the insurer to indemnify the insured for any losses sustained to his or her property. Property insurance is included in many different types of coverage, including homeowners' coverage. Fire insurance and flood insurance are both types of property insurance. Property insurance, however, covers far more perils than fire and flood and frequently includes windstorm, lightning, rain, hail, and similar natural catastrophes.

Property insurance generally comes in two forms—actual cash value (the initial cost minus accrued depreciation) or replacement cost (the cost of replacing the article at the date of loss rather than at its depreciated value). Therefore, most replacement-cost policies require higher premiums than actual-cash-value policies.

Title Insurance

The primary purpose behind title insurance is to provide coverage to the insured for any loss that may result due to a defect in the title to property (not losses due to defects in or damage to the property itself). An insured is obligated to prove the nature and amount of the loss incurred, and the insurer then indemnifies the insured against only that loss. In many instances, a problem with a title results in no damages or only insubstantial ones.

Suppose a title insurer issues a policy of title insurance for a parcel of land but fails to disclose an easement over the south ten feet of the property. If the title policy insured ownership of the entire parcel to the policyholder, the policyholder would be entitled to indemnification for only the loss in value due to the existence of the unknown easement. Very likely an easement for five or ten feet would be relatively insignificant with respect to the total value of the property. In contrast, if such an undisclosed easement divided the property in half, the value of the remaining parcels might be dramatically affected.

Title insurance comes in a variety of forms, including the owner's policy, the lender's policy, and the American Land Title Association (ALTA) policy. The owner's policy tries to meet the needs of real estate buyers, the lender's policy protects the interest of the financing entity in a real estate transaction, and the ALTA policy provides the maximum protection to the insured. Because of its extensive coverage the ALTA policy is substantially greater in cost per dollar of coverage than other title policies.

Workers' Compensation

Workers' compensation, like unemployment insurance, is highly regulated. All states have regulatory agencies whose purpose is to ensure that employees have a source of compensation for work-related injuries. In most instances, the acceptance of workers' compensation benefits provided by statute precludes the employee from suing the employer for negligence. Workers' compensation, in general, provides benefits without regard to fault of the injured party. In other words, even though the employee was negligent in not abiding by the safety rules and regulations established by the employer, she is still entitled to workers' compensation benefits in the event of injury. As with unemployment insurance, the statutory framework in reference to workers' compensation claims must be extensively analyzed in light of relevant court decisions. Workers' compensation insurance is discussed in Chapter 19

Automobile Insurance

Perhaps nowhere in our court system is more litigation threatened or initiated than in reference to liability arising out of motor vehicle accidents. Automobile insurance, with all its variations, possesses most of the attributes of the other types of insurance. Automobile insurance is discussed in some detail in Chapter 17.

DEFENSES AN INSURANCE COMPANY CAN RAISE AGAINST ITS INSURED

The issuance of an insurance policy begins when an insured or his agent fills out an application. The primary purpose of the application is to answer certain relevant questions surrounding the issuance of the policy. A health insurance application, for example, deals primarily with the applicant's previous medical history. The insurer needs this information to

© Cengage Learning 2012

EXHIBIT C–3   *Defenses Insurer Can Raise*

- Insured makes material misrepresentation in application
- Insured fails to cooperate with insurer in dealing with claim
- Insured fails to give timely notice to insurer of potential claim
- Insured commits intentional act.

determine whether any preexisting conditions should be excluded from the policy as well as to assess the overall insurability of the applicant.

Misrepresentations

If an applicant makes any material misrepresentations relating to any risks that are insured, the insurer may be able to void the policy should the insured make any claim relating to those risks (see Exhibit C–3). If the applicant attempts to conceal material facts or deliberately misrepresent material issues in the application, she may be denied any coverage whatsoever and may be relegated to, at most, reimbursement of the premiums paid to date. Many policies provide that after two years have elapsed since issuance of the policy, the insurer cannot use any error or misrepresentation on the application to void the insurance contract.

Failure to Abide by Terms of Policy

A policy can also be voided by the insured's failure to abide by the terms of the policy. Insureds are most likely to be at odds with their insurance company in one of two ways. The first involves the insured's duty to cooperate with the insurer in dealing with the claim. The second involves the policy's provisions requiring the insured to give prompt notice of any potential claim.

Failure to Cooperate

An insured potentially violates the duty to cooperate if he refuses to give a statement to the insurance company, refuses to make books and records available (where applicable), or refuses to allow the insurance company to enter his premises for inspection purposes in the case of a fire or property damage claim. The insured also violates the duty to cooperate when she is sued and fails to participate in the discovery process by refusing to attend depositions, answer interrogatories, respond to requests for admissions, or assist in the production of documents.

Failure to Notify

Failure to notify an insurance company of a claim is a second potential point of contention between insureds and their insurance companies. Although most policies require reasonable notice, some attempt to set an outer time limit by which any claim must be reported. Before an insured can be said to have violated the duty to give notice, he must know or have reason to know that a claim is forthcoming. What might appear, for example, to be a minor motor vehicle collision with no property damage and no personal injury could nevertheless result in a subsequent claim. If the insured reasonably believes that no damage occurred and no claim will be made, failure to advise the carrier about the accident will not give the insurance company grounds for denying coverage.

In a similar vein, the insured has a duty to advise the insurance company of any suit that is actually filed against him. If the carrier is unable to answer the complaint because of the insured's failure to notify it in a timely manner and a default judgment is entered, the insurer can attempt to deny coverage. Alternatively, the insurer might seek reimbursement for the damages it sustained as a result of the default judgment against the insured. Suppose an insured, through his own inaction, allows a default judgment to be entered against him. The carrier may then be relieved of the responsibility of paying the judgment, or may be allowed to attempt to set aside the judgment as far as it relates to its duty to indemnify the insured.

Intentional Acts

Most insurance policies exempt coverage for intentional acts of the insured. Such acts include intentionally setting fire to insured property, suicide (although many life insurance policies cover suicide if committed after a fixed period of time following the issuance of the policy), intentionally using a motor vehicle to cause damage, or intentionally assaulting a third party.

Reservation of Rights

An insurer may find it difficult to immediately determine whether it has a right to deny coverage under the policy. Therefore, most insurance carriers, until they are sure they have a right to deny coverage, will defend the insured under a reservation of rights. Here the insurer advises the insured that coverage may not be available but promises to defend the insured until that determination is made. In many cases the insurer will institute a declaratory-judgment action seeking a court determination regarding the issue of coverage. If an insurer proceeds under a reservation of rights, it may later withdraw from representation of the insured and seek reimbursement for its defense costs.

Insurer's Actions

An insurance carrier can by its own actions lose its right to assert a defense against an insured. In such cases the insurer will be deemed to have waived its rights to contest the policy and may, in some circumstances, be estopped (prevented) from asserting defenses because of its prior acts.

As with all areas of insurance, court rulings and statutory enactments affecting the policy in question must be carefully researched. In some instances the plain wording of the policy and the insurer's actions have been deemed wrongful and in violation of "public policy." Public policy attempts to reconcile legislative enactments, prior court decisions, and the public good in overriding provisions perceived as inequitable. Public-policy requirements will be read into an insurance policy, and terms and conditions conflicting with public policy will either be ignored or deemed unenforceable. Provisions in a policy that exclude members of an insured's family from coverage, for example, may be deemed in violation of public policy and therefore unenforceable by the insurer.

APPENDIX D

© Cengage Learning 2012

Sample Insurance Policy

No. 323—Drive Other Car

No. 334—Emergency Road Service

No. 335—Additional Living Expense

No. 368—Car Rental Reimbursement

No. 303—Underinsured Motorist Coverage

Section IV—Inland Marine

Conditions—Applicable to Section IV

Section V—Umbrella

If applicable (if described in the Declarations with a premium charge), see Section V index.

Special State Provisions, Mutual Conditions—If applicable to the Company and its State of Location as stated in the Declarations

DEFINITIONS APPLICABLE TO SEC. I, II, IV

The following definitions apply to Sections I, II and IV; they do not apply to Sections III or V:

Throughout these sections we, us and our mean the Company named in the Declarations. You and your mean the person named in the Declarations and that person's spouse if a resident of the same household. You and your also refer to a partnership, corporation, estate or trust named in the Declarations.

Bodily Injury means physical injury or death to a person caused by an **occurrence**.

Business means a trade, profession or occupation, other than **farming** or **custom farming. Business** includes rental of all or any part of an **insured location** to others, or held for rental by you other than:

1. Your **residence premises** if rented occasionally;

2. Garages or stables, if not more than three (3) car spaces or stalls are rented or held for rental;

3. One-, two-, three-, or four-family **dwellings** described in the Declarations; or

4. Your farm.

Business does not include:

1. The operation of roadside stands principally for the sale of produce raised on the **insured location**; or

2. Newspaper delivery, baby-sitting, lawn care or similar activities normally performed by minors, when the activity is not the principal occupation of any **insured.**

Custom Farming means the use of any draft animal or **mobile agricultural machinery** in connection with **farming** operations for others for any charge.

Dwelling means a one-, two-, three-, or four-family **dwelling** listed in the Declarations, including its grounds and private garages.

Farm Employee means someone employed by you whose duties are in connection with the maintenance or use of the **insured location** as a farm, including the maintenance or use of your farm equipment. **Farm employee** does not include you, your spouse, or a minor child of either, but does include exchange labor.

Farm Personal Property means your personal property which is usual and incidental to the operation of a farm and is used on your farm. It includes livestock, poultry, **mobile agricultural machinery**, tools, supplies, equipment, and harvested crops used in or resulting from your **farming** operation. It includes property being purchased under an installment plan whether or not you have title to the property.

Farming means the production of fruit, nut or field crops, or the raising or keeping of livestock, poultry, fish, fur-bearing animals or bees. It includes wholesale but not retail sales, except incidental retail sales of your unprocessed farm products with the resulting gross income being less than 25 percent of your combined **farming** gross income.

Insured means you and if residents of your household:

1. Your **relatives**; and

2. Minors in the care of those named above.

Under Section II of this policy, **insured** also means a person while operating machinery, watercraft, or, in charge of your domestic or farm animals with your permission in your operations covered by this policy.

Insured Location means

1. All locations listed in the Declarations where you maintain a farm or residence, including private approaches;

2. Locations acquired by you during the policy period where you maintain a farm or residence, including private approaches;

3. Individual or family cemetery plots or burial vaults;

4. A location in which you temporarily reside but do not own; and

5. Vacant land owned by you and listed in the Declarations or acquired by you during the policy period.

Insured Location does not include property on which a **business** is conducted.

Medical Expenses means reasonable charges for medical, surgical, x-ray, dental, ambulance, hospital, professional nursing and prosthetic devices.

Mobile Agricultural Machinery means a land vehicle, including any machinery or attached apparatus, whether or not self-propelled, usual to the operation of a farm and used exclusively for agricultural purposes, not subject to registration and designed for use principally off public roads.

Mobile agricultural machinery includes implements of husbandry which are defined as a vehicle or piece of equipment or machinery designed for agricultural purposes, used primarily in the conduct of agricultural operations and used principally off the highway.

Motor Vehicle means a motorized land vehicle, trailer, or semi-trailer (including any attached machinery or apparatus) designed principally for travel on public roads. The following are not considered **motor vehicles** unless they are being towed by or carried on a **motor vehicle**:

1. A utility, boat, camping or travel trailer;

2. **Mobile agricultural machinery**;

3. **Recreational motor vehicles**;

4. Any equipment which is designed for use principally off public roads and not subject to registration or licensing.

Occurrence means an unexpected and unintended event, including continuous or repeated exposure to conditions, which results in **bodily injury** or **property damage** during the policy period. All **bodily injury** and **property damage** resulting from a common cause shall be considered the result of one **occurrence**.

Personal Property means personal property usual and incidental to the use of the **dwelling premises** as a **dwelling**.

Property Damage means injury to or destruction of tangible property caused by an **occurrence**.

Recreational Motor Vehicle or Recreational Vehicle means any motorized vehicle designed for recreation, principally used off public roads, and not subject to licensing.

Relative means a person related to you by blood, marriage, or adoption who is a resident of your household, including a ward or foster child.

Residence Employee means someone employed by you who performs duties in connection with the maintenance or use of the **residence premises**. This includes a person who performs duties for you elsewhere of a similar nature not in connection with your **business** or **farming**.

Residence Premises means a one-, two-, three-, or four-family **dwelling** which is your principal residence, including its grounds, and private garages. **Residence premises** also means that part of any other building which is your principal residence but does not include any portion used for **business**

GENERAL CONDITIONS APPLICABLE TO SEC. I, II, III, & IV

Unless otherwise indicated, the following conditions are applicable to Sections I, II, III, and IV:

1. **Agreement.** We will provide the insurance described in this policy and Declarations if you have paid the premium and have complied with the policy provisions and conditions. This policy is divided into four sections, some with multiple coverages. You have only the coverages for which you have paid premium. These coverages are indicated in the Declarations and are subject to the indicated limits of insurance.

READ THE DECLARATIONS TO DETERMINE WHICH COVERAGES PERTAIN TO YOU

2. **Abandonment of Property.** We need not pay for nor accept any property abandoned by an **insured**.

3. **Appraisal** (Not applicable to liability coverages). If you and we fail to agree on the amount of loss, either one can demand that the amount of loss be set by appraisal. If either makes a written demand for appraisal, each shall select a competent, independent appraiser and notify the other of the appraiser's identity within 20 days of receipt of the written demand. The two appraisers shall then select a competent, impartial umpire. If the two appraisers are unable to agree upon an umpire within 15 days, you or we can ask a judge of a court of record in the state where the **residence premises** is located to select an umpire. The appraisers shall then set the amount of the loss. If the appraisers submit a written report of an agreement to us, the amount agreed upon shall be the amount of the loss. If the appraisers fail to agree within a reasonable time,

they shall submit their differences to the umpire. Written agreements signed by any two of these three shall set the amount of the loss. Each appraiser shall be paid by the party selecting that appraiser. Other expenses of the appraisal and the compensation of the umpire shall be shared equally.

4. **Assignment**. Assignment of this policy shall not be valid unless we give our written consent.

5. **Audit Premium**. The premium stated in the Declarations shall be computed according to our rules and rating plans. The premium is for insurance from the inception date in the Declarations (12:01 a.m.) to the expiration date in the Declarations (12:01 a.m.); date and time being at your **residence premises**. This premium, however, is an estimated premium only. We shall be permitted to examine and audit your books and records during the policy period and within three (3) years after the final termination of the policy, to obtain information about the premium basis of this insurance. The earned premium for the insurance shall be computed according to our rules and rating plans. If the earned premium exceeds the estimated premium you paid, you shall pay us the excess; if the earned premium is less, we shall return the overpayment to you.

6. **Bankruptcy of an Insured**. Bankruptcy or insolvency of an **insured** shall not relieve us of our obligations under this policy.

7. **Cancellation** You may cancel this entire policy by mailing to us written notice stating when this cancellation shall be effective. Our cancellation rights appear on back pages of this policy labelled "Cancellation".

8. **Concealment or Fraud**. We will not provide coverage if any **insured** has intentionally concealed or misrepresented any material fact or circumstance relating to this insurance.

9. **Death**. Upon your death, we will continue through the current policy period to insure any member of your household who is an **insured** at the time of your death. We will also insure:

    a. With respect to your property, the person having proper temporary custody of the property until appointment and qualification of a legal representative; or

    b. The legal representative of the deceased, but only with respect to the premises and property of the deceased covered under the policy at the time of death.

10. **Declarations**. By acceptance of this policy, you agree that the Declarations indicate the coverages you purchased. This policy embodies the only agreements existing between you and us or any of our agents relating to this insurance.

11. **Deductible Clause**. Loss from each **occurrence** shall be adjusted separately. The deductible stated in the Declarations shall be subtracted from each adjusted loss or the limit of insurance, whichever is less. Under the special limits applicable to Coverage C, however, the deductible shall be subtracted from only the adjusted loss.

12. **Dividends or Credits**. Any obligation of ours for dividend or credit shall not in any way extend or change the policy period.

13. **Inspection and Audit**. We shall be permitted to inspect and audit your insured property and operation at any time. We are not obligated, however, to conduct inspections and any inspection or report shall not be considered a representation that the operation or property is safe.

14. **Liberalization Clause**. If we adopt any revision which would broaden the coverage under this policy without payment of additional premium within 60 days prior to or during the policy period, the broadened coverage will immediately apply to this policy.

15. **Loss Payment**. (Not applicable to liability coverages). We will adjust all losses with you. Payment for loss will be made within 60 days after we receive your signed, sworn statement of loss and ascertainment of the loss is made either by agreement with you, entry of a final judgment, or the filing of an appraisal award with us. Actual cash value in this policy means replacement cost less depreciation.

16. **Mortgage Clause**. (Limited to Sections I and IV). The word "mortgagee" includes a trustee of a deed of trust.

    If a mortgagee is named in this policy, any loss payable under Sections I or IV shall be paid to the mortgagee and you, as interests appear. If more than one mortgagee is named, the order of payment shall be the same as the order or precedence of the mortgages.

If we deny your claim, that denial shall not apply to a valid claim of the mortgagee, if the mortgagee:

a. Notifies us of any change in ownership, occupancy or substantial change in risk of which the mortgagee is aware;

b. Pays any premium due under this policy on demand if you have neglected to pay the premium; and

c. Submits a signed, sworn statement of loss within 60 days after receiving notice from us of your failure to do so. Policy conditions relating to Appraisal, Suit Against Us and Loss Payment apply to the mortgagee.

If the policy is cancelled by us, notice shall be mailed to the mortgagee at least 10 days before the date cancellation takes effect.

If we pay the mortgagee for any loss and deny payment to you:

a. We are subrogated to all the rights of the mortgagee granted under the mortgage on the property; or

b. At our option, we may pay to the mortgagee the whole principal on the mortgage plus any accrued interest. In this event, we shall receive a full assignment and transfer.

Subrogation shall not impair the right of the mortgagee to recover the full amount of the mortgagee's claim.

17. **No Benefit to Bailee**. We will not recognize any assignment or grant any coverage for the benefit of any person or organization holding, storing or transporting property for a fee regardless of any other provision of this policy.

18. **Nonduplication of Insurance Benefits**. No person entitled to benefits under any coverage of this policy shall recover duplicate benefits for the same elements of loss under other coverages of this policy or other policies written by us.

19. **Our Option**. If we give you written notice within 30 days after we receive your signed, sworn statement of loss, we may:

a. Take all or any part of the property at the agreed or appraised value; or

b. Repair or replace any part of the property damaged with equivalent property. We will not be liable for any loss resulting from delay in repair or choice of repairmen.

20. **Policy Period**. This policy applies only to **occurrences** which take place during the policy period.

21. **Policy Renewals**. Subject to our consent, you may renew this policy for successive periods by payment to us of the premium we require to renew the policy. Premium payment for any renewal period shall be due on the expiration of the preceding policy period.

22. **Policy Termination**. If you fail to pay the premium when due, the policy shall terminate on the expiration date of the policy without any notice or action by us.

23. **Subrogation—Our Right to Recover Payment**.

a. If we make payment under this policy and the person to or for whom payment was made has a right to recover damages, we will be subrogated to that right (have that right transferred to us). That person must do whatever is necessary to enable us to exercise our rights and must do nothing after the loss to prejudice our rights.

b. If we make a payment under this policy, and the person to or for whom payment was made recovers damages from another, that person must hold the proceeds of the recovery in trust for us and must reimburse us to the extent of our payment.

24. **Suit Against Us**. No action shall be brought against us unless there has been compliance with the policy provisions. No one shall have any right to join us as a party to any action against an **insured**. Further, no action with respect to liability coverages shall be brought against us until the obligation of the **insured** has been determined by final judgment or agreement signed by us.

25. **Terms of Policy to Conform to Statute**. Terms of this policy which are in conflict with the statutes of the state where the policy is issued are hereby amended to conform to such statutes.

26. **Waiver or Change of Policy Provisions**. A waiver or change of any provision of this policy must be in writing by us to be valid. Our request for an appraisal or examination shall not waive any of our rights.

SECTION I—PROPERTY INSURANCE

We cover the property insured under Section I against direct physical loss only for specified perils. The perils and our limit of liability applicable to each coverage are indicated in the Declarations.

COVERAGE A

Your Dwelling(s)

We cover the following:

1. The **dwelling** on the **residence premises** shown in the Declarations used principally as your private residence, including structures attached to the dwelling and outdoor equipment pertaining to the **dwelling** and materials and supplies located on or adjacent to the **residence premises** for use in the construction, alteration or repair of the **dwelling** or private garage on the **residence premises**.

2. Your **dwelling(s)** other than the **dwelling** on the **residence premises**, shown in the Declarations and used principally as a private residence, including structures attached to and outdoor equipment pertaining to them and materials and supplies on these **dwelling premises** for the construction, alteration or repair of them or their private garages.

Coverage for outdoor radio and television antennas, aerials, and satellite receivers, including their lead-in wiring, masts, and towers, is subject to a maximum payment of $250, unless such equipment is specifically insured elsewhere for a greater amount. Fences within 250 feet of the **dwelling** on the **residence premises** are covered. Field and pasture fences are excluded.

We cover detached private garages and storage sheds pertaining to the above **dwelling(s)**. Coverage for these structures shall not exceed ten percent (10%) of the amount of the insurance specified for the applicable **dwelling** as an additional amount of insurance. We do not cover these structures if used for **business**, professional or **farming** purposes. We also do not cover any garage or storage shed rented to someone other than a tenant of the **dwelling**.

COVERAGE B

Additional Living Expense

If a loss covered under Coverage A of this policy makes the **dwelling** uninhabitable, we pay the following not to exceed the applicable limit stated in the Declarations:

1. **Additional Living Expense.** Any necessary increase in living expenses incurred by you so that your family can maintain its normal standard of living. Payment shall be for the shortest time required to repair or replace the premises or, if you permanently relocate, the shortest time required for your household to settle elsewhere. This period of time is not limited by expiration of this policy.

2. **Fair Rental Value.** The fair rental value of the **dwelling premises**. Payment shall be for the shortest time required to repair or replace the part of the premises rented or held for rental. This period of time is not limited by expiration of this policy. Fair rental value shall not include any expenses that do not continue while part of the **dwelling premises** rented or held for rental is uninhabitable.

3. **Prohibited Use.** If a civil authority prohibits you from use of the **dwelling premises** as a result of direct damage to neighboring premises by a peril insured against in this policy, we cover any resulting additional living expenses or fair rental value loss incurred by you for a period not exceeding two weeks during which use is prohibited. We do not cover loss or expense due to cancellation of a lease or agreement. No deductible applies to Coverage B.

COVERAGE C

Personal Property

We cover **personal property** owned or used by any **insured** while it is anywhere in the world. At your request, we will cover personal property owned by others while the property is in that part of the **residence premises** occupied exclusively by an **insured**. Your **personal property** in a newly acquired principal residence is covered only for thirty days immediately after you begin to move the property there. If your **personal property** is distributed between your **residence premises** and this newly acquired principal residence, the limit of liability shall apply at each location in the proportion that the value at each location bears to the total value of all property distributed between the two locations.

If you have more than one **dwelling** insured under Coverage A of this policy a different Coverage C limit of liability applies to each **dwelling**. These limits are stated in the Declarations. The limit applicable to one insured **dwelling** can not be applied to a loss at another insured **dwelling**.

Our limit of liability for your **personal property** usually situated at your **dwelling premises** insured under Coverage A, located at other than your principal **dwelling** on the **residence premises,** is five percent (5%) of the limit of liability for that **dwelling premises** insured under Coverage A, unless the Declarations indicate you have purchased additional coverage. Any additional coverage is limited to the amount indicated for that particular location.

1. **Special Limits of Liability**. These limits do not increase the Coverage C limit of liability.

    The special limit for each following category is the total limit for each **occurrence** for all property in that category:

    a. $200 on money, bank notes, numismatic property, bullion, gold other than gold-ware, silver other than silverware, platinum, coins, medals, stamps, and other philatelic property;

    b. $1,000 on securities, accounts, deeds, evidences of debt, letters of credit, notes other than bank notes, manuscripts, passports and tickets;

    c. $1,000 on watercraft, including their trailers, furnishings, equipment, and outboard motors. We do not cover any loss by windstorm or hail to this property unless it is inside a fully enclosed building;

    d. $1,000 on utility trailers not otherwise insured;

    e. $1,000 on grave markers;

    f. $1,000 for loss by theft of jewelry, watches, furs, precious and semi-precious stones;

    g. $1,000 for loss by theft of firearms;

    h. $2,500 for loss by theft of silverware, silver-plated ware, goldware, gold-plated ware and pewterware.

2. **Property Not Insured**. We do not insure under Coverage C:

    a. **Farm personal property**;

    b. Animals, birds, fish or pets;

    c. Motorized land vehicles and parts, including **mobile agricultural machinery** except

vehicles used to service your **dwellings** and not licensed for road use, such as power lawnmowers;

d. Aircraft and parts;

e. Property of roomers, tenants and boarders not related to an **insured**;

f. **Business** personal property, including, but not limited to office equipment, supplies, furnishings, merchandise, samples, tools, and **business** papers and records;

g. **Recreational vehicles**, trailer homes and campers;

h. Any **personal property** located at any **dwellings** which are owned by you and not insured under Section I;

i. Articles separately described and specifically insured by this or other insurance.

3. **Supplementary Coverages**. The following supplementary coverages do not increase the applicable limit of liability under this policy:

    a. Consequential loss. We also cover loss to property insured under Coverage C while at the **insured location** due to change in temperature as a result of physical damage to the building or equipment therein caused by a peril insured against.

    b. Credit Card, Bank Transfer Card, Counterfeit Currency and Forgery. We will pay up to $1,000 for:

    (1) The legal obligation of an **insured** to pay because of the theft or unauthorized use of credit cards or bank transfer cards issued to or registered in any **insured's** name. We do not cover credit card or bank card use if any **insured** has not complied with all terms and conditions under which the card was issued;

    (2) Loss suffered by an **insured** caused by forgery or alteration of any check or negotiable instrument;

    (3) Loss suffered by an **insured** through acceptance in good faith of counterfeit United States or Canadian paper currency.

We do not cover losses resulting from **business** pursuits or dishonesty of any **insured**.

COVERAGE D

Farm Personal Property

We cover your unscheduled **farm personal property** on the **insured location**. This coverage is further extended for your **farm personal property** away from the **insured location** except while:

1. Stored in or being processed in manufacturing plants, public elevators, warehouses, seed houses, or drying plants;

2. In transit by common or contract carrier; or

3. In public sales barns or sales yards.

We will cover **farm personal property** leased, rented or borrowed by you to conduct your **farming** operation. This **farm personal property** may not be available for your regular use and may not be used on a co-operative exchange basis. This coverage is excess over insurance which the owner has on the property.

1. **Livestock Coverage**. We cover your **livestock** for the specified perils only if death occurs.

   Livestock is defined as cattle, horses, mules, swine, poultry, donkeys, goats and sheep. Dogs, cats and fur-bearing animals are not covered. Our limit of liability shall in no case exceed the actual cash value of the livestock subject to the maximum per head limit stated in the Declarations. Death must result within fifteen (15) days from the date of **occurrence**.

2. **Limited Crop Coverage**. Hay, straw and fodder are covered for loss caused by peril 1 (fire) only not to exceed the amount stated in the Declarations in any one stack or building. If a stack or hay building is exposed within 125 feet by another stack or building, the applicable limit shall apply to the aggregate of all such exposed stacks or buildings. For example, if stack Y is 100 feet from stack X and stack Z is 100 feet from stack Y but 200 feet from stack X, the aggregate limit applicable to stacks X, Y and Z is the Coverage D stack limit stated in the Declarations.

3. **Coinsurance Clause**. You must maintain insurance on all your eligible unscheduled **farm personal property** to the extent of at least eighty percent (80%) of the actual cash value at the time of loss and no less than at the time of our auditing or taking inventory. For example, if at the time of loss your unscheduled **farm personal property** is worth $100,000, then the amount of insurance must be at least $80,000. If you fail to keep this agreed percentage of coverage, you will share in each loss in addition to the deductible. We will pay the proportion of each loss represented by the amount you did insure at the time of loss divided by the amount you should have insured.

   If the aggregate claim for any loss under this coverage is less than two percent (2%) of the total amount of insurance under Coverage D, you will not be required to furnish an inventory of the undamaged property. This does not mean we waive any of our rights concerning the application of this coinsurance clause.

4. **Inspection and Audit**. We shall be permitted to inspect and audit your insured **farm personal property** at any reasonable time.

5. **Coverage Limitation to Records and Electronic Data Processing Property**. Our liability for loss to:

   a. Books of account, manuscripts, abstracts, drawings, card index systems and other records except electronic data processing records shall not exceed the cost of blank books, cards or other blank material, plus the cost of labor incurred by you for transcribing or copying such records;

   b. Film, tape, disc, drum, cell and other magnetic recording or storage media for electronic data processing shall not exceed the cost of such media in unexposed or blank form.

6. **Exclusions**. Coverage D does not cover:

   a. **Personal property**;

   b. Animals, other than **livestock**;

   c. Accounts, bills, currency, deeds, evidences of debt, money and securities;

   d. Vegetables (except threshed peas and beans), root crops, bulbs, fruits, cotton, tobacco and silage;

   e. Permanently installed irrigation pumps, buried water lines; and permanently installed or portable sprinkler lines and sprinkler equipment (including any sprinkler's electrical equipment);

   f. Fences, sawmill equipment, windmills, wind chargers and their towers, private power, light and telephone poles, radio and television towers and antennas, vehicles primarily designed and licensed for road use other than wagons and trailers designed for **farming** purposes and used principally on the insured premises;

g. Trucks, automobiles, housetrailers, motorcycles, watercraft, **recreational motor vehicles,** aircraft, or their parts or accessories;

h. Standing growing crops or stubble. However, 10% of the amount specified for Coverage D will cover standing corn, wheat, oats, barley, rye, flax, soybeans and other grains against loss by fire only;

i. Grain, seeds, peas, beans, hay, straw, and fodder unless loss is caused by peril 1 (fire);

j. Structures and buildings except portable buildings on skids in an amount not to exceed $300 per building;

k. Any damage arising from wear and tear, freezing, mechanical breakdown or failure;

l. Under collision or overturn coverage: damage to tires, unless damaged by the same cause as other loss covered under Coverage D;

m. Bee boards or their larvae and bees;

n. Loss to **livestock** caused by the direct or indirect result of fright, freezing, running into fences or other objects, running into streams or ditches, or smothering;

o. Livestock losses caused by collision with any **insured's** vehicle or with the roadbed; or

p. Property which is separately described and specifically insured in whole or in part by this or any other insurance.

COVERAGE E

Additional Buildings

We cover your **dwellings,** barns, buildings, fences and structures listed on the schedule of additional buildings.

1. **Materials and Supplies.** Coverage on a building or structure is extended to cover all materials and supplies on the premises or adjacent to them intended to be used in the construction, alteration or repair of such building or structure.

2. **Coverage on Buildings.** Coverage on buildings includes permanent fixtures and sheds attached to the described buildings, but excluding fences.

3. **Utility Poles.** Coverage on private utility poles includes attached switch boxes, fuse boxes, and other electrical equipment mounted on the poles.

4. **Fences and Similar Structures**. Our liability for loss to fences, corrals, pens, chutes and feed racks shall not be for a greater proportion of any loss than the amount of insurance bears to the total value of that particular property at the time of loss.

5. **New Construction.** We will pay up to $5,000 per **occurrence** for loss to newly constructed additional dwellings, barns, or buildings when erected on the **insured location**. This includes all materials and supplies on the premises to be used in the construction. This coverage shall cease sixty (60) days from the date construction was begun or the policy expiration date, whichever occurs first. For additional coverage, you must request it and pay the required premium. This extension does not cover additions, alterations or repairs to existing dwellings, barns or buildings. Perils 1–9 apply to New Construction Coverage.

   Coverage to outdoor radio and television antennas, aerials, and satellite receivers including their lead-in wiring, masts and towers, is subject to a maximum payment of $250, unless such equipment is specifically insured for a greater amount.

SECTION I—ADDITIONAL COVERAGES

No deductible applies to these additional coverages.

1. **Debris Removal.** We will pay the reasonable expense incurred by you in the removal of debris of covered property provided coverage is afforded for the peril causing the loss. Debris removal expense is included in the limit of liability applying to the damaged property. When the amount payable for the actual damage to the property plus the expense for debris removal exceeds the limit of liability for the damaged property, an additional 5% of that limit of liability will be available to cover debris removal expense.

2. **Reasonable Repairs.** We will pay the reasonable costs incurred by you for necessary repairs made solely to protect covered property from further damage provided coverage is afforded

for the peril causing the loss. This coverage does not increase the limit of liability applicable to the property being repaired.

3. **Trees, Shrubs and Other Plants** (Limited to Coverage A—Your Dwellings). We cover trees, shrubs, plants and lawns within 250 feet of the **dwelling premises** for loss caused by the following perils: fire or lightning, explosion, riot or civil commotion, aircraft, vehicles not owned or operated by a resident of the **dwelling premises**, vandalism or malicious mischief or theft. The limit of liability for this coverage shall not exceed five percent (5%) of the limit of liability specified for the Coverage A **dwelling** at the same **dwelling premises**. Our limit of liability for any one tree, shrub or plant is $500. We do not cover property grown for **business** or **farming** purposes under this paragraph. This coverage shall not increase the applicable Coverage A limit under your policy.

4. **Refrigerated Products.** If Coverage C applies to your policy, we will pay an amount not to exceed $500 for loss or damage to contents of a freezer or refrigerator at the **residence premises**. This coverage does not apply to **farm personal property**. If a different amount is stated in the Declarations, that amount applies. The loss or damage must be caused by a change in temperature resulting from:

   a. Interruption of electrical service to refrigeration equipment caused by damage to the generating or transmission equipment which results in a breakdown in the system; or

   b. Mechanical or electrical breakdown of the refrigeration system.

   You must exercise diligence in inspecting and maintaining refrigeration equipment in proper working condition. If interruption of electrical service, mechanical or electrical breakdown is known, you must exercise all reasonable means to protect the insured property from further damage.

5. **Fire Department Service Charge.** We will pay up to $300 for your liability assumed by contract or agreement for fire department charges incurred when the fire department is called to save or protect covered property from a peril insured against. No deductible applies to this coverage. Coverage afforded under this clause applies only if the covered property is not located within the limits of the city, municipality or protection district furnishing such fire department response. This coverage does not apply to property located in Arizona.

SECTION I—PERILS INSURED AGAINST

We cover for direct physical loss to property insured caused by the following perils:

1. **Fire** or **lightning**.

2. **Removal**. When property is removed because it is endangered by other insured perils, we pay for direct loss from any cause for accidental loss to that property while it is being removed and for thirty (30) days after removal to a proper place.

3. **Windstorm** or **hail**.

   a. This peril does **not** include loss to the interior or contents of a building caused by rain, snow, sleet, sand or dust unless the direct force of wind or hail damages the building causing an opening in a roof or wall through which the rain, snow, sleet, sand, or dust gets in;

   b. This peril does **not** include loss caused directly or indirectly by frost, cold weather, ice (other than hail), snowstorm or sleet, all whether driven by wind or not;

   c. This peril does **not** include loss to watercraft and their trailers, furnishings, equipment and outboard motors while outside a fully enclosed building.

4. **Explosion. This peril does not** include:

   a. Concussion unless caused by explosion;

   b. Electrical arcing;

   c. Water hammer;

   d. Rupture or bursting of steam boilers, steam pipes, steam turbines, steam engines, or water pipes, if owned by, leased or actually operated under the control of an **insured**;or

   e. Rupture or bursting due to expansion or swelling of the contents of any building or structure, caused by or resulting from water;

   f. Rupture or bursting of rotating parts of machinery caused by centrifugal force; or

   g. Shock waves caused by aircraft, including a sonic boom.

5. **Riot** or **civil commotion**.

6. **Aircraft**, including self-propelled missiles and spacecraft.

7. **Vehicles**. This peril does **not** cover loss:

   a. To a fence, driveway, walk, or structure insured under Coverage E, caused by a vehicle owned or operated by you, your employees or by a resident of the premises; or

   b. To any **motor vehicle** or trailer.

   NOTE: Loss by Perils 6 (Aircraft) and 7 (Vehicles) includes only direct loss by actual physical contact of an aircraft or vehicle with the covered property.

8. **Smoke**, meaning sudden and accidental damage from smoke.

   This peril does **not** include loss caused by smoke from agricultural smudging or industrial operations.

9. **Vandalism or malicious mischief**, meaning only the willful and malicious damage to or destruction of the property covered.

   This peril does **not** cover:

   a. Loss if the **dwelling** has been vacant or unoccupied for more than thirty (30) consecutive days immediately before the loss. A **dwelling** being constructed is not considered vacant or unoccupied;

   b. Wear and tear caused by tenants or members of their household.

10. **Theft**, including attempted theft and loss of property from a known location when it is likely that the property has been stolen.

    Property of a student who is an **insured** is covered while at a residence away from home only if the student has been there at any time during the forty-five (45) days immediately before the loss.

    The term "theft" shall **not** include escape, inventory shortage, wrongful conversion or embezzlement.

    This peril does **not** include loss:

    a. Committed by any **insured**;

    b. In or to a building under construction;

    c. Of materials, tools and supplies for use in the construction of a building until it is completed and occupied;

    d. From any part of a **dwelling premises** rented by an **insured** to other than an **insured**;

    e. Of property while in the custody of the postal service or similar government or private business;

    f. Caused by tenants, their employees, or members of their households.

    In the event of loss by theft, you shall give immediate notice to the nearest law enforcement officer. We will not pay any reward you offer for the return or recovery of any stolen property.

11. **Breakage of glass or safety glazing** material which is part of the covered building. This coverage extends to storm doors and storm windows in summer storage. This peril does **not** include loss if the building has been vacant more than thirty (30) consecutive days immediately before the loss. A building being constructed is not considered vacant.

12. **Weight of ice, snow**, or **sleet** which causes damage to a building or property contained in a building. This peril does **not** include loss to an awning, fence, patio, pavement, swimming pool, foundation, retaining wall, bulkhead, pier, wharf, or dock.

13. **Collapse** of a building or any part of a building.

    This peril does **not** include loss to an awning, fence, patio, pavement, swimming pool, underground pipe, flue, drain, cesspool, septic tank, foundation, retaining wall, bulkhead, pier, wharf or dock unless the loss is a direct result of the collapse of a building. Collapse does **not** include: settling, cracking, shrinking, bulging or expansion.

14. **Accidental discharge or overflow** of water or steam from within a plumbing, heating or air conditioning system or from within a household appliance. We also pay for tearing out and replacing any part of the covered **dwelling** necessary to repair the system or appliance from which the water or steam escaped.

    This peril does **not** include loss:

    a. To a **dwelling** caused by continuous or repeated see page or leakage for more than thirty (30) days;

    b. On the **dwelling premises**, if the **dwelling** has been vacant for more than thirty (30) consecutive days immediately before the loss. A **dwelling** being constructed is not considered vacant;

c. To the system or appliance from which the water or steam escaped;

d. Caused by or resulting from freezing; or

e. On the **dwelling premises** caused by accidental discharge or overflow which occurs off the **dwelling premises**.

15. **Sudden or accidental tearing apart, cracking, burning** or **bulging** of a steam or hot water heating system, an air conditioning system, or an appliance for heating water.

   We do **not** cover loss caused by or resulting from freezing under this peril.

16. **Falling objects**. This peril does **not** include loss to the interior of a building or property contained in the building unless the roof or an exterior wall of the building is first damaged by a falling object. This peril does not include loss to outdoor equipment, awnings, fences, and retaining walls. Damage to the falling object itself is not included.

17. **Freezing of a plumbing, heating or air conditioning** system or of a household appliance.

   This peril does not include loss on the **dwelling premises** while the **dwelling** is vacant, unoccupied, or being constructed unless you have:

   a. Maintained heat in the building; or

   b. Shut off the water supply and drained the system and appliances of water.

18. **Sudden and accidental damage from artificially generated electrical current**.

   This peril does **not** include loss to a tube, transistor or other electronic components.

19. **Collision with another object or overturn**. This peril does not apply to **livestock**. Impact with the ground or roadbed is not considered a collision.

20. **Electrocution**. This peril applies only to **livestock**.

21. **Attack by dogs or wild animals**. This peril applies only to **livestock**. It does **not** include attack by dogs owned by you or any person residing on the insured location.

22. **Accidental shooting**. This peril applies only to **livestock**. This peril does not include loss caused by any **insured**, employees of an **insured**, or persons residing on the **insured location**.

23. **Loading, unloading, collision or overturn while in transit**. This peril applies only to **livestock**. Impact with the ground or roadbed is not considered a collision.

24. **Drowning**. This peril applies only to **livestock** and excludes swine under thirty (30) days old and poultry.

25. **All risk**.

   We insure for all risks of physical loss to the property insured **except**:

   a. Those losses excluded under **"Exclusions Applicable to Section I"**;

   b. Freezing of a plumbing, heating or air conditioning system or of a household appliance, or by discharge, leakage or overflow from within the system or appliance caused by freezing, while the **dwelling** is vacant, unoccupied or being constructed unless you have used reasonable care to:

   (1) Maintain heat in the building; or

   (2) Shut off the water supply and drained the system and appliances of water.

   c. Freezing, thawing, pressure or weight of water or ice, whether driven by wind or not, to a fence, pavement, patio, swimming pool, foundation, retaining wall, bulkhead, pier, wharf or dock;

   d. Theft in or to a building under construction, or of materials, tools and supplies for use in the construction until the building is completed and occupied;

   e. Vandalism and malicious mischief or breakage of glass and safety glazing materials if the building has been vacant or unoccupied for more than thirty (30) consecutive days immediately before the loss. A building being constructed is not considered vacant or unoccupied;

   f. Continuous or repeated see page or leakage of water or steam for more than thirty (30) days within a plumbing, heating or air conditioning system or from within a household appliance;

   g. Wear and tear; marring; deterioration; inherent vice; latent defect; mechanical breakdown; rust; mold; wet or dry rot; contamination;

smog; smoke from agricultural smudging or industrial operations; settling, cracking, shrinking, bulging, or expansion of pavements, patios, foundations, walls, floors, roofs or ceilings; loss caused by birds, vermin, rodents, insects or domestic animals. If any of these cause water to escape from a plumbing, heating or air conditioning system or household appliance, we cover loss caused by the water. We also cover the cost of tearing out and replacing any part of a building necessary to replace the system or appliance. We do **not** cover loss to the system or appliance from which this water escaped.

If Peril 25 applies to Coverage C, the following additional exclusions also apply:

h. Breakage of eye glasses, glassware, statuary, bric-a-brac, porcelains, and similar fragile articles, other than jewelry, watches, bronzes, cameras, and photographic lenses. These items are covered, however, if breakage results from Perils 1 through 10 or 13 through 16;

i. Dampness of atmosphere or extremes of temperature unless the direct cause of loss is rain, snow, sleet or hail;

j. Loss arising from refinishing, renovating or repairing property other than watches, jewelry and furs;

k. Collision other than collision with a land vehicle; sinking, swamping or stranding of watercraft, including their trailers, furnishings, equipment and outboard motors.

Under items g and a through d above any ensuing loss not excluded is covered.

EXCLUSIONS APPLICABLE TO SECTION I

We do not cover loss under Section I resulting directly or indirectly from:

1. **Ordinance or law**, meaning enforcement of any ordinance or law regulating the construction, repair, or demolition of a building or other structure, unless specifically provided under this policy.

2. **Earth movement**, including but not limited to earthquake, landslide, mudflow, earth sinking, rising or shifting. Direct loss by fire, explosion, theft, or breakage of glass or safety glazing materials resulting from earth movement is covered.

3. **Water damage**, meaning:
   a. Flood, surface water, waves, tidal water, overflow of a body of water, or spray from any of these, whether or not driven by wind;
   b. Water which backs up through sewers or drains;
   c. Water below the surface of the ground, including water which exerts pressure on, or seeps or leaks through a building, sidewalk, driveway, foundation, swimming pool or other structure. Direct loss by fire, explosion or theft resulting from water damage is covered.

4. **Volcanic eruption**.

5. **Neglect**, meaning neglect of an **insured** to use all reasonable means to save and preserve property at and after the time of loss, or when property is endangered by a peril insured against.

6. **War**, including undeclared war, civil war, insurrection, rebellion, revolution, warlike act by military force or military personnel, destruction or seizure for use for any purpose by any governmental authority, and including any consequence of any of these. Discharge of a nuclear weapon shall be deemed a warlike act even if accidental.

7. **Power, heating or cooling failure** unless the failure results from physical damage to power, heating or cooling equipment situated on the **dwelling premises** where the loss occurs. This failure must be caused by a peril insured against.

8. **Depreciation, decay, deterioration, change in temperature or humidity, loss of market**, or from any other consequential or indirect loss of any kind.

9. **Any sound reproducing, receiving or transmitting equipment** designed for use as an eight-track player, cassette player, citizens band radio, two-way mobile radio or telephone, scanning monitor, radar detection or similar device, or any tape, wire, record, disc, or other medium for use with any such device while any of this property is in or upon any motorized vehicle, farm equipment, boat or aircraft, and capable of being operated by power supplied from these vehicles. These devices are covered if factory installed in

mobile agricultural machinery insured under Coverage D.

10. **Nuclear hazard**, meaning any nuclear reaction, radiation, or radioactive contamination, all whether controlled or uncontrolled or however caused, or any consequence of any of these. Loss caused by the nuclear hazard shall not be considered loss caused by fire, explosion, or smoke, whether these perils are specifically named or otherwise included within the perils insured against in Section I.

The above exclusions, 1 through 10, apply even if the following contribute to the loss: faulty, inadequate or defective planning; zoning; development; maintenance of property on or off the insured location by any person or organization.

11. **Any damage caused intentionally** by or at the direction of any **insured**.

CONDITIONS APPLICABLE TO SECTION I

1. **Insurable Interest and Limit of Liability**. Even if more than one person has an insurable interest in the property covered, we shall not be liable:

   a. To the **insured** for an amount greater than the **insured's** interest; nor

   b. For more than the applicable limit of liability.

2. **Your Duty after Loss**. In case of a loss to which this insurance may apply, you must see that the following duties are performed:

   a. Give written notice to us or our agent, as soon as practicable, and also give notice to the police if loss is suspected to be in violation of a law. In case of loss under the credit or bank card coverage, also notify the issuing card company;

   b. Protect the property from further damage, make reasonable and necessary repairs required to protect the property and keep an accurate record of repair expenditures;

   c. Prepare an inventory of damaged property showing in detail, the quantity, description, actual cash value and amount of loss. Attach to the inventory all bills, receipts and related documents that substantiate the figures in the inventory;

   d. As often as we may reasonably require, exhibit the damaged property and submit to examination under oath and subscribe the same;

   e. Within sixty (60) days after our request, submit to us your signed, sworn statement of loss which sets forth the following information to the best of your knowledge and belief:

      (1) The time and cause of loss;

      (2) The interest of the **insured** and all others in the property involved and all encumbrances on the property;

      (3) Other insurance which may cover the loss;

      (4) Changes in title or occupancy of the property during the term of the policy;

      (5) Specifications of any damaged building and detailed estimates for repair of the damage;

      (6) An inventory of damaged property as described above;

      (7) Receipts for additional living expenses incurred and records supporting any fair rental value loss; and

      (8) Evidence or affidavit supporting a claim under the credit card or bank card coverage stating the amount and cause of loss.

3. **Loss Settlement**. Subject to the applicable limits stated in the Declarations, covered property losses are settled as follows:

   a. **Personal Property,** structures that are not buildings, **farm personal property**, and buildings insured under Coverage E, at actual cash value at the time of loss but not exceeding the amount necessary to repair or replace;

   b. Floor coverings, domestic appliances, awnings, outdoor antennas and outdoor equipment, whether or not attached to the buildings, at actual cash value at the time of loss but not exceeding the amount necessary to repair or replace;

   c. Buildings insured under Coverage A:

      (1) When the full cost of repair or replacement for loss to a building under Coverage A is less than $1500, Coverage A is extended to include the full cost of

repair or replacement without deduction for depreciation.

   (2) If the limit of liability on the damaged building is less than 80% of its replacement cost at the time of the loss, we pay the larger of the following:

     (a) Actual cash value of the damaged part of the building; or

     (b) That proportion of the replacement cost of the damaged part which our limit of liability on the building bears to 80% of the full current cost of the building.

   (3) If the limit of liability on the damaged building is at least 80% of its replacement cost at the time of loss we pay the full cost of repair or replacement of the damaged part without deduction for depreciation, but not more than the smallest of the following amounts:

     (a) The limit of liability applicable to the building;

     (b) The cost to repair or replace the damage on the same premises using materials of equivalent kind and quality to the extent practicable; or

     (c) The amount actually and necessarily spent to repair or replace the damage.

   (4) When the cost to repair or replace exceeds 5% of the applicable limit of liability on the damaged building, we are not liable for more than the actual cash value of the loss until actual repair or replacement is completed. You may make a claim for the actual cash value amount of the loss before repairs are made. A claim for any additional amount payable under this provision must be made and construction started within one hundred and eighty (180) days after the loss.

4. **Increased Hazard**. We shall not be liable for any loss to property insured under this policy occurring while the hazard is increased by any means within the control or knowledge of any **insured**.

5. **Loss to a Pair or Set**. In case of a loss to a pair or set, we may elect to:

  a. Repair or replace any part or restore the pair or set to its value before the loss; or

  b. Pay the difference between the actual cash value of the property before and after the loss.

6. **Glass Replacement**. Covered loss for breakage of glass shall be settled on the basis of replacement with safety glazing materials when required by ordinance or law.

7. **Waiver of Subrogation**. You may waive in writing before a loss all right of recovery against any person. If not waived, we may require an assignment of rights for a loss to the extent that payment is made by us.

8. **Other Insurance**. If you are carrying other insurance on the property to which this policy applies, the coverage under this policy is null and void. We may permit other insurance, however, by endorsement to this policy. If other insurance is permitted, we will not be liable for a greater portion of any loss than our pro rata share in excess of any deductible.

9. **Vacancy**. When a building insured under this policy has been vacant, unoccupied or abandoned for a period of six (6) consecutive months at the initial inception date of this policy or any time after that, our liability is reduced fifty (50) percent. Outbuildings, which are in a seasonal state of vacancy or unoccupancy due to normal practices of **farming** operations, are not considered vacant or unoccupied as defined in the policy and therefore, our liability is not reduced under the provisions of this clause.

ENDORSEMENTS APPLICABLE TO SECTION I

Each of the following endorsements may be purchased by your payment of an additional premium. All policy provisions apply to these endorsements unless an endorsement specifically states otherwise. **An endorsement applies only when it is listed in the Declarations and you pay this premium**.

No. 111 Replacement Cost—Personal Property.

Losses under Coverage C shall be settled at replacement cost without deduction for depreciation.

Property Not Eligible

Property listed below is not eligible for replacement cost settlement. Any loss shall be settled at actual cash value at the time of loss but not exceeding the amount necessary to repair or replace.

1. Antiques, fine arts, paintings, statues and other articles which by their inherent nature cannot be replaced with new articles.

2. Articles whose age or history contribute substantially to their value, including but not limited to memorabilia, souvenirs, and collectors items.

3. Personal property of others.

4. Articles not maintained in good or workable condition.

5. Articles that are outdated or obsolete and are stored or not being used.

Replacement Cost

1. We will pay not more than the smallest of the following amounts:

   a. Replacement cost at time of loss without deduction for depreciation;

   b. The full cost of repair at time of loss;

   c. 400% of the actual cash value at time of loss;

   d. Any special limit of liability applicable under Coverage C; or

   e. The total limit of liability applicable to Coverage C.

2. When the replacement cost for the entire loss under this endorsement exceeds $500, we will pay no more than the actual cash value for the loss or damage until the actual repair or replacement is completed.

3. You may make a claim for loss on an actual cash value basis and then make claim within 180 days after the loss for any additional liability in accordance with this endorsement.

4. This endorsement also covers domestic appliances, floor coverings, awnings, outdoor antennas, and outdoor equipment pertaining to a **dwelling** insured under Coverage A.

No. 114 Borrowed Equipment Endorsement.

We cover under Coverage D loss to **mobile agricultural machinery** in which you have no interest, provided such machinery has been borrowed by either you or **your employees** and is actually being used in the conduct of your own farm operation, is not available for your regular use, and is not used on a cooperative exchange basis. This coverage, however, shall apply as excess over any insurance which the owner has on this borrowed property. Our limit of liability per **occurrence** under this endorsement is stated in the Declarations.

No. 120 Inflation Guard Endorsement.

It is agreed that the Limit of Liability specified in the Declarations for Section I—Property under Coverage A (Dwelling), Coverage B (Additional Living Expense) and Coverage C (Personal Property), shall be increased at the same rate as the increase in the Company Index as developed monthly from available Governmental and Appraisal Company Indices and kept on file in the Home Office.

In no event will the limit of liability be less than the amount specified in the Declarations.

At each renewal date after this endorsement becomes effective, the amount of insurance on the above coverages will be corrected to the nearest $100 in accordance with the above factor and renewal premium will be adjusted accordingly.

No. 130 Elimination of Livestock under Coverage D.

There is no coverage for livestock under Coverage D.

No. 171 Glass Deductible Waived.

No deductible will apply to glass breakage to the building(s) insured under Coverage A of Section I.

No. 183 Guaranteed Replacement Cost Endorsement

We agree that our limit of liability for buildings insured under Coverage A is not limited by the amount shown on the Declarations page provided:

1. You have insured your **dwelling** and other structures to 100% of their replacement costs as we determine based on the accuracy of information you furnish, and you pay the premium we require;

2. You accept the property insurance adjustment condition in paragraph 1 above, agree to accept any annual adjustment, and pay the additional premium charged;

3. You notify us within ninety (90) days of the start of any additions or other physical changes which increase the value of your **dwelling** or other structures on the dwelling premises by $5,000.00 or more, and pay the additional premium charged.

Losses under this endorsement are covered for the full cost of repair or replacement of the damaged part without deduction for depreciation, but not more than the amount actually and necessarily spent to repair or replace the damage on the same premises using materials of equivalent kind and quality to the extent practical.

Parts c(1), (2) and (3) of the loss settlement clause of "Conditions Applicable to Section I" are deleted. This endorsement is void if you fail to comply with its provisions.

SECTION II—YOUR LIABILITY PROTECTION

COVERAGE F

Liability

If a claim is made or a suit is brought against any **insured** for damages because of **bodily injury** or **property damage** caused by an **occurrence** to which this coverage applies, we will:

1. Pay up to our limit of liability for the damages for which the **insured** is legally liable;

2. Provide a defense at our expense by counsel of our choice. We may make any investigation and settlement of any claim or suit that we decide is appropriate. Our obligation to defend any claim or suit ends when the amount we pay for damages equals our limit of liability.

COVERAGE G

Premises Medical

We will pay the necessary medical and funeral expenses incurred within three years from the date of an **occurrence** causing **bodily injury**. This coverage does not apply to you or regular residents of your household other than **residence employees**. As to others, this coverage applies only:

1. To a person on the **insured location** with the permission of any **insured**; or

2. To a person off the **insured location**, if the **bodily injury**:

    a. Arises out of a condition in the **insured location** or the ways immediately adjoining;

    b. Is caused by the activities of any **insured**;

    c. Is caused by the activities of a **farm** or **residence employee** in the course of employment by an **insured**;

    d. Is caused by an animal owned by or in the care of any **insured**;

e. Is sustained by any **residence employee** and arises out of and in the course of employment.

No payment shall be made under Coverage G unless the person to or for whom such payment is made shall have signed an agreement that the amount of such payment shall be applied toward the settlement of any claim, or the satisfaction of any judgment for damages entered in the person's favor against any **insured** because of **bodily injury** to which Coverage F of this policy applies. (This paragraph is not applicable if this policy is issued in Arizona.)

COVERAGE H

Employer's Liability

If a claim is made or suit brought against you or your **relatives** because of **bodily injury** caused by an **occurrence** sustained by any **farm employee** arising out of and in the course of employment by you, we will:

1. Pay up to our limit of liability for the damages for which you are legally liable;

2. Provide a defense at our expense by counsel of our choice. We may make any investigation and settle any claim or suit that we decide is appropriate. Our obligation to defend any claim or suit ends when the amount we pay for damages resulting from the **occurrence** equals our limit of liability.

COVERAGE I

Medical Payments for Farm Employees

We will pay the necessary **medical** and funeral expenses incurred within three years from the date of **occurrence** to or for each **farm employee** who sustains **bodily injury** caused by an **occurrence** arising out of and in the course of employment by you.

No payment shall be made under Coverage I unless the person to or for whom such payment is made shall have signed an agreement that the amount of such payment shall be applied toward the settlement of any claim, or the satisfaction of any judgment for damages entered in the person's favor because of **bodily injury** to which Coverage H of this policy applies.

COVERAGE J

Medical Payments (Named Persons)

We will pay the necessary **medical** and funeral expenses incurred within three years from the date of **occurrence** to or for each person named in Coverage J of the Declarations, who sustains **bodily injury** caused by an **occurrence**.

No payment shall be made under Coverage J unless the person to or for whom such payment is made shall have signed an agreement that the amount of such payment shall be applied toward the settlement of any claim, or the satisfaction of any judgment for damages entered in the person's favor against any **insured** because of **bodily injury** to which Coverage F or H of this policy applies.

COVERAGE K

Death of Livestock by Collision

We will pay, subject to the limits of liability stated in the Declarations, for loss by death of any cattle, horse, or hybrid thereof, hog, sheep or goat owned by you and not otherwise covered, caused by collision between such animal and a **motor vehicle**, provided:

1. The **motor vehicle** is not owned or operated by an **insured** or any **insured's** employee;
2. The animal is within a public highway and is not being transported;
3. Death to the animal occurs within fifteen days after the date of the collision.

We further extend this coverage to include the death of livestock when killed by any train, provided you first present a claim in your name to the railroad company involved.

COVERAGE L

Custom Farming

Coverage F also covers your **custom farming**.

Coverage L does **not** apply to:

1. Any damage or injury to the land or crops upon which the **custom farming** is performed or is to be performed, arising from:
   a. The mixing or application of fertilizers, herbicides, pesticides, fungicides, or other chemical treatment of real property, seeds or crops;
   b. Any goods, products, or their containers manufactured, sold, handled or distributed by or on behalf of any **insured**.
2. Injury or damage resulting from:
   a. A delay in or lack of performance by or on behalf of any **insured** of any contract or agreement, written or oral; or

b. The failure of any **insured's** products or work performed by or on behalf of any **insured** to meet the level of performance, quality, fitness or result warranted or represented by any insured.

COVERAGE M

Damage to Property of Others

We will pay for **property damage** to property of others caused by an **insured**. We will not pay for **property damage**:

1. Caused intentionally by any **insured** who is thirteen (13) years of age or older;
2. To property owned by or rented to any **insured**, a tenant of any **insured**, or a resident of any **insured's** household; or
3. Arising out of:
   a. Any **business**;
   b. The ownership, maintenance, use, loading or unloading of a **motor vehicle**, watercraft, or aircraft;
   c. Theft, mysterious disappearance, or loss of use;
   d. Mechanical or electrical breakdown, wear and tear, latent defect or inherent vice;
4. To tires.

Coverage M is subject only to the above exclusions and not to the general exclusions applicable to Section II.

Limit of Liability.

Our limit of liability under Coverage M for **property damage** arising out of any **occurrence** shall not exceed the lesser of:

1. The actual cash value of the damaged property at the time of the loss; or
2. What it would then cost to repair or replace the damaged property with other of like kind and quality; or
3. The limit of liability stated in the Declarations for Coverage M.

If Section I of this policy also applies to a loss under Coverage M, Section I is primary and Coverage M is excess. You must pay any applicable Section I deductible before Coverage M applies.

We may pay for the loss in money or may repair or replace the property and may settle the claim for loss to property either with the owner or with you. Any property paid for or replaced shall, at our option, become our property.

We have no obligation under Coverage M to provide a defense against any claim or suit brought against any insured.

SECTION II—ADDITIONAL COVERAGES

Section II includes the following:

1. **Fire Legal Liability**. Coverage F is extended to cover **property damage** to a lodging place and its furnishings rented to, occupied or used by or in the care of an **insured** if such **property damage** arises out of fire, smoke or explosion. For purposes of this fire legal coverage, **insured** shall include only you and those persons listed in Paragraphs (1) and (2) of the definition of **insured**. The care, custody and control exclusion does not apply to this extension of coverage.

2. **Newly Acquired Locations**. Section II is extended to cover locations you acquire by ownership or leasehold if similar to premises or **dwellings** described in the Declarations, if you notify us of these acquisitions on or prior to the next renewal date of this policy. The insurance afforded to these acquisitions is limited to the insurance applicable to the locations already described in the Declarations.

   This extension of coverage does not apply to loss for which you have other valid and collectible insurance. You must pay any additional premium required because of the application of this insurance to such newly acquired locations.

SECTION II—ADDITIONAL PAYMENTS

Under Coverages F and H, we will pay the following expenses in addition to our limits of liability, but our obligation for these payments ceases when our obligation to defend ends:

1. Expenses for first aid to others incurred by any insured for bodily injury covered under this policy. We will not pay for first aid to you or any other insured;

2. Expenses incurred by us and costs taxed against any **insured** in any suit we defend;

3. Premiums on bonds required in a suit defended by us, but not for bond amounts greater than the limit of liability provided by this policy. We are not obligated to apply for or furnish any bond;

4. Reasonable expenses incurred by any **insured** at our request, including actual loss of earnings (but not loss of other income) up to $50 per day for assisting us in the investigation or defense of any claim or suit;

5. Interest on the entire judgment which accrues after entry of that part of the judgment which does not exceed the limit of liability that applies and before we pay, tender or deposit in court that part of the judgment which does not exceed the limit of liability that applies.

EXCLUSIONS APPLICABLE TO SECTION II

The following exclusions apply to all coverages under Section II except Coverage M. Section II does not cover **bodily injury** or **property damage**:

1. Arising from any **insured's business** activities or any professional service;

2. Arising from any location which an **insured** owns, rents, leases, or controls, other than an **insured location**. This exclusion does not apply to **bodily injury** of **residence employees** arising out of and in the course of employment by an **insured**;

3. Which is intentionally caused by any **insured**;

4. Arising from the maintenance, operation, use, loading or unloading of any of the following which any **insured** owns, borrows, rents, leases or operates:

   a. Any aircraft, except model aircraft of the hobby variety not used or designed for the transportation of people or cargo;

   b. Any **motor vehicle**, coverage however, applies on the **insured location** if the **motor vehicle** is not licensed for road use because it is used exclusively on the **insured location**;

   c. Any watercraft:

      (1) If powered by an inboard or inboard-outboard motor of more than fifty (50) horsepower;

      (2) If a sailing vessel twenty-six (26) feet or more in overall length.

   Exclusion 4.c. does not apply while the watercraft is stored on the **insured location**.

d. Any **recreational vehicle** if the **bodily injury** or **property damage** occurs away from the **insured location**. Exclusion 4.d. does not apply to golf carts while used for golfing purposes.

Exclusions 4.c. and 4.d. do not apply to watercraft or **recreational vehicles** borrowed or rented by an **insured** for less than 10 days. Damage to the borrowed or rented **recreational vehicle** or watercraft, however, is not covered. Exclusion 4 does not apply to **bodily injury** sustained by a **residence employee** in the course of employment.

5. Arising out of the use of any aircraft, **motor vehicle, mobile agricultural machinery,** watercraft or **recreational vehicle,** while being used in or following any prearranged or organized racing, speed or stunting activity or in practice or preparation for any such contest or activity;

6. Which results from liability arising out of any contract or agreement;

7. Arising out of **custom farming** when total receipts exceed $10,000 in a calendar year. This exclusion does not apply if coverage is indicated under Coverage L in the Declarations;

8. Caused by or resulting from declared or undeclared war, civil war, insurrection, rebellion, revolution, warlike act by a military force or military personnel, destruction or seizure or use for any government purpose, and including any consequence of these. Discharge of a nuclear weapon shall be deemed a warlike act even if accidental;

9. Resulting from any act or omission of a **residence** or **farm employee** who is also an **insured** while away from the **insured location,** if the employee is under the control and direction of some person other than an **insured**;

10. Caused by a substance released or discharged from an aircraft owned or operated by an **insured** in connection with dusting or spraying operations;

11. Caused by any goods, products or containers manufactured, processed, sold, handled or distributed by an **insured,** except farm products raised on the **insured location**. Loss arising out of the failure of seed sold by an **insured** to conform to the variety, purpose or quality specified by the insured, however, is not covered. The term "seed" means seeds, bulbs, plants, roots, tubers, cuttings or other similar means of plant propagation;

12. Arising out of the discharge, dispersal, release or escape of smoke, vapors, soot, fumes, acids, alkalis, toxic chemicals, liquids or gases, waste materials or other irritants, contaminants, or pollutants into or upon land, the atmosphere or any water course or body of water. This exclusion does not apply to:

    a. Crop damage resulting from the accidental above ground contact with herbicides, pesticides, fungicides and fertilizers caused by the application of the same to an insured site which results in actual damages within one growing season of said application.

    b. Bodily injury resulting from the accidental above ground contact with herbicides, pesticides, fungicides and fertilizers caused by the application of the same to an insured site which results in medical treatment within one year (365 days) of said application.

13. Sustained by you or any **insured** as defined in paragraphs (1) and (2) of the definition of **insured**;

14. Arising out of a violation of a criminal law, except traffic violations, if committed by any **insured**;or

15. With respect to which any **insured** under this policy is also an **insured** under a nuclear energy liability policy issued by a nuclear energy liability insurance association, mutual atomic energy liability underwriters, nuclear insurance association of Canada, or any similar organization, or would be an **insured** under any such policy but for its termination upon exhaustion of its limits of liability;

16. Arising out of the entrustment by the **insured** of a **motor vehicle** to any person; coverage, however, applies on the **insured location** if the **motor vehicle** is not licensed for road use because it is used exclusively on the **insured location**.

    Exclusion 16 does not apply to bodily injury sustained by a residence employee in the course of employment.

    Section II does not cover:

17. Property owned by, used by, rented to, or in the care, custody or control of any **insured** or his

employees, or as to which any **insured** or his employees exercise physical control for any purpose (This exclusion is the care, custody and control exclusion referred to in **Section II Additional Coverages—Fire Legal Liability**.);

18. Any **property damage** to work completed by or for an **insured**, any damage arising out of such work, or out of the materials, parts, or equipment furnished in connection with such work;

19. Any **property damage** to goods or products, including containers, which an **insured** manufactures, sells, handles, raises or distributes;

20. Damages claimed for the withdrawal, inspection, repair, replacement, or loss of use of your products, or work completed by or for you or for any property of which such products or work form a part, if such products, work or property are withdrawn from the market or from use because of any known or suspected defect or deficiency;

21. Punitive or exemplary damages;

22. **Bodily injury** to any person eligible to receive any benefits required to be provided or voluntarily provided by any **insured** under any worker's compensation, nonoccupational disease, disability or occupational disease law;

23. **Property damage** to an **insured location** arising out of the alienation (for example, selling, leasing, separating, etc.) of that location;

24. **Bodily injury** under Coverage G sustained by any person residing on the **insured location** except a **residence employee**;

25. Under Coverages G, I and J:

    a. **Bodily injury** involving hernia or back injury, unless it is of recent origin, it is accompanied by pain, it was immediately preceded by some accidental strain suffered in the course of employment, and it did not exist prior to the date of the alleged injury;

    b. Any person while conducting his **business** on the **insured location,** including the employees of that person;

    c. **Bodily injury** to the extent that any medical expenses are paid or payable under the provision of any:

       (1) Auto or premises insurance;

       (2) Accident, disability, or hospitalization insurance;

       (3) Medical or surgical reimbursement plan prepaid or otherwise;

       (4) National, state or other governmental plan; or

       (5) Worker's compensation or similar law.

26. Under Coverages F and G, **bodily injury** sustained by any **farm employee** arising out of employment;

27. Loss of use of property which has not been physically injured or destroyed, resulting from:

    a. A delay in or lack of performance by or on your behalf of any contract or agreement; or

    b. The failure of your products or work performed by or on your behalf to meet the level of performance, quality, fitness or durability warranted or represented by you;

28. **Bodily injury** or **property damage** which arises out of the transmission of:

    a. Acquired Immune Deficiency Syndrome (AIDs); or

    b. Genital herpes, syphilis, gonorrhea or other venereal disease caused wholly or in part by the acts of an **insured, farm employee,** or **residence employee**;

29. Any **bodily injury** sustained by any person arising out of or resulting from the molesting of minors by:

    a. any **insured**,

    b. any **farm employee** or **residence employee** of any **insured**, or

    c. any volunteer

    We shall not have any duty to defend any suit against the **insured** seeking damages on account of such **bodily injury.**

CONDITIONS APPLICABLE TO SECTION II

1. **Duties after Loss.** In case of an accident or **occurrence**, the **insured** shall perform the following duties:

   a. Give written notice to us or our agent as soon as practicable, which sets forth:

      (1) The identity of the policy and **insured**;

      (2) Reasonable available information on the time, place and circumstances of the accident or **occurrence**;

(3) Names and addresses of any claimants and witnesses.

b. Immediately forward to us every notice, demand, summons or other process relating to the accident or **occurrence**;

c. At our request, assist in:

(1) Making settlement;

(2) The enforcement of any right of contribution or indemnity against any person or organization who may be liable to any **insured**;

(3) The conduct of suits and attend hearings and trials;

(4) Securing and giving evidence and obtaining the attendance of witnesses.

d. The **insured** shall not, except at the **insured's** own cost, voluntarily make any payment, assume any obligation or incur any expense other than for first aid to others at the time of the **bodily injury**;

e. Under Coverage M—Damage to the Property of Others—submit to us within 60 days after the loss, a sworn statement of loss and exhibit the damaged property, if within the **insured's** control.

2. **Duties of an Injured Person**—Coverages G, I and J. The injured person or someone acting on behalf of the injured person shall:

a. Give us a written proof of claim, under oath if required, as soon as practicable;

b. Execute authorization to allow us to obtain copies of medical reports and records; and

c. Submit to physical examination by a physician selected by us when and as often as we reasonably require.

3. **Cooperation of Insured**—If any **insured** fails to cooperate with us or send us legal papers as required, we have the right to refuse any further coverage for the **occurrence** or loss.

4. **Payment of Claim**. Any payment under Section II is not an admission of liability by any **insured** or us.

5. **Limits of Liability**—Coverages F and H. Regardless of the number of:

a. **insureds** under this policy,

b. persons or organizations sustaining **bodily injury** or **property damage,** or

c. claims made,

Our liability for each **occurrence** is subject to the following limitations:

a. Our total combined single limit of liability under Coverage F for all **bodily injury** and **property damage** resulting from one **occurrence** shall not exceed the applicable limit of liability stated in the Declarations.

b. Our total limit of liability under Coverage H for all **bodily injury** resulting from one **occurrence** shall not exceed the applicable limit stated in the Declarations.

c. **Products Liability Limits**. The per **occurrence** combined single limit of liability for **bodily injury** and **property damage** caused by farm products produced on the **insured location** is also the total limit of our liability for all such **occurrences** during the policy period.

6. **Limits of Liability**—Coverages G, I and J. The limit of liability for Coverages G, I and J as stated in the Declarations as applicable to each person is our limit of liability for all expenses incurred by or on behalf of each person who sustains **bodily injury** resulting from an **occurrence**. Subject to the limit of liability for each person, our total limit of liability for each occurrence for **bodily injury** sustained by two or more persons is the per **occurrence** limit of liability stated in the Declarations.

7. **Other Insurance**—The insurance under Section II is excess over any other valid and collectible insurance except insurance written specifically to cover as excess over the limits of liability that apply in this policy.

ENDORSEMENTS APPLICABLE TO SECTION II

Each of the following endorsements may be purchased by your payment of an additional premium. All policy provisions apply to these endorsements unless an endorsement specifically states otherwise. **An endorsement applies only when it is listed in the Declarations and you pay this premium**.

No. 204 Employer's Nonownership Liability Endorsement.

We agree that Coverage F of Section II covers the liability of you and any of your executive officers arising out of the use of any **nonowned motor vehicle** used in your farm or household **business** by any person other than you.

1. **Definitions**.

   In this endorsement only, **nonowned motor vehicle** means a land motor vehicle, trailer or semi-trailer not owned by, registered in the name of, hired or leased by, or loaned to you.

2. **Application of Insurance**.

   a. This endorsement does not apply to any **motor vehicle** owned by any of your executive officers or their spouses.

   b. This insurance does not apply to any **motor vehicle** owned by or registered in the name of a partner if your **business** is in the form of a partnership.

3. **Other Insurance**.

   This insurance shall be excess insurance over any other valid and collectible insurance.

SECTION III—AUTOMOBILE DEFINITIONS

The following definitions apply to Section III:

Throughout this section, we, us, and our mean the Company named in the Declarations. You and your mean the person named in the Declarations and that person's spouse if a resident of the same household. You and your also refer to a partnership, corporation, estate, or trust named in the Declarations.

Bodily Injury means physical injury or death to a person caused by an occurrence.

Insured means:

1. Under Coverages N, R, S and T with respect to an **insured vehicle**:

   a. You and any **relative**;

   b. Anyone using an **insured vehicle** within the scope of your permission or within the scope of permission of your adult **relative**;

   c. Any person or organization legally responsible for the **insured vehicle,** provided the use of the **insured vehicle** is by you or with your permission and within the scope of such permission.

2. Under Coverage N with respect to a **nonowned vehicle,** you or your **relatives** when operating a **nonowned vehicle,** or when that vehicle is operated by your agent and with your permission and within the scope of such permission.

Insured Vehicle means:

1. Any vehicle shown in the Declarations;

2. Under Coverages N, P and Q, any private passenger automobile, pickup, panel truck, farm truck, van, motorcycle or motorhome, ownership of which is acquired by you during the policy period;

3. If you have Coverages S and T, any private passenger automobile, pickup, panel truck, farm truck, **trailer,** camper, van or motorhome, ownership of which is acquired by you during the policy period provided the vehicle falls within the year model limitation indicated in the Declarations.

   The vehicles in 2 and 3 above are not insured vehicles unless we insure all of your vehicles and you ask us to insure the newly acquired vehicle during the policy period or within 30 days of its acquisition, whichever is shorter. A newly acquired vehicle includes a vehicle which replaces one shown in the Declarations.

4. A **temporary substitute vehicle** which is a **motor vehicle** or **trailer** you do not own while temporarily used as a substitute for a vehicle described in the Declarations when that vehicle cannot be used because of breakdown or servicing;

5. Under Coverage N only, any **trailer** while attached to a vehicle described in the Declarations. Also included is a **trailer** while being used with a **temporary substitute vehicle**.

Medical Expenses means reasonable charges for medical, surgical, x-ray, dental, ambulance, hospital, professional nursing, and prosthetic devices.

Motor Vehicle means a motorized land vehicle designed principally for travel on public roads. The term motor vehicle does not include a **trailer**.

Nonowned Vehicle means a **trailer** or **motor vehicle** not exceeding two-tons in capacity operated by you or your **relatives** or in the custody of you or your **relatives** provided the actual use is with the permission of the owner. This vehicle must not be owned by you or your **relatives** or be available for regular use by you or your **relatives**.

Occupying means in, on or getting in or out of.

Occurrence means an accident arising out of the ownership, maintenance or use of a **motor vehicle,** including continuous or repeated exposure to conditions, which results in unexpected **bodily injury**

or **property damage** during the policy period. All **bodily injury** and **property damage** resulting from a common cause shall be considered the result of one **occurrence**.

Property Damage means injury to or destruction of tangible property caused by an **occurrence**.

Relative means a person related to you by blood, marriage or adoption who is a resident of your household, including a ward or foster child.

Trailer means a vehicle designed for towing by a private passenger automobile or farm truck. It also includes a farm wagon, farm semi-trailer or farm implement while towed by an **insured vehicle. Trailer** does not include vehicles used:

1. To haul passengers;
2. As an office, store or for display purposes;
3. As a permanent residence.

SECTION III—COVERAGES

COVERAGE N

Liability

If a claim is made or a suit is brought against any insured for damages because of **bodily injury** or **property damage** arising out of an **occurrence** involving an **insured vehicle** or a **nonowned vehicle,** we will:

1. Pay up to our limit of liability for the damages for which the **insured** is legally liable;
2. Provide a defense at our expense by counsel of our choice. We may make any investigation and settlement of any claim or suit that we decide is appropriate. Our obligation to defend any claim or suit ends when the amount we pay for damages equals our limit of liability.

Additional Payments

We will pay the following in addition to our limits of liability, but our obligation for these payments ceases when our obligation to defend ends:

1. Expenses for first aid to others incurred by any **insured** for **bodily injury** covered under this policy. We will not pay for first aid to you or any other **insured**;
2. Expenses incurred by us and costs taxed against any **insured** in any suit we defend;
3. Premiums on bonds required in a suit defended by us, but not for bond amounts greater than the limit of liability provided by this policy. We will also pay up to $250 for the premium of any bail bond required of an **insured** because of an arrest in connection with an accident resulting from the use of an **insured vehicle**. We are not obligated to apply for or furnish any bond;
4. Reasonable expenses incurred by any **insured** at our request, including actual loss of earnings (but not loss of other income) up to $50 per day for assisting us in the investigation or defense of any claim or suit;
5. Interest on the entire judgment which accrues after entry of that part of the judgment which does not exceed the limit of liability that applies and before we pay, tender or deposit in court that part of the judgment, which does not exceed the limit of liability that applies.

COVERAGE P

Uninsured Motorist

See the back pages of this Section III entitled "Uninsured Motorist Coverage".

COVERAGE Q

Medical Payments

We will pay the necessary **medical** and funeral expenses incurred within three (3) years from the date of **occurrence** to each **insured** who sustains **bodily injury** caused by an **occurrence**.

The following are **insureds** under Coverage Q:

1. You or any person **occupying** an **insured vehicle** with your permission or the permission of an adult **relative** and sustaining **bodily injury** caused by an **occurrence** resulting from the use of this **insured vehicle**;
2. You or your **relatives** sustaining **bodily injury** caused by an **occurrence** while **occupying** a **nonowned vehicle**;
3. Any person sustaining **bodily injury** while **occupying** a **nonowned vehicle,** if the **bodily injury** results from:
   a. Its operation by you or on your behalf by a private chauffeur or domestic servant;
   b. Its operation by a **relative**.
4. You and your **relatives** sustaining **bodily injury** while a pedestrian or a bicyclist when struck by a **motor vehicle** or **trailer**.

No payment shall be made under this coverage unless the person to or for whom such payment is made shall first execute a written agreement that the amount of the payment shall be applied toward the settlement of any claim, or the satisfaction of any judgment of damages entered in the person's favor against any **insured** because of **bodily injury** to which Coverage N or P of this policy applies. (This paragraph is not applicable if this policy is issued in Arizona.)

COVERAGE R

Fire and Theft Only

We will pay for any direct and accidental loss of, or damage to, your **insured vehicle** and its equipment caused by:

1. Fire, lightning or windstorm;

2. Smoke or smudge due to a sudden, unusual and faulty operation of any heating equipment serving the premises in which the vehicle is located;

3. The stranding, sinking, burning, collision or derailment of any conveyance in or upon which the vehicle is being transported; or

4. Theft.

If Coverage R applies to your **insured vehicle**, it will also extend to a **nonowned vehicle**.

COVERAGE S

Comprehensive

We will pay for any direct and accidental loss of, or damage to, your **insured vehicle** and its equipment not caused by collision or rollover. Loss or damage from missiles, falling objects, theft, collision with animals, or accidental glass breakage are comprehensive losses.

If Coverage S applies to your **insured vehicle,** it will also extend to a **nonowned vehicle**.

COVERAGE T

Collision and Roll Over

We will pay for direct and accidental loss to your **insured vehicle** and its equipment when it is hit by or hits another vehicle, or object, or rolls over. We will waive any applicable deductible if the collision involves **insured vehicles** of two or more of our policyholders. If Coverage T applies to your **insured vehicle**, it will also extend to a **nonowned vehicle**.

Additional Payments

1. **Loss to Luggage**.

   If as a result of other loss covered under Coverages R, S or T, damage results to clothing or personal luggage, including contents of the luggage being transported by the insured vehicle, we will pay up to $200 for this loss. Exclusion 13 does not apply to this coverage.

2. **Loss of Use by Theft—Reimbursement**.

   Following a theft of an **insured vehicle** covered under Coverage R or S, we will reimburse you for expenses up to $25 a day to a maximum of $500 incurred for the rental of a substitute automobile including taxi cabs. This reimbursement is limited to such expense incurred during the period commencing 48 hours after the theft has been reported to us and the police, and terminating, regardless of expiration of the policy period, on the date the automobile is returned to you and on such earlier date as we make or offer settlement for this theft.

EXCLUSIONS APPLICABLE TO SECTION III

Section III does not cover:

1. Any **insured** while using any vehicle to carry persons for a fee. This exclusion does not apply to a share-the-expense car pool;

2. Any **insured** for any vehicle rented or leased to others;

3. Any **insured** while using any vehicle in a prearranged race, speed contest, or other competition, or preparation for any of these activities;

4. Any damages which are intentionally caused by any **insured**;

5. Any nonowned vehicle while an insured is using it in the business of selling, repairing, servicing, storing or parking **motor vehicles,** including road testing and delivery;

6. Any damage caused by nuclear reaction, radiation, or radioactive contamination;

7. Any radar or similar detection device; any device or instrument designed for the recording, reproduction, amplification, receiving, or transmitting of sound, radio waves, microwaves, or television signals; or tapes, records, or other discs designed for use with this equipment.

This exclusion does not apply to a device or instrument if it is permanently installed in the dash or console opening;

8. Damages caused by declared or undeclared war, invasion, insurrection, civil war, other assumption of power, or confiscation by a duly constituted governmental or civil authority;

9. Exemplary or punitive damages;

10. **Bodily injury** to anyone eligible to receive benefits which an **insured** either provides or is required to provide under any worker's compensation or occupational disease law;

11. Any damages arising out of the ownership, maintenance or use of any type of emergency vehicle; gas, oil, or newspaper delivery truck; logging truck; or any nonfarm commercial truck;

12. Under Coverage N, **bodily injury** sustained by:

    a. You;

    b. The operator of the **insured vehicle**, or the residents of the operator's household who are related to the operator by blood, marriage or adoption, including a ward or foster child.

13. Under Coverage N, damage to property owned or transported by any **insured**;

14. Under Coverage N, damage to property rented to, used by, or in the care, custody or control of an **insured**. This exclusion does not apply to **property damage** to a residence or private garage rented to an **insured**;

15. Under Coverages N, and P, liability arising out of any contract or agreement;

16. Under Coverage Q, **bodily injury** sustained while an **insured vehicle** is used as a residence or temporary living quarters;

17. Under Coverage Q, **bodily injury** sustained by a person engaged in the maintenance or repair of an **insured vehicle**;

18. Under Coverage Q, **bodily injury** to anyone eligible to receive benefits under any:

    a. Automobile or premises insurance affording benefits for medical expenses;

    b. Worker's compensation, disability benefits or similar law;

    c. National, state or other governmental plan.

19. Under Coverages R, S and T, any loss by collapse, explosion or implosion of any tank or container;

20. Under Coverages R, S and T, any equipment or accessories contained in a motorhome, camper unit or trailer unless the equipment or accessories are built in and form a permanent part of the vehicle;

21. Under Coverages, R, S and T, loss caused by recall of an **insured vehicle**;

22. Tires, unless damaged concurrent with other loss covered under Coverages R, S, or T;

23. Damages caused by wear and tear, freezing, mechanical or electrical breakdown or failure other than burning of wiring, unless the damage results from other loss covered under Coverages R, S, or T.

CONDITIONS APPLICABLE TO SECTION III

1. **Out of State Insurance.** If you have liability insurance under this policy and if you are traveling in a state or province which has a compulsory insurance, financial responsibility, or similar law affecting nonresidents, we will automatically provide the legally required minimum amounts and types of coverages if your policy does not already provide these coverages, or the limits stated in the Declarations whichever are greater, with respect to the operation or use of the insured vehicle in that state or province. The required coverage, however, will be excess over any other collectible insurance.

2. **Two or More Vehicles.** When two or more vehicles are covered by this policy, the policy terms will apply separately to each. A vehicle, however, and an attached **trailer** will be considered one vehicle under Coverages N, P and Q and separate vehicles under Coverages R, S and T; any deductible will be applied to each vehicle.

    The maximum limits of liability set forth in Paragraphs 3 and 10 of these conditions shall not be increased in any way by this paragraph.

3. **Other Vehicle Insurance in the Company.** If this policy and any other vehicle insurance policy issued to you by this company apply to the same **occurrence**, the maximum limit of our liability under all of the policies will not exceed the highest applicable limit of liability under any one policy. This is the most we will pay regardless of the number of **insureds**, claims made, **insured vehicles** or premiums.

4. **Duties after Loss**. In case of an accident or **occurrence,** the **insured** shall perform the following duties:

 a. Give written notice to us or our agent as soon as practicable, which sets forth:

   (1) The identity of the policy and **insured**;

   (2) Reasonably available information on the time, place and circumstances of the accident or **occurrence**;

   (3) Names and addresses of any claimants and witnesses;

 b. Immediately forward to us every notice, demand, summons or other process relating to the accident or **occurrence**;

 c. At our request, assist in:

   (1) Making settlement;

   (2) The enforcement of any right of contribution or indemnity against any person or organization who may be liable to any **insured;**

   (3) The conduct of suits and attend hearings and trials;

   (4) Securing and giving evidence and obtaining the attendance of witnesses.

 d. The **insured** shall not, except at the **insured's** own cost, voluntarily make any payment, assume any obligation or incur any expense other than for first aid to others at the time of the **occurrence**.

5. **Duties after Loss—Coverages R, S, and T**. In the case of the loss to which this insurance applies, you shall perform the following duties:

 a. Give written notice to us or our agent, as soon as practicable, and also give notice to the police if loss is suspected to be in violation of a law;

 b. Protect the property from further damage, make reasonable and necessary repairs required to protect the property and keep an accurate record of repair expenditures. If you fail to do these things, further damage is not insured under this policy;

 c. Prepare an inventory of damaged property showing in detail, the quantity, description, actual cash value and amount of loss. Attach to the inventory all bills, receipts, and related

documents that substantiate the figures in the inventory;

 d. As often as we may reasonably require, exhibit the damaged property and submit to examination under oath and subscribe the same;

 e. Within sixty (60) days after our request, submit to us your signed, sworn statement of loss which sets forth the following information to the best of your knowledge and belief:

   (1) The time and cause of loss;

   (2) The interest of the **insured** and all others in the **insured vehicle** involved and all encumbrances on the **insured vehicle**;

   (3) Other insurance which may cover the loss;

   (4) Changes in title of the **insured vehicle** during the term of the policy.

6. **Duties of an Injured Person—Coverages P and Q**. The injured person or someone acting on behalf of the injured person shall:

 a. Give us a written proof of claim, under oath if required, as soon as practicable;

 b. Execute authorization to allow us to obtain copies of medical reports and records; and

 c. The injured person shall submit to physical examination by a physician selected by us when and as often as we reasonably require.

7. **Cooperation of Insured**. If any **insured** fails to cooperate or send us legal papers as required, we have the right to refuse any further protection for the **occurrence** or loss.

8. **Territory**. This policy applies only to **occurrences** within the United States of America and Canada. Section III Coverages are extended for trips into that part of the Republic of Mexico lying not more than 100 miles from the nearest boundary line of the United States of America. If applicable to your insured vehicle, our liability for Coverages R, S and T will be determined on the basis of cost at the nearest United States point.

 WARNING: Automobile accidents in the Republic of Mexico are considered a criminal offense, rather than a civil matter. The insurance provided by this policy will not meet the Mexican automobile insurance requirements. If you are in an automobile accident in Mexico and have not purchased insurance through a licensed Mexican insurance company you may be jailed and may have your automobile impounded.

9. **Payment of Claim.** Any payment under Section III is not an admission of liability by any **insured** or us.

10. **Limits of Liability.** Regardless of the number of:

    a. **insureds** or vehicles insured under this policy,

    b. persons or organizations sustaining **bodily injury** or **property damage,** or

    c. claims made,

    our liability for each **occurrence** is subject to the following limitations:

    a. Our total combined single limit of liability under Coverage N for all **bodily injury** and **property damage** resulting from any one **occurrence**, shall not exceed the applicable limit of liability stated in the Declarations.

    b. Under Coverage Q the **medical** limit for each person is our limit of liability for all expenses incurred by or on behalf of each person who sustains **bodily injury** resulting from an **occurrence**.

    c. Under Coverages R, S, and T, our limit of liability will be the actual cash value of the stolen or damaged property at the time of loss. If the loss is a part of that stolen or damaged property, we will pay the actual cash value of that part at the time of loss or what it would cost to repair or replace the part with like kind and quality.

11. We will apply the combined single limit of liability to provide any separate limits required by law for **bodily injury** or **property damage.** This provision, however, will not increase our total limit of liability.

12. **Other Insurance.** The insurance under Section III is excess over any other valid and collectible insurance except insurance written specifically to cover as excess over the limits of liability that apply in this policy.

13. **Loss Payable Clause.** This clause is applicable only if a lienholder is named in the Declarations.

    a. We will pay you and the lienholder named in the policy for loss to an **insured vehicle,** as interest may appear.

    b. Section III covers the interest of the lienholder unless the loss results from fraudulent acts or omissions on your part.

    c. We may cancel the policy during the policy period. Notice of cancellation shall be mailed to the lienholder at least ten (10) days before the date the cancellation takes effect.

    d. If we make any payment to the lienholder, we will obtain his rights against any other party.

COVERAGE P

Uninsured Motorist Coverage

We will pay damages which an **insured** is legally entitled to recover from the owner or operator of an **uninsured motor vehicle** because of **bodily injury** sustained by an **insured** and caused by an **occurrence.** The owner's or operator's liability for these damages must arise from the ownership, maintenance or use of the **uninsured motor vehicle.**

The following additional definitions apply to Coverage P:

1. **Insured** means:

    a. You and any **relative**;

    b. Anyone occupying an **insured vehicle**; or

    c. Anyone **occupying** a **nonowned vehicle** while operated by you or any **relative.**

2. **Uninsured motor vehicle** means a **motor vehicle** or **trailer**:

    a. To which a **bodily injury** liability bond or policy does not apply at the time of the **occurrence**;

    b. For which an insuring or bonding company denies coverage or is or becomes insolvent; or

    c. Which is a hit-and-run vehicle and neither the driver nor the owner can be identified. The hit-and-run vehicle must hit an **insured,** and **insured vehicle** or a vehicle which an **insured** is **occupying**;

    d. Which is insured by a **bodily injury** liability bond or policy at the time of the **occurrence** but its limit of **bodily injury** liability is less than the minimum limit for **bodily injury** specified by the financial responsibility law of the state in which your **insured vehicle** is principally garaged.

3. An **uninsured motor vehicle** does not include any **motor vehicle** or **trailer**:

   a. Owned by any governmental unit or agency; (Not applicable if this policy is issued in Arizona.)

   b. Designed for use mainly off public roads while not on public roads;

   c. Used as a residence;

   d. Owned by or furnished for the regular use of you or any **relative**; or

   e. Which is an **insured vehicle**.

Exclusions

In addition to the general exclusions of Section III, the following exclusions apply to Coverage P. Coverage P does not apply to:

1. **Bodily injury** sustained by any **insured** while **occupying** a **motor vehicle** or **trailer** without the permission of the owner.

2. The direct or indirect benefit of any insurer or self-insured under any worker's compensation, disability benefits or similar law.

Conditions

In addition to the general conditions applicable to Section III, the following conditions apply to Coverage P only.

1. **Limits of Liability.** Our total limit of liability under Coverage P for all **bodily injury** resulting from one **occurrence** shall not exceed the applicable limit of liability stated in the Declarations.

2. **Nonstacking of Limits.** Regardless of the number of **insured vehicles**, **insureds**, policies of insurance with us, claims made or vehicles involved in the **occurrence**, the most we will pay for all damages resulting from any **occurrence** is the limit of liability shown in the Declarations subject to reduction as outlined in the next paragraph.

3. **Reduction of Amounts Payable.** Amounts payable for damages under Coverage P will be reduced by:

   a. All sums paid by or on behalf of persons or organizations who may be legally responsible for the **bodily injury** to which this coverage applies. This includes all amounts paid under the liability coverage of this or any other policy;

   b. The sum of all amounts payable under any worker's compensation, disability, or similar law;

   c. All sums paid under medical payments or death benefits coverages of any policy issued by us. Any payment under this coverage to or for an **insured** will reduce any amount that person is entitled to receive under this policy's liability coverages.

4. **Hit-and-run Accident.** At our request, the **insured** shall make available for inspection any **motor vehicle** or **trailer** which the **insured** occupied at the time of a hit-and-run accident. The **insured** must notify the police within twenty-four (24) hours of a hit-and-run accident.

5. **Arbitration.**

   a. If we and an **insured** disagree whether the **insured** is legally entitled to recover damages from the owner or driver of an **insured motor vehicle** or do not agree as to the amount of damages, either party may make a written demand for arbitration. In the event, each party will select an arbitrator. The two arbitrators will select a third. If they cannot agree upon a third arbitrator within thirty (30) days, either may request that selection be made by a judge of a court having jurisdiction. Each party will pay the expenses it incurs and bear the expenses of the third arbitrator equally.

   b. Unless both parties agree otherwise, arbitration will take place in the county in which the **insured** lives. Local rules of law as to arbitration procedure and evidence will apply. A decision agreed to by two of the arbitrators will be binding.

6. **Trust Agreement.** If a claim or payment is made under this coverage:

   a. We will be entitled to reimbursement of payments we have made to an **insured** to be taken from the proceeds of any judgment or settlement;

   b. An **insured** will hold in trust all rights or recovery for us against any person or organization. That person will also do whatever is proper to secure those rights and do nothing after the loss to prejudice any rights of recovery;

c. If we make the request in writing, the **insured** must take any necessary or appropriate action to recover damages from any other person or organization through any representative we designate. Any action may be taken in the **insured's** name and in the event of recovery, we will be reimbursed for any expenses, costs, and attorney fees we incur; and

d. The **insured** must execute and deliver any document to us that may be appropriate for the purpose of securing the rights and obligations for the **insured** and for us as established by this provision.

7. **Payment of loss**. We have the option to pay any amount due under this coverage as follows:

a. To the **insured**;

b. If the **insured** is deceased, to the **insured's** surviving spouse; or

c. To a person authorized by law to receive such payment, or to a person who is legally entitled to recover the damages which the payment represents.

8. **Nonbinding Judgments**. No judgment resulting from a suit brought without our written consent is binding on us, either in determining the liability of the **uninsured motor vehicle** operator or owner or the amount of damages to which the **insured** is entitled.

ENDORSEMENTS APPLICABLE TO SECTION III

Each of the following endorsements may be purchased by your payment of an additional premium. All policy provisions apply to these endorsements unless an endorsement specifically states otherwise. **An endorsement applies only when it is listed in the Declarations, and you pay this premium.**

No. 323 Drive Other Car.

Coverage N of Section III is amended to cover you while you are operating a **motor vehicle** that does not qualify as a **nonowned vehicle**, provided you have the permission of the owner of the vehicle. This endorsement does not cover a **motor vehicle**:

1. Owned in whole or in part by you or any relative;

2. Registered in your name or in the name of any relative;

3. Used in transporting persons or property for hire.

This endorsement shall not cover the owner of the motor vehicle you are driving.

No. 334 Emergency Road Service.

We will pay for reasonable and necessary towing and labor expense, but not to exceed $40, caused by the disablement of your **insured vehicle**, provided the expense is incurred at the place of disablement. No deductible applies to this coverage.

No. 335 Additional Living Expense.

If loss exceeds the applicable deductible to your **insured vehicle** we will pay for your reasonable and necessary additional living expense incurred as a result of the disablement of your vehicle due to loss covered under Coverages S or T. The maximum we will pay for this additional living expense is $75 per day up to a maximum of $300 per disablement. The loss must occur more than 100 miles from the place of principal garaging for this additional living expense coverage to apply. No deductible applies to this coverage.

No. 368 Car Rental Reimbursement.

If a loss exceeds the applicable deductible to the **insured vehicle** under Coverages S or T, we agree to reimburse you for:

1. The expense incurred by you for the rental fee (excluding all other charges) of a substitute automobile from a car rental agency or garage; or

2. The expense incurred by you for taxicabs during a period starting at 12:01 a.m. on the date following:

a. The date of loss if as a direct result of this loss the **insured vehicle** cannot be operated under its own power; or

b. If the **insured vehicle** is operable, the date you authorize repairs and deliver the vehicle to the repair shop.

In no event, however, shall we be liable for more than $25 per day to a maximum of $500 for taxicab or for rental fees.

Regardless of the policy period, our liability for taxicab or rental fees shall end on the earliest of the following:

1. Upon completion of repair or replacement of property lost or damaged;

2. Upon such date as we make or tender settlement for the loss or damage.

This coverage shall not apply in the event of a theft of the **insured vehicle** for which reimbursement of transportation expense is provided elsewhere in this policy.

No. 303 Underinsured Motorist Coverage.

Coverage P is changed to include Underinsured Motorist Coverage.

We will pay damages which an **insured** is legally entitled to recover from the owner or operator of an **underinsured motor vehicle** because of **bodily injury** sustained by an **insured** and caused by an **occurrence**. The owner's or operator's liability for these damages must arise from the ownership, maintenance or use of the **underinsured motor vehicle**.

The following additional definitions apply to Coverage P:

1. **Insured** means:
   a. You and any **relative**;
   b. Anyone **occupying** an **insured vehicle**;or
   c. Anyone **occupying** a **nonowned vehicle** while operated by you or any **relative**.

2. **Underinsured motor vehicle** means a **motor vehicle** or **trailer** for which the sum of all liability bonds or policies applicable to an **occurrence** is less than the amount of damages an **insured sustains** because of **bodily injury** caused by that **occurrence**.

3. An **underinsured motor vehicle** does not include any **motor vehicle** or **trailer**:
   a. Owned or operated by a self-insured as defined by any applicable **motor vehicle** law; (Not applicable if this policy is issued in Arizona).
   b. Owned by any governmental unit or agency;
   c. Designed for use mainly off public roads while not on public roads;
   d. Used as a residence;
   e. Owned by you or any **relative,** or furnished or available for regular use by you or any **relative**;
   f. Which is an **insured vehicle**;
   g. Which is insured by a **bodily injury** liability bond or policy at the time of the **occurrence** but its limit of **bodily injury** liability is less than the minimum limit for **bodily injury** specified by the financial responsibility law of the state in which your **insured vehicle** is principally garaged.

Exclusions

In addition to the general exclusions of Section III, the following exclusions apply to Coverage P. Coverage P does not apply to:

1. **Bodily injury** sustained by any **insured** while **occupying** a **motor vehicle** or **trailer** without the permission of the owner.

2. The direct or indirect benefit of any insurer or self-insured under any worker's compensation, disability benefits or similar law.

Conditions

In addition to the general conditions applicable to Section III, the following conditions apply to Coverage P only.

1. **Limits of Liability**.

   Our total limit of liability Coverage P for all **bodily injury** resulting from one **occurrence** shall not exceed the applicable limit of liability stated in the Declarations.

2. **Nonstacking of Limits**.

   Regardless of the number of **insured vehicles, insureds,** policies of insurance with us, claims made or vehicles involved in the **occurrence,** the most we will pay for all damages resulting from any **occurrence** is the limit of liability shown in the Declarations subject to reduction as outlined in the next paragraph.

3. **Reduction of Amounts Payable**. Amounts payable for damages under Coverage P will be reduced by:
   a. The sum of all amounts payable under any worker's compensation, disability, or similar law;
   b. All sums paid under medical payments or death benefits coverages of any policy issued by us.

   Any payment under this coverage to or for an **insured** will reduce any amount that person is entitled to receive under this policy's liability coverages.

4. **Hit-and-run Accident**. At our request, the **insured** shall make available for inspection any **motor vehicle** or **trailer** which the **insured** occupied at the time of a hit-and-run accident. The **insured** must notify the police within twenty-four (24) hours of a hit-and-run accident.

5. **Arbitration**.

   a. If we and an **insured** disagree whether the **insured** is legally entitled to recover damages from the owner or driver of an **underinsured motor vehicle** or do not agree as to the amount of damages, either party may make a written demand for arbitration. In this event, each party will select an arbitrator. The two arbitrators will select a third. If they cannot agree upon a third arbitrator within thirty (30) days, either may request that selection be made by a judge of a court having jurisdiction. Each party will pay the expenses it incurs and bear the expenses of the third arbitrator equally;

   b. Unless both parties agree otherwise, arbitration will take place in the county in which the **insured** lives. Local rules of law as to arbitration procedure and evidence will apply. A decision agreed to by two of the arbitrators will be binding.

6. **Trust Agreement**. If a claim or payment is made under this coverage:

   a. We will be entitled to reimbursement of payments we have made to an **insured** to be taken from the proceeds of any judgment or settlement;

   b. An **insured** will hold in trust all rights of recovery for us against any person or organization. That person will also do whatever is proper to secure those rights and do nothing after the loss to prejudice any rights of recovery;

   c. If we make the request in writing, the **insured** must take any necessary or appropriate action to recover damages from any other person or organization through any representative we designate. Any action may be taken in the **insured's** name and in the event of recovery, we will be reimbursed for any expenses, costs, and attorney fees we incur; and

   d. The **insured** must execute and deliver any document to us that may be appropriate for the purpose of securing the rights and obligations for the **insured** and for us as established by this provision.

7. **Payment of Loss**. We will pay only after all liability bonds or policies applicable to the **occurrence** have been exhausted by judgments or payments. We have the option to pay any amount due under this coverage as follows:

   a. To the **insured**;

   b. If the **insured** is deceased, to the **insured's** surviving spouse;

   c. To a person authorized by law to receive such payment, or to a person who is legally entitled to recover the damages which the payment represents.

8. **Nonbinding Judgments**. No judgment resulting from a suit brought without our written consent is binding on us, either in determining the liability of the **underinsured motor vehicle** operator or owner or the amount of damages to which the **insured** is entitled.

SECTION IV—INLAND MARINE

The coverage under this section applies as indicated by endorsements attached to and listed in the Declarations. All policy provisions apply to these endorsements unless an endorsement specifically states otherwise.

CONDITIONS APPLICABLE TO SECTION IV

1. **Your Duty after Loss**. In case of a loss to which this insurance may apply, you must see that the following duties are performed:

   a. Give written notice to us or our agent, as soon as practicable, and also give notice to the police if loss is suspected to be in violation of a law;

   b. Protect the property from further damage, make reasonable and necessary repairs required to protect the property and keep an accurate record of repair expenditures;

   c. Prepare an inventory of damaged property showing in detail the quantity, description, actual cash value and amount of loss. Attach to the inventory all bills, receipts, and related documents that substantiate the figures in the inventory;

   d. As often as we may reasonably require, exhibit the damaged property and submit to examination under oath and subscribe the same;

e. Within sixty (60) days after our request, submit to us your signed, sworn statement of loss which sets forth the following information to the best of your knowledge and belief:

(1) The time and cause of loss;

(2) The interest of the **insured** and all others in the property involved and all encumbrances on the property;

(3) Other insurance which may cover the loss;

(4) Changes in title during the term of the policy;

(5) Specifications of any damaged property and detailed estimates for repair of the damage;

(6) An inventory of damaged property as described above.

2. **Loss to a Pair or Set**. In case of a loss to a pair or set, we may elect to:

a. Repair or replace any part of or restore the pair or set to its value before the loss; or

b. Pay the difference between the actual cash value of the property before and after the loss.

3. **Valuation**. We shall not be liable beyond the actual cash value of the property at the time of any loss or the applicable endorsement limit, whichever is less. In no event shall we be liable for more than what it would cost to repair or replace the property with material of like kind and quality.

4. **Other Insurance**. The insurance under Section IV is excess over any other valid and collectible insurance except insurance written specifically to cover as excess over the limits of liability that apply in this policy.

Special State Provision

Our state of location as stated in the Declarations will determine which of the following special provisions apply to your policy. Read the provisions following the applicable state heading to determine which paragraphs apply to you.

1. **Arizona**

A. **Cancellation Sections I, II and IV**

You may cancel Sections I, II and IV of this policy at any time by returning it to us or by notifying us in writing of the date cancellation takes effect. The date of cancellation must not be earlier than the date you mail or deliver notice to us. If you cancel, the refund premium, if any, will be computed in accordance with the customary short rate tables and procedures.

We may cancel this policy only for the reasons stated in this condition by notifying you in writing of the date cancellation takes effect. This cancellation must be mailed to you at your last mailing address known by us. Proof of mailing will be sufficient proof of notice.

(1) When you have not paid the premium, whether payable to us or to our agent, we may cancel at any time by notifying you at least ten (10) days before the date cancellation takes effect.

(2) When this policy has been in effect for less than sixty (60) days and is not a renewal with us, we may cancel for any reason by notifying you at least ten (10) days before the date cancellation takes effect.

(3) When this policy has been in effect for sixty (60) days or more, or at any time if it is a renewal with us, we may cancel:

(a) If there has been a material misrepresentation of fact which if known to us would have caused us not to issue the policy, or

(b) If the risk has changed substantially since the policy was issued. This can be done by notifying you at least ten (10) days before the date cancellation takes effect.

(c) **Nonrenewal**. We may elect not to renew Sections I, II and IV of this policy. We must do so by mailing written notice to you at least thirty (30) days before the expiration date of this policy. This notice will be sent to your last mailing address known by us. Proof of mailing will be sufficient proof of notice.

(4) When this policy is cancelled, the premium for the period from the date of cancellation to the expiration date will be refunded to you.

If the return premium is not refunded with the notice of cancellation of when this policy is returned to us, we will refund it within a reasonable time after the cancellation takes effect.

If we cancel, the refund premium, if any, will be computed on a pro-rata basis.

B. Cancellation Section III

You may cancel Section III of this policy by returning it to us or by written notice mailed or delivered to us. The notice must give us the date to cancel which must not be earlier than the date you mail or deliver it to us.

We may cancel by mailing a notice of cancellation or termination to you at the address shown in the Declarations or by delivery of the notice. The notice will give the date the cancellation is effective. It will be mailed to you at least ten (10) days before the cancellation effective date.

Proof of mailing a notice is proof of notice.

If you cancel, the refund of premium, if any, will be computed in accordance with customary short rate tables and procedures. If we cancel, the refund, if any, will be computed on a pro rata basis. Any unearned premium may be returned at the time of cancellation or within a reasonable time thereafter. Delay in the return of unearned premium does not effect the cancellation.

The policy will automatically terminate at the end of the policy period if you or your representative do not accept our offer to renew or continue it. Your failure to pay the required renewal or continuation premium by the renewal or continuation date means that you have declined our offer.

If you obtain other insurance on your covered auto, any similar insurance provided by this policy will terminate as to that auto on the effective date of other insurance.

After this policy has been in effect for sixty (60) days, or if it is a renewal, we will not cancel or decline renewal unless:

(1) You fail to pay the premium when it is due;

(2) The policy was obtained through fraudulent misrepresentation;

(3) You or any other person who regularly drives the auto have:

    (a) Had his or her driver's license suspended or revoked during the policy period;

    (b) Become permanently disabled either mentally or physically, and do not submit a doctor's certificate testifying to his or her ability to drive;

    (c) Been convicted during the three years just before the effective date of the policy or during the policy period of:

        (1) Criminal negligence resulting in death, homicide or assault in connection with the use of a motor vehicle.

        (2) Driving while under the influence of alcohol or drugs.

        (3) Leaving the scene of an accident.

        (4) Reckless driving, or

        (5) Lying to obtain a driver's license.

Even if this policy has been in effect for sixty (60) days or if it is a renewal, we retain unlimited right to cancel if:

    a. This policy insures four or more autos;

    b. The auto is used in the auto business.

    c. The auto is available to the public for hire or is rented to others; or

    d. The auto insured has a load capacity of 1,500 pounds or more.

Grace Period. A grace period of seven (7) days is allowed for the payment of premium due except the first. An initial payment on the renewal of a policy is not a first payment of premium.

If the premium due is not received by the end of the grace period, a cancellation notice will be mailed to you at the address shown in the Declarations. The cancellation will be effective on the date the notice is mailed to you.

2. New Mexico

Cancellation. You may cancel this entire policy by mailing to us written notice stating when this cancellation shall be effective. We may change or cancel this entire policy or any portion of it, by mailing it to you at the address shown in the Declarations, written notice stating when not less than ten (10) days thereafter the change or cancellation shall be effective. Payment or tender of unearned premium is not a condition of cancellation. The mailing of notice shall be sufficient proof of notice and the effective date and hour of cancellation stated in the notice shall become the end of the policy period. Delivery of this written notice, either by you or by us shall be equivalent to mailing.

If you cancel, earned premiums shall be computed according to our customary short rate table and procedure. If we cancel, earned premiums shall be computed pro rata. Premium adjustment may be made at this time or as soon after as is practical. Our check mailed or delivered shall be sufficient tender of any refund of premium.

SECTION V
YOUR PERSONAL AND/OR FARM AND RANCH UMBRELLA

[This portion of the policy has been omitted.]

SCHEDULE OF VEHICLES

AUTOMOBILE - ADDITIONAL POLICY DECLARATIONS

POLICY NO.   2SAMPLE   DOE, PERRY AND PAULINE   5/30/20XX

BILLING TERM 5/30/20XX TO 5/30/20XX

LIABILITY LIMITS   MEDICAL LIMITS

B.I.   100,000 EA PER   10,000 EA PER
       300,000 EA OCC   50,000 EA OCC
P.D.   50,000 EA OCC

UNINSURED MOTORIST   UNDERINSURED MOTORIST

B.I.   15,000 EA PER   B.I.   15,000 EA PER
       30,000 EA OCC   30,000 EA OCC

MATERIAL DAMAGE

ITEM	YR	MAKE	TYPE	COMP	COLL	LIAB PREM	MAT DAM PREM	LIEN
01	91	CHEV	S-102X	ACV*	500 DED	710.40	533.70	00000

SERIAL NUMBER 1GC#S19Z0M123456

* ACTUAL CASH VALUE

TOTAL ANNUAL PREMIUM 5 1244.10 TOTAL

* MATERIAL DAMAGE COVERAGE APPLIES ONLY TO VEHICLES SHOWN ON THE SCHEDULE OF VEHICLES INSURED FOR MATERIAL DAMAGE. NEWLY ACQUIRED VEHICLE(S) MUST BE REPORTED TO THE COMPANY OR AGENT WITHIN 30 DAYS OF ACQUISITION OR THE POLICY PERIOD, WHICHEVER IS SHORTER, IF MATERIAL DAMAGE COVERAGE IS DESIRED.

* NEWLY ACQUIRED VEHICLES COVERAGE FOR COMP. OR COLL. APPLICABLE ONLY TO VEHICLES WITH MODEL YEAR 8 YEARS OLD OR LESS FROM CURRENT CALENDAR YEAR.

ISSUE DATE 2/01/20XX

DOE, PERRY & P.
10505 N. 89TH ST.
SUITE 600
SCOTTSDALE, AZ 85253
POLICY TERM 1/09/20XX 12:01 A.M. TO 1/09/20XX 12:01 A.M.

POLICY NUMBER 14311501
COUNTY 07   AGENT 468
TERM 1 YR   ONG, BRIAN

INSURANCE IS PROVIDED ONLY WITH RESPECT TO THOSE COVERAGES DESIGNATED BELOW BY EITHER PREMIUM OR THE WORD INCLUDED, BUT ONLY TO THE EXTENT SET FORTH IN THE SPECIFIC FORMS AND ENDORSEMENTS MADE A PART OF THE POLICY. COVERAGE IS AS SPECIFIED ON ATTACHED ADDITIONAL POLICY DECLARATION SHEETS.

SECTION I - PROPERTY COVERAGE EFF 1/09/20XX 1,271.40
SECTION II - LIABILITY COVERAGE EFF 1/09/20XX 180.80
SECTION III - AUTOMOBILE COVERAGE 00
SECTION IV - INLAND MARINE COVERAGE EFF 1/09/20XX 36.60
SECTION V - UMBRELLA COVERAGE EFF 1/09/20XX 353.00

TOTAL ANNUAL PREMIUM   1,841.80

ENDORSEMENTS-
391 (06-90) 111 120 114 F02A
438-BFU (5-42) EM-L (10-80) 401
30 (5-42) 408 L93 L95(11/89) L9
L97(11/89) L99(11/89) L30

LEGAL LOCATION-
REFER TO SCHEDULE OF LOCATIONS   LO
MORTGAGE CLAUSE- IF A MORTGAGE AND/OR LOSS PAYABLE CLAUSE(S) SHALL BE APPLICABLE.

36822 SEC I
DEER VALLEY CR UN
P.O. BOX 8000
PHOENIX, AZ 85066

THE INSURANCE AFFORDED BY THIS POLICY AS INDICATED WITHIN THIS DECLARATION SUPERSEDES AND REPLACES ALL INSURANCE PREVIOUSLY AFFORDED BY THIS POLICY. ASSIGNMENT OF THIS POLICY SHALL NOT BE VALID UNLESS WE GIVE OUR WRITTEN CONSENT.

_____

COUNTERSIGNATURE   *SEE ATTACHED SCHEDULE(S)*

SCHEDULE OF ADDITIONAL DWELLINGS, PERSONAL PROPERTY, AND OUTBUILDINGS

AS144   ADDITIONAL POLICY DECLARATION

POLICY NO. 14311501   DOE, PERRY & P.   2/01/20XX

BILLING TERM 1/09/20XX TO 1/09/20XX

ITEM NO.	TYPE	DESCRIPTION	DED	PERIL	INSURANCE AMOUNT	PREMIUM AMOUNT	MORT. NO.
01	F.P.P.	FARM PERSONAL PROP.	100	1-24	16,275	109.00	
01	DWELLING	GUEST HOUSE	100	25	40,000	180.00	
04	DWELLING	EMPLOYEE MOBILE	100	1-9	3,000	13.00	
02	OUTBUILDING	HAY SHED	100	1-9	3,000	17.90	
03	OUTBUILDING	PIPE BARN	100	1-9	5,000	29.90	
04	OUTBUILDING	TENNIS CRT WNDSCRN	100	1-9	1,000	6.00	
05	OUTBUILDING	TENNIS COURT FENCNG	100	1-9	4,000	23.90	
06	OUTBUILDING	TENNIS COURT LGHTNG	100	1-9	5,000	29.90	
07	OUTBUILDING	STORAGE SHED	100	1-9	8,000	58.40	
01	ELEC. MOTOR	400AMP ELEC PANEL	100	25	3,000	64.70	
02	ELEC. MOTOR	WELL PMP MTRS#M729	100	25	2,000	43.10	
TOTALS					90,275	575.80	

80 PERCENT COINSURANCE ON ALL ELEC. MOTOR ITEMS.

REFERENCE ADDITIONAL INSUREDS, ADDRESSES OR DESCRIPTIONS

(ITEM 02)   '71 NATIONAL M/H, S#3856, 12' X 60'

(ITEM 03)   '74 PARK MANOR M/H, S#FPA-4173-E, 14' X 70'

(ITEM 04)   '72 STREAMLINE TRAVEL TRAILER, S# D25S2984, 8' X 26'

SPECIAL LIMITS OF LIABILITY ARE AS FOLLOWS—

- -

COV D HAY, STRAW, AND FODDER, PER STACK OR BUILDING $10,000

COV D HORSE, CATTLE, MULE OR DONKEY, PER HEAD $ 500

COV D SWINE, SHEEP, OR GOAT, PER HEAD $ 100

END 114 BORROWED EQUIPMENT - SAME AS THE FARM P.P. LIMIT

SCHEDULE OF SECTION II

ADDITIONAL POLICY DECLARATION

POLICY NO. 14311501   DOE, PERRY & P.   2/01/20XX

BILLING TERM 1/09/20XX TO 1/09/20XX

LIABILITY TERMS $300,000   BI-PD MEDICAL LIMITS   5,000 EA. PER.
                                      EA. OCC.   25,000 EA. OCC.

ITEM	DESCRIPTION	AMT. OF INS. OR OTHER	ANNUAL PREMIUM
	LEGAL DESCRIPTION		
01	REFER TO SCHEDULE OF LOCATIONS	10 ACRES CROP	180.80
	-FOR ADDITIONAL LOCATIONS SEE SCHEDULE OF LOCATIONS		
	COV. F,G,M		INCL

TOTAL PREMIUM   180.80

SPECIAL LIMITS OF LIABILITY ARE AS FOLLOWS

- -

COV M DAMAGE TO PROPERTY OF OTHERS, PER OCC. $500

SCHEDULE OF SECTION IV

ADDITIONAL POLICY DECLARATION   AS145

POLICY NO. 14311501   DOE, PERRY & P.   2/01/20XX

BILLING TERM 1/09/20XX TO 1/09/20XX

OTHER SCHEDULED PERSONAL PROPERTY.

ITEM	DESC & SERIAL NO	FORMS	DED. AMOUNT	AMOUNT OF INSURANCE	TOTAL PREMIUM
02	FEATHERED VASE	K	NIL	185	1.00
03	FISHING BOY	K	NIL	165	1.00
04	MORNING AIR	K	NIL	2,800	5.50
05	MOTHER AND COLT	K	NIL	2,500	5.00
06	FRIENDS	K	NIL	475	1.00
07	ECLIPSE	K	NIL	1,800	3.60
08	XEROX COPIER	K	NIL	750	1.50
09	TRS80 II MICRO CMPT 025717	X	NIL	1,000	9.00
10	TRS80 II DISK SYSTM 123601	X	NIL	700	6.30
11	TRS80 MDL 4 DM PRTR	X	NIL	300	2.70

*** TOTAL   36.60 ***
   FORMS TABLE

   K = 401
   X = 408

SCHEDULE OF SECTION V—UMBRELLA

AS1455   2/01/20XX

ADDITIONAL POLICY DECLARATION

POLICY 14311501   NAMED INSURED PERRY & PAULINE DOE
BILLING TERM 1/09/20XX TO 1/09/20XX

LIABILITY LIMIT - $2,000,000 EACH OCCURRENCE
                       $2,000,000 EACH AGGREGATE

SELF-INSURED RETENTION - $1,000

SCHEDULE OF UNDERLYING INSURANCE

PREMISES AND OPERATIONS LIABILITY -

(X) SECTION II
( ) OTHER POLICIES -

AUTOMOBILE LIABILITY -

( ) SECTION III
(X) OTHER POLICIES -

TYPE OF
POLICY

UM / UIM LIAB

                                                        ANNUAL PREMIUM - $353.00

ENDORSEMENTS - L9 L21

SCHEDULE OF LOCATIONS

ADDITIONAL POLICY DECLARATION

                                                                          AS141

POLICY NO. 14311501   DOE, PERRY & P.   2/01/20XX
ITEM   DWELLING

NO.	LOCATION	ACRES	TYPE	NO.
01	S29 T6N R3E			02
02	X-REF WITH ALL BUILDINGS			01
03	S29 T6N R3E	10	ACRES	01

GLOSSARY

A

abnormally dangerous activity Activity for which a defendant is strictly liable if someone is injured; characterized as an activity having a high degree of risk of serious harm that cannot be eliminated with due care and whose value is outweighed by its dangerous attributes.

absolute privileges Absolute defense to defamation, regardless of defendant's motives.

abuse of process Use of litigation devices for improper purposes.

accrual Time at which a statute of limitations begins to run, usually at the time the plaintiff is injured.

action in trespass (*vi et armis*) Early cause of action involving serious, forcible breaches of peace that evolved to encompass even minor physical contact; no showing of fault was required.

actual cause Cause in fact of the plaintiff's injuries.

actual malice Acting with knowledge of the falsity of one's statement or with reckless disregard as to the truth or falsity of one's statement.

additur When the trial court increases a jury award or orders a new trial because the jury's award of damages is inadequate.

adhesion contract Standardized contract characterized by the unequal bargaining power of the parties and the lack of negotiation regarding the terms of the contract.

affirmative defense Any defense that a party asserts for which it bears the burden of proof.

answer A pleading in which the defendant responds to the plaintiff's complaint.

appeal Formal request by a party asking a higher court to review the decision of a lower court.

appropriation Use of the value of plaintiff's name or picture for defendant's financial gain.

assault Intentional causing of an apprehension of harmful or offensive contact.

assumption of risk Defense that the plaintiff voluntarily consented to take the chance that harm would occur if he engaged in certain conduct.

attractive nuisance Dangerous condition on the defendant's property that is likely to induce children to trespass.

at-will employee Employee who, because of the nature of his employment contract, can be discharged at any time for any reason.

automobile-guest statutes Laws holding a driver of a vehicle liable to a guest in his car only under circumstances of extreme misconduct.

avoidable-consequences rule Obligation of a plaintiff to minimize (mitigate) her damages.

B

bailee One who is temporarily entrusted with the custody of goods.

bailor One who entrusts her goods to the temporary custody of another.

battery Intentional infliction of a harmful or offensive contact upon a person.

bench trial Trial before a judge.

beyond a reasonable doubt Standard of proof requiring a showing of almost absolute certainty for each element.

black-letter law Legal principles generally accepted by the legal community.

breach of duty Failure to conform to the required standard of care.

business invitee One who enters the land for a purpose connected with the business dealings of the possessor.

C

case law Case-by-case decision making by the court.

certification of a class Court's agreement to allow one or more members of the class to serve as representatives for the other members of the class.

challenge for cause Request to remove a potential juror because of his alleged inability to decide the case impartially.

charging the jury Process in which the judge instructs the jurors in rules of law they are to apply.

chattels Personal property.

class action Suit in which representative members of a class sue on behalf of other members of the class.

closing argument Final statement made by an attorney that summarizes the evidence.

collateral-source rule The collateral-source rule precludes the admission of evidence to the jury regarding payment of benefits such as Social Security, Medicare, pension payments and vacation and/or sick pay to the injured party from a source other than the tortfeasor. The rule gives the plaintiff the ability to recover twice for damages.

comparative negligence   Defense that the plaintiff's recovery should be reduced in direct proportion to the plaintiff's percentage of contribution to her own injuries.

compensatory damages   Damages designed to compensate the plaintiff; consist of both general and special damages.

complaint   An initial pleading filed on behalf of the plaintiff, the purpose of which is to provide the defendant with the material elements of the plaintiff's demand.

concurrent tortfeasors   Tortfeasors who independently cause the plaintiff injury.

contribution   Partial reimbursement of a tortfeasor who has paid more than her pro rata share of the damages.

contributory negligence   Defense that the plaintiff contributed to his own injuries and should therefore be barred from recovery.

conversion   Substantial interference with another's property to the extent that justice demands payment for the full value of the property.

coordination of benefits provision   Policy provision that precludes payment to the insured if the insured has other insurance available.

counterclaim   A claim presented by a defendant in opposition to the plaintiff's claim.

covenant not to sue   Promise by a plaintiff not to sue a particular defendant.

cross-appeal   Appeal filed after an appeal is filed by the opposing party.

cross-claim   A claim brought by a defendant against a co-defendant in the same action.

cross-examination   Examination of a witness called by the opposing party.

custodian of the records   The person in an organization who knows about its filing system and records.

D

deadly force   Force likely to cause death or serious bodily injury.

deceit   Common law cause of action equated with intentional misrepresentation; also referred to as fraud.

declaratory judgment action   Action in which the court renders an opinion as to a matter of law or in reference to the rights of the parties but does not order any action to be taken.

defamation   Statement that tends to harm the reputation of another, encompassing both libel and slander.

default judgment   Judgment entered due to lack of opposition on behalf of the opposing party.

defective warning   Defect arising out of a manufacturer's failure to give adequate warnings or directions for use. In other words, it is the warning that is defective rather than the product.

demand letter   A letter detailing a client's damages and setting forth the reasons for his or her demand.

demurrer   Motion for dismissal based on a defect in the form or content of a complaint.

deposition   Oral examination of a witness under oath.

derivative claim   Claim derived from underlying claim (e.g., loss of consortium).

design defect   Defect arising out of a manufacturer's use of an unreasonably dangerous design.

direct examination   Examination by the attorney that called the witness.

directed verdict   Dismissal of a case because of the opposing party's failure to meet the requisite burden of proof.

disclosure statement   A document each party is required to prepare and serve on opposing parties shortly after a lawsuit commences. This document must contain certain categories of information about that party's case.

discounting an award   Reducing an award to its present value.

discovery   Process through which parties try to find out as much as possible about the other side's case.

discretionary function   Act of a government employee requiring the use of judgment.

duty   Legal obligation to act reasonably and that arises out of our relationship to others.

E

economic loss   Diminution in the value of a product.

excess judgment   Judgment for more than the insured's policy limits.

exemplary damages   Damages designed to punish the defendant and to deter similarly situated wrongdoers (also known as punitive damages).

express warranty   Express representation by a seller that a product possesses certain qualities.

F

fair market value   Amount property could be sold for on the open market.

false imprisonment   Intentional confinement of another.

false light   Representing the plaintiff to the public in a way that would be highly offensive to a reasonable person.

family-purpose doctrine   Doctrine that makes the owner of a car liable for the tortious acts of family members committed while driving.

fault insurance   Automobile insurance coverage where the insurance carrier of the vehicle pays for damages to the vehicle's occupants and others only if the driver of the vehicle was responsible for the injuries sustained.

fellow-servant rule   Doctrine that shields employers from liability for damages incurred for injuries to an employee due to the negligence of a co-worker.

fiduciary relationship   Relationship based on trust and confidence that imposes an obligation to act in good faith; an example is the attorney-client relationship.

G

general damages   Damages that generally result from conduct engaged in by the defendant.

general verdict   Verdict in which a jury decides issues of liability and damages.

Good Samaritan statutes   Law providing that anyone who provides medical assistance is not liable for damages arising from that assistance as long as care is provided in good faith and does not constitute gross negligence.

governmental function   Tasks typically performed by a governmental entity.

I

immunity   Absolute defense derived from the defendant's status (e.g., a government official) or relationship to the plaintiff (e.g., spouse of the plaintiff).

implied warranty   Representations as to a product's qualities that are implied by virtue of the product being offered for sale.

imputed negligence   Negligence that is charged or attributed to another.

indemnification   Total acceptance of financial responsibility by one tortfeasor for another.

independent contractor   Someone hired to do a job who works at his own pace, in his own way, under his own supervision.

informed consent   Knowledgeable consent based on disclosure of all relevant facts that allows one to make an informed decision.

injurious falsehood   False disparagement of a plaintiff's business, product, or property rights.

innuendo   Use of extrinsic facts to convey the defamatory meaning of a statement.

intentional tort   Tort in which the tortfeasor intends to bring about a particular consequence or knows with substantial certainty that a result will occur.

interrogatories   Written questions submitted to the opposing party that that party must answer in writing and under oath.

intervening cause   Act that contributes to the plaintiff's injuries but does not relieve the defendant of liability.

invitees   Persons invited by possessor of land onto her property for the purpose of conducting business.

J

joint and several liability   Liability for an entire loss if the loss is indivisible.

joint enterprise   Two or more persons who agree to a common goal or purpose, share a common pecuniary interest, and have an equal right to control the direction of the enterprise.

joint tortfeasors   Those who act together to cause the plaintiff's injury.

judgment notwithstanding the verdict (JNOV)   A decision that the verdict reached was contrary to the evidence and the law.

jurisdiction   Power to hear a particular kind of case.

L

last-clear-chance doctrine   Doctrine that allows the plaintiff to recover in a contributory-negligence system despite the plaintiff's negligence.

latent defect   Defect that is invisible or not readily discoverable.

libel   Written defamatory statements.

licensee   Person who has possessor's consent to be present on land.

loss of consortium   Loss of services, including companionship, sex, and earnings outside of the home.

M

manufacturing defect   Defect arising out of a deviation in the manufacturing process.

motion for a new trial   Motion requesting a new trial based on an alleged error committed by the trial judge.

motion for a protective order   Motion that protects a party from having to disclose privileged information.

motion for summary judgment   Motion requesting that the court enter a judgment on the party's behalf because there is no material fact at issue.

motion in limine   Motion to prevent evidence from being presented to the jury.

motion to compel   Motion to force the opposing party to comply with a request for discovery.

N

necessity Privilege that justifies the defendant's harming of the plaintiff's property in an effort to prevent great harm to the defendant or others.

negligence Conduct that creates an unreasonable risk of harm to another.

no-fault insurance Automobile insurance coverage where the insurance carrier of the vehicle pays for damages to the vehicle's occupants irrespective of whether or not the driver of the vehicle was responsible for the injuries sustained.

nolo contendere Pleas of "no contest"; not an admission of guilt.

nominal damages Damages awarded when liability is shown but no actual damages are proved.

nuisance Substantial and unreasonable interference with a plaintiff's interest; includes public and private nuisance.

O

objective standard Comparison of a defendant's conduct to that of a reasonable person.

opening statements Statements made by counsel to the jury at the beginning of trial.

overrule To deny an objection.

P

parasitic damages Damages attached to physical injury, (e.g., mental suffering).

patent defect Defect that is visible or readily discoverable.

pecuniary Monetary; that which can be valued in terms of money.

peremptory challenge Request to remove a potential juror for no articulated reason.

preempts Prohibits a state tort law claim due to a federal enactment.

preponderance of the evidence Standard of proof requiring a showing that each element is more probable than not.

present value Value of money paid now to compensate for future earnings, based on the assumption that money received today is worth more than money received in the future because of the investment potential of money.

presumed damages Damages that ordinarily stem from a defamatory statement and that do not require the showing of actual harm.

pretrial conference Conference involving the judge and parties at which issues and procedures for the trial are clarified and efforts are made at settlement.

primary coverage Insurance providing initial coverage for all damages up to the limits of the policy.

private necessity Privilege that justifies the defendant's harming of the plaintiff's property in order to protect his own interests or those of a few private citizens.

privity Requirement that the plaintiff must contract directly with the defendant in order to recover for losses.

product liability The liability of a manufacturer, seller, or other supplier of a chattel which, because of a defect, causes injury to a consumer, a user, or in some cases a bystander. Liability can be based on any of three theories of recovery: (1) negligence, (2) warranty, or (3) strict liability.

professional rescuers doctrine Limits or bars the liability of tortfeasors to professional rescuers such as police officers and firefighters who sustained injuries as a result of ordinary negligence.

proprietary function Function performed by the government that could just as easily be performed by a private entity.

proximate cause Legal cause of the plaintiff's injuries; emphasis is on the concept of foreseeability.

public figure One who has achieved persuasive fame or notoriety or who becomes involved in a public controversy.

public invitee One who enters the land for the purpose for which the land is held open to the public.

public necessity Privilege that justifies the defendant's harming of the plaintiff's property in an effort to prevent great harm to the public as a whole or to a substantial number of persons.

public policy Policy of the public or a community which dictates the norms of the community based on its beliefs and values regarding justice, fairness, and equality.

publication Hearing or seeing of a defamatory statement by someone other than the plaintiff.

punitive damages Damages designed to punish the defendant (also known as exemplary damages) and to deter others from engaging in reckless or egregious misconduct.

Q

qualified privileges Privilege that applies only when a defendant acts on the basis of certain well-defined purposes.

R

reformation of a policy Construing a policy to provide the minimum coverage required by statute.

release Agreement to absolve a defendant of all liability.

remitted When the trial court lowers the jury's award of damages or orders a new trial because the damages awarded were excessive.

request for medical examination   Request that the opposing party be examined by a physician chosen by the party making the request.

request for production of documents   Request for document in possession of the opposing party.

requests for admissions   Request by one party asking the other party to admit certain facts.

res judicata   Legal principle stating that issues litigated cannot be relitigated at a later time.

rescue doctrine   Doctrine under which anyone who negligently causes harm to a person or property may be liable to one who is injured in an effort to rescue the imperiled person or property.

respondeat superior doctrine   Doctrine that makes an employer liable for the tortious acts of employees committed in the scope and furtherance of their employment (vicarious liability).

restitution   Compensation for a crime given to the victim.

S

satisfaction   Payment of a judgment.

scheduled injuries   Injuries, such as loss of sight or of an appendage, for which stated benefits are paid.

secondary coverage   Insurance that provides coverage for damages incurred but that does not do so until the limits of the primary policy have been exhausted.

single-limit coverage   Insurance coverage providing a single amount of recovery that is available for damages.

slander   Oral defamatory statements.

slander of title   False disparagement of the plaintiff's property rights.

slander per se   Slander in which pecuniary harm can be assumed.

slippery-slope argument   Argument that once you take a first step in allowing something in one instance, you are in danger of sliding the "slippery slope" into a bottomless pit of circumstances requiring comparable treatment.

special damages   Damages that are unique to the plaintiff.

special harm   Harm of a pecuniary nature.

special verdict   Verdict in which the jury is required to answer special interrogatories, which the judge must review to determine who the prevailing party is.

split-limits coverage   Insurance coverage that sets forth a maximum amount an individual can recover for damages and an aggregate amount available for damages independent of the total claims involved.

stacking of policies   Using one or more policies to provide coverage for the same incident.

statute of limitations   Statute that limits the time period in which a claim can be filed.

statute of repose   Statute of limitations in product liability cases that limits the time period during which suit can be filed; statute of limitations in reference to sale of products.

strict liability   Liability imposed without a showing of intent or negligence.

structured settlement   Agreement to pay damages in installments rather than a lump sum.

subjective standard   Use of the defendant's own subjective perceptions to determine whether the defendant behaved reasonably.

subrogation   The right of an insurer to institute suit in the name of the insured against the responsible party to collect for monies paid by the insurer to the insured.

superseding cause   Act that contributes to the plaintiff's injuries to the extent that the defendant is relieved of liability.

survival action   Action that remains available after the decedent's death.

sustain   To grant an objection.

T

tort   Civil wrong for which victim receives compensation in the form of damages.

tortfeasor   One who has committed a tort.

trade libel   False disparagement of the plaintiff's goods or business.

transferred-intent doctrine   Intent with respect to one person (or tort) is transferred to another person (or tort).

trespass on the case   Early cause of action involving injuries inflicted indirectly and requiring some showing of fault.

trespass to chattels   Intentional interference with another's use or possession of chattels.

trespass to land   Intentionally entering or wrongfully remaining on another's land.

U

umbrella policy   Policy that provides a secondary source of coverage after the deductible has been paid, usually coordinated with the limits of the underlying policy.

unavoidably unsafe products   Products incapable of being made safe for their ordinary and intended use.

V

verification   Affidavit indicating that the plaintiff has read the complaint and to the best of her knowledge believes it to be true.

vicarious liability   Liability for the tortious acts of another.

voir dire   Process of jury selection involving the use of challenges for cause and peremptory challenges.

W

warranty of fitness for a particular purpose   Implied warranty that goods are suitable to be used for a particular (noncustomary) purpose.

warranty of merchantability   Implied warranty that goods are fit for the ordinary purpose for which they are used.

wrongful-death action   Action brought by third parties to recover for losses they suffered as a result of the decedent's death.

INDEX